FINANCIAL ACCOUNTING: A FOCUS ON INTERPRETATION AND ANALYSIS

FINANCIAL ACCOUNTING: A FOCUS ON INTERPRETATION AND ANALYSIS

Sixth Edition

Richard F. Kochanek
University of Connecticut

A. Douglas Hillman
Drake University

Noah P. Barsky
Villanova University

THOMSON

Australia · Canada · Mexico · Singapore · Spain · United Kingdom · United States

Financial Accounting: A Focus on Interpretation and Analysis
Richard F. Kochanek, A. Douglas Hillman, and Noah P. Barsky

Executive Editors:
Michele Baird, Maureen Staudt &
Michael Stranz

Project Development Manager:
Linda de Stefano

Marketing Coordinators:
Lindsay Annett and Sara Mercurio

Production/Manufacturing Supervisor:
Donna M. Brown

Pre-Media Services Supervisor:
Dan Plofchan

Rights and Permissions Specialists:
Kalina Hintz and Bahman Naraghi

Cover Image
Getty Images*

The Adaptable Courseware Program consists of products and additions to existing Thomson products that are produced from camera-ready copy. Peer review, class testing, and accuracy are primarily the responsibility of the author(s).

Financial Accounting: A Focus on Interpretation and Analysis / Richard F. Kochanek, A. Douglas Hillman, and Noah P. Barsky – Sixth Edition
p. 000
ISBN 0-759-33811-6

International Divisions List

Asia (Including India):
Thomson Learning
(a division of Thomson Asia Pte Ltd)
5 Shenton Way #01-01
UIC Building
Singapore 068808
Tel: (65) 6410-1200
Fax: (65) 6410-1208

Australia/New Zealand:
Thomson Learning Australia
102 Dodds Street
Southbank, Victoria 3006
Australia

Latin America:
Thomson Learning
Seneca 53
Colonia Polano
11560 Mexico, D.F., Mexico
Tel (525) 281-2906
Fax (525) 281-2656

Canada:
Thomson Nelson
1120 Birchmount Road
Toronto, Ontario
Canada M1K 5G4
Tel (416) 752-9100
Fax (416) 752-8102

UK/Europe/Middle East/Africa:
Thomson Learning
High Holborn House
50-51 Bedford Row
London, WC1R 4L$
United Kingdom
Tel 44 (020) 7067-2500
Fax 44 (020) 7067-2600

Spain (Includes Portugal):
Thomson Paraninfo
Calle Magallanes 25
28015 Madrid
España
Tel 34 (0)91 446-3350
Fax 34 (0)91 445-6218

PREFACE

The Sixth Edition of Financial Accounting focuses on analysis and interpretation while retaining the basics of relevant accounting processes. The focus on analyzing and interpreting real-life financial statements is a key part of this text. This begins with an analysis of Intel in the Introduction Chapter.

We have incorporated significant amounts of real world data into the text and problems. In addition, we have increased our major thrust of user analysis in the text and problems. We have done a very careful review of comments from our users and taken a hard look at exactly what is important for the introductory student. Because of this, we have been able to add significantly to use of real- world companies for analysis while significantly shortening the length of chapters and the overall text.

Chapters 6 through 18 include an analysis and interpretation focus of the text called a "Comprehensive Analysis Problem." The first of these problems appears in Chapter 6. We present the systematic methodology for doing these problems in the body of Chapter 6 using Dell Computer. The analysis uses a "Linked Spreadsheet." Each chapter through 18 contains a problem based on an actual company with a "Linked Spreadsheet" designed to help the student develop their analytical skills. The companies used in this series of problems include many that are familiar to the students such as Coca-Cola, Nike, Harley-Davidson, Reebok, and Starbucks.

Chapters 1 through 18 each contain an "Analyzing Information" section. This section presents information from financial statements of real-life companies. Then, we raise sets of user-oriented questions about this information and develop answers to these questions. We lead the student through the thought process necessary to respond to the real-life questions. End-of-chapter problems based on actual companies allow students to practice their new skills. We updated all of these sections with new companies and current financial data. We have used the experience and comments of our users to improve the "Analyzing Information" sections.

Our overall objective in our revisions is to focus on four standards of excellence: relevance, simplicity, clarity, and a vision of the future direction of accounting education.

Relevance

- Is a topic worthy of student and instructor time?

- Does an issue recognize changes in the business world?

- Is there a real-life application that will add excitement and meaning to the presentation?

Simplicity

- Are the chapters as concise as they can be with adequate coverage?

- Does an example or illustration cover all essential issues as simply and directly as possible?

- Are numbers easy to follow and understand?

- Are sections of the text written as simply and directly as possible?

Clarity
- Does the writing style use active voice and short sentences to achieve readability?

- Are illustrations effectively integrated into and explained by the text material?

- Does the text design allow key elements to be easily identified?

Vision
- Is the topic covered from a user perspective and supported by real-world examples?

- Are technical procedures linked to major business issues for a broader understanding of business and accounting concepts?

- Does the chapter pedagogy help students "learn to learn," enabling them to face future career demands?

- Do end-of-chapter materials include problems that require students to form judgments and interpretations?

RESPONSE TO CHANGES IN ACCOUNTING EDUCATION

We face a time of change in accounting education. From a pedagogical standpoint, the following are some of the most important overall changes in the Sixth Edition.

ONE OF THE MOST VISIBLE CHANGES YOU WILL NOTICE IS THE START OF THE TEXT. Most accounting texts begin with a long list of accounting concepts and analysis of business transactions. In our "Introduction to Using Accounting Information," we introduce students to planning, reporting, and assessment activities that each manager faces. To apply our discussion to real-life, we use 2004 data for Intel as an illustrative company in this introduction. **Our focus** is simple: total revenues and expenses on the income statement, and total assets, liabilities, and owners' equity on the balance sheet. **Our goal** is to create an interest in the uses of accounting *before* discussing the details. End-of-chapter problems in the Introduction involve analyzing Home Depot, Yahoo!, GAP, Limited Brands, Safeway, Inc., Whole Foods Market, Wal-Mart and Target.

Developments in the Sixth Edition include:

1. The financial accounting section now includes a new "Comprehensive Analysis Problem" in each chapter from 6 through 18. The first of these problems appears in Chapter 6. We present the systematic methodology for doing these problems in the body of Chapter 6 using Dell Computer. The analysis uses a "Linked Spreadsheet" contained on a diskette included with the text. Then each chapter through 18 contains a problem based on an actual company with a "Linked Spreadsheet" designed to help the student develop their analysis skills. The companies used in this series of problems include many that are familiar to the students such as Coca-Cola, Nike, Harley-Davidson, Reebok, and Starbucks.

2. Each financial accounting chapter includes a user perspective to analyzing financial information. In each "Analyzing Information" section, we present real-world data that highlights topics presented in that chapter. We then raise important questions about that data and take the student through an answer to each question. Walking through this analysis of real-world situations will help the student become a better user of financial statement information.

3. We have expanded real-life applications. *We now have a text that retains sound coverage of the accounting process but also includes an unprecedented amount of actual company data and a user orientation.*

4. Chapter introductions focus on the business issues underlying accounting concepts and applications that we will cover in that chapter. New data brings current real-world situations to the chapters.

5. We have continued to focus on readability and an active-voice writing style. We use short, concise sentences and text sections. This improves a text that students already rave about for its ease of learning.

6. We clearly identify major accounting issues in each chapter to focus on important concepts. After reading each chapter, students understand which issues are important.

7. We mark and integrate Learning Goals throughout the text and learning package. We mark all exercises and problems with the appropriate learning goals.

8. There is an extensive choice of assignment materials, including the following:

    a. All new *"Analyzing Information"* problems require analysis of real-world financial statement data from a user perspective. These problems follow the analysis format developed in the "Analyzing Information" section of the chapter. Complimenting these problems are the brand new "Comprehensive Analysis Problems" with Linked Spreadsheets at the end of Chapters 6–18.

    b. This edition adds new World-Wide-Web based problems that allow the student to use the web to obtain the data to do the analysis of the financial information.

    c. *Business Decision and Communication Problems* focus on forming judgments and developing writing skills.

    d. *Ethical Dilemmas* are cases that encourage sensitivity to potential conflicts of interest.

    e. Summary *Practice Cases* integrate accounting concepts for each chapter.

    f. *Practice Sets* integrate accounting concepts for major sections of the textbook. It is no longer necessary to buy separate practice sets. We have included two practice sets in the text.

    g. End-of-chapter exercises contain an extensive selection having a single Learning Goal. These allow each instructor to customize the course.

    h. Problems have multiple Learning Goals, which integrate topics in each chapter.

9. An improved design that enhances the learning features.

THE TEXTBOOK

The introductory accounting course is usually a student's first exposure to business terms and issues. Presenting accounting concepts in a logical and careful order is critical to capturing and enhancing student interest. Offering an extensive and varied set of self-test and end-of-chapter materials is essential to maximizing student learning. Each chapter of the Sixth Edition uses creative pedagogical features consistently to create student excitement about accounting.

Pedagogical Features for Each Chapter

1. The textbook presents specific, clearly stated Learning Goals throughout. Each chapter begins with a list of the Learning Goals. Each Learning Goal appears next to the appropriate material in the chapter. The end-of-chapter items show the Learning Goals covered.

2. The Understanding Business Issues section helps students appreciate the *real-world significance* of each chapter.

3. We use an *active-voice writing style* that fosters reading interest and comprehension.

4. Pages are uncluttered and feature a design that draws attention to key concepts and highlights important relationships.

5. We continue to key text discussion and explanations to chapter illustrations by using boxed reference numbers. This permits students to link explanations and illustrations easily.

6. The "Analyzing Information" section of each chapter leads the student through a *user analysis* of real-world financial statement information.

7. *Real-life company* examples throughout apply the accounting concepts to actual practice.

8. An end-of-chapter Learning Goals Review captures the main points of each topic studied in the chapter.

9. Demonstration Problems contain *Solution Approach* sections, usually for each requirement. This is a unique feature of our text that we were the first to develop. Each Solution Approach contains hints and discussion of the logical thought process that students should use in solving the problem. This feature will help the student in learning-to-learn. Studying the Demonstration Problem is an excellent chapter review.

Learning Features for the Entire Text

1. The textbook uses a master chart of accounts for all illustrations and problems. We print this in the front and back endpapers for easy reference.

2. The Sixth Edition contains two Practice Sets (usable after Chapters 3 or 4, and 10) that integrate and review major sections of the text. This allows the potential use of three practice sets without the student purchasing extra materials. These are full feature practice sets, comparable in coverage to separately purchased practice sets.

3. Appendix B includes a summary set of financial statements and explanatory notes for a hypothetical company. In the margins are boxed explanations of all important items. In Appendix B, we emphasize a *user's analysis* of published annual financial statements.

ORGANIZATION OF THE TEXTBOOK

Part I: "The Accounting Model" (Chapters 1–5)

Part I develops the basic accounting model using a simplified corporate form. Chapters 1–4 explain and illustrate the concepts, techniques, and steps in the accounting cycle. We introduce the statement of cash flows early in the text.

Part II: "Internal Control and Income Measurement Issues" (Chapters 6–10)

Part II introduces internal controls and cash accounting issues. Chapters then cover income measurement and valuation issues relating to receivables, short-term financing, inventories, and long-term assets.

Part III: "Financing and Investing Issues" (Chapters 11–14)

Chapters 11 and 12 discuss the corporation as a unique form of business organization. We discuss accounting for the issuance of bonds and investments in bonds and stocks (Chapters 13 and 14) using both the straight-line and the effective interest methods.

Part IV: "Reporting and Analysis Issues" (Chapters 15–18)

Chapter 15 illustrates the statement of cash flows, using a unique introduction that shows interrelationships among the financial statements. Chapter 16 discusses financial statement analysis with an emphasis on the significance and interpretation of the results. Chapter 17 describes and illustrates consolidated statements. The section concludes with Chapter 18 on international accounting and financial reporting issues.

End-of-Book Appendices

The textbook includes three appendixes. Appendix A considers basic income tax procedures, using flow diagrams to present an overview of income tax computations. It also introduces interperiod income tax allocation. Appendix B contains a summary of basic financial statements and explanatory notes for a hypothetical company. Appendix C contains the coverage of present value concepts and tables for four basic present value techniques.

In addition to the textbook, the teaching package includes a remarkable set of teaching tools for the instructor and tools of learning for the student.

FOR THE INSTRUCTOR

The textbook authors have taken primary responsibility for these parts of the package. This brings a consistency to these materials that cannot be achieved when nonauthors develop these supplementary materials.

Solutions Manual

The text authors prepare the Solutions Manual. Included are solutions for Questions for Group Learning, Exercises, Problems, Practice Cases, Business Decision and Communication Problems, Ethical Dilemmas, and Practice Sets.

Electronic Teaching Media

A series of electronic slide presentations developed using PowerPoint is available for many chapters.

Test Resource Manual

The test bank includes 30 true/false, 50 multiple-choice questions, and 15–20 short problems for each chapter. We also include solutions with supporting computations for selected items. Approximately one-half of the multiple-choice items are conceptual and one-half are problem oriented. We reference all test items to chapter Learning Goals.

Computerized Test Bank

All test items are available in computerized format for use on Windows systems. The software can generate multiple versions of each exam with answer keys. The system also allows instructors to edit existing questions and add new ones.

ACKNOWLEDGMENTS

We would like to thank all text users (both professors and students) who have given us many valuable comments. Your ideas have contributed greatly to this significant revision. We also wish to express our thanks to our accounting professors who taught us both accounting concepts and professional/ethical responsibilities.

We would also like to express our very deep appreciation to the staff at Thomson Learning who have worked so diligently on this project. Developing and publishing a principles of accounting text is a tremendous undertaking.

Richard Kochanek
Storrs, Connecticut

Douglas Hillman
Des Moines, Iowa

Noah Barsky
Villanova, Pennsylvania

ABOUT THE AUTHORS

RICHARD F. KOCHANEK, Ph.D., is an emeritus professor of accounting in the School of Business at the University of Connecticut. Professor Kochanek received his B.B.A. and MBA degrees from the University of Massachusetts and his Ph.D. from the University of Missouri. He joined the accounting faculty at the University of Connecticut in 1972.

Although he has taught a variety of undergraduate and graduate courses, his primary teaching responsibility has been the accounting principles course. Professor Kochanek has received every outstanding teaching award the University of Connecticut offers. These include outstanding accounting professor, outstanding professor in the School of Business, the United Technologies Corporation outstanding undergraduate teaching award, outstanding MBA professor, and the Alumni Award for the outstanding teacher at the University of Connecticut. He was one of the first four faculty named as "University Teaching Fellows".

Professor Kochanek has published in *The Accounting Review, Accounting Horizons, Management Accounting, The CPA Journal*, and *Financial Executive*. He is a recipient of the Competitive Manuscript Contest Award of the American Accounting Association. Professor Kochanek has been a faculty intern with Price Waterhouse, and has conducted executive seminars in financial reporting issues for banks, insurance companies, manufacturing companies, and public accounting firms.

A. DOUGLAS HILLMAN, Ph.D., CMA, is the Aliber Professor of Accounting at Drake University in Des Moines, Iowa. He obtained a bachelor of arts degree in accounting from Augustana College in Rock Island, Illinois, in 1965. He received his master of science degree in accounting from the University of Denver in 1967, and at the University of Missouri—Columbia in 1970 he was awarded a doctor of philosophy degree in accounting. Dr. Hillman has been a professor of accounting at Drake since 1970; he is a certified management accountant.

Professor Hillman's foremost teaching emphasis is in the principles of accounting course. His secondary teaching emphasis is in cost and managerial accounting at both undergraduate and graduate levels. He also teaches in the CPA Review and Certified Property and Casualty Underwriter Programs at Drake. Professor Hillman has been recognized on numerous occasions for his teaching excellence. He has received the outstanding teacher award from the College of Business at Drake University. He has served as Director of Graduate Studies in Business and Director of the School of Accounting while at Drake.

Professor Hillman has published and presented papers in the *Accounting Review*, at the American Accounting Association meetings, and at numerous regional meetings, and he has been a regular contributor to the Certified Management Accounting examination. He does consulting in accounting information systems for small business and is a member of the American Accounting Association, the Institute of Management Accountants, and the Institute of Certified Management Accountants. He has served on committees of the American Accounting Association, the Federation of Schools of Accounting, and the Institute of Management Accountants. And he is the past chairman of the Information System/MAS Section of the American Accounting Association.

NOAH P. BARSKY, Ph.D., CPA, CMA, is an associate professor of accountancy in the College of Commerce and Finance at Villanova University. Professor Barsky received his B.S. and M.S. in accounting from Penn State University and his Ph.D. from the University of Connecticut. He joined the faculty at Villanova University in 1998.

Professor Barsky has taught a variety of financial and managerial accounting courses at four different universities. He was recognized as the 2003 Villanova University Teacher of the year and has received other awards for his teaching and scholarship.

Professor Barsky is an active member of the American Accounting Association, the American Institute of CPAs, and the Institute of Management Accountants. He has given research presentations at numerous national meetings of academic and professional associations. He has also authored five books and published articles in the *Journal of Accounting, Auditing and Accountability, Issues in Accounting Education* and *Strategic Finance*.

CONTENTS IN BRIEF

CONTENTS

Appendices

THE ACCOUNTING MODEL

INTRODUCTION TO USING ACCOUNTING INFORMATION

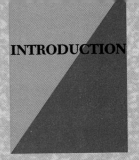

Chapter Thought

"A rock pile ceases to be a rock pile the moment a single man contemplates it, bearing within him the image of a cathedral."

Saint Exupery

LEARNING GOALS

After studying Introduction, you should be able to:

1. Define *accounting*

2. Identify users of accounting information.

3. Define *accounting entity* and compare different types of business ownership.

4. Identify the purpose and explain the types of information contained in the (1) balance sheet, (2) income statement, and (3) statement of cash flows.

5. Analyze information contained in the financial statements to identify favorable and unfavorable trends for real-life companies.

UNDERSTANDING BUSINESS ISSUES

WELCOME TO ACCOUNTING! We are very excited about showing you concepts which you can use to make business decisions. Many students approach the study of accounting with a sense of apprehension. Please don't worry. Our goals in this text are: (1) focus only on important concepts, (2) explain everything as simply and clearly as possible, and most important, (3) enable you to **use** accounting concepts in your personal life and career. Who knows, perhaps you may even choose to major in accounting. The following cartoon shows how attractive a career in accounting may be:

"It's the old story. I was in the middle of a successful acting career when I was bitten by the accounting bug."

Drawing by Leo Cullum; © 1992
The New Yorker Magazine, Inc.

But, let's not get ahead of ourselves.

Most accounting texts begin with a long list of accounting concepts and analysis of business transactions. We are going to save some of these details for later. Right now, it is more important that you understand and identify two major classes of business activities:

1. **Business planning activities each manager faces.** These are activities involving (a) operating the business each day (operating activities), (b) investing the resources of the business in income producing assets (investing activities), and (c) obtaining financial resources (financing activities).

2. **Business reporting and assessment activities each manager faces.** These include preparing and interpreting reports which summarize the results of business activities. The main summary accounting reports are the (a) balance sheet, (b) income statement, and (c) statement of cash flows.

To apply our discussion to real-life, we will use Intel Corporation as an illustrative company in this Introduction to Using Accounting Information. Intel is the world's leading producer of microprocessors. During the period from January 1, 1994, to December 31, 2004, total sales of microprocessors for Intel grew from $11.5 billion to $34.2 billion. The number of Intel-employees grew from 32,600 in 1994 to 85,000 in 2004. Investment in research and development has increased from 1.0 billion in 1994 to 4.8 billion in 2004. This is truly a record of significant accomplishment. Throughout this entire text, we will show you how to interpret accounting information for actual companies you are familiar with.

Business Planning Activities

Individual Point of View

While in high school, you had to develop goals and personal objectives for your life after graduation. These included choices for careers, colleges, and courses. Setting goals and objectives is the starting point for developing a plan of action.

Now, as a college student, you face basic planning activities in managing your financial affairs each day. Questions you must periodically ask include:

1. How much cash will I need for personal expenses such as food, clothing, and supplies to survive each day? How much can I earn from summer and part-time jobs to offset these expenses? (These represent operating decisions.)

2. How much cash will I need for college tuition, fees, and books each year? If I need a car, how much will it cost? (These represent investing decisions you are making in your future.)

3. How will I obtain the cash resources necessary to meet my investing and operating requirements (not met from summer and part-time jobs)? Possible sources include proceeds from loans and scholarships, and assistance from parents. (These represent financing decisions.)

Business Point of View

Business leaders also need to establish and continually review organizational goals and objectives. From an operating perspective, management must plan and control the business activities. **Planning** is a process that includes the following phases:

1. Developing assumptions about the future environment the business will operate in and the competition it will face.

2. Establishing goals and objectives for the business.

3. Making decisions about courses of action for the business.

4. Developing and putting plans into action.

5. Evaluating the results based on the action plans.

Budgeting and controlling are part of the planning process. A **budget** is a financial plan for a future period. **Controlling** is the process of measuring and evaluating actual performance and taking corrective action. For example, the sales manager may receive a report that shows planned sales (budgeted) compared to actual sales. Based on the evaluation, managers take appropriate action.

Net sales of microprocessors have grown from $4,779 million in 1991 to $34,209 million in 2004. The following chart illustrates the growth in net sales from 1991 to 2004.

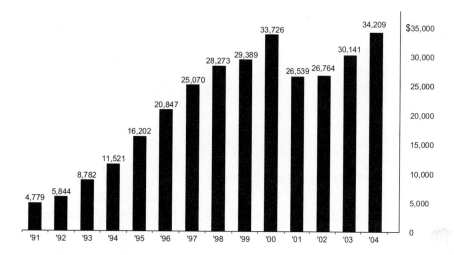

Intel Corporation
Consolidated Net Sales (millions)

To continue this dramatic growth, management has sought to find new growth markets. This objective is summarized in the following statement from the 2004 annual report:

> *Worldwide growth is our story for 2004, a year in which more than 75% of our revenue came from geographies outside the Americas, up from 57% just five years ago. The digital transformation is only beginning to reach the billions of people in countries where the build-out of the communications and computing infrastructure is in its infancy.*

Management of Intel faces basic planning activities in managing the future growth of the Company. Questions management must periodically ask include:

1. How much cash will the business generate from sales of microprocessors? How much cash will they need to purchase manufacturing materials, to pay employees, to pay advertising and operating costs, and to pay income taxes? (These represent <u>operating</u> decisions.)

2. How much cash will the business need for investments in new plants and expansion into new markets? (These represent <u>investing</u> decisions the business is making in its future.)

3. How will the business obtain cash resources necessary to meet investing and operating requirements? Possible sources include borrowing money from financial institutions and issuing additional shares of ownership stock to investors. A possible use includes paying borrowed money back when it is due. (These represent <u>financing</u> decisions.)

To illustrate the magnitude of these decisions for Intel, for 2004, the total dollar amounts for each of these three activities were:

1.	Net cash *inflow* from operating activities	$13,119,000,000
2.	Net cash *outflow* for investing activities	$(5,032,000,000)
3.	Net cash *outflow* for financing activities	$(7,651,000,000)

BUSINESS REPORTING AND ASSESSMENT ACTIVITIES

The ultimate purpose of this book is to enable you to use accounting information to make business decisions. In chapters 1-4 you will learn about the basic financial statements a business prepares and the accounting records from which they prepare them. In this Introduction, we are more concerned with showing you (1) an overview of the financial statements and (2) how to begin to interpret this information. We will introduce information about the accounting records in Chapter 1

The Accounting Information System

Learning Goal 1   Define accounting.

Accounting is an information system. It generates financial information about a business that users rely on to make decisions. Exhibit I.1 shows the flow of data and information in a typical accounting information system. The first step is to (1) *collect* financial and other economic data. After gathering the data, we must measure the data and record it. Just as physical measurements allow us to learn about the world around us, economic measurements allow us to evaluate a business. We make accounting measurements in financial terms. Next, we (2) *process* the data by organizing and storing it for use in reporting. Finally, we summarize the accounting data into reports that (3) *communicate* information to financial statement users.

An **accounting information system** is the resources and procedures in a business that changes economic data into financial information. Managers use this information to make decisions and to report the results of the business to other external users and internal users.

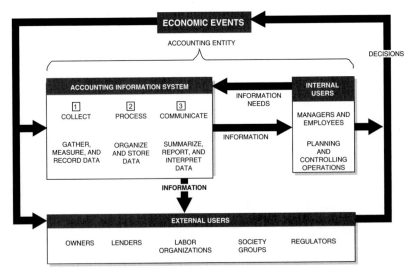

EXHIBIT **I.1**

The Accounting Information System

Users of Accounting Information

Learning Goal 2   Identify users of accounting information.

As we can see in Exhibit I.1 the accounting information system serves *users* inside and outside the business organization. **Management accounting** is the part of accounting that provides information to internal users. **Financial accounting** is the part that provides information to external users. The users' information needs should determine the design of the reports prepared by the system.

Internal Users (Management Accounting)

Internal users are those people within an organization who make decisions affecting the business. Accounting information has two roles in these decisions. First, it shows the need for action. Second, it provides a basis for choosing among alternatives. For example, after comparing the profitability of a business with competitors, management may first observe that our costs are higher. As a result, management might ask: "By how much will the use of different new types of factory equipment enable us to be more efficient and reduce costs?"

External Users (Financial Accounting)

In addition to managers who run the business internally, various other groups *outside* the company need information about a business. We refer to these interest groups as **external users**. This is because, unlike managers, the external user groups do not have direct access to the records of the business. Instead, they depend on management to provide information. Exhibit I.2 summarizes the external user interest groups and the types of business information they require.

Owners hope the value of their investment will increase. Owners may be individuals, institutions such as pension funds, or employees who have purchased ownership shares. They use financial statements to assess the current and long-term profitability of the business.

Lenders or *creditors* are individuals or institutions, such as a bank or insurance company, who lend money to a business. Lenders use financial statements to determine whether a business seeking a loan has the ability to make interest payments and to repay the loan.

Labor organizations such as unions have an interest in increased wages, benefits, and jobs. They use financial statements to assess the current and long-term profitability of the business.

Customers want to know if the business can supply a high quality product at a fair price. They use financial statements to help assess the ability of the business to deliver these products on a timely basis.

Society groups want to know if the business leaders are ethical and environmentally responsible. Information in the financial statements showing business expenditures for environmental and social programs help users assess the responsibility of management in these areas.

Governmental regulatory agencies such as tax authorities also use accounting reports. For example, businesses prepare income tax returns with information taken from the accounting records.

EXTERNAL USER INTEREST GROUPS	TYPES OF INFORMATION REQUIRED
Owners—Current & Prospective	• What is the current and long-term profitability of the business? • How does an investment in this business compare with other alternatives?
Lenders (Creditors)	• What is the current and long-term profitability of the business? • What is the ability of the company to pay amounts owed on time? • If the company were forced to go out of business, will we get our money back?
Labor Organizations	• What is the current and long-term profitability of the business? • What is the ability of the business to pay increased wages and benefits? • What is the ability of the business to support new jobs?
Customers	• Does the business offer competitively priced high quality products? • Does the business finance customer purchases? • Does the business support the customer with product warranties and service? • Will the business be able to supply products on a continual basis?
Society Groups	• Does the business have responsible manufacturing and business practices? • Is the business environmentally responsible? • Does management maintain high ethical standards?
Government Regulatory Agencies	• Does the company have responsible financial reporting and disclosures? • Does the company maintain accurate and complete financial records? • Is the company in compliance with regulatory requirements?

EXHIBIT 1.2

External User Interest Groups for a Business

Primary Financial Statements

We have described the role of accounting information in decision making. Now we are ready to introduce and begin to interpret three primary financial statements business organizations prepare:

1. Balance sheet

2. Income statement

3. Statement of cash flows

At this point, we want to show you an *overview* of the broad classes of information these three statements contain. In order to understand the basis for the financial statements, we must first explain the entity concept and discuss different types of business organizations.

The Entity Concept

Learning Goal 3   Define accounting entity and compare different types of business ownership.

Accounting reports summarize the activities of a business unit for which users must make decisions. The accounting concept that identifies the unit is called the *entity* concept. It is defined as follows:

An **accounting entity** is any organization unit for which we gather and process financial and economic data for the purpose of decision making.

An accounting entity may be a large company like Intel or it may be a local grocery store. We must develop a set of records and financial statements for *each* entity before we can make a decision on that business unit.

Types of Business Organization

Businesses organize in one of three ways: single proprietorship, partnership, or corporation.

Single proprietorship is a business owned by one person. Many small retail stores and service businesses operate as single proprietorships. They are the most numerous type of business entities in the United States. For accounting purposes, we treat a single proprietorship as an entity separate from its owner. Legally, however, the business owner is personally responsible for any debts incurred by the business. If the business fails, the owner must pay any claims against the business from his or her personal property.

In a **partnership**, two or more people choose to join in a business venture to earn and share profits. Many people such as doctors, lawyers, and accountants form partnerships. Like a single proprietorship, the partnership is an accounting entity separate from its owners. Legally, any partner is responsible for debts the business incurs. Partnerships are formed by contract or oral agreement. They dissolve upon the death of a partner or upon the closing of the business.

Corporations are legal entities issued a charter by a state. Most corporations have multiple owners, who buy ownership shares in the company called capital stock. Owners can sell or transfer ownership shares from one stockholder to another without affecting the operation of the corporation. This allows a corporation to operate after the death or retirement of its founders. Because a corporation is a separate legal entity, it is accountable for its own acts and its own debts. The owners have limited liability. If a corporation ceases operation, the most an owner can lose is the amount of his or her investment in the corporation. Limited liability of stockholders and the easy transfer of stock ownership enable corporations to attract large amounts of resources to invest. Most large companies such as Intel are corporations. In this text, we focus on corporations as a type of business organization.

Financial Statements

Learning Goal 4   Identify the purpose and explain the types of information contained in the (1) balance sheet, (2) income statement, and (3) statement of cash flows.

The primary financial statements are the balance sheet, the income statement, and the statement of cash flows. The following sections discuss the purpose of each statement and the types of information each shows. At this point in the text, we will focus only on major categories in the financial statements. We will introduce details for each category in Chapter 1

Balance Sheet

The **balance sheet** summarizes assets, liabilities, and owners' equity as of a specific moment in time. Exhibit I.3 shows the comparative balance sheets for Intel as of December 25, 2004, and December 27, 2003.

INTEL CORPORATION
(1) COMPARATIVE BALANCE SHEETS
(2) December 25, 2004 And December 27, 2003
(in millions)

	December 25 2004	December 27 2003
(3) Total assets	$ 48,143	$ 47,143
(4) Total liabilities	$ 9,564	$ 9,297
(5) Total owners' equity	38,579	37,846
(6) Total liabilities and owners' equity	$ 48,143	$ 47,143

Explanations of numbered items:

(1) Balance sheet summarizes assets, liabilities, and owners' equity at a specific moment in time.
(2) Dates covered for Intel are as of December 25, 2004, and December 27, 2003.
(3) Assets are economic resources or items of value owned by the business.
(4) Liabilities are debts of the business. They represent the creditors' claims against the assets.
(5) Owners' equity is the sum of all ownership claims against assets of the business.
(6) For a balance sheet, total assets must equal total liabilities plus total owners' equity. This is the basic accounting equation. **(ASSETS = LIABILITIES + OWNERS' EQUITY)**

EXHIBIT **I.3**

Comparative Balance Sheets for Intel with Explanations of Financial Statement Items

---

Assets are the *economic resources* or items of value a business owns. Specific examples for Intel include cash, inventories of microprocessors, and buildings. **Liabilities** are claims against the assets by creditors. For example, Intel may have purchased office supplies on credit. The amounts owed as of a balance sheet date represent debts or liabilities. **Owners' equity** is the sum of all claims against the assets by the owners. As we will explain more completely later, owners' equity increases by additional owner investment and by profits the business has from operations. Owners' equity decreases by losses from operations. Owners' equity is a *residual* interest. If a company goes out of business, the creditors have first claim on the assets of the company before owners receive any money.

For a balance sheet, total assets must equal total liabilities plus total owners' equity. We refer to this equality as the *basic accounting equation*. The following must always be true for any business:

ASSETS   =   LIABILITIES + OWNERS' EQUITY
(Economic resources)   (Claims on assets)

For Intel, total assets of $48,143 million equal total liabilities of $9,564 million and total owners' equity of $38,579 million on December 25, 2004. The balance sheet shows the financial position of a business on a specific date. It informs the reader how much resources (assets) a business has and who provided the financing, creditor sources (liabilities) or owner sources (owners' equity).

Income Statement

The **income statement** presents the results of operations for a period of time. Exhibit I.4 shows the comparative income statements for Intel for the 2004 fiscal year ended December 25, 2004, and the 2003 fiscal year ended December 27, 2003. In the income statement, we compare total revenues and total expenses.

Companies end their fiscal year at different times. Most retail companies (such as Target, GAP, Inc., and Lands' End) end their financial reporting year at the end of January. This corresponds to the end of the busy holiday season. A period of 12 consecutive months selected by a business as the reporting period for annual reports is called a **fiscal year**. For Target, January 29, 2005, is the end of the 2004 fiscal year.

Businesses have an increase in assets when they perform services or sell goods. We call these inflows of assets **revenues**. Businesses use assets or incur liabilities when earning revenues. We call these outflows of assets or increases in liabilities **expenses**. Revenues and expenses are the result of operating activities. For Intel in 2004, total revenues were $34,209 million and total expenses were $26,693 million.

When total revenues exceed total expenses, we call the difference between revenues and expenses **net income**. In this case, the business operates at a profit. When total expenses exceed total revenues, we call the difference between revenues and expenses a **net loss**. For Intel in fiscal 2004, revenues exceeded expenses and net income was $7,516 million.

INTEL CORPORATION
(1) COMPARATIVE INCOME STATEMENTS
(2) For The Years Ended December 25, 2004, And December 27, 2003
(*in millions*)

	Years Ended	
	December 25 2004	December 27 2003
(3) Total revenues	$34,209	$30,141
(4) Total expenses	26,693	24,500
(5) Net income	$ 7,516	$ 5,641

Explanations of numbered items:

(1) Income statement compares revenues and expenses for a period of time.
(2) Periods of time covered for Intel are the years ended December 25, 2004, (fiscal 2004), and December 27, 2003, (fiscal 2003).
(3) Total revenues for Intel are the total increases in assets from sales of product.
(4) Total expenses for Intel are the total assets used or liabilities incurred in the process of generating revenues.
(5) The difference between revenues and expenses for a period is net income (if revenues exceed expenses) or net loss (if expenses exceed revenues).

EXHIBIT I.4

Comparative Income Statements for Intel with Explanations of Financial Statement Items

Statement of Cash Flows

Overall, the **statement of cash flows** shows all of the reasons why cash on the balance sheet changed from one date to another. The statement of cash flows presents the cash flows from operating, investing, and financing activities for a period of time. Exhibit I.5 shows the comparative cash flow statements for Intel for the years ended December 25, 2004, and December 27, 2003.

Net cash from *operating activities* shows the difference between cash received from revenues and cash paid for expenses on the income statement. Cash from operating activities is the main source of cash inflow for many businesses. Net cash from *investing activities* shows the cash outflows from buying new long-term assets and the cash inflows from selling old long-term assets used in the business. Examples of investing activities include buying and selling land, buildings, and equipment. Net cash from *financing activities* shows the net cash inflow or outflow from additional financing a business needs to pay for operating and investing activities. Examples of financing activities include issuing (or buying back) additional shares of ownership stock and issuing (or retiring) long-term debt.

For Intel in fiscal 2004, net cash provided by operating activities was $13,119 million. Net cash used by investing activities was $(5,032) million. Net cash used by financing activities was $(7,651) million. The result of these three cash inflows and outflows was an overall increase in cash for Intel of $436 million. This increased the cash balance from $7,971 million at the beginning of the year to $8,407 million at the end.

INTEL CORPORATION
(1) COMPARATIVE STATEMENTS OF CASH FLOWS
(2) For the Years Ended December 25, 2004, And December 27, 2003
(in millions)

	Years Ended	
	December 25 2004	December 27 2003
(3) Net cash provided by (used by) operating activities	$13,119	$11,515
(4) Net cash provided by (used by) investing activities	(5,032)	(7,090)
(5) Net cash provided by (used by) financing activities	(7,651)	(3,858)
(6) Net increase (decrease) in cash	$ 436	$ (567)
Cash balance, beginning of year	7,971	7,404
Cash balance, end of year	$ 8,407	$ 7,971

Explanations of numbered items:

(1) Statement of cash flows summarizes cash inflows and outflows from operating, investing, and financing activities for a period of time.

(2) Periods of time covered for Intel are the years ended December 25, 2004 (fiscal 2004), and December 27, 2003 (fiscal 2003).

(3) Cash flows from operating activities include cash receipts and cash payments from transactions that relate to net income on the income statement.

(4) Cash flows from investing activities include cash receipts and cash payments from transactions that relate to (1) buying and selling plant assets, (2) buying and selling investment securities, and (3) lending money and collecting on the loans.

(5) Cash flows from financing activities include cash receipts and cash payments from transactions that relate to (1) obtaining resources from owners and providing them a return on their investment and (2) obtaining resources from creditors and repaying amounts borrowed.

(6) The net result of operating, investing, and financing cash flows for a period represents the net increase or decrease in the amount of cash the business has.

EXHIBIT **I.5**

Comparative Statements of Cash Flows for Intel with Explanations of Financial Statement Items

PUBLISHED ANNUAL FINANCIAL REPORTS

A primary objective of studying financial accounting is to understand and interpret published financial reports. Throughout this textbook, we will use many real-life company examples. In addition to the financial statements, the annual financial report contains many other items of interest to financial statement users. In this section, we will discuss the letter to stockholders, management's discussion and analysis of operations and financial condition, and the report of the independent accountant.

Letter to Stockholders

At the beginning of the published annual report for most corporations, the chief officers include a *letter to stockholders*. The purpose of the letter is to give the chairman of the board and the president a chance to comment on the operating results of the past year, the financial condition at the end of the year, and prospects and plans for the future. The letter to stockholders gives financial statement users an overview of the company's recent performance. The following excerpts from the 2004 letter to stockholders for Intel Corporation highlight record performance levels.

Intel Corporation

Excerpts from Letter to Stockholders (2004 Annual Report)

To Our Stockholders

We ended 2004 with double-digit revenue gains, and robust demand for Intel® architecture products across all geographies. Our new products, global presence and investments in manufacturing capacity allowed us to post record revenue for 2004 of $34.2 billion, up 13.5% from 2003. Net income for 2004 was $7.5 billion, up 33% from 2003. During the year, we paid record cash dividends of $1 billion, announced two doublings of our cash dividend and used $7.5 billion to repurchase 301 million shares of common stock. We are optimistic going into 2005 and expect continued growth based on the momentum of our current products and the introduction of dual-core microprocessors across a range of platforms.

Management's Discussion and Analysis (MDA)

The Securities and Exchange Commission (SEC) is an independent federal agency which governs companies that sell securities to investors on stock exchanges. For many companies, the tone of the letter to stockholders is positive and encouraging about the future. The SEC believes that somewhere in the annual report, management should prepare a detailed explanation of any favorable or unfavorable trends. The SEC requires companies to address these areas in a special section of the annual report called *management's discussion and analysis (MDA)*.

The management's discussion and analysis section of the annual report provides the financial statement user with a more detailed explanation of changes in operating results and financial position. The first part of the MDA discusses the results of operations, comparing the current year with preceding years. Other parts of the MDA discuss the financial condition and liquidity of the company. The SEC also requires companies to discuss future trends and cash needs. The following excerpts from the 2004 MDA discuss the future outlook for Intel.

Intel Corporation

Excerpts from Management's Discussion and Analysis (MDA) (2004 Annual Report)

Outlook

Our future results of operations and the other forward-looking statements contained in this filing, including this MD&A, involve a number of risks and uncertainties—in particular, the statements regarding our goals and strategies, new product introductions, plans to cultivate new businesses, market segment share and growth rate assumptions, future economic conditions and recovery in the communications businesses, revenue, pricing, gross margin and costs, capital spending, depreciations and amortization, research and development expenses, potential impairment of investments, the tax rate and pending tax and legal proceedings.

We believes that we have the product offerings, facilities, personnel, and competitive and financial resources for continued business success, but future revenues, costs, gross margins and profits are all influenced by a number of factors, including those discussed above, all of which are inherently difficult to forecast.

The Report of the Independent Accountant

The financial statements of a company show management's view of the firm. Management has the primary responsibility for the fairness of presentation and the degree of disclosure in the financial statements and accompanying explanatory notes. The role of the independent accountant is to provide a check on the financial reporting of management. The result of the examination by the independent accountant is a report that comments on both the scope of the examination and the opinion on the financial statements.

Exhibit I.6 shows the report of independent accountants taken from the *2004 Annual Report of Intel*. The independent public accounting firm of Ernst & Young used by Intel is

---

Report of Ernst & Young LLP
Independent auditors

The Board of Directors and Stockholders, Intel Corporation

We have audited the accompanying consolidated balance sheets of Intel Corporation as of December 25, 2004 and December 27, 2003, and the related consolidated statements of income, stockholders' equity, and cash flows for each of the three years in the period ended December 25, 2004. These financial statements are the responsibility of the Company's management. Our responsibility is to express an opinion on these financial statements based on our audits.

We conducted our audits in accordance with generally accepted auditing standards. Those standards require that we plan and perform the audit to obtain reasonable assurance about whether the financial statements are free of material misstatement. An audit includes examining, on a test basis, evidence supporting the amounts and disclosures in the financial statements. An audit also includes assessing the accounting principles used and significant estimates made by management, as well as

evaluating the overall financial statement presentation. We believe that our audits provide a reasonable basis for our opinion.

In our opinion, the financial statements referred to above present fairly, in all material respects, the consolidated financial position of Intel Corporation at December 25, 2004 and December 27, 2003, and the consolidated results of its operations and its cash flows for each of the three years in the period ended December 25, 2004, in conformity with generally accepted accounting principles.

Ernst & Young LLP

San Jose, California
February 15, 2005

EXHIBIT **I.6**

Report of Independent Accountants from 2004 Annual Report of Intel Corporation

one of the largest public accounting firms in the world. Explanations of items in Exhibit I.6 follow:

1. The report of independent accountants addresses either the board of directors or the stock-holders of the company, or both, rather than management.

2. The introductory paragraph specifies the financial statements audited, acknowledges that the financial statements are the primary responsibility of management, and states that the responsibility of the independent accountant is to express an opinion on the statements.

3. The second paragraph states the auditor's responsibility to provide reasonable—not absolute—assurance that the financial statements are free from material errors and irregularities. In addition, a brief description of what an audit is introduces some important concepts involved in an audit.

4. We call the third paragraph the opinion paragraph. In this paragraph, the auditor states whether the financial statements fairly present the financial position, results of operations, and cash flows in conformity with generally accepted accounting principles. For Intel, the 2004 independent accountant's report states that the financial statements fairly present the results of operations and financial condition. We frequently call this an *unqualified* or *clean opinion*. If the financial statements do not fairly present this information, then the auditor must provide additional paragraphs to specify their reservations and concerns.

ANALYZING INFORMATION

Learning Goal 5   Analyze information contained in the financial statements to identify favorable and unfavorable trends for real-life companies.

One goal of this text is to show you how to use accounting information to make decisions. This is best done in a series of small steps. So far, we have looked at the information contained in the balance sheet, income statement, and statement of cash flows. Now we will show you the first steps in analyzing and interpreting the balance sheet and income statement. We will expand these steps and add the statement of cash flows in later chapters.

Common-Size Statements

Frequently, it is much easier to see relationships if we show financial statement items in percentages instead of dollars. In a **common-size statement**, we express each item in the statement as a percent of the total for that statement. In a balance sheet, we set both total assets and total liabilities + owners' equity each at 100%. We then divide each statement item amount by the total amount. This expresses each item as a percent of the total. In an income statement, we set total revenues at 100%. Then, we divide all income statement item amounts by total revenues to express each item as a percent of total revenues. As you will see, common-size statements allow the user to quickly observe trends over time for one company or to compare different companies. We show balance sheets and income statements with common-size percents for Intel in Exhibits I.7 and I.8

Balance Sheet Analysis

To make the analysis easy to follow, we will first state questions you might ask for the balance sheet. Then we will examine appropriate information from the balance sheet and indicate whether the

INTEL CORPORATION
COMPARATIVE COMMON-SIZE BALANCE SHEETS
December 25, 2004 And December 27, 2003
(*in millions*)

	December 25 2004	December 27 2003	Common-size Percentages	
			December 25 2004	December 27 2003
Total assets	$ 48,143	$ 47,143	100.0%*	100.0%*
Total liabilities	$ 9,564	$ 9,297	19.9%	19.7%
Total owners' equity	38,579	37,846	80.1%	80.3%
Total liabilities and owners' equity	$ 48,173	$ 47,143	100.0%*	100.0%*

* Always set at 100% in a common-size balance sheet.

EXHIBIT **I.7**

Comparative Common-size Balance Sheets for Intel

percentage or trend is favorable or unfavorable. Often, the identification of an item as favorable or unfavorable is just the beginning of our analysis. We will refine our questions as we go through the text. Exhibit I.7 shows the comparative balance sheets with additional columns showing common-size percentages. In a common-size balance sheet, we always set total assets and total liabilities + owners' equity each equal to 100%. To illustrate a common-size percent computation, total liabilities as of December 25, 2004, as a percent of total liabilities and owners' equity is 19.9% ($9,564 ÷ $48,143).

Question 1. Are total assets for a company higher or lower this year versus last year? In comparing different companies (which we will do later), which company has higher total assets?

Analysis 1. For Intel, total assets at December 25, 2004 ($48,143 million) are greater than the total at December 27, 2003 ($47,143 million). At this point, we cannot say whether the decrease in total assets is favorable or unfavorable. Later in this analysis, we will relate the increase in assets on the balance sheet to the change in revenues on the income statement to reach a conclusion.

Question 2. What is the percent change in total assets from last year to this year?

Analysis 2. We can compute a percent change in total assets from the prior year as follows:

$$\textbf{Percent change} = 100 \times \frac{\text{Dollar Amount of Change}^*}{\text{Dollar Amount for Prior Year}} \qquad {}^*\text{current year} - \text{prior year}$$

In this case, the percent increase in total assets from December 27, 2003, to December 25, 2004, is:

$$2.1\% = 100 \times \frac{\$1,000^*}{\$47,143} \qquad {}^* \$48,143 - \$47,143$$

This allows us to see the that the total assests for Intel have increased 2.1%. As we will see later in the Demonstration Problem for this Introduction, the growth percents help us to compare different companies.

Question 3. Is the percent of total liabilities to total liabilities + owners' equity increasing or decreasing? As a result, is there more or less risk that a business could not pay its debts?

Analysis 3. In Exhibit I.7 refer to the common-size percent for liabilities. The percent of liabilities has increased from 19.7% on December 27, 2003, to 19.9% on December 25, 2004. This is a relatively small increase. Overall, Intel has a modest liability percent.

Income Statement Analysis

One of the primary concerns of many financial statement users is the profitability of a business. Exhibit I.8 shows the comparative income statements with additional columns showing common-size percentages. In a common-size income statement, we always set total revenues equal to 100%. To illustrate a common-size percent computation, total expenses as a percent of total revenues for the 2004 fiscal year is 78.0% ($26,693 ÷ $34,209).

Question 1. Are total revenues for a company higher or lower this year versus last year?

Analysis 1. For Intel, total revenues in fiscal 2004 ($34,209 million) are greater than the total for fiscal 2003 ($30,141 million). The increase in total revenues indicates more ability of Intel to grow. To remain in business, every company needs to continue sales to existing customers and attract new customers. Generally, an increase in total revenues for a business is *favorable*.

Question 2. What is the percent change in total revenues from last year to this year?

Analysis 2. We can compute a percent change in total revenues from the prior year as follows:

$$\text{Percent change} = 100 \times \frac{\text{Dollar Amount of Change}^*}{\text{Dollar Amount for Prior Year}} \qquad {}^*\text{current year} - \text{prior year}$$

In this case, the percent increase in total revenues from fiscal 2003 to fiscal 2004 is:

$$13.5\% = 100 \times \frac{\$4,068^*}{\$30,141} \qquad {}^* \$34,209 - \$30,141$$

Total revenues for Intel have increased 13.5% from 2003 to 2004.

INTEL CORPORATION
COMPARATIVE COMMON-SIZE INCOME STATEMENTS
For The Years Ended December 25, 2004, And December 27, 2003
(*in millions*)

	Years Ended		Common-size Percentages	
	December 25 2004	December 27 2003	December 25 2004	December 27 2003
Total revenues	$ 34,209	$ 30,141	100.0%*	100.0%*
Total expenses	26,693	24,500	78.0%	81.3%
Net Income	$ 7,516	$ 5,641	22.0%	18.7%

* Always set at 100% in a common-size income statement.

EXHIBIT **I.8**

Comparative Common-size Income Statements for Intel

Question 3. Is the percent of total expenses to total revenues increasing or decreasing from last year to this year?

Analysis 3. The percent of expenses to revenues has decreased from 81.3% in 2003 to 78.0% in 2004. The result is an increase in net income as a percent of revenues from 18.7% in 2003 to 22.0% in 2004. This is *favorable*.

We can combine the revenue growth percent with the increase in net income percentage of total revenues to say: "Overall, it is *favorable* that Intel could increase total revenues by 13.5%. It is also *favorable* that the expense percent decreased and the net income percent increased from 18.7% in 2003 to 22.0% in 2004." It would be helpful to have information about competing companies in order to make comparisons of expense and net income percents. In the Demonstration Problem at the end of this Introduction, we will show an example comparing two companies in the same industry (Apple Computer, Inc. and Gateway Computer).

Integrative Balance Sheet and Income Statement Analysis

In our analysis so far, we observed that both total assets and total revenues for Intel increased in fiscal 2004 from 2003. Now, we need to combine this information to assess the overall efficiency of Intel.

Question 1. Is the business operating efficiently by using the least amount of asset investment to generate a given level of total revenues?

Analysis 1. We can answer this question for Intel by dividing total revenues by average total assets for each year. Average assets for a year are simply ending assets plus beginning assets divided by 2. For this computation, we need to know that for Intel, total assets as of December 25, 2002 were $44,224 million. The computations are:

	Fiscal 2004	**Fiscal 2003**
$\dfrac{\text{Total Revenues}}{\text{Average Total Assets}}$	$\dfrac{\$34,209}{\$47,643^*} = 0.72$ times	$\dfrac{\$30,141}{\$45,684^{**}} = 0.66$ times

* ($48,143 + $47,143) ÷ 2
** ($47,143 + $44,224) ÷ 2

The resulting number represents the number of times the investment in average total assets turns over during a year. This number is a ratio called **total asset turnover**. A higher number for the total asset turnover ratio is more favorable since it shows that a business is operating with a smaller asset investment to generate a given level of total revenues. For Intel, the total asset turnover ratio increased from 0.66 times in 2003 to 0.72 times in 2004. In general, this is an *favorable* trend. The Company is operating more efficiently.

Concluding Comment

This is the start of our efforts to analyze and interpret accounting information. It is important to note that at this point, we are only making some general observations based on limited information. As we develop our understanding of accounting concepts throughout this text, we will refine our questions and interpretations.

LEARNING GOALS REVIEW

1. Define *accounting*.

Accounting is an information system. An accounting information system is the resources and procedures that turn the effects of economic events into financial information. In an accounting information system, we (1) collect data, (2) process the data, and (3) communicate information to users.

2. Identify users of accounting information.

People both inside and outside a company use accounting information to make decisions. Internal users are the company's managers. External users include owners (both current and prospective), lenders, labor organizations, customers, society groups, and government regulatory agencies.

3. Define *accounting entity* and compare different types of business ownership.

An accounting entity is any organization unit for which we gather financial and economic data and process it for the purpose of making decisions. We must develop a separate set of accounting records for each business unit.

The basic types of business ownership are the single proprietorship, partnership, and corporation. A single proprietorship is a business owned by one person. A partnership is a business with two or more owners who voluntarily join in a business venture. A corporation is a legal entity separate from its owners. It is accountable for its own actions and debts.

4. Identify the purpose and explain the types of information contained in the (1) balance sheet, (2) income statement, and (3) statement of cash flows.

The balance sheet summarizes the assets, liabilities, and owners' equity of a business as of a specific moment in time. The income statement shows the revenues and expenses for a period of time. The statement of cash flows presents the cash flows from operating, investing, and financing activities for a period of time.

5. Analyze information contained in the financial statements to identify favorable and unfavorable trends for real-life companies.

Frequently, we can see relationships and trends easier when we convert financial statements to common-size percents. In a balance sheet, we set both total assets and liabilities + owners' equity equal to 100%. In an income statement, we set total revenues equal to 100%. Then, we divide all individual statement amounts by the totals to express each item as a percent of the totals. To begin our analysis of financial statements in this text, we ask a series of questions that primarily focus on (1) are financial statement dollar totals increasing or decreasing? and (2) are common-size percents for financial statement items increasing or decreasing? If possible, we then try to identify changes as favorable or unfavorable.

DEMONSTRATION PROBLEM

Using Accounting Information

Comparing Apple Computer, Inc. and Gateway, Inc.

Apple Computer, Inc. and Gateway, Inc. both manufacture and sell computers. Listed below are comparative balance sheets and income statements with common-size percents for the 2004 and 2003 fiscal years (in millions).

APPLE COMPUTER AND GATEWAY INC.
COMPARATIVE COMMON-SIZE BALANCE SHEETS
2004 And 2003
(in millions)

	Apple Computer				Gateway Inc.			
	As of Sept. 30, 2004	As of Sept. 30, 2004	As of Sept. 30, 2003	As of Sept. 30, 2003	As of Dec. 31, 2004	As of Dec. 31, 2004	As of Dec. 31, 2003	As of Dec. 31, 2003
	$	%	$	%	$	%	$	%
Total assets	$ 8,050.0	100.0%	$ 6,815.0	100.0%	$ 1,771.8	100.0%	$ 2,028.4	100.0%
Total liabilities	$ 2,974.0	36.9%	$ 2,592.0	38.0%	$ 1,526.8	86.2%	$ 1,306.4	64.4%
Total owners' equity	$ 5,076.0	63.1%	$ 4,223.0	62.0%	$ 245.0	13.8%	$ 722.0	35.6%
Total liabilities and owners' equity	$ 8,050.0	100.0%	$ 6,815.0	100.0%	$ 1,771.8	100.0%	$ 2,028.4	100.0%

APPLE COMPUTER AND GATEWAY INC.
COMPARATIVE COMMON-SIZE INCOME STATEMENTS
2004 And 2003
(in millions)

	Apple Computer				Gateway Inc.			
	For Year Ended Sept. 30, 2004	For Year Ended Sept. 30, 2004	For Year Ended Sept. 30, 2003	For Year Ended Sept. 30, 2003	For Year Ended Dec. 31, 2004	For Year Ended Dec. 31, 2004	For Year Ended Dec. 31, 2003	For Year Ended Dec. 31, 2003
	$	%	$	%	$	%	$	%
Total revenues	$ 8,279.0	100.0%	$ 6,207.0	100.0%	$ 3,649.7	100.0%	$ 3,402.4	100.0%
Total expenses	$ 8,003.0	96.7%	$ 6,138.0	98.9%	$ 4,217.3	115.6%	$ 3,917.2	115.1%
Net income (loss)	$ 276.0	3.3%	$ 69.0	1.1%	$ (567.6)	-15.6%	$ (514.8)	-15.1%

Required

BALANCE SHEET QUESTIONS (LG 4, 5):

1. At the end of 2004 which company has higher total assets in dollars?

2. From 2003 to 2004 which company had the largest growth percent in total assets? (*Hint*: For this answer, compute a percent change in total assets from 2003 to 2004 for each company).

3. At the end of 2004, which company has more risk in terms of liabilities? Briefly explain.

INCOME STATEMENT QUESTIONS (LG 4, 5):

4. For the 2004 reporting year, which company had higher total revenues in dollars?

5. From 2003 to 2004, which company had the largest growth percent in total revenues? (*Hint*: For this answer, compute a percent change in total revenues from 2003 to 2004 for each company).

6. For the 2004 reporting year, which company had the lowest percent of total expenses to total revenues?
   As a result, which company had e highest percent of net income to total revenues?

7. From 2003 to 2004, which company was able to reduce expenses as a percent of total revenues better? (*Hint*: For this answer, examine the comparative common size 2003 and 2004 total expense percents for each company).

INTEGRATIVE BALANCE SHEET AND INCOME STATEMENT QUESTION (LG 4, 5):

8. For 2004, which company is operating more efficiently by using the least amount of asset investment to generate a given level of revenues? Briefly explain. (*Hint*: For this answer, you will need to compute *total asset turnover* ratios for both companies).

SOLUTION

Solution Approach 1-8

In all of the problems in this chapter, we use a format for financial statements similar to Exhibit I.7 (Balance Sheet) and I.8 (Income Statement). In the financial statements you will analyze, we show comparative dollar amounts for two years. In addition, we also calculate common-size percents for each year. In a common-size balance sheet, we set total assets and total liabilities + owners' equity at 100%. In a common-size income statement, we set total revenues at 100%. To express all other financial statement amounts as a percent of these totals, divide the financial statement amount by the total.

    Guidelines for Rounding Calculations: When making calculations, keep everything simple by (1) rounding to nearest thousands or millions *before* you divide and (2) by rounding your answer to no more than two decimal places. Using assumed numbers, look at the following calculations:

Complete calculation:	$2,555,633 ÷ $3,256,272 = 0.784834
Numbers rounded to nearest thousand (two decimal place answer):	$2,555.6 ÷ $3,256.3 = 0.78
Numbers rounded to nearest thousand (one decimal place answer):	$2,555.6 ÷ $3,256.3 = 0.8
Numbers rounded to nearest million (two decimal place answer):	$2.6 ÷ $3.3 = 0.79
Numbers rounded to nearest million (one decimal place answer):	$2.6 ÷ $3.3 = 0.8

    The decision to round numbers to nearest thousands or millions and to round answers to two or one decimal places depends on the size of the numbers you are working with and the level of accuracy you need. In this Demonstration Problem, we round all financial statement amounts to millions and all percent computations to one decimal place. In Exhibits I.7 and I.8 we rounded financial statement amounts to nearest millions and percent computations to one decimal place. It is important to be comfortable with a number of different rounding formats that you will encounter in real-life.

Requirement 1

Apple Computer ($8,050.0 million for Apple versus $1,771.8 million for Gateway).

Requirement 2

Apple Computer : $18.1\% = 100 \times \dfrac{\$1,235.0}{\$6,815.0}$ $^* \$8,050.0 - \$6,815.0 = \$1,235$

Gateway Computer : $12.7\% = 100 \times \dfrac{\$(256.6)}{\$2,028.4}$ $^* \$1,771.8 - \$2,028.4 = \$(256.6)$

Apple Computer increased its total assets by a 18.1%. Gateway decreased assets by (12.7%).

Requirement 3

Apple Computer has less risk since it has a lower percent of liabilities (Apple's liabilities are 36.9% of total liabilities + owners' equities as of September 30, 2004, versus 86.2% for Gateway as of December 31, 2004).

Requirement 4

Apple Computer has higher total revenues ($8,279.0 million for Apple versus $3,649.7 million for Gateway).

Requirement 5

Apple Computer : $33.4\% = 100 \times \dfrac{\$2,072.0^*}{\$6,207.0}$ $^* \$8,279.7 - \$6,207.0 = \$2,072.0$

Gateway Computer : $7.3\% = 100 \times \dfrac{\$247.3^*}{\$3,402.4}$ $^* \$3,649.7 - \$3,402.4 = \$247.3$

Gateway and **Apple Computer** have both increased total revenues in 2004. We can view the dramatic increase in total revenues for Apple as *favorable*.

Requirement 6

Apple Computer had the lowest expense percent, (96.7% for Apple versus 115.6% for Gateway). Gateway is operating at a net loss in both 2004 and 2003.

Requirement 7

Apple Computer decreased total expenses as a percent of total revenues from 98.9% in 2003 to 96.7% in 2004. This is *favorable*. Gateway increased total expenses from 115.1% in 2003 to 115.6% in 2004. This is *unfavorable*.

Requirement 8

Solution Approach

$$\textbf{Total Asset Turnover} = \frac{\text{Total Revenues}}{\text{Average Total Assets}^*} \quad ^*(\text{ending assests} + \text{beginning assests}) \div 2$$

Apple Computer : $1.11 \text{ times} = \dfrac{\$8,279.0^*}{\$7,432.5}$ $^*\$8,050.0 + \$6,815.0 \div 2 = \$7,432.5$

Gateway Computer : $1.92 \text{ times} = \dfrac{\$3,649.7^*}{\$1,900.1}$ $^*\$1,771.8 + \$2,028.4 \div 2 = \$1,900.1$

Gateway has a higher total asset turnover ratio. Gateway is operating more efficiently by using a smaller proportionate investment in total assets to generate total revenues. This is *favorable*. In contrast, the lower total asset turnover ratio for Apple means it is using a higher proportionate investment in assets to generate revenues.

GLOSSARY

accounting An information system that generates financial information about a business.

accounting entity Any organization unit for which financial and economic data are gathered and processed for the purpose of decision making.

accounting information system The resources and procedures in a firm that change the results of economic data into financial information.

assets Economic resources or items of value a business owns.

balance sheet The financial statement that summarizes a firm's assets, liabilities, and owners' equity as of a specific date.

budget A financial plan for a future period.

common-size statement Statements where we express each item in the statement as a percent of the total for that statement.

controlling Process of measuring and evaluating actual performance and taking corrective action.

corporation Legal entities issued a charter by a state. Multiple owners buy ownership shares in the company called capital stock.

expenses The outflow of assets or incurring of liabilities that occur in the process of generating revenues.

external users Groups outside the company such as owners and creditors that need information about a business.

financial accounting Part of the accounting system that provides information to external users.

fiscal year A period of 12 consecutive months selected by a business as the reporting year for annual reports.

income statement The financial statement that compares revenues and expenses for a period of time to determine net income or net loss.

internal users People within a business who need accounting information.

liabilities The debts of a business; creditors' claims against the assets.

management accounting Part of the accounting system that provides information to internal users.

net income The difference between revenues and expenses for a period of time if revenues exceed expenses.

net loss The difference between revenues and expenses for a period of time if expenses exceed revenues.

owners' equity The sum of all claims against the assets by the owners of a business.

partnership A business where two or more people join together to earn and share profits.

planning A process that includes developing assumptions about the future, establishing goals, making decisions about courses of action, putting plans into action, and evaluating results.

revenues The source of an increase in assets from performing services or selling goods.

single proprietorship A business owned by one person.

statement of cash flows The financial statement that reports the events that cause inflows and outflows of cash during the period.

total asset turnover The number of times the investment in average total assets turns over during a year.

QUESTIONS FOR GROUP LEARNING

QI-1. List the phases involved in the planning process.

QI-2. For a business, identify and explain the three types of cash flows that must be managed.

QI-3. Define accounting.

QI-4. What is the difference between internal and external users of accounting information? Identify the types of external users, and describe how they may use accounting information.

QI-5. What are the three types of business organizations? What is the difference between them in relation to the personal liability of the owners?

QI-6. What are the three primary financial statements of a business? Briefly explain what information each financial statement discloses.

QI-7. A practicing accountant tells you that the balance sheet can be thought of as a photograph, and the income statement and statement of cash flows can be viewed as motion pictures. Is this statement true? Briefly explain.

QI-8. What is the basic accounting equation? Briefly explain what each of the three elements of the accounting equation represent.

QI-9. You are having a discussion with a fellow student in your accounting class concerning analyzing financial statements. Your friend believes that because the balance sheet and income statement are separate, the analysis of each statement completely ignores the other. You believe that information from both financial statements must be viewed as a whole. Who is correct? Briefly explain.

QI-10. In analyzing two companies in the same industry, you note that both companies have total revenues of $20 million. Company 1 has total assets of $10 million on its balance sheet. Company 2 has $5 million of total assets. Based only on this information, which Company would you view more favorably? Briefly explain.

EXERCISES

EI-11. Users of accounting information (LG 2) The persons or groups listed below use the financial reports or accounting records of Sunbelt Travel. Identify each as an external or internal user of accounting information.

1. The loan manager of a bank to which Sunbelt has applied for a 90-day loan.

2. Brenda Weiss, who owns 100 shares of Sunbelt common stock.

3. The president of Sunbelt.

4. The regional director of the Internal Revenue Service.

5. Shane Kelly, the corporation's planning manager.

6. Van Mantoya, the corporation's budget director.

7. Audrey Josey, who has a sum of money lent to the company.

8. Dawn Denby, tour director for Sunbelt.

EI-12. Entity concept (LG 3) Irvin Stein owns a checking account, a savings account, a residence with personal property, Stein's Camera Repair Center, and Capital City Audio Sales. How many accounting entities are involved? Name them.

EI-13. Balance sheet relationships for real-life companies (LG 4) Listed below are amounts in millions from 2004 annual reports of companies in different industries. Fill in the missing amounts.

Company	Total Assets	Total Liabilities	Owners' Equity
Walt Disney	$53,902.0	?	$26,081.0
Estée Lauder	3,708.1	$1,974.6	?
Hershey Foods	3,797.5	?	1,089.3
H.J. Heinz	?	7,983.0	1,894.2
Nike	7,891.6	?	4,781.7
Wm. Wrigley	3,166.7	988.0	?

EI-14. Income statement relationships for real-life companies (LG 4) Listed below are amounts in millions from 2004 annual reports of companies in different industries. Fill in the missing amounts.

Company	Total Revenues	Total Expenses	Net Income (Loss)
Walt Disney	$30,752.0	$28,407.0	?
Estée Lauder	5,790.4	5,448.3	?
Hershey Foods	?	3,838.3	590.9
H.J. Heinz	8,414.5	?	804.3
Nike	12,253.1	11,307.5	?
Wm. Wrigley	3,648.6	?	493.0

EI-16. Statement of cash flows relationships for real-life companies (LG 4) Listed below are amounts in millions from 2004 annual reports of companies in different industries. Fill in the missing amounts.

Company	Net Cash Provided by (Used by) Operating Activities	Net Cash Provided by (Used by) Investing Activities	Net Cash Provided by (Used by) Financing Activities	Increase (Decrease) in Cash
Walt Disney	$4,370.0	$(1,484.0)	$(2,701.0)	?
Estée Lauder	667.3	(208.0)	?	243.3
Hershey Foods	?	(362.7)	(494.7)	(59.9)
H.J. Heinz	1,249.0	?	(643.9)	344.0
Nike	1,514.4	(946.5)	(398.5)	?
Wm. Wrigley	?	(482.3)	(146.2)	96.0

EI-17. Analyzing balance sheets for real-life companies (LG 5)

    a. For each of the companies listed in Exercise I-13, compute total liabilities as a percent of total liabilities + owners' equity.

    b. Which company has the highest percent of liabilities?

    c. Generally, is a higher percent for liabilities favorable or unfavorable? Briefly explain.

EI-17. Analyzing income statements for real-life companies (LG 5)

    a. For each of the companies listed in Exercise I-14, calculate total expenses as a percent of total revenues.

    b. Which company has the highest percent of expenses?

    c. Generally, is a higher percent for expenses favorable or unfavorable? Briefly explain.

EI-18. Analyzing statements of cash flows for real-life companies (LG 5)

    a. For each of the companies listed in Exercise I-15, add cash provided by operating activities and cash provided by (used by) investing activities together.

    b. Which company has the largest amount of net cash *outflow* from these two activities?

    c. Briefly explain why you believe this net cash outflow may be unfavorable.

PROBLEMS

PI-19. Analyzing Home Depot (LG 4, 5) Home Depot, Inc. is a leading home improvement store. Listed below are comparative balance sheets and income statements with common-size percents for 2005 and 2004 (in millions).

HOME DEPOT, INC.
COMPARATIVE COMMON-SIZE BALANCE SHEETS
2005 And 2004
(in millions)

	Home Depot			
	As of Jan. 31, 2005	As of Jan. 31, 2005	As of Jan. 31, 2004	As of Jan. 31, 2004
	$	%	$	%
Total assets	$ 38,907.0	100.0%	$ 34,437.0	100.0%
Total liabilities	$ 14,749.0	37.9%	$ 12,030.0	34.9%
Total owners' equity	$ 24,158.0	62.1%	$ 22,407.0	65.1%
Total liabilities and owners' equity	$ 38,907.0	100.0%	$ 34,437.0	100.0%

HOME DEPOT, INC.
COMPARATIVE COMMON-SIZE INCOME STATEMENTS
2005 And 2004
(in millions)

	Home Depot			
	For Year Ended Jan. 31, 2005	For Year Ended Jan. 31, 2005	For Year Ended Jan. 31, 2004	For Year Ended Jan. 31, 2004
	$	%	$	%
Total revenues	$ 73,094.0	100.0%	$ 64,816.0	100.0%
Total expenses	$ 68,093.0	93.2%	$ 60,512.0	93.4%
Net income (loss)	$ 5,001.0	6.8%	$ 4,304.0	6.6%

REQUIRED
Balance sheet questions:

1. Are total assets higher or lower in 2005 compared to 2004?

2. What is the percent change in total assets from 2005 to 2004? (*Hint:* For this answer, compute a percent change in total assets from 2004 to 2005).

3. Is the percent of total liabilities to total liabilities + owners' equity increasing or decreasing from 2004 to 2005? As a result, does the company have more or less risk? Briefly explain.

INCOME STATEMENT QUESTIONS:

4. Are total revenues higher or lower in 2005 compared to 2004?

5. What is the percent change in total revenues from 2004 to 2005?

6. Is the percent of total expenses to total revenues increasing or decreasing from 2004 to 2005? (*Hint*: For this answer, examine the comparative common size 2004 and 2005 total expense percents for each company).

INTEGRATIVE BALANCE SHEET AND INCOME STATEMENT QUESTION:

7. Is the company operating more or less efficiently in 2005 compared to 2004 in terms of total asset investment needed to generate total revenues? Briefly explain. Total assets at the end of 2003 were $30,011.0 million. (*Hint*: For this answer, you will need to compute *total asset turnover* ratios for both years).

PI-20. Analyzing yahoo! Inc. (LG 4, 5) yahoo is a rapidly growing internet site. Listed below are comparative balance sheets and income statements with common-size percents for 2004 and 2003 (in millions).

YAHOO! INC.
COMPARATIVE COMMON-SIZE BALANCE SHEETS
2004 And 2003
(in millions)

	Yahoo			
	As of Dec. 31, 2004	As of Dec. 31, 2004	As of Dec. 31, 2003	As of Dec. 31, 2003
	$	%	$	%
Total assets	$ 9,178.2	100.0%	$ 5,931.7	100.0%
Total liabilities	$ 2,076.8	22.6%	$ 1,568.2	26.4%
Total owners' equity	$ 7,101.4	77.4%	$ 4,363.5	73.6%
Total liabilities and owners' equity	$ 9,178.2	100.0%	$ 5,931.7	100.0%

YAHOO! INC.
COMPARATIVE COMMON-SIZE INCOME STATEMENTS
2004 And 2003
(in millions)

	Yahoo			
	For Year Ended Dec. 31, 2004	For Year Ended Dec. 31, 2004	For Year Ended Dec. 31, 2003	For Year Ended Dec. 31, 2003
	$	%	$	%
Total revenues	$ 3,574.5	100.0%	$ 1,625.1	100.0%
Total expenses	$ 2,734.9	76.5%	$ 1,387.2	85.4%
Net income (loss)	$ 839.6	23.5%	$ 237.9	14.6%

REQUIRED
Balance sheet questions:

1. Are total assets higher or lower in 2004 compared to 2003?

2. What is the percent change in total assets from 2003 to 2004? (*Hint:* For this answer, compute a percent change in total assets from 2000 to 2001).

3. Is the percent of total liabilities to total liabilities + owners' equity increasing or decreasing from 2003 to 2004? As a result, does the company have more or less risk? Briefly explain.

INCOME STATEMENT QUESTIONS:

4. Are total revenues higher or lower in 2004 compared to 2003?

5. What is the percent change in total revenues from 2003 to 2004?

6. Is the percent of total expenses to total revenues increasing or decreasing from 2003 to 2004? (*Hint:* For this answer, examine the comparative common size 2003 and 2004 total expense percents for each company).

INTEGRATIVE BALANCE SHEET AND INCOME STATEMENT QUESTION:

7. Is the company operating more or less efficiently in 2004 compared to 2003 in terms of total asset investment needed to generate total revenues? Briefly explain. Total assets at the end of 2002 were $2,790.2 million. (*Hint:* For this answer, you will need to compute *total asset turnover* ratios for both years).

PI-21. Comparing GAP and Limited Brands (LG 5) The GAP, Inc. and Limited Brands, Inc. both operate in the retailing clothing business. Listed below are comparative balance sheets and income statements with common-size percents for 2005 and 2004 (in millions).

REQUIRED
BALANCE SHEET QUESTIONS:

1. At the end of 2005, which company has higher total assets in dollars?

2. From 2004 to 2005, which company had the largest growth percent in total assets? (*Hint:* For this answer, compute a percent change in total assets from 2004 to 2005 for each company).

3. At the end of 2005, which company has more risk in terms of liabilities? Briefly explain.

INCOME STATEMENT QUESTIONS:

4. For 2005, which company had higher total revenues in dollars?

5. For 2005, which company had the lowest percent of total expenses to total revenues? As a result, which company had the highest percent of net income to total revenues?

6. From 2004 to 2005, which company was able to reduce expenses as a percent of total revenues better? (*Hint:* For this answer, examine the comparative common size 2004 and 2005 total expense percents for each company).

INTEGRATIVE BALANCE SHEET AND INCOME STATEMENT QUESTION:

7. For 2005, which company is operating more efficiently by using the least amount of asset investment to generate a given level of revenues? Briefly explain why the nature of each company's business may help to explain the ratio results. (*Hint:* For this answer, you will need to compute *total asset turnover* ratios for both companies).

GAP, INC. AND LIMITED BRANDS, INC.
COMPARATIVE COMMON-SIZE BALANCE SHEETS
2005 And 2004
(in millions)

	Gap				Limited Brands			
	As of Jan. 31, 2005	As of Jan. 31, 2005	As of Jan. 31, 2004	As of Jan. 31, 2004	As of Jan. 31, 2005	As of Jan. 31, 2005	As of Jan. 31, 2004	As of Jan. 3 2004
	$	%	$	%	$	%	$	%
Total assets	$ 10,048.0	100.0%	$ 10,343.0	100.0%	$ 6,089.0	100.0%	$ 7,873.0	100.0
Total liabilities	$ 5,112.0	50.9%	$ 5,560.0	53.8%	$ 3,754.0	61.7%	$ 2,607.0	33.1
Total owners' equity	$ 4,936.0	49.1%	$ 4,783.0	46.2%	$ 2,335.0	38.3%	$ 5,266.0	66.9
Total liabilities and owners' equity	$ 10,048.0	100.0%	$ 10,343.0	100.0%	$ 6,089.0	100.0%	$ 7,873.0	100.0

GAP, INC. AND LIMITED BRANDS, INC.
COMPARATIVE COMMON-SIZE INCOME STATEMENTS
2005 And 2004
(in millions)

	Gap				Limited Brands			
	For Year Ended Jan. 31, 2005	For Year Ended Jan. 31, 2005	For Year Ended Jan. 31, 2004	For Year Ended Jan. 31, 2004	For Year Ended Jan. 31, 2005	For Year Ended Jan. 31, 2005	For Year Ended Jan. 31, 2004	For Year Ended Jan. 3 2004
	$	%	$	%	$	%	$	%
Total revenues	$ 16,267.0	100.0%	$ 15,854.0	100.0%	$ 9,408.0	100.0%	$ 8,934.0	100.0
Total expenses	$ 15,117.0	92.9%	$ 14,824.0	93.5%	$ 8,703.0	92.5%	$ 8,217.0	92.0
Net income (loss)	$ 1,150.0	7.1%	$ 1,030.0	6.5%	$ 705.0	7.5%	$ 717.0	8.0

PI-22. Comparing Safeway, Inc. and Whole Foods Market (LG 5) Safeway, Inc. is a leading regional food retailer. Whole Foods Market is a fast growing company. Listed below are comparative balance sheets and income statements with common-size percents for 2004 and 2003 (in millions).

SAFEWAY, INC AND WHOLE FOODS MARKET
COMPARATIVE COMMON-SIZE BALANCE SHEETS
2004 And 2003
(in millions)

	Safeway				Whole Foods			
	As of Dec. 31, 2004	As of Dec. 31, 2004	As of Dec. 31, 2003	As of Dec. 31, 2003	As of Sep. 30, 2004	As of Sep. 30, 2004	As of Sep. 30, 2003	As of Sep. 30, 2003
	$	%	$	%	$	%	$	%
Total assets	$ 15,388.4	100.0%	$ 15,096.7	100.0%	$ 1,521.0	100.0%	$ 1,196.8	100.0%
Total liabilities	$ 11,081.5	72.0%	$ 11,452.4	75.9%	$ 571.4	37.6%	$ 420.6	35.1%
Total owners' equity	$ 4,306.9	28.0%	$ 3,644.3	24.1%	$ 949.6	62.4%	$ 776.2	64.9%
Total liabilities and owners' equity	$ 15,388.4	100.0%	$ 15,096.7	100.0%	$ 1,521.0	100.0%	$ 1,196.8	100.0%

SAFEWAY, INC AND WHOLE FOODS MARKET
COMPARATIVE COMMON-SIZE INCOME STATEMENTS
2004 And 2003
(in millions)

	Safeway				Whole Foods			
	For Year Ended Dec. 31, 2004	For Year Ended Dec. 31, 2004	For Year Ended Dec. 31, 2003	For Year Ended Dec. 31, 2003	For Year Ended Sep. 30, 2004	For Year Ended Sep. 30, 2004	For Year Ended Sep. 30, 2003	For Year Ended Sep. 30, 2003
	$	%	$	%	$	%	$	%
Total revenues	$ 35,822.9	100.0%	$ 35,552.7	100.0%	$ 3,865.0	100.0%	$ 3,148.6	100.0%
Total expenses	$ 35,262.7	98.4%	$ 35,722.5	100.5%	$ 3,735.5	96.6%	$ 3,044.9	96.7%
Net income (loss)	$ 560.2	1.6%	$ (169.8)	-0.5%	$ 129.5	3.4%	$ 103.7	3.3%

REQUIRED

BALANCE SHEET QUESTIONS:

1. At the end of 2004, which company has higher total assets in dollars?

2. From 2003 to 2004, which company had the largest growth percent in total assets? (*Hint*: For this answer, compute a percent change in total assets from 2003 to 2004 for each company).

3. At the end of 2004, which company has more risk in terms of liabilities? Briefly explain.

INCOME STATEMENT QUESTIONS:

4. For 2004, which company had higher total revenues in dollars?

5. For 2004, which company had the lowest percent of total expenses to total revenues? As a result, which company had the highest percent of net income to total revenues?

6. From 2003 to 2004, why did net income for Safeway increase in dollar amount despite only a small increase in total revenues? Briefly explain.

INTEGRATIVE BALANCE SHEET AND INCOME STATEMENT QUESTION:

7. For 2004, which company is operating more efficiently by using the least amount of asset investment to generate a given level of revenues? Briefly explain. (*Hint*: For this answer, you will need to compute *total asset turnover* ratios for both companies).

PI-23. Comparing Wal-Mart and Target (LG 5) Target Corporation and Wal-mart Stores, Inc. both operate general merchandise chains. Listed below are comparative balance sheets and income statements with common-size percents for 2005 and 2004 (in millions).

TARGET CORP AND WAL-MART STORES
COMPARATIVE COMMON-SIZE BALANCE SHEETS
2005 And 2004
(in millions)

	Target				Wal-Mart			
	As of Jan. 31, 2005	As of Jan. 31, 2005	As of Jan. 31, 2004	As of Jan. 31, 2004	As of Jan. 31, 2005	As of Jan. 31, 2005	As of Jan. 31, 2004	As of Jan. 31, 2004
	$	%	$	%	$	%	$	%
Total assets	$ 32,293.0	100.0%	$ 31,392.0	100.0%	$ 120,223.0	100.0%	$ 104,912.0	100.0%
Total liabilities	$ 19,264.0	59.7%	$ 20,327.0	64.8%	$ 70,827.0	58.9%	$ 61,289.0	58.4%
Total owners' equity	$ 13,029.0	40.3%	$ 11,065.0	35.2%	$ 49,396.0	41.1%	$ 43,623.0	41.6%
Total liabilities and owners' equity	$ 32,293.0	100.0%	$ 31,392.0	100.0%	$ 120,223.0	100.0%	$ 104,912.0	100.0%

TARGET CORP AND WAL-MART STORES
COMPARATIVE COMMON-SIZE INCOME STATEMENTS
2005 And 2004
(in millions)

	Target				Wal-Mart			
	For Year Ended Jan. 31, 2005	For Year Ended Jan. 31, 2005	For Year Ended Jan. 31, 2004	For Year Ended Jan. 31, 2004	For Year Ended Jan. 31, 2005	For Year Ended Jan. 31, 2005	For Year Ended Jan. 31, 2004	For Year Ended Jan. 31, 2004
	$	%	$	%	$	%	$	%
Total revenues	$ 46,839.0	100.0%	$ 48,163.0	100.0%	$ 287,989.0	100.0%	$ 258,681.0	100.0%
Total expenses	$ 43,641.0	93.2%	$ 46,322.0	96.2%	$ 277,722.0	96.4%	$ 249,627.0	96.5%
Net income (loss)	$ 3,198.0	6.8%	$ 1,841.0	3.8%	$ 10,267.0	3.6%	$ 9,054.0	3.5%

REQUIRED

Balance sheet questions:

1. At the end of 2005, which company has higher total assets in dollars?

2. From 2004 to 2005, which company had the largest growth percent in total assets? (*Hint*: For this answer, compute a percent change in total assets from 2004 to 2005 for each company).

3. At the end of 2005, which company has more risk in terms of liabilities? Briefly explain.

INCOME STATEMENT QUESTIONS:

4. For 2005, which company had higher total revenues in dollars?

5. For 2005, which company had the lowest percent of total expenses to total revenues? As a result, which company had the highest percent of net income to total revenues?

6. From 2004 to 2005, which company was able to reduce expenses as a percent of total revenues better? (*Hint*: For this answer, examine the comparative common size 2004 and 2005 total expense percents for each company).

INTEGRATIVE BALANCE SHEET AND INCOME STATEMENT QUESTIONS:

7. For 2005, which company is operating more efficiently by using the least amount of asset investment to generate a given level of revenues? Briefly explain. (*Hint*: For this answer, you will need to compute *total asset turnover* ratios for both companies).

AN ACCOUNTING INFORMATION SYSTEM

CHAPTER

1

Chapter Thought

"When you can measure what you are speaking about, and express it in numbers, you know something about it."

Lord Kelvin, 1824–1907

LEARNING GOALS

After studying Chapter 1, you should be able to:

1. Identify generally accepted accounting principles (GAAP) and the groups that help develop them.

2. Identify the importance of ethics in accounting.

3. Construct the accounting equation and define *assets, liabilities,* and *owners' equity.*

4. Analyze business transactions using the accounting equation.

5. Prepare simple versions of the four basic financial statements.

6. Analyze financial statement information for real-life companies.

UNDERSTANDING BUSINESS ISSUES

Businesses as diverse as Intel, Coca-Cola, and Panera Bread have much in common. Although they operate in different industries and produce different products, they all have common needs for information. Each must be able to assess its performance and financial position and make decisions about the future. Accounting information is the basis for such evaluations and decisions.

Decisions based on accounting information affect how businesses operate. For example, Panera Bread decides the number of loaves of bread to bake using records of how many loaves it usually sells each day. The price of each loaf depends on the costs of making the dough, baking it, and wrapping it. Every group in the production chain, from the farmer to the retailer, relies on accounting information to figure its costs.

In the Introduction to this text, we provided an overview of the accounting information system. In this chapter, we begin to develop the procedures used to gather, record, classify, and summarize accounting data. We start by providing some background on accounting and the accounting profession. Then we turn to the basic concepts of the accounting model. Using this information, we start our study of the measurements accountants make and the reports they create from them. Our study of the accounting cycle spans the first four chapters.

DEVELOPMENT OF ACCOUNTING PRINCIPLES

Learning Goal 1   Identify generally accepted accounting principles (GAAP) and the groups that help develop them.

What financial information is communicated depends on the needs of users and on the business environment. Accounting is an old discipline, with its roots in the beginnings of civilization. Reporting requirements have evolved over the centuries. They are currently shaped by professional authoritative bodies and by government agencies. In this section, we will briefly describe the history of accounting and identify the groups that influence modern accounting practice.

History of Accounting

Some of the world's first documents date from 5000 BC. The need to account for holdings of wealth prompted the development of a form of writing referred to as script. Babylonian textile mills, in about 600 BC, kept production control records and paid workers based upon how much cloth they produced. In 1494, an Italian monk named Luca Pacioli included a section on book-keeping in a mathematics textbook. This was the first known printed description of *double-entry* bookkeeping.

In early America, accounting generally served to maintain a firm's records of business dealings with its customers. As the United States moved toward an industrial economy, the rise of large companies created requirements for more accounting information. New inventions brought forth new products. Accounting methods and techniques had to be developed to meet these changes. Today, corporations communicate information to users of financial information in a wide variety of forms. These range from printed annual reports to press releases over the internet.

The Major Accounting Bodies

The National Corporation Act was passed in England in 1845 to regulate businesses. One effect of the act was the development of accounting principles. When the industrial revolution began in the United States in the mid-1880s, accounting practices were disorganized and not standardized. In response, accounting groups modeled on the English Institute of Chartered Accountants were formed to develop uniform accounting principles.

Currently, three major authoritative bodies are the American Institute of Certified Public Accountants (AICPA), the Financial Accounting Standards Board (FASB), and the Securities and Exchange Commission (SEC). The first two are private-sector organizations. The SEC is a federal government agency. In addition, other organizations help develop standards that affect current accounting practices.

American Institute of Certified Public Accountants (AICPA)

The **American Institute of Certified Public Accountants (AICPA)** was created in 1936. Its formation created the basic authority for certified public accountants in the United States. The AICPA played a very active role in the development of accounting guidelines from 1937 to 1973.

In 1937, the AICPA created the Committee on Accounting Procedure, which issued a series of *Accounting Research Bulletins (ARBs)*. These bulletins were issued to standardize accounting practices. In 1959, this committee was replaced by the *Accounting Principles Board (APB)*. Starting in 1962, the APB, an arm of the AICPA, began to publish a new set of pronouncements, entitled *Opinions of the Accounting Principles Board (APB Opinions)*. By the time the APB was replaced in 1973, it had issued 31 opinions.

Financial Accounting Standards Board (FASB)

In mid-1973, an independent private body, the **Financial Accounting Standards Board (FASB)**, replaced the APB. It assumed responsibility for issuing financial accounting standards. The AICPA remains the primary source for auditing standards for independent auditors.

The FASB began to issue standards in 1973. It is now the independent nongovernmental body that develops and issues standards for financial accounting. Pronouncements of the FASB are called **Statements of Financial Accounting Standards (SFAS)**. The Statements of Financial Accounting Standards are more commonly called FASB Statements. The FASB also issues *Statements of Financial Accounting Concepts*. These form the basic conceptual framework for all accounting.

Governmental Accounting Standards Board (GASB)

Accounting standards for state and local governments are set by the **Governmental Accounting Standards Board (GASB)**, established in 1984. This is an organization similar to the FASB. The GASB is authorized to issue *Statements of Governmental Accounting Standards*.

Sarbanes-Oxley Act of 2002

The Sarbanes-Oxley Act of 2002, sponsored by US Senator Paul Sarbanes and US Representative Michael Oxley, represents one of the biggest changes to federal securities laws since the New Deal. It came as a result of the large corporate financial scandals involving Enron, WorldCom, Global Crossing and Arthur Andersen. Effective in 2004, *all* publicly-traded companies are required to submit an annual report of the effectiveness of their internal accounting controls to the Securities and Exchange Commision (SEC). The major provisions of the Sarbanes Oxley Act (SOX) include criminal and civil penalities for noncompliance violations, certification of internal auditing by external auditors, and increased disclosure regarding all financial statements.

Securities and Exchange Commission (SEC)

The **Securities and Exchange Commission (SEC)** was created by the Securities Exchange Act of 1934. The SEC has the legal authority to set accounting methods for firms whose shares of stock are sold on the stock exchanges. The law requires that such companies report to the SEC with details about their operations. The SEC, a federal agency, has broad powers over the amount and type of information to be included and the methods used to develop it. Since its creation in 1934, the SEC has concentrated on protecting investors. It has given high priority to public disclosure of fair and accurate financial information. It has left the task of issuing detailed accounting rules to the accounting profession. However, the SEC keeps a watchful eye on the private bodies and does not hesitate to exercise its influence when necessary.

Generally Accepted Accounting Principles (GAAP)

Accountants call the standards they follow **generally accepted accounting principles (GAAP)**. These principles are designed to make financial information more useable. The principles assure users that the accounting information has been assembled in a standard way. This makes the accounting information comparable between companies. The principles arise in two ways. They may be practices that have been accepted by most or all accountants. Or they may be statements issued by the accounting organizations described above. They are broad rules that accountants use to measure, categorize, and report business activities. New pronouncements continue to be issued in response to changes in business practice, the economic environment, or demands of users.

ETHICS AND ACCOUNTING

Learning Goal 2   Identify the importance of ethics in accounting.

To save money, a manager orders employees to disregard safety measures. Pollution control measures for another business meet the letter of the law but still pollute the streams near their plant. Another business designs advertising that is technically correct but misleading. Are the managers of these businesses acting in an ethical manner? What is legal may not be ethical. Ethical issues come about in business from competing interests. The desire to maximize profit may not always be fair to all parties involved.

Ethical conduct is fair and socially desirable. Each person's definition of ethical conduct varies. Experience, cultural background, and political beliefs affect a person's definition. It often requires a level of behavior above the minimum level required by the law.

Ethics is the process that individuals use to evaluate their conduct in light of moral principles and values.

Ethical standards often become part of the law. For example, once bribery was common practice for corporate officials. In many countries, bribery is still legal. To ensure that a corporation with ethical principles is not at a disadvantage, in 1977 the United States passed the Foreign Corrupt Practices Act. This law prohibits a U.S. corporation from bribing a foreign public official. Management must use control measures that prevent business bribes to foreign officials.

As students in accounting, it is important that you learn to recognize ethical dilemmas. A commitment to high ethical standards is a requirement in the accounting profession. To help you develop a concern for ethical issues, the textbook presents a short ethical case for discussion after each chapter's problems.

BUILDING THE ACCOUNTING INFORMATION SYSTEM

We introduced the primary financial statements and how they can be used in decision making in the Introduction to the text. Now we are ready to start our study of the process accountants use to gather, record, summarize, report and interpret business information.

The Accounting Equation

Learning Goal 3   Construct the accounting equation and define *assets, liabilities,* and *owners' equity.*

The financial status of an accounting entity at any moment in time is described by the accounting equation. The accounting equation (assets = liabilities + owners' equity) expresses the relationship of the assets of an entity to the claims (equities) against those assets. This relationship is shown on the balance sheet.

Assets

The **assets** of a business are everything of value held by the business. We interpret the word *value* to mean the future usefulness to a business. Examples of assets are cash, accounts receivable, supplies on hand, land, buildings, and trucks. Accounts receivable are amounts owed to the business by customers who purchased goods and services on credit.

An asset is recorded on the books of the entity at its actual full cost. The full cost is the amount the entity agrees to pay. This is true even though it may not have been fully paid for in cash. Accounting principles and concepts that affect the measurement of assets are the cost principle, the going-concern concept, the objectivity principle, and the stable dollar concept. These concepts are discussed next.

The Cost Principle

Assets are valued and recorded according to the cost principle. The **cost principle** requires that assets be recorded at the price originally paid to acquire them, called *historical cost*. This may not be the amount that would have to be paid if the asset were purchased currently. For example, assume a business agrees to buy land for $20,000 in cash. We record the land at $20,000 even if the initial asking price is $25,000. Ten years later, if the land had appreciated to $30,000, the accounting records would still show $20,000.

The Going-concern Concept

Under the **going-concern concept**, accountants assume that a company will continue to operate indefinitely unless there is evidence to the contrary. This is one reason that historical costs are not changed to reflect changes in market prices. The assets used in the business were not acquired for sale, but for operations. Thus, market values are generally not used in valuing assets for a going concern. If plans are to sell or liquidate a business, the going-concern concept no longer applies. Then a departure from the cost principle may be justified.

The Objectivity Principle

Another reason that assets are recorded at historical cost is the **objectivity principle**. This principle states that whenever possible, amounts used to record business transactions should be based on objective evidence. A *business document* normally serves as objective evidence. Examples of business documents include copies of checks, receipts for payment, and supplier's invoices. The accountant uses these documents as a basis for recording accounting information.

The Stable Dollar Concept

The **stable dollar concept** assumes that the dollar is sufficiently free from changes in purchasing power to be used as the basic unit of measure in accounting. When inflation is high, changes in purchasing power cause historical cost amounts to be less meaningful. In such cases, *price-level adjusted statements* may be prepared to convert the historical cost dollars into current purchasing power dollars.

Equities

Equities are claims against the total assets of a business. For every asset that exists, someone has a claim to it. Therefore, total claims to assets must equal total assets. The two major types of equities are liabilities and owners' equities.

Liabilities

Liabilities (debts) are claims against the assets of the business by nonowners. A business owes its liabilities to creditors. Examples of liabilities are accounts payable and wages owed to employees. Accounts payable are promises to pay for goods and services bought on credit. We record liabilities at the amount of cash that would be needed to pay off the debt.

Owners' Equity

Owners' equity is the sum of all claims against business assets by the owners. Owners' equity is equal to the excess of total assets over total liabilities. *Net worth* is another name for owners' equity. In times of financial difficulty, creditors' claims to assets must be paid before the owners' claims. Thus, owners' equity claims are secondary (or *residual*). The amount of owners' equity may change for one of four reasons: owners' investment, revenues, expenses, and dividends. Exhibit 1.1 is a

CHANGES IN OWNERS' EQUITY

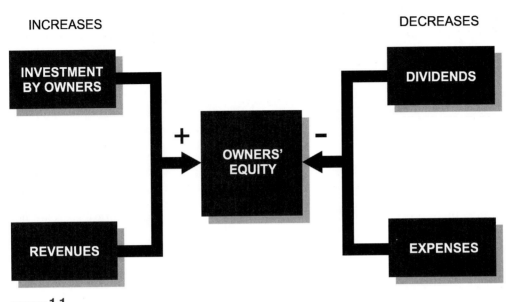

EXHIBIT **1.1**

Four Transactions that Increase and Decrease Owners' Equity

summary of the ways in which owners' equity changes. There are two primary components of owners' equity for a corporation: common stock and retained earnings.

Owners' Investment

Owners' equity increases when owners invest assets in a business. For a corporation, owners typically invest cash and receive shares of common stock. **Common stock** shows the amount of the owners' investment in a corporation. The owners are frequently referred to as *stockholders.* The investment by owners increases assets (cash) and increases owners' equity (common stock). Although there are several types of stock a corporation may issue, the most frequent type is *common stock.* We want to make our introduction to accounting as simple as possible and also agree with what you see when you look at financial statements for real-life corporations. Therefore, in Chapters 1–10, we will assume that when owners invest assets in a business, they receive ownership shares of *common stock* in return.

Retained Earnings

Retained earnings represents the cumulative total of net income, net loss, and dividends since the start of the corporation. There are three basic items that increase or decrease retained earnings: (1) revenues, (2) expenses, and (3) dividends.

Revenues

Businesses have an increase in assets when they perform services for or sell goods to customers. These inflows of assets are called **revenues**. The increase in assets may be either cash or accounts receivable. The **realization principle** states that the business earns revenues when it performs services or delivers goods. Thus, we record revenues when an inflow of assets from operating activities occurs. Note that earning revenue does not require the receipt of cash. Earning revenues causes an increase in the assets and the equity of the owners in the business. Therefore, earning revenues also increases owners' equity (retained earnings). We measure the amount of revenue by the value of the assets received.

Expenses

Businesses consume assets or incur liabilities while earning revenues. These outflows of assets or incurrence of liabilities in operating the business are called **expenses**. A business incurs expenses to earn revenues. Thus, expenses are also a result of operating activities. Expenses decrease assets, or increase liabilities, as well as decrease owners' equity (retained earnings). We measure the amount of the expense by the cost of the asset that expired or the amount of the liability incurred. If revenues are greater than expenses for a period of time, the result is a **net income**. If expenses are greater than revenues, the result is a **net loss**.

Dividends

The most frequent payment by a corporation to its owners is for cash dividends. **Dividends** are a distribution of net income to its owners. A corporation's board of directors (the corporation's policy making group elected by owners) must declare a dividend before it is paid. The declaration and payment of a cash dividend to owners reduces assets (cash) and reduces owners' equity (retained earnings). Dividends are not an expense and do not appear on the income statement.

Equating Assets and Equities

Because equities are the total claims against assets, *total assets must equal total equities*. Exhibit 1.2 shows this relationship. As we learned in the last section, we divide equities into two types—those of creditors (liabilities) and those of owners (owners' equity). Therefore, the following basic accounting equation must always be true:

$$\textbf{ASSETS} = \textbf{LIABILITIES} + \textbf{OWNERS' EQUITY}$$

Net assets, a term often used in business, are found by rearranging the terms in the accounting equation:

$$\textbf{ASSETS} - \textbf{LIABILITIES} = \textbf{NET ASSETS} \text{ (equal to owners' equity)}$$

As events occur that change individual assets, liabilities, and owners' equity, we enter these changes into the accounting records. To make these entries, we must analyze the effects of these events (called *transactions*) on the accounting entity. We can use the accounting equation to do this analysis. The next section illustrates the use of the accounting equation in analyzing transactions.

FOR EACH BUSINESS ENTITY:

ASSETS   =   EQUITIES

(Economic resources used in the business)

LIABILITIES   +   OWNERS' EQUITY

(Creditor claims or interest in assets)

(Owner claims or interest in assets)

Common Stock
(Investment by owners in entity)

Retained Earnings
(Cumulative net income, net loss, and dividends)

EXHIBIT 1.2

Accounting Equation

Analyzing Transactions Using the Accounting Equation

Learning Goal 4   Analyze business transactions using the accounting equation.

All businesses go through a start-up phase in which owners make an initial cash investment. The business next acquires assets to operate and then starts operations. The transactions involved in starting Recycle Consultants, Inc. illustrate this cycle. (We will refer to these transactions throughout the rest of this chapter.)

Transaction	2007		
(1)	Dec.	1	Recycle Consultants, Inc. was organized to provide environmental consulting. Owners invested $90,000 and received shares of common stock in Recycle Consultants, Inc.
(2)		5	Purchased land and a building for $70,000 in cash. The land cost $20,000 and the building cost $50,000.
(3)		9	Received furniture purchased on open charge account from Atlantic Furniture for $8,000.
(4)		16	Completed consulting services for the city of Ames and received $4,000 in cash.
(5)		18	Paid the entire amount owed to Atlantic Furniture.
(6)		23	Completed consulting services for the city of Boone and sent a bill for $2,000.
(7)		26	Paid $1,400 in cash for advertising that had appeared in *The City Administrator*, a magazine distributed to city managers.
(8)		27	Collected $1,500 in cash from the city of Boone for services billed on December 23.
(9)		30	Received a bill for $600 for utilities used during December.
(10)		31	Recycle Consultants declared and paid a total of $1,000 in cash dividends to owners.

Analysis of Transactions: Effect on Accounting Equation

Since each transaction that a business engages in affects its financial position, transactions can be analyzed by use of the basic accounting equation. To illustrate the use of the accounting equation as a tool in analyzing transactions, consider the ten transactions Recycle Consultants made during December, 2007.

TRANSACTION 1   CASH INVESTMENT BY OWNER.

Owners made an initial cash investment of $90,000 and received shares of common stock. The asset Cash has increased by $90,000. The investment also creates an increase in owners' equity of $90,000. For this corporation, we record it as common stock. We use the accounting equation to analyze this transaction as follows:

ASSETS	=	LIABILITIES	+	OWNERS' EQUITY
Cash +$90,000	=			Common Stock +$90,000

The accounting equation is in balance. Total assets are $90,000, and total liabilities and owners' equity are $90,000. To accumulate the effects of the transactions on the accounting equation, we can construct a simple columnar schedule. The schedule will have a column for each element of the accounting equation. All ten transactions are summarized in Exhibit 1.3. As you study each individual transaction, please refer to Exhibit 1.3 to see the cumulative effect of each transaction.

TRANSACTION 2   ASSETS PURCHASED FOR CASH.

Recycle purchased land and a building for cash. The purchase of the land and building will increase the asset Land by $20,000 and increase the asset Building by $50,000. These increases are offset by a decrease in another asset, Cash, of $70,000. Thus, there is no change in total assets and no change in total equities, as follows:

ASSETS		=	LIABILITIES	+	OWNERS' EQUITY
Cash	−$70,000				
Land	+$20,000				
Building	+$50,000				

Since this transaction only caused a change in the composition of the assets, total assets are still $90,000 and total equities are still $90,000.

TRANSACTION 3   ASSETS PURCHASED ON ACCOUNT.

On December 9, Recycle purchased furniture and promised to pay for it in the future. The purchase has increased the firm's assets by the cost of the furniture, $8,000. It has also created a liability, Accounts Payable, to Atlantic Furniture of $8,000. There was an increase in assets of $8,000, and an increase in liabilities of $8,000. This keeps the accounting equation in balance.

ASSETS		=	LIABILITIES	+	OWNERS' EQUITY
Furniture	+$8,000	=	Accounts		
			Payable +$8,000		

This transaction has caused an equal increase in total assets and total liabilities.

TRANSACTION 4   REVENUE EARNED FOR CASH.

The company completed consulting services for Ames for a cash fee of $4,000. Since it completed the work, it has earned the revenue. A revenue causes an increase in assets and an increase in owners' equity. Here, the asset Cash increased by $4,000; owners' equity increased by the same amount. This shows the increase in the owners' share of the assets.

ASSETS		=	LIABILITIES	+	OWNERS' EQUITY
Cash	+$4,000	=			Retained
					Earnings +$4,000

Earning a revenue causes both an asset and owners' equity (retained earnings) to increase by the same amount.

TRANSACTION 5   LIABILITY PAID WITH CASH.

On December 9, Recycle purchased an asset, furniture, but did not pay for it at that time. On December 18, Recycle sent a check for $8,000 to pay the amount owed. This causes an $8,000 decrease in the asset Cash and the same decrease in the liability Accounts Payable:

ASSETS		=	LIABILITIES	+	OWNERS' EQUITY
Cash	−$8,000	=	Accounts		
			Payable −$8,000		

This transaction caused an equal decrease in assets and liabilities.

TRANSACTION 6 REVENUE EARNED ON ACCOUNT.

The firm completed a second consulting contract on December 23. It billed the client but did not receive payment. The revenue is earned because Recycle completed the service. Again, earning revenue causes an increase in assets and owners' equity (retained earnings). Since the revenue earned was on account, Accounts Receivable increased instead of Cash. Using the accounting equation, the analysis appears as follows:

ASSETS	=	LIABILITIES	+	OWNERS' EQUITY
Accounts Receivable +$2,000	=			Retained Earnings +$2,000

Assets increased by $2,000 and retained earnings increased by $2,000.

TRANSACTION 7 EXPENSE INCURRED FOR CASH.

The company paid $1,400 in cash for advertising that appeared in a magazine. This causes a decrease in the asset Cash. Since the advertising has already appeared, Recycle has received the benefit. When assets decrease and the firm receives a current benefit, the company incurs an expense. The expense results in a decrease in owners' equity (retained earnings). We again use the accounting equation to analyze the transaction:

ASSETS	=	LIABILITIES	+	OWNERS' EQUITY
Cash −$1,400	=			Retained Earnings −$1,400

Assets decreased by $1,400 and retained earnings decreased by $1,400.

TRANSACTION 8 RECEIVABLE COLLECTED IN CASH.

Recycle received a check for $1,500 from Boone in partial payment of its account. Cash increases by $1,500, and Accounts Receivable decreases by the same amount. Note that there is no revenue now, because the company recorded the revenue when the service was performed. Again, we analyze the transaction with the accounting equation as follows:

ASSETS	=	LIABILITIES	+	OWNERS' EQUITY
Cash +$1,500	=			
Accounts Receivable −$1,500				

One asset increased by the same amount that another asset decreased.

TRANSACTION 9 EXPENSE INCURRED ON ACCOUNT.

During December, the company used utilities at a cost of $600. Thus, the firm has received the benefit. The utility company billed Recycle, but Recycle has not paid. This causes an increase in Accounts Payable and a decrease in owners' equity (retained earnings). Because of incurring the expense, the owners' claim to assets decreases. We use the accounting equation to analyze the transaction as follows:

ASSETS	=	LIABILITIES	+	OWNERS' EQUITY
		Accounts Payable +$600		Retained Earnings −$600

TRANSACTION 10   CASH DIVIDENDS DECLARED AND PAID.

Recycle Consultants, Inc. declared and paid a $1,000 cash dividend to owners. Cash decreases by $1,000. Owners' equity (retained earnings) decreases by $1,000. Using the accounting equation, the analysis appears as follows:

ASSETS	=	LIABILITIES	+	OWNERS' EQUITY
Cash −$1,000	=			Retained
				Earnings −$1,000

Exhibit 1.3 summarizes the effect of each transaction on the accounting equation. The balances show the status of each element of the equation. As of December 31, 2007, the accounting equation is in balance. Total assets are $93,600 ($15,100 + $500 + $20,000 + $50,000 + $8,000). Total equities are also $93,600 ($600 + $90,000 + $3,000).

Four Basic Financial Statements

Learning Goal 5   Prepare simple versions of the four basic financial statements.

In the Introduction to this text, we examined the balance sheet, income statement, and statement of cash flows. Now we add a fourth financial statement, the statement of owners' equity. In this simple illustration, we can prepare all four financial statements from the information in Exhibit 1.3.

Income Statement

The difference between revenues and expenses for a period is **net income**. If expenses exceed revenues, the difference is **net loss**. We report the details of revenue and expense in an **income statement**. Many users believe that the income statement is the most important statement. It reports whether the business met its profit objective. Net income is important to creditors because it shows the firm's ability to earn profits to pay its debts. Owners are interested in net income because the market value of the firm's common stock and cash dividends to owners are related to profits.

Exhibit 1.4 shows Recycle Consultants' income statement for December, 2007. We get the income and expense information from the owners' equity column of the schedule in Exhibit 1.3. The income statement shows the totals of each type of revenue. For Recycle, there was only one source of revenue: fees earned of $6,000. Next, the statement lists the totals of each type of expense. Recycle incurred two expenses: advertising of $1,400 and utilities of $600. Finally, the statement shows the difference between revenues and expenses as net income of $4,000. Net income increases the owners' interest in the business. Thus, we carry the $4,000 net income over to the statement of owners' equity.

The heading on *all* financial statements contains three lines of information:

1. The name of the business.

2. The name of the statement.

3. The date of the statement or period of time covered.

Here, the income statement shows the results of operations for the month ended December 31, 2007.

Transaction	Date	Effect on Accounting Equation	ASSETS					=	LIABILITIES	+	OWNERS' EQUITY		Explanation of Change in Owners' Equity
			Cash	Accounts Receivable	Land	Building	Furniture	=	Accounts Payable	+	Common Stock	Retained Earnings	
	2007 Dec.												
(1)	1	+A: +OE	+$ 90,000					=		+	+ $90,000		Investment
(2)	5	+A: -A	- 70,000		+$20,000	+$50,000							
		Balances	$ 20,000		$20,000	$50,000		=			$90,000		
(3)	9	+A: +L					+$8,000		+$8,000				
		Balances	$ 20,000		$20,000	$50,000	$8,000	=	$8,000	+	$90,000		
(4)	16	+A: +OE	+ 4,000									+ $4,000	Revenue
		Balances	$ 24,000		$20,000	$50,000	$8,000	=	$8,000	+	$90,000	+ $4,000	
(5)	18	-A: -L	- 8,000						- 8,000				
		Balances	$ 16,000		$20,000	$50,000	$8,000	=	$ 0	+	$90,000	+ $4,000	
(6)	23	+A: +OE		+$2,000								+ 2,000	Revenue
		Balances	$ 16,000	$2,000	$20,000	$50,000	$8,000	=	$ 0	+	$90,000	+ $6,000	
(7)	26	-A: -OE	- 1,400									- 1,400	Expense
		Balances	$ 14,600	$2,000	$20,000	$50,000	$8,000	=	$ 0	+	$90,000	+ $4,600	
(8)	27	+A: -A	+ 1,500	- 1,500									
		Balances	$ 16,100	$ 500	$20,000	$50,000	$8,000	=	$ 0	+	$90,000	+ $4,600	
(9)	30	+L: -OE							+ 600			- 600	Expense
		Balances	$ 16,100	$ 500	$20,000	$50,000	$8,000	=	$ 600	+	$90,000	+ $4,000	
(10)	31	-A: -OE	- 1,000									- 1,000	Dividend
		Balances	$ 15,100	$ 500	$20,000	$50,000	$8,000	=	$ 600	+	$90,000	+ $3,000	

EXHIBIT 1.3

Summarized Accounting Equation

Statement of Owners' Equity

The **statement of owners' equity** reports the changes in the owners' interest in the assets during the period. The statement begins with the owners' equity at the end of the last period. We then *add* any new investments by owners during the period and the period's net income. Finally, we *subtract* any dividends declared to get the owners' equity at the end of this period. The period used for the statement of owners' equity must be the same as that for the income statement.

Exhibit 1.4 shows the statement of owners' equity for Recycle Consultants, Inc. Since December was the first month of operations, there was no beginning common stock. We add the initial investment of $90,000 in common stock. To determine ending retained earnings, we add the net income from the income statement, $4,000. Then, we subtract the dividends of $1,000. This makes ending retained earnings $3,000. Total ending owners' equity is common stock $90,000 plus retained earnings $3,000 equals $93,000. We carry the $93,000 forward to the owners' equity section of the balance sheet.

Classified Balance Sheet

The **balance sheet** summarizes assets, liabilities, and owners' equity at a specific moment in time. The balance sheet is an expansion of the accounting equation. Since it shows the company's financial position, we can also call this statement a *statement of financial position*.

To make balance sheet information easier to interpret, we group or *classify* similar information together. The classification and the order of the items depend on tradition, the type of business, and the anticipated use of the balance sheet. Recycle Consultants' balance sheet classifies assets by their length of service. It classifies liabilities by when they must be paid. This is the most common method of classification.

> Statement **classification** is the arrangement of financial statement items into groupings that have some common basis. This permits subtotals for these similar items and interpretation of the information.

Assets are divided into two primary categories: (1) current and (2) property, plant, and equipment. **Current assets** include cash and other assets that the company expects to convert into cash within one year. It also includes assets that will be used in the operation of the business within one year, such as office supplies. We list current assets in descending order of their expected conversion into cash (liquidity). The **property, plant, and equipment** category includes assets used over a long period in the operation of the business. They are not held for the purpose of reselling them later. We list them in their order of permanence with the most permanent asset first.

Liabilities are classified as either current or long-term. **Current liabilities** include debts that must be paid within one year. We list them in their probable order of payment with those to be paid first shown first. **Long-term liabilities** include debts that are not due during the next year.

The form of business organization determines the reporting of owners' equity. A corporation, such as Recycle Consultants, Inc., reports owners' equity as shown in Exhibit 1.4. Exhibit 1.4 shows the balance sheet for Recycle Consultants, Inc. We list each asset and liability from Exhibit 1.3, with its ending balance.

Statement of Cash Flows

A fourth financial statement reports the cash flows during a period. It classifies the flows of cash as either *operating, investing, or financing* activities. This statement is the **statement of cash flows**. It shows all the reasons why the balance in cash changed during the accounting period.

Exhibit 1.5 shows Recycle Consultants' statement of cash flows for the month of December, 2007. The cash column of Exhibit contains the information used to construct the statement of cash flows. Note that cash received from customers is not equal to revenues—Recycle has not collected $500 of the revenues from a customer. Also, the utilities expense does not appear on the statement

RECYCLE CONSULTANTS, INC.
INCOME STATEMENT
FOR THE MONTH ENDED DECEMBER 31, 2007

Revenues
Fees revenue $ 6,000
Expenses
Advertising expense $ 1,400
Utilities expense   600
  Total expenses   2,000
Net income $ 4,000

RECYCLE CONSULTANTS, INC.
STATEMENT OF OWNERS' EQUITY
FOR THE MONTH ENDED DECEMBER 31, 2007

Common stock, December 1, 2007 $ 0
Add: Investments by owners   90,000
  Common stock, December 31, 2007 $ 90,000
Retained earnings, December 1, 2007 $ 0
Add: Net income   4,000
Deduct: Dividends   (1,000)
  Retained earnings, December 31, 2007   3,000
Owners' equity, December, 31, 2007 $ 93,000

RECYCLE CONSULTANTS, INC.
BALANCE SHEET
DECEMBER 31, 2007

ASSETS

Current assets
Cash $ 15,100
Accounts receivable   500
  Total current assets $ 15,600
Property, plant, and equipment
Land $ 20,000
Building   50,000
Furniture   8,000
  Total property, plant, and equipment   78,000
Total assets $ 93,600

LIABILITIES

Current liabilities
Accounts payable $ 600

OWNERS' EQUITY

Common stock $ 90,000
Retained earnings   3,000
  Total owners' equity   93,000

Total liabilities and owners' equity $ 93,600

EXHIBIT **1.4**

Financial Statements for Recycle Consultants, Inc.

because Recycle has not paid the cash. Normally net cash provided by operating activities on the statement of cash flows will not equal net income.

RECYCLE CONSULTANTS, INC.
STATEMENT OF CASH FLOWS
FOR THE MONTH ENDED DECEMBER 31, 2007

Cash flows from operating activities		
Cash received from customers	$ 5,500	
Cash paid for advertising	(1,400)	
Net cash provided by operating activities		$ 4,100
Cash flows from investing activities		
Purchase of land	$ (20,000)	
Purchase of building	(50,000)	
Purchase of furniture	(8,000)	
Net cash used in investing activities		(78,000)
Cash flows from financing activities		
Proceeds from issuance of common stock	$ 90,000	
Dividends paid	(1,000)	
Net cash provided by financing activities		89,000
Net increase in cash		$ 15,100
Cash at beginning of month		0
Cash at end of month		$ 15,100

EXHIBIT **1.5**

Statement of Cash Flows for Recycle Consultants, Inc.

The purchase of land, buildings, and furniture are investing activities. They have all caused cash outflows this month. The initial investment by owners is a financing activity. It caused a cash inflow during the month. Dividends caused a financing outflow. A more extensive discussion of the statement of cash flows appears in Chapter 15.

ANALYZING INFORMATION

Learning Goal 6   Analyze financial statement information for real-life companies.

In the Introduction to the text, we asked some basic financial statement interpretation questions. The real-life company examples in the Introduction covered two fiscal years. Now, we will look at and interpret a company's results over a longer period of time. We will examine Amazon.com for the years 2004-2001. First, we will look at the income statement. Then, we will examine the balance sheet. Finally, we will relate the two financial statements together.

Income Statement Analysis

Exhibit 1.6 shows comparative income statements for the fiscal years 2004-2001. For each year, we show the dollar amount and the common-size percent. For example, in 2004 total expenses for Amazon.com were $6,332.6 million and were 91.5% ($6,332.6 ÷ $6,921.1) of total revenues. In a common-size income statement, we always set total revenues equal to 100%. We will follow the same question and answer approach we used in the Introduction.

Question 1. Are total revenues for Amazon higher or lower over the four year period?

Analysis 1. For Amazon, total revenues in fiscal 2004 ($6,921,100,000) are significantly higher than the total for fiscal 2001 ($3,122,400,000). Over the four year period, total revenues have steadily and dramatically increased.

AMAZON.COM, INC.
COMPARATIVE COMMON-SIZE INCOME STATEMENTS
For The Years Ended December 31, 2004, 2003, 2002, 2001
(*in millions*)

	2004	2004	2003	2003	2002	2002	2001	2001
	$	%	$	%	$	%	$	%
Total revenues	$ 6,921.1	100.0%	$ 5,263.7	100.0%	$ 3,932.9	100.0%	$ 3,122.4	100.0%
Total expenses	$ 6,332.6	91.5%	$ 5,228.4	99.3%	$ 4,082.0	103.8%	$ 3,689.7	118.2%
Net income (loss)	$ 588.5	8.5%	$ 35.3	0.7%	$ (149.1)	-3.8%	$ (567.3)	-18.2%

EXHIBIT **1.6**

Comparative Common-size Income Statements for Amazon.com, Inc., 2004-2001

Question 2. What is the percent change in total revenues from 2001 to 2004?

Analysis 2. The percent increase in total revenues from fiscal 2001 to fiscal 2004 is:

$$121.7\% = 100 \times \frac{\$3,798,700,000^*}{\$3,122,400,000} \qquad {}^* \$6,921,100,000 - \$3,122,400,000$$

Total revenues for Amazon increased 121.7% from 2001 to 2004.

Question 3. Is the percent of total expenses to total revenues increasing or decreasing over the four year period?

Analysis 3. The percent of expenses to revenues decreased from 118.2% in 2001 to 91.5% in 2004. The result is a net income percent of 8.5% in 2004. Amazon.com, Inc. has two *favorable* trends over the four-year period. First, total revenues have increased sharply. Second, the net loss percent has changed from (18.2)% in 2001 to a net income of 8.5% in 2004.

Balance Sheet Analysis

Exhibit 1.7 shows comparative balance sheets as of December 31, 2004-2001. For each year, we show the dollar amount and the common-size percent. For example, in 2004 total liabilities for Amazon.com, Inc. were $3,475.7 million and were 107.0% ($3,475.7 ÷ $3,248.5) of total liabilities and owners' equity. In a common-size balance sheet, we always set total assets, and total liabilities and owners' equity equal to 100%.

Question 1. Are total assets for Amazon.com higher or lower over the four year period?

Analysis 1. For Amazon.com, total assets at December 31, 2004 ($3,248,500,000) are significantly higher than the total at December 31, 2001 ($1,637,600,000).

Question 2. What is the percent change in total assets from 2001 to 2004?

Analysis 2. In this case, the percent increase in total assets from December 31, 2001, to December 31, 2004, is:

$$98.4\% = 100 \times \frac{\$1,610,900,000^*}{\$1,637,600,000} \qquad {}^* \$3,248,500,000 - \$1,637,600,000$$

As with total revenues, the total assets for Amazon have increased significantly over the four year period.

AMAZON.COM, INC.
COMPARATIVE COMMON-SIZE BALANCE SHEETS
December 31, 2004, 2003, 2002, 2001
(*in millions*)

	2004	2004	2003	2003	2002	2002	2001	2001
	$	%	$	%	$	%	$	%
Total assets	$ 3,248.5	100.0%	$ 2,162.0	100.0%	$ 1,990.4	100.0%	$ 1,637.6	100.0%
Total liabilities	$ 3,475.7	107.0%	$ 3,198.1	147.9%	$ 3,343.2	168.0%	$ 3,077.6	187.9%
Total owners' equity	$ (227.2)	-7.0%	$(1,036.1)	-47.9%	$(1,352.8)	-68.0%	$(1,440.0)	-87.9%
Total liabilities and owners' equity	$ 3,248.5	100.0%	$ 2,162.0	100.0%	$ 1,990.4	100.0%	$ 1,637.6	100.0%

EXHIBIT **1.7**

Comparative Common-size Balance Sheets for Amazon.com, Inc., 2004-2001

Question 3. Is the percent of total liabilities to total liabilities + owners' equity increasing or decreasing? As a result, is there more risk that Amazon could not pay its debts?

Analysis 3. In Exhibit 1.7, refer to the common-size percent for liabilities each year. The percent of liabilities decreased sharply from 187.9% in 2001 to a low of 107.0% in 2004. Although improved in 2004, the high percent of liabilities over the entire four-year period is very *unfavorable*.

Integrative Income Statement and Balance Sheet Analysis

In our analysis so far, we observed that both total revenues and total assets for Amazon increased significantly from 2001 to 2004. Now, we need to combine this information to assess the overall efficiency of Amazon.

Question 1. Is Amazon operating efficiently by using the least amount of asset investment to generate a given level of total revenues?

Analysis 1. We can answer this question for Amazon by dividing total revenues by total average assets for each year. Average assets for a year are simply ending assets plus beginning assets divided by 2. The computations for 2004, 2003, and 2002 are:

Fiscal 2004
$$\frac{\$6,921,100,000}{\$2,705,250,000^*} = 2.56 \text{ times}$$

Fiscal 2003
$$\frac{\$5,263,700,000}{\$2,076,200,000^{**}} = 2.54 \text{ times}$$

Fiscal 2002
$$\frac{\$3,932,900,000}{\$1,814,000,000^{***}} = 2.17 \text{ times}$$

$$^*(\$3,248,500,000 + \$2,162,000,000) \div 2$$
$$^{**}(\$2,162,000,000 + \$1,990,400,000) \div 2$$
$$^{***}(\$1,990,400,000 + \$1,637,600,000) \div 2$$

The resulting number is a ratio called *total asset turnover*. A higher number for the total asset turnover ratio is more favorable since it shows that a business is operating with a smaller asset investment to generate a given level of total revenues. For Amazon, the total asset turnover ratio increased from 2.17 times in 2001 to 2.56 times in 2004. This is a *favorable* trend. Amazon is operating more efficiently.

LEARNING GOALS REVIEW

1. **Identify generally accepted accounting principles (GAAP) and the groups that help develop them.**

   Generally accepted accounting principles are the accounting standards that make financial information useful for the users. The major professional organizations that help develop accounting principles are the American Institute of Certified Public Accountants (AICPA), the Financial Accounting Standards Board (FASB), and the Securities and Exchange Commission (SEC).

2. **Identify the importance of ethics in accounting.**
    Ethics is the process individuals use to evaluate their conduct in light of moral principles and values. It is important to the credibility of accounting information.

3. **Construct the accounting equation and define *assets*, *liabilities*, and *owners' equity*.**
    The accounting equation can be stated as follows:

    Assets = Liabilities + Owners' Equity

    The accounting equation requires that everything of value owned by a business (its assets) equals all of the claims against the business (its equities). There are two types of claims against the assets. Liabilities are the claims of nonowners, and owners' equity are the claims of owners.

4. **Analyze business transactions using the accounting equation.**
    Each transaction must be recorded in the accounting records in a way to keep the accounting equation in balance. This means that the record of the change caused by the transaction must have at least two parts. Thus, whenever an asset increases, some other asset decreases, or a liability or owners' equity increases, and vice versa. Whenever a liability or owners' equity increases, some other liability or owners' equity decreases or an asset increases, and vice versa.

5. **Prepare simple versions of the four basic financial statements.**
    The four basic financial statements are the income statement, statement of owners' equity, balance sheet, and statement of cash flows. The income statement shows revenues and expenses for a period. The statement of owners' equity summarizes the changes in common stock and retained earnings for the period. The balance sheet shows the financial position at the end of the period. The statement of cash flows shows the inflows and outflows of cash for the period.

6. **Analyze financial statement information for real-life companies.**
    Frequently, we can see relationships and trends easier when we convert financial statements to common-size percents.

DEMONSTRATION PROBLEM

Accounting Information

On March 5, 2007, Willus Corporation was formed to publish stories for magazines. The following events took place during March.

2007

Mar.	5	Owners invested $10,000 and received shares of common stock in Willus Corporation.
	8	Rented a small office for use in writing and paid rent for March of $500 in cash.
	17	Purchased computer for $5,000. Paid the store $500 cash and signed a note payable in six months for the balance.
	18	Purchased computer software for $600 on open account.
	19	Sold a story to a magazine for $2,000 in cash.
	20	Paid $200 of the amount owed on the computer software.
	28	Sold a completed story to a magazine for $500 on account.
	30	Received a bill for photos used in the two stories sold this month. The bill was $400.

REQUIRED

1. **(LG 3)** Set up a columnar worksheet similar to Exhibit 1.3. Across the top, write out the accounting equation. Enter the following items in columns, making sure to enter them under the proper accounting equation element: Cash, Accounts Receivable, Computer System, Accounts Payable, Notes Payable, Common Stock, and Retained Earnings.

2. **(LG 4)** Analyze each of the transactions using the accounting equation, and enter those that affect the business in the proper columns. Use Exhibit 1.3 as a model.

3. **(LG 5)** Prepare the four basic financial statements as of March 31, 2007.

SOLUTION

Requirements 1 and 2

> **Solution Approach**
>
> Across a piece of columnar paper, write the accounting equation. Then under the asset side of the equation, enter each of the asset items (there are three). Do the same with the liabilities (two) and owners' equity (two). Then begin analyzing each transaction. Use the accounting equation as a tool. Remember that each transaction must change items in the equation so that the equation remains in balance. Total assets must be equal to total liabilities and owners' equity after each transaction is recorded.

Date		Effect on Accounting Equation	ASSETS			=	LIABILITIES		+	OWNERS' EQUITY		Explanation of Change in Owners' Equity
			Cash +	Accounts Receivable +	Computer System =		Accounts Payable +	Notes Payable +		Common Stock +	Retained Earnings	
2007 Mar.	5	+A: +OE	+ $ 10,000			=			+	+$10,000		Investment
	8	-A: -OE	- 500						+		- $ 500	Expense
		Balances	$ 9,500 +			=			+	$10,000 +	$ (500)	
	17	+A: -A, +L	- 500		+ $5,000			+ $4,500				
		Balances	$ 9,000 +		$5,000	=		+ $4,500 +		$10,000 +	$ (500)	
	18	+A: +L			+ 600		+$600					
		Balances	$ 9,000 +		$5,600	=	$600	+ $4,500 +		$10,000 +	$ (500)	
	19	+A: +OE	+ 2,000						+		+ 2,000	Revenue
		Balances	$ 11,000		$5,600	=	$600	+ $4,500 +		$10,000 +	$1,500	
	20	-A: -L	- 200				- 200					
		Balances	$ 10,800 +		$5,600	=	$400	+ $4,500 +		$10,000 +	$1,500	
	28	+A: +OE		+ $500					+		+ 500	Revenue
		Balances	$ 10,800 +	$500 +	$5,600	=	$400	+ $4,500 +		$10,000 +	$2,000	
	30	+L: -OE					+ 400				- 400	Expense
		Balances	$ 10,800 +	$500 +	$5,600	=	$800	+ $4,500 +		$10,000 +	$1,600	

Requirement 3

> **Solution Approach**
>
> In preparing the financial statements, start with the income statement. List the revenue first, then the expenses. Subtract the expenses from the revenue to get net income. Second, prepare the statement of owners' equity. Carry the net income over from the

income statement. Third, prepare the balance sheet. The assets should be classified as either current or property, plant, and equipment. Both of the liabilities are current. Last, prepare the statement of cash flows. Use the cash column of the schedule to identify the cash flows.

WILLUS CORPORATION
INCOME STATEMENT
FOR THE MONTH ENDED MARCH 31, 2007

Revenues
Fees revenue		$2,500

Expenses
Photo expense	$400	
Rent expense	500	
Total expenses		900
Net income		$1,600

WILLUS CORPORATION
STATEMENT OF OWNERS' EQUITY
FOR THE MONTH ENDED MARCH 31, 2007

Common stock, March 1, 2007	$ 0	
Add: Investments by owners	10,000	
Common stock, March 31, 2007		$ 10,000
Retained earnings, March 1, 2007	$ 0	
Add: Net income	1,600	
Deduct: Dividends	0	
Retained earnings, March 31, 2007		1,600
Owners' equity, March 31, 2007		$11,600

WILLUS CORPORATION
BALANCE SHEET
MARCH 31, 2007
Assets

Current assets
Cash	$10,800	
Accounts receivable	500	
Total current assets		$ 11,300

Property, plant, and equipment
Computer system		5,600
Total assets		$ 16,900

Liabilities

Current liabilities
Accounts payable	$ 800	
Notes payable	4,500	
Total liabilities		$ 5,300

Owners' Equity
Common stock	$10,000	
Retained earnings	1,600	
Total owners' equity		11,600
Total liabilities and owners' equity		$ 16,900

WILLUS CORPORATION
STATEMENT OF CASH FLOWS
FOR THE MONTH ENDED MARCH 31, 2007

Cash flows from operating activities		
Cash received from customers	$ 2,000	
Cash paid for rent	(500)	
Net cash provided by operating activities		$ 1,500
Cash flows from investing activities		
Purchase of computer system	$ (700)	
Net cash used by investing activities		(700)
Cash flows from financing activities		
Proceeds from issuance of stock	$ 10,000	
Net cash provided by financing activities		10,000
Net increase in cash		$ 10,800
Cash at beginning of month		0
Cash at end of month		$ 10,800

GLOSSARY

American Institute of Certified Public Accountants (AICPA) The national organization of certified public accountants that was the major source of accounting standards from 1937 to 1973.

asset A thing of value owned by an economic enterprise.

balance sheet The financial statement that summarizes a firm's assets, liabilities, and owners' equity as of a specific date.

classification Grouping of similar elements of the accounting equation in a financial statement.

common stock Amount of investment by owners in the corporation.

cost principle The accounting principle that requires assets to be recorded at the price originally paid for them.

current assets Cash and other assets that will be consumed or converted into cash within one year.

current liabilities Liabilities to be paid within one year.

dividends Distributions of net income to owners.

equities Claims against the total assets of a business.

ethics The process that individuals use to evaluate their conduct in light of moral principles and values.

expenses The outflow of assets or incurring of liabilities that occur in the process of generating revenues.

Financial Accounting Standards Board (FASB) The current independent private body that issues accounting concepts and standards statements for financial accounting in the private sector.

generally accepted accounting principles (GAAP) Standards used by accountants to make financial information more meaningful.

going-concern concept The accounting concept that an entity will continue to operate indefinitely unless there is evidence to the contrary.

Governmental Accounting Standards Board (GASB) The current independent private body that issues accounting concepts and standards statements for state and local governments.

income statement The financial statement that compares revenues and expenses for a period of time to determine net income or loss.

liabilities The debts of an enterprise; creditors' claims against the assets.

long-term liabilities Liabilities such as bonds payable that are not due to be paid for more than one year in the future.

net assets Total assets minus total liabilities.

net income The difference between revenues and expenses for a period.

net loss The difference between revenues and expenses for a period if expenses exceed revenues.

objectivity principle The accounting principle that whenever possible the amounts used in recording transactions should be based on objective source documents.

owners' equity The sum of all ownership claims against assets of an enterprise.

property, plant, and equipment Long-lived assets that are used in the operation of a firm and are not held for resale.

realization principle The accounting principle that the business earns revenues when it performs services or delivers goods.

retained earnings Cumulative total of net income, net loss, and dividends since the start of the corporation.

revenues The source of an increase in assets from performing services or delivering a product.

Securities and Exchange Commission (SEC) The federal government agency with legal authority to prescribe accounting methods for firms whose stock or bonds are sold to the public on the exchanges.

stable dollar concept The accounting concept that the dollar is free enough from changes in purchasing power to be used as the basic measuring unit.

statement of cash flows The financial statement that reports the events that cause inflows and outflows of cash during the period.

Statements of Financial Accounting Standards (SFAS) Titles of the authoritative pronouncements of the Financial Accounting Standards Board.

statement of owners' equity The financial statement that reports the changes in the owners' interest in the assets of the firm during the period.

QUESTIONS FOR GROUP LEARNING

Q1- 1. What is the primary reason for recording accounting information?

Q1- 2. What are the three major authoritative bodies in accounting? What role has each played in the development of accounting principles?

Q1- 3. What are generally accepted accounting principles (GAAP)? How do these principles arise?

Q1- 4. What are ethics? Why is the study of ethics important?

Q1- 5. What are the characteristics of an asset? A liability? An owners' equity item?

Q1- 6. What are the classifications of assets? Of liabilities? Explain how to determine when an item falls into each classification.

Q1- 7. What are the four basic financial statements? What does each report?

Q1- 8. What is a business transaction? Can there be a business transaction that does not change two or more elements of the accounting equation? Explain.

EXERCISES

E1- 9. **The accounting equation (LG 3)** Provide the missing amounts below:

Current Assets	Property, Plant, and Equipment	Current Liabilities	Long-term Liabilities	Owners' Equity
$ 6,000	$ 19,000	$ 5,000	$10,000	$?
30,000	60,000	?	30,000	50,000
?	100,000	10,000	40,000	80,000
20,000	?	5,000	30,000	25,000
20,000	36,000	10,000	?	21,000

E1-10. **Changes in the accounting equation (LG 3)** Every transaction results in at least two changes in the accounting equation. For each of the following changes, list the other three types of changes that may have occurred to keep the equation in balance. The first is done as an example.

   a. An increase in an asset. *Answer:* A decrease in another asset, an increase in a liability, or an increase in owners' equity.

   b. An increase in a liability.

   c. A decrease in an asset.

   d. An increase in owners' equity.

   e. A decrease in a liability.

E1-11. **Using the accounting equation to analyze a transaction (LG 4)** Dave Company purchased $800 in office supplies, promising to pay in 30 days. Identify the two parts of the accounting equation that changed and indicate if they increased or decreased and by how much. Does this keep the accounting equation in balance?

E1-12. **Using the accounting equation to analyze a transaction (LG 4)** Tolland Services purchased a computer system for $8,000, paying cash. Identify the two parts of the accounting equation that changed and indicate if they increased or decreased and by how much. Does this keep the accounting equation in balance?

E1-13. **Analysis of balance sheet transactions (LG 3, 4)** Listed below are several transactions for Ralph Company. Analyze the transactions in terms of the accounting equation in a form similar to Exhibit 1.3, disregarding balances.

2007

Jun.	4	Owners invested $15,000 in cash and received shares of common stock.
	8	Purchased $600 in office supplies on account, promising to pay in 30 days.
	12	Bought a used truck at a cost of $4,000, paying cash.

E1-14. **Analysis of revenue and expense transactions (LG 3, 4)** Listed below are several transactions for Quickoil Company. Analyze the transactions in terms of the accounting equation in a form similar to Exhibit 1.3, disregarding balances.

2007		
Aug.	1	Paid rent on office space for August in cash, $800.
	11	Completed services for a customer and received $1,000 cash.
	15	Received a bill for advertising that had appeared in the newspaper $150. No payment was made.
	26	Completed services for a customer and sent a bill for $900.

E1-15. **Balance sheet classification (LG 5)** Identify each of the following as (1) a current asset, (2) property, plant, and equipment, (3) a current liability, (4) a long-term liability, or (5) owners' equity:

a. Accounts payable

b. Accounts receivable

c. Buildings

d. Cash

e. Delivery equipment

f. Common stock

g. Land

h. Notes payable (due June 17, 2009)

i. Notes receivable (due 60 days from current date)

j. Office supplies

k. Store equipment

E1-16. **Preparation of balance sheet (LG 5)** The following alphabetical list of information is taken from the records of Delightful Doughnuts Company for December 31, 2007:

Accounts payable	$12,000
Accounts receivable	28,000
Building	80,000
Cash	10,000
Delivery equipment	15,000
Common stock	52,000
Retained earnings	31,000
Land	40,000
Merchandise inventory	30,000
Notes payable (due April 1, 2008)	18,000
Notes payable (due July 1, 2011)	90,000

Prepare a balance sheet.

E1-17. **Preparation of financial statements (LG 5)** Barsky Company was formed on January 1, 2007. The following alphabetical list of information is taken from the records on December 31, 2007:

Accounts payable	$20,000
Accounts receivable	11,000
Advertising expense	8,000
Cash	15,000
Common stock	50,000
Dividends	5,000
Fees revenue	94,000
Land	50,000
Rent expense	18,000
Trucks	25,000
Utilities expense	6,000
Wages expense	30,000
Wages payable	4,000

Prepare an income statement, a statement of owners' equity, and a balance sheet from this information.

PROBLEMS

P1-18. Using the accounting equation for real-life companies (LG 3) Listed below are the assets, liabilities, and owners' equities of several major U.S. corporations (in millions of dollars).

	Wal-Mart	Nike	Johnson & Johnson	IBM
Total current assets	$28,200.0	$?	$15,450.0	$42,461.0
Total noncurrent assets	?	2,194.3	15,871.0	?
Total assets	83,400.0	?	?	?
Total current liabilities	27,200.0	?	7,140.0	?
Total long-term liabilities	?	538.4	?	15,963.0
Total owners' equity	35,100.0	3,494.5	18,808.0	23,614.0
Total liabilities and owners' equity	?	5,819.6	?	88,313.0

REQUIRED

Compute the missing numbers for each corporation.

P1-19. Computing net income, owners' equity, and missing balance sheet amount (LG 3) The loan officer from a bank is considering a loan request from Willington Company. No new investments in common stock were made by owners during 2007. He has obtained the following figures as of December 31, 2007, from the company:

Cash	$ 7,000
Fees revenue	44,000
Dividends	9,000
Supplies expense	4,000
Accounts receivable	?
Utilities expense	7,000
Accounts payable	4,000
Land	8,000
Rent expense	12,000
Supplies on hand	1,000
Owners' equity, January 1, 2007	5,000

REQUIRED

1. Compute the net income for the year ended December 31, 2007.

2. Compute total owners' equity on December 31, 2007.

3. Compute the total of liabilities and owners' equity on December 31, 2007.

4. Compute the amount of accounts receivable on December 31, 2007.

P1-20. Preparing financial statements (LG 5) Vernon Service, Inc. was formed on January 1, 2007, with an initial investment by shareholders of $40,000. The following information is available for Vernon Service, Inc. as of December 31, 2007:

Advertising expense	$ 5,000
Cash	9,000
Land	26,000
Wages expense	36,000
Accounts payable	7,000
Utilities expense	18,000
Service revenue	65,000
Automobiles	11,000
Notes payable (short-term)	6,000
Accounts receivable	13,000
Common stock	40,000

REQUIRED
Prepare the following financial statements:
a. Income statement for the year ended December 31, 2007.

b. Statement of owners' equity for the year ended December 31, 2007.

c. Balance sheet at December 31, 2007.

P1-21. Preparing financial statements for The Boeing Company (LG 5) Boeing is the world's largest aerospace company and commercial jet maker. Selected information (in millions) for the year ended December 31, 2004, is shown below.

Cash	$ 3,204.0
Expenses	50,585.0
Accounts payable	17,989.0
Dividends	648.0
Other current liabilities	2,846.0
Revenues	52,457.0
Other current assets	4,636.0
Noncurrent assets	38,863.0
Long-term liabilities	21,842.0
Accounts receivable	7,260.0
Owners' equity (January 1, 2004)	10,062.0

REQUIRED
Prepare the following financial statements:
a. Income statement for the year ended December 31, 2004.

b. Statement of owners' equity for the year ended December 31, 2004.

c. Balance sheet at December 31, 2004.

P1-22. **Analyzing transactions using the accounting equation and preparing a balance sheet (LG 3-5)** Dunbar, Inc. formed a new business to offer writing services to other businesses. Following are the transactions for the month of April 2007, when management was organizing the business. They planned to begin offering services in May 2007.

2007

Apr.	3	Owners invested $20,000 in cash in the new business and received shares of common stock.
	10	Purchased a word processing system at a cost of $2,000. The purchase was on account.
	16	Purchased supplies costing $400, on account, for use in the business.
	22	Bought an old compact car to use to deliver work to customers. Paid $450 cash for the car.
	24	Purchased some additional supplies, paying cash of $100.
	30	Paid the amount owed on the word processing system.

REQUIRED

1. Analyze the transactions and record them on a form similar to that shown in Exhibit 1.3.

2. Prepare a balance sheet as of April 30, 2007.

P1-23. **Analyzing transactions using the accounting equation (LG 3, 4)** Leanne, Inc. was formed to design and install small business computer systems. Following are transactions for December 2007, the first month of operations.

2007

Dec.	3	Owners invested $25,000 and received shares of common stock.
	6	Purchased a computer system for $11,000 on account. Promised to pay the seller by the end of the month.
	11	Purchased office supplies costing $1,000 using cash.
	14	Paid rent of $1,500 in cash for the month of December on a small office.
	20	Completed the installation of a computer system for a client. Received the total fee of $2,000 in cash.
	22	Received a bill in the amount of $500 for an advertisement that had appeared in the local business newspaper.
	27	Completed the installation of another computer system on account and billed the client $4,000.
	28	Paid $1,500 of cash dividends to owners.
	29	Paid the $11,000 owed on the computer system purchased on December 6.

REQUIRED

Analyze the transactions and record them on a form similar to that shown in Exhibit 1.3.

P1-24. **The accounting equation and the financial statements (LG 3, 5)** On January 1, 2007, Yah Company had total assets of $80,000 and total liabilities of $20,000. During 2007, the company had total revenues of $70,000 and total expenses of $50,000. Also during 2007, the cash dividends of $10,000 were declared and paid. On December 31, 2007, total assets were $100,000.

REQUIRED
Calculate the following amounts:

1. Owners' equity on January 31, 2007.

2. Net income for the year 2007.

3. Owners' equity on December 31, 2007.

4. Total liabilities on December 31, 2007.

P1-25. **Analyzing Target Corp. for the Period 2005-2002 (LG 6)** Target Corporation is one of the largest retail discount chains. The company has its headquarters in Minneapolis, Minnesota. Listed below are comparative income statements and balance sheets with common-size percents for 2005-2002 (in millions).

TARGET CORP.
COMPARATIVE COMMON-SIZE INCOME STATEMENTS
For The Years Ended January 31, 2005, 2004, 2003, 2002
(*in millions*)

	2005 $	2005 %	2004 $	2004 %	2003 $	2003 %	2002 $	2002 %
Total revenues	$ 46,839.0	100.0%	$ 48,163.0	100.0%	$ 43,917.0	100.0%	$ 39,888.0	100.0%
Total expenses	$ 43,641.0	93.2%	$ 46,322.0	96.2%	$ 42,263.0	96.2%	$ 38,520.0	96.6%
Net income (loss)	$ 3,198.0	6.8%	$ 1,841.0	3.8%	$ 1,654.0	3.8%	$ 1,368.0	3.4%

TARGET CORP.
COMPARATIVE COMMON-SIZE BALANCE SHEETS
January 31, 2005, 2004, 2003, 2002
(*in millions*)

	2005 $	2005 %	2004 $	2004 %	2003 $	2003 %	2002 $	2002 %
Total assets	$ 32,293.0	100.0%	$ 31,392.0	100.0%	$ 28,603.0	100.0%	$ 24,154.0	100.0%
Total liabilities	$ 19,264.0	59.7%	$ 20,327.0	64.8%	$ 19,160.0	67.0%	$ 16,294.0	67.5%
Total owners' equity	$ 13,029.0	40.3%	$ 11,065.0	35.2%	$ 9,443.0	33.0%	$ 7,860.0	32.5%
Total liabilities and owners' equity	$ 32,293.0	100.0%	$ 31,392.0	100.0%	$ 28,603.0	100.0%	$ 24,154.0	100.0%

REQUIRED
Income statement questions:
1. Are total revenues for Target higher or lower over the four year period?
2. What is the percent change in total revenues from 2002 to 2005?
3. Is the percent of total expenses to total revenues increasing or decreasing over the four year period?

Balance sheet questions:
4. Are total assets for Target higher or lower over the four year period?
5. What is the percent change in total assets from 2002 to 2005?
6. Is the percent of total liabilities to total liabilities + owners' equity increasing or decreasing? As a result, is there more risk that Target could not pay its debts?

Integrative income statement and balance sheet questions:
7. Is Target operating more or less efficiently from 2003 to 2005 by using the least amount of asset investment to generate a given level of total revenues?

P1-26. **Analyzing Wal-Mart Stores for the Period 2005-2002 (LG 6)** Wal-Mart is one of the largest retail stores in the world. Listed below are comparative income statements and balance sheets with common-size percents for 2005-2002 (in millions).

WAL-MART STORES
COMPARATIVE COMMON-SIZE INCOME STATEMENTS
For The Years Ended January 31, 2005, 2004, 2003, 2002
(in millions)

	2005	2005	2004	2004	2003	2003	2002	2002
	$	%	$	%	$	%	$	%
Total revenues	$ 287,989.0	100.0%	$ 258,681.0	100.0%	$ 246,525.0	100.0%	$ 204,011.0	100.0%
Total expenses	$ 277,722.0	96.4%	$ 249,627.0	96.5%	$ 238,486.0	96.7%	$ 197,419.0	96.8%
Net income (loss)	$ 10,267.0	3.6%	$ 9,054.0	3.5%	$ 8,039.0	3.3%	$ 6,592.0	3.2%

WAL-MART STORES
COMPARATIVE COMMON-SIZE BALANCE SHEETS
January 31, 2005, 2004, 2003, 2002
(in millions)

	2005	2005	2004	2004	2003	2003	2002	2002
	$	%	$	%	$	%	$	%
Total assets	$ 120,223.0	100.0%	$ 105,405.0	100.0%	$ 92,900.0	100.0%	$ 81,549.0	100.0%
Total liabilities	$ 70,827.0	58.9%	$ 61,782.0	58.6%	$ 53,439.0	57.5%	$ 46,357.0	56.8%
Total owners' equity	$ 49,396.0	41.1%	$ 43,623.0	41.4%	$ 39,461.0	42.5%	$ 35,192.0	43.2%
Total liabilities and owners' equity	$ 120,223.0	100.0%	$ 105,405.0	100.0%	$ 92,900.0	100.0%	$ 81,549.0	100.0%

REQUIRED
Income statement questions:

1. Are total revenues for Wal-Mart higher or lower over the four year period?

2. What is the percent change in total revenues from 2002 to 2005?

3. Is the percent of total expenses to total revenues increasing or decreasing over the four year period?

Balance sheet questions:

4. Are total assets for Wal-Mart higher or lower over the four year period?

5. What is the percent change in total assets from 2002 to 2005?

6. Is the percent of total liabilities to total liabilities + owners' equity increasing or decreasing? As a result, is there more risk that Wal-Mart could not pay its debts?

Integrative income statement and balance sheet questions:

7. Is Wal-Mart operating more or less efficiently from 2003 to 2005 by using the least amount of asset investment to generate a given level of total revenues?

PRACTICE CASE

Analyzing transactions and preparing financial statements (LG 3-6) Tony Cycle Rental, Inc. opened in June, 2007. During the first month of operations the following events took place:

2007

Jun.	2	Owners invested $60,000 cash in Tony Cycle Rental and received shares of common stock.
	5	Purchased 25 bicycles to be rented to customers at a total cost of $7,500. Made a down payment of $2,000 in cash and signed a six-month note payable for the $5,500 remaining balance.
	7	Paid $1,000 rent on a store for June in cash.

8	Purchased $500 in bicycle repair supplies on account and promised to pay before the end of the month.
11	Paid a local printer $200 cash for advertising flyers, which were distributed to motels and stores in the area.
16	Rented 10 bicycles to a local convention organizer who promised to pay $1,200 in a week.
20	Rented bicycles to a vacationing family for $600 cash.
23	Received $800 in cash from the convention organizer who had rented the bicycles on June 16.
26	Paid $400 cash on account for the supplies purchased on June 8.
30	Paid a part-time worker $800 for June.

REQUIRED

1. At the top of columnar paper write out the accounting equation. Set up columns on a work sheet similar to that in Exhibit 1.3 and enter the following items making sure to enter them under the proper accounting equation element: cash, accounts receivable, repair supplies, bicycles, accounts payable, notes payable (short-term), common stock, and retained earnings.

2. Analyze each of the events using the accounting equation and enter those that affect the business in the proper columns (as in Exhibit 1.3).

3. Prepare the following financial statements:

   a. Income statement for the month ended June 30, 2007.

   b. Statement of owners' equity for the month ended June 30, 2007.

   c. Balance sheet as of June 30, 2007.

   d. Statement of cash flows for the month ended June 30, 2007.

BUSINESS DECISION AND COMMUNICATION PROBLEM

Comparing balance sheets to make a loan decision Assume you are a loan officer for the New London Bank. Two home decorating businesses each request a loan of $100,000. The purpose of each loan is to construct a building for use as a showroom. The only information you have been provided to evaluate the loan requests are the following balance sheets:

WAFEEK'S HOME DESIGNS
BALANCE SHEET
DECEMBER 31, 2007
ASSETS

Current assets	
Cash	$ 90,000
Accounts receivable	20,000
Decorating supplies	10,000
Total current assets	$ 120,000
Property, plant, and equipment	
Land	80,000
Total assets	$ 200,000

LIABILITIES

Current liabilities

Accounts payable	$ 10,000
Notes payable	5,000
Salaries payable	1,000
Total current liabilities	$ 16,000

OWNERS' EQUITY

Owners' equity	184,000
Total liabilities and owners' equity	$ 200,000

OSCAR'S HOME DESIGNS
BALANCE SHEET
DECEMBER 31, 2007

ASSETS

Current assets

Cash	$ 10,000
Accounts receivable	70,000
Decorating supplies	40,000
Total current assets	$ 120,000

Property, plant, and equipment

Land	80,000
Total assets	$ 200,000

LIABILITIES

Current liabilities

Accounts payable	$ 80,000
Notes payable	70,000
Salaries payable	20,000
Total current liabilities	$ 170,000

OWNERS' EQUITY

Owners' equity	30,000
Total liabilities and owners' equity	$ 200,000

REQUIRED

Using only the information contained in the two balance sheets prepare a written evaluation of the two loan requests. Address your memo to Helen Synodi, president of the New London Bank.

ETHICAL DILEMMA

Ethics in recording transactions (LG 2) You own and operate a company that keeps the accounting records and prepares financial statements for small businesses. One of your clients who is the sole owner of a company has purchased a new car with company funds for her spouse's personal use. She suggests in a discussion with you that she wants the car recorded as a company asset. She explains that she will be applying for a loan soon and needs to keep the assets of her business as high as possible. She suggests that if you cannot handle this problem she is sure that she can find an accountant who will account for the car as a business asset.

REQUIRED

Discuss the alternatives that you may follow and the ethical considerations in this situation.

INTERNET SEARCH

One of the organizations described as contributing to Generally Accepted Accounting Standards is the Financial Accounting Standards Board. Access the FASB's web site at http://www.fasb.org/ and write a short report describing the mission of the FASB.

CHAPTER

2

PROCESSING BUSINESS TRANSACTIONS

"I am only one; but I am still one. I cannot do everything, but still I can do something. I will not refuse to do the something I can do."

Helen Keller

LEARNING GOALS

After studying Chapter 2, you should be able to:

1. Define the term *account*.

2. Identify commonly used accounts and describe a chart of accounts.

3. State the rules for the use of debits and credits.

4. Analyze transactions using debits and credits in T accounts.

5. Describe the function of a general ledger and the information contained in ledger accounts.

6. Explain the purpose of a journal and enter transactions in a general journal.

7. Describe the steps in posting transactions from the general journal to the general ledger.

8. Prepare a trial balance and use it to prepare financial statements.

9. Analyze financial statement information for real-life companies.

UNDERSTANDING BUSINESS ISSUES

In June 2005, Viacom struck a deal to buy children's web company Neopets, Inc. for $160 million. Throughout the process of arranging the business purchase, management in the companies involved needed accounting information. Questions arose such as the following. What are the estimated total revenues for the new combined companies? How much will costs need to be cut to make each combined company competitive? In what areas is it possible to reduce costs? How much should the acquiring company pay for the company being taken over? How should each combination be financed?

Managers use accounting systems to record and process data from transactions into meaningful reports. They use these reports to make decisions such as those described in the two cases above. In

64

Chapter 2, we begin our study of how management uses accounting systems to produce financial reports. Our main interest in this chapter is processing business transactions.

This chapter first examines the accumulation of transaction data in accounts using *debits* and *credits*. Then the chapter shows how to analyze and record transactions using a *double-entry* system. To integrate these concepts, we then explain how these procedures form the *accounting cycle*. We conclude by analyzing real-life accounting information.

OVERVIEW OF A SIMPLE ACCOUNTING SYSTEM

Accounting systems produce information for decision making by processing data from business transactions into meaningful reports. Exhibit 2.1 presents an overview of the information flow for a simple accounting system. The input into the accounting system is the transaction data contained in business documents such as a sales invoice. Transaction processing includes recording the transaction in a journal and then transferring the information to an account in the general ledger. The output of the accounting system is financial reports. With this overview in mind, we will now examine the parts of the accounting system.

Accumulating Transaction Data: The Account

In Chapter 1 we used the accounting equation to analyze transactions for Recycle Consultants, Inc. The form we used in Exhibit 1-3 would not be feasible for even a small business. Clearly, another method must be used to accumulate transaction data. In the following sections, we show how accounts and a double-entry accounting system can solve this problem.

What is an Account?
Learning Goal 1   Define the term *account*.

An **account** is a recording device used for sorting accounting data into similar groupings. We use accounts to record increases and decreases for each item about which we wish to accumulate information. Accountants place all transactions affecting a single item in the same account. Each asset, liability, and owners' equity item on the financial statements will have a separate account. In the case of Recycle Consultants, asset accounts are needed for cash, accounts receivable, furniture, land, and building. The only liability account is Accounts Payable. Owners' equity on the balance sheet consists of two primary accounts: Common Stock and Retained Earnings. Recycle Consultants will also use temporary accounts: fees revenue, expenses and dividends. Temporary accounts accumulate information for a particular period. As we shall see in Chapter 4, these accounts are closed to Retained Earnings at year-end.

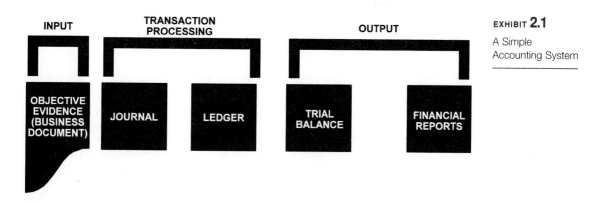

INPUT   TRANSACTION PROCESSING   OUTPUT

OBJECTIVE EVIDENCE (BUSINESS DOCUMENT)   JOURNAL   LEDGER   TRIAL BALANCE   FINANCIAL REPORTS

EXHIBIT **2.1**
A Simple Accounting System

Accounts Commonly Used in Business

Learning Goal 2   Identify commonly used accounts and describe a chart of accounts.

Financial statements report the balances in accounts. To make it easier to prepare financial statements, each item that appears on a statement should have a separate account. Although businesses select accounts that match their information needs, some accounts are used by most businesses.

Asset Accounts

Businesses maintain a separate account for each type of asset that they own. Assets are frequently divided into two categories: current and long-term. Current assets consist of cash and other assets expected to be converted into cash or to be consumed in the operation of the business within one year. Long-term assets are used in the operation of the business over a period longer than one year. One common classification of long-term assets is property, plant, and equipment, or plant assets.

CURRENT ASSETS

Most businesses have the following *current asset* accounts:

Cash

A business uses the Cash account to record any asset that a bank will accept as a deposit and that is acceptable as a means of payment. Cash includes coins, currency, and checks.

Accounts Receivable

Businesses use an Accounts Receivable account to record amounts due from customers for services rendered, or merchandise sold.

Notes Receivable

Notes receivable are formal written promises to receive a fixed amount of money at a future date. They represent a more formal promise than accounts receivable.

Prepaid Expenses

Prepaid expenses include services and supplies that will be consumed during the next year. They are assets because they have future usefulness in the business operations. As the business uses them they become an expense. Each type of prepaid expense is recorded in a separate account. The following are some examples of prepaid expenses:

- We group together office supplies such as paper and pencils under the account title Office Supplies. The cost of unused supplies at any point in time represents the asset office supplies.

- Businesses take out insurance policies for protection against certain types of loss. They must pay the insurance premium in advance for future coverage. The unexpired portion of the premium is an asset called prepaid insurance.

- Businesses may rent equipment and buildings. Rental agreements often require a payment of rent in advance of the use. These advance payments represent future benefits through the use of the equipment or building. The payments that relate to a future period are an asset called prepaid rent.

LONG-TERM ASSETS

Assets whose benefits to the company extend beyond the next year are *long-term assets*. The major classification of long-term assets is *property, plant, and equipment*. The following are examples of property, plant, and equipment accounts used by most businesses:

Land

We record the cost of land actively being used in the operation of the business in the Land account. Land is a permanent asset. Although it is often purchased with buildings on it, we record the cost of the land in a separate account from the cost of the buildings. We separate these two assets because the land does not depreciate over time, whereas the building does.

Buildings

The Buildings account includes the cost of structures the business owns and uses in its operations. Buildings are long-term assets that will provide benefits over several accounting periods.

Equipment

Businesses have different accounts to record the cost of equipment used in operations. For example, the Office Equipment account may include the cost of word processors, furniture, and file cabinets. An account called Store Equipment records such assets as display cabinets and store counters.

Liability Accounts

Liability accounts record increases and decreases in amounts a business owes its creditors. Like asset accounts, we separate liability accounts into current and long-term.

CURRENT LIABILITIES

Current liabilities are amounts the business owes and must pay within a one-year period. Most businesses show the following current liabilities:

Accounts Payable

Businesses record the debts they incur when they purchase assets on short-term credit in the Accounts Payable account. These debts usually are payable within 30 to 60 days.

Notes Payable

The Notes Payable account includes formal written promises by the business to pay money to its creditors. Notes payable arise from the purchase of assets or when a company borrows money.

Other Liability Accounts

Businesses often owe money for other reasons. For example, businesses record wages owed in a Wages Payable account.

LONG-TERM LIABILITIES

Liabilities that will not require payment within the next year are long-term liabilities. The number and titles of these accounts depend on the type of borrowing that the business has done. The following examples are common to many businesses:

Mortgage Payable

A mortgage payable is a debt the business owes for which it pledges specific assets as security. The Mortgage Payable account initially records the amount borrowed (principal) of the mortgage.

Bonds Payable

To raise funds, some businesses borrow money by issuing bonds. *Bonds* are long-term promises to repay amounts borrowed. They usually extend over a period of 10 to 30 years. The Bonds Payable account includes the principal amount of the long-term bonds. We record interest owed in a separate account.

Owners' Equity Accounts

Owners' equity accounts show claims of the business owners to the assets of the firm. The illustration in Chapter 1 showed changes including investments by the owners, revenues, expenses, and dividends. For easier reporting, accountants record these different types of changes in separate accounts, as follows.

Common Stock

The common stock account for a corporation shows the owners' interest in the business assets. We record the initial investment and any additional investment in this account.

Retained Earnings

Cumulative total of net income, net loss, and dividends since the start of the corporation.

Revenues

Revenues cause an increase in owners' equity. We recognize **revenue** when there is an inflow of assets from performing a service or selling a product. The assets received usually are cash or accounts receivable.

We use separate revenue accounts to record the amounts earned during a period. If we recorded revenues directly as increases in Retained Earnings, it would be difficult to separate revenues from other changes in Retained Earnings. Keep in mind that revenues are increases in the owners' equity. They are first recorded in revenue accounts. Titles of revenue accounts identify the reason for the asset inflow—for example, Sales Revenue, Commissions Revenue, Consulting Fees Revenue, and Interest Revenue. We will transfer the amounts to the Retained Earnings account at the end of the period. We will study this transfer process in Chapter 4

Expenses

Expenses cause decreases in owners' equity. We record an **expense** when the business uses an asset or service in order to produce revenue. The amount of the expense is equal to the cost of the asset consumed or the liability incurred.

Accountants create different expense accounts to accumulate the amounts of different types of expenses. The title of the account should show the cause of the expense. The number of accounts a business uses depends on the detail the owner or manager wishes the reports to show. Remember, expenses are actually decreases in owners' equity. Although first recorded in expense accounts, we transfer the amounts to the Retained Earnings account at the end of the period. Typical expense accounts include Salaries Expense, Rent Expense, and Supplies Expense. To understand expenses better, we must understand the difference between a cost and an expense.

> A **cost** is the amount given up to purchase an asset. A cost becomes an expense when the purchased item is used in producing revenue and is no longer an asset.

The cost of a resource that benefits future operations is an asset. When the asset loses its potential to produce future revenue, the cost expires. At this point, it becomes an *expense*. We can conclude the following:

Assets = Unexpired Costs (to be used to produce future revenue)

Expenses = Expired Costs (used in producing this period's revenue)

For example, office supplies purchased for future use are assets. As they are used, they are expensed.

Dividends

Dividends represent distributions of company earnings to owners. Dividends reduce retained earnings and total owners' equity.

The Chart of Accounts

The **chart of accounts** is the complete listing of the account titles to be used by the entity. The account number assigned to each account shows the classification and order in which the accounts are used in the financial statements. In setting up a chart of accounts, it is important to first decide what types of information are needed. Then we establish a separate account for each type of information. The more detail a business desires, the more accounts it will have in its chart of accounts. For example, if managers only want to know total revenues, one revenue account is enough. If they want to know the revenue from each type of service performed, they need a separate revenue account for each type of service. Businesses review their chart of accounts periodically to ensure that the accounts selected meet their information needs.

Exhibit 2.2 shows a chart of accounts for Recycle Consultants, Inc. Management selects enough accounts to give the detail for sound decision making. The account titles describe the activities of the business.

The accountant assigns an *account number* to each account in the system. The account number shows the order and the classification of the accounts. The various digits can show account classification, division within a business, or geographical location. Recycle Consultants, Inc. uses a three-digit account number. Large businesses with many departments and divisions may need many more digits. Many computerized systems allow for 15 or more digits in an account number. A complete chart of all accounts used in this text are included inside the front and rear covers of this text.

RECYCLE CONSULTANTS, INC.
CHART OF ACCOUNTS

ASSET ACCOUNTS (100-189)

Current Assets (100-143)
101	Cash
111	Accounts Receivable

Property, Plant, and Equipment (150-189)
151	Land
153	Building
171	Furniture

LIABILITY ACCOUNTS (200-299)

Current Liabilities (200-249)
201	Accounts Payable

Long-term Liabilities (250-299)

OWNERS' EQUITY ACCOUNTS (300-399)
331	Common Stock
360	Retained Earnings
372	Dividends

REVENUE ACCOUNTS (400-499)
423	Fees Revenue

EXPENSE ACCOUNTS (500-949)
616	Advertising Expense
721	Utilities Expense

EXHIBIT **2.2**

Recycle Consultants, Inc. Chart of Accounts

The T Account

A *T account* is a way of noting the changes to an account during a period of time. It is named for its shape. Each T account consists of three parts: (1) the left side, or debit side; (2) the right side, or credit side; and (3) the title of the account, written across the top:

Account Title	
Left side (the debit side)	Right side (the credit side)

We use the two sides for recording increases and decreases to the account. Increases are placed on one side of the T and decreases are placed on the other. The T account used to record the cash transactions for Recycle Consultants, Inc. for December would look like this:

		Cash			
12/01	Owners' investment	90,000	12/05	Asset purchase	70,000
12/16	Revenue	4,000	12/18	Liability payment	8,000
12/27	Receivable collection	1,500	12/26	Expense payment	1,400
			12/31	Dividends	1,000
	Balance	15,100			

Notice the balance line at the bottom of the T account. The **balance of an account** is the difference between the total of the debit entries and the total of the credit entries.

Actual accounting records do not use this simple T account. We use T accounts only for teaching purposes. It is easier to illustrate the effects of transactions on an account with T accounts. A more formal account notation appears later in this chapter.

Debits and Credits

Learning Goal 3   State the rules for the use of debits and credits.

Originally the terms *debit* and *credit* had a meaning related to debtor and creditor accounts. Today, *debit* simply describes the left side of an account and *credit* the right side of an account. *Debiting* is placing an amount on the left side of an account. *Crediting* is placing an amount on the right side of an account. A *debit entry* is an amount on the left side of an account. A *credit entry* is an amount on the right side of an account. The abbreviation for debit is Dr.; for credit, Cr.

The left side of any account is the **debit** side, and the right side is the **credit** side.

We base the rules for the use of debits and credits on the accounting equation. From the accounting equation, we know that assets must always equal liabilities plus owners' equity. Also, when we record a transaction, it must be done in such a way that debits equal credits. We derive the rules for increasing and decreasing accounts by putting the accounting equation together with accounts, as follows:

ASSETS (Resources Owned by a Business)		=	**LIABILITIES** (Creditors' Claims to Assets)		+	**OWNERS' EQUITY** (Owners' Claims to Assets)	
Debit increase	Credit decrease		Debit decrease	Credit increase		Debit decrease	Credit increase

Remember that in the accounting equation, assets are on the left side and liabilities and owners' equities are on the right side. The rule then states that debit (left-side) entries, increase assets. Credit (right-side) entries increase liabilities and owners' equity. For example, assume a transaction causes a $100 increase in assets and a $100 increase in liabilities. We record the increase in assets with a $100 entry to the debit side of an asset account We record the increase in liabilities with a $100 entry to the credit side of a liability account. The accounting equation remains in balance. We also have recorded an equal amount of debits and credits.

An easy way to remember the rules is to remember the position of the account in the equation. Assets are on the left side of the accounting equation. We therefore increase them by entries to the left (debit) side of the T account. Liabilities and owners' equity are on the right side of the accounting equation. We increase them by entries to the right (credit) side of the T account. We can sum this up with the following debit/credit rules:

Debit an account to record:	Credit an account to record:
An increase of an asset	A decrease of an asset
A decrease of a liability	An increase of a liability
A decrease in owners' equity	An increase in owners' equity

When we calculate the balance of an account, we have a *debit balance* when debits exceed credits and a *credit balance* when credits exceed debits. Asset accounts have a normal debit balance. Liability and owners' equity accounts have a normal credit balance.

Since revenue, expense, and withdrawals accounts record changes in owners' equity, they use the debit/credit rules for owners' equity accounts. Revenue accounts record increases in owners' equity. Thus, we *increase a revenue account with credits* and *decrease a revenue account with debits*. Revenue accounts have a normal credit balance.

Expenses record decreases in owners' equity. The more expenses there are, the less owners' equity there is. Thus, we *increase an expense account with debits* and *decrease an expense account with credits*. Expense accounts have a normal debit balance.

The Dividends account also records decreases in owners' equity. We increase Dividends with debits and decrease Dividends with credits. The Dividends account has a normal debit balance.

Exhibit 2.3 shows the relationship the rules of debits and credits have to the accounting equation. Assets are on the left side of the equation, and debits (left-side entries) increase assets. Liabilities and owners' equity are on the right side of the equation, and credits (right-side entries) increase them. Since an increase in owners' equity is a credit and revenues increase owners' equity, credits increase

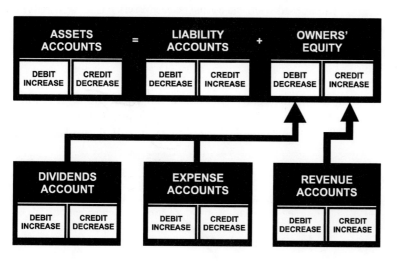

EXHIBIT **2.3**

Debit/Credit Rules and the Accounting Equation

revenues. Since a decrease in owners' equity is a debit and expenses decrease owners' equity, debits increase expenses. Dividends also reduce owners' equity. We increase the Dividends account with debits. Placing the debit/credit rules in a T account also will help us learn them.

Account Title	
Debit Side	**Credit Side**
Increase assets	Decrease assets
Increase dividends	Decrease dividends
Increase expenses	Decrease expenses
Decrease liabilities	Increase liabilities
Decrease common stock	Increase common stock
Decrease revenues	Increase revenues
Decrease retained earnings	Increase retained earnings

Take the time now to study how each type of account is increased and decreased. We will use these rules in the next section to analyze the same transactions for Recycle Consultants, Inc. that we studied in Chapter 1. (Throughout the chapter, these entries are printed in bold in the T accounts.)

Analyzing Transactions with the Debit/Credit Rules
Learning Goal 4   Analyze transactions using debits and credits in T accounts.

In this section, we will illustrate how to increase and decrease accounts using the debit and credit rules. We return to the transactions for Recycle Consultants, Inc. *These are the same transactions that we used to analyze the accounting equation in* Chapter 1 To analyze a transaction, we suggest you do the following steps:

1. Identify the accounts that change.

2. Identify the amount of the changes and whether they are increases or decreases.

3. Use the rules to decide whether to debit or credit each account.

TRANSACTION 1   CASH INVESTMENT BY OWNERS.

On December 1, 2007, investors invested $90,000 in cash to start Recycle Consultants, Inc. In exchange, Recycle issued shares of common stock to these owners.

T ACCOUNT		EXPLANATION
Cash		
12/01 90,000		The debit of $90,000 to Cash increases the account. Cash is an asset account, and debits increase assets.
Common Stock		
	12/01 90,000	The credit of $90,000 to Common Stock increases this account because it is an owners' equity account.

It is important to note that the total debits to record the transaction equal the total credits. When total debits equal total credits in a transaction, the accounting equation remains in balance. The necessity for each transaction to have equal debits and credits is called **double-entry accounting**.

TRANSACTION 2   ASSETS PURCHASED FOR CASH.

On December 5, Recycle purchased land and a building, paying cash. The land cost $20,000 and the building cost $50,000.

T ACCOUNT				EXPLANATION
Cash				
12/01	90,000	**12/05**	**70,000**	A credit of $70,000 to Cash is a decrease because Cash is an asset.
Land				
12/05	**20,000**			Land is debited for $20,000. A debit to the asset account Land records an increase.
Building				
12/05	**50,000**			The Building account increases. Since Building is an asset, the increase requires a debit.

TRANSACTION 3   ASSETS PURCHASED ON ACCOUNT.

On December 9, Recycle purchased furniture on account at a cost of $8,000.

T ACCOUNT				EXPLANATION
Furniture				
12/09	**8,000**			The debit of $8,000 to the asset account Furniture increases the account.
Accounts Payable				
		12/09	8,000	Credits to liability accounts cause increases. Accounts Payable is a liability. Thus, the $8,000 credit to Accounts Payable increases the account.

TRANSACTION 4   REVENUE EARNED FOR CASH.

On December 16, Recycle Consultants completed a consulting engagement for the city of Ames. Recycle received $4,000 in cash for its services.

T ACCOUNT				EXPLANATION
Cash				
12/01	90,000	12/5	70,000	Cash increases because of the collection. Since cash is an asset, a debit records the increase.
12/16	**4,000**			
Fees Revenue				
		12/16	4,000	Since the services are complete, the revenue has been earned. Revenue increases owners' equity, so a credit is necessary.

TRANSACTION 5   LIABILITY PAID WITH CASH.

Recycle owed $8,000 to a supplier for the furniture purchased on December 9. On December 18, it paid this debt in full.

T ACCOUNT				EXPLANATION
Cash				
12/01	90,000	12/05	70,000	Cash decreases because of the payment. Since cash is an asset, a credit records the decrease.
12/16	4,000	**12/18**	**8,000**	
Accounts Payable				
12/18	**8,000**	12/09	8,000	Paying the liability reduces it. Liabilities are reduced with debits.

TRANSACTION 6   REVENUE EARNED ON ACCOUNT.

On December 23, Recycle completed another consulting contract for the city of Boone in the amount of $2,000. Since Recycle completed the service, it earned the revenue. Instead of paying in cash, Boone agreed to pay in the future. The asset Recycle received is an account receivable.

	T ACCOUNT			EXPLANATION
	Accounts Receivable			
12/23	**2,000**			Since the client agreed to pay cash in the future, Recycle has an increase in the asset Accounts Receivable. We increase assets with a debit.
	Fees Revenue			
		12/16	4,000	Since the service is complete, Recycle has earned the revenue. We record increases in revenue with a credit.
		12/23	**2,000**	

TRANSACTION 7   EXPENSE INCURRED FOR CASH.

On December 26, Recycle paid $1,400 in cash for advertising. Since the advertising has appeared, Recycle has received the benefit and incurred the expense.

	T ACCOUNT			EXPLANATION
	Cash			
12/01	90,000	12/05	70,000	The payment of cash causes a decrease in the asset Cash. We record decreases in assets with credits.
12/16	4,000	12/18	8,000	
		12/26	**1,400**	
	Advertising Expense			
12/26	**1,400**			Since Recycle has received the advertising benefit, the cost is an expense. We record increases in expenses with debits.

TRANSACTION 8   RECEIVABLE COLLECTED IN CASH.

On December 27, Recycle received a check for $1,500 from the city of Boone, which owed the firm money. Since Recycle recorded the revenue when it completed the service to Boone, this $1,500 is not additional revenue. Instead, Recycle is collecting the account receivable. The form of the asset changes from an account receivable to cash.

	T ACCOUNT			EXPLANATION
	Cash			
12/01	90,000	12/05	70,000	The receipt of cash causes an increase in the asset Cash. We record increases in assets with debits.
12/16	4,000	12/18	8,000	
12/27	**1,500**	12/26	1,400	
	Accounts Receivable			
12/23	2,000	**12/27**	**1,500**	When a customer pays all or a part of the amount it owes on account, Accounts Receivable decreases. Since Accounts Receivable is an asset, we record the decrease with a credit.

TRANSACTION 9   EXPENSE INCURRED ON ACCOUNT.

On December 30, Recycle received a bill for the utilities used during the month. The cost of the utilities used was $600. Since Recycle received the benefit, it records an expense even though it has not paid the amount.

| **T ACCOUNT** | | | | **EXPLANATION** |

		Accounts Payable		
12/18	8,000	12/09	8,000	Recycle has incurred an additional liability. The credit of
		12/30	**600**	$600 increases the liability Accounts Payable.

	Utilities Expense	
12/30	**600**	We record the increase in the expense with a debit.

TRANSACTION 10   DIVIDENDS PAID TO OWNERS.

At the end of December, Recycle paid $1,000 of dividends to its owners. This reduces the assets of the business and reduces their interest in the assets.

| **T ACCOUNT** | | | | **EXPLANATION** |

		Cash		
12/01	90,000	12/05	70,000	The use of cash to pay dividends decreases the asset
12/16	4,000	12/18	8,000	Cash. Credits record decreases in assets. Thus, we credit
12/27	1,500	12/26	1,400	the asset Cash.
		12/31	**1,000**	

	Dividends	
12/31	**1,000**	Dividends paid to owners decrease owners' equity. Decreases in owners' equity require debits. We record the debit in the Dividends account.

The General Ledger Account

Learning Goal 5   Describe the function of a general ledger and the information contained in ledger accounts.

The T form of an account allows us to concentrate on the debits and credits while learning. Actual business practice uses a more complete form of the account. Whether the accounting system is manual or computerized, the account contains certain information. It normally includes the date, an explanation of the entry, the page number of the source of the information (or "PR" for "page reference"), and columns for amounts. These columns are for the debit or credit amounts of the entries and for the cumulative balance after each entry. The actual format may differ among businesses. Exhibit 2.4 shows the Cash account for Recycle Consultants, Inc. as of December 31, 2007. This is the format of the account used in this text. Remember that for a transaction to take place a debit or credit entry to one account must be offset by a credit or debit entry to another (or

						Cash			Acct. No. 101
								Balance	
Date			**Explanation**	**PR**	**Debit**	**Credit**	**Debit**	**Credit**
2007								
Dec.	1			J1	90,000		90,000	
	5			J1		70,000	20,000	
	16			J1	4,000		24,000	
	18			J1		8,000	16,000	
	26			J1		1,400	14,600	
	27			J1	1,500		16,100	
	31			J1		1,000	15,100	

EXHIBIT **2.4**

A Typical Account

more than one) account. Thus each line in the Cash account in Exhibit 2.4 is an entry that must be offset by an entry in another account. This is the essence of *double-entry* accounting.

The collection of all accounts for an accounting entity is called a **general ledger**. It is a categorical record of all transactions. The formal name of an account is a *ledger account*. The ledger may be in the form of a book with a separate page for each account. In today's computerized world, it is more likely that the ledger will be on-line at most businesses.

Processing Transactions

In the last section, we used the transactions of Recycle Consultants, Inc. to study the use of debits and credits to record changes in accounts. Although we could keep records with only ledger accounts, this process is not used for several reasons. First, we record part of the transaction in one account and the other part in another account. Thus, recording transactions in the ledger accounts does not enable a person to see the entire business transaction.

At a future date, it might be difficult to remember why a certain account was debited or credited without seeing the other parts of the transaction. Second, it would be easy to make an error such as forgetting to record the debit or credit part of the business transaction.

This section covers the accounting steps of journalizing and posting. These two processes enable us to establish more detailed records while minimizing errors in the recording process.

The Journal

Learning Goal 6   Explain the purpose of a journal and enter transactions in a general journal.

The *journal* is the record keeping device in which we first record transactions. It is a chronological record of transactions. It provides in one place a complete history of all transactions, recorded in the order they occurred. The journal also includes detailed descriptions of each transaction not kept in the ledger. Business managers and accountants often want to view a transaction in its entirety. Since we record debit and credit entries in different accounts, reconstructing any single transaction would be difficult using only the ledger. Therefore, we first record all entries in a journal, a book of original entry. Then, we transfer the information to a ledger. The simplest form of journal is called the **general journal**.

Using a journal prevents errors that might go undetected if we entered transactions directly and only into the ledger. It would be difficult to find a missing debit or credit or an incorrect ledger entry. The journal entry contains the debit and credit in the same place. This helps in locating discrepancies.

Journalizing

Journalizing is recording transactions in the general journal, a book of original entry. The record of a transaction in the journal is called a *journal entry*.

Exhibit 2.5 shows the first transaction of Recycle Consultants, Inc. entered in a general journal. The following sequence of steps corresponds to the numbers in the figure:

1. Write the year at the top of the Date column.

2. Enter the month of the first transaction recorded on this page. It is not necessary to write the month again on this page unless it changes.

3. Enter the date of each transaction.

4. Place the title of the account debited in the Accounts and Explanations column against the date line. To eliminate confusion, *the account title written in the journal entry should be the exact title of the account as it appears in the ledger*.

5. Enter the amount of the debit in the Debit amount column.

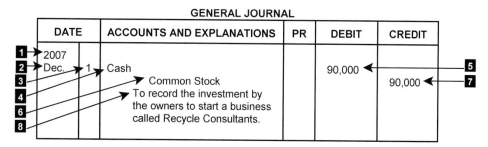

GENERAL JOURNAL

	DATE		ACCOUNTS AND EXPLANATIONS	PR	DEBIT	CREDIT	
1	2007						
2	Dec.	1	Cash		90,000		**5**
3			Common Stock			90,000	**7**
4			To record the investment by				
6			the owners to start a business				
8			called Recycle Consultants.				

EXHIBIT **2.5**

A Typical Journal Entry

---

6. Indent the title of the account credited a few spaces from the Date column.

7. Enter the amount of the credit in the Credit column.

8. Write the explanation on the next line, indenting from the left a few spaces. It should contain all the essential information about the journal entry—this is a reference to the relevant source document, check number, cash receipt number, and so on.

   In journals, ledger accounts, and trial balances—which we will discuss shortly—two zeros or a dash in the cents column indicate that the cents are zero. We may write an amount "2,375.00" or "2,375–." In financial statements, it is preferable to use zeros for items having no cents. In this book, most examples contain whole dollar amounts. Thus the text often omits the cents column in statements, journals, and ledgers. We do not write dollar signs in journals and ledger accounts. We use them in all formal statements and reports.

Posting

Learning Goal 7 Describe the steps in posting transactions from the general journal to the general ledger.

The journal *does not replace* the ledger account. Rather, it is where we record transactions *as they occur*. In the sequence that makes up the accounting cycle, we first journalize business transactions in the journal and then post them to the general ledger.

   Posting is transferring amounts in the journal to the correct accounts in the general ledger.

Exhibit 2.6 illustrates how to post the December 1 entry, shown in Exhibit 2.5 from the general journal to the ledger. We normally post daily. The sequence of steps to post from the journal to ledger accounts follows.

1. Locate the ledger account for the debit entry.

2. Write the year (2007) at the top of the Date column in the ledger account. Then enter the date (Dec. 1), the journal page (J1), and the debit amount ($90,000) in the debit column of the Cash account in the ledger. Remember that we do not use dollar signs in journals or ledgers. Determine the effect of the transaction on the account balance, and place the appropriate value in the Balance column. In this case, the debit balance is $90,000.

3. Enter the ledger account number for the debit entry (101) in the posting reference (PR) column of the journal. This cross-references the journal and the ledger. *The presence of the account number here shows that we posted the item. Do not insert this reference until after posting.*

4. Find the ledger account for the credit entry.

5. Write the year (2007) at the top of the Date column. Enter the date (Dec. 1), the journal page (J1), and the credit amount ($90,000) in the credit column of the Common Stock account in

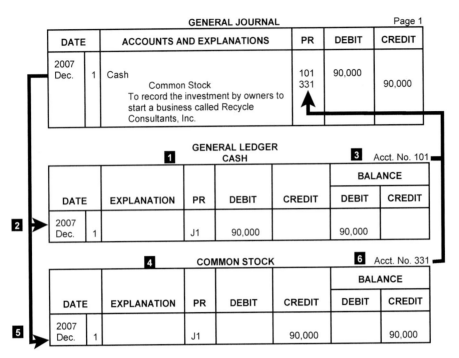

EXHIBIT **2.6**

The Posting Process

GENERAL JOURNAL Page 1

DATE		ACCOUNTS AND EXPLANATIONS	PR	DEBIT	CREDIT
2007 Dec.	1	Cash 　　　Common Stock 　　　To record the investment by owners to 　　　start a business called Recycle 　　　Consultants, Inc.	101 331	90,000	90,000

GENERAL LEDGER
CASH   Acct. No. 101

DATE		EXPLANATION	PR	DEBIT	CREDIT	BALANCE DEBIT	BALANCE CREDIT
2007 Dec.	1		J1	90,000		90,000	

COMMON STOCK   Acct. No. 331

DATE		EXPLANATION	PR	DEBIT	CREDIT	BALANCE DEBIT	BALANCE CREDIT
2007 Dec.	1		J1		90,000		90,000

the ledger. Determine the effect of the transaction, and place the appropriate value in the Balance column. In this case, the credit balance is $90,000.

6. Enter the ledger account number for the credit entry (331) in the posting reference (PR) column of the journal. The cross-reference in the journal shows that the posting to the ledger is complete.

We do not usually use explanations in the ledger accounts. The cross-reference to the journal page permits a person to quickly find complete information on the transaction.

Illustration of Journalizing and Posting

We again will use the transactions of Recycle Consultants, Inc. to study the journalizing and posting of transactions. Recycle's ten transactions for December were as follows:

2007

Dec.	1	Investors invested $90,000 to start Recycle Consultants, Inc. In exchange, Recycle, Inc. issued shares of common stock to these owners.
	5	Purchased land and a building for $70,000 in cash. The land cost $20,000 and the building cost $50,000.
	9	Received furniture purchased on open charge account from Atlantic Furniture for $8,000.
	16	Completed consulting services for the city of Ames and received $4,000 in cash.
	18	Paid the entire amount owed to Atlantic Furniture.
	23	Completed consulting services for the city of Boone and sent a bill for $2,000.
	26	Paid $1,400 in cash for advertising that had appeared in The City Administrator, a magazine distributed to city managers.
	27	Collected $1,500 in cash from the city of Boone for services billed on December 23.
	30	Received the utility bill for $600 for utilities used during December.
	31	Recycle paid $1,000 of dividends to its owners.

PROCESSING BUSINESS TRANSACTIONS 79

	Date		Accounts and Explanations	PR	Debit	Credit
	2007 Dec.	1	Cash	101	90,000	
			Common Stock	331		90,000
			To record the investment by owners to start a business called Recycle Consultants, Inc.			
		5	Land	151	20,000	
			Building	153	50,000	
			Cash	101		70,000
			To record the purchase of land and building for cash.			
		9	Furniture	171	8,000	
			Accounts Payable	201		8,000
			To record the purchase of furniture on account.			
		16	Cash	101	4,000	
			Fees Revenue	423		4,000
			To record cash revenue earned from consulting for city of Ames.			
		18	Accounts Payable	201	8,000	
			Cash	101		8,000
			To record payment on account			
		23	Accounts Receivable	111	2,000	
			Fees Revenue	423		2,000
			To record revenue earned on account from city of Boone.			
		26	Advertising Expense	616	1,400	
			Cash	101		1,400
			To record cash payment for advertising expense incurred.			
		27	Cash	101	1,500	
			Accounts Receivable	111		1,500
			To record partial collection of account from city of Boone.			
		30	Utilities Expense	721	600	
			Accounts Payable	201		600
			To record receipt of bill for utilities used during December.			
		31	Dividends	372	1,000	
			Cash	101		1,000
			To record dividends paid to owners.			

EXHIBIT **2.7**

General Journal of Recycle Consulants, Inc.

First, we journalize these transactions in the general journal as shown in Exhibit 2.7 Posting references shown in the PR column are not entered until after posting to the general ledger. *A blank line separates each journal entry.* Second, we post the journal entries from the general journal to the general ledger accounts as shown in Exhibit 2.8 When the posting of each entry is complete, we enter the appropriate posting references.

Take the time now to carefully study this illustration. Note how the process fits our definition of double-entry accounting. The journal entry for each transaction has an equality of total debits and total credits.

Preparing a Trial Balance

Learning Goal 8 Prepare a trial balance and use it to prepare financial statements

Periodically, we test the accuracy of the journalizing and posting process by preparing a **trial balance**. The steps in preparing a trial balance are:

1. List each ledger or "T" account and place the ending debit or credit balance in the appropriate amount column.

GENERAL LEDGER

Cash — Acct. No. 101

Date		Explanation	PR	Debit	Credit	Balance Debit	Balance Credit
2007 Dec.	1		J1	90,000		90,000	
	5		J1		70,000	20,000	
	16		J1	4,000		24,000	
	18		J1		8,000	16,000	
	26		J1		1,400	14,600	
	27		J1	1,500		16,100	
	31		J1		1,000	15,100	

Accounts Receivable — Acct. No. 111

Date		Explanation	PR	Debit	Credit	Balance Debit	Balance Credit
2007 Dec.	23		J1	2,000		2,000	
	27		J1		1,500	500	

Land — Acct. No. 151

Date		Explanation	PR	Debit	Credit	Balance Debit	Balance Credit
2007 Dec.	5		J1	20,000		20,000	

Building — Acct. No. 153

Date		Explanation	PR	Debit	Credit	Balance Debit	Balance Credit
2007 Dec.	5		J1	50,000		50,000	

Furniture — Acct. No. 171

Date		Explanation	PR	Debit	Credit	Balance Debit	Balance Credit
2007 Dec.	9		J1	8,000		8,000	

Accounts Payable — Acct. No. 201

Date		Explanation	PR	Debit	Credit	Balance Debit	Balance Credit
2007 Dec.	9		J1		8,000		8,000
	18		J1	8,000			0
	30		J1		600		600

Common Stock — Acct. No. 331

Date		Explanation	PR	Debit	Credit	Balance Debit	Balance Credit
2007 Dec.	1		J1		90,000		90,000

Dividends — Acct. No. 372

Date		Explanation	PR	Debit	Credit	Balance Debit	Balance Credit
2007 Dec.	31		J1	1,000		1,000	

Fees Revenue — Acct. No. 423

Date		Explanation	PR	Debit	Credit	Balance Debit	Balance Credit
2007 Dec.	16		J1		4,000		4,000
	23		J1		2,000		6,000

Advertising Expense — Acct. No. 616

Date		Explanation	PR	Debit	Credit	Balance Debit	Balance Credit
2007 Dec.	26		J1	1,400		1,400	

Utilities Expense — Acct. No. 721

Date		Explanation	PR	Debit	Credit	Balance Debit	Balance Credit
2007 Dec.	30		J1	600		600	

EXHIBIT 2.8

General Ledger of Recycle Consultants, Inc.

RECYCLE CONSULTANTS, INC.
TRIAL BALANCE
DECEMBER 31, 2007

Acct. No.	Account Title	Debits	Credits
101	Cash	$ 15,100	
111	Accounts Receivable	500	
151	Land	20,000	
153	Building	50,000	
171	Furniture	8,000	
201	Accounts Payable		$ 600
331	Common Stock		90,000
372	Dividends	1,000	
423	Fees Revenue		6,000
616	Advertising Expense	1,400	
721	Utilities Expense	600	
	Totals	$ 96,600	$ 96,600

=

These amounts must be equal for the trial balance to be correct

EXHIBIT 2.9

Trial Balance for Recycle Consultants, Inc.

RECYCLE CONSULTANTS, INC.
TRIAL BALANCE
DECEMBER 31, 2007

Acct. No.	Account Title	Debits	Credits
101	Cash	$ 15,100	
111	Accounts Receivable	500	
151	Land	20,000	
153	Building	50,000	
171	Furniture	8,000	
201	Accounts Payable		$ 600
331	Common Stock		90,000
372	Dividends	1,000	
423	Fees Revenue		6,000
616	Advertising Expense	1,400	
721	Utilities Expense	600	
	Totals	$ 96,600	$ 96,600

RECYCLE CONSULTANTS, INC.
INCOME STATEMENT
FOR THE MONTH ENDED DECEMBER 31, 2007

Revenues		
Fees revenue		$ 6,000
Expenses		
Advertising expense	$ 1,400	
Utilities expense	600	
Total expenses		2,000
Net income		$ 4,000

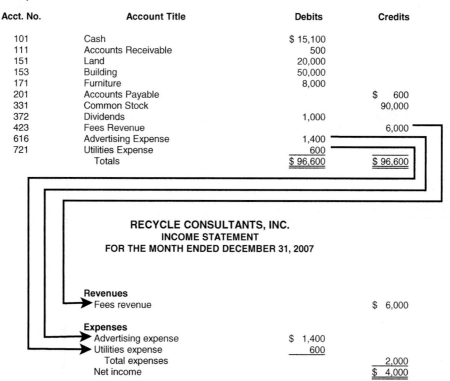

EXHIBIT 2.10

Preparing the Income Statement

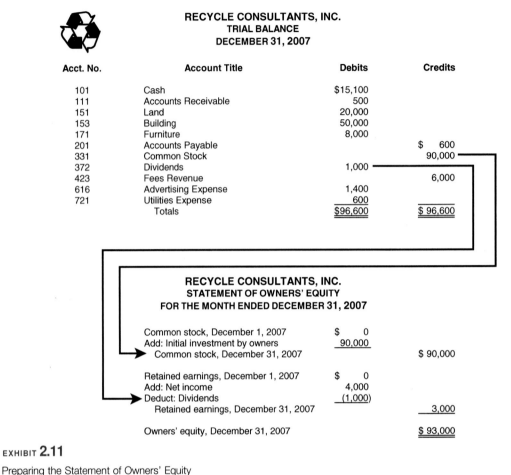

EXHIBIT 2.11

Preparing the Statement of Owners' Equity

2.   Total the debit column and the credit column.

3.   Compare the totals to see that the debit and credit columns are equal.

We prepare a trial balance after the journalizing and posting is complete. Exhibit 2.9 illustrates the trial balance on December 31, 2007, for Recycle Consultants, Inc.

   The trial balance *only* verifies that the total debits in the general ledger are equal to the total credits. A trial balance will not detect an error such as a missing transaction. Neither will it detect an entry that debits or credits the wrong account. Remember that *the trial balance only shows that the total debits in the general ledger are equal to the total credits.* If the total of the debits equals the total of the credits, we assume that the processing is accurate. We then prepare the financial statements.

Preparing Financial Statements

At this point, we prepare the financial statements using the balances in the trial balance. Exhibit 2.10 uses the trial balance to prepare the income statement. Exhibit 2.11 illustrates preparation of the statement of owners' equity, and Exhibit 2.12 the balance sheet. In each exhibit, the arrows show the trial balance data used to prepare the financial statement. The format of the balance sheet is known as the *report form.* This places the liabilities and owners' equity below the assets. The *account form* places them side by side. Businesses commonly use both forms. The text will use the report form because it fits the page format better.

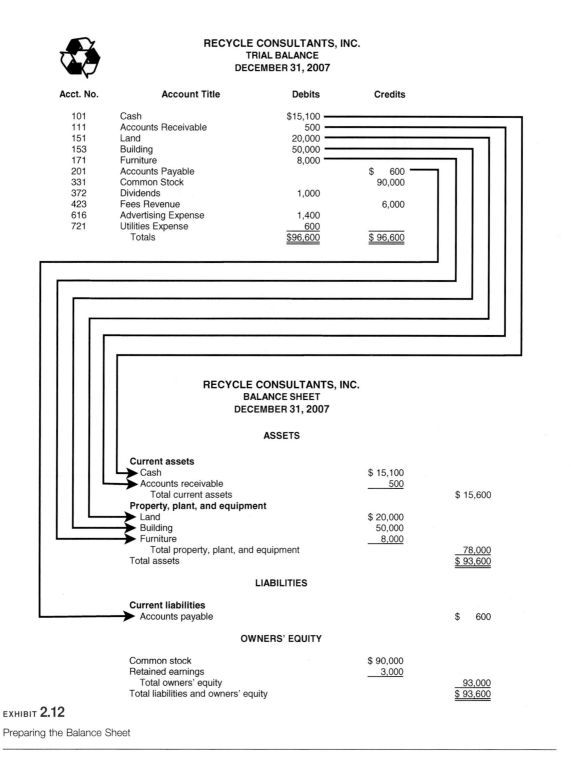

EXHIBIT 2.12

Preparing the Balance Sheet

The Accounting Cycle

The **accounting cycle** is a series of steps used to collect, process, and communicate financial information. Accountants call it a cycle because they repeat the steps each accounting period. We can think of the counting cycle as a flow. In the next two chapters, we will study the remaining steps of the accounting cycle.

TYCO INTERNATIONAL, LTD.
COMPARATIVE COMMON-SIZE INCOME STATEMENTS
For The Years Ended September 30, 2004, 2003, 2002, 2001
(in millions)

	2004	2004	2003	2003	2002	2002	2001	2001
	$	%	$	%	$	%	$	%
Total revenues	$ 40,153.0	100.0%	$ 36,801.3	100.0%	$ 35,589.8	100.0%	$ 34,002.1	100.0%
Total expenses	$ 37,274.0	92.8%	$ 35,821.7	97.3%	$ 44,769.3	125.8%	$ 30,538.1	89.8%
Net income (loss)	$ 2,879.0	7.2%	$ 979.6	2.7%	$ (9,179.5)	-25.8%	$ 3,464.0	10.2%

EXHIBIT **2.13**

Comparative Common-Size Income Statements for Tyco International, 2004-2001

ANALYZING INFORMATION

Learning Goal 9   Analyze financial statement information for real-life companies.

In this chapter, we will analyze the financial statements of Tyco International, LTD for the years 2004-2001. Tyco is an industry leader in telecommunications and electronics, healthcare and specialty products, fire and security systems, and flow control valves.

Income Statement Analysis

Exhibit 2.13 shows comparative income statements for the fiscal years 2004-2001. For each year, we show the dollar amount and the common-size percent.

Question 1. Are total revenues for Tyco higher or lower over the four year period?

Analysis 1. For Tyco, total revenues in fiscal 2004 ($40,153,000,000) are higher than the total for fiscal 2001 ($34,002,100,000). Revenues for Tyco have increased in each year of our analysis.

Question 2. What is the percent change in total revenues from 2001 to 2004?

Analysis 2. The percent increase in total revenues from fiscal 2001 to fiscal 2004 is:

$$18.1\% = 100 \times \frac{\$6,150,900,000^*}{\$34,002,100,000} \qquad {}^*\$40,153,000,000 - \$34,002,100,000$$

Total revenues for Tyco increased by 18.1% from 2004 to 2001.

Question 3. Is the percent of total expenses to total revenues increasing or decreasing over the four year period?

Analysis 3. For 2004, 2003, and 2001 total revenues are greater than total expenses. This is *favorable*. Total expenses as a percent of total revenues reached a high of 125.8% in 2002. The expense percent decreased to 97.3% of revenues in 2003 and 92.8% in 2004. The lower expense ratio in 2003 and 2004 indicates that management is having success in reducing expenses. The result is that net income as a percent of total revenues increased from 2.7% in 2003 to 7.2% in 2004.

Balance Sheet Analysis

Exhibit 2.14 shows comparative balance sheets as of September 30, 2004-2001. For each year, we show the dollar amount and the common-size percent.

Question 1. Are total assets for Tyco higher or lower over the four year period?

Analysis 1. For Tyco, total assets at September 30, 2004 ($63,667,000,000) are lower than the total at September 30, 2001 ($70,413,200,000).

TYCO INTERNATIONAL, LTD.
COMPARATIVE COMMON-SIZE BALANCE SHEETS
September 30, 2004, 2003, 2002, 2001
(in millions)

	2004	2004	2003	2003	2002	2002	2001	2001
	$	%	$	%	$	%	$	%
Total assets	$ 63,667.0	100.0%	$ 63,545.0	100.0%	$ 65,457.5	100.0%	$ 70,413.2	100.0%
Total liabilities	$ 33,375.0	52.4%	$ 37,176.0	58.5%	$ 41,376.2	63.2%	$ 39,332.9	55.9%
Total owners' equity	$ 30,292.0	47.6%	$ 26,369.0	41.5%	$ 24,081.3	36.8%	$ 31,080.3	44.1%
Total liabilities and owners' equity	$ 63,667.0	100.0%	$ 63,545.0	100.0%	$ 65,457.5	100.0%	$ 70,413.2	100.0%

EXHIBIT **2.14**

Comparative Common-Size Balance Sheets For Tyco International, 2004-2001

Question 2. What is the percent change in total assets from 2001 to 2004?

Analysis 2. In this case, the percent decrease in total assets from September 30, 2001, to September 30, 2004, is:

$$(9.6)\% = 100 \times \frac{\$6,746,200,000^*}{\$70,413,200,000} \qquad ^*\$63,667,000,000 - \$70,413,200,000$$

The total assets for Tyco have decreased over the four year period.

Question 3. Is the percent of total liabilities to total liabilities + owners' equity increasing or decreasing? As a result, is there more risk that Tyco could not pay its debts?

Analysis 3. In Exhibit 2.14 refer to the common-size percent for liabilities each year. The percent of liabilities increased from 55.9% in 2001 to 52.4% in 2004. As of September 30, 2004, 52.4% of all the assets of Tyco are financed by creditors. The increasing percent of liabilities indicates more risk that Tyco may not meet debt payments when they come due.

Integrative Income Statement and Balance Sheet Analysis

In our analysis so far, we observed that both total assets and total revenues for Tyco increased significantly from 2001 to 2004. Now, we need to combine this information to assess the overall efficiency of Tyco.

Question 1. Is Tyco operating efficiently by using the least amount of asset investment to generate a given level of total revenues?

Analysis 1. We can answer this question for Tyco by dividing total revenues by average total assets for each year. Average assets for a year are simply ending assets plus beginning assets divided by 2. The computations for 2004, 2003, and 2002 are:

Fiscal 2004   **Fiscal 2003**   **Fiscal 2002**

$$\frac{\$40,153,000,000}{\$63,606,000,000^*} = 0.63 \text{ times} \quad \frac{\$36,801,300,000}{\$64,501,250,000^{**}} = 0.57 \text{ times} \quad \frac{\$35,589,800,000}{\$67,935,350,000^{***}} = 0.52 \text{ times}$$

$$^* \quad (\$63,667,000,000 + \$63,545,000,000) \div 2$$
$$^{**} \quad (\$63,545,000,000 + \$65,457,500,000) \div 2$$
$$^{***} \quad (\$65,457,500,000 + \$70,413,200,000) \div 2$$

The resulting number is a ratio called *total asset turnover*. A higher number for the total asset turnover ratio is more favorable. For Tyco, the total asset turnover ratio increased from 0.52 times in 2002 to 0.63 times in 2004. In general, this is a *favorable* trend. Comparatively, Tyco currently operating more efficiently than in the past.

LEARNING GOALS REVIEW

1. **Define the term *account*.**
   An account is a recording device used for sorting accounting information into similar groups.

2. **Identify commonly used accounts and describe a chart of accounts.**
   Typical current asset accounts are Cash, Accounts Receivable, and Prepaid Expenses. Typical property, plant, and equipment asset accounts are Land and Buildings. Current liability accounts include Accounts Payable and Wages Payable. Long-term liability accounts include Mortgages Payable. Owners' equity accounts include Common Stock, Retained Earnings, Dividends, revenues, and expenses. A chart of accounts is a listing of all the accounts used in an entity's system.

3. **State the rules for the use of debits and credits.**
   Entries on the debit (left) side or credit (right) side of an account increase and decrease the account. Debits increase assets, dividends, and expenses, and decrease liabilities, common stock, retained earnings, and revenues. Credits increase liabilities, common stock, retained earnings, and revenues, and decrease assets, dividends, and expenses.

4. **Analyze transactions using debits and credits in T accounts.**
   To analyze a transaction: (1) identify the accounts that change; (2) identify the amount of the changes and whether they are increases or decreases; and (3) use the rules to decide whether the change is a debit or a credit.

5. **Describe the function of a general ledger and the information contained in ledger accounts.**
   The general ledger contains all of the accounts for an accounting entity. It is a record of information sorted by financial statement items. Typically the information includes the dates of each transaction, the page numbers of the journal from which the amounts were transferred, the debit or credit amounts of the transactions, and the account balance.

6. **Explain the purpose of a journal and enter transactions in a general journal.**
   The general journal contains a complete record of each business transaction in one place. We first record data in the journal. To enter a transaction in the journal, write the date of the transaction, the title of the account debited, and the debit amount on the first line. If more than one account is being debited, enter the second debit account and amount on the next line. Then, on the next line, indent and write in the title of the account being credited and the credit amount. If additional credits are to be entered, complete those. When all of the debits and credits are entered, indent a few spaces and write an explanation for the entry. The format for the journal entry is shown in Exhibit 2-5.

7. **Describe the steps in posting transactions from the general journal to the general ledger.**
   Posting is the process of transferring the data from the journal to the ledger. To perform this procedure, follow these six steps: (1) Locate the debit entry ledger account in the journal. (2) In the ledger account, enter the date, the journal entry page number, and the debit amount. Then enter a new balance for the account. (3) Enter the account number for the debit entry in the posting reference column of the journal. (4) Locate the credit entry ledger account. (5) Enter the transaction date, the journal entry page number, and the credit amount. Then enter the new balance. (6) Enter the account number for the credit entry in the posting reference column of the journal.

8. **Prepare a trial balance and use it to prepare financial statements.**

   A trial balance is a test of the equality of debits and credits in the general ledger. Prepare a trial balance by listing the accounts and their balances. If the total of the debit and credit columns is equal, the general ledger is in balance. The revenue and expense accounts listed in the trial balance provide information for the income statement. The common stock and dividends in the trial balance and net income provide the information for the statement of owners' equity. The asset and liability accounts from the trial balance and end-of-period capital from the statement of owners' equity provide information for the balance sheet.

9. **Analyze financial statement information for real-life companies.**

   In Chapter 2, we used the analysis questions from the Introduction to evaluate the performance of Tyco over the period 2001 to 2004.

DEMONSTRATION PROBLEM

Processing Transactions

Computer Services, Inc. began in November 2007. On November 30, 2007, its balance sheet appeared as follows:

COMPUTER SERVICES, INC.
BALANCE SHEET
NOVEMBER 30, 2007
Assets

Current assets		
Cash		$10,000
Accounts receivable		800
Office supplies		200
Total assets		$11,000
Liabilities		
Current liabilities		
Accounts payable		$ 500
Owners' Equity		
Common stock	$ 9,300	
Retained earnings	1,200	
Total owners' equity		10,500
Total liabilities and owners' equity		$11,000

During December 2007, the business engaged in the following transactions:

2007

Dec.	5	Purchased office supplies in the amount of $300 on account.
	7	Paid $700 in office rent for the month of December.
	10	Hired a receptionist to begin work on December 15.
	17	Paid the amount owed on open account on November 30.
	19	Performed computer services for cash in the amount of $900.
	21	Collected $600 of amounts owed on account.
	27	Purchased land for a future store at a cost of $8,000 and signed a three-year note for the total amount owed.
	29	Billed customers $1,800 for services rendered during the month.
	31	Paid the receptionist $500 in wages for the last half of December.
	31	Computer Services declared and paid $1,000 cash dividends to its owners.

REQUIRED

1. **(LG 1, 2)** Develop a chart of accounts for Computer Services and assign account numbers.

2. **(LG 3, 6)** Journalize the transactions in a general journal.

3. **(LG 5, 7)** Post the journal entries to the general ledger.

4. **(LG 8)** Prepare a trial balance.

5. **(LG 8)** Prepare an income statement and a statement of owners' equity for the month ended December 31, 2007, and a balance sheet as of December 31, 2007.

SOLUTION

Requirement 1

> ## Solution Approach
>
> In setting up a chart of accounts, read through the transactions and identify the accounts that will be necessary. Select titles that describe the items that will be recorded in each account. In assigning the account numbers, set up a structure that places the accounts in the order that they will appear in the financial statements: assets, liabilities, common stock, retained earnings, dividends, revenues, and expenses. Also, assign the numbers so that the accounts are properly classified as to current and long-term. Leave space between numbers to add additional accounts as the business expands.

COMPUTER SERVICES, INC.
CHART OF ACCOUNTS

Asset Accounts (100–189)	
Current Assets (100–143)	
101	Cash
111	Accounts Receivable
135	Office Supplies
Property, Plant, and Equipment (150–189)	
151	Land

Liability Accounts (200–299)	
Current Liabilities (200–249)	
201	Accounts Payable
Long-term Liabilities (250–299)	
252	Notes Payable—Long-term

Owners' Equity Accounts (300–399)	
331	Common Stock
360	Retained Earnings
372	Dividends

Revenue Accounts (400–499)	
423	Professional Fees Revenue

Expense Accounts (500–949)	
705	Wages Expense
715	Rent Expense

Requirement 2

GENERAL JOURNAL   Page 1

Date		Accounts and Explanations	PR	Debit	Credit

2007 Dec.	5	Office Supplies
		    Accounts Payable
		    To record purchase of office supplies on
		    account.
			135
			201
				300	300

	7	Rent Expense
		    Cash
		    To record payment of December rent.
			715
			101
				700	700

	17	Accounts Payable
		    Cash
		    To record payment on account.
			201
			101
				500	500

	19	Cash
		    Professional Fees Revenue
		    To record cash revenue earned.
			101
			423
				900	900

	21	Cash
		    Accounts Receivable
		    To record collection on account.
			101
			111
				600	600

	27	Land
		    Notes Payable—Long-term
		    To record purchase of land by signing a long-
		    term note.
			151
			252
				8,000	8,000

	29	Accounts Receivable
		    Professional Fees Revenue
		    To record revenue earned on account.
			111
			423
				1,800	1,800

	31	Wages Expense
		    Cash
		    To record payment of wages.
			705
			101
				500	500

	31	Dividends
		    Cash
		    To record dividends paid to owners
			372
			101
				1,000	1,000

Requirement 3

Solution Approach

Transfer the debit and credit amounts for each of the transactions to the appropriate accounts in the general ledger. After this is completed, enter the account number in the posting reference column of the journal.

GENERAL LEDGER

Cash   Acct. No. 101

Date		Explanation	PR	Debit	Credit	Balance Debit	Balance Credit
2007							
Nov.	30	Balance				10,000	
Dec.	7		J1		700	9,300	
	17		J1		500	8,800	
	19		J1	900		9,700	
	21		J1	600		10,300	
	31		J1		500	9,800	
	31		J1		1,000	8,800	

Accounts Receivable   Acct. No. 111

Date		Explanation	PR	Debit	Credit	Balance Debit	Balance Credit
2007							
Nov.	30	Balance				800	
Dec.	21		J1		600	200	
	29		J1	1,800		2,000	

Office Supplies   Acct. No. 135

Date		Explanation	PR	Debit	Credit	Balance Debit	Balance Credit
2007							
Nov.	30	Balance				200	
Dec.	5		J1	300		500	

Land   Acct. No. 151

Date		Explanation	PR	Debit	Credit	Balance Debit	Balance Credit
2007							
Dec.	27		J1	8,000		8,000	

Accounts Payable   Acct. No. 201

Date		Explanation	PR	Debit	Credit	Balance Debit	Balance Credit
2007							
Nov.	30	Balance					500
Dec.	5		J1		300		800
	17		J1	500			300

Notes Payable—Long-term   Acct. No. 252

Date		Explanation	PR	Debit	Credit	Balance Debit	Balance Credit
2007							
Dec.	27		J1		8,000		8,000

Common Stock

Acct. No. 331

Date		Explanation	PR	Debit	Credit	Balance Debit	Balance Credit
2007 Nov.	30	Balance					9,300

Retained Earnings

Acct. No. 360

Date		Explanation	PR	Debit	Credit	Balance Debit	Balance Credit
2007 Nov.	30	Balance					1,200

Dividends

Acct. No. 372

Date		Explanation	PR	Debit	Credit	Balance Debit	Balance Credit
2007 Dec.	31		J1	1,000		1,000	

Professional Fees Revenue

Acct. No. 423

Date		Explanation	PR	Debit	Credit	Balance Debit	Balance Credit
2007 Dec.	19		J1		900		900
	29		J1		1,800		2,700

Wages Expense

Acct. No. 705

Date		Explanation	PR	Debit	Credit	Balance Debit	Balance Credit
2007 Dec.	31		J1	500		500	

Rent Expense

Acct. No. 715

Date		Explanation	PR	Debit	Credit	Balance Debit	Balance Credit
2007 Dec.	7		J1	700		700	

Requirement 4

COMPUTER SERVICES, INC.
TRIAL BALANCE
DECEMBER 31, 2007

Acct. No.	Account Title	Debits	Credits
101	Cash	$ 8,800	
111	Accounts Receivable	2,000	
135	Office Supplies	500	
151	Land	8,000	
201	Accounts Payable		$ 300
252	Notes Payable—Long-term		8,000
331	Common Stock		9,300
360	Retained Earnings		1,200
372	Dividends	1,000	
423	Professional Fees Revenue		2,700
705	Wages Expense	500	
715	Rent Expense	700	
	Totals	$21,500	$21,500

Requirement 5

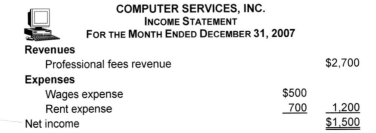

COMPUTER SERVICES, INC.
INCOME STATEMENT
FOR THE MONTH ENDED DECEMBER 31, 2007

Revenues		
Professional fees revenue		$2,700
Expenses		
Wages expense	$500	
Rent expense	700	1,200
Net income		$1,500

COMPUTER SERVICES, INC.
STATEMENT OF OWNERS' EQUITY
FOR THE MONTH ENDED DECEMBER 31, 2007

Common stock, December 1, 2007	$9,300	
Add: Investments by owners	0	
Common stock, December 31, 2007		$ 9,300
Retained earnings, December 1, 2007	$1,200	
Add: Net income	1,500	
Deduct: Dividends	(1,000)	
Retained earnings, December 31, 2007		1,700
Owners' equity, December 31, 2007		$11,000

COMPUTER SERVICES, INC.
BALANCE SHEET
DECEMBER 31, 2007

Assets

Current assets		
Cash	$8,800	
Accounts receivable	2,000	
Office supplies	500	
Total current assets		$11,300
Property, plant, and equipment		
Land		8,000
Total assets		$19,300

Liabilities

Current liabilities		
Accounts payable		$ 300
Long-term liabilities		
Notes payable—long-term		8,000
Total liabilities		$ 8,300

Owners' Equity

Common stock	$ 9,300	
Retained earnings	1,700	
Total owners' equity		11,000
Total liabilities and owners' equity		$19,300

GLOSSARY

account A recording device used for sorting accounting information into similar groupings.

accounting cycle A series of steps repeated during each accounting period that enables an accounting entity to record, classify, and summarize financial information.

balance of an account The difference between the total of the debits and the total of the credits in an account.

chart of accounts The complete listing of the account titles to be used by the entity.

cost The amount given up to purchase an asset.

credit The amount shown on the right side of an account, or the process of placing an amount on the right side of an account.

debit The amount shown on the left side of an account or the process of placing an amount on the left side of an account.

double-entry accounting A system of recording both the debit and credit entries of each transaction.

expense Expired cost of the resource used in the production of revenue during a specific period.

general journal The accounting record in which a transaction is first recorded. It is called a book of original entry.

general ledger The collection of all accounts for an accounting entity.

journalizing The process of recording a transaction, analyzed in terms of its debits and credits, in a record of original entry referred to as a journal.

posting The process of transferring an amount recorded in the journal to the indicated account in the ledger.

revenue A term describing the source of inflows of assets received in exchange for services rendered, sales of products or merchandise, and earnings from interest and dividends on investments.

trial balance A statement that shows the name and balance of all ledger accounts arranged according to whether they are debits or credits. The total of the debits must equal the total of the credits in this statement.

QUESTIONS FOR GROUP LEARNING

Q2-1. Define the term *account*. Identify the parts of an account.

Q2-2. What are the major classifications of accounts commonly used in business? List some commonly used examples of each type.

Q2-3. Define *revenue*. Does the receipt of cash by a business indicate that revenue has been earned? Explain.

Q2-4. Define *expense*. Does the payment of cash by a business indicate that an expense has been incurred? Explain. Are withdrawals an expense? Explain.

Q2-5. What factors should a business consider in setting up a chart of accounts? What factors should it consider in selecting a title for an account and assigning account numbers?

Q2-6. State the rules of debit and credit for assets, liabilities, owners' capital, owners' withdrawals, revenues, and expenses. Would it be possible to have a general ledger in balance if the rules of debit and credit were reversed? Explain.

Q2-7. When an account is debited, does the balance of the account always increase? Explain.

Q2-8. What is the purpose of a general ledger? The general ledger is often called a categorical record of transactions. Why?

Q2-9. What is the purpose of a journal? The journal is often called a chronological record of transactions. Why?

Q2-10. Describe the analytical process that is used for each transaction. List the information found in each journal entry.

Q2-11. Why are journal entries posted to accounts when each journal entry already contains the details of a complete transaction?

Q2-12. What is the purpose of a trial balance? What cannot be determined from a trial balance?

Q2-13. Discuss the nature and purpose of the income statement.

Q2-14. What item is common to each of the following pairs of financial statements: (a) The income statement and the statement of owners' equity? (b) The statement of owners' equity and the balance sheet as of the beginning of an accounting period? (c) The statement of owners' equity and the balance sheet as of the end of an accounting period?

EXERCISES

E2-15. Setting up a chart of accounts (LG 1, 2) Tom Cleaning is a corporation that does house cleaning. They intend to keep the business simple by performing only one type of service, house cleaning. They intend to buy a van to travel to jobs. They know that they must buy supplies to do the cleaning. They plan to hire two employees, and do some advertising. They will perform services either for cash or on account. A local vendor of supplies has agreed to sell to Tom Cleaning on credit. Set up a chart of accounts for Tom Cleaning.

E2-16. Rules of debit and credit (LG 3) Following are six T accounts. Each represents a type of account. For each of the numbers 1 through 12, indicate whether an entry in that position would be an increase or a decrease.

Asset		Liability		Common Stock	
1	2	3	4	5	6

Dividends		Revenue		Expense	
7	8	9	10	11	12

E2-17. Recording transactions in the accounts (LG 4) On April 2, 2007, Nicole Rich, attorney, paid office rent for two months in advance at the rate of $600 per month. On the same date, she purchased an item of office equipment for $2,000 in cash. Determine the account titles to be used and record these transactions directly in the T accounts.

E2-18. Analyzing transactions with T accounts (LG 4) Scott Company began business on October 31, 2007. Analyze the following transactions for November and enter the debits and credits directly in T accounts. You will need the following T accounts: Cash, Office Supplies, Office Furniture, Accounts Payable, Service Revenue, and Advertising Expense. Enter a beginning cash balance of $10,000 in the Cash T account.

2007

Nov.	11	Purchased office furniture at a cost of $2,000 and paid cash.
	15	Purchased office supplies on account at a cost of $500.
	20	Performed services for clients and received $1,000.
	27	Received a bill for television advertising that had appeared, $300.

E2-19. Analysis of transactions (LG 4) The March 2007 transactions of O'Neill Travel Service, Inc., are as follows:

2007

Mar.	1	Paid $400 for an advertisement that had appeared in the travel section of the *Register*.
	5	Arranged a round-the-world trip for Mr. and Mrs. Oliver Stone. Collected commission of $400 in cash from the steamship company.
	10	Arranged fly-now, pay-later Asian trips for several clients. Far East Air agreed to a commission of $1,000 for services rendered but had not paid it.
	12	Placed another advertisement in the *Register* for $400; this account is payable in ten days.
	20	Global Travel paid $1,500 dividends to its owners.
	25	Collected $1,000 from Far East Air.

Following the example below for the March 1 transaction, analyze each transaction.
EXAMPLE

Mar. 1	a.	Advertising is an expense. Increases in expenses are recorded by debits.
		Debit Advertising Expense for $400.
	b.	The asset Cash was decreased. Decreases of assets are recorded by credits.
		Credit Cash for $400.

E2-20. Journalizing transactions (LG 6) Journalize the following transactions for Falmouth Tax Service.

2007

Mar.	7	Purchased office supplies on account in the amount of $600.
	9	Paid $600 for advertising in the local paper.
	15	Paid $500 of the amount owed on the office supplies.

E2-21. Posting transactions (LG 7) Following is the journal for Ted Music. Set up ledger accounts as shown in Exhibit 2.2 and post the transactions. Assume a beginning Cash balance of $3,000.

	GENERAL JOURNAL			Page 4
Date	**Explanation**	**PR**	**Debit**	**Credit**
2007				
Aug. 8	Repair Expense		300	
	Cash			300
	To record the payment for repairs to a typewriter.			
14	Advertising Expense		100	
	Cash			100
	To record purchase of fliers for cash.			
28	Advertising Expense		200	
	Accounts Payable			200
	To record receipt of bill for advertising that had appeared.			

E2-22. Preparing a trial balance (LG 8) Following is a list of accounts for Sara Company and their normal balances as of December 31, 2007. Prepare a trial balance.

Accounts Payable	$ 800
Accounts Receivable	2,000
Delivery Equipment	8,000
Cash	8,000
Fees Revenue	32,000
Common Stock	7,200
Dividends	1,500
Store Supplies	500
Store Supplies Expense	3,000
Cleaning Expense	2,000
Wages Expense	15,000

E2-23. Effect of errors on trial balance (LG 8) Quick Accountants began work on January 2, 2007. Unfortunately, they made several errors that were discovered by the auditor during the year-end review. For each error described in the following list, indicate the effect of the error (by filling out a solution form like that illustrated next). Treat each error separately; do not attempt to relate the errors to one another.

Suggested Solution Form

GENERAL JOURNAL
Page 4

Error	Would the December 31, 2007, trial balance be out of balance?		If yes, by how much?	Which would be larger?	
	Yes	No		Debit Total	Credit Total
a.					
b.					
etc.					

ERRORS

a. The company bought a cash register for $1,000 and paid cash. The debit was posted twice in the Asset account. The Cash credit was posted correctly.

b. A debit to the Cash account of $3,121 was posted as $3,112.

c. Cash collections of $6,000 from customers in settlement of their accounts were not posted to the Accounts Receivable account but were posted correctly to the Cash account.

d. A purchase of office supplies for $450 for cash was recorded as a debit to Cash and a credit to Office Supplies.

E2-24. Identifying the financial statements on which trial balance amounts appear (LG 8)
Following is a list of accounts appearing in Manchester Company's trial balance. For each, indicate the financial statement on which it would appear.

a.	Wages Expense	b.	Common Stock
c.	Building	d.	Professional Fees Revenue
e.	Cash	f.	Supplies Expense
g.	Accounts Payable	h.	Dividends
i.	Accounts Receivable	j.	Prepaid Rent
k.	Trucks	l.	Wages Payable
m.	Commissions Revenue	n.	Rent Expense

E2-25. Preparing financial statements from a trial balance (LG 8) The trial balance of Betsy Copy Company as of December 31, 2007, the end of the current accounting year, is as follows:

BETSY COPY COMPANY
TRIAL BALANCE
DECEMBER 31, 2007

Acct. No.	Account Title	Debits	Credits
101	Cash	$ 10,000	
135	Office Supplies	3,000	
141	Prepaid Insurance	1,000	
171	Office Equipment	30,000	
201	Accounts Payable		$ 1,000
202	Notes Payable		4,000
331	Common Stock		14,000
360	Retained Earnings		11,000
372	Dividends	2,000	
416	Copying Revenue		68,000
705	Salaries Expense	30,000	
711	Rent Expense	12,000	
718	Office Supplies Expense	4,000	
721	Utilities Expense	6,000	
	Totals	$98,000	$98,000

Prepare an income statement, a statement of owners' equity, and a balance sheet for Betsy Copy Company. No new investment was made during the year.

PROBLEMS

P2-26. Designing a chart of accounts (LG 1, 2) The accountant for Audi Company set up the following chart of accounts:

Assets

101	Cash
102	Prepaid Insurance
103	Equipment
104	Accounts Receivable
105	Accounts Payable
106	Notes Payable
107	Utilities Expense
108	Repairs Expense

Liabilities and Owners' Equities

201	Buildings
202	Office Supplies Expense
203	Office Supplies
204	Land
205	Common Stock
206	Retained Earnings
207	Professional Fees Revenue

Income Statement

302	Wages Payable
303	Wages Expense
304	Insurance Expense
305	Rent Expense
306	Advertising Expense
307	Service Revenue
308	Dividends

REQUIRED

Using the same accounts that Audi's accountant used, design a chart of accounts in good form.

P2-27. Analyzing transactions and entering in T accounts (LG 4) Pat Delivery, Inc. has set up the following accounts:

101	Cash	372	Dividends
111	Accounts Receivable	413	Service Revenue
167	Delivery Equipment	603	Delivery Salaries Expense
201	Accounts Payable	614	Rent Expense—Trucks
331	Common Stock	616	Advertising Expense

During April, 2007, the first month of operations, the following transactions occurred.

2007

Apr.	1	Owners invested $60,000 cash to start Pat Delivery, Inc.
	4	Purchased equipment to be used in deliveries for $1,000, paying cash.
	7	Paid $500 for April's rent on a truck to be used in deliveries.
	10	Received a bill for $100 for advertisements in home shopper papers in local area.
	14	Billed a client $2,000 for deliveries completed.
	17	Paid the April 10 bill for the advertising.
	20	Made deliveries for a client and received $1,000 cash.
	26	Received $1,500 from the April 14 billings to customers.
	29	Paid delivery employees $1,500 for the month's work.
	30	Pat Delivery paid $600 dividends to its owners.

REQUIRED

1. Set up T accounts for the accounts provided.

2. Analyze the transactions and enter the appropriate debits and credits directly into the T accounts.

3. Determine the account balances as of April 30, 2007

P2-28. Performing accounting sequence steps (LG 3, 5-8) The following transactions occurred during October 2007 at Gus Repair Company:

2007

Oct.	1	Owners invested $60,000 in cash to start Gus Repair Company.
	5	Paid $200 for two days' rental of test equipment used on a repair job.
	10	Purchased United States Government bonds as a short-term investment for $8,000 in cash.
	15	Collected $2,000 in cash on completion of repair work not previously billed.
	18	Signed an agreement with Western College to repair computers for $5,000. The work is to be completed during November and December.
	25	Gus Repair Company paid $500 dividends to its owners.
	27	Paid $900 for repair materials used on jobs during the month.
	29	Paid $3,000 in salaries and wages.
	30	Completed computer repair work for Joseph Reynolds in the amount of $1,000. Reynolds promised to pay for the work on November 15.

Use the following account titles and numbers:

101	Cash	411	Repair Revenue
105	Short-term Investments	620	Repair Materials Expense
111	Accounts Receivable	705	Salaries and Wages Expense
331	Common Stock	711	Rental Expense
372	Dividends		

REQUIRED

1. Journalize the transactions. Assign numbers to the journal pages.

2. Post to general ledger accounts.

3. Prepare a trial balance.

P2-29. Preparing financial statements using a trial balance (LG 8) Lopez Fashions began business on December 1, 2007. Following are the accounts and their normal balances as of December 31, 2007. The accounts are listed in alphabetical order. The capital balance is Lopez's initial investment.

Accounts Payable	$ 8,000	Office Supplies Expense	200
Accounts Receivable	12,000	Prepaid Insurance	2,000
Advertising Expense	500	Professional Fees Revenue	40,000
Building	120,000	Rent Expense	1,500
Cash	15,000	Salaries Expense	8,000
Equipment	20,000	Salaries Payable	1,500
Insurance Expense	1,200	Utilities Expense	600
Land	30,000	Common Stock	63,500
Notes Payable—Long-term	100,000	Dividends	1,000
Office Supplies	1,000	Retained Earnings	0

REQUIRED

1. Prepare a trial balance as of December 31, 2007.

2. Prepare an income statement for the month ended December 31, 2007.

3. Prepare a statement of owners' equity for the month ended December 31, 2007.

4. Prepare a balance sheet as of December 31, 2007.

P2-30. Preparing financial statements using a trial balance (LG 8) Agway Company began business on January 1, 2007. Following are the accounts and their normal balances taken from the general ledger as of January 31, 2007. The accounts are listed in alphabetical order. The balance in Agway's common stock is the owners' initial investment.

Accounts Payable	$ 7,300	Office Equipment	5,000
Accounts Receivable	15,000	Office Salaries Expense	2,500
Advertising Expense	3,600	Prepaid Insurance	1,200
Cash	12,000	Salaries Payable	700
Commissions Revenue	30,000	Supplies	800
Insurance Expense	300	Supplies Expense	1,500
Land	10,000	Utilities Expense	700
Mortgages Payable	50,000	Common Stock	51,000
Notes Receivable	5,000	Dividends	1,400
Office Building	80,000	Retained Earnings	0

REQUIRED

1. Prepare a trial balance as of January 31, 2007.

2. Prepare an income statement for the month ended January 31, 2007.

3. Prepare a statement of owners' equity for the month ended January 31, 2007.

4. Prepare a balance sheet as of January 31, 2007.

P2-31. Performing accounting sequence steps (LG 3-8) Mad Medics, opened an office for the practice of medicine. During May 2007, the following transactions occurred:

2007

May	1	Owners invested $90,000 in cash to start Mad Medics. In exchange, owners received shares of common stock.
	4	Purchased $2,000 of medical supplies on account from State Medical Supply.
	5	Paid $1,500 for May rent of building.
	6	Purchased medical equipment from Hamer, Inc., and paid $3,000.
	8	Paid $1,000 for miscellaneous general expenses.
	9	Received $10,000 in cash for professional services rendered but not previously billed.
	14	Paid on account $1,500 to State Medical Supply.
	24	Mailed statements to the following patients for services rendered:

Charlie Smith $ 500

Ken Nelson   1,000

	28	Paid $300 for office cleaning for May.
	29	Mad Medics paid $1,200 dividends to its owners.
	30	Received on account $300 in cash from Charlie Smith and $400 from Ken Nelson.

Use the following account titles and numbers:

101	Cash		360	Retained Earnings
111	Accounts Receivable		372	Dividends
138	Medical Supplies		424	Medical Service Revenue
159	Equipment		711	Rent Expense—Building
201	Accounts Payable		725	Cleaning Expense
331	Common Stock		791	Miscellaneous General Expense

REQUIRED

1. Journalize the transactions.

2. Post to the general ledger. (Assign numbers to the journal pages.)

3. Prepare a trial balance.

4. Prepare an income statement, a statement of owners' equity, and a balance sheet.

P2-32. Preparing and analyzing financial statements for Merck & Co., Inc. (LG 8, 9) Merck is one of the world's largest pharmaceutical companies. Merck develops, produces and distributes human and animal health products. Selected information (in millions) for the year ended December 31, 2004, is shown below.

Revenues	$22,938.6		
Other current assets	6,968.7	Dividends	3,310.7
Noncurrent assets	29,097.6	Other current liabilities	2,181.2
Long-term liabilities	13,540.5	Accounts receivable	3,627.7
Cash	2,878.8	Owners' equity (January 1, 2004)	15,576.4
Expenses	17,125.2	Other payments to owners (stock buy back)	790.9
Accounts payable	9,562.9		

REQUIRED

1. Determine the net income for the year ended December 31, 2004.

2. Prepare a statement of owners' equity for the year ended December 31, 2004.

3. Prepare a balance sheet at December 31, 2004.

4. Compute the percent of net income to total revenues for Merck. Pfizer's net income to total revenues was 25.3%. Which company was more profitable in 2004?

5. Compute the percent of total liabilities to total liabilities and owners' equity for Merck. Pfizer's percent of total liabilities is 50.2%. Which company uses more debt as a source of financing as of the end of fiscal 2004?

P2-33. Analyzing Merck & Co., Inc. for the Period 2004-2001 (LG 9) Merck is one of the largest pharmaceutical companies. The company has its headquarters in Whitehouse Station, New Jersey. Listed below are comparative income statements and balance sheets with common-size percents for 2004-2001 (in millions).

MERCK & CO. INC.
COMPARATIVE COMMON-SIZE INCOME STATEMENTS
For The Years Ended December 31, 2004, 2003, 2002, 2001
(in millions)

	2004	2004	2003	2003	2002	2002	2001	2001
	$	%	$	%	$	%	$	%
Total revenues	$ 22,938.6	100.0%	$ 22,485.9	100.0%	$ 51,790.3	100.0%	$ 47,715.7	100.0%
Total expenses	$ 17,125.2	74.7%	$ 15,655.0	69.6%	$ 44,640.8	86.2%	$ 40,433.9	84.7%
Net income (loss)	$ 5,813.4	25.3%	$ 6,830.9	30.4%	$ 7,149.5	13.8%	$ 7,281.8	15.3%

MERCK & CO. INC.
COMPARATIVE COMMON-SIZE BALANCE SHEETS
December 31, 2004, 2003, 2002, 2001
(in millions)

	2004	2004	2003	2003	2002	2002	2001	2001
	$	%	$	%	$	%	$	%
Total assets	$ 42,572.8	100.0%	$ 40,587.5	100.0%	$ 47,561.2	100.0%	$ 44,006.7	100.0%
Total liabilities	$ 25,284.6	59.4%	$ 25,011.1	61.6%	$ 29,360.7	61.7%	$ 27,956.6	63.5%
Total owners' equity	$ 17,288.2	40.6%	$ 15,576.4	38.4%	$ 18,200.5	38.3%	$ 16,050.1	36.5%
Total liabilities and owners' equity	$ 42,572.8	100.0%	$ 40,587.5	100.0%	$ 47,561.2	100.0%	$ 44,006.7	100.0%

REQUIRED

INCOME STATEMENT QUESTIONS:

1. Are total revenues for Merck higher or lower over the four year period?

2. What is the percent change in total revenues from 2001 to 2004?

3. Is the percent of total expenses to total revenues increasing or decreasing over the four year period?

BALANCE SHEET QUESTIONS:

4. Are total assets for Merck higher or lower over the four year period?

5. What is the percent change in total assets from 2001 to 2004?

6. Is the percent of total liabilities to total liabilities + owners' equity increasing or decreasing? As a result, is there more risk that Merck could not pay its debts?

INTEGRATIVE INCOME STATEMENT AND BALANCE SHEET QUESTIONS:

7.   Is Merck operating efficiently by using the least amount of asset investment to generate a given level of total revenues?

P2-34. Preparing and analyzing financial statements for Abbott Labs (LG 8, 9) Abbott Labs is a leading pharmaceutical firm. Selected information (in millions) for the year ended December 31, 2004, is shown below.

Revenues	$19,680.0	Expenses	16,444.1
Other current assets	4,781.0	Dividends	1,982.4
Noncurrent assets	18,033.0	Current liabilities	6,825.6
Long-term liabilities	7,616.1	Accounts receivable	4,727.9
Cash	1,225.6	Owners' equity (January 1, 2004)	13,072.3

REQUIRED

1.   Determine the net income for the year ended December 31, 2004.

2.   Prepare a statement of owners' equity for the year ended December 31, 2004.

3.   Prepare a balance sheet at December 31, 2004.

4.   Compute the percent of net income to total revenues for Abbott Labs. Pfizer's net income to total revenues was 25.3%. Which company was more profitable in 2004?

5.   Compute the percent of total liabilities to total liabilities and owners' equity for Abbott Labs. Pfizer's percent of total liabilities is 50.2%. Which company uses more debt as a source of financing as of the end of fiscal 2004?

6.   In the problem data, "other current assets" are $4,781.0 million. Included in total current assets is cash of $1,225.6 million and accounts receivable of $4,727.9 million. What individual asset do you think accounts for most of the "other current assets" of $4,781.0 million?

P2-35. Analyzing Abbott Labs, Inc. for the Period 2004-2001 (LG 9) Abbott Labs is one of the largest pharmaceutical firms. The company has its headquarters in Abbott Park, Illinois. Listed below are comparative income statements and balance sheets with common-size percents for 2004-2001 (in millions).

ABBOTT LABS, INC.
COMPARATIVE COMMON-SIZE INCOME STATEMENTS
For The Years Ended December 31, 2004, 2003, 2002, 2001
(in millions)

	2004	2004	2003	2003	2002	2002	2001	2001
	$	%	$	%	$	%	$	%
Total revenues	$ 19,680.0	100.0%	$ 19,680.6	100.0%	$ 17,684.7	100.0%	$ 16,285.3	100.0%
Total expenses	$ 16,444.1	83.6%	$ 16,927.4	86.0%	$ 14,891.0	84.2%	$ 14,734.9	90.5%
Net income (loss)	$ 3,235.9	16.4%	$ 2,753.2	14.0%	$ 2,793.7	15.8%	$ 1,550.4	9.5%

ABBOTT LABS, INC.
COMPARATIVE COMMON-SIZE BALANCE SHEETS
December 31, 2004, 2003, 2002, 2001
(in millions)

	2004	2004	2003	2003	2002	2002	2001	2001
	$	%	$	%	$	%	$	%
Total assets	$ 28,767.5	100.0%	$ 26,715.3	100.0%	$ 24,259.1	100.0%	$ 23,296.4	100.0%
Total liabilities	$ 14,441.7	50.2%	$ 13,643.0	51.1%	$ 13,594.5	56.0%	$ 14,237.0	61.1%
Total owners' equity	$ 14,325.8	49.8%	$ 13,072.3	48.9%	$ 10,664.6	44.0%	$ 9,059.4	38.9%
Total liabilities and owners' equity	$ 28,767.5	100.0%	$ 26,715.3	100.0%	$ 24,259.1	100.0%	$ 23,296.4	100.0%

REQUIRED

INCOME STATEMENT QUESTIONS:

1. Are total revenues for Abbott Labs higher or lower over the four year period?

2. What is the percent change in total revenues from 2001 to 2004?

3. Is the percent of total expenses to total revenues increasing or decreasing over the four year period?

BALANCE SHEET QUESTIONS:

4. Are total assets for Abbott Labs higher or lower over the four year period?

5. What is the percent change in total assets from 2001 to 2004?

6. Is the percent of total liabilities to total liabilities + owners' equity increasing or decreasing? As a result, is there more risk that Abbott Labs could not pay its debts?

INTEGRATIVE INCOME STATEMENT AND BALANCE SHEET QUESTIONS:

7. Is Abbott Labs operating efficiently by using the least amount of asset investment to generate a given level of total revenues?

PRACTICE CASE

Processing business transactions (LG 1-3, 5-8) Herman Shows, Inc., began business near the end of November 2007 to entertain children. The balance sheet for the business as of November 30, 2007, is as follows:

HERMAN SHOWS, INC.
BALANCE SHEET
NOVEMBER 30, 2007
Assets

Current assets		
Cash		$20,000
Supplies		2,000
Total assets		$22,000

Liabilities

Current liabilities		
Accounts payable		$ 1,000

Owners' Equity

Common stock	$ 17,000	
Retained earnings	4,000	
Total owners' equity		21,000
Total liabilities and owners' equity		$22,000

During December 2007, Herman Shows engaged in the following transactions:

2007

Dec.	2	Purchased supplies at a cost of $500 and paid cash.
	5	Paid $800 rent for December for a car to travel to shows.
	8	Received a bill for $200 for advertising that had appeared in the local paper.
	10	Owners invested an additional $2,000 in cash in the business and received shares of common stock.
	12	Performed for a birthday and collected $200 in cash.
	16	Paid $600 on the account owed at the beginning of December.
	20	Performed at another party and gave a bill for $1,000 to the host, who promised to pay in seven days.
	26	Purchased a car for use in the business at a cost of $6,000. Paid $1,000 in cash and signed a six-month note payable for the balance of $5,000.
	27	Collected $400 of the amount owed from the December 20 performance.
	28	Paid a student who had been helping at the shows $100 in cash.
	30	Herman paid $500 of cash dividends to owners.

REQUIRED

1. Develop a chart of accounts for Herman Shows, Inc. and assign account numbers. (Hint: You will need 13 accounts.)

2. Open ledger accounts and use the November 30, 2007, balance sheet to enter beginning balances in the appropriate accounts.

3. Journalize the transactions in a general journal.

4. Post the journal entries to the general ledger.

5. Prepare a trial balance.

6. Prepare an income statement and a statement of owners' equity for the month ended December 31, 2007, and a balance sheet as of December 31, 2007.

BUSINESS DECISION AND COMMUNICATION PROBLEM

Commenting on a chart of accounts A friend of yours, Jay Harrison, has begun a new business. The accountant he hired has prepared the following chart of accounts:

Assets

101 Cash
102 Accounts Receivable
103 Accounts Payable
104 Land
105 Office Supplies
106 Office Supplies Expense
107 Retained Earnings

Liabilities

201 Wages Payable
202 Wages Expense
203 Buildings
204 Dividends

Revenues

401 Service Revenue
402 Common Stock

Expenses

701 Advertising Expense
702 Rent Expense
703 Utilities Expense
704 Repairs Expense

REQUIRED

Write a memo to Jay commenting on the appropriateness of the chart of accounts. If the chart of accounts needs correcting, prepare a corrected chart of accounts.

ETHICAL DILEMMA

Neglecting to record expenses You are the chief accountant for the largest division of your company. On December 21, your boss, the divisional president, comes to you and asks a "small favor." He requests that you not record any bill for an expense that comes in until January 1. He said that there would be no problem because none of the bills must be paid until January 1. He suggests that this will help make "your team's" performance look good. The division has shown steady growth over the past five years, and "we" need to keep up the good work. As he leaves your office, he says that good divisional performance also will help support his consideration of your upcoming raise. The division's net income is the basis for your boss's compensation.

REQUIRED

Discuss the impact of your boss's request on the income statement for the current year and the balance sheet at year-end. Should you go along with his request? Explain what other choices you have besides doing the "favor."

INTERNET PROBLEM

Frater Luca Bartolomes Pacioli is known as the father of accounting. Using the Association of Chartered Accountants web site, http://www.acaus.com/history/, briefly describe what is known about financial records in Mesopotamia around 3500 BC. Also, discuss the role the Luca Pacioli played in the early days of accounting.

ADJUSTING ENTRIES

CHAPTER

3

"Sure bet: Anything delayed will get further delayed."

Robert Half

LEARNING GOALS

After studying chapter 3, you should be able to:

1. Explain (a) the accounting period assumption, (b) cash versus accrual accounting, (c) the matching principle, and (d) the materiality concept.

2. Explain the purpose of adjusting entries.

3. Describe and prepare adjusting entries for prepaid expenses.

4. Define *depreciation expense* and prepare entries to record it.

5. Describe and prepare adjusting entries for unearned revenues.

6. Describe and prepare adjusting entries to record accrued revenues.

7. Describe and prepare adjusting entries to record accrued expenses.

8. Analyze financial statement information for real-life companies.

UNDERSTANDING BUSINESS ISSUES

As transactions occur, we journalize the effects and post them to the general ledger. Since we use the general ledger account balances at the end of the period to prepare financial statements, these balances must be accurate. *Adjusting entries* ensure that the general ledger balances properly show the following:

- The revenues earned.
- The expenses incurred.
- The assets owned.
- The liabilities owed.
- The owners' equity in the business.

For example, assume McDonald's Corporation purchases napkins for $500,000 on January 1, 2007. McDonald's debits Paper Supplies and credits Cash for $500,000. On December 31, 2007, a count shows that $100,000 worth of napkins remain unused. Thus, on December 31, 2007, the company really has an expense of $400,000 and an asset of $100,000. Since it does not make an entry every time it uses some napkins, an adjusting entry is necessary. If McDonald's makes no adjusting entry on December 31, 2007, the amount for paper supplies expense on 2007's income statement would be understated by $400,000. The December 31, 2007, balance sheet would overstate the asset paper supplies by $400,000. An adjusting entry will improve the accuracy of both the income statement and balance sheet.

Chapter 3 begins by examining four accounting issues related to measuring business income. The chapter then uses another business, Metro Delivery, Inc., to illustrate adjusting entries.

MEASURING BUSINESS INCOME

Learning Goal 1   Explain (a) the accounting period assumption, (b) cash versus accrual accounting, (c) the matching principle, and (d) the materiality concept.

Users of financial statements need information about income for many of their decisions. In measuring income, the accountant must resolve many issues to provide meaningful information. This section discusses four of these issues: (1) the accounting period assumption, (2) cash basis versus accrual basis accounting, (3) the matching principle, and (4) the materiality concept.

The Accounting Period

Without the idea of an *accounting period*, the only time we would know the true income of a company such as McDonald's Corporation is when it goes out of business. At that point, the company would sell its assets and pay its debts. We could then compare its ending cash balance with its balance at start-up. The problem with this approach is that financial statement users need information more frequently to make decisions.

To permit periodic reporting to users, we divide the life of a company into shorter periods of time, usually one year. This division of a business's life into equal time intervals is called the **accounting period assumption**.

Besides annual statements, companies also prepare reports for shorter periods. For internal use, monthly statements are common. As the reporting period gets shorter, the difficulty of accurately measuring business income increases. This is true because many transactions overlap these short time periods.

Cash Accounting Versus Accrual Accounting

There are two methods of accounting used to decide when a business should record revenues and expenses—the cash basis and the accrual basis. Under the **cash basis**, a business records revenues when it receives the cash. The firm records expenses when it pays out cash. The cash basis is simple to apply, but it usually does not produce good information. For example, using a strict cash basis, a McDonald's restaurant would expense a set of "Golden Arches" in the accounting period the company pays for them. The income statement for that period would be misleading. Income would be low due to the large amount of expense. In following years, the income statement would show no expense from the ongoing benefit of the sign. The balance sheet would understate assets because no asset for the "Golden Arches" appears.

The **accrual basis** states that a business should recognize revenues when it performs a service or sells a product. It then matches with these revenues all expenses incurred to generate the revenues.

Using accrual basis accounting, we would divide the cost of the "Golden Arches," and assign it as an expense over the accounting periods benefitted. Thus, the measurement of income for a single period would be more accurate. The balance sheet would more accurately reflect the financial position. Generally accepted accounting principles (GAAP) require that businesses use the accrual basis.

The Matching Principle and Materiality Concept

Accrual accounting determines business income by *matching* revenues and expenses. The **matching principle** states that income information is better when we assign expenses to the same accounting period that we earn the revenues. Exhibit 3.1 illustrates the relationship of the accounting period assumption and the matching principle.

Most revenue and expense transactions fit neatly into one accounting period. Still, some transactions affect the revenues and expenses of more than one accounting period. To apply accrual accounting and the matching principle, journal entries are necessary at the end of the accounting period to adjust the accounts. The rest of the chapter illustrates the types of adjusting entries necessary to better measure income and report financial position.

The materiality concept permits an exception to adjusting entries. If the amount is small, the **materiality concept** allows us to skip the adjustment. For example, the unused paper clips in a person's desk at year-end are an asset. It is possible, but not practical, to count these and include them in the office supplies adjustment. Because of the item's small cost, failure to include them in the adjustment will have no material effect on the financial statements.

Materiality depends on whether the failure to show the item will affect decisions of an informed statement user. Materiality addresses either the size or the nature of the item. In terms of size, an item costing $100 may be material in a small business. But an item costing $1,000 may be immaterial in a multimillion-dollar business. The accountant along with management must determine whether an item's cost is material.

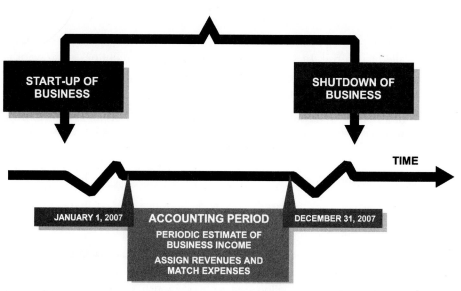

EXHIBIT **3.1**

Business Income: The Accounting Period and the Matching Principle

ADJUSTING ENTRIES

Learning Goal 2   Explain the purpose of adjusting entries.

Matching revenues and expenses requires adjustment of transactions whose effects span more than one accounting period. **Adjusting entries** are journal entries that update the general ledger accounts to state revenues, expenses, assets, liabilities, and owners' equity more accurately.

Adjusting entries always involve at least one income statement account and one balance sheet account. In preparing adjusting entries, the amounts of cash receipts and cash payments for the period do not change. Therefore, we *never adjust the Cash account in an adjusting entry.* For example, assume that on December 1, 2007, we pay rent for the next three months in the amount of $1,500 ($500 per month). In preparing the financial statements for the month ended December 31, 2007, we would want to show $500 as an expense on the income statement for December. Also, we want to show $1,000 as an asset on the balance sheet as of December 31, 2007. We need an adjusting entry on December 31, 2007, to reflect these changes in the accounts. Note that the amount of cash paid out as of December 31, 2007, is correct and does not need adjustment. We paid out cash of $1,500 on December 1, 2007, and we decreased the cash account on that date.

Illustration of Adjusting Entries

To illustrate the adjusting process, we will examine the December transactions for Metro Delivery, Inc. Assume that Metro Delivery started business on December 1, 2007. This corporation picks up and delivers letters and packages for local companies. The unadjusted trial balance taken from Metro Delivery's general ledger appears in Exhibit 3.2 along with other information needed to make the adjusting entries. We call it an unadjusted trial balance because we have not yet journalized and posted adjustments.

In the sections that follow, we will analyze the adjustments using T accounts and journalize them. In Chapter 4, we will prepare the financial statements for Metro Delivery, Inc. using the adjusted balances.

Deferrals

One type of adjustment is called a deferral. In a **deferral**, there is a cash payment or cash receipt in the current period. However, we defer a portion of the expense or revenue until a future accounting period. We make this type of adjustment in two cases:

1. When we pay the cost of a benefit in advance, we usually record the cost as an asset. Then we must allocate these costs as expenses to the periods that receive the benefits.

2. When we receive a cash revenue in advance, we usually record the amount as a liability. Then we must allocate these amounts as revenues to the periods in which we earn the revenues.

Prepaid Expenses

Learning Goal 3   Describe and prepare adjusting entries for prepaid expenses.

A **prepaid expense adjustment** requires the allocation of a previously paid and recorded cost between the current and future periods. Metro Delivery has two assets that fit this category: prepaid insurance and office supplies. The adjusting entry allocates a portion of the recorded asset

METRO DELIVERY, INC.
UNADJUSTED TRIAL BALANCE
DECEMBER 31, 2007

Acct. No.	Account Title	Debits	Credits
101	Cash	$ 6,500	
111	Accounts Receivable	2,100	
115	Notes Receivable	1,200	
135	Office Supplies	300	
141	Prepaid Insurance	600	
169	Trucks	26,000	
201	Accounts Payable		$ 1,000
231	Unearned Rent		600
331	Common Stock		32,000
372	Dividends	500	
420	Trucking Revenue		7,500
705	Wages Expense	1,600	
711	Rent Expense—Building	1,400	
721	Heat and Light Expense	200	
726	Gas and Oil Expense	700	
	Totals	$ 41,100	$ 41,100

Other information required for adjustments:
a. Insurance premium of $600 for a comprehensive one-year policy was paid in cash on December 1, 2007.
b. During December, $300 of office supplies were purchased for cash. As of December 31, 2007, a physical count revealed that $100 in office supplies remained on hand.
c. Two trucks costing $13,000 each were purchased on December 1, 2007. Each truck has an estimated life of five years and an estimated residual value of $1,000 ($2,000 in total) at the end of that period. The trucks are to be depreciated over the five-year period by the straight-line method.
d. Metro Delivery signed an agreement on December 1, 2007, to rent a truck on weekends to Tom's Floral Shop. Metro Delivery collected rent of $600 in advance for six months starting December 1, 2007.
e. Metro Delivery received a $1,200 note receivable on December 11; 2007. The note has a stated interest rate of 15% and is due in 30 days on January 10, 2007.
f. Wages of $80 for Monday, December 31, 2007, have not been paid or recorded.
g. Estimated income taxes accrued are $900.

EXHIBIT **3.2**

Unadjusted Trial Balance and Supplementary Information for Metro Delivery, Inc.

---

cost to an expense of the current accounting period. This will then show the proper asset balance remaining for future accounting periods.

Each prepaid expense adjustment involves one asset account and one expense account. We follow three steps in preparing adjusting entries (we use the same three steps in analyzing *all* of the adjustments):

1. Identify the accounts requiring adjustment and determine their unadjusted balances.

2. Determine the correct (adjusted) balance in each account requiring adjustment.

3. Prepare the adjusting entry to bring the accounts into agreement with the balances computed in step 2. Enter the words "Adjusting Entries" above the first adjustment in the journal.

Adjustment of Prepaid Insurance

Metro Delivery paid a premium of $600 for a one-year insurance policy effective December 1, 2007. At December 31, Metro needs an adjustment to divide the insurance cost between the current period and the next period.

Step 1.   On December 1, 2007, the company purchased a one-year insurance policy, paying $600 in cash. Looking at the December 31, 2007, unadjusted trial balance, we see that the Prepaid Insurance account still has a balance of $600. Also, since Insurance Expense does not appear, it must have a zero balance. From this, we can assume that Metro debited Prepaid Insurance and credited Cash to record the transaction on December 1, 2007. Since one month has passed, some insurance cost has expired. Metro has incurred insurance expense and has less prepaid insurance. Thus, the two accounts requiring adjustment are Insurance Expense and Prepaid Insurance. We can use T accounts to help visualize the effect of the adjustment. At this point the T accounts would appear as follows:

(Asset Account)		**(Expense Account)**	
Prepaid Insurance		**Insurance Expense**	
Balance	600	Balance	0

Step 2.   The next step is to calculate the correct balance for each account. We calculate the monthly insurance expense by dividing the total cost, $600, by 12 months. Thus, the monthly expense is $50 ($600 ÷ 12). Since Metro has used one month of insurance coverage, the Insurance Expense account balance should be $50. Eleven months' coverage remains as of December 31, 2007. The balance in Prepaid Insurance should be $550 ($50 × 11). Exhibit 3.3 depicts the allocation of total cost to the two accounting periods.

Step 3.   We can add this information to the T accounts to help visualize the adjusting entry needed. (Throughout the chapter, these adjusting entries are printed in bold in the T accounts.)

(Asset Account)			**(Expense Account)**		
Prepaid Insurance			**Insurance Expense**		
Balance	600		Balance	0	
	12/31	**50**	**12/31**	**50**	
Balance	550		Balance	50	

   The asset account Prepaid Insurance must decrease by $50 from its unadjusted balance of $600 down to $550. We record decreases in assets with credits. Insurance Expense must increase by $50 from its unadjusted balance of $0 up to $50. We record increases in expenses with debits. Thus, the adjusting entry to update the accounts is a debit to the Insurance Expense account and a credit to the Prepaid Insurance account for $50. We would journalize the following adjusting entry and post it to the general ledger:

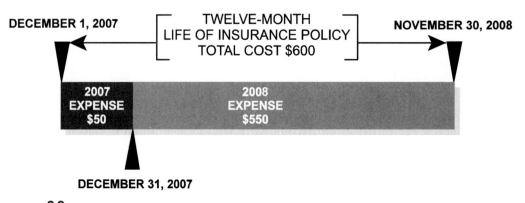

EXHIBIT 3.3

Allocation of Insurance Cost

| GENERAL JOURNAL | | | | Page 4 | |
Date		Accounts and Explanations	PR	Debit	Credit
2007					
Dec.	31	Insurance Expense	719	50	
		Prepaid Insurance	141		50
		To record insurance expense for December.			

After we post the adjusting entry, the ledger accounts and financial statements will show the up-to-date balances calculated in step 2. If we made no adjusting entry, the income statement would show no insurance expense. The income statement then would overstate net income by $50. The balance sheet would report prepaid insurance as $600. This would overstate assets by $50. Since we add net income to owners' equity, the balance sheet also will report $50 more owners' equity than is correct. This example shows that adjusting entries are necessary to improve the accuracy of *both* the income statement and balance sheet.

Adjustment of Office Supplies

In the trial balance in Exhibit 3.2, the Office Supplies account has a debit balance of $300 as of December 31, 2007. This amount represents the amount of office supplies available for use during December. The adjusting information in Exhibit 3.2 states that $100 of office supplies were on hand on December 31, 2007.

Step 1.   On December 31, 2007, the Office Supplies account (an asset) has an unadjusted debit balance of $300. Since the Office Supplies Expense account (an expense) is not in the trial balance, it must have a balance of $0.

Step 2.   The amount of office supplies expense for December should be $200 ($300 - $100). Metro Delivery had $300 of office supplies available for use during December. At the end of December, Metro had only $100 of supplies left unused. We then assume that the difference of $200 represents the office supplies used during December. Thus, the balance in Office Supplies Expense should be $200. The balance in the asset account Office Supplies should be $100. This is the amount of supplies on hand on December 31, 2007.

Step 3.   The following T accounts summarize the thought process in determining the adjustment.

(Asset Account)				(Expense Account)		
Office Supplies				**Office Supplies Expense**		
Balance	300			Balance	0	
		12/31	200	12/31	200	
Balance	100			Balance	200	

The adjusting entry requires a debit to Office Supplies Expense and a credit to Office Supplies for $200 as follows:

| GENERAL JOURNAL | | | | Page 4 | |
Date		Accounts and Explanations	PR	Debit	Credit
2007					
Dec.	31	Office Supplies Expense	718	200	
		Office Supplies	135		200
		To record supplies used during December.			

The adjusting entry for office supplies accomplishes two objectives: (1) It recognizes the physical use of $200 of office supplies as an expense for the month of December, and (2) it shows $100 as the correct amount of office supplies remaining as an asset as of December 31, 2007.

If we made no adjusting entry, December's income statement would show no office supplies expense. The income statement would understate expenses by $200 and overstate net income by $200. The balance sheet would show the asset office supplies at $300. This would overstate total assets by $200. Owners' equity would also be overstated by $200 due to the overstatement of net income.

Depreciation Expense

Learning Goal 4   Define *depreciation expense* and prepare entries to record it.

The previous examples illustrate how the costs of short-term assets are allocated to the periods in which they are consumed. Similarly, we must allocate the costs of assets with a life greater than one year over the periods of use. This is a **depreciation adjustment**. The periodic expired cost of such long-term assets as equipment, trucks, and buildings is depreciation expense. We record it in an adjusting entry.

> The portion of the cost of a property, plant, and equipment asset assigned to the accounting period is called **depreciation expense**.

Metro Delivery requires one adjustment to record the depreciation expense on its two trucks. It purchased the trucks on December 1, 2007, for $13,000 each. The estimated useful life of each truck is five years, or 60 months. Management estimates each truck will have a residual value of $1,000 at the end of its useful life. **Residual value** (or *salvage* value) is the estimated price for which an asset may be sold when it is no longer serviceable to the business. The use of each truck for five years has a net cost to the company of $12,000 ($13,000 - $1,000). We spread this net cost over the five years of use as depreciation expense.

Step 1.   On December 31, 2007, the Trucks account (an asset) has a balance of $26,000, which represents the cost of the two trucks. The company has used the trucks for one month. Thus, we should recognize part of their cost as an expense of December. We will use two new accounts to record depreciation on the trucks. We debit the depreciation expense for the period to Depreciation Expense—Trucks. We credit an account called Accumulated Depreciation—Trucks.

The **Accumulated Depreciation** account is a new account. It accumulates the total depreciation expense taken on long-lived assets. Instead of using it, we could directly credit the Trucks account. However, by crediting the Accumulated Depreciation account instead, the Trucks account continues to show the original cost. We call the Accumulated Depreciation account a **contra account**. It gets its name because its balance is opposite that of the related account. We deduct it from the Trucks account in the balance sheet to show the undepreciated cost of the asset.

On December 31, 2007, the Depreciation Expense—Trucks account (an expense) has an unadjusted balance of $0 and the Accumulated Depreciation—Trucks account (a contra asset account) has an unadjusted balance of $0. Both accounts have no balance because Metro has never recorded depreciation on the trucks.

Step 2.   Several methods are available to calculate the periodic depreciation expense. In this chapter, we will compute depreciation using the **straight-line method** of depreciation. Straight-line depreciation assigns a uniform portion of the cost as an expense to each period. The formula is as follows:

$$\frac{\text{Cost} - \text{Residual Value}}{\text{Estimated Months of Useful Life}} = \text{Depreciation per Month}$$

The depreciation expense for December for each of the two trucks is as follows:

$$\frac{\text{Cost of } \$13,000 - \text{Residual value of } \$1,000}{60 \text{ months}} = \$200 \text{ depreciation per month for each truck}$$

The amount of the depreciation expense for the two trucks for December should be $400. Since this is the first accounting period that the trucks are depreciated, the balance in Accumulated Depreciation—Trucks should also be $400.

Step 3.   The following T accounts summarize the adjustment process for this situation.

(Expense Account) **Depreciation Expense—Trucks**		**(Contra Asset Account)** **Accumulated Depreciation— Trucks**	
Balance	0	Balance	0
12/31	**400**	**12/31**	**400**
Balance	400	Balance	400

The following adjusting entry is recordéd in the general journal and posted to the general ledger:

GENERAL JOURNAL					Page 4
Date		Accounts and Explanations	PR	Debit	Credit
2007					
Dec.	31	Depreciation Expense—Trucks	759	400	
		Accumulated Depreciation—Trucks	170		400
		To record depreciation for December.			

The adjusting entry for depreciation accomplishes two objectives: (1) It assigns $400 as depreciation expense in the income statement for December, and (2) it shows $400 as the balance in accumulated depreciation on the balance sheet as of December 31, 2007.

We record depreciation for each month of the trucks' useful life in the Accumulated Depreciation—Trucks account. The balance reflects the total depreciation to date. The cost of the trucks and the accumulated depreciation are shown on the balance sheet on December 31, 2007, as follows:

Property, plant, and equipment
Trucks	$26,000	
Deduct: Accumulated depreciation–trucks	400	$25,600

We refer to the difference between the cost of the trucks and the balance in accumulated depreciation ($25,600) as the *book value* of the trucks. This amount represents the undepreciated cost of the long-lived asset.

After adjustment the next month on January 31, 2008, the ledger accounts for the asset Trucks and the contra asset Accumulated Depreciation—Trucks would look as follows:

(Asset Account)
Trucks   Acct. No. 169

Date		Explanation	PR	Debit	Credit	Balance Debit	Balance Credit
2007							
Dec.	1		J1	26,000		26,000	

(Contra Asset Account)
Accumulated Depreciation—Trucks   Acct. No. 170

Date		Explanation	PR	Debit	Credit	Balance Debit	Balance Credit
2007							
Dec.	31	Adjusting	J4		400		400
2008							
Jan.	31	Adjusting	J8		400		800

The balance sheet on January 31, 2008, would show the cost of the trucks and the accumulated depreciation as follows:

Property, plant, and equipment

Trucks	$26,000	
Deduct: Accumulated depreciation–trucks	800	$25,200

Unearned Revenues

Learning Goal 5   Describe and prepare adjusting entries for unearned revenues.

Many businesses have transactions in which they receive cash before they earn the revenue. For example, an airline receives the cash for tickets in advance of a flight. Initially, the business usually records these **unearned revenues** in liability accounts. The company is obligated to perform a service or provide a product before it can recognize the revenue as earned. At the end of the accounting period, we must adjust these liability accounts. The adjustment transfers any revenue earned from the liability to the revenue account. Such **unearned revenue adjustments** allocate the previously recorded revenue between current and future accounting periods.

ADJUSTMENT OF UNEARNED RENT On December 1, 2007, Metro Delivery signed an agreement to rent a truck on weekends to Tom's Floral Shop. Metro Delivery collected rent of $600 in advance for six months starting December 1, 2007. To account for the receipt of $600 on December 1, 2007, Metro debited Cash and credited a liability account, Unearned Rent, for $600.

Step 1.   On December 31, 2007, the Unearned Rent account (a liability) has an unadjusted credit balance of $600. Since the Rent Revenue account does not appear in the trial balance, we assume it has an unadjusted balance of $0.

Step 2.   The amount of revenue earned for December should be $100 ($600/6 months). Since five months' rent remain unearned, the balance in the liability account Unearned Rent should be $500 ($100 × 5 months).

Step 3.   The following T accounts summarize the adjustment process:

(Liability Account) **Unearned Rent**		**(Revenue Account)** **Rent Revenue**	
	Balance 600		Balance 0
12/31 100			12/31 100
	Balance 500		Balance 100

The following entry records the adjustment in the general journal:

GENERAL JOURNAL					Page 4
Date		Accounts and Explanations	PR	Debit	Credit
2007 Dec.	31	Unearned Rent	231	100	
		Rent Revenue	430		100
		To record rent earned during December.			

The adjusting entry for rent earned accomplishes two objectives: (1) It assigns $100 as the proper amount of rent revenue in the income statement for December, and, (2) it shows $500 as the correct amount of the unearned rent remaining as a liability on the balance sheet as of December 31, 2007.

After we post the adjusting entry, the ledger accounts and the financial statements will show the correct balances calculated in step 2 above. If we made no adjusting entry, December's income statement would show no rent revenue. As a result, it would understate revenues by $100 and understate net income by $100. On the balance sheet, the liability account Unearned Rent would have a balance of $600. This would overstate total liabilities by $100. Since net income is ultimately transferred to owners' equity, this amount is also understated by $100.

Accruals

Another group of adjustments are **accruals**. They recognize revenues and expenses that have accumulated or *accrued* during the accounting period. At the end of the period, we must record these accruals, which have accumulated but *have not been recorded*. Metro Delivery has one accrued revenue and two accrued expenses. These require adjustment as of December 31, 2007.

Accrued Revenues
Learning Goal 6   Describe and prepare adjusting entries to record accrued revenues.

Accrued revenues are revenues earned in the current period, but not yet collected in cash or recorded in the accounts. To adjust for accrued revenues, we increase both a revenue account and an asset account. The accrued revenue adjustment for Metro Delivery is for interest revenue earned but unrecorded as of December 31, 2007.

ADJUSTMENT FOR ACCRUED INTEREST REVENUE On December 11, 2007, Metro Delivery made a $1,200 loan to a customer. The customer signed a 30-day, 15%, interest-bearing note. To record the note on December 11, Metro debited the asset account Notes Receivable and credited Cash for $1,200. During December, interest revenue has accrued on the note receivable, but Metro has not recorded it. We must record this interest earned so that it appears as a revenue on the income statement and an asset on the balance sheet.

Step 1.   On December 31, 2007, the Interest Revenue account and the Interest Receivable account (an asset) both have unadjusted balances of $0. Both accounts have a $0 balance because Metro has recorded no interest earned on the note receivable. Interest earned on the note receivable accumulates with the passage of time. Metro will receive the interest on the maturity date, January 10, 2008. To record the interest accrued during December, we must enter it in the Interest Revenue account. We also must set up an asset account called Interest Receivable. This account will show the interest earned during the 20 days in December 2007, but not yet received.

Step 2.   To calculate the interest on the note receivable, we will use the following simple interest formula:

$$\text{Interest} = \text{Principal} \times \text{Interest Rate} \times \frac{\text{Elapsed Time in Days}}{360}$$

We can compute the elapsed time in days for December 2007 as follows:

Number of days in December	31
Deduct: Date of note	11
Elapsed days in December	20

The unrecorded interest accrued through December 31, 2007, is as follows:

$$\text{Interest} = \$1{,}200 \times 0.15 \times \frac{20}{360}$$
$$= \$10$$

The interest rate given is always an annual rate. Whenever we multiply the principal by the interest rate, we get the interest for one year. In this case it is $180 ($1,200 × 0.15). We must then multiply the interest for one year by the elapsed fraction of a year (20/360) to determine the interest for 20 days. We use a 360-day year in the text to simplify the calculation. Thus, Interest Receivable and Interest Revenue should be $10.

Step 3.   The following T accounts summarize the adjustment process for unrecorded interest revenue.

(Revenue Account) Interest Revenue			(Asset Account) Interest Receivable		
	Balance	0		Balance	0
	12/31	10		12/31	10
	Balance	10		Balance	10

We record the adjusting entry in the general journal as follows:

		GENERAL JOURNAL			Page 4
Date		Accounts and Explanations	PR	Debit	Credit
2007 Dec.	31	Interest Receivable	117	10	
		Interest Revenue	431		10
		To record interest revenue accrued during December 12-31, 2007.			

After we have posted the adjusting entry, the ledger accounts and the financial statements will show the correct balances calculated in step 2 above. If Metro made no adjusting entry, the income statement would show no interest revenue for December. Revenues would be understated by $10 and net income understated by $10. The balance sheet would understate the asset account Interest Receivable by $10. Since net income is ultimately transferred to owners' equity, this amount is also understated by $10.

The adjusting entry for interest revenue accomplishes two objectives: (1) It recognizes $10 as the proper amount of interest revenue on the income statement for December, and (2) it shows $10 as the correct amount of the asset interest receivable on the balance sheet as of December 31, 2007.

Accrued Expenses

Learning Goal 7   Describe and prepare adjusting entries to record accrued expenses.

At the end of an accounting period, a company may have incurred or accumulated expenses that have not been paid in cash or recorded. These unpaid and unrecorded expenses are called **accrued expenses**. We must make adjusting entries to record them by debiting an expense account and by crediting a liability account to reflect the expense and the obligation. Examples of accrued expenses include salaries earned by employees and income taxes accrued.

ADJUSTMENT FOR ACCRUED WAGES EXPENSE Metro Delivery pays its employees each Friday for the current week. It normally records this expense at that time by a debit to Wages Expense and a credit to Cash. If December 2007 ended on a Monday, Metro would have incurred one day's wages that were unrecorded and unpaid. To properly recognize all wages expense and show the correct liabilities, Metro must make an adjusting entry for accrued wages.

Step 1.   Assume that on December 31, 2007, the Wages Expense account has an unadjusted balance of $1,600. This represents the amount of wages expensed and paid during December 2007. The Wages Payable account (a liability) has an unadjusted balance of $0. It is an **accrued liability** (a liability for an expense incurred in the current accounting period but not payable until a future period).

Step 2.   If the weekly wages are $400, we will assume that the daily wages are $80 ($400 ÷ 5). The balance of Wages Expense for December should be $1,680. This is the $1,600 incurred and paid during the first four weeks plus the $80 for Monday, December 31. The balance of the liability account Wages Payable should be $80. This is the amount owed as of December 31, 2007.

Step 3.   The following T accounts summarize the adjusting process for unrecorded wages expense.

(Expense Account)			(Liability Account)	
Wages Expense			**Wages Payable**	
Balance	0		Balance	0
12/07	400		**12/31**	**80**
12/14	400		Balance	80
12/21	400			
12/28	400			
12/31	**80**			
Balance	1,680			

The entry to record the adjustment in the general journal is as follows:

		GENERAL JOURNAL			Page 4
Date		**Accounts and Explanations**	**PR**	**Debit**	**Credit**
2007					
Dec.	31	Wages Expense	705	80	
		Wages Payable	205		80
		To record wages expense accrued for December 31, 2007.			

After we have posted the adjusting entry, the ledger accounts and the financial statements will show the correct balances calculated in step 2 above. If we made no adjusting entry, wages expense for December would be the unadjusted balance of $1,600. As a result, we would understate expenses by $80 and overstate net income by $80. The balance sheet would show the liability account Wages Payable understated by $80. Therefore, total liabilities would be understated by $80. Since net income is ultimately transferred to owners' equity, this amount is overstated by $80.

The adjusting entry for wages accomplishes two objectives: (1) It recognizes $1,680 as the proper amount of wages expense in the income statement for the month of December, and (2) it shows $80 as the correct amount of the liability, Wages Payable, on the balance sheet as of December 31, 2007.

ADJUSTMENT FOR ACCRUED INCOME TAXES As a corporation, Metro Delivery is also liable for income taxes. The adjustment for income taxes is another example of an accrued expense adjustment. It is an accrual since it is an incurred but unrecorded expense. The corporation is liable for income taxes on income earned in a period. To achieve proper matching of revenues and expenses, we must accrue the expense in the same period that the income is reported. We again use the three steps for analyzing an adjustment.

Step 1.   The accounts used are Income Tax Expense and Income Taxes Payable. Both have unadjusted balances of zero.

Step 2.   Metro Delivery, Inc. estimates its income taxes for the period to be $900. It must record this amount in both the expense and liability accounts.

Step 3.   The following T accounts summarize the adjustment process for unrecorded income tax expense.

(Expense Account) Income Tax Expense		(Liability Account) Income Taxes Payable	
Balance 0		Balance 0	
12/31 900		**12/31 900**	
Balance 900		Balance 900	

We record the adjusting entry in the general journal as follows:

GENERAL JOURNAL				Page 4	
Date		Accounts and Explanations	PR	Debit	Credit
2007 Dec.	31	Income Tax Expense	901	900	
		Income Taxes Payable	215		900
		To record estimated income taxes accrued.			

The income tax expense of $900 appears in the income statement. We deduct it from income before income taxes to determine net income. Income taxes payable of $900 appears in the balance sheet as a current liability.

Summary of Adjusting Entries

We classify adjustments into two broad groups: deferrals and accruals. Exhibit 3.4 reviews the three types of deferrals and two types of accruals. In this chapter, we studied the analysis process for working out the adjusting entries. Exhibit 3.5 shows this adjusting process as a flowchart. We first ask if the adjustment is a deferral or an accrual. Based on the answer to that question, we ask another question, make a calculation, and make the entry.

	Kind of Adjustment	Brief Description	Adjusting Entry
Deferrals (Cash payment or receipt precedes expense or revenue recognition)	Prepaid Expense *Assumption:* The original debit is made to an asset account.	A prepaid item that benefits two or more periods; it is necessary to allocate expense to appropriate periods.	Dr. _____ Expense (E) Cr. Prepaid _____ (A)
	Depreciation.	The systematic allocation of the historical cost of long-lived asset to the periods benefitted.	For a depreciable property, plant, and equipment item: Dr. Depreciation Expense (E) Cr. Accumulated Depreciation (Contra A)
	Unearned revenue *Assumption:* The original credit is made to a liability account.	A revenue item that is collected in advance of the period(s) earned; it is necessary to allocate the revenue to the appropriate period in which it is earned.	Dr. Unearned _____ (L) Cr. _____ Revenue (R)
Accruals (Expense or revenue recognition precedes cash payment or receipt)	Accrued revenue.	Revenue earned in a given period but not yet collected or recorded.	Dr. _____ Receivable (A) Cr. _____ Revenue (R)
	Accrued expense.	Expense incurred in a given period but not yet paid or recorded.	Dr. _____ Expense (E) Cr. _____ Payable (L)

Codes used: A, asset; R, revenue; E, expense; L, liability; Contra A, contra asset account.

EXHIBIT **3.4**

Summary of Deferrals and Accruals

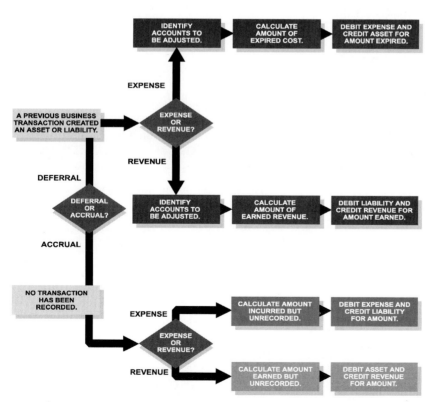

EXHIBIT **3.5**

Summary of Adjusting Entries

ANALYZING INFORMATION

Learning Goal 8   Analyze financial statement information for real-life companies.

In Chapter 3, we expand our analysis to include more integrative income statement and balance sheet questions. We compare Pfizer and Johnson & Johnson.

Income Statement Analysis

Exhibit 3.6 shows comparative income statements for 2004 and 2003 for Pfizer and Johnson & Johnson. For each year, we show the dollar amount and the common-size percent.

Question 1. For 2004, which company has higher total revenues? Are total revenues for each company higher or lower over the two year period?

Analysis 1. Pfizer's revenues ($52,516,000,000) are higher than Johnson & Johnson's ($47,348,000,000). For both companies, revenues have increased from 2003 to 2004.

Question 2. What is the percent change in total revenues from 2003 to 2004 for each company?

Analysis 2. The percent change in total revenues is:

$$\textbf{Pfizer} \qquad 16.2\% = 100 \times \frac{\$7,328,000,000^*}{\$45,188,000,000} \qquad {}^* \$52,516,000,000 - \$45,188,000,000$$

$$\textbf{Johnson \&} \atop \textbf{Johnson} \qquad 13.1\% = 100 \times \frac{\$5,486,000,000^*}{\$41,862,000,000} \qquad {}^* \$47,348,000,000 - \$41,862,000,000$$

In terms of total revenues, Pfizer is slightly larger and is growing slightly faster that Johnson & Johnson.

Question 3. Is the percent of total expenses to total revenues for each company increasing or decreasing over the two year period?

Analysis 3. Pfizer was able to reduce total expenses from 91.3% of total revenues in 2003 to 78.4% in 2004. This is *favorable*. Johnson & Johnson's expense percent decreased slightly from 82.8% of revenues in 2003 to 82.0% in 2004. Net income as a percent of total revenues is called **profit margin**. For 2004, Pfizer's profit margin of 21.6% is higher than Johnson & Johnson's of 18.0%.

Balance Sheet Analysis

Exhibit 3.7 shows comparative balance sheets as of December 31, 2004, and 2003. For each year, we show the dollar amount and the common-size percent.

PFIZER AND JOHNSON & JOHNSON
COMPARATIVE COMMON-SIZE INCOME STATEMENTS
For the Years Ended December 31, 2004, 2003
(in millions)

	Pfizer				Johnson & Johnson			
	2004	2004	2003	2003	2004	2004	2003	2003
	$	%	$	%	$	%	$	%
Total revenues	$ 52,516.0	100.0%	$ 45,188.0	100.0%	$ 47,348.0	100.0%	$ 41,862.0	100.0%
Total expenses	$ 41,155.0	78.4%	$ 41,278.0	91.3%	$ 38,839.0	82.0%	$ 34,665.0	82.8%
Net income (loss)	$ 11,361.0	21.6%	$ 3,910.0	8.7%	$ 8,509.0	18.0%	$ 7,197.0	17.2%

EXHIBIT 3.6

Comparative Common-Size Income Statements for Pfizer and Johnson & Johnson 2004-2003

PFIZER AND JOHNSON & JOHNSON
COMPARATIVE COMMON-SIZE BALANCE SHEETS
December 31, 2004, 2003
(in millions)

	Pfizer				Johnson & Johnson			
	2004	2004	2003	2003	2004	2004	2003	2003
	$	%	$	%	$	%	$	%
Total assets	$ 123,684.0	100.0%	$ 116,775.0	100.0%	$ 53,317.0	100.0%	$ 48,263.0	100.0%
Total liabilities	$ 55,406.0	44.8%	$ 51,398.0	44.0%	$ 21,504.0	40.3%	$ 21,394.0	44.3%
Total owners' equity	$ 68,278.0	55.2%	$ 65,377.0	56.0%	$ 31,813.0	59.7%	$ 26,869.0	55.7%
Total liabilities and owners' equity	$ 123,684.0	100.0%	$ 116,775.0	100.0%	$ 53,317.0	100.0%	$ 48,263.0	100.0%

EXHIBIT **3.7**

Comparative Common-Size Balance Sheets for Pfizer and Johnson & Johnson 2004-2003.

Question 1. For 2004, which company has higher assets? Are total assets for each company higher or lower over the two year period?

Analysis 1. Pfizer's assets ($123,684,000,000) are higher than Johnson & Johnson's ($53,317,000,000). Total assets for both companies have increased from 2003 to 2004.

Question 2. What is the percent change in total assets from 2003 to 2004 for each company?

Analysis 2. The percent increase in total assets from 2003 to 2004 for each company is:

Pfizer $5.9\% = 100 \times \dfrac{\$6,909,000,000^*}{\$116,775,000,000}$ $^* \$123,684,000,000 - \$116,775,000,000$

Johnson & Johnson $10.5\% = 100 \times \dfrac{\$5,054,000,000}{\$48,263,000,000}$ $^* \$53,317,000,000 - \$48,263,000,000$

Question 3. Is the percent of total liabilities to total liabilities + owners' equity increasing or decreasing? As a result, is there more risk that each company could not pay its debts?

Analysis 3. In Exhibit 3.7, refer to the common-size percent for liabilities each year. The percent of liabilities for Pfizer in 2004 (44.8%) is higher than for Johnson & Johnson (40.3%). Overall, Pfizer is relying more on debt as a source of financing than Johnson & Johnson. Thus, Pfizer has more risk.

Integrative Income Statement and Balance Sheet Analysis

In this section we will add a new measure to look at the relationship between profitability on the income statement and asset investment on the balance sheet.

Question 1. Are the companies operating efficiently by using the least amount of asset investment to generate a given level of total revenues?

Analysis 1. We can answer this question by dividing total revenues by average total assets for each year. The computations for both companies in 2004 are:

$$\textbf{Pfizer} \qquad\qquad \textbf{Johnson \& Johnson}$$

$$\frac{\$52,516,000,000}{\$120,229,500,000^*} = 0.44 \text{ times} \qquad \frac{\$47,348,000,000}{\$50,790,000,000^{**}} = .093 \text{ times}$$

$$^* \quad (\$123,684,000,000 + \$116,775,000,000) \div 2$$
$$^{**} \quad (\$53,317,000,000 + \$48,263,000,000) \div 2$$

The resulting number is a ratio called *total asset turnover*. A higher number for the total asset turnover ratio is more favorable. Some companies will have a higher or lower asset turnover due to the nature of the industry. Both Pfizer and Johnson & Johnson have large investments in assets such as plant and equipment. As a result, Johnson & Johnson has a relatively low asset turnover ratio of 0.93 times. Pfizer's is lower at 0.44 times.

Question 2. Are the companies operating efficiently by using the least amount of asset investment to generate a given level of *net income*?

Analysis 2. We can answer this question by dividing net income by total average assets for each year. The resulting ratio is called **return on assets (ROA)**. Return on assets provides a basic measure for evaluating profitability by relating net income to the total assets employed in a company. The computations for both companies in 2004 are:

<table>
<tr><th>Pfizer</th><th>Johnson & Johnson</th></tr>
<tr><td>$\dfrac{\$11,361,000,000}{\$120,229,500,000\,*} \times 100 = 9.5\%$</td><td>$\dfrac{\$8,509,000,000}{\$50,790,000,000\,**} \times 100 = 16.8\%$</td></tr>
</table>

$$* \quad (\$123,684,000,000 + \$116,775,000,000) \div 2$$
$$** \quad (\$53,317,000,000 + \$48,263,000,000) \div 2$$

A higher number for the return on assets percent is more favorable. In this case, Johnson & Johnson's ROA of 16.8% is more favorable than Pfizer's ROA of 9.5%.

APPENDIX 3A
DEFERRALS ORIGINALLY RECORDED TO INCOME STATEMENT ACCOUNTS

Learning Goals After Studying Appendix 3A, you should be able to:

A1. Prepare an adjusting entry for a deferral when the original transaction is recorded in an income statement account.

UNDERSTANDING BUSINESS ISSUES

Accountants may initially record a prepaid expense or unearned revenue in a balance sheet (permanent) account or in an income statement (temporary) account. The examples in Chapter 3 assumed that we recorded the original transaction in a permanent account. Now we will study the adjustment process if we recorded the original transaction in a temporary account. We can still use the same three steps to aid in the analysis of the adjustment.

Learning Goal A1 Prepare an adjusting entry for a deferral when the original transaction is recorded in an income statement account.

Alternative Treatment of Prepaid Insurance

On December 1, 2007, Metro Delivery paid $600 for a one-year insurance policy. Instead of recording the transaction with a debit to Prepaid Insurance, it would be equally correct to debit Insurance Expense. Recording the original debit to either account is correct. With the proper adjustment, the financial statements will show the same result in either case. The adjustment is different from that studied in the chapter because the $600 is now in an expense account.

Step 1. Assume that Metro debited Insurance Expense for $600 on December 1, 2007. The Prepaid Insurance account (an asset) will have an unadjusted balance of $0 on December 31, 2007. The Insurance Expense account (an expense) will have an unadjusted debit balance of $600.

Step 2. It is important to see that the correct insurance expense for the month and the correct prepaid insurance at the end of the month do not change. The amount of insurance expense for December still should be $50 ($600 ÷ 12 months). The balance in the asset account Prepaid Insurance still should be $550 ($50 × 11 months).

Step 3. The following T accounts summarize the determination of the adjustment for this situation. (Throughout, the adjusting entry appears in bold in the T accounts.)

(Asset Account) Prepaid Insurance				(Expense Account) Insurance Expense		
Balance	0			Balance	600	
12/31	**550**				**12/31**	**550**
Balance	550			Balance	50	

The adjusting entry to update the accounts requires a debit to Prepaid Insurance and a credit to Insurance Expense for $550. We record the following adjusting entry in the general journal:

GENERAL JOURNAL					Page 4
Date		Accounts Titles and Explanations	PR	Debit	Credit
2007 Dec.	31	Prepaid Insurance	141	550	
		Insurance Expense	719		550
		To record the unexpired insurance premium.			

After posting the adjusting entry, the ledger accounts and the financial statements will show the correct balances calculated in step 2 above. If we made no adjusting entry, insurance expense for the month of December would be $600. As a result, the income statement would overstate expenses by $550 and understate net income by $550. On the balance sheet, the asset prepaid insurance would have a balance of $0 and cause total assets to be understated by $550. Since net income is transferred to owners' equity, owners' equity is understated by $550.

The alternative adjusting entry for insurance accomplishes two objectives: (1) It shows $50 as the proper amount of insurance expense in the income statement for December, and (2) shows $550 as the correct amount of the prepaid insurance remaining as an asset on the balance sheet as of December 31, 2007. Although the adjusting entry is different, the ending balances are the same as before.

Alternative Treatment of Unearned Rent

On December 1, 2007, Metro Delivery signed an agreement to rent a truck on weekends to Tom's Floral Shop. Metro Delivery collected rent of $600 in advance for six months starting December 1, 2007. To account for the receipt of $600 on December 1, 2007, assume Metro debited Cash and— *instead* of crediting Unearned Revenue—credited the revenue account Rent Revenue.

Step 1. On December 31, 2007, the Rent Revenue account has an unadjusted credit balance of $600 and the Unearned Revenue account (a liability) has an unadjusted balance of $0.

Step 2. Once again, the desired ending account balances are the same as before. The amount of rent earned for December should be $100 ($600 ÷ 6 months). The remaining balance in the liability account Unearned Rent should be $500 ($100 × 5 months).

Step 3.   The following T accounts summarize the adjustment process:

(Liability Account) Unearned Rent		
Balance	0	
12/31	500	
Balance	500	

(Revenue Account) Rent Revenue		
	Balance	600
12/31	500	
	Balance	100

The following adjusting entry records the adjustment:

	GENERAL JOURNAL			Page 4

Date	Accounts Titles and Explanations	PR	Debit	Credit
2007 Dec. 31	Rent Revenue	430	500	
	Unearned Rent	231		500
	To record remaining portion of unearned rent on truck.			

After we have posted the adjusting entry, the ledger accounts and the financial statements will show the correct balances calculated in step 2 above. If we made no adjusting entry, rent revenue for the month of December would be the entire $600. As a result, the income statement would overstate revenues by $500 and overstate net income by $500. On the balance sheet, the liability Unearned Rent would have a balance of $0. This would understate total liabilities by $500. Since net income is ultimately transferred to owners' equity, this amount would also be overstated.

The alternative adjusting entry for rent revenue accomplishes two objectives: (1) It records $100 as the proper amount of rent revenue in the income statement for the month of December, and (2) it shows $500 as the correct amount of the unearned rent as a liability on the balance sheet as of December 31, 2007.

LEARNING GOALS REVIEW

1. **Explain (a) the accounting period assumption, (b) cash versus accrual accounting, (c) the matching principle, and (d) the materiality concept.**
   The accounting period assumption states that users of financial information require periodic reports. Thus, we divide the life of a business into 12-month reporting periods. Cash-basis accounting recognizes revenues and expenses when the cash is exchanged. Under accrual-basis accounting, we recognize revenues and expenses when benefits are exchanged. The matching principle matches revenues earned during a period against the expenses incurred to generate the revenues. The materiality concept allows accountants to ignore adjustments for insignificant or trivial items. If failure to disclose an item would be misleading to a user of information, that item is material.

2. **Explain the purpose of adjusting entries.**
   Adjusting entries update the ledger accounts to include revenues that have been earned and expenses that have been incurred. They also state assets, liabilities, and owners' equity at their proper amounts.

3. **Describe and prepare adjusting entries for prepaid expenses.**
   At the end of the accounting period, portions of certain assets have either expired or been physically used up. A prepaid expense adjustment transfers the amount consumed from an asset account to an expense account.

4. **Define *depreciation expense* and prepare entries to record it.**
   Depreciation expense is the portion of the cost of a property, plant, and equipment asset

assigned to the accounting period. To compute the expense using the straight-line method, divide the cost minus residual value by the useful life. Debit this amount to the appropriate expense account, and credit the contra asset Accumulated Depreciation.

5. **Describe and prepare adjusting entries for unearned revenues.**
   Unearned revenues are usually recorded in liability accounts when received. Unearned revenue adjustments allocate the previously recorded revenue to current and future accounting periods.

6. **Describe and prepare adjusting entries to record accrued revenues.**
   Accrued revenue adjustments recognize revenues that have accumulated or accrued during the accounting period. To adjust for accrued revenues, record increases in revenue and asset accounts.

7. **Describe and prepare adjusting entries to record accrued expenses.**
   Accrued expense adjustments recognize expenses that have accumulated or accrued during the accounting period. To adjust for accrued expenses, record increases in expense and liability accounts.

8. **Analyze financial statement information for real-life companies.**
   Chapter 3 introduces a ratio called return on assets (ROA) which provides a basic measure for evaluating profitability relative to total asset investment. ROA equals net income divided by average total assets.

A1. **Prepare an adjusting entry for a deferral when the original transaction is recorded in an income statement account.**
   For a prepaid expense initially debited to an expense account, debit an asset and credit the expense for the asset portion left. For an unearned revenue initially credited to a revenue account, debit the revenue and credit a liability for the portion unearned.

DEMONSTRATION PROBLEM

Adjustments for Deferrals and Accruals

Selected unadjusted account balances from the trial balance of Game Parlor, Inc. for the year ended December 31, 2007, are as follows:

GAME PARLOR, INC.
PARTIAL UNADJUSTED TRIAL BALANCE
DECEMBER 31, 2007

Account Title	Debits	Credits
Cash	$1,000	
Prepaid Rent	4,800	
Game Systems	2,000	
Accumulated Depreciation—Game Systems		$ 800
Notes Payable		1,000
Unearned Rent		450

Adjustment data for the year ended December 31, 2007, are as follows:

a. The balance in Prepaid Rent represents payment in advance for renting office space. On January 1, 2007, Game Parlor, Inc. paid $4,800 cash for the next 16 months' rent.
b. Twenty computer game systems were purchased on account on September 1, 2005. Each system cost $100, has an estimated residual value of $10, and is expected to have a useful life of 3 years. The straight-line depreciation method is used.

c. The balance in Notes Payable represents a 12% interest-bearing note dated December 16, 2007, and due in 60 days.

d. On August 1, 2007, Game Parlor, Inc. received a check for $450 as payment for nine months' rental of some extra games.

REQUIRED (LG 3-7)

Using T accounts, determine the journal entries needed to adjust the accounts as of December 31, 2007.

SOLUTION

Solution Approach

Use the three steps discussed in the chapter to analyze each situation.

1. Identify the accounts to be adjusted and determine their unadjusted balances.

2. Determine the correct balance in each account requiring adjustment.

3. Determine the adjusting entry to bring the accounts into agreement with the corrected balances computed in step 2.

A. Adjustment for Prepaid Rent

Step 1. On December 31, 2007, the Prepaid Rent account (an asset) has an unadjusted debit balance of $4,800. The Rent Expense account (an expense) must have an unadjusted balance of $0.

Step 2. The amount of rent expense for the year ended December 31, 2007, should be $3,600 [($4,800 ÷ 16 months) × 12 months]. The balance in the asset account Prepaid Rent should be $1,200 ($300 × 4).

Step 3. The following T accounts summarize the adjustment process for this situation. (The adjusting entry appears in bold in each of the accounts.)

(Asset Account) Prepaid Rent			(Expense Account) Rent Expense		
Balance	4,800		Balance	0	
		12/31 3,600	12/31	3,600	
Balance	1,200		Balance	3,600	

B. Adjustment for Depreciation

Step 1. On December 31, 2007, the Depreciation Expense—Game Systems account (expense) has an unadjusted balance of $0. The Accumulated Depreciation—Game Systems account (contra asset) has an unadjusted credit balance of $800. This balance is from depreciation taken in 2005 and 2006.

Step 2. The total cost of the 20 game systems is $2,000. The expected residual value of the game systems is $200, or (20 × $10). The amount of the depreciation expense for the game systems for the year ended December 31, 2007, should be $600 [($2,000 - $200) ÷ 36 months × 12].

Step 3. The following T account summarizes the adjustment process. (The adjusting entry appears in bold.)

(Expense Account) Depreciation Expense— Game Systems			(Contra Asset Account) Accumulated Deprecation— Game Systems		
				12/31/05	200
				12/31/06	600
Balance	0			Balance	800
12/31/07	**600**			**12/31/07**	**600**
Balance	600			Balance	1,400

C. Adjustment for Interest Expense

Step 1.   On December 31, 2007, the Interest Expense account (an expense) and the Interest Payable account (a liability) both have unadjusted balances of $0. Both accounts have a $0 balance because we have recognized no interest expense on the note payable. Interest on the note payable accumulates with the passage of time.

Step 2.   To calculate the interest on the note payable, we use the following formula for simple interest:

$$\text{Interest} = \text{Principal} \times \text{Interest Rate} \times \frac{\text{Elapsed Time in Days}}{360}$$

The elapsed time in days for December 2007 is:

Number of days in December	31
Deduct: Date of note	16
Elapsed days in December	15

The unrecorded interest expense accrued through December 31, 2007,

$$\text{Interest} = \$1,000 \times 0.12 \times \frac{15}{360} = \$5$$

Step 3.   The following T accounts summarize the adjustment process for unrecorded interest expense. (The adjusting entry is in bold.)

(Expense Account) Interest Expense			(Liability Account) Interest Payable		
Balance	0		Balance		0
12/31	**5**		**12/31**		**5**
Balance	5		Balance		5

D. Adjustment for Rent Revenue

Step 1.   On December 31, 2007, the Unearned Rent account (a liability) has an unadjusted credit balance of $450 and the Rent Revenue account (a revenue) has an unadjusted balance of $0.

Step 2.   The amount of rent earned for the year ended December 31, 2007, should be $250 [($450 ÷ 9 months) × 5 months)]. The remaining balance in the liability account Unearned Rent should be $200 ($50 × 4 months).

Step 3.   The following T accounts summarize the adjustment process. (The adjusting entry is in bold.)

(Liability Account) Unearned Rent			(Revenue Account) Rent Revenue		
		Balance	450	Balance	0
12/31	**250**			**12/31**	**250**
		Balance	200	Balance	250

GLOSSARY

accounting period assumption   The division of a business's life into shorter periods of time to permit periodic reporting.

accrual basis   The basis of accounting that assumes a business realizes revenue at time of the sale of goods or services. A business recognizes expenses at the time it receives benefits or consumes an asset in the production of revenue.

accruals   Adjustments that update unrecorded revenues earned and expenses incurred and also the related asset or liability.

accrued expenses   Expenses that have been incurred in a given period but that have not yet been paid or recorded.

accrued liability   The liability for an expense that has been incurred but not yet paid or recorded.

accrued revenues   Revenues that have been earned in a given period but that have not yet been collected or recorded.

Accumulated Depreciation   An account that reveals all past depreciation expense recorded on a depreciable item of property, plant, and equipment.

adjusting entries   Journal entries made to update revenue, expense, asset, and liability accounts as required by the accrual basis of accounting.

book value   The difference between the original cost of a depreciable item of property, plant, and equipment and its related accumulated depreciation.

cash basis   The basis of accounting that recognizes revenue at the time cash is received and expenses in the period of the payment.

contra account   An account used to record the negative portion of a related account.

deferrals   A classification of adjustments that includes prepaid expenses, depreciation, and unearned revenue adjustments. These are called deferrals because we defer the recognition of a portion of expense or revenue until a future period.

depreciation adjustment   An adjustment that assigns a portion of the cost of a long-lived asset to the periods benefitted.

depreciation expense   The amount of property, plant, and equipment cost that is assigned to a given period.

matching principle   A basic accounting principle that requires comparing revenues of a period with the expenses incurred to earn them.

materiality concept   An accounting concept that requires an item large enough and significant enough to influence decision makers to be separately identified in accounting statements.

prepaid expense adjustment   An adjustment that allocates a prepaid item between the current period and a future period.

profit margin   The percentage contribution of a sales dollar to net income. We compute it by dividing net income by total revenues.

residual value   The estimated salvage value or resale value that an item of property, plant, and equipment should have at the end of its estimated useful life.

return on assets (ROA)   The measure of the amount a company earns on each dollar of asset investment. We compute it by dividing net income by average total assets.

straight-line method of depreciation   A method that allocates the cost less residual value of a depreciable asset equally over the estimated useful life of the asset.

unearned revenue adjustment   An adjustment that allocates an advance collection of a revenue between the current period and a future period.

unearned revenues   Revenue payments received before they are earned (that is, before goods or services are exchanged for them).

QUESTIONS FOR GROUP LEARNING

Q3-1. Describe the accounting period assumption. How does it relate to the matching principle?

Q3-2. The adjustment process is really a question of measuring net income first and balance sheet items second. From an income measurement point of view, why is it important to match all incurred expenses against all earned revenue to determine net income?

Q3-3. (a) What purpose do adjusting entries serve? (b) What types of events make adjusting entries necessary?

Q3-4. Most adjustments are grouped into two categories—deferrals and accruals. Discuss these terms and indicate what kinds of adjustments would fall in each group.

Q3-5. Does the need to make adjusting entries at the end of a period mean that errors were made in the accounts during the period? Discuss.

Q3-6. Define the following terms: (a) accrued revenues, (b) accrued expenses, (c) prepaid expenses, (d) depreciation, (e) unearned revenues.

Q3-7. (a) What is a contra account? (b) Name one contra account involved in adjusting entries. (c) What is the specific purpose of the contra account you just named?

Q3-8. State where you would classify the following on the balance sheet: (a) prepaid insurance, (b) unearned rent, (c) interest receivable, (d) wages payable.

Q3-9. During 2007, Jablonsky Company prepaid its premiums on one-year, two-year, and three-year property insurance policies. The company recorded the premium payments in an account that it calls Prepaid Property Insurance.

    a. At the close of 2007, will the necessary adjusting entry be a deferral or an accrual?

    b. Which of the following types of accounts will be affected by the adjusting entry required at the end of the year: asset, liability, revenue, or expense?

Q3-10. At the end of the fiscal year, a company has a 150-day, interest-bearing note payable that had been issued to a supplier 90 days earlier.

    a. Is the interest on the note as of the end of the current year a deferral or an accrual?

    b. Which of the following types of accounts is affected by the related adjusting entry at the end of the current year: asset, liability, revenue, or expense?

    c. Assuming that the company does not pay the note until maturity, what fraction of the total interest should it allocate to the year in which it pays the note?

Q3-11. (**Appendix**) There are two alternative approaches for first recording deferrals. Describe each approach for a situation involving an unearned revenue. Also state how the adjusting entry process would differ under each approach.

EXERCISES

E3-12. Applying the matching principle (LG 1) Florida Company makes rent payments every three months for the next three-month period beginning that day. Florida has made the following rent payments applicable to 2007:

November 1, 2006	$1,200
February 1, 2007	1,500
May 1, 2007	1,500
August 1, 2007	1,800
November 1, 2007	1,800

Calculate the rent expense that should be shown on the income statement for the year ended December 31, 2007.

E3-13. Prepaid expense adjustment (LG 2, 3) Willenborg Company began operations on January 1, 2007. During the year it purchased $3,300 in office supplies and debited the asset account Office Supplies. On December 31, 2007, a count of office supplies on hand showed $400. Prepare the required December 31, 2007, adjusting entry in general journal form.

E3-14. Prepaid expense adjustments (LG 3) The trial balance of Arnold Company on December 31, 2007, included the following account balances before adjustments:

Prepaid Insurance	$1,800
Advertising Supplies	2,500
Prepaid Rent	1,200
Office Supplies	4,000

a. On November 1, 2007, the company purchased a two-year comprehensive insurance policy for $1,800.

b. Advertising supplies on hand totaled $300.

c. On September 1, 2007, the company paid one year's rent in advance.

d. The office supplies inventory on December 31 was $800.

Journalize the adjusting entries. Explanations are not required for this exercise.

E3-15. Depreciation adjustment (LG 4) Montana Company purchased a new van on January 1, 2007, for $34,000. The van had an estimated useful life of five years and a residual value at the end of that time of $4,000.

1. What is the amount of depreciation expense for 2007?

2. What is the balance in the Accumulated Depreciation—Vans account at the end of 2007? 2008?

3. What will be the book value of the vans on the balance sheet of December 31, 2007? December 31, 2008?

4. Why is the depreciation amount credited to Accumulated Depreciation—Vans rather than directly to Vans?

E3-16. Adjustment for unearned revenue (LG 5) Chopper Bike Magazine Company credited Unearned Subscription Revenue for $120,000 received from subscribers to its new monthly magazine. All subscriptions were for 12 issues. The initial issue was mailed during August 2007.

  1. Make the adjusting journal entry on December 31, 2007.

  2. Suppose the initial issue was mailed during January 2007 and the last issue in December. Is an adjusting journal entry needed on December 31, 2007?

E3-17. Accrued expense adjustment (LG 7) Ocean Company employs six clerks at a weekly salary of $250 each. The clerks are paid on Friday, the last day of a five-day work week. Make the adjusting journal entry, assuming that the accounting period ended (a) on a Monday or (b) on a Wednesday.

E3-18. Accrued revenue adjustment (LG 6) On April 15, 2007, Hopi Company received a 30-day, 12% note for $12,000 from a customer. Make a journal entry to adjust Hopi Company's books on April 30.

E3-19. Various accrual adjustments (LG 6, 7) Prepare adjusting journal entries from the following information pertaining to the accounts of Reeves Company at the end of September 2007. (Explanations are not required.)

  a. Accrued rent receivable is $650.

  b. Accrued interest payable is $200.

  c. Accrued taxes payable are $500.

  d. Accrued wages payable are $1,900.

  e. Reeves rented a trenching machine during September from Quality Equipment Rent Company at $50 per hour. It used the machine for 140 hours during the month. The company had made an initial payment of $2,500 to Quality Equipment Rent Company for the rental of the machine. It debited the payment to Equipment Rent Expense.

  f. Accrued interest on investment in municipal bonds is $700.

  g. Estimated income taxes accrued are $2,200.

E3-20. Various adjustments (LG 3, 4, 6, 7) Make the end-of-month adjusting journal entries for Mary Company for the following items (explanations not required):

  a. The debit balance of the Prepaid Insurance account is $2,400. Of this amount, $300 is expired.

  b. The Office Supplies account has a balance of $2,300; $300 of supplies are on hand.

  c. Depreciation on store equipment is $600.

  d. Accrued salaries and wages payable total $700.

  e. Accrued interest receivable is $90.

  f. Accrued interest payable is $180.

E3-21. Various adjustments (LG 3-7) The accountant for Speers Company unexpectedly disappeared just before the close of the company's accounting year. In his haste to leave, he did not have a chance to discuss what adjusting entries would be necessary at the end of the year, December 31, 2007. Fortunately, however, he did jot down a few notes that provided some leads. The following are his notes:

a. Depreciation on furniture and equipment for the year is $7,000.

b. Insurance in the amount of $2,900 expired for the year. The unadjusted balance in Prepaid Insurance is $3,500.

c. The unadjusted balance in Unearned Revenue is $4,200. $2,000 has been earned.

d. The company has received no bill from the car rental agency for a salesperson's car. The bill is estimated to be $6,100 for the year.

e. Four days' salaries will be unpaid at year-end; total weekly (five days') salary is $6,000.

f. Estimated income taxes accrued are $1,700.

On the basis of the information available, prepare adjusting journal entries with brief explanations.

E3-22. Calculation of information from adjustment data (LG 3)

1. The balance sheets of Marge Company as of December 31, 2007 and 2008, showed office supplies totaling $3,000 and $4,000, respectively. During 2008, office supplies totaling $7,000 were purchased. What was the amount of office supplies expense for the year 2008?

2. The balances of the Prepaid Insurance account of Rome Company were as follows:

December 31, 2007	$ 1,000
December 31, 2008	1,200

The company debits Prepaid Insurance for all insurance premiums when it makes cash payments. The income statement for 2008 showed insurance expense of $2,600. What was the total cash expenditure for insurance premiums during 2008?

E3-23. (Appendix) Alternative approaches of accounting for prepaid expense (LG A1) Mary Sunshine is opening a hair styling salon and has ordered subscriptions to some popular magazines to put in her waiting room. She must pay for the 12-month subscriptions in advance. On April 1, 2007, she sends checks totaling $480 to the various publishers. The part-time bookkeeper she has hired to manage her billings has the option of making the entry on April 1, 2007, as in Case 1 or as in Case 2.

Case 1

GENERAL JOURNAL   Page 4

Date			Accounts Titles and Explanations	PR	Debit	Credit
2007 Apr.	1		Prepaid Magazine Subscriptions		480	
			Cash			480
			To record payment for 12-month magazine subscriptions.			

Case 2

GENERAL JOURNAL   Page 4

Date			Accounts Titles and Explanations	PR	Debit	Credit
2007 Apr.	1		Magazine Subscription Expense		480	
			Cash			480
			To record payment for 12-month magazine subscriptions.			

Make the adjusting journal entry as of December 31, 2007, assuming (a) the bookkeeper used the Case 1 method and (b) the bookkeeper used the Case 2 method.

E3-24. (Appendix) Alternative approaches of accounting for unearned revenue (LG A1)
Diane Corporation received rent of $4,800 for one year beginning August 1, 2007. They recorded the transaction as follows:

	GENERAL JOURNAL			Page 4
Date	**Accounts Titles and Explanations**	**PR**	**Debit**	**Credit**
2007 Aug. 1	Cash		4,800	
	Rent Revenue			4,800
	To record receipt of rent for one year.			

1. What adjusting journal entry is required on December 31, 2007?

2. What balance sheet account could have been credited on August 1, 2007, instead of Rent Revenue?

3. Based on your answer to question 2, what adjusting journal entry would then be necessary?

PROBLEMS

P3-25. Analyzing adjustments (LG 3, 7) Mexico Corporation had prepared the following unadjusted trial balance as of December 31, 2007:

MEXICO CORPORATION
UNADJUSTED TRIAL BALANCE
DECEMBER 31, 2007

Acct. No.	Account Title	Debits	Credits
101	Cash	$ 2,100	
111	Accounts Receivable	7,000	
115	Notes Receivable	8,000	
136	Store Supplies	900	
151	Land	18,000	
155	Store Building	90,000	
156	Accumulated Depreciation—Store Building		$ 4,000
201	Accounts Payable		5,000
230	Unearned Revenue		1,200
331	Common Stock		106,800
372	Dividends	6,000	
410	Revenue		80,000
615	Rent Expense—Store Equipment	21,000	
621	Delivery Expense	8,000	
705	Salaries Expense	36,000	
	Totals	$197,000	$197,000

Mexico began business on January 1, 2006. The following data was available on December 31, 2007.

a. The balance in Notes Receivable is for a single $8,000 note from a customer dated December 16, 2007. The 60-day note, due February 14, 2008, carries an interest rate of 15%.

b. A count of the store supplies showed $400 of unused supplies remaining.

c. Mexico acquired the store building when the business began. It estimated that the building has a useful life of 20 years and a residual value of $10,000. The straight-line depreciation method is used.

d. Salaries in the amount of $800 have been earned as of December 31, 2007, but are unrecorded.

e. Mexico has not yet earned $300 of the amount shown in the Unearned Revenue account.

f. Income taxes accrued are estimated to be $4,000.

REQUIRED

For each of the required adjustments draw T accounts for the two accounts affected. Follow the three-step process used in the chapter to determine the adjusting entry. Journalize the adjusting entries.

P3-26. Adjusting entries from a trial balance and added data (LG 3-7) The unadjusted trial balance of Storrs Company, Inc. contained the following accounts as of December 31, 2007.

STORRS COMPANY, INC.
PARTIAL UNADJUSTED TRIAL BALANCE
DECEMBER 31, 2007

Acct. No.	Account Title	Debits	Credits
135	Office Supplies	$ 2,000	
141	Prepaid Insurance	5,200	
143	Prepaid Advertising	8,000	
231	Unearned Rent		$ 12,000
430	Rent Revenue		222,000
431	Interest Revenue		1,950
705	Wages Expense	51,000	

Additional information includes the following:

a. Interest that had accrued on notes receivable at December 31, 2007, amounted to $400.

b. The count of office supplies on hand at December 31, 2007, was $400.

c. The insurance records show that $2,000 of insurance has expired during 2007.

d. The company had prepaid an advertising contract of $8,000. Sixty percent of this contract has been used, and the remainder will be used in the following year.

e. Wages due to employees of $1,900 have accrued as of December 31, 2007.

f. The portion of rent collected in advance that will not be earned until 2008 amounted to $5,200.

REQUIRED

1. Open the accounts listed in the trial balance and record the balance in the appropriate column as of December 31, 2007. Also, open the following accounts and enter zero balances:

117	Interest Receivable	718	Office Supplies Expense
205	Wages Payable	719	Insurance Expense
616	Advertising Expense		

2. Journalize the adjusting entries and post to the appropriate accounts. Assign the journal page number 10. In the accounts, identify the postings by writing "Adjusting" in the explanation columns.

P3-27. Adjusting entries for deferrals and accruals (LG 3-7) After an analysis of the accounts and the other records of Sea Corporation, the following information is made available for the year ended December 31, 2007:

a. The Office Supplies account has a debit balance of $2,000. Office supplies on hand at December 31 total $600.

b. The Prepaid Rent account has a debit balance of $19,500. Included in this amount is $1,500 paid in December 2007 for the following January; $18,000 has expired.

c. The Prepaid Insurance account has a debit balance of $1,320. It consists of the following policies purchased during 2007:

Policy No.	Date of Policy	Life of Policy	Premium
C3PX	August 1	1 year	$720
Y206	December 1	6 months	600

d. At the close of the year, two notes receivable were on hand:

Date	Face Value	Life of Note	Interest Rate (%)
November 1	$ 5,000	120 days	12
December 1	6,000	90 days	15

e. At the close of the year, two notes payable were outstanding:

Date	Face Value	Life of Note	Interest Rate (%)
October 2	$4,000	180 days	15
November 1	9,000	90 days	12

f. Salaries and wages accrued totaled $1,800.

g. The Unearned Rent account has a credit balance of $24,000 for receipt of cash for a one-year lease effective June 1, 2007.

h. The Store Equipment account has a debit balance of $33,000. The equipment has an estimated useful life of 10 years and a residual value of $3,000. Sea Corporation acquired all store equipment on January 1, 2006.

i. Income taxes accrued are estimated to be $5,000.

REQUIRED
Prepare the adjusting journal entries required at December 31, 2007. (Explanations are not necessary.)

P3-28. Preparation of adjusting entries and financial statements (LG 3-7) The unadjusted trial balance for Poland Corporation for December 31, 2007, is shown below:

POLAND CORPORATION
UNADJUSTED TRIAL BALANCE
DECEMBER 31, 2007

Acct. No.	Account Title	Debits	Credits
101	Cash	$ 20,000	
111	Accounts Receivable	27,000	
115	Notes Receivable	8,000	
135	Office Supplies	5,700	
142	Prepaid Rent	9,300	
171	Office Equipment	12,000	
172	Accumulated Depreciation—Office Equipment		$ 1,000
201	Accounts Payable		8,000
233	Unearned Service Revenue		4,000
331	Common Stock		30,700
360	Retained Earnings		8,000
372	Dividends	1,600	
413	Service Revenue		124,800
616	Advertising Expense	26,000	
705	Salaries Expense	39,600	
720	Postage Expense	3,000	
721	Utilities Expense	9,300	
725	Cleaning Expense	15,000	
	Totals	$176,500	$176,500

No additional investments were made during the year. On December 31, 2007, the following data was accumulated for use in adjusting entries.

a. The company loaned $8,000 to a key customer. The customer signed a 15%, note dated November 16, 2007.

b. The company made two rent payments during the year on its office. On January 1, 2007, it paid $3,000 for six months' rent beginning on that date. On July 1, 2007, it paid $6,300 for nine months' rent beginning on that date.

c. Salaries earned by employees as of December 31, 2007, but unpaid were $2,000.

d. The company bought all its office equipment on January 1, 2006. The equipment had an estimated useful life of 10 years and a total estimated residual value of $2,000. The company uses the straight-line depreciation method.

e. The company received service revenue of $4,000 in advance on September 1, 2007. Eighty percent of this amount has been earned as of December 31, 2007.

f. A count of office supplies showed $800 remaining unused on December 31, 2007.

g. Income taxes accrued are estimated to be $4,845.
  Accounts in addition to those in the trial balance that will be used are as follows:

117	Interest Receivable	715	Rent Expense
205	Salaries Payable	718	Office Supplies Expense
215	Income Taxes Payable	754	Depreciation Expense—Office Equipment
431	Interest Revenue	901	Income Tax Expense

REQUIRED

1. Open general ledger accounts for the accounts in the trial balance and the list and enter the December 31, 2007, unadjusted balances.

2. Journalize the necessary adjusting entries for December 31, 2007.

3. Post the adjusting entries to the general ledger.

4. Prepare an adjusted trial balance as of December 31, 2007.

5. Prepare an income statement and statement of owners' equity for the year ended December 31, 2007, and a balance sheet for December 31, 2007.

P3-29. Adjustments and effect on statements (LG 2-7) Certain unadjusted account balances from the trial balance of Viola Consulting for the year ended December 31, 2007, are given below:

VIOLA CONSULTING
PARTIAL UNADJUSTED TRIAL BALANCE
DECEMBER 31, 2007

Acct. No.	Account Title	Debits	Credits
111	Accounts Receivable	$ 50,000	
115	Notes Receivable	6,000	
135	Office Supplies	1,800	
141	Prepaid Insurance	3,000	
173	Automobiles	26,500	
174	Accumulated Depreciation—Automobiles		$ 4,500
202	Notes Payable		8,000
231	Unearned Rent		3,300
235	Unearned Professional Fees		4,200
423	Professional Fees Revenue		180,000
705	Salaries Expense	125,500	
721	Utilities Expense	9,500	

Adjustment data on December 31, are as follows:

a. A count of office supplies on hand on December 31, 2007, showed $500 remaining.

b. The company owns two automobiles. They were purchased on January 1, 2006. They have an estimated useful life of five years, and the total residual value of the two cars is $4,000. The company uses straight-line depreciation.

c. The company has not received the utilities bill for December. It estimates that the cost of utilities used is $600.

d. The company accepted a $6,000, 90-day note from a customer dated December 1, 2007. The note carries an interest rate of 15%. No interest has been recorded.

e. The balance in Prepaid Insurance represents a 12-month policy effective April 1, 2007.

f. Property taxes accrued but unrecorded are $2,000.

g. Salaries earned by employees as of December 31 but unrecorded are $600.

h. Viola had leased some unused equipment to another company. It received a $3,300 payment for six months' rent on September 1.

i. On November 1, 2007, Viola borrowed $8,000 from the local bank. It signed a 120-day note at 9% interest. The company has recorded no interest.

j. On December 1, Viola signed a contract to provide consulting services for a client. The client paid $4,200 on that date. As of December 31, Viola had provided 60% of the services.

k. Income taxes accrued are estimated to be $14,000.

REQUIRED
Using the format shown below:

1. Record adjusting journal entries.

2. Indicate the financial statement classification where each account in the entry would appear.

3. Show the amount that would be reported on the financial statement for each account after the adjusting entry is posted.

Item	Adjusting Journal Entry December 31, 2007			Financial Statement Classification	Amount Reported on Financial Statement
a.	Office Supplies Expense	1,300		Expense	$1,300
	Office Supplies		1,300	Current asset	500

P3-30. (Appendix) Adjustments for transactions initially recorded in income statement (temporary) accounts (LG A1) Solar Company prepared the following unadjusted trial balance as of December 31, 2007:

SOLAR COMPANY
UNADJUSTED TRIAL BALANCE
DECEMBER 31, 2007

Acct. No.	Account Title	Debits	Credits
101	Cash	$ 9,000	
111	Accounts Receivable	5,000	
115	Notes Receivable	6,000	
141	Prepaid Insurance	1,800	
151	Land	14,000	
153	Building	80,000	
201	Accounts Payable		$ 6,000
331	Common Stock		66,800
360	Retained Earnings		30,000
372	Dividends	7,000	
410	Revenue		98,000
621	Delivery Expense	14,000	
705	Salaries Expense	40,000	
715	Rent Expense	15,000	
718	Office Supplies Expense	9,000	
	Totals	$200,800	$200,800

Solar began business on January 1, 2007. The following data was available on December 31, 2007:

a. Salaries in the amount of $1,800 have been earned as of December 31, 2007, but are unrecorded.

b. A count of the office supplies showed $1,400 of supplies remaining unused.

c. Solar has not yet earned $2,300 of the amount included in Revenue.

d. The balance in Notes Receivable is for a single $6,000 note from a customer dated December 1, 2007. The note is due January 30, 2008, and carries an interest rate of 12%.

e. Solar acquired the building when the business began. It estimated that the building has a useful life of 20 years and a residual value of $10,000. The company uses straight-line depreciation.

f. The balance in Rent Expense represents 15 months' rent paid in advance on March 1, 2007.

g. The company took out a 12-month insurance policy effective August 1, 2007, and paid $1,800 in cash.

REQUIRED

Journalize the necessary adjustments in general journal form.

P3-31. Evaluation and restatement of financial statements to conform to accrual basis of accounting (LG 2-7) Owners invested $50,000 cash to start Conservative Parking Lot, Inc. in downtown Hartford on January 1, 2007. Conservative Parking completed its first month in business and desires a $40,000 bank loan in order to expand the business. They plan to pay the loan back at the end of one year. You are a loan officer at Rockville Bank. On your request, they have prepared a set of financial statements for their first month in business. The financial statements are as follows (ignore income taxes):

CONSERVATIVE PARKING LOT, INC.
INCOME STATEMENT
FOR THE MONTH ENDED JANUARY 31, 2007

Parking lot revenues		$ 24,000
Expenses:		
Advertising expense	$ 12,000	
Wages expense	3,000	
Rent expense	48,000	
Office supplies expense	6,000	
Insurance expense	2,520	
Total expenses		71,520
Net loss		$ (47,520)

CONSERVATIVE PARKING LOT, INC.
STATEMENT OF OWNERS' EQUITY
FOR THE MONTH ENDED JANUARY 31, 2007

Common stock, January 1, 2007	$ 0	
Add: Initial investment by owners	50,000	
Common stock, January 31, 2007		$ 50,000
Retained earnings, January 1, 2007	$ 0	
Deduct: Net loss	(47,520)	
Dividends	(1,000)	
Retained earnings (deficit), January 31, 2007		(48,520)
Owners' equity, January 31, 2007		$ 1,480

CONSERVATIVE PARKING LOT, INC.
BALANCE SHEET
JANUARY 31, 2007
Assets

Current assets:		
Cash		$ 19,480
Liabilities		
Current liabilities:		
Advance payments from customers		$ 18,000
Owners' Equity		
Common stock	$ 50,000	
Retained earnings (deficit)	(48,520)	
Total owners' equity		1,480
Total liabilities and owners' equity		$ 19,480

In reviewing the financial statements, you request that Conservative Parking provide some additional information regarding the treatment of certain financial statement accounts. Conservative Parking provides the following information:

Parking lot revenues

Revenues collected in cash. — $24,000

Other revenue information

Revenues from customers on account that Conservative Parking did not record since cash was not received. — $31,000

Cash collections from customers paying for six months in advance on January 1, 2007. — $18,000

Wages expense

Wages paid to four parking lot attendants for first half of January. (Wages of $3,000 earned during second half of January will be paid in February.) — $3,000

Office supplies

Parking lot tickets and office supplies purchased for cash on January 2, 2007. (At the end of January, $4,800 of supplies remain in inventory.) — $6,000

Prepaid insurance

Premium on liability insurance policy for the period January 1, 2007, to July 1, 2007. — $2,520

Prepaid parking lot rent

Amount paid on January 1, 2007, to rent a parking lot in downtown Hartford for 12 months. (Comparable lots were renting for an average monthly rent of $6,000.) — $48,000

Advertising campaign expenditures

Cost of extensive advertising during the first two weeks in January to advertise the parking lot (Conservative Parking took out full-page newspaper ads and feels that the advertising campaign will help to generate business for years to come.) — $12,000

REQUIRED

1. Restate the financial statements using the accrual basis of accounting. (Hint: Look at the existing financial statements to see how transactions have been recorded. Then, think about the adjustment you need to correct the recorded transaction.)

2. Based on the restated financial statements how would you respond to Conservative Parking's request for a $40,000 loan payable in one year?

P3-32. Evaluation and restatement of financial statements to conform to accrual basis of accounting (LG 2-7) Owners invested $50,000 cash to start Generous Parking Lot, Inc. in downtown Los Angeles on January 1, 2007. Generous has completed its first month in business and desires a $40,000 bank loan in order to expand its business. They are extremely excited about the business based on its success in the first month of operations. They plan to pay the loan back at the end of one year. You are a loan officer at First Bank of Los Angeles. Upon your request, Generous has prepared a set of financial statements for its first month in business. The financial statements are as follows (ignore income taxes):

In reviewing the financial statements, you request that Generous provide some additional information regarding the treatment of certain financial statement accounts. Generous provides the following information:

GENEROUS PARKING LOT, INC.
INCOME STATEMENT
FOR THE MONTH ENDED JANUARY 31, 2007

Parking lot revenues	$ 73,000
Expenses:	
Wages expense	3,000
Net income	$ 70,000

GENEROUS PARKING LOT, INC.
STATEMENT OF OWNERS' EQUITY
FOR THE MONTH ENDED JANUARY 31, 2007

Common stock, January 1, 2007	$ 0	
Add: Initial investment	50,000	
Common stock, January 31, 2007		$ 50,000
Retained earnings, January 1, 2007	$ 0	
Add: Net income	70,000	
Deduct: Dividends	(10,000)	
Retained earnings, January 31, 2007		60,000
Owners' Equity, January 31, 2007		$110,000

GENEROUS PARKING LOT, INC.
BALANCE SHEET
JANUARY 31, 2007
Assets

Current assets		
Cash	$ 10,480	
Accounts receivable	31,000	
Office supplies	6,000	
Prepaid insurance	2,520	
Total current assets		$ 50,000
Property, plant, and equipment		
Prepaid parking lot rent	$ 48,000	
Advertising campaign expenditures	12,000	
Total property, plant, and equipment		60,000
Total assets		$ 110,000
Owners' Equity		
Common stock	$ 50,000	
Retained earnings	60,000	
Total owners' equity		$ 110,000

Parking lot revenues

Revenues collected in cash.	$24,000
Revenues from customers on account.	31,000
Cash collections from customers paying for six months in advance on January 1, 2007.	18,000
Total	$73,000

Wages expense

Wages paid to four parking lot attendants for first half of January. (Wages of $3,000 earned during second half of January will be paid in February.)	$ 3,000

Office supplies

Parking lot tickets and office supplies purchased for cash on January 2, 2007. (At the end of January, $4,800 of supplies remain in inventory.)	$ 6,000

Prepaid insurance

Premium on liability insurance policy for the period January 1, 2007 to July 1, 2007.	$ 2,520

Prepaid parking lot rent

Amount paid on January 1, 2007, to rent a parking lot in downtown Los Angeles
for 12 months. (Comparable lots were renting for an average monthly rent of
$6,000.)   <u>$48,000</u>

Advertising campaign expenditures

Cost of extensive advertising during the first two weeks in January to advertise
the parking lot. (Generous took out full-page newspaper ads and feels that the
advertising campaign will help to generate business for years to come.)   <u>$12,000</u>

REQUIRED

1. Restate the financial statements using the accrual basis of accounting. (Hint: Look at the existing financial statements to see how transactions have been recorded. Then, think about the adjustment you need to correct the recorded transaction.)

2. Based on the restated financial statements how would you respond to the company's request for a $40,000 loan payable in one year?

P3-33. Analyzing Advanced Micro Devices and Texas Instruments (LG 8) Listed below are comparative income statements and balance sheets with common-size percents for 2004-2003 (in millions).

ADVANCED MICRO DEVICES AND TEXAS INTRUMENTS
COMPARATIVE COMMON-SIZE INCOME STATEMENTS
For the Years Ended December 31, 2004, 2003
(in millions)

	Advanced Micro Devices				Texas Instruments			
	2004	2004	2003	2003	2004	2004	2003	2003
	$	%	$	%	$	%	$	%
Total revenues	$ 5,001.4	100.0%	$ 3,519.2	100.0%	$ 12,580.0	100.0%	$ 9,834.0	100.0%
Total expenses	$ 4,910.2	98.2%	$ 3,793.7	107.8%	$ 10,719.0	85.2%	$ 8,636.0	87.8%
Net income (loss)	$ 91.2	1.8%	$ (274.5)	-7.8%	$ 1,861.0	14.8%	$ 1,198.0	12.2%

ADVANCED MICRO DEVICES AND TEXAS INTRUMENTS
COMPARATIVE COMMON-SIZE BALANCE SHEETS
December 31, 2004, 2003
(in millions)

	Advanced Micro Devices				Texas Instruments			
	2004	2004	2003	2003	2004	2004	2003	2003
	$	%	$	%	$	%	$	%
Total assets	$ 7,844.2	100.0%	$ 7,094.3	100.0%	$ 18,299.0	100.0%	$ 15,510.0	100.0%
Total liabilities	$ 4,834.1	61.6%	$ 4,656.0	65.6%	$ 3,236.0	19.9%	$ 3,646.0	23.5%
Total owners' equity	$ 3,010.1	38.4%	$ 2,438.3	34.4%	$ 13,063.0	80.1%	$ 11,864.0	76.5%
Total liabilities and owners' equity	$ 7,844.2	100.0%	$ 7,094.3	100.0%	$ 16,299.0	100.0%	$ 15,510.0	100.0%

REQUIRED

Income statement questions:

1. For 2004, which company has higher total revenues? Are total revenues for each company higher or lower over the two year period?

2. What is the percent change in total revenues from 2003 to 2004 for each company?

3. Is the percent of total expenses to total revenues for each company increasing or decreasing over the two year period?

Balance sheet questions:

4. For 2004, which company has higher assets? Are total assets for each company higher or lower over the two year period?

5. What is the percent change in total assets from 2003 to 2004 for each company?

6. Is the percent of total liabilities to total liabilities + owners' equity increasing or decreasing? As a result, is there more risk that each company could not pay its debts?

Integrative income statement and balance sheet questions:

7. Are the companies operating efficiently by using the least amount of asset investment to generate a given level of total revenues? Compute total asset turnover for each company for 2004.

8. Are the companies operating efficiently by using the least amount of asset investment to generate a given level of net income? Compute return on assets (ROA) for each company for 2004.

PRACTICE CASE

End-of-period adjusting entries (LG 2-7) Certain unadjusted account balances from the trial balance of New York Consulting, Inc. for the year ended December 31, 2007, are given below:

NEW YORK CONSULTING, INC.
PARTIAL UNADJUSTED TRIAL BALANCE
DECEMBER 31, 2007

Account Title	Debits	Credits
Cash	$ 40,000	
Office Supplies	4,000	
Prepaid Rent	24,000	
Office Equipment	32,000	
Accumulated Depreciation—Office Equipment		$ 2,000
Notes Payable		12,000
Unearned Professional Fees		18,000
Professional Fees Revenue		436,000
Salaries Expense	165,000	

Adjustment data for the year ended December 31, 2007, are as follows:

a. A count of office supplies on hand on December 31, 2007, revealed that $600 of supplies were left.

b. Office equipment was purchased on account on May 1, 2006. The equipment has a residual value of $2,000 and an expected useful life of 10 years. The straight-line depreciation method is used.

c. The balance in Notes Payable represents a 15%, interest-bearing note dated November 1, 2007, and is due in 90 days.

d. On November 1, 2007, New York Consulting, Inc. received a check for $18,000 as an advance payment for six months of management consulting services. The services are performed uniformly over time.

e. As of December 31, 2007, salaries of $3,000 have been earned but will not be paid until January 4, 2008.

f. The balance in the Prepaid Rent account represents payment in advance for renting office space. On October 1, 2007, $24,000 was paid in cash for rent for the next 10 months.

REQUIRED

1. Prepare the adjusting journal entries needed to correct the accounts as of December 31, 2007.

2. For each situation in a. through f., state the dollar amount and the effect on each of the following financial statement amounts if the required adjusting entry were not made. For example, would the amount be overstated, understated, or unaffected?
Total assets as of December 31, 2007.
Total liabilities as of December 31, 2007.
Total owners' equity as of December 31, 2007.
Total revenues for the year ended December 31, 2007.
Total expenses for the year ended December 31, 2007.

BUSINESS DECISION AND COMMUNICATION PROBLEM

Accounting for amortization of videocassettes by Video Village Corporation (LG 1-8) Video Village is a leading video rental chain. One of the largest assets on the balance sheet for Video Village is the videocassette rental inventory. In order to properly match revenues and expenses, Video Village must expense a portion of the videocassettes each year. This process is called "amortization" and is essentially the same as depreciation. In computing the yearly amortization, management must estimate the period of time the videocassettes will be useful and in demand. In the section below, we show the note to the financial statements on videocassette amortization for 2007.

2007 Annual Report: Videocassette Rental Inventory

Videocassettes are recorded at cost and amortized over their estimated economic life with no provision for salvage value. Those videocassettes which are considered base stock ("non-hits") are amortized over thirty six months on a straight-line basis. Beginning January 1, 2007 (*the start of the current reporting period*), economic life and the related amortization for new release feature films, which are frequently ordered in large quantities to satisfy initial demand ("hits"), were revised to approximately 36 months on an accelerated basis.

During the six-month period ended December 31, 2006 (*the previous reporting period*), the economic life of "hits" and related amortization period approximated nine months on a straight-line basis with no salvage value. The Company has determined that the economic useful life and related amortization for these "hits" more closely approximates 36 months on an accelerated basis with no provision for salvage value.

In your role as a financial analyst, your supervisor, Mr. Stuart Brown desires your opinion about the change in amortization period starting as of January 1, 2007.

REQUIRED

Write a memo to Mr. Stuart Brown. In the memo, start by summarizing both the new and old amortization policies for videocassettes. Second, express your opinion as to whether the new amortization policy will cause net income to be higher or lower for 2007 and explain why. Finally, discuss whether or not the new amortization policy is an improvement over the old in terms of the overall "fairness" of financial reporting.

ETHICAL DILEMMA

Extending useful life of assets to raise net income You are the chief accountant for a regional chain of retail shoe stores. The main agenda item at the June 2007 executive committee meeting was the current year's anticipated net income. As a part of that discussion, the president brought up the estimated life used to depreciate plant assets. He asked you what estimated life was used to calculate annual depreciation expense. He said that it was important because the company would be applying for a major loan in July. Thus, he wanted to show the highest net income possible. You stated that the company used an average life of 20 years to depreciate plant assets. You also stated that most companies in your industry use the same estimated useful life. The president says that he believes that 30 years would be a more reasonable estimate. He adds that "after all it is only an estimate." The conversation has put obvious pressure on you to use the longer useful life. This will give a lower depreciation expense and a higher reported net income on the financial statements presented to the bank for the loan.

REQUIRED

Describe what alternative actions are available to you. Discuss the ethical implications of each.

INTERNET PROBLEM

Access Starbucks Coffee's most recent financial statements at www.starbucks.com. Using these financial statements answer the following questions.

1. Over the three-year period shown in the Consolidated Statement of Income, are total revenues increasing or decreasing?

2. What is the percentage change in total revenues from the first year shown to the last year shown?

3. Using the Consolidated Balance Sheet, are total sets higher or lower in the later year?

4. What is the percentage change in total assets from the earliest year to the latest year shown?

COMPLETION OF THE ACCOUNTING CYCLE

CHAPTER

4

"Our bodies are where we stay; Our souls are what we are"   Cecil Baxter

LEARNING GOALS

After studying Chapter 4, you should be able to:

1. List all of the steps in the accounting cycle.

2. Explain the purpose of a work sheet.

3. Prepare a work sheet.

4. Prepare financial statements from the work sheet.

5. Record adjusting entries from the work sheet.

6. Explain the purpose of closing entries.

7. Record closing entries from the work sheet.

8. Explain the purpose of a postclosing trial balance and prepare one.

9. Analyze financial statement information for real-life companies.

UNDERSTANDING BUSINESS ISSUES

The accountant has three tasks at the end of an accounting period: (1) preparing adjusting entries to correct the accounts, (2) preparing the financial statements for the accounting period, and (3) preparing the accounts for the next period. To help, the accountant frequently uses a *work sheet*, an informal tool used to organize and sort information for the formal financial statements.

In this chapter we will learn to use the work sheet by continuing the illustration for Metro Delivery, Inc. introduced in Chapter 3. After completing the work sheet and preparing the financial statements, we will prepare the accounts for the next accounting period. This last step involves preparing closing entries. Closing entries clear the revenue, expense, and dividends accounts for the next period's transactions.

We also continue our real-life company analysis. We will show how to disaggregate the *return on assets* (ROA) ratio into its components: the *profit margin* percent and the *total asset turnover* ratio.

Review of the Accounting Cycle

Learning Goal 1   List all of the steps in the accounting cycle.

Chapters 1 through 3 introduced the steps completed during the accounting period and the adjusting entries that are prepared at the end. This chapter completes our study of the accounting cycle.

Exhibit 4.1, reviews the sequence of steps within the accounting cycle. The work sheet is an extra step in the accounting cycle, added after the preparation of the unadjusted trial balance. The adjusting entries must still be journalized and posted.

Illustration of the Accounting Cycle Continued: Metro Delivery, Inc.

We will now continue the illustration of Metro Delivery, Inc. which we started in Chapter 3. The next step in the accounting cycle is preparing the work sheet. To provide a convenient reference, Exhibit 4.2 reproduces the trial balance and supplementary information shown previously in Exhibit 3.2.

The Work Sheet

Learning Goal 2   Explain the purpose of a work sheet.

Accountants use the end-of-period **work sheet** to bring together information needed to prepare the financial statements. The work sheet is not a financial statement, nor is it a substitute for one. Instead, it is a working paper that bridges the gap between the accounting records and the financial statements. It permits us to determine the effect of the end-of-period adjustments and the amount of net income or net loss for the period. The work sheet allows the calculation of net income before journalizing and posting adjustments. It does not, however, eliminate the need to journalize and post the adjusting entries. The work sheet reduces the chances of overlooking an adjustment and helps check the arithmetic accuracy of the end-of-period work.

Exhibit 4.3 shows a pictorial overview of the work sheet. Exhibit 4.3 also summarizes a series of sequential steps to complete a work sheet. Exhibit 4.4 shows the completed work sheet for Metro Delivery.

Overview of the Work Sheet

In Exhibit 4.3, steps 1–5 show the order we follow in completing the work sheet. We will explain each of these steps in detail in the next section.

Five Steps to Preparing the Work Sheet
Learning Goal 3   Prepare a work sheet.

We can summarize the work sheet preparation in five steps. Review Exhibit 4.3 as you read each step:

1. Enter the heading at the top of the work sheet. Enter the account numbers, titles, and general ledger account balances in the Trial Balance columns. We take these amounts directly from the general ledger accounts.

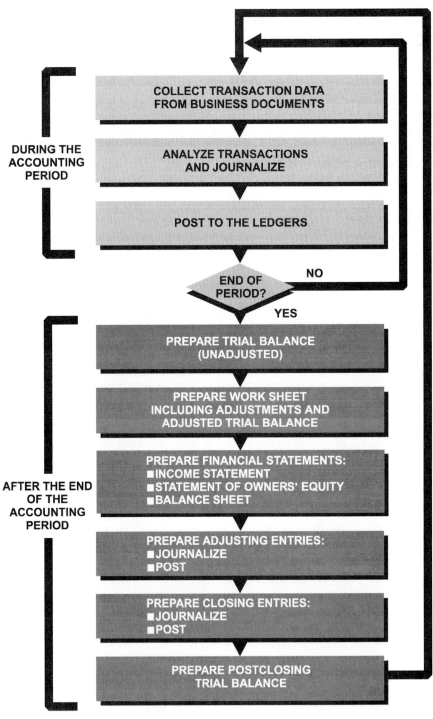

EXHIBIT 4.1

The Accounting Cycle

2. Enter the adjustments in the Adjustments columns.

3. Calculate the adjusted trial balance in the Adjusted Trial Balance columns.

METRO DELIVERY, INC.
UNADJUSTED TRIAL BALANCE
DECEMBER 31, 2007

Acct. No.	Account Title	Debits	Credits
101	Cash	$ 6,500	
111	Accounts Receivable	2,100	
115	Notes Receivable	1,200	
135	Office Supplies	300	
141	Prepaid Insurance	600	
169	Trucks	26,000	
201	Accounts Payable		$ 1,000
231	Unearned Rent		600
331	Common Stock		32,000
372	Dividends	500	
420	Trucking Revenue		7,500
705	Wages Expense	1,600	
711	Rent Expense—Building	1,400	
721	Heat and Light Expense	200	
726	Gas and Oil Expense	700	
	Totals	$ 41,100	$ 41,100

Other information required for adjustments:
a. Insurance premium of $600 for a comprehensive one-year policy was paid in cash on December 1, 2007.
b. During December, $300 of office supplies were purchased for cash. As of December 31, 2007, a physical count revealed that $100 in office supplies remained on hand.
c. Two trucks costing $13,000 each were purchased on December 1, 2007. Each truck has an estimated life of five years and an estimated residual value of $1,000 ($2,000 in total) at the end of that period. The trucks are to be depreciated over the five-year period by the straight-line method.
d. Metro Delivery signed an agreement on December 1, 2007, to rent a truck on weekends to Tom's Floral Shop. Metro Delivery collected rent of $600 in advance for six months starting December 1, 2007.
e. Metro Delivery received a $1,200 note receivable on December 11, 2007. The note has a stated interest rate of 15% and is due in 30 days on January 10, 2008.
f. Wages of $80 for Monday, December 31, 2007, have not been paid or recorded.
g. Estimated income taxes accrued are $900.

EXHIBIT **4.2**

Unadjusted Trial Balance and Supplementary Information for Metro Delivery, Inc.

---

4. Extend the amounts in the Adjusted Trial Balance columns to the Income Statement columns or Balance Sheet columns.

5. Subtotal the four financial statement columns of the work sheet. Determine the amount that will balance the Income Statement and Balance Sheet columns. Enter this amount below the subtotals to balance the columns.

We will now describe and illustrate each step in detail using the unadjusted account balances for Metro Delivery, Inc. contained in Exhibit 4.2.

Step 1.   Enter the Work Sheet Heading and Insert the Account Numbers, Account Titles, and Account Balances in the Trial Balance Columns.

The heading for the Metro Delivery, Inc. work sheet should look like this:

METRO DELIVERY, INC.
Work Sheet
For the Month Ended December 31, 2007

Enter the trial balance account numbers, titles, and balances directly from the general ledger. Enter the account titles in the space provided and the balances in the Trial Balance. Total (or *foot*) the debit and credit Trial Balance columns.

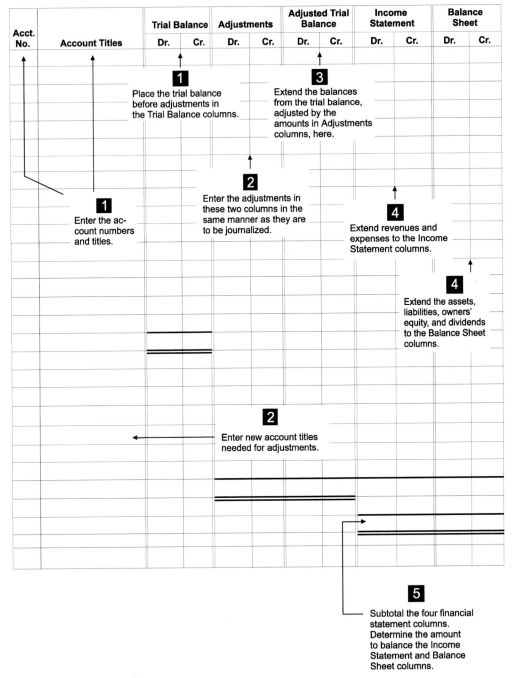

EXHIBIT 4.3

Pictorial Overview of a Work Sheet

METRO DELIVERY, INC.
WORK SHEET
FOR THE MONTH ENDED DECEMBER 31, 2007

Acct. No.	Account Titles	Trial Balance Dr.	Cr.	Adjustments Dr.	Cr.	Adjusted Trial Balance Dr.	Cr.	Income Statement Dr.	Cr.	Balance Sheet Dr.	Cr.
101	Cash	6,500				6,500				6,500	
111	Accounts Receivable	2,100				2.100				2,100	
115	Notes Receivable	1,200				1,200				1,200	
135	Office Supplies	300			(b) 200	100				100	
141	Prepaid Insurance	600			(a) 50	550				550	
169	Trucks	26,000				26,000				26,000	
201	Accounts Payable		1,000				1,000				1,000
231	Unearned Rent		600	(d) 100			500				500
331	Common Stock		32,000				32,000				32,000
360	Retained Earnings		0				0				0
372	Dividends	500				500				500	
420	Trucking Revenue		7,500				7,500		7,500		
705	Wages Expense	1,600		(f) 80		1,680		1,680			
711	Rent Expense— Building	1,400				1,400		1,400			
721	Heat and Light Expense	200				200		200			
726	Gas and Oil Expense	700				700		700			
	Totals	41,100	41,100								
719	Insurance Expense			(a) 50		50		50			
718	Office Supplies Expense			(b) 200		200		200			
759	Depreciation Expense— Trucks			(c) 400		400		400			
170	Accumulated Depreciation—Trucks				(c) 400		400				400
430	Rent Revenue				(d) 100		100		100		
117	Interest Receivable			(e) 10		10				10	
431	Interest Revenue				(e) 10		10		10		
205	Wages Payable				(f) 80		80				80
901	Income Tax Expense			(g) 900		900		900			
215	Income Taxes Payable				(g) 900		900				900
	Totals			1,740	1,740	42,490	42,490	5,530	7,610	36,960	34,880
	Net Income for the Month							2,080			2,080
	Totals							7,610	7,610	36,960	36,960

5
The difference between the Income Statement columns is net income.

5
Net income should also balance the difference between the Balance Sheet columns.

EXHIBIT **4.4**

Completed Work Sheet

Step 2.   Enter the Adjustments in the Adjustments Columns.

To speed the preparation of financial statements, enter the adjustments in the work sheet before journalizing them in the general journal. The seven adjustments for Metro Delivery, discussed in Chapter 3, are as follows:

- Adjustment (a): To adjust for expired insurance.

- Adjustment (b): To adjust for office supplies used.

- Adjustment (c): To adjust for depreciation of the trucks.

- Adjustment (d): To adjust for the rent that is earned.

- Adjustment (e): To adjust for the accrued interest revenue.

- Adjustment (f): To adjust for the accrued wages expense.

- Adjustment (g): To adjust for accrued income tax expense.

We cross-reference each adjusting entry with identification key letters. This enables us to match the debit for each adjustment with its credit. If an account to be debited or credited is not in the Trial Balance, add its title below the Trial Balance totals. In the case of Metro Delivery, we recorded accounts such as Insurance Expense, Office Supplies Expense, and Depreciation Expense—Trucks in this manner.

Step 3.   Calculate the Adjusted Trial Balance in theAdjusted Trial Balance Columns.

Next, we calculate the **adjusted trial balance**. We combine the amounts for each account in the Trial Balance columns and the Adjustments columns. We call this horizontal combination **cross-footing**. The process we use is:

- If there are *no* adjustments to an account, extend a debit trial balance amount to the Debit column of the adjusted trial balance and extend a credit trial balance amount to the Credit column of the adjusted trial balance. Examples of these entries are the Cash *debit* balance of $6,500 and the Accounts Payable *credit* balance of $1,000.

- If an account that requires an adjustment has a debit balance in the trial balance, *add* its *debit* adjustments or *subtract* its *credit* adjustments. If the result is a debit, extend it to the Adjusted Trial Balance Debit column. If the result is a credit, extend it to the Credit column. For example, we adjusted the debit balance of Wages Expense in the trial balance by the debit of $80. We extend the resulting debit of $1,680 to the Debit column of the adjusted trial balance. In contrast, we adjusted the $300 debit balance of Office Supplies in the trial balance by a credit of $200. We extend the resulting debit of $100 to the Adjusted Trial Balance Debit column.

- If the account that requires an adjustment has a credit balance in the trial balance, *add* its *credit* adjustments or *subtract* its *debit* adjustments. If the result is a credit, extend the adjusted balance to the Credit column. If the result is a debit, extend it to the Debit column. In the case of Metro Delivery, we adjusted the Unearned Rent credit balance of $600 by a debit of $100. We extended the credit balance of $500 to the Credit column of the adjusted trial balance.

- For the amounts listed below the trial balance, extend the adjustments directly to the appropriate Adjusted Trial Balance column.

The amounts in the Adjusted Trial Balance columns will be the same as the general ledger balances *after* we journalize and post adjusting entries. After each account has been cross-footed, we total the Adjusted Trial Balance Debit column and the Credit column. If the column totals match, your work sheet is mathematically accurate to this point. If not, locate and correct the error.

Step 4.   Extend the Amounts in the Adjusted Trial Balance Columns to the Income Statement Columns or to the Balance Sheet Columns.

Once the adjusted trial balance is in balance, extend the balance for each account to the Debit or Credit column of the Income Statement or Balance Sheet columns. Extend each amount to one and only one column. *No figure is ever extended to more than one place.* Enter expense and revenue account balances in the Income Statement columns. Enter asset, liability, common stock, retained earnings, and dividends account balances in the Balance Sheet columns.

Step 5.   (A) Subtotal the Four Financial Statement Columns of the Work Sheet. (B) Determine the Amount That Will Balance the Income Statement and Balance Sheet Columns. (C) Enter this Amount below the Subtotals to Balance the Columns.

For the final step, subtotal the four financial statement columns. The difference between the subtotals of the Income Statement columns is the net income or net loss for the period. If the subtotal of the Credit column exceeds the subtotal of the Debit column, then the business has earned a *net income*. A business has incurred a *net loss* if expenses exceed revenues. When this happens, the subtotal of the Income Statement Debit column exceeds the subtotal of the Income Statement Credit column. For Metro Delivery, the net income is $2,080.

Revenue (income statement credit column total)	$7,610
Deduct: Expenses (income statement debit column total)	5,530
Net income	$2,080

Enter this amount on the work sheet twice. Enter it as a debit in the Income Statement columns. Then enter it as a credit in the Balance Sheet columns. Write the label "Net income for the month" in the Account Title column on the same line. Adding this amount to the Income Statement Debit column balances the Income Statement columns. When we add it to the Balance Sheet Credit column, we are including the increase in owners' equity from net income in the balance sheet totals. This is necessary because the balance in the Retained Earnings account does *not* include net income for the period.Adding the net income figure to the Balance Sheet Credit column balances the Balance Sheet columns. We enter a loss on the work sheet in the Income Statement Credit column and the Balance Sheet Debit column just below the column subtotals. Exhibit 4.4 shows how the work sheet should look after the completion of step 5.

If the differences between the Income Statement columns and the Balance Sheet columns are not the same, there is an error in the work sheet. Errors can occur if we calculated totals incorrectly or extended account balances to the wrong columns. The completed work sheet assists in (1) preparing the financial statements, (2) journalizing and posting of adjusting entries, and (3) preparing closing entries. We will examine each in the next three sections.

PREPARING THE FINANCIAL STATEMENTS FROM THE WORK SHEET

Learning Goal 4   Prepare financial statements from the work sheet.

After completing the work sheet, we prepare the income statement from the amounts in the Income Statement columns of the work sheet. We prepare the statement of owners' equity and balance sheet from the amounts in the Balance Sheet columns. Exhibit 4.5, 4.6, and 4.7 show the financial statements for Metro Delivery for December.

METRO DELIVERY, INC.
INCOME STATEMENT
FOR THE MONTH ENDED DECEMBER 31, 2007

Revenues		
Trucking revenue	$ 7,500	
Rent revenue	100	
Interest revenue	10	
Total revenues		$ 7,610
Expenses		
Wages expense	$ 1,680	
Rent expense—building	1,400	
Office supplies expense	200	
Insurance expense	50	
Heat and light expense	200	
Gas and oil expense	700	
Depreciation expense—trucks	400	
Total expenses		4,630
Net income before income taxes		$ 2,980
Income tax expense		900
Net income		$ 2,080

EXHIBIT **4.5**

Income Statement

METRO DELIVERY, INC.
STATEMENT OF OWNERS' EQUITY
FOR THE MONTH ENDED DECEMBER 31, 2007

Common stock, December 1, 2007	$ 0	
Add: Initial investment by owners	32,000	
Common stock, December 31, 2007		$ 32,000
Retained earnings, December 1, 2007	$ 0	
Add: Net income	2,080	
Deduct: Dividends	(500)	
Retained earnings, December 31, 2007		1,580
Total owners' equity, December 31, 2007		$ 33,580

EXHIBIT **4.6**

Statement of Owners' Equity

METRO DELIVERY, INC.
BALANCE SHEET
DECEMBER 31, 2007

Assets

Current assets		
Cash	$ 6,500	
Accounts receivable	2,100	
Notes receivable	1,200	
Interest receivable	10	
Office supplies	100	
Prepaid insurance	550	
Total current assets		$ 10,460
Property, plant, and equipment		
Trucks	$ 26,000	
Deduct: Accumulated depreciation	400	25,600
Total assets		$ 36,060

Liabilities

Current liabilities		
Accounts payable	$ 1000	
Wages payable	80	
Unearned rent	500	
Income taxes payable	900	
Total current liabilities		$ 2,480

Owners' Equity

Common stock	$ 32,000	
Retained earnings	1,580	
Total owners' equity		33,580
Total liabilities and owners' equity		$ 36,060

EXHIBIT **4.7**

Balance Sheet

RECORDING ADJUSTING ENTRIES

Learning Goal 5   Record adjusting entries from the work sheet.

After preparing the financial statements, we journalize the adjusting entries. We take the adjusting entries directly from the Adjustments columns of the work sheet. After we have posted the adjusting entries, the general ledger account balances will correspond to the amounts in the Adjusted Trial Balance columns. Exhibit 4.8 illustrates recording of the adjusting entries. The account numbers in the posting reference column verify that posting is complete.

CLOSING THE REVENUE, EXPENSE, AND DIVIDENDS ACCOUNTS

Learning Goal 6   Explain the purpose of closing entries.

Revenue, expense, and dividends accounts accumulate changes in the owners' equity during an accounting period. At the end of the period, we must transfer these changes in owners' equity to the retained earnings account. This procedure, called *closing the books*, also reduces the balances in the

GENERAL JOURNAL

Date		Account Titles and Explanations	PR	Debit	Credit

2007
Dec.
	31	Adjusting Entries
		Insurance Expense
		    Prepaid Insurance
		    To record insurance expense for
		    December.
			719
			141
				50	50

	31	Office Supplies Expense
		    Office Supplies
		    To record supplies used during
		    December.
			718
			135
				200	200

	31	Depreciation Expense—Trucks
		    Accumulated Depreciation—Trucks
		    To record the depreciation for
		    December.
			759
			170
				400	400

	31	Unearned Rent
		    Rent Revenue
		    To record rent earned during
		    December.
			231
			430
				100	100

	31	Interest Receivable
		    Interest Revenue
		    To record interest revenue accrued
		    during December 12-31, 2007.
			117
			431
				10	10

	31	Wages Expense
		    Wages Payable
		    To record wages expense accrued
		    for December 31, 2007.
			705
			205
				80	80

	31	Income Tax Expense
		    Income Taxes Payable
		    To record estimated income taxes
		    accrued.
			901
			215
				900	900

EXHIBIT **4.8**

Adjusting Entries

revenue, expense, and dividends accounts to zero. This sets up the accounts to accumulate changes in owners' equity for the next period.

The revenue, expense, and dividends accounts are closed at the end of a period. For this reason, these accounts are often called temporary owners' equity accounts, or **nominal accounts**. **Real (or permanent) accounts** are accounts that appear in the balance sheet. These accounts are not closed at the end of a period. They carry amounts forward from one period to the next.

We call the journal entries that transfer the balances of nominal accounts to retained earnings **closing entries**. The closing entries serve two primary purposes: (1) they close the nominal accounts to zero balances so that they are ready to accumulate information for the new accounting period, and (2) they transfer the net income or net loss for the current period and the dividends account to retained earnings.

To close the books, first we transfer (*close*) the revenue and expense accounts to Income Summary. Finally, we close Income Summary and the dividends account to retained earnings.

Four Steps in Preparing Closing Entries Directly from the Work Sheet

Learning Goal 7   **Record closing entries from the work sheet.**

We can make the closing entries directly from the work sheet in the following four-step sequence:

1. Debit each account in the Income Statement Credit column, and credit their sum (the subtotal in the Credit column) to the Income Summary account.

2. Credit each account in the Income Statement Debit column, and debit their sum (the subtotal in the Debit column) to the Income Summary account.

3. After posting entries 1 and 2, the balance of Income Summary represents the net income or the net loss. Transfer this amount to Retained Earnings.

4. Close the balance of Dividends to Retained Earnings. *The balance in the Dividends account is never closed to the Income Summary.* The amount in the Dividends account is not an expense and has nothing to do with determining income.

Using the work sheet, let's study the closing process for Metro Delivery, Inc.

Recording Closing Entries Directly from the Work Sheet

We record closing entries in the general journal directly from the work sheet using the four-step sequence outlined on the previous page.

Step 1.   Close the Revenue Accounts to Income Summary

Debit each revenue account in the Income Statement Credit column. Credit their sum (the subtotal in the Credit column) to Income Summary. This transfers the total revenues into the Income Summary account and reduces each revenue account to a zero balance.

Trucking Revenue				Income Summary		
12/31	7,500	Balance	7,500		12/31	7,610
		Balance	0			

Rent Revenue			
12/31	100	Balance	100
		Balance	0

Interest Revenue			
12/31	10	Balance	10
		Balance	0

Step 2.   Close the Expense Accounts to Income Summary

Credit each expense account in the Income Statement Debit column. Debit their sum (the subtotal in the Debit column) to Income Summary. This transfers the total expenses into the Income Summary account and reduces each expense account to a zero balance.

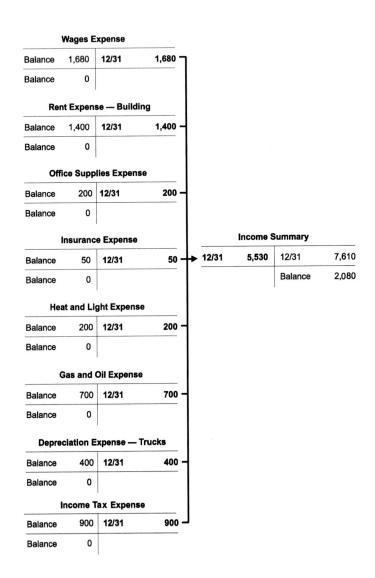

Step 3.   Close Income Summary to Retained Earnings

After posting entries 1 and 2, the balance of Income Summary is equal to the net income or the net loss. Now transfer it to Retained Earnings. In the Metro Delivery example, there is a credit balance of $2,080. To close the Income Summary account, debit it for this amount. The credit is to Retained Earnings. This increases the Retained Earnings account.

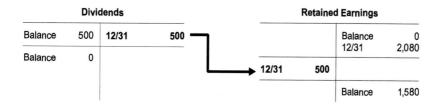

Income Summary					Retained Earnings		
12/31	5,530	12/31	7,610		Balance		0
					12/31		2,080
12/31	2,080	Balance	2,080				
		Balance	0		Balance		2,080

Step 4.   Close Dividends to Retained Earnings

Close the balance of Dividends to Retained Earnings. Since the dividends account has a debit balance, close it with a credit. The debit is to Retained Earnings. This reduces the retained earnings account by the amount of dividends.

Dividends					Retained Earnings		
Balance	500	12/31	500		Balance		0
					12/31		2,080
Balance	0						
				12/31	500		
					Balance		1,580

Exhibit 4.9 summarizes the closing procedure. It shows the flow of account balance information from the revenue and expense accounts to the Income Summary account. Then the flow goes from the Income Summary account to the retained earnings account. Finally, the flow is from the dividends account directly to the retained earnings account.

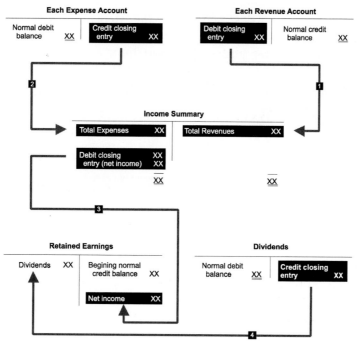

EXHIBIT **4.9**

The Closing Procedure Flow

GENERAL JOURNAL

Date		Account Titles and Explanations	PR	Debit	Credit
2007		Closing Entries			
Dec.	31	Trucking Revenue	420	7,500	
		Rent Revenue	430	100	
		Interest Revenue	431	10	
		Income Summary	999		7,610
		To close revenue accounts.			
	31	Income Summary	999	5,530	
		Wages Expense	705		1,680
		Rent Expense—Building	711		1,400
		Office Supplies Expense	718		200
		Insurance Expense	719		50
		Heat and Light Expense	721		200
		Gas and Oil Expense	726		700
		Depreciation Expense—Trucks	759		400
		Income Tax Expense	901		900
		To close expense accounts.			
	31	Income Summary	999	2,080	
		Retained Earnings	360		2,080
		To transfer net income to the retained earnings account.			
	31	Retained Earnings	360	500	
		Dividends	372		500
		To close the dividends account to the retained earnings account.			

EXHIBIT **4.10**

Closing Entries

Exhibit 4.10 shows the closing entries recorded in the Metro Delivery general journal. When we record these entries, we enter the caption "Closing Entries" on the journal page under the adjusting entries. After journalizing, post the closing entries to the general ledger.

THE POSTCLOSING TRIAL BALANCE

Learning Goal 8   Explain the purpose of a postclosing trial balance and prepare one.

After posting the closing entries, we prepare a *postclosing trial balance* from the general ledger. Exhibit 4.11 shows the postclosing trial balance for Metro Delivery. Only real accounts have balances at this time. Thus, *the accounts in the postclosing trial balance are the same as those in the balance sheet.* The postclosing trial balance tests the debit and credit equality of the general ledger before the next accounting period.

METRO DELIVERY, INC.
POSTCLOSING TRIAL BALANCE
DECEMBER 31, 2007

Acct. No.	Account Title	Debits	Credits
101	Cash	$ 6,500	
111	Accounts Receivable	2,100	
115	Notes Receivable	1,200	
117	Interest Receivable	10	
135	Office Supplies	100	
141	Prepaid Insurance	550	
169	Trucks	26,000	
170	Accumulated Depreciation—Trucks		$ 400
201	Accounts Payable		1,000
205	Wages Payable		80
215	Income Taxes Payable		900
231	Unearned Rent		500
331	Common Stock		32,000
360	Retained Earnings		1,580
	Totals	$36,460	$36,460

EXHIBIT **4.11**

Postclosing Trial Balance

ANALYZING INFORMATION

Learning Goal 9   Analyze financial statement information for real-life companies.

In Chapter 3, we introduced a ratio called *return on assets (ROA)*. This ratio asks "is a company operating efficiently by using the least amount of asset investment to generate a given level of net income?" To study changes in the rate of return on assets (ROA), we can disaggregate or separate the ROA ratio into two components: *profit margin* and *total asset turnover*. The profit margin percent (net income ÷ total revenues) measures a firm's ability to control the level of expenses relative to revenues. The total asset turnover ratio (revenues ÷ average total assets) measures a firm's ability to generate revenues from a given level of total asset investment. Disaggregating ROA into its two components allows the user to see the reasons for an increase or decrease in ROA. The relationship of profit margin, total asset turnover, and ROA is as follows:

$$\begin{array}{ccc} \text{PROFIT} & & \text{TOTAL ASSET} & & \text{RETURN ON} \\ \text{MARGIN} & \times & \text{TURNOVER} & = & \text{ASSETS (ROA)} \end{array}$$

$$\text{Return on Assets (ROA) Disaggregated} = \frac{\text{Net income}}{\text{Total revenues}} \times \frac{\text{Total revenues}}{\text{Average total assets}} = \frac{\text{Net income}}{\text{Average total assets}}$$

Observe that total revenues is used in both the profit margin and total asset turnover ratio formulas. By removing this common element from both formulas, return on assets (ROA) is net income divided by average total assets. To see why disaggregating ROA is useful in analyzing a company, look at the following results and computations for Apple Computer, Dell Computer, and Gateway Computer:

2004 FISCAL YEAR RESULTS:

	Total Revenues	Net Income	Average Total Assets
Apple	$ 8,279,000,000	$ 276,000,000	$ 7,432,500,000
Dell	$ 49,205,000,000	$ 3,043,000,000	$ 21,263,000,000
Gateway	$ 3,649,734,000	$ (567,818,000)	$ 1,900,112,500

ROA (disaggregated):

		PROFIT MARGIN	x	TOTAL ASSET TURNOVER	=	RETURN ON ASSETS (ROA)
Apple Computer	=	$\dfrac{\$\ \ 276{,}000{,}000}{\$\ \ 8{,}279{,}000{,}000}$	x	$\dfrac{\$\ \ 8{,}279{,}000{,}000}{\$\ \ 7{,}432{,}500{,}000}$	=	$\dfrac{\$\ \ 276{,}000{,}000}{\$\ \ 7{,}432{,}500{,}000}$
		3.334% x		1.114 =		3.713%
Dell Computer	=	$\dfrac{\$\ \ 3{,}043{,}000{,}000}{\$\ 49{,}205{,}000{,}000}$	x	$\dfrac{\$\ 49{,}205{,}000{,}000}{\$\ 21{,}263{,}000{,}000}$	=	$\dfrac{\$\ \ 3{,}043{,}000{,}000}{\$\ 21{,}263{,}000{,}000}$
		6.184% x		2.314 =		14.311%
Gateway Computer	=	$\dfrac{\$\ \ (567{,}818{,}000)}{\$\ \ 3{,}649{,}734{,}000}$	x	$\dfrac{\$\ \ 3{,}649{,}734{,}000}{\$\ \ 1{,}900{,}112{,}500}$	=	$\dfrac{\$\ \ (567{,}818{,}000)}{\$\ \ 1{,}900{,}112{,}500}$
		–15.558% x		1.921 =		–29.883%

Analyzing the results of the ROA analysis, we see that Gateway Computer had the lowest ROA (-29.883%), Apple was in the middle with (3.713%) and Dell Computer had the highest (14.311%). We can understand more about each company's performance when we look at the components of ROA, profit margin, asset turnover.

Dell had the highest total asset turnover, (2.314 times). This means that Dell generated about $2.31 in revenues for each dollar invested in assets. The management of this company was efficient in the use of assets in generating revenues. Apple had the lowest total asset turnover (1.114 times). They were only able to generate $1.11 in revenues for each dollar invested in assets. They were not as effective in generating revenues with their investment in assets. Gateway was the next lowest at 1.921 times.

Looking at profit margin, we see that Dell, Apple, and Gateway had different profit margins, Dell (6.184%), Apple (3.334%), and Gateway (-15.558%). This means, for example, that Dell generated 6.18 cents, Apple earned 3.33 cents and Gateway lost 15.56 cents in net income for each dollar of sales revenue. Since profit margin measures the efficiency in the control of operating expenses, the ratios indicate that management of Dell conducted their operations with higher efficiency. Gateway lost 15.56 cents in net income for each dollar of revenue. This indicates that Gateway and Apple were less efficient in operations than Dell.

By putting these two pieces of information (profit margin and total asset turnover) together, we can gain a better understanding of each company's performance. Dell had the highest profit margin, as well as the highest total asset turnover, resulting in a favorable return on assets of 14.311%. Apple had both lower profit margin and Asset turnover than Dell. Of the three companies, Gateway performed the worst.

The breakdown of return on assets into its component parts, *profit margin* and *total asset turnover*, points out that a company can work towards achieving a higher return on assets in two ways. First, the company can work to increase its profit margin by selling at a higher markup and/or controlling costs. Second, the company can also work to increase the revenues it generates from a given level of investment in assets. Return on assets is a product of profit margin and total asset turnover.

LEARNING GOALS REVIEW

1. List all of the steps in the accounting cycle.

    1. Collect business information from business documents.

    2. Analyze and journalize transactions.

    3. Post transactions to ledgers.

    4. Prepare an unadjusted trial balance.

    5. Prepare a work sheet.

    6. Prepare financial statements.

    7. Journalize and post adjusting entries.

    8. Journalize and post closing entries.

    9. Prepare postclosing trial balance.

2. Explain the purpose of a work sheet.

The work sheet is a working paper from which we prepare financial statements. It permits the accountant to calculate the effect of the end-of-period adjustments and determine the amount of net income or net loss for the period before journalizing and posting those adjustments to the ledger.

3. Prepare a work sheet.

There are five steps in preparing the work sheet:

    1. Enter the headings at the top of the work sheet. Enter the account numbers, titles, and general ledger account balances in the Trial Balance columns.

    2. Enter the adjustments in the Adjustments columns.

    3. Calculate the adjusted trial balance in the Adjusted Trial Balance columns.

    4. Extend the amounts in the Adjusted Trial Balance columns to the Income Statement columns or Balance Sheet columns.

    5. Subtotal the four financial statement columns of the work sheet. Determine the amount that will balance the Income Statement and Balance Sheet columns.

4. Prepare financial statements from the work sheet.

After completing the work sheet, we prepare the income statement from the amounts in the Income Statement columns of the work sheet. We then prepare the statement of owners' equity and balance sheet from the Balance Sheet columns.

5. Record adjusting entries from the work sheet.

Although we enter the adjustments on the work sheet, we must still journalize and post the adjusting entries. We take the adjusting entries directly from the Adjustments columns of the work sheet.

6. Explain the purpose of closing entries.

Closing entries serve two primary purposes. (1) They close the temporary or nominal accounts to zero balances so that they are ready to accumulate information in the new accounting period. (2) They transfer the net income or net loss for the current accounting period to the retained earnings account. They also close the dividends account to the retained earnings account.

7. Record closing entries from the work sheet.

We can make the closing entries directly from the work sheet in the following four-step sequence:

1. Debit each account in the Income Statement Credit column, and credit their sum (the subtotal in the Credit column) to the Income Summary account.

2. Credit each account in the Income Statement Debit column, and debit their sum (the subtotal in the Debit column) to the Income Summary account.

3. Transfer the balance of Income Summary to the retained earnings account.

4. Close the balance of the dividends account to the retained earnings account.

8. Explain the purpose of a postclosing trial balance and prepare one.

We prepare the postclosing trial balance after posting the closing entries. It contains only real or permanent accounts. The postclosing trial balance tests the debit and credit equality of the general ledger before the next accounting period.

9. Analyze financial statement information for real-life companies.

We can disaggregate or separate the return on assets (ROA) ratio into two components: *profit margin* and *total asset turnover*. The profit margin percent (net income ÷ total revenues) measures a firm's ability to control the level of expenses relative to revenues. The total asset turnover ratio (revenues ÷ average total assets) measures a firm's ability to generate revenues from a given level of total asset investment. Disaggregating ROA into its two components allows the user to see the reasons for changes in ROA.

DEMONSTRATION PROBLEM

Preparing a Work Sheet for a Company with a Net Loss

College Cab, Inc. provides a transportation service for students at a large university. The company was formed on January 1, 2005, when owners invested $40,000 in the business. At December 31, 2007, the firm prepared the following unadjusted trial balance:

COLLEGE CAB, INC.
UNADJUSTED TRIAL BALANCE
DECEMBER 31, 2007

Acct. No.	Account Title	Debits	Credits
101	Cash	$ 34,200	
111	Accounts Receivable	800	
135	Office Supplies	400	
141	Prepaid Insurance	5,400	
173	Automobiles	34,000	
174	Accumulated Depreciation—Automobiles		$ 12,000
201	Accounts Payable		850
202	Notes Payable		1,600
231	Unearned Rent		750
331	Common Stock		40,000
360	Retained Earnings		22,000
372	Dividends	1,000	
410	Revenues		54,000
705	Wages Expense	28,000	
711	Rent Expense—Building	15,000	
721	Heat and Light Expense	1,400	
726	Gas and Oil Expense	11,000	
	Totals	$131,200	$131,200

Other information required for adjustments follows:

a. Paid an insurance premium of $5,400 for a comprehensive 18-month insurance policy in cash on January 1, 2007.

b. During the year, the company purchased $400 of office supplies for cash. As of December 31, 2007, a physical count revealed that remaining office supplies on hand amounted to $50.

c. College Cab signed an agreement on November 1, 2007, to rent a vehicle on a part-time basis on weekends to Sue's Bridal Shop. College Cab collected rent of $750 in advance for three months starting November 1, 2007.

d. Four automobiles costing $8,500 each were purchased on January 1, 2005. Each automobile has an estimated life of five years and an estimated residual value of $1,000 ($4,000 in total) at the end of that period. The automobiles are depreciated uniformly over the five-year period by the straight-line method.

e. College Cab issued a $1,600 note payable on December 1, 2007. The note has an interest rate of 15% and is due in 60 days on January 30, 2008.

f. Wages of $120 for Monday, December 31, 2007, have not been paid or recorded.

g. The estimated income tax refund receivable due to a net loss is $3,000. This results in an income tax credit instead of an income tax expense.

REQUIRED
Prepare a work sheet for College Cab, Inc. for the year ended December 31, 2007.

SOLUTION

Solution Approach

Follow the five steps discussed in the chapter to prepare the work sheet.

1. Enter the headings at the top of the work sheet. Enter the account numbers, titles, and general ledger account balances in the Trial Balance columns.

2. Enter the adjustments in the Adjustments columns.

3. Calculate the adjusted trial balance in the Adjusted Trial Balance columns.

4. Extend the amounts in the Adjusted Trial Balance columns to the Income Statement columns or Balance Sheet columns.

5. Subtotal the four financial statement columns of the work sheet. Determine the amount that will balance the Income Statement and Balance Sheet columns.

Supporting calculations and comments for adjusting entries follow:

a. ($5,400 ÷ 18 months) × 12 months = $3,600 insurance expense for 2007.

b. $400 Office Supplies - $50 supplies left = $350 office supplies expense for 2007.

c. ($750 ÷ 3 months) × 2 months = $500 rent earned for 2007.

d. $8,500 - $1,000 = $7,500 ÷ 5 years = $1,500 depreciation expense per automobile for one year × 4 automobiles = $6,000.

e. $1,600 × 0.15 × 30/360 = $20 interest expense for 30 days.

f. Accrued wages = $120.

g. Accrued income tax refund receivable = $3,000.

Solution to Demonstration Problem

COLLEGE CAB, INC.
WORK SHEET
FOR THE YEAR ENDED DECEMBER 31, 2007

Acct. No.	Account Titles	Trial Balance Dr.	Trial Balance Cr.	Adjustments Dr.	Adjustments Cr.	Adjusted Trial Balance Dr.	Adjusted Trial Balance Cr.	Income Statement Dr.	Income Statement Cr.	Balance Sheet Dr.	Balance Sheet Cr.
101	Cash	34,200				34,200				34,200	
111	Accounts Receivable	800				800				800	
135	Office Supplies	400			(b) 350	50				50	
141	Prepaid Insurance	5,400			(a) 3,600	1,800				1,800	
173	Automobiles	34,000				34,000				34,000	
174	Accumulated Depreciation—Automobiles		12,000		(d) 6,000		18,000				18,000
201	Accounts Payable		850				850				850
202	Notes Payable		1,600				1,600				1,600
231	Unearned Rent		750	(c) 500			250				250
331	Common Stock		40,000				40,000				40,000
360	Retained Earnings		22,000				22,000				22,000
372	Dividends	1,000				1,000				1,000	
410	Revenues		54,000				54,000		54,000		
705	Wages Expense	28,000		(f) 120		28,120		28,120			
711	Rent Expense—Building	15,000				15,000		15,000			
721	Heat and Light Expense	1,400				1,400		1,400			
726	Gas and Oil Expense	11,000				11,000		11,000			
	Totals	131,200	131,200								
719	Insurance Expense			(a) 3,600		3,600		3,600			
718	Office Supplies Expense			(b) 350		350		350			
430	Rent Revenue				(c) 500		500		500		
755	Depreciation Expense—Automobile			(d) 6,000		6,000		6,000			
852	Interest Expense			(e) 20		20		20			
204	Interest Payable				(e) 20		20				20
205	Wages Payable				(f) 120		120				120
119	Income Tax Refund Receivable			(g) 3,000		3,000				3,000	
901	Income Tax Expense (Credit)				(g) 3,000		3,000		3,000		
	Totals			13,590	13,590	140,340	140,340	65,490	57,500	74,850	82,840
	Net loss for the year								7,990	7,990	
	Totals							65,490	65,490	82,840	82,840

GLOSSARY

adjusted trial balance A trial balance prepared after the adjusting entries are journalized and posted.

closing entries The journal entries that close the nominal accounts to capital at the end of a period—that is, reduce these accounts to a zero balance and transfer net income to capital.

cross-footing Horizontal addition or subtraction across columns.

dividends Distribution of net income, whether earned in the current period or in past periods.

nominal accounts Temporary accounts that measure part of the change in owners' equity during a period.

real accounts Accounts that are not closed at the end of a period and that appear in the balance sheet.

work sheet An orderly and systematic method of collecting information needed to prepare financial statements

QUESTIONS FOR GROUP LEARNING

Q4-1. Identify the steps an accountant would take at the end of an accounting period. Why is each step taken?

Q4-2. (a) What is the purpose of the work sheet? (b) Can the work of the accountant be completed without the use of the work sheet?

Q4-3. (a) Why are the parts of each entry in the Adjustment columns cross-referenced with either letters or numbers? (b) How is the amount to be extended into another column determined?

Q4-4. (a) What determines the column into which an amount in the Adjusted Trial Balance Column is to be extended? (b) Is the work sheet foolproof?

Q4-5. Student A argues that since the work sheet has columns headed Income Statement and Balance Sheet there is no need to prepare any end-of-period statement except the statement of owners' equity. Student B counters that a formal balance sheet, income statement, and statement of owners' equity should be prepared. With which student do you agree? Why?

Q4-6. Since adjustments are entered on the work sheet, does this step eliminate the need to journalize the adjustments and post them to the ledger accounts? Why or why not?

Q4-7. Is it possible to prepare the formal financial statements from a work sheet containing only trial balance and adjustments columns? Explain.

Q4-8. What is the purpose of closing entries? Describe the steps in closing.

Q4-9. (a) When would the amounts in Depreciation Expense and in Accumulated Depreciation be the same in the Adjusted Trial Balance column of the work sheet? (b) When would these amounts be different?

EXERCISES

E4-10. Partial work sheet (LG 3) Column totals for the partially completed work sheet of Falmouth Company are shown below:
Complete the work sheet.

Account Title		Income Statement		Balance Sheet	
		Dr.	Cr.	Dr.	Cr.
Totals		45,000	60,000	150,000	135,000

E4-11. Work sheet completion (LG 3) Tolland Care Company's adjusted trial balance, taken from the work sheet for the year ended December 31, 2007, was as follows:

TOLLAND CARE COMPANY
ADJUSTED TRIAL BALANCE
DECEMBER 31, 2007

Account Title	Debits	Credits
Cash	$ 70,000	
Accounts Receivable	25,000	
Equipment	60,000	
Accumulated Depreciation		$ 20,000
Accounts Payable		12,000
Notes Payable		16,000
Income Taxes Payable		5,700
Common Stock		82,000
Dividends	2,500	
Service Revenue		105,000
Heat and Light Expense	7,000	
Wages Expense	62,500	
Depreciation Expense	8,000	
Income Tax Expense	5,700	
Totals	$ 240,700	$ 240,700

Enter the adjusted trial balance on a work sheet and complete the work sheet.

E4-12. Work sheet and income statement (LG 3, 4) Following is the trialbalance of Theodore, Inc. for the month of June, the first month of operations (ignore income taxes):

THEODORE, INC.
TRIAL BALANCE
JUNE 30, 2007

Account Title	Debits	Credits
Cash	$ 9,000	
Accounts Receivable	2,500	
Service Supplies	900	
Accounts Payable		$ 1,000
Common Stock		10,000
Dividends	100	
Service Revenue		3,200
Advertising Expense	350	
Miscellaneous Expense	500	
Communication Expense	250	
Wages Expense	600	
Totals	$14,200	$14,200

Supplementary data on June 30 were as follows:

a. Service supplies on hand were $700.

b. Wages earned by employees but not paid were $300.

1. Enter the trial balance on a work sheet.

2. Complete the work sheet for June.

3. Prepare an income statement for the month.

E4-13. Work sheet with adjustments and discussion (LG 3) The books of Eastham Movie Theater, Inc. are closed annually on December 31. The company obtains revenue from admission fees and from a refreshment stand that is leased on a concession basis. Its general ledger showed the following unadjusted balances on December 31, 2007:

Cash	$ 30,200
Theater Supplies	4,600
Prepaid Insurance	3,200
Prepaid Rent	8,400
Projection Equipment	64,000
Accumulated Depreciation	15,000
Accounts Payable	5,000
Common Stock	62,700
Dividends	500
Admissions Revenue	48,000
Concession Revenue	18,200
Wages Expense	31,000
Heat And Light Expense	3,000
Miscellaneous Expense	4,000

Supplementary Data

a. Theater supplies on hand based on physical count total $600.

b. The balance of the Prepaid Insurance account represents the premium on a four-year insurance policy, effective January 1, 2007.

c. Rent expense for the year was $5,400.

d. The projection equipment has an expected useful life of 12 years and an estimated salvage value of $4,000. No equipment was acquired during the year.

e. Wages earned by employees but unpaid on December 31 were $900.

f. Estimated income taxes payable are $3,000.

   1. Enter the trial balance on a work sheet.

   2. Complete the work sheet.

   3. Why is the difference between the totals of the Income Statement columns and the Balance Sheet columns the same amount?

E4-14. Adjusting, closing, and future-year entries for accruals (LG 5, 7) Diane Company incurred the following transactions during 2007:

2007

Nov.	1	Received a 12%, 90-day note receivable for $7,200 dated today in exchange for an account receivable.
Dec.	1	Issued a 13%, 60-day note payable dated today in the amount of $3,600 to eliminate an account payable.
	31	The year ended on Tuesday. Weekly wages are $1,500, and Flyers has a five-day work week that ends on Friday.

   1. Journalize the transactions, adjusting entries, and closing of the nominal accounts created. No explanations are necessary.

   2. Prepare journal entries to record payment of the weekly wages, collection of the note receivable, and payment of the note payable in January 2008. (Wages are paid each Friday.)

E4-15. Adjusting entries and their statement effect (LG 4, 5) The following information is taken from Leanne Company's books as of December 31, 2007:

	Trial Balance Amount		**Adjustment Data**	
1.	Prepaid Insurance	$ 4,800	Expired insurance	$ 2,000
2.	Prepaid Rent	9,000	Rent paid in advance as of end of year	2,000
3.	Wages Expense	18,000	Accrued wages	1,000
4.	Interest Expense	900	Accrued interest	200
5.	Unearned Rent	6,500	Rent earned	2,500
6.	Interest Revenue	3,000	Accrued interest	800

For each account: (a) prepare the adjusting journal entry (omit explanations); (b) state the amount to be shown in the income statement; (c) state the amount to be shown in the balance sheet.

E4-16. Closing entries (LG 7) The following income statement has been prepared:

POLAR COMPANY
INCOME STATEMENT
FOR THE YEAR ENDED APRIL 30, 2007

Revenue		
Storage fees revenue		$ 62,000
Expenses		
Office rent expense	$ 9,000	
Salaries expense	30,000	
Miscellaneous expense	3,000	
Total expenses		42,000
Net income before income taxes		$ 20,000
Income tax expense		5,400
Net income		$14,600

During the year, the company paid $3,000 in dividends. Journalize closing entries necessary for Polar Company.

E4-17. Closing entries (LG 7, 8) The adjusted trial balance for Fast Car, Inc. for the year ended December 31, 2007, is shown below:

FAST CAR, INC.
ADJUSTED TRIAL BALANCE
DECEMBER 31, 2007

Acct. No.	Account Title	Debits	Credits
101	Cash	$ 30,000	
111	Accounts Receivable	3,000	
141	Prepaid Insurance	2,500	
173	Automobiles	40,000	
174	Accumulated Depreciation—Automobiles		$ 12,000
201	Accounts Payable		1,000
202	Notes Payable		2,000
215	Income Taxes Payable		7,500
331	Common Stock		20,000
360	Retained Earnings		16,500
372	Dividends	1,000	
413	Service Revenue		77,000
430	Rent Revenue		500
705	Wages Expense	28,000	
711	Rent Expense—Building	10,000	
718	Office Supplies Expense	2,000	
721	Heat and Light Expense	1,500	
726	Gas and Oil Expense	11,000	
901	Income Tax Expense	7,500	
	Totals	$136,500	$ 136,500

1. Prepare the closing entries for the year ended December 31, 2007.

2. Prepare a postclosing trial balance as of December 31, 2007.

E4-18. Effect of errors in adjustments on statements (LG 4) The inexperienced accountant for Sunny Company prepared the following condensed income statement for the year ended December 31, 2007, and the condensed balance sheet as of the same date (ignore income taxes):

SUNNY COMPANY
INCOME STATEMENT
FOR THE YEAR ENDED DECEMBER 31, 2007

Service revenue		$60,000
Operating expenses:		
Insurance expense	$ 4,000	
Miscellaneous expense	2,000	
Wages expense	25,000	31,000
Net income		$29,000

SUNNY COMPANY
BALANCE SHEET
DECEMBER 31, 2007
Assets

Cash		$ 6,000
Accounts receivable		15,000
Office supplies		3,000
Equipment		50,000
Total assets		$74,000
Liabilities		
Accounts payable		$10,000
Owners' Equity		
Common stock	$10,000	
Retained earnings	54,000	
Total owners' equity		64,000
Total liabilities and owners' equity		$74,000

The accountant overlooked the following items in preparing the statements:

a. Depreciation of equipment (acquired January 1, 2007): estimated life, 10 years; no salvage value.

b. Wages earned by employees that have not been paid, $1,000.

c. Office supplies on hand, $400.

    1. Journalize all necessary adjusting entries. No explanations are necessary.

    2. Prepare corrected classified financial statements after all adjustments have been made.

PROBLEMS

P4-19. Work sheet and end-of-period statements (no adjustments) (LG 3,4) Linda Computer Services, Inc. adjusted trial balance, taken from the work sheet for the month ended July 31, 2007, was as follows:

LINDA COMPUTER SERVICES, INC.
ADJUSTED TRIAL BALANCE
JULY 31, 2007

Account Title	Debits	Credits
Cash	$ 13,000	
Accounts Receivable	8,000	
Office Supplies	2,000	
Prepaid Insurance	1,600	
Land	20,000	
Building	76,000	
Accumulated Depreciation—Building		$ 10,000
Accounts Payable		5,000
Notes Payable (due November 1, 2007)		3,000
Income Taxes Payable		4,000
Notes Payable (due July 31, 2009)		9,000
Common Stock		56,600
Retained Earnings		20,000
Dividends	1,000	
Service Revenue		40,000
Heat and Light Expense	2,800	
Telephone Expense	600	
Wages Expense	10,000	
Office Supplies Expense	8,000	
Insurance Expense	600	
Depreciation Expense—Building	300	
Wages Payable		300
Interest Expense	100	
Interest Payable		100
Income Tax Expense	4,000	
Totals	$148,000	$148,000

REQUIRED

1. Enter the adjusted trial balance on a work sheet using the appropriate two columns.

2. Complete the work sheet.

3. Prepare an income statement, a statement of owners' equity, and a balance sheet.

P4-20. Completion of a work sheet (LG 3) The general ledger of Perfect Lawn Company showed the following balances at December 31, 2007. The books are closed annually on December 31. The company obtains revenue from its lawn services.

Account Title	Debits	Credits
Cash	$ 20,000	
Lawn Supplies	12,000	
Prepaid Insurance	10,000	
Prepaid Rent	12,000	
Lawn Equipment	85,000	
Accumulated Depreciation—Lawn Equipment		$22,000
Accounts Payable		40,000
Common Stock		6,000
Retained Earnings		10,000
Dividends	3,000	
Lawn Service Revenue		88,000
Wages Expense	16,000	
Maintenance Expense	3,000	
Utilities Expense	2,500	
Telephone Expense	500	
Miscellaneous Expense	2,000	
Totals	$166,000	$166,000

Supplementary data include the following:

a. Lawn supplies on hand, based on a physical count, totaled $1,000.

b. The balance of the Prepaid Insurance account represents the premium on a four-year insurance policy, effective January 1, 2007.

c. Rent expense for the year was $9,000.

d. The lawn equipment has an expected life of 10 years and a residual value of $5,000. No equipment was acquired during the year.

e. Salaries earned by employees but unpaid on December 31 were $500.

f. Estimated income taxes payable are $8,000.

REQUIRED

1. Enter the trial balance on a work sheet.

2. Complete the work sheet.

3. Why is the difference between the totals of the Income Statement columns and the totals of the Balance Sheet columns the same amount?

P4-21. **The complete accounting cycle (LG 3-5, 7, 8)** On April 1, 2007, Larry Repairing, Inc. started business. During April the following transactions were completed (ignore income taxes):

2007		

Apr.	1	Owners invested $20,000 to start Larry Repairing, Inc. Shares of common stock were issued to owners.
	2	Paid $500 for office supplies. Debited office supplies.
	3	Purchased secondhand office equipment for $1,000 in cash.
	4	Issued a check for $400 for April rent. Debited rent expense.
	5	Paid a premium of $240 for an insurance policy for 12 months on the equipment, effective April 1. Debited prepaid insurance.
	9	Purchased repair supplies on account as follow (debited repair supplies):

		Fulton and Sams, Inc.	$ 600
		Hintze Supply Company	700
		Total	$ 1,300

	15	Received $5,000 for repair work completed but not previously billed.
	19	Completed additional repair work and sent out bills, as follows:

		Ed Easley	$ 1,000
		Dale Martin	1,400
		Total	$ 2,400

	21	Paid $200 for the telephone service for the month.
	24	Paid the following creditors:

		Fulton and Sams, Inc.	$ 500
		Hintze Supply Company	400
		Total	$ 900

	28	Received cash from customers to apply on account, as follows:

		Ed Easley	$ 800
		Dale Martin	900
		Total	$ 1,700

	30	Expert Repairing declared and paid $1,500 in dividends to owners.

Supplementary data as of April 30, 2007, were as follows:

a. The insurance premium paid on April 5 is for one year.

b. A physical count shows that office supplies on hand total $200 and repair supplies on hand total $300.

c. The office equipment has an estimated useful life of five years with $100 salvage value. Use straight-line depreciation.

REQUIRED

1. Open the following accounts in the general ledger: Cash, 101; Accounts Receivable, 111; Office Supplies, 135; Repair Supplies, 137; Prepaid Insurance, 141; Office Equipment, 171; Accumulated Depreciation—Office Equipment, 172; Accounts Payable, 201; Common Stock, 331; Retained Earnings, 360; Dividends, 372; Repair Revenue, 411; Rent Expense, 615; Repair Supplies Expense, 620; Office Supplies Expense, 718; Insurance Expense, 719; Communication Expense, 722; Depreciation Expense—Office Equipment, 754; Income Summary, 999.

2. Record all the transactions in the general journal, post to the general ledger, and enter the general ledger account balances directly in the Trial Balance columns of the work sheet. No explanations are necessary.

3. Complete the work sheet.

4. Prepare an income statement, a statement of owners' equity, and a balance sheet.

5. Journalize adjusting journal entries in the general journal. No explanations are necessary.

6. Post the adjusting journal entries from the general journal to thegeneral ledger.

7. Prepare closing entries in the general journal and post to the general ledger.

8. Prepare a postclosing trial balance.

P4-22. Closing entries and postclosing trial balance (LG 7, 8) The trial balance of Storrs Company on December 31, 2007, follows:

STORRS COMPANY
ADJUSTED TRIAL BALANCE
DECEMBER 31, 2007

Acct. No.	Account Title	Debits	Credits
101	Cash	$12,000	
111	Accounts Receivable	6,000	
135	Supplies	3,000	
159	Equipment	35,000	
201	Accounts Payable		$10,000
215	Income Taxes Payable		2,000
331	Common Stock		16,500
360	Retained Earnings		20,000
372	Dividends	500	
410	Revenue		31,000
616	Advertising Expense	2,000	
620	Supplies Expense	4,000	
705	Salaries Expense	12,000	
791	Miscellaneous Expense	3,000	
901	Income Tax Expense	2,000	
	Totals	$79,500	$79,500

REQUIRED

1. Set up ledger accounts for Common Stock, Retained Earnings, Dividends, for each revenue and expense account listed in the trial balance, and the Income Summary account (Acct. No. 999). Enter the account balances.

2. Journalize the closing entries and post to the accounts (assign a page number to the journal).

3. Prepare a postclosing trial balance at the end of the fiscal year, December 31, 2007.

P4-23. Disaggregating ROA for Coca-Cola Company and Anheuser-Busch (LG 9) You are given the following results for Coca-Cola and Anheuser-Busch for the 2004 fiscal year:

2004 FISCAL YEAR RESULTS:

	Total Revenues	Net Income	Average Total Assets
Coca-Cola	$21,962,000,000	$4,847,000,000	$29,334,500,000
Anheuser-Busch	14,934,000,000	2,240,300,000	15,431,450,000

REQUIRED

1. Compute the profit margin percent, total asset turnover ratio, and return on total assets ratio for each company using the following format to disaggregate ROA:

$$\text{PROFIT MARGIN} \times \text{TOTAL ASSET TURNOVER} = \text{RETURN ON ASSETS (ROA)}$$

2. Comment briefly on the reasons why ROA is higher for one company than the other.

P4-24. Disaggregating ROA for Motorola and Nokia (LG 9) You are given the following results for Motorola and Nokia for the 2004 fiscal year:

2004 FISCAL YEAR RESULTS:

	Total Revenues	Net Income	Average Total Assets
Motorola	$31,323,000,000	$1,532,000,000	$ 31,493,500,000
Nokia	39,931,895,000	4,561,189,000	30,894,996,000

REQUIRED

1. Compute the profit margin percent, total asset turnover ratio, and return on total assets ratio for each company using the following format to disaggregate ROA:

$$\text{PROFIT MARGIN} \times \text{TOTAL ASSET TURNOVER} = \text{RETURN ON ASSETS (ROA)}$$

2. Comment briefly on the reasons why ROA is higher for one company than the other.

PRACTICE CASE

Completion of the accounting cycle (LG 3-5, 7, 8) Andy Car Service, Inc. provides minor repairs on cars directly at the customer's home or business through the use of a mobile repair truck. The company was formed on July 1, 2006, when owners invested $10,000 in the business. At December 31, 2007, the following unadjusted trial balance was prepared from the general ledger:

ANDY CAR SERVICE, INC.
TRIAL BALANCE
DECEMBER 31, 2007

Acct. No.	Account Title	Debits	Credits
101	Cash	$ 36,000	
111	Accounts Receivable	4,000	
137	Repair Supplies	9,000	
141	Prepaid Insurance	2,400	
169	Trucks	18,000	
170	Accumulated Depreciation—Trucks		$ 1,000
201	Accounts Payable		2,000
202	Notes Payable		3,600
233	Unearned Service Revenue		5,000
331	Common Stock		10,000
360	Retained Earnings		10,400
372	Dividends	2,000	
411	Repair Revenue		80,000
705	Wages Expense	29,000	
711	Rent Expense—Building	5,000	
721	Utilities Expense	2,000	
726	Gas and Oil Expense	4,600	
	Totals	$112,000	$112,000

Other information required for adjustments follows:

a. An insurance premium of $2,400 for a comprehensive 12-month insurance policy was paid in cash on May 1, 2007.

b. Andy Car Service received $5,000 in cash on December 1, 2007, from customers who purchased gift certificates for car repairs. The gift certificates are good for a one-year period. During the month of December 2007, $3,000 of the gift certificates were redeemed and the repair services were rendered.

c. During the year, $9,000 of repair supplies were purchased for cash. As of December 31, 2007, a physical count revealed that remaining repair supplies on hand amounted to $1,000.

d. A truck costing $18,000 was purchased on July 1, 2006. The truck has an estimated life of eight years and an estimated salvage value of $2,000. The truck is depreciated by the straight-line method.

e. Wages of $200 for the partial week ended December 31, 2007, have not been paid or recorded.

f. Andy Car Service issued a $3,600 note payable on November 1, 2007. The note has an interest rate of 10% and is due in 180 days.

g. Income taxes are estimated at $8,000.

REQUIRED

1. Prepare a work sheet for Andy Car Service, Inc. for the year ended December 31, 2007.

2. Prepare an income statement, statement of owners' equity, and balance sheet for the year ended December 31, 2007.

3. Journalize all adjusting entries.

4. Journalize the closing entries.

BUSINESS DECISION AND COMMUNICATION PROBLEM

Disaggregating ROA for three companies in different industries: Hershey Foods (candy), Lowes (building/home supplies), and Walt Disney (entertainment) (LG 9) You work as an investment advisor for Adams Investments. Your supervisor, Pam Adams has given you the following results for Hershey Foods, Lowes, and Walt Disney for the 2004 fiscal year:

2004 FISCAL YEAR RESULTS:

	Total Revenues	Net Income	Average Total Assets
Hershey Foods	$ 4,429,248,000	$ 590,879,000	$ 3,690,035,500
Lowes	36,464,000,000	2,176,000,000	20,125,500,000
Walt Disney	30,752,000,000	2,345,000,000	51,945,000,000

Pam Adams has asked you to develop answers to the following questions:

1. Compute the profit margin percent, total asset turnover ratio, and return on total assets ratios for each company using the following format to disaggregate ROA:

$$\begin{array}{ccc} \text{PROFIT} \\ \text{MARGIN} \end{array} \times \begin{array}{c} \text{TOTAL ASSET} \\ \text{TURNOVER} \end{array} = \begin{array}{c} \text{RETURN ON} \\ \text{ASSETS (ROA)} \end{array}$$

2. Which company has the highest profit margin? Comment briefly on the reasons why profit margin is higher for this company.

3. Which company has the highest total asset turnover? Comment briefly on the reasons why total asset turnover is highest for this company.

4. Which company has the highest return on assets? Comment briefly on the reasons why total assets is higher for this company..

REQUIRED
Write a memo to Pam Adams addressing these items.

ETHICAL DILEMMA

Changing the company's accounting methods to raise net income You are an accountant working for a computer consulting company that operates as a proprietorship. The owner is worried about the unchanged level of income over the past three years. The primary source of revenue is consulting assignments. The main expense is wages and salaries of the employees. Depreciation on computer equipment is also a major expense. You have been appointed by the chief financial officer to a planning committee. The charge to the committee is to consider ways to improve the performance of the company.

At the first meeting, the discussion begins with suggestions on monitoring the efficiency of the staff. A member suggests that the firm could delay some planned acquisition of new computers. One of the committee members, a good friend of the chief financial officer, suggests that a quick way to increase the income of the firm is to change some of the accounting methods that are being used. He states that "after all, many of the items are estimates anyway." One of the suggestions is to increase the estimated useful lives of the computer equipment. Also, he suggested that the business could accrue revenues for work on jobs that have been started but not completed. He stated that in both cases the company has been very conservative in the past. These changes he said "would give a quick boost to income."

REQUIRED
What would be the financial implications of the committee member's suggestions? What alternative actions are available to you? Discuss the ethical implications of each.

PRACTICE SET I (CHAPTERS 1–4)

This Practice Set May Be Assigned after Chapter 3 or 4

Environmentally Sound was formed as a corporation on December 1, 2007. The purpose of the business was to assist in properly disposing of toxic wastes. An accounting firm has helped set up the accounting system You have been hired part-time to keep the accounting records. You will be responsible for journalizing and posting the transactions, adjustments, and preparing financial statements.

The accounting records used by the business include the general journal and the general ledger. The chart of accounts designed by the accounting firm is as follows:

101 Cash	372 Dividends
111 Accounts Receivable	413 Service Revenue
137 Supplies	616 Advertising Expense
141 Prepaid Insurance	705 Wages Expense
159 Equipment	711 Rent Expense—Building
160 Accumulated Depreciation—Equipment	718 Supplies Expense
169 Trucks	719 Insurance Expense
170 Accumulated Depreciation—Trucks	721 Utilities Expense
201 Accounts Payable	722 Communication Expense
202 Notes Payable	723 Repairs Expense
204 Interest Payable	726 Gas and Oil Expense
205 Wages Payable	753 Depreciation Expense—Equipment
215 Income Taxes Payable	759 Depreciation Expense—Trucks
233 Unearned Service Revenue	852 Interest Expense
331 Common Stock	901 Income Tax Expense
360 Retained Earnings	999 Income Summary (If assigned after *Chapter 4*)

During December, Environmentally Sound completed the following transactions:

2007

Dec.	1	Environmentally Sound was formed with an initial investment by shareholders of $50,000. Shares of common stock were issued to owners.
	2	Paid $1,000 for December's rent on a building in which to operate the business.
	2	Paid $3,600 for a used truck for use in the business. The estimated useful life is two years. The truck is not expected to have any value at the end of its useful life.
	3	Purchased equipment at a cost of $5,000 on account. The equipment has an estimated useful life of four years and a salvage value of $200.
	6	Purchased supplies on account from the following suppliers:

Storage Supply Co.	$200
Shore Chemicals	400
Absorbent Materials	100
Total	$700

	8	Paid $600 for a six-month insurance policy effective December 1, 2007.
	10	Billed customers for work completed during the week as follows:

Bend Platers	$2,000
Green Yard Service	1,000
House Painters, Inc.	2,200
Total	$5,200

10	Paid $300 for an advertisement placed in the Sunday business section of the local newspaper announcing the opening of Environmentally Sound. The advertisement will appear in the paper on December 12, 2007.
13	Received $400 from a customer for services not previously billed.
14	Paid $300 for repairs on the truck.
15	Decided to pay employees twice monthly on the 1st and 15th of each month. Paid $800 to employees for the first half of December.
16	Borrowed $8,000 from the First State Bank signing a 12%, 120-day note dated today.
17	Paid Storage Supply Co. the $200 owed on account.
17	Billed customers for services completed during the week as follows:

Bend Platers	$2,000
Green Yard Service	1,000
House Painters, Inc.	2,200
Total	$5,200

20	Received cash of $1,000 from Green Yard Service on account.
21	Paid Shore Chemicals the $400 owed on account.
22	Purchased $300 additional repair supplies from Storage Supply Co. on account.
22	Received $1,000 cash from Bend Platers on account.
23	Received $900 from Hills Manufacturing for services to be rendered during the remainder of December and January.
27	Received $600 cash from customers for services completed but not previously billed.
28	Paid the $5,000 owed for the equipment purchased on December 3.
28	Paid $150 for gasoline purchased during December.
29	Paid $100 telephone bill for the month of December.
30	Received the utility bill in the amount of $200 for December's utilities.

Adjustment Data?

a. Accrue $800 wages expense for the last half of December.

b. A physical count shows supplies on hand total $400.

c. Record the expiration of one month's insurance.

d. As of December 31, 2007, $300 of the amount received from Hills Manufacturing had been earned.

e. Accrue interest on the note to First State Bank.

f. Record depreciation on the truck and equipment.

g. Estimated income taxes accrued are $900.

Requirements When Assigned after Chapter 3

1. Open general ledger accounts for the accounts listed in the chart of accounts.

2. Journalize the transactions in the general journal.

3. Post to the general ledger.

4. Prepare an unadjusted trial balance.

5. Journalize and post adjustments.

6. Prepare an adjusted trial balance.

7. Prepare an income statement, a statement of owners' equity, and a balance sheet.

Requirements When Assigned after Chapter 4

1. Open general ledger accounts for the accounts listed in the chart of accounts.

2. Journalize the transactions in the general journal.

3. Post to the general ledger.

4. Enter the trial balance on a work sheet and complete the work sheet.

5. Prepare an income statement, a statement of owners' equity, and a balance sheet.

6. Journalize and post adjustments.

7. Journalize and post closing entries.

8. Prepare a postclosing trial balance.

ACCOUNTING FOR A MERCHANDISING BUSINESS

CHAPTER

5

"The whole art of teaching is only the art of awakening the natural curiosity of young minds for the purpose of satisfying it afterwards.

Anatole France

LEARNING GOALS

After studying Chapter 5, you should be able to:

1. Show the difference between the calculation of net income for service and merchandising businesses.

2. Identify the sales revenue accounts and calculate net sales revenue.

3. Distinguish between a periodic and a perpetual inventory system.

4. Calculate cost of goods sold for the period.

5. Prepare a multiple-step income statement and compare it to a single-step income statement.

6. Describe the classifications of operating expenses.

7. Describe the updating of the Merchandise Inventory account at the end of the period using closing entries and complete the work sheet.

8. Explain how the net price method enables managers to control the cost of buying merchandise.

9. Analyze financial statement information for real-life companies.

UNDERSTANDING BUSINESS ISSUES

So far in this book, we have studied accounting methods and financial statements for service companies. In chapters 1 through 4, we used service companies such as Recycle Consultants and Metro Delivery. These businesses earned their revenues by providing a service.

Many businesses, such as The Gap, Inc., Circuit City, and Wal-Mart earn revenue by buying goods and reselling them to customers. They are called *merchandising businesses*. The financial information provided by a merchandiser is different from that of a service company. One major cost incurred by a merchandising business is *cost of goods sold*. The 2004 fiscal year financial statements for The Gap, Inc., showed sales of merchandise of $16,267 million. The cost of that merchandise to

The Gap., Inc. was $9,886 million, which represents 60.8% of sales. The cost of goods sold is a major cost that appears on the income statement of a merchandising company.

In this chapter, we will study the accounts used to record the transactions for a merchandising company. We also will look at the differences in the work sheet and the financial statements for a merchandiser. Our focus is on the additional information contained in the accounting system of a merchandising business.

INCOME CALCULATION FOR A MERCHANDISING BUSINESS

Learning Goal 1   Show the difference between the calculation of net income for service and merchandising businesses.

There are important differences between calculating income for a service business and for a merchandising business. Exhibit 5.1 compares the major income statement categories for a service business and a merchandising business. The amounts used are for Metro Delivery and TeleVideo Distributors. Net income for the year ended December 31, 2007, for both businesses equals the difference between revenues and expenses. But the merchandising business has different types of revenue and expense items on its income statement. **Cost of goods sold** is the cost to the merchandising firm of the goods sold to customers during a period of time. The difference between cost of goods sold and net sales revenue is **gross margin on sales** (or simply gross margin). Gross margin gives us information on the ability to sell merchandise at a price greater than its cost. We deduct operating expenses from gross margin to calculate **net operating margin**. Net operating margin measures management's ability to control operating expenses such as salaries, supplies, and utilities. *Other revenues* and *other expenses* are items that do not relate to the primary source of revenue. Examples include rent revenue and interest expense. We will now study each part of the income statement for TeleVideo Distributors in detail.

NET SALES REVENUE

Learning Goal 2   Identify the sales revenue accounts and calculate net sales revenue.

Merchandising businesses maintain three accounts to collect sales transaction data. In this section we examine the Sales account and trade discounts, the Sales Returns and Allowances account, and the Sales Discounts account. We calculate *net sales revenue* using the balances in these accounts at the end of the period.

Sales

Sales are transactions in which we exchange goods for cash or a promise to pay at a later date. The revenue account **Sales** records total or *gross sales* of merchandise. We record sales of merchandise by debiting Cash or Accounts Receivable and crediting the Sales account. A copy of an invoice showing a sale to J&Z Movie Rentals for $200 on account appears in Exhibit 5.2. The journal entry for the sale to J&Z Movie Rental on account would be as follows:

2007					
Dec.	6		Accounts Receivable	200	
			Sales		200
			Sold merchandise on account to J&Z Movie Rentals.		

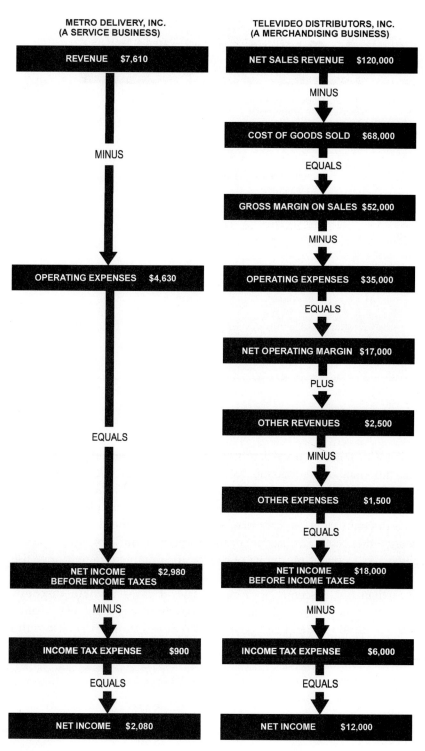

**METRO DELIVERY, INC.
(A SERVICE BUSINESS)**

REVENUE $7,610

MINUS

OPERATING EXPENSES $4,630

EQUALS

NET INCOME $2,980
BEFORE INCOME TAXES

MINUS

INCOME TAX EXPENSE $900

EQUALS

NET INCOME $2,080

**TELEVIDEO DISTRIBUTORS, INC.
(A MERCHANDISING BUSINESS)**

NET SALES REVENUE $120,000

MINUS

COST OF GOODS SOLD $68,000

EQUALS

GROSS MARGIN ON SALES $52,000

MINUS

OPERATING EXPENSES $35,000

EQUALS

NET OPERATING MARGIN $17,000

PLUS

OTHER REVENUES $2,500

MINUS

OTHER EXPENSES $1,500

EQUALS

NET INCOME $18,000
BEFORE INCOME TAXES

MINUS

INCOME TAX EXPENSE $6,000

EQUALS

NET INCOME $12,000

EXHIBIT **5.1**

Comparison of Income Statements for Service and Merchandising Businesses

The debit to Accounts Receivable records an increase in an asset. The credit to Sales, a revenue account, records the gross increase in owners' equity. We record the entire sale price of the goods as revenue. Later in this chapter we will see how to calculate the total cost of the goods which were sold.

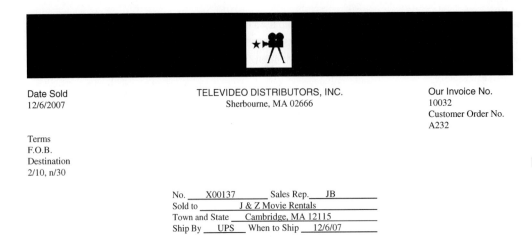

Date Sold 12/6/2007		TELEVIDEO DISTRIBUTORS, INC. Sherbourne, MA 02666		Our Invoice No. 10032 Customer Order No. A232	

Terms
F.O.B.
Destination
2/10, n/30

No. ___X00137___ Sales Rep.___JB___
Sold to _____J & Z Movie Rentals_____
Town and State ___Cambridge, MA 12115____
Ship By ___UPS___ When to Ship ___12/6/07___

Item No.	Shipper's Check	Quantity	Description	Price	Amount
67181	✓	11	Titanic	$10	$110
4979	✓	6	Star Wars	$15	90
			Total		$200

EXHIBIT 5.2

Sales Invoice

Trade Discounts

Businesses often print a catalog with standard price lists of their goods. To offer different prices to various groups of customers, they may offer discounts from these list prices. The discount may depend on the class of buyer (wholesaler or retailer) or the quantity ordered. This type of discount is called a **trade discount** and is a percentage reduction from a list price. We calculate the invoice price by subtracting the trade discount from the list price. We then record the transaction at the invoice price. We do not record either the trade discount or the list price in the accounting records. Granting trade discounts eliminates frequent reprinting of catalogs or printing different price lists for different classes of buyers.

If a business gives more than one discount on a single sale, it gives a **chain discount**. In calculating the invoice price, we apply each discount successively to the declining balance. Assume that TeleVideo's h as a cash sale to Sight and Sound Video Stores for merchandise with a list price of $625 less trade discounts of 20% and 10%. TeleVideo computes the invoice price as follows:

List price	$625
Less 20% discount (0.20 × $625)	125
Remainder	$500
Less 10% discount (0.10 × $500)	50
Invoice price	$450

Another way to compute the invoice price is to multiply the list price by the complements of the discounts. In this case, $625 × 0.80 × 0.90 = $450. Because we record the sale at the invoice price, there is no need to record trade discounts in the accounts.

Sales Returns and Allowances

A customer may return merchandise because it is defective or broken. Or the customer may request a *price allowance* because the goods were not as ordered. The effect of an entry to record a return or allowance is the opposite of a sale. We debit an account called **Sales Returns and Allowances**, a contra account to Sales. The Sales account shows management total sales and its contra account shows the returns and allowances. If J&Z Movie Rentals returned five copies of Titanic, order number 67181, the journal entry would be as follows (see invoice in Exhibit 5.2 for the price):

2007					
Dec.	9	Sales Returns and Allowances		50	
		Accounts Receivable			50
		Defective merchandise was returned by J&Z Movie Rentals.			

TeleVideo issues a business form called a **credit memorandum** to J&Z Movie Rentals. The seller is advising the customer that it has credited the customer's account on its books. A separate account keeps track of the amount of sales returns and allowances so that management has information on the extent of the returns. Either a return or an allowance indicates that a problem exists for the selling company. It is delivering merchandise that does not meet customer expectations. If this happens too frequently, a business will lose customers. By keeping track of sales returns and allowances, we can alert management to potential problems.

Sales Discounts

The invoice shows the terms of a sale of merchandise on credit. Often a business offers a discount to customers who pay within a stated time period. We call this reduction a **cash discount**. Businesses do this to speed up the cash inflow. This allows the business to buy new merchandise or meet other obligations.

We compute cash discounts on the invoice amount. The invoice shows the payment terms. For example, the sales invoice in Exhibit 5.2 shows sales terms of *2/10, n/30*. We read this as "two ten, net thirty." The buyer may deduct 2% from the invoice amount by paying the account within 10 days from the date of the invoice. The buyer may instead pay the total (or *net*) invoice price within 30 days from the date of the invoice. The **discount period** is the period in which the discount is available. Other common credit terms are *n/30* (net invoice price due in 30 days after invoice date) and *n/10 EOM* (net invoice price due 10 days after the end of the month).

To show how important the cash discount is, we can convert the discount into its equivalent annual interest rate. Assuming terms of 2/10, n/30, the cost to the customer of waiting the additional 20 days is high. The loss of the 2% discount amounts to 0.1% per day (2% ÷ 20), or 36% per 360-day year (0.1% x 360).

Since a discount reduces the cash received from the sale, we debit it to **Sales Discounts**, a contra account to Sales. When we offer discounts, the customer has the choice of paying either the full amount of the invoice or the reduced amount. The seller does not know at the time of the sale whether the customer is going to take the discount. If the seller receives payment within the discount period, it records the collection as follows:

2007						
Dec.	16	Cash			147	
		Sales Discounts			3	
		Accounts Receivable				150
		Received payment from J&Z Movie Rentals for the				
		sale of December 6 less the 2% cash discounts:				
		Gross sale price	$200			
		Merchandise returned	50			
		Accounts receivable balance	$150			
		2% cash discount	3			
		Cash received	$147			

Note that the sales discount applies only to the $150 of merchandise actually kept.

Calculating Net Sales Revenue

At the end of the accounting period, we use the balances in the Sales account and its two contra accounts, Sales Returns and Allowances and Sales Discounts, to determine net sales revenue. The following partial income statement for TeleVideo Distributors shows the calculation of net sales revenue using assumed amounts:

Gross sales revenue		$125,000
Deduct: Sales returns and allowances	$ 3,000	
Sales discounts	2,000	5,000
Net sales revenue		$120,000

Sales Taxes Payable

Most states levy a sales tax on certain types of merchandise. They levy the tax on the customer but require the seller to collect the tax. The seller periodically remits the tax to the appropriate governmental unit. To illustrate, assume that a state levies a retail sales tax of 4% on all sales in the state. If Sight and Sound Video sells a tape it bought from TeleVideo for $50 cash, it would have to collect $52. We record this transaction as follows:

2007						
Dec.	30	Cash			52	
		Sales				50
		Sales Tax Payable				2
		To record cash sales with a 4% sales tax.				

Although Sight and Sound collects the sales taxes, the amount belongs to the state government. The company must create a liability for the amount payable to the state government. It is a current liability. The company must file a sales tax return, usually each month. At the time the company files the return, it pays the sales tax. The entry debits Sales Taxes Payable and credits Cash.

MERCHANDISE INVENTORY SYSTEMS

Learning Goal 3   Distinguish between a periodic and a perpetual inventory system.

Merchandising firms keep a stock of goods on hand for sale to customers. We call this stock of goods *merchandise inventory*. Accounting for inventory may use two alternative systems, periodic or perpetual. Under the **periodic inventory system**, we determine the cost of goods sold and the ending inventory balance only at the end of each accounting period. This is the system we introduce in this chapter. We start by using a periodic inventory system because it is an easier way to learn the basics of accounting for a merchandising business.

Under the **perpetual inventory system**, we determine the cost of the product sold and the inventory balance on hand at each sale. As a result, perpetual inventory produces a continuous record of cost of goods sold and inventory on hand. Chapter 11 presents the perpetual inventory system. In the past, the type of merchandise sold often determined which inventory system to use. Sellers of high-cost, low-volume items such as automobiles, furniture, or appliances used perpetual inventory systems. It was easy to keep track of each sale. Businesses selling high-volume, low-cost merchandise, such as hardware stores or supermarkets, found it more efficient to use the periodic inventory system. Computers have blurred this distinction. Using bar codes and point-of-sale terminals, any business can maintain daily inventory balances and cost of sales information for diverse types of high-volume merchandise.

COST OF GOODS SOLD ACCOUNTS: PERIODIC INVENTORY SYSTEM

Learning Goal 4   Calculate cost of goods sold for the period.

Earlier, Exhibit 5.1 showed cost of goods sold as a deduction from net sales revenue to determine gross margin on sales. In this section we begin by describing the accounts used to record purchases of merchandise. Then we explain how to calculate cost of goods sold.

Purchases

The periodic inventory system uses a separate **Purchases** account to record the cost of all merchandise bought for resale. We do not record the purchase of operating supplies or store equipment in the Purchases account. During the accounting period, we debit the Purchases account with the cost of each purchase of merchandise. The Purchases account is a record of the cost of the goods purchased during the period. A typical journal entry to record a purchase of merchandise on account of $800 from Lyon Studio is as follows:

2007					
Dec.	5	Purchases		800	
		Accounts Payable			800
		Purchases merchandise on account, terms 1/10, n/30.			

Transportation In

The invoice price of goods may include the cost of transportation from the seller's place of business to the buyer's. If so, we make no separate record of the transportation costs—we debit the entire cost to purchases. If the seller does not include the transportation cost, we must decide who is responsible for this cost. Normally, the *owner of the goods during transit* is responsible for freight costs. To decide ownership, we refer to the *F.O.B.* (free on board) *terms* of the transaction. Two common F.O.B. terms are as follows:

F.O.B. shipping point means that title (ownership) to goods passes to the buyer when the seller turns the shipment over to a common carrier (party transporting goods). This means that the *buyer* is the owner during transit and is responsible for transportation costs.

F.O.B. destination means that title to goods passes to the buyer at the destination. This means that the *seller* is the owner during transit and is responsible for transportation costs.

The following table helps explain the ownership and responsibility for transportation costs.

F.O.B. Terms	Ownership during Transit	Responsibility for Transportation Costs
F.O.B. shipping point	Buyer	Buyer
F.O.B. destination	Seller	Seller

When the cost of transportation is the responsibility of the buyer, it debits the cost to **Transportation In**. We add this account balance to purchases in the income statement to find the gross delivered cost of purchases. Assuming a company purchases goods F.O.B. shipping point, it will make the following entry when it pays the freight bill.

2007					
Dec.	7	Transportation In		50	
		Cash			50
		Paid freight charges on merchandise purchased.			

Purchases Returns and Allowances

Goods bought for resale may be defective, broken, or not of the quality or quantity ordered. We may return them for credit, or the seller may make an adjustment by reducing the original price. In either case, the buyer makes the following entry:

2007					
Dec.	8	Accounts Payable		100	
		Purchases Returns and Allowances			100
		Returned defective merchandise to vendor: Lyon Studio.			

Purchases Returns and Allowances is a contra account to Purchases. We could accomplish the same result by crediting Purchases directly. But, top management can control operations more effectively by having separate information on returns. For example, excessive returns might result from poor decisions by managers in charge of purchasing. Or it might pinpoint problems with particular suppliers. Information about returns and allowances is important for controlling operations.

Purchases Discounts

We use the **Purchases Discounts** account to record cash discounts allowed for payments made within the discount period. It is a contra account to Purchases. An entry for payment within the discount period is as follows:

2007						
Dec.	13	Accounts Payable			700	
		Cash				693
		Purchases Discounts				7
		Paid for merchandise purchased on December 5 less discount:				
		Gross sale price	$800			
		Merchandise returned	100			
		Accounts payable balance	$700			
		1% payable discount	7			
		Cash paid	$693			

Net Cost of Purchases

The **net cost of purchases** is the invoice cost of purchases plus transportation in, minus purchases returns and allowances and purchases discounts. The calculation for TeleVideo Distributors is as follows:

Purchases		$65,000	
Transportation in		5,000	
Gross delivered cost of purchases		$70,000	
Deduct: Purchases returns and allowances	$2,000		
Purchases discounts	4,000	6,000	
Net cost of purchases			$64,000

Merchandise Inventory

The periodic inventory system records merchandise purchased for resale at *invoice cost* in the Purchases account. An account called **Merchandise Inventory** shows the cost of merchandise on hand at the end of each accounting period. We determine the ending inventory amount by taking a physical count of the units on hand and pricing them at their respective unit costs. During the accounting period, the amount in the Merchandise Inventory account is the beginning inventory balance. At the end of the period, we remove the beginning inventory balance and replace it by the new ending inventory amount.

In the periodic inventory system, journal entries to change the inventory balance are necessary at the end of the accounting period. Some accountants treat these as closing entries and others view them as adjusting entries. The method used has a minor impact on the work sheet and the closing entries, as we illustrate later in this chapter. We remove the beginning inventory balance by a debit to Income Summary and a credit to the Merchandise Inventory account. We set up the new ending inventory amount by a debit to Merchandise Inventory and a credit to Income Summary. After posting of the entries, the Merchandise Inventory account in the general ledger of TeleVideo Distributors appears as follows:

		Merchandise Inventory					Acct. No. 130	
						Balance		
Date		**Explanation**	**PR**	**Debit**	**Credit**	**Debit**	**Credit**	
2006 Dec.	31			15,000		**1** 15,000		
2007 Dec.	31				**2** 15,000	0		
	31			**3** 11,000		11,000		

1 The debit balance of $15,000 is the cost of the merchandise inventory on hand as of December 31, 2006 (the beginning inventory for 2007).

2 The credit posting of $15,000 temporarily reduces the account to zero.

3 The debit posting of $11,000 is the cost of the merchandise inventory on hand as of December 31, 2007 (the ending inventory). This amount will remain unchanged in the account until we change the account again on December 31, 2008.

Calculating Cost of Goods Sold

We can now look at the cost of goods sold section of TeleVideo Distributors' income statement for the year ended December 31, 2007. We add the beginning inventory to the net cost of purchases to arrive at the cost of goods available for sale. Then we deduct the ending inventory to arrive at the *cost of goods sold*, as follows:

Cost of goods sold:			
Merchandise inventory, January 1, 2007*			$ 15,000
Purchases		$ 65,000	
Transportation in		5,000	
Gross delivered cost of purchases		$ 70,000	
Deduct: Purchases returns and allowances	$2,000		
Purchases discounts	4,000	6,000	
Net cost of purchases			64,000
Cost of goods available for sale			$ 79,000
Deduct: Merchandise inventory,			
December 31, 2007			11,000
Cost of goods sold			$ 68,000

* Same as merchandise inventory December 31, 2006

Gross Margin on Sales

The *gross margin on sales* is the difference between net sales revenue and cost of goods sold. The term *gross* means that we must still deduct the expenses necessary to operate the business to arrive at the net operating margin. We can summarize the net sales and cost of goods for TeleVideo Distributors into a partial income statement for the year ended December 31, 2007, as follows. This shows the determination of gross margin on sales.

Net sales revenue	$ 120,000
Cost of goods sold	68,000
Gross margin on sales	$ 52,000

MULTIPLE-STEP INCOME STATEMENT

Learning Goal 5   Prepare a multiple-step income statement and compare it to a single-step income statement.

Exhibit 5.4 shows the income statement for TeleVideo Distributors. This form of income statement is the **multiple-step income statement** because it provides several intermediate margin figures before net income. Management decisions require this detail. Therefore, businesses use the multiple-step format for internal reporting.

Operating Expenses

Learning Goal 6   Describe the classifications of operating expenses.

Operating expense accounts record the expired costs of goods or services used in operating the business. Examples are salaries, postage, computer services, utilities, and insurance. Opening an

TELEVIDEO DISTRIBUTORS, INC.
INCOME STATEMENT
FOR THE YEAR ENDED DECEMBER 31, 2007

Gross sales revenue			$ 125,000
Deduct: Sales returns and allowances		$ 3,000	
Sales discounts		2,000	5,000
Net sales revenue			$ 120,000
Cost of goods sold:			
Merchandise inventory, January 1, 2007		$ 15,000	
Purchases	$ 65,000		
Transportation in	5,000		
Gross delivered cost of purchases	$ 70,000		
Deduct: Purchases returns and allowances	$ 2,000		
Purchases discounts	4,000	6,000	
Net cost of purchases		64,000	
Cost of goods available for sale		$ 79,000	
Deduct: Merchandise inventory, December 31, 2007		11,000	
Cost of goods sold			68,000
Gross margin on sales			$ 52,000
Operating expenses:			
Selling expenses:			
Sales salaries expense	$ 12,000		
Rent expense—warehouse	6,000		
Advertising expense	3,000		
Transportation out expense	2,500		
Total selling expenses		$ 23,500	
General and administrative expenses:			
Office salaries expense	$ 7,000		
Rent expense—office equipment	500		
Utilities expense	1,000		
Depreciation expense—office building	3,000		
Total general and administrative expenses		11,500	
Total operating expenses			35,000
Net operating margin			$ 17,000
Other revenues:			
Rent revenue		$ 2,500	
Other expenses:			
Interest expense		1,500	1,000
Net income before income taxes			$ 18,000
Income tax expense			6,000
Net income			$ 12,000

EXHIBIT **5.4**

Multiple-Step Income Statement for a Merchandising Company

account for each type of operating expense allows analyses and comparisons for cost control. The amount of detail shown—that is, the number of accounts opened—depends on the size and type of the business and on the needs of management.

We classify operating expenses into selling or general and administrative categories. Expenses incurred in packaging, advertising, selling, and delivering the product are **selling expenses**. We classify other operating expenses as **general and administrative expenses**. Examples include office expenses, computer services, executive salaries, and the portion of rent and insurance that applies to the administrative function.

Net Operating Margin

Net operating margin measures the net income from the major operating function of the business. In Exhibit 5.4, we deduct the total operating expenses of $35,000 from the gross margin on sales of $52,000 to arrive at the net operating margin of $17,000.

Other Revenue and Other Expenses

We classify revenue and expenses that do not relate to the principal activity of the business as **other revenue and other expenses**. These sections of the income statement serve a valuable function. They permit calculation of net operating margin without its being distorted by these nonoperating items.

Income Tax Expense

Corporations pay income taxes. Exhibit 5.4 shows that net income before income taxes is $18,000. Estimated income tax expense for the year is $6,000. After deducting income tax expense, net income for TeleVideo Distributors is $12,000.

SINGLE-STEP INCOME STATEMENT

A common alternative to the multiple-step income statement format is the *single-step* format. Under the **single-step income statement**, we deduct the total expenses from the total revenues in one step. Most published financial statements for large corporations are in a single-step format. Exhibit 5.5 shows a single-step income statement for TeleVideo Distributors.

WORK SHEET FOR A MERCHANDISING BUSINESS

Learning Goal 7   Describe the updating of the Merchandise Inventory account at the end of the period using closing entries and complete the work sheet.

The work sheet for a merchandising business is similar to that for a service business. The only difference between the two is that the merchandiser includes a line for Merchandise Inventory on its work sheet. Under the periodic inventory system, we must record the new merchandise inventory balance based on a physical count at the end of the year. We can use either closing entries or adjusting entries to do this. This section illustrates inventory changes as closing entries. Appendix 5A focuses on inventory changes treated as adjusting entries. **Your instructor will assign one of these two methods for you to study.**

TELEVIDEO DISTRIBUTORS, INC.
INCOME STATEMENT
FOR THE YEAR ENDED DECEMBER 31, 2007

Revenues		
Net sales		$ 120,000
Other revenues		2,500
Total revenues		$ 122,500
Expenses		
Cost of goods sold	$ 68,000	
Selling expenses	23,500	
General and administrative expenses	11,500	
Other expenses	1,500	
Total expenses		104,500
Net income before income taxes		$ 18,000
Income tax expense		6,000
Net income		$ 12,000

EXHIBIT **5.5**

Single-Step Income Statement for a Merchandising Company

Inventory Changes Treated as Closing Entries

Exhibit 5.6 shows a partial work sheet with inventories. (The complete work sheet shown in Exhibit 5.8 and closing entries illustrated in this chapter also use this approach.) The debit balance of $15,000 in the Merchandise Inventory account in the trial balance is the beginning inventory amount. We transfer this amount to the Income Statement Debit column. It is an addition in the computation of cost of goods available for sale. We enter the ending inventory of $11,000 in the Income Statement Credit column. It is a deduction from the cost of goods available for sale. We also enter the ending inventory in the Balance Sheet Debit column. It is an asset on the balance sheet. The closing journal entries will remove the beginning inventory amount and enter the new ending inventory amount. We will show them later in the chapter.

TELEVIDEO DISTRIBUTORS, INC.
INCOME STATEMENT
FOR THE YEAR ENDED DECEMBER 31, 2007

Account Titles	Trial Balance Dr.	Trial Balance Cr.	Adjustments Dr.	Adjustments Cr.	Adjusted Trial Balance Dr.	Adjusted Trial Balance Cr.	Income Statement Dr.	Income Statement Cr.	Balance Sheet Dr.	Balance Sheet Cr.
Cash										
Accounts Receivable										
Merchandise Inventory	15,000				15,000		15,000	11,000	11,000	

Extend the **beginning inventory** in the trial balance to the Adjusted Trial Balance and the Income Statement Debit columns.

Enter the **ending inventory** in the Income Statement Credit column.

Also enter the **ending inventory** in the Balance Sheet Debit column.

EXHIBIT **5.6**

Partial Work Sheet for a Merchandising Company Inventory Changes Treated as Closing Entries

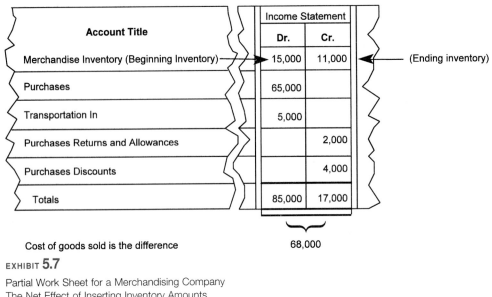

Account Title	Income Statement	
	Dr.	Cr.
Merchandise Inventory (Beginning Inventory)	15,000	11,000
Purchases	65,000	
Transportation In	5,000	
Purchases Returns and Allowances		2,000
Purchases Discounts		4,000
Totals	85,000	17,000

(Ending inventory)

Cost of goods sold is the difference   68,000

EXHIBIT **5.7**

Partial Work Sheet for a Merchandising Company
The Net Effect of Inserting Inventory Amounts

Frequently, students have difficulty seeing the net effect of placing inventory amounts on the work sheet. We enter both the beginning and ending inventory amounts in the Income Statement columns because we use both amounts to compute cost of goods sold. This also includes the net effect of cost of goods sold in the Income Statement columns of the work sheet. We can see this by looking at the partial Income Statement columns of the work sheet in Exhibit 5.7. They show *only* the accounts that make up cost of goods sold.

Statements Prepared from the Work Sheet

We use the work sheet in Exhibit 5.8 to prepare the income statement illustrated in Exhibit 5.4, the statement of owners' equity in Exhibit 5.9, and the classified balance sheet in Exhibit 5.10.

Closing Entries

The procedure for recording the closing entries in a merchandising business is essentially the same as that in a service business. The only difference involves the accounts introduced in this chapter. We prepare the closing entries from the work sheet. Exhibit 5.11 shows these closing entries. After posting the closing entries, all the revenue, expense, and merchandise accounts (except Merchandise Inventory) have zero balances. Closing entries have changed the balance in the Merchandise Inventory account from the beginning amount to the ending amount.

MANAGEMENT CONTROL: THE EXCEPTION PRINCIPLE

Learning Goal 8   Explain how the net price method enables managers to control the cost of buying merchandise.

Managers who practice the control principle of **management by exception** devote their energies to activities that differ from expectations. These exceptions might include cost

TELEVIDEO DISTRIBUTORS, INC.
WORK SHEET
FOR THE YEAR ENDED DECEMBER 31, 2007

Acct. No.	Account Titles	Trial Balance Dr.	Trial Balance Cr.	Adjustments Dr.	Adjustments Cr.	Adjusted Trial Balance Dr.	Adjusted Trial Balance Cr.	Income Statement Dr.	Income Statement Cr.	Balance Sheet Dr.	Balance Sheet Cr.
101	Cash	20,000				20,000				20,000	
111	Accounts Receivable	27,000				27,000				27,000	
130	Merchandise Inventory	15,000				15,000		15,000	11,000	11,000	
157	Office Building	70,000				70,000				70,000	
158	Accumulated Depreciation—Office Building		7,000		(a)3,000		10,000				10,000
201	Accounts Payable		18,000				18,000				18,000
252	Notes Payable—Long-Term		26,000				26,000				26,000
331	Common Stock		30,000				30,000				30,000
360	Retained Earnings		27,000				27,000				27,000
372	Dividends	1,000				1,000				1,000	
401	Sales		125,000				125,000		125,000		
402	Sales Returns and Allowances	3,000				3,000		3,000			
403	Sales Discounts	2,000				2,000		2,000			
501	Purchases	65,000				65,000		65,000			
502	Transportation in	5,000				5,000		5,000			
503	Purchases Returns and Allowances		2,000				2,000		2,000		
504	Purchases Discounts		4,000				4,000		4,000		
602	Sales Salaries Expense	12,000				12,000		12,000			
611	Rent Expense—Warehouse	6,000				6,000		6,000			
616	Advertising Expense	3,000				3,000		3,000			
617	Transportation Out Expense	2,500				2,500		2,500			
703	Office Salaries Expense	7,000				7,000		7,000			
712	Rent Expense—Office Equip.	500				500		500			
721	Utilities Expense	1,000				1,000		1,000			
803	Rent Revenue		2,500				2,500		2,500		
852	Interest Expense	1,500				1,500		1,500			
	Totals	241,500	241,500								
752	Depreciation Expense—Office Building			(a)3,000		3,000		3,000			
901	Income Tax Expense			(b)6,000		6,000		6,000			
215	Income Taxes Payable				(b)6,000		6,000				6,000
	Totals			9,000	9,000	250,500	250,500	132,500	144,500	129,000	117,000
	Net income for the year							12,000			12,000
	Totals							144,500	144,500	129,000	129,000

EXHIBIT **5.8**

Work Sheet for a Merchandising Company

overruns, excessive overtime, and missed deadlines. When applying this principle to accounting, managers want to isolate items that identify operating inefficiencies. They can then focus their attention on the areas that might require corrective action. An alternative method for recording cash discounts—the net price method—is an application of the principle of management by exception.

TELEVIDEO DISTRIBUTORS, INC.
STATEMENT OF OWNERS' EQUITY
FOR THE YEAR ENDED DECEMBER 31, 2007

Common stock, December 31, 2007		$ 30,000
Retained earnings, January 1, 2007	$ 27,000	
Add: Net income	12,000	
Deduct: Dividends	(1,000)	
Retained earnings, December 31, 2007		38,000
Total owners' equity, December 31, 2007		$ 68,000

EXHIBIT **5.9**

Statement of Owners' Equity for a Merchandising Company

TELEVIDEO DISTRIBUTORS, INC.
BALANCE SHEET
DECEMBER 31, 2007

Assets

Current Assets		
Cash	$ 20,000	
Accounts receivable	27,000	
Merchandise inventory	11,000	
Total current assets		$ 58,000
Property, plant, and equipment		
Office building	$ 70,000	
Deduct: Accumulated depreciation	10,000	
Total property, plant, and equipment		60,000
Total assets		$ 118,000

Liabilities

Current liabilities		
Accounts payable	$ 18,000	
Income taxes payable	6,000	
Total current liabilities		$ 24,000
Long-term liabilities		
Notes payable		26,000
Total liabilities		$ 50,000

Owners' Equity

Common stock	$ 30,000	
Retained earnings	38,000	
Total owners' equity		68,000
Total liabilities and owners' equity		$ 118,000

EXHIBIT **5.10**

Balance Sheet for a Merchandising Company

Net Price Method

Earlier in the chapter, we recorded all purchases at gross prices, a practice called the **gross price method**. This method accumulates the volume of discounts taken in the Purchases Discounts account. However, management's interest is not in the amount of discounts taken, but rather in the exceptions, the *discounts not taken*. A balance in an account called Purchases Discounts Lost shows the missed opportunity to decrease cost of goods sold.

The alternative procedure for recording purchases discounts is the **net price method**, also called the *purchases discounts lost method*. Under this method, we record purchases at net—invoice price minus discount. If we lose a discount, we enter it in a special Purchases Discounts Lost account. The method does not use the Purchases Discounts account.

2007			Closing Entries			
Dec.	31		Merchandise Inventory	130	11,000	
			Sales	401	125,000	
			Purchases Returns and Allowances	503	2,000	
			Purchases Discounts	504	4,000	
			Rent Revenue	803	2,500	
			Income Summary	999		144,500
			To record the ending inventory and to close the revenue and the credit balance merchandise accounts.			
	31		Income Summary	999	132,500	
			Merchandise Inventory	130		15,000
			Sales Returns and Allowances	402		3,000
			Sales Discounts	403		2,000
			Purchases	501		65,000
			Transportation In	502		5,000
			Sales Salaries Expense	602		12,000
			Rent Expense—Warehouse	611		6,000
			Advertising Expense	616		3,000
			Transportation Out Expense	617		2,500
			Office Salaries Expense	703		7,000
			Rent Expense—Office Equipment	712		500
			Utilities Expense	721		1,000
			Depreciation Expense—Office Building	752		3,000
			Interest Expense	852		1,500
			Income Tax Expense	901		6,000
			To close the beginning inventory, the expense, and the debit balance merchandise accounts.			
	31		Income Summary	999	12,000	
			Retained Earnings	360		12,000
			To transfer net income to retained earnings			
	31		Retained Earnings	360	1,000	
			Dividends	372		1,000
			To close dividends to retained earnings			

EXHIBIT **5.11**

Closing Entries for a Merchandising Company

To illustrate the accounting for discounts lost, assume that we make a purchase of $5,000 in merchandise on July 5. The terms are 2/10, n/30, and we pay the invoice on July 15. The entries for the purchase and payment assuming we make the payment within the discount period are as follows:

2007						
Jul.	5		Purchases		4,900	
			Accounts Payable			4,900
			Purchases merchandise on account ($5,000 less 2%).			
	15		Accounts Payable		4,900	
			Cash			4,900
			Paid for merchandise purchased on July 5.			

If the invoice were not paid until July 30, the entries would be as follows:

2007					
Jul.	5	Purchases	4,900	
		Accounts Payable		4,900
		Purchased merchandise on account.		
	30	Accounts Payable	4,900	
		Purchases Discounts Lost	100	
		Cash		5,000
		Paid for merchandise purchased on July 5.		

Under the net price method, the debit to Purchases is $4,900 whether or not the discount is lost. The lost discount of $100 appears in a separate account. The loss of available discounts may result from a weakness in the organization. The business may lack bank credit or it may be slow in processing invoices for payment. We classify the Purchases Discounts Lost account balance under other expenses in the income statement.

There are some disadvantages to recording purchases at the net price: (1) it does not report the amount of discounts taken separately in the income statement; (2) statements from creditors do not match the net of discount amounts recorded in accounts payable; (3) there are increased clerical costs and inconveniences; and (4) it requires an adjusting entry at the end of the period to record the lapsed discount portion of unpaid invoices. This entry debits Purchases Discounts Lost and credits Accounts Payable. However, for many firms, the stronger managerial control with the net price method outweighs these disadvantages.

ANALYZING INFORMATION

Learning Goal 9   Analyze financial statement information for real-life companies.

Now we will analyze the income statement for retailing companies in more detail. In this section, we will analyze The Gap, Inc. In the end-of chapter materials, we will analyze Home Depot (Exercise 5-27), Limited Brands versus The Talbots, Inc. (Problem 5-34), and Walgreen Company versus CVS Corporation (Problem 5-35).

Exhibit 5.12 shows comparative income statements for 2004, 2003, and 2002 for The Gap, Inc. For each year, we show the dollar amount and the common-size percent. Our focus in earlier chapters was on total revenues and total expenses. Now we replace revenues with *net sales* and closely examine changes in *gross margin* and *net operating margin*.

Question 1. Are net sales for The Gap, Inc. higher or lower over the three year period?

Analysis 1. Net sales have increased from $14,454,700,000 in 2002 to $16,267,000,000 in 2004.

Question 2. What is the percent change in net sales from 2002 to 2004?

Analysis 2. The percent increase in net sales is:

$$12.5\% = 100 \times \frac{\$1,812,300,000^*}{\$14,454,700,000} \qquad {}^*\$16,267,000,000 - \$14,454,700,000$$

Question 3. Is the percent of cost of goods sold to net sales increasing or decreasing over the three year period? As a result, is the gross margin percent increasing or decreasing?

Analysis 3. The Gap, Inc.'s cost of goods sold as a percent of net sales decreased from 66.0% in 2002 to 60.8% in 2004. The result is a gross profit margin of 39.2% in 2004. This is *favorable*.

THE GAP, INC.
COMPARATIVE COMMON-SIZE PARTIAL INCOME STATEMENTS
For The Years Ended January 29, 2005, January 31, 2004, and February 1, 2003
(in millions)

	Fiscal Year					
	2004	2004	2003	2003	2002	2002
	$	%	$	%	$	%
Net sales	$ 16,267.0	100.0%	$ 15,854.0	100.0%	$ 14,454.7	100.0%
Cost of goods sold	$ 9,886.0	60.8%	$ 9,886.0	62.4%	$ 9,541.6	66.0%
Gross margin	$ 6,381.0	39.2%	$ 5,968.0	37.6%	$ 4,913.1	34.0%
Operating expenses	$ 4,401.0	27.1%	$ 4,089.0	25.8%	$ 3,900.5	27.0%
Operating margin	$ 1,980.0	12.2%	$ 1,879.0	11.9%	$ 1,012.6	7.0%
Other revenues	$ -	0.0%	$ -	0.0%	$ -	0.0%
Other expenses	$ 108.0	0.7%	$ 196.0	1.2%	$ 211.7	1.5%
Income before taxes	$ 1,872.0	11.5%	$ 1,683.0	10.6%	$ 800.9	5.5%
Income taxes	$ 722.0	4.4%	$ 653.0	4.1%	$ 323.4	2.2%
Net income (loss)	$ 1,150.0	7.1%	$ 1,030.0	6.5%	$ 477.5	3.3%

EXHIBIT **5.12**

Comparative Common-size Income Statements for the Gap, Inc.

Gross margin is an important measure of the pricing policy, basic cost structure of a company, and the efficiency of operations. The increase in the gross margin percent could have been caused by a combination of (1) increased sales prices, (2) decreased cost of goods sold, or (3) a different mix of products sold. From the information shown, we cannot determine the exact reason for the increase in the gross margin percent.

Question 4. Is the percent of operating expenses to net sales increasing or decreasing over the three year period? As a result, is the operating margin percent increasing or decreasing?

Analysis 4. Operating expenses as a percent of net sales increased slightly from 27.0% in 2002 to 27.1% in 2004. This trend is *unfavorable*. The sharp decrease in the cost of goods sold percent resulted in an increase in the operating margin from 7.0% in 2002 to 12.2% in 2004.

Question 5. Is the percent of other revenues and other expenses to net sales increasing or decreasing over the three year period? As a result, is the net income percent (or profit margin) increasing or decreasing?

Analysis 5. Other expenses as a percent of net sales have decreased from 1.5% in 2002 to 0.7% in 2004. Over the three-year period, the net income percent has increased from 3.3% in 2002 to 7.1% in 2004.

APPENDIX 5A
INVENTORY CHANGES TREATED AS
ADJUSTING ENTRIES

UNDERSTANDING BUSINESS ISSUES

In the chapter, we recorded these inventory changes as a part of closing entries. Some accountants prefer to treat these inventory changes as adjusting entries. We will explain and illustrate this alternative approach in this appendix. Your instructor will assign one of these approaches for you to study.

Learning Goal A1   Describe the procedures for updating the Merchandise Inventory account at the end of the period using adjusting entries.

INVENTORY CHANGES TREATED AS ADJUSTING ENTRIES

We must record the new merchandise inventory balance and remove the old inventory balance. Exhibit A5.1 shows a partial work sheet with inventory changes treated as adjusting entries. Adjusting entry (a) removes the beginning inventory amount from the Merchandise Inventory account and debits Income Summary. Adjusting entry (b) establishes the new inventory amount in the Merchandise Inventory account and credits Income Summary.

After extending the adjustments, the amounts appearing in the Income Statement and Balance Sheet columns will be *exactly the same* as in Exhibit 5.6. Both the beginning and ending inventory amounts needed to compute cost of goods sold appear in the Income Statement columns. The ending inventory amount, which is an asset on the balance sheet, appears in the Balance Sheet Debit column.

When recording inventory changes as adjustments, we include the journal entries needed to change the inventory balance as part of the adjusting entries. In Exhibit A5.1, note that we do not combine the Income Summary debit and credit balances as we extend them. We need the separate amounts to prepare the cost of goods sold section. We carry the merchandise inventory line across the work sheet in the same manner as any other asset.

TELEVIDEO DISTRIBUTORS, INC.
PARTIAL WORK SHEET
FOR THE YEAR ENDED DECEMBER 31, 2007

Account Titles	Trial Balance Dr.	Cr.	Adjustments Dr.	Cr.	Adjusted Trial Balance Dr.	Cr.	Income Statement Dr.	Cr.	Balance Sheet Dr.	Cr.
Cash										
Accounts Receivable										
Merchandise Inventory	15,000		(b)11,000	(a)15,000	11,000				11,000	
Totals	241,500	241,500								
Income Summary			(a)15,000	(b)11,000	15,000	11,000	15,000	11,000		

Adjustment (a) removes $15,000 of asset value above and debits it to Income Summary.

Adjustment (b) adds $11,000 of asset value above and credits it to Income Summary.

Unlike other work sheet items, both the debit and credit are extended to the Adjusted Trial Balance and Income Statement columns.

EXHIBIT **A5.1**

Partial Work Sheet for a Merchandising Company
Inventory Changes Treated as Closing Entries

LEARNING GOALS REVIEW

1. **Show the difference between the calculation of net income for service and merchandising businesses.**

   Cost of goods sold is the cost of the merchandise sold to customers during a period of time. The difference between cost of goods sold and net sales revenue is gross margin on sales. We then deduct operating expenses from gross margin to calculate net operating margin. Adding other revenues and deducting other expenses gives net income or net loss before income taxes.

2. **Identify the sales revenue accounts and calculate net sales revenue.**

   The sales revenue accounts are Sales, Sales Returns and Allowances, and Sales Discounts. Deducting the balances in Sales Returns and Allowances and Sales Discounts from the balance in Sales gives net sales revenue.

3. **Distinguish between a periodic and a perpetual inventory system.**

   Under the periodic inventory system, we calculate the cost of goods sold and the inventory balance only at the end of each accounting period. Under the perpetual inventory system, we determine the cost of the product sold and the inventory balance on hand as we record each sale during the accounting period.

4. **Calculate cost of goods sold for the period.**

   We add the Purchases and Transportation In accounts to compute the gross delivered cost of purchases. From this amount, subtract the balances in the Purchases Returns and Allowances account and Purchases Discounts account to find the net cost of purchases. We add the net cost of purchases to the inventory balance from the beginning of the period to get the cost of goods available for sale. From this total, we subtract the ending inventory balance, resulting in the cost of goods sold during the period.

5. **Prepare a multiple-step income statement and compare it with a single-step income statement.**

   The multiple-step income statement provides net sales, gross margin, net operating margin, and net income in steps. Because this detail is necessary for management decisions, internal reporting uses this format. The single-step income statement deducts total expenses from total revenues in one step. Study Exhibits 5.4 and 5.5 for format.

6. **Describe the classifications of operating expenses.**

   Operating expenses are expired costs incurred for goods or services used in operating the business. We classify these expenses into selling or general and administrative categories.

7. **Describe the updating of the Merchandise Inventory account at the end of the period using closing entries and complete the work sheet.**

   We extend the beginning inventory in the trial balance to the Adjusted Trial Balance and the Income Statement Debit columns. We enter the ending inventory in the Income Statement Credit column and in the Balance Sheet Debit column. The rest of the work sheet is the same. The closing entries remove the beginning balance and insert the ending balance in Merchandise Inventory.

8. **Explain how the net price method enables managers to control the cost of buying merchandise.**

   The net price method identifies the discounts the company has been offered but has not taken. This procedure records purchases at net invoice price minus cash discount. We enter discounts not taken in a Purchases Discounts Lost account. This makes it easy for managers to identify whether the company is taking advantage of available discounts. The loss of available discounts may indicate a problem such as lack of bank credit or slowness in processing invoices for payment.

9. **Analyze financial statement information for real-life companies.**

   Two important measures for a retail company are gross margin and operating margin. Gross margin equals net sales minus cost of goods sold. Operating margin equals gross margin less operating expenses.

A1. **Describe the updating of the Merchandise Inventory account at the end of the period using adjusting entries.**

   One adjusting entry removes (credits) the amount of the beginning inventory from the Merchandise Inventory account and debits Income Summary. Another adjusting entry establishes the new inventory amount by debiting the Merchandise Inventory account and crediting Income Summary. Since we need both amounts to compute cost of goods sold, we extend both debit and credit amounts in the Income Summary to the Adjusted Trial Balance columns and also to the Income statement columns.

DEMONSTRATION PROBLEM

Preparing a Single-step Income Statement and Journalizing Closing Entries for a Merchandising Business

The adjusted trial balance of Tiny Tots Sales Company for the year ended December 31, 2007, appears as follows:

Account Title	Debits	Credits
Cash	$ 23,000	
Accounts Receivable	63,000	
Merchandise Inventory, January 1, 2007	14,000	
Office Supplies	1,200	
Land	20,000	
Store Building	90,000	
Accumulated Depreciation—Store Building		$ 18,000
Accounts Payable		34,000
Salaries Payable		700
Income Taxes Payable		10,000
Common Stock		61,500
Retained Earnings		63,100
Dividends	2,000	
Sales		169,500
Sales Returns and Allowances	1,300	
Sales Discounts	800	
Purchases	85,000	
Transportation In	1,100	
Purchases Returns and Allowances		500
Purchases Discounts		200
Sales Salaries Expense	14,000	
Advertising Expense	6,000	
Depreciation Expense—Store Building	9,000	
Office Salaries Expense	11,000	
Rent Expense—Office Building	5,000	
Office Supplies Expense	1,300	
Rent Revenue		600
Interest Expense	400	
Income Tax Expense	10,000	
Totals	$ 358,100	$ 358,100

A physical count on December 31, 2007, reveals that $8,100 of merchandise inventory remains on hand.

REQUIRED (LG 5, 7)

1. Prepare a single-step income statement for the year ended December 31, 2007.

2. Assuming that Tiny Tots Sales Company handles inventory changes as closing entries, prepare all of the journal entries required to close the accounts as of December 31, 2007.

SOLUTION

Requirement 1

Revenues
 Net sales
 Other revenues
  Total revenues
Expenses
 Cost of goods sold
 Selling expenses
 General and administrative expenses
 Other expenses
  Total expenses

TINY TOTS SALES COMPANY
INCOME STATEMENT
FOR THE YEAR ENDED DECEMBER 31, 2007

Revenues		
Net sales		$167,400
Other revenues		600
Total revenues		$168,000
Expenses		
Cost of goods sold	$91,300	
Selling expenses	29,000	
General and administrative expenses	17,300	
Other expenses	400	
Total expenses		138,000
Net income before income taxes		$ 30,000
Income tax expense		10,000
Net income		$ 20,000

Solution Approach

Supporting schedule for cost of goods sold:

Cost of goods sold:		
Merchandise inventory, January 1, 2007		$ 14,000
Purchases	$ 85,000	
Transportation in	1,100	
Gross delivered cost of purchases	$ 86,100	
Deduct: Purchases returns and allowances	$ 500	
Purchases discounts	200	700
Net cost of purchases		85,400
Cost of goods available for sale		$ 99,400
Deduct: Merchandise inventory, December 31, 2007		8,100
Cost of goods sold		$ 91,300

Requirement 2

2007			Closing Entries			
Dec.	31		Merchandise Inventory		8,100	
			Sales		169,500	
			Purchases Returns and Allowances		500	
			Purchases Discounts		200	
			Rent Revenue		600	
			Income Summary			178,900
			To record the ending inventory and close the revenue and the credit balance merchandise inventory accounts.			
			Income Summary		158,900	
			Merchandise Inventory			14,000
			Sales Returns and Allowances			1,300
			Sales Discounts			800
			Purchases			85,000
			Transportation In			1,100
			Sales Salaries Expense			14,000
			Advertising Expense			6,000
			Depreciation Expense—Store Building			9,000
			Office Salaries Expense			11,000
			Rent Expense—Office Building			5,000
			Office Supplies Expense			1,300
			Interest Expense			400
			Income Tax Expense			10,000
			To close the beginning inventory, the expense, and the debit balance merchandise accounts.			
	31		Income Summary		20,000	
			Retained Earnings			20,000
			To transfer net income to retained earnings.			
	31		Retained Earnings		2,000	
			Dividends			2,000
			To close dividends to retained earnings.			

GLOSSARY

cash discount A deduction from the invoice price of goods allowed if payment is made within a specified period of time.

chain discount A multiple percentage reduction from a list price to arrive at the invoice price with each discount in the chain applied successively to the declining balance.

cost of goods sold The cost to the merchandising firm of the goods sold to customers during a period of time. It is calculated by adding net purchases to the beginning inventory to derive the cost of goods available for sale and then deducting from this sum the ending inventory.

credit memorandum A business form issued to a customer to advise that his or her account has been credited for a return of merchandise or for an allowance for defective merchandise.

discount period The period in which the cash discount is available.

F.O.B. destination A term indicating that the title to goods passes when the goods arrive at their destination. The owner of the goods while in transit—the seller—should bear the cost of freight.

F.O.B. shipping point A term indicating that the title to goods passes when the seller places the goods on the common carrier (railroad or truck). The owner of the goods while in transit—the buyer—should bear the cost of the freight.

general and administrative expenses The general office, accounting, personnel, credit and collection expenses, and rent and insurance for management.

gross margin on sales The excess of net sales revenue over the cost of goods sold.

gross price method Accounting for cash discounts by accumulating the amount of the discounts taken in Sales Discounts and in Purchases Discounts accounts.

management by exception A management principle that when applied to accounting isolates accounts and amounts that may indicate operating inefficiencies. It focuses the manager's attention on areas that require corrective action.

Merchandise Inventory An account that shows the cost of merchandise on hand. The ending inventory of one period becomes the beginning inventory of the next period.

multiple-step income statement An income statement on which cost of goods sold and the expenses are subtracted in steps to arrive at net income.

net cost of purchases The cost of all merchandise bought for sale, including transportation in, but reduced by purchases returns and allowances and purchases discounts.

net operating margin The excess of gross margin over operating expenses.

net price method Procedures that apply the principle of management by exception. We record purchases at net of cash discount prices. We record discounts lost in a separate account.

operating expenses The cost of goods or services expired or used in operating the business, excluding cost of goods sold.

other revenue and other expenses Items of ordinary revenue and expense that arise from a source other than the basic business purpose of the company.

periodic inventory system Determining the amount of merchandise on hand at the end of each accounting period by counting the goods on hand and making a list showing physical quantities and cost.

perpetual inventory system A system in which a continuous record of merchandise on hand is maintained.

Purchases An account debited for the cost of merchandise bought for resale.

Purchases Discounts An account credited with amounts of invoice price allowed for payment within the stated discount period. It is a contra account to Purchases.

Purchases Returns and Allowances An account credited for cost of merchandise returned to a vendor or for allowances for defective merchandise purchases received. It is a contra account to Purchases.

Sales An account credited for the selling price of merchandise sold.

Sales Discounts An account debited for the amounts that customers deduct from the invoice price when making payment within the stated discount period.

Sales Returns and Allowances An account debited for the selling price of merchandise returned by customers or allowances for defective merchandise kept by customers.

selling expenses The expenses of preparing and storing goods for sale, promoting sales, making sales, and delivering goods to customers.

single-step income statement An income statement form in which we add cost of goods sold and the expenses together and subtract the total in one step from revenue to arrive at net income.

trade discount A percentage reduction in a list price that results in the net price or invoice price. Unlike the cash discount, it is not recorded in the accounts.

transportation in Freight, express, or other transportation costs on merchandise purchased for resale.

QUESTIONS FOR GROUP LEARNING

Q5-1. Why is the income statement for a merchandising business more complicated than for a service business?

Q5-2. Student A says that because cost of goods sold is an item that can't be controlled by management, there is little need to be concerned with it. Do you agree? Give examples to support your answer.

Q5-3. Sales discounts cause a business to collect less cash from sales. Why, then, would a company offer them to its customers? Does management really want customers to take advantage of sales discounts? Why or why not?

Q5-4. How does a trade discount differ from a cash discount?

Q5-5. What are the differences between periodic and perpetual inventory systems? Describe briefly.

Q5-6. Estimates indicate that billions of dollars in sales are lost in the United States each year because of shoplifting. How does this loss affect the cost of goods sold for businesses that use the periodic inventory system?

Q5-7. Why not debit the Purchases account for all purchases, including store supplies, advertising supplies, and postage stamps, for example?

Q5-8. How does the use of contra accounts for purchases returns and allowances and for purchases discounts strengthen managerial control in a business?

Q5-9. If a company in Pittsburgh sells to a buyer in Williamsport, Pennsylvania, F.O.B. destination, when does title transfer? Why? Whose responsibility are freight costs?

Q5-10. Marge Company uses a periodic inventory system and adjusts and closes its accounting records on a calendar-year basis. Is the inventory amount on an unadjusted trial balance taken on December 31 the beginning or ending inventory figure? Why?

Q5-11. Is the normal balance for each of the following accounts a debit or a credit: Sales Discounts, Purchases, Sales, Transportation In, Purchases Discounts, Sales Returns and Allowances, Purchases Returns and Allowances, and Merchandise Inventory?

Q5-12. What is the difference between selling expenses and general and administrative expenses? Between operating expenses and other expenses?

Q5-13. In what columns of the work sheet are the elements that make up cost of goods sold found?

Q5-14. How does a multiple-step income statement differ from a single-step income statement?

Q5-15. How can the use of management by exception be applied to strengthen managerial control over purchases discounts?

EXERCISES

E5-16. **Journalizing sales transactions (LG 2)** Car Perfect Company is an auto parts retailer. The company gives all customers 2/10, n/30 terms. Journalize the following transactions for February 2007.

2007		
Feb.	4	Sold merchandise on account to South Company at an invoice price of $1,400. Charged sales tax of 5% on the sale.
	7	Sold merchandise on account to Crankfast Company at an invoice price of $2,000. Charged no sales tax on the sale, since East Company took delivery of the merchandise in another state.
	9	Crankfast Company returned $600 of unsatisfactory merchandise. Credited their account.
	15	Received payment in full from Crankfast Company.
	22	Received payment in full from South Company.

E5-17. **Journalizing purchases transactions (LG 4)** Whole Food Company is a wholesaler of food products. Journalize the following transactions for April 2007.

2007		
Apr.	5	Purchased $2,000 in products on account from Plains Company, F.O.B. shipping point, 2/10, n/30.
	7	Purchased $1,000 in products on account from Growers Inc., F.O.B. destination, 1/10, n/30.
	9	Paid a $100 freight bill on the purchase from Plains Company.
	10	Found $200 of the product from Growers, Inc., to be spoiled and returned it for credit.
	14	Paid Plains Company the amount due in full.
	25	Paid Growers, Inc., the amount due in full.

E5-18. **Trade discounts (LG 2)** Arizona Company sold merchandise to Texas Supply with a list price of $20,000 and a trade discount of 20% and 10%. Cash discount terms were 1/10, n/30. The invoice date was April 8, 2007. Journalize the sale on April 8 and payment on April 17, 2007.

E5-19. **Sales discounts: partial payment (LG 2)** Casio, Inc., grants customer discounts on partial payments made within the discount period. On June 10, 2007, the company sold merchandise to Jean Stubs for $22,000, terms 2/10, n/30. On June 20, 2007, Stubs sent the company a check for $14,700. On July 8, 2007, Stubs sent a check for the balance due. Journalize the sale and both collection entries on Casio's books.

E5-20. **Computation of net sales, net purchases, cost of goods sold, and gross margin on sales (LG 2, 4)** The following information is taken from the books of Thomas Company:

Merchandise inventory, January 1, 2007	$ 1,900
Merchandise inventory, January 31, 2007	2,000
Sales	18,000
Transportation in	400
Purchases discounts	300
Sales returns and allowances	200
Purchases	5,600
Sales discounts	100
Purchases returns and allowances	400

Compute for January 2007: (a) net sales, (b) net purchases, (c) cost of goods sold, (d) gross margin on sales.

E5-21. Calculation of gross sales (LG 4, 5) The following information is from the books of Rosman Company:

Merchandise inventory, beginning	$ 6,000
Net cost of purchases	31,000
Total operating expenses	15,000
Other revenues	500
Merchandise inventory, ending	5,000
Net income	4,000

Calculate the gross sales for the period.

E5-22. Inventories in the work sheet (Instructor to choose approach) (LG 7 or A1) Following is a section of the work sheet of Cruz Company:

	Trial Balance		Adjustments		Adjusted Trial Balance		Income Statement		Balance Sheet	
	Dr.	Cr.	Dr.	Cr.	Dr.	Cr.	Dr.	Cr.	Dr.	Cr.
Cash	5,000				5,000				5,000	
Accounts Receivable	12,000				12,000				12,000	
Merchandise Inventory										

Beginning inventory is $20,000. Ending inventory is $17,000.
Answer *either* requirement 1 or 2 as directed by your instructor:

1. Assuming that inventory is treated as closing entries, enter the beginning and ending inventory amounts in the appropriate columns.

2. Assuming that inventory is treated as adjusting entries, prepare the necessary adjusting entries in the work sheet and transfer the amounts to the appropriate columns.

E5-23. **Determination of missing income statement amounts (LG 5)** The following financial data pertain to Kona, Oahu, and Hilo Companies. Fill in the missing amounts for each company:

	Kona Company	Oahu Company	Hilo Company
Sales	$ 50,000	$?	$?
Merchandise inventory, beginning	4,000	6,000	?
Purchases	30,000	?	40,000
Transportation in	2,000	3,000	?
Gross delivered cost of purchases	?	30,000	?
Purchases returns and allowances	1,000	500	2,000
Purchases discounts	2,000	?	4,000
Net cost of purchases	?	?	39,000
Cost of goods available for sale	?	34,000	?
Merchandise inventory, ending	3,000	4,000	6,000
Cost of goods sold	?	?	41,000
Gross margin on sales	?	25,000	?
Total operating expenses	?	?	15,000
Net operating margin	9,000	17,000	?
Other revenue	500	?	3,000
Other expenses	2,500	1,000	2,000
Net income before income taxes	?	18,000	15,000

E5-24. **Multiple-step income statement (LG 5)** The following selected adjusted account balances were taken from the work sheet of Paris Company for the year ended December 31, 2007:

Account Title	Debits	Credits
Sales		$ 60,000
Sales Returns and Allowances	$ 00	
Sales Discounts	1,300	
Purchases	20,000	
Transportation In	1,000	
Purchases Returns and Allowances		1,400
Purchases Discounts		1,600
Selling Expenses	15,000	
General and Administrative Expenses	10,000	
Other Revenues		800
Other Expenses	1,000	
Income Tax Expense	4,000	

Merchandise Inventory balances were as follows:

January 1, 2007	$ 4,000
December 31, 2007	3,000

Prepare a multiple-step income statement.

E5-25. **Closing entries (LG 7)** Journalize the closing entries for the account balances in E5-24. (If your instructor uses the adjusting entry approach, also journalize necessary adjusting entries.)

E5-26. **Recordkeeping of purchases: net price method (LG 8)** On June 5, 2007, Linda Company, which uses the net price method, purchased merchandise for $9,000, terms 2/10, n/30. The invoice was paid on July 1, 2007.

1. Journalize the purchase and the payment of the invoice.

2. Is the net cost of purchases the same under both the gross and the net price methods? show your computations.

3. Assume that Linda desires to take advantage of all purchases discounts. Is there any advantage in using the gross price method of recording the purchase of merchandise?

E5-27.   Analyzing The Home Depot (LG 9) The Home Depot was founded in 1978 in Atlanta, Georgia. Currently, The Home Depot is the world's largest home improvement retailer and ranks among the largest retailers in the United States. Listed below are comparative income statements for the fiscal years 2004-2002 (in millions).

HOME DEPOT, INC.
COMPARATIVE COMMON-SIZE PARTIAL INCOME STATEMENTS
For The Years Ended January 30, 2005, February 1, 2004, and February 2, 2003
(in millions)

	Fiscal Year					
	2004	2004	2003	2003	2002	2002
	$	%	$	%	$	%
Net sales	$ 73,094.0	100.0%	$ 64,816.0	100.0%	$ 58,247.0	100.0%
Cost of goods sold	$ 48,664.0	66.6%	$ 44,236.0	68.2%	$ 40,139.0	68.9%
Gross margin	$ 24,430.0	33.4%	$ 20,580.0	31.8%	$ 18,108.0	31.1%
Operating expenses	$ 16,504.0	22.6%	$ 13,734.0	21.2%	$ 12,278.0	21.1%
Operating margin	$ 7,926.0	10.8%	$ 6,846.0	10.6%	$ 5,830.0	10.0%
Other revenues	$ -	0.0%	$ -	0.0%	$ -	0.0%
Other expenses	$ 14.0	0.0%	$ 3.0	0.0%	$ (42.0)	-0.1%
Income before taxes	$ 7,912.0	10.8%	$ 6,843.0	10.6%	$ 5,872.0	10.1%
Income taxes	$ 2,911.0	4.0%	$ 2,539.0	3.9%	$ 2,208.0	3.8%
Net income (loss)	$ 5,001.0	6.8%	$ 4,304.0	6.6%	$ 3,664.0	6.3%

1.   Are net sales for Home Depot higher or lower over the three year period?

2.   What is the percent change in net sales from 2002 to 2004?

3.   Is the percent of cost of goods sold to net sales increasing or decreasing over the three year period? As a result, is the gross margin percent increasing or decreasing?

4.   Is the percent of operating expenses to net sales increasing or decreasing over the three year period? As a result, is the operating margin percent increasing or decreasing?

5.   Is the percent of other revenues and other expenses to net sales increasing or decreasing over the three year period? As a result, is the net income percent (or profit margin) increasing or decreasing?

PROBLEMS

P5-28.   Use of merchandising accounts (LG 2, 4) Diane Company had the following transactions for 2007.

2007

Feb.	4	Purchased merchandise from Mankato Company at a list price of $5,000; terms n/30, F.O.B. shipping point. A trade discount of 10%, 20% was given.
	6	Paid Overnight Express $150 for delivery cost of the purchase of February 4.
	6	Upon inspection, noted that merchandise invoiced at $1,000 in the Mankato shipment was the wrong model. Returned the incorrect merchandise by Overnight Express collect as authorized by Mankato Company.
	8	Sold merchandise to Susan Sexton in amount of $2,000; terms 2/10, n/30, F.O.B. shipping point.
	18	Received a check from Susan Sexton in total payment of her purchase of February 8.
	19	Sold merchandise to Dale Karn in amount of $1,500; terms 2/10, n/30, F.O.B. destination.
	19	Paid $200 to Overnight Express for delivery of merchandise to Karn.
	20	Karn reported that an item in the shipment was defective; it was agreed that Karn would retain the item and receive a credit of $100.
	28	Received a check from Dale Karn for amount due.
Mar.	5	Paid Mankato Company the amount due on the purchase of February 4.

REQUIRED

Journalize the above transactions using the gross price method.

P5-29. Partial income statement (LG 4) MO Company had the following balances in its general ledger accounts at September 30, 2007, the end of its fiscal year:
The merchandise inventory determined by physical count on September 30, 2007, was $30,000.

Account Title	Debits	Credits
Merchandise Inventory	$ 27,000	
Sales		$ 700,000
Sales Discounts	5,000	
Purchases	360,000	
Transportation In	8,000	
Purchases Returns and Allowances		7,000
Purchases Discounts		3,000
Transportation Out Expense	10,000	

REQUIRED

Prepare a partial income statement through gross margin for the year ended September 30, 2007.

P5-30. Income statement and closing entries(LG 5, 7) The adjusted trial balance of Russ Crow Company on December 31, 2007, included the following accounts:

Account Title	Debits	Credits
Sales		$ 670,000
Sales Returns and Allowances	$ 4,000	
Sales Discounts	11,000	
Purchases	410,000	
Transportation In	8,000	
Purchases Returns and Allowances		6,000
Purchases Discounts		5,000
Sales Salaries Expenses	166,000	
Advertising Expense	12,000	
Transportation Out Expense	4,000	
Administrative Salaries Expense	32,000	
Office Supplies Expense	5,000	
Depreciation Expense—Office Equipment	2,000	
Interest Revenue		1,500
Interest Expense	8,500	
Income Tax Expense	5,000	

Merchandise inventory balances are as follows:

January 1, 2007	$27,000
December 31, 2007	24,000

REQUIRED

1. Prepare an income statement for 2007. Use the multiple-step format.

2. Prepare closing entries. (If your instructor requires the adjusting entries approach, also prepare adjusting entries.)

P5-31. Journalizing transactions for retail store (LG 2-5) Mary Hanks operates a music shop called Pop Music Company. She carries charge accounts for a few customers and offers cash discounts of 2/10, n/30 to encourage prompt payment. Inventory on hand on January 1, 2007, was $4,000. Following are the transactions for January 2007.

2007		
Jan.	6	Purchased compact discs from Columbia Supply at a list price of $5,000. Terms were 1/10, n/30, F.O.B. destination. A trade discount of 20%, 10% was given.
	7	Purchased cassette tapes from Warner Entertainment at an invoice price of $3,000, terms 2/10, n/30, F.O.B. shipping point.
	9	Paid $200 for advertising that had appeared in the local paper.
	10	Compact discs, with a list price of $600, from Columbia Supply were defective. They were returned for a credit. Columbia agreed to pay the freight.
	12	Paid the freight charges of $100 on shipment from Warner Entertainment.
	15	Cash sales for the first half of the month totaled $5,200.
	15	Sales on account for the first half of the month totaled $2,000.
	17	Paid the amount owed to Warner Entertainment.
	18	Two customers who had purchased compact discs on account for $100 returned them.
	20	Paid a delivery company $200 for delivery of merchandise to customers during the month.
	24	Customers owing $1,400 made payments less the discount.
	27	Received the utility bill for the month on the store, $300.
	28	Paid $400 in wages to sales clerks and $200 to a part-time office clerk for the month.
	30	Cash sales for the second half of the month totaled $5,000.
	30	Sales on account for the second half of the month totaled $1,000.
	31	Estimated income taxes accrued are $600.

A count of inventory on hand on January 31, 2007, showed $3,000 remaining. The beginning balance in cash was $5,000.

REQUIRED

1. Journalize the transactions in general journal form.

2. Open the following accounts and post the journal entries.

101	Cash	503	Purchases Returns and Allowances
111	Accounts Receivable	504	Purchases Discounts
201	Accounts Payable	602	Sales Wages Expense
215	Income Taxes Payable	616	Advertising Expense
401	Sales	621	Delivery Expense
402	Sales Returns and Allowances	625	Utilities Expense
403	Sales Discounts	703	Office Wages Expense
501	Purchases	901	Income Tax Expense
502	Transportation In		

3. Prepare a multiple-step income statement.

P5-32. **Completion of a work sheet, preparation of statements, adjusting and closing entries (LG 2, 4-7)** Following is the trial balance of Macrosoft Company on December 31, 2007, the end of the fiscal year:

Acct. No.	Account Title	Debits	Credits
101	Cash	$ 21,000	
111	Accounts Receivable	40,000	
130	Merchandise Inventory	15,000	
136	Store Supplies	30,000	
165	Store Equipment	150,000	
166	Accumulated Depreciation—Store Equipment		$ 40,000
201	Accounts Payable		30,000
202	Notes Payable (due 2008)		10,000
231	Unearned Rent		3,000
331	Common Stock		60,000
360	Retained Earnings		38,000
372	Dividends	2,000	
401	Sales		352,000
403	Sales Discounts	5,000	
501	Purchases	196,000	
502	Transportation In	4,000	
504	Purchases Discount		3,000
602	Sales Salaries Expense	40,000	
703	Office Salaries Expense	20,000	
711	Rent Expense*	16,000	
721	Utilities Expense*	7,000	
803	Rent Revenue		10,000
	Totals	$546,000	$546,000

* Classified as general and administrative expense.

The merchandise inventory at December 31, 2007, is $12,000. Data for adjustments are as follows:

a. Store supplies on hand have a valuation of $3,000.

b. Depreciation of store equipment for 2004 is $12,000.

c. Interest of $1,000 is accrued on notes payable.

d. Salaries earned as of December 31 but not due to be paid until January are $3,000; they are equally divided between sales salaries and office salaries.

e. The last quarterly rent collection for November, December, and January was credited to Unearned Rent when collected on November 1, 2007.

f. Estimated income tax expense is $10,000.

REQUIRED

1. Enter the above balances in a work sheet and complete the work sheet. Use the approach for inventory changes your instructor prefers.

2. Prepare (a) a multiple-step income statement, (b) a statement of owners' equity, and (c) a balance sheet. No additional shares of common stock were sold during the year.

3. Journalize the adjusting and the closing entries.

P5-33. **Recording purchases net of discount (LG 8)** The following transactions were completed by Fonz Company during July 2007:

2007		
Jul.	2	Purchased merchandise from the Goss Company for $1,000, terms 2/10, n/30, F.O.B. destination.
	3	Purchased merchandise on account from the Willi Company for $600, terms 2/10, n/30, F.O.B. shipping point.
	4	Paid freight charges of $30 on the merchandise purchased from Willi Company.
	5	Received a $50 credit (gross amount) for defective merchandise returned to Willi Company.
	11	Paid Goss Company.
	31	Paid Willi Company.

REQUIRED

1a. Journalize the transactions using the gross price method.

1b. Prepare the cost of goods sold section of the income statement. Assume the following inventories: July 1, $300; July 31, $400.

2a. Journalize the transactions using the net price method.

2b. Prepare the cost of goods sold section of the income statement. Assume inventories are identical to those in Part 1b.

3. Under the net price method, how are purchases discounts lost classified in the income statement?

P5-34. Analyzing Limited Brands, Inc. and The Talbot's, Inc. (LG 9) Limited Brands and The Talbot's are large clothing retailers. Listed below are comparative partial income statements for 2004-2003 (in millions).

LIMITED BRANDS, INC. AND THE TALBOT'S, INC.
COMPARATIVE COMMON-SIZE PARTIAL INCOME STATEMENTS
For 2004 And 2003 Fiscal Years
(in millions)

	Limited Brands				The Talbot's			
	2004	2004	2003	2003	2004	2004	2003	2003
	$	%	$	%	$	%	$	%
Net sales	$ 9,408.0	100.0%	$ 8,934.0	100.0%	$ 1,697.8	100.0%	$ 1,624.3	100.0%
Cost of goods sold	$ 6,030.0	64.1%	$ 5,683.0	63.6%	$ 1,093.0	64.4%	$ 1,001.6	61.7%
Gross margin	$ 3,378.0	35.9%	$ 3,251.0	36.4%	$ 604.8	35.6%	$ 622.7	38.3%
Operating expenses	$ 2,351.0	25.0%	$ 2,288.0	25.6%	$ 462.7	27.3%	$ 453.1	27.9%
Operating margin	$ 1,027.0	10.9%	$ 963.0	10.8%	$ 142.1	8.4%	$ 169.6	10.4%

REQUIRED

1. For 2004, which company has higher net sales? Are net sales for each company higher or lower over the two year period?

2. What is the percent change in net sales from 2003 to 2004 for each company?

3. Is the percent of cost of goods sold to total net sales for each company increasing or decreasing over the two year period? As a result, is the gross margin percent increasing or decreasing?

4. Is the percent of operating expenses to net sales for each company increasing or decreasing over the two year period? As a result, is the operating margin percent increasing or decreasing?

P5-35. Analyzing Walgreen Company and CVS Corporation (LG 9) Walgreen Company is the oldest major U.S. drugstore chain. CVS ranks number one in drugstore count. Listed below are comparative partial income statements for 2004-2003 (in millions).

WALGREEN COMPANY AND CVS CORPORATION
COMPARATIVE COMMON-SIZE PARTIAL INCOME STATEMENTS
For 2004 And 2003 Fiscal Years
(in millions)

	Walgreen				CVS			
	2004	2004	2003	2003	2004	2004	2003	2003
	$	%	$	%	$	%	$	%
Net sales	$ 37,508.2	100.0%	$ 32,505.4	100.0%	$ 30,594.3	100.0%	$ 26,588.0	100.0%
Cost of goods sold	$ 27,310.4	72.8%	$ 23,706.2	72.9%	$ 22,563.1	73.7%	$ 19,725.0	74.2%
Gross margin	$ 10,197.8	27.2%	$ 8,799.2	27.1%	$ 8,031.2	26.3%	$ 6,863.0	25.8%
Operating expenses	$ 8,071.7	21.5%	$ 6,950.9	21.4%	$ 6,576.5	21.5%	$ 5,439.4	20.5%
Operating margin	$ 2,126.1	5.7%	$ 1,848.3	5.7%	$ 1,454.7	4.8%	$ 1,423.6	5.4%

REQUIRED

1. For 2004, which company has higher net sales? Are net sales for each company higher or lower over the two year period?

2. What is the percent change in net sales from 2003 to 2004 for each company?

3. Is the percent of cost of goods sold to total net sales for each company increasing or decreasing over the two year period? As a result, is the gross margin percent increasing or decreasing?

4. Is the percent of operating expenses to net sales for each company increasing or decreasing over the two year period? As a result, is the operating margin percent increasing or decreasing?

PRACTICE CASE

Preparing a multiple-step income statement, statement of owners' equity, and balance sheet for a merchandising business (LG 4, 5). The adjusted trial balance of Paris Hilton Fashion Company for the year ended December 31, 2007, appears as follows:

Account Title	Debits	Credits
Cash	$ 35,000	
Accounts Receivable	50,000	
Merchandise Inventory, January 1, 2007	30,000	
Office Supplies	3,000	
Land	25,000	
Store Building	80,000	
Accumulated Depreciation—Store Building		15,000
Accounts Payable		20,000
Salaries Payable		1,000
Income Taxes Payable		3,000
Notes Payable, due December 2009		60,000
Common Stock		70,000
Retained Earnings		39,000
Dividends	1,000	
Sales		225,000
Sales Returns and Allowances	4,000	
Sales Discounts	3,000	
Purchases	99,000	
Transportation In	2,500	
Purchases Returns and Allowances		600
Purchases Discounts		900
Sales Salaries Expense	27,000	
Advertising Expense	37,000	
Depreciation Expense—Store Building	7,000	
Office Salaries Expense	15,000	
Rent Expense—Office Building	6,000	
Office Supplies Expense	3,000	
Interest Revenue		1,000
Interest Expense	5,000	
Income Tax Expense	3,000	
Totals	$ 335,500	$ 335,500

A physical count on December 31, 2007, reveals that $20,000 of merchandise inventory remains on hand. No additional investments were made by stockholders during 2007.

REQUIRED

1. Prepare a multiple-step income statement for the year ended December 31, 2007.

2. Prepare a statement of owners' equity for the year ended December 31, 2007.

3. Prepare a balance sheet as of December 31, 2007.

BUSINESS DECISION AND COMMUNICATION PROBLEM

Improving Profitability Tees Unlimited is a retail clothing store. The president, Sam Tees, is concerned about the losses that the company is incurring. He has given you the following income statement and has asked for your advice.

TEES UNLIMITED
INCOME STATEMENT
FOR THE YEAR ENDED DECEMBER 31, 2007

Gross sales revenues			$ 50,000
Deduct: Sales returns and allowances			10,000
Net sales revenue			$ 40,000
Cost of goods sold:			
Merchandise inventory, January 1, 2007		$ 20,000	
Purchases	$ 50,000		
Deduct: Purchases returns and allowances	7,000		
Net cost of purchases		43,000	
Cost of goods available for sale		$ 63,000	
Deduct: Merchandising inventory, December 31, 2007		30,000	
Cost of goods sold			33,000
Gross margin on sales			$ 7,000
Operating expenses:			
Selling expenses		$ 8,000	
General and administrative expenses		3,000	
Total operating expenses			11,000
Net loss			$ (4,000)

REQUIRED

Prepare a memo to Sam Tees suggesting areas that he might consider to improve the profitability of the store.

ETHICAL DILEMMA

Predating Sales Transactions You are the accountant for a small wholesaler of gifts. The president of the company has come to you with a request. He asks that you date some sales transactions December 31, 2007. The transactions in question were shipped to the buyers F.O.B. shipping point on January 3, 2008. The president indicates that it will hurt no one since he is the only user of the statements. You are aware that the company will be applying for a loan in late January 2008.

REQUIRED

Identify the effects on the financial statements of the owner's request. Discuss the ethical considerations of his request.

INTERNAL CONTROL AND CASH

"Every luxury must be paid for, and everything is a luxury, starting with being in the world."

Cesar Pavese

LEARNING GOALS

After studying Chapter 6, you should be able to:

1. Define *internal control* and describe the three elements of internal control.

2. Describe the procedures involved in internal control of cash

3. Describe the operation of an imprest petty cash fund.

4. Interpret a monthly bank statement and prepare a bank reconciliation.

5. Record journal entries required to adjust the Cash account after the bank reconciliation.

6. Analyze financial statement information for real-life companies

UNDERSTANDING BUSINESS ISSUES

One of the main responsibilities of management is keeping the data that make up the financial statements safe and accurate. To do this, management maintains a system of controls called an *internal control structure*. It safeguards the assets and provides accurate data.

Cash is the most *liquid* and easily stolen asset of a business. It may be hard for an employee or outsider to steal plant assets or inventory. These assets tend to be large and carry identification numbers. But coins and currency have instant cash value and no marks to show who owns them. An employee can easily transfer cash from one person or place to another. Today, most banks and brokerage houses provide customers access to their accounts over the internet. With electronic cash transfer capabilities, the amounts of cash theft can be huge.

Cash is also the most *flexible* asset. A company with cash can hire employees, purchase inventory, and add to plant assets. A company with cash may remain in business despite the loss of a key executive or sales contract. It will not survive if it loses the ability to generate cash.

Flows of cash through a business can be very large. In 2004, $19,945 million in cash flowed into and $19,656 million in cash flowed out of Wal-Mart Stores, Inc. It is important to have effective controls to assure the proper handling and recording of cash.

This chapter introduces internal control and discusses its importance. It presents two popular internal control procedures for cash. These include the operation of a petty cash fund and the reconciliation of the bank statement. We end the chapter by analyzing cash for real-life companies.

INTERNAL CONTROL STRUCTURE

Learning Goal 1   Define internal controland describe the three elements of internal control.

The word *control* means to regulate. To function effectively, a business must have a structure of internal control. **Internal control** includes the policies and procedures for protecting assets from improper use. It also includes the detection and prevention of errors or irregularities in accounting.[1]

Internal controls are not the same in every company. They depend on the type of business and its size. Small companies rely heavily on the owner's everyday oversight of the company's activities. Larger companies must rely on the policies and procedures by which the business operates. All businesses base their internal control systems on the same elements.

Elements of the Internal Control Structure

The American Institute of Certified Public Accountants'*Statement on Auditing Standards No. 55* identifies three elements of the internal control structure: (1) the control environment, (2) the accounting system, and (3) the control procedures.[2]

The Control Environment

The *control environment* consists of management's policies and actions that enable the business to meet its goals. It includes the attitude of management, owners, and others about the importance of internal controls. Management's philosophy and operating style affect its ability to maintain an effective internal control system.

For example, the control environment includes management's attitude toward ethical behavior. Management shows this attitude by setting and adhering to a formal code of conduct. It also shows its attitude toward ethics by the way it monitors employees'behavior and handles unethical behavior. Open lines of communication that encourage the reporting of unethical behavior show management's desire for ethical conduct. An atmosphere that encourages ethical behavior promotes good internal control.

---

[1] *Statement on Auditing Standards (SAS) No. 55,* "Consideration of the Internal Control Structure in a Financial Statement Audit,"AICPA Professional Standards (New York: AICPA, 1988), section 319, paragraph 6.

[2] SAS No. 55, section 319, paragraph 8.

The organizational structure of management affects internal control. Management's methods of monitoring and following up on performance also affect the control environment. Typically, an audit committee of the board of directors is part of the control environment. This committee, composed of outside members of the board of directors, oversees management's policies and practices.

The Accounting System

The *accounting system* consists of the methods and records used to identify, assemble, classify, analyze, record, and report a firm's transactions. Methods and records that will identify and record all transactions in the proper time period are part of an effective internal control system. The accounting system should classify the transactions and measure their value. A quality system leads to the proper presentation of transactions and disclosure in the firm's financial statements.

The Control Procedures

Control procedures provide reasonable assurance that the business will safeguard its assets and record its transactions accurately. The nature of the business, and its size and complexity, affect the design of control procedures. The following are basic procedures used to promote effective internal control:

- *Proper authorization of transactions and activities* Only certain persons should have the authority to start transactions. In a computerized system, only those who use the appropriate codes can enter transaction data.

- *Separation of duties* Companies should assign different persons the responsibility of authorizing transactions, recording transactions, and holding assets. In a cash receipts system, the same person or department should not receive the cash and also record the transaction. No one person should have the chance to both steal assets and conceal the theft by falsifying records.

- *Design and use of adequate source documents and records* The business should have reasonable assurance that it is recording all valid transactions. For example, the shipping department should use prenumbered shipping documents. When the accounting department collects these documents, it can determine whether all documents are accounted for, which allows it to verify that it has recorded all shipments.

- *Adequate safeguards over access to and use of assets and records* Only authorized persons should have access to assets, either physically or indirectly through records. Only authorized persons should be able to make bank deposits or write checks. The same person should not have access to both the physical assets and the records for those assets.

- *Periodic independent review of internal controls* Independent parties should make regular reviews of performance and recorded amounts. These reviews should include clerical checks, reconciliations, and comparisons of the physical assets with recorded amounts. We can use computer programs to compare the quantities shown on receiving reports with the quantities billed. Only when the amounts match will the program print a check. Users should review computer generated reports for completeness and reasonableness. Many larger companies have *internal audit departments* to periodically check whether employees are following proper procedures and controls are functioning properly.

To be effective, management must be committed to and fully support a strong internal control system. Exhibit 6.1 summarizes the elements of the internal control structure.

ELEMENTS OF THE INTERNAL CONTROL STRUCTURE

Control Environment

- ▸ Management's philosophy and operating style.
- ▸ The organizational structure.
- ▸ The audit committee of the board of directors.
- ▸ Methods of assigning authority and responsibility.
- ▸ Methods for controlling performance.
- ▸ Management's policies and practices.

Accounting System

- ▸ Identification and recording of all valid transactions.
- ▸ Proper classification of transactions.
- ▸ Proper measurement of the dollar amount of transactions.
- ▸ Assignment of transactions to proper time periods.
- ▸ Proper presentation of financial statements and notes.

Control Procedures

- ▸ Proper authorization of transactions and activities.
- ▸ Separation of duties.
- ▸ Documents and records that ensure proper recording.
- ▸ Adequate safeguards over access to and use of assets and records.
- ▸ Review of the internal control system by internal audit department.

SOURCE: *SAS No.* 55, *section* 319, paragraph 8.

EXHIBIT **6.1**

Elements of the Internal Control Structure

CONTROL STRUCTURE FOR CASH

Learning Goal 2   Describe the procedures involved in internal control of cash.

Cash includes deposits in checking and savings accounts and any item that a bank customarily accepts for immediate deposit. It also includes coins, currency, cashier's checks, money orders, and certain credit card sales invoices. Notes receivable, IOUs, and checks dated in the future are examples of items not considered to be cash for accounting purposes.

From a control point of view, it is not the balance sheet cash amount that represents the cash control problem. The real challenge is to control the large inflows and outflows of cash that occur during the year. As an illustration, Exhibit 6.2 shows the cash inflows and outflows for Wal-Mart Stores, Inc. for fiscal 2004. During 2004, the cash balance for Wal-Mart increased from $5,199 million to $5,488 million. However, the challenge for the management of Wal-Mart was to control cash inflows of $19,945 million and the cash outflows of $19,656 million. In following sections, we will discuss principles and procedures to assist management in controlling cash.

Cash Control

Cash is easily subject to theft or misuse. We must design safeguards to prevent the following:

- Theft of cash receipts concealed by failure to record the transaction in the journal. For example, an employee may sell scrap and waste material for cash and not report it.

Cash balance at January 31,2004 (fiscal 2004 beginning)	$ 5,199

PLUS

Cash Inflows

Net cash provided by operating activities	$ 15,044
Proceeds from borrowings	4,041
Cash received from other sources	860
Total cash inflows	$ 19,945

MINUS

Cash Outflows

Payments for property, plant and equipment	$ 12,893
Repurchase of common stock from shareholders	4,549
Cash dividends paid	2,214
Total cash outflows	$ 19,656

EQUALS

Cash balance at January 31, 2005 (fiscal 2004 end)	$ 5,488

EXHIBIT **6.2**

Wal-Mart Stores, Inc. Cash Flows for Fiscal 2004 (In millions)

- Improper recording of the receipt of cash. For example, an employee may keep cash received from a customer. He or she may conceal the theft by debiting Sales Returns and Allowances instead of Cash.

- Recording false debits to expense accounts or other accounts to cover fraudulent cash withdrawals. For example, a branch supervisor may carry a terminated employee's name on the payroll for several additional pay periods. The supervisor forges the endorsement of the former employee and cashes these payroll checks.

- Theft of cash by computer. For example, an employee may transfer cash to an unauthorized account by changing the computer program. Today, many companies transfer funds via the Internet.

We must have certain basic controls to prevent the misuse of cash. We must clearly establish individual responsibility for each step in the flow of cash. On receipt, we should endorse all checks and stamp them *For deposit only* to prevent their misuse. We should deposit total cash receipts intact daily. *Intact* means that we should not pay any bills from the cash collected that day. We should make all payments by company check and not out of cash receipts. We should use automated control devices, like cash registers, wherever possible.

Proper internal control of cash requires certain fundamental steps, including the following:

- Clear separation of duties and responsibilities among those who handle and account for cash.

- Provision of the equipment necessary for cash control.

- Definite written instructions that control authorization for payment of cash.

- Organization of the flow and recording of documents so that, whenever possible, the work of one employee is automatically verified by another. We should separate the handling of cash from the recordkeeping. No one person should both receive or disburse cash and also record it in the cash journals.

- Periodic testing to see if internal controls are operating effectively. For example, at unannounced times, someone should compare recorded cash receipts with cash on hand and recent deposits.

- Establishment of controls over access to computers and computer programs.

Electronic Transfers of Cash

Electronic cash transfers involve cash receipts and disbursements by computer as opposed to cash or check. One type of electronic cash transfer system businesses use is *point-of-sale*. Point-of-sale is a cash receipt system that allows customers to transfer cash from personal bank accounts at the time of sale. Customer information is entered into the computer system by inserting debit cards and entering the customer's personal identification number. After verifying the encoded information and whether the customer has sufficient funds to pay for the purchase, bank computers reduce the customer's account and increase the store's account. Since employees do not have to handle cash, point-of-sale systems enhance control of cash receipts from sales transactions. In recent years, customers have become comfortable in using such direct transfer systems.

Petty Cash

Learning Goal 3   Describe the operation of an imprest petty cash fund.

For adequate internal control, we should deposit total cash receipts intact daily. We should normally make disbursements by check. However, sometimes payment by check is impractical. For example, payments for postage, taxi fares, and minor supplies may require currency. We should set up a special **petty cash fund** for these payments. We place the fund in the custody of one person. A receipt signed by the person receiving the cash (a **petty cash voucher**) supports each payment. The voucher shows the purpose of the expenditure, the date, and the amount (see Exhibit 6.3).

To establish the petty cash fund, we write a check to the order of the fund custodian. He or she cashes it at the bank and puts the currency in a locked drawer. The journal entry to record the establishment of a petty cash fund of $500 by High Company is as follows:

2007				
Aug.	3	Petty Cash	500	
		Cash		500
		To establish petty cash fund.		

Safekeeping of the money and the signed vouchers is the responsibility of the custodian.

When the cash in the found approaches a predetermined minimum, or at the end of each accounting period, we replenish the fund. The signed petty cash vouchers are evidence of the disbursements. Assume that on August 31 2007, High Company's petty cash fund consists of cash and signed receipts for the following expenditures:

PETTY CASH VOUCHER

No.   324

| X | PAY IN CASH |

All expenditures paid in cash
must be explained and
receipted for on this voucher

VERIFIED
MH

CASHIER:

August 15,   20 07

PAY ____ Jim Brady _____

____ Thirty-five and 75/100 ---------------DOLLARS

CHARGE ___ Postage Expense ___   ACCOUNT NO___ 720 ___

DESCRIPTION ____ Special Mailings _____

APPROVED FOR PAYMENT	RECEIVED PAYMENT
Norma Gravski	*Jim Brady*

EXHIBIT **6.3**

Petty Cash Voucher

Cash	$ 47
Postage	112
Outstide telephone calls	54
Supplies for exibition both at regional sales meeting	114
Blank form pads	12
Transportation in on purchases	159
Total	$ 498
Shortage	2
Total to be accounted for	$ 500

We issue the custodian a check for $453 ($500 - $47) to restore the fund to its original cash balance of $500. The entry to record this check is as follows:

2007					
Aug	31	Postage Expense		112	
		Telephone Expense		54	
		Sales Promotion Expense		114	
		Office Supplies Expense		12	
		Transportation In		159	
		Cash Over and Short*		2	
		Cash			453
		To replenish the petty cash fund.			

*See the next section.

Since the entry does not debit or credit Petty Cash, the Petty Cash account in the general ledger remains at its original balance of $500. The method described here is the **imprest petty cash system**. We advance a fixed amount of money in trust to a custodian. There are no further debits or credits to Petty Cash unless we either increase or decrease the amount of the fund. Thus, the $500 balance is *imprest* upon the account. An increase or decrease in the fund requires an additional debit or credit to Petty Cash.

We should replenish the fund at the end of each accounting period, even when it is above the minimum cash balance. This will record all the expenses incurred during the period. It also will bring the amount of currency and coins on hand up to the balance of the Petty Cash account. We should make unannounced inspections at intervals to determine that the amount of cash plus receipted vouchers is equal to the fund balance.

Cash Over and Short

In the foregoing illustration, we found a cash shortage of $2 when replenishing the petty cash fund. Also, the daily count of cash in the cash registers may differ from the cash register readings. If the records do not disclose a clerical error, we may assume that an error in making change caused the overage or shortage. We should enter the discrepancy in the books as a debit or a credit to the **Cash Over and Short** account. To illustrate, assume that a cash register tape shows cash sales for the day of $1,000. The count shows the cash on hand to be $1,003. This account should only reflect minor discrepancies in the cash total. The journal entry to record the cash sales based on the cash register total, the cash based on the actual count, and the cash overage is as follows:

```
2007
Nov.  30  Cash                              1,003
              Sales                                    1,000
              Cash Over and Short                          3
          To record cash sales and cash overage.
```

If the cash count showed $996, we would debit the Cash Over and Short account for $4.

We classify cash over and short on the income statement as a general and administrative expense if it has a debit balance. If it has a credit balance, we classify it as other revenue. We should investigate overages and shortages of material amounts.

Bank Checking Account

Most transactions ultimately involve the receipt or payment of cash, often in the form of a check. The bank checking account of a business operates in the same way as a personal checking account. An **check** is a written order directing a bank to pay a specified amount of money to the order of a payee. An essential part of the internal control system is that only a selected person or persons should have the authority to sign checks.

The depositor fills out a *deposit ticket* each time he or she makes a bank deposit. The deposit ticket lists each check deposited, the date of the deposit, and the account number into which the deposit was made. The deposit tickets are evidence for the depositor of the amount of money deposited in the bank.

The Bank Statement

Learning Goal 4   Interpret a monthly bank statement and prepare a bank reconciliation.

Banks send depositors a monthly statement along with the cancelled checks and notices of bank debits and credits. The bank statement shows the activities for the month. It should list, at a minimum, the following information:

- The beginning balance.
- The deposits received.
- The checks paid.
- Other debits and credits to the account.
- The ending balance.

Exhibit 6.4 shows the September 2007 bank statement of Clearwater Company. Following are some common transactions reported on a bank statement:

Service Charge

Unless depositors keep a specified minimum balance in the bank, banks often impose **service charge** for their costs of handling the account.

Debit Memo

A **debit memo** describes a bank deduction from the depositor's account. An example would be a customer's check previously deposited but uncollectible (**nonsufficient funds or NSF**). The bank reports this with a debit memo. It is a debit memo to the bank because the bank reduces its liability to the depositor. From the depositor's point of view, it is a reduction in the bank balance and a credit—*not a debit*—to the Cash account in the ledger.

Credit Memo

A **credit memo** describes a bank credit. The bank statement usually shows it in the Deposits column. For example, the bank may collect a note receivable left at the bank by a depositor. It is a credit memo to the bank because the bank increases its liability to the depositor. From the depositor's point of view, it is an increase in the bank balance and a debit—*not a credit*—to the Cash account in the ledger.

Certified Check

When the depositor requests a **certified check**, the bank immediately deducts the amount of the check from the depositor's balance. This procedure assures the payee that the bank will pay the check.

Interest

Some banks pay interest based on daily balances in checking accounts.

Reconciliation Procedure

The use of a business checking account is essential to the control of cash. A business should deposit total receipts intact daily. They should make all payments by check. This will mean that for each entry in the depositor's Cash account, there should be a counterpart in the bank's books. Although the bank's entries are made at different times, the bank, an outside organization, is keeping a separate and independent record of cash.

THE BANK OF CONNECTICUT

HARTFORD, CONNECTICUT

Statement of Account for:

Clearwater Company
20 Post Road
Tolland, Connecticut 06084

Account No.	12-8832-00
Period Ending	September 30, 2007
Page	1

Balance from last statement	$ 386.50	**Withdrawals**	$	1,439.78
Number of deposits	9	**Bank service charge**	$	5.40
Deposits	$1,262.08	**Interest**	$	0.84
Number of withdrawals	17	**New balance this statement**	$	204.24

Date	Transaction		Checks & Debits	Deposits & Credits	Balance
09-02	Deposit			82.20	468.70
09-03	Deposit			56.72	525.42
	Check	637	49.00		476.42
	Check	638	238.60		237.82
09-04	Deposit			102.54	340.36
	Check	640	200.16		140.20
	Check	644	118.37		21.83
09-05	Deposit			108.72	130.55
	Check	641	86.50		44.05
	Check	642	25.75		18.30
09-06	Deposit			112.50	130.60
	Debit memo-nonsufficient funds	645	21.20		109.40
	Check		18.30		91.10
09-16	Credit memo-collection note			497.00	588.10
	Check	647	10.00		578.10
	Check	650	67.60		510.50
09-18	Deposit			86.80	597.30
	Check	646	110.00		487.30
	Check	648	180.00		307.30
	Check	649	138.20		169.10
09-27	Deposit			103.62	272.72
	Check-certified	651	100.00		172.72
	Check	653	9.80		162.92
09-30	Deposit			112.18	275.10
	Check	655	15.68		259.42
	Check	656	50.62		208.80
	Service charge		5.40		203.40
	Interest			0.84	204.24

Checks and other debits:

#637	49.00	#645	18.30	#651	100.00	
638	238.60	646	110.00	653	9.80	
640	200.16	647	10.00	655	15.68	
641	86.50	648	180.00	656	50.62	
642	25.75	649	138.20		21.20	
644	118.37	650	67.60		5.40	

EXHIBIT **6.4**

Bank Statement for Clearwater Company

The records of the depositor and of the bank normally will not agree at the end of the month. Items will appear on one record but not on the other. In some cases, there is a time lag in recording deposits and checks. There may be bank charges and credits of which the depositor is unaware. There may also be errors or irregularities. We must reconcile the two balances and determine the

adjusted cash balance. The **bank reconciliation** is a statement that shows the items that account for the difference between the Cash account balance and the bank statement balance. One of its primary purposes is to strengthen internal control over cash. We prepare it as follows:

1. Compare deposits shown on the bank statement with debits in the Cash account. We call deposits made too late in the month to be credited by the bank on the current statement **deposits in transit**. We should inspect the bank reconciliation for the previous month for any deposits in transit at the end of that period. They should appear as the early deposits of the current period.

2. Compare checks paid and returned by the bank (cancelled checks) with the credit entries in the Cash account. Checks that have not yet been presented by the payees to the bank for payment are **outstanding checks**. We should inspect the previous bank reconciliation to see that outstanding checks from that reconciliation have now cleared the bank on this statement.

3. Compare special debits and credits made by the bank—usually reported in debit or credit memos—with the depositor's books to see if they have already been recorded.

4. List any errors in the bank's or the depositor's records that become apparent during completion of Steps 1-3.

Exhibit 6.5 shows the overall format for a bank reconciliation. All items in the *Per Books* section require entries in the general journal or special cash journals to adjust the books. Items in the *Per Bank* section do not require entries in the depositor's books. They may require action to see that the bank records them.

NAME
BANK RECONCILIATION
DATE

Per Books				Per Bank			
Cash balance per ledger, date			$XXX	Cash balance per bank statement, date			$XXX
Add:				Add:			
1. Any increases in cash already recorded by the bank but not yet recorded by the firm.				1. Any increases in cash already recorded by the firm but not yet recorded by the bank.			
Example: Collection of note by bank	$XX			Example: Deposits in transit	$XX		
2. Any error in the firm's books that failed to record an increase in cash or that improperly decreased cash.				2. Any error by the bank that failed to record an increase in cash or that improperly decreased cash.			
Example: Check from customer for $90 entered as $70	XX	XX		Example: Another depositor's check incorrectly charged to this depositor's account		XX	XX
Subtotal			$XXX	Subtotal			$XXX
Deduct:				Deduct:			
1. Any decreases in cash already recorded by the bank but not yet recorded by the firm.				1. Any decreases in cash already recorded by the firm but not yet recorded by the bank.			
Example: Bank sewice charges	$XX			Example: Outstanding checks	$XX		
2. Any error in the firm's books that failed to record a decrease in cash or that improperly increased cash.				2. Any error by the bank that failed to record a decrease in cash or that improperly increased cash.			
Example: Check issued in pavment to a creditor for $462 entered as $426	XX	XX		Example: Firm's deposit of $679 entered by the bank as $697		XX	XX
Adjusted cash balance, date			$XXX	Adjusted cash balance, date			$XXX

EXHIBIT **6.5**

Format for a Bank Reconciliation

We will study the preparation of a bank reconciliation with Clearwater Company's bank statement for September (shown in Exhibit 6.4 In Clearwater's August 2007 bank reconciliation, the firm listed a deposit of $82.20 made on August 30 as a deposit in transit. Outstanding checks on August 31 were as follows:

Check No.	Amount	Check No.	Amount
637	$ 49.00	641	$ 86.50
638	238.60	642	25.75
639	15.00	643	5.00
640	201.06	644	118.37

The Cash account of Clearwater Company showed activity in September as follows:

	Deposits*		Payments
Date	Amount	Check No.	Amount
Sept. 2	$ 56.72	645	$ 18.30
3	102.54	646	110.00
4	108.72	647	10.00
5	112.30	648	180.00
17	86.80	649	138.20
26	103.62	650	67.60
27	112.18	651	100.00
30	421.50	652	30.20
		653	9.80
		654	21.50
		655	15.68
		656	50.62
		657	9.85
		658	3.72

* As indicated earlier, effective internal control requires daily deposit of cash receipts intact. To shorten the illustration, we do not follow this practice after the deposit of September 5 (recorded September 6 on the bank statement).

The balance in the Cash account on September 30, 2007, is $68.33. The balance for September 30 shown on the bank statement in Exhibit 6.4 is $204.24. As Clearwater's accountant, assume we know the following facts when studying the bank statement:

1. The debit memorandum dated September 6 for $21.20 represented a customer's check from Ann Lanier included in an earlier deposit and returned marked "NSF."Clearwater has not yet charged this check back to the customer's account.

2. The credit memorandum for $497 dated September 16 represents a $500 credit less $3 collection fee. The bank collected a note receivable for Clearwater. There was no interest on the face value of this note.

3. The $100 certified check on September 27 was for check no. 651 certified for Clearwater Company on that date. It was among the checks returned as paid by the bank. Even if it were not paid, we would not include it as an outstanding check on September 30. The bank deducted it from Clearwater's balance on the date of certification.

We then verify that the deposit in transit on August 31 appears on the September bank statement. The next task is to trace the August 31 outstanding checks and checks written in

September to the bank statement. We list those that have not cleared as outstanding checks. Then we prepare a bank reconciliation, as shown in Exhibit 6.6 Numbered items are explained as follows:

1. Clearwater Company had a note receivable from a customer made out for its maturity value due on September 16. Since the customer had an account at the same bank, Clearwater delivered the note to the bank with a request that it be collected. The bank, after securing permission from the customer, debited the customer's account on September 16 for $500 and credited Clearwater's. There was a $3 charge for this service. Clearwater has not recorded either the $500 credit or the $3 charge. So we add the note proceeds less the service charge to the balance per books.

2. The bank has credited the interest earned on this checking account. Clearwater has not recorded it. We add it to the balance per books.

3. When we traced the checks clearing the bank to the books, we discovered that we recorded check no. 640 in payment for equipment repairs in error as $201.06. The correct amount, as shown on the bank statement and the cancelled check, is $200.16. Since the credit to the Cash account was $.90 greater than it should have been, we add this amount to the balance per books.

4. As indicated earlier, the bank returned a customer's check for $21.20 marked "NSF." When we received it from the customer, we added it to the Cash account and deposited it in the bank. Since the bank rejected it for deposit, we now must deduct it from the balance per books.

5. We have not entered the monthly bank service charge in the books. We must deduct it from the balance per books.

6. The bank received the deposit of September 30 in the amount of $421.50 too late to include it in this bank statement. We add it to the balance per bank statement. It should appear as the first deposit on the October statement.

7. We compare the checks previously listed as outstanding and those paid by the bank in September. This shows that two checks listed on the bank reconciliation had not yet reached the bank. Checks no. 639 and 643 were outstanding on August 31 and still did not clear the bank in September. Sometimes the person or company receiving a check does not deposit it—even though this is not sound financial practice. If these two checks remain outstanding for another month or two, there is a chance that the recipient has lost them. We should write or call to ask about them.

CLEARWATER COMPANY
BANK RECONCILIATION
September 30, 2007

Cash balance per ledger.				Cash balance per bank		
September 30			$ 68.33	statement, September 30		$204.24
Add: Customer.note collected by bank	**1** $500.00			Add: Deposit in transit		**6** 421.50
Deduct: Collection charge	3.00	$497.00		Subtotal		$625.74
Interest earned on account Error		**2** 0.84		Deduct: Outstanding checks **7**		
in check no. 640		**3** 0.90	498.74	No. 639	$15.00	
			$567.07	643	5.00	
Deduct: Customer's NSF check		**4** $ 21.20		652	30.20	
Bank service charge		**5** 5.40	26.60	654	21.50	
				657	9.85	
				658	3.72	85.27
Adjusted cash balance,				Adjusted cash balance,		
September 30			$540.47	September 30		$540.47

EXHIBIT **6.6**

Bank Reconciliation for Clearwater Company

Recording the Adjustments

Learning Goal 5   Record journal entries required to adjust the Cash account after the bank reconciliation.

The adjustments made to the cash balance of the *Per Books* section in the bank reconciliation require journal entries. This will update Clearwater Company's accounts so that the Cash account balance agrees with the adjusted balance in the reconciliation. Other ledger account balances are also affected. We can make all adjustments in one compound entry or in separate entries as follows:

2007					
Sep.	30	Cash		497.00	
		Collection Fee Expense		3.00	
		Notes Receivable			500.00
		To record collection of customer note made out for face value.			
	30	Cash		0.84	
		Interest Revenue			0.84
		To record interest on checking account.			
	30	Cash		0.90	
		Repairs Expense			0.90
		To record error in check no. 640 written for $200.16 but recorded at $201.06.			
	30	Accounts Receivable, Ann Lanier		21.20	
		Cash			21.20
		To record customer's NSF check.			
	30	Bank Service Charge Expense		5.40	
		Cash			5.40
		To record cost of checking account service.			

After posting the entries, the Cash account will have a new balance of $540.47. This also updates the other affected accounts.

Only the items from the reconciliation that either increase or decrease the balance per books need to be entered in the journal. The depositor has already recorded the items that increase or decrease the balance per bank. They require *no adjusting entry*. The bank reconciliation strengthens internal control over cash by highlighting all differences between the accounts and the bank's records. It also shows that the balances for both the bank and the Cash account reconcile to the adjusted cash figure at the end of each month.

ANALYZING INFORMATION

Learning Goal 6   Analyze financial statement information for real-life companies.

In looking at balance sheets of real-life companies, you will notice that the first asset listed is usually "cash and cash equivalents." Cash equivalents are short-term, highly liquid investments. They must be readily convertible into cash and have an original maturity of three months or less. Examples of items frequently included as a cash equivalent are investments in U.S. treasury bills, bank time deposits, and money market funds.

In analyzing cash and cash equivalents on the balance sheet, users frequently focus on whether the amount is higher or lower than the previous year. The size of the cash balance may be misleading since it is easily manipulated for a balance sheet date. For example, cash on a balance sheet date may be increased by not paying bills or by borrowing money for a short period of time. Rather than looking at the amount of cash on a given date, it is more useful to look at cash inflows and outflows for the year. This information is shown in the Statement of Cash Flows. We will analyze this statement in detail later in the text.

At this point, our analysis of cash will focus on any restrictions that might exist on the cash balance and on any concerns on where it is invested. For example, many people reading this text have bank accounts with "free checking" as long as a minimum account balance is maintained. Many businesses must maintain a similar bank balance called a *compensating balance* to support free bank services or borrowing under a line of credit. If the bank balance falls below the required compensating balance amount, the business could face the risk of increased bank costs or loss of a borrowing source. As an illustration, let's look at the following information on cash from the 2004 annual report of Avon Products, Inc.:

AVON PRODUCTS, INC

Balance Sheet (in millions)	December 31	
	2004	2003
Current assets:		
Cash, including cash equivalents of $401.2 and $373.8	769.6	694.0

Notes to Financial Statements:

Cash and Equivalents—Cash equivalents are stated at cost plus accrued interest, which approximates fair value. Cash equivalents are high quality, short-term money market instruments with an original maturity of three months or less and consist of time deposits with a number of U.S. and non-U.S. commercial banks and money market fund investments.

Debt—...At December 31, 2004 revolving credit of $600.0, of which none was outstanding. Such lines have covenants including one requiring the interest coverage ratio to exceed 4:1. Avon is in compliance with all covenants.

Question. Do you have any concerns over where cash equivalents have been invested? If the business must maintain a certain covenants is Avon satisfy the requirement?

Answer. Avon is minimizing the risk of investing funds in a single bank by using a number of different financial institutions. Currently, Avon is meeting its covenants.

COMPREHENSIVE ANALYSIS CASE

From the very start of this text, we have been analyzing information for real-life companies. Starting with this chapter, we will introduce a *Comprehensive Analysis Case*. Our text includes Comprehensive Case Analysis problems in the end-of-chapter assignments for Chapters 6-18 The purpose of these problems is to take you through a complete analysis for real-life companies.

Comprehensive Analysis Case Questions Analyzing Dell, Inc. for the Period 2004-2002

The comparative income statements and balance sheets with common-size percents for Dell for the period 2004-2002 (in millions) are shown on the next page. Also included are selected *ratio* statistics. Financial statement ratios show the relative size of one financial statement item to another. We discuss these ratios in detail in Chapter 16 if you wish additional background.

DELL INC.
COMPARATIVE COMMONSIZE INCOME STATEMENTS
For The Years Ended Jan. 30, 2004, Jan. 31, 2003, and Feb. 1, 2002
(in millions)

	2004	2004	2003	2003	2002	2002
	$	%	$	%	$	%
Revenues	$ 41,444.0	100.0%	$ 35,404.0	100.0%	$ 31,168.0	100.0%
Cost of goods sold	$ 33,892.0	81.8%	$ 29,055.0	82.1%	$ 25,661.0	82.3%
Gross margin	$ 7,552.0	18.2%	$ 6,349.0	17.9%	$ 5,507.0	17.7%
Operating expenses:						
Selling and administrative expenses	$ 3,544.0	8.6%	$ 3,050.0	8.6%	$ 2,784.0	8.9%
Research and development	$ 464.0	1.1%	$ 455.0	1.3%	$ 452.0	1.5%
Other expense	$ -	0.0%	$ -	0.0%	$ -	0.0%
Other expense	$ -	0.0%	$ -	0.0%	$ 482.0	1.5%
Total operating expenses	$ 4,008.0	9.7%	$ 3,505.0	9.9%	$ 3,178.0	11.9%
Operating income	$ 3,544.0	8.6%	$ 2,844.0	8.0%	$ 1,789.0	5.7%
Interest expense	$ 14.0	0.0%	$ -	0.0%	$ -	0.0%
Other expense (income)	$ (194.0)	-0.5%	$ (183.0)	-0.5%	$ 58.0	0.2%
Income before income taxes	$ 3,724.0	9.0%	$ 3,027.0	8.5%	$ 1,731.0	5.6%
Income taxes	$ 1,079.0	2.6%	$ 905.0	2.6%	$ 485.0	1.6%
Net income (loss) before unusual items	$ 2,645.0	6.4%	$ 2,122.0	6.0%	$ 1,246.0	4.0%
Nonrecurring losses (gains) net of tax	$ -	0.0%	$ -	0.0%	$ -	0.0%
Net income (loss)	$ 2,645.0	6.4%	$ 2,122.0	6.0%	$ 1,246.0	4.0%

DELL INC.
COMPARATIVE COMMONSIZE BALANCE SHEETS
Jan. 30, 2004, Jan. 31, 2003, and Feb. 1, 2002
(in millions)

	2004	2004	2003	2003	2002	2002
	$	%	$	%	0	%
ASSETS						
Current:						
Cash & cash equivalents	$ 4,317.0	22.4%	$ 4,232.0	27.4%	$ 3,641.0	26.9%
Short-term investments	$ 835.0	4.3%	$ 406.0	206%	$ 273.0	2.0%
Accounts receivable, net	$ 3,635.0	18.8%	$ 2,586.0	16.7%	$ 2,269.0	16.8%
Inventory	$ 327.0	1.7%	$ 306.0	2.0%	$ 278.0	2.1%
Other current assets	$ 1,519.0	7.9%	$ 1,394.0	9.0%	$ 1,416.0	10.5%
Other current assets	$ -	0.0%	$ -	0.0%	$ -	0.0%
Total current assets	$ 10,633.0	55.1%	$ 8,924.0	57.7%	$ 7,877.0	58.2%
Fixed:						
Property & equipment, net	$ 1,517.0	7.9%	$ 913.0	5.9%	$ 826.0	6.1%
Long-term investments	$ 6,770.0	35.1%	$ 5,267.0	34.0%	$ 4,373.0	32.3%
Intangibles & goodwill	$ -	0.0%	$ -	0.0%	$ -	0.0%
Other assets	$ 391.0	2.0%	$ 366.0	2.4%	$ 459.0	3.4%
Total assets	$ 19,311.0	100.0%	$ 15,470.0	100.0%	$ 13,535.0	100.0%
LIABILITIES						
Current:						
Short-term debt	$ -	0.0%	$ -	0.0%	$ -	0.0%
Accounts payable	$ 9,935.0	51.4%	$ 6,282.0	40.6%	$ 7,519.0	55.6%
Unearned income	$ -	0.0%	$ -	0.0%	$ -	0.0%
Other current liabilities	$ 961.0	15.3%	$ 2,651.0	54.4%	$ -	0.0%
Other current liabilities	$ -	0.0%	$ -	0.0%	$ -	0.0%
Total current liabilities	$ 10,896.0	56.4%	$ 8,933.0	57.7%	$ 7,519.0	55.6%
Long-term debt	$ 505.0	2.6%	$ 506.0	3.3%	$ 520.0	3.8%
Other noncurrent liabilities	$ 538.0	2.8%	$ 1,158.0	7.5%	$ 802.0	5.9%
Other noncurrent liabilities	$ 1,092.0	5.7%	$ -	0.0%	$ -	0.0%
Total liabilities	$ 13,031.0	67.5%	$ 10,597.0	68.5%	$ 8,841.0	65.3%
OWNERS' EQUITY						
Total owners' equity	$ 6,280.0	32.5%	$ 4,873.0	31.5%	$ 4,694.0	34.7%
Total liabilities and owners' equity	$ 19,311.0	100.0%	$ 15,470.0	100.0%	$ 13,535.0	100.0%

(Note: percents may not add to 100 due to rounding)

DELL INC.
RATIO ANALYSIS SUMMARY
For fiscal years 2004, 2003, 2002

	2004	2003	2002
SHORT-TERM LIQUIDITY RATIOS			
Current Ratio (Current Assets/Current Liabilities)	0.98	1.00	1.05
Quick Ratio (Cash + ST Invest + AR)/Current Liabilities	0.81	0.81	0.82
LONG-TERM SOLVENCY (LEVERAGE) RATIO			
Total Debt Ratio (Total Liabilities/Total Assets)	67.48%	68.50%	65.32%
ACTIVITY (TURNOVER) RATIOS			
Accounts Receivable Turnover 1 (Revenues/Average AR)	13.32	14.58	
Accounts Receivable Turnover 2 (Revenues/Year-end AR)	11.40	13.69	13.74
Inventory Turnover 1 (CGS/Average Inventory)	107.08	99.50	
Inventory Turnover 2 (CGS/Year-end Inventory)	103.65	94.95	92.31
Total Asset Turnover (Revenues/Average Total Assets)	2.38	2.44	
PROFITABILITY RATIOS			
Gross Profit Margin (GP/Rev)	18.22%	17.93%	17.67%
Operating Profit Margin (Pretax Income/Rev)	8.55%	8.03%	5.74%
Net Profit Margin (Return on Sales) (ROS) (NI/Rev)	6.38%	5.99%	4.00%
Return on Total Assets (ROA) (NI/Average Total Assets)	15.21%	14.63%	

As in previous chapters, we list a series of questions to guide your analysis. We will list all questions first to show the overall scope of our analysis. We then lead you through responses for these questions. The end-of-chapter Comprehensive Analysis Case for Chapter 6 is Intel.

Income Statement Questions:

1. Are total revenues higher or lower over the three-year period?

2. What is the percent change in total revenues from 2002 to 2004?

3. Is the percent of cost of goods sold to total revenues increasing or decreasing over the three-year period? As a result, is the gross margin percent increasing or decreasing?

4. Is the percent of total operating expenses to total revenues increasing or decreasing over the three-year period? As a result, is the operating income percent increasing or decreasing?

5. Is the percent of net income to total revenue increasing or decreasing over the three-year period?

Balance Sheet Questions:

6. Are total assets higher or lower over the three-year period?

7. What is the percent change in total assets from 2002 to 2004?

8. What are the largest asset investments for the company over the three-year period?

9. Are the largest asset investments increasing faster or slower than the percent change in total revenues?

10. Is the percent of total liabilities to total liabilities + owners' equity increasing or decreasing? Therefore, is there more or less risk that the company could not pay its debts?

Integrative Income Statement and Balance Sheet Question:

11. Is the company operating more or less efficiently by using the least amount of asset investment to generate a given level of total revenues? Note that the "total asset turnover" ratio is computed and included in the "ratio analysis summary."

Ratio Analysis Questions (Refer to Chapter 16 for Additional Ratio Explanation)

Short-term Liquidity Ratios (Assess ability to pay current liabilities)

12. **Current Ratio** This ratio shows current assets available to pay current liabilities. We compute this ratio as follows: Current Assets/Current Liabilities. We ask the question: Is the *current ratio* better (higher) or worse (lower) in the most current year compared to prior years?

13. **Quick Ratio** This ratio shows liquid assets available to pay current liabilities. We compute this ratio as follows: (Cash + Short-term Investments + Accounts Receivable)/Current Liabilities. We ask the question: Is the *quick ratio* better (higher) or worse (lower) in the most current year compared to prior years?

14. **Accounts Receivable Turnover 1 (Based on average receivables)** This ratio shows the number of times the company turns average receivables into cash during a period. We compute this ratio as follows: Revenues/Average Accounts Receivable. (Note that we can only calculate the average ratio for the two most recent years because we do not know accounts receivable for 2001.) We ask the question: Is the *accounts receivable turnover ratio 1* (based on *average* receivables) better (higher) or worse (lower) in the most current year compared to prior years?

15. **Accounts Receivable Turnover 2 (Based on year-end receivables)** This ratio bases receivable turnover on year-end instead of average receivables. We do this to assess if year-end trends in receivables are better or worse than the average. This is important to assess recent changes that may cause concern. (Note that we can calculate the year-end ratio for all three years since we do not use an average.) We compute this ratio as follows: Revenues/Year-end Accounts Receivable. We ask the question: Is the 2004 *accounts receivable turnover ratio 2* (based on *year-end* receivables) better or worse than the 2004 ratio based on an *average*?

16. **Inventory Turnover 1 (Based on average inventory)** This ratio shows the number of times inventory turns over during a period. We prefer a smaller inventory investment and a higher inventory turnover. We compute this ratio as follows: Cost of Goods Sold/Average Inventory. (Note that we can calculate the average ratio only for the two most recent years.) We ask the question: Is the *inventory turnover ratio 1* (based on *average* inventory) better (higher) or worse (lower) in the most current year compared to prior years?

17. **Inventory Turnover 2 (Based on year-end inventory)** This ratio bases inventory turnover on year-end versus inventory. We do this to assess if year-end trends in inventory are better or worse than the average. This is important to assess recent changes that may cause concern. We compute this ratio as follows: Cost of Goods Sold/Year-end Inventory. (Note that we can calculate the year-end ratio for all three years since we do not use an average.) We ask the question: Is the 2004 *inventory turnover ratio 2* (based on *year-end* inventory) better (higher) or worse (lower) than the 2004 ratio based on an *average*?

Profitability Ratio (Assess return on total assets)
18. **Return on Total Assets (ROA)** This ratio measures the amount a firm earns on a dollar of investment in assets. We compute this ratio as follows: Net Income/Average Total Assets. (Note that we can calculate the average ratio for the two most recent years.) We ask the question: Is the *return on total assets (ROA) ratio* better (higher) or worse (lower) in the most current year compared to prior years?

Comprehensive Analysis Case Responses Analyzing Dell Computer Corporation for the Period 2004-2002

Income Statement Responses:
1. Total revenues in 2004 are greater than the total for 2002.

2. The percent increase in total revenues from 2002 to 2004 is:

$$33.0\% = 100 \times \frac{\$10,276,000,000^*}{\$31,168,000,000} \quad {}^*\$41,444,000,000 - 31,168,000,000$$

Total revenues increased 33.0% from 2002 to 2004.

3. The cost of goods sold percent decreased from 82.3% in 2002 to 81.8% in 2004. As a result, the gross margin percent increased from 17.7% in 2002 to 18.2% in 2004. This is a *favorable* trend.

4. The percent of total operating expenses to total revenues decreased from 11.9% in 2002 to 9.7% in 2004. This is *favorable*. The result was an increase in the operating income percent from 5.7% in 2002 to 8.6% in 2004.

5. The percent of net income to total revenues increased from 4.0% in 2002 to 6.4% in 2004. This is an *favorable* trend.

Balance Sheet Responses:

6. Total assets at January 30, 2004 are greater than the total at February 1, 2002.

7. In this case, the percent increase in total assets from February 1, 2002 to January 30, 2004 is:

$$42.7\% = 100 \times \frac{\$5,776,000,000^*}{\$13,535,000,000} \quad {}^*19,311,000,000 - 13,535,000,000$$

As with total revenues, the total assets have increased over the three-year period.

8. The largest investments for the company other than cash are long-term investments and receivables. These two items make up 53.9% of the company's assets at the end of the most recent year.

9. Since the largest asset investment is in long-term investments, which is a non-liquid asset, we will perform our analysis on accounts receivable. The percent increase in accounts receivable between 2002 and 2004 is:

$$60.2\% = 100 \times \frac{\$1,366,000,000^*}{\$2,269,000,000} \quad {}^*3,635,000,000 - 2,269,000,000$$

The largest asset investment (accounts receivable) is growing at a faster rate than the total revenues increase. This is *unfavorable* because Dell is not collecting its accounts receivables as fast as it is growing revenues.

10. On the balance sheet, refer to the common-size percent for total liabilities each year. The percent of total liabilities increased from 65.3% in 2002 to 67.5% in 2004. In general, it is favorable to decrease the percent of total liabilities + owners'equity. Therefore, the trend is *unfavorable* between 2002 and 2004. Considering Dell's large amount of cash and long-term investments as of January 30, 2004, the percent of total liabilities (67.5%) is less of a problem.

Integrative Income Statement and Balance Sheet Response:

11. This company is operating less efficiently in 2004 than in 2002. We conclude this by comparing the total asset turnover (see *total asset turnover* ratio) for the two years. This ratio decreased from 2.44 times in 2003 to 2.38 times in 2004. Each dollar of investment in assets generated a lower amount of revenues in 2004 than in 2003. This is *unfavorable*.

Ratio Analysis Responses:

12. The current ratio for this company is worse in 2004 compared to the two previous years. In 2004, the current ratio was 0.98. This is a decrease from 1.00 in 2003 and a decrease from 1.05 in 2002. This is *unfavorable*.

13. The quick ratio for this company is worse in 2004 compared to 2002. In 2004, the quick ratio was 0.81. This is a decrease from 0.82 in 2002. This is *unfavorable*.

14. The accounts receivable turnover ratio 1 is worse this year compared to the previous year. In 2004, the accounts receivable turnover ratio 1 is 13.32 times. This is an decrease from 14.58 times in 2003. This is *unfavorable*.

15. For the year ended January 30, 2004, the 2004 accounts receivable turnover 2 (based on year-end receivables) is worse at 11.40 times compared to the 2004 accounts receivable turnover 1 (based on average receivables) at 13.32 times. Dell is collecting its receivables slower.

16. The inventory turnover ratio 1 is better in 2004 compared to the previous year. In 2004, the inventory turnover ratio 1 is 107.08 times. This is an increase from 99.50 times in 2003. This is *favorable*.

17. For the year ended January 30, 2004, the 2004 inventory turnover ratio 2 (based on year-end inventory) at 103.65 times is worse than the 2004 inventory turnover ratio 1 (based on average inventory) at 107.08 times. Dell is increasing its investment in inventories. This is *unfavorable*.

18. The return on total assets (ROA) ratio is better in 2004 than in 2003. In 2004, the ROA is 15.21%. This is a increase from 14.63% in 2003. This is *favorable*.

LEARNING GOALS REVIEW

1. Define internal control and describe the three elements of internal control.

Internal control is a set of policies and procedures designed to provide reasonable assurance that we prevent or detect errors or irregularities on a timely basis. Internal control also protects assets from improper use. The elements of the internal control structure are the control environment, the accounting system, and the control procedures.

Basic procedures for internal control include proper authorization of transactions and activities; separation of duties; design and use of adequate documents and records; adequate safeguards over access to and use of assets and records; and periodic internal review of performance and proper valuation of recorded amounts.

2. Describe the procedures involved in internal control of cash.

To prevent the misuse of funds, we must establish individual responsibility for each step in the flow of cash. On receipt, we should endorse all checks *For deposit only*. We should deposit total cash receipts intact daily and make payments by company check, not with cash. We should separate handling cash from recording cash transactions. The work of one employee should be automatically verified by another. Periodic testing should determine whether internal controls are working effectively. We should control access to computers and computer programs.

3. Describe the operation of an imprest petty cash fund.

To establish the petty cash fund, we write a check to the order of the fund custodian, who cashes it at the bank. The custodian is responsible for the safekeeping of the money and the signed receipts for the cash, called petty cash vouchers. Whenever cash is disbursed, a voucher is completed and signed by the custodian and the person receiving payment. When we replenish the fund, we record the expenses evidenced by the vouchers.

Unannounced inspections should be held to verify that the amount of cash plus vouchers equals the fund balance.

4. Interpret a monthly bank statement and prepare a bank reconciliation.

Exhibit 6.4 shows a bank statement. The bank reconciliation involves preparing a statement such as the one shown in Exhibit 6.5 using four steps: (1) Compare deposits shown on the bank statement with debits in the Cash account. (2) Compare the cancelled checks with the credit entries in the Cash account. (3) Compare the bank's special debits and credits with the company's books to see if the amounts have already been recorded. (4) List any errors in the bank's or the depositor's records that become apparent during the first three steps.

5. **Record journal entries required to adjust the Cash account after the bank reconciliation.**

   Make entries to update the company's accounts so that the Cash balance agrees with the adjusted balance in the bank reconciliation. We make entries for the items from the reconciliation that either increase or decrease the balance per books.

6. **Analyze financial statement information for real-life companies.**

   Our analysis of cash focuses on any restrictions that might exist on the cash balance and on any concerns on where it is invested. Do you have any concerns over where cash equivalents have been invested? If the business must maintain a minimum compensating bank balance, does the existing cash balance satisfy the requirement?

DEMONSTRATION PROBLEM

Bank Reconciliation

The following information comes from the records of HotFire Stove Company for the month of May 2007

Other Information

As of April 30, 2007, checks no. 274 for $350 and no. 281 for $760 were outstanding, and a deposit made on April 30, 2007, in the amount of $500 had not yet been recorded by the bank. The credit memo on May 21, 2007, is for the collection of a note receivable by the bank including $15 in interest. Returned with the May 31, 2007, bank statement was an NSF check for $330. HotFire had received this check from a customer named John Trivo and had deposited it on May 17, 2007. They had not recorded the NSF check on the records of HotFire Stove Company as of May 31, 2007.

Date		Explanation	Debit	Credit	Balance Debit	Balance Credit
2007						
Apr.	30	Balance			9,160	
May		Summary of Deposits	6,140			
		Summary of Payments		8,630		
May	31	Balance			6,670	

Deposits

Date		Debit Cash
2007		
May	2	960
	8	1,020
	16	750
	24	1,540
	31	1,870
		6,140

Payments

Date		Check No.	Credit Cash
2007			
May	1	282	710
	1	283	560
	7	284	860
	14	285	1,230
	17	286	470
	23	287	1,790
	29	288	880
	29	289	1,450
	31	290	680
			8,630

The Bank of Alaska
Fairbanks, Alaska

Statement of Account for:

HotFire Stove Company	Account No.		88-5294-0001
27 Ice Lane	Period Ending		May 31, 2007
Fairbanks, Alaska	Page		1

Balance from last statement	$ 9,770	**Withdrawals**	$ 7,280
Number of deposits	6	**Bank service charge**	$ 10
Deposits	$ 5,385	**Interest**	$ 32
Number of withdrawals	9	**New balance this statement**	$ 7,897

Date	Transaction		Checks & Debits	Deposits & Credits	Balance
05-01	Deposit			500	10,270
	Check	281	760		9,510
05-03	Deposit			960	10,470
	Check	274	350		10,120
	Check	283	560		9,560
05-07	Check	282	710		8,850
05-09	Deposit			1,020	9,870
	Check	284	860		9,010
05-17	Deposit			750	9,760
05-21	Credit memo-collection of note			615	10,375
	Debit memo-nonsufficient funds check		330		10,045
	Check	286	470		9,575
05-23	Check-certified	287	1,790		7,785
05-25	Deposit			1,540	9,325
05-30	Check	289	1,450		7,875
05-31	Interest			32	7,907
	Service charge		10		7,897

Checks and other debits:

#274	350	#284	860		330
281	760	286	470		10
282	710	287	1,790		
283	560	289	1,450		

REQUIRED

1. **(LG 4)** Prepare a bank reconciliation as of May 31, 2007.

2. **(LG 5)** Prepare general journal entries to adjust the accounting records.

SOLUTION

Requirement 1

Solution Approach

1. Begin the bank reconciliation by entering the unadjusted cash balances per books and per bank as of the reconciliation date, May 31, 2007. The focus of the reconciliation procedure is to determine the items that account for the difference between the book balance and bank balance. You may follow these steps:

> **a.** Compare the deposits recorded by the bank with the deposits recorded on the books to determine any deposits in transit. Any deposits unrecorded by the bank should be added to the bank balance.
>
> **b.** Compare the checks deducted by the bank with the checks written by the company to determine any checks outstanding. Any checks outstanding should be deducted from the bank balance.
>
> **c.** Add to the book balance credit memo items on the bank statement not recorded on the company's records.
>
> **d.** Deduct from the book balance any debit memo items not recorded on the company's records.
>
> **e.** Prove that the adjusted cash balance per books is equal to the adjusted cash balance per bank.
>
> **2.** Base the journal entries needed to adjust the cash account on the items in the reconciliation that either increase or decrease the balance per books.

HOTFIRE STOVE COMPANY
Bank Reconciliation
May 31, 2007

Per Books

Cash balance per ledger, May 31, 2007			$ 6,670
Add:	Customer note collected by bank, including interest of $15.	$ 615	
	Interest earned on acccount.	32	647
			$ 7,317
Deduct: NSF customer check		$ 615	
	Bank service charge.	10	340
Adjusted cash balance, May 31, 2007			$ 6,977

Per Bank

Cash balance per bank statement, May 31, 2007			$ 7,897
Add:	Deposit in Transit		1,870
	Subtotal		$ 9,767
Deduct: Outstanding checks:			
	No. 285	$ 1,230	
	No. 288	880	
	No. 290	680	2,790
Adjusted cash balance, May 31, 2007			$ 6,977

Requirement 2

General Journal

2007					
May	31	Cash		615	
			Notes Receivable		600
			Interest Revenue		15
			To record note collected by bank.		
	31	Cash		32	
			Interest Revenue		32
			To record interest earned on bank account.		
	31	Accounts Receivable, John Trivo		330	
			Cash		330
			To record customer's NSF check		
	31	Bank Service Charge Expense		10	
			Cash		10
			To record cost of checking account.		

GLOSSARY

adjusted cash balance The true cash balance resulting from reconciling the difference between the balance reported by the bank and the amount shown on the depositor's books.

bank reconciliation A statement showing the specific items that account for the differences between the balance reported by the bank and the amount shown on the depositor's books.

Cash Over and Short An income statement account that measures the amount of the discrepancy in the physical count of cash and the cash register readings or shortages or overages in the petty cash fund.

certified check A depositor's check, payment of which is guaranteed by a bank by its endorsement on the face of the check. The bank deducts the amount of the check from the depositor's balance when it certifies the check.

check An order written by a depositor directing a bank to pay a specified amount of money to the order of the payee.

credit memo A bank's memo explaining an addition to the bank balance not caused by a deposit.

debit memo A bank's memo explaining a deduction from the depositor's account.

deposits in transit Deposits made too late in the month to be credited by the bank on the current statement.

imprest petty cash system A petty cash fund system in which the balance of the petty cash account remains unchanged because a specified amount is advanced to a custodian in trust.

internal control A set of policies and procedures designed to provide reasonable assurance that errors or irregularities will be prevented or detected on a timely basis and that assets will be protected from improper use.

NSF check A customer's check that has been deposited but did not clear on presentation for payment because of "nonsufficient funds." The customer's bank balance was less than the amount of the check.

outstanding checks Checks sent to payees but not yet presented to the depositor's bank for payment.

petty cash fund A separate cash fund used for cash disbursements when payment by check is impractical.

petty cash voucher A signed receipt that shows the purpose of a petty cash expenditure, the date, and the amount.

service charge A monthly charge that may be imposed by the bank to cover its costs of handling an account or when the account falls below a specified balance.

QUESTIONS FOR GROUP LEARNING

Q6-1. Define internal control and state the three elements of the internal control structure.

Q6-2. List five internal control procedures.

Q6-3. What specific items qualify to be included in the term cash? What is a basic rule to determine whether or not an item is part of cash?

Q6-4. Why is it important to involve two or more persons in the handling and recording of cash receipts?

Q6-5. Why is it an advantage to deposit total cash receipts intact and to make all disbursements by check?

Q6-6. (a) What is a petty cash fund? (b) How does the imprest petty cash system operate? (c) Why should the petty cash fund always be replenished at the end of each accounting period?

Q6-7. Explain the matching relationships between the cash records of the bank and those of the depositor.

Q6-8. Explain the following terms: certified check, service charge, NSF, debit memo, credit memo.

Q6-9. Explain the effect, if any, on the bank statement balance of each of the following bank reconciliation items:

    a. Outstanding checks total $323.

    b. The bank recorded a $650 deposit as $560.

    c. The service charge for the month was $7.

    d. Deposits in transit total $800.

    e. A note payable of $500 made to the bank by the depositor became due and was deducted y the bank.

Q6-10. (a) How often should bank reconciliations be prepared? (b) What are the steps to be followed when preparing the bank reconciliation? (c) Which items must be journalized? (d) What do you think is the most important function of a bank reconciliation?

EXERCISES

E6-11. **Internal control (LG 1, 2)** A college friend of yours is opening a laundry business. He plans to employ several people part time. He understands that controls will be necessary for him to meet his business goals. He knows that you are studying accounting and has asked you for some assistance. Specifically, he wants to know where he should start so that the controls will assist in meeting his goals.

E6-12. **Petty cash transactions (LG 3)** On December 1, 2007 Mesa Company established an imprest petty cash fund of $1,000. On December 31, 2007, the petty cash fund consisted of cash and other items as follows:

Currency and coins		$403
Receipted petty cash vouchers for:		
Transportation in	$217	
Telephone	34	
Postage	210	
Office supplies	138	599
Total		$1,002

1. Prepare a general journal entry to establish the fund on December 1, 2007.

2. Assuming that the fund was replenished, prepare the necessary general journal entry on December 31, 2007.

3. The treasurer of Mesa Company feels that the fund does not have to be replenished on December 31, 2007, since a relatively large cash balance remains in the fund. Assuming that Mesa's fiscal year ends on December 31, briefly explain whether the fund must be replenished.

E6-13. **Cash over and short (LG 3)** Arch Records has a change fund of $50 in the cash register to start each day. At the end of the day on April 10, 2007, the cash register tape showed cash sales of $562. The total amount of cash and checks in the register was $606. Is there a cash shortage or overage? Compute it and prepare a general journal entry to record cash sales for the day.

E6-14. **Items on the bank reconciliation (LG 4)** Indicate which of the following items pertaining to the banking activities of Cubs Company should be (a) added to the balance per bank statement, (b) deducted from the balance per bank statement, (c) added to the balance per books, or (d) deducted from the balance per books:

1. Bank service charges.

2. Deposits in transit.

3. Outstanding checks.

4. Credit for a customer note collected by the bank.

5. A customer's check returned marked NSF.

6. Check for $68 incorrectly entered in the accounting records journal as $86.

7. Check for $86 incorrectly entered in the accounting records journal as $68.

8. Deposit of Bears Company credited in error to the Cubs Company.

9. A check made out by the Packer Company charged in error to the Cubs Company's account.

10. Interest earned on an interest-bearing checking account.

E6-15. **Simple bank reconciliation (LG 4)** Carol's Care Center's Cash account shows a balance of $2,498 as of June 30, 2007. The balance on the bank statement on that date is $3,193. Checks for $160, $230, and $70 are outstanding. The bank statement shows a charge for $67, with a cancelled check enclosed, that belongs to another company. The statement shows a credit of $350 for the maturity value of a note receivable that was left with the bank for collection. No collection fee is charged by the bank. A customer's NSF check for $48 was returned with a debit memo. What is the true cash balance as of June 30?

E6-16. **Recording reconciliation items (LG5)** Following is a bank reconciliation for Pennypack Computer City

PENNYPACK COMPUTER CITY
BANK RECONCILIATION
OCTOBER 31, 2007

Cash balance per ledger, October 31		541.91	Cash balance per bank, October 31		$1,049.28
Add Error in check no. 407 for			Add: Deposit in transit		210.50
office rent	$ 5.00		Subtotal		$1,259.78
Note collected by bank	200.00		Deduct: Outstanding checks		585.62
Interest on account	5.85	210.85			
Subtotal		$ 752.76			
Deduct: NSF customer check	$ 75.60				
Service charge	3.00	78.60			
Adjusted cash balance, October 31		$ 674.16	Adjusted cash balance, October 31	$ 674.16	

In general journal form, make all entries required by this reconciliation.

E6-17.   Finding reconciliation errors (LG 4) The accountant for Spector Corporation has completed the bank reconciliation and finds that it does not balance. The adjusted cash balance per books is $6,000. The adjusted cash balance per bank is $5,050. He wonders if the deposit of $600 made on the 31st of last month that appears on this month's bank statement is part of the reason. He has added it to the per books section of the reconciliation. He is sure that all outstanding checks have been deducted from the per bank section. One of these checks in the amount of $300 was outstanding at the end of last month. The bank deducted a $350 check from Spector Corporation account in error. Since Spector did not write the check, he did not include it in the reconciliation. Show the changes that must be made to correct the bank reconciliation.

E6-18.   Bank reconciliation and journal entries (LG 4, 5) The accountant for the Rodeo Drive Bootery has the following data for the bank reconciliation of May 31, 2007:

Balance per bank statement	$ 8,200
Balance per Cash account	8,030
NSF check from customer returned by bank	160
Deposit made on May 3 1 not credited by bank	2,300
Check no. 882 for $450 entered in the books as $540	90
Outstanding checks total	3,400
Debit memo for note payable of $800 plus interest that the	
bank collected for holder of note	860

Prepare a bank reconciliation and the entries (in general journal form) to adjust the accounts.

PROBLEMS

P6-19.   Internal control system (based on an actual occurrence) (LG 2) At the Dakota City public swimming pool, swimmers rent lockers from the locker room attendant for $1 per visit. Several popular brands of candy bars are kept at the locker room entrance for sale to the swimmers. All cash collected is placed in a metal cash box that is locked in the locker room when the pool is closed. When the locker room attendant is absent, she turns the box over to one of the lifeguards to collect cash and make change for locker rentals or candy sales. An assistant city recreation supervisor stops by every few days to deliver more candy and to take out cash for deposit to the city's bank account. There are no signatures for receipt of candy or for cash taken out for deposit.

One day in August, the city recreation supervisor noticed a full box of candy on the back seat of a lifeguard's car. Becoming suspicious, she compared total swimming pool operations with the same period to date last year. Although the number of swimmers had increased by about 20%, cash receipts were several hundred dollars less than for the same period last year. Obviously, someone was stealing candy or cash (or both).

REQUIRED

1. Point out the internal control weaknesses in the present system.

2. Suggest some steps that the city recreation supervisor might take to correct this situation. She cannot hire additional employees.

P6-20. **Internal control system (based on an actual occurrence) (LG 2)** An employee of Waukee Company, who takes the daily bank deposit to the bank each evening, stole the deposit of February 3. It contained $320 in cash and 10 checks totaling $540. Since he could not cash the checks, he held them until February 19 and inserted them in that deposit, taking out $540 of the cash. Because he was a longstanding employee, the owner had made out deposit tickets in duplicate and let him take both the original and duplicate copy to the bank. It was the owner's usual practice to place the duplicate copy in a file of deposit slips upon returning from the bank each evening.

REQUIRED

1. How is Waukee likely to discover the theft? What valid evidence will he have?

2. What action can the company take to lessen future chances of this type of loss?

P6-21. **Petty cash fund (LG 3)** Sanders Company established a petty cash fund of $1,000 by issuing a check to the fund custodian on November 20, 2007. On November 30, management desired to prepare financial statements for internal use and replenished the fund in order to record the expenditures. The content of the fund on November 30 was as follows:

Currency and coins		$ 500
Receipted petty cash vouchers for:		
Transportation in for merchandise	$ 280	
Sales promotion	180	
Postage paid on outgoing mail	35	495
Total		$ 995

On December 31, the fund was again replenished. On that date, the contents were:

Currency and coins		$ 252
Receipted petty cash vouchers for:		
Repairs to office equipment	$ 180	
Transportation in for merchandise	260	
Christmas sales promotion	250	
Postage paid on outgoing mail	60	750
Total		$ 1,002

After two months of experience with the fund, management has decided to reduce the fund to about 30 days' requirements. It ordered a reduction to $750 on December 31.

REQUIRED

1. Prepare a general journal entry to establish the fund.

2. Prepare a general journal entry to replenish the fund on November 30.

3. Prepare a general journal entry to replenish and reduce the fund on December 31.

P6-22. **Bank reconciliation: routine items (LG 4, 5)** The Cash account of Dunes Company showed a balance of $4,398 on July 31, 2007. The bank statement showed a balance of $4,700. Other differences between the firm's Cash account and the bank's records are as follows:

a. A deposit of $650 made on July 31 was not included on the bank statement.

b. The following items were included with the bank statement:

    1. A debit memo for $80 with a customer's NSF check that the firm had included in its deposit of July 28.

    2. A debit memo for $50 for safe deposit box rental.

    3. A cancelled check for $330 drawn by another company charged by the bank against Southwest Company by mistake.

c. Check number 607 was made out correctly for $142 in payment for office supplies but was entered in the accounting records as $124. It was returned with the statement.

d. Outstanding checks on July 31 totaled $1,430.

REQUIRED

1. Prepare a bank reconciliation as of July 31, 2007.

2. Prepare entries in general journal form as required by the reconciliation.

P6-23. **Bank reconciliation: tracing items to statements (LG 4, 5)** Dodge Company had a Cash account balance of $2,835 on April 12, 2007. A special bank statement requested by the auditors for that date showed a balance of $5,680. At the end of March there were no deposits in transit. There were three checks outstanding on March 31 as follows:

Check Number	Amount
620	$ 10
621	460
622	360

Deposits made and checks written in the first 12 days of April were as follows:

Deposits		Payments	
Date	Amount	Check Number	Amount
Apr. 1	$340	623	$ 115
2	420	624	90
3	110	625	1,120
4	80	626	140
5	970	627	680
8	480	628	320
9	420	629	540
10	360	630	760
11	250	631	60
12	400	632	160

On the bank statement of April 12, the deposit of April 12 had not yet been credited. Cancelled checks of Dodge Company returned with the bank statement were in the amounts of $10, $460, $115, $90, $1,210, $140, $680, $760, and $60. Also returned with the bank statement were the following:

a. A credit memo for $2,060 representing a customer note receivable for $2,000 plus interest collected by the bank for Dodge.

b. A debit memo for $10 for the note collection fee.

c. A $95 customer check marked NSF.

d. Comparison of cancelled checks with the accounting records revealed that check no. 625 was written for $1,210 in payment for store equipment. It was incorrectly entered in the accounting records as $1,120.

REQUIRED

1. Prepare a bank reconciliation as of April 12, 2007.

2. Prepare the entries needed to adjust the books (use general journal form).

P6-24. **Determining a cash theft (LG 2, 3)** Eagles Company had poor internal control over its cash transactions. Facts about its cash position at June 30, 2007, were as follows:

a. The Cash account showed a balance of $15,375, which included cash receipts for the past four days not yet taken to the bank for deposit.

b. A credit memo for $1,800 representing a customer note receivable collected by the bank did not appear on the books of the company.

c. The bank statement balance was $15,035.

d. Checks outstanding were no. 595 for $140, no. 622 for $180, no. 649 for $300, no. 7835 for $325, no. 7837 for $260, and no. 7843 for $175. Checks no. 595, 622, and 649 were claimed to be written in 1995 in payment for advertising at a trade fair that year, but there is no proof of this.

The cashier took all of the cash on hand in excess of $1,000 and then prepared the following reconciliation:

Balance per books, June 30, 2007			$15,375
Add:	Checks outstanding		
	No. 7835	$325	
	No. 7837	260	
	No. 7837	175	660
			$16,035
Deduct: Cash on hand not deposited			1,000
Balance per bank, June 30, 2007			$15,035
Deduct: Note proceeds not recorded			1,800
True cash balance, June 30, 2007			$13,235

REQUIRED

1. How much did the cashier take? (Hint: A starting place would be to prepare a corrected bank reconciliation.)

2. How did the cashier attempt to conceal the theft?

3. Taking only the information given, identify two specific aspects of internal control that were apparently missing.

P6-25.   Bank reconciliation: based on bank statement and company records (LG 4, 5) The following Cash account from the general ledger and other pertinent information come from the records of The Hop Shop for the month of June 2007. The bank statement is shown on the next page.

Date		Explanation	Debit	Credit	Balance Debit	Balance Credit
2007						
May	31	Balance			770	
Jun.		Summary of Deposits	3,480			
		Summary of Payments		3,032		
	30	Balance			1,218	

Deposits

Date		Debit Cash
2007		
Jun.	5	450
	11	584
	18	838
	22	786
	30	822
		3,480

Payments

Date		Check No.	Credit Cash
2007			
Jun.	4	155	88
	4	156	140
	4	157	262
	8	158	578
	13	159	1,180
	18	160	296
	27	161	33
	27	162	64
	29	163	391
			3,032

Other Information

As of May 31, 2007, checks no. 149 for $ 120 and no. 154 for $ 146 were outstanding, and a deposit mailed to the bank on May 31, 2007, in the amount of $980 had not yet been recorded by the bank. The credit memo on June 25, 2007, is for the collection of a note receivable by the bank including $10 in interest and a bank collection fee of $3. Returned with the June 30, 2007, bank statement was an NSF check for $310. This check had been received from a customer named Dave Drier and had been deposited on June 23, 2007. The NSF check had not been reflected on the records of The Hop Shop as of June 30, 2007.

REQUIRED

1.   Prepare a bank reconciliation as of June 30, 2007.

2.   Prepare general journal entries to adjust the accounting records.

P6-26.   Analyzing cash for Wildcat Company (LG 6) For a recent year, Wildcat Company had a cash balance of $645,000. A note to the financial statements included the following comments on credit arrangements and compensating balance requirements for the Company:

Notes Payable to Banks

The Company has formal short-term lines of credit with lending banks aggregating $47,000,000, with interest payable at or below prime. At the end of the current year, $35,000,000 of borrowings are outstanding. The use of these lines is restricted to the extent that the Company is required to liquidate its indebtedness to individual banks for a 30-day

West Bank

Denver, Colorado

Statement of Account for:

The Hop Shop	Account No.	2233-66-944
11 Mountain Drive	Period Ending	June 30, 2007
Dry Springs, Colorado	Page	1

Balance from last statement	$ 56	**Withdrawals**	$ 2,330
Number of deposits	6	**Bank service charge**	$ 9
Deposits	$ 4,045	**Interest**	$ 4
Number of withdrawals	9	**New balance this statement**	$ 1,766

Date	Transaction		Checks & Debits	Deposits & Credits	Balance
06-01	Check	149	120		(64)
	Check	154	146		(210)
	Debit memo-overdraft charge		20		(230)
06-03	Deposit			980	750
06-06	Deposit			450	1,200
	Check	156	140		1,060
	Check	157	262		798
06-09	Check	155	88		710
06-12	Deposit			584	1,294
06-19	Deposit			838	2,132
	Check	159	1,180		952
06-23	Deposit			786	1,738
	Debit memo-nonsufficient funds check		310		1,428
06-25	Credit memo-collection of note			407	1,835
06-27	Check-certified	162	64		1,771
06-30	Interest			4	1,775
	Service charge		9		1,766

Checks and other debits:

#149	120		#157	262	20
154	146		159	1,180	310
155	88		162	64	9
156	140				

period each year. At times, the Company borrows amounts in excess of the lines on a short-term basis. At the end of last year, $6,600,000 of borrowings were outstanding.

As part of the borrowing arrangements, the Company is expected to maintain average compensating cash balances, which are based on a percentage of the available credit line by bank and the percentages vary by bank. The amount of compensating balances required for credit lines in effect at the end of the current year was an average of $975,000. The Company is in substantial compliance with the compensating balance requirements. Funds on deposit with the lending banks are subject to withdrawal; however, the availability of the short-term lines of credit is dependent upon the maintenance of sufficient average compensating balances.

Required

Comment on any concerns you may have on the adequacy of the cash balance for Wildcat Company.

PRACTICE CASE

Internal control and cash transactions (LG 2, 3, 4, 5) Charles Scott is the owner of a bicycle sales shop called Charlie's Cycle Center. The business employs six salespersons and one office employee named Dan Hands. Dan is a personal friend of Charles and has been a trusted employee since the business started three years ago. The following Cash account from the general ledger and other pertinent information come from the records of Charlie's Cycle Center for the month of October 2007:

						Balance	
Date		Explanation	PR	Debit	Credit	Debit	Credit
2007							
Sep.	30	Balance				42,974	
Oct.	5			7,452		50,426	
	12			8,377		58,803	
	19			6,195		64,998	
	26			9,114		74,112	
	31				14,257	59,855	

(Cash — Acct. No. 101)

Racine, Wisconsin

Statement of Account for:

Charlie's Cycle Center
4835 Lake Street
Racine, Wisconsin

Account No.   99-492-6661
Period Ending   October 31, 2007
Page   1

Balance from last statement	$ 45,573	Withdrawals	$ 15,541
Number of deposits	1	Bank service charge	$ 18
Deposits	$ 23,366	Interest	$ 0
Number of withdrawals	12	New balance this statement	$ 53,380

Date	Transaction		Checks & Debits	Deposits & Credits	Balance
10-01	Check	932	929		44,644
10-02	Debit memo-nonsufficient funds check		455		44,189
	Check	931	1,103		43,086
10-05	Check	933	2,433		40,653
10-12	Check	934	756		39,897
	Check	935	1,228		38,669
10-19	Check	937	892		37,777
10-21	Check	936	521		37,256
10-22	Check	938	1,322		35,934
10-26	Check	939	3,449		32,485
10-30	Check	940	1,785		30,700
	Check	941	668		30,032
10-31	Deposit			23,366	53,398
	Service charge		18		53,380

Checks and other debits:

#931	1,103	#935	1,228	#939	3,449
932	929	936	521	940	1,785
933	2,433	937	892	941	668
934	756	938	1,322		18

Deposits		Payments		
Date	**Debit Cash**	**Date**	**Check No.**	**Credit Cash**
2007		2007		
Oct. 5	7,452	Oct. 2	933	2,433
12	8,377	5	934	756
19	6,195	9	935	1,228
26	9,114	11	936	521
	31,138	16	937	892
		18	938	1,232
		22	939	3,449
		24	940	1,785
		26	941	668
		30	942	1,293
				14,257

Other Information

As of September 30, 2007, checks no. 24 for $567, no. 931 for $1,103, and no. 932 for $929 were outstanding. Check no. 24 had been written in December 2000 and was never cashed. There were no unrecorded bank deposits or bank charges at the end of September. Examination of the checks returned with the October 31, 2007, bank statement revealed that a check written by Peg Girotti in the amount of $455 in payment for a bicycle purchased in September 2007 had been returned by the bank due to nonsufficient funds. Check number 938 was written in payment of Accounts Payable.

Until the beginning of October 2007, Charles Scott had personally taken responsibility for recording and depositing cash receipts, writing out all checks for payment, and preparing the bank reconciliation at the end of each month. As of October 1, 2007, Dan Hands was put in charge of all of these duties.

Dan instituted a practice of counting the amount of cash and checks in the cash register at the end of each day and reconciling the amount to the cash register tape. The two amounts were the same each day. At the end of each day, the cash and checks were placed in a file cabinet located in the basement of the store. At the end of each week, Dan made a summary entry in the cash receipts journal debiting Cash and crediting Sales. Cash receipts for October 29, 30, and 31 in the amount of $3,421 have not been recorded yet. Dan felt that since there was an adequate balance in the checking account, he would make the bank deposit only once at the end of the month.

Dan removed all of the cash and the customer checks from the file cabinet on October 31, 2007. He personally made the bank deposit of $23,366 at the end of that day and made sure that the bank recorded it as being received. Dan has tried to prepare the bank reconciliation for the month of October several times. However, he is having difficulty reconciling the book and bank balances. Charles Scott is concerned because he feels that, based on sales for the month of October 2007, the bank cash balance should be higher than $53,380.

REQUIRED
1. Prepare a bank reconciliation as of September 30, 2007.

2. Determine the correct cash balance that should appear as an adjusted cash balance as of October 31, 2007, and compute the missing amount of cash.

3. Prepare general journal entries to adjust the accounting records as of October 31, 2007.

4. Prepare a list of internal control recommendations for Charlie's Cycle Center.

BUSINESS DECISION AND COMMUNICATION PROBLEM

Internal control over cash (LG 1, 2, 3) Frank Morgan, the owner of a small retail gift shop, hires you to review the shop's internal control procedures for handling cash. After observing the office procedures and talking with employees, you have developed the following notes.

The business has one employee who does all of the accounting. In order to stimulate sales, the shop encourages customers to open charge accounts with the store. Customers make their payments by mail. A store clerk brings the unopened payments to the accounting clerk each morning when the mail arrives. The accounting clerk opens the receipts and makes journal entries to record the collections. The accounting clerk then puts the checks in a safe. The sales clerk puts each day's cash receipts, along with the cash register tape, in the safe each night. Once a week, the accounting clerk takes all the receipts and makes out a bank deposit slip. The accounting clerk then takes the deposit to the bank. After making the deposit, the accounting clerk uses the cash register tapes to journalize the cash sales.

The accounting clerk writes and signs checks to pay bills when the business receives them. If the shop must make small payments, the sales clerk pays these using currency in the cash register.

The accounting clerk reconciles the bank statement when it arrives each month. Sometimes the adjusted balance on the per books side does not agree with the adjusted balance on the per bank side. When this occurs, the accounting clerk makes an entry to bring the Cash balance in agreement with the adjusted balance per bank.

Required
Prepare a memo to Frank Morgan recommending changes in the internal control procedures for cash.

ETHICAL DILEMMA

Theft by the petty cash clerk (LG 3, 4) You work in the marketing department of a wholesale food company. Periodically you entertain customers. When you return to the office, you give a copy of the bill to the petty cash clerk, who reimburses you for the cost of the entertainment. Each time, the petty cash clerk asks you to sign a petty cash voucher that he has made out in pencil. Several times when you walk by the petty cash clerk's desk, you note that he is erasing and writing on the petty cash vouchers. The petty cash clerk is a longtime employee of the company and is highly trusted. You have never seen him taking any money out of the petty cash fund. You know that periodically the office manager makes surprise counts on the fund to check it. But you notice that the petty cash clerk always seems to have the latest in fashion and seems to spend a large amount of money in comparison to his salary.

Required
Identify the potential problems with the observed practice and state what you should do.

COMPREHENSIVE ANALYSIS CASE INTEL CORPORATION

Analyzing Intel for the Period 2004-2002 Listed below are comparative income statements and balance sheets with common-size percents for 2004-2002 (in millions). Also included are selected ratio statistics. Please provide a brief explanation for your answer to each question.

INTEL
COMPARATIVE COMMON-SIZE INCOME STATEMENTS
For The Years Ended December 31, 2004, 2003, 2002
(in millions)

	2004 $	2004 %	2003 $	2003 %	2002 $	2002 %
Revenues	$ 34,209.0	100.0%	$ 30,141.0	100.0%	$ 26,764.0	100.0%
Cost of goods sold	$ 14,463.0	42.3%	$ 13,047.0	43.3%	$ 13,446.0	50.2%
Gross margin	$ 19,746.0	57.7%	$ 17,094.0	56.7%	$ 13,318.0	49.8%
Operating expenses:						
Sales, marketing, general administrative	$ 4,659.0	13.6%	$ 4,278.0	14.2%	$ 4,334.0	16.2%
Research and development	$ 4,778.0	14.0%	$ 4,360.0	14.5%	$ 4,034.0	15.1%
Other expense	$ 179.0	0.5%	$ 923.0	3.1%	$ 568.0	2.1%
Other expense	$ -	0.0%	$ -		$ -	0.0%
Total operating expenses	$ 9,616.0	28.1%	$ 9,561.0	31.7%	$ 8,936.0	33.4%
Operating income	$ 10,130.0	29.6%	$ 7,533.0	25.0%	$ 4,382.0	16.4%
Net interest expense (income)	$ (289.0)	-0.8%	$ (192.0)	-0.6%	$ (194.0)	-0.7%
Other expense (income)	$ 2.0	0.0%	$ 283.0	0.9%	$ 372.0	1.4%
Income before income taxes	$ 10,417.0	30.5%	$ 7,442.0	24.7%	$ 4,204.0	15.7%
Income taxes	$ 2,901.0	8.5%	$ 1,801.0	6.0%	$ 1,087.0	4.1%
Net income (loss) before unusual items	$ 7,516.0	22.0%	$ 5,641.0	18.7%	$ 3,117.0	11.6%
Other losses (gains) net of tax	$ -	0.0%	$ -	0.0%	$ -	0.0%
Net income (loss)	$ 7,516.0	22.0%	$ 5,641.0	18.7%	$ 3,117.0	11.6%

INTEL
COMPARATIVE COMMON-SIZE INCOME STATEMENTS
December 31, 2004, 2003, 2002
(in millions)

	2004 $	2004 %	2003 $	2003 %	2002 0	2002 %
ASSETS						
Current:						
Cash & cash equivalents	$ 8,407.0	17.5%	$ 7,971.0	16.9%	$ 7,404.0	16.7%
Short-term investments	$ 8,765.0	18.2%	$ 8,193.0	17.4%	$ 5,183.0	11.7%
Accounts receivable, net	$ 2,999.0	6.2%	$ 2,960.0	6.3%	$ 2,574.0	5.8%
Inventory	$ 2,621.0	5.4%	$ 2,519.0	5.3%	$ 2,276.0	5.1%
Other current assets	$ 1,266.0	2.6%	$ 1,239.0	2.6%	$ 1,488.0	3.4%
Other current assets	$ -	0.0%	$ -	0.0%	$ -	0.0%
Total current assets	$ 24,058.0	50.0%	$ 22,382.0	48.5%	$ 18,925.0	42.8%
Fixed:						
Property & equipment, net	$ 15,768.0	32.8%	$ 16,661.0	35.3%	$ 17,847.0	40.4%
Long-term investments	$ 3,219.0	6.7%	$ 2,380.0	5.0%	$ 1,234.0	2.8%
Intangibles & goodwill	$ 3,719.0	7.7%	$ 3,705.0	7.9%	$ 4,330.0	9.8%
Other assets	$ 1,379.0	2.9%	$ 1,515.0	3.2%	$ 1,888.0	4.3%
Total assets	$ 48,143.0	100.0%	$ 47,143.0	100.0%	$ 44,224.0	100.0%
LIABILITIES						
Current:						
Short-term debt	$ 201.0	0.4%	$ 224.0	0.5%	$ 436.0	1.0%
Accounts payable	$ 1,943.0	4.0%	$ 1,660.0	3.5%	$ 1,543.0	3.5%
Accrued salaries and benefits	$ 1,858.0	3.9%	$ 1,559.0	3.3%	$ 1,287.0	2.9%
Unearned revenue	$ 592.0	1.2%	$ 633.0	1.3%	$ 475.0	1.1%
Other current liabilities	$ 3,412.0	7.1%	$ 2,803.0	5.9%	$ 2,854.0	6.5%
Total current liabilities	$ 8,006.0	16.6%	$ 6,879.0	14.6%	$ 6,595.0	14.9%
Long-term debt	$ 703.0	1.5%	$ 936.0	2.0%	$ 929.0	2.1%
Deferred income tax liabilities	$ 855.0	1.8%	$ 1,482.0	3.1%	$ 1,232.0	2.8%
Other long -term liabilities	$ -	0.0%	$ -	0.0%	$ -	0.0%
Total liabilities	$ 9,564.0	19.9%	$ 9,297.0	19.7%	$ 8,756.0	19.8%
OWNERS' EQUITY						
Total owners' equity	$ 38,579.0	80.1%	$ 37,846.0	80.3%	$ 35,468.0	80.2%
Total liabilities and owners' equity	$ 48,143.0	100.0%	$ 47,143.0	100.0%	$ 44,224.0	100.0%

(Note: percents may not add to 100 due to rounding)

INTEL
RATIO ANALYSIS SUMMARY
For The Years Ended December 31, 2004, 2003, 2002

	2004	2003	2002
SHORT-TERM LIQUIDITY RATIOS			
Current Ratio (Current Assets/Current Liabilities)	3.00	3.33	2.87
Quick Ratio (Cash + Short-term Investments + Accounts Receivable)/Current Liabilities	2.52	2.78	2.30
Accounts Receivable Turnover 1 (Revenues/Average Accounts Receivable)	11.48	10.89	
Accounts Receivable Turnover 2 (Revenues/Year-end Accounts Receivable)	11.41	10.18	10.40
Inventory Turnover 1 (Cost Goods Sold/Average Inventory)	5.63	5.44	
Inventory Turnover 2 (Cost Goods Sold/Year-end Inventory)	5.52	5.18	5.91
LONG-TERM SOLVENCY (LEVERAGE) RATIO			
Total Debt Ratio (Total Liabilities/Total Assets)	19.87%	19.72%	19.80%
PROFITABILITY RATIOS			
Gross Profit Margin (Gross Margin/Revenues)	57.72%	56.71%	49.76%
Operating Profit Margin (Operating Income/Revenues)	29.61%	24.99%	16.37%
Net Profit Margin (Return on Sales) (ROS) (Net Income/Revenues)	21.97%	18.72%	11.65%
Total Asset Turnover (Revenues/Average Total Assets)	0.72	0.66%	
Return on Total Assets (ROA) (Net Income/Average Total Assets)	15.78%	12.35%	

REQUIRED

Income statement questions:

  1. Are total revenues higher or lower over the three-year period?

  2. What is the percent change in total revenues from 2002 to 2004?

  3. Is the percent of cost of goods sold to total revenues increasing or decreasing over the three-year period? As a result, is the gross margin percent increasing or decreasing?

  4. Is the percent of total operating expenses to total revenues increasing or decreasing over the three-year period? As a result, is the operating income percent increasing or decreasing?

  5. Is the percent of net income to total revenue increasing or decreasing over the three-year period?

Balance sheet questions:

  6. Are total assets higher or lower over the three-year period?

  7. What is the percent change in total assets from 2002 to 2004?

  8. What are the largest asset investments for the company over the three-year period?

  9. Are the largest asset investments increasing faster or slower than the percent change in total revenues?

  10. Is the percent of total liabilities to total liabilities + owners'equity increasing or decreasing? As a result, is there more or less risk that the company could not pay its debts?

Integrative income statement and balance sheet question:

  11. Is the company operating more or less efficiently by using the least amount of asset investment to generate a given level of total revenues? Note that the "total asset turnover" ratio is computed and included in the "ratio analysis summary."

Ratio analysis questions:

  12. Is the *current ratio* better or worse in the most current year compared to prior years?

  13. Is the *quick ratio* better or worse in the most current year compared to prior years?

  14. Is the *accounts receivable turnover ratio 1* (based on *average* receivables) better or worse in the most current year compared to prior years?

  15. Is the 2004 *accounts receivable turnover ratio 2* (based on *year-end* receivables) better or worse than the 2004 ratio based on an *average*?

  16. Is the *inventory turnover ratio 1* (based on *average* inventory) better or worse in the most current year compared to prior years?

  17. Is the 2004 *inventory turnover ratio 2* (based on *year-end* inventory) better or worse than the 2004 ratio based on an *average*?

  18. Is the *return on total assets (ROA) ratio* better or worse in the most current year compared to prior years?

ACCOUNTS RECEIVABLE AND BAD DEBTS EXPENSE

"When you put your hand in a flowing stream, you touch the last that has gone by before and the first of what is still to come."

Leonardo Davinci

LEARNING GOALS

After studying Chapter 7, you should be able to:

1. Identify and classify receivables on the balance sheet.

2. Explain why accountants must provide for uncollectible accounts to match revenues and expenses on the income statement and to present accounts receivable on the balance sheet.

3. Journalize entries under the allowance method to record the bad debts adjustment, write off uncollectible accounts, and recover bad debts.

4. Estimate uncollectible accounts using approaches based on sales and receivables.

5. Journalize entries under the direct write-off method to write off uncollectible accounts and recover bad debts.

6. Compare the allowance and direct write-off methods as they affect the income statement and the balance sheet.

7. Record credit card sales.

8. Identify the internal control issues involved with accounts receivable.

9. Analyze financial statement information for real-life companies.

UNDERSTANDING BUSINESS ISSUES

Extending credit and selling on account is common for most companies. When times are hard, attractive credit terms may be the key to business survival. Many manufacturing companies have created their own financing subsidiaries. For example, at December 31, 2004, total receivables for Caterpillar, Inc., were 47.5% of 2004 sales revenues. Of Caterpillar's $14,367 million in receivables, $6,510 (45.3%)were issued by its financing subsidiary.

For many companies, accounts receivable is one of the largest assets on the balance sheet. Managing the investment in receivables and ensuring prompt collection is critical for business survival. The following table shows accounts receivable as a dollar amount and as a percent of total assets for selected companies in different industries at the end of a recent year.

Company	Total Accounts Receivable (in millions)	Accounts Receivable as a Percent of Total Assets
Manpower, Inc.	$3,324.3	56.9%
Nike	2,285.2	30.0%
Caterpillar	14,367.0	33.3%
Hewlett-Packard Co.	21,754.0	28.6%
Georgia Pacific	2,040.0	8.4%
Neiman Marcus	560.8	22.0%
Best Buy	343.0	4.0%

We begin this chapter with a broad overview of types of receivables. We discuss alternative methods of accounting for uncollectible accounts. Important topics include recognizing bad debts expense and valuation of accounts receivable. We also cover accounting for credit card sales, internal control of accounts receivable, and analysis of receivables.

CLASSIFYING RECEIVABLES

Learning Goal 1   Identify and classify receivables on the balance sheet.

Receivables are claims against individuals or companies for the future receipt of cash or other assets. There are two broad categories:

1. **Trade receivables** arise from the sale of goods or services to customers.

2. **Nontrade receivables** arise from other sources.

Trade receivables are normally collectible within one year (or one operating cycle, if longer than a year). We should show them as current assets on the balance sheet. We should show nontrade receivables collectible in the current period separately from trade receivables. Examples of nontrade receivables include cash advances to employees and loans to subsidiaries.

CLASSIFYING TRADE RECEIVABLES

The three classes of trade receivables are accounts receivable, notes receivable, and credit card receivables.

Accounts receivable are claims against customers for sales made on account with specified credit terms. Accounts receivable are the major focus of this chapter.

Notes receivable are claims supported by written, formal promises to pay. Notes can arise from trade or nontrade arrangements. We will discuss accounting for notes receivable in Chapter 8

Credit card receivables arise from sales made with nonbank credit cards, such as American Express. Banks do not accept nonbank credit card sales slips directly for deposit. We record sales using *bank* credit cards, such as VISA or MasterCard, as cash sales. Banks accept these signed credit card sales slips directly for deposit.

PROVIDING FOR UNCOLLECTIBLE ACCOUNTS

The Allowance Method

Most businesses will lose some money on credit sales. In determining its credit policy, a business must reach a balance between extra sales due to liberal credit and a reasonable amount of uncollectible accounts. Most companies with many sales on account have a credit department. This department examines the credit history of customers, establishes customer credit limits, and follows up on unpaid accounts.

Bad Debts Expense

Learning Goal 2   Explain why accountants must provide for uncollectible accounts to match revenues and expenses on the income statement and to present accounts receivable on the balance sheet.

Regardless of how well the credit department screens customers, some accounts may prove uncollectible. A **bad debt** is an account receivable that proves uncollectible. One problem in accounting for such accounts is determining the accounting period for recognizing bad debt losses.

Remember that the central goal of the *accrual basis* of accounting is to *match* revenues with expenses for a period of time. Therefore, we should recognize the **bad debts expense** during the same period when we recognize the sales revenues. However, at the time credit sales are made, the business does not know which customers will not subsequently pay their accounts. In order to currently match revenues with expenses, it must make an *estimate* of the amount of accounts receivable that will prove uncollectible. This estimate becomes the basis for matching bad debts expense with current sales revenue. Recording estimated bad debts expense at the end of each accounting period is called the **allowance method** of accounting for bad debts.

The allowance method also results in a better presentation of accounts receivable on the balance sheet. Instead of showing accounts receivable at their gross amount, the amount of estimated uncollectible accounts is deducted from the balance in accounts receivable on the balance sheet. As a result, accounts receivable are shown at the net amount expected to be collected from customers (**net realizable value**). If we report accounts receivable at their gross value without adjusting for the estimated uncollectible portion, we would overstate both total assets and total owners' equity.

Learning Goal 3   Journalize entries under the allowance method to record the bad debts adjustment, write off uncollectible accounts, and recover bad debts.

We estimate and record bad debts expense in an end-of-period adjusting entry. Assume that on December 31, 2007, after its first year of operations, the credit department of Moulin Rouge Company determines that $600 is a reasonable estimate of 2007 bad debts expense. The adjusting general journal entry recorded on December 31, 2007, and the posting of the entry to the general ledger accounts are shown in Exhibit 7.1

Bad debts expense is an operating expense on the income statement, and we close the account to Income Summary. **Allowance for Doubtful Accounts** is a contra asset to Accounts Receivable on the balance sheet. Since $600 is an estimate not related to specific customers' accounts, we must make the credit to the contra account and not to Accounts Receivable. A credit to Accounts

2007
Dec. 31   Bad Debts Expense   731   600
                  Allowance for Doubtful Accounts   112   600
               To record bad debts expense for 2007

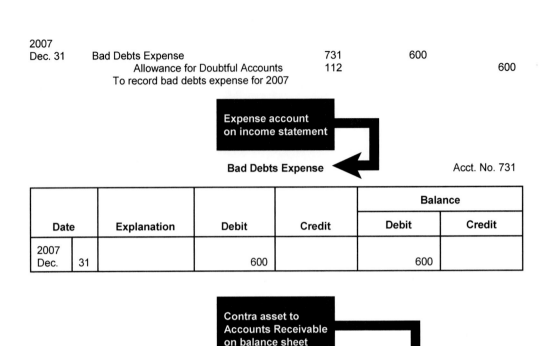

| Bad Debts Expense | | | | | Acct. No. 731 |

				Balance	
Date	Explanation	Debit	Credit	Debit	Credit
2007 Dec. 31		600		600	

| Allowance for Doubtful Accounts | | | | | Acct. No. 112 |

				Balance	
Date	Explanation	Debit	Credit	Debit	Credit
2007 Dec. 31			600		600

EXHIBIT **7.1**

Recording the Bad Debts Adjustment

Receivable would also require a posting to a specific customer's subsidiary ledger account. Using assumed amounts, Moulin Rouge's year-end balance sheet would appear as follows:

MOULIN ROUGE COMPANY
PARTIAL BALANCE SHEET
DECEMBER 31, 2007
Assets

Current assets
Cash $2,000
Accounts receivable $8,000
Deduct: Allowance for doubtful accounts   600   7,400
Notes receivable   1,000

The $7,400 represents the net cash expected to be received (net realizable value) when the accounts receivable are collected.

The advantages of the allowance method are that (1) it more properly matches revenues with expenses on the income statement and (2) we report accounts receivable on the balance sheet at the net estimated amount that will be collected. Both financial statements are improved by the use of the allowance method.

Writing off Uncollectible Accounts

Determining that an account is uncollectible is complex. Only after we have made many collection efforts should we write off the debt. As we determine actual accounts receivable to be uncollectible, we debit Allowance for Doubtful Accounts and credit Accounts Receivable. Note that we debit the contra account because the bad debts adjusting entry has already recognized the expense. A debit to Bad Debts Expense at the time of write-off would record the expense twice—when we estimated the expense and again when we wrote it off.

Assume that on January 15, 2008, Moulin Rouge Company determines that a claim of $80 against John Elton is uncollectible. The entry to record the write-off of this account is as follows:

```
2008
Jan.   15    Allowance for Doubtful Accounts                        80
                  Accounts Receivable, John Elton                            80
                  To write off receivable from John Elton as uncollectible.
```

The entry to write off the uncollectible account on January 15, 2008, is *not* a bad debts expense for 2008. The expense was previously recorded by the adjusting entry of December 31, 2007. Also, the entry does not change the net realizable value of the receivables on January 15, 2008. We can see this in the following comparison of amounts for Moulin Rouge Company *before* and *after* the write-off:

	Balances before Write-off	Write-off	Balances after Write-off
Accounts receivable	$ 8,000	$ (80)	$ 7,920
Deduct: Allowance for doubtful accounts	600	(80)	520
Net realizable value	$ 7,400		$ 7,400

The write-off equally reduces *both* Accounts Receivable and Allowance for Doubtful Accounts. The net realizable value of accounts receivable remains the same. The impact on the financial statements occurs *in the year the bad debt is recognized, not in the year of the write-off.*

Recovery of Bad Debts

An account that we have written off may later be recovered in part or in full. We reverse the entry made to write off the account for the amount recovered or expected to be recovered. Assume that on November 1, 2008 John Elton pays the entire $80 he owes. The required journal entries are as follows:

```
2008
Nov.   1    Accounts Receivable, John Elton                        80
                  Allowance for Doubtful Accounts                          80
                  To reinstate the account of John Elton previously written off.
       1    Cash                                                    80
                  Accounts Receivable, John Elton                          80
                  To record payment received from John Elton.
```

The debit and the credit to Accounts Receivable cancel each other. They are necessary to maintain a complete record of all transactions with the customer. Such a record is important in deciding to grant credit in the future.

Estimating the Amount of Bad Debts Expense

Learning Goal 4   Estimate uncollectible accounts using approaches based on sales and receivables.

Management must make a careful estimate of the amount of its uncollectible accounts based on judgment and past experience. There are two commonly used alternative approaches to estimating bad debts: the *income statement approach* and the *balance sheet approach*.

Estimate Based on Sales (The Income Statement Approach)

The **income statement approach** answers the question: How much bad debts expense is associated with this year's sales? This approach, also referred to as the *percentage of sales approach*, bases bad debts expense on dollar volume of sales. Typically, we base the expense on a percentage of net sales (sales less sales returns and allowances). If the proportion of sales on credit changes greatly from year to year, it may be desirable to base the expense on a percentage of net credit sales only.

The income statement approach is simple to apply. The focus is on the amount of bad debts expense on the income statement. Thus, we ignore any existing balance in the Allowance for Doubtful Accounts when computing the expense amount. If the estimates of bad debts are consistently too large or too small over a number of years, the Allowance for Doubtful Accounts balance could be severely misstated. This would cause the net realizable receivables on the balance sheet to be distorted. For this reason, management should periodically reexamine the percentage figure it uses to estimate bad debts.

To illustrate the income statement approach, assume that Winwood Company's past bad debts have indicated that 0.5% (one-half of 1%) of net credit sales are uncollectible. Net credit sales for 2007 are $200,000, and there is a credit balance of $150 in Allowance for Doubtful Accounts before adjustments are made. The bad debts expense for 2007 is $1,000 (0.005 × $200,000). We base the computation of bad debts expense on sales. We ignore any existing balance in Allowance for Doubtful Accounts under the income statement approach. Therefore, the $150 balance in the allowance account is not part of the computation of the bad debts expense. The adjusting journal entry to record estimated bad debts expense is as follows:

```
2007
Dec.   31    Bad Debts Expense                                    1,000
                    Allowance for Doubtful Accounts                        1,000
                 To record bad debts expense for 2007 based on credit sales.
```

After this entry is posted, Bad Debts Expense and Allowance for Doubtful Accounts would appear as follows:

Bad Debts Expense   Acct. No. 731

Date		Explanation	Debit	Credit	Balance Debit	Balance Credit
2007 Dec.	31		1,000		1,000	

		Allowance for Doubtful Accounts			Acct. No. 112	

Date		Explanation	Debit	Credit	Balance Debit	Balance Credit
2007 Dec.	31	Credit balance				150
	31			1,000		1,150

After the adjusting entry is posted to Allowance for Doubtful Accounts, its balance is $1,150. This amount is different from the $1,000 amount in Bad Debts Expense for the year. It is not an error, since the two accounts measure different things:

1. Bad Debts Expense measures the estimated uncollectible portion of the current year's sales on account.

2. Allowance for Doubtful Accounts measures the estimated uncollectible accounts receivable without regard to when the sales were made.

Estimate Based on Receivables (The Balance Sheet Approach)

The **balance sheet approach** seeks an answer to the question: How large a valuation allowance do we need in order to show net receivables at the estimated amount to be collected? This approach requires adjusting the balance of Allowance for Doubtful Accounts to an amount that will show accounts receivable at their net realizable value. We use the balance sheet item Accounts Receivable, rather than the income statement item Sales, as the base for the adjustment.

Under this approach, we find the desired balance of Allowance for Doubtful Accounts by either of two procedures: (1) applying an estimated percentage to the current receivables balance, or (2) aging the accounts receivable in terms of the amount of time specific receivables have remained unpaid. Since we determine a *specific desired balance* for the allowance account under this approach, we must consider the existing balance in this account. The debit to Bad Debts Expense is the amount needed to produce the desired balance in the allowance account.

Use of a Percentage to Obtain Desired Allowance Balance

If we know from the past what percentage of accounts receivable may prove uncollectible, we can use this percentage to determine the desired allowance balance. For example, assume that Simon Company knows from previous years that 3% of its outstanding receivables will be uncollectible. As of December 31, 2007, Simon Company has an Accounts Receivable balance of $60,000 and a *credit* balance of $100 in Allowance for Doubtful Accounts. Its desired credit balance in the allowance account is $1,800 ($60,000 × 0.03). Since the allowance account already has a credit balance of $100, Simon needs $1,700 more. The required adjusting entry is as follows:

2007				
Dec.	31	Bad Debts Expense	1,700	
		Allowance for Doubtful Accounts		1,700
		To increase the allowance account to the desired balance ($1,800 - $100 previous credit balance).		

After this entry is posted, the Bad Debts Expense and Allowance for Doubtful Accounts would appear as follows:

Bad Debts Expense   Acct. No. 731

Date		Explanation	Debit	Credit	Balance	
					Debit	Credit
2007 Dec.	31		1,700		1,700	

Allowance for Doubtful Accounts   Acct. No. 112

Date		Explanation	Debit	Credit	Balance	
					Debit	Credit
2007 Dec.	31	Credit balance				100
	31			1,700		1,800

Normally, Allowance for Doubtful Accounts has a credit balance. But if past estimates of uncollectible accounts have been too low, the allowance may have a debit balance. This results when we write off more accounts than we provide for. If the existing allowance balance for Simon Company had been a *debit* balance of $100 instead of a credit balance, the required adjusting entry amount would have been $1,900 ($1,800 + $100). After this entry is posted, the allowance account would contain the desired credit balance of $1,800.

Aging the Accounts Receivable to Obtain the Desired Allowance Balance

Aging the accounts receivable considers the number of days that have elapsed *since the due date*. Many companies use an **aging schedule**, like the one shown in Exhibit 7.2 for Simon Company, to make the analysis easier.

SIMON COMPANY
ANALYSIS OF ACCOUNTS RECEIVABLE BY AGE
DECEMBER 31, 2007

Customer's Name	Total Balance	Not Yet Due	Days Past Due			
			1-30 Days	31-60 Days	61-90 Days	Over 90 Days
J. Cash	$ 900	$ 800	$ 100			
E. Harris	1,800	1,000	500	$ 300		
R. McEntire	200				$ 200	
R. Travis	300	100	200			
H. Williams	800				300	$ 500
Others	56,000	45,100	4,200	3,000	2,000	1,700
Totals	$ 60,000	$ 47,000	$ 5,000	$ 3,300	$ 2,500	$ 2,200

EXHIBIT **7.2**

An Aging Schedule Analysis of Accounts Receivable by Age

To create an aging schedule, we list all accounts in the accounts receivable subsidiary ledger and their balances in the Customer's Name and Total Balance columns. Next, we divide into age classifications the amounts that make up each balance in the Total Balance column. Then we extend each amount to the appropriate columns. For example, if $100 of the total amount J. Cash owes originated on November 20, 2007, and the terms were 2/10, n/30, the amount would have been due on December 20. As of December 31, 2007, J. Cash's $100 would be 11 days past due. Therefore, it would fall in the 1-30 days past due category. The aging of accounts receivable for Simon Company shows that of the $60,000 total amount, $47,000 are current and $13,000 ($5,000 + $3,300 + $2,500 + $2,200) are past due.

We use the analysis in Exhibit 7.2 to determine the desired balance for Allowance for Doubtful Accounts. We apply percentage estimates based on previous experience to the total amount in each column of the aging schedule. The estimated percent uncollectible increases rapidly as the account becomes increasingly past due. The computation to determine expected uncollectible items for Simon Company is as follows:

Account Status	Amount	Estimated Percent Uncollectible	Allowance for Doubtful Accounts
Not yet due	$47,000	1	$ 470
Past due:			
1-30 days	5,000	4	200
31-60 days	3,300	10	330
61-90 days	2,500	20	500
Over 90 days	2,200	50	1,100
Total accounts receivable	$60,000		
Total balance needed in allowance account			$2,600

On the basis of this summary, an estimated $2,600 of the outstanding accounts receivable on December 31 is uncollectible. Consequently, Allowance for Doubtful Accounts requires a balance of $2,600.

If Simon Company has a present *credit* balance in Allowance for Doubtful Accounts of $100 remaining from earlier periods, the adjusting entry amount will be for $2,500 ($2,600 - $100). The adjusting journal entry is as follows:

2007				
Dec.	31	Bad Debts Expense	2,500	
		Allowance for Doubtful Accounts		2,500
		To increase the allowance account to the desired		
		balance ($2,600 - $100 previous credit balance).		

The aging method gives a better estimate of the allowance for doubtful accounts because the estimate is based on a study of individual customer accounts rather than on a blanket percentage of a single general ledger account balance. The analysis of accounts receivable aids management not only in the accounting for uncollectible accounts but also in making credit decisions. Interpreting this information for credit decisions, management should also compare the current analysis of accounts receivable by age with those of earlier periods.

NOT PROVIDING FOR UNCOLLECTIBLE ACCOUNTS: THE DIRECT WRITE-OFF METHOD

Learning Goal 5   Journalize entries under the direct write-off method to write off uncollectible accounts and recover bad debts.

If a company cannot reasonably estimate the amount of bad debts expense, it must use the **direct write-off method** for recording bad debts expense.[1] Using the data for the Moulin Rouge Company example, the January 15, 2008 entry to write off John Elton's account under the direct write-off method is as follows:

2008				
Jan.	15	Bad Debts Expense	80	
		Accounts Receivable, John Elton		80
		To write off receivable from John Elton as uncollectible.		

Under the direct write-off method, we recognize the expense in the *period of write-off* rather than in the period of the sale. Therefore, an improper matching of revenues and expenses on the income statement may occur. It may also cause the receivables as shown in the balance sheet to be overstated, since there is no allowance for uncollectible accounts. Such a departure from the matching principle is justified if the amount of losses cannot be reasonably estimated.[2]

Assume again that on November 1, 2008, John Elton pays the entire amount owed. The required journal entries under the direct write-off method are as follows:

2008				
Nov.	1	Accounts Receivable, John Elton	80	
		Bad Debts Recovered		80
		To reinstate the account of John Elton previously written off.		
	1	Cash	80	
		Accounts Receivable, John Elton		80
		To record payment received from John Elton.		

Bad Debts Recovered is a cost recovery account that is often considered to be a revenue account. Its balance should be reported in the Other Revenue section of the income statement. Alternatively, Bad Debts Recovered could be shown as a contra account to Bad Debts Expense.

---

[1] In this method, the company does not record any expense until a specific receivable is written off. It does not use Allowance for Doubtful Accounts, and it makes no end-of-period adjusting entry for estimated expense.

[2] *SFAS No. 5*, paragraph 8. This statement provides for accrual of loss contingencies only if the loss is probable and its amount can be reasonably estimated.

A COMPARISON OF THE ALLOWANCE AND DIRECT WRITE-OFF METHODS

Learning Goal 6   Compare the allowance and direct write-off methods as they affect the income statement and the balance sheet.

Exhibit 7.3 compares the two methods of recording bad debts expense. Assume the following data:

Accounts Receivable (debit balance, January 1, 2007)	$ 30,000
Allowance for Doubtful Accounts (credit balance, January 1, 2007)	1,000
All sales on account during 2007	205,000
Sales returns and allowances during 2007	5,000
Cash collections on account during 2007	150,000
Accounts receivable written off as uncollectible during 2007	800
Bad debts recovered (previously written off as uncollectible) during 2007	300

The basis for estimating bad debt expenses is 1% × (Sales - Sales Returns and Allowances).

Under the allowance method estimated bad debts is shown as an expense in the same accounting period that the revenues are recognized. Under the direct write-off method, bad debts expense consists of accounts receivable that were actually written off during the accounting period. Generally, the allowance method provides a better matching of revenues and expenses on the income statement than the direct write-off method.

Using the allowance method, the balance sheet shows the amount of accounts receivable the company expects to collect. This figure is calculated by deducting the allowance for doubtful accounts from the gross amount of accounts receivable. This total is the net realizable value of the accounts receivable. Under the direct write-off method, accounts receivable are shown at their gross value since there is no allowance for uncollectible accounts. Therefore, the balance sheet under the direct write-off method tends to overstate total assets. Since no estimate of bad debts expense is made under the direct write-off method, total owners' equity is also overstated.

FINANCIAL STATEMENT DISCLOSURESFOR TRADE RECEIVABLES

To show a real-life application of the allowance method and the disclosure of receivables on the balance sheet, we use Tiffany & Company. Tiffany has an international reputation as a retailer of high quality jewelry. Exhibit 7.4 shows the current asset section of the balance sheet as of January 31, 2004 and 2003. Net accounts receivable represent approximately 13.1% of current assets as of January 31, 2004. Tiffany & Co. shows accounts receivable at net realizable value and discloses the allowance balance at the end of each year. Assume that notes to Tiffany's financial statements give the following explanation for the change in the allowance account during the reporting year ending on January 31, 2004:

Balance at beginning of period, January 31, 2003	$ 8,258,000
Add: Bad debts expense for year	1,255,000
Deduct: Uncollectible accounts written off	(2,521,000)
Balance at end of period, January 31, 2004	$ 6,992,000

Transactions (Jan. 1-Dec. 31, 2007)	Allowance Method		Direct Write-off Method	

All sales on account	Accounts Receivable 205,000
	  Sales
		205,000	Accounts Receivable 205,000
			  Sales
				205,000

Sales returns and allowances	Sales Returns and
	  Allowances 5,000
	    Accounts Receivable
		5,000	Sales Returns and
			  Allowances 5,000
			    Accounts Receivable
				5,000

Cash collections on account	Cash 150,000
	  Accounts Receivable
		150,000	Cash 150,000
			  Accounts Receivable
				150,000

Accounts receivable written off as uncollectible	Allowance for Doubtful
	  Accounts 800
	    Accounts Receivable
		800	Bad Debts Expense 800
			  Accounts Receivable
				800

Bad debts recovered	Accounts Receivable 300
	  Allowance for Doubtful
	    Accounts
	Cash 300
	  Accounts Receivable
		300
		
		300
			Accounts Receivable 300
			  Bad Debts Recovered
			
			Cash 300
			  Accounts Receivable
				300
				
				300

Adjusting entry, December 31, 2007 [($205,000 − $5,000) × .01 = $2,000]	Bad Debts Expense 2,000
	  Allowance for Doubtful
	    Accounts
		2,000	(No entry is made.)	

Closing entry, December 31, 2007	Sales 205,000
	  Sales Returns and
	    Allowances
	  Bad Debts Expense
	  Income Summary
		5,000
		2,000
		198,000
			Sales 205,000
			Bad Debts Recovered 300
			  Sales Returns and
			    allowances
			  Bad Debts Expense
			  Income Summary
				5,000
				800
				199,500

Income Statement Account Balances for Year Ended December 31, 2007	Revenues
	  Sales
	  Sales returns and
	    allowances
	Operating expenses:
	  Bad debts expense
		$205,000
		
		5,000
		
		2,000
			Revenues
			  Sales
			  Sales returns and
			    allowances
			Operating expenses:
			  Bad debts expense
			Other revenues:
			  Bad debts recovered
				$205,000
				
				5,000
				
				800
				
				300

Balance Sheet Presentation of Accounts Receivable as of December 31, 2007	Current assets:
	  Accounts receivable
	  Deduct: Allowance for
	    doubtful accounts
	  Net realizable value
		$79,200
		
		2,500
		$76,700
			Current assets:
			  Accounts receivable
				$79,200

EXHIBIT **7.3**

Comparison of Allowance and Direct Write-off Methods

TIFFANY & CO.
Balance Sheet (current assets)
(*in thousands*)

	January 31	
	2004	**2003**
Current assets		
Cash and cash equivalents	$ 276,115	$ 156,197
Accounts receivable, less allowances of $6,992 and $8,258	177,033	157,441
Inventories	871,251	732,088
Other current assets	23,683	24,662
Total current assets	$1,348,082	$1,070,388

EXHIBIT **7.4**

Trade Receivables on Balance Sheet for Tiffany & Co.

We can compute total or gross accounts receivable by adding the allowance balance to net accounts receivable. Gross accounts receivable are $184,025,000 ($177,033,000 + $6,992,000) as of January 31, 2004, and $165,699,000 ($157,441,000 + $8,258,000) as of January 31, 2003. During fiscal 2003, $2,521,000 of accounts receivable were written off as uncollectible. In an adjusting entry, estimated bad debts of $1,255,000 were provided for.

CREDIT CARD SALES

Learning Goal 7   Record credit card sales.

Most retail firms accept credit cards. Credit cards enable consumers to make purchases without paying cash immediately or establishing credit with individual stores. From the retailer's point of view, credit cards eliminate the need to check credit ratings and to collect cash from individual customers. Credit card companies charge retailers a fee of 2-6% of credit card sales. However, retail firms receive cash payment faster than if they sell on account and then collect from customers.

For bank credit cards such as VISA or MasterCard, the bank accepts copies of the signed **credit card sales slips** as deposits just like cash. Therefore, each deposit increases the bank account balance of the business. To illustrate, assume that a business has bank credit card sales on April 6, 2007, of $10,000. The bank charges a 5% credit card fee. These sales would be recorded as follows:

2007					
Apr.	6	Cash		9,500	
		Credit Card Fees Expense		500	
		Sales			10,000
		To record bank credit card sales less a 5% credit card expense.			

Banks do not usually accept credit card sales slips on nonbank credit cards such as American Express. Instead, the retailer sends the credit card slips to the credit card company for payment. Therefore, we debit a receivable from the credit card company instead of cash. Because the credit card company assumes the risk of collecting from the customer, the credit card receivable does not require a bad debts allowance. The entry on April 6, 2007, to record American Express credit card sales of $10,000 with a 5% credit card fee is as follows:

2007					
Apr.	6	Accounts Receivable, American Express		9,500	
		Credit Card Fees Expense		500	
		Sales			10,000
		To record bank credit card sales less a 5% credit card expense.			

The entry to record the receipt of cash from the credit card company on April 15, 2007, is as follows:

2007					
Apr.	15	Cash		9,500	
		Accounts Receivable, American Express			9,500
		To record cash receipt from American Express.			

OPPOSITE BALANCES IN ACCOUNTS RECEIVABLE AND ACCOUNTS PAYABLE

In the accounts receivable subsidiary ledger, the customers' accounts normally have debit balances. Sometimes an overpayment, a sales return or allowance after a customer has paid an account, or an advance payment may create a credit balance. Assume that there is a net debit balance of $29,600 in an accounts receivable subsidiary ledger consisting of 100 accounts, as follows:

98 accounts with a debit balance	$ 30,000
2 accounts with a credit balance	400
Net debit balance of 100 accounts receivable	$ 29,600

The debit amount of $30,000 and the credit amount of $400 would appear on the balance sheet as follows:

Current assets		**Current liabilities**	
Accounts receivable	$30,000	Credit balances in customer accounts	$400

The controlling account balance of $29,600 should not be used in the balance sheet. It would conceal the current liability of $400, which should be shown with the caption "**credit balances in customer accounts**." The accounts payable subsidiary ledger is similar. If it contains creditors' accounts with debit balances, the balance sheet should show the total of accounts with debit balances as a current asset. For example, a net balance in the Accounts Payable controlling account of $88,600 (with subsidiary ledger accounts having debit balances that total $1,400) would appear in the balance sheet as follows:

Current assets		**Current liabilities**	
Debit balances in creditor accounts	$1,400	Accounts payable	$90,000

INTERNAL CONTROL OF ACCOUNTS RECEIVABLE

Learning Goal 8   Identify the internal control issues involved with accounts receivable.

Most companies receive cash collections on account by mail. Usually checks received are made payable to the business. It is still possible for an employee to forge endorsements and deposit the checks in bank accounts the employee has control over. Therefore, it is important that there is a separation of duties in handling incoming payments. Employees who keep the accounts receivable records should not have access to cash or make bank deposits. For example, one employee could have the responsibilities of opening the mail and making bank deposits. He or she would send customer remittance slips to another employee in the accounting department, who would compare the slip with a copy of the original sales invoice and credit the customer's account. A supervisor could prepare the monthly bank reconciliation.

A supervisor should authorize recording sales returns and allowances, discounts, and bad debts write-offs. He or she should separate the cash receipt and cash disbursement functions. The supervisor should make an independent check to see that the account balance statements sent to customers are in agreement with the accounts receivable records and periodically review overdue accounts. Control over receivables begins with properly approved sales orders. It continues through the remaining steps in the credit process: approval of credit terms, recording shipment, customer billing, recording the receivable and collection, and approval of subsequent adjustments.

ANALYZING INFORMATION

Learning Goal 9   Analyze financial statement information for real-life companies.

To illustrate the analysis of accounts receivable, we will use Sharper Image Corporation. Sharper Image is one of the nation's large sellers of merchandise customers. Since the company makes substantial sales on credit, receivables and bad debts are an important consideration. Following is selected assumed information (in thousands) for the years ended December 31, 2004 and 2003:

	2004	2003
SHARPER IMAGE CORPORATION		
For the year ended December 31:		
Net sales	$ 630,084	$ 498,702
Bad debts expense	5,800	4,650
As of December 31:		
Gross accounts receivable	$ 22,462	$ 13,564
Deduct: Allowance for doubtful accounts	1,266	967
Accounts receivable, net of allowance	$ 21,196	$ 12,597

Question 1. Is the percent of bad debts expense to net sales increasing or decreasing over time?

Analysis 1. On the *income statement*, it is important to look at the relationship between net sales and bad debts expense. For example, if sales are increasing and bad debts expense is decreasing, it may indicate that a company's collection experience is improving (*favorable*) or it may indicate that the current expense estimate is too low (*unfavorable*). In either case, the trend would cause the analyst to ask for an explanation from management.

For Sharper Image, the dollar amount of bad debts expense increased from 2003 to 2004. The dollar amount of net sales increased from 2003 to 2004. The percent of bad debts expense to net sales is 0.92% in 2004 ($5,800 ÷ $630,084) and 0.93% in 2003 ($4,650 ÷ $498,702). It appears that management believes that a smaller percent of 2004 sales may prove uncollectible than in 2003. A question we may raise is: are increased sales for 2004 a result of selling to customers with a higher credit risk?

Question 2. Is the percent of the allowance for doubtful accounts to gross accounts receivable increasing or decreasing over time?

Analysis 2. On the *balance sheet*, it is important to look at the relationship between the allowance for doubtful accounts and gross accounts receivable. For example, if gross receivables are increasing and the allowance balance is decreasing, it may indicate that a company's collection experience is improving (*favorable*) or it may indicate that the current allowance amount is too low (*unfavorable*). In either case, we would ask for an explanation.

For Sharper Image, the dollar amount of both gross accounts receivable and the allowance balance increased from 2003 to 2004. The percent of the allowance for doubtful accounts to gross accounts receivable is 5.6% in 2004 ($1,266 ÷ $22,462) and 7.1% in 2003 ($967 ÷ $13,564). It appears that management feels that a smaller percent of receivables at the end of 2004 may prove uncollectible than at the end of 2003. A question we may ask: is the decreased allowance percent an indication of improvement in collecting existing receivables next year?

A comprehensive review of all issues dealing with accounts receivable for Manpower, Inc. is shown in Problem 7-33.

LEARNING GOALS REVIEW

1. **Identify and classify receivables on the balance sheet.**

   Receivables fall into two broad categories: trade receivables and nontrade receivables. There are three classes of trade receivables: accounts receivable, notes receivable, and credit card receivables.

2. **Explain why accountants must provide for uncollectible accounts to match revenues and expenses on the income statement and to present accounts receivable on the balance sheet.**

   The goal of accrual-basis accounting is to match revenues with expenses. Estimated losses from uncollectible accounts should be recognized as an expense during the period when sales are recognized. Making this adjustment shows accounts receivable at the amount the company actually expects to collect.

3. **Journalize entries under the allowance method to record the bad debts adjustment, write off uncollectible accounts, and recover bad debts.**

   The adjusting entry records the estimate of bad debts as a debit to Bad Debts Expense and a credit to Allowance for Doubtful Accounts. The write-off of uncollectible accounts debits Allowance for Doubtful Accounts and credits Accounts Receivable. The recovery of accounts written off debits Accounts Receivable and credits Allowance for Doubtful Accounts. A second entry debits Cash and credits Accounts Receivable.

4. **Estimate uncollectible accounts using approaches based on sales and receivables.**

   An estimate based on sales (income statement approach) multiplies sales or net sales by a percentage estimate of bad debts. We ignore any existing balance in Allowance for Doubtful Accounts when computing bad debts expense in the income statement approach. The estimate based on receivables (balance sheet approach) determines the desired balance of the allowance account by examining the collectibility of accounts receivable. We use either a percentage or an aging schedule of accounts receivable. We add or subtract the existing balance in Allowance for Doubtful Accounts when computing bad debts expense in the balance sheet approach.

5. **Journalize entries under the direct write-off method to write off uncollectible accounts and recover bad debts.**

   Under the direct write-off method, we debit Bad Debts Expense when a specific receivable becomes uncollectible. We credit Accounts Receivable for that amount. There is no allowance for doubtful accounts and no end-of-period adjusting entry. To recover bad debts, we debit Accounts Receivable for the amount recovered and credit Bad Debts Recovered. Then we debit Cash and credit Accounts Receivable.

6. **Compare the allowance and direct write-off methods as they affect the income statement and the balance sheet.**

   The allowance method results in a better matching of revenues and expenses on the income statement. The allowance method shows estimated bad debts as an expense in the same accounting period that the revenues are recognized. Under the direct write-off method, bad debts expense consists of accounts receivable that were actually written off during the accounting period. The balance sheet under the allowance method shows the amount of accounts receivable the company expects to collect. Under the direct write-off method, it shows accounts receivable at their gross value.

7. **Record credit card sales.**

   A business that accepts a bank credit card treats the transaction as a cash sale. It debits Credit Card Fees Expense for the credit card fee and debits Cash for the balance of the sales amount. It credits Sales for the total sales amount. In a transaction using a nonbank credit card, the company debits Credit Card Fees Expense for the fee and Accounts Receivable, (Credit Card Company) for the remaining balance.

8. **Identify the internal control issues involved with accounts receivable.**

   Duties should be separated so that one employee's work can be checked and verified by another employee's work. For example, those who maintain records of accounts receivable should not have access to cash. A supervisor should authorize recording returns and allowances, discounts, and write-offs of bad debts. A responsible supervisor should review delinquent accounts. Activities at all stages of sales and collections should require proper authorization and verification.

9. **Analyze financial statement information for real-life companies.**

   In analyzing the bad debts on the income statement, compute and observe the trend in bad debts expense as a percent of net sales. In analyzing the allowance account on the balance sheet, compute and observe the trend in the allowance for doubtful accounts as a percent of gross accounts receivable.

DEMONSTRATION PROBLEM

Allowance Method Versus Direct Write-Off Method of Accounting for Bad Debts

Bizet Company sells musical instruments on credit. It provides for uncollectible accounts using a percentage of 6% of accounts receivable on December 31, 2007, to determine the desired allowance balance. On January 1, 2007, the trial balance showed the following selected account balances:

Accounts Receivable	$40,000
Allowance for Doubtful Accounts (credit)	2,400

During 2007, the following summary transactions occurred:

a. Sales on account were $300,000.

b. Accounts of Mozart Company written off on August 1, 2007, as uncollectible totaled $3,000.

c. Collections from customers on account were $260,000.

REQUIRED

1. **(LG 3, 4)** Prepare the general journal entries to write off the accounts receivable determined to be uncollectible during 2007 and the adjusting entry for bad debts as of December 31, 2007.

2. **(LG 3)** Show the presentation of accounts receivable in the current assets section of the balance sheet after the adjusting entry on December 31, 2007.

3. **(LG 3, 4)** Assume that Bizet Company used the allowance method, but used the income statement approach to estimate bad debts. Two percent of sales have proven to be uncollectible. Determine the amount of bad debts expense for 2007.

4. **(LG 5)** Assuming that Bizet Company had used the direct write-off method for bad debts:

   a. Prepare the general journal entry to write off accounts receivable determined to be uncollectible during 2007.

   b. For 2007, what amount would appear on the income statement for bad debts expense?

   c. Show the presentation of accounts receivable in the current assets section of the balance sheet as of December 31, 2007.

SOLUTION

Solution Approach

1, 2. When using an allowance method based on a percentage of accounts receivable, we must consider any existing balance in the allowance account in determining the amount of bad debts expense. This is because the objective of the balance sheet approach is to present accounts receivable at their net realizable value.

3. When using an allowance method based on a percentage of net sales, we ignore any existing balance in the allowance account in determining the amount of bad debts expense. This is because the objective of this approach is to associate bad debts expense directly with dollar volume of sales.

4. Under the direct write-off method, we recognize bad debts in the period when the account receivable is determined to be uncollectible.

Requirement 1

Solution Approach

$40,000 + $300,000 - $3,000 - $260,000 = $77,000 ending accounts receivable;
$77,000 × .06 = $4,620 desired allowance balance;
$4,620 + $600 (debit allowance balance) = $5,220 bad debts expense.

2007				
Aug.	1	Allowance for Doubtful Accounts	3,000	
		Accounts Receivable, Mozart Company		3,000
		To write off receivable from Mozart Company as uncollectible.		
Dec.	31	Bad Debts Expense	5,220	
		Allowance for Doubtful Accounts		5,220
		To increase the allowance account to the desired balance ($4,620 + $600 previous debit balance).		

Requirement 2

Current assets

Accounts receivable	$ 77,000
Deduct: Allowance for doubtful accounts	4,620
Net realizable value	$ 72,380

Requirement 3

$300,000 \times .02 = \$6,000.$

Requirement 4

a.	2007				
	Aug.	1 Bad Debts Expense		3,000	
		Accounts Receivable, Mozart Company			3,000
		To write off receivable from Mozart Company as uncollectible.			
b.	$3,000				
c.		**Current assets**			
		Accounts receivable	$77,000		

GLOSSARY

aging A method of classifying individual receivables by age groups, according to time elapsed from due date.

aging schedule A columnar work sheet showing the individual receivables by age groups, according to time elapsed from due date. The amounts for each age group are also totaled, and the percentage of each group to the total receivables is computed to aid in determining the allowance for doubtful accounts.

Allowance for Doubtful Accounts A valuation account contra to Accounts Receivable showing the amount of estimated uncollectible accounts as of a given date.

allowance method A method that estimates bad debt expense at the end of each accounting period.

bad debt An uncollectible account receivable.

Bad Debts Expense An expense account showing the estimated uncollectible credit sales for a given time period if the allowance method is used, or actual write-offs if the direct write-off method is used.

Bad Debts Recovered A revenue account (or cost recovery account) that is credited for the recovery of an account receivable previously written off under the direct write-off method.

balance sheet approach A method of estimating the adjusted amount needed in Allowance for Doubtful Accounts; the estimate is based on the balance sheet item, accounts receivable.

credit balances in customer accounts A liability item representing the amounts due customers because of overpayment or a sales return made after payment had been made.

credit card sales slip A signed voucher prepared from a sale on a credit card. The item verifies the sale and serves as an invoice.

direct write-off method A method in which bad debts expense is not recognized until the period in which the receivable proves uncollectible.

income statement approach A method of estimating the bad debts expense for a given period; the estimate is based on an income statement item, sales.

net realizable value The estimated collectible amount of accounts receivable.

nontrade receivable A receivable arising from a source other than sales of merchandise or sales of ordinary services.

trade receivable A claim against a customer arising from sales of merchandise or sale of ordinary services.

DISCUSSION QUESTIONS

Q7-1. Explain why trade receivables collectible in 16 months may be properly shown as a current asset on the balance sheet.

Q7-2. How does the matching principle affect the disclosure of trade receivables on the balance sheet?

Q7-3. (a) What is the function of the Allowance for Doubtful Accounts account? (b) What methods may be used to estimate its amount? (c) How is this account shown on the balance sheet?

Q7-4. What is the difference between the income statement approach and the balance sheet approach in estimating bad debts expense? What are the advantages and disadvantages of each?

Q7-5. A company attempting to state its accounts receivable at net realizable value may have to set up accounts other than Allowance for Doubtful Accounts. Can you think of any other possible contra accounts for Accounts Receivable? When would such accounts be useful?

Q7-6. What kind of account (asset, liability, expense, and so on) is Allowance for Doubtful Accounts? Is its normal balance a debit or a credit? What action is taken if its normal balance becomes negative?

Q7-7. Rockwood Company, which had accounts receivable of $75,822 and a balance in Allowance for Doubtful Accounts of $3,814 on January 1, 2007, wrote off a past due account of Mark Slater in 2007 for $680.

    a. What effect will the write-off have on the total current assets of the company? Why?

    b. What effect will the write-off have on 2007 net income? Why?

Q7-8. A company systematically adjusts its allowance for doubtful accounts at the end of each year by adding a fixed percent of the year's sales minus sales returns and allowances. After five years, the credit balance in Allowance for Doubtful Accounts has become disproportionately large in relation to the balance in Accounts Receivable. What are two possible explanations for the large balance?

Q7-9. When a company adjusts the balance in its allowance for doubtful accounts to a percentage of accounts receivable, the balance of the allowance account will tend to be partially self-correcting, provided that there is only a small error in the percentage rate that is being applied. The bad debts expense for certain years, on the other hand, may contain sizable errors. What are the reasons for this situation?

Q7-10. Credit card sales on other than bank credit cards result in a debit to a receivable account. Why?

Q7-11. How does the valuation of receivables arising from nonbank credit card sales differ from the valuation of other trade receivables?

Q7-12. (a) What are some reasons why credit balances occur in individual accounts receivable accounts? (b) How are such balances presented in the balance sheet?

Q7-13. Identify the internal control procedures applicable to accounts receivable.

Q7-14. At what point in the time sequence of selling and collecting does the bad debts expense occur? Discuss.

Q7-15. Tomlinson Company had a debit balance in its Allowance for Doubtful Accounts account before adjustments. Does this mean an error had been made? Discuss.

EXERCISES

E7-16. **Balance sheet classification of receivables (LG 1)** Fort Pierce Company had the following items in its adjusted trial balance as of December 31, 2007.

Account Title	Debits	Credits
Accounts Receivable	$80,000	
Allowance for Doubtful Accounts		$1,500
Accounts Receivable, American Express	10,000	
Notes Receivable (due October 1, 2010)	52,000	
Interest Receivable	1,450	
Notes Receivable, Officers (due 2009)	18,500	

1. Prepare a partial balance sheet showing how you recommend that the foregoing should be reported using generally accepted accounting principles.

2. Explain why you classified each item as you did.

E7-17. **Journalizing entries under the allowance method (LG 3)** Palm Company, which uses an Allowance for Doubtful Accounts account, had the following transactions involving uncollectible accounts in 2007 and 2008:

2007

Dec.	31	Recorded estimated bad debts expense of $5,000.

2008

Jun.	12	Wrote off Jack Sweeney's account receivable of $1,120 as uncollectible.
Aug.	1	Jack Sweeney won the state lottery and paid the amount due of $1,120.

Journalize the transactions.

E7-18. **Recording bad debts expense by use of the allowance method (LG 3, 4)** Sunshine Company had sales on credit of $900,000 during 2007, with accounts receivable of $250,000 and a credit balance of $400 in Allowance for Doubtful Accounts at the end of the year. Record the bad debts expense for the year, using each of the following methods for the estimate:

a. Allowance for doubtful accounts is to be increased to 5% of accounts receivable.

b. Bad debts expense is estimated to be 1% of sales on credit.

c. Allowance for doubtful accounts is to be increased to $8,500, as indicated by an aging schedule.

E7-19.   Recording bad debts by use of the allowance method (LG 3, 4) Latasha Company had sales on credit of $900,000 and cash sales of $150,000 during 2007. At the end of the year, there was a debit balance in Accounts Receivable of $80,000 and a debit balance in Allowance for Doubtful Accounts of $800. Record the bad debts expense for the year, using each of the following methods for the estimate:

   a. Allowance for doubtful accounts is to be increased to 4% of accounts receivable.

   b. Bad debts expense is estimated to be 0.6% of credit sales.

   c. Allowance for doubtful accounts is to be increased to $6,700, as indicated by aging the accounts receivable.

E7-20.   Recording bad debts expense, write-off, and balance sheet presentation under the allowance method (LG 3, 4) The trial balance of Sinatra Company included the following accounts on June 30, 2007, the end of the company's fiscal year:

Accounts Receivable	$ 140,000
Allowance for Doubtful Accounts (credit)	550
Sales	700,000

Uncollectible accounts are estimated at 6% of accounts receivable.

   1. Make the adjusting entry to record the bad debts expense.

   2. Show the presentation of accounts receivable and allowance for doubtful accounts in the June 30, 2007 balance sheet.

   3. Give the entry to write off the account of an insolvent customer, Samuel Davids, for $1,300 on July 3, 2007.

   4. Show the presentation of accounts receivable and allowance for doubtful accounts in the balance sheet prepared immediately after the write-off on July 3, 2007.

E7-21.   Aging accounts receivable and recording bad debts expense under the allowance method (LG 3, 4) The accounts receivable subsidiary ledger of Steel Pier Distributing Company shows the following data on December 31, 2007 (the general ledger showed a $200 debit balance in Allowance for Doubtful Accounts before adjustments):

Name of Customer	Invoice Date	Amount
Atlantic Company	May 2, 2007	$ 1,000
Margate Company	August 15, 2007	650
Ventnor Company	December 8, 2007	400
	October 2, 2007	700
Cape May Company	March 3, 2007	600
Avalon Company	November 11, 2007	775
	November 20, 2007	325
LBI Company	September 4, 2007	500
	July 10, 2007	900
Others	December 5, 2007	41,000

Terms of sale are n/30.

   1. Prepare an aging schedule.

   2. Compute the estimated uncollectible amount based on the following rates:

	Estimated Percent Uncollectible
Accounts not due	2
Accounts past due	
1-30 days	6
31-60 days	15
61-90 days	30
91-120 days	40
121-365 days	70

3. Record the bad debts expense.

E7-22. **Journalizing entries under the direct write-off method (LG 5)** Doors Company uses the direct write-off method of accounting for bad debts expense. The company had the following transactions involving uncollectible accounts in 2007:

2007

Apr.	18	Wrote off Tom Petty's account of $1,000 as uncollectible. The merchandise had been sold in 2006.
Nov.	28	Recovered $450 from Tom Petty

Journalize the transactions in general journal form.

E7-23. **Comparing the allowance and direct write-off methods (LG 6)** Assume the following data for Polo Company for the year ended December 31, 2007:

Accounts receivable, January 1, 2007	$ 100,000
Sales on account during 2007	520,000
Sales returns and allowances	10,000
Total expenses during 2007 (other than bad debts expense)	420,000
Cash collections on account (not including bad debts recovered)	510,000
Accounts written off as uncollectible	5,000
Bad debts recovered (previously written off as uncollectible in 2006)	1,000

Compute each of the amounts listed below under the assumption that Polo Company uses (1) the direct write-off method of recording bad debts and (2) the allowance method of recording bad debts. Under the allowance method, assume that there was a beginning credit balance of $7,000 in Allowance for Doubtful Accounts and that bad debts are estimated at 6% of the ending balance in Accounts Receivable.

a. Net sales for 2007.

b. Bad debts expense for 2007.

c. Net income for 2007

d. The amount shown for net accounts receivable on the balance sheet prepared as of December 31, 2007.

E7-24. **Accounting for credit card sales (LG 7)** Bennett Corporation makes sales on account only to customers who charged purchases on credit cards from Bankco Company (a bank credit card) and Marksman Card Company (a nonbank credit card). These two credit card companies each charge a fee of 4%. On December 12, 2007 customers of Bennett Corporation charged merchandise to these credit cards as follows:

Bankco Company	$ 35,000
Marksman Card Company	12,000

Journalize these sales on the books of Bennett Corporation.

E7-25. **Balance sheet disclosure of receivables with credit balances (LG 1)** Masaba Company maintains a controlling account entitled Receivables, the balance of which was $76,700 on December 31, 2007. The subsidiary ledger and other information reveal the following:

470 trade accounts (debit balances)	$58,200
8 trade accounts (credit balances)	900
9 trade notes	12,400
4 loans to the president and vice-presidents (due June 30, 2011)	7,000
Allowance for doubtful accounts	4,600

Show how this information should be reported on the balance sheet.

E7-26. **Internal control of accounts receivable (LG 8)** O'Brien Company has asked you to review the internal control procedures over accounts receivable. In the course of your examination, you discover the following:

1. One employee who has been with the company for 20 years is responsible for maintaining the accounts receivable records and also counting and depositing cash receipts each day. The company president states that this employee is so loyal that he has never taken a vacation.

2. O'Brien Company maintains a policy of customer satisfaction. All employees are authorized to issue immediate cash refunds to customers who are not satisfied with their purchases by taking cash from the cash register.

3. Aging of the accounts receivable indicates that $17,000 of the total receivable balance of $60,000 is past due. Included in the past due accounts is a $5,000 account receivable from a personal friend of the company president that was due seven years ago. The O'Brien Company uses the direct write-off method but has never written off an account receivable.

Based on the preceding information, prepare a list of recommendations concerning internal control of receivables.

E7-27. **Chapter integrating and review exercise: Computing cash received from customers (LG 1-3)** The Cash account page in the general ledger of the Somerton Company has been temporarily misplaced. The following account data are available:

	December 31		Year 2008
	2008	**2007**	
Accounts Receivable, Trade	$70,000	$60,000	
Allowance for Doubtful Accounts	5,000	5,900	
Sales			$610,000
Sales Discounts			9,000

During 2008, accounts receivable of $4,000 were written off as uncollectible, and one account of $700, previously written off in 2007, was collected and recorded in the following manner:

Accounts Receivable	700	
Allowance for Doubtful Accounts		700
Cash	700	
Accounts Receivable		700

Compute the cash received from customers during 2008.

PROBLEMS

P7-28. **Journalizing entries under the allowance method (LG 3)** Good Eats Baking Company uses an allowance approach for doubtful accounts. The following selected transactions involving uncollectible accounts occurred in 2006 and 2007:

2006

Dec.	31	Recorded estimated bad debts expense of $3,600.

2007

Apr.	16	Wrote off the $500 balance owed by Sam's Diner, which was bankrupt.	
Jun.	10	Reinstated the account of Mary's Lunch, which had been written off in October 2006 as uncollectible. Recorded the receipt of a check for $600 in full payment of her account.	
Nov.	4	Performed an analysis of all accounts outstanding and wrote off the following accounts as uncollectible:	
		Adams Eatery	$200
		Sally's Coffee	80
		Jenny's Deli	220
Dec.	2	Received $180 of the $400 balance owed by Donny's Bar and wrote off the remaining balance as uncollectible.	

REQUIRED

Record the transactions in general journal form.

P7-29. **Journalizing entries under the allowance method: Using estimates based on both sales and receivables (LG 3, 4)** The Allowance for Doubtful Accounts account of Packard Company showed a credit balance of $2,900 on December 31, 2006, before adjustments were made. The bad debts expense for 2006 was estimated at 2% of the sales on credit of $900,000 for the year. The following transactions occurred during the next two years:

2007

May	12	Wrote off May Weston's $4,200 account as uncollectible.
Sep.	28	Wrote off Jane Eastman's account of $3,500 as uncollectible.
Oct.	29	Received a check for $1,700 in final settlement of May Weston's account written off in May. She had been adjudged bankrupt by the courts.
Dec.	31	An analysis of accounts receivable by age indicated that accounts doubtful of collection totaled $18,000. (Note that the method of estimating bad debts expense has been changed from an emphasis on sales to receivables.)

2008

Aug.	21	Wrote off D. A. Dawson's $6,900 account as uncollectible.
Dec.	31	Estimated that uncollectible accounts receivable totaled $17,000.

REQUIRED

1. Record In General Journal Form Transactions And Events, Including Adjusting Entries, For December 31, 2006, 2007, and 2008.

2. Post to a ledger account for Allowance for Doubtful Accounts. (*Hint*: Complete this step as you do requirement 1.)

P7-30. **Recording various accounts receivable transactions using the allowance method (LG 3, 4, 7)** During November and early December 2007, Kendrick Company had the following sales and receivable transactions (all sales were made on account and, except on credit cards, carried terms of 2/10, n/30):

2007

Nov.	1	Sold merchandise to Bat Eason for $2,660 on invoice no. 1001.
	2	Sold merchandise to C. Faison for $9,400 on invoice no. 1002.
	7	Credited C. Faison for returned merchandise with an invoice price of $1,400.
	9	Received a check from Bat Eason for the amount due on invoice no. 1001.
	10	Sold merchandise to Verree Company for $3,200 on invoice no. 1003.
	13	Received $862.40 in cash from Verree Company in partial payment of invoice no. 1003. Discounts are allowed on partial payments.
	14	Received a check for the amount due from C. Faison.
	15	Sold merchandise to Dick Bracey Company for $18,000 on invoice no. 1004.
	23	Received a check from Dick Bracey Company for the amount due on invoice no. 1004.
	30	Sold merchandise to Annie Leigh Company for $12,600 on invoice no. 1005.
	30	Sold merchandise to Three F Company for $15,000 on invoice no. 1006.
	30	Summary bank credit card sales for November were $12,800; nonbank credit card sales on American Express for November were $14,200. A fee of 6% is charged for each of these sales.
	30	Estimated the bad debts expense for November to be 3.6% of credit sales less sales returns and allowances (excluding credit card accounts receivable).
Dec.	8	Received a notice that Verree Company had been adjudged bankrupt. The balance of its account was therefore regarded as uncollectible.

REQUIRED

1. Journalize the transactions in general journal form.

2. Post all entries (*excluding credit card sales*) to the Accounts Receivable controlling and subsidiary accounts. Post credit card receivables to appropriate accounts.

3. Prepare a schedule of accounts receivable after the December 8, 2007, transaction is recorded.

P7-31. Journalizing entries and preparing an income statement under the direct write-off method (LG 5) Most of the sales of Al's Auto Parts are on a cash basis. As a result, Al's uses the direct write-off method to account for the relatively few bad debts the business experiences. Before Al's considered any uncollectible account transactions, the following selected account balances appeared in a trial balance as of the year end, December 31, 2007:

	Debit	Credit
Accounts Receivable	$ 76,000	
Accounts Payable		$ 80,000
Cost of Goods Sold	520,000	
Common Stock		200,000
Operating Expenses	130,000	
Sales		760,000
Sales Returns	22,000	

The following transactions involving uncollectible accounts occurred on December 31, 2007, after the trial balance was prepared:

a. Received notice that Gramling's Service Station had closed and that the owner, Larry Gramling had left the country. As a result, $5,000 of accounts receivable from Gramling were written off as uncollectible.

b. Received a check for $1,500 from Hal Wyman in full payment of his account, which had been written off in 2006 when Wyman's Texaco went out of business. Mr. Wyman recently won the state lottery and wanted to pay past debts.

c. Estimated that $3,000 of the sales for 2007 will prove uncollectible.

REQUIRED

1. Record in general journal form the entries for uncollectible accounts required in transactions (a) through (c) above.

2. Assuming the journal entries have been recorded and posted, prepare an income statement for the year ended December 31, 2007.

3. Compute the amount of accounts receivable that will be shown on the balance sheet prepared as of December 31, 2007.

P7-32. **Comparing the allowance method with the direct write-off method (LG 6)** On December 31, 2007, Cooky's Pizza Sauce showed the following on its trial balance:

Accounts Receivable	$40,000
Allowance for Doubtful Accounts (credit)	400

After making an analysis of the accounts receivable on December 31, 2007, Cooky estimated the accounts doubtful of collection at $1,640. During the year 2008, the following transactions occurred:

a. Sales on account were $165,200.

b. Accounts written off as uncollectible totaled $1,600.

c. Collections from customers on account were $150,000.

d. A customer whose account had been previously written off paid $200 in full payment of his balance.

On December 31, 2008, Cooky estimated the accounts doubtful of collection at $1,800.

REQUIRED

1. Set up ledger accounts for accounts receivable and allowance for doubtful accounts; record the balances as of December 31, 2007, in these accounts, and then post the entries for 2007 and 2008 directly into these accounts.

2. Compute the bad debts expense deduction for the income statement for the year 2008, using (a) the direct write-off method and (b) the allowance method.

P7-33. **Comprehensive analysis of accounts receivable for Manpower, Inc. (LG 9)** Manpower, Inc. is the largest non-governmental employment services organization in the world. Following is selected information (in thousands) for Manpower, Inc. for the 2004, 2003, and 2002 fiscal years.

	2004	2003	2002
For the year ended June 30:			
Net sales	$14,930,000	$12,184,500	$10,610,900
Bad debts expense	27,200	16,700	18,200
As of the year end:			
Accounts receivable, net of allowance	$3,234,300	$2,710,800	$2,293,300
Allowance for doubtful accounts	91,400	79,100	81,900

REQUIRED

1. Comment briefly on the trend in net sales for Manpower. Is the company growing over the three- year period?

2. Comment briefly on the relationship between the growth in net sales and the growth in accounts receivable over the three-year period. Does the relationship between sales growth and receivable growth seem reasonable?

3. For bad debts, does Manpower use the allowance method or the direct write-off method? Briefly explain.

4. As of the end of fiscal 2004, compute the gross amount of accounts receivable.

5. As of the end of fiscal 2004, compute the net realizable value of accounts receivable.

6. For 2004, prepare the journal entry to record the bad debts expense estimate.

7. For 2004, prepare the journal entry to write off uncollectible accounts (note: you will have to use the information provided above to compute this amount).

8. Identify the year that Manpower had the largest estimate of bad debts expense.

9. Compute bad debts expense as a percent of net sales for each year. Comment on the trend in the percent from 2002 to 2004.

10. Compute the allowance for doubtful accounts as a percent of gross accounts receivable for each year. Comment on the trend in the percent from 2002 to 2004.

11. In 2004, if Manpower used the direct write-off method, what amount would appear on the income statement for bad debts expense?

12. At the end of 2004, if Manpower used the direct write-off method, what amount would appear on the balance sheet for net accounts receivable?

PRACTICE CASE

Accounts receivable and bad debts expense (LG 1, 3-7) Dick's Stereo Ultimate sells high-end stereo equipment. The average price of a stereo system is $4,000. To assist customers in financing their purchases, the following sales terms are available:

a. Immediate payment in full by cash or check. A discount of 2% of the sales invoice is allowed to encourage cash payment at the point of sale.

b. Payment using a credit card. Issuing institutions charge the retailer a fee of 4% for accepting and collecting credit card receivables.

c. Payment of the sales invoice price within 30 days from the invoice date on an interest-free basis. As of December 31, 2006, the balances in selected current asset accounts were as follows:

	Debit	Credit
Cash	$ 90,000	
Accounts Receivable	130,000	
Allowance for Doubtful Accounts		$ 6,500
Accounts Receivable—Credit Cards	7,000	

During the year 2007, the following summary transactions occurred:

a. Sales on a cash basis totaled $180,000 (before discounts).

b. Credit card sales using bank credit cards totaled $180,000 and using nonbank credit cards totaled $50,000.

c. Sales on open 30-day account totaled $440,000.

d. Cash collections on open account were $365,000 and from nonbank credit cards were $44,000.

e. The $5,200 account of Ron Murphy was written off as uncollectible.

f. Received a check from Phil Ressler for $2,600 in full payment of his account, which had been written off as uncollectible in September 2006.

g. Don Johnson returned an amplifier he did not like for a credit to his account in the amount of $3,200. Johnson did not have any previous balance in his account and has agreed to apply the credit to a new amplifier, which is on special order.

h. Increased the allowance to 8% of the accounts receivable outstanding as of December 31, 2007. (Do not consider the $3,200 credit balance in transaction g.)

REQUIRED
1. Journalize the transactions in general journal form.

2. Based on the accounts given in the problem, prepare the current asset section of the balance sheet as of December 31, 2007.

3. If Dick's Stereo Ultimate used the direct write-off method of accounting for bad debts, compute the amount of total current assets as of December 31, 2007.

BUSINESS DECISION AND COMMUNICATION PROBLEM

Effect of alternative methods for bad debts on financial statements (LG 6) Debra's Dolls was incorporated on January 1, 2007. After completing its first year of operations, the trial balance included the following selected accounts at December 31, 2007:

Sales Revenues	$900,000
Cost of Goods Sold	600,000
Operating Expenses	160,000
Accounts Receivable	500,000

To increase sales its first year, Tom Manchester, the sales manager, decided to sell to customers to whom competing firms had refused to extend credit. Tom Manchester expresses the belief that strong collection efforts will result in the collection of all of the accounts. He feels that an allowance for doubtful accounts is not necessary and that the direct write-off method should be used. Pat Vernon, credit manager, estimates that 30% of the accounts receivable as of December 31, 2007 will not be collected. She recommends that an allowance account be established.

Debra Tomany has asked you to prepare a memo to her covering the following issues:

1. A comparison of net income for the year ended December 31, 2007, assuming that uncollectible accounts are (a) provided by the allowance method and (b) not provided for. Briefly explain which net income figure best matches revenues and expenses.

2. A comparison of net accounts receivable shown on the balance sheet assuming that uncollectible accounts are (a) provided for by the allowance method and (b) not provided for. Briefly explain which alternative results in a better balance sheet presentation of accounts receivable.

3. Your recommendations along with a discussion of any concerns you have regarding the business.

REQUIRED

Prepare a written response in the form of a memo addressed to Debra Tomany, President.

ETHICAL DILEMMA

Disclose to casino customers that some gambling debts will not be collected? (LG 3) In a recent year, a large hotel chain generated about one-third of its revenues from casino operations. Assume that you have been placed in charge of financial reporting for the hotel chain at a substantial salary. The president feels that the current allowance for doubtful casino accounts of $8 million (20% of casino accounts receivable) sends the message to customers that the hotel does not expect them to pay their gambling debts. Therefore, the president has asked you to remove the allowance account and simply show the casino accounts receivables at their gross value.

REQUIRED

Prepare a short written response.

COMPREHENSIVE ANALYSIS CASE SUN MICROSYSTEMS, INC.

Analyzing Sun Microsystems, Inc. for the Period 2004-2002 Listed below are comparative income statements and balance sheets with common-size percents for 2004-2002 (in millions). Also included are selected ratio statistics. Please provide a brief explanation for your answer to each question. The "acquired in-process technology" expenses in the income statement represent the write-off of purchased technology costs that no longer have any benefit to the company.

REQUIRED

Income statement questions:

1. Are total revenues higher or lower over the three-year period?

2. What is the percent change in total revenues from 2002 to 2004?

3. Is the percent of cost of goods sold to total revenues increasing or decreasing over the three-year period? As a result, is the gross margin percent increasing or decreasing?

4. Is the percent of total operating expenses to total revenues increasing or decreasing over the three-year period? As a result, is the operating income percent increasing or decreasing?

5. Is the percent of net income to total revenue increasing or decreasing over the three-year period?

Balance sheet questions:

6. Are total assets higher or lower over the three-year period?

7. What is the percent change in total assets from 2002 to 2004?

8. What are the largest asset investments for the company over the three-year period?

SUN MICROSYSTEMS INC.
COMPARATIVE COMMON-SIZE INCOME STATEMENTS
For The Years Ended Jan. 30, 2004, 2003, 2002
(in millions)

	2004 $	2004 %	2003 $	2003 %	2002 $	2002 %
Revenues	11,185.0	100.0%	11,434.0	100.0%	12,496.0	100.0%
Cost of goods sold	6,669.0	59.6%	6,492.0	56.8%	7,580.0	60.7%
Gross margin	4,516.0	40.4%	4,942.0	43.2%	4,916.0	39.3%
Operating expenses:						
Sales, marketing, general administrative	3,317.0	29.7%	3,329.0	29.1%	3,812.0	30.5%
Research and development	1,926.0	17.2%	1,837.0	16.1%	1,835.0	14.7%
Other expense	463.0	4.1%	2,500.0	21.9%	517.0	4.1%
Other expense	-	0.0%	-	0.0%	-	0.0%
Total operating expenses	5,706.0	51.0%	7,666.0	67.0%	6,164.0	49.3%
Operating income	(1,190.0)	-10.6%	(2,724.0)	-23.8%	(1,248.0)	-10.0%
Net interest expense (income)	37.0	0.3%	43.0	0.4%	58.0	0.5%
Other expense (income)	(1,664.0)	-14.9%	(114.0)	-1.0%	(258.0)	-2.1%
Income before income taxes	437.0	3.9%	(2,653.0)	-23.2%	(1,048.0)	-8.4%
Income taxes	825.0	7.4%	776.0	6.8%	(461.0)	-3.7%
Net income (loss) before unusual items	(388.0)	-3.5%	(3,429.0)	-30.0%	(587.0)	-4.7%
Other losses (gains) net of tax	-	0.0%	-	0.0%	-	0.0%
Net income (loss)	(388.0)	-3.5%	(3,429.0)	-30.0%	(587.0)	-4.7%

SUN MICROSYSTEMS INC.
COMPARATIVE COMMON-SIZE BALANCE SHEETS
June 30, 2004, 2003, 2002
(in millions)

	2004 $	2004 %	2003 $	2003 %	2002 $	2002 %
ASSETS						
Current:						
Cash & cash equivalents	2,141.0	14.8%	2,015.0	15.5%	2,024.0	12.3%
Short-term investments	1,460.0	10.1%	1,047.0	8.1%	861.0	5.2%
Accounts receivable, net	2,623.0	18.1%	2,514.0	19.4%	3,454.0	20.9%
Inventory	464.0	3.2%	416.0	3.2%	591.0	3.6%
Other current assets	615.0	4.2%	787.0	6.1%	847.0	5.1%
Other current assets	-	0.0%	-	0.0%	-	0.0%
Total current assets	7,303.0	50.4%	6,779.0	52.2%	7,777.0	47.1%
Fixed:						
Property & equipment, net	2,210.0	15.2%	2,517.0	19.4%	2,453.0	14.8%
Long-term investments	4,118.0	28.4%	2,886.0	22.2%	2,979.0	18.0%
Intangibles & goodwill	533.0	3.7%	417.0	3.2%	2,286.0	13.8%
Other assets	339.0	2.3%	386.0	3.0%	1,027.0	6.2%
Total assets	14,503.0	100.0%	12,985.0	100.0%	16,522.0	100.0%
LIABILITIES						
Current:						
Short-term debt	257.0	1.8%	-	0.0%	205.0	1.2%
Accounts payable	2,987.0	20.6%	2,409.0	18.6%	2,783.0	16.8%
Accrued salaries and benefits	-	0.0%	-	0.0%	-	0.0%
Unearned revenue	-	0.0%	1,720.0	13.2%	-	0.0%
Other current liabilities	1,869.0	12.9%	-	0.0%	2,069.0	12.5%
Total current liabilities	5,113.0	35.3%	4,129.0	31.8%	5,057.0	30.6%
Long-term debt	2,395.0	16.5%	1,531.0	11.8%	1,664.0	10.1%
Deferred income tax liabilities	-	0.0%	-	0.0%	-	0.0%
Other long-term liabilities	557.0	3.8%	834.0	6.4%	-	0.0%
Total liabilities	8,065.0	55.6%	6,494.0	50.0%	6,721.0	40.7%
OWNERS' EQUITY						
Total owners' equity	6,438.0	44.4%	6,491.0	50.0%	9,801.0	59.3%
Total liabilities and owners' equity	14,503.0	100.0%	12,985.0	100.0%	16,522.0	100.0%

(Note: percents may not add to 100 due to rounding)

SUN MICROSYSTEMS INC.
RATIO ANALYSIS SUMMARY
For The Years Ended Jan. 30, 2004, 2003, 2002

	2004	2003	2002
SHORT-TERM LIQUIDITY RATIOS			
Current Ratio (Current Assets/Current Liabilities)	1.43	1.64	1.54
Quick Ratio (Cash + Short-term Investments + Accounts Receivable)/Current Liabilities	1.22	1.35	1.25
Accounts Receivable Turnover 1 (Revenues/Average Accounts Receivable)	4.35	3.83	
Accounts Receivable Turnover 2 (Revenues/Year-end Accounts Receivable)	4.26	4.55	3.62
Inventory Turnover 1 (Cost Goods Sold/Average Inventory)	15.16	12.89	
Inventory Turnover 2 (Cost Goods Sold/Year-end Inventory)	14.37	15.61	12.83
LONG-TERM SOLVENCY (LEVERAGE) RATIO			
Total Debt Ratio (Total Liabilities/Total Assets)	55.61%	50.01%	40.68%
PROFITABILITY RATIOS			
Gross Profit Margin (Gross Margin/Revenues)	40.38%	43.22%	39.34%
Operating Profit Margin (Operating Income/Revenues)	-10.64%	-23.82%	-9.99%
Net Profit Margin (Return on Sales) (ROS) (Net Income/Revenues)	-3.47%	-29.99%	-4.70%
Total Asset Turnover (Revenues/Average Total Assets)	0.81	0.78	
Return on Total Assets (ROA) (Net Income/Average Total Assets)	-2.82%	-23.24%	

9. Are the largest asset investments increasing faster or slower than the percent change in total revenues?

10. Is the percent of total liabilities to total liabilities + owners' equity increasing or decreasing? As a result, is there more or less risk that the company could not pay its debts?

Integrative income statement and balance sheet question:

11. Is the company operating more or less efficiently by using the least amount of asset investment to generate a given level of total revenues? Note that the "total asset turnover" ratio is computed and included in the "ratio analysis summary."

Ratio analysis questions:

12. Is the *current ratio* better or worse in the most current year compared to prior years?

13. Is the *quick ratio* better or worse in the most current year compared to prior years?

14. Is the *accounts receivable turnover ratio 1* (based on *average* receivables) better or worse in the most current year compared to prior years?

15. Is the 2004 *accounts receivable turnover ratio 2* (based on *year-end* receivables) better or worse than the 2004 ratio based on an *average*?

16. Is the *inventory turnover ratio 1* (based on *average* inventory) better or worse in the most current year compared to prior years?

17. Is the 2004 *inventory turnover ratio 2* (based on *year-end* inventory) better or worse than the 2004 ratio based on an *average*?

18. Is the *return on total assets (ROA) ratio* better or worse in the most current year compared to prior years?

Accounts receivable and bad debts expense questions (Chapter 7 focus):

19. Based on the information in the financial statements, is selling on account important for Sun Microsystems? Explain briefly.

Information for questions 20-24:

Supplemental footnote information on accounts receivable are as follows:
Assumed reconciliation of the allowance for doubtful accounts for each year is (in millions):

	2004	2003	2002
Beginning balance	$ 30.3	$ 30.4	$ 30.5
Add: Bad debts expense for year	20.0	50.4	50.6
Deduct: Accounts written off	10.3	50.5	50.7
Ending balance	$ 40.0	$ 30.3	$ 30.4

20. Compute the gross value of accounts receivable at the end of 2004.

21. What journal entry was made at the end of 2004 to provide for estimated bad debts?

22. What journal entry was made in 2004 to write-off uncollectible accounts receivable?

23. What concern do you have about the bad debt adjustment for 2004?

24. What concern do you have about the allowance for doubtful accounts balance as of June 30, 2004?

SHORT-TERM FINANCING

CHAPTER

8

"To educate a man in mind and not in morals is to educate a menace to society."

Theodore Roosevelt

LEARNING GOALS

After studying Chapter 8, you should be able to:

1. Define *promissory note* and explain its characteristics.

2. Make calculations for promissory notes.

3. Compute the annual effective interest rate on a note.

4. Record the issuance of notes payable and related end-of-period adjusting entries.

5. Record the receipt of notes receivable and related end-of-period adjusting entries.

6. Calculate the cash proceeds from discounting notes receivable and record the transaction.

7. Analyze financial statement information for real-life companies.

UNDERSTANDING BUSINESS ISSUES

At various times, most businesses need to grant more generous sales terms and to borrow money on a short-term basis to finance investments in receivables and inventories. They must plan carefully to prevent the debt from becoming too great a burden on the company. For example, Kmart Corp., was the second largest discount retailer in the U.S. throughout the 1990s. By 1999, Kmart faced sluggish sales and strong competition from Wal-Mart Stores, Inc. One result was that Kmart's inventories grew from 83.5% of current assets at the end of 1998 to 87% of current assets at the end of 1999. The company took on debt to meet suppliers' bills. In January 2002, Kmart filed for Chapter 11 bankruptcy.

As a more personal example of financing needs, borrowing to pay for college costs has soared in the past few years. Many students are graduating from college with a large debt burden. For example, repaying a $50,000 loan at 8% interest over ten years comes to a monthly payment of $644. With your expected starting salary after college, could you meet living expenses and also pay $644 per month on college loans?

To show short-term financing transactions from both the debtor (borrower) and creditor (lender) points of view, this chapter discusses both notes payable and notes receivable. We begin by calculating interest and determining an annual effective interest rate. Next we consider accounting for notes payable used in short-term financing. Finally, we examine accounting for short-term notes receivable.

THE SHORT-TERM FINANCING DECISION

Businesses must often use some form of short-term financing. Most firms maintain lines of credit with banks under which they can borrow money up to specified limits. For example, as of December 31, 2001, Kmart Corp. maintained lines of credit of $1.6 million. These agreements required the company to maintain a minimum weekly cash balance each quarter. By the first quarter of 2002, Kmart failed to meet this covenant, and its ability to borrow was substantially impaired.

Financing decisions are important to running a business. When various financing methods are available to a company, the financial manager must consider the following factors:

1. The interest cost of each method.

2. Whether the financing method will continue to be available to the firm.

3. The possible effects on the availability and cost of alternative sources of money, both short-term and long-term.

The financial manager should choose the method that will consistently generate the desired short-term funds at the lowest possible overall cost. The interest rate that a firm must pay to obtain funds depends on a combination of factors including its reputation, the size of the loan, its past record of financial integrity and earnings performance, and its prospects for the future.

PROMISSORY NOTES

Description of Promissory Notes

Learning Goal 1   Define *promissory note* and explain its characteristics.

A **promissory note** is an unconditional written promise to pay a definite sum of money on demand or at a future date. The person signing the note and promising to pay is the *maker* of the note. The person promised the payment is the *payee*. Exhibit 8.1 shows a promissory note. The major characteristics of a promissory note are as follows:

- It must be in writing and signed by the maker.

- It must contain an unconditional promise to pay a certain sum of money.

- It may be payable to a *bearer* (person holding the note) or to a stated person (the payee).

- It must be payable either on demand or at a specified future time.

- It may or may not be interest bearing.

From the maker's point of view, the note illustrated in Exhibit 8.1 is a liability. The maker records it by crediting Notes Payable. From the payee's point of view, the same note is an asset. The payee records the note by debiting Notes Receivable. A note may also be **negotiable**. This means that the owner may transfer the note to another person. The owner transfers a note by endorsing it

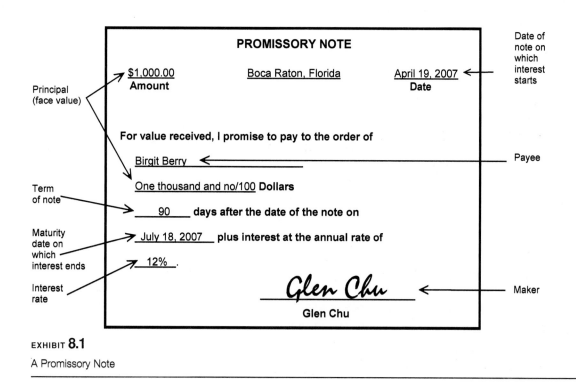

EXHIBIT 8.1

A Promissory Note

and delivering it to the new owner. An *endorsement* is a signature on the back of the note that assigns the rights of the note to another party.

Computations for Promissory Notes

Learning Goal 2   Make calculations for promissory notes.

Maturity Date of Notes

The **maturity date** is the date on which payment of a note is due. Following are alternative ways of stating a maturity date:

1. A specific future date. For example, a note dated April 3 with a stated maturity date of April 28.

2. A specific number of months or years after the date on the note. For example, a two-year note dated April 3, 2007, is due on April 3, 2009. A three-month note dated April 30, 2007, is due on the last day of July (July 31, 2007).

3. A specific number of days after the date on the note. For example, a 20-day note dated April 3 is due on April 23.

If the term of the note is expressed in days, the maturity date is determined by counting the exact number of days after the date of the note. In computing the maturity date, it is important to *exclude the date of the note* and *include the maturity date*. The date of the note in Exhibit 8.1 is April 19. The maturity date is July 18. We determine the maturity date of this 90-day note as follows:

	Number of Days	Cumulative Days
Total days in month note is dated (April)	30	
Deduct: Date of note in April	<u>19</u>	
Number of days note runs in April (excluding April 19)	11	11
Add: Number of days to make up term of note (90 days):		
May	31	42
June	30	72
July (90 days minus 72 days)	18*	90

*Maturity date of 90-day note dated April 19, 2007, is July 18, 2007.

Computing Interest on Notes

Interest is the charge made for the use of money. Interest is an expense to the borrower and a revenue to the lender. **Simple interest** is computed on the original principal (face value) of a note. Interest amounts that have accrued in past periods are not included in the amount on which we calculate simple interest. The formula for computing interest is:

$$\text{Interest} = \text{Principal} \times \text{Rate of Interest} \times \text{Time}$$

Using the note in Exhibit 8.1 the amount of interest on the $1,000, 12%, 90-day note is:

$$
\begin{array}{ccccccc}
\text{Interest} & = & \text{Principal} & \times & \text{Rate of Interest} & \times & \text{Time} \\
\$30 & = & \$1,000 & \times & 0.12 & \times & 90/360
\end{array}
$$

For notes with maturities stated in days, the actual number of days of the note term is used as the numerator. In this textbook we use a 360-day business year as the denominator to simplify interest calculations. If the maturity date is stated in months or years, we use fractions of years or years for the time. For example, interest on a $1,000, 12%, five-month note is:

$$
\begin{array}{ccccccc}
\text{Interest} & = & \text{Principal} & \times & \text{Rate of Interest} & \times & \text{Time} \\
\$50 & = & \$1,000 & \times & 0.12 & \times & 5/12
\end{array}
$$

Interest on a $1,000, 12%, two-year note is:

$$
\begin{array}{ccccccc}
\text{Interest} & = & \text{Principal} & \times & \text{Rate of Interest} & \times & \text{Time} \\
\$240 & = & \$1,000 & \times & 0.12 & \times & 2 \text{ (yrs)}
\end{array}
$$

Maturity Value of a Note

The **maturity value** of a note is the principal amount of the note plus interest to maturity. The maturity value represents the total proceeds of a note the payee will receive at the maturity date. The maturity value of the note in Exhibit 8.1 is:

$$
\begin{array}{ccccc}
\text{Maturity Value} & = & \text{Principal} & + & \text{Interest} \\
\$1,030 & = & \$1,000 & + & \$30
\end{array}
$$

Annual Percentage Rate (APR) or Annual Effective Interest

Learning Goal 3   Compute the annual effective interest rate on a note.

The federal *Truth in Lending Law*, enacted in 1969, requires lenders to disclose the **annual effective interest rate** or the annual percentage rate (APR) on loans. Determining the effective interest rate or APR can be very simple or quite complex. Here, we will illustrate two simple cases.

First, a loan that carries a 1½% monthly rate (as many monthly charge accounts do) would have an APR of 18% (12 × 1½%). It may be necessary in some cases to approximate the annual effective interest rate. This is particularly true when prospective loan customers are not given the APR and must select a single financing method.

The second case occurs when merchandise is bought on the installment basis where payments are made over several months. If the effective interest rate is not stated, it is important to approximate the APR. The approximation assumes that each payment includes an equal reduction in the principal. Thus the average outstanding debt is one-half the original principal. We then calculate the APR by dividing the interest for one year by the average outstanding principal.

To illustrate this approximation, assume that we buy merchandise costing $1,000. We agree to pay this amount in 24 equal monthly installments of $50 each. The APR calculation is as follows:

1.   Average outstanding principal = $1,000 ÷ 2 = $500.

2.   Annual interest cost:
     Total interest for two years = ($50 × 24) – $1,000 = $200.
     Interest for one year = $200 ÷ 2 = $100.

3.   Approximation of APR is:
     $100 ÷ $500 = 20% per year.

NOTES PAYABLE

Learning Goal 4   Record the issuance of notes payable and related end-of-period adjusting entries.

Notes payable are amounts payable to creditors supported by formal written promises to pay. We may record all notes payable in a single Notes Payable account in the general ledger. We can show supplementary details including name of payee, interest rate, and terms of the note in the explanation column as follows:

			Notes Payable				Acct. No. 202
						Balance	
Date		**Explanation**	**Debit**	**Credit**	**Debit**	**Credit**	
2007							
Nov.	15	A. Coops, 12%, 60 days		2,000		2,000	
	20	B. Bosch, 11%, 30 days		500		2,500	
Dec.	3	F. Piller, 10%, 90 days		1,000		3,500	
	10	B. Bosch (paid)	500			3,000	

Issuance of Notes for Property, Plant, and Equipment

The following example illustrates the recording of notes payable in the acquisition of property, plant, and equipment. Assume that on July 10, 2007, Ace Company buys a copying machine from Triangle Company at a cost of $4,000. The creditor agrees to take a 90-day, 12% note dated that day for the purchase price. Ace would record this transaction as follows:

```
2007
Jul.    10    Office Equipment                                    4,000
                  Notes Payable                                            4,000
                  To record the purchase of a copying machine and the issuance of a
                  12%, 90-day note dated July 10, 2007, to Triangle Company.
```

On October 8, 2007, Ace records the payment of the note and interest to Triangle Company as follows:

```
2007
Oct.     8    Notes Payable                                       4,000
              Interest Expense                                      120
                  Cash                                                     4,120
                  To record the payment of a 12%, 90-day note and interest to the
                  Triangle Company ($120 = $4,000 × 0.12 × 90/360).
```

Issuance of Notes for Merchandise

Creditors may require a business to issue interest-bearing notes if the business cannot make payment within the normal credit period. We first record all merchandise purchases involving the issuance of notes in the Accounts Payable account and the accounts payable subsidiary ledger. This allows management to know the volume of business done with individual suppliers. Assume that on October 11, 2007, Ace Company purchases merchandise costing $3,600 from Boone Company. It issues a 12%, 45-day note payable to the supplier dated the same day. Ace pays the note and interest on November 25, 2007. It records these transactions as follows:

```
2007
Oct.    11    Purchases                                           3,600
                  Accounts Payable, Boone Company                         3,600
                  To record merchandise purchased from Boone Company

        11    Accounts Payable                                    3,600
                  Notes Payable                                            3,600
                  To record the issuance of a 12%, 45-day note dated October 11,
                  2007, to Boone Company.

Nov.    25    Notes Payable                                       3,600
              Interest Expense                                       54
                  Cash                                                     3,654
                  To record payment of a note and interest to the Boone Company
                  ($54 = $3,600 × 0.12 × 45/360).
```

Issuance of Notes in Settlement of Open Accounts

A firm may issue a note to obtain an extension of time to pay an open account payable. The entry for the issuance of a note in settlement of an open account payable is the same as the second entry dated October 11.

Issuance of Notes to Borrow from Banks

Banks and other lenders handle notes in two ways:

1. They may lend money on a **note bearing interest on face value**. In this case the borrower receives the face value of the note and pays the face value plus the accumulated interest on the maturity date.

2. They may lend money on a note where the amount of interest on face value is subtracted in advance. This is a **note payable discounted on face value**. The borrower receives the face value less the total interest amount but pays the full face value of the note on the maturity date. The amount of interest deducted in advance is the *bank discount.*

   Bank discount is the amount of interest deducted in advance from the face value of the note. We compute the discount as follows:

$$\text{Discount} = \text{Face Value} \times \text{Rate of Interest} \times \text{Discount Period}$$

Issuance of a Note Bearing Interest on Face Value

On March 1, 2007, Ace Company borrowed $10,000 from the First National Bank. It signed a 12%, 60-day note dated the same day. On April 30 it paid the bank the note and interest. Ace records the issuance and payment of the note as follows:

2007					
Mar.	1	Cash		10,000	
		Notes Payable			10,000
		To record a 12%, 60-day note dated March 1, 2007, issued to the First National Bank.			
Apr.	30	Notes Payable		10,000	
		Interest Expense		200	
		Cash			10,200
		To record payment of a 12%, 60-day note issued to the First National Bank ($200 = $10,000 × 0.12 × 60/360).			

Issuance of a Note Payable Discounted on Face Value

On May 1, 2007, Ace Company borrowed money from the City National Bank. Ace discounted on face value its own $10,000, 60-day note dated the same day at the discount rate of 12%. Ace received $9,800, or $10,000 less a discount of $200. Ace makes the following entry to record the initial borrowing:

2007					
May	1	Cash		9,800	
		Discount on Notes Payable		200	
		Notes Payable			10,000
		To record payment of a note dated May 1, 2007, issued to City National Bank discounted on face value at 12% for 60 days ($200 = $10,000 × 0.12 × 60/360).			

The $200 discount is the interest deducted at the time of the borrowing. We debit it to Discount on Notes Payable. **Discount on Notes Payable** should appear on the balance sheet as a contra account to (subtracted from) Notes Payable. On the date the note is issued, the carrying value of the note (here $9,800, or $10,000 - $200), is the net amount of cash received from the lender. As the term of the note expires, we recognize the expired portion of the discount as interest expense.

At the maturity date, June 30, 2007, Ace makes a journal entry recognizing that the discount of $200 has now become interest expense. This entry is as follows:

```
2007
Jun.    30    Interest Expense                                        200
                    Discount on Notes Payable                                200
                To record interest expense.
```

Also, Ace must pay the face amount of the note, as follows:

```
2007
Jun.    30    Notes Payable                                         10,000
                    Cash                                                   10,000
                To record payment of a discounted note to City National Bank.
```

If Ace Company issued the note on December 16, 2007, and closed its books on December 31, 2007, an adjusting entry would be necessary. The adjustment transfers 15/60, or one-fourth, of the discount amount to interest expense on December 31, 2007. Then at maturity in 2008, Ace recognizes the remaining part of the discount as an expense.

Effective Interest Calculation

Learning Goal 3   Compute the annual effective interest rate on a note.

Whenever a business borrows money, it is important for management to know the true cost of the loan. In both the March 1 and May 1 bank loans, the amount Ace Company paid at maturity was $200 more than the amount it received. However, Ace had the use of $10,000, or the full face value of the note bearing interest on face value (the March 1 bank loan). By comparison, Ace had the use of only $9,800 from the discounted note (the May 1 bank loan). We compute the annual effective interest rate (in the following equation) on a discounted note as follows:

$$I = \frac{D}{P} \times \frac{360}{T}$$

where D = The amount of the discount.

P = The net proceeds.

360 = Days in the year.

T = The term of the note in days.

The annual effective interest rate for the note discounted on face value is not 12%. Rather, it is 12.24%, calculated as follows:

$$i = \frac{\$200}{\$9,800} \times \frac{360}{60} = 0.12249 \text{ or } 12.24\%$$

From this analysis, Ace's management would know that it was less costly to borrow with the March 1 note.

End-of-period Adjusting Entries for Notes Payable

It is necessary to make adjusting entries for the interest expense on notes payable that are written in one accounting period and mature in a later period. We will study two kinds of adjustments: (1) the accrual of interest on a note payable bearing interest on its face, and (2) recording the interest expense on a discounted note payable.

Assume that Adjusto Company has the following accounts in its general ledger as of December 31, 2007. The two notes remain outstanding on December 31 and thus will require adjusting entries for interest expense.

Notes Payable   Acct. No. 202

Date		Explanation	Debit	Credit	Balance Debit	Balance Credit
2007 Dec.	1 1	Florida Bank, 12%, 45 days Texas Bank, discounted at 12%, 45 days		5,000 10,000		5,000 15,000

Discount on Notes Payable   Acct. No. 203

Date		Explanation	Debit	Credit	Balance Debit	Balance Credit
2007 Dec.	1	Discount on Texas Bank note	150		150	

At December 31, 2007, Adjust to must make the following two adjusting entries: Comments on these entries follow:

2007						
Dec.	31	Interest Expense		**1**	50	
		Interest Payable				50
		To record accrued interest on the note issued to Florida Bank.				
	31	Interest Expense		**2**	100	
		Discount on Notes Payable				100
		To record interest on the note discounted at the Texas Bank.				

1. The Florida Bank note has accrued 30 days' interest at 12%. The interest calculation is $5,000 × 0.12 × 30/360 = $50.

2. The Second adjusting entry transfers interest from the discount on Notes Payable account to the Interest Expense account. The interest calculation is $10,000 × 0.12 × 30/360 = $100.

We now look at the entries when Adjusto pays these two notes. On January 15, 2008, it makes the following entry when it pays the Florida Bank note:

```
2008
Jan.    15    Notes Payable                                              5,000
              Interest Payable                                              50
              Interest Expense                                             25
                    Cash                                                            5,075
              To record payment of a 12%, 45-day note to the Florida Bank.
```

The $5,075 credit to Cash includes the payment of two liabilities already on the books—Notes Payable and Interest Payable. The interest expense of $25 ($5,000 $\times$ 0.12 $\times$ 15/360) is the interest Adjusto incurred from January 1, 2008, to January 15, 2008. When Adjusto pays the Texas Bank the $10,000 discounted note, they make the following entries:

```
2008
Jan.    15    Interest Expense                                           50
                    Discount on Notes Payable                                   50
              To transfer the remainder of the discount amount to Interest
              Expense.

        15    Notes Payable                                          10,000
                    Cash                                                        10,000
              To record payment of the note to the Texas Bank.
```

NOTES RECEIVABLE

Learning Goal 5   Record the receipt of notes receivable and related end-of-period adjusting entries.

Many businesses require promissory notes for sales of merchandise on credit. Financial institutions also receive notes receivable when they lend money. We record promissory notes from customers in an account called **Notes Receivable**. In a business that accepts only a few notes, the business can record the name of the maker, the interest rate, and the term in the explanation column of the account. A Notes Receivable account is shown as follows:

		Notes Receivable			Acct. No. 115	
					Balance	
Date		**Explanation**	**Debit**	**Credit**	**Debit**	**Credit**
2007 Nov.	1	C. Anson, 12%, 45 days	700		700	
Dec.	16	C. Anson, paid note		700	0	
	20	B. Barker, 11%, 90 days	400		400	

Each debit posting indicates that we have acquired an asset, a note receivable, from a customer. The credit entry indicates that a particular note has been settled by payment. Credits will also be recorded if a note has been dishonored (not paid) or renewed (matured and replaced by a new note).

Receipt of a Note for a Sale

Assume that on March 3, 2007, Potter Company sells merchandise to John Rawson. Potter receives a 12%, 90-day note dated the same day for $1,000. Potter makes the following entries:

2007
Mar.   3   Accounts Receivable, John Rawson   1,000
                Sales   1,000
                To record sale of merchandise on account to John Rawson.

        3   Notes Receivable   1,000
                Accounts Receivable, John Rawson   1,000
                To record the receipt of a 12%, 90-day note dated March 3, 2007,
                from John Rawson in settlement of account.

The first entry causes the customer's account in the accounts receivable subsidiary ledger to contain a complete record of all credit sales transactions. This information is useful to management in making decisions about collection efforts and further extension of credit.

On June 1, 2007, when Potter Company receives payment in full from John Rawson, it makes the following entry:

2007
Jun.   1   Cash   1,030
                Notes Receivable   1,000
                Interest Revenue   30
                To record receipt of payment from John Rawson for note and
                interest due today ($30 = $1,000 × 0.12 × 90/360).

Receipt of a Note in Settlement of an Open Account

Businesses often require customers to substitute notes for open accounts when customers do not pay the accounts on time. The entry for such notes is the same as Potter Company's second journal entry on March 3.

Dishonor of a Note Receivable by the Maker

If a note cannot be collected at maturity, it is a **dishonored note**. The maker has **defaulted** on the note. If the maturity date of a note passes without collection, we should make an entry transferring the face value of the note plus any uncollected interest to the Accounts Receivable account.

Assume that on June 1, 2007, Mark Biggs issued a 10%, 60-day note for $3,000 to Potter Company. At the maturity date, July 31, 2007, Biggs fails to pay the amount of the note and interest. At that time, Potter Company makes the following entry:

2007
Jul.   31   Accounts Receivable, Mark Biggs   3,050
                Notes Receivable   3,000
                Interest Revenue   50
                To record the dishonor of a 10%, 60-day note from Mark Biggs.

Why does Potter recognize $50 as revenue and credit the Interest Revenue account? Under the accrual concept, Potter has earned the interest. It is a valid claim against Biggs, the maker of the note. If the face value of the note is collectible, then so is the interest. Why does Potter allow the item to remain as a valid account receivable? The fact that Potter has not collected the note at its maturity does not mean it is uncollectible. Most business firms assume that, in the absence of evidence to the contrary, notes are ultimately collectible.

End-of-period Adjusting Entries for Notes Receivable

The adjusting entries for interest on notes receivable parallel the adjusting entries for interest on notes payable. To illustrate these adjusting entries, assume that Emerson Company has the following account in its general ledger as of December 31, 2007:

Notes Receivable					Acct. No. 115
				Balance	
Date	Explanation	Debit	Credit	Debit	Credit
2007 Nov. 1	Linda Wilson, 10%, 90 days	6,000		6,000	

At December 31, 2007, Emerson Company makes the following adjusting entry:

2007		
Dec. 31	Interest Receivable	100
	Interest Revenue	100
	To record the accrued interest on the Linda Wilson note at 10% for 60 days ($100 = $6,000 × 0.10 × 60/360).	

Emerson makes the following entry on January 30, 2008, when it collects the note:

2008		
Jan. 30	Cash	6,150
	Notes Receivable	6,000
	Interest Receivable	100
	Interest Revenue	50
	To record collection of a 10%, 90-day note and interest from Linda Wilson.	

The debit of $6,150 to Cash represents the collection of two receivables already on the books—a note receivable and interest receivable. It also includes a revenue, interest revenue, of $50, which it earned for the period January 1, 2008, through January 30, 2008.

Discounting Customer's Notes Receivable

Turning all forms of receivables into cash as soon as possible is important. Businesses may obtain immediate cash from customer notes receivable by *discounting* them at a bank. When a business discounts the note it assumes a contingent liability. If the maker of the note fails to pay the bank at the maturity date, the firm that has discounted the note must make payment to the bank.

> A **contingent liability** is an amount that may become a liability in the future if certain events occur. A note endorser's potential obligation to pay the note if it is dishonored is an example of a contingent liability.

Determining the Cash Proceeds on a Discounted Note

Learning Goal 6 Calculate cash proceeds from discounting notes receivable and record the transaction.

The amount the bank will collect on a discounted note on the maturity date is the maturity value of the note. The discount the bank deducts is a discount rate applied to the maturity value for the remaining period of the note to maturity. The bank discount subtracted from the maturity value is the **cash proceeds** received by the discounter. To compute the proceeds of a discounted note, we do the following:

1. Determine the maturity value of the note (the principal plus the total interest to maturity).

2. Find the discount period for which the bank will hold the note (the number of days from the discount date to the maturity date).

3. Compute the discount by multiplying the maturity value by the bank discount rate for the discount period.

4. Deduct the bank discount from the maturity value to find the cash proceeds.

Assume that on April 1, 2007, Fuller Company receives from Edward Grande, in settlement of an account receivable, a 12%, 60-day note dated that day for $6,000. Fuller records this transaction as follows:

```
2007
Apr.  1   Notes Receivable                                      6,000
              Accounts Receivable, Edward Grande                        6,000
              To record receipt of a 12%, 60-day note dated April 1, 2007, in
              settlement of a past-due open account of Edward Grande.
```

On April 11, 2007, Fuller Company, needing short-term funds, decides to discount Grande's note at the bank's rate of 14%. We calculate the proceeds as follows:

1.	Maturity value of note:		
	Face value	$6,000	
	Total interest to maturity ($6,000 × 0.12 × 60/360)	120	
	Maturity value of note		$ 6,120
	Due date	May 31	
2.	Discount period:		
	April 11 - April 30 (not counting April 11)	19 days	
	May 1 - May 31 (including May 31)	31 days	
	Discount period	50 days	
3.	Bank discount at 14% for 50 days on the maturity value:		
	($6,120 × 0.14 × 50/360)		119
4.	Net cash proceeds		$ 6,001

Recording the Proceeds

The entry on Fuller Company's books to record the discounting of the Grande note is as follows:

2007

Apr.	11	Cash		6,001	
			Notes Receivable Discounted		6,000
			Interest Revenue		1

To record the discounting of Edward Grande's 12%, 60-day note
at the bank at 14%.

The **Notes Receivable Discounted** account is used to indicate that Fuller Company is contingently liable. Having endorsed the note, Fuller must pay the note if Grande does not. Fuller Company must pay the $6,000 contingent liability plus the $120 interest, plus any **protest fee**(additional bank charges). The obligation Fuller Company assumes is contingent on Grande's failure to pay. We therefore refer to the account as a **contingent liability account**

Presentation of Notes Receivable on the Balance Sheet

In preparing financial statements, **full disclosure** of all essential facts such as contingent liabilities is of critical importance. Assume that on April 30 the Notes Receivable account shows a balance of $10,000 (including the $6,000 note discounted on April 11). The balance sheet prepared on that date may disclose the contingent liability by offsetting notes receivable discounted against notes receivable in the balance sheet as follows:

FULLER COMPANY
PARTIAL BALANCE SHEET
APRIL 30, 2007
Assets

Current assets		
Notes receivable	$10,000	
Deduct: Notes receivable discounted	6,000	
Net notes receivable		$4,000

Alternatively, the balance sheet prepared on that date may disclose the contingent liability by a supplementary note, as follows:

FULLER COMPANY
PARTIAL BALANCE SHEET
APRIL 30, 2007
Assets

Current assets	
Notes receivable (see Note 6)	$4,000

Note 6: The company is contingently liable for notes receivable discounted in the amount of $6,000.

Entries at Maturity
Elimination of Contingent Liability

On May 31, 2007, the note's maturity date, Fuller makes an entry to eliminate the contingent liability as follows:

2007

May	31	Notes Receivable Discounted		6,000	
			Notes Receivable		6,000

To eliminate the contingent liability on Grande's note, which was
discounted on April 11, 2007.

As of this date, the contingent liability no longer exists. Either the maker pays the note, or the contingent liability becomes a real liability. Also, as of May 31, 2007, a valid negotiable instrument (a note receivable) ceases to exist. Therefore, this entry must be made at the maturity date.

Payment of a Discounted Note

The bank normally does not notify the discounter that the maker has paid the note. Therefore, if the discounter does not receive notification of dishonor from the bank, it assumes that the maker paid the note at the maturity date. This releases the discounter from the contingent liability. Since it made an entry recording the elimination of the contingent liability on the maturity date, no entry is required.

Nonpayment of a Discounted Note

Assume that the bank advises Fuller on May 31, 2007, that Grande has defaulted. The bank charges a protest fee of $8. Fuller makes the following entry to record payment of the face value of the note, the interest, and the protest fee:

2007					
May	31	Accounts Receivable, Edward Grande		6,128	
		Cash			6,128
		To record payment of Edward Grande's note, which was discounted and is now dishonored:			
		Protest fee	$ 8		
		Interest	120		
		Face Value	6,000		
		Total debited in subsidiary ledger to Edward Grande	$ 6,128		

Fuller debits Accounts Receivable in the entry recording the cash payment. The fact that Grande dishonored the note does not mean that it will be uncollectible. Grande may pay at a later date. The account remains open in the general ledger and the accounts receivable subsidiary ledger until it is settled or determined to be uncollectible and written off.

Internal Control for Notes Receivable

Because of the negotiability of notes receivable, companies should use internal control measures similar to those for checks. We should employ the following internal control measures for notes receivable:

- Written procedures for the receipt, recording, and storage of notes receivable, including separation of duties.

- Written instructions that clearly state which employees have the authority to endorse notes receivable.

- A filing and records system to ensure that action is taken to collect notes when they reach maturity.

- Unannounced examinations of notes receivable records and comparison with the actual file of notes to verify that they agree.

- Proper security to prevent unauthorized access to computerized notes receivable records, such as special passwords to gain access to the computer files and periodic changing of the passwords.

ANALYZING INFORMATION

Learning Goal 7   Analyze financial statement information for real-life companies.

In Chapter 6 our analysis of cash included comparing a minimum compensating bank balance requirement with an existing cash balance. Frequently, compensating bank balances are required to support a *short-term, revolving line of credit*. Under a revolving line of credit, a bank promises to advance cash on demand to a business up to a maximum limit. Usually, the business is required to pay down the credit line to a zero balance for a certain number of days each year. The purpose of the pay down requirement is to ensure that the business has the ability and intent to pay off the loan. Businesses use revolving credit lines to meet seasonal needs such as the financing of inventory and receivables during peak sales periods. For longer term acquisitions of plant and equipment, a more permanent source of financing such as issuing common stock or long-term debt is more appropriate.

To illustrate the analysis of short-term financing sources, we will use The Bombay Company. The Bombay Company markets furniture and accessories in shopping malls throughout the United States and Canada. Bombay Company ended its 2003 reporting year on January 31, 2004. The following is summarized from the note on debt in the 2003 annual report:

> The Company has an unsecured revolving credit agreement with a group of banks aggregating $75 million at January 31, 2004 of which $62 million is committed. The credit facility is for working capital and letter of credit purposes, primarily to fund seasonal merchandise purchases, and bears interest at market rates based on prime. The credit agreement restricts dividend payments, and requires the maintenance of various financial ratios and the payment of negotiated fees. The revolving credit agreement expires July 5, 2005 and is expected to be renewed under similar terms. At January 31, 2004, there were $6,840,000 in letters of credit outstanding under the credit facility, issued principally in conjunction with overseas merchandise purchases. Interest expense and negotiated fees for Fiscal 2003, Fiscal 2002 and Fiscal 2001 totaled $1,086,000, $617,000 and $889,000, respectively.

Question. Overall, the user wants to determine the availability and adequacy of the credit sources. The following issues may be raised. What is the percent of the credit line used up as of the balance sheet date? When does the credit line expire? Is it likely that it will be renewed? Are there any credit line requirements that are not being met? Is the credit line sufficient to meet the short-term financing needs of the business?

Answer. In the case of The Bombay Company, 9.1% ($6,840,000 ÷ $75,000,000) of the *total credit lines* is used up as of January 31, 2004. We would want to ask management if the total amount of credit available is sufficient to meet future needs. A second concern is that the credit line agreements expire on July 5, 2005. Although the Company states that renewal will not be a problem, we would want to ask management to provide further evidence that the credit arrangements will continue. However, we would also want to ask specifically what financial ratios and dividend restrictions must be met to satisfy the credit agreements.

LEARNING GOALS REVIEW

1. **Define *promissory note* and explain its characteristics.**

    A promissory note is an unconditional written promise to pay a specified sum to the order of a designated person or to bearer at a fixed or determinable future time or on demand. It may or may not be interest bearing.

2. **Make calculations for promissory notes.**

A note expressed in years or months matures on the corresponding date in the maturity year or month. If the term of the note is in days, find the maturity date by counting forward the specified number of days after the date of the note. To compute simple interest per period, multiply the principal times the interest rate per period times the term of the note. The maturity value of a note is the principal plus interest.

3. **Compute the annual effective interest rate on a note.**

Multiply a monthly rate by 12 to find the approximate annual rate. If a monthly rate is not given, we can make an approximation. Subtract the principal from the total amount of payments to find the total interest paid. Divide by the number of years to find the interest per year. Divide the interest per year by the average outstanding debt to find the approximate percentage rate.

4. **Record the issuance of notes payable and related end-of-period adjusting entries.**

Businesses issue notes to acquire assets or to borrow money. They can use either a note bearing interest on face value or a note payable discounted on face value. In the latter case, the lender reduces the cash amount by any discount. We record the discount in the Discount on Notes Payable account. At the maturity date, we credit this account and debit Interest Expense for the amount. At the end of the accounting period, an adjusting entry is necessary to transfer the expired amount of interest from Discount on Notes Payable to the Interest Expense account.

5. **Record the receipt of notes receivable and related end-of-period adjusting entries.**

When we receive a note for a sale, we first debit Accounts Receivable and credit Sales. Then we debit Notes Receivable and credit Accounts Receivable to record the receipt of the note. We record the collection of a note as a debit to Cash and a credit to Notes Receivable and Interest Revenue. When interest accrues, we debit it to Interest Receivable and credit Interest Revenue.

6. **Calculate the cash proceeds from discounting notes receivable and record the transaction.**

We calculate cash proceeds in four steps: (1) Determine the maturity value (principal plus interest). (2) Find the discount period (the number of days from the discount date to the maturity date). (3) Compute the discount by multiplying the maturity value by the stipulated bank discount rate by the discount period. (4) Deduct the discount from the maturity value. To record the discounting, we debit Cash for the amount of the net cash proceeds. We credit Notes Receivable Discounted for the face value of the note and credit Interest Revenue for the difference.

7. **Analyze financial statement information for real-life companies.**

We need to determine the availability and adequacy of the credit sources. The following issues may be raised. What is the percent of the credit line used up as of the balance sheet date? When does the credit line expire? Is it likely that it will be renewed? Are there any credit line requirements that are not being met? Is the credit line sufficient to meet the short-term financing needs of the business?

DEMONSTRATION PROBLEM

Notes Payable and Notes Receivable Transactions

Chicago Company sells special sets of gourmet cooking pans to fine restaurants. Sales terms normally are cash payment at the time of the sale. In limited cases, it accepts a note with a term no longer than 45 days. During 2007, Chicago completed the following selected transactions:

2007

Aug.	12	Purchased 60 sets of cooking pans from TopPan Company on account; total invoice price $48,000; terms 2/10, n/30.
Sep.	10	Gave TopPan Company a 10%, 30-day note dated September 10, 2007, in settlement of the purchase on August 12.
	28	Sold two sets of cooking pans with a total invoice price of $1,400 to Hugo Bissel. Accepted a 45-day, 12% note dated today from Mr. Bissel.
Oct.	8	Discounted at 13% at the New Bank & Trust the note from Hugo Bissel dated September 28.
	10	Borrowed cash to pay the note payable to TopPan Company. Discounted at 11% its own $48,000, 30-day note dated this day, made out to the Jersey Bank fot the maturity value.
	10	Paid TopPan Company the amount due on the note dated September 10, which matures today.
Nov.	10	Paid the note due the Jersey Bank dated October 10.
	12	Maturity date of Hugo Bissel note discounted at New Bank & Trust. Since Chicago received no notice from the bank, it assumed that Bissel paid the amount due to the bank.

REQUIRED

(**LG 2, 4-6**) Record the transactions in general journal form.

SOLUTION

2007

Aug.	12	Purchases	48,000.00	
		Accounts Payable, TopPan Company		48,000.00
		To record merchandise purchased from TopPan Company, terms 2/10, n/30.		
Sep.	10	Accounts Payable, TopPan Company	48,000.00	
		Notes Payable		48,000.00
		To record issuance of a 10%, 30-day note dated September 10, 2007, to TopPan Company.		
	28	Accounts Receivable, Hugo Bissel	1,400.00	
		Sales		1,400.00
		To record sale of merchandise on account to Hugo Bissel.		
	28	Notes Receivable	1,400.00	
		Accounts Receivable, Hugo Bissel		1,400.00
		To record the receipt of a 12%, 45-day note dated September 28, 2007, from Hugo Bissel in settlement of account.		
Oct.	8	Cash	1,403.04	
		Notes Receivable Discounted		1,400.00
		Interest Revenue		3.04
		To record the discounting of Hugo Bissel's 12%, 45-day note at New Bank & Trust at 13%.		

Solution Approach

Maturity Date of Note from Hugo Bissel	Number of Days	Cumulative Days
Total days in month note is dated (September)	30	
Deduct: Date of note in September	28	
Number of days note runs in September (excluding September 28)	2	2
Add: Number of days to make up term of note (45 days):		
October	31	33
November (45 days minus 33 days)	12 *	45

* Maturity date of a 45-day note dated September 28, 2007, is November 12, 2007.

Calculation of Proceeds:
1. Maturity value: $1,400 + ($1,400 \times 0.12 \times 45/360)$ — $1,421.00
2. Discount period:

October 8-31 (not counting October 8)	23 days
November 1-12 (including November 12)	12 days
Discount period	35 days

3. Bank discount at 13% for 35 days on the maturity value:
   $1,421 \times 0.13 \times 35/360$ — 17.96
4. Net cash proceeds — $1,403.04

Oct.	10	Cash	47,560.00	
		Discount on Notes Payable	440.00	
		Notes Payable		48,000.00
		To record on a note dated October 10, 2007, issued to Jersey Bank discounted on face value at 11% for 30 days ($440 = $48,000 \times 0.11 \times 30/360$).		
	10	Notes Payable	48,000.00	
		Interest Expense	400.00	
		Cash		48,400.00
		To record payment of a 10%, 30-day note issue to TopPan Company ($400 = $48,000 \times 0.10 \times 30/360$).		
Nov.	10	Interest Expense	440.00	
		Discount on Notes Payable		440.00
		To record interest expense.		
	10	Notes Payable	48,000.00	
		Cash		48,000.00
		To record payment of discounted note to the Jersey Bank.		
	12	Notes Receivable Discounted	1,400.00	
		Notes Receivable		1,400.00
		To eliminate the contingent liability on Bissel's note, which was discounted on October 8, 2007.		

Solution Approach

The entry on November 12, 2007, removes the contingent liability and is made regardless of whether the maker of the note pays the bank or not.

Glossary

annual effective interest rate The true interest rate computed on only the remaining balance of an unpaid debt for the specific time period, usually stated as an annual fraction.

bank discount An amount subtracted in advance from a maturity value to determine net cash proceeds as of the present time.

cash proceeds The amount of cash that is received when a firm discounts a note at a bank.

contingent liability An amount that may become a liability in the future *if* certain events occur.

contingent liability account An account in which a contingent liability is recorded.

defaulted Having failed to pay the amount owed on a negotiable instrument at its maturity.

discount on Notes Payable A contra account to the Notes Payable account; it represents the interest that was deducted from the face amount of the note. The discount on the notes payable amount is allocated to the applicable periods to which the interest expense belongs.

dishonored note A note not paid by the maker at the maturity date.

full disclosure A concept requiring that all essential facts about an item (or activity) be shown in applicable financial statements. An example is the disclosure of contingent liabilities.

interest The price of credit; a rental charge for the use of money.

maturity date The date on which a note is due and payable.

maturity value The amount payable (or receivable) on a note at its maturity date; it includes face value plus any stated interest.

negotiable A characteristic of a document that permits it to be transferred for value received by endorsement to another person.

note bearing interest on face value A note with a specified interest rate with interest to be paid at maturity in addition to the face value of the note.

note payable discounted on face value A note payable issued for its maturity value that includes interest; the interest is deducted as a bank discount from face value at the time the note is issued.

notes payable Amount payable to creditors supported by formal written promises to pay.

Notes Receivable An account for claims against individuals or companies supported by formal written promises to pay. A note receivable may be either a trade note or a non-trade note.

Notes Receivable Discounted An account that discloses the contingent liability for customers' notes that have been discounted.

promissory note An unconditional written promise to pay a specified sum of money to the order of a designated person, or to bearer, at a fixed or determinable future time or on demand.

protest fee A fee charged by a bank or financial institution for a note that is dishonored (not paid) at maturity.

simple interest Interest on the original principal only.

QUESTIONS FOR GROUP LEARNING

Q8-1.   Discuss the managerial factors that a company must consider in determining what method of short-term financing should be used.

Q8-2.   What is a negotiable promissory note? What does the term *negotiable* indicate?

Q8-3.   What is the meaning of APR? Why is APR significant?

Q8-4.   Describe briefly how a person can calculate the effective interest rate (APR) on a note discounted on face value at the bank. Give an example.

Q8-5.   Is it better for a company to borrow money on a note discounted on face value at 12% or on a note bearing interest on the face at 12%? Explain.

Q8-6.   Under what conditions would a company issue notes? Give four examples where notes are issued very frequently.

Q8-7.   Explain the following terms and procedures for notes receivable:

    a. Discounting a note receivable.

    b. Bank discount rate.

    c. Contingent liability.

    d. Proceeds.

    e. Maturity value.

    f. A dishonored note receivable.

Q8-8.   The following account balances appear in the general ledger of the Handy Company:

Notes Receivable		Notes Payable	
90,000			40,000

Notes Receivable Discounted	
	25,000

    a. What is the total amount of customers' notes outstanding?

    b. What amount of customers' notes is in Handy Company's possession?

    c. What amount of customers' notes has been discounted?

    d. What is Handy Company's contingent liability on discounted notes?

    e. How would these accounts be shown on the balance sheet?

Q8-9.   Explain full disclosure. Why is full disclosure important?

Q8-10.   Why should the Notes Receivable Discounted account and the Notes Receivable account be eliminated at maturity date regardless of whether a discounted note is paid?

Q8-11.   (a) What is a contingent liability? (b) What amounts must a person who is contingently liable on an interest-bearing note pay if the maker dishonors the note on its due date?

EXERCISES

E8-12. **Determining maturity date of notes (LG 2)** Following is information about eight notes:

Date of Note	Term of Note
June 16, 2007	30 days
July 16, 2007	30 days
April 30, 2007	90 days
May 2, 2007	120 days
July 14, 2007	180 days
September 2, 2007	3 months
March 30, 2007	3 months
May 3, 2007	2 years

Compute the maturity date of each note.

E8-13. **Determining maturity value of notes (LG 2)** Following is information about five notes:

Date of Note	Term of Note	Interest Rate	Principal
March 4, 2007	150 days	9%	$4,000
April 15, 2007	60	12	2,000
August 24, 2007	45	9	4,000
September 23, 2007	120	9	3,300
November 10, 2007	90	10	3,000

Determine the maturity date and maturity value of each note.

E8-14. **Calculating effective interest rates (LG 3)** Determine the annual percentage rate for the following credit situations (calculate each):

a. Jason, Inc., borrows money on the basis of a 1 ¼% interest rate each month.

b. Grant, Inc., purchases merchandise costing $2,520; this amount is to be paid in 24 equal monthly installments of $125 each (which include interest).

c. On June 1, 2007, Marge Casey borrowed money from the Tolland Bank by discounting on face value her own $8,000, 90-day note payable at a discount rate of 10%. The amount of cash received was $7,800.

E8-15. **Recording notes payable transactions with interest on face value (LG 4)** The following were among the transactions of Hartford Company for 2007 and 2008.

2007

Jan.	2	Purchased $15,000 of merchandise from Karla Company and issued a 12%, 45-day note dated today.
Feb.	16	Paid note and interest due Karla Company.
Mar.	15	Issued a 12%, 90-day note dated today to Pierce Company in settlement of an open account of $9,000.
Jun.	13	Paid Pierce Company $6,000 on principal and all the interest on the $9,000 note for the preceding 90 days; issued a new 14%, 60-day note for the balance of the principal.
Aug.	12	Paid the remaining amount due Pierce Company.
Dec.	1	Issued a 12%, 45-day note dated today to Polk Company in settlement of an open account of $15,000.

2008

Jan.	15	Paid the amount due Polk Company.

Journalize the transactions, including any necessary adjusting entries on December 31, 2007.

E8-16. Calculating and recording interest on notes payable (LG 2, 4) Information regarding two notes payable issued for merchandise by Lincoln Company follows:

Date of Note	Term of Note	Interest Rate	Principal
October 15, 2007	90 days	14%	$12,000
November 5, 2007	60	11	6,000

Roosevelt adjusts and closes the books on December 31, 2007. Compute the total simple interest to be credited to the Interest Payable account and prepare the necessary adjusting entry.

E8-17. Recording notes payable discounted at face value (LG 4) The following were among the transactions of Roosevelt Company for 2007 and 2008:

2007

Aug.	3	Issued its own 90-day note, made out to the Ohio Bank in the maturity amount of $9,000, and discounted it at a rate of 12%.
Nov.	1	Paid the Ohio Bank the amount due.
Dec.	16	Issued its own 60-day note, made out to the Iowa Bank in the maturity amount of $9,000, and discounted it at a rate of 12%.

2008

Feb.	14	Paid the amount due the Iowa Bank.

Journalize the transactions, including all necessary adjusting entries. Assume books are closed each December 31.

E8-18. Recording issuance of notes to borrow from banks and calculating effective interest rates (LG 3, 4) The following notes payable transactions occurred for Clarke Company:

2007

Nov.	1	Borrowed $9,000 from the Vernon Bank, issuing a 10%, 90-day note.
	1	Borrowed from the Manchester Bank, discounting on face value, its own $9,000, 90-day note at the discount rate of 10%.

2008

Jan.	30	Paid the notes due to the Vernon Bank and the Manchester Bank.

1. Journalize the transactions on the books of the Clarke Company, including any necessary adjusting entries on December 31, 2007.

2. Calculate the annual effective interest rates on the Vernon Bank and Manchester Bank notes.

E8-19. Recording notes receivable transactions (LG 5) The following were among the transactions of Bundy Company for 2007 and 2008:

2007		
Apr.	19	Sold merchandise for $5,400 to Gretzky and received a 10%, 60-day note dated today.
Jun.	18	Collected the amount due from Gretzky.
	21	Received a 12%, 120-day note dated today from Messier in settlement of an open account for $4,000.
Oct.	19	Messier dishonored his note.
Nov.	16	Received a 12%, 90-day note dated today from Ed Snider in settlement of an open account of $3,600.
2008		
Feb.	14	Collected the note and interest from Snider.

Journalize the transactions, including any necessary adjusting entries on December 31, 2007.

E8-20. Calculating and recording accrued interest on notes receivable (LG 2, 5) Information regarding three notes receivable held by Boosh Company follows:

Date of Note	Term of Note	Interest Rate	Principal
November 1, 2007	120 days	11%	$7,200
November 16, 2007	90	12	3,600
December 1, 2007	45	9	4,200

The books are closed on December 31, 2007. Compute the total simple interest to be debited to the Interest Receivable account and prepare the necessary adjusting entry.

E8-21. Discounting a customer's note receivable paid by the customer (LG 5, 6) Spectrum Company completed the following transactions in 2007 and 2008:

2007		
Oct.	8	Received a $1,800, 90-day, 10% note dated today in full settlement of the Hextall account.
Dec.	5	Discounted the above note at 12% at the Vorhees Bank.
2008		
Jan.	6	The October 8 note was paid at maturity.

Journalize the transactions on the books of Spectrum Company.

E8-22. Discounting a customer's note receivable dishonored by the customer (LG 5, 6) On September 5, 2007, Dunstan Company sold $5,400 of merchandise on account to Berne Company and received a 12%, 90-day note. This note was discounted at 15% on October 20, 2007, at the Foxhall Bank. At maturity date, Berne Company dishonored the note, and Dunstan Company paid the maturity value plus a $15 protest fee. Journalize the transactions on the books of Dunstan Company.

E8-23. Recording note transaction: maker and payee (LG 4, 5, 6) Lou Blue received from Fred Red a 10%, 120-day note for $3,000 dated March 3, 2007, in settlement of an open account. Thirty days later, Blue discounted Red's note with Money Bank at 12%. Red paid the note at maturity. Journalize the transactions on the books of both Blue and Red.

E8-24. Describing transactions from account data (LG 5) Six transactions related to a sale to a customer are recorded in the following T accounts. Describe each transaction.

Cash				Accounts Receivable				Notes Receivable		
(c)	912	(d)	944	(a)	900	(b)	900	(b)	900	(e)	900
(f)	989			(d)	944	(f)	944				

Notes Receivable Discounted				Sales			Interest Revenue		
(e)	900	(c)	900		(a)	900		(c)	12
								(f)	45

PROBLEMS

P8-25. Calculating and recording accrued interest on notes payable (LG 2, 5) Following is information regarding four notes issued by Brazil Company:

Date of Note	Term of Note	Interest Rate	Principal
July 11, 2007	240 days	11%	$ 4,000
November 1, 2007	150	12	12,000
November 16, 2007	120	10	14,000
December 5, 2007	90	9	5,000

REQUIRED

Assume that Brazil Company closes the books each December 31. Compute the total amount of accrued interest payable and make the necessary adjusting entry as of December 31, 2007.

P8-26. Determining approximate APR (LG 3) Cleanworld Sales sells standard washing machines for $800 in cash or on terms of $150 a month for six months. In order to meet competition, Cleanworld Sales is considering changing its credit terms to $75 a month for 12 months.

REQUIRED

Compute the approximate effective annual interest rate (APR) under (a) the present plan and (b) the proposed plan. Assume that each installment includes a uniform monthly reduction in the principal. (c) Which credit terms would the buyer prefer? (d) Which terms would the seller prefer?

P8-27. Recording notes payable transactions (LG 2, 4) Razor Company completed the following transactions during 2007 and 2008 (the fiscal year ends December 31):

2007

Jan.	2	Purchased $9,000 of merchandise from Lightning Company, issuing an 11%, 45-day note dated today.
Feb.	16	Paid the Lightning Company the amount due for the note and interest.
Jun.	1	Borrowed $14,000 from Ray Bank, issuing a 12%, 30-day note.
Jul.	1	Paid the Ray Bank the amount due.
Nov.	22	Issued to Goals Company a 9%, 90-day note dated today for $6,000 in settlement of an open account.
Dec.	16	Discounted at 11% its own $18,000, 60-day note, made out to the Sun Bank for the maturity value.

2008

Feb.	14	Paid the Sun Bank the amount due.
	20	Paid the amount due to Goals Company for the note issued on November 22, 2007.

REQUIRED

Journalize the transactions, including all necessary adjusting entries. Assume books are closed each December 31.

P8-28. **Determining cost of credit (LG 2, 4)** Legends Company negotiated a 90-day loan (reference 1) with the Dallas Bank. The loan was paid on its due date (reference m). Legends Company arranged for another 90-day loan (reference x) with the Boone Bank, which was also paid when due (reference y).

	Cash				Notes Payable to Bank				Interest Expense	
(l)	9,000	(m)	9,200	(m)	9,000	(l)	9,000	(m)	200	
(x)	8,800	(y)	9,000	(y)	9,000	(x)	9,000	(x)	200	

REQUIRED

1. Describe the type of negotiable instrument used by (a) the Dallas Bank and (b) the Boone Bank.

2. Which loan is more favorable to Legends Company? Why?

P8-29. **Recording notes receivable transactions (LG 5, 6)** During 2007 and 2008, Pixal Camera Company completed the following selected transactions:

2007

Sept.	14	Accepted a partial payment of $500 and a $9,000, 12%, 120-day note dated September 14, 2007, from Jane Deer in settlement of her account.
Nov.	3	Sold 15 model BB5 cameras to Mall Pictures on account; total invoice price $3,600; terms n/30.
Dec.	3	Accepted a $3,600, 10%, 60-day note dated December 3, 2007, from Mall Pictures in settlement of their account.
	28	Discounted at 12% at the Texas First Bank the note from Mall Pictures dated December 3, 2007.

2008

Jan.	12	Jane Deer failed to pay the amount of the note and the interest due today. In a phone call, Deer promises that she can send a check for the maturity value in 10 days.
	22	As promised, Jane Deer delivers a check in the amount of $9,360 in payment of her past due account.
Feb.	1	Since notice protesting the Mall Pictures note was not received, it was assumed that it had been paid.

REQUIRED

Journalize the transactions, including all necessary adjusting entries. Assume books are closed each December 31.

P8-30. **Comprehensive notes receivable transactions (LG 5, 6)** During 2007, Ted's Tire Company completed the following transactions, among others:

2007

Mar.	8	Sold merchandise to Marty Dare on account; invoice price $3,000; terms 2/10, n/30.	
	10	Accepted a $4,200, 12%, 60-day note dated this day in settlement of a past due account of Rose Van.	
	15	Accepted a $5,600, 9%, 45-day note dated this day in settlement of an open account of Al Pal.	
Apr.	7	Marty Dare gave a 12%, 90-day note dated this day in full settlement of his account (March 8 sale).	
	29	Al Pal's note of March 15 was dishonored.	
May	9	Received a check from Rose Van for $1,000 plus the full amount of the interest due on the March 10th note and accepted a new 12%, 60-day note for $3,200.	
	10	Discounted at 14% at the Hartford Bank the note from Marty Dare dated April 7.	
	21	Discounted at 12% at the Vernon Bank the note from Rose Van dated May 9.	
Jul.	6	Since notice protesting the Marty Dare note was not received, it was assumed that it had been paid.	
	8	Received notice that Rose Van had dishonored her note of May 9. Paid the bank the maturity value of the note plus a protest fee of $20.	
Aug.	7	Received payment from Rose Van of the maturity value of her dishonored note, the protest fee, and interest on both at 12% for 30 days beyond the maturity date.	
	31	Wrote off the Al Pal account receivable of as uncollectible. Used the allowance method.	

REQUIRED

Record the transactions in general journal form.

P8-31.   **Selecting best source of short-term credit (LG 3, 7)** The following two sources of credit were available to Weinrich Company:

a. The Patrick Bank agreed to accept on a discount basis the Weinrich Company's one-year note made out for the maturity value of $20,000 discounted at a 20% rate.

b. The Barber Bank agreed to loan cash of $16,000 on a note with interest at 12% for one year added to the $16,000, making the principal of the note $17,920. The note is to be paid off in monthly installments of $1,493.33 over 12 months.

REQUIRED

Which method of credit should Weinrich Company choose and why? Support your reasons with appropriate calculations.

P8-32.   **Interpretation of short-term borrowing and credit arrangement note for The Neiman Marcus Group (LG 7)** Neiman Marcus ended its 2004 reporting year on July 31, 2004. On that date, total assets were $2,545.8 million and total liabilities were $1,164.9 million. Of the total liabilities, $727.7 million were current. Of the total assets, accounts receivable were $551.7 million and inventories of goods for sale were $720.3 million. For the year ended July 31, 2004, the Company reported net earnings of $204.8 million and paid cash dividends on common stock of $18.9 million. The following note to the financial statements on short-term borrowings and credit arrangements is taken from the 2004 annual report of Neiman Marcus.

Long-term Liabilities

The Company has a five year, $350 million revolving credit facility which expires in July, 2009. The revolving credit facility contains, among other restrictions, provisions requiring maintenance of certain leverage and fixed charge ratios.

In addition to its revolving credit facility, the Company borrows from other banks on an uncommitted basis. Such borrowings are included in notes payable and current maturities of long-term liabilities.

REQUIRED

How do you feel about the availability of short-term credit financing for Neiman Marcus as of July 31, 2004? Include a discussion of all of the factors which support your conclusion.

PRACTICE CASE

Short-term financing Watson (LG 2, 4-6) Watson Company sells high-quality garden tractors to lawn-care companies. During 2007, the Watson Company completed the following selected transactions:

2007

Jun.	21	Purchased 10 garden tractors from Tuff Machine, Inc. on account; total invoice price $36,000; terms 2/10, n/30.
Jul.	21	Gave Tuff Machine, Inc. a 12%, 30-day note dated July 21, 2007, in settlement of the June 21 purchase.
	28	Sold one garden tractor to Lemek Lawns on account; invoice price was $5,200; terms n/30.
Aug.	19	Borrowed cash to pay the note payable to Tuff Machine, Inc. Discounted at 13% its own $36,000, 60-day note, made out to the City Bank for the maturity value.
	20	Paid Tuff Machine, Inc. for the July 21 note.
	27	Received a phone call from Lew Lemek asking if he could give a 30-day, 12% note for the purchase on July 28, 2007. Accepted the note dated today.
Sep.	3	Sold five tractors to Green Acres for a total of $21,000. Accepted a 60-day, 12% note dated today.
	10	Discounted at 13% at the Friendly Finance Company the note from Green Acres dated September 3, 2007.
	26	The note receivable from Lemek Lawns dated August 27, 2007, was dishonored.
Oct.	18	Paid $36,000 to the City Bank for the amount borrowed on August 19, 2007.
Nov.	2	Since notice protesting the note from Green Acres discounted on September 10 was not received, it was assumed that it had been paid.
Dec.	15	Wrote off the receivable balance from Lemek Lawns as uncollectible. Used the allowance method.

REQUIRED

Journalize the transactions.

BUSINESS DECISION AND COMMUNICATION PROBLEM

Extended credit terms (LG 2, 6) You are currently a vice president at Farm Equipment Company, which supplies tractors and other equipment to farmers. Because of a decrease in demand, inventories of tractors have increased. Jane McCandless, sales manager, feels that she has a solution to decreased sales and a weak cash position. She proposes that the company should offer to sell the tractors by having customers sign three-year, noninterest-bearing notes for the full purchase price. Farm Equipment could then discount the notes receivable at a bank in order to obtain immediate cash. Jane feels that the economic situation will turn around in three years, and that farmers could pay at that time. Charlie Checker, the president of the company, asks you to evaluate Jane's suggestion.

REQUIRED

Prepare a memo to the president in which you evaluate the plan.

ETHICAL DILEMMA

Interest calculation procedure (LG 2) You are in charge of customer receivable and supplier payable records for Fabulous Vacations. Due to the extended period of time over which customer collections are received and supplier payments are made, interest is usually charged on receivables and payables. Your supervisor has told you that beginning next month, the number of days in a year used to calculate interest will be changed, as follows:

	Number of days in a Year
Customer accounts receivable	360
Supplier accounts payable	365

Previously, a 360-day year was used for all interest calculations.

REQUIRED

Explain the motivation behind the change. Is this ethical?

COMPREHENSIVE ANALYSIS CASE THE COCA-COLA COMPANY

Analyzing The Coca-Cola Company for the Period 2004-2002 Listed below are comparative income statements and balance sheets with common-size percents for 2004-2002 (in millions). Also included are selected ratio statistics. Please provide a brief explanation for your answer to each question.

REQUIRED

Income statement questions:

1. Are total revenues higher or lower over the three-year period?

2. What is the percent change in total revenues from 2002 to 2004?

3. Is the percent of cost of goods sold to total revenues increasing or decreasing over the three-year period? As a result, is the gross margin percent increasing or decreasing?

4. Is the percent of total operating expenses to total revenues increasing or decreasing over the three-year period? As a result, is the operating income percent increasing or decreasing?

5. Is the percent of net income to total revenue increasing or decreasing over the three-year period?

Balance sheet questions:

6. Are total assets higher or lower over the three-year period?

7. What is the percent change in total assets from 2002 to 2004?

8. What are the largest asset investments for the company over the three-year period?

9. Are the accounts receivable increasing faster or slower than the percent change in total revenues?

10. Is the percent of total liabilities to total liabilities + owners' equity increasing or decreasing? As a result, is there more or less risk that the company could not pay its debts?

Integrative income statement and balance sheet question:

11. Is the company operating more or less efficiently by using the least amount of asset investment to generate a given level of total revenues? Note that the "total asset turnover" ratio is computed and included in the "ratio analysis summary".

COCA-COLA CO
COMPARATIVE COMMON-SIZE INCOME STATEMENTS
For The Years Ended Dec. 31, 2004, 2003, 2002
(in millions)

	2004 $	2004 %	2003 $	2003 %	2002 $	2002 %
Revenues	21,962.0	100.0%	21,044.0	100.0%	19,564.0	100.0%
Cost of goods sold	7,638.0	34.8%	7,762.0	36.9%	7,105.0	36.3%
Gross margin	14,324.0	65.2%	13,282.0	63.1%	12,459.0	63.7%
Operating expenses:						
Sales, marketing, general administrative	8,626.0	39.3%	8,061.0	38.3%	7,001.0	35.8%
Research and development	-	0.0%	-	0.0%	-	0.0%
Other expense	-	0.0%	-	0.0%	-	0.0%
Other expense	-	0.0%	-	0.0%	-	0.0%
Total operating expenses	8,626.0	39.3%	8,061.0	38.3%	7,001.0	35.8%
Operating income	5,698.0	25.9%	5,221.0	24.8%	5,458.0	27.9%
Net interest expense (income)	196.0	0.9%	178.0	0.8%	199.0	1.0%
Other expense (income)	(720.0)	-3.3%	(452.0)	-2.1%	(240.0)	-1.2%
Income before income taxes	6,222.0	28.3%	5,495.0	26.1%	5,499.0	28.1%
Income taxes	1,375.0	6.3%	1,148.0	5.5%	1,523.0	7.8%
Net income (loss) before unusual items	4,847.0	22.1%	4,347.0	20.7%	3,976.0	20.3%
Other losses (gains) net of tax	-	0.0%	-	0.0%	926.0	4.7%
Net income (loss)	4,847.0	22.1%	4,347.0	20.7%	3,050.0	15.6%

COCA-COLA CO
COMPARATIVE COMMON-SIZE BALANCE SHEETS
Dec. 31, 2004, 2003, 2002
(in millions)

	2004 $	2004 %	2003 $	2003 %	2002 $	2002 %
ASSETS						
Current:						
Cash & cash equivalents	6,707.0	21.4%	3,362.0	12.3%	2,126.0	8.7%
Short-term investments	61.0	0.2%	120.0	0.4%	219.0	0.9%
Accounts receivable, net	2,171.0	6.9%	2,091.0	7.6%	2,097.0	8.6%
Inventory	1,420.0	4.5%	1,252.0	4.6%	1,294.0	5.3%
Other current assets	1,735.0	5.5%	1,571.0	5.7%	1,616.0	6.6%
Other current assets	-	0.0%	-	0.0%	-	0.0%
Total current assets	12,094.0	38.6%	8,396.0	30.7%	7,352.0	30.0%
Fixed:						
Property & equipment, net	6,091.0	19.4%	6,097.0	22.3%	5,911.0	24.1%
Long-term investments	6,252.0	20.0%	5,538.0	20.3%	4,991.0	20.4%
Intangibles & goodwill	3,836.0	12.2%	3,989.0	14.6%	3,553.0	14.5%
Other assets	3,054.0	9.7%	3,322.0	12.1%	2,694.0	11.0%
Total assets	31,327.0	100.0%	27,342.0	100.0%	24,501.0	100.0%
LIABILITIES						
Current:						
Short-term debt	6,021.0	19.2%	2,906.0	10.6%	2,655.0	10.8%
Accounts payable	4,751.0	15.2%	4,980.0	18.2%	4,686.0	19.1%
Accrued salaries and benefits	-	0.0%	-	0.0%	-	0.0%
Unearned revenue	-	0.0%	-	0.0%	-	0.0%
Other current liabilities	199.0	0.6%	-	0.0%	-	0.0%
Total current liabilities	10,971.0	35.0%	7,886.0	28.8%	7,341.0	30.0%
Long-term debt	1,157.0	3.7%	2,517.0	9.2%	2,701.0	11.0%
Deferred income tax liabilities	450.0	1.4%	337.0	1.2%	399.0	1.6%
Other long-term liabilities	2,814.0	9.0%	2,512.0	9.2%	2,260.0	9.2%
Total liabilities	15,392.0	49.1%	13,252.0	48.5%	12,701.0	51.8%
OWNERS' EQUITY						
Total owners' equity	15,935.0	50.9%	14,090.0	51.5%	11,800.0	48.2%
Total liabilities and owners' equity	31,327.0	100.0%	27,342.0	100.0%	24,501.0	100.0%

(Note: percents may not add to 100 due to rounding)

COCA-COLA CO
RATIO ANALYSIS SUMMARY
For The Years Ended Dec. 31, 2004, 2003, 2002

	2004	2003	2002
SHORT-TERM LIQUIDITY RATIOS			
Current Ratio (Current Assets/Current Liabilities)	1.10	1.06	1.00
Quick Ratio (Cash + Short-term Investments + Accounts Receivable)/Current Liabilities	0.81	0.71	0.61
Accounts Receivable Turnover 1 (Revenues/Average Accounts Receivable)	10.31	10.05	
Accounts Receivable Turnover 2 (Revenues/Year-end Accounts Receivable)	10.12	10.06	9.33
Inventory Turnover 1 (Cost Goods Sold/Average Inventory)	5.72	6.10	
Inventory Turnover 2 (Cost Goods Sold/Year-end Inventory)	5.38	6.20	5.49
LONG-TERM SOLVENCY (LEVERAGE) RATIO			
Total Debt Ratio (Total Liabilities/Total Assets)	49.13%	48.47%	51.84%
PROFITABILITY RATIOS			
Gross Profit Margin (Gross Margin/Revenues)	65.22%	63.12%	63.68%
Operating Profit Margin (Operating Income/Revenues)	25.94%	24.81%	27.90%
Net Profit Margin (Return on Sales) (ROS)(Net Income/Revenues)	22.07%	20.66%	15.59%
Total Asset Turnover (Revenues/Average Total Assets)	0.75	0.81	
Return on Total Assets (ROA)(Net Income/Average Total Assets)	16.52%	16.77%	

Ratio analysis questions:

12. Is the *current ratio* better or worse in the most current year compared to prior years?

13. Is the *quick ratio* better or worse in the most current year compared to prior years?

14. Is the *accounts receivable turnover ratio 1* (based on *average* receivables) better or worse in the most current year compared to prior years?

15. Is the 2004 *accounts receivable turnover ratio 2* (based on *year-end* receivables) better or worse than the 2004 ratio based on an *average*?

16. Is the *inventory turnover ratio 1* (based on *average* inventory) better or worse in the most current year compared to prior years?

17. Is the 2004 *inventory turnover ratio 2* (based on *year-end* inventory) better or worse than the 2004 ratio based on an *average*?

18. Is the *return on total assets (ROA) ratio* better or worse in the most current year compared to prior years?

CHAPTER 9

INVENTORIES AND COST OF GOODS SOLD

LEARNING GOALS

After studying Chapter 9, you should be able to:

1. Identify costs that should be included in inventory.

2. Journalize entries to account for inventory transactions under the periodic and perpetual inventory systems.

3. Compute the cost of ending inventory and the cost of goods sold using (a) the specific identification method; (b) the weighted average cost method; (c) the first-in, first-out (FIFO) method; and (d) the last-in, first-out (LIFO) method under the periodic inventory system.

4. Compute the cost of ending inventory and the cost of goods sold using (a) the moving average cost method; (b) the first-in, first-out (FIFO) method; and (c) the last-in,

first-out (LIFO) method under the perpetual inventory system.

5. State the impact on the income statement and the balance sheet of using alternative inventory cost flow assumptions.

6. Apply the lower-of-cost-or-market (LCM) rule to inventory valuation.

7. Estimate the cost of ending inventory by using (a) the gross margin method and (b) the retail inventory method.

8. Determine the effects of an inventory error on the income statement and the balance sheet.

9. Analyze financial statement information for real-life companies.

UNDERSTANDING BUSINESS ISSUES

We introduced inventories and cost of goods sold for a merchandising firm in Chapter 5. For both merchandising and manufacturing companies, inventories are a major asset on the balance sheet and cost of goods sold is the major expense on the income statement. For example, the table below shows recent information about inventories and cost of goods sold for companies in different lines of business.(Dollar amounts in millions)

Company	BALANCE SHEET		INCOME STATEMENT	
	Total Inventories	Percentage of Total Assets	Cost of Goods Sold	Percentage of Sales Revenue
Dell Computer (computers)	$ 327.0	1.7%	$ 33,892.0	81.8%
Neiman Marcus (retail clothing)	720.3	28.3	2,321.1	65.5
Nike, Inc. (footwear)	1,633.6	20.7	7,001.4	57.1
Toys "Я" Us (toy retailer)	2,286.0	22.4	7,849.0	67.9
Wal-Mart Stores (discount store)	26,612.0	25.4	198,747.0	76.8
Winn-Dixie Stores (grocery store)	991.6	37.9	7,819.1	73.5

Inventories are the largest current asset for most merchandising and manufacturing companies. Assigning a value to the ending inventory is important in order to fairly present the company's financial position. For the income statement, determining cost of goods sold is important in matching expenses and revenues. This chapter deals with inventory valuation and shows how it directly affects income. We illustrate and compare both the periodic and perpetual inventory systems. We also cover methods for estimating the cost of ending inventory and the effect of inventory errors on the financial statements.

COSTS TO INCLUDE IN INVENTORY

Learning Goal 1   Identify costs that should be included in inventory.

A merchandising firm like Wal-Mart buys a finished product and sells it to a customer. Inventory for a merchandising firm consists of all goods owned and held for sale in the normal course of business. We originally record inventories at cost. The **cost of an inventory item** includes all expenditures incurred to bring the item to its existing condition and location. Cost consists of the invoice price of the merchandise (less purchase discounts), plus transportation, insurance while in transit, and any other expenses to get the merchandise to the place of business. Merchandise inventory is shown as a current asset because a business normally will use it in operations within one year.

If purchased goods are in transit, we include the goods in inventory if title has passed to the buyer. Therefore, the inventory of the buyer includes goods purchased *F.O.B. shipping point* even if the buyer has not received them. In some cases, goods may be on hand but not included in inventory. An example common in the retailing industry is goods held by a seller on consignment. In a *consignment* arrangement, the owner of the goods (the *consignor*) transfers goods to a retailing company (the *consignee*). The consignee sells the goods on the owner's behalf but does not take title to the goods. Therefore, the consignee does not include these goods in inventory.

A manufacturing firm like Dell Computer, Inc., produces products in addition to selling products. A manufacturing firm has three major types of inventories: (1) materials inventory to be used to produce product, (2) work-in-process inventory for the cost of items partly completed, and (3) finished goods inventory, for units completed and ready for sale. We show the three types of inventory as current assets.

INVENTORY SYSTEMS

Learning Goal 2   Journalize entries to account for inventory transactions under the periodic and perpetual inventory systems.

Two alternative systems for recording inventory transactions are the periodic and perpetual systems. Chapter 5 illustrated the **periodic inventory system**. To review this method briefly, we record acquisitions of merchandise inventory by debits to a Purchases account. When we record sales, we do not record any decrease in the Merchandise Inventory account or record any cost of goods sold. Under the periodic inventory system, we make journal entries to the Merchandise Inventory account only at the end of the accounting period. These end-of-period entries transfer out the beginning inventory amount and establish the new ending inventory amount. We calculate cost of goods sold at the end of the accounting period as follows:

$$
\begin{array}{rl}
 & \text{Beginning Inventory} \\
+ & \underline{\text{Purchases (net)}} \\
= & \text{Cost of Goods Available for Sale} \\
- & \underline{\text{Ending Inventory}} \\
= & \text{Cost of Goods Sold}
\end{array}
$$

The **perpetual inventory system** continually updates the Merchandise Inventory account. Journal entries record merchandise receipts, the cost of merchandise sold, and merchandise returns. A separate Cost of Goods Sold general ledger account records the cost of the inventory items sold at the time of each sale. To compare the journal entries to record merchandise transactions under both inventory systems, assume the following data for Logo Company for April 2007:

2007			
Apr.	1	Total inventory on hand at cost	$300
	9	Purchases of merchandise on account	700
	12	Return of a defective merchandise item	100
	23	Sales on account (cost of goods sold is $500)	800
	30	Total inventory on hand at cost	400

Exhibit 9.1 shows the general journal entries to record the transactions and a partial income statement under both the periodic and perpetual inventory systems.

The periodic inventory system uses individual accounts to record purchases and purchases returns and allowances. We transfer all merchandise accounts (including the beginning and ending inventory amounts) individually to Income Summary at the end of the accounting period. The net effect of closing all merchandise accounts is to accumulate the cost of goods sold in the Income Summary account.

In a perpetual inventory system, we debit the Merchandise Inventory account directly for each purchase of merchandise. We credit the Merchandise Inventory account for each return. Each time merchandise is sold, we must make an entry to record the cost of the goods sold and the decrease in inventory. This entry debits Cost of Goods Sold and credits Merchandise Inventory for the cost of the merchandise sold. The cost of goods sold for an accounting period is the balance in the Cost of Goods Sold account. At the end of the period, we close this account by debiting Income Summary and crediting Cost of Goods Sold. Since

Transactions	Periodic System	Perpetual System

April 9, 2007
Purchase
Merchandise
on account.
	Purchases 700
	   Accounts Payable 700
		Merchandise Inventory 700
		   Accounts Payable 700

April 12, 2007
Return defective
items.
	Accounts Payable 100
	   Purchases Returns
	      and Allowances 100
		Accounts Payable 100
		   Merchandise
		      Inventory 100

April 23, 2007
Sell merchandise
on account.
	Accounts Receivable 800
	   Sales 800
	Note: We do not determine the cost of goods
	sold at this time but at the end of the period
		Accounts Receivable 800
		   Sales 800
		Cost of Goods Sold 500
		   Merchandise
		      Inventory 500

April 30, 2007
Closing entries.
	Sales 800
	   Income Summary 800
	Income Summary 500
	Merchandise Inventory
	   (ending) 400
	Purchases Returns
	   and Allowances 100
	      Merchandise Inventory
	         (beginning) 300
	      Purchases 700
		Sales 800
		   Income Summary 800
		Income Summary 500
		   Cost of Goods Sold 500

**Income Statement
for the Month Ended
April 30, 2007**
	Sales $800
	Cost of goods sold:
	  Merchandise inventory,
	    April 1, 2007 $300
	  Purchases $700
	  Deduct: Returns 100
	    Net cost of purchase 600
	  Cost of goods
	    available for sale $900
	  Deduct: Merchandise
	    inventory, April 30, 2007 400
	    Cost of goods sold $500
	Gross margin $300
		Sales $800
		Cost of goods sold 500
		Gross margin $300

EXHIBIT **9.1**

Periodic and Perpetual Inventory Systems Compared

we update the Merchandise Inventory account continuously, the ending balance is the amount that should be on hand. We must take a physical inventory at least once a year to compare inventory records to actual quantities.

Perpetual inventory systems enable managers to constantly monitor inventories on hand. The use of computers and bar-coding has greatly decreased the cost of maintaining perpetual inventory systems. Today, both large and small companies use perpetual inventory systems extensively.

INVENTORY COSTING METHODS

Assigning a cost to units in ending inventory is easy when the costs per unit do not change. However, in the real world, the cost of most items changes constantly. Determining the ending inventory cost valuation is relatively simple when we can identify each item acquired with its specific cost. This is the *specific identification method*. It may be used for high-priced items such as automobiles, diamonds, and works of art. For most high-volume, low-priced business inventories, such as computer chips, specific identification is not feasible. As an alternative, most companies use one of the following three cost flow assumptions:

1. **Average cost flow assumption** assumes that the cost of inventory items sold is a *weighted average* of the costs incurred to acquire those items. The cost of the units remaining in inventory at the end of the accounting period is the same weighted average cost per item.

2. **First-in, first-out (FIFO)** is an assumption that the cost of the earliest (oldest) goods on hand is the cost of the first inventory item(s) sold. As a result, FIFO assumes that the cost of the units remaining in ending inventory is the cost of the latest inventory items acquired.

3. **Last-in, first-out (LIFO)** is an opposite cost flow assumption from FIFO. LIFO assumes that the cost of the latest (newest) goods on hand is the cost of the first inventory item(s) sold. As a result, LIFO assumes that the cost of the units remaining in ending inventory is the cost of the earliest inventory items acquired.

The three cost flow assumptions may be used in both periodic and perpetual inventory systems. The chapter illustration of these methods assumes the following information for a company's purchases and sales of designer sunglasses for April 2007:

PURCHASES AND SALES INFORMATION FOR APRIL
DESIGNER SUNGLASSES, STOCK NUMBER 701

	Units	Unit Cost	Total Cost	Specific Identification of Units Remaining in April 30 Inventory
Inventory, April 1	60	$40	$ 2,400	25 units
Purchases				
April 5	90	50	4,500	30
April 16	150	60	9,000	35
Total goods available for sale	300		$ 15,900	
Sales				
April 12	100			
April 28	110			
Total units sold	210			
Inventory, April 30	90			90 units

Periodic Inventory System

Learning Goal 3   Compute the cost of ending inventory and the cost of goods sold using the specific identification, weighted average cost, FIFO, and LIFO methods under the periodic inventory system.

With the periodic inventory system, we determine the ending inventory value by first taking a physical count of the units on hand. We then price the units at cost using either the specific identification method or one of the cost flow assumptions. The periodic system assumes that purchased goods not on hand have been sold. Losses due to theft or breakage are included in the cost of goods sold since the units are not part of ending inventory.

The Specific Identification Method

The **specific identification method** requires that we assign each inventory item a specific name or number and cost. Based on information provided for designer sunglasses, the specific identification cost of the 90 units in *ending inventory* on April 30 is:

SPECIFIC IDENTIFICATION ENDING INVENTORY VALUATION
(90 UNITS)

Purchase Lot	Units	Unit Cost	Total Cost
April 1 inventory	25	$40	$ 1,000
April 5 purchase	30	50	1,500
April 16 purchase	35	60	2,100
Ending inventory	90		$ 4,600

We compute the *cost of goods sold* by deducting the specific identification ending inventory valuation from the cost of goods available for sale, as follows:

SPECIFIC IDENTIFICATION OF GOODS SOLD
(210 UNITS)

Cost of goods available for sale (300 units)	$ 15,900
Deduct: Ending inventory at specific identification (90 units)	4,600
Cost of goods sold	$ 11,300

Specific identification is feasible when a business handles small numbers of high-cost and easily distinguishable inventory items. A major deficiency of the method is the difficulty of keeping track of purchases and sales of specific units. Usually, we substitute other cost flow assumptions for specific identification.

Weighted Average Method

Weighted average inventory costing values all units at the same weighted average cost computed at the end of each period. We compute the weighted average unit cost by dividing the total cost of goods available for sale by the total units available for sale. The computation of the weighted average unit cost for April 2007 is as follows:

Purchase Lot	Units	Unit Cost	Total Cost
April 1 inventory	60	$40	$ 2,400
April 5 purchase	90	50	4,500
April 16 purchase	150	60	9,000
Total goods available for sale	300		$ 15,900

$$\text{Weighted Average Unit Cost} = \frac{\text{Cost of Goods Available for Sale}}{\text{Units Available for Sale}}$$

$$= \frac{\$15,900}{300}$$

$$= \$53$$

The cost assigned to the *ending inventory* is:

WEIGHTED AVERAGE ENDING INVENTORY VALUATION
(90 UNITS)

At weighted average unit cost (90 units at $53)	$ 4,770

We compute the *cost of goods sold* by deducting the weighted average ending inventory valuation from the cost of goods available for sale, as follows:

WEIGHTED AVERAGE COST OF GOODS SOLD
(210 UNITS)

Cost of goods available for sale (300 units)	$ 15,900
Deduct: Ending inventory at weighted average (90 units × $53)	4,770
Cost of goods sold	$ 11,130

First-in, First-out (FIFO) Method

Under the periodic inventory system, FIFO costing assumes that the *earliest* inventory costs incurred are the *first* ones transferred out when units are sold. *This cost flow assumption relates only to the method of accounting and <u>not to the actual physical flow of goods</u>.* FIFO matches the first costs with revenue. As a result, the balance sheet shows the most recent costs for inventory.

Under FIFO, we value the 90 pairs of sunglasses on hand on April 30, 2007, at the cost of the most recent lot purchased on April 16. Since the last purchase made was large enough to make up the entire ending inventory, we value all 90 units at $60 per unit. Therefore, the cost assigned to the *ending inventory* is as follows:

FIFO ENDING INVENTORY VALUATION
(90 UNITS)

Purchase Lot	Units	Unit Cost	Total Cost
April 16 purchase	90	$60	$ 5,400
Ending inventory	90		$ 5,400

We compute the *cost of goods sold* by deducting the FIFO ending inventory valuation from the cost of goods available for sale, as follows:

FIFO COST OF GOODS SOLD
(210 UNITS)

Cost of goods available for sale (300 units)	$ 15,900
Deduct: Ending inventory at FIFO (90 units)	5,400
Cost of goods sold	$ 10,500

The following diagram shows a summary of the FIFO ending inventory and cost of goods sold computations.

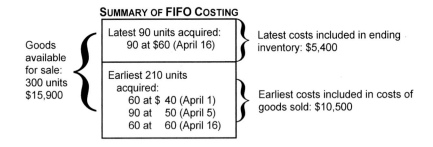

Last-in, First-out (LIFO) Method

Under the periodic inventory system, LIFO costing assumes that the *latest* inventory costs incurred are the *first* ones transferred out when units are sold. As with FIFO, *this cost flow assumption relates only to the method of accounting and <u>not to the actual physical flow of goods</u>.* LIFO matches the latest costs with revenue. As a result, the balance sheet shows the earliest costs for inventory.

Under LIFO, we value the 90 pairs of sunglasses on hand April 30, 2007, at the costs of the earliest lots acquired. The earliest lot, beginning inventory (60 units), is not large enough to make up the ending inventory (90 units).

Therefore, we include sufficient units from the first April purchase to make up the ending inventory. The cost assigned to the *ending inventory* is:

LIFO ENDING INVENTORY VALUATION
(90 UNITS)

Purchase Lot	Units	Unit Cost	Total Cost
April 1 inventory	60	$40	$ 2,400
April 5 purchase	30	50	1,500
Ending inventory	90		$ 3,900

We compute the *cost of goods sold* by deducting the LIFO ending inventory valuation from the cost of goods available for sale, as follows:

LIFO COST OF GOODS SOLD
(210 UNITS)

Cost of goods available for sale (300 units)	$ 15,900
Deduct: Ending inventory at LIFO (90 units)	3,900
Cost of goods sold	$ 12,000

The following diagram shows a summary of the ending inventory and cost of goods sold computations under LIFO.

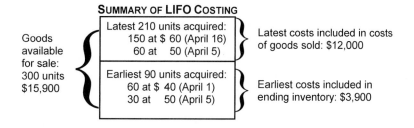

SUMMARY OF LIFO COSTING

Goods available for sale: 300 units $15,900	Latest 210 units acquired: 150 at $ 60 (April 16) 60 at 50 (April 5)	Latest costs included in costs of goods sold: $12,000
	Earliest 90 units acquired: 60 at $ 40 (April 1) 30 at 50 (April 5)	Earliest costs included in ending inventory: $3,900

Perpetual Inventory System

Learning Goal 4   Compute the cost of ending inventory and the cost of goods sold using the moving average cost, FIFO, and LIFO methods under the perpetual inventory system.

The perpetual inventory system provides continuous updated information about items on hand. The system keeps an inventory record for each inventory item. As we purchase or sell units, we update the inventory record for the item to show the quantity and value on hand.

Prior to the widespread use of computers, perpetual inventory records were costly to maintain. Although many companies still keep some inventories on a periodic basis, computers ease the burden of maintaining perpetual records. This is especially true when the business uses devices such as optical scanners and bar coding.

Moving Average Method

Exhibit 9.2 illustrates a perpetual inventory record using the **moving average inventory costing** method. This method prices units at a continuous weighted average cost. We compute a new weighted average unit cost each time we purchase merchandise. It is not necessary to compute a new cost after each sale because sales do not change the unit cost. We use this average unit cost for sales until we purchase additional units at a different cost. For example, the purchase of 90 units on April 5 requires a new unit cost computation of $46 (see computation (a) in Exhibit 9.2 The purchase of April 16 requires a new unit cost of $56.50 (see computation (b) in Exhibit 9.2

The cost of goods sold is the sum of the Total Cost column in the Sold section of the inventory record. For these sunglasses, the *cost of goods sold* is as follows:

MOVING AVERAGE COST OF GOODS SOLD
(210 UNITS)

Sale of April 12 (100 units at $46.00)	$ 4,600
Sale of April 28 (110 units at $56.50)	6,215
Cost of goods sold	$10,815

The cost assigned to *ending inventory* from the Total Cost column in the Balance section of the inventory record is as follows:

MOVING AVERAGE ENDING INVENTORY VALUATION
(90 UNITS)

At moving average unit cost, 90 units at $56.50 $5,085

ITEM: DESIGNER SUNGLASSES, STOCK NUMBER 701, LOCATION L-7

Date		Purchased			Sold			Balance		
		Quantity	Unit Cost	Total Cost	Quantity	Unit Cost	Total Cost	Quantity	Unit Cost	Total Cost
2007										
Apr.	1							60	40.00	2,400
	5	90	50	4,500				150	46.00	6,900 (a)
	12				100	46.00	4,600	50	46.00	2,300
	16	150	60	9,000				200	56.50	11,300 (b)
	28				110	56.50	6,215	90	56.50	5,085
Totals		240		13,500	210		10,815	90		5,085

(a)
60 at $40 = $2,400
90 at 50 = 4,500
150          $6,900

Average = $46 = ($6,900 ÷ 150)

(b)
50 at $46 = $ 2,300
150 at 60 =   9,000
200          $11,300

Average = $56.50 = ($11,300 ÷ 200)

EXHIBIT **9.2**

Perpetual Inventory Record (Moving Average)

First-in, First-out (FIFO) Method

Exhibit 9.3 illustrates a perpetual inventory record using the FIFO costing method. As we receive each shipment of goods, we record its quantity, unit cost, (perpetual basis) and total cost as a separate lot. Each time we sell goods, we transfer out the costs of the earliest goods. FIFO assumes that the cost of the 100 units sold on April 12 consists of 60 units in beginning inventory on April 1 and 40 units from the April 5 purchase. The cost of the 110 units sold on April 28 consists of the remaining 50 units from the April 5 purchase and 60 units from the April 16 purchase.

For FIFO applied on a perpetual basic, the *cost of goods sold* is:

FIFO COST OF GOODS SOLD
(210 UNITS)

Sale of April 12 (100 units)	
(60 units × $40 = $2,400) + (40 units × $50 = $2,000)	$ 4,400
Sale of April 28 (110 units)	
(50 units × $50 = $2,500) + (60 units × $60 = $3,600)	6,100
Cost of goods sold	$ 10,500

The cost assigned to *ending inventory* is:

FIFO ENDING INVENTORY VALUATION
(90 UNITS)

Purchase lot	Units	Unit cost	Total Cost
April 16 purchase	90	$60	$5,400
Ending inventory	90		$5,400

ITEM: DESIGNER SUNGLASSES, STOCK NUMBER 701, LOCATION L-7

Date		Purchased Quantity	Unit Cost	Total Cost	Sold Quantity	Unit Cost	Total Cost	Balance Quantity	Unit Cost	Total Cost
2007										
Apr.	1							60	40	2,400
	5	90	50	4,500				60	40	
								90	50	6,900
	12				60	40	2,400			
					40	50	2,000	50	50	2,500
	16	150	60	9,000				50	50	
								150	60	11,500
	28				50	50	2,500			
					60	60	3,600	90	60	5,400
Totals		240		13,500	210		10,500	90		5,400

EXHIBIT 9.3

Perpetual Inventory Record (FIFO)

Last-in, First-out (LIFO) Method

Exhibit 9.4 illustrates a perpetual inventory record using the LIFO costing method. As we receive each shipment of goods, we record its quantity, unit cost, and total cost as a separate lot. Each time we sell goods, we transfer out the costs of the latest goods on hand *at the time of the sale*. LIFO assumes that the cost of the 100 units sold on April 12 consists of 90 units from the April 5 purchase and 10 units from beginning inventory on April 1. The cost of the 110 units sold on April 28 consists of 110 units from the April 16 purchase.

For LIFO applied on a perpetual basis, the *cost of goods sold* is:

LIFO Cost of Goods Sold
(210 units)

Sale of April 12 (100 units)
(90 units × $50 = $4,500) + (10 units × $40 = $400) $ 4,900
Sale of April 28 (110 units)
(110 units × $60 = $6,600)   6,600
Cost of goods sold $11,500

The cost assigned to *ending inventory* is:

LIFO Ending Inventory Valuation
(90 units)

Purchase Lot	Units	Unit Cost	Total Cost
April 1 inventory	50	$40	$ 2,000
April 16 purchase	40	60	2,400
Ending inventory	90		$ 4,400

ITEM: DESIGNER SUNGLASSES, STOCK NUMBER 701, LOCATION L-7

Date		Purchased			Sold			Balance		
		Quantity	Unit Cost	Total Cost	Quantity	Unit Cost	Total Cost	Quantity	Unit Cost	Total Cost
2007										
Apr.	1							60	40	2,400
	5	90	50	4,500				60	40	
								90	50	6,900
	12				90	50	4,500			
					10	40	400	50	40	2,000
	16	150	60	9,000				50	40	
								150	60	11,000
	28				110	60	6,600	50	40	
								40	60	4,400
Totals		240		13,500	210		11,500	90		4,400

EXHIBIT **9.4**

Perpetual Inventory Record (LIFO)

Periodic and Perpetual Systems Compared

The value of the ending inventory and the cost of goods sold is identical under the FIFO periodic and the FIFO perpetual inventory systems. In both systems, we value the ending inventory units at the cost of the most recently acquired units.

Under LIFO costing, however, the valuations of the cost of goods sold and ending inventory may differ under periodic and perpetual. With periodic, we assume that costs at the beginning of the period are in the ending valuation. With the perpetual system, we may have used the beginning costs as we recorded sales. At each sale, LIFO assumes that we assign the latest costs incurred to goods sold.

The following table illustrates the different results of LIFO costing with the perpetual and periodic inventory systems for the sunglasses example:

	LIFO	
	Periodic Inventory	**Perpetual Inventory**
Inventory, April 1	$ 2,400 *	$ 2,400 *
Purchases	13,500	13,500
Total goods available for sale	$ 15,900	$ 15,900
Inventory, April 30	3,900	4,400
Cost of goods sold	$ 12,000	$ 11,500

*These beginning LIFO inventory amounts are the same for this illustration but are not likely to be the same in the future (see the April 30 inventory).

Similarly, the weighted average (periodic system) and the moving average (perpetual system) costing methods yield different results. Using the sunglasses example, the results are as follows:

	Average	
	Weighted Average Periodic Inventory	**Moving Average Perpetual Inventory**
Inventory, April 1	$ 2,400 *	$ 2,400 *
Purchases	13,500	13,500
Total goods available for sale	$ 15,900	$ 15,900
Inventory, April 30	4,770	5,085
Cost of goods sold	$ 11,130	$ 10,815

*These beginning weighted average inventory amounts are the same for this illustration but are not likely to be the same in the future (see the April 30 inventory).

COST FLOW ASSUMPTIONS COMPARED

Learning Goal 5   State the impact on the income statement and the balance sheet of using alternative inventory cost flow assumptions.

The *cost flow assumption* can have a significant effect on the results in the financial statements if prices are changing. The price of the sunglasses rose significantly, from $40 to $60 in the month of April. Using the data from the periodic system, we can illustrate the effect of rising prices on the income statement and balance sheet. We will make five additional assumptions:

1. The selling price for each of the 210 units sold is $90.

2. Operating expenses for the month are $4,000.

3. The company collects all revenues and pays all expenses in cash.

4. The income tax rate is 30%.

5. The beginning balance sheet amounts as of April 1 consisted of the following:

Cash	$10,000		
Inventory	2,400	Owners' equity	$12,400
Total assets	$12,400	Total owners' equity	$12,400

Exhibit 9.5 shows the income statement and balance sheet effects of using periodic FIFO, average cost, and LIFO.

INCOME STATEMENT

	FIFO	Average Cost	LIFO
Sales (210 units at $90)	$ 18,900	$ 18,900	$ 18,900
Cost of goods sold	10,500	11,130	12,000
Gross margin	$ 8,400	$ 7,770	$ 6,900
Operating expenses	4,000	4,000	4,000
Net income before income taxes	$ 4,400	$ 3,770	$ 2,900
Income tax expense	1,320	1,131	870
Net income	$ 3,080	$ 2,639	$ 2,030

BALANCE SHEET

	FIFO	Average Cost	LIFO
Cash	$ 10,080*	$ 10,269	$ 10,530
Inventory	5,400	4,770	3,900
Total assets	$ 15,480	$ 15,039	$ 14,430
Owners' equity	$ 15,480†	$ 15,039	$ 14,430

*Beginning cash ($10,000) + Sales ($18,900) - Purchases ($13,500) - Operating expense ($4,000) - Income tax expense ($1,320).
†Beginning owners' equity ($12,400) + Net income ($3,080).

EXHIBIT **9.5**

Effect of Alternative Inventory Cost Flow Assumptions on Income Statement and Balance Sheet

During a period of rising prices, FIFO costing results in the lowest cost of goods sold and highest reported net income. This occurs because older (lower) costs are matched with revenues. The greater profit shown under FIFO is misleading. This is because we must replace the units sold with units purchased at a current (higher) cost. In addition, the higher reported net income under the FIFO method will result in higher income taxes. Note that cash on the balance sheet is lowest under FIFO. This is a result of higher income tax payments. In times of rising prices, the net income reported under LIFO is the lowest of the three methods. This occurs because the cost of goods sold is greatest. However, it is a more accurate determination of net income since relatively current (higher) costs are matched with current revenues. During a period of falling prices, FIFO results in the highest cost of goods sold and lowest net income. LIFO gives opposite results.

Ending inventory appears in the balance sheet as a current asset. Therefore, the choice of cost flow assumption also affects this statement. A disadvantage of LIFO is that the balance sheet shows an inventory amount at earlier and out-of-date costs. In the sunglasses example, the balance sheet inventory amount shown under LIFO is $3,900 compared to $5,400 for FIFO. Since inventory is a significant current asset we must consider the method the company uses to assign inventory cost when analyzing the balance sheet.

LIFO: Additional Considerations

The notes to the financial statements are an integral part of the financial statements. Frequently, the notes contain important information that we must consider when evaluating the balance sheet and income statement. Exhibit 9.6 shows the current assets section of the balance sheet and the inventory note from the 2004 annual report of Caterpillar, Inc. As of December 31, 2004, total inventory on the balance sheet amounts to $4,675 million and comprises 22.4% of current assets. The inventory note to the financial statements reveals that Caterpillar has used mostly LIFO for inventory valuation. Many large companies use different inventory cost flow assumptions in their various divisions. A competing company, Deere & Company, uses LIFO for approximately 70% of inventories and FIFO for the remainder.

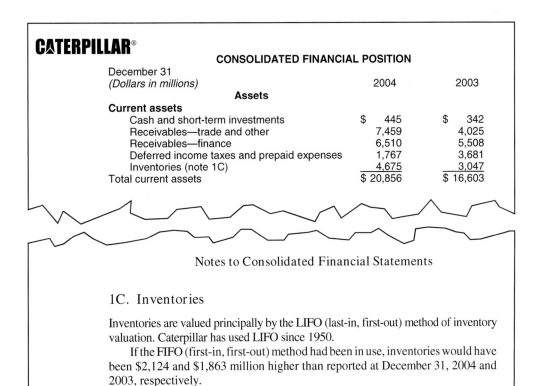

CATERPILLAR®

CONSOLIDATED FINANCIAL POSITION

December 31
(Dollars in millions)

	2004	2003
Assets		
Current assets		
Cash and short-term investments	$ 445	$ 342
Receivables—trade and other	7,459	4,025
Receivables—finance	6,510	5,508
Deferred income taxes and prepaid expenses	1,767	3,681
Inventories (note 1C)	4,675	3,047
Total current assets	$ 20,856	$ 16,603

Notes to Consolidated Financial Statements

1C. Inventories

Inventories are valued principally by the LIFO (last-in, first-out) method of inventory valuation. Caterpillar has used LIFO since 1950.

If the FIFO (first-in, first-out) method had been in use, inventories would have been $2,124 and $1,863 million higher than reported at December 31, 2004 and 2003, respectively.

EXHIBIT **9.6**

Current Assets Section of Balance Sheet and Inventory Note for Caterpillar, Inc.

Caterpillar has used LIFO since 1950. Using LIFO over an extended period of rising prices means that the inventory value shown on the balance sheet will probably be understated. This occurs because LIFO values the units at the earliest costs. For Caterpillar, Inc., the understatement is very large. The approximate current replacement cost of the inventory exceeds the LIFO inventory value by $2,124 million as of December 31, 2004. This means that the approximate replacement cost of the *total* inventory as of December 31, 2004, is $6,799 million ($4,675 + $2,124). This is 45.4% greater than the inventory amount shown on the balance sheet! In evaluating balance sheets of companies using LIFO, reference to the inventory note is important. The notes allow us to determine the total current value of the inventory.

Another problem with LIFO occurs when inventory quantities are reduced in a given year. When this happens, cost of goods sold will include relatively old costs accumulated in prior years. The resulting use of low-cost inventory quantities (called a *LIFO liquidation*) causes a lower cost of goods sold and a corresponding increase in net income and income tax expense for the period. Although companies using LIFO in a period of rising prices generally report lower profits (and pay less in income taxes), reducing inventory quantities from prior years can raise profits and taxes dramatically.

LOWER-OF-COST-OR-MARKET (LCM)

Learning Goal 6   Apply the lower-of-cost-or-market (LCM) rule to inventory valuation.

The various cost flow assumptions we have discussed are means of determining an inventory cost. Certain conditions decrease the value of some of the items in inventory. We should show the loss of value as an expense and as a decrease in inventory value in the period the loss occurs. To do this, accountants use a valuation concept known as **lower-of-cost-or-market (LCM)**. The term **market** means the cost of replacing the inventory items as of the balance sheet date. We also refer to it as **replacement cost**.

The process of valuing the inventory at LCM occurs at the end of the accounting period. We first determine cost by using any of the cost flow assumptions. Then we apply the LCM method (1) to each item individually, (2) to each major inventory category, or (3) to the entire inventory. Exhibit 9.7 shows the computation of lower of cost or market. The valuation under each procedure is as follows:

1. Applying LCM to each item individually, we would report the inventory as $5,200. This basis for LCM always produces the lowest possible inventory valuation.

2. Applying LCM to the inventory by major categories, we would report it as $5,500. This basis for LCM produces an inventory valuation that is equal to or greater than in **1** and equal to or smaller than in **3**.

3. Applying LCM to the inventory in total, we would report it as $5,800. This basis for LCM always produces the highest possible LCM inventory valuation.

						1	**2**	**3**
							Basis for LCM	
Item	Quantity	Unit Cost	Unit Market Price	Total Cost	Total Market	Item	Major Category	Total Inventory
Beach towels:								
Large	100	$10	$9	$ 1,000	$ 900	$ 900		
Regular	200	4	6	800	1,200	800		
Subtotal				$ 1,800	$ 2,100		$ 1,800	
Sunscreen:								
High protection	400	6	5	$ 2,400	$ 2,000	2,000		
Medium protection	300	4	3	1,200	900	900		
Low protection	200	3	4	600	800	600		
Subtotal				$ 4,200	$ 3,700		3,700	
Totals				$ 6,000	$ 5,800			$ 5,800
Inventory at lower of cost or market						$ 5,200	$ 5,500	$ 5,800

EXHIBIT 9.7

Application of Lower-of-Cost-or-Market (LCM)

The accounting procedures for recording the chosen LCM valuation may involve a direct reduction to the Inventory account or the use of a valuation (contra) account. More advanced courses cover the procedures.

INVENTORY ESTIMATION METHODS

Learning Goal 7   Estimate the cost of ending inventory by using the (a) gross margin method and (b) the retail inventory method.

Taking a physical inventory is often costly and time consuming. For some purposes—such as preparing monthly financial statements—accountants use an estimate. For example, a note in the annual financial report of Walgreen Company states:

> Cost of sales is primarily derived based upon point-of-scale scanning information with an estimate for shrinkage and adjusted based on periodic inventories.

The two common methods of estimating are the gross margin method and the retail inventory method.

Gross Margin Method

The **gross margin method** uses the historical average gross margin percent to estimate ending inventory. We compute the gross margin percent by dividing gross margin by net sales. Accountants frequently use the gross margin method to check on the accuracy of a physical count or to determine the amount of inventory stolen or destroyed in a fire. We estimate the ending inventory using the following three steps:

1. Compute the *cost of goods available for sale* by adding beginning inventory, net purchases, and transportation in.

2. Compute the *estimated cost of goods sold* by multiplying the net sales by an estimated cost of goods sold percent. The estimated cost of goods sold percent is 100% minus the average gross margin percent.

3. Compute the *cost of the estimated ending inventory* by subtracting estimated cost of goods sold (step **2**) from goods available for sale (step **1**).

Assume that Kelly's General Stores has averaged a gross margin of 40% of net sales. Since gross margin is 40% of sales, cost of goods sold as a percent of sales is 60% (100% – 40%). For the year ended December 31, 2007, the following information for Kelly's is available:

Inventory, January 1, 2007	$ 30,000
Purchases	140,000
Purchases returns and allowances	4,000
Transportation in	1,000
Sales	205,000
Sales returns and allowances	5,000

Using the three steps in the gross margin method, we compute the estimated ending inventory on December 31, 2007, as follows:

GROSS MARGIN METHOD OF ESTIMATING ENDING INVENTORY

1 Goods available for sale		
Inventory, January 1, 2007		$ 30,000
Purchases	$ 140,000	
Deduct: Purchases returns allowances	(4,000)	
Add: Transportation in	1,000	137,000
Total goods available for sale		$167,000
2 Estimated cost of goods sold		
Sales	$ 205,000	
Deduct: Sales returns and allowances	(5,000)	
Net sales	$ 200,000	
Multiply by cost of goods sold percent	× 0.60	
Estimated cost of goods sold		120,000
3 Estimated inventory, December 31, 2007		$ 47,000

Retail Inventory Method

The **retail inventory method** uses the current relationship between goods available for sale at *cost prices* and goods available for sale at *retail* (selling) prices to estimate ending inventory. Businesses use it where it is relatively easy to maintain records of inventory at both cost and retail prices. Department stores frequently use the retail method in preparing monthly or quarterly financial statements. The method estimates the ending inventory using the following four steps:

1. Compute the *goods available for sale* at both *cost* and *retail* prices.

2. Compute the *cost-to-retail* percent by dividing "goods available for sale at cost" by "goods available for sale at retail".

3. Compute *ending inventory at retail* by deducting net sales from goods available for sale at retail.

4. Compute *estimated ending inventory* at cost by multiplying ending inventory at retail (step **3**) by the cost-to-retail percent (step **2**).

Following is an example of the retail method using assumed data for Texas Department Store:

RETAIL METHOD OF ESTIMATING ENDING INVENTORY

	Cost	Retail
1 Goods available for sale		
Inventory, January 1, 2007	$ 28,000	$ 40,000
Add: Net purchases	182,000	260,000
Total goods available for sale	$210,000	$300,000
2 Cost-to-retail percent: $\frac{\$210,000}{\$300,000} = 70\%$		
3 Ending inventory at retail:		
Deduct: Net sales		250,000
Ending inventory at retail		$ 50,000
4 Estimated inventory at cost: ($50,000 × 0.70)	$ 35,000	

Evaluation of Estimating Methods

Both gross margin and retail inventory methods use a calculation of the cost of goods sold percent. The gross margin method uses past experience as a basis. The retail inventory method uses current experience. The gross margin method may be less reliable because past experience may be different from current experience. Both methods enable the company to prepare frequent financial statements without a physical count or perpetual inventory records. However, they do not eliminate the need for a physical count at least once a year.

CONSISTENCY IN THE APPLICATION OF INVENTORY VALUATION PROCEDURES

A business may use different procedures to value various classes of inventory. *Consistency* is most important. The company should follow the selected method consistently from year to year in each class. Inconsistency in inventory costing would make year-to-year comparisons of operating results and financial position meaningless.

Whatever the method of inventory valuation chosen, a company should follow it **consistently** from year to year.

The principle of consistency does not mean we cannot change from one accounting method to another. However, if we make such changes, notes to the financial statements should explain the nature of the change, the reason for the change, and the effect of the change on income, and why the new principle is preferable.

INVENTORY ERRORS

Learning Goal 8 Determine the effects of an inventory error on the income statement and the balance sheet.

An error in determining ending inventory will result in errors in cost of goods sold, gross margin, net income, current assets, and owners' equity. The ending inventory in one accounting period becomes the beginning inventory for the next period. Therefore, cost of goods sold, gross margin, and net income will have counterbalancing errors in the subsequent accounting period. Assuming no further errors are made, all balance sheet items will be correct at the end of the second period.

We can illustrate the effect of inventory errors on various financial statement items. Exhibit 9.8 shows the effect on cost of goods sold and selected financial statement items. It assumes that the 2007 ending inventory is understated by $1,000.

	2007	2008
Cost of goods sold		
Beginning inventory	correct	−1,000
Add: Purchases	correct	correct
Goods available for sale	correct	−1,000
Deduct: Ending inventory	−1,000	correct
Cost of goods sold	+1,000	−1,000
Financial statement balances		
Gross margin on income statement	−1,000	+1,000
Net income on income statement	−1,000	+1,000
Current assets (inventory) on balance sheet	−1,000	correct
Owners' equity on balance sheet	−1,000	correct

EXHIBIT **9.8**

Effect of Ending Inventory Error

The understatement of ending inventory in 2007 causes an overstatement of cost of goods sold. This in turn understates gross margin and net income for 2007. Since we close net income to owners' equity, that section of the balance sheet is also understated at the end of 2007. The understatement of inventory understates the current assets section.

The 2007 ending inventory is also the 2008 beginning inventory. In 2008, the understatement of beginning inventory causes both goods available for sale and cost of goods sold to be understated. This overstates gross margin and net income. By the end of 2008, the balance sheet shows the inventory and owners' equity at the correct amounts. The inventory on the balance sheet is correct because a new count has been used at the end of 2008. Owners' equity is now correct. The understatement of net income in 2007 is offset by an equal overstatement of net income in 2008.

INTERNAL CONTROL OVER INVENTORY

Just as separation of duties is important for the control of cash, it is also important for the control of inventory. Both cash and items in inventory are subject to loss, theft, and faulty record keeping. Lack of control over inventory leads to poor decisions by management.

Lack of controls over inventories can seriously damage a business. An excessive inventory is expensive to carry. Studies indicate that inventory carrying costs such as taxes, insurance, and warehousing may be 25% of the purchase price. This excludes the potential lost earnings (interest) on money tied up in inventories. On the other hand, a business must have sufficient items and quantities to provide customers with good service.

Maintaining a proper balance to avoid both inventory shortages and excesses requires organization and planning. Control must provide for day-to-day comparisons of projected purchases of inventory with current sales volume.

ANALYZING INFORMATION

Learning Goal 9   Analyze financial statement information for real-life companies.

To illustrate the analysis of inventories, we will use the information about Caterpillar shown in Exhibit 9.6 Caterpillar has used LIFO for a number of years and provides an excellent example of how financial information can be affected by inventory valuation methods.

Question 1. Considering the costing method in use, is the amount shown for cost of goods sold on the income statement representative of the current value of the goods sold? As a result, is there a good matching of revenues and current cost of goods sold on the income statement?

Analysis 1. Generally, LIFO provides the best matching of revenues and costs of goods sold on the income statement. This is because LIFO charges to cost of goods sold relatively recent and current costs. This will be true both when prices are rising or falling. Since Caterpillar uses LIFO, it is matching revenues with relatively current costs of goods sold on its income statement. Therefore, there is a good matching of revenues and current costs.

Question 2. Considering the costing method in use, is the amount shown for inventory on the balance sheet representative of the inventory's current value?

Analysis 2. Generally, LIFO results in an understated balance sheet inventory value in a period of rising prices. In assessing the current asset position of a company, it is important to determine the current inventory value. For Caterpillar, this means adding the excess of FIFO inventory value ($2,124 million) to the LIFO value ($4,675 million) to determine the total inventory current value ($6,799 million). If the inventory were to be used as collateral for a loan, indicating the inventory current value of $6,799 million instead of the carrying cost of $4,675 million is important.

The excess of FIFO cost over LIFO cost is the *LIFO reserve*. The LIFO reserve indicates cumulatively how much extra cost the company has charged to cost of goods sold since it began using LIFO. Therefore, it can also be used to estimate how much income taxes the company has saved through using LIFO. Assuming an income tax rate of 30%, Caterpillar has saved approximately $637.2 million ($2,124 million × 30%) since it began using LIFO in 1950. This is because the higher costs charged against revenues has resulted in lower income and therefore lower income tax expense.

A comprehensive review of all issues dealing with inventories is shown for Winn-Dixie in Problem 9-33 and for Wm. Wrigley Jr. Company in Problem 9-34. The Business Decision and

Communication Problem addresses inventory valuation issues for Pennzoil Company. The Comprehensive Analysis Case involves Molson-Coors Brewing Company.

LEARNING GOALS REVIEW

1. **Identify costs that should be included in inventory.**

   Merchandise inventory consists of all goods owned and held for sale in the normal course of business. The cost of an inventory item includes all expenditures incurred to bring the item to its existing condition and location. The inventory of a manufacturing firm includes materials inventory to be used in making products, the cost of items partly completed (work-in-process inventory), and finished goods inventory.

2. **Journalize entries to account for inventory transactions under the periodic and perpetual inventory systems.**

   In a periodic inventory system, we record purchases with a debit to Purchases and a credit to Accounts Payable. We debit the cost of merchandise inventory returned to Accounts Payable and credit it to Purchases Returns and Allowances. We calculate cost of goods sold at the end of the accounting period. Under a perpetual inventory system, we debit purchases of inventory to Merchandise Inventory and credit them to Accounts Payable. We debit the cost of returned inventory to Accounts Payable and credit it to Merchandise Inventory. When the business sells inventory, we debit Cost of Goods Sold and credit Merchandise Inventory for the cost of goods sold amount.

3. **Compute the cost of ending inventory and the cost of goods sold using (a) the specific identification method; (b) the weighted average cost method; (c) the first-in, first-out (FIFO) method; and (d) the last-in, first-out (LIFO) method under the periodic inventory system.**

   Under all methods, we deduct the cost assigned to ending inventory from cost of goods available for sale to determine cost of goods sold. (a) Specific identification determines total ending inventory cost by summing the costs of the specific items on hand. (b) The weighted average method computes a weighted average unit cost by dividing cost of goods available for sale by units available for sale. We multiply this weighted average by the number of units to find ending inventory. (c) The FIFO method assigns the latest unit costs to ending inventory units. (d) The LIFO method assigns the earliest unit costs to ending inventory units.

4. **Compute the cost of ending inventory and the cost of goods sold by using (a) the moving average cost method; (b) the first-in, first-out (FIFO) method; and (c) the last-in, first-out (LIFO) method under the perpetual inventory system.**

   Under all methods, the cost assigned to ending inventory is the cost of units not transferred out to cost of goods sold. (a) Under the moving average cost method, we cost units sold at a continuous weighted average cost. This average changes whenever additional units are purchased at a different cost. (b) Under the FIFO method, we assume the units sold during the period are from the oldest remaining batches. (c) Under the LIFO method, we assume the units sold during the period are from the latest remaining batches on hand at the time of each sale.

5. **State the impact on the income statement and balance sheet of using alternative inventory cost flow assumptions.**

   When prices are rising, FIFO results in the lowest cost of goods sold and highest reported net income. However, the higher reported net income under FIFO will result in higher income taxes. In contrast, the net income reported under LIFO would be lowest. On the balance sheet, LIFO states ending inventory at relatively old costs. FIFO states ending inventory at relatively current costs.

6. **Apply the lower-of-cost-or-market (LCM) rule to inventory valuation.**
    The lower-of-cost-or-market rule states that inventory should be recorded at either the replacement cost or the cost to acquire the inventory, whichever is less. At the end of the accounting period, we compare that cost for each item, category, or total inventory to the replacement cost, or market. If the market value is less, we adjust the inventory value to market.

7. **Estimate the cost of ending inventory by using (a) the gross margin method and (b) the retail inventory method.**
    (a) The gross margin method estimates cost of goods sold by multiplying the net sales by the estimated cost percent (100% minus the gross margin percent). We subtract the estimated cost of goods sold from the cost of goods available for sale to determine the estimated ending inventory. (b) The retail inventory method deducts the sales during the period from the total goods available for sale priced at retail. We convert this inventory at retail to cost by applying the cost percent (ratio of cost of goods available for sale to their retail price).

8. **Determine the effects of an inventory error on the income statement and the balance sheet.**
    An error in determining ending inventory will result in errors in the items computed from inventory: cost of goods sold, gross margin, net income, current assets, and owners' equity. Since the ending inventory for one period becomes the beginning inventory for the next period, that period will show counterbalancing errors in cost of goods sold, gross margin, and net income. At the end of the second period, all balance sheet items will be correct if no further errors have been made.

9. **Analyze financial statement information for real-life companies.**
    Overall, we want to assess the impact of inventory methods on the income statement and the balance sheet. Questions we may ask are: (1) Is there a good matching of revenues and current cost of goods sold on the income statement? (2) Is the amount shown for inventory on the balance sheet representative of the inventory's current value?

DEMONSTRATION PROBLEM

Periodic and Perpetual Inventory Systems

Jogger Company had the following beginning inventory, purchases, and sales of running shoes during the month of August 2007:

2007

Aug.	1	Balance on hand is 100 pairs of shoes at $10 per pair.
	4	Sold 50 pairs of shoes at $25 per pair.
	23	Purchased 200 pairs of shoes at $17.50 per pair.
	27	Sold 130 pairs of shoes at $28 per pair.

REQUIRED

1. **(LG 3)** Assuming that Jogger Company uses the periodic inventory system, determine ending inventory and cost of goods sold, using (a) the weighted average cost flow assumption, (b) the FIFO cost flow assumption, and (c) the LIFO cost flow assumption.

2. **(LG 4)** Assuming that Jogger Company uses the perpetual inventory system, determine ending inventory and cost of goods sold, using (a) the moving average cost flow assumption, (b) the FIFO cost flow assumption, and (c) the LIFO cost flow assumption.

SOLUTION

Solution Approach

1. Begin by computing the total units and the total cost of the units available for sale. Price the units in ending inventory under the various cost flow assumptions to determine the value of the ending inventory. Subtract the ending inventory amount from the cost of goods available for sale to determine the cost of goods sold.

2. Set up perpetual inventory records similar to Exhibits 9.2 9.3 and 9.4

Requirement 1

Basic computations: determination of (1) cost of goods available for sale, (2) units sold, and (3) units in ending inventory:

	Units	Unit Cost	Total Cost
Beginning inventory	100	$10.00	$1,000
Purchases:			
August 23	200	17.50	3,500
1. Total goods available for sale	300		$ 4,500

	Units
Sales:	
August 4	50
27	130
2. Total units sold	180
3. Inventory, August 31 (units)	120

a. *Weighted average on a periodic basis*

$$\text{Weighted average unit cost} = \frac{\$4,500}{300} = \$15.$$

**WEIGHTED AVERAGE ENDING INVENTORY VALUATION
(120 UNITS)**

At weighted average unit cost, 120 units at $15	$ 1,800

**WEIGHTED AVERAGE COST OF GOODS SOLD
(180 UNITS)**

Cost of goods available for sale (300 units)	$ 4,500
Deduct: Ending inventory at weighted average (120 units)	1,800
Cost of goods sold	$ 2,700

b. *FIFO on a Periodic Basis*

FIFO ENDING INVENTORY VALUATION
(120 UNITS)

Purchase Lot	Units	Unit Cost	Total Cost
August 23 purchase	120	$17.50	$2,100
Ending inventory	120		$2,100

FIFO COST OF GOODS SOLD
(180 UNITS)

Cost of goods available for sale (300 units)	$ 4,500
Deduct: Ending inventory at FIFO (120 units)	2,100
Cost of goods sold	$ 2,400

c. *LIFO on a Periodic Basis*

LIFO ENDING INVENTORY VALUATION
(120 UNITS)

Purchase Lot	Units	Unit Cost	Total Cost
August 1 inventory	100	$10.00	$ 1,000
August 23 purchase	20	$17.50	350
Ending inventory	120		$1,350

LIFO COST OF GOODS SOLD
(180 UNITS)

Cost of goods available for sale (300 units)	$ 4,500
Deduct: Ending inventory at LIFO (120 units)	1,350
Cost of goods sold	$ 3,150

Requirement 2

a. *Moving average on a perpetual basis*

PERPETUAL INVENTORY RECORD (MOVING AVERAGE)
Item: Running shoes (Pairs)

Date	Ref.	Purchased (or Received) Quantity	Unit Cost	Total Cost	Sold (or Issued) Quantity	Unit Cost	Total Cost	Balance Quantity	Unit Cost	Total Cost
2007										
Aug. 1 Balance								100	10.00	1,000
4					50	10.00	500	50	10.00	500
23		200	17.50	3,500				250	16.00*	4,000
27					130	16.00	2,080	120	16.00	1,920
Totals		200		3,500	180		2,580	120		1,920

$$*\frac{\$500 + \$3,500}{50 + 200} = \$16.$$

	Units	Total Cost
Ending inventory (120 × $16.00)	120	$1,920
Cost of goods sold ($500 + $2,080)	180	$2,580

b. *FIFO on a perpetual basis*

PERPETUAL INVENTORY RECORD (FIFO)
Item: Running shoes (Pairs)

Date		Ref.	Purchased (or Received)			Sold (or Issued)			Balance		
			Quantity	Unit Cost	Total Cost	Quantity	Unit Cost	Total Cost	Quantity	Unit Cost	Total Cost
2007											
Aug.	1	Balance							100	10.00	1,000
	4					50	10.00	500	50	10.00	500
	23		200	17.50	3,500				50	10.00	
									200	17.50	4,000
	27					50	10.00	500			
						80	17.50	1,400	120	17.50	2,100
Totals			200		3,500	180		2,400	120		2,100

	Units	Total Cost
Ending inventory (120 × $17.50)	120	$2,100
Cost of goods sold ($500 + $500 + $1,400)	180	$2,400

c. *LIFO on a perpetual basis*

PERPETUAL INVENTORY RECORD (LIFO)
Item: Running shoes (Pairs)

Date		Ref.	Purchased (or Received)			Sold (or Issued)			Balance		
			Quantity	Unit Cost	Total Cost	Quantity	Unit Cost	Total Cost	Quantity	Unit Cost	Total Cost
2007											
Aug.	1	Balance							100	10.00	1,000
	4					50	10.00	500	50	10.00	500
	23		200	17.50	3,500				50	10.00	
									200	17.50	4,000
	27					130	17.50	2,275	50	10.00	
									70	17.50	1,725
Totals			200		3,500	180		2,775	120		1,725

	Units	Total Cost
Ending inventory [(50 × $10.00) + (70 × $17.50)]	120	$1,725
Cost of goods sold ($500 + $2,275)	180	$2,775

GLOSSARY

average cost flow assumption The cost of both items sold and items in ending inventory is assumed to consist of weighted average unit cost.

consistency The concept that uniformity-with full disclosure for any departures-from year to year, especially in inventory pricing, cost allocation, and financial statement presentation, is essential for meaningful comparisons.

cost of an inventory item The expenditures incurred in bringing an inventory item to its existing condition and location.

first-in, first-out (FIFO) inventory costing A method of determining the cost of goods on hand and the cost of goods sold, based on the assumption that the cost flows of the units sold are in the order in which they were acquired.

gross margin method A method of estimating inventory value by deducting the estimated cost of goods sold from the total cost of goods available for sale. We compute the estimated cost of goods sold by multiplying net sales by the cost of goods sold percent.

last-in, first-out (LIFO) inventory costing A costing method based on the assumption that the cost of goods sold should be calculated on prices paid for the most recently acquired units, and that the units on hand consist of the oldest units acquired.

lower-of-cost-or-market (LCM) An inventory valuation method by which units are valued at the lower of either original acquisition cost or replacement cost (market).

market In LCM, the cost of replacing an item at the balance sheet date.

moving average inventory costing A perpetual inventory costing method by which the cost of each purchase is added to the cost of units on hand, and the total cost is divided by the total quantity on hand to find the new average unit price each time new merchandise is received at a different price.

periodic inventory system Determining the amount of merchandise on hand at the end of each accounting period by counting the goods on hand and making a list showing physical quantities and cost.

perpetual inventory system A system in which a continuous record of merchandise on hand is maintained.

replacement cost The current cost of replacing inventory items, using the usual sources of supply and usual quantities.

retail inventory method A method of estimating inventory value in which the ratio of the cost of goods available at cost and goods available at retail is used to convert the inventory valued at retail to cost.

specific identification inventory costing An inventory costing method by which the unit cost is identified specifically with the purchase lot from which the inventory item comes.

weighted average inventory costing A costing method by which the ending inventory and the cost of goods sold are priced at the end of each accounting period at a unit cost computed by dividing the total cost of goods available for sale by the physical units available for sale.

QUESTIONS FOR GROUP LEARNING

Q9-1. How do the perpetual and the periodic inventory systems differ? Does the perpetual inventory system eliminate the need for a physical inventory count? Explain.

Q9-2. A fresh fruit store would normally try to sell the first cases of fruit received first. As a result, must the FIFO inventory costing method also be used? Explain.

Q9-3. Explain the effect on the balance sheet valuation and on the income determination of the use of LIFO as compared with FIFO (a) if prices have risen during the year, and (b) if prices have fallen during the year.

Q9-4. Under the LIFO inventory costing method, explain why using periodic or perpetual inventory systems may result in different amounts for cost of goods sold. Why does this not occur under FIFO?

Q9-5. During a period of rising prices, which inventory costing method would management select in order to achieve each of the following objectives:

    a. Highest amount of net sales on income statement.

    b. Highest amount of gross margin.

    c. Highest amount of net income on income statement.

    d. Current value for inventory on balance sheet.

    e. Lowest amount of income taxes for the owner.

Q9-6. Explain why the inventory costing method chosen has an impact on both the income statement and the balance sheet.

Q9-7. In a period of changing prices, is it possible to select an inventory costing method that optimizes the presentation on both the income statement and the balance sheet? Explain.

Q9-8. Define the term *market* as used in LCM inventory valuation. What are reasons that a business would price inventory at LCM?

Q9-9. Compare the gross margin method with the retail inventory method.

Q9-10. An audit of the records of Roenick Company showed that the ending inventory on December 31, 2007, was overstated by $7,000. What was the effect of the error on the income statements for 2007 and 2008? What was the overall effect for the two-year period, assuming no further errors were made in inventories?

Q9-11. Why is it important that the selected inventory cost flow method be applied consistently from year to year? Does compliance with the principle of consistency preclude a change from FIFO to LIFO?

Q9-12. How would overstatements or understatements of inventory affect net income in the period in which the error was made? In the following year?

EXERCISES

E9-13. **Computation of inventory cost (LG 1)** Vanna's Dress Shop purchased 50 high-style dresses from Fashion Designers of Paris. Each dress had a list price of $300. A 2% discount was allowed because Vanna's paid cash at the time of the delivery. The buyer paid shipping and insurance charges and they amounted to $200. Each dress will have a retail price of $600 in Vanna's Dress Shop. Cost of a special newspaper ad to advertise the dresses was $90. Vanna's hired extra sales staff on opening day at a cost of $400 to help sell the dresses. Compute the total cost of the dresses that Vanna's will record in its Merchandise Inventory account prior to any sales transactions. Assume that Vanna's uses a perpetual inventory system.

E9-14. **Journal entries for periodic and perpetual inventory systems (LG 2)** Make general journal entries to record the following transactions under (a) a periodic inventory system and (b) a perpetual inventory system. There is no beginning merchandise inventory.

2007

May	4	Received 500 calculators from AddFast Company at a cost of $2 each, terms n/10.
	6	Returned 30 defective calculators to AddFast Company for full credit.
	8	Sold 180 calculators for $5 each.
	14	Paid AddFast Company the balance due on the account.

E9-15. **Income statement using specific identification (LG 3)** In October 2007, Guten Company began buying and selling printing presses. Transactions for October, during which the cost to purchase a press increased, were as follows:

2007

Oct.	3	Purchased machine no. 1 for $14,000.
	7	Purchased machine no. 2 for $26,000.
	10	Purchased machine no. 3 for $17,000.
	24	Sold machine no. 1 for $35,000.
	28	Sold machine no. 3 for $40,000.

Prepare an income statement for the month of October through gross margin on sales, using the specific identification method of inventory costing.

E9-16. **Income determination using specific identification (LG 3)** Using the data in E9-15, assume that instead of selling machine no. 1 on October 24, Guten Company sold machine no. 2. What dollar impact would this decision have on gross margin for the month of October?

E9-17. **Inventory valuation and cost of goods sold assuming FIFO and LIFO (LG 3)** The beginning inventory, purchases, and sales of hairbrushes by Pattison Store for the month of July 2007 were as follows:

2007

Jul	1	Inventory on hand consisted of 100 units at $3 each.
	10	Sold 50 units at $10.
	11	Purchased 40 units at $5 each.
	17	Purchased 70 units at $6 each.
	20	Sold 50 units at $11 each.
	27	Purchased 60 units at $8 each.
	29	Sold 40 units at $11 each.

Compute the July 31 inventory valuation and July cost of goods sold using (a) periodic FIFO and (b) periodic LIFO.

E9-18. **Recordkeeping on perpetual records using FIFO and LIFO (LG 4)** The Soapy Sales Company buys and sells washing machines. Purchases and sales during June 2007 are shown below.

Date	Purchases	Sales
2007		
Jun. 3	80 units at $300	
11		150 units
14	70 units at 310	
18	90 units at 315	
20		60 units
25	95 units at 325	
28		170 units

The inventory on June 1 consisted of 100 units at $290 each. Enter the beginning inventory on a perpetual inventory record and record the transactions using the FIFO assumption. Repeat the process, changing the assumption to LIFO.

E9-19. **Inventory valuation and cost of goods sold assuming weighted average (LG 3)** The following data are from purchase invoices and sales tickets for a notebook at Hendrix College bookstore during April 2007:

	Purchases				Sales	
Date	Quantity	Cost		Date	Quantity	
Apr. 4	400	$1.40		Apr. 8	240	
13	300	1.50		11	120	
25	200	1.60		19	200	
				22	100	

The balance on April 1 was 200 notebooks at a cost of $1.20 each. Using the weighted average assumption (periodic system), compute (a) inventory valuation on April 30 and (b) cost of notebooks sold in April.

E9-20. **Recordkeeping with perpetual inventory using moving average (LG 4)** Record on a perpetual inventory record the activity of the following item stocked and sold by Byberry Community College bookstore during November 2007. Use the moving average cost flow assumption.

2007

Nov.	1	Balance on hand is 300 units at a cost of $3 each.
	8	Sold 100 units.
	11	Purchased 200 units at $4 each.
	22	Sold 300 units.
	28	Purchased 400 units at $5 each.

E9-21. **Effect of inventory cost flow assumptions on income statement (LG 3, 5)** Surf Tech Company was formed on January 1, 2007, for the purpose of selling personal computers to college students. Summary information regarding purchases, sales, and operating expenses during 2007 and 2008 is as follows:

2007

Purchased 400 computers at a unit cost of $600 each.

Sold 350 computers at a sales price of $1,000 each.

Operating expenses for the year totaled $50,000. The income tax rate is 30%.

2008

Purchased 450 computers at a unit cost of $800 each.

Sold 400 computers at a sales price of $1,000 each.

Operating expenses for the year totaled $50,000. The income tax rate is 30%.

Prepare income statements for 2007 and 2008 assuming (a) the FIFO cost flow assumption is used and (b) the LIFO cost flow assumption is used. Briefly comment on which inventory cost flow assumption results in a better matching of revenues and expenses for 2007 and for 2008.

E9-22. Three LCM valuations and their effect on gross margin (LG 6) Sack Time Beds compiled the following information for its inventory of August 31, 2007, the end of the accounting year:

| | | Units | |
Item	Quantity	Cost	Market
Frames:			
Type F-1	100	$14	$15
Type F-12	200	26	27
Type F-15	60	21	20
Spring (sets):			
Type S-1	500	6	8
Type S-12	1,000	10	9
Type S-15	300	8	6

Compute the ending inventory at the lower of cost or market, applied to each item, to each category, and to the entire inventory. Briefly explain what the effect of each application of LCM has on the gross margin in the current year and in the following year.

E9-23. Estimation of inventory by gross margin method (LG 7) The entire inventory of New Mexico Toy Company was destroyed by fire on June 22, 2007. The books of the company (kept in a fireproof vault) showed the value of goods on hand on June 1 to be $80,000. Transactions for the period June 1 through June 22 resulted in the following amounts:

Sales	$280,000	Purchases returns	$2,000
Sales returns	4,000	Transportation in	1,000
Purchases	160,000		

The rate of gross margin on net sales for the previous three years averaged 30%. Determine the cost of the inventory destroyed by the fire.

E9-24. **Estimation of inventory by the retail method (LG 7)** Phoenix Traders estimates its merchandise inventory when preparing monthly financial statements. The following information was available on April 30:

	Cost	Retail
Merchandise inventory, April 1	$ 75,000	$100,000
Purchases during April (net)	345,000	600,000
Sales during April (net)		520,000

Compute the estimated inventory on April 30 using the retail inventory method.

E9-25. **Inventory errors (LG 8)** At the end of the 2007 reporting year, Walnut Company made an error in pricing its inventory under the periodic inventory system. As a result, ending inventory was overstated by $4,000. Assuming that the error was never discovered and corrected, what effect would the error have on each of the following financial statement amounts for 2007 and 2008?

	2007	2008
Purchases	_____	_____
Cost of goods sold	_____	_____
Gross margin	_____	_____
Inventory (end-of-year balance sheet)	_____	_____
Owners' equity (end-of-year)	_____	_____

PROBLEMS

P9-26. **Journal entries for a perpetual inventory system (LG 2)** Manders Company maintains perpetual inventory records. It receives all purchases F.O.B. destination and makes returns at the supplier's expense. Following are summary data from the records for January 2007, the first month of operations:

Total purchases (on account)	$340,000
Total returns of defective merchandise for credit	6,000
Operating expenses (paid in cash)	130,000
Total sales (on account)	470,000
Cost of goods sold per stock records	240,000

REQUIRED

1. Prepare summary general journal entries dated January 31 to record purchases, purchase returns, sales, and operating expenses.

2. Journalize all closing entries, including the transfer of net income to retained earnings.

P9-27. **Computation of inventory and cost of goods sold: periodic inventory system (LG 3)** Omaha Community College bookstore had the following beginning inventory and purchases of mechanical pencils during 2007:

Date 2007	Units	Unit Cost	Total Cost
Inventory, January 1, 2007	800	$1.00	$ 800
Purchases:			
January 3	700	1.10	770
April 5	600	1.15	690
August 20	900	1.40	1,260
December 2	1,000	1.68	1,680
Total goods available for sale	4,000		$ 5,200

A physical count of mechanical pencils at December 31, 2007, reveals that 1,600 pencils are left. Therefore, it was assumed that 2,400 pencils were sold during 2007.

REQUIRED

Under the periodic inventory system, determine: the ending inventory and cost of goods sold, using (1) the weighted average cost flow method, (2) the FIFO cost flow method, and (3) the LIFO cost flow method.

P9-28. **Recordkeeping with perpetual inventory (LG 4)** Ultimate Tools uses a perpetual inventory system. During May 2007, the company experienced the following activity with a wrench, stock number W-100:

2007

May	1	Balance on hand is 200 units at $8 each.
	6	Sold 160 units.
	10	Received 160 units at $8.75 each.
	24	Sold 180 units.
	30	Received 80 units at $9.50 each.

REQUIRED

Record the beginning balance and the May activity on perpetual inventory records, and determine: the ending inventory valuation and the cost of goods sold, using (1) the moving average cost flow assumption, (2) the FIFO cost flow assumption, and (3) the LIFO cost flow assumption.

P9-29. **Effect of cost flow assumptions on financial statements in a period of rising prices(LG 3, 5)** On June 1, 2007, investors established E.P. Company with an investment of $80,000 in cash. Purchases and sales of an item during the month are shown below:

2007

June	1	Purchased 3,000 units at $10.
	10	Sold 1,800 units at $20.
	13	Purchased 2,000 units at $12.
	17	Sold 2,000 units at $20.
	22	Purchased 2,500 units at $14.
	29	Sold 2,200 units at $20.

Operating expenses were $40,000. The company completed cash settlements on all transactions by the end of the month. There were 1,500 units remaining in inventory on June 30, 2007.

REQUIRED

1. Compute the cost assigned to ending inventory (periodic system) and the cost of goods sold using (a) FIFO and (b) LIFO.

2. Prepare income statements and balance sheets based on each of the foregoing two methods of inventory valuation. The income tax rate is 30%.

3. Explain why the different methods yield different results.

4. What factors should E.P. consider in its choice of inventory valuation method?

5. Which method would you recommend? Explain.

6. FIFO reflects price increases of goods on hand in net income, but these are not real profits because, as the inventory is depleted, replacement costs will be higher. Do you agree? Explain.

P9-30. **Estimation of inventories by the gross margin and retail inventory methods (LG 7)** Selected data for two companies are as follows:

Company A

Inventory, September 1, 2007	$180,000
Net purchases during September	500,000
Net sales during September	900,000

Average gross margin percent for the past three years has been 30% of sales.

Company B

Net sales	$620,000
Purchases at cost	320,000
Purchases at retail	520,000
Inventory, June 1, 2007 (cost)	100,000
Inventory, June 1, 2007 (retail)	180,000

REQUIRED

1. Estimate the September 30 inventory of Company A using the gross margin method.

2. Estimate the June 30 inventory of Company B using the retail method.

P9-31. **Effect of overstatement of ending inventory and failure to record purchases (LG 8)** Mozart Company uses a periodic inventory system. Summary income statements for the years ended 2007 and 2008 are shown below (ignore income taxes for this problem):

	2007	2008
Sales revenue	$80,000	$75,000
Cost of goods sold	52,000	41,000
Gross margin	$28,000	$34,000
Operating expenses	20,000	20,000
Net income	$ 8,000	$14,000

The president of Mozart Company is disturbed that although total sales revenue increased in 2008, net income decreased to approximately 50% of 2007. In reviewing the accounting records and supporting documents, she discovers that two separate errors were made in recording inventory transactions at the end of 2007 that were never discovered in 2008. First, during the inventory count at the end of 2007, $3,000 of inventory was counted twice. Second, $5,000 of inventory purchased at the end of 2007 was not recorded as a purchase and was not counted as part of inventory as of December 31, 2007. The $5,000 of merchandise was shipped F.O.B. shipping point on December 26, 2007, and did not arrive until January 2, 2008, when it was recorded as a purchase in 2008.

REQUIRED

1. Prepare corrected income statements for 2007 and 2008.

2. Explain what effect each of the errors will have on the following balance sheet amounts as of December 31, 2007, and December 31, 2008:

   a. Total assets.

   b. Total liabilities.

   c. Total owners' equity.

P9-32. Effect of inventory errors (LG 8) At Saddle Company, where a periodic inventory system is used, the December 31, 2007, inventory was undervalued by $20,000. This occurred when the company failed to include some merchandise that it had received and recorded in the Purchases account. As a result, additional orders were placed at the beginning of 2008, resulting in a duplication of items on hand that was not corrected until return of the merchandise three months later for credit. The company's short-term borrowing rate to finance the unnecessary purchase was 12% per year. Saddle Company paid transportation costs of $80 for the return.

REQUIRED

1. What was the effect of the error on the net income for 2007?

2. What was the effect of the error on 2008 net income? Support your answer with assumptions and computations.

3. What was the ultimate effect of the error on the owners' equity?

P9-33. Comprehensive analysis of inventory for Winn-Dixie (LG 9) Assume that as of June 30, 2004, Winn-Dixie listed total merchandise inventories of $991.6 million on the balance sheet. The inventory total was $1,046.9 million as of June 25, 2003. A note to the financial statements included the following information on inventories:

INVENTORY VALUATION:
Inventory cost is determined using the last-in, first-out (LIFO) method for inventories. The excess of FIFO cost over LIFO cost was $219,700 and $214,547 at June 30, 2004 and June 25, 2003 respectively.

REQUIRED

1. As of June 30, 2004, what is the approximate current value of total inventories for Winn-Dixie?

2. If Winn-Dixie were applying for a bank loan, what amount would the Company like to disclose as the total inventory value?

3. Assuming an average income tax rate of 30%, approximately how much has Winn-Dixie saved in income taxes since it started using LIFO? (Hint: the excess of replacement cost over LIFO cost represents the additional amount charged to cost of goods sold over the years. This difference is sometimes referred to as the *LIFO reserve*.)

4. Assuming an average income tax rate of 30%, approximately how much has Winn-Dixie saved in income taxes in 2004 as a result of using LIFO? (Hint: the excess of replacement cost over LIFO cost is a cumulative amount.)

5. Assume Winn-Dixie experiences a sharp decrease in inventory quantities in 2005 and has a LIFO liquidation.

a. Would this cause 2005 cost of goods sold to be higher or lower? Explain briefly.

b. Would this cause 2005 net income to be higher or lower? Explain briefly.

c. Would this cause 2005 income taxes to be higher or lower? Explain briefly.

P9-34. **Comprehensive analysis of inventory for Wm. Wrigley Jr. Company (LG 9)**
Wm. Wrigley Jr. Company has manufactured chewing gum since 1891. As of December 31, 2004, Wrigley Company listed total merchandise inventories of $398,107,000 on the balance sheet. Total current assets on December 31, 2004, were $1,505,910,000. For 2004, net sales was $3,648,592,000 and cost of goods sold was $1,609,978,000. The following inventory note is taken from Wrigley's 2004 annual financial report:

Inventories

Inventories are valued at cost on a last-in, first-out (LIFO) basis for U.S. companies and at the lower of cost (principally first-in, first-out basis) or market for international associated companies. Inventories totaled $398,107,000 and $349,968,000 at December 31, 2004 and 2003, respectively, including $137,471,000 and $129,431,000, respectively, valued at cost on a LIFO basis. If current costs had been used, such inventories would have been $1,952,000 and $5,173,000 higher than reported at December 31, 2004 and 2003, respectively.

REQUIRED

1. For the year ended December 31, 2004, is the amount shown for cost of goods sold on the income statement representative of the current value of the goods sold? Briefly explain.

2. For the year ended December 31, 2004, compute cost of goods sold as a percent of net sales. If the Company had a LIFO liquidation in 2004, would the cost of goods sold percent be higher or lower?

3. As of December 31, 2004, what is the approximate current value of total inventories for Wrigley Company?

4. As of December 31, 2004, what is the approximate current value of inventories valued on a LIFO basis for Wrigley Company?

5. If Wrigley were applying for a bank loan, what amount would the Company like to disclose as an inventory value?

6. Assuming an average income tax rate of 30%, approximately how much has Wrigley saved in income taxes since it started using LIFO?

PRACTICE CASE

Inventories and cost of goods sold (LG 3-5) Medical Style Company was incorporated on December 1, 2007, to sell nursing uniforms. Medical Style Company had the following transactions during the month of December 2007:

2007

Dec.	1	Purchased 50 nursing uniforms on account from Hospital Supply Company at $38 each, terms n/10.
	4	Sold 35 uniforms at $52 each for cash.
	6	Returned 5 defective uniforms to Hospital Supply Company for full credit.
	11	Paid the balance due Hospital Supply Company.
	16	Purchased 70 uniforms on account from Hospital Supply Company at $40 each, terms n/30.
	22	Sold 74 uniforms at $60 each for cash.
	24	Purchased 50 uniforms on account from Hospital Supply Company at $45 each, terms n/30.
	31	Operating expenses for the month of December totaled $750.
	31	A physical count revealed that 56 uniforms were on hand at the end of the month.

REQUIRED

1. Assuming that Medical Style Company uses the periodic inventory system, prepare an income statement for the month ended December 31, 2007, using (a) the FIFO cost flow assumption and (b) the LIFO cost flow assumption. The income tax rate is 30%.

2. Assuming that Medical Style Company uses the perpetual inventory system, prepare an income statement for the month ended December 31, 2007, using (a) the FIFO cost flow assumption and (b) the LIFO cost flow assumption.

3. Briefly explain why the periodic and perpetual inventory systems may yield the same or different results for cost of goods sold for (a) the FIFO cost flow assumption and (b) the LIFO cost flow assumption.

4. Assuming that a periodic inventory system is used, which inventory cost flow assumption would you recommend if the president of the business, Marge Berkel, desired:

   a. to report the highest amount of net income?

   b. to show inventory on the balance sheet at relatively current values?

   c. to report the largest amount of owners' equity?

   d. to pay the smallest amount of personal income taxes?

BUSINESS DECISION AND COMMUNICATION PROBLEM

Comparison of inventory cost flow methods for Pennzoil Company with competing oil companies (LG 9) You have taken a job as an investment analyst specializing in oil stocks. In reviewing a recent annual report of Pennzoil Company, you read the following information concerning inventory methods(assumed data):

Inventories

Substantially all inventories are reported at cost using the last in, first out ("LIFO") method, which is lower than market. Inventories valued on the LIFO method totaled $156,400,000 at the end of the current year. The current cost of these inventories was approximately $170,700,000.

Your supervisor is interested in how selected financial statement items compare for Pennzoil Company and its competitors. Assume for this problem that costs are rising and that most other companies in the oil industry are using FIFO.

REQUIRED

Write a memo to your supervisor, Reggie Leach. In your memo, discuss ways in which the amounts shown in the financial statements for the following items may or may not be comparable for Pennzoil and its competitors for the current year.

1. Cost of goods sold.

2. Net income.

3. Income tax expense.

4. Current assets.

5. Owners' equity.

ETHICAL DILEMMA

Managing reported net income under LIFO (LG 5) You are the chief accountant for a major chemical company. Your company has used LIFO consistently during a period of rising prices. Currently, the units in ending inventory are valued far below their current cost. The president of the company calls you into his office on December 1, 2007, and comments that net income for the year ended December 31, 2007, will be very low compared to previous years. He asks you to defer all new purchases of inventory until January 2008 and to decrease the inventory on hand to levels that are below the amount considered acceptable for the company.

REQUIRED
What is the motivation behind the president's request? How would you respond?

COMPREHENSIVE ANALYSIS CASE MOLSON-COORS BREWING COMPANY

Analyzing Molson-Coors Brewing Company for the Period 2004-2002 Listed below are comparative income statements and balance sheets with common-size percents for 2004-2002 (in millions). Also included are selected ratio statistics. Please provide a brief explanation for your answer to each question.

MOLSON COORS BREWING COMPANY
COMPARATIVE COMMON-SIZE INCOME STATEMENTS
For the year ended Dec. 26, 2004, Dec. 28, 2003, and Dec. 29, 2002
(In millions)

	2004 $	2004 %	2003 $	2003 %	2002 $	2002 %
Revenues	$ 4,305.8	100.0%	$ 4,000.1	100.0%	$ 3,776.3	100.0%
Cost of goods sold	$ 2,741.7	63.7%	$ 2,586.8	64.7%	$ 2,414.5	63.9%
Gross margin	$ 1,564.1	36.3%	$ 1,413.3	35.3%	$ 1,361.8	36.1%
Operating expenses:						
Sales, marketing, general administrative	$ 1,223.2	28.4%	$ 1,106.0	27.6%	$ 1,057.2	28.0%
Research and development	$ -	0.0%	$ -	0.0%	$ -	0.0%
Other expense	$ (7.5)	-0.2%	$ -	0.0%	$ 6.3	0.2%
Other expense	$ -	0.0%	$ -	0.0%	$ -	0.0%
Total operating expenses	$ 1,215.7	28.2%	$ 1,106.0	27.6%	$ 1,063.5	28.2%
Operating income	$ 348.4	8.1%	$ 307.3	7.7%	$ 298.3	7.9%
Net interest expense (income)	$ 53.1	1.2%	$ 61.9	1.5%	$ 49.7	1.3%
Other expense (income)	$ (12.9)	-0.3%	$ (8.4)	-0.2%	$ (8.0)	-0.2%
Income before income taxes	$ 308.2	7.2%	$ 253.8	6.3%	$ 256.6	6.8%
Income taxes	$ 95.2	2.2%	$ 79.1	2.0%	$ 94.9	2.5%
Net income (loss) before unusual items	$ 213.0	4.9%	$ 174.7	4.4%	$ 161.7	4.3%
Other losses (gains) net of tax	$ 16.2	0.4%	$ -	0.0%	$ -	0.0%
Net income (loss)	$ 196.8	4.6%	$ 174.7	4.4%	$ 161.7	4.3%

MOLSON COORS BREWING COMPANY
COMPARATIVE COMMON-SIZE BALANCE SHEETS
Dec. 26, 2004, Dec. 28, 2003, and Dec. 29, 2003
(In millions)

	2004 $	2004 %	2003 $	2003 %	2002 $	2002 %
ASSETS						
Current:						
Cash & cash equivalents	$ 123.0	2.6%	$ 19.4	0.4%	$ 59.2	1.4%
Short-term investments	$ -	0.0%	$ -	0.0%	$ -	0.0%
Accounts receivable, net	$ 825.1	17.7%	$ 751.1	16.9%	$ 726.4	16.9%
Inventory	$ 234.8	5.0%	$ 209.5	4.7%	$ 215.2	5.0%
Other current assets	$ -	0.0%	$ -	0.0%	$ -	0.0%
Other current assets	$ 85.3	1.8%	$ 98.8	2.2%	$ 53.1	1.2%
Total current assets	$ 1,268.2	27.2%	$ 1,078.8	24.3%	$ 1,053.9	24.5%
Fixed:						
Property & equipment, net	$ 1,445.6	31.0%	$ 1,450.8	32.6%	$ 1,380.2	32.1%
Long-term investments	$ 140.6	3.0%	$ 193.6	4.4%	$ 300.3	7.0%
Intangibles & goodwill	$ 1,471.8	31.6%	$ 1,348.5	30.3%	$ 1,256.2	29.2%
Other assets	$ 331.3	7.1%	$ 373.0	8.4%	$ 306.8	7.1%
Total assets	$ 4,657.5	100.0%	$ 4,444.7	100.0%	$ 4,297.4	100.0%
LIABILITIES						
Current:						
Short-term debt	$ 38.5	0.8%	$ 91.2	2.1%	$ 144.0	3.4%
Accounts payable	$ 1,055.5	22.7%	$ 984.9	22.2%	$ 1,003.8	23.4%
Accrued salaries and benefits	$ 82.9	1.8%	$ 57.6	1.3%	$ -	0.0%
Unearned revenue	$ -	0.0%	$ -	0.0%	$ -	0.0%
Other current liabilities	$ -	0.0%	$ -	0.0%	$ -	0.0%
Total current liabilities	$ 1,176.9	25.3%	$ 1,133.7	25.5%	$ 1,147.8	26.7%
Long-term debt	$ 893.7	19.2%	$ 1,160.0	26.1%	$ 1,383.4	32.2%
Deferred income tax liabilities	$ 149.9	3.2%	$ 195.5	4.4%	$ 668.3	15.6%
Other long-term liabilities	$ 799.0	17.2%	$ 688.2	15.5%	$ 116.0	2.7%
Total liabilities	$ 3,019.5	64.8%	$ 3,177.4	71.5%	$ 3,315.5	77.2%
OWNERS' EQUITY						
Total owners' equity	$ 1,638.0	35.2%	$ 1,267.3	28.5%	$ 981.9	22.8%
Total liabilities and owners' equity	$ 4,657.5	100.0%	$ 4,444.7	100.0%	$ 4,297.4	100.0%

(Note: percents may not add to 100 due to rounding)

MOLSON COORS BREWING COMPANY
RATIO ANALYSIS SUMMARY
For the year ended Dec. 26, 2004, Dec. 28, 2003, and Dec. 29, 2002

	2004	2003	2002
SHORT-TERM LIQUIDITY RATIOS			
Current Ratio (Current Assets/Current Liabilities)	1.08	0.95	0.92
Quick Ratio (Cash + Short-term Investments + Accounts Receivable)/Current Liabilities	0.81	0.68	0.68
Accounts Receivable Turnover 1 (Revenues/Average Accounts Receivable)	5.46	5.41	
Accounts Receivable Turnover 2 (Revenues/Year-end Accounts Receivable)	5.22	5.33	5.20
Inventory Turnover 1 (Cost Goods Sold/Average Inventory)	12.34	12.18	
Inventory Turnover 2 (Cost Goods Sold/Year-end Inventory)	11.68	12.35	11.22
LONG-TERM SOLVENCY (LEVERAGE) RATIO			
Total Debt Ratio (Total Liabilities/Total Assets)	64.83%	71.49%	77.15%
PROFITABILITY RATIOS			
Gross Profit Margin (Gross Margin/Revenues)	36.33%	35.33%	36.06%
Operating Profit Margin (Operating Income/Revenues)	8.09%	7.68%	7.90%
Net Profit Margin (Return on Sales) (ROS) (Net Income/Revenues)	4.57%	4.37%	4.28%
Total Asset Turnover (Revenues/Average Total Assets)	0.95	0.92	
Return on Total Assets (ROA) (Net Income/Average Total Assets)	4.32%	4.00%	

REQUIRED

Income statement questions:

1. Are total revenues higher or lower over the three-year period?

2. What is the percent change in total revenues from 2002 to 2004?

3. Is the percent of cost of goods sold to total revenues increasing or decreasing over the three-year period? As a result, is the gross margin percent increasing or decreasing?

4. Is the percent of total operating expenses to total revenues increasing or decreasing over the three-year period? As a result, is the operating income percent increasing or decreasing?

5. Is the percent of net income to total revenue increasing or decreasing over the three-year period?

Balance sheet questions:

6. Are total assets higher or lower over the three-year period?

7. What is the percent change in total assets from 2002 to 2004?

8. What are the largest asset investments for the company over the three-year period?

9. Are the property, plant and equipment increasing faster or slower than the percent change in total revenues?

10. Is the percent of total liabilities to total liabilities + owners' equity increasing or decreasing? As a result, is there more or less risk that the company could not pay its debts?

Integrative income statement and balance sheet question:

11. Is the company operating more or less efficiently by using the least amount of asset investment to generate a given level of total revenues? Note that the "total asset turnover" ratio is computed and included in the "ratio analysis summary".

Ratio analysis questions:

12. Is the *current ratio* better or worse in the most current year compared to prior years?

13. Is the *quick ratio* better or worse in the most current year compared to prior years?

14. Is the *accounts receivable turnover ratio 1* (based on *average* receivables) better or worse in the most current year compared to prior years?

15. Is the 2004 *accounts receivable turnover ratio 2* (based on *year-end* receivables) better or worse than the 2004 ratio based on an *average*?

16. Is the *inventory turnover ratio 1* (based on *average* inventory) better or worse in the most current year compared to prior years?

17. Is the 2004 *inventory turnover ratio 2* (based on *year-end* inventory) better or worse than the 2004 ratio based on an *average*?

18. Is the *return on total assets (ROA) ratio* better or worse in the most current year compared to prior years?

Inventory questions (Chapter 9 focus):

Assume a note to the financial statements included the following information on inventories:

Inventories:

Inventories are stated at the lower of cost or market. Cost is determined by the last-in, first-out (LIFO) method for substantially all inventories.

The excess of replacement cost over LIFO cost was $46.2 million and $42.8 million at December 31, 2004 and December 31, 2003 respectively.

19. As of December 31, 2004, and December 31, 2003, what are the approximate current values of total inventories for Molson-Coors?

20. If Molson-Coors used FIFO, would the current ratio for 2004 be higher or lower? Explain briefly.

21. If Molson-Coors used FIFO, would the total revenues for 2004 be higher or lower? Explain briefly.

22. If Molson-Coors used FIFO, would the gross margin percent for 2004 be higher or lower? (Assume there are no LIFO liquidations in 2004.) Explain briefly.

23. If Molson-Coors used FIFO, would the total owners' equity at December 31, 2004 be higher or lower (Ignore income tax)? Explain briefly.

24. If Molson-Coors used FIFO, would the inventory turnover ratio for 2004 be higher or lower (Ignore income tax)? (Assume there are no LIFO liquidations in 2004.) Explain briefly.

LONG-TERM ASSETS

CHAPTER

10

 "Wishing to be friends is quick work, but friendship is a slow-ripening fruit"

Aristotle

LEARNING GOALS

After studying Chapter 10, you should be able to:

1. Determine the cost of tangible plant assets.

2. Define *depreciation* and explain factors that affect the computation of depreciation.

3. Compute depreciation using the (a) straight-line method, (b) the production unit method, (c) the double declining-balance method, and (d) the sum-of-the-years'-digits method.

4. Explain the difference between revenue expenditures and capital expenditures.

5. Record revisions of depreciation expense.

6. Record the sale, retirement, or exchange of tangible plant assets.

7. Discuss accounting issues for natural resources and compute depletion.

8. Explain the accounting issues associated with intangible assets and compute amortization

9. Analyze financial statement information for real-life companies.

UNDERSTANDING BUSINESS ISSUES

Businesses use various types of long-term assets in their operations. These assets provide benefits for more than one accounting period. Long-term assets fall into three groups:

1. *Tangible plant assets*, such as land, buildings, machinery, equipment, and trucks.

2. *Natural resources*, such as those found in mining, oil and gas, and forestry.

3. *Intangible assets*, such as patents, computer software development costs, and the excess of purchase price over the fair value of a business acquired (called *goodwill*).

In this chapter, we first illustrate types of long-term assets used by some well known companies. Then we discuss how to determine the costs of long-term assets and record their acquisition. We explain alternative methods for allocating the cost of long-term assets over their useful lives. We describe the accounting for disposal and retirement of tangible assets. Finally, we examine accounting issues associated with natural resources and intangible assets.

TYPES OF LONG-TERM ASSETS

Tangible plant assets are long-term assets that businesses acquire for use in operations. They are not intended for resale to customers. For example, on its balance sheet Federal Express lists a computer purchased for its own use as a tangible plant asset. A computer manufactured by IBM for sale to customers is part of inventory on its balance sheet. We use the term **property, plant, and equipment** to describe all tangible plant assets such as land, buildings, and equipment.

Natural resources are long-term assets with a value that decreases through use or sale. An example of a natural resource is timber maintained by Sunoco Products Company for making packaging material.

Intangible assets are long-term assets that do not have physical substance. They are useful because of special rights or advantages they provide. An example of an intangible asset is rights to the name, likeness, and portrait of Walt Disney held by The Walt Disney Corporation.

Companies in different industries require varying amounts of investments in long-term assets. To illustrate this, recent balance sheet information about investments in long-term assets (dollar amounts in millions) for selected companies is as follows:

Company	Tangible Assets $ Total	Tangible Assets % of Assets	Natural Resources $ Total	Natural Resources % of Assets	Intangible Assets $ Total	Intangible Assets % of Assets
Sunoco	$ 974	41%	$35	2%	$360	15%
Walt Disney Company	16,482	31	–	0	19,781	37
Wendy's International	1,640	79	–	0	41	2
Deere & Company	2,162	7	–	0	995	3

Using the matching concept, we allocate the cost of most long-term assets to the accounting periods they benefit. The expense titles used for the allocation of different types of long-term assets are as follows:

Type of Balance Sheet Asset Account	Type of Income Statement Expense Account
Tangible plant assets:	
Land	None
Buildings, machinery, and equipment	Depreciation
Natural resources	Depletion
Intangible assets	Amortization

TANGIBLE PLANT ASSETS

Cost of Tangible Plant Assets

Learning Goal 1   Determine the cost of tangible plant assets.

We initially record a tangible plant asset in the accounting records at the amount paid for it. The cost includes the purchase price (less any cash discount) plus all other reasonable and necessary expenditures to prepare the asset for use in operations. Therefore, the cost of a computer includes such costs as transportation, special wiring, installation, and test runs. The cost of a building includes permit fees, excavation and grading costs, architectural and engineering fees, and construction costs. In some cases firms construct assets for their own use. Interest expense on loans used to finance construction is part of the asset cost. We debit the interest cost to the plant asset.[1] For example, in 2004 total interest cost for The Walt Disney Company was $624 million. Of this amount, $7 million was debited to plant assets instead of to interest expense.

We do not include costs associated with damage to an asset during its preparation for use as part of the acquisition cost of the asset. For example, it might cost $100 to repair a computer monitor that was dropped during installation. We record this cost, which results from negligent actions, as an expense of the current accounting period.

Assume that a company buys a computer with a list price of $5,000 at terms of 2/10, n/60, with freight paid by the buyer. Installing the computer requires special electrical wiring and the construction of a computer desk. We debit these expenditures to the asset account. The total asset cost includes the following:

Purchase price	$ 5,000
Deduct: Cash discount	100
Net purchase price	$ 4,900
Transportation	125
Cost of writing	75
Construction of a special desk	300
Total asset cost	$ 5,400

Sometimes, companies acquire long-term assets by gift or in exchange for capital stock. In these cases, we value the assets on the basis of the amount of cash that would be required to buy them (**fair market value**). When we acquire used plant assets, we debit the asset account with all expenditures incurred in getting the asset ready for use.

The cost of land includes brokers' fees, legal fees, and transfer taxes. We also include costs of preparing the land for use, such as grading, clearing, and the removal of unwanted existing structures. We reduce the cost by amounts received for scrap and salvage. Land appears separately on the balance sheet because it is not subject to depreciation. However, improvements to land—lighting, parking areas, fencing—that deteriorate through use are subject to depreciation. We should record these items in a separate account, Land Improvements.

Subsidiary Records

It is usually necessary for management to have specific information about each long-term asset. We need this to compute depreciation, make disposal and replacement decisions, and maintain a log of repairs and maintenance. Exhibit 10.1 shows a sample equipment record for Tony's Garage.

---

[1] *Statement of Financial Accounting Standards (SFAS) No. 34,* "Capitalization of Interest Cost" (as amended by SFAS Statements *No. 58* and 62) (Norwalk, CT: FASB, October 1979).

```
┌─────────────────────────────────────────────────────────────────────────────────┐
│ TONY'S GARAGE                                                                     │
│                                                                                   │
│ EQUIPMENT RECORD                        ASSET         CLASS        ACCT.          │
│                                         NO.   1252    NO.   14     NO.   169      │
│ NAME OF ASSET        Tow Truck                                                    │
├───────────────────────────────────────────────────────────────┬─────────────────┤
│ Made by    Northern Motors      Manufacturer's                 │   Location      │
│                                 Serial No. 1BS50216            │                 │
│ Purchased                       Purchase                       │                 │
│ from  Great Truck Sales         Guarantee 12 months           │   Downtown      │
│                                                                │   Service       │
│ Year 2007      Model Heavy Duty      Acquisition Cost $27,000  │   Station       │
│                                                                │                 │
│ Estimated      Depreciation          Estimated                │                 │
│ Life 5 Yrs.    Rate 20%    Per Year   Residual Value $7,000    │                 │
│                                                                │                 │
│ Insurance                                                                        │
│ Carried    Great American Insurance                                              │
└──────────────────────────────────────────────────────────────────────────────────┘
```

ACCUMULATED DEPRECIATION						COST		
Year	Annual Amt.	To Date	Net Asset Value	Date	DESCRIPTION	Posting Ref.	Debit	Credit	Balance
2007	4,000	4,000	23,000	12/31		169	27,000		27,000
2008	4,000	8,000	19,000	12/31					

EXHIBIT **10.1**

Equipment Record

Depreciation of Tangible Plant Assets

Learning Goal 2   Define depreciation and explain factors that affect the computation of depreciation.

To match revenues and expenses, we must allocate the cost of each plant asset to expense over its estimated useful life. **Depreciation** is the process of allocating the cost of an asset to the periods the asset benefits. It is important to note that depreciation is a cost allocation process, not a valuation process. Therefore, the emphasis in depreciation is on the systematic recognition of depreciation expense on the income statement.

Factors in Estimating Depreciation Expense

Three factors affect the computation of periodic depreciation expense. They are **(1)** the initial cost, **(2)** the estimated residual value, and **(3)** the estimated useful life. Exhibit 10.2 illustrates these three factors and the computation of depreciation expense using the straight-line method.

Initial Cost

The *initial cost* is the net purchase price plus all reasonable and necessary expenditures to get the asset ready for use. In Exhibit 10.2 the initial cost of the tow truck includes the purchase price, tow lift, special paint, and sales tax. The total debit to the asset account is $27,000.

Estimated Residual Value

The expected cash receipts when the asset is ultimately scrapped, sold, or traded is the **residual value** (or *salvage value*). The residual value is an estimate. If we expect a plant asset to have no residual value when it is retired, we should depreciate the total cost. The estimated residual value should be reduced by expenditures for dismantling or removing the asset at the end of its use.

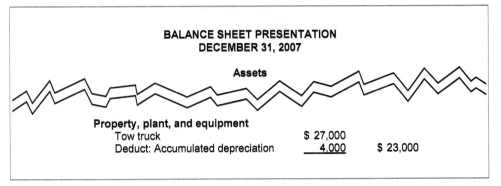

EXHIBIT **10.2**

Factors in Estimating Depriciation Expense Straight-line Method

In Exhibit 10.2 the estimates of residual value for the tow truck range from $9,000 to $2,000. When estimating residual value, the accountant tries to select the most reasonable estimate (in this case, $7,000). We deduct the estimated residual value from the cost of the asset to determine its

depreciable cost. The depreciable cost of the tow truck is $20,000 ($27,000 - $7,000). We then allocate the depreciable cost over the estimated useful life of the asset.

Estimated Useful Life (EUL)

The **estimated useful life (EUL)** is the number of years or service units expected from the asset. A number of factors limit the useful lives of tangible plant assets. These include wear and tear through normal use, repair and maintenance, climate and use conditions, and obsolescence.

In Exhibit 10.2 Tony's Garage chose five years as the most reasonable estimate of the useful life of the tow truck. Using the straight-line depreciation method discussed in Chapter 3 the yearly depreciation expense is $4,000 ($20,000 ÷ 5 years). We record depreciation by an adjusting entry at the end of each accounting period.

On the balance sheet the accumulated depreciation balance is deducted from the asset cost. The net amount represents the undepreciated cost of the asset and is called the **book value** (or *carrying value* or *undepreciated cost*) of the asset.

Methods of Computing Depreciation

Learning Goal 3 Compute depreciation using the straight-line, production unit, double declining-balance, and sum-of-the-years'-digits methods.

A number of methods exist to calculate periodic depreciation. Each may give a significantly different result. We should base the method selected in any specific instance on a careful evaluation of all the factors involved. These include estimated useful life, intensity of use, changes in technology, and revenue-generating potential. Alternative depreciation methods include (1) the straight-line method, (2) the production unit method, and (3) accelerated methods, including the double declining-balance and the sum-of-the-years'-digits methods.

Straight-line Method

With the **straight-line method**, we allocate an equal amount of asset cost to each accounting period. The straight-line method is simple to use. It is the method most commonly used by companies for external financial reporting purposes. It assumes uniform levels of operating efficiency, repair and maintenance, and revenue contributions for each period of the asset's EUL. The formula for the straight-line method is as follows:

$$\frac{\text{Cost} - \text{Estimated Residual Value}}{\text{Estimated Useful Life}} = \text{Depreciation Expence}$$

Assume we purchase a machine costing $17,000, with an EUL of five years and an estimated residual value of $2,000, on January 1, 2007. Following is the annual depreciation expense:

$$\frac{\$17,000 - \$2,000}{5 \text{years}} = \$3,000 \text{ per year}$$

We can also compute straight-line depreciation by use of a *straight-line rate*. We calculate this by dividing 100% by the number of years in the EUL. In this situation:

$$\frac{100\%}{5 \text{ years}} = 20\% \text{ per year}$$

$$0.20 \times (\$17,000 - \$2,000) = \$3,000 \text{ per year}$$

The following depreciation schedule summarizes the annual depreciation expense, the accumulated depreciation balance, and the asset's book value at the end of each year:

DEPRECIATION SCHEDULE
(STRAIGHT-LINE METHOD)
Annual Depreciation

Date	Asset Cost	Depreciation Rate		Depreciable Cost		Depreciation Expense	Accumulated Depreciation	Asset Book Value
Jan. 1, 2007	$17,000							$17,000
Dec. 31, 2007		20%	×	$15,000	=	$3,000	$ 3,000	14,000
Dec. 31, 2008		20%	×	15,000	=	3,000	6,000	11,000
Dec. 31, 2009		20%	×	15,000	=	3,000	9,000	8,000
Dec. 31, 2010		20%	×	15,000	=	3,000	12,000	5,000
Dec. 31, 2011		20%	×	15,000	=	3,000	15,000	2,000

Production Unit Method

With the **production unit method**, we compute the depreciation of an asset on its *units of output*. The units of output may be units produced, miles driven, hours in service, or some other measure. For this method, we need a reasonably accurate estimate of total units of output for the asset. Assume that the machine in the previous example can produce an estimated output of 100,000 units over its useful life. Following is the depreciation cost per unit for our example:

$$\frac{\text{Cost} - \text{Estimated Residual Value}}{\text{Estimated Useful Life in units}} = \text{Depreciation Expense per Unit}$$

$$\frac{\$17,000 - \$2,000}{100,000 \text{ units}} = \$0.15 \text{ per unit}$$

We calculate depreciation expense for a period as follows:

$$\text{Depreciation Expense per Unit} \times \text{Units Produced during Period} = \text{Depreciation Expense}$$

If we produce 20,000 units the first year, 30,000 the second, 25,000 the third, 15,000 the fourth, and 10,000 the fifth, the depreciation schedule is as follows:

DEPRECIATION SCHEDULE
(PRODUCTION UNIT METHOD)
Annual Depreciation

Date	Asset Cost	Depreciation Per Unit		Number of Units		Depreciation Expense	Accumulated Depreciation	Asset Book Value
Jan. 1, 2007	$17,000							$17,000
Dec. 31, 2007		$0.15	×	20,000	=	$3,000	$ 3,000	14,000
Dec. 31, 2008		0.15	×	30,000	=	4,500	7,500	9,500
Dec. 31, 2009		0.15	×	25,000	=	3,750	11,250	5,750
Dec. 31, 2010		0.15	×	15,000	=	2,250	13,500	3,500
Dec. 31, 2011		0.15	×	10,000	=	1,500	15,000	2,000

The production unit method does not depend on time as the other depreciation methods do. In the production unit method, there is a direct relationship between the use of the asset and the amount of depreciation expense. This method is appropriate where a business uses assets in varying amounts each year.

Accelerated Methods

The use of **accelerated methods** results in larger depreciation expense amounts in the early years of an asset's life and decreasing amounts in later years. These methods assume that assets depreciate more rapidly in the early years of their lives, when the asset is more efficient and technologically up-to-date. We base the accelerated methods on the passage of time. Two common accelerated methods are (1) the double declining-balance method and (2) the sum-of-the-years' digits method.

Double Declining-Balance Method

In the *declining-balance method*, we apply a uniform depreciation rate to the remaining asset book value (cost less accumulated depreciation). The most common form of the declining balance method uses twice the straight-line rate. This method is the **double declining-balance method (DDB)**. We do not deduct residual value in the computation of double declining-balance depreciation. However, we cannot depreciate the asset below residual value. The steps in the double declining-balance method are:

1. Calculate a straight-line depreciation rate for the asset.

2. Multiply the straight-line rate by 2.

3. Multiply the previous asset book value by the doubled rate to determine depreciation expense for the year.

In the case of the machine purchased for $17,000, the computation of double declining-balance depreciation for the first year is:

1. 100% ÷ 5 years = 20% per year (straight-line rate).

2. 20% × 2 = 40%.

3. 40% × $17,000 = $6,800 depreciation expense for the first year.

The double declining-balance method is the only method in which the asset's residual value is ignored in the calculation. We do not consider estimated residual value in computing DDB depreciation until the end of the asset's life. In the last year, we must limit depreciation expense to the amount that will bring the asset's book value down to the estimated residual value. The double declining-balance method depreciation schedule is:

DEPRECIATION SCHEDULE
(DOUBLE DECLINING-BALANCE METHOD)

Date	Asset Cost	Depreciation Rate		Previous Asset Book Value		Depreciation Expense	Accumulated Depreciation	Asset Book Value
Jan. 1, 2007	$17,000							$17,000
Dec. 31, 2007		40%	×	$17,000	=	$6,800	$ 6,800	10,200
Dec. 31, 2008		40%	×	10,200	=	4,080	10,880	6,120
Dec. 31, 2009		40%	×	6,120	=	2,448	13,328	3,672
Dec. 31, 2010		40%	×	3,672	=	1,469	14,797	2,203
Dec. 31, 2011		($2,203 - $2,000)			=	203*	15,000	2,000

*In the last year, depreciation is limited to the amount needed to reduce the asset's book value to its residual value. $203 = $2,203 (previous book value) - $2,000 (residual value).

Sum-of-the-Years'-Digits Method

Another accelerated depreciation method based on time is the **sum-of-the-years'-digits method (SYD)**. Using this method, we calculate depreciation for a year by multiplying the cost less the asset's residual value by a fraction. The fraction's denominator is the sum of the digits representing the life of the asset. For the machine with a five-year life, the sum of the years' digits is 15 $(1 + 2 + 3 + 4 + 5)$. The fraction's numerator is the individual year of the asset's life in reverse order. The formula for the sum-of-the-years'-digits method is as follows:

$$(\text{Cost} - \text{Estimated Residual Value}) \times \frac{\text{Individual Year (reverse order)}}{\text{Sum of the Years' Digits}}$$

Using this formula, we can calculate the first year's depreciation expense for the machine in our example:

$$(\$17,000 - \$2,000) \times \frac{5}{15} = \$5,000$$

Following is the sum-of-the-years'-digits depreciation schedule for the machine:

DEPRECIATION SCHEDULE
(SUM-OF-THE-YEARS'-DIGITS METHOD)

Date	Asset Cost	Sum-of-the-Years'-Digits Fraction		Depreciable Cost		Depreciation Expense	Accumulated Depreciation	Asset Book Value
Jan. 1, 2007	$17,000							$17,000
Dec. 31, 2007		5/15	×	$15,000	=	$5,000	$ 5,000	12,000
Dec. 31, 2008		4/15	×	15,000	=	4,000	9,000	8,000
Dec. 31, 2009		3/15	×	15,000	=	3,000	12,000	5,000
Dec. 31, 2010		2/15	×	15,000	=	2,000	14,000	3,000
Dec. 31, 2011		1/15	×	15,000	=	1,000	15,000	2,000

We can also calculate the sum of the years' digits (S) using the following formula:

$$S = \frac{n(n + 1)}{2}$$

where n = estimated useful life (EUL). For example:

$$S = \frac{5(5 + 1)}{2} = \frac{30}{2} = 15$$

Comparison of Depreciation Methods

For the machine costing $17,000 in our example, Exhibit 10.3 shows a graphic comparison of depreciation expense under the various methods. The straight-line method gives uniform depreciation charges over the life of the asset. Most companies use the straight-line method to depreciate some of their plant assets. Depreciation under the production unit method varies each year in relation to the usage of the asset. As a result, there is no uniform pattern. Production unit depreciation is best suited for situations in which the business uses plant assets in varying amounts from year to year. Boise Cascade Corporation and Murphy Oil Corporation use the production unit method.

The accelerated methods provide the highest amount of depreciation expense in the early years. They are most appropriate for assets that decrease most in revenue-generating ability during the first few years of ownership. Caterpillar, Inc. uses accelerated depreciation methods. Double-declining balance gives the highest depreciation in the first year because of the higher rate (40%) and higher base ($17,000, compared to $15,000). Under sum-of-the-years'-digits, depreciation declines evenly each year.

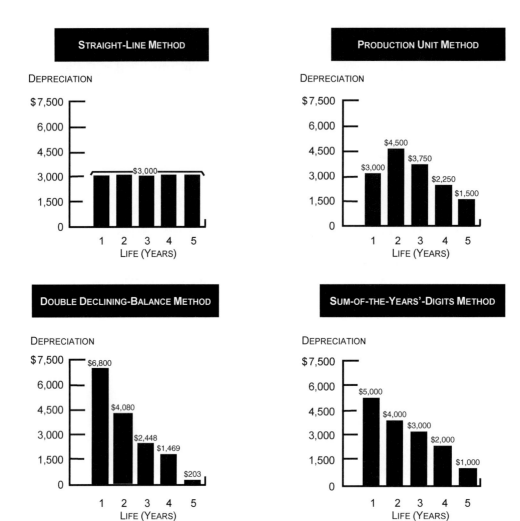

EXHIBIT **10.3**

Comparison of Depreciation Expense Under Different Depreciation Methods

Exhibit 10.4 shows a comparison of the asset's book value under the various methods. All four methods begin with the same asset book value ($17,000) and end with the same residual value ($2,000). However, different patterns of depreciation charges result in differing book values over the life of the asset. Assuming equal investments in plant assets, companies using the straight-line method will generally show the highest asset book value on the balance sheet.

COMPARISON OF ASSET BOOK VALUE

Year	Straight-Line	Production Unit	Accelerated Methods	
			Double Declining-Balance	Sum-of-the-Years'-Digits
Jan. 1, 2007	$17,000	17,000	$17,000	$17,000
Dec. 31, 2007	14,000	14,000	10,200	12,000
Dec. 31, 2008	11,000	9,500	6,120	8,000
Dec. 31, 2009	8,000	5,750	3,672	5,000
Dec. 31, 2010	5,000	3,500	2,203	3,000
Dec. 31, 2011	2,000	2,000	2,000	2,000

EXHIBIT **10.4**

Comparison of Asset Book Value Under Different Depreciation Methods

Depreciation for Partial Accounting Periods

Frequently, businesses purchase or retire assets at some time during the accounting period. Usually we compute depreciation to the nearest month. Since depreciation is an estimate, we do not often count the exact number of days of the asset's use. A common method is to take a full month of depreciation if we purchase the asset on or before the fifteenth of the month. We take no depreciation for the month in which we purchase the asset after the fifteenth. Assuming that we purchase the machine in the example on October 7, 2007, depreciation expense for 2007 (three months) using the straight-line method is as follows:

2007   (Straight-line depreciation for 3 months of asset life year 1):

$$\frac{\$17,000 - \$2,000}{5 \text{ years}} \times \frac{3}{12} = \$750$$

Straight-line depreciation expense for 2008 (12 months) is $3,000.

For the accelerated methods, we must also compute depreciation for the fraction of the year used. Recall the purchase of the machine on October 7, 2007. Exhibit 10.3 shows depreciation for each full year of the asset's life. The computation of depreciation expense for 2007 (3 months) and 2008 (12 months) using the double-declining balance method is as follows:

2007   (Double declining-balance depreciation for 3 months of asset life year 1)

$$\$6,800 \times \frac{3}{12} = \$1,700$$

2008   (Double declining-balance depreciation for 12 months)

1. (Depreciation for remaining 9 months of asset life year 1)

$$\$6,800 \times \frac{9}{12} = \$5,100$$

2. (Depreciation for 3 months of asset life year 2)

$$\$4,080 \times \frac{3}{12} = \$1,020$$

3. $5,100 + $1,020 = $6,120

The same process applies to future years and to the sum-of-the-years'-digits method. Under the double declining-balance method, we can simplify the depreciation computation for 2008. First we compute the asset's book value as of January 1, 2008. Then we multiply this amount by the DDB rate to calculate 2008 depreciation, as follows: ($17,000 - $1,700) × 40% = $6,120. There is no parallel simplification for the sum-of-the-years'-digits method.

Modified Accelerated Cost Recovery System (MACRS) for Income Tax Reporting

For income tax reporting, we also deduct depreciation in order to compute taxable income. However, the amount of the *cost recovery deduction* (depreciation deduction) shown on the tax return may be different than the amount shown on the income statement. For income tax reporting, businesses generally use the **modified accelerated cost recovery system (MACRS)**. This system applies to tangible property placed in service after 1986. It requires that we compute a cost recovery deduction over a specified period of years for different classes of property. Generally, the recovery periods specified under MACRS are shorter than the estimated useful lives used for financial reporting purposes.

The accelerated cost recovery rates and the short recovery time periods are an incentive for businesses to invest in new assets. Cost recovery deductions for tax purposes are not usually acceptable for financial reporting purposes.

Selection of Depreciation Method

Many businesses use one depreciation method for income tax reporting and a different method for financial reporting. For income tax purposes, management should select the depreciation method that minimizes taxes in the current accounting period. The MACRS method generally provides the greatest amount of deductions in the early years of an asset's life. This results in the lowest amount of taxable income.

For financial reporting purposes, the objective is to select a depreciation method that most correctly matches revenues and expenses. The straight-line method is simple to apply and works well where the assets undergo about the same use each year. The production unit method is most appropriate for assets subject to varying amounts of use in each accounting period. This is important where the loss in the asset's usefulness depends on some measure of its use, such as units produced, rather than on the passing of time. The accelerated methods are based on the idea that the service provided by a tangible plant asset is greatest in the early years of use. Depreciation under the accelerated methods for these assets results in a more accurate matching of expense and revenue. They also take into account the fact that as an asset gets older, it requires more maintenance. The increasing maintenance expenses in later years are offset by the diminishing depreciation expense. This helps equalize the total expense of the asset and achieves a better matching of expense with revenue.

Revenue and Capital Expenditures

Learning Goal 4   Explain the difference between revenue expenditures and capital expenditures.

We may classify expenditures made to acquire, improve, maintain, or expand tangible plant assets as *revenue expenditures* or *capital expenditures*. A revenue expenditure results in an addition to an expense account. A capital expenditure increases the book value of an asset.

Revenue expenditures benefit only the current accounting period. We make revenue expenditures for the purpose of maintaining the asset in satisfactory operating condition. Examples include ordinary repairs, maintenance, or replacement of minor parts. These expenditures do not increase the serviceability of the asset beyond the original estimated life. We recognize these normal maintenance costs as expenses in the current period.

Capital expenditures are significant costs that benefit two or more accounting periods. They may be (1) initial costs of acquiring tangible plant assets, or (2) costs incurred subsequent to the purchase of plant assets, such as additions, betterments, or extraordinary repairs. Capital expenditures make the plant asset more valuable or extend its useful life. As discussed previously in this chapter, we debit (**capitalize**) the initial costs of acquiring plant assets to the appropriate asset account.

Additions are expenditures that enhance usefulness by enlarging an existing plant asset. An example would be the construction of a new wing on an existing factory building. *Betterments* are expenditures for changes in assets that increase or improve services. For example, the installation of an improved air conditioning system in an office building would be a betterment. We capitalize these by debiting the appropriate asset account.

Extraordinary repairs are significant expenditures that extend the useful life of a plant asset or change its estimated salvage value. An example is a major overhaul of an aircraft engine to extend its useful life. We treat expenditures for extraordinary repairs as capital expenditures. However, we debit extraordinary repairs to an accumulated depreciation account. This debit to Accumulated Depreciation cancels past depreciation charges and increases the book value of the asset. We then depreciate the increased book value over the revised estimated asset life.

For example, assume that the $17,000 machine in previous illustrations receives a complete overhaul at the beginning of the year 2010. The overhaul, at a cost of $2,500, adds two years to the original estimated useful life (EUL) of five years. The general journal entry to record the overhaul is as follows:

```
2010
Jan.   1   Accumulated Depreciation—Machinery              2,500
                 Cash                                               2,500
               To record the overhaul of a machine.
```

When we make any capital expenditure—an addition, betterment, or extraordinary repair—on an asset already in service, there is a change in the book value. Therefore, we need to prepare a new depreciation schedule.

Revisions of Depreciation Expense

Learning Goal 5   Record revisions of depreciation expense.

The periodic depreciation expense may require revision as the result of (1) an extraordinary repair that extends the original EUL, or (2) errors in the EUL or estimated residual value. In either case, we allocate the remaining book value over the new estimate of the asset's remaining life.[2] To illustrate a revision of depreciation expense, we use the previous example for the $17,000 machine. We placed it in service on January 1, 2007, and overhauled it at a cost of $2,500 on January 1, 2010. In addition to adding two years to the EUL of five years, we revise the estimated residual value from $2,000 to $2,300. Following is the calculation of the revised depreciation expense (straight-line method):

Original cost		$ 17,000
Accumulated depreciation recorded for prior years (2007, 2008, 2009) =		
($3,000 × 3 years)	$ 9,000	
Deduct: Reduction in accumulated depreciation due to overhaul	2,500	6,500
Adjusted book value		$ 10,500
Deduct: Estimated residual value		2,300
New depreciable cost		$ 8,200
New annual depreciation expense, based on remaining useful life of 4 years		
($8,200 ÷ 4)		$ 2,050

The Delta Air Lines, Inc. example shown in Exhibit 10.5 shows the revision of depreciation expense for a real-life company. In this example, Delta increased the estimated lives of its airplanes from 15 years to 20 years in fiscal 1993. In addition, in 1993 the estimated residual value of the airplanes was reduced from 10% of cost to only 5%. The impact of both of these changes was to reduce depreciation expense and increase reported operating income as the following summary shows:

CHANGES IN ESTIMATED USEFUL LIFE OF AIRPLANES: DELTA AIR LINES (AMOUNTS IN MILLIONS)

Year (Revision)	Operating Income (Loss) BEFORE Decrease in Depreciation Expense	DECREASE in Depreciation Expense	Operating Income (Loss) AFTER Decrease in Depreciation Expense
1993 (15 to 20 years)	$(609)	$ 34	$(575) = $(609) + 34

---

[2] *Opinions of the Accounting Principles Board (APB) No. 20, "Accounting Changes"* (New York: AICPA, July 1971), defines such a change as a change in accounting estimate and requires footnote disclosure in the financial statements.

The following notes describing depreciable lives and residual values are taken from the 2001 and 1993 annual financial reports of Delta Air Lines, Inc. Before the revisions in 1993, Delta was depreciating its airplanes over a 15-year life with a residual value of 10% of cost. After the changes, Delta is now depreciating its airplanes over a 20-year life with a residual value of only 5% of cost. The result is a decrease in depreciation expense and an increase in reported earnings. Paying attention to the information disclosed in the notes to financial statements is important in trying to assess reasons for net income changes.

2001 Annual Report
Depreciation and Amortization: Flight equipment is depreciated on a straight-line basis to residual values (5% of cost) over a 20-year period from the dates placed in service (unless earlier retirement of the aircraft is planned).

1993 Annual Report
Depreciation and Amortization: Prior to April 1, 1993, substantially all of the Company's flight equipment was being depreciated on a straight-line basis to residual values (10% of cost) over a 15-year period from dates placed in service. As a result of a review of its fleet plan, effective April 1, 1993, the Company increased the estimated useful lives of substantially all of its flight equipment. Flight equipment that was not already fully depreciated is now depreciated on a straight-line basis to residual values (5% of cost) over a 20-year period from dates placed in service. The effect of this change was a $34.3 million decrease in depreciation expense and a $22 million ($.44 per common share) decrease in net loss for the year ended June 30, 1993.

EXHIBIT **10.5**

Revisions of Asset Lives and Depreciation Expense: Delta Air Lines

For 1993, the impact of the increase in estimated life from 15 to 20 years and the decrease in residual value from 10% to 5% is reduced by the fact that Delta made the change only for the last three months of fiscal 1993. If the change had been made at the beginning of the year, the decrease in depreciation expense in 1993 would have been approximately four times $34 million or $136 million.

Disposals of Tangible Plant Assets
Learning Goal 6   Record the sale, retirement, or exchange of tangible plant assets.

We may dispose of a tangible plant asset by retiring, selling, or trading it in as part of the purchase price of a replacement. The accounting treatment of sales and retirements is similar. Trade-ins are somewhat different.

Sale or Retirement of Tangible Plant Assets

When we dispose of an asset, we make an entry to remove the appropriate amounts from the asset and the accumulated depreciation accounts. Assume that a company acquired a truck with a five-year EUL on January 1, 2007, at a cost of $20,000. It has no residual value. We record depreciation on a straight-line basis at the rate of $4,000 annually. We illustrate three situations, together with the methods of accounting for the disposal of the truck.

Example 1: Sale of Asset at a Price Equal to Book Value Assume we sell the truck on October 1, 2011, for $1,000. The first entry records the depreciation for the current year up to the date of sale:

2011					
Oct.	1	Depreciation Expense—Trucks	663	3,000	
		Accumulated Depreciation—Trucks	170		3,000
		To record depreciation on trucks for the nine-month period Jan. 1, 2011, to Oct. 1, 2011.			

The Accumulated Depreciation account now has a credit balance of $19,000, as shown below.

Accumulated Depreciation—Trucks Acct. No. 170

Date		Explanation	PR	Debit	Credit	Balance Debit	Balance Credit
2007							
Dec.	31		J73		4,000		4,000
2008							
Dec.	31		J85		4,000		8,000
2009							
Dec.	31		J97		4,000		12,000
2010							
Dec.	31		J109		4,000		16,000
2011							
Oct.	1		J119		3,000		19,000

The book value of the truck is $1,000, computed as follows:

Cost at acquisition	$20,000
Deduct: Accumulated depreciation	19,000
Book value	$ 1,000

Following is the entry to record the sale:

2011
Oct. 1 Cash ... 1,000
Accumulated Depreciation—Trucks ... 19,000
Trucks ... 20,000
To record sale of truck.

This entry records the receipt of cash, eliminates the accumulated amount from the Accumulated Depreciation account, and reduces the asset account by the original cost of the truck.

Example 2: Sale of Asset at a Price Above Book Value Assume we sell the truck on October 1, 2011, for $1,200. The entry to record the depreciation for the current year up to the date of sale is the same as in Example 1. The following entry records the sale:

2011
Oct. 1 Cash ... 1,200
Accumulated Depreciation—Trucks ... 19,000
Trucks ... 20,000
Gain on Disposal of Plant Assets ... 200
To record sale of truck at a gain computed as follows:
Cost of truck ... $20,000
Deduct: Accumulated depreciation ... 19,000
Book value of truck ... $ 1,000
Amount received ... 1,200
Gain on disposal ... $ 200

A gain results when the proceeds are greater than the book value; a loss results when they are less.

Example 3: Sale of Asset at a Price Below Book Value Assume we sell the truck on October 1, 2011, for $400 in cash. Again, the entry to record the depreciation applicable to the year of sale is the same as in Example 1. The entry to record the sale is as follows:

2011					
Oct.	1	Cash		400	
		Accumulated Depreciation—Trucks		19,000	
		Loss on Disposal of Plant Assets		600	
		Trucks			20,000

To record sale of truck at a loss computed as follows:

Cost of truck	$ 20,000
Deduct: Accumulated depreciation	19,000
Book value of truck	$ 1,000
Amount received	400
Loss on disposal	$ 600

In the three previous examples, we received some cash at the time of disposal. If the truck had simply been retired (same as sold for $0), the loss would equal book value.

Exchange of Tangible Plant Assets

When we exchange a plant asset for a new asset, two situations are possible. Most frequently, we trade the old asset in on the purchase of a similar plant asset. Sometimes, the trade-in is on a dissimilar asset. The accounting issue in exchanges involves whether to recognize gains and losses. In exchanges of dissimilar items, we recognize all gains and losses. We will discuss exchanges of dissimilar assets first because the accounting procedures involved are easier to understand.

Exchange of Dissimilar Tangible Plant Assets

After we bring the accumulated depreciation up to date, we compare the book value of the old asset with its trade-in allowance. We recognize a gain if the trade-in allowance is greater than the book value, a loss if it is less. When the book value and the trade-in allowance are equal, there is no gain or loss.

Example 1: Trade-in Allowance the Same as Book Value Assume we exchange a computer that cost $5,000 with accumulated depreciation of $4,500 for a delivery truck with a cash price of $12,000. The trade-in allowance is $500. We pay cash of $11,500. We record the new asset at the cash payment plus the fair market value of the old asset. The journal entry is as follows:

2011					
Sep.	1	Delivery Truck		12,000	
		Accumulated Depreciation—Computer		4,500	
		Cash			11,500
		Computer			5,000

To record trade-in of old computer for delivery truck.

We calculate the cash payment of $11,500 as follows:

Selling price of the new asset	$ 12,000
Trade-in allowance on the old asset	500
Cash payment	$ 11,500

There is no gain or loss in this example because the trade-in allowance is the same as the book value.

Example 2: Trade-in Allowance Less than Book Value Assume the computer in Example 1 has a trade-in allowance of $300. We record a loss because the computer's book value of $500 is greater than the fair market value of $300. The entry is as follows:

2011				
Sep.	1	Delivery Truck	12,000	
		Accumulated Depreciation—Computer	4,500	
		Loss on Disposal of Plant Assets	200	
		Cash		11,700
		Computer		5,000

To record trade-in of computer at a loss, computed as follows:

Cost of old asset	$ 5,000
Accumulated depreciation to date of trade-in	4,500
Book value	$ 500
Trade-in allowance	300
Loss on trade-in	$ 200

Example 3: Trade-in Allowance Greater than Book Value Assume we exchange the computer in Example 1 for a delivery truck with a trade-in allowance of $800. We record a gain because the fair market value of $800 is greater than the book value of $500. The entry is as follows:

2011				
Sep.	1	Delivery Truck	12,000	
		Accumulated Depreciation—Computer	4,500	
		Cash		11,200
		Computer		5,000
		Gain on Disposal of Plant Assets		300

To record trade-in of computer at a gain, computed as follows:

Cost of old asset	$ 5,000
Accumulated depreciation to date of trade-in	4,500
Book value	$ 500
Trade-in allowance	800
Gain on trade-in	$ 300

Exchange of Similar Tangible Plant Assets

In many cases, we trade a tangible plant item in on a similar asset—one that has essentially the same function as the old asset. The Accounting Principles Board views the new, similar asset as continuing the same stream of earnings as the old one.[3] A gain is not appropriate because the same stream of earnings continues. The Board's Opinion further states that when a loss results from an exchange of assets, we should recognize the entire loss on the transaction.[4] If the loss were not recorded, it would be necessary to record the new asset at more than its fair market value. This would be inconsistent with generally accepted accounting principles.

---

[3] *APB No. 29, "Accounting for Nonmonetary Transactions"* (New York: AICPA. May 1973), paragraph 21.
[4] *APB No. 29,* paragraph 22.

Exchange at a Loss

In Example 2 in the preceding section, assume we trade in the old computer on a new computer instead of a delivery truck. Since a loss of $200 results from the exchange, we recognize the loss. The entry is similar to the one shown in Example 2 and we record it as follows:

2011				
Sep.	1	Computer (new)	12,000	
		Accumulated Depreciation—Computer (old)	4,500	
		Loss on Disposal of Plant Assets	200	
		Cash		11,700
		Computer (old)		5,000

To record trade-in of computer at a loss, computed as follows:

Cost of old asset	$ 5,000
Accumulated depreciation to date of trade-in	4,500
Book value	$ 500
Trade-in allowance	300
Loss on trade-in	$ 200

Exchange at a Gain

We do not record a gain on exchanges of similar assets. Using data from Example 3, assume that we trade in the old computer for a new computer. A trade-in allowance of $800 is given on the old computer. Cash of $11,200 is paid. The entry to record the trade-in on a similar asset is:

2011				
Sep.	1	Computer (new)	11,700	
		Accumulated Depreciation—Computer (old)	4,500	
		Cash		11,200
		Computer (old)		5,000

To record trade-in of old computer for new computer. The valuation of the new computer is computed as follows:

Book value of old computer	$ 500
Cash paid	11,200
Total given up for new computer	$ 11,700

The cost recorded for the new computer is equal to the book value of the old computer plus the cash paid. This is the same as the cash price of the new computer ($12,000) less the gain that is not recognized ($300). We compensate for not recognizing the gain in current income by having $300 less to depreciate over the EUL of the new asset.

NATURAL RESOURCES

Learning Goal 7   Discuss accounting issues for natural resources and compute depletion.

Another class of long-term assets is **natural resources**. Examples include mineral deposits, oil wells, and timber tracts. As we extract the resource, we reduce its asset value. The primary accounting task is to measure the periodic charge to operations for the exhaustion or expiration of a natural resource, or its **depletion**. We determine periodic depletion in a manner similar to the production unit method of depreciation. It is a debit to the Depletion Cost account or an inventory account and a credit to the Accumulated Depletion account. In the balance sheet, we classify accumulated depletion as a contra account deducted from the natural resource account.

Depletion of Natural Resources

We usually calculate the periodic depletion charge on an output basis similar to the production unit method of recording depreciation. For example, if the asset is a mineral measured in tons:

$$\frac{\textbf{Cost} - \textbf{Residual Value}}{\textbf{Estimated Tons to be Mined}} = \textbf{Depletion Cost per Ton}$$

Assume that a mine costs $180,000 and contains an estimated 400,000 tons of ore. We estimate that the net residual value is $20,000. The depletion charge per unit is:

$$\frac{\$180,000 - \$20,000}{400,000} = \$0.40 \textbf{ per ton}$$

Depletion of natural resources is not the same as the depreciation of a long-term tangible plant item. Unlike depreciation, depletion provides an inventory of goods that can be sold. Normally, a merchandising firm buys its inventory. A production firm—for example, a mining company—incurs certain costs to produce an inventory. All costs directly involved in production of inventory (including depletion costs) are **inventoriable costs**. They are not expenses of a period but become a part of the cost of inventory. As such, we carry them as assets until they appear in the income statement as cost of goods sold. Continuing with our previous mining example, if we mine 10,000 tons during an accounting period and sell 8,000 tons, the cost of goods sold is as follows:

Cost of goods sold:
Depletion (10,000 tons × $0.40)	$ 4,000
Other costs of production (assumed to be $1 per ton)	10,000
Total cost of production ($14,000 ÷ 10,000 tons = $1.40 per ton)	$14,000
Deduct: Ending inventory (2,000 tons × $1.40 per ton)	2,800
Cost of goods sold (8,000 tons × $1.40 per ton)	$11,200

The journal entries to record these events depend on whether we use a perpetual or a periodic inventory system. In either case, we show the inventory valuation (here $2,800) as a current asset in the balance sheet. Cost of goods sold ($11,200) appears in the income statement. The mine appears as a long-lived asset in the balance sheet at cost minus accumulated depletion ($180,000 - $4,000 = $176,000).

INTANGIBLE ASSETS

Learning Goal 8   Explain the accounting issues associated with intangible assets and compute amortization.

Intangible assets are long-term rights that have a future value to a business. Some intangibles, such as patents, copyrights, franchises, and leaseholds, can be readily identified and their cost measured. Others, such as goodwill, are not specifically identifiable or measurable. The process of estimating and recording the periodic expiration of an intangible asset is **amortization**. It is similar to computing and recording depreciation by the straight-line method. We compute the amortization by dividing the asset cost by the legal life or the EUL, whichever is shorter. However, the period of amortization should not exceed 40 years.[5] The entry is usually a debit to an amortization expense account and a credit directly to the asset account.

Patents

The United States Patent Office grants **patents**—exclusive rights to the owners to produce and sell their inventions or discoveries—for a period of 17 years. We include all the costs of acquiring a patent from others in the intangible asset account Patents. We amortize the cost of a patent over the useful economic life of the asset or 17 years, whichever is shorter. If the patent is for a nonmanufacturing function, the accounting entry is as follows:

2007					
Dec.	31	Patent Amortization Expense		1,000	
		Patents			1,000
		To record amortization of patents for 2007.			

Research and Development Costs

In the past, some companies capitalized expenditures for research and development as intangible assets and amortized them as described earlier in this section. Other companies treated all research and development expenditures as expenses of the current accounting period. To resolve this lack of uniformity, the Financial Accounting Standards Board ruled that the costs of research and development performed by a company should be debited to expense accounts in the period incurred.[6] This includes the cost of patents resulting from a company's own research and development expenditures.

Computer Software Development Costs

Companies can spend significant amounts of money to develop computer software programs. In the past, some firms that developed computer software for sale or lease to others expensed the development costs as they incurred them; others capitalized some of the development costs. The impact of expensing versus capitalizing is quite dramatic for some companies. For example, a company called Comserve (a maker of software systems for manufacturing companies) capitalized computer software costs and reported a net income of $2.2 million. If it had expensed these software development costs, it would have reported a *loss* of $1 million instead.

The Financial Accounting Standards Board ruled that software producers must expense costs incurred in creating a computer software product until technological feasibility is established for the product. We establish technological feasibility upon completion of a detailed program design or working model. Thereafter, we capitalize and amortize all software costs.[7]

---

[5] *APB No. 17, "Intangible Assets"* (New York: AICPA, August 1970), paragraphs 24, 26, 28, and 29.
[6] *SFAS No. 2, "Accounting for Research and Development Costs"* (Norwalk, Conn.: FASB, June 1975), paragraph 11.
[7] *SFAS No. 86, "Accounting for the Costs of Computer Software to Be Sold, Leased, or Otherwise Marketed"* (Norwalk, Conn.: FASB, August 1985).

Goodwill

Goodwill is a general term used to describe the ability of a firm to realize higher than normal earnings. We record goodwill only in the acquisition of all or part of another company. Goodwill is that intangible asset represented by the excess of purchase price over the fair market value of assets acquired. The amount paid for goodwill is usually a result of bargaining between the buyer and the seller.

Exhibit 10.6 shows selected information taken from the 2000 annual report of AT & T Corporation and provides a dramatic illustration of goodwill. Of the $45 billion paid for MediaOne Group, Inc., only $25 billion was for the fair value of net assets acquired. The excess paid of $20 billion represents the amount identified as goodwill. On December 31, 1999, goodwill for AT & T Corporation was approximately 4.4% of total assets. On December 31, 2000, goodwill for AT & T Corporation was approximately 13.0% of total assets. Each year AT & T will assess whether this goodwill has been impaired, and, if so, write it down by that amount.

Other Intangible Assets

A **copyright** is an exclusive right to publish a literary or artistic work. For the life of the creator plus 50 years, it gives the owner, or heirs, the exclusive rights to reproduce and sell the work. We record the copyright at cost and amortize it over its useful economic life.

A **franchise** is a monopolistic right to render a service or to produce a good. A right to operate a bus line or a railroad or the exclusive use of a television transmitting channel is a valuable asset to the owner. Businesses use franchises to grant a dealer the exclusive privilege to sell the manufacturer's product within a defined geographical area. Examples are McDonald's, Dunkin' Donuts, and Holiday Inns. We amortize the cost of obtaining the franchise over its estimated useful life or 40 years, whichever is shorter.

Leases are rights to the use of land, buildings, equipment, or other property that belong to others. Title to improvements made to leased property by a lessee reverts to the lessor when the lease is over. Thus the lessee records the cost of such improvements in an intangible asset account, Leasehold Improvements. We amortize leasehold improvements over their estimated useful lives or the remaining term of the lease, whichever is the shorter period.

AT & T CORPORATION
Selected Financial Statement Information
For the Years Ended December 31, 2000 And 1999
(in millions)

	December 31 2000	December 31 1999
Income Statement (for the year ended)		
Net income	$ 4,669	$ 3,428
Balance Sheet (as of the year end)		
Goodwill	$ 33,240	$ 7,808
Total assets	$242,223	$169,406

2000 Annual Report: Notes to Financial Statements

Acquisition of MediaOne Group, Inc.: In February 2000, the Company completed the acquisition of the worldwide animal health business of MediaOne for approximately $45 billion. The acquisition was accounted for under the purchase method of accounting. The purchase price exceeded the net assets acquired by $25 billion.

EXHIBIT **10.6**

Goodwill Illustration for AT & T Corporation: Acquisition of MediaOne Group, Inc.

ANALYZING INFORMATION

Learning Goal 9   Analyze financial statement information for real-life companies.

We report property, plant, and equipment items on the balance sheet at cost less accumulated depreciation, depletion, or amortization. Additional disclosures in the notes to the statements usually include specific asset categories, estimated useful lives, and the methods of depreciation applied. Exhibit 10.7 shows the presentation of intangible assets and property, plant, and equipment on the balance sheet and the related footnote information for Dillard's Inc.

Question. The statement user wants to assess whether the assumptions used in computing depreciation and amortization expense are reasonable. Overall questions include: (1) Are the methods, asset lives, and residual values used to allocate asset cost reasonable? (2) If the methods, asset lives, or residual values are changed during the year, what is the impact on reported net income? (3) If some interest expense has been capitalized and debited to an asset account, what is the total amount of interest cost for the period?

DILLARD'S INC.
Selected Financial Statement Information
For the Years Ended January 31, 2004, and February 1, 2003
(*in millions*)

	2004	2003
Income Statement (for the year ended)		
Depreciation and amortization	$ 290.7	$ 301.4
Interest expense	$ 181.1	$ 189.8
Income tax expense	$ 6.7	$ 72.3
Net income	$ 9.3	$ (398.4)
Balance Sheet (as of the year end)		
Total property and equipment, net	$ 3,197.5	$ 3,370.5
Total assets	$ 6,411.1	$ 6,675.9

Annual Report for year ended February 3, 2001: Notes to Financial Statements

Property and Equipment
Property and equipment owned by the Company is stated at cost less accumulated depreciation and amortization. For tax reporting purposes, accelerated depreciation or cost recovery methods are used and the related deferred income taxes are included in noncurrent deferred income taxes in the consolidated balance sheets. For financial reporting purposes, depreciation is computed by the straight-line method over estimated useful lives of:

Building and leasehold improvements	20– 40 years
Furniture, fixtures and equipment	3–10 years

Capitalized Interest
Interest on borrowed funds is capitalized during construction of property and is amortized by charges to earnings over the depreciable lives of the related assets. Interest of $2.6 million, $2.5 million, and $5.4 million was capitalized during 2004, 2003, and 2002, respectively.

EXHIBIT **10.7**

Financial Statement Disclosure of Property, Plant, and Equipment and Related Items: Dillard's. Inc.

Answer. For Dillard's, depreciation is computed using the straight-line method. If an accelerated method was used, depreciation expense would be higher and reported net income would be lower. No mention is made of any changes in estimated asset lives. In the Delta Air Lines example discussed earlier, the increase in the asset lives decreased depreciation expense significantly.

Fixed interest payments on debt are an obligation companies must meet each year. Creditors want to know the firm's ability to pay annual interest charges. We may compute a ratio called *times interest earned* by dividing net income + income tax expense + interest expense by interest cost. The resulting number tells us how many times interest expense was covered during a period. A high ratio is more favorable. In computing the ratio, it is important to divide by the *total* interest cost for the period. If interest has been capitalized, only the net interest appears on the income statement. Usually, the amount of interest capitalized appears in a note to the financial statements. In the case of Dillard's, the total interest cost is $183,700,000 ($181,100,000 + $2,600,000) and the times interest earned ratio based on total interest cost for 2004 is:

Times interest earned based on total interest cost:

(Net Income	+	Income Tax Expense	+	Interest Expense)	÷	Total Interest Cost
($9,300,000	+	$6,700,000	+	$181,100,000)	÷	$183,700,000

= 1.07 times

If we based the ratio on net interest cost, the times interest earned ratio would be misleadingly higher as shown by the following computation:

Times interest earned based on net interest cost shown on Income Statement:

(Net Income	+	Income Tax Expense	+	Interest Expense)	÷	Net Interest Cost
($9,300,000	+	$6,700,000	+	$181,100,000)	÷	$181,100,000

= 1.09 times

LEARNING GOALS REVIEW

1. Determine the cost of tangible plant assets.

The acquisition cost of a tangible plant asset is the purchase price less any cash discount plus all other reasonable and necessary expenditures to prepare the asset for use in operations. Interest on construction financing is also a cost of acquiring a tangible asset. We value long-term assets acquired other than by a cash or credit purchase at fair market value.

2. Define depreciation and explain factors that affect the computation of depreciation.

Depreciation is the process of allocating the cost of an asset to the periods benefited. We depreciate the asset over the course of its estimated useful life. To determine the depreciable cost, we deduct the residual value from the cost.

3. Compute depreciation using the (a) straight-line method, (b) the production unit method, (c) the double declining-balance method, and (d) the sum-of-the-years'-digits method.

a. Under the straight-line method, depreciation expense for each year is: (Cost - Estimated Residual Value) ÷ Estimated Useful Life.

b. Under the production unit method, the depreciation per unit produced is: (Cost - Estimated Residual Value) ÷ Estimated useful life in units. We multiply the depreciation per unit by the number of units produced during the period to find the depreciation expense for the period.

c. Under the declining-balance method, we apply a uniform depreciation rate in each period to the remaining book value. The rate under the double declining-balance method (DDB) is twice the straight-line rate. We do not deduct residual value.

d. Under the sum-of-the-years'-digits method, we multiply the cost less the estimated residual value by a fraction. The numerator is the number of years remaining (including the current year) and the denominator is the sum of digits represented by the estimated useful life of the asset.

4. Explain the difference between revenue expenditures and capital expenditures.
Revenue expenditures benefit only a current accounting period. Therefore they are expenses of the current accounting period. Capital expenditures are significant costs that benefit two or more accounting periods. Capital expenditures may be acquisition costs, additions, betterments, or extraordinary repairs. We debit acquisition costs, additions, and betterments to the asset account. We debit extraordinary repairs to the accumulated depreciation account.

5. Record revisions of depreciation expense.
If an estimate of asset useful life changes, we allocate the remaining book value over the new estimate of the asset's remaining life. If estimated salvage value changes, we subtract the new salvage value from book value to find the new depreciable cost. We divide the new depreciable cost by the remaining useful life to determine the new depreciation amount.

6. Record the sale, retirement, or exchange of tangible plant assets.
When an asset is sold or retired, we first bring the depreciation up to date. The book value of the asset is the cost minus the accumulated depreciation. If the sale price equals book value, there is no gain or loss. If the asset is sold for more than book value, there is a gain on disposal. If the asset is sold for less than book value, there is a loss on disposal. In an exchange of dissimilar plant assets, we recognize both gains and losses. In an exchange of similar assets, we recognize a loss but not a gain. We deduct the gain from the cost of the new asset.

7. Discuss accounting issues for natural resources and compute depletion.
The primary accounting task is to measure depletion. We record periodic depletion by a debit to Depletion Cost or an inventory account and a credit to Accumulated Depletion. On the balance sheet we show accumulated depletion as a contra account deducted from the cost of the resource. Depletion cost per unit is (Cost - Residual Value) ÷ Estimated Number of Units. We multiply this per-unit charge by the number of units removed during the accounting period to find the depletion for the period.

8. Explain the accounting issues associated with intangible assets and compute amortization
We compute the amount to be amortized annually by dividing the asset cost by the legal life or the estimated useful life, whichever is shorter. The entry is usually a debit to an amortization expense account and a credit directly to the appropriate asset account. We record goodwill only in connection with purchase of all or part of a business. In that case, goodwill is the excess of the purchase price over the fair market value of assets acquired.

9. Analyze financial statement information for real-life companies.
Questions we may ask are: (1) Are the methods, asset lives, and residual values used to allocate asset cost reasonable? (2) If the methods, asset lives, or residual values are changed during the year, what is the impact on reported net income? (3) If some interest expense has been capitalized and debited to an asset account, what is the total amount of interest cost for the period?

DEMONSTRATION PROBLEM

Long-term Asset Transactions

Classic Corvette Company restores used sports cars for auto enthusiasts. During 2007, 2008, and 2009, Classic Corvette Company had the following transactions involving a precision metal grinder used to resurface engine parts. All expenditures were in cash.

2007

Jan.	1	Purchased a used precision metal grinder for $41,600. At this time, similar used grinders were selling for $46,000. Paid delivery charges of $400, installed a special foundation for the grinder at a cost of $700, paid $300 to have wiring on the grinder motor replaced, and paid $200 to repair a control on the grinder that was accidentally damaged during installation. The grinder has an estimated useful life of eight years and an expected residual value of $3,000. The straight-line method is used for financial reporting purposes.
Oct.	15	Paid $180 for ordinary maintenance repairs on the grinder.
Dec.	31	Recorded depreciation for 2007.

2008

Jan.	1	Purchased an attachment for the grinder that would enable the machine to work on a greater variety of engine parts. The attachment costs $1,000 and does not extend the useful life of the machine beyond the original estimate or change the estimated residual value.
	3	Paid $2,500 for a major overhaul of the motor on the grinder. It is expected that the overhaul will add three years to the original estimated life of eight years. The estimate of residual value is revised to $1,500.
Dec.	31	Recorded depreciation for 2008.

2009

Jul.	1	Decided that it would cost less if engine parts were sent out to an independent machine shop for grinding. Traded the grinding machine for a used tow truck valued at $48,000. A trade-in allowance of $39,000 was allowed on the grinder and $9,000 was paid in cash.

REQUIRED

Record the preceding transactions in general journal form (**LG 1, 3-6**).

SOLUTION

Solution Approach

Record tangible plant assets at acquisition cost. Therefore, ignore the market value of similar used grinders ($46,000). Capitalize all reasonable and necessary expenditures to prepare the asset for use in operations. The $200 repair charge on January 1 was due to a negligent action. Treat it as a revenue expenditure (expensed). Total costs capitalized are $43,000 ($41,600 + $400 + $700 + $300).

2007					
Jan.	1	Grinder		43,000	
		Cash			43,000
		Purchase of used precision metal grinder.			
	1	Repairs Expense		200	
		Cash			200
		Repairs due to damage of grinding machine during installation.			

Solution Approach

Treat costs of ordinary maintenance as revenue expenditures (expensed).

2007
Oct.   15   Repairs Expense   180
                 Cash   180
                 Ordinary maintenance on grinding machine.

Solution Approach

$43,000 - $3,000 = $40,000 ÷ 8 years = $5,000.

2007
Dec.   31   Depreciation Expense   5,000
                 Accumulated Depreciation—Grinder   5,000
                 Depreciation expense for 2007.

Solution Approach

Capitalize expenditures that enlarge or improve a plant asset by debiting the appropriate asset account.

2008
Jan.   1   Grinder   1,000
                 Cash   1,000
                 Purchased attachment for grinder.

Solution Approach

Treat extraordinary repairs that extend the useful life or capacity of a plant asset and/or change the estimated residual value as capital expenditures. Record extraordinary repairs by a debit to Accumulated Depreciation.

2008
Jan.   3   Accumulated Depreciation—Grinder   2,500
                 Cash   2,500
                 To record overhaul of grinder motor.

Solution Approach

Original cost		$43,000
Add: Attachment		1,000
Subtotal		$44,000
Deduct:		
Accumulated depreciation recorded in prior years (2007)	$ 5,000	
Deduct: Reduction in accumulated depreciation due to overhaul	2,500	2,500
Adjusted book value		$41,500
Deduct: Revised residual value		1,500
New depreciable cost		$40,000
New annual depreciation expense, based on remaining useful life of 10 years		
(original life of 8 years + increase of 3 years - 1 year already taken) =		
($40,000 ÷ 10)		$ 4,000

2008				
Dec.	31	Depreciation Expense—Grinder	4,000	
		Accumulated Depreciation—Grinder		4,000
		Depreciation expense for 2008.		

Solution Approach

When an asset is disposed of, the first journal entry should be to record depreciation for the current year up to the date of sale. $4,000 × 6/12 = $2,000.

2009				
Jul.	1	Depreciation Expense—Grinder	2,000	
		Accumulated Depreciation—Grinder		2,000
		To record depreciation on grinder for first six months in 2009.		

Solution Approach

First determine account balances in old plant asset and accumulated depreciation accounts. A useful way to do this is to construct T accounts as follows:

Grinder			Accumulated Depreciation—Grinder		
1/1/07	43,000		1/3/08	2,500	12/31/07 5,000
1/1/08	1,000				12/31/08 4,000
					7/1/09 2,000
Balance	44,000				Balance 8,500

In a trade-in for a dissimilar item, record the new asset at fair market value. Remove the cost of the old asset and related accumulated depreciation balances. We must recognize a gain in the case of a trade-in of dissimilar plant assets. Compute it as follows:

Cost of old asset	$ 44,000
Deduct: Accumulated depreciation to date	8,500
Book value	$ 35,500
Trade-in allowance	39,000
Gain on trade-in	$ 3,500

2009					
Jul.	1		Tow Truck	48,000	
			Accumulated Depreciation—Grinder	8,500	
			Grinder		44,000
			Cash		9,000
			Gain on Disposal of Plant Assets		3,500
			To record trade-in of grinder for tow truck.		

GLOSSARY

accelerated methods Depreciation methods that result in larger expense during the early years of asset life, with gradually decreasing expense in later years.

amortization General term to cover write-down of assets; it is most commonly used to describe periodic allocation of costs of intangible assets to expense.

book value The net amount at which an asset is carried on the books or reported in the financial statements. It is the asset's cost at acquisition reduced by the amount of its total depreciation recorded to date. Also called carrying value and undepreciated cost.

capital expenditures Payments or promises to make future payments for assets that will benefit more than one accounting period. They are carried forward as assets.

capitalize To increase the property, plant, and equipment book value for expenditures that increase the EUL or the valuation of such an asset.

copyright An exclusive right to reproduce and sell a literary or artistic work.

depletion The process of estimating and recording periodic charges to operations because of the exhaustion of a natural resource.

depreciable cost The net cost of an asset to be recorded as expense over its estimated useful life.

depreciation Allocating the cost of an asset to the periods the asset benefits.

double declining-balance method (DDB) An accelerated depreciation method in which a constant rate—twice that of the straight-line rate—is applied to carrying value to compute annual charges.

estimated useful life (EUL) An estimate, made at the time of acquisition, of the term of usefulness of an asset (may be in years, working hours, or units of output).

fair market value Value determined by informed buyers and sellers based usually on current invoice or quoted prices.

franchise A monopolistic right granted by a government or other entity to produce goods or render services.

goodwill A general term embodying a variety of intangible factors relating to the reputation of a firm and its ability to generate above-normal earnings. It is measured by the excess of sales price over fair market value at acquisition date.

intangible assets Long-term assets that have no physical substance, but whose ownership is expected to contribute to operations.

inventoriable costs All costs directly involved in the production of inventory (including depletion costs and patent amortization costs).

lease The right to use, for a fixed period of time, property belonging to others.

modified accelerated cost recovery system (MACRS) A method of tax deductions to recover the cost of depreciable property.

natural resources Long-term assets with physical substance whose value to the firm is diminished through use or sale.

patent The exclusive right to exploit a method or a product over a legal life of 17 years.

production unit method A method of depreciation based on a fixed rate per unit of output determined by estimating the total units of output.

property, plant, and equipment Tangible plant assets whose use will provide benefits over more than one accounting period; these include land, buildings, and machinery.

residual value The amount of asset cost that is expected to be recovered when the asset is ultimately scrapped, sold, or traded in; also called salvage value.

revenue expenditures Expenditures that benefit the current period only and are debited to expense.

straight-line method A depreciation method that allocates a uniform portion of the depreciable asset cost to each accounting period over the estimated useful life of the asset.

sum-of-the-years'-digits method (SYD) An accelerated depreciation method in which annual depreciation expense is determined by multiplying cost less residual value by a fraction.

tangible plant assets Long-term assets with physical substance, such as land, buildings, machinery, or equipment.

QUESTIONS FOR GROUP LEARNING

Q10-1. Define the term long-term assets. What groups of assets are included in this term? Give examples of each.

Q10-2. (a) List some expenditures other than the purchase price that make up the cost of tangible plant assets. (b) Why are cash discounts excluded from the cost of tangible plant assets?

Q10-3. (a) What distinguishes a capital expenditure from a revenue expenditure? (b) What is the impact on the financial statements if this distinction is not properly made?

Q10-4. Student A maintains that if a tangible plant asset has a fair market value greater than its cost after one year of use, no depreciation need be recorded for the year. Student B insists that the fair market value is irrelevant in this context. Indicate which position you support and give your reasons.

Q10-5. What are some factors that must be considered when choosing a depreciation method?

Q10-6. Since the total amount to be depreciated cannot exceed the cost of the asset, does it make any difference which method is used in calculating the periodic depreciation charges? Explain.

Q10-7. Does the recording of depreciation have any relation to the accounting standard of matching revenue and expenses? Explain.

Q10-8. Describe the conditions that might lead to the use of each of the following methods of depreciation: (a) straight-line, (b) units of production, (c) accelerated.

Q10-9. What procedures should be followed in computing depreciation on assets held for part of a month?

Q10-10. What is the relationship, if any, between the amount of annual depreciation expense on tangible plant assets and the amount of money available for new plant assets?

Q10-11. What accounting problems result (a) from the exchange of a tangible plant asset? (b) From the sale of a plant asset?

Q10-12. (a) Distinguish among the terms depreciation, depletion, and amortization. (b) How is the periodic depletion charge determined?

Q10-13. Is depletion an operating expense? How does depletion cost reduce net income?

Q10-14. (a) What are intangible assets? (b) What factors must be considered when the cost of intangibles is (1) recorded? (2) amortized? (c) Is a contra account used for accumulated amortization?

Q10-15. According to current accounting standards, how are (a) research and development costs and (b) computer software development costs each treated in the financial statements?

EXERCISES

E10-16. Amount of debit to asset account (LG 1) Diane's Deli made the following expenditures on the acquisition of a new delivery van:

Invoice cost ($25,000) less 2 % cash discount	$24,500
Transportation charges	570
Repair of dent when Sal backed into a tree	700
Special paint and lights	500
Adding custom shelves	2,425
Sales tax	1,000

What is the amount of the total debit to the Delivery Van account?

E10-17. Recordkeeping: An acquisition (LG 1) Greg's Computers purchased office equipment for $6,000 subject to terms of 2/10, n/30. Record the purchase and the payment of the invoice within the discount period.

E10-18. Recording the cost of a new plant (LG 1) During 2007, Bartley Manufacturing purchased a lot on which an existing building was located. The total cost of the lot and building was $160,000. The company paid $10,000 to have the building torn down and $6,000 to grade the lot. Proceeds from materials sold from the building were $3,000. To construct a new building, the company paid $3,500,000 to Santini Construction Company. In addition, a parking lot was constructed at a cost of $60,000. All transactions were in cash. Prepare a single journal entry dated December 31, 2007, to record the above transactions.

E10-19. Depreciation: all methods (full year) (LG 3) On January 2, 2007, Fly Fast Airlines bought a new aircraft for $5,000,000. At the end of its EUL, it is expected to have a residual value of $800,000. Fly Fast estimates that the aircraft will be used in its operations for 16 years. Record, in general journal form, the depreciation adjustment at December 31, 2007, under each of the following assumptions:

a. The straight-line method is used.

b. The double declining-balance method is used.

c. The production unit method is used. It is estimated that the new aircraft has a useful life of 80,000 flying hours. It was flown 2,200 hours in 2007.

E10-20. Partial-year depreciation: three methods (partial year plus full year) (LG 3) Valley Company began business on July 1, 2007, with two new machines. Data for the machines are as follows:

Machine	Cost	Estimated Residual Value	EUL (Years)
X	$ 75,000	$ 15,000	5
Y	126,000	16,000	10

Compute the depreciation expense for calendar years 2007 and 2008 by each of the following methods: (a) straight-line, (b) sum-of-the-years'-digits, and (c) double declining-balance.

E10-21. **Revenue and capital expenditures (LG 4)** For each of the following items, indicate whether the payment is a revenue or a capital expenditure and identify the account debited.

a. Expenditure for installing machinery.

b. Expenditure for trial run of new machinery.

c. Expenditure for insurance on machinery after it is in operation.

d. Payment of delinquent taxes on a newly purchased building (taxes were delinquent at the date of purchase of the building).

e. Expenditure for extensive plumbing repairs to make a newly purchased building usable.

f. Sales tax paid on new machinery just purchased.

g. Payment for the right to operate a Holiday Inn.

h. Expenditure for a major overhaul that restores an aircraft engine to its original condition and extends its useful life.

i. Expenditure for an addition to a building that is leased for 20 years.

j. Amount paid for a business in excess of the appraised value of the net assets.

k. Ordinary repair to an aircraft engine after it is in operation.

l. Expenditure for leaflet to advertise new services available because of new machinery.

m. Interest on money borrowed to construct a new building.

E10-22. **Revision of depreciation expense (LG 5)** Tops Company purchased a Ferrari sports car on July 1, 2007, as an incentive for the sales staff. The top salesperson in a particular month has the use of the car in the following month. The Ferrari cost $200,000. It was estimated that the car would have a useful life of seven years and a residual value of $60,000. The straight-line method is used. On January 1, 2009, inspection of the car indicated that the original estimate of useful life was too long considering the driving habits of the Tops sales staff. As a result the total life of the car was revised to only six years, and the residual value was revised to $26,000. Compute the amount of depreciation expense recognized in 2007, 2008, and 2009.

E10-23. **Overhaul and new depreciation amount (LG 5)** The Scoops Delight acquired a new freezer on January 1, 2007, at an installed cost of $60,000. The freezer had an estimated useful life of eight years and a residual value of $6,000. Two years later, on January 1, 2009, the freezer was completely overhauled at a cost of $12,000. These improvements were expected to increase the total useful life from eight years to twelve years. Residual value remains at $5,000. Prepare, in general journal form, all entries pertaining to this freezer except closing entries from acquisition through December 31, 2009. The company uses the straight-line method of depreciation.

E10-24. **Sale of a used asset (LG 6)** On July 1, 2007, Big O Corporation sold for $35,000 cash a piece of drilling machinery that had been in use since January 3, 1998. The original cost of the machine was $134,000. Big O has recorded $12,000 of straight-line depreciation annually through December 31, 2006. In general journal form, record the sale.

E10-25. **Trade-in on a similar and a dissimilar item (LG 6)** On April 2, 2007, Norfolk Freight purchased a new forklift truck for $14,000 cash. It estimated the truck to have a useful life of five years and a residual value of $2,000. At the end of 2007, Norfolk concluded that the truck was the wrong model, and it was traded in for a similar truck that had a cash price (and fair market value) of $24,000.

1. Record the purchase on April 2, 2007, and the depreciation adjustment on December 31, 2007 (straight-line depreciation).

2. Record the trade-in using the following assumptions:

   a. The dealer gave a fair value trade-in allowance of $13,500; Norfolk paid the balance in cash.

   b. The dealer gave a fair value trade-in allowance of $8,000; Norfolk paid the balance in cash.

3. Using the assumptions in requirement 2 above, record the trade-in on a parcel of land that had a fair market price of $20,000.

E10-26. **Computation of depletion cost (LG 7)** Gold Mines purchased a piece of land and the mineral rights for $3,200,000. Company engineers estimate that the property contains 600,000 tons of ore and that Gold can sell the land for $200,000 when it completes mining operations. In the first year, Gold mined 120,000 tons of ore. Compute depletion cost for the first year.

E10-27. **Cost allocation for long-term assets (LG 2, 7, 8)** Indicate which word—depreciation, depletion, or amortization—should be used to identify the allocation of the following expenditures. Place an "N" next to expenditures that are expensed or for which cost allocation procedures do not apply.

a. Cash registers used in the business.

b. Land.

c. Computers acquired for resale.

d. Special foundations constructed for machines used in the business.

e. Excess of purchase price over fair market value of businesses acquired (goodwill).

f. Patents.

g. Delivery truck.

h. Extraordinary repairs that extend the life of a machine used in the business.

i. Timber tracts for a lumber company.

j. Computer software developmental costs incurred prior to completing a detailed program design or working model.

k. Research and development costs.

l. Cost of paving and painting lines on company parking lot.

m. Expenditures for trial runs to test new automated machines.

E10-28. **Amortization of franchise (LG 8)** Station KHUT received a franchise to transmit on channel 89.3 for eight years. The accounting, legal, clerical, and consultant fees for obtaining this franchise amounted to $120,000. These costs were recorded as an intangible asset, Franchise, on April 1, 2007. Make adjusting entries to record amortization of the franchise in the fiscal years ending December 31, 2007 and 2008.

E10-29. **Amortization of patent (LG 8)** On July 1, 2007, Inlet Lobster purchased a patent for a new freezing process at a cost of $48,000. It is estimated that the patent will give it an advantage over its competitors for the next three years. In general journal form, record the amortization adjustments for the years ended December 31, 2007, and December 31, 2008.

PROBLEMS

P10-30. **Determining the cost of tangible plant assets (LG 1)** Rega Recordings purchased a new digital tape recorder on August 1, 2007, for use in the business. The list price of the tape recorder was $28,000. After considerable negotiations, the manufacturer agreed to sell the tape recorder to Rega Recordings for $28,000 with a 2% discount for cash payment on delivery. Competing recording studios had recently paid $30,000 for a similar tape recorder. Sales taxes on the tape recorder amounted to $7,600, delivery charges were $70, and labor charges to install the tape recorder amounted to $300. When the tape recorder was being carried through the parking lot a van belonging to a recording group under contract to Rega Recordings was accidentally scratched. The cost of repainting the van was $900 and was paid by the company. Ordinary maintenance on the tape recorder during 2007 amounted to $700. Rega Recordings took advantage of the cash discount offered for immediate cash payment on the tape recorder and paid all other expenditures in cash.

REQUIRED

1. Determine the amount that should be properly recorded as a debit to the Tape Recorder asset account.

2. For the year ended December 31, 2007, compute the total amount of expenses associated with the tape recorder, other than depreciation expense, which would appear on the income statement for Rega Recordings.

P10-31. **Depreciation for several years: three methods (LG 3)** Lazy Days Mine has the following information about its plant assets at the end of 2007:

	Building	Excavating Equipment	Sorting Equipment
Date acquired	January 1, 2001	January 7, 2006	January 3, 2006
Cost	$ 900,000	$ 680,000	$ 405,000
Estimated residual value	$ 150,000	$ 100,000	$ 45,000
EUL in years	30	8	9
Method of depreciation	SL	DDB	SYD

REQUIRED

1. Compute the balance in the Accumulated Depreciation account for each category of plant assets at the beginning of calendar year 2007.

2. Prepare the adjusting entries for depreciation as of December 31, 2007.

P10-32. **Entries over the life of a plant asset: SYD depreciation (LG 1, 3, 6)** Quick Cleaners purchased a carpet cleaning system in 2007. Significant events concerning this system were as follows:

2007

Jun.	5	Received equipment at an invoice price of $140,000, 2/10, n/30; recorded liability at net amount.
	15	Paid for the account payable balance.
	19	Paid $7,600 for installation costs.
	28	Paid $7,200 for testing and debugging.
Jul.	1	The cleaning system was placed in full operation. It was estimated that the cleaning system had an EUL of eight years with a residual value of $8,000. It is to be depreciated by the straight-line method.
Aug.	22	Paid $800 for minor repairs.
Dec.	31	Recorded depreciation for 2007.

2008

Jul.	8	Paid $900 for minor repairs.
Dec.	31	Recorded depreciation for 2008.

2009

Jul.	3	Having decided that the cleaning system was not required, management sold it for $124,000 cash.

REQUIRED

In general journal form, record the above events.

P10-33. **Exchange for similar and dissimilar items (LG 6)** Amy's Limo purchased a Lincoln limousine on July 1, 2007, at a cost of $67,000. Amy's estimated it to have a useful life of eight years and a residual value of $5,000. Amy's uses the double declining-balance method of depreciation. After the depreciation was recorded on December 31, 2007, Amy's decided that the Lincoln was not the correct model so it was traded in on a Cadillac limousine priced at a fair market value of $94,000 on January 2, 2008.

REQUIRED

Record the exchange on January 2, 2008, under the following independent assumptions:

1. The dealer gives a fair value trade-in allowance of $62,000; Amy's pays the balance in cash.

2. The dealer gives a fair value trade-in allowance of $52,000; Amy's pays the balance in cash.

3. Same as the problem and requirement 1 except that Amy's traded in the limousine for a boat with a fair market price of $94,000.

P10-34. **Depletion and inventoriable costs (LG 7)** On October 1, 2007, Panhandle Oil, Inc. purchased a tract of land and the oil rights to it for $24,800,000. Company engineers estimate that 1,000,000 barrels of oil will be extracted from this deposit over a period of about two years. It is further estimated that dismantling the drilling rig will cost $100,000, and resale of the land will bring in $300,000. Panhandle began drilling operations in October and by December 31, 2007, the well had produced 300,000 barrels of oil. Panhandle had sold 185,000 barrels of this production in 2007, and 115,000 barrels remained in inventory on December 31, 2007. Labor, materials, depreciation, and other costs in addition to depletion incurred in production operations amounted to $1,080,000. Oil sold in 2007 brought an average selling price of $45 per barrel.

REQUIRED

Compute the following for this well:

1. The depletion cost in 2007.

2. The cost of oil sold in 2007.

3. The gross margin on 2007 sales.

4. The valuation to be placed on the December 31, 2007, inventory.

P10-35. **Revenue expenditure or capital expenditure for long-term assets (LG 1, 4, 8)**
During 2007, Keystone Company incurred expenditures described in the independent cases that follow:

- **Case 1** Constructed a new addition to the manufacturing plant at a cost of $900,000. Additional costs include architectural fees of $65,000, building permit fees of $5,500, interest expense of $9,000 during construction on bank loans used to finance construction costs, and $11,300 for education programs to train employees who will work in the new addition. Completed the building on December 31, 2007.

- **Case 2** Spent $790,000 for research and development during 2007 in an attempt to develop a new computer printer that will be introduced into the product line next year. The printer has the potential to become a best-seller.

- **Case 3** Spent $920,000 for the development of new computer software for sale to others during the year. Of this amount, $400,000 was incurred after a working model had been developed. The remainder was spent in the initial design stages of the software product. It is expected that the software product will be introduced next year.

- **Case 4** Purchased a patent on a solar energy cell for $432,000 on March 1, 2007. Began to manufacture and sell the product on that date. The patent has a remaining legal life of 12 years and an estimated economic life of 6 years due to rapid changes in technology. Gross sales revenue from the sale of the energy cell during 2007 totaled $800,000.

REQUIRED

Explain whether each of the expenditures described above should be treated as a revenue or capital expenditure during 2007. If you feel that the costs represent a capital expenditure, state whether the expenditure will result in the recognition of (a) a tangible plant asset, (b) a natural resource asset, or (c) an intangible asset on the balance sheet as of December 31, 2007. If possible, also state the amount of the long-term asset on the balance sheet as of December 31, 2007.

P10-36. **Analyzing long-term assets for Vail Resorts (LG 9)** Vail Resorts is the premier mountain resort company in North America. Selected data in millions are:

FOR THE YEAR ENDED JULY 31, 2004:

Net income (loss)	$(5.9)
Income tax expense	0.0
Interest expense (net)	47.5

As of July 31, 2004:

Property and Equipment, net	$968.8
Total assets	1,534.0

Notes to Financial Statements: Capitalized Interest

Interest capitalized on real estate development for the year ended July 31, 2004, was $1.6 million.

REQUIRED

1. Is investing in long-term assets a significant issue for Vail? Briefly explain.

2. Compute times interest earned using total interest cost for the year.

3. Compute times interest earned using net interest expense for the year.

4. Briefly state and explain why answer #2 or #3 is more correct.

P10-37. **Analyzing long-term assets for Wal-Mart Stores, Inc. (LG 9)** Wal-Mart Stores, Inc. is one of the world's largest discount retail chains. Selected information (in millions) for the fiscal year ended on January 31, 2004 are:

For the year ended January 31, 2004:

Net income	$9,054
Income tax expense	5,118
Interest expense (net)	996

As of January 31, 2004:

Property and Equipment, net	$58,530
Total assets	104,912

Notes to Financial Statements: Capitalized Interest

Interest expense capitalized as a component of construction costs was $144 million in 2004.

REQUIRED

1. Is investing in long-term assets a significant issue for Wal-Mart? Briefly explain.

2. Compute times interest earned using total interest cost for the year.

3. Compute times interest earned using net interest expense for the year.

4. Briefly state and explain why answer #2 or #3 is more correct.

PRACTICE CASE

Long-term assets (LG 1, 3-6) Shapes Fitness Center promises a new body in six months or a full refund of its membership fee. To help make the promise a reality, they seek out and invest in the latest bodybuilding machines. During 2007, 2008, and 2009, Shapes Fitness Center had the following transactions involving the "Wonder Body" machine manufactured by a company in Sweden. All expenditures were for cash.

2007

Jul.	1	Purchased a new "Wonder Body" machine for $83,000. At this time, machines claiming similar results were selling for $80,000. Paid delivery charges from Sweden of $1,900, installed a special foundation for the machine at a cost of $1,200, paid $300 to have a new electrical circuit for the machine installed, and paid $200 to repair a lever on the machine that was damaged when the machine was accidentally dropped during installation. The machine has an estimated useful life of 10 years and an expected residual value of $6,400. The straight-line method is used for financial reporting purposes.
Dec.	31	Recorded depreciation for 2007.

2008

Jan.	1	Purchased an attachment for the machine that would enable it to condition additional body parts. The attachment costs $8,000 and does not extend the useful life of the machine beyond the original estimate, but increases the estimated residual value to $9,040.
Oct.	3	Replaced all of the belts in the machine at a cost of $500. This was considered to be a normal maintenance procedure.
Dec.	31	Recorded depreciation for 2008.

2009

Jan.	1	Paid $6,300 for a major overhaul of the machine. It is expected that the overhaul will add 1 ½ years to the original estimated life of 10 years. The estimated residual value is revised to $12,000.
Jul.	1	Decided that the machine was not meeting its stated performance standards. Traded the machine in on a similar machine made in France. The new machine cost $102,000. A trade-in allowance of $87,275 was allowed on the old machine, and $14,725 was paid in cash.

REQUIRED

In general journal form, record the transactions listed above.

BUSINESS DECISION AND COMMUNICATION PROBLEM

Interpretation of depreciation note for Caterpillar, Inc. (LG 9) A recent annual report of Caterpillar, Inc., contained the following notes concerning the impact on financial statements of using alternative depreciation methods (dollars in millions):

Depreciation

Depreciation is computed principally using accelerated methods. If the straight-line method had always been used, "Land, buildings, machinery, and equipment—net" would have been $633 million higher than reported at the end of the year.

Buildings, machinery, and equipment at December 31, by major classification were as follows (dollars in millions):

Buildings	$2,226
Machinery and equipment	2,900
Patterns, dies, jigs, etc.	452
Furniture and fixtures	472
Transportation equipment	25
Construction-in-process	642
Equipment owned and leased out	289
	$7,006
Deduct: Accumulated depreciation	3,609
Buildings, machinery, and equipment—net	$3,397

REQUIRED

You are a stock analyst employed by a stock brokerage company. Ed Time, your supervisor, has asked you to respond to the following questions he has concerning Caterpillar, Inc. Prepare a memo answering his questions.

1. What type of depreciation method does Caterpillar use for financial reporting purposes?

2. As of the year-end, what was the amount of total investment in buildings, machinery, and equipment for Caterpillar?

3. As of the year-end, what was the total book value of buildings, machinery, and equipment for Caterpillar?

4. As of the year-end, buildings, machinery, and equipment net of depreciation total $3,394 million for Caterpillar. If straight-line depreciation had always been used, compute the amount of buildings, machinery, and equipment net of depreciation as of the year-end.

5. Because of its depreciation policy for financial reporting over the years, has Caterpillar tended to maximize or minimize reported net income? Explain briefly.

6. Why do you suppose Caterpillar included the note explaining the impact of using alternative depreciation methods?

ETHICAL DILEMMA

Depreciation policies (LG 2) You are the chief accountant for Wayne Instrument Manufacturing. The company has faced a significant decrease in customer orders. There is no sign of improvement over the next few years due to depressed economic conditions. Past depreciation policy has been to use the sum-of-the-years'-digits method for computer manufacturing equipment. An estimated useful life of five years and a residual value of 5% of asset cost has been assumed. The president has asked you to change depreciation policies to the following:

1. Straight-line method.

2. Useful life of 20 years.

3. Residual value of 25% of asset cost.

REQUIRED

Describe the impact of the new depreciation policies on reported net income. How would you respond?

COMPREHENSIVE ANALYSIS CASE BEST BUY CO., INC.

Analyzing Best Buy Co. Inc. for the Period 2004-2002 Best Buy is the nation's largest volume specialty retailer selling consumer electronics, computers, software, and appliances. The Company is ranked 78th in the Fortune 500. Listed below are comparative income statements and balance sheets with common-size percents for 2004-2002 (in millions). Also included are selected ratio statistics. Please provide a brief explanation for your answer to each question.

REQUIRED

Income statement questions:

  1. Are total revenues higher or lower over the three-year period?

  2. What is the percent change in total revenues from 2002 to 2004?

  3. Is the percent of cost of goods sold to total revenues increasing or decreasing over the three-year period? As a result, is the gross margin percent increasing or decreasing?

  4. Is the percent of total operating expenses to total revenues increasing or decreasing over the three-year period? As a result, is the operating income percent increasing or decreasing?

  5. Is the percent of net income to total revenue increasing or decreasing over the three-year period?

Balance sheet questions:

  6. Are total assets higher or lower over the three-year period?

  7. What is the percent change in total assets from 2002 to 2004?

  8. What are the largest asset investments for the company over the three-year period?

  9. Are the inventories increasing faster or slower than the percent change in total revenues?

  10. Is the percent of total liabilities to total liabilities + owners' equity increasing or decreasing? As a result, is there more or less risk that the company could not pay its debts?

Integrative income statement and balance sheet question:

  11. Is the company operating more or less efficiently by using the least amount of asset investment to generate a given level of total revenues? Note that the "total asset turnover" ratio is computed and included in the "ratio analysis summary".

Ratio analysis questions:

  12. Is the *current ratio* better or worse in the most current year compared to prior years?

  13. Is the *quick ratio* better or worse in the most current year compared to prior years?

  14. Is the *accounts receivable turnover ratio 1* (based on *average* receivables) better or worse in the most current year compared to prior years?

  15. Is the 2004 *accounts receivable turnover ratio 2* (based on *year-end* receivables) better or worse than the 2004 ratio based on an *average*?

  16. Is the *inventory turnover ratio 1* (based on *average* inventory) better or worse in the most current year compared to prior years?

  17. Is the 2004 *inventory turnover ratio 2* (based on *year-end* inventory) better or worse than the 2004 ratio based on an *average*?

  18. Is the *return on total assets (ROA) ratio* better or worse in the most current year compared to prior years?

BEST BUY CO INC
COMPARATIVE COMMON-SIZE INCOME STATEMENTS
For the years ended Feb. 28, 2004, Mar. 1, 2003, and Mar. 2, 2002
(*in millions*)

	2004 $	2004 %	2003 $	2003 %	2002 $	2002 %
Revenues	$ 24,547.0	100.0%	$ 20,946.0	100.0%	$ 19,597.0	100.0%
Cost of goods sold	$ 18,350.0	74.8%	$ 15,710.0	75.0%	$ 15,167.0	77.4%
Gross margin	$ 6,197.0	25.2%	$ 5,236.0	25.0%	$ 4,430.0	22.6%
Operating expenses:						
Sales, marketing, general administrative	$ 4,893.0	19.9%	$ 4,226.0	20.2%	$ 3,493.0	17.8%
Research and development	$ -	0.0%	$ -	0.0%	$ -	0.0%
Other expense	$ -	0.0%	$ -	0.0%	$ -	0.0%
Other expense	$ -	0.0%	$ -	0.0%	$ -	0.0%
Total operating expenses	$ 4,893.0	19.9%	$ 4,226.0	20.2%	$ 3,493.0	17.8%
Operating income	$ 1,304.0	5.3%	$ 1,010.0	4.8%	$ 937.0	4.8%
Net interest expense (income)	$ 8.0	0.0%	$ -	0.0%	$ 1.0	0.0%
Other expense (income)	$ -	0.0%	$ (4.0)	0.0%	$ -	0.0%
Income before income taxes	$ 1,296.0	5.3%	$ 1,014.0	4.8%	$ 936.0	4.8%
Income taxes	$ 496.0	2.0%	$ 392.0	1.9%	$ 366.0	1.9%
Net income (loss) before unusual items	$ 800.0	3.3%	$ 622.0	3.0%	$ 570.0	2.9%
Other losses (gains) net of tax	$ 95.0	0.4%	$ 523.0	2.5%	$ -	0.0%
Net income (loss)	$ 705.0	2.9%	$ 99.0	0.5%	$ 570.0	2.9%

BEST BUY CO INC
COMPARATIVE COMMON-SIZE BALANCE SHEETS
Feb. 28, 2004, Mar. 1, 2003, and Mar. 2, 2002
(*in millions*)

	2004 $	2004 %	2003 $	2003 %	2002 $	2002 %
ASSETS						
Current:						
Cash & cash equivalents	$ 2,600.0	30.1%	$ 1,914.0	25.0%	$ 1,855.0	25.2%
Short-term investments	$ -	0.0%	$ -	0.0%	$ -	0.0%
Accounts receivable, net	$ 343.0	4.0%	$ 322.0	4.2%	$ 326.0	4.4%
Inventory	$ 2,607.0	30.1%	$ 2,046.0	26.7%	$ 2,258.0	30.6%
Other current assets	$ 174.0	2.0%	$ 585.0	7.6%	$ 172.0	2.3%
Other current assets	$ -	0.0%	$ -	0.0%	$ -	0.0%
Total current assets	$ 5,724.0	66.2%	$ 4,867.0	63.5%	$ 4,611.0	62.5%
Fixed:						
Property & equipment, net	$ 2,244.0	25.9%	$ 2,062.0	26.9%	$ 1,897.0	25.7%
Long-term investments	$ -	0.0%	$ -	0.0%	$ -	0.0%
Intangibles & goodwill	$ 514.0	5.9%	$ 462.0	6.0%	$ 773.0	10.5%
Other assets	$ 170.0	2.0%	$ 272.0	3.5%	$ 94.0	1.3%
Total assets	$ 8,652.0	100.0%	$ 7,663.0	100.0%	$ 7,375.0	100.0%
LIABILITIES						
Current:						
Short-term debt	$ 368.0	4.3%	$ 1.0	0.0%	$ 7.0	0.1%
Accounts payable	$ 3,833.0	44.3%	$ 3,472.0	45.3%	$ 3,723.0	50.5%
Accrued salaries and benefits	$ 300.0	3.5%	$ 320.0	4.2%	$ -	0.0%
Unearned revenue	$ -	0.0%	$ -	0.0%	$ -	0.0%
Other current liabilities	$ -	0.0%	$ -	0.0%	$ -	0.0%
Total current liabilities	$ 4,501.0	52.0%	$ 3,793.0	49.5%	$ 3,730.0	50.6%
Long-term debt	$ 482.0	5.6%	$ 828.0	10.8%	$ 813.0	11.0%
Deferred income tax liabilities	$ -	0.0%	$ -	0.0%	$ -	0.0%
Other long-term liabilities	$ 247.0	2.9%	$ 312.0	4.1%	$ 311.0	4.2%
Total liabilities	$ 5,230.0	60.4%	$ 4,933.0	64.4%	$ 4,854.0	65.8%
OWNERS' EQUITY						
Total owners' equity	$ 3,422.0	39.6%	$ 2,730.0	35.6%	$ 2,521.0	34.2%
Total liabilities and owners' equity	$ 8,652.0	100.0%	$ 7,663.0	100.0%	$ 7,375.0	100.0%

(Note: percents may not add to 100 due to rounding)

BEST BUY CO INC
RATIO ANALYSIS SUMMARY
For the years ended Feb. 28, 2004, Mar. 1, 2003, and Mar. 2, 2002

	2004	2003	2002
SHORT-TERM LIQUIDITY RATIOS			
Current Ratio (Current Assets/Current Liabilities)	1.27	1.28	1.24
Quick Ratio (Cash + Short-term Investments + Accounts Receivable)/Current Liabilities	0.65	0.59	0.58
Accounts Receivable Turnover 1 (Revenues/Average Accounts Receivable)	73.83	64.65	
Accounts Receivable Turnover 2 (Revenues/Year-end Accounts Receivable)	71.57	65.05	60.11
Inventory Turnover 1 (Cost Goods Sold/Average Inventory)	7.89	7.30	
Inventory Turnover 2 (Cost Goods Sold/Year-end Inventory)	7.04	7.68	6.72
LONG-TERM SOLVENCY (LEVERAGE) RATIO			
Total Debt Ratio (Total Liabilities/Total Assets)	60.45%	64.37%	65.82%
PROFITABILITY RATIOS			
Gross Profit Margin (Gross Margin/Revenues)	25.25%	25.00%	22.61%
Operating Profit Margin (Operating Income/Revenues)	5.31%	4.82%	4.78%
Net Profit Margin (Return on Sales) (ROS) (Net Income/Revenues)	2.87%	0.47%	2.91%
Total Asset Turnover (Revenues/Average Total Assets)	3.01	2.79	
Return on Total Assets (ROA) (Net Income/Average Total Assets)	8.64%	1.32%	

PRACTICE SET II(CHAPTERS 1-10)

Global Sales was incorporated on January 1, 2005. The purpose of the business is to sell recycling containers that allow different types of trash to be segregated. The public accounting firm of Left & Right, located in Cherry Hill, New Jersey, established an accounting system and set up a chart of accounts (which follows the accounts used in this textbook) on January 1, 2005. You have been asked to assist in preparing the financial statements for 2007. The following unadjusted balance as of December 31, 2007 is provided:

GLOBAL SALES, INC.
UNADJUSTED TRIAL BALANCE
DECEMBER 31, 2007

Acct No.	Account Title	Debits	Credits
101	Cash	$ 87,400	
102	Petty Cash	500	
105	Short-term Investments	100,000	
111	Accounts Receivable	200,000	
112	Allowance for Doubtful Accounts		$ 4,000
115	Notes Receivable	50,000	
130	Merchandise Inventory	150,000	
141	Prepaid Insurance	7,200	
142	Prepaid Rent	45,000	
165	Store Fixtures	62,000	
166	Accumulated Depreciation—Store Fixtures		8,000
177	Computer System	15,000	
178	Accumulated Depreciation—Computer System		9,600
201	Accounts Payable		120,000
202	Notes Payable		30,000
203	Discount on Notes Payable	1,200	
230	Unearned Revenue		8,000
252	Notes Payable—Long-term		200,000
331	Common Stock		100,000
360	Retained Earnings		115,900
372	Dividends	26,000	
401	Sales		1,182,000
402	Sales Returns and Allowances	5,000	
403	Sales Discounts	7,000	
501	Purchases	800,000	
602	Sales Salaries Expense	85,000	
616	Advertising Expense	110,000	
617	Transportation Out Expense	14,000	
625	Utilities Expense	5,800	
703	Office Salaries Expense	18,000	
802	Interest Revenue		11,600
	Totals	$1,789,100	$1,789,100

Adjustment Data

a. On December 31, 2007, the petty cash fund consisted of cash and other items as follows:

Currency and coins	$162
Office supplies expense	335
Total	$497

Record the entry to replenish petty cash.

b. On December 31, 2007, Global Sales management determined that the account receivable balance of $2,200 from Scott Teeter is uncollectible. Record the entry to write off the account receivable.

c. After Global Sales wrote off the account receivable from Scott Teeter an aging of the remaining accounts receivable indicated that a total of $6,400 will prove uncollectible. Record the bad debts adjustment.

d. Notes receivable consisted of the following two notes:Accrue interest on the two notes.

Date of Note	Term of Note	Interest Rate	Principal
October 2, 2007	120 days	12%	$ 30,000
November 16, 2007	90 days	11	20,000

e. The company uses the last-in, first-out (LIFO) cost flow assumption for inventories. It uses a periodic inventory system. Cost information for the beginning inventory and 2007 purchases is as follows:

Date	Quantity	Unit Cost	Total Cost
January 1, 2007 (beginning inventory)	6,000	$25	$150,000
March 10, 2007	8,000	35	280,000
July 2, 2007	10,000	38	380,000
October 18, 2007	3,500	40	140,000
Total goods available for sale	27,500		$950,000
Sales	19,700		
Inventory, December 31, 2007	7,800		

Compute the ending inventory value and enter it in the appropriate work sheet columns. Assume that the company treats inventory changes as closing entries.

f. The company paid the prepaid insurance policy in advance for 18 months on January 1, 2007.

g. The monthly rent for the store is $3,000. The company paid rent for the next 15 months on January 1, 2007.

h. Depreciation information is as follows:

Asset	Residual Value	Depreciation Method	EUL (Years)
Store fixtures	$ 2,000	Straight-line	15
Computer system	1,000	Double declining-balance	5

i. On September 15, 2007, Global Sales borrowed cash from Smith Bank. The company discounted at 12% a $30,000, 120-day note dated September 15, 2007, made out for the maturity value. Recognize the interest expense on the note for 2007.

j. A customer named Stuart Brown made an advance payment of $8,000 for containers on November 12, 2007. As of December 31, 2007, the company had delivered $5,200 of containers. It will fill the remainder of the order in 2008.

k. On July 1, 2007, Global Sales Management arranged for a five-year loan for $200,000 from Kelly Bank. Interest at 10% is payable annually on July 1. Accrue interest for six months in 2007.

l. Estimated income taxes are $54,300.

Requirements

1. Enter the trial balance on a work sheet and complete the work sheet.

2. Prepare an income statement, a statement of owners' equity, and a classified balance sheet.

3. Journalize adjustments.

4. Journalize closing entries.

5. Prepare responses to the following:

    a. Management asks you to compute the amounts of the following items if the company used FIFO instead of LIFO in 2007. (Assume a 35% income tax rate on additional income.)

        1. Net income for 2007.

        2. Merchandise inventory as of December 31, 2007.

        3. Retained earnings as of December 31, 2007.

    b. Management asks you to explain the probable reasons why the public accounting firm of Left & Right specified a shorter life and different depreciation method for the computer system than for the store fixtures.

    c. If Global Sales used the direct write-off method for bad debts instead of the allowance approach:

        1. Would total current assets as of December 31, 2007, be higher or lower? By how much?

        2. Would net income for the year ended December 31, 2007, be higher or lower? By how much?

PART three

FINANCING AND INVESTING ISSUES

CORPORATIONS: PAID-IN CAPITAL

"Find something you love to do and you'll never have to work a day in your life."

Harvey Mackay

LEARNING GOALS

After studying Chapter 11, you should be able to:

1. Define *corporation* and state the advantages and disadvantages of using the corporate form of organization.

2. Identify the sources of stockholders' equity.

3. Explain the key terms used to define and measure the elements of paid-in capital.

4. Distinguish between the two main classes of stock for a corporation.

5. Account for the issuance of stock for cash and for noncash assets.

6. Prepare the stockholders' equity section of the balance sheet.

7. Analyze financial statement information for real-life companies.

UNDERSTANDING BUSINESS ISSUES

Businesses organized as corporations generate the vast majority of revenue of all businesses in the United States. As an example, Coca-Cola Company reported total revenues of $22 billion and net income of $4.8 billion in 2004. Producing that net income was sales of 17.8 billion cases of soft drinks. Every day consumption of Coca-Cola soft drinks was approximately 1.3 billion eight-ounce servings in 2004. Coca-Cola sells its product in more than 200 countries throughout the world.

One feature of a corporation that makes this level of activity possible is the ability to attract large amounts of investment capital. Corporations raise this capital through the sale of shares of capital stock. As of December 31, 2004, Coca-Cola had approximately 2,409.3 million shares of common stock outstanding. When valued at the year-end closing market price of approximately $42 per share, the total market value for the company was almost $101.2 billion! Besides such giants as Coca-Cola, many smaller companies organize as corporations. Therefore, being familiar with the special issues of accounting for a corporation is important for users of financial information.

This chapter discusses why businesses choose to incorporate. We examine the accounting practices related to the formation of a corporation. The primary difference in accounting for corporations is recording stock transactions. We introduce the sources of corporate capital, the different classes of stock, and the terms used to measure stock. We also describe the journal entries to record the issuance of stock.

THE CORPORATION AS A FORM OF BUSINESS ORGANIZATION

Learning Goal 1   Define *corporation* and state the advantages and disadvantages of using the corporate form of organization.

A **corporation** is a group of persons authorized to act as a separate legal entity. The corporation has the same privileges and responsibilities as a person. This means that a corporation, acting through corporate officials, may enter into contracts, sue or be sued in court, and own, buy, and sell property.

In most states, the formation of a corporation requires the filing of an application containing the *articles of incorporation*. After approving the application, the state grants a corporate **charter**. The charter is a contract between the state and the incorporators authorizing the corporation to conduct business. The corporation then sells and issues ownership shares of stock to investors. Small family businesses with only a few owners are *closely held* companies. *Publicly held* companies are larger corporations owned by many investors.

Organization of a Corporation

Exhibit 11.1 is an overview of the organization of a corporation. We divide the ownership of a corporation into shares of stock. Large numbers of individual investors can purchase and own shares of stock. We call these individual investors *stockholders* or *shareholders*. The shares of stock of large, publicly held companies trade on organized stock exchanges.

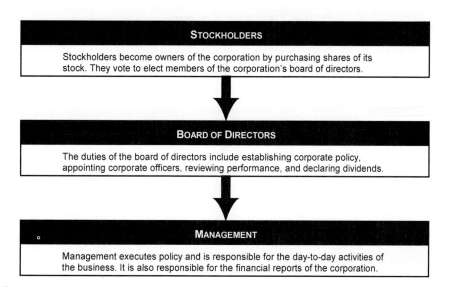

STOCKHOLDERS

Stockholders become owners of the corporation by purchasing shares of its stock. They vote to elect members of the corporation's board of directors.

BOARD OF DIRECTORS

The duties of the board of directors include establishing corporate policy, appointing corporate officers, reviewing performance, and declaring dividends.

MANAGEMENT

Management executes policy and is responsible for the day-to-day activities of the business. It is also responsible for the financial reports of the corporation.

EXHIBIT 11.1

Organization of a Corporation

Stockholders

Stockholders usually purchase shares of stock for economic benefit. Two of the most common economic benefits of owning shares of stock in a corporation are (1) the receipt of periodic cash distributions from the corporation's earnings, called **dividends**, and (2) the gains resulting from selling shares at more than their purchase price. Generally, stockholders do not participate directly in the operation of the corporation. Instead, they vote to elect directors. The **directors** are responsible for establishing broad corporate policy and protecting the interests of the stockholders.

Ownership of shares of stock in a corporation carries certain rights and privileges. Some companies issue more than one class of stock, such as common stock and preferred stock. (We will discuss different classes of stock later in the chapter.) Certain basic rights that usually attach to shares of common stock are as follows:

1. The right to vote at stockholder meetings.

2. The right to sell or dispose of shares of stock.

3. The right to participate in corporate profits by receiving dividends when the board of directors declares them.

4. The right to maintain one's percentage ownership if the corporation increases the number of shares outstanding (called the *preemptive right*).

5. The right to participate in the distribution of assets that remain after the corporation pays creditors if the corporation liquidates.

Board of Directors

The *board of directors* establishes broad corporate policies and oversees the overall performance of the company. It does not participate in day-to-day operations. Generally, selected officers of the company and *outside directors* who are not employees of the company make up the board. Outside directors provide an independent and objective assessment of the performance of management. Composition of some sample boards of directors for large companies is as follows:

Company	Total Number of Directors	Composition of Directors	
		Company Officers	Outside Directors
Coca-Cola	15	1	14
PepsiCo	13	2	11
Toys "Я" Us	11	4	7
Wal-Mart	14	4	10
Walt Disney	12	2	10

Management

The *management* of the corporation operates the company. It follows the overall corporate objectives and policy guidelines established by the board of directors. Management is responsible for preparing all information included in the annual report to stockholders.

Advantages of Incorporation

When investors form a business, the type of business organization they choose—single proprietorship, partnership, or corporation—requires evaluation of several issues. The corporate form has several advantages, as follows:

Ability to Generate Capital Investment

By dividing the ownership of a corporation into shares of stock, we spread ownership among a large number of investors. The ability to sell shares at small amounts per share to many different stockholders means that a corporation can raise large amounts of capital.

Ease of Transfer of Ownership Rights

A stockholder has the right to sell his or her shares of stock anytime. A transfer of ownership of shares from one stockholder to another does not affect the corporation. The shares of larger corporations trade on organized stock exchanges such as the *New York Stock Exchange*. The following shows a typical newspaper summary of stock information for Coca-Cola on a certain day:

52-Week High	Low	Stock	Dividend	Dividend Yield %	P/E Ratio	Sales 100's	High	Low	Close	Change
53 1/2	38 5/16	KO	$1.12	2.69%	20.85	6611	41 7/8	41 5/8	41 5/8	+1/8

In the previous 52-week period, Coca-Cola sold for a high of $53.50 and a low of $38.3125 per share. Coca-Cola pays a dividend of $1.12 per share. This provides a dividend yield percent of 2.69% based on the closing market price per share. The P/E ratio (stock price ÷ net income per share) is the number of times net income per share Coca-Cola is selling for. Generally, a higher number means that investors expect high earnings growth for a company in the future. On that day, investors sold approximately 6,611,000 shares of Coca-Cola common stock. Other investors purchased these shares at a price per share ranging from a high of $41.875 to a low of $41.625. Coca-Cola common stock closed at $41.625 per share. This was a increase of $0.125 from the previous trading day.

Continuity of Life

The life of the corporation is "perpetual," or forever. The withdrawal or death of one stockholder does not affect the life or existence of the corporation. In contrast, partnerships dissolve upon the death or retirement of a partner. This continuity enables corporation managers to make plans based on the best long-term interest of the business.

Limited Liability

The stockholders in a corporation are not personally liable for debts the corporation cannot pay. If a corporation gets into serious financial difficulty and declares bankruptcy, its shares of stock may become worthless. The stockholders will lose their investment in the corporation. However, creditors cannot make a claim on the personal assets of the stockholders to satisfy the corporation's unpaid debts. This feature of a corporation— **limited liability**—means that the maximum amount stockholders can lose is the amount of their original investment in the corporation.

Professional Management

Most large corporations have many stockholders. The stockholders hope that the price of the shares will increase and/or they will receive dividends. The individual stockholders usually do not have the time, expertise, or desire to manage the company on a day-to-day basis. Instead, they delegate the responsibility and authority for operating the corporation to the officers of the corporation. As a result, each corporation can select personnel who will best manage the business. The corporation can replace managers who do not perform as expected.

Disadvantages of Incorporation

The corporate form of business organization has the following disadvantages. We must consider these before deciding to incorporate.

Costs of Incorporation

The state in which the corporation forms generally charges an incorporation fee. The legal work involved in starting a corporation usually requires the services of an attorney. They must design and print stock certificates. We record these initial costs as a debit to an intangible asset account called *Organization Costs*.

Increased Regulation

Of the three types of business organizations, the corporate form is the most difficult to establish. State laws require a corporate charter, a lengthy and costly procedure. After receiving a charter, corporations must file periodic reports. Publicly held companies and those whose shares trade on organized stock exchanges must file quarterly and annual reports with the stock exchanges and with the Securities and Exchange Commission (SEC). An independent Certified Public Accountant must audit the annual financial reports.

Double Taxation

Many feel that a disadvantage of most corporations is *double taxation* of income. A corporation usually pays state and federal taxes first on its own corporate income. Then, if it distributes some of the earnings to stockholders as dividends, the shareholders must again pay tax. Owners of sole proprietorships and partnerships only pay tax on their earnings.

Separation of Ownership and Management Functions

Theoretically, a number of checks and balances in the functions of the board of directors protect the interests of the stockholders. Unfortunately, occasionally management makes decisions that benefit a few individuals rather than the stockholders as a group. Because stockholders are not generally aware of the day-to-day operations of the corporation, they may not discover such actions in time to correct them at stockholder meetings. Often, selling their stock is the only way stockholders can express dissatisfaction with management.

AN OVERVIEW OF STOCKHOLDERS' EQUITY

Until this point in the text, *owners' equity* or *stockholders' equity* was comprised of only common stock and retained earnings. We will expand this now. Stockholders' equity for a corporation comes from several different sources. It is important that we identify and account for each of these sources.

Sources of Stockholders' Equity: A Summary

Learning Goal 2   Identify the sources of stockholders' equity.

There are two separate components of the stockholders' equity section for a corporation: paid-in capital and retained earnings. Exhibit 11.2 is an overview of the sources of stockholders' equity for a corporation.

Paid-in capital for a corporation is the entire corporate investment. This includes all assets received from the issuance of stock to stockholders. Sometimes businesses call this section

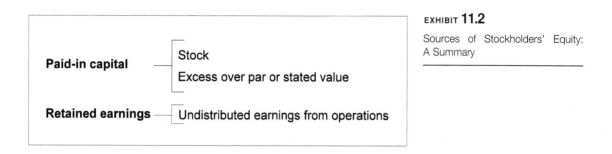

EXHIBIT 11.2

Sources of Stockholders' Equity: A Summary

contributed capital. Retained earnings are the undistributed earnings retained by the business and reinvested in the corporation. The retained earnings balance equals all of the net income since the business began operations less all of the net losses and dividend distributions to stockholders.

PAID-IN CAPITAL

The paid-in capital portion of stockholders' equity includes the classes of stock and any excess paid-in capital above *par* or *stated value* received. We account separately for each of these sources of stockholders' equity. We disclose each source in the stockholders' equity section of the balance sheet.

Key Terms

Learning Goal 3   Explain the key terms used to define and measure the elements of paid-in capital.

We use certain key terms to define and measure paid-in capital. These terms are *authorized stock, issued stock, treasury stock, outstanding stock, par value, no-par value, stated value, legal capital*, and *market value*. Understanding these key terms is important. We discuss each in this section.

Authorized, Issued, and Outstanding Shares of Stock

The corporation's charter authorizes it to issue a designated number of shares of stock. The maximum number of shares of each class of stock that the corporation may issue according to its charter is the **authorized stock**. The corporation usually secures authorization to issue enough shares of stock to allow for both present and future capital needs. The total number of shares of any given class of stock issued cannot exceed the number of shares authorized.

Owners of the corporation receive stock in exchange for their investment of cash or other assets in the business. **Issued stock** refers to the number of shares of stock sold or transferred to stockholders. At times, the company may choose to reacquire shares of stock it once issued to stockholders. This **treasury stock** consists of shares of the corporation's own stock that it issued and later reacquired but has not formally canceled.

Outstanding stock is the number of shares of a class of stock issued and still in the hands of stockholders. Shares of stock repurchased by the company (treasury stock) or given back to the company by a stockholder (donated capital) are no longer outstanding. We deduct these shares from the number of shares issued to calculate shares outstanding. Consider the following example showing the status of shares authorized, issued, and outstanding immediately after different common stock transactions:

Date		Stock Transactions	Number of Common Shares		
			Authorized	Issued	Outstanding
2007					
Jan.	1	Authorization to issue 100,000 shares of common stock.	100,000	0	0
Feb.	1	Issued 70,000 shares of common stock for cash.	100,000	70,000	70,000
Mar.	1	Reacquired 10,000 shares of common stock from stockholders (treasury stock).	100,000	70,000	60,000
Apr.	1	Sold 5,000 shares of treasury stock reacquired on March 1.	100,000	70,000	65,000

The example illustrates that the number of shares *issued* changes only when we sell or transfer unissued shares. The number of shares *outstanding* may be equal to or less than the number of shares issued. If there are treasury shares, we deduct the number of treasury shares from the number of shares issued to determine shares outstanding. If there are no treasury shares, the number of shares issued and outstanding is equal.

Par Value

Par value refers to a dollar amount assigned to each share of stock in the corporation's charter. Corporations print it on each stock certificate. Par value represents the legal capital of the company. *Legal capital* (discussed later) is the minimum amount of capital that state law requires be left in the corporation to protect creditors.

The par value of a stock may be set at any amount agreed upon by the organizers of the corporation. It is *not* an indication of the market value or worth of the stock. In some states, issuing stock at a price below par value is illegal. In this textbook, we always assume that the corporation issues shares of stock at par value or more.

No-Par Value And Stated Value

Because of various difficulties involved with par value stock, some companies issue **no-par value stock** This stock does not have an assigned par value. For example, McDonald's Corporation preferred stock is no-par stock. For stock without a par value, the corporate directors may assign a **stated value** to each share. Once assigned, we account for a stated value as if it were a par value.

Legal Capital

The legal liability of stockholders is limited. Therefore, creditors need protection. **Legal capital** is the minimum amount of capital that must be left in the corporation for the protection of creditors. The designation of legal capital limits the amount of assets that a corporation can pay out to stockholders. Legal capital provides a cushion of capital to protect creditors. State laws vary considerably. However, most states determine legal capital as follows:

1. On par value stock: the par value of all issued shares.

2. On no-par stock with a stated value: the stated value of all issued shares.

3. On no-par, no stated value stock: the total proceeds from the original issuance of all issued shares.

Market Value

The market value of a share of stock is not its par or stated value. **Market value** is the actual price in dollars that a share will bring at the time its owner offers it for sale. (A corporation sells its stock initially. Later stock sales involve third parties, not the corporation.) Market value reflects both (1) general economic and political factors and (2) expectations of investors about the future growth and earning ability of a corporation.

Classes of Stock

Learning Goal 4   Distinguish between the two main classes of stock for a corporation.

Until this point in the text, the only class of stock discussed was common stock. In addition, a corporation may issue shares of preferred stock. Exhibit 11.3 shows a common stock certificate of The Coca-Cola Company.

Common Stock

If a corporation issues only one class of stock, then all shares are common stock. **Common stock** is the *residual class of ownership* in the corporation. This means that if the corporation ceases operations and liquidates, they pay claims by creditors and preferred stockholders on the assets of the company before those of the common stockholders.

Although common stockholders have a residual interest in the corporation, they are the controlling owners of the company. Common stockholders vote and elect the board of directors. Common stockholders receive dividends on their shares only after preferred stockholders receive their dividends. However, unlike most preferred stocks, common stocks have no stated maximum dividend. If the company is successful, common stockholders may receive substantial economic benefits.

Preferred Stock

Preferred stock is a class of corporate ownership that generally has two forms of preference: (1) Holders of preferred stock receive their dividends before holders of common stock receive theirs (the *earnings preference*). (2) If the corporation must liquidate its assets, holders of preferred stock can make claims to the corporation's assets before holders of common stock can (the *preference as to assets upon liquidation*).

EXHIBIT 11.3

Face of a Stock Certificate for Coca-Cola Company

Preferred stock has a stated dividend rate. This rate is frequently a percentage of its par value. For example, 10% preferred stock with a par value of $50 pays an annual dividend of $5 ($50 × 0.10). Sometimes they directly state the dividend rate, such as "$1 preferred stock." The annual dividend rate is $1. Preferred stockholders receive the stated dividend before any payment goes to common stockholders. Preferred stockholders generally do not receive dividends beyond the stated amount.

Most preferred stock is **cumulative**. This means that undeclared dividends accumulate. Accumulated undeclared dividends are **dividends in arrears**. The corporation must pay both the current dividend and the dividends in arrears before common stockholders receive any dividends. Corporations sometimes issue **noncumulative preferred stock**. The dividends on noncumulative shares do not accumulate if the corporation does not declare them. The next chapter contains a detailed discussion of dividends and how we account for them.

Recording Stock Transactions

Learning Goal 5   Account for the issuance of stock for cash and for noncash assets.

The *Securities Act of 1933* requires certain large corporations that issue stock to the public in interstate markets to file a registration statement with the SEC. Companies often use *underwriters* (syndicates of banks or brokerage firms) to help them sell their stock. Announcements that the shares of stock are available for sale appear in advertisements similar to the one in Exhibit 11.4. The SEC restricts official advertising to a booklet of facts called a *prospectus*. The ad announces only that the stock is available for sale. It states where a person may obtain the prospectus. The ad in Exhibit 11.4 announces that 4,400,000 common shares of Merkert American Corporation are for sale at $15 per share. It also lists the underwriters that can provide a copy of the prospectus. We will now illustrate the accounting for various types of paid-in capital transactions.

This announcement is neither an offer to sell not a solicitation of an offer to buy these securities. The offer is made only by the Prospectus.

December 15, 2004

4,400,000 Shares

Merkert American Corporation

Common Stock

Price $15.00 Per Share

Wheat First Union
A Division of Wheat First Securities, Inc.

Cleary Gull Reiland & McDevitt Inc.

Scott & Stringfellow, Inc.

EXHIBIT **11.4**

Typical Announcement of Stock for Sale

Issuance of Par Value Common Stock

On February 2, 2007, Kheel Corporation, a marine supply business, received its charter authorizing the issuance of 200,000 shares of common stock with a $2.50 par value.

Memorandum Entry to Record Charter Data

The initial entry may be a simple memorandum narrative statement made in the general journal and the stock accounts. It notes basic data taken from the corporate charter. It may include the name of the corporation, the date of incorporation, the nature of the business, and the number and classes of shares authorized.

Common Stock Issued at Par for Cash

On February 2, 2007, Kheel Corporation issued 40,000 shares of common stock at par value for cash. We record this transaction as follows:

2007				
Feb.	2	Cash	100,000	
		Common Stock		100,000
		To record the issuance of 40,000 shares of $2.50 par value common stock at par value.		

Common Stock Issued at Par for Cash and Noncash Assets

On February 11, 2007, Kheel Corporation issued 36,000 shares for $40,000 in cash plus land and buildings having a fair cash value of $10,000 and $40,000, respectively. A key issue in this transaction is proper valuation of the land and buildings at their current fair cash value. We record this transaction as follows:

2007				
Feb.	11	Cash	40,000	
		Land	10,000	
		Buildings	40,000	
		Common Stock		90,000
		To record the issuance of 36,000 shares of $2.50 par value common stock at par value in exchange for cash and noncash assets.		

After the preceding transactions, the stockholders' equity section of the Kheel Corporation balance sheet shows the following:

Stockholders' Equity
Paid-in capital:
Common stock, $2.50 par value, 200,000 shares
authorized, 76,000 shares issued $190,000

Common Stock Issued at a Premium for Cash

On November 4, 2007, Kheel Corporation issued 40,000 shares of common stock at $2.70 per share. (The market price changed. It depends on many factors such as the condition of the corporation and expectations for future profits.) The entry for this transaction is as follows:

2007					
Nov.	4	Cash		108,000	
		Common Stock			100,000
		Paid-in Capital—Excess over Par Value, Common			8,000
		To record the issuance of 40,000 shares of $2.50 par value common stock at $2.70 per share.			

We record the $8,000 in a separate paid-in capital account, **Paid-in Capital—Excess over Par Value, Common**. Thus, we record only the legal capital amount in the Common Stock account. Both Common Stock and Paid-in Capital—Excess over Par Value, Common are paid-in capital accounts (see Exhibit 11.2). Both appear in the balance sheet under the stockholders' equity subsection, paid-in capital. Immediately following the issuance of the 40,000 shares for $108,000, the stockholders' equity section of the balance sheet appears as follows:

Stockholders' Equity

Paid-in capital:	
Stock:	
Common stock, $2.50 par value, 200,000 shares	
authorized, 116,000 shares issued	$290,000
Additional paid-in capital:	
Paid-in capital—excess over par value, common	8,000
Total paid-in capital	$298,000

Issuance of No-Par Common Stock

The following examples illustrate the accounting for no-par value stock. On March 1, 2007, Village Corporation's television cable company received its charter authorizing the issuance of 100,000 no-par value common shares. On March 5, 2007, Village Corporation issued for cash 10,000 shares of its no-par common stock at $6 per share.

Stock Issued with No Stated Value

No-par stock may be "pure" no-par. That is, it has no stated value (the entire proceeds in this case become the legal capital). Or the board of directors may set a stated value per share for the no-par stock. In the latter case, we record the stock the same way we record par value stock. Assuming that the no-par stock has no stated value, the entry to record the issuance would be as follows:

2007					
Mar.	5	Cash		60,000	
		Common Stock			60,000
		To record issuance of 10,000 shares of no-par, no stated value stock at $6 per share.			

Stock Issued with a Stated Value

The board of directors of Village Corporation sets a stated value of $5 for each share of no-par common stock. The entry would be as follows:

```
2007
Mar.    5   Cash                                                    60,000
                Common Stock                                                50,000
                Paid-in Capital—Excess over Stated Value, Common            10,000
                    To record the issuance of 10,000 shares of no-par, $5 stated
                    value stock at $6 per share.
```

The stated value amount typically becomes the legal capital. It is the amount credited to Common Stock. Both credit items are in the paid-in capital subsection of the stockholders' equity section of Village Corporation's balance sheet.

Issuance of Preferred Stock

The accounting for the issuance of preferred stock parallels that of common stock. To illustrate, assume that in addition to the 100,000 shares of no-par common stock discussed in the previous section, the state also authorizes Village Corporation to issue 30,000 shares of $10 par value, 15% preferred shares. The 15% is the annual dividend rate based on par value. Annual dividends on this preferred stock are $1.50 ($10 × 0.15) per share. On March 5, 2007, Village Corporation issued 10,000 shares of preferred stock for $11 per share cash. The entry to record this sale is as follows:

```
2007
Mar.    5   Cash                                                   110,000
                Preferred Stock                                            100,000
                Paid-in Capital—Excess over Par Value, Preferred            10,000
                    To record the issuance of 10,000 shares of $10 par value
                    preferred stock at $11 per share.
```

Note that for the two accounts credited, we substitute the word *preferred* for *common* in their titles. Both accounts are part of paid-in capital.

Disclosure of Paid-in Capital on the Balance Sheet

Learning Goal 6   Prepare the stockholders' equity section of the balance sheet.

To illustrate the balance sheet disclosure of paid-in capital accounts, we will use the two transactions of Village Corporation previously illustrated. These are as follows:

• The issuance of 10,000 shares of no-par common stock, stated value $5 per share, for $6 per share.

• The issuance of 10,000 shares of $10 par value, 15% preferred stock for $11 per share.

In addition, assume that as of December 31, 2007, Village Corporation has a balance of $50,000 in Retained Earnings. Exhibit 11.5 shows the stockholders' equity section of the balance sheet as of December 31, 2007.

Detailed Sources of Stockholders' Equity

Exhibit 11.2 presented an overview of the sources of stockholders' equity. To summarize the concepts covered in this chapter, Exhibit 11.6 presents a more detailed version of the sources of stockholders' equity. We expand these sources further in the next chapter.

VILLAGE CORPORATION
PARTIAL BALANCE SHEET
DECEMBER 31, 2007

Stockholders' Equity

Paid-in capital
Stock:

Preferred stock, 15%, $10 par value, 30,000 shares authorized, 10,000 shares issued		$ 100,000	
Common stock, no-par value, stated value established at $5 per share; 100,000 shares authorized, 10,000 shares issued		50,000	
Total stock			$ 150,000
Additional paid-in capital:			
Paid-in capital—excess over par value, preferred	$ 10,000		
Paid-in capital—excess over stated value, common	10,000		
Total additional paid-in capital			20,000
Total paid-in capital			$ 170,000
Retained earnings			50,000
Total stockholders' equity			$ 220,000

EXHIBIT **11.5**

Stockholder's Equity:a Partial Balance Sheet

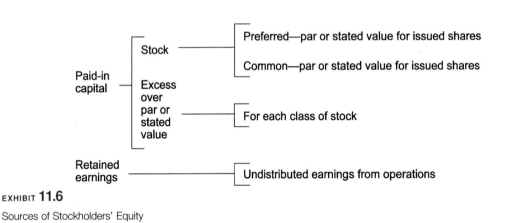

EXHIBIT **11.6**

Sources of Stockholders' Equity

ANALYZING INFORMATION

Learning Goal 7   Analyze financial statement information for real-life companies.

Exhibit 11.7 shows the stockholders' equity section of the balance sheet for The Walt Disney Company. The paid-in capital and retained earnings information are from the 2004 annual report of Disney. The Company ends its financial reporting year on September 30.

Question. As of the end of fiscal 2004 and 2003, what are the (1) total number of common shares authorized, (2) total number of common shares issued, (3) total number of common shares

THE WALT DISNEY COMPANY
STOCKHOLDERS' EQUITY
(*ALL DOLLAR AMOUNTS IN MILLIONS*)

Paid-in Capital:
Stock:
Preferred stock, $0.01 par value

100.0 million shares authorized, none issued	$ 0	$ 0
Common stock, $0.01 par value		
3,600 million shares authorized, 2,040 million		
and 2,044 million shares issued	20	20
Total stock	$ 20	$ 20
Additional paid-in capital	12,427	12,134
Total paid-in capital	$ 12,447	$ 12,154
Retained earnings	15,732	13,817
Accumulated other comprehensive loss	(236)	(653)
Total	$ 27,943	$ 25,318
Deduct: Cost of shares repurchased (treasury shares:		
101.6 million and 86.7 million shares)	(1,862)	(1,527)
Total stockholders' equity	$ 26,081	$ 23,791

EXHIBIT **11.7**

Stockholders' Equity Section of Balance Sheet for the Walt Disney Company as of September 30, 2004 and 2003

outstanding, and (4) total market value of common shares outstanding? The closing prices of each common share was $22.55 (9/30/04) and $20.17 (9/30/03).

Answer.

	September 30	
	2004	**2003**
1. Total number of common shares authorized	3,600,000,000	3,600,000,000
2. Total number of common shares issued	2,040,000,000	2,044,000,000
3. Total number of common shares outstanding		
2004 (2,040,000,000 -101,600,000)	1,938,400,000	
2003 (2,044,000,000 - 86,700,000)		1,957,300,000
4. Total market value of common shares outstanding		
2004 ($22.55 × 1,938,400,000 shares)	$43,710,920,000	
2003 ($20.17 × 1,957,300,000 shares)		$39,478,741,000

We compute the shares outstanding by subtracting the treasury shares from the issued shares. Treasury shares represent shares of stock that were once issued and then repurchased by the company.

LEARNING GOALS REVIEW

1. **Define *corporation* and state the advantages and disadvantages of using the corporate form of organization.**

    A corporation is a group of persons authorized to act as a separate legal entity. Shares of stock represent fractional elements of ownership for a corporation. The stockholders seldom participate directly in the operation of the corporation. Rights of ownership include the right to vote at stockholders' meetings, the right to participate in profits, the preemptive right, and the right to participate in the distribution of assets if they liquidate the corporation. The board of directors establishes broad corporate policy and protects the interests of stockholders. The management of the corporation manages the business within the overall corporate objectives and policies established by the directors. Management prepares the information included in the annual report to stockholders.

Advantages of the corporate form of organization include the ability to generate capital investment, ease of transferring ownership rights, continuity of life, limited liability, and professional management. The disadvantages include the costs of incorporation, increased regulation, double taxation, and separation of the ownership and management functions.

2. **Identify the sources of stockholders' equity.**
The stockholders' equity of a corporation includes paid-in capital and retained earnings. Paid-in capital may be stock and any excess received for stock over par. Retained earnings are the undistributed earnings of the business.

3. **Explain the key terms used to define and measure the elements of paid-in capital.**
Authorized stock is the maximum number of shares of each class of stock the corporation may issue according to its charter. Issued stock is shares of stock sold or transferred to stockholders. Treasury stock is stock that the company has reacquired from shareholders but not formally canceled. Outstanding stock is the number of shares of a class of stock issued and still in the hands of stockholders. Par value is the face amount of a share of stock. No-par value stock is stock with no assigned par value. Stated value is a value assigned by the directors to stock with no par value. Legal capital is the minimum amount of capital that must be left in the corporation for the protection of creditors. Market value is the actual price that a share will bring when offered for sale.

4. **Distinguish between the two main classes of stock for a corporation.**
The two major classes of stock are common stock and preferred stock. If the company has only one class of stock, it is common stock. Common stock represents the residual class of ownership in the corporation. Preferred stock represents a type of ownership with a dividend preference and a preference as to assets in case of liquidation. Preferred stock carries a stated dividend rate, often with any undeclared dividends accumulating. If they liquidate the corporation, the preferred stockholders receive payment before common stockholders.

5. **Account for the issuance of stock for cash and for noncash assets.**
To record the issuance of common stock at par, debit the asset received and credit Common Stock for the par value. If a company issues stock at a premium, we debit the asset and credit Common Stock for the par value. We credit the difference to Paid-in Capital—Excess over Par Value.

6. **Prepare the stockholders' equity section of the balance sheet.**
First we add the par value for preferred stock and the par value for common stock to arrive at total stock. For both kinds of stock, the balance sheet shows the par value, number of shares authorized, and number of shares issued. Then we show all other sources of paid-in capital. This includes paid-in capital in excess of par on both preferred and common stock. We add retained earnings to the total amount of paid-in capital to determine total stockholders' equity.

7. **Analyze financial statement information for real-life companies.**
We compute the shares outstanding by subtracting the treasury shares from the issued shares. Treasury shares represent shares of common stock that were once issued and then repurchased by the company. To determine the total market value of a firm's stock, we multiply the market price per share by the number of shares outstanding.

DEMONSTRATION PROBLEM

Stock Transactions and Preparing a Balance Sheet for a Corporation

After successfully managing several formal wear stores, Karin Belsito decided to open a store selling bridal gowns and dresses for formal occasions. Many of her friends were confident she would be a success and expressed a desire to invest in the company. To attract sufficient capital, the business organized as a corporation. Called NiteStyle Corporation, the company operates in Boston, Massachusetts. The following transactions involving the common stock of the company took place during March 2007:

2007

Mar.	1	Received a charter authorizing the issuance of 300,000 shares of $1 par value common stock.
	2	Issued for cash 60,000 shares of common stock at $2.50 per share. The shares were purchased by Karin (50,000 shares) and her brother Joel (10,000 shares).
	12	Issued for cash 20,000 shares of common stock at $3.00 per share.
	15	Purchased some used store fixtures and display racks at Eric's Liquidation Emporium. The store equipment had a cost to the previous owner of $29,000 and had a current fair market value of $18,000. The owner, Eric, wanted payment in cash, but agreed to accept 6,000 shares of common stock as payment for the equipment.
	30	Joel Belsito sold 500 of the shares he purchased on March 2, 2007, to a friend named Shane O'Neill for $2.90 per share.

REQUIRED

1. **(LG 5)** Journalize the transactions in general journal form.

2. **(LG 7)** Prepare a classified balance sheet for NiteStyle Corporation as of March 31, 2007.

SOLUTION

Requirement 1

> ## Solution Approach
>
> In recording stock transactions, an overall point to remember is that we must maintain a separation between the two component parts of stockholders' equity: paid-in capital and retained earnings. We should also clearly label separate accounts designating the different sources of paid-in capital.

2007
Mar. 1 Memorandum entry: Received charter authorizing the issuance of
300,000 shares of $1 par value common stock.

Mar.	2	Cash	150,000	
		Common Stock		60,000
		Paid-in Capital—Excess over Par Value, Common		90,000
		To record issuance of 60,000 shares of $1 par value common stock at $2.50 per share.		

Record the par value representing the legal capital in the Common Stock account, the remainder in the excess over par account.

Mar.	12	Cash	60,000	
		Common Stock		20,000
		Paid-in Capital—Excess over Par Value, Common		40,000

To record issuance of 20,000 shares of common stock at $3.00 per share.

	15	Store Equipment	18,000	
		Common Stock		6,000
		Paid-in Capital—Excess over Par Value, Common		12,000

To record issuance of 6,000 shares of common stock in exchange for store equipment with a fair value of $18,000.

We should value assets received in exchange for shares of stock at current cash value.

| Mar. | 30 | No journal entry is made on the books of the corporation |

After it issues shares of stock, the corporation does not record subsequent exchanges of shares between investors. However, the corporation must cancel the old stock certificates and issue new ones for the appropriate number of shares in the name of the new owner.

Requirement 2

NITESTYLE CORPORATION
BALANCE SHEET
MARCH 31, 2007
Assets

Current assets		
Cash		$ 210,000
Total current assets		$ 210,000
Property, plant, and equipment		
Store equipment		18,000
Total assets		$ 228,000

Liabilities
Stockholders' Equity

Paid-in capital		
Stock:		
Common stock, $1 par value, 300,000 shares authorized, 86,000 shares issued	$ 86,000	
Additional paid-in capital:		
Paid-in capital—excess over par value, common	142,000	
Total paid-in capital		228,000
Total liabilities and stockholders' equity		$ 228,000

GLOSSARY

authorized stock The maximum number of shares of each class of stock the corporation may issue according to its charter.

charter The legal document issued by a state that includes the articles of incorporation and certificate of incorporation.

common stock The residual class of ownership if more than one class of stock is issued; if only one class, then all shares are treated alike, and that stock is called common stock.

corporation A group of persons authorized to act as a separate legal entity.

cumulative preferred stock The class of preferred stock on which undeclared dividends are accumulated and must be paid together with the current dividends before any dividend payment can be made on common stock.

directors Elected representatives of the stockholders who establish policies for the corporation.

dividend A distribution of some portion of net income in the form of cash, stock, or other corporate property to its stockholders.

dividends in arrears Accumulated undeclared preferred dividends.

issued stock The stock sold or transferred to stockholders.

legal capital The minimum amount of capital that state law requires be left in the corporation for the protection of creditors. It cannot be paid out to the stockholders.

limited liability A legal concept by which the creditors of a corporation cannot hold the stockholders personally liable for the debts of the corporation.

market value The amount that a share of stock will bring if the stock is sold.

noncumulative preferred stock A class of preferred stock on which a dividend not declared (passed) in any one year is lost.

no-par value stock Stock without an indicated par value.

outstanding stock Stock in the hands of the stockholders and not in the treasury of the corporation. It is issued stock minus any treasury stock of a given class.

paid-in capital The entire investment in a corporation by others, including all assets received from the issuance of stock and all gifts or donations of assets to the corporation.

Paid-in Capital—Excess over Par Value, Common An account for the part of capital paid in by stockholders that is not credited to the stock accounts and is usually not a part of legal capital .

par value The nominal or face value printed on a stock certificate, representing the minimum amount to be paid to the issuing corporation by the original purchaser.

preferred stock A class of stock having various preferences, two of which are preference as to dividends and preference as to assets in liquidation.

stated value A value assigned to each share of no-par value stock by the directors of the corporation.

treasury stock A corporation's own stock issued and fully paid for, and later reacquired by the corporation.

QUESTIONS FOR GROUP LEARNING

Q11-1. What advantages and disadvantages should a business group consider in determining whether to incorporate?

Q11-2. Differentiate between the following terms: *common stock* and *preferred stock*; *par value* and *stated value*; *market value* and *no-par value*.

Q11-3. What is the meaning of the following: *limited liability, excess over par value, excess over stated value, and paid-in capital?*

Q11-4. Describe the function of the board of directors in a corporation.

Q11-5. What is the legal responsibility of the owner of a majority of the stock of a corporation to pay its debts if the corporation gets into financial difficulties?

Q11-6. What is treasury stock? Explain how treasury stock affects the computation of issued and outstanding shares of stock.

Q11-7. Does a corporation earn revenue by selling its stock at an amount in excess of par value? Explain.

Q11-8. What is the meaning of *no-par value*? What are some reasons for a firm to seek authorization to issue no-par stock?

Q11-9. A corporation's charter authorizes 20,000,000 shares of $0.10 par value common stock. Why do you think the par value was set so low?

Q11-10. In which form of business organization is ownership most readily transferable? Explain why.

Q11-11. Distinguish between "authorized and unissued stock" and "issued and outstanding stock."

Q11-12. Student A says that if she were buying stock, she would purchase only stock having a par value. Student B prefers no-par stock. Discuss.

Q11-13. What is legal capital? How is it determined? How does it differ from paid-in capital?

Q11-14. Big Bank Company has 1,000,000 shares of $1 par value stock authorized, 700,000 shares issued, and 520,000 shares outstanding. How many treasury shares does it have?

EXERCISES

E11-15. Identifying sources of stockholders' equity (LG 2) Savanna Corporation had the following selected account balances on a postclosing trial balance prepared as of December 31, 2007.

Accounts Receivable.	$ 34,000
Common Stock ($4 par value)	300,000
Notes Payable (due May 2010)	60,000
Paid-in Capital—Excess over Par Value, Common	75,000
Preferred Stock ($50 par value)	500,000
Retained Earnings	220,000

   1. Indicate the proper balance sheet classification of each of the accounts.

   2. As of December 31, 2007, prepare the stockholders' equity section of the balance sheet for Savanna Corporation.

E11-16. Identifying key terms used to define and measure elements of paid-in capital (LG 3) Using the information contained in Exercise 11-15, compute each of the amounts below as of December 31, 2007:

   1. Total amount of legal capital for all classes of stock.

   2. Total amount of paid-in capital.

3. Total number of common shares issued.

4. Total number of common shares outstanding.

5. Average price per share received for the common shares issued.

E11-17. Identifying key terms used to define and measure elements of paid-in capital (LG 3) The paid-in capital section of the balance sheet for Copper Company as of December 31, 2007, is as follows:

Stockholders' Equity

Paid-in capital

Stock:

Preferred stock, cumulative, 11%, $40 par value 100,000 shares authorized, 80,000 shares issued and outstanding. $ 3,200,000

Common stock, no par, no stated value, 500,000 shares authorized, 70,000 shares issued and outstanding   700,000 $ 3,900,000

Additional paid-in capital:

Paid-in capital—excess over par value, preferred stock   600,000

Total paid-in capital $ 4,500,000

Compute each of the following amounts as of December 31, 2007.

1. The number of shares of (a) preferred and (b) common stock issued.

2. The number of shares of (a) preferred and (b) common stocks outstanding.

3. The total amount of legal capital of (a) preferred and (b) common stock.

4. The average issue price per share of the (a) preferred and (b) common stock.

5. The total annual dividend requirement on the preferred stock.

E11-18. Recording common stock transactions (LG 5) Elder Corporation was authorized to issue 20,000 shares of common stock. Record in general journal form the issue of 9,000 shares for cash at $6 a share on January 7, 2007, assuming:

1. That the shares have a $1 par value.

2. That the shares have no par and no stated value.

3. That the shares have no par value but have a stated value of $2.

E11-19. Recording par value common stock (LG 5) LeftField Corporation, organized on August 31, 2007, was authorized to issue 300,000 shares of $5 par value common stock; it had the following transactions:

2007		
Sep.	25	Issued for cash 50,000 shares at $8.00 a share.
Nov.	11	Issued for cash 20,000 shares at $9.00 a share.

Record the transactions in general journal form.

E11-20. Issuing common stock for cash and noncash items (LG 5) True Products Corporation is authorized to issue 800,000 shares of $5 par value common stock. The following transactions occurred in sequence:

1. Issued for cash 50,000 shares at par value.

2. Issued 40,000 shares in exchange for a factory building and land valued at $190,000 and $16,000, respectively.

3. Issued for cash 20,000 shares at $5.50 a share.

4. Issued for cash 15,000 shares at $6 a share.

Record the transactions in general journal form using transaction numbers instead of dates.

E11-21. Calculating the cash collections from stock transactions (LG 2, 4) Mitchell Corporation was authorized to issue 100,000 shares of no-par value common stock with a $20 stated value and 20,000 shares of 12% preferred stock, $100 par value. At the end of the first year of operations, Mitchell Corporation's trial balance included the following account balances:

Preferred Stock	$ 1,420,000
Common Stock	980,000
Paid-In Capital—Excess Over Par Value, Common	374,000

How much cash has been collected from the stock transactions?

E11-22. Recording common stock transactions (LG 5) Holdum Sales Corporation received its charter on August 7, 2007, authorizing the issuance of 200,000 shares of no-par value common stock. The stock had a stated value of $5 per share. The following transactions took place during August:

2007

Aug.	7	Issued 30,000 shares of common stock at $10 per share for cash.

Record the foregoing transaction in general journal form.

E11-23. Preparing paid-in capital section of balance sheet (LG 6) On December 31, 2007, the ledger of Satelite Electronics Company included, among others, the following account balances:

Notes Receivable	$ 24,000
Merchandise Inventory	85,000
Common Stock ($10 par value)	300,000
Preferred Stock ($100 par value, authorized and issued 5,000 shares)	500,000
Paid-in Capital—Excess over Par Value, Preferred Stock	50,000
Building	225,000
Paid-in Capital—Excess over Par Value, Common Stock	120,000

Prepare the paid-in capital portion of the stockholders' equity section of the balance sheet as of December 31, 2007. The authorized common shares are 200,000.

PROBLEMS

P11-24. **Identifying key terms and computing elements of paid-in capital (LG 2, 3)** The stockholders' equity section of the balance sheet for Tastyfoods Company as of December 31, 2007, is as follows:

Stockholders' Equity

Paid-in capital
Stock:

Preferred stock, cumulative, 10%, $30 par value 100,000 shares authorized, 15,000 shares issued and outstanding		$?	
Common stock, $5 par value, 500,000 shares authorized, 30,000 shares issued and outstanding		?	
Total stock			$?
Additional paid-in capital:			
Paid-in capital—excess over par value, preferred	$100,000		
Paid-in capital—excess over par value, common	?		
Total additional paid-in capital		?	
Total paid-in capital			$ 730,000
Retained earnings			?
Total stockholders' equity			$ 770,000

REQUIRED

1. Compute each of the unknown amounts in the stockholders' equity section above.

2. Compute each of the following amounts as of December 31, 2007:

   a. The total amount of legal capital of (1) preferred and (2) common stock.

   b. The average issue price per share of the (1) preferred and (2) common stock.

   c. The total annual dividend requirement on the preferred stock.

P11-25. **Identifying key terms and computing elements of paid-in capital (LG 2, 3)** The stockholders' equity section of the balance sheet for Waterloo Nurseries as of December 31, 2007, is as follows:

Stockholders' Equity

Paid-in capital
Stock:

$2 preferred stock, $10 par value, 100,000 shares authorized, 20,000 shares issued and outstanding		$?	
Common stock, stated value $10, 200,000 shares authorized, 80,000 shares issued and outstanding		?	
Total stock			$1,000,000
Additional paid-in capital:			
Paid-in capital—excess over par value, preferred		$?	
Paid-in capital—excess over stated value, common		400,000	
Total additional paid-in capital			800,000
Total paid-in capital			$?
Retained earnings			900,000
Total stockholders' equity			$?

REQUIRED

1. Compute each of the unknown amounts in the stockholders' equity section above.

2. Compute each of the following amounts as of December 31, 2007:

   a. The total amount of legal capital of (1) preferred and (2) common stock.

   b. The average issue price per share of the (1) preferred and (2) common stock.

   c. The total annual dividend requirement on the preferred stock.

P11-26. **Recording common stock transactions and calculating account balances (LG 5,6)** Thai Foods, Inc., was organized on January 2, 2007, with authority to issue 200,000 shares of $10 par value common stock. The following transactions occurred during the year:

2007

Jan.	4	Issued for cash 6,000 shares at par value.
Mar.	18	Issued for cash 20,000 shares at $14 per share.
Apr.	1	Issued 35,000 shares for land and building with a fair market value of $540,000. One-sixth of the total valuation was allocable to the land.
Jul.	5	Purchased equipment for $90,000 in cash.
Dec.	16	Issued 10,000 shares for cash at $16 per share.

REQUIRED

1. Record the transactions in general journal form.

2. Determine the balances in the Common Stock and the Paid-in Capital-Excess over Par Value, Common accounts. Set up T accounts for these two accounts to support your calculations.

P11-27. **Recording stock transactions and preparing the paid-in capital portion of a balance sheet (LG 5, 6)** The following selected transactions occurred at the newly formed Riverboat Corporation:

2007

Jul.	1	Received a charter authorizing the issuance of 20,000 shares of $50 par value preferred stock and 200,000 shares of $2 par value common stock.
	5	Issued for cash 40,000 shares of common stock at $10 per share.
	8	Issued 500 shares of common stock to an incorporator for a patent that he had perfected, valued at $7,500.
	18	Issued 2,000 shares of preferred stock at $51 per share.
	31	Issued common stock at $12 per share for equipment valued at $54,000.

REQUIRED

1. Journalize the transactions in general journal form.

2. Post the transactions to appropriate ledger accounts.

3. Prepare the paid-in capital portion of the stockholders' equity section of the Riverboat balance sheet as of July 31, 2007.

P11-28. **Recording various stock transactions and preparing the stockholders' equity section of a balance sheet (LG 5, 6)** A summary of the paid-in capital portion of the stockholders' equity section of the balance sheet for Camp Company on July 1, 2007, was as follows:

Stockholders' Equity

Paid-in capital

Stock:

Preferred stock, $50 par value	$ 200,000	
Common stock, $1 par value	300,000	
Total stock		$ 500,000
Additional paid-in capital:		
Paid-in capital—excess over par value, preferred	$ 40,000	
Paid-in capital—excess over par value, common	50,000	
Total additional paid-in capital		90,000
Total paid-in capital		$ 590,000

The following transactions occurred during the next three months:

2007

Jul.	1	Issued for cash 5,000 shares of preferred stock at $55 a share.
	1	Issued for cash 50,000 shares of common stock at $6 a share.
	19	Issued for cash 10,000 shares of common stock at $8 a share.
Aug.	1	Issued for cash 20,000 shares of preferred stock at $60 a share.
	2	Issued 1,000 shares of preferred stock in payment for a patent valued at $60,000.
Sep.	30	Issued 10,000 shares of common stock in exchange for land and a building appraised at $25,000 and $60,000, respectively.

REQUIRED

1. Open ledger accounts for the stockholders' equity items; enter the balances from the partial stockholders' equity section.

2. Journalize the foregoing transactions.

3. Post the journal entries to the stockholders' equity accounts only.

4. Prepare the stockholders' equity section of the balance sheet as of September 30, 2007 (authorized shares: preferred, 100,000; common, 700,000). Assume that retained earnings on September 30, 2007, were $400,000.

P11-29. **Reconstructing journal entries for stock transactions (LG 5)** Kid Glove Stores was formed on May 1, 2007. There were two transactions involving issuance of shares of preferred stock: (1) 4,000 shares were issued in exchange for equipment, and (2) 1,000 shares were issued for cash at $70 per share. Selected general ledger accounts for Kid Glove Stores show the following activity for the first month of operations:

Cash		Preferred Stock ($50 Par Value)	
200,000			200,000
70,000			50,000

		Paid-in Capital—Excess over Par Value, Preferred	
Equipment			
280,000			80,000
			20,000

		Common Stock ($5 Par Value)	
			125,000

		Paid-in Capital—Excess over Par Value, Common	
			75,000

REQUIRED

1. Reconstruct the journal entries made for stock transactions during May 2007.

2. As of May 31, 2007, compute the following amounts:

a. Total number of (1) preferred and (2) common shares outstanding.

b. Total amount of legal capital for all classes of stock.

c. Total amount of paid-in capital for Kid Glove Stores.

P11-30. **Interpreting stockholders' equity information for Anheuser-Busch Company (LG 2, 3, 7)** The 2004 annual report of Anheuser-Busch showed the following information concerning stockholders' equity as of the end of its fiscal year, December 31, 2004 and 2003 (dollar amounts and number of shares stated in millions):

ANHEUSER-BUSCH COMPANIES
STOCKHOLDERS' EQUITY
(ALL DOLLAR AMOUNTS IN MILLIONS)

	December 31	
	2004	**2003**
Paid-in Capital:		
Common stock, $1.00 par value		
Authorized, 950,000,000 shares		
Issued,1,463,000,000 and 1,457,900,000 shares	$ 1,463.0	$ 1,457.9
Additional paid-in capital	1,425.3	1.194.0
Total paid-in capital	$ 2,888.3	$ 2,651.9
Retained Earnings	15,407.2	13,935.4
Total	$ 18,295.5	$ 16,587.3
Deduct: Cost of shares repurchased (treasury shares)		
678,000,000 and 644,800,000 shares	14,638.5	12,939.0
Nonowner changes in shareholder equity	(988.9)	(890.3)
Total stockholders' equity	$ 2,668.1	$ 2,758.0

REQUIRED

1. As of the end of fiscal 2004 and 2003, what are the total number of common shares authorized?

2. Does it appear that any additional shares were issued in the fiscal year ending December 31, 2004? If so, how many?

3. Based on the data for December 31, 2004, what was the average issue price for common shares?

4. As of the end of 2004 and 2003, what are the total number of common shares outstanding?

5. Compute the total market value of common shares outstanding as of December 31, 2004 and 2003. The closing prices of each common share was $50.73 (12/31/04) and $52.68 (12/31/03).

6. If Anheuser-Busch reacquires 10,000,000 additional shares of its common stock on January 1, 2005, how many issued shares will it have after the acquisition? How many outstanding shares will it have after the acquisition?

P11-31. **Interpreting stockholders' equity information for Kellogg Company (LG 2, 3, 7)** The 2004 annual report of Kellogg Company showed the following information concerning stockholders' equity as of the end of its fiscal year, December 31, 2004 and 2003 (dollar amounts and number of shares stated in millions):

KELLOGG COMPANY
STOCKHOLDERS' EQUITY
(ALL DOLLAR AMOUNTS IN MILLIONS)

	December 31	
	2004	2003
Paid-in Capital:		
Common stock, $0.25 par value		
Authorized, 1,000,000,000 shares		
Issued, 415,451,198 and 415,451,198 shares	$ 103.8	$ 103.8
Additional paid-in capital	0.0	24.5
Total paid-in capital	$ 103.8	$ 128.3
Retained Earnings	2,701.3	2,247.7
Total	$ 2,805.1	$ 2,376.0
Deduct: Cost of shares repurchased (treasury shares)		
2,428,824 and 5,751,578 shares	108.0	203.6
Accumulated other comprehensive income (loss)	(439.9)	(729.2)
Total stockholders' equity	$ 2,257.2	$ 1,443.2

REQUIRED

1. As of the end of fiscal 2004 and 2003, what are the total number of common shares authorized?

2. Does it appear that any additional shares were issued in the fiscal year ending December 31, 2004? If so, how many?

3. Based on the data for December 31, 2004, what was the average issue price for common shares?

4. As of the end of 2004 and 2003, what are the total number of common shares outstanding?

5. Compute the total market value of common shares outstanding as of December 31, 2004 and 2003. The closing prices of each common share were $44.66 (12/31/04) and $38.08 (12/31/03).

6. If Kellogg sells 1,000,000 shares of its treasury stock on January 1, 2005, how many issued shares will it have after the sale? How many outstanding shares will it have after the sale of the treasury shares?

Practice Case

Corporations: Paid-in capital (LG 1-3, 5, 6) As the manager of the interior design department of a large furniture store, Lisa Simpson has had a very successful career. Lisa now wishes to open her own home interior design store in Boca Raton, Florida. To attract sufficient capital, she forms the new company as a corporation named Sofisticate Designs Company. The following transactions involving the common stock of the company took place during August 2007, the first month of operations:

2007

Aug.	1	Received a charter authorizing the issuance of 500,000 shares of $1 par value common stock.
	6	Issued for cash 150,000 shares of common stock at $1.60 per share. The shares were purchased by Lisa (100,000 shares) and her husband Paul (50,000 shares).
	20	Issued for cash 30,000 shares of common stock at $4 per share.
	21	Exchanged 10,000 shares of common stock for equipment having a fair market value of $48,000.
	29	Barry Broden sold his 1,500 shares of common stock to a business associate named George Generas for $3.50 per share.

REQUIRED

1. Journalize the transactions in general journal form.

2. Prepare a classified balance sheet for Sofisticate Designs Company as of August 31, 2007.

3. Describe some of the advantages that Lisa will gain by using the corporate form of organization and some of the disadvantages she will experience.

4. What other sources of equity will Lisa have in the future that have not been used so far?

Business Decision and Communication Problem

The decision to incorporate (LG 1, 2) Rob Snyder owns three very successful coffee shops in Kansas City. He wants to expand to Denver but needs additional money to finance the expansion.

Currently, Rob's business operates as a sole proprietorship. Rob believes that he should probably incorporate, although he is not sure he knows what the major advantages of incorporation are. If he does incorporate, Rob is uncertain about what type or types of shares of stock he should use. Rob does not understand the difference between preferred and common stock. He is confused about how stock with a par value differs from no-par stock.

Rob has called you, his longtime accountant, asking for information on the issues described above. You promise to prepare a memo providing the information Rob wants.

REQUIRED

Draft a memo for Rob covering the points he raised.

Ethical Dilemma

Valuing assets acquired for stock (LG 5) Jonathan Black is a close friend of Jane Bedard, president of Nebraska Milling Company. Nebraska Milling plans to expand and needs a building site. Black has offered to exchange a piece of land he owns for 12,000 shares of Nebraska's common stock.

Nebraska's stock does not trade on a stock exchange and no shares have sold recently. The most recent appraisal for the property was approximately two years ago. Currently, the market for real estate is quite depressed and the market value of Black's property has probably declined by about 20%.

Jane decides to use the old appraisal value to record the transaction. She reasons that this will make the asset side of Nebraska's balance sheet look better, without any cost to the corporation. The paid-in capital portion of stockholders' equity will also increase. Jane believes that the real estate market will turn around soon and the piece of property will appreciate rapidly.

REQUIRED
Has Jane behaved ethically? Explain

COMPREHENSIVE ANALYSIS CASE CIRCUIT CITY STORES, INC.

Analyzing Circuit City Stores, Inc. for the Period 2004-2002 Circuit City is a leading retailer of consumer electronics, computers, software, and appliances. Listed below are comparative income statements and balance sheets with common-size percents for 2004-2002 (in millions). Also included are selected ratio statistics. Please provide a brief explanation for your answer to each question.

REQUIRED
Income statement questions:
1. Are total revenues higher or lower over the three-year period?

2. What is the percent change in total revenues from 2002 to 2004?

3. Is the percent of cost of goods sold to total revenues increasing or decreasing over the three-year period? As a result, is the gross margin percent increasing or decreasing?

4. Is the percent of total operating expenses to total revenues increasing or decreasing over the three-year period? As a result, is the operating income percent increasing or decreasing?

5. Is the percent of net income to total revenue increasing or decreasing over the three-year period?

Balance sheet questions:
6. Are total assets higher or lower over the three-year period?

7. What is the percent change in total assets from 2002 to 2004?

8. What are the largest asset investments for the company over the three-year period?

9. Are the largest asset investments increasing faster or slower than the percent change in total revenues?

10. Is the percent of total liabilities to total liabilities + owners' equity increasing or decreasing? As a result, is there more or less risk that the company could not pay its debts?

Integrative income statement and balance sheet question:
11. Is the company operating more or less efficiently by using the least amount of asset investment to generate a given level of total revenues? Note that the "total asset turnover" ratio is computed and included in the "ratio analysis summary".

Ratio analysis questions:
12. Is the *current ratio* better or worse in the most current year compared to prior years?

13. Is the *quick ratio* better or worse in the most current year compared to prior years?

CIRCUIT CITY STORES INC.
COMPARATIVE COMMON-SIZE INCOME STATEMENTS
For the years ended Feb. 28, 2004, 2003, 2002
(in millions)

	2004 $	2004 %	2003 $	2003 %	2002 $	2002 %
Revenues	$ 9,745.4	100.0%	$ 9,953.5	100.0%	$ 13,107.9	100.0%
Cost of goods sold	$ 7,518.1	77.1%	$ 7,603.2	76.4%	$ 10,376.2	79.2%
Gross margin	$ 2,227.3	22.9%	$ 2,350.3	23.6%	$ 2,731.7	20.8%
Operating expenses:						
Sales, marketing, general administrative	$ 2,259.5	23.2%	$ 2,344.6	23.6%	$ 2,372.9	18.1%
Research and development	$ -	0.0%	$ -	0.0%	$ -	0.0%
Other expense	$ -	0.0%	$ -	0.0%	$ -	0.0%
Other expense	$ -	0.0%	$ -	0.0%	$	0.0%
Total operating expenses	$ 2,259.5	23.2%	$ 2,344.6	23.6%	$ 2,372.9	18.1%
Operating income	$ (32.2)	-0.3%	$ 5.7	0.1%	$ 358.8	2.7%
Net interest expense (income)	$ 1.8	0.0%	$ 1.1	0.0%	$ 5.8	0.0%
Other expense (income)	$ (32.7)	-0.3%	$ (62.4)	-0.6%	$ -	0.0%
Income before income taxes	$ (1.3)	0.0%	$ 67.0	0.7%	$ 353.0	2.7%
Income taxes	$ (0.5)	0.0%	$ 25.5	0.3%	$ 134.1	1.0%
Net income (loss) before unusual items	$ (0.8)	0.0%	$ 41.5	0.4%	$ 218.9	1.7%
Other losses (gains) net of tax	$ 88.5	0.9%	$ (64.5)	-0.6%	$ -	0.0%
Net income (loss)	$ (89.3)	-0.9%	$ 106.0	1.1%	$ 218.9	1.7%

CIRCUIT CITY STORES INC.
COMPARATIVE COMMON-SIZE BALANCE SHEETS
Feb. 28, 2004, 2003, 2002
(in millions)

	2004 $	2004 %	2003 $	2003 %	2002 $	2002 %
ASSETS						
Current:						
Cash & cash equivalents	$ 783.5	21.6%	$ 884.7	23.3%	$ 1,251.5	27.6%
Short-term investments	$ -	0.0%	$ -	0.0%	$ -	0.0%
Accounts receivable, net	$ 579.7	16.0%	$ 775.3	20.4%	$ 726.6	16.0%
Inventory	$ 1,517.3	41.8%	$ 1,409.7	37.1%	$ 1,633.3	36.0%
Other current assets	$ 38.6	1.1%	$ 33.2	0.9%	$ 41.3	0.9%
Other current assets	$ -	0.0%	$ -	0.0%	$ -	0.0%
Total current assets	$ 2,919.1	80.3%	$ 3,102.9	81.7%	$ 3,652.7	80.5%
Fixed:						
Property & equipment, net	$ 585.9	16.1%	$ 649.6	17.1%	$ 853.8	18.8%
Long-term investments	$ -	0.0%	$ -	0.0%	$ -	0.0%
Intangibles & goodwill	$ -	0.0%	$ -	0.0%	$ -	0.0%
Other assets	$ 128.0	3.5%	$ 46.6	1.2%	$ 32.9	0.7%
Total assets	$ 3,633.0	100.0%	$ 3,799.1	100.0%	$ 4,539.4	100.0%
LIABILITIES						
Current:						
Short-term debt	$ 1.1	0.0%	$ 1.4	0.0%	$ 112.3	2.5%
Accounts payable	$ 1,172.5	32.3%	$ 1,278.7	33.7%	$ 1,529.0	33.7%
Accrued salaries and benefits	$ -	0.0%	$ -	0.0%	$ -	0.0%
Unearned revenue	$ -	0.0%	$ -	0.0%	$ -	0.0%
Other current liabilities	$ 3.1	0.1%	$ -	0.0%	$ -	0.0%
Total current liabilities	$ 1,176.7	32.4%	$ 1,280.1	33.7%	$ 1,641.3	36.2%
Long-term debt	$ 22.7	0.6%	$ 11.2	0.3%	$ 14.1	0.3%
Deferred income tax liabilities	$ -	0.0%	$ -	0.0%	$ 149.6	3.3%
Other long-term liabilities	$ 209.6	5.8%	$ 166.2	4.4%	$ -	0.0%
Total liabilities	$ 1,409.0	38.8%	$ 1,457.5	38.4%	$ 1,805.0	39.8%
OWNERS' EQUITY						
Total owners' equity	$ 2,224.0	61.2%	$ 2,341.6	61.6%	$ 2,734.4	60.2%
Total liabilities and owners' equity	$ 3,633.0	100.0%	$ 3,799.1	100.0%	$ 4,539.4	100.0%

(Note: percents may not add to 100 due to rounding)

CIRCUIT CITY STORES INC.
RATIO ANALYSIS SUMMARY
For the years ended Feb. 28, 2004, 2003, 2002

	2004	2003	2002
SHORT-TERM LIQUIDITY RATIOS			
Current Ratio (Current Assets/Current Liabilities)	2.48	2.42	2.23
Quick Ratio (Cash + Short-term Investments + Accounts Receivable)/Current Liabilities	1.16	1.30	1.21
Accounts Receivable Turnover 1 (Revenues/Average Accounts Receivable)	14.38	13.25	
Accounts Receivable Turnover 2 (Revenues/Year-end Accounts Receivable)	16.81	12.84	18.04
Inventory Turnover 1 (Cost Goods Sold/Average Inventory)	5.14	5.00	
Inventory Turnover 2 (Cost Goods Sold/Year-end Inventory)	4.95	5.39	6.35
LONG-TERM SOLVENCY (LEVERAGE) RATIO			
Total Debt Ratio (Total Liabilities/Total Assets)	38.78%	38.36%	39.76%
PROFITABILITY RATIOS			
Gross Profit Margin (Gross Margin/Revenues)	22.85%	23.61%	20.84%
Operating Profit Margin (Operating Income/Revenues)	-0.33%	0.06%	2.74%
Net Profit Margin (Return on Sales) (ROS) (Net Income/Revenues)	-0.92%	1.06%	1.67%
Total Asset Turnover (Revenues/Average Total Assets)	2.62	2.39	
Return on Total Assets (ROA) (Net Income/Average Total Assets)	-2.40%	2.54%	

14. Is the *accounts receivable turnover ratio 1* (based on *average* receivables) better or worse in the most current year compared to prior years?

15. Is the 2004 *accounts receivable turnover ratio 2* (based on *year-end* receivables) better or worse than the 2004 ratio based on an *average*?

16. Is the *inventory turnover ratio 1* (based on *average* inventory) better or worse in the most current year compared to prior years?

17. Is the 2004 *inventory turnover ratio 2* (based on *year-end* inventory) better or worse than the 2004 ratio based on an *average*?

18. Is the *return on total assets (ROA) ratio* better or worse in the most current year compared to prior years?

Stockholders' equity questions (Chapter 11 focus)

19. Assume Circuit City Stores issues additional shares of common stock for $2,000,000 on June 1, 2004. What impact would this have on the total debt ratio on that date (increase, decrease, no impact)? Briefly explain.

20. Assume Circuit City Stores issues additional shares of common stock for $2,000,000 on June 1, 2004. What impact would this have on the retained earnings balance on that date (increase, decrease, no impact)? Briefly explain.

21. Assume Circuit City Stores issues additional shares of common stock for $2,000,000 on June 1, 2004. What impact would this have on the total amount of paid-in capital on that date (increase, decrease, no impact)? Briefly explain.

22. Assume Circuit City Stores issues additional shares of common stock for $2,000,000 on June 1, 2004. What impact would this have on the amount of total assets on that date (increase, decrease, no impact)? Briefly explain.

ADDITIONAL STOCKHOLDERS' EQUITY TRANSACTIONS AND INCOME DISCLOSURES

LEARNING GOALS

After studying Chapter 12, you should be able to:

1. Define *retained earnings* and describe factors that affect them.

2. Account for cash dividends and describe their effects on assets and stockholders' equity.

3. Account for stock dividends and stock splits and describe their effects on assets and stockholders' equity.

4. Account for treasury stock transactions and describe their impact on the balance sheet.

5. Calculate book value per share and explain its significance.

6. Explain how we report discontinued operations and extraordinary items.

7. Calculate earnings per share.

8. Analyze financial statement information for real-life companies.

UNDERSTANDING BUSINESS ISSUES

The two parts of stockholders' equity for a corporation are paid-in capital and retained earnings. Both are sources of capital that management is responsible for investing wisely. Exhibit 11.7 in Chapter 11 shows the total paid-in capital for the Walt Disney Company as of September 30, 2004, was $12,447 million. This amount represents the total sources of capital contributed by investors. As of September 30, 2004, retained earnings for the Walt Disney Company were $15,732 million. This is the net income earned by Walt Disney Company since its incorporation, less net losses and dividend distributions. Disney's retained earnings are larger than the total amount of its paid-in capital. Retained earnings represent 29% of the *total* of liabilities and stockholders' equity as of September 30, 2004. Clearly, retained earnings are an important source of capital for the Walt Disney Company.

This chapter continues the discussion of corporations. We begin by describing how to account for transactions that affect retained earnings. We then describe additional transactions that affect stockholders' equity. These include paying cash dividends, declaring stock dividends and stock splits, and reacquiring the corporation's stock. The chapter concludes with income statement disclosures for nonrecurring items and a discussion of how to compute earnings per share.

RETAINED EARNINGS

Learning Goal 1   Define retained earnings and describe factors that affect them.

-Earnings that a corporation has not paid out to its stockholders as dividends are **retained earnings**. Retained earnings are cumulative net income of past years minus net losses and dividends declared during those years. *Reinvested earnings, retained income, accumulated earnings, and earnings retained for use in the business are alternative terms used for retained earnings.* If cumulative losses and dividend distributions exceed earnings, the Retained Earnings account will have a debit balance. We show this in the balance sheet as a deduction, or **deficit**, in the stockholders' equity section.

Exhibit 12.1 shows a statement of retained earnings for General Mills, Inc. for the year ended May 30, 2004. Net income increases the beginning balance of $3,079 million by $1,055 million. Cash dividends on common stock totaling $412 million decrease it. The ending retained balance is $3,722 million.

The primary factors that affect retained earnings are as follows:

1. Net income or net loss.
2. Restrictions of retained earnings.
3. Prior period adjustments.
4. Dividends.

We will discuss each of these in this section.

Net Income and Net Loss

At the end of the year, we close the net income or net loss for a corporation to the Retained Earnings account. For General Mills, Inc., assume that all of 2004's revenues and expenses have been closed to Income Summary. The entry to close net income to Retained Earnings is as follows:

GENERAL MILLS, INC.
STATEMENT OF RETAINED EARNINGS
FOR THE YEAR ENDED MAY 30, 2004
(*ALL DOLLAR AMOUNTS IN MILLIONS*)

Retained earnings, beginning of year	$ 3,079
Add: Net income	1,055
Subtotal	$ 4,134
Deduct: Cash dividends, common stock	412
Retained earnings, end of year	$ 3,722

EXHIBIT **12.1**

Statement of Retained Earnings for General Mills, Inc. for the Year Ended May 30, 2004

```
2004
May    30   Income Summary                                    1,055,000,000
                    Retained Earnings                                              1,055,000,000
                    To close net income to retained earnings.
```

Restrictions on Retained Earnings

Corporations may be required or want to restrict part of the retained earnings balance. The creation of **restricted retained earnings** (sometimes called *appropriations*) tells the financial statement reader that they may not pay out this part of retained earnings as dividends. The total amount of retained earnings remains the same. However, a corporation may declare dividends only from the unrestricted retained earnings balance. The board of directors makes restrictions on retained earnings for two broad purposes:

1. *Required Retained Earnings Restrictions* Required restrictions comply with legal or contract limits on dividend distributions. They ensure that corporations maintain a minimum level of stockholders' equity. Both dividend distributions and treasury stock purchases decrease assets available to pay liabilities. As a condition of a loan agreement, a bank may require a limit on the amount of retained earnings that may flow out of the corporation as dividends. Many states place limits on the amount of treasury stock a firm may buy back.

2. *Voluntary Retained Earnings Restrictions* Voluntary restrictions show the reasons why management wishes to restrict dividend distributions. Examples include restrictions on dividends because of plant expansion plans or business contingencies such as a pending lawsuit. Both actions will require the use of corporate assets—the first to pay for the plant expansion, the second to pay attorneys' fees or damages if the suit is lost. Corporations must retain these assets rather than use them to pay dividends.

We usually disclose restrictions of retained earnings in a note to the financial statements. As an example of a required restriction of retained earnings, the following note appears in the 1994 annual report of US AIR Group.

US AIR Group: Notes to Financial Statements (1994 annual report)
Dividend Restrictions

The Company, organized under the laws of the State of Delaware, is subject to statutory restrictions on the payment of dividends. At December 31, 1994, the Company's retained earnings was exhausted and therefore, under Delaware law, the Company is legally restricted from paying dividends on all outstanding common and preferred stock issuances.

At December 31, 1994, US AIR Group has a retained earnings *deficit* of $2,417.5 million. Total assets on this date are $6,808.0 million. Therefore, the negative retained earnings balance is a significant problem for the Company. The note states that under these conditions, the Company is legally restricted from paying any dividends. Creditors who have loaned US AIR Group money wish to protect their investment by placing limits on possible dividend distributions.

By 1997, US AIR Group has a retained earnings deficit of only $1,280 million with total assets of $8,372 million. This has caused the dividend restriction to be removed. The following note appears in the 1997 annual report stating that there is no dividend restriction.

US AIR Group: Notes to Financial Statements (1997 annual report)
Dividend Restrictions

The Company, organized under the laws of the State of Delaware, is subject to statutory restrictions on the payment of dividends. As of December 31, 1997, the Company does not believe that Delaware Law placed any material restrictions on the Company's ability to pay dividends on or repurchase or redeem its capital stock.

Prior Period Adjustments

A company may make an error in preparing the financial statements of one accounting period that they do not discover until a later period. We treat the correction of the error, if material, as an adjustment to the beginning retained earnings balance.[1] This is a **prior period adjustment**. Under generally accepted accounting principles, we do not include the correction of the error in the income statement.

For an illustration, assume that Sweet Tomato Company records $50,000 too much income tax expense for 2007. Therefore, it will understate net income and ending retained earnings by $50,000. If it discovers the error on March 1, 2008, after closing the books for 2007, it makes the correcting entry as follows:

2008					
Mar.	1	Income Taxes Payable		50,000	
		Retained Earnings			50,000
		To correct error in computing income tax expense for 2007.			

We show the prior period adjustment on the statement of retained earnings. The correction appears as an adjustment to the beginning retained earnings balance. Using assumed amounts for beginning retained earnings, net income, and dividends, Exhibit 12.2 shows Sweet Tomato Company's statement of retained earnings for 2008.

SWEET TOMATO COMPANY
STATEMENT OF RETAINED EARNINGS
FOR THE YEAR ENDED DECEMBER 31, 2008

Retained earnings, January 1, 2008 (as previously reported)	$ 700,000
Add: Prior period adjustment	
(credit to correct for overstatement of income tax expense in 2007)	50,000
Retained earnings, January 1, 2008 (as adjusted)	$ 750,000
Add: Net income (2008)	200,000
Subtotal	$ 950,000
Deduct: Cash dividends, common stock (2008)	100,000
Retained earnings, December 31, 2008	$ 850,000

EXHIBIT **12.2**

Illustration of Prior Period Adjustment on Statement of Retained Earnings

---

[1] *Statement of Financial Accounting Standards (SFAS) No. 16,* "Prior Period Adjustments" (Norwalk, Conn.: Financial Accounting Standards Board, 1977), paragraphs 10-12.

Dividends

The declaration of a **dividend** decreases retained earnings. Dividends may include the distribution of cash, stock, or other corporate property to the stockholders. The board of directors formally declares a dividend. The entry in the board's minutes of the meeting shows the declaration date, date of record, and payment date.

The payment of a cash dividend decreases cash. Thus, *both* unrestricted retained earnings and cash must be available for distribution. Only the board of directors has the authority to declare a dividend. Once the board takes formal action, *the dividend immediately becomes a current liability* of the corporation.

Cash Dividends

Learning Goal 2   Account for cash dividends and describe their effects on assets and stockholders' equity.

Cash Dividends on Common Stock

We state the dividend on common stock as a specified amount per share. The Coca-Cola Company has paid quarterly dividends for 84 consecutive years. One of their more recent dividends was declared on February 17, 2005. Coca Cola will mail the holder of 100 shares of common stock on March 15, 2005, a check for $28.00 ($0.28 per share × 100 shares) on April 1, 2005. An investor who buys the stock by March 15, 2005, the record date, will receive the dividend. An investor who buys stock after the record date is said to buy the stock **ex-dividend**—that is, without the right to receive the latest declared dividend. During the interval between March 15, 2005, and April 1, 2005, the company prepares the list of eligible stockholders. Usually an independent *transfer agent* does this function. These are banks or trust companies that also handle the recording, issuance, and transfer of stock certificates.

Because of dividend priorities, it is a good idea to have a separate Dividends account for each class of stock. We debit these dividends accounts each time we declare a dividend. Assume that The Coca Cola Company has 1,000,000 shares of common stock outstanding. It would record the declaration and payment of the quarterly dividend of 28 cents per share as follows:

2005					
Feb	17	Dividends—Common Stock		280,000	
		Dividend Payable—Common Stock			280,000
		To record declaration of a cash dividend of 28 cents per share on 1,000,000 shares of common stock outstanding.			
Apr	1	Dividends Payable—Common Stock		280,000	
		Cash			280,000
		To record payment of the dividend declared on Feb 1.			

The company needs no journal entry on Mar. 15, 2005, the date of record. If it prepares a balance sheet between Feb. 1 and Apr. 1, it classifies the Dividends Payable—Common Stock account as a current liability. At the end of the year, if the company declares four quarterly dividends of the same amount, the Dividends—Common Stock account would have a debit balance of $1,120,000. We close all dividends accounts into the Retained Earnings account at the end of the year. For Coca Cola Company, this entry would be:

2005				
Dec.	31	Retained Earnings	1,120,000	
		Dividends—Common Stock		1,120,000
		To close the Dividends account.		

Cash Dividends on Preferred Stock

Preferred stock has certain dividend *preferences*. We must pay a stated amount per share to the preferred stockholders before making any dividend distribution to holders of common stock.

For **cumulative preferred stock**, undeclared dividends accumulate. We must pay the accumulated (past) dividends plus the current dividend on preferred stock before paying any dividend on common stock. These dividends not declared in past periods on cumulative preferred stock are **dividends in arrears**. If the preferred stock is *noncumulative*, the stockholder loses a dividend not formally declared by the board of directors.

Companies typically declare preferred dividends semiannually. To illustrate, assume that on July 1, 2007, Columbia Corporation has outstanding 1,000 shares of 12%, cumulative preferred stock. It has a par value of $100. Columbia did not declare semiannual dividends on the preferred stock during 2006. This means that $12,000 (12% × $100,000) of dividends are in arrears as of July 1, 2007. We calculate the preferred dividend of $18,000 as follows:

Preferred dividends in arrears (12% × $100,000)	$ 12,000
Current semiannual preferred dividends (½ × $12,000)	6,000
Total preferred dividend declared	$ 18,000

The journal entry to record the declaration of this dividend is as follows:

2007					
Jul.	1	Dividends—Preferred Stock		18,000	
		Dividends Payable—Preferred Stock			18,000
		To record the declaration of the preferred dividend, which includes the current semiannual dividend plus the dividends in arrears for 2006.			

The payment of the liability results in a debit to Dividends Payable—Preferred Stock and a credit to Cash.

Stock Dividends

Learning Goal 3   Account for stock dividends and stock splits and describe their effects on assets and stockholders' equity.

A corporation may issue a **stock dividend** to its existing stockholders. This results in the issuance of additional shares of its authorized stock without investment of any assets by the stockholders. There are various reasons for the declaration of a stock dividend, such as:

- A desire to give stockholders some measure of the company's success.

- A need to conserve available cash.

- A desire by the directors to reduce the market price of the stock.

- A desire to increase the permanent capitalization of the company by converting part of the retained earnings into stock.

A *cash dividend* decreases both the assets and stockholders' equity of a corporation. A *stock dividend* simply transfers a certain amount of retained earnings to paid-in capital accounts. Declaring and distributing a stock dividend does not affect either *total assets* or *total stockholders' equity*. The change is within the stockholders' equity section (retained earnings decreases and paid-in capital increases). To illustrate stock dividends, assume that Topps Corporation's stockholders' equity at December 31, 2007, is as follows:

Stockholders' Equity

Paid-in capital

Common stock, $10 par value, 100,000 shares authorized, 10,000 shares issued and outstanding	$ 100,000
Paid-in capital—excess over par value, common	20,000
Total paid-in capital	$ 120,000
Retained earnings	280,000
Total stockholders' equity	$ 400,000

Recording Small Stock Dividends

Small stock dividends involve less than 20-25% of the number of shares previously outstanding. The American Institute of Certified Public Accountants (AICPA) recommends that we transfer an amount equal to the market value of the stock from retained earnings to paid-in capital.[2] The reasoning is that a small stock dividend will not change the market value significantly. Therefore, the market value shows the economic effect of the stock dividend better than does the par or stated value. The transfer of retained earnings to paid-in capital *capitalizes* retained earnings.

Assume that on January 1, 2008, the directors of Topps Corporation declare a 10% stock dividend distributable on January 30 to the stockholders of record on January 15. The stock dividend will result in the issuance of 1,000 (10,000 × 0.10) new common shares. Assume the market value of the common stock before the stock dividend is $30 per share. The amount of retained earnings transferred (capitalized) is $30,000 (1,000 shares × $30). The entries to record the declaration and stock issuance are:

2008					
Jan.	1	Stock Dividends—Common		30,000	
		Stock Dividends to Be Issued—Common			10,000
		Paid-in Capital—Excess over Par Value, Common			20,000
		To record declaration of 1,000 share common stock dividend.			
Jan.	30	Stock Dividends to Be Issued—Common		10,000	
		Common Stock			10,000
		To record issuance of common stock dividend.			

If we prepare a balance sheet between January 1 and January 30, we show the Stock Dividends to Be Issued—Common account as part of paid-in capital. It is not a liability because its reduction will result in an increase in common stock, not a decrease in a current asset. We close the Stock Dividends—Common account to Retained Earnings at the end of the year.

Recording Large Stock Dividends

Large stock dividends involve issuance of more than 20-25% of the number of shares previously outstanding. The AICPA recommends that for large stock dividends, we should transfer the par or stated value of the stock from retained earnings to paid-in capital.[3] The market value should decrease significantly, since we issue a large number of additional shares.

Assume instead that on January 1, 2008, the directors of Topps Corporation declare a 50% stock dividend. It is distributable on January 30 to the stockholders of record on January 15. The

---

[2] *Accounting Research Bulletin (ARB) No. 43,* "Restatement and Revision of Accounting Research Bulletins" (New York: American Institute of Certified Public Accountants, 1953), Chapter 7, Section B, paragraphs 10 and 13. The question of whether to use 20% or 25% depends on whether the stock dividend influences the market price if a rate higher than 20% is used.

[3] *ARB No. 43,* paragraph 11.

stock dividend results in the issuance of 5,000 (10,000 × 0.50) new common shares. The amount of retained earnings transferred (capitalized) is $50,000 (5,000 shares × $10). The entries to record the declaration and stock issuance are as follows:

2008					
Jan.	1	Stock Dividends—Common		50,000	
		Stock Dividend to Be Issued—Common			50,000
		To record declaration of 5,000 share common stock dividend.			
	30	Stock Dividend to Be Issued—Common		50,000	
		Common Stock			50,000
		To record issuance of common stock dividend.			

Effect of Stock Dividends

Using the 10% stock dividend example for Topps Corporation, Exhibit 12.3 shows the effect of stock dividends on stockholders' equity. Unlike a cash dividend, the corporation distributes no assets to stockholders in a stock dividend. Therefore, there is no impact on either the corporation's total assets or its total stockholders' equity. Total stockholders' equity of $400,000 is the same before and after the stock dividend. The only effects of a stock dividend are an increase in outstanding shares, a decrease in retained earnings, and an increase in paid-in capital.

Exhibit 12.4 shows the effect of a stock dividend on the equity interest of an individual stockholder owning 10% of the outstanding shares. The stockholder's ownership percentage of the company remains the same before and after a stock dividend.

A stock dividend may be significant to the stockholder even if the equity interest in the company does not change. If the stock does not drop in value, the stockholder gains the market

	Stockholders' Equity		
	Immediately before Declaration (12/31/07)	Immediately after Declaration (1/1/08)	Immediately after Issuance (1/30/08)
Paid-in capital			
Common stock, $10 par	$100,000	$100,000	$110,000
Stock dividend to be issued	0	10,000	0
Paid-in capital—excess over par, common	20,000	40,000	40,000
Total paid-in capital	$120,000	$150,000	$150,000
Retained earnings	280,000	250,000	250,000
Total stockholders' equity	$400,000	$400,000	$400,000
Shares outstanding	10,000	10,000	11,000

EXHIBIT **12.3**

Effect of 10% Stock Dividend on Stockholders' Equity

	Stockholders' Equity		
	Immediately before Declaration (12/31/07)	Immediately after Declaration (1/1/08)	Immediately after Issuance (1/30/08)
Shares outstanding	10,000	10,000	11,000
Shares owned by stockholder owning 10% of outstanding shares	1,000	1,000	1,100
Ownership percentage	10%	10%	10%
Equity in company ($400,000 × 10%)	$40,000	$40,000	$40,000

EXHIBIT **12.4**

Effect of 10% Stock Dividend on an Individual Stockholder's Equity Interest in Company

value of the new shares received. If the corporation maintains the same cash dividend per share amount, the stockholder gains the future dividends on the additional shares.

A stock dividend provides certain advantages to the corporation. It is a way of giving something to stockholders without having to distribute assets. The company can use the cash retained for expansion or other purposes. A large stock dividend allows the corporation to reduce the market price of its shares to attract more investors.

Stock Split

Another way to reduce the market price of a stock is by a stock split. In a **stock split**, we decrease the par or stated value per share and increase the number of shares issued. The total paid-in capital and retained earnings remain the same. We make a notation in the Common Stock account to show the new par or stated value per share.

Assume, for example, that a corporation has outstanding 500,000 shares of $10 par value common stock. The current market price of the stock is $175 per share. The corporation wishes to lower the stock price to make it more affordable to investors. The corporation reduces the par value from $10 to $5 and increases the number of shares from 500,000 to 1,000,000. This "two-for-one split" should result in a decrease of the market price by one-half. We record the stock split either by a memorandum notation in the journal and Common Stock account or by the following journal entry:

2008

Jan.   1   Common Stock ($10 par value)   5,000,000
                  Common Stock ($5 par value)   5,000,000
              To record a 2-for-1 split, increasing the number of
              outstanding shares from 500,000 to 1,000,000 and reducing
              par value from $10 to $5.

Both stock dividends and stock splits change the number of shares outstanding. Neither changes total stockholders' equity nor the proportionate ownership interest of each stockholder. A stock dividend requires a transfer from retained earnings to paid-in capital. A stock dividend increases the Common Stock account by the par or stated value of the dividend shares. A stock split changes the par or stated value of the common stock without changing the total dollar balances of any accounts.

Over a period of years, repeated stock dividends and splits can result in large increases in the number of shares held by a stockholder. Exhibit 12.5 shows the cumulative impact of stock dividends and splits for The Coca-Cola Company. Assume an investor purchased one share of Coca-Cola common stock when the company was incorporated in 1919. As of December 31, 2004,

Year	Activity	Cumulative Shares
1919	purchase 1 share	1
1927	1-for-1 stock dividend	2
1935	4-for-1 stock split	8
1960	3-for-1 stock split	24
1965	2-for-1 stock split	48
1968	2-for-1 stock split	96
1977	2-for-1 stock split	192
1986	3-for-1 stock split	576
1990	2-for-1 stock split	1,152
1992	2-for-1 stock split	2,304
1996	2-for-1 stock split	4,608

EXHIBIT **12.5**

Cumulative Impact of Stock Splits and Stock Dividends for the Coca-Cola Company

he or she would own 4,608 shares of common stock. At the market price of $41.64 per share, the original investment of one share would be worth $191,877 as of December 31, 2004!

TREASURY STOCK AND OTHER CORPORATE CAPITAL CONCEPTS

Treasury Stock

Learning Goal 4   Account for treasury stock transactions and describe their impact on the balance sheet.

A corporation may repurchase some of its own stock. We call such stock **treasury stock**. The treasury stock may be reissued at a later date. While in the treasury, it has issued but not outstanding status. Therefore, it does not have voting or *cash* dividend rights.

Corporations frequently purchase their own stock to distribute to their employees in place of other compensation. For example, during 2001, The Coca-Cola Company reacquired approximately 38 million shares of its common stock. The acquisition of treasury stock reduces both the assets and the stockholders' equity. We show the Treasury Stock account in the stockholders' equity section as a deduction from total paid-in capital and retained earnings.

Recording the Purchase of Treasury Stock

The cost method is the most commonly used method for recording the purchase of treasury stock. We debit the Treasury Stock account for the cost of the shares acquired. To illustrate the cost method, assume that on August 1, 2007, Ell Corporation reacquires 1,000 shares of its own $5 par value common stock at $8 per share. The entry to record this reacquisition is as follows:

```
2007
Aug.    1   Treasury Stock—Common                              8,000
                Cash                                                    8,000
                To record purchase of 1,000 shares of own common
                stock at $8 per share.
```

The purchase of the 1,000 shares of common stock reduces cash and stockholders' equity by $8,000. It also reduces the number of shares outstanding. It does not reduce the number of issued shares. To illustrate these points, Exhibit 12.6 shows balance sheets for Ell Corporation before and after the purchase of the treasury stock.

Recording Reissuance of Treasury Stock

Reissuance Above Cost

We record the reissuance of treasury stock by a credit to Treasury Stock for the *cost of the shares*. We record the difference between the cost and the issue price of treasury stock as a paid-in capital item (*never a gain*). We credit it to Paid-in Capital from Treasury Stock Transactions. To illustrate, assume that on October 1, 2007, Ell Corporation reissued 100 shares for $10 per share. The entry for reissuance is:

```
2007
Oct.    1   Cash (100 shares × $10)                            1,000
                Treasury Stock—Common (100 shares × $8)                 800
                Paid-in Capital from Treasury Stock Transactions, Common  200
                Reissued 100 shares of treasury stock at $10 per share.
```

BEFORE PURCHASE OF TREASURY STOCK
ELL CORPORATION
BALANCE SHEET
AUGUST 1, 2007
Assets

Cash	$ 50,000
Other assets	300,000
Total assets	$ 350,000

Stockholders' Equity

Common stock, $5 par value, 50,000 shares authorized and issued	$ 250,000
Retained earnings	100,000
Total stockholders' equity	$ 350,000

AFTER PURCHASE OF TREASURY STOCK
ELL CORPORATION
BALANCE SHEET
AUGUST 1, 2007
Assets

Cash ($50,000 - $8,000)	$ 42,000
Other assets	300,000
Total assets	$ 342,000

Stockholders' Equity

Common stock, $5 par value, 50,000 shares authorized and issued, **of which 1,000 shares are held in the treasury**	$ 250,000
Retained earnings	100,000
Subtotal	$ 350,000
Deduct: Cost of treasury stock	**8,000**
Total stockholders' equity	$ 342,000

EXHIBIT **12.6**

Before and After Balance Sheet Effects and Disclosure of Treasury Stock Purchase

---

Reissuance Below Cost

The entry to record the issuance of treasury stock below cost depends on any existing additional paid-in capital accounts. To illustrate, assume that on November 1, 2007, Ell Corporation reissues another 100 shares of treasury stock for $7 per share. Since Paid-in Capital from Treasury Stock Transactions has a previous balance, we debit the difference of $100 to this account as follows:

2007					
Nov.	1	Cash (100 shares × $7)		700	
		Paid-in Capital from Treasury Stock Transactions, Common		100	
		Treasury Stock—Common (100 shares × $8)			800
		Reissued 100 shares of treasury stock at $7 per share.			

If Paid-in Capital from Treasury Stock Transactions does not exist, we debit the excess to any paid-in capital account arising from the same class of stock. If no such accounts exist, we debit the difference to Retained Earnings.

Book Value of Common Stock

Learning Goal 5   Calculate book value per share and explain its significance.

Book value per share is the stockholders' equity on a per-share basis. We compute book value for each class of stock by dividing stockholders' equity for that class by the number of shares of stock outstanding. The stockholders' equity for a class of stock depends on the respective owners' claims to the assets if the company is liquidated.

Stockholders' Equity

Paid-in capital

Common stock, $1 par value; 100,000 shares issued and outstanding	$ 100,000
Additional paid-in capital—excess over par value, common stock	180,000
Total paid-in capital	$ 280,000
Retained earnings	200,000
Total stockholders' equity	$ 480,000

Book value per common share

$$\frac{\$480,000 \text{ (Total Stockholders' Equity)}}{100,000 \text{ Common Shares Outstanding}} = \$4.80$$

EXHIBIT **12.7**

Computation of Book Value per Common Share

When Only One Class of Stock Is Outstanding

If we have only one class of stock outstanding, we calculate book value as follows:

$$\text{Book Value per Share} = \frac{\text{Total Stockholders' Equity}}{\text{Shares Outstanding}}$$

Exhibit 12.7 illustrates the computation of book value per common share.

When More than One Class of Stock Is Outstanding

When more than one class of stock is outstanding, it is necessary to first determine the liquidation claims of each class of stock. *If they give no liquidation value for preferred stock, we assume it has a liquidation claim equal to its total par value plus dividends in arrears.* **Important: Use this assumption for all end-of-chapter exercises and problems.**

Exhibit 12.8 illustrates the computation of book value per preferred share and per common share. The exhibit assumes that the company has not paid preferred dividends for the current year.

Significance of Book Value per Share

Book value per share is of limited significance. Book value does not equal market value for a share of stock. Book value per share is the amount each stockholder would receive per share if the company liquidated all assets and liabilities at book values. However, the valuations on the books do not usually equal current market values. Therefore, the book value of a share of stock may be more or less than the market value. To illustrate this point, the following are book values and market values per common share for five well-known companies on March 31, 2005:

	Book Value per Common Share	Market Value per Common Share
Coca-Cola Company	$ 6.61	$ 41.95
Intel	6.17	23.49
General Motors Company	49.10	29.50
Toys "Я" Us	19.87	25.83
Walt Disney Company	13.18	28.35

Investors still calculate book value and compare it with the estimated market value of the firm's assets. They use this figure and other data to determine limits to what they may be willing to offer for the stock.

Stockholders' Equity

Paid-in capital
  Stock:
    Preferred stock, 10%, $50 par value;
      1,000 shares issued and outstanding $ 50,000
    Common stock, $1 par value;
      100,000 shares issued and outstanding   100,000
        Total stock $ 150,000
    Additional paid-in capital:
      Paid-in capital—excess over par value, preferred stock $ 30,000
      Paid-in capital—excess over par value, common stock   180,000
        Total additional paid-in capital   210,000
        Total paid-in capital $ 360,000
Retained earnings   200,000
Total stockholders' equity $ 560,000

  1. **Book value per preferred share**

$$\frac{\$50,000 \text{ (Preferred Par)} + \$5,000 \text{ (Dividends)}}{1,000 \text{ Preferred Shares Outstanding}} = \frac{\$55,000}{1,000} = \$55$$

  2. **Book value per common stock**

$$\frac{\$560,000 \text{ (Total Stockholders' Equity)} - \$55,000 \text{ (Preferred Equity)}}{100,000 \text{ Common Shares Outstanding}} = \frac{\$505,000}{100,000}$$
$$= \$5.05$$

EXHIBIT **12.8**

Computation of Book Value per Preferred Share and per Common Share

Expanded View of Stockholders ' Equity

To summarize the concepts covered so far in Chapters 11 and 12, Exhibit 12.9 presents an expanded version of Exhibits 11.2 and 11.6 The two sources of stockholders' equity are paid-in capital and retained earnings.

REPORTING INCOME INFORMATION

Learning Goal 6   Explain how we report discontinued operations and extraordinary items.

Net income is the financial statement item that receives the most attention. Users of financial statements look most closely at the *quality* of a company's reported net income. The following factors reflect the quality of a company's net income:

  1. *The accounting methods and estimates used by a company to prepare its financial statements.* For example, assume that two companies in the same industry make a $1 million investment in new computer equipment. Company A depreciates the equipment over an estimated life of 10 years using the straight-line method. Company B, recognizing rapid changes in technology, depreciates the equipment over an estimated life of 5 years using the double declining-balance method. The result is that Company B will show a higher (more realistic) figure for depreciation expense and a lower (more correct) net income figure. By using more conservative accounting methods, Company B has a higher quality net income figure than Company A, according to some financial statement users.

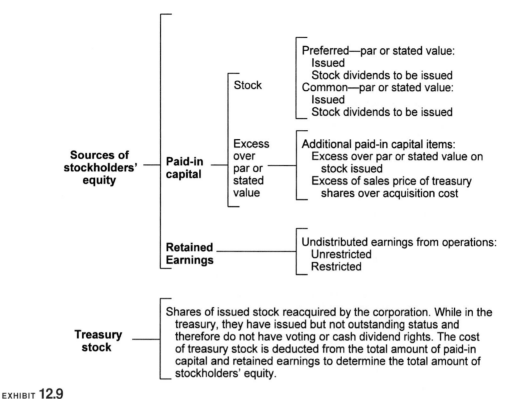

EXHIBIT **12.9**

Expanded View of Stockholders' Equity

2. *The number and size of nonrecurring revenue and expense items on the income statement.* Financial statement users focus on historical trends in net income to predict future results. Nonrecurring income and expense items, such as a gain on the sale of a major segment of the business or a loss from a tornado, can distort trends in earnings. To make interpretation of the income statement more meaningful, we should clearly indicate and disclose these nonrecurring items.

In this section, we discuss the disclosure of nonrecurring items on the income statement. These are discontinued operations, and extraordinary gains and losses.

Discontinued operations, and extraordinary gains and losses all affect the net income and may affect income tax expense. Interpreting these items in the income statement is easier if we show the income taxes related to each nonrecurring item with the item. Note in Exhibit 12.10 that we show all items *after income from continuing operations* net of income taxes. We call this technique **intraperiod tax allocation**. With a loss, we reduce the loss by the income tax savings caused by the loss. We assume a 40% corporate income tax rate to keep the illustration simple.

Continuing Operations

Financial statement users want know the income from the continuing operations of a business. We show this in section **[1]** in Exhibit 12.10 Income from continuing operations of $180,000 is the income from business segments that will operate in the future. It is a key income number financial

DIVERSIFIED CORPORATION
INCOME STATEMENT
FOR THE YEAR ENDED DECEMBER 31, 2007

1 Revenues		$900,000
Costs and expenses		600,000
Income from continuing operations before taxes		$300,000
Income tax expense (40% income tax rate)		120,000
Income from continuing operations		$180,000
2 Discontinued operations:		
Income from operations of discontinued segment		
(net of $12,000 income taxes)	$ 18,000	
Gain on disposal of assets of discontinued segment		
(net of $24,000 income taxes)	36,000	54,000
Income before extraordinary item and cumulative effect		
of a change in accounting principle		$234,000
3 Extraordinary item:		
Loss from uninsured hurricane damage		
(net of $52,000 income taxes)		(78,000)
Net income		$ 156,000
4 Earnings per common share (100,000 shares outstanding):		
Income from continuing operations		$ 1.80
Discontinued operations		.54
Extraordinary loss		(.78)
Net income		$ 1.56

EXHIBIT **12.10**

Income Statement Showing Discontinued Operations, Extraordinary Item, and Cumulative Effect of a Change in Accounting Principle

statement users look at to estimate future earnings for the company. We deduct income tax expense of $120,000 ($300,000 × 40%) to compute income from continuing operations.

Discontinued Operations

Large companies often operate in different lines of business and serve different classes of customers. A line of business or class of customer may qualify as a business segment. When management decides to dispose of a business segment, we must report the results for that segment separately on the income statement. We report the financial results of these segments in a special section labeled **discontinued operations**. Section **[2]** in Exhibit 12.10 is an example of this.

Note that there are two elements in the discontinued operations section.(1) We show the operating income or loss on discontinued operations for the period. This is income or loss from operating the segment from the start of the year to the disposal date. We show the income of $18,000 net of related income taxes of $12,000. This means that the operating income before taxes for the discontinued segment was $30,000 ($18,000 + $12,000). (2) We show the gain on disposal of $36,000. This represents the after-tax gain realized when we sold the segment during 2007. We show it separately from the income (loss) from operations.

Extraordinary Items

Extraordinary items are gains and losses that are *both* unusual and infrequent.[4] Section **[3]** shows an extraordinary loss from uninsured hurricane damage. We show the after-tax loss of $78,000 net of its related tax savings of $52,000.

---

[4] *Opinions of the Accounting Principles Board No. 30*, "Reporting the Results of Operations" (New York: AICPA, June 1973), paragraph 20.

We apply the "unusual and infrequent" criterion by taking into account the environment in which the firm operates. For example, a loss from a flood in an area where floods are common would not qualify as extraordinary. Instead, we would show this loss as a separate item in the income from continuing operations section of the income statement. Examples of items that we usually treat as extraordinary are: (1) uninsured losses from earthquakes and fires; (2) gains or losses from early retirement of debt; (3) gains or losses resulting from the passing of a new law; and (4) gains or losses from foreign governments taking business property.

Reporting Earnings per Share

Section [4] of Exhibit 12.10 shows information on *earnings per share*. The relatively simple earnings per share computation here involves dividing the net income amounts by the 100,000 common shares outstanding throughout the year. We should show separate earnings per share figures for each of the following:

- Income from continuing operations.
- Discontinued operations.
- Extraordinary items.
- Net income.

We explain how to compute earnings per share in more detail in the next section.

EARNINGS PER SHARE (EPS)

Learning Goal 7   Calculate earnings per share.

The purpose of **earnings per share (EPS)** is to express net income for the period on a per-common-share basis. Financial statement readers use earnings per share to judge the performance of a company. We show earnings per common share or net loss per common share on the face of the income statement.

Under *FASB Statement No. 128*, the computation and presentation of earnings per share depend on whether the company has a simple or a complex capital structure. In a simple capital structure, there are no debt or equity securities outstanding that could dilute (decrease) earnings per share. An example of a potentially dilutive security is shares of preferred stock that have a conversion option into common stock. In a complex capital structure, potentially dilutive securities exist. *FASB Statement No. 128* provides rules regarding the treatment of these securities when calculating earnings per share. In the following sections, we present examples of earnings per share calculations for a simple and a complex capital structure.

Simple Capital Structure

For a simple capital structure, we compute basic earnings per share on net income *minus preferred dividends*. **Basic earnings per share** excludes dilutive securities and is computed by dividing income by weighted average common shares. The calculation is as follows:

$$\text{Basic Earnings per Share} = \frac{\text{Net Income} - \text{Dividends on Preferred Stock}}{\text{Weighted Average Number of Common Shares Outstanding during the Period}}$$

To illustrate the basic earnings per share calculation for a simple capital structure, assume the following for Sanders Corporation:

		Shares
Net income for 2007	$60,000	
Shares of stock:		
12% Preferred stock, $100 par value, nonconvertible 1,000 shares issued and outstanding during 2007		1,000
Common stock, $1 par:		
Issued and outstanding on January 1, 2007		12,000
Additional shares issued on April 1, 2007		4,000

We base the calculation of basic earnings per share on the *weighted average* number of common shares outstanding. In this example, the number of common shares has changed during the year. The company issued additional shares on April 1, 2007. Therefore, we calculate the weighted average number of shares as follows:

Weighted average common shares outstanding from:	
January 1, 2007, through March 31, 2007	
(12,000 shares × ¼ year)	3,000
April 1, 2007, through December 31, 2007,	
[(12,000 + 4,000) × ¾ year]	12,000
Weighted average common shares outstanding during 2007	15,000

Basic earnings per share for 2007 is as follows:

$$\text{Basic Earnings per Share} = \frac{\$60,000 - 12,000^*}{15,000 \text{ weighted average common shares}}$$

$$= \$3.20 \text{ per share}$$

$$^*1,000 \times \$100 \times 0.12 = \$12,000$$

If there were no preferred shares outstanding in the example, then basic earnings per share for 2007 would be $4 ($60,000 ÷ 15,000 shares).

Complex Capital Structure

In a complex capital structure, a variety of convertible debt and equity securities that have the potential to dilute (decrease) earnings per share may exist. We have a complex set of rules for recognizing the potential dilution resulting from convertible securities. Advanced accounting courses cover these rules in detail. In this textbook, we state how to treat potentially dilutive securities.

For companies with a complex capital structure, we present two earnings per share figures:

1. **Basic earnings per share** is EPS based on the weighted average number of common shares outstanding.

2. **Diluted earnings per share** reflects the maximum potential dilution possible in earnings per share. We base this EPS on the weighted average number of common shares outstanding plus all dilutive potential common shares that were outstanding during the period.

Assume the previous information for Sanders Corporation with the addition of a second class of preferred stock. The preferred stock is convertible into shares of common stock. It has the following characteristics:

	Shares
12% Preferred stock, $50 par, each share convertible into 10 shares of common stock, 1,000 shares issued and outstanding during 2007	1,000

Sanders Corporation now has a complex capital structure due to the existence of the convertible preferred stock. The convertible preferred stock shares do not enter the computation of basic earnings per share. However, to show the maximum potential dilution in EPS, we assume the holders convert the convertible preferred shares into shares of common to calculate diluted earnings per share. The following shows the calculations of both EPS numbers.

Basic Earnings per Share

To compute basic earnings per share, we must subtract the dividend requirements on both classes of preferred stock from net income. We calculate basic earnings per share as follows:

$$\text{Basic Earnings per Share} = \frac{\$60,000 - 18,000^*}{15,000 \text{ weighted average common shares}}$$

$$= \$2.80 \text{ per share}$$

$$^*1,000 \times \$100 \times 0.12 = \$12,000$$

$$1,000 \times \$50 \times 0.12 = \$6,000$$

$$12,000 + \$6,000 = \$18,000$$

Diluted Earnings per Share

To compute diluted earnings per share, we assume the holders convert the convertible preferred shares into shares of common stock. Therefore, we make two changes in the preceding computation. First, we do not subtract the dividends on the *convertible* preferred stock from net income in the numerator. If the preferred shares are assumed converted into common, there would be no preferred dividend requirement. Second, we increase the number of shares of common stock in the denominator by the number of additional shares assumed issued in the conversion. The additional number of common shares is 10,000 (1,000 preferred shares 10 shares of common each). Diluted earnings per share is as follows:

$$\text{Diluted Earnings per Share} = \frac{\$60,000 - 12,000^*}{15,000 \text{ weighted average common shares } + 10,000 \text{ common shares for preferred shares assumed converted}}$$

$$= \$1.92 \text{ per share}$$

$$^* \ 1,000 \times \$100 \times 0.12 = \$12,000$$

The bottom of the income statement shows net income and the two earnings per share amounts as follows:

Net income	$ 60,000
Earnings per share of common stock	
Basic	$ 2.80
Diluted	$ 1.92

Nonrecurring items such as extraordinary items may also exist. If so, we also report basic and diluted EPS amounts for each of the nonrecurring items.

ANALYZING INFORMATION

Learning Goal 8   Analyze financial statement information for real-life companies.

Exhibit 12.11 shows information for Target and Talbots on items we have discussed in Chapters 11 and 12. Both companies end their financial reporting year on January 31.

Question. What are the major differences you can observe in comparing Target and Talbot's? Which company would you view as more successful?

Answer. (a) Overall Observations: Both companies have relatively low par values per share. Talbot's has issued a greater percentage of its authorized shares than Target. Talbot's has repurchased more common shares for the treasury. Target book value per share is higher than Talbot's. The common stocks of both companies are selling for much more than the book value. Talbot's has a dividend yield of 1.36% compared to Target of 0.64%. **(b) Performance Evaluation:** There is a difference in the profitability and return on assets between the two companies. Talbot's has a profit margin percent of 6.08% (versus 4.02% for Target). We could view Talbot's as more successful.

Selected Information (as of January 31, 2004)	Target	Talbot's
Par value per share	$ 0.0833	$ 0.01
Number of shares authorized	6,000,000,000	200,000,000
Number of shares issued	911,808,051	76,245,075
Number of shares in treasury	0	19,569,569
Number of shares outstanding	911,808,051	56,675,506
Book value per common share	$ 14.638	$ 11.03
Market price per share	$ 37.96	$ 32.50
Cash dividend per common share	$ 0.32	$ 0.44
Dividend yield	0.64%	1.36%
Profit margin % (Net income ÷ Net sales)	4.02%	6.08%
Return on assets (ROA) (Net income ÷ Average total assets)	5.93%	9.91%
Earnings per share (EPS)	$ 2.06	$ 1.73
Price earnings (P/E) ratio (Market price per share ÷ Earnings per share)	18.43 times	18.79 times

EXHIBIT **12.11**

Common Stock Information for Target and Talbot's

LEARNING GOALS REVIEW

1. **Define *retained earnings* and describe factors that affect them.**
   Retained earnings are undistributed earnings arising from profitable operations. The primary factors that affect retained earnings are net income or net loss, restrictions of retained earnings, prior period adjustments, and cash and stock dividends.

2. **Account for cash dividends and describe their effects on assets and stockholders' equity.**
   Cash dividends decrease assets and stockholders' equity, since they are a distribution of corporate assets to stockholders. We debit a dividends account and credit Dividends Payable to record the declaration of a cash dividend. We debit Dividends Payable and credit Cash to record the payment of a cash dividend.

3. **Account for stock dividends and stock splits and describe their effects on assets and stockholders' equity.**

For stock dividends involving less than 20-25% of the shares outstanding, we debit Stock Dividends for the current market value of the stock times the number of shares to be issued. For a stock dividend involving more than 20-25% of the outstanding shares, we use the par value of the stock for the debit to Stock Dividends. A stock split is an increase in the number of shares outstanding. In a stock split, we reduce the par value per share and issue additional shares. Stock dividends and stock splits do not affect total assets or total stockholders' equity.

4. **Account for treasury stock transactions and describe their impact on the balance sheet.**
   The purchase of treasury stock reduces total assets and total stockholders' equity. We debit Treasury Stock and credit Cash for the cost of treasury shares purchased. To record the reissuance of treasury stock above cost, we credit the excess received to Paid-in Capital from Treasury Stock Transactions. To record the reissuance below cost, we debit the Paid-in Capital from Treasury Stock Transactions or the Retained Earnings account for the difference between the cost and the issuance price.

5. **Calculate book value per share and explain its significance.**
   Book value represents the amount each stockholder would receive if the company liquidated all assets and liabilities at book value. If only common stock is outstanding, we compute book value per share by dividing total stockholders' equity by the number of common shares outstanding. If both preferred and common stock are outstanding, we first compute the liquidation claim of the preferred stock. We add any dividends in arrears to the liquidation claims of the preferred stock. We divide the total by the number of preferred shares to compute book value. We divide the remaining stockholders' equity by the common shares outstanding to compute common book value per share. Since book value is not equal to market value, the book value per share may be of limited significance.

6. **Explain how we report discontinued operations and extraordinary items.**
   We report discontinued operations and extraordinary items on the income statement after income from continuing operations. We show these items net of related income taxes. Discontinued operations are disposals of lines of business or classes of customers. Extraordinary items are gains and losses that are both unusual and infrequent.

7. **Calculate earnings per share.**
   To compute earnings per share for a simple capital structure, we first subtract any preferred dividends from net income. We divide this amount by the weighted average number of common shares outstanding during the period. A complex capital structure involves the computation of two earnings per share figures: basic and diluted. To compute basic earnings per share, we subtract dividends on any preferred stock from net income. We divide the difference by the weighted average number of common shares. For fully diluted earnings per share, we assume that all convertible securities are converted into common stock. First, we do not subtract the dividends on the *convertible* preferred stock from net income in the numerator. Second, we increase the number of shares of common stock in the denominator by the number of additional shares assumed issued in the conversion.

8. **Analyze financial statement information for real-life companies.**
   One of the objectives of most companies is to provide continuing and increasing returns to its stockholders. Generally, investors are willing to pay a higher price/earnings multiple for a company with higher profitability, efficient use of assets, and good prospects for continued sales and earnings growth.

DEMONSTRATION PROBLEM

Stockholders' Equity Transactions, Preparing the Stockholders' Equity Section, and Computing Book Value per Share

The stockholders' equity section of Lisa Corporation's balance sheet as of December 31, 2006, follows:

Stockholders' Equity

Paid-in capital
  Stock:
    Preferred stock, 12% cumulative, $20 par value 50,000 shares

authorized, 5,000 shares issued	$ 100,000
Common stock, $2 par value; 200,000 shares authorized, 70,000 shares	
issued	140,000
Total stock	$ 240,000
Additional paid-in capital:	
Paid-in capital—excess over par value, common stock	210,000
Total paid-in capital	$ 450,000
Retained earnings	380,000
Total stockholders' equity	$ 830,000

Selected transactions for Lisa Corporation for 2007 are as follows:

2007

Jan.	3	Declared a 100% stock dividend on common stock. The dividends are distributable on February 9, 2007, to stockholders of record on January 31, 2007. The market price per share of the common stock on January 3, 2007, is $18.
Feb.	9	Distributed the stock dividend.
Jun.	12	Purchased 8,000 shares of own common stock at $10 per share.
Nov.	5	Sold 3,000 of the treasury shares at $11.50 per share.
Dec.	12	Declared a cash dividend of $.20 per share on the common stock and $2.40 per share on the preferred. The dividends are payable on January 9, 2008, to stockholders of record on December 31, 2007.
	31	Net income for 2007 was $102,000. Closed this amount to Retained Earnings.
	31	Closed the Dividends accounts.

REQUIRED

1. **(LG 2-4)** Journalize the selected stockholders' equity transactions that occurred during 2007.

2. **(LG 1-4)** Prepare the stockholders' equity section of the balance sheet as of December 31, 2007.

3. **(LG 5)** Compute the book value per share of the common stock as of December 31, 2007.

4. **(LG 1)** Assume that state law requires that Lisa Corporation restrict retained earnings for the cost of treasury stock held. Prepare a note to the financial statements as of December 31, 2007, that describes this required retained earnings restriction.

SOLUTION

Requirement 1

Solution Approach

In the case of a large stock dividend, the amount of retained earnings we transfer to paid-in capital is the par or stated value per share. Do not consider the $18 market price of common stock in the case of a large stock dividend. The amount of retained earnings capitalized is as follows:

Common shares issued and outstanding	70,000
× Stock dividend percentage (100%)	1.00
Number of common shares to issue	70,000
× Par value of common stock per share	$ 2.00
Amount of retained earnings transferred to Paid-in Capital	$140,000

2007

Jan.	3	Stock Dividends—Common	140,000	
		Stock Dividends to Be Issued		140,000
		To record declaration of stock dividend.		

If Lisa prepares a balance sheet between January 3 and February 9, disclose the Stock Dividends to Be Issued account as part of paid-in capital, not as a liability.

Feb.	9	Stock Dividend to Be Issued—Common	140,000	
		Common Stock		140,000
		To record issuance of stock dividend.		
Jun.	12	Treasury Stock—Common	80,000	
		Cash		80,000
		Purchased 8,000 shares of own common stock at $10 per share.		

Treasury shares are issued but are no longer outstanding. The balance in Treasury Stock appears as a deduction from the total amount of stockholders' equity on the balance sheet. Debit Treasury Stock for the cost of the treasury shares.

Nov.	5	Cash	34,500	
		Treasury Stock—Common		30,000
		Paid-in Capital from Treasury Stock Transactions, Common		4,500
		Reissued 3,000 shares of treasury stock at $11.50 per share.		

Reduce the Treasury Stock account for the cost of the treasury shares sold. Credit any excess to a paid-in capital account.

Dec.	12	Dividends—Preferred Stock	12,000	
		Dividends Payable—Preferred Stock		12,000
		To record declaration of annual dividend on preferred stock for 2007 (0.12 × $20 par value per share × 5,000).		
	12	Dividends—Common Stock	27,000	
		Dividends Payable—Common Stock		27,000
		To record declaration of 20-cents-a-share cash dividend on 135,000 shares of common stock.		

Computation of common shares outstanding:

Shares outstanding on Jan. 1, 2007	70,000
Shares issued in 100% stock dividend on Feb. 9, 2007	70,000
Shares reacquired on Jun. 12, 2007	(8,000)
Treasury shares reissued on Nov. 5, 2007	3,000
Shares outstanding on Dec. 12, 2007	135,000

Note that the 5,000 treasury shares are not outstanding and are not entitled to receive cash dividends.

Dec.	31	Income Summary	102,000	
		Retained Earnings		102,000
		To close net income to Retained Earnings.		
	31	Retained Earnings	179,000	
		Stock Dividends—Common		140,000
		Dividends—Preferred Stock		12,000
		Dividends—Common Stock		27,000
		To close Dividends accounts to Retained Earnings.		

Requirement 2

Solution Approach

To determine account balances, prepare selected summary T accounts even if the problem requirements do not call for them.

Common Stock		
	Balance	140,000
	2/9	140,000
	Balance	280,000

Retained Earnings				
12/31	179,000	Balance	380,000
		12/31	102,000
		Balance	303,000

Paid-in Capital—Excess over Par Value, Common

	Balance	210,000

Treasury Stock—Common				
6/12	80,000	11/5	30,000
Balance	50,000		

Paid-in Capital from Treasury Stock Transactions, Common

	11/5	4,500

Stockholders' Equity

Paid-in capital

Stock:

Preferred stock, 12% cumulative, $20 par value; 50,000 shares authorized, 5,000 shares issued	$ 100,000	
Common stock, $2 par value; 200,000 shares authorized, 140,000 shares issued of which 5,000 shares are held in treasury	280,000	
Total stock		$ 380,000
Additional paid-in capital:		
Paid-in capital—excess over par value, common stock	$ 210,000	
Paid-in capital from treasury stock transactions, common	4,500	
Total additional paid-in capital		214,500
Total paid-in capital		$ 594,500
Retained earnings		303,000
Total paid-in capital and retained earnings		$ 897,500
Deduct: Cost of treasury stock—common		50,000
Total stockholders' equity		$ 847,500

ADDITIONAL STOCKHOLDERS' EQUITY TRANSACTIONS

Requirement 3

Solution Approach

Assume that the preferred stockholders have a claim on assets in liquidation of an amount equal to par value plus any dividends in arrears. We base the book value computation on the number of shares outstanding on the balance sheet date.

Total stockholders' equity	$847,500
Deduct: Equity of preferred stockholders	100,000
Total equity of common stockholders	$747,500
Number of common shares outstanding (140,000 - 5,000)	135,000
Book value per share ($747,500 ÷ 135,000 shares)	$ 5.54

Requirement 4

Solution Approach

In the case of treasury stock, the company pays out cash to specific stockholders and reduces the shares of stock outstanding. The purpose of the restriction of retained earnings in the amount of the treasury stock is to prevent the company from paying out dividends greater than the current balance in Retained Earnings less the cost of the treasury stock.

Note XX: Restriction of retained earnings.
As of December 31, 2007, the total balance in Retained Earnings is $303,000. Of this total $50,000 is restricted due to purchases of treasury stock in this amount and is not available for distribution as dividends. Unrestricted retained earnings are $253,000.

GLOSSARY

basic earnings per share The earnings per share amount calculated by dividing the net income for the period by the weighted common shares outstanding.

book value per share The amount that a stockholder would receive on a per-share basis if assets were sold at no gain or loss; the portion of the stockholders' equity assigned to a class of stock divided by the number of shares of that class of stock issued and outstanding.

complex capital structure A corporate structure in which potentially dilutive securities are outstanding.

cumulative preferred stock The class of preferred stock on which undeclared dividends are accumulated and must be paid together with the current dividends before any dividend payment can be made on common stock.

deficit The negative retained earnings caption used in the balance sheet to indicate that the retained earnings balance is negative.

diluted earnings per share The earnings per share amount calculated by dividing the applicable net income for the period by the common stock outstanding, plus other securities with conversion privileges that could decrease earnings per share.

discontinued operations Business segments, involving a line of business or class of customers, that the company plans to eliminate. A section of the income statement in which we report the financial results of such segments.

dividend A distribution of some portion of net income in the form of cash, stock, or other corporate property by a corporation to its stockholders.

dividends in arrears The amount of dividends on cumulative preferred stock not declared or in arrears for any dividend period or periods.

earnings per share Net income for the period stated on a per-share basis.

ex-dividend Stock purchased without the right to receive the latest declared but unpaid dividend.

extraordinary items Gains or losses that are both unusual and infrequent.

intraperiod tax allocation Allocation of income taxes to normal and nonrecurring items on the income statement.

prior period adjustment Adjustment to beginning retained earnings balance to correct for past error.

restricted retained earnings The portion of retained earnings not available for dividends.

retained earnings Cumulative net income minus net losses and dividends declared.

simple capital structure A corporate structure in which there are no debt or equity securities outstanding with the potential to dilute earnings per share.

stock dividend The issuance by a corporation of additional shares of its authorized stock without additional investment by the stockholders. A stock dividend may be classified as large (more than 20-25% of the number of shares previously outstanding) or small (less than 20-25% of the number of shares previously outstanding).

stock split An increase in the number of shares of stock outstanding without a change in the total par or total stated value of the outstanding shares (usually the par or stated value per share will be decreased).

treasury stock A company's own stock previously issued and outstanding but reacquired by purchase or gift or in settlement of a debt.

QUESTIONS FOR GROUP LEARNING

Q12-1.   Since it represents earnings retained for use in the business, is the Retained Earnings account an asset? Explain.

Q12-2.   What is the meaning of the following terms: (a) retained earnings? (b) restricted retained earnings? (c) deficit?

Q12-3.   Differentiate between the following pairs of terms: (a) cash dividend and stock dividend; (b) book value per share and market value per share; (c) cumulative stock and noncumulative stock; (d) restricted retained earnings and unrestricted retained earnings; (e) stock dividend and stock split.

Q12-4.   The following quotation is adapted from the notes to the financial statements of a large company:"Retained earnings of $28,200,000 are restricted from payment of cash dividends on common stock because of a promissory note agreement. Further restrictions of $1,600,000 are made to cover the cost of the company's own common stock reacquired." What is the significance of this note to a long-term creditor?

Q12-5.   (a) What is a stock dividend? (b) What conditions prompt its declaration?

Q12-6.   How does a stock dividend affect: (a) the total stockholders' equity? (b) the total assets? (c) the book value per share? (d) the market price per share?

Q12-7.   (a) What is treasury stock? (b) Why do corporations buy back their own shares? (c) How does the reacquisition of a company's own shares affect its net assets?

Q12-8.   (a) Why do some states place certain restrictions on treasury stock acquisitions? (b) How is the purchase of treasury stock recorded? (c) How is the sale of treasury stock recorded? (d) How does the sale of treasury stock affect the income statement?

Q12-9.   Would you expect the market value of a company's stock to equal its book value? Explain your answer.

Q12-10.   What is the purpose of intraperiod tax allocation?

Q12-11.   State the two criteria for extraordinary items. Where are extraordinary items shown on the income statement?

Q12-12.   Explain the difference between a simple capital structure and a complex capital structure with regard to computing earnings per share.

Q12-13.   Discuss the treatment of preferred stocks that are not convertible into shares of common stock in computing basic and diluted earnings per share.

Q12-14.   Discuss the treatment of preferred stocks that are convertible into shares of common stock in computing basic and diluted earnings per share.

EXERCISES

E12-15.   **Determining the effect of transactions on retained earnings (LG 1)** Indicate the effect—increase, decrease, no effect—of each of the following transactions on *total* retained earnings of the Case Company:

   a. The board of directors declared a 5% stock dividend to be issued one month from the current date.

   b. Issued the stock dividend declared in transaction a.

   c. Wrote off accounts receivable against the allowance for doubtful accounts.

   d. Paid accounts payable.

   e. Collected accounts receivable.

   f. Issued $1 par value common stock at $5 a share.

   g. Restricted retained earnings for contingencies.

   h. Issued $50 par value preferred stock at $57 a share.

   i. Purchased machinery on open account.

   j. Issued long-term notes and received cash in return.

E12-16.   **Recording cash dividends (LG 2)** Rizzo Corporation has 100,000 shares of common stock outstanding. On June 5, 2007, the board of directors declared a $.25 per share dividend payable on July 10, 2007, to stockholders of record on June 24, 2007. Prepare the necessary journal entries on each of the foregoing dates.

E12-17. **Calculating dividends (LG 2)** Ben B Corporation had the following stockholders' equity during 2007.

12% preferred stock, $100 par value	$200,000
Common stock, $10 par value	300,000
Total stockholders' equity	$500,000

Assume that Ben B Corporation has $140,000 available for dividends during 2007 and that the preferred stock is cumulative and dividends are in arrears for the entire year of 2006. Calculate the amount that would be payable to preferred shareholders and to common shareholders if $140,000 is declared for the total dividends.

E12-18. **Recording a small stock dividend (LG 3)** Wafeek Corporation had the following stockholders' equity on August 2, 2007.

Common stock, $5 par value; 500,000 shares authorized, 300,000 shares issued and outstanding	$ 1,500,000
Retained earnings	2,000,000
Total stockholders' equity	$ 3,500,000

On August 2, 2007, the board of directors declared a 10% stock dividend to be issued on September 5, 2007, to stockholders of record on August 21, 2007. The market price of the common stock at date of declaration of the dividend was $19 per share.

1. Prepare the necessary journal entries on each of the foregoing dates.

2. What is the total stockholders' equity after the foregoing entries are made?

E12-19. **Effects of stock dividends and stock splits (LG 3)** Socks Corporation was incorporated in 1999 with 400,000 authorized shares of $1 par value common stock. On January 20, 1999, 200,000 shares of common stock were sold at $4 per share. Socks has issued no other shares of stock. The corporation was a huge success, and as of January 1, 2007, the common stock is selling for $60 per share and Retained Earnings has a credit balance of $2,000,000. Management wishes to reduce the market price of the common stock and is considering either (a) issuing a 100% stock dividend or (b) issuing a two-for-one stock split in which the par value of the common stock would be reduced from $1 to $.50 per share.

1. Prepare the necessary journal entries to record both alternatives (a) and (b).

2. For both alternatives (a) and (b), compute each of the following amounts after the stock dividend or stock split is issued:

a. Total amount of legal capital.

b. Total amount of paid-in capital.

c. Total amount of retained earnings.

d. Total amount of stockholders' equity.

e. Market price per share at which the common stock should be selling.

E12-20. **Recording treasury stock transactions (LG 4)** The stock of DSM Corporation consists of $2 par value common stock. Record the following events, occurring in sequence (using letters instead of dates in the journal):

a. The issuance of 20,000 shares at $9 a share.

b. The reacquisition of 500 shares at $10 a share.

c. The reissuance of all the treasury stock at $12 per share.

E12-21. **Recording treasury stock transactions (LG 4)** On July 1, 2007, Jacob Corporation had the following stockholders' equity:

Common stock, $1 par value, 40,000 shares authorized, issued and outstanding	$40,000
Paid-in capital—excess over par value, common	175,000
Retained earnings	610,500

The following selected transactions took place during July and August 2007:

2007

Jul.	7	Reacquired 1,000 shares of own common stock at $20 per share.
Aug.	12	Reissued 200 treasury shares for $24 per share.
	23	Reissued 200 treasury shares for $19 per share.
	30	Reissued the remaining 600 shares to employees for $17 per share.

Prepare journal entries to record the foregoing transactions.

E12-22. **Recording stock and cash dividends with treasury stock (LG 2, 3)** The stockholders' equity section of Cherry Company's balance sheet shows the following:

Common stock, $1 par value, 200,000 shares authorized, 100,000 shares issued	$100,000
Retained earnings	200,000
Total stockholders' equity	$300,000

Record each of the following events, occurring in sequence (using letters instead of dates in the journal):

a. The declaration of a 15% stock dividend; the market price of the stock is $9 per share.

b. The issuance of the dividend.

c. The acquisition of 200 shares of the company's own stock for $10 a share.

d. The reissuance of 100 of the reacquired shares for $13 a share.

e. The declaration of a $.25-per-share cash dividend.

f. The payment of the cash dividend.

E12-23. **Calculating book value per share (LG 5)** The condensed balance sheet of E-Z Company as of December 31, 2007, contained the following items:

Total assets	$520,000
Total liabilities	$100,000
Preferred stock, 12%, $50 par value; cumulative, 2,000 shares issued	100,000
Common stock, no-par value; $1 stated value, 200,000 shares issued	200,000
Paid-in capital—excess over par value, preferred stock	10,000
Paid-in capital—excess over stated value, common stock	15,000
Retained earnings	95,000
Total liabilities and stockholders' equity	$520,000

The liquidating value of the preferred stock is equal to the par value plus any dividends in arrears.

1. Determine the book value per share of common stock, assuming that there are no dividends in arrears as of December 31, 2007.

2. Calculate the book value per share of common stock, assuming that dividends on the preferred stock are in arrears for the years 2006 and 2007.

E12-24. **Preparing a stockholders' equity section (LG 1-4)** Atlas Company had the following selected account balances on its ledger as of December 31, 2007:

Paid-in Capital from Treasury Stock Transactions, Common	$25,000
Preferred Stock (12% cumulative, $100 par value, issued 8,600 of 50,000 authorized shares)	860,000
Common Stock ($5 stated value; issued 58,000 of 300,000 authorized shares)	290,000
Retained Earnings	480,000
Treasury Stock—Common (600 shares)	28,000
Paid-in Capital—Excess over Stated Value, Common	96,000
Bonds Payable (due 2017)	200,000

Prepare the stockholders' equity section of the balance sheet as of December 31, 2007.

E12-25. **Income statement disclosures (LG 6)** You assemble the following information for Felix Company for the year ended December 31, 2007:

Net sales	$1,700,000
Costs and expenses	1,400,000
Income from operations on discontinued segment	90,000
Loss on disposal of discontinued segment	(20,000)
Extraordinary gain on lawsuit	100,000

Prepare the income statement for the company for the year ended December 31, 2007. Assume a 30% income tax rate on all items. Ignore earnings per share disclosures.

E12-26. **Calculating earnings per share for a simple capital structure (LG 7)** The 2007 net income after taxes of Starr Corporation was $46,000. During 2007, Starr Corporation had the following shares of capital stock outstanding:

	Shares
Shares of capital stock:	
Preferred stock, 5%, $100 par value, nonconvertible, 4,000 shares issued and outstanding during 2007.	4,000
Common stock, $1 par value:	
Issued and outstanding on January 1, 2007	20,000
Additional shares issued on July 1, 2007	8,000

Calculate earnings per share for 2007.

E12-27. **Calculating earnings per share for a complex capital structure (LG 7)** The 2007 net income after taxes of Lennon Corporation was $223,500. During 2007, Lennon Corporation had the following shares of capital stock outstanding:

	Shares
Shares of capital stock:	
Preferred stock, 12%, $100 par, nonconvertible, 2,000 shares issued and outstanding during 2007	2,000
Preferred stock, 11%, $100 par, each share convertible into 8 shares of common stock, 1,000 shares issued and outstanding during 2007	1,000
Common stock, $1 par:	
Issued and outstanding on Jan. 1, 2007	30,000
Additional shares issued on Oct. 1, 2007	10,000

Calculate basic and diluted earnings per share for 2007.

PROBLEMS

P12-28. Journalizing various stockholders' equity transactions (LG 1-4) TK Company was organized on January 1, 2007, with authority to issue 50,000 shares of no-par value common stock and 12,000 shares of 12% cumulative preferred stock, $50 par value. During 2007, the following selected transactions occurred in this sequence:

a. Issued 8,000 shares of common stock for cash at $14 per share. The board of directors sets a stated value of $10 per share for the common stock.

b. Issued 2,000 shares of preferred stock at $60 per share.

c. Acquired 400 shares of common stock for $4,000 from the estate of a deceased stockholder.

d. Reissued the 400 shares of the treasury stock at $12 per share.

e. Declared a 12% annual dividend on preferred stock.

f. Paid the preferred dividend.

g. Declared a 10% stock dividend on the common stock. The current market value per share is $16.

h. Distributed the stock dividend.

i. Closed the 2007 end-of-the year credit balance of $150,000 in the Income Summary account. (Make the closing entry.)

REQUIRED
Prepare the journal entries to record the transactions using letters in place of dates.

P12-29. Journalizing various stockholders' equity transactions and preparing a stockholders' equity section (LG 1, 2, 4) The stockholders' equity section of Regan Company's balance sheet as of December 31, 2006, was as follows:

Stockholders' Equity

Paid-in capital	
Stock:	
Preferred stock, 15%, $50 par value; 6,000 shares authorized and issued	$ 300,000
Common stock, $4 par value; 150,000 shares authorized and issued	600,000
Total stock	$ 900,000
Paid-in capital—excess over par value, common stock	85,000
Total paid-in capital	$ 985,000
Retained earnings	800,000
Total stockholders' equity	$ 1,785,000

Selected transactions for 2007 occurred in the following sequence:

a. Declared a total annual cash dividend of $120,000 for 2007. (The preferred stock is cumulative; there are no dividends in arrears.)

b. Paid the dividend declared in transaction a.

c. Purchased 2,000 shares of its own common stock for $8 a share.

d. Reissued 500 shares of treasury stock for $10 a share.

e. Reissued 400 shares of treasury stock for $9 a share.

f. Earnings from operations for the year after income taxes were $200,000. (Make the closing entry. Also close the dividends accounts.)

REQUIRED

1. Prepare general journal entries to record the transactions using letters in place of dates.

2. Enter the December 31, 2006, balances in ledger accounts. Post the journal entries to these and other newly created *stockholders' equity accounts* only.

3. Prepare the stockholders' equity section of the balance sheet as of December 31, 2007.

P12-30. **Determining book value per share (LG 5)** The condensed balance sheet data of East Company as of December 31, 2007, were as follows:

Total assets	$900,000
Total liabilities	$150,000
Preferred stock, 10%, $50 par value; cumulative, 4,000 shares issued	200,000
Common stock, no-par value; $10 stated value, 35,000 shares issued	350,000
Paid-in capital—excess over par value, preferred stock	10,000
Paid-in capital—excess over stated value, common stock	40,000
Retained earnings	150,000
Total liabilities and stockholders' equity	$900,000

REQUIRED

1. Determine the book value per share of common stock, assuming that there are no dividends in arrears. The liquidation value of the preferred stock is equal to the par value plus any dividends in arrears.

2. Calculate the book value per share of common stock, assuming that dividends on the preferred stock are in arrears for the years 2005, 2006, and 2007.

3. What is the significance of the book value per share?

4. What is the interrelationship between book value per share and market value per share?

P12-31. **Income statement disclosures (LG 6)** You assemble the following information for Johnson Company for the year ended December 31, 2007:

Net sales	$1,900,000
Costs and expenses	1,500,000
Income from operations on discontinued segment	400,000
Gain on disposal of discontinued segment	300,000
Extraordinary loss on lawsuit	200,000

REQUIRED

1. Prepare the income statement for the company for the year ended December 31, 2007. Assume a 30% income tax rate on all items. Assume 100,000 weighted average common shares were outstanding in order to compute earnings per share.

2. Based on the income statement, briefly comment on your assessment of Johnson Company's 2007 operating results.

P12-32. Calculating earnings per share for a simple capital structure (LG 7) Assume the following for Bear Company:

	Shares
Shares of stock:	
Preferred stock, 12%, $100 par, nonconvertible,	
6,000 shares issued and outstanding during 2007	6,000
Common stock, $0.25 par:	
Issued and outstanding on January 1, 2007	50,000
Additional shares issued on July 1, 2007	12,000
Shares reacquired on October 1, 2007	4,000

Net income for 2007:

Income before extraordinary items	$264,500
Extraordinary gain	23,100
Net income	$287,600

REQUIRED

Calculate earnings per share for 2007 on income before extraordinary items, on the extraordinary gain, and on net income.

P12-33. Calculating earnings per share for a complex capital structure (LG 7) The net income after taxes of Campus Company for 2007 was $234,000. During 2007, the following shares of capital stock were outstanding:

	Shares
Shares of capital stock:	
Preferred stock, 12%, $50 par, nonconvertible, 4,000 shares	
issued and outstanding during 2007	4,000
Preferred stock, 10%, $100 par, each share convertible into	
15 shares of common stock, 1,000 shares issued and outstanding	
during 2007	1,000
Common stock, $1 par:	
Issued and outstanding on January 1, 2007	60,000
Additional shares issued on July 1, 2007	40,000

REQUIRED

1. Calculate basic earnings per share for 2007.

2. Calculate diluted earnings per share for 2007.

PRACTICE CASE

Corporations: Retained earnings, dividends, treasury stock, and book value (LG 1-5) The stockholders' equity section of Mini Corporation as of December 31, 2006, follows:

Stockholders' Equity

Paid-in capital	
Stock:	
Preferred stock, 10% cumulative, $50 par value; 50,000 shares authorized, 4,000 shares issued	$200,000
Common stock, $1 par value; 400,000 shares authorized, 90,000 shares issued	90,000
Total stock	$290,000
Additional paid-in capital:	
Paid-in capital—excess over par value, common stock	160,000
Total paid-in capital	$450,000
Retained earnings	500,000
Total stockholders' equity	$950,000

The following selected transactions occurred in 2007:

2007

Feb.	7	Declared a 10% stock dividend on common stock. The dividends are distributable on March 14, 2007, to stockholders of record on March 1, 2007. The market price per share of the common stock on February 5, 2007, is $8.
Mar.	14	Distributed the stock dividend.
Apr.	19	Purchased 10,000 shares of its own common stock at $9 per share.
May	9	Discovered that depreciation expense for 2006 had been incorrectly computed. Instead of the amount recorded of $55,000, the correct amount should have been $30,000. Made a journal entry to correct the error. Ignore income tax effects.
Oct.	5	Sold 3,000 of the treasury shares at $10 per share.
Dec.	17	Declared a cash dividend of $.20 per share on the common stock and $5 per share on the preferred. The dividends are payable on January 10, 2008, to stockholders of record on December 31, 2007.
	31	Net loss for 2007 was $64,000. Closed this amount to Retained Earnings.
	31	Closed the dividends accounts.

REQUIRED

1. Journalize the selected stockholders' equity transactions that occurred during 2007.

2. Prepare the stockholders' equity section of the balance sheet as of December 31, 2007.

3. Compute the book value per share of the common stock as of December 31, 2007. Assume the liquidation value of the preferred stock is equal to its par value and there are no dividends in arrears.

4. Assume state laws require that retained earnings be restricted for the cost of treasury stock held. Prepare a note to the financial statements as of December 31, 2007, that describes this retained earnings restriction.

BUSINESS DECISION AND COMMUNICATION PROBLEM

Comprehensive Comparison of Apple Computer and Dell Computer (LG 8) Selected information for Apple Computer and Dell Computer are shown below. Apple ends its financial reporting year on September 25 and Dell ends its year on January 30. All results below are for the 2004 reporting year.

Selected Information (end of 2004 reporting year)	Apple	Dell
Par value per common share	no par value	$0.01
Preferred stock	none	$0.01
Number of common shares authorized	900,000,000	7,000,000,000
Number of common shares issued	391,443,617	2,721,000,000
Number of common shares in treasury	none	165,000,000
Number of common shares outstanding	391,443,617	2,556,000,000
Total stockholders' equity	$5,076,000,000	6,280,000,000
Market price per share	37.15	33.44
Cash dividend per common share for 2004	none	none
Net sales for 2004	8,279,000,000	41,444,000,000
Net income (loss) for 2004	276,000,000	2,645,000,000
Earnings (loss) per share (EPS) for 2004	0.74	1.03
Average total assets during 2004	7,432,500,000	17,390,500,000

You are currently an investment analyst. Pat Burns, a client, calls you to ask the following questions about the two companies.

1. Pat Burns would like a comparison of measurements for Apple and Dell. She requests that you provide her the following measurements. (Note: Some of the formulas required for the measures are shown in Exhibit 12.11

    a. Book value per common share.

    b. Dividend yield percent.

    c. Profit margin percent.

    d. Return on assets (ROA).

    e. Price earnings (P/E) ratio.

2. What are the major differences you can observe in comparing Apple and Dell? Which company would you view as more successful? Please explain.

3. Assume that in 2005, both companies purchase 20,000,000 of their own common shares. What impact will the purchase of the treasury shares have on each of the following items (increase, decrease, or no effect)?

    a. Total stockholders' equity.

    b. Number of common shares issued.

    c. Number of common shares outstanding.

    d. Total retained earnings.

REQUIRED
Write a memo to Pat Burns addressing her questions about Apple and Dell.

ETHICAL DILEMMA

Proposed change in accounting method to increase net income You are president of a company that manufactures building materials. Your company is currently facing a decrease in sales due to a decline in new home construction. Projected net income for the current year is significantly below last year. Overall, you believe the economy will improve and sales will be up next year. Some of your managers believe that this would be a good time to change the accounting method for depreciation from double declining-balance to straight-line and sell a segment of the business at a gain. The result of these two actions would increase final net income to record levels.

REQUIRED
Would the proposed increase in final net income necessarily be viewed as positive by financial statement users? Discuss what factors should enter into your decision to change accounting methods and sell a segment of the business.

COMPREHENSIVE ANALYSIS CASE PFIZER, INC.

Analyzing Pfizer, Inc. for the Period 2004-2002 Pfizer, Inc. discovers, develops, manufacturers, and markets health care products and services over the world. Founded in 1849, Pfizer, Inc. serves customers in more than 150 countries. Listed below are comparative income statements and balance sheets with common-size percents for 2004-2002 (in millions). Also included are selected ratio statistics. Please provide a brief explanation for your answer to each question.

REQUIRED

Income statement questions:

1. Are total revenues higher or lower over the three-year period?

2. What is the percent change in total revenues from 2002 to 2004?

3. Is the percent of cost of goods sold to total revenues increasing or decreasing over the three-year period? As a result, is the gross margin percent increasing or decreasing?

4. Is the percent of total operating expenses to total revenues increasing or decreasing over the three-year period? As a result, is the operating income percent increasing or decreasing?

5. Is the percent of net income to total revenue increasing or decreasing over the three-year period?

Balance sheet questions:

6. Are total assets higher or lower over the three-year period?

7. What is the percent change in total assets from 2002 to 2004?

8. What are the largest asset investments for the company over the three-year period?

9. Are the largest asset investments increasing faster or slower than the percent change in total revenues?

10. Is the percent of total liabilities to total liabilities + owners' equity increasing or decreasing? As a result, is there more or less risk that the company could not pay its debts?

Integrative income statement and balance sheet question:

11. Is the company operating more or less efficiently by using the least amount of asset investment to generate a given level of total revenues? Note that the "total asset turnover" ratio is computed and included in the "ratio analysis summary".

Ratio analysis questions:

12. Is the *current ratio* better or worse in the most current year compared to prior years?

13. Is the *quick ratio* better or worse in the most current year compared to prior years?

14. Is the *accounts receivable turnover ratio 1* (based on *average* receivables) better or worse in the most current year compared to prior years?

15. Is the 2004 *accounts receivable turnover ratio 2* (based on *year-end* receivables) better or worse than the 2004 ratio based on an *average*?

16. Is the *inventory turnover ratio 1* (based on *average* inventory) better or worse in the most current year compared to prior years?

17. Is the 2004 *inventory turnover ratio 2* (based on *year-end* inventory) better or worse than the 2004 ratio based on an *average*?

18. Is the *return on total assets (ROA) ratio* better or worse in the most current year compared to prior years?

Stockholders' equity questions (Chapter 12 focus):

19. Assume Pfizer acquires 100,000 shares of its own common stock (treasury stock) for $6,000,000 on June 1, 2005. What impact would this have on the total debt ratio on that date (increase, decrease, no impact)? Briefly explain.

20. Assume Pfizer acquires 100,000 shares of its own common stock (treasury stock) for $6,000,000 on June 1, 2005. What impact would this have on the retained earnings balance on that date (increase, decrease, no impact)? Briefly explain.

21. Assume Pfizer acquires 100,000 shares of its own common stock (treasury stock) for $6,000,000 on June 1, 2005. What impact would this have on the total amount of stockholders' equity on that date (increase, decrease, no impact)? Briefly explain.

22. Assume Pfizer acquires 100,000 shares of its own common stock (treasury stock) for $6,000,000 on June 1, 2005. What impact would this have on the amount of total assets on that date (increase, decrease, no impact)? Briefly explain.

PFIZER INC.
COMPARATIVE COMMON-SIZE INCOME STATEMENTS
For the years ended Dec. 31, 2004, 2003, 2002
(in millions)

	2004 $	2004 %	2003 $	2003 %	2002 $	2002 %
Revenues	$ 52,516.0	100.0%	$ 45,188.0	100.0%	$ 32,373.0	100.0%
Cost of goods sold	$ 7,541.0	14.4%	$ 9,832.0	21.8%	$ 4,045.0	12.5%
Gross margin	$ 44,975.0	85.6%	$ 35,356.0	78.2%	$ 28,328.0	87.5%
Operating expenses:						
Sales, marketing, general administrative	$ 16,903.0	32.2%	$ 15,242.0	33.7%	$ 10,846.0	33.5%
Research and development	$ 7,684.0	14.6%	$ 7,131.0	15.8%	$ 5,176.0	16.0%
Other expense	$ 2,264.0	4.3%	$ 6,110.0	13.5%	$ 510.0	1.6%
Other expense	$ 3,364.0	6.4%	$ -	0.0%		
Total operating expenses	$ 30,215.0	57.5%	$ 28,483.0	63.0%	$ 16,532.0	51.1%
Operating income	$ 14,760.0	28.1%	$ 6,873.0	15.2%	$ 11,796.0	36.4%
Net interest expense (income)	$ 347.0	0.7%	$ -	0.0%	$ -	0.0%
Other expense (income)	$ 406.0	0.8%	$ 3,610.0	8.0%	$ -	0.0%
Income before income taxes	$ 14,007.0	26.7%	$ 3,263.0	7.2%	$ 11,796.0	36.4%
Income taxes	$ 2,665.0	5.1%	$ 1,621.0	3.6%	$ 2,609.0	8.1%
Net income (loss) before unusual items	$ 11,342.0	21.6%	$ 1,642.0	3.6%	$ 9,187.0	28.4%
Other losses (gains) net of tax	$ (19.0)	0.0%	$ (2,268.0)	-5.0%	$ 61.0	0.2%
Net income (loss)	$ 11,361.0	21.6%	$ 3,910.0	8.7%	$ 9,126.0	28.2%

PFIZER INC.
COMPARATIVE COMMON-SIZE BALANCE SHEETS
Dec. 31, 2004, 2003, 2002
(in millions)

	2004 $	2004 %	2003 $	2003 %	2002 $	2002 %
ASSETS						
Current:						
Cash & cash equivalents	$ 1,808.0	1.5%	$ 1,520.0	1.3%	$ 1,878.0	4.1%
Short-term investments	$ 18,738.0	15.1%	$ 10,432.0	8.9%	$ 10,673.0	23.0%
Accounts receivable, net	$ 9,367.0	7.6%	$ 9,166.0	7.8%	$ 6,184.0	13.3%
Inventory	$ 6,660.0	5.4%	$ 5,837.0	5.0%	$ 4,249.0	9.2%
Other current assets	$ 3,121.0	2.5%	$ 2,786.0	2.4%	$ 1,797.0	3.9%
Other current assets	$ -	0.0%	$ -	0.0%	$ -	0.0%
Total current assets	$ 39,694.0	32.1%	$ 29,741.0	25.5%	$ 24,781.0	53.5%
Fixed:						
Property & equipment, net	$ 18,385.0	14.9%	$ 18,287.0	15.7%	$ 10,712.0	23.1%
Long-term investments	$ 3,873.0	3.1%	$ 6,142.0	5.3%	$ 5,161.0	11.1%
Intangibles & goodwill	$ 57,007.0	46.1%	$ 58,656.0	50.2%	$ 2,121.0	4.6%
Other assets	$ 4,725.0	3.8%	$ 3,949.0	3.4%	$ 3,581.0	7.7%
Total assets	$ 123,684.0	100.0%	$ 116,775.0	100.0%	$ 46,356.0	100.0%
LIABILITIES						
Current:						
Short-term debt	$ 11,266.0	9.1%	$ 8,818.0	7.6%	$ 8,669.0	18.7%
Accounts payable	$ 8,256.0	6.7%	$ 8,975.0	7.7%	$ 5,861.0	12.6%
Accrued salaries and benefits	$ -	0.0%	$ -	0.0%	$ -	0.0%
Unearned revenue	$ -	0.0%	$ -	0.0%	$ -	0.0%
Other current liabilities	$ 6,936.0	5.6%	$ 5,864.0	5.0%	$ 4,025.0	8.7%
Total current liabilities	$ 26,458.0	21.4%	$ 23,657.0	20.3%	$ 18,555.0	40.0%
Long-term debt	$ 7,279.0	5.9%	$ 5,755.0	4.9%	$ 3,140.0	6.8%
Deferred income tax liabilities	$ 12,632.0	10.2%	$ 13,238.0	11.3%	$ 364.0	0.8%
Other long-term liabilities	$ 9,037.0	7.3%	$ 8,748.0	7.5%	$ 4,347.0	9.4%
Total liabilities	$ 55,406.0	44.8%	$ 51,398.0	44.0%	$ 26,406.0	57.0%
OWNERS' EQUITY						
Total owners' equity	$ 68,278.0	55.2%	$ 65,377.0	56.0%	$ 19,950.0	43.0%
Total liabilities and owners' equity	$ 123,684.0	100.0%	$ 116,775.0	100.0%	$ 46,356.0	100.0%

(Note: percents may not add to 100 due to rounding)

PFIZER INC.
RATIO ANALYSIS SUMMARY
For the years ended Dec. 31, 2004, 2003, 2002

	2004	2003	2002
SHORT-TERM LIQUIDITY RATIOS			
Current Ratio (Current Assets/Current Liabilities)	1.50	1.26	1.34
Quick Ratio (Cash + Short-term Investments + Accounts Receivable)/Current Liabilities	1.13	0.89	1.01
Accounts Receivable Turnover 1 (Revenues/Average Accounts Receivable)	5.67	5.89	
Accounts Receivable Turnover 2 (Revenues/Year-end Accounts Receivable)	5.61	4.93	5.23
Inventory Turnover 1 (Cost Goods Sold/Average Inventory)	1.21	1.95	
Inventory Turnover 2 (Cost Goods Sold/Year-end Inventory)	1.13	1.68	0.95
LONG-TERM SOLVENCY (LEVERAGE) RATIO			
Total Debt Ratio (Total Liabilities/Total Assets)	44.80%	44.01%	56.96%
PROFITABILITY RATIOS			
Gross Profit Margin (Gross Margin/Revenues)	85.64%	78.24%	87.51%
Operating Profit Margin (Operating Income/Revenues)	28.11%	15.21%	36.44%
Net Profit Margin (Return on Sales) (ROS) (Net Income/Revenues)	21.63%	8.65%	28.19%
Total Asset Turnover (Revenues/Average Total Assets)	0.44	0.55	
Return on Total Assets (ROA) (Net Income/Average Total Assets)	9.45%	4.79%	

LONG-TERM LIABILITIES

"There is only one success—to be able to spend your own life in your own way."

Christopher Morley

LEARNING GOALS

After studying Chapter 13, you should be able to:

1. Define the term *bond* and state why corporations may choose to issue bonds rather than stock.

2. Account for bonds issued at face value on an interest date.

3. Explain why bonds sell at a premium or a discount and calculate the sales price of a bond to yield a given rate.

4. Account for the issuance and bond interest expense of bonds issued at a premium.

5. Account for the issuance and bond interest expense of bonds issued at a discount.

6. Account for the accrual of bond interest expense, the issuance of bonds between interest dates, the retirement of bonds, and the conversion of bonds into common stock.

7. Explain the features of mortgage notes payable.

8. Analyze financial statement information for real-life companies.

UNDERSTANDING BUSINESS ISSUES

Many firms need to raise large amounts of cash to invest in new assets. For example, in 2004, Dell Computer spent $525 million on new property and equipment. To finance these expenditures, Dell used several financing sources. On January 28, 2005, Dell had financed $505 million or 11.19% of its total assets with a variety of long-term liabilities.

Long-term liabilities are obligations that have maturity dates beyond the next year or operating cycle. The maturity dates of some long-term debt range up to 30 years. For example, the due dates on Dell's long-term debt as of January 28, 2005, range from 2005 to 2028.

In Chapter 8, we discussed short-term sources of financing. Chapters 11 and 12 discussed stock and retained earnings as sources of investment funds. This chapter looks at long-term liabilities as another source of financing for a business. We will study two types of long-term debt—bonds and mortgages.

BONDS PAYABLE

Learning Goal 1   Define the term bond and state why corporations may choose to issue bonds rather than stock.

One way businesses borrow long-term funds is the issuance of bonds. A **bond** is a written promise to pay a specific sum of money on a specified future date. The bond must be payable to the order of a specific person or the bearer of the bond. The purchaser of a bond, a **bondholder** , is a creditor of the corporation. Each bondholder receives a **bond certificate** that provides written evidence of the corporation's obligation to the bondholder.

Corporations usually issue bonds in denominations of $1,000 each. Thus, a bond issue of $500,000 consists of 500 bonds. Like shares of stock, investors may buy and sell bonds on organized exchanges. Unlike shares of stock, bonds have a fixed maturity date. The issuer must repay the face value of the bond at maturity. Except currently maturing amounts, we show bonds payable as a long-term liability on the balance sheet. Bonds maturing in the next year are current liabilities.

The issuer makes periodic payments of interest to the bondholders to compensate them for the use of their money. Periodic bond interest payments are usually semiannual (twice a year). A contract between the corporation issuing bonds and the bondholders that contains all relevant privileges, restrictions, and other provisions is a **bond indenture.**

Classification of Bonds

A corporation may issue several kinds of bonds to meet its financing needs. Most bonds are **registered bonds**. Corporations issue these bonds in the name of the bondholder. The issuing company or its transfer agent keeps records of who owns the bonds. They mail interest checks directly to the registered owner of the bond.

Bonds may be secured by corporation assets or unsecured. When a corporation pledges part of its assets as security, it is a **secured bond**. If the corporation fails to pay interest or principal, the bondholder has the right to the pledged assets. A specific pledge of assets does not back **unsecured bonds** (called **debenture bonds**). Corporations issue debenture bonds based on the general credit of the company.

Bonds may have other special features. **Serial bonds** mature in installments instead of at the end of a fixed time period. With a **callable bond**, the corporation has the option of retiring (calling) the bonds before maturity. In other cases, the bondholder has an option to exchange the bonds for shares of capital stock (**convertible bonds**). The bond agreement may require the issuing corporation to make regular deposits to a **sinking fund**, a fund created to retire the bonds. Corporations include certain of these provisions to make the bonds more attractive to investors.

Bonds Compared to Stock

Most companies use several sources of financing. Some financing is stock and some is bonds. There are a variety of reasons why a corporation issues bonds instead of stock. Exhibit 13.1 compares bonds to stock.

Bonds	Stock
Bondholders are creditors.	Stockholders are owners.
Bonds Payable is a long-term liability account.	Stock is a stockholders' equity account.
Bondholders, along with other creditors, have primary claims on assets in liquidation.	Stockholders have residual claims on assets in liquidation.
Interest is typically a fixed charge. It must be paid or the creditors can begin bankruptcy proceedings.	Dividends are not fixed charges. Even preferred dividends are at best only *contingent charges*. These are paid if income is sufficient and if declared by the corporate board of directors.
Interest is an expense.	Dividends are not expenses. They are distributions of net income.
Interest is deductible in arriving at both taxable and business income.	Dividends are not deductible in arriving at taxable or business income.
Bonds do not carry voting rights.	All stock carries voting rights unless expressly denied by contract, as is usually the case with preferred stock.

EXHIBIT **13.1**

Comparison of Bonds to Stock

Three important reasons for the use of bonds are financial leverage, corporate income tax rules, and the funds produced for reinvestment. **Financial leverage** occurs when a company invests borrowed money within the business to earn a higher rate than the borrowing cost. For example, assume a business can borrow money at 10% and use it in the operation of the business to earn 15%. It returns 10% to the lenders and the extra earnings benefit the stockholders. This company is using financial leverage.

Corporate tax rules also affect the choice between bonds and stock. Currently, bond interest is a tax deductible expense. This means that the interest paid to bondholders reduces income tax expense. Dividends on stock are not expenses and are not tax deductible. Therefore, the after-tax cost of interest on bonds is less than the cost of comparable dividends.

The top of Exhibit 13.2 illustrates how leverage and income taxes affect the choice of financing methods. The example assumes that the corporation needs $500,000 to purchase additional assets. Currently the company has 100,000 shares of $10 par value common stock outstanding and no bonds. The company forecasts net income before interest expense and income taxes to be $400,000 per year. The income tax rate is 40%. The company is considering two financing plans.

Plan 1:   Issue $500,000 of $10 par value common stock. For simplicity, we assume the company issues 50,000 shares at par.

Plan 2:   Issue $500,000 of 10% bonds at face value.

The results in Exhibit 13.2 show that income taxes are lower under plan 2. The use of bonds creates a $50,000 tax-deductible expense. This reduces the income taxes that the company pays. It also reduces net income because the $50,000 return to the providers (interest expense) appears on the income statement. However, since there are no new common stockholders, the projected earnings per share is higher with plan 2 (bonds). Despite the lower net income, there are 50,000 fewer shares of stock outstanding. This causes earnings per share to be higher with plan 2.

FINANCING EFFECT ON
NET INCOME AND EARNINGS PER SHARE

	Plan 1 Issue Stock	Plan 2 Issue Bonds
Net income before interest and income taxes	$ 400,000	$ 400,000
Deduct: Interest expense ($500,000 × 0.10)	0	50,000
Net income before income taxes	$ 400,000	$ 350,000
Deduct: Income taxes (assumed rate of 40%)	160,000	140,000
Net income	$ 240,000	$ 210,000
Earnings per share on common stock:		
Plan 1 (150,000 shares outstanding)	$ 1.60	
Plan 2 (100,000 shares outstanding)		$ 2.10

FINANCING EFFECT ON
AMOUNT AVAILABLE FOR REINVESTMENT

	Plan 1 Issue Stock	Plan 2 Issue Bonds
Net income (from above)	$ 240,000	$ 210,000
Deduct: (Cash dividends paid on common stock:		
Plan 1 (150,000 shares × $1)	150,000	
Plan 2 (100,000 shares × $1)		100,000
Amount available for reinvestment after cash dividends	$ 90,000	$ 110,000

EXHIBIT **13.2**

Effects of Leverage and Income Taxes: Common Stock Versus Bond Financing

Another consideration is the amount of funds available for reinvestment in other projects within the business. *Funds available for reinvestment* is the increase in assets from net income after subtracting dividends. The bottom of Exhibit 13.2 shows this calculation. Under either plan, the corporation pays $50,000 to the providers of the $500,000 in funds used.

Plan 1:	$1 per share dividend on 50,000 additional shares of stock	$50,000
Plan 2:	10% interest on $500,000 in bonds	$50,000

However, in plan 2 the $50,000 in interest is tax deductible. As Exhibit 13.2 shows, it reduces income taxes by $20,000. Thus, the after-tax cost of interest is only $30,000 ($50,000 - $20,000). Plan 1 requires the company to pay an extra $50,000 in dividends on the stock from after-tax earnings. Thus, plan 1 costs the company $50,000.

Plan 1 requires that the company pay a total of $150,000 in dividends out of the $240,000 in net income. Since plan 2 has fewer shares of stock outstanding, it requires only $100,000 in dividends. Thus, though the net income is $30,000 lower under plan 2, the company will pay out $50,000 less in dividends. With plan 2 there will be more assets available for reinvestment than with plan 1.

Why would a company use stock financing when it could issue bonds? One reason is that financial leverage works positively only when they can invest the funds at a higher return than the borrowing cost. If interest rates are too high, leverage will work against the company. Also, if net income decreases, the required interest and principal payments may be difficult to make. Stock does not have the requirement of annual payments to the investors, nor is there principal to be repaid. Stocks and bonds both have their advantages. Thus, companies use a mixture of stock and bond financing. The decision involves projections of future levels of income and interest rates and management's ability to deal with risk.

Issuing Bonds at Face Value

Learning Goal 2   Account for bonds issued at face value on an interest date.

Authorizing the Bond Issue

After management decides to issue bonds, many decisions remain. For example, it must determine the exact amount to be borrowed, the maturity date, and any assets pledged. Management must also determine the **stated interest rate** (or *contract interest rate*) for the bonds. This is the rate that we multiply by the face value to get the periodic cash interest payments.

Management prepares a written report for the board of directors. This report summarizes the proposed features of the bonds, the use of the funds, and the means of retiring the bond issue. The board of directors then passes a resolution recommending to the stockholders that the bonds be issued. Next, the stockholders vote on the proposal. Authorization of the bond issue requires no formal journal entry. We should make a memorandum in the Bonds Payable account showing the total amount authorized. We will need this information when preparing the balance sheet, since a firm should disclose the total authorization and the amount issued.

Accounting for Bonds Issued at Face Value

In the following example, a corporation issues bonds at **face value** (sometimes called *issuance at par*) on an interest date. Suppose that Brigade Corporation stockholders approve a bond issue of $200,000. Brigade will issue 10-year, 9% debenture bonds. Amerson will pay the interest semiannually on May 1 and November 1. The company closes its books on December 31. Assume that the corporation issues all of the authorized bonds on May 1, 2007, at 100 or face value (100 means 100% of face value). Following are the entries to record the issue and the first interest payment. We also show the adjusting entry on December 31 and the entry for the first 2008 interest payment:

2007					
May	1	Cash		200,000	
		Bonds Payable			200,000
		To record the issuance of 9% bonds due			
		April 1, 2014.			
Nov.	1	Interest Expense		9,000	
		Cash			9,000
		To record the payment of interest on the			
		bonds for six months.			

Dec.	31	Interest Expense	3,000	
		Interest Payable		3,000
		To record the accrual of bond interest for two months.		

2008				
May	1	Interest Expense	6,000	
		Interest Payable	3,000	
		Cash		9,000
		To record payment of semiannual interest.		

Comments on these entries follow:

1. The Bonds Payable account is a long-term liability since they will not repay it for ten years.

2. The entries to record the bond interest expense are very similar to those recording interest expense on notes payable discussed in previous chapters.

3. The adjusting entry for accrued bond interest is similar to the recording of accrued interest on notes payable. Interest payable is a current liability on the December 31, 2007, balance sheet.

4. In computing bond interest in this book, we divide each year into 12 equal months (30-day month time).

Why Bonds Sell at a Discount or Premium

Learning Goal 3   Explain why bonds sell at a premium or a discount and calculate the sales price of a bond to yield a given rate.

The prevailing market interest rate on bonds of a comparable grade may be higher or lower than the stated interest rate on the bonds being issued. If the market rate is higher than the stated rate, investors will offer less than the face value of the bonds. The difference between the issue price and the face value is the **discount**. This discount plus receipts of the semiannual interest will give the investors a return on their investments approximating the prevailing market interest rate. If the stated interest rate is higher than the current market rate, investors will offer a **premium** (an amount greater than the face value). The issue price of the bond determines the rate of return the investor will earn. This rate is also the effective cost of borrowing to the firm. We call this rate of return the **effective rate** or *yield rate* of interest. The important point is that premium and discount arise because of a difference between the average market rate of interest on a comparable bond and the stated rate on the bonds. Exhibit 13.3 shows this relationship.

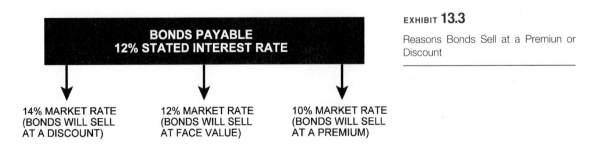

EXHIBIT **13.3**

Reasons Bonds Sell at a Premiun or Discount

Calculating the Exact Sales Price of Bonds to Yield a Given Rate

We can calculate the exact price that an investor must pay for the bonds to yield a given rate using *present values*. To illustrate the computation, assume that a company will issue five-year, 12% bonds with a face value of $100,000. The bonds pay interest semiannually. Thus, there will be 10 interest periods. Assume the company issues the bonds at a price to yield 10% (or 5% every six months). The calculation of the issue price involves the determination of the *present value at the issue date* of two *separate* cash flows: (1) the face amount of the bonds discounted at the market rate, and (2) the interest payments discounted at the market rate (see Appendix C at the back of this textbook for a review of present value concepts). This calculation is as follows.

1. **Present value of face amount of $100,000**
   $100,000 (a single sum) will be paid in 10 periods
      at a market rate of 5% ($100,000 × 0.614) $ 61,400
2. **Present value of 10 interest payments of $6,000**
   Ten $6,000 interest payments (an annuity) at a
      market rate of 5% ($6,000 × 7.722)   46,332
   Total price to yield 10% annually $107,732

The following comments explain the calculation of the sales price of the bond:

- It helps to decide whether the selling price will be above or below par *before* calculating the sales price. Here, the stated interest rate on the bonds is 12% compared to a market interest rate of 10%. Since the stated interest rate is greater than the current market interest rate, investors will pay a premium for the bonds.

- The interest rate used to calculate the sales price of a bond is always the *market* interest rate. Here the annual market interest rate is 10%. Since interest payments on the bonds are semiannual, we use the semiannual market rate of 5%. Since the rate is semiannual, we must state the number of time periods the same way. Therefore, we use 10 semiannual periods to calculate the sales price.

- There are two cash flows that the bondholders will receive on the bond. They will receive the face value of the bond, $100,000, when the bond matures at the end of five years (10 semiannual periods). This is a *single flow* of cash. We find the present value factor of 0.614 by looking up the present value of a single sum of $1 for 10 periods at 5% in Table C-2 in Appendix C.

- The second flow of cash that the bondholders will receive consists of the ten semiannual interest payments of $6,000. They will receive these payments at the end of each of the ten semiannual periods. This is an *ordinary annuity*. We find the present value factor of 7.722 by looking up the present value of an ordinary annuity of $1 for 10 periods at 5% in Table C-4 in Appendix C.

- The sum of the two present values ($107,732) is the sales price of the bonds that will yield a market rate of return on the bonds of 10% (or 5% every six months).

Methods of Amortizing Premium and Discount

In accounting for bond interest expense, we must write off the premium or discount to expense over the remaining life of the bond issue. We call this procedure amortization. Two methods of **amortization** are available for this write-off: (1) the *straight-line method*, and (2) the *effective interest method*.

Theoretically, bond interest expense should be measured by the amount of the effective interest. The effective interest is equal to the effective rate multiplied by the carrying value of the bonds at the beginning of each interest period. The **carrying value** is the face value plus unamortized premium or minus unamortized discount. This method is the **effective interest method of amortization**. The Accounting Principles Board states in *APB Opinion No. 21* that the effective interest method is the correct method. However, *Opinion No. 21* allows the straight-line method if the results are not materially different from those using the effective interest method. The **straight-line method** recognizes equal interest expense each period.

Bonds Issued at a Premium

Learning Goal 4   Account for the issuance and bond interest expense of bonds issued at a premium.

First we will study the issuance and recording of interest expense for bonds issued at a premium. *Your instructor should tell you which of the interest amortization methods (straight-line or effective interest) you should use. Study that part of this section.*

Assume that on July 1, 2007, the stockholders of Mankato Corporation authorized the issuance of $100,000 in debenture bonds. The stated interest rate is 12% with interest payable June 30 and December 31. The bonds are due June 30, 2012.

Issuance

Assume that Mankato Corporation issued all the bonds on July 1, 2007, for $107,732. This price gives an effective interest rate of 10% (see the previous calculation). The journal entry to record the issuance is as follows:

2007					
Jul.	1	Cash		107,732	
		Bonds Payable			100,000
		Premium on Bonds Payable			7,732
		To record the issuance of 12% bonds due June 30, 2012.			

Statement Disclosure

A balance sheet prepared on July 1, 2007, would show bonds payable and premium on bonds payable as follows:

Long-term liabilities
12% Bonds payable, due June 30, 2012	$100,000
Add: Premium on bonds payable	7,732
Total long-term liabilities	$107,732

The face value plus the unamortized premium is the *carrying value*.

Recording Interest

Since bond interest is payable semiannually, we would record six months' interest on June 30 and December 31 of each year. To measure interest expense properly, each interest entry must amortize part of the premium.

Straight-line Method of Amortization

Under the straight-line amortization method, we *record equal amounts of bond interest expense each period.* Exhibit 13.4 shows a bond interest table for the Mankato Corporation bond using the straight-line amortization method. The cash interest payment will be $6,000 ($100,000 × 0.12 × ½) for each six-month period. The premium amortization using the straight-line method is one-tenth of the total premium each six months. We divide by 10 because the five-year bond will be outstanding for 10 semiannual interest periods. The bond interest expense is the cash interest payment minus the premium amortization. Note that we must adjust the amortization in the last period to completely amortize the premium.

We record the bond interest expense for the first six-month period ending December 31, 2007, as follows:

2007					
Dec.	31	Interest Expense		5,227	
		Premium on Bonds Payable		773	
		Cash			6,000
		To record the semiannual bond interest payment and amortization.			

Exhibit 13.4 shows that each interest expense entry will have similar amounts. The $7,732 in premium represents a reduction in interest over the five-year life of the bonds. Thus, each time we record interest expense we must reduce the interest expense by part of the premium.

We can calculate the interest expense in another way to prove the $5,227 semiannual bond interest figure. The difference between the total cash the company must pay out over the life of the bond and the total cash it receives is its total interest expense. Mankato Corporation received $107,732 for the bonds, and it will pay out a total of $160,000 ($100,000 for face value and $60,000 for interest). The difference,

Face Value   __$100,000__   Periods   __5 years__

Stated Rate   __12%__   Effective rate __10%__

Payable   __Semiannually__

(A) Semiannual Interest Period	(B) Carrying Value at Beginning	(C) Bond Interest Expense (Col. D - Col. E)	(D) Cash Interest Payment (Face × 6%)	(E) Premium Amortization (Premium ÷ 10)	(F) Carrying Value at End (Col. B - Col. E)
At issuance					$ 107,732
1	$ 107,732	$ 5,227	$ 6,000	$ 773	106,959
2	106,959	5,227	6,000	773	106,186
3	106,186	5,227	6,000	773	105,413
4	105,413	5,227	6,000	773	104,640
5	104,640	5,227	6,000	773	103,867
6	103,867	5,227	6,000	773	103,094
7	103,094	5,227	6,000	773	102,321
8	102,321	5,227	6,000	773	101,548
9	101,548	5,227	6,000	773	100,775
10	100,775	5,225	6,000	775*	100,000
Totals		$ 52,268	$ 60,000	$ 7,732	

*Adjusted to compensate for rounding errors.

EXHIBIT **13.4**

Interest Expense and Premium Amortization: Straight-line Method

$52,268, is Mankato's total interest expense for the five years. This amount divided by ten semiannual periods gives the $5,227 of interest expense per period. We calculate this as follows:

Future cash payments

Face value of bonds at maturity	$100,000
Total interest ($100,000 × 0.12 × 5)	60,000
Total cash payments	$160,000
Cash received from issuance	107,732
Interest expense five years	$ 52,268
Net semiannual interest expense	
$52,268 ÷ 10 semiannual periods = $5,227	

Each entry reduces the bond premium account. Balance sheets prepared beginning December 31, 2007, show a smaller carrying value as we amortize the premium. At maturity, the Premium on Bonds Payable account will have a zero balance. The carrying value of the bonds will be equal to the face value. The entry to record the retirement at maturity is:

2012				
Jun.	30	Bonds Payable	100,000	
		Cash		100,000
		To record retirement of 12% debenture bonds payable at maturity.		

Effective Interest Method of Amortization

The effective interest method of amortization measures the bond interest expense using the effective interest rate determined by the issue price. Exhibit 13.5 shows the calculation of the bond interest

Face Value $100,000   Periods   5 years

Stated Rate   12%   Effective rate   10%

Payable   Semiannually

(A) Semiannual Interest Period	(B) Carrying Value at Beginning	(C) Bond Interest Expense (Col. B × 5%)	(D) Cash Interest Payment (Face × 6%)	(E) Premium Amortization (Col. D – Col. C)	(F) Carrying Value at End (Col. B - Col. E)
At issuance					$ 107,732
1	$ 107,732	$ 5,387	$ 6,000	$ 613	107,119
2	107,119	5,356	6,000	644	106,475
3	106,475	5,324	6,000	676	105,799
4	105,799	5,290	6,000	710	105,089
5	105,089	5,254	6,000	746	104,343
6	104,343	5,217	6,000	783	103,560
7	103,560	5,178	6,000	822	102,738
8	102,738	5,137	6,000	863	101,875
9	101,875	5,094	6,000	906	100,969
10	100,969	5,031*	6,000	969	100,000
Totals		$ 52,268	$ 60,000	$ 7,732	

*Adjusted to compensate for rounding errors.

EXHIBIT **13.5**

Interest Expense and Premium Amortization: Effective Interest Method

expense and premium amortization for each interest period. With the effective interest method of amortization, we first calculate the bond interest expense. This is equal to the carrying value at the beginning of the period times the effective interest rate for six months. We always calculate the cash interest payment in the same way, face value times stated interest rate for six months. Then, the amount of amortization is the difference between the bond interest expense and the cash interest payment.

The journal entry for the December 31, 2007, interest payment is as follows:

2007				
Dec.	31	Interest Expense ($107,732 × 0.05)	5,387	
		Premium on Bonds Payable (balance entry)	613	
		Cash ($100,000 × 0.06)		6,000
		To record the semiannual bond interest		
		payment and amortization.		

This entry reduces the balance in Premium on Bonds Payable and the carrying value of the bonds. The bond interest expense for the six-month period ending June 30, 2008, uses this *new* carrying value times the effective interest rate. Thus, we would expect the bond interest expense to decrease in the next six-month period. Take the time now to follow the calculation in Exhibit 13.5 for several interest periods. The bond interest expense for the period ending June 30, 2008, uses the new carrying value, $107,119, times the effective interest rate. The journal entry would be:

2008				
Jun.	30	Interest Expense ($107,119 × 0.05)	5,356	
		Premium on Bonds Payable (balance entry)	644	
		Cash ($100,000 × 0.06)		6,000
		To record the semiannual bond interest		
		payment and amortization.		

Comparison of Straight-line and Effective Interest Methods

Exhibit 13.6 summarizes the straight-line and effective interest methods of amortization. Both methods will have the same cash interest payments.

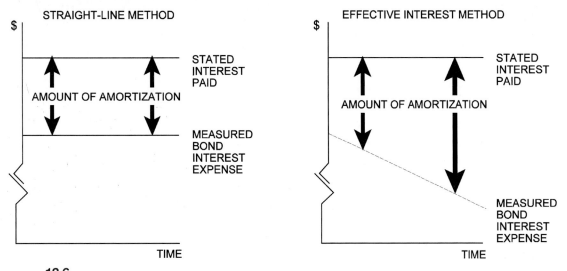

EXHIBIT **13.6**

Straight-line and Effective Interest Methods for Bonds Issued at a Premium

Interest Period	Straight-line Amortization	Effective Interest Method Amortization
1	$5,227 ÷ $107,732 = 4.85%	$5,387 ÷ $107,732 = 5%
2	$5,227 ÷ $106,959 = 4.89%	$5,356 ÷ $107,119 = 5%
3	$5,227 ÷ $106,186 = 4.92%	$5,324 ÷ $106,475 = 5%
4	$5,227 ÷ $105,413 = 4.96%	$5,290 ÷ $105,799 = 5%

EXHIBIT **13.7**

Comparison of Effective Interest rates for Straight-line and Effective Interest Methods of Amortization

The two methods differ in the amount of bond interest expense recorded in each period. The straight-line method results in a constant amount of bond interest expense each period. The effective interest method produces a constant rate of expense on the carrying value of the bonds. You can see this also if you compare Exhibit 13.4 and Exhibit 13.5. The total amount of bond interest expense recognized by the straight-line method and the effective interest method is the same over the five-year period.

When we use the straight-line method, both the amount of the bond interest expense and the amount of the amortization are uniform over time. Exhibit 13.7 shows that dividing the bond interest expense by the carrying value of the bonds each year gives us an increasing effective interest rate. When we use the effective interest method, the amount of bond interest expense decreases over time. Exhibit 13.7 shows that if we divide the bond interest expense by the carrying value, the resulting effective interest rate is constant. The straight-line method is simple and easy to use. The effective interest method is more theoretically correct. It shows a *constant effective rate of interest* on a bond carrying value that is decreasing over time.

Bonds Issued at a Discount

Learning Goal 5   Account for the issuance and bond interest expense of bonds issued at a discount.

When the stated rate of interest is below the market interest rate, bonds sell at a discount. Assume that on July 1, 2007, the stockholders of Hastings Corporation authorized the issuance of $100,000 in 12% debenture bonds payable. The interest dates are June 30 and December 31. The bonds are five-year bonds due on June 30, 2012.

Issuance

Assume that when Hastings Corporation issues the bonds on July 1, 2007, the annual market interest rate is 14%. The price the bonds should sell for is $92,944 and is computed as follows:

1. **Present value of face amount of $100,000**
   $100,000 (a single sum) will be paid in 10 periods
   at a market rate of 7% ($100,000 × 0.508) $ 50,800
2. **Present value of 10 interest payments of $6,000**
   Ten $6,000 interest payments (an annuity) at a
   market rate of 7% ($6,000 × 7.024)   42,144
   Total price to yield 14% annually $ 92,944

The marketplace bid the price of the bonds down (discount) because investors demanded a rate of return (14%) higher than the stated rate on the Hastings bonds (12%). Following is the journal entry to record the issuance:

2007
Jul.   1   Cash   92,944

              Discount on Bonds Payable   7,056

                   Bonds Payable   100,000

                   To record the issuance of 12% bonds due
June 30, 2012.

Statement Disclosure

If Hastings Corporation prepared a balance sheet on July 1, 2007, it would show the bonds payable and discount on bonds payable as follows:

     Long-term liabilities

         12% Bonds payable, due June 30, 2012 $100,000

         Deduct: Discount on bonds payable   7,056

              Total long-term liabilities $ 92,944

For a discount, the face value of the bonds minus the discount is the carrying value.

Recording Interest

Since the bond interest is payable semiannually on June 30 and December 31, we record interest expense every six months beginning December 31, 2007. Each interest expense entry must amortize part of the discount to measure bond interest expense properly.

Straight-line Amortization

Using the straight-line method, we record equal amounts of bond interest expense each period. Exhibit 13.8 shows the bond interest table for the Hastings Corporation bond using

Face Value $100,000   Periods   5 years

Stated Rate   12%   Effective rate 14%

Payable   Semiannually

(A) Semiannual Interest Period	(B) Carrying Value at Beginning	(C) Bond Interest Expense (Col. D + Col. E)	(D) Cash Interest Payment (Face × 6%)	(E) Discount Amortization (Discount ÷ 10)	(F) Carrying Value at End (Col. B + Col. E)
At issuance					$ 92,944
1	$ 92,944	$ 6,706	$ 6,000	$ 706	93,650
2	93,650	6,706	6,000	706	94,356
3	94,356	6,706	6,000	706	95,062
4	95,062	6,706	6,000	706	95,768
5	95,768	6,706	6,000	706	96,474
6	96,474	6,706	6,000	706	97,180
7	97,180	6,706	6,000	706	97,886
8	97,886	6,706	6,000	706	98,592
9	98,592	6,706	6,000	706	99,298
10	99,298	6,706	6,000	702*	100,000
Totals		$ 67,056	$ 60,000	$7,056	

*Adjusted to compensate for rounding errors.

EXHIBIT **13.8**

Interest Expense and Discount Amortization: Straight-line Method

straight-line amortization. The discount is the difference between the face value and the issue price, $7,056 ($100,000 - $92,944). We assign an equal portion of this discount to each interest period. Since the Hastings bond will be outstanding for the full five years, this is one-tenth of the discount, or $706 ($7,056 ÷ 10). The cash interest payment is $6,000 ($100,000 × 0.12 × ½) for each six-month period. The bond interest expense is the total of the cash payment and the discount amortization. Note that we must adjust the amortization in the final period to completely amortize the discount.

The entry on December 31, 2007, to record the first interest payment is as follows:

2007					
Dec.	31	Interest Expense		6,706	
		Discount on Bonds Payable			706
		Cash			6,000
		To record the semiannual bond interest payment and amortization.			

Exhibit 13.8 shows that each bond interest expense entry would be similar. It would record $6,706 in bond interest expense and amortize $706 in discount. The $7,056 in discount represents an increase in the interest expense over the five-year life of the bonds. Thus, each time we record interest expense we must increase the interest expense by part of the discount.

The difference between the total cash the company must pay out for the bond and the total cash it receives is its total interest expense. Hastings Corporation received $92,944 for the bonds but they will pay out $160,000. The difference, $67,056, is its total interest expense for the five years. We calculate this as follows:

Future cash payments	
Face value of bonds at maturity	$100,000
Total interest ($100,000 × 0.12 × 5)	60,000
Total cash payments	$160,000
Cash received from issuance	92,944
Interest expense for five years	$ 67,056
Net semiannual interest expense	
$67,056 ÷ 10 semiannual periods = $6,706	

Effective Interest Method of Amortization

The calculation of bond interest expense for a bond issued at a discount using the effective interest method of amortization is the same as with a premium. Exhibit 13.9 shows the bond interest expense and amortization calculation for each interest period. Carefully study the first three periods.

We calculate bond interest expense by multiplying the beginning of the period carrying value by the effective interest rate for six months. The issue price of this bond set an effective interest rate of 14% per year. For period 1, the beginning carrying value is $92,944. Multiplying this by the effective interest rate for six months, 7%, we get a bond interest expense of $6,506. We always calculate the cash interest payment the same way: face amount times stated rate times the time. For Hastings, this is $6,000 ($100,000 × 0.12 × ½).

Face Value ___$100,000___   Periods ___5 years___

Stated Rate ___12%___   Effective rate ___14%___

Payable ___Semiannually___

(A) Semiannual Interest Period	(B) Carrying Value at Beginning	(C) Bond Interest Expense (Col. B × 7%)	(D) Cash Interest Payment (Face × 6%)	(E) Discount Amortization (Col. C - Col. D)	(F) Carrying Value at End (Col. B + Col. E)
At issuance					$ 92,944
1	$ 92,944	$ 6,506	$ 6,000	$ 506	93,450
2	93,450	6,542	6,000	542	93,992
3	93,992	6,579	6,000	579	94,571
4	94,571	6,620	6,000	620	95,191
5	95,191	6,663	6,000	663	95,854
6	95,854	6,710	6,000	710	96,564
7	96,564	6,759	6,000	759	97,323
8	97,323	6,813	6,000	813	98,136
9	98,136	6,870	6,000	870	99,006
10	99,006	6,994*	6,000	994	100,000
Totals		$ 67,056	$ 60,000	$ 7,056	

*Adjusted to compensate for rounding errors.

EXHIBIT **13.9**

Interest Expense and Discount Amortization: Effective Interest Method

The amount of amortization is the difference between the bond interest expense and the cash payment. The journal entry to record the December 31, 2007, bond interest expense is as follows:

```
2007
Dec.  31   Interest Expense                      6,506
                Discount on Bonds Payable                    506
                Cash                                       6,000
           To record the semiannual bond interest
           payment and amortization.
```

This entry reduces the balance in Discount on Bonds Payable. This, in turn, increases the carrying value of the bonds. Thus, we would expect the bond interest expense to increase in the next six-month period. Looking at Exhibit 13.9 we can see that this is true. The bond interest expense for the period ending June 30, 2008, uses the new carrying value, $93,450, times the effective interest rate.

Comparison of Straight-line and Effective Interest Methods

Exhibit 13.10 is an overview of the entire life of the Hastings Corporation bond issue. It highlights the differences between the two amortization methods. When we use the straight-line method, the bond interest expense and the discount amortization are the same for each period. With the effective interest method, the bond interest expense and the discount amortization increases over time.

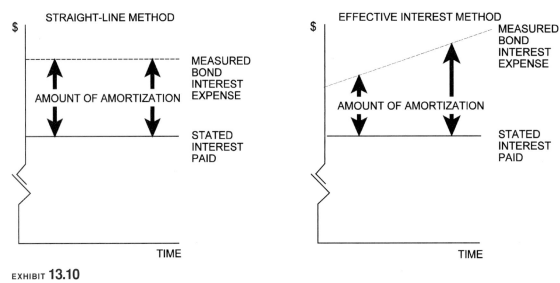

EXHIBIT **13.10**

Straight-line and Effective Interest Methods for Bonds issued at a Discount

Other Bond Payable Items

Learning Goal 6   Account for the accrual of bond interest expense, the issuance of bonds between interest dates, the retirement of bonds, and the conversion of bonds into common stock.

Several other items are common to many bond payable situations. In this section we will study five of these items (1) accrual of interest, (2) issuance between interest dates, (3) retirement of bonds at maturity and (4) before maturity, and (5) conversion of bonds into stock.

Accrual of Interest

If an interest payment date does not coincide with the accounting period end, accruing interest expense is necessary. As we have learned already, every time we record bond interest expense we must amortize the premium or discount. As in the previous illustration, assume that Hastings Corporation issues 12% debenture bonds at $92,944. However, assume that the authorization date is November 1, 2007, and the interest payment dates are April 30 and October 31. Assume straight-line amortization. The bond table in Exhibit 13.8 is still appropriate.

The first interest payment period is from November 1, 2007, to April 30, 2008. Since this interest period covers two accounting periods, we must make an adjusting entry on December 31, 2007. Assuming the straight-line method of amortization, Exhibit 13.8 shows the bond interest expense for the six-month period is $6,706. Since two months of the interest period falls in 2007, we must accrue one-third of the interest expense in 2007. The journal entry for the accrual is as follows:

2007				
Dec.	31	Interest Expense ($6,706 × 2/6)	2,235	
		Discount on Bonds Payable ($706 × 2/6)		235
		Interest Payable ($6,000 × 2/6)		2,000
		To record accrual of interest and the		
		amortization of 2 months' discount.		

Note that we only compute the bond interest expense each six months. The *interest for a shorter period* is the pro rata portion of the six months' interest. The entry for the payment of interest on April 30, 2008, is as follows:

2008					
Apr.	30	Interest Expense ($6,706 × 4/6)		4,471	
		Interest Payable ($6,000 × 2/6)		2,000	
		Discount on Bonds Payable ($706 × 4/6)			471
		Cash ($100,000 × 0.12 × ½)			6,000
		To record payment of semiannual interest and			
		amortization of 4 months' discount.			

Issuance Between Interest Dates

A more complex problem is the issuance of bonds between interest dates. In this illustration, we will show the straight-line amortization method. The general principle is the same for both amortization methods.

A corporation's stockholders may authorize bonds, but the corporation may not issue them until a later date. The current market conditions may not be favorable for issue. Or the corporation may issue some bonds and hold the rest until a specific need for the funds arises.

Bonds carry an inherent promise to pay not only the face value at maturity but six months' interest at each interest date. When issuing bonds between interest dates, interest since the last interest date accrues to the date of issuance. In these cases, it is customary for the investor to pay the issue price plus an amount equal to the accrued interest. In turn, the first interest payment to the bondholder will be for one full interest period-six months' interest. This returns to the bondholder the accrued interest he or she paid in plus the interest earned. This practice allows corporations to avoid the expense of computing and paying interest for fractional periods.

Problem Data

Assume that on June 30, 2007, the stockholders of TennTech Corporation authorized issuance of $100,000 of 12% debenture bonds. Interest is payable semiannually on June 30 and December 31. The bonds are due June 30, 2012. TennTech issued the bonds on September 1, 2007, for 100 plus accrued interest. We can compute the cash TennTech receives as follows:

Issue price of the bonds ($100,000 × 1.00)	$100,000
Accrued interest ($100,000 × 0.12 × 2/12)	2,000
Total cash received	$102,000

On December 31, 2007, the purchaser of the bonds will receive an interest payment of $6,000. The payment includes a return of the $2,000 that the investor paid for accrued interest on September 1. Exhibit 13.11 illustrates this accrual and payment of interest.

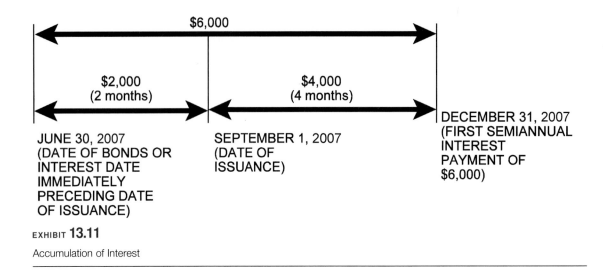

EXHIBIT **13.11**

Accumulation of Interest

Journal Entry to Record the Issue

TennTech Corporation records the bond issuance as follows:

```
2007
Sep.    1    Cash                                    102,000
                    Bonds Payable                                   100,000
                    Interest Payable                                  2,000
             To record the issuance of bonds at 100 plus
             accrued interest.
```

We credit the accrued interest to a current liability account since we must repay it on the next interest date.

Recording Bond Interest Expense

On the next interest payment date, we record the interest expense from the date of issue. We also record the return of the accrued interest paid in by the buyer, as follows:

```
2007
Dec.    31    Interest Expense                        4,000
             Interest Payable                         2,000
                    Cash                                            6,000
             To record the payment of semiannual interest
             at 12% on bonds payable.
```

The entry for the interest payment reflects the amounts shown in Exhibit 13.11. The semiannual cash payment includes a return of $2,000 for the accrued interest sold to the investor. It also includes $4,000 for interest incurred by TennTech for the four months' use of the money. If amortization is necessary, the **amortization period** is the period from the date of issuance to the maturity date only.

Retirement of Bonds Payable

The borrowing company may retire its outstanding bonds at the maturity date by paying the face value in cash. The entry to record the retirement *at maturity* is a debit to Bonds Payable and a credit to Cash for the face value. Other methods of bond **retirement**, discussed next, include: (1) the retirement of all or part of a bond issue before the bonds are due and (2) the conversion of bonds payable into capital stock.

Retirement of Bonds Before Maturity

If interest rates fall, a corporation may wish to retire all or part of its outstanding bonds before maturity. Management may decide to retire the bonds early if it has excess cash. This will decrease the fixed charges for the bond interest. A corporation may retire bonds early in different ways. The bonds may contain a call provision*call provision*, or the issuer may purchase them on the open market. For bonds to be *callable* the indenture agreement must contain a provision permitting the issuing corporation to redeem the bonds by paying a specified price. The price is usually slightly above face value.

Retirement of bonds at a price less than the carrying value adjusted to the date of retirement results in a gain. The issuer incurs a loss if the retirement cost exceeds the adjusted carrying value. We classify material gains and losses on the early retirement of bonds payable in the income statement as extraordinary items.

Assume that Greensboro Corporation issues $100,000 in 12% bonds on July 1, 2007, at $106,000. The bonds pay interest semiannually on June 30 and December 31 and are due June 30, 2012. Management decides to retire all of the debenture bonds after the interest payment on June 30, 2009. The company pays 104 for the bonds. The bond accounts as of June 30, 2009, are as follows:

GENERAL LEDGER

Bonds Payable   Acct. No. 261

Date		Explanation	PR	Debit	Credit	Balance Debit	Balance Credit
2007 Jul.	1				100,000		100,000

Premium on Bonds Payable   Acct. No. 266

Date		Explanation	PR	Debit	Credit	Balance Debit	Balance Credit
2007 Jul.	1				6,000		6,000
Dec.	31			600			5,400
2008 Jun.	30			600			4,800
Dec.	31			600			4,200
2009 Jun.	30			600			3,600

The carrying value of the liability at the retirement date is $103,600 ($100,000 + $3,600). Thus, if Greensboro Corporation pays $104,000 ($100,000 × 1.04) for the bonds, it has a loss on early retirement of $400 ($103,600 - $104,000). We would record the early retirement as follows:

2009				
Jun.	30	Bonds Payable	100,000	
		Premium on Bonds Payable	3,600	
		Loss on Retirement of Bonds Payable	400	
		Cash		104,000
		To record retirement of debenture bonds at 104.		

Conversion of Bonds into Common Stock

To make bonds more attractive, the bond agreement may give investors the option of exchanging their bonds for stock of the issuing company. The option usually allows the conversion of a bond into a specified number of shares. These bonds, called *convertible bonds*, offer an investor the fixed return of interest initially. Then, by conversion, they offer the chance to share in profitable operations through stock ownership. Conversion is at the option of the bondholder. If earnings are unfavorable, the bondholder can continue to hold the bonds and collect interest.

Assume that the bonds of Greensboro Corporation in the last example were convertible bonds. The conversion feature allowed the bondholder to convert each $1,000 bond into 50 shares of $5 par value common stock. Assume that instead of the company retiring the bonds on June 30, 2009, the bondholders converted their bonds into common stock. The corporation would issue 5,000 shares of common stock [($100,000 ÷ $1,000) × 50]. Greensboro would make the following entry:

2009					
Jun.	30	Bonds Payable		100,000	
		Premium on Bonds Payable		3,600	
		Common Stock			25,000
		Paid-in Capital—Excess over Par Value, Common			78,600
		To record conversion of bonds into common stock, 50 shares of stock per $1,000 bond.			

Since holders converted all of the bonds, we must remove the balance in both the bond and premium accounts. We credit the Common Stock account for the par value of the shares issued. We credit a paid-in capital account for the difference.

MORTGAGE NOTES PAYABLE

Learning Goal 7   Explain the features of mortgage notes payable.

Another long-term liability is mortgage notes payable, sometimes called mortgages payable. A **mortgage note payable** involves the issuance of a long-term note with an assignment of an interest in property to the seller. The property serves as collateral in case the purchaser defaults on the payment of the long-term obligation.

We usually pay mortgages in equal periodic installments. Part of the payment represents interest expense on the remaining liability balance and the remainder represents a reduction in the mortgage liability. As an illustration, Exhibit 13.12 shows the first five monthly payments for a $100,000, 12%, 10-year mortgage taken out on January 1, 2007. Monthly payments are $1,435. Interest expense decreases each month as payments reduce the mortgage liability. Note that this is the same as the effective interest method. The journal entry to record the first mortgage payment is as follows:

2007					
Feb.	1	Interest Expense		1,000	
		Mortgage Payable		435	
		Cash			1,435
		To record mortgage payment.			

(1) Monthly Payment Date	(2) Liability Balance at Beginning of Month	(3) Monthly Interest Expense* (1% × Col. 2)	(4) Monthly Payment	(5) Reduction in Liability Balance (Col. 3 - Col. 4)	(6) Liability Balance at End of Month
Jan. 1					$100,000
Feb. 1	$100,000	$1,000	$1,435	$435	99,565
Mar. 1	99,565	996	1,435	439	99,126
Apr. 1	99,126	991	1,435	444	98,682
May 1	98,682	987	1,435	448	97,234
Jun. 1	98,234	982	1,435	453	97,781

* Rounded to the nearest dollar

EXHIBIT **13.12**

Partial Monthly Mortgage Table: $100,000, 12%, Ten-year Mortgage

ANALYZING INFORMATION

Learning Goal 8   Analyze financial statement information for real-life companies.

In previous chapters, we have pointed out that higher levels of debt on the balance sheet involve greater risk. The difficulty is that a company with excessive amounts of debt financing may not be able to meet periodic interest payments and repayment of the face value on the maturity date. We have also shown how to compute the *times interest earned ratio*. This ratio is an indicator of the ability of a company to meet its fixed interest payments. Exhibit 13.13 shows liability and owners' equity information along with related footnote information for a sample company called Great

GREAT SNEAKER, INC.
SUMMARIZED BALANCE SHEET INFORMATION: LIABILITIES AND STOCKHOLDERS' EQUITY
NOVEMBER 30, 2007
(*in thousands*)

	$	%
Current liabilities	$ 46,570	20.7%
Long-term liabilities:		
7 3/4% convertible debentures due 2007	50,000	22.3
Mandatorily redeemable 7.5% preferred stock	100,000	44.6
Total liabilities	$ 196,570	87.6%
Stockholders' equity	27,893	12.4
Total liabilities and stockholders' equity	$ 224,463	100.0%

2007 Annual Report: Notes to Financial Statements (Excerpts):
Convertible Subordinated Debentures The debentures were issued in 2000 and mature in 2010. The fair market of the debentures at November 30, 2007 was $34.5 million.
7.5% Preferred Stock One million shares of preferred stock were issued in 1998. If the 7.5% dividends on the preferred stock are in arrears, the rate increases to 8.625%. The Company is required to redeem 350,000 shares of preferred stock on August 31, 2009, and 162,500 shares on each August 31 thereafter until all shares are redeemed. If the Company fails to redeem the preferred shares when required, the dividend rate on the shares increases to 10.125%.

EXHIBIT **13.13**

Financial Statement Disclosure of Long-term Liabilities:Great Sneaker,Inc.

Sneaker, Incorporated. Revenues for Great Sneaker, Inc. have decreased from $800 million to $500 million over the past two years. The Company has experienced net losses in both years.

Question. The statement user needs to assess whether the company will be able to pay its debt obligations. Especially important is information contained in the notes to the financial statements regarding terms and maturity dates for the debt. Overall questions include: (1) Is the level of total debt the Company has manageable? (2) Does it seem likely that the Company can meet interest and principal payments in light of the terms and maturity dates of the indenture conditions? (3) If the Company needs additional financing, would you recommend lending to or investing in it?

Answer. Great Sneaker, Inc. faces a very difficult situation. (1) Total liabilities are 87.6% of total equities on November 30, 2007. This is a very high percent. (2) Revenues have declined significantly and that the Company has been incurring losses. Therefore, a large amount of cash from operations to meet interest and debt payments does not exist. (3) In addition to interest and dividend payments, the Company must begin to redeem the preferred stock in 2009. If the Company fails to redeem the preferred shares, the dividend rate increases significantly. The convertible debt is due in 2010. These dates are coming up soon and the Company does not have much time to turn the profit picture around. Since the Company has so much debt, issuing additional debt to raise cash is probably not possible. Considering the decrease in revenues, issuing additional shares of stock is most likely not an option.

LEARNING GOALS REVIEW

1. **Define the term *bond* and state reasons why corporations may choose to issue bonds rather than stock.**

   A bond is a written promise to pay a specific sum of money on a specified future date. The major classifications of bonds are registered, secured, and unsecured bonds. Registered bonds are issued in the name of the bondholder and require an endorsement to transfer. Secured bonds are bonds that pledge some part of the corporate assets as security for the bonds. Unsecured bonds, or debenture bonds, pledge no such security and rely upon the corporation's general credit. A corporation may choose to issue bonds because they provide access to sources of funds that it would not have through a stock issue. Bonds may offer financial leverage, bringing stockholders additional returns. There is leverage if the borrowed funds earn a rate of return greater than the borrowing cost. Bond interest expense is deductible in arriving at both taxable and business income.

2. **Account for bonds issued at face value on an interest date.**

   When issuing the bonds, we debit Cash for the amount received and credit Bonds Payable. When making an interest payment we debit Interest Expense and credit Cash.

3. **Explain why bonds sell at a premium or a discount and calculate the sales price of a bond to yield a given rate.**

   Bonds sell at a premium or discount when they pay a different rate of interest than prevailing market rates for bonds of comparable risk. If the prevailing market rate is higher than the stated rate on the bonds, investors will offer less than the face value of the bonds (a discount). If the prevailing market rate is lower than the stated rate on the bonds, investors will offer more than the face value (a premium). To calculate the sales price of a bond to yield a given market rate, we compute the present value of the face amount of the bond and of the interest payments, discounted at the market interest rate. The sum of the two present values is the total price to yield the market interest rate.

4. Account for the issuance and bond interest expense of bonds issued at a premium.

We record the issuance of bonds at a premium by debiting Cash for the proceeds, crediting Bonds Payable for the face value, and crediting Premium on Bonds Payable for the excess. We record the interest expense by debiting Interest Expense and Premium on Bonds Payable and crediting Cash. The credit to Cash is equal to the face value of the bond times the stated interest rate for the period. We can determine the debit to Premium on Bonds Payable by either the straight-line method or the effective interest method of amortization. The straight-line method assigns an equal portion of the premium to each interest period. The interest expense is the cash payment minus the premium amortization. The effective interest method calculates the interest expense by multiplying the carrying value of the bond by the effective interest rate on the bond. The premium amortization is the difference between the interest expense and the cash payment.

5. Account for the issuance and bond interest expense of bonds issued at a discount.

We record the issuance of bonds at a discount by crediting Bonds Payable for the face value and debiting Cash for the proceeds and Discount on Bonds Payable for the difference. We record the interest expense by debiting Interest Expense and crediting Discount on Bonds Payable and Cash. The credit to Cash is equal to the face value of the bond times the stated interest rate for the period. We can determine the credit to Discount on Bonds Payable by either the straight-line method or the effective interest method of amortization. The straight-line method assigns an equal portion of the discount to each interest period. The interest expense is the cash payment plus the discount amortization. The effective interest method calculates the interest expense by multiplying the carrying value of the bond by the effective interest rate on the bond. The discount amortization is the difference between the interest expense and the cash payment.

6. Account for the accrual of bond interest expense, the issuance of bonds between interest dates, the retirement of bonds, and the conversion of bonds into common stock.

Accruing bond interest expense involves a debit to Interest Expense and a credit to Interest Payable. It also requires amortization of premium or discount by the appropriate debit or credit. Issuance of bonds between interest dates requires the investor to pay the accrued interest since the last interest payment date. This is in addition to the price of the bond. The issuer returns the accrued interest paid in as a part of the first interest payment. To record the retirement of bonds before maturity, we reduce the Bonds Payable account and the premium or discount accounts. We record a gain or loss on retirement as the difference between the carrying value and the cash paid. To record the conversion of bonds into common stock, we transfer the carrying value of the bonds into Common Stock and Paid-in Capital—Excess over Par Value, Common.

7. Explain the features of mortgage notes payable.

A mortgage note payable involves the issuance of a long-term note by the purchaser. The note assigns an interest in property to the seller as collateral in case the purchaser defaults on the payment of the long-term obligation. Mortgages are paid in monthly installments. Part of the payment is for interest expense on the remaining liability balance and the remainder of the payment reduces the mortgage liability.

8. Analyze financial statement information for real-life companies.

Questions we may ask are: (1) Is the level of total debt the company has manageable? (2) Does it seem likely that the company can meet interest and principal payments in light of the terms and maturity dates of the indenture conditions? (3) If the company needs additional financing, would you recommend lending to or investing in it?

DEMONSTRATION PROBLEM

Bond Issuance, Conversion, and Retirement

On January 1, 2007, Lexican Company issued 10-year 12% convertible bonds with a face value of $800,000. Interest is payable semiannually on June 30 and December 31. Lexican uses the straight-line amortization method. Each $1,000 bond is convertible into 90 shares of $10 par value common stock at the option of the bondholder. Transactions involving the bonds during 2007 and 2008 are as follows:

2007

Jan.	1	Issued all of the bonds at 98.
Jun.	30	Paid the semiannual interest and amortized the discount.
Dec.	31	Paid the semiannual interest and amortized the discount.

2008

Jan.	1	Holders of bonds with a face value of $600,000 converted their bonds into shares of common stock.
Jun.	30	Paid the semiannual interest and amortized the discount on the remaining bonds.
Jul.	1	Purchased the remaining bonds on the open market at 103 and retired the bonds.

REQUIRED

(LG 5, 6) Prepare journal entries to record the transactions involving bonds during 2007 and 2008.

SOLUTION

> ## Solution Approach
>
> To keep track of the changing balances in the bond-related accounts, we recommend the use of summary T accounts. The solution shows the updated T accounts after each transaction.

2007					
Jan.	1	Cash		784,000	
		Discount on Bonds Payable		16,000	
		Bonds Payable			800,000
		To record the issuance of 12% convertible bonds due December 31, 2016.			

Bonds Payable			Discount on Bonds Payable		
	1/1/07	800,000	1/1/07	16,000	

Jun.	30	Interest Expense		48,800	
		Discount on Bonds Payable			800
		Cash			48,000
		To record semiannual bond interest payment and amortization. The amount of amortization is $16,000 \div 20$ semiannual periods = $800.			

Bonds Payable			Discount on Bonds Payable			
	1/1/07	800,000	1/1/07	16,000	6/30/07	800
			Balance	15,200		

Dec.	31	Interest Expense	48,800	
		Discount on Bonds Payable		800
		Cash		48,000
		To record semiannual bond interest payment and amortization.		

Bonds Payable			Discount on Bonds Payable			
	1/1/07	800,000	1/1/07	16,000	6/30/07	800
			Balance	15,200	12/31/07	800
			Balance	14,400		

2008				
Jan.	1	Bonds Payable	600,000	
		Discount on Bonds Payable		10,800
		Common Stock ($10 par value)		540,000
		Paid-in Capital—Excess over Par Value, Common		49,200
		To record conversion of bonds into common stock.		

Computations:
Discount on Bonds Payable: $14,400 \times 600/800 = \$10,800$ balance canceled.
Common Stock: ($600,000 \div \$1,000) = 600$ bonds $\times 90$ shares per bond =
54,000 shares of common stock $\times \$10$ par = \$540,000 par value.
Paid-in Capital—Excess of Par Value, Common: The amount necessary to balance the entry.

Bonds Payable			Discount on Bonds Payable			
1/1/08	600,000	1/1/07	800,000	1/1/07	16,000	6/30/07	800
		Balance	200,000	Balance	15,200	12/31/07	800
				Balance	14,400	1/1/08	10,800
				Balance	3,600		

Jun.	30	Interest Expense	12,200	
		Discount on Bonds Payable		200
		Cash		12,000
		To record semiannual bond interest payment and amortization.		

Bonds Payable			Discount on Bonds Payable			
1/1/08	600,000	1/1/07	800,000	1/1/07	16,000	6/30/07	800
		Balance	200,000	Balance	15,200	12/31/07	800
				Balance	14,400	1/1/08	10,800
				Balance	3,600	6/30/08	200
				Balance	3,400		

Jul.	1	Bonds Payable	200,000	
		Loss on Retirement of Bonds Payable	9,400	
		Discount on Bonds Payable		3,400
		Cash		206,000
		To record retirement of bonds payable at 103.		

Computations:
Discount on Bonds Payable: $3,400 balance in account.
Cash: $200,000 \times 1.03 = \$206,000$.
Loss on Retirement of Bonds Payable: The amount necessary to balance the entry.

GLOSSARY

amortization The periodic writing off of the premium or discount on bonds payable. This write-off decreases or increases interest expense. We use either the straight-line method or the effective interest method.

amortization period The period for which the premium or discount should be amortized. It spans the period from the date of issuance of the bonds to the maturity date.

bond A written promise to pay a specified sum of money on a specified future date to a person named in the bond certificate or to the bearer.

bond certificate Written evidence that a loan has been made to a corporation. It contains the written promise to pay a specific sum of money on a specified future date to the person named in the certificate or to the bearer.

bondholder A creditor who has lent money and has received a bond certificate as evidence of the loan.

bond indenture A contract between the corporation issuing bonds and the bondholders, containing all relevant privileges, restrictions, covenants, and other provisions.

bond sinking fund A special fund in which assets are set aside for the purpose of retiring bonds.

callable bond A bond that gives the issuing corporation an option to retire before maturity at a specified price on specific dates.

carrying value The face or principal amount of the bonds payable plus the unamortized premium or minus the unamortized discount.

convertible bond A bond that contains a provision entitling the bondholder to exchange the bond for capital stock of predetermined amount (at the bondholder's option).

debenture bonds Often referred to as debentures. They are unsecured bonds carrying no pledge of collateral.

discount The amount by which the face value of bonds exceeds the price received for the bonds on issuance. It arises because the stated rate of interest is lower than the going market rate of interest on bonds with similar risk.

effective interest method of amortization A method of amortizing premium or discount on bonds payable in which periodic amortization is the difference between the effective interest expense determined by multiplying the effective interest rate by the bond carrying value at the beginning of the interest period and the stated interest calculated on the face of the bonds.

effective rate The cost of borrowing money determined by the issue price.

face value The principal or par amount of bonds that will be repaid on the maturity date.

financial leverage The practice of borrowing money and using the borrowed funds in the business to earn a higher rate of return than the borrowing rate.

long-term liabilities Obligations that are due to be paid after the coming year or operating cycle.

mortgage notes payable Long-term notes issued with a pledge of specified property, plant, and equipment for the loan.

premium The excess of the price received for bonds payable above face value. It arises because the stated rate of interest is higher than the market rate of interest on bonds of similar risk.

registered bond A bond whose owner's name is recorded by the issuing corporation. To transfer to another individual, it must be endorsed and a request filed to have the owner's name changed on the records of the issuing corporation.

retirement The payment of the principal amount at maturity or at an earlier date.

secured bond A bond for which the issuing corporation pledges some part of the firm's assets as security .

serial bonds Bonds that mature in periodic installments and are paid at stated intervals of time.

sinking fund A fund created to retire bonds.

stated interest rate The rate of interest on the bond certificate that is paid on the principal or face amount at interest dates. It is also the contract rate.

straight-line method A method of amortizing bond premium or discount in equal amounts at interest dates over the term of the bonds. Straight-line recognizes equal interest expense during each period.

unsecured bonds Bonds for which there is no pledge of assets for security. These bonds also are debenture bonds or often simply debentures.

QUESTIONS FOR GROUP LEARNING

Q13-1. Distinguish between stated and effective interest rates on bonds.

Q13-2. On January 1, 2007, Atlanta Sales Company issued 10-year, 10% bonds having a face value of $2,000,000. The proceeds to the company were $1,900,000. Thus, on January 1, 2007, the bonds had a market price of 95% of face value. Explain the nature of the $100,000 difference between the face value and the market value of the bonds on January 1, 2007.

Q13-3. Justify the classification of bonds payable and interest payable as liabilities.

Q13-4. What is the difference between stock and bonds?

Q13-5. Define the following terms: (a) *registered bonds*, (b) *secured bonds*, (c) *unsecured bonds*, (d) *serial bonds*, (e) *convertible bonds*.

Q13-6. A corporation needs cash to acquire property, plant, and equipment. It is considering two alternative sources: additional common stock and 10% bonds. (a) What are some of the factors involved in this decision? (b) Will the decision affect the present common stockholders? Discuss.

Q13-7. (a) Why does the buyer of a bond between interest dates pay the seller for accrued interest on the bond? (b) Is the accrued interest included in the stated purchase price of the bond?

Q13-8. List two ways that bonds can be retired.

Q13-9. Does the total amount of premium or discount amortized over the life of a bond differ if the effective interest method is used instead of the straight-line method? What is the difference between the two methods?

Q13-10. *APB Opinion No. 21* states that the effective interest method should be used in amortizing premium and discount on long-term debt instruments. From a theoretical point of view, state why this method is superior to the straight-line method.

Q13-11. Why isn't the stated interest rate on bonds always equal to the market interest rate, thereby eliminating bond discount or bond premium?

Q13-12. (a) What is the difference to the issuing corporation between common stock issued at a premium and bonds issued at a premium? (b) Does revenue result from either?

EXERCISES

E13-13. **Issuing bonds payable at face value and recording interest (LG 2)** On the date of authorization, January 1, 2007, Sweeney Corporation issued 20-year, 12% bonds to financial corporations with a face value of $300,000 at 100. Interest is payable each January 1 and July 1.

    1. Record the issuance of the bonds.

    2. Record the first interest payment.

    3. Record the accrued interest expense on December 31, 2007.

    4. Record the payment of semiannual interest on January 1, 2008.

E13-14. **Premium and discount concepts (LG 3)** Fill in the proper response: premium or discount.

    a. If the market rate of interest exceeds a bond's stated interest rate, the bond will sell at a _____.

    b. If a bond's stated interest rate exceeds the market rate of interest, the bond will sell at a _____.

    c. In computing the carrying value of a bond, unamortized _____ is subtracted from the face value of the bond.

    d. In computing the carrying value of a bond, unamortized _____ is added to the face value of the bond.

    e. If a bond sells at a _____, an amount in excess of the face value of the bond is received on the date of issuance.

    f. If a bond sells at a _____, an amount less than the face value of the bond is received on the date of issuance.

E13-15. **Calculation of bond issue price (requires familiarity with present value concepts) (LG 3)** ACE Corporation is considering issuing $100,000 in 10%, 10-year bonds payable. The bonds will pay interest on April 30 and October 31. Calculate the issue price assuming ACE issues the bonds on the authorization date in each of the following situations.

    a. The market interest rate on bonds of similar risk is 9%.

    b. The market interest rate on bonds of similar risk is 11%

E13-16. **Issuance of bonds at premium: straight-line amortization method (LG 4)** On the date of authorization, January 1, 2007, Blue Corporation issued 10-year, 12% bonds with a face value of $1,000,000 at 104. Interest is payable each January 1 and July 1.

    1. Record the issuance of the bonds.

    2. Record the first interest payment and amortization of the premium by the straight-line method.

3. Record the accrued interest expense and amortization of the premium on December 31, 2007.

4. Prepare a schedule proving the interest cost for 2007 by the straight-line amortization method.

E13-17. **Issuance of bonds at premium: effective interest method of amortization (LG 4)** On the date of authorization, July 1, 2007, Escape Corporation issued 20-year, 12% bonds with a face value of $600,000, for $647,856, which is a price to yield 11%. Interest is payable each January 1 and July 1.

1. Record the issuance of the bonds.

2. Record the accrued interest expense and amortization of the premium on December 31, 2007, by the effective interest method.

3. Record the interest payment on July 1, 2008, and amortization of the premium by the effective interest method.

E13-18. **Issuance of bonds at discount: straight-line amortization (LG 5)** On the date of authorization, July 1, 2007, Toy Corporation issued 10 year, 12% bonds with a face value of $2,000,000 at 95. Interest is payable June 30 and December 31.

1. Record the issuance of the bonds.

2. Record the first interest payment and amortization of the discount by the straight-line method.

3. Prepare a schedule proving the interest cost for 2007 by the straight-line amortization method.

E13-19. **Issuance of bonds at discount: effective interest method of amortization (LG 5)** On the date of authorization, July 1, 2007, Colorado Company issued 10-year, 11% bonds with a face value of $2,000,000, for $1,880,700, which is a price to yield 12%. Interest is payable June 30 and December 31.

1. Record the issuance of the bonds on July 1, 2007.

2. Record the December 31, 2007, and June 30, 2008, interest payments with accompanying amortization, using the effective interest method of amortization.

E13-20. **Issuance of bonds between interest dates (LG 6)** On November 1, 2007, Queen Corporation issued 12% bonds with a face value of $800,000 for $800,000 plus accrued interest. The bonds mature on July 1, 2011, and interest is paid each June 30 and December 31. Prepare all the entries relating to the bond issue during 2007.

E13-21. **Accrual of interest: straight-line amortization (LG 6)** Kelly Corporation issued $400,000 in 9%, 10-year bonds on July 31, 2007, at 106. Interest is payable on July 31 and January 31.

1. Record the issuance of the bonds.

2. Record the accrual of bond interest expense on December 31, 2007.

3. Record the interest payment on January 31, 2008.

E13-22. **Convertible bonds (LG 6)** On July 1, 2005, South Corporation issued $200,000 of 10-year, 12% convertible bonds at 102 to Big Investment Company. Each $10,000 bond is convertible into 1,000 shares of South Corporation $1 par value common stock. It is now July 1, 2007, and Big is considering converting its bonds into common stock. The balance in the Premium on Bonds Payable account is now $3,200.

1. Why would a bondholder decide to convert bonds into common stock?

2. Assume that Big converts its bonds into common stock on July 1, 2007. Make the appropriate entry on South Corporation's books.

3. Amounts supplied by creditors and stockholders are both on the same side of the balance sheet. Will conversion by Big change South Corporation's balance sheet? Explain.

E13-23. **Early retirement of bonds (LG 6)** On July 1, 2007, UTAH Corporation issued 10-year, 12% bonds with a face value of $200,000 at 104. Interest dates are June 30 and December 31. On December 31, 2008, after making the interest payment, UTAH Corporation purchased its own bonds on the open market at 102. Prepare the journal entry to record the early retirement, assuming straight-line amortization.

E13-24. **Issuance of and monthly payments on mortgage payable (LG 7)** Eagle Company purchased an office building for use in its business for $80,000 on June 1, 2007. They paid $10,000 in cash and took out a 15-year, 15% mortgage in the amount of $70,000. The monthly mortgage payments are $980, and the first payment is due on July 1, 2007. Prepare the journal entries to record receipt of the mortgage proceeds on June 1, 2007, and the monthly mortgage payments on July 1, and August 1, 2007, on the books of Eagle Company.

PROBLEMS

P13-25. **Issuance of bond at discount: straight-line amortization method (LG 5)** On March 1, 2007, the authorization date, the Lefty Company issued 10-year, 12% debenture bonds with a face value of $100,000 for $97,900. Interest is payable each March 1 and September 1. The company closes its books on December 31. It made the following selected transactions and adjustments:

2007

Mar.	1	Issued all the bonds for cash.
Sep.	1	Paid the semiannual interest.
Dec.	31	Accrued the bond interest.

2008

Mar.	1	Paid the semiannual interest.
Sep.	1	Paid the semiannual interest.
Dec.	31	Accrued the bond interest.

2017

Mar.	1	Paid the semiannual interest.
	1	Paid the bonds outstanding at maturity.

REQUIRED

Record the foregoing transactions. (Assume that Lefty amortizes the discount by the straight-line method each time it records the bond interest expense.)

P13-26. **Issuance of bonds at premium between interest dates: straight-line amortization method (LG 4, 6)** On May 1, 2007, the stockholders of CAT Corporation authorized the issuance of 20-year, 10% debenture bonds with a face value of $300,000. The bonds mature on May 1, 2027, and interest is payable each May 1 and November 1.

2007

Jun.	1	Issued all the bonds for $305,975 plus accrued interest.
Nov.	1	Paid the semiannual interest. (Assume that Anthony amortizes the premium on bonds payable by the straight-line method each time it records the bond interest expense.)
Dec.	31	Accrued the bond interest.
	31	Closed the Interest Expense account.

2008

May	1	Paid the semiannual interest.
Nov.	1	Paid the semiannual interest.
Dec.	31	Accrued the bond interest.
	31	Closed the Interest Expense account.

REQUIRED

Make journal entries to record the foregoing transactions.

P13-27. **Issuance of bonds at premium: effective interest method of amortization (LG 4)** On July 1, 2007, Yankee Corporation issued 10-year, 10% bonds with a face value of $500,000 for $532,700, which is a price to yield 9%. Interest is payable June 30 and December 31.

2007

Jul.	1	Issued all the bonds for cash.
Dec.	31	Paid the semiannual interest and recorded the proper amortization.

2008

Jun.	30	Paid the semiannual interest and recorded the proper amortization.
Dec.	31	Paid the semiannual interest and recorded the proper amortization.

REQUIRED

1. Prepare a bond interest table for the first four interest periods (round to whole dollars).

2. Prepare journal entries to record the foregoing transactions, assuming that the effective interest method of amortization is used

P13-28. **Preparing an amortization table and recording various bond transactions by effective interest method (requires familiarity with present value techniques) (LG 3, 5, 6)** On May 1, 2007, the authorization date, Jenkins Corporation issued five-year, 10% bonds with a face value of $200,000 at a price to yield 11%. Interest is payable each May 1 and November 1. The company closes its books on December 31 and uses the effective interest method of amortization. It made the following selected transactions and adjustments:

2007

May	1	Issued all the bonds for cash.
Nov.	1	Paid the semiannual interest.
Dec.	31	Accrued the bond interest.

2008

May	1	Paid the semiannual interest.
Nov.	1	Paid the semiannual interest.
Dec.	31	Accrued the bond interest.

2012

May	1	Paid the bonds outstanding at maturity (assume last interest payment is recorded).

REQUIRED

1. Determine the issue price and prepare a bond table for two years (round to nearest whole dollar).

2. Journalize the foregoing transactions.

P13-29. **Bond calculations and interpretations: effective interest method of amortization (requires familiarity with present value techniques) (LG 3, 5)** On January 1, 2007, Atlanta Company issued 10-year, 10% bonds with a face value of $2,000,000. Interest is payable semiannually on June 30 and December 31. At the time the bonds were sold, the market interest rate on competing bonds was 12%.

REQUIRED

1. Based on the information contained in the problem, would you expect the bonds to sell at a premium or a discount? Explain your answer.

2. Determine the total amount of cash proceeds received from the sale of the bonds on January 1, 2007.

3. Calculate the amount of total interest paid in cash on the bonds during 2007.

4. Calculate the amount of total interest paid out on the bonds over the 10-year bond life.

5. Calculate the total bond interest expense that appears on the income statement for 2007. Assume the effective interest method of amortization.

6. Calculate the total amount of interest expense that will be recognized over the 10-year bond life.

7. On the balance sheet prepared as of December 31, 2007, determine the carrying value of the bonds in the long-term liability section.

P13-30. **Analyzing Information (LG 8)** Partial balance sheet information for Penny Pincher Discount Stores is listed below. For the past three years, total revenues have been steady at $4,000,000 per year. Net income has been constant at $60,000 each year.

PENNY PINCHER DISCOUNT STORES
SUMMARIZED BALANCE SHEET INFORMATION: LIABILITIES AND STOCKHOLDERS' EQUITY
DECEMBER 31, 2007
(*in thousands*)

	$	%
Current liabilities	$ 100,000	%
Long-term liabilities:		
Bonds payable	300,000	
Notes payable	300,000	
Total liabilities	$ 700,000	%
Stockholders' equity		
14% Preferred stock	$ 500,000	%
Common stock	200,000	
Retained earnings	600,000	
Total stockholders' equity	$1,300,000	%
Total liabilities and stockholders' equity	$2,000,000	%

Notes to Financial Statements (Debt and Preferred Stock) The bonds payable are 14%, 10-year debentures issued in 2000. The bonds mature in 2010. The long-term notes have a 16% interest rate and mature in July 2009. The 14% preferred stock contains a redemption condition under which the total amount must be paid back to stockholders on March 1, 2009.

REQUIRED

1. Do you agree with the way in which management has classified the liability and stockholder equity items on the balance sheet? If not, prepare a new balance sheet with correct classification.

2. Compute the missing common size percents for your new balance sheet.

3. Is the level of total debt the Company has manageable? Explain briefly.

4. Does it seem likely that the Company can meet interest and principal payments in light of the terms and maturity dates of the debt?

5. If the Company needs additional financing, would you recommend lending to or investing in it?

PRACTICE CASE

Bonds payable (LG 4,6) On January 1, 2007, the stockholders of Hawk Company authorized issuance of 10-year, 12% convertible bonds with a face value of $800,000. Interest is payable semiannually on June 30 and December 31. Hawk uses the straight-line amortization method. Each $1,000 bond is convertible into 85 shares of $5 par value common stock at the option of the bondholder. Transactions involving the bonds during 2007 and 2008 were as follows:

REQUIRED

2007

Jan.	1	Issued all of the bonds at 105.
Jun.	30	Paid the semiannual interest and amortized the premium.
Dec.	31	Paid the semiannual interest and amortized the premium.

2008

Jan.	1	Holders of bonds with a face value of $700,000 converted their bonds into shares of common stock.
Jun.	30	Paid the semiannual interest and amortized the premium on the remaining bonds.
Jul.	1	Hawk Company purchased the remaining bonds on the open market at 96 and retired the bonds.

Prepare journal entries to record the transactions involving bonds during 2007 and 2008.

BUSINESS DECISION AND COMMUNICATION PROBLEM

Financing with stock or bonds (LG 1) Debbie Silver, the president of Arizona Apparel, has hired you as a consultant. She has developed a successful retail clothing business in Tucson. She currently operates one store in a suburban shopping mall and is considering opening a second store in another mall. Arizona Apparel is organized as a corporation.

You have studied the current operations of her proposed new store and have developed the following information. Last year's income before taxes was $700,000. There are currently 300,000 shares of common stock outstanding. Debbie and her husband own 60% of the outstanding stock in the business. There are no other owners with large holdings of the stock. The stock is currently selling on the market at $10 per share. Debbie estimates that the new store would require an investment of $500,000. She projects that the new store would earn an income before interest and taxes of $150,000 per year. The business has a tax rate of 30%.

She has identified two alternative methods of financing the store that she would like you to review. First, the business has additional shares of authorized common stock that it could issue. Second, the business could issue debenture bonds. She has studied the market and believes that a 10% interest rate paid semiannually on 20-year bonds would be appropriate. You find that the current market interest rate for bonds of similar companies is 10%.

Required

Write a memo to Debbie Silver discussing the advantages and disadvantages of the two alternatives. Include calculations of the impact on net income and earnings per share of issuing stock versus bonds.

Ethical Dilemma

Presentation of bond premium on a balance sheet (LG 4) You own your own small public accounting firm. One of your audit clients has come to you to discuss the presentation of the balance sheet for his company. He has $2,000,000 in 20-year bonds outstanding. The company issued the bonds at a premium of $400,000 five years ago. In preparing the balance sheet, you have told the client that the unamortized premium balance must be added to the face value in long-term liabilities. The client instead wants to show the premium on bonds payable as part of paid-in capital in stockholders' equity. He said that he does not believe that adding it to bonds payable is appropriate because he will only have to pay back the face value at maturity. He said that he is concerned that adding it to bonds payable will overstate the liabilities of his company. As your discussion continues, your client becomes more insistent and indicates that he will take his business elsewhere if you do not agree. The fees that you collect from this client annually are substantial. Loss of his business would have a significant impact on your business' income.

Required

Discuss the effects and appropriateness of your client's request. What action should you take?

Comprehensive Analysis Case Harley Davidson, Inc.

Analyzing Harley Davidson, Inc. for the Period 2004-2002 The only major American-based motorcycle manufacturer and a leading supplier of premium quality, heavyweight motorcycles to the global market. Listed below are comparative income statements and balance sheets with common-size percents for 2004-2002 (in millions). Also included are selected ratio statistics. Please provide a brief explanation for your answer to each question.

Additional Information:

A significant portion of Harley-Davidson's accounts receivables is attributed to current finance receivables. These amounts were $656.4 million, $530.9 million, and $441.0 million for the fiscal years ending December 31, 2004, 2003, and 2002, respectively. A significant portion of other fixed assets are attributable to long-term finance receivables. These amounts were $379.3 million, $234.1 million, and $354.9 million for the fiscal years ending December 31, 2004, 2003, and 2002, respectively.

Required

Income statement questions:

1. Are total revenues higher or lower over the three-year period?

2. What is the percent change in total revenues from 2002 to 2004?

3. Is the percent of cost of goods sold to total revenues increasing or decreasing over the three-year period? As a result, is the gross margin percent increasing or decreasing?

4. Is the percent of total operating expenses to total revenues increasing or decreasing over the three-year period? As a result, is the operating income percent increasing or decreasing?

5. Is the percent of net income to total revenue increasing or decreasing over the three-year period?

Balance sheet questions:

6. Are total assets higher or lower over the three-year period?

7. What is the percent change in total assets from 2002 to 2004?

8. What are the largest asset investments for the company over the three-year period?

9. Are the largest asset investments increasing faster or slower than the percent change in total revenues?

10. Is the percent of total liabilities to total liabilities + owners' equity increasing or decreasing? As a result, is there more or less risk that the company could not pay its debts?

Integrative income statement and balance sheet question:

11. Is the company operating more or less efficiently by using the least amount of asset investment to generate a given level of total revenues? Note that the "total asset turnover" ratio is computed and included in the "ratio analysis summary."

Ratio analysis questions:

12. Is the *current ratio* better or worse in the most current year compared to prior years?

13. Is the *quick ratio* better or worse in the most current year compared to prior years?

14. Is the *accounts receivable turnover ratio 1* (based on *average* receivables) better or worse in the most current year compared to prior years?

15. Is the 2004 *accounts receivable turnover ratio 2* (based on *year-end* receivables) better or worse than the 2004 ratio based on an *average*?

16. Is the *inventory turnover ratio 1* (based on *average* inventory) better or worse in the most current year compared to prior years?

17. Is the 2004 *inventory turnover ratio 2* (based on *year-end* inventory) better or worse than the 2004 ratio based on an *average*?

18. Is the *return on total assets (ROA) ratio* better or worse in the most current year compared to prior years?

Finance receivables and debt financing (Chapter 13 focus):

19. Based on the information in the financial statements, is selling on account important for Harley Davidson? Explain briefly.

21. As of December 31, 2004, what is the percent of total receivables (both accounts receivable and finance receivables) as a percent of total assets?

22. Most of the long-term debt on the balance sheet is issued to obtain funds to provide for financing to customers. If Harley's ability to issue additional debt was sharply reduced, what would be the likely impact on total revenues in the future?

23. Assume market interest rates rise sharply in 2005 and Harley's existing debt has a fixed interest rate of 7%. Would the market value of the debt rise or fall as a result? Please explain.

HARLEY DAVIDSON
COMPARATIVE COMMON-SIZE INCOME STATEMENTS
For The Years Ended December 31, 2004, 2003, 2002
(in millions)

	2004 $	2004 %	2003 $	2003 %	2002 $	2002 %
Revenues	$ 5,015.0	100.0%	$ 4,624.0	100.0%	$ 4,091.0	100.0%
Cost of goods sold	$ 3,116.0	62.1%	$ 2,959.0	64.0%	$ 2,673.0	65.3%
Gross margin	$ 1,899.0	37.9%	$ 1,665.0	36.0%	$ 1,418.0	34.7%
Operating expenses:						
Selling, general, and engineering	$ 727.0	14.5%	$ 684.0	14.8%	$ 639.0	15.6%
Total operating expenses	$ 727.0	14.5%	$ 684.0	14.8%	$ 639.0	15.6%
Operating income	$ 1,172.0	23.4%	$ 981.0	21.2%	$ 779.0	19.0%
Financial Services (Income) Expense	$ (189.0)	-3.8%	$ (167.0)	-3.6%	$ (104.0)	-2.5%
Other expense (income), net	$ (19.0)	-0.4%	$ (17.0)	-0.4%	$ (4.0)	-0.1%
Income before income taxes	$ 1,380.0	27.5%	$ 1,165.0	25.2%	$ 887.0	21.7%
Income taxes	$ 490.0	9.8%	$ 405.0	8.8%	$ 306.0	7.5%
Net income (loss)	$ 890.0	17.7%	$ 760.0	16.4%	$ 581.0	14.2%

HARLEY DAVIDSON
COMPARATIVE COMMON-SIZE BALANCE SHEETS
December 31, 2004, 2003, 2002
(in millions)

	2004 $	2004 %	2003 $	2003 %	2002 $	2002 %
ASSETS						
Current:						
Cash & cash equivalents	$ 275.0	5.0%	$ 329.0	6.7%	$ 281.0	7.3%
Marketable Securities	$ 1,337.0	24.4%	$ 993.0	20.2%	$ 515.0	13.3%
Accounts receivable, net	$ 121.0	2.2%	$ 112.0	2.3%	$ 109.0	2.8%
Current Portion of finance receivables, net	$ 1,207.0	22.0%	$ 1,002.0	20.4%	$ 856.0	22.2%
Inventory	$ 227.0	4.1%	$ 208.0	4.2%	$ 218.0	5.6%
Deferred Income Taxes	$ 61.0	1.1%	$ 51.0	1.0%	$ 41.0	1.1%
Other current assets	$ 38.0	0.7%	$ 33.0	0.7%	$ 47.0	1.2%
Total current assets	$ 3,266.0	59.6%	$ 2,728.0	55.4%	$ 2,067.0	53.5%
Fixed:						
Property, plant & equipment, net	$ 1,025.0	18.7%	$ 1,046.0	21.3%	$ 1,032.0	26.7%
Finance receivables, net	$ 905.0	16.5%	$ 736.0	15.0%	$ 590.0	15.3%
Goodwill	$ 59.0	1.1%	$ 54.0	1.1%	$ 50.0	1.3%
Other assets	$ 228.0	4.2%	$ 358.0	7.3%	$ 122.0	3.2%
Total assets	$ 5,483.0	100.0%	$ 4,922.0	100.0%	$ 3,861.0	100.0%
LIABILITIES						
Current:						
Accounts payable	$ 244.0	4.5%	$ 224.0	4.6%	$ 227.0	5.9%
Accrued Expenses and other liabilities	$ 433.0	7.9%	$ 408.0	8.3%	$ 380.0	9.8%
Current portion of finance debt	$ 495.0	9.0%	$ 324.0	6.6%	$ 383.0	9.9%
Total current liabilities	$ 1,172.0	21.4%	$ 956.0	19.4%	$ 990.0	25.6%
Finance debt	$ 800.0	14.6%	$ 670.0	13.6%	$ 380.0	9.8%
Deferred Income Taxes	$ 51.0	0.9%	$ 126.0	2.6%	$ 29.0	0.8%
Other long-term liabilities	$ 241.0	4.4%	$ 213.0	4.3%	$ 228.0	5.9%
Total liabilities	$ 2,264.0	41.3%	$ 1,965.0	39.9%	$ 1,627.0	42.1%
OWNERS' EQUITY						
Total owners' equity	$ 3,219.0	58.7%	$ 2,957.0	60.1%	$ 2,234.0	57.9%
Total liabilities and owners' equity	$ 5,483.0	100.0%	$ 4,922.0	100.0%	$ 3,861.0	100.0%

(Note: percents may not add to 100 due to rounding)

HARLEY DAVIDSON
RATIO ANALYSIS SUMMARY
For The Years Ended December 31, 2004, 2003, 2002

	2004	2003	2002
SHORT-TERM LIQUIDITY RATIOS			
Current Ratio (Current Assets/Current Liabilities)	2.79	2.85	2.09
Quick Ratio (Cash + Short-term Investments + Accounts Receivable)/Current Liabilities	1.48	1.50	0.91
Accounts Receivable Turnover 1 (Revenues/Average Accounts Receivable)	43.05	41.85	
Accounts Receivable Turnover 2 (Revenues/Year-end Accounts Receivable)	41.45	41.29	37.53
Inventory Turnover 1 (Cost Goods Sold/Average Inventory)	14.33	13.89	
Inventory Turnover 2 (Cost Goods Sold/Year-end Inventory)	13.73	14.23	12.26
LONG-TERM SOLVENCY (LEVERAGE) RATIO			
Total Debt Ratio (Total Liabilities/Total Assets)	41.29%	39.92%	42.14%
PROFITABILITY RATIOS			
Gross Profit Margin (Gross Margin/Revenues)	37.87%	36.01%	34.66%
Operating Profit Margin (Operating Income/Revenues)	23.37%	21.22%	19.04%
Net Profit Margin (Return on Sales) (ROS) (Net Income/Revenues)	17.75%	16.44%	14.20%
Total Asset Turnover (Revenues/Average Total Assets)	0.96	1.05	
Return on Total Assets (ROA) (Net Income/Average Total Assets)	17.11%	17.31%	

INVESTMENTS IN STOCKS AND BONDS

"The secret of success is constancy to purpose."

Disraeli Benjamin

LEARNING GOALS

After studying Chapter 14, you should be able to:

1. Define *short-term investments* and explain what types of securities are included in this classification.

2. Account for short-term investments in stocks (trading securities).

3. Account for short-term investments in bonds (trading securities).

4. Account for investments in available-for-sale securities.

5. Apply the equity method for long-term investments in stock where there is significant influence.

6. Account for investments in bonds held-to-maturity purchased at a premium and a discount.

7. Record bonds purchased between interest dates.

8. Analyze financial statement information for real-life companies.

UNDERSTANDING BUSINESS ISSUES

In the last three chapters, we discussed obtaining sources of cash by issuing stocks and bonds. Sometimes corporations use cash to invest in the stocks and bonds of other companies. For example, as of June 30, 2004, Microsoft had $16.0 billion in cash and cash equivalents, $44.6 billion in short-term investments, and $12.2 billion in long-term investments. The combined investments accounted for 79% of the total assets of Microsoft on the same date. Following are some of the reasons why companies invest in stocks and bonds of other companies:

1. To maximize net income by reducing uninvested cash balances.

2. To become closer to suppliers and customers.

3. To buy an interest in another company to gain access to its customers, products, markets, or technology.

4. To buy an interest in another company with the goal of eventually taking over the company.

In this chapter, we discuss the accounting issues related to investments in stocks and bonds: (1) determining the acquisition cost, (2) recording the investment, (3) recording dividend and interest receipts, (4) recording sales of securities, and (5) valuing securities on the balance sheet.

OVERVIEW OF ACCOUNTING FOR CERTAIN DEBT AND EQUITY SECURITIES: FASB NO. 115

The accounting treatment for investments in many debt and equity securities is covered by *FASB Statement No. 115*, issued in May 1993.[1] Overall, the Statement requires most investment securities to be valued at market value on each balance sheet date. Under former accounting rules, most investment securities were valued at historical cost or at lower of cost or market. One of the reasons for the change to "mark to market" valuation was the financial failure of a significant number of banks in the early 1990s. These failures resulted in financial losses for depositors and investors. Many failed banks held large amounts of investments in debt securities which had significantly declined in value. Under existing GAAP, the debt securities were still reported on the balance sheet at cost despite a decline in market value. Showing the decline in market value of the securities on the financial statements would have alerted users to the problem earlier. Requiring that these investment securities be shown at market value is an attempt to improve the financial reporting process.

FASB Statement No. 115 applies to *both* debt and equity securities with readily determinable fair values. Securities are classified into three categories: (1) held-to-maturity securities, (2) trading securities, and (3) available-for-sale securities. In this chapter, we will illustrate each type of security. Exhibit 14.1 shows a summary of the types of securities in the three categories and the accounting treatment we use for each category:

We present this summary first so that you see an overview of the three security categories. Our goal in this chapter is to explain the basic accounting concepts for investments in stocks and bonds. In our discussion, we will show you many real-life company illustrations.

Security Category	Accounting Treatment
Held-to-Maturity (Debt securities only that will be held to maturity date.)	➤ Show on the balance sheet at amortized cost.
Trading Securities (Debt and equity securities which are purchased and sold for short-term profits.)	➤ Show on the balance sheet at fair market value. ➤ Report changes in *unrealized* gain or losses on the income statement. ➤ When actually sold, *realized* gain or loss is difference between selling price and adjusted cost.
Available-for-Sale (All debt and equity securities not classified as held-to-maturity or trading securities.)	➤ Show on the balance sheet at fair market value. ➤ Report changes in *unrealized* gains and losses as a part of Accumulated Other Comprehensive Income, separate component of stockholders' equity. ➤ When actually sold, *realized* gain or loss is difference between selling price and original cost.

EXHIBIT **14.1**

Summary of Accounting Treatment for Investment Securities by Category: *FASB Statement No. 115*

---

[1] *Statement of Financial Accounting Standards (SFAS) No. 115*, "Accounting for Certain Investments in Debt and Equity Securities" (Norwalk, Conn.: Financial Accounting Standards Board, May 1993).

SHORT-TERM INVESTMENTS

Learning Goal 1   Define short-term investments and explain what types of securities are included in this classification.

Many companies have seasonal patterns of cash outflows and inflows. For example, a manufacturer of lawn mowers has cash outflows during the fall and winter months when they produce the mowers. The company has cash inflows during the spring and summer months when they sell the mowers. Companies should invest seasonal cash excesses immediately in order to maximize net income. They can sell these investments when they need cash to pay their bills.

Short-term investments are investments (1) that are readily saleable securities and (2) that management intends to sell within one year. If securities meet *both* of these requirements, we classify the investments as a current asset on the balance sheet. From a disclosure point of view, *all* three categories of securities under *FASB Statement No. 115* (held-to-maturity, trading, and available-for-sale) may be classified as a short-term investment as long as they meet the two criteria. Long-term investments may also be in readily saleable securities. However, we would not include them as a short-term investment if management intends to hold them for longer than one year.

According to generally accepted accounting principles (GAAP), we show highly liquid investments with original maturities of three months or less to the investing firm as *cash and cash equivalents* on the balance sheet. Since the investments are highly liquid and have a short maturity date, the cost carrying amount approximates fair value.

We list short-term investments that do not qualify as cash equivalents as a separate item in the current assets section of the balance sheet. Exhibit 14.2 illustrates the disclosure of cash and cash equivalents, and short-term investments for Microsoft Corporation.

MICROSOFT CORPORATION
PARTIAL BALANCE SHEET
JUNE 30, 2004, AND 2003
(*in millions*)

Cash and Short-term Investments

Cash and equivalents:	2004	2003
Cash	$ 5,407	$ 2,571
Commercial paper	4,109	774
Municipal securities	1,043	348
Corporate notes and bonds	1,010	828
U.S. government and agency securities	4,083	1,889
Certificates of deposit	330	28
Cash and equivalents	$ 15,982	$ 6,438
Short-term investments:		
Commercial paper	$ 3,177	100
Municipal securities	4,125	8,992
Corporate notes and bonds	16,264	22,408
U. S. government and agency securities	20,959	10,841
Certificates of deposit	85	269
Short-term investments	$ 44,610	$42,610
Cash and short-term investments	$ 60,592	$49,048

EXHIBIT **14.2**

Cash and Cash Equivalents, and Short-term Investements: Microsoft Corporation

Short-Term Investments in Stocks (Trading Securities)

Learning Goal 2 Account for short-term investments in stocks (trading securities).

We purchase and sell **trading securities** for their short-term profit potential. The holding period for these securities is frequently just a few days or in some cases hours. For many companies, investing in stocks of other companies on a very short-term basis is too risky. Therefore, as a short-term investment, most nonfinancial firms invest only in high quality debt securities with a short maturity date. Short-term investments in stocks will primarily be in financially strong companies known as *blue-chip* stocks. In this section, we show how to account for investments in stocks which are classified as trading securities.

Recording Purchases

We initially record all investments in the accounting records at cost. **Cost** includes the stock price plus brokerage fees. To illustrate this, assume that on November 1, 2007, Nike, Inc. purchases 1,000 shares of IBM common stock at $120 per share and pays a brokerage fee of $1,400. The entry to record the purchase is:

2007					
Nov.	1	Short-term Investments (Trading Securities) IBM Stock		121,400	
		Cash			121,400
		To record purchase of 1,000 shares of IBM			
		Corporation common stock at $120 plus commission			
		of $1,400.			

Recording Cash Dividend Receipts

Assume that on December 1, 2007, Nike, Inc. receives a cash dividend of $1.00 per share on the IBM stock. The entry to record the dividend receipt is:

2007				
Dec.	1	Cash	1,000	
		Dividend Revenue		1,000
		To record receipt of dividend from IBM Corporation		
		(1,000 shares × $1.00).		

We classify **Dividend Revenue** under other revenue on the income statement. Dividends do not accrue as interest does. Therefore, we usually do not record dividends until we receive them.

Recording Stock Dividends or Stock Splits

In addition to cash dividends, a corporation may issue additional shares of stock as a *stock dividend*, or a *stock split*. The additional shares an investing company receives are not revenue to it. Only a memorandum entry is necessary to record the increase in the number of shares owned. The carrying value of each share decreases as a result of stock dividends or splits. As an example, assume IBM declared and issued a 100% stock dividend (a two-for-one split would be treated in the same way) on December 31, 2007. Nike, Inc., would receive an additional 1,000 shares of IBM stock on December 31, 2007, and would make a note in its general journal as follows:

2007
Dec.   31   Memorandum Entry: Received today 1,000 additional shares of stock in IBM
              Corporation, representing a 100% stock dividend. The cost per share of the stock is
              recomputed as follows:

Old Number of Shares	New Number of Shares
1,000	2,000
Total Cost	**New Cost per Share**
$121,400	$60.70

Recording Sales

Assume that Nike, Inc. sells all 1,000 shares of IBM common stock on December 15, 2007 (ignore the stock dividend in the previous section). The sales price is $130 per share less a commission of $1,500. The entry to record the sale is:

2007
Dec.   15   Cash   128,500
                    Short-term Investments (Trading Securities) IBM
                        Stock   121,400
                    Realized Gain on Investments   7,100
                    To record the sale of 1,000 shares of IBM
                    Corporation common stock at $130 less commission
                    of $1,500.

The **Realized Gain on Investments** account reflects the difference between the net sales proceeds and the investment cost. We call it a realized gain because the actual sale and collection of cash has occurred.

Valuation and Subsequent Sale of Trading Securities

FASB Statement No. 115 requires that we show investments in trading securities at market value on each balance sheet. To illustrate this, assume that Nike, Inc. had the following two investments in stocks (trading securities) as of December 31, 2007:

Short-term Investments (Trading Securities), December 31, 2007

Security	Acquisition Cost	Market Value	Unrealized Gain (Loss)
Coca-Cola Common Stock	$ 80,000	$ 86,000	$ 6,000
Wendy's Common Stock	60,000	58,000	(2,000)
Total	$140,000	$144,000	$ 4,000

The difference between the total cost of $140,000 and the total current market of $144,000 is a $4,000 net **unrealized gain on investments**. The gain is unrealized because Nike, Inc. has not sold the securities as of December 31, 2007. Under *FASB Statement No.115*, we recognize *both* unrealized gains and losses on *trading securities* on the income statement. We record the following entry on December 31, 2007, to adjust the trading securities to market and show the net unrealized gain:

```
2007
Dec.    31    Short-term Investments (Trading Securities) Coca-Cola Stock    6,000
                  Short-term Investments (Trading Securities) Wendy's
                     Stock                                                          2,000
                  Unrealized Gain on Investments                                    4,000
               To revalue trading securities to market value and
               recognize holding gain in income.
```

We show the unrealized gain of $4,000 on the 2007 income statement. The balance sheet as of December 31, 2007, will report total short-term investments at current market value, $144,000.

Assume that on January 10, 2008, Nike sells all of the Coca-Cola shares for $84,000 and all of the Wendy's shares for $59,000, net of commissions. The adjusted cost basis of both investments is now the market values on December 31, 2007. The entries to record the two sales are:

```
2008
Jan.    10    Cash                                                          84,000
              Realized Loss on Investments                                   2,000
                  Short-term Investments (Trading Securities) Coca-
                     Cola Stock                                                    86,000
               To record the sale of Coca-Cola common stock carried at
               $86,000 for $84,000, net of commissions.

        10    Cash                                                          59,000
                  Short-term Investments (Trading Securities) Wendy's
                     Stock                                                          58,000
                  Realized Gain on Investments                                     1,000
               To record the sale of Wendy's common stock carried at
               $58,000 for $59,000, net of commissions.
```

It is important to observe that with trading securities, the basis for the realized gain or loss when we sell the securities is the adjusted cost at the last balance sheet date. When preparing the next balance sheet, the investing company goes through the same market valuation process for trading securities.

SHORT-TERM INVESTMENTS IN BONDS (TRADING SECURITIES)

Learning Goal 3   Account for short-term investments in bonds (trading securities).

As a short-term investment, many companies invest in high-grade corporate bonds or U.S. government debt. These relatively secure investments minimize the risk of losing principal. The accounting for short-term investments in bonds, which are classified as trading securities, is almost identical to stocks. The only differences are: (1) interest revenue on bonds replaces dividend revenue on stocks and (2) we must accrue interest on balance sheet dates. For bonds held as a short-term investment, we do not amortize bond premiums or discounts.

Recording Purchases

Assume that on November 1, 2007, General Motors purchases 12% bonds of IBM Corporation with a face value of $100,000 at 98. The bonds pay interest on May 1 and November 1, and they mature in five years. General Motors intends to only hold the bonds for a short period of time and classifies the bonds as trading securities. Brokerage fees are $500. The entry to record the purchase is:

```
2007
Nov.    1   Short-term Investments (Trading Securities) IBM Bonds    98,500
                Cash                                                          98,500
                To record purchase of 12%, $100,000  IBM
                Corporation bonds at 98 plus commission of $500.
```

Recording Interest Accruals and Receipts

By contract, the issuer must pay interest on the bonds it issues. Therefore, the investor should accrue interest when preparing financial statements. General Motors makes the following entry for accrued interest on December 31, 2007:

```
2007
Dec.   31   Interest Receivable                                      2,000
                Interest Revenue                                             2,000
                To accrue interest on  IBM Corporation bonds for
                two months ($100,000 × 0.12 × 2/12).
```

If General Motors held the bonds on the next interest payment date, May 1, 2008, the entry to record the cash receipt of semi-annual interest would be:

```
2008
May     1   Cash                                                     6,000
                Interest Receivable                                          2,000
                Interest Revenue                                             4,000
                To record receipt of semi-annual interest on IBM
                Corporation bonds  ($100,000 × 0.12 × 6/12).
```

When investors purchase bonds as a short-term investment, they do not amortize any premium or discount. This is acceptable because the length of the investment period is not known. Also, since the bonds will be held for only a short time, the effects of amortization are not significant.

Valuation of Trading Securities

We show both bond and stock investments in trading securities at market value on the balance sheet. To illustrate, assume that the IBM Corporation bonds are trading at 97 on December 31, 2007. The following schedule shows an unrealized loss of $1,500:

Short-term Investments (Trading Securities), December 31, 2007

Security	Acquisition Cost	Market Value	Unrealized Gain (Loss)
IBM Corporation Bonds	$98,500	$97,000	$(1,500)

We report the unrealized loss on trading securities on the income statement. The following entry on December 31, 2007, adjusts the trading securities to market and shows the unrealized loss:

2007
Dec.   31   Unrealized Loss on Investments   1,500
                    Short-term Investments (Trading Securities) IBM
                        Bonds   1,500
                    To revalue trading securities to market value and
                    recognize holding loss in income.

Recording Sales

Assume that General Motors sells the IBM bonds on February 1, 2008, at 98 plus accrued interest for three months. Brokerage fees are $500. The entry to record the sale is:

2008
Feb.   1   Cash ($97,500 net proceeds + $3,000 interest)   100,500
                    Accrued Interest Receivable   2,000
                    Interest Revenue   1,000
                    Short-term Investments (Trading Securities) IBM
                        Bonds   97,000
                    Realized Gain on Investments   500
                    To record the sale of IBM Corporation bonds at 98 plus
                    accrued interest less $500 brokerage fees.

The Realized Gain on Investments account reflects the difference between the net sales proceeds and the adjusted investment cost. The net sales proceeds are $97,500 = ($100,000 × 0.98 = $98,000 - $500 fees) . The adjusted cost from December 31, 2007, is $97,000. We call it a realized gain because the actual sale and collection of cash has occurred.

INVESTMENTS IN AVAILABLE-FOR-SALE SECURITIES

Learning Goal 4   Account for investments in available-for-sale securities.

FASB Statement No. 115 classifies equity and debt securities that are neither trading securities nor held-to-maturity securities as **available-for-sale securities**. Companies may acquire securities in this category as a short-term or long-term investment. Securities which the firm intends to sell within one year are shown as current assets. Securities we intend to hold for beyond one year are long-term investments. For available-for-sale bonds held as a long-term investment, we should amortize any premium or discount. Later in this chapter, we show you the amortization procedures for bonds held-to-maturity. The accounting for available-for-sale equity and debt securities is similar to trading securities except:

1. We report unrealized gains and losses on available-for-sale securities as part of Accumulated Other Comprehensive Income, which is a *separate component of stockholders' equity.* (For trading securities, we show unrealized gains and losses on the income statement.)

2. When we actually sell available-for-sale securities, the realized gain or loss is the difference between the selling price and *original cost.* (For trading securities, the realized gain or loss is the difference between selling price and *adjusted cost.*)

The entries to purchase available-for-sale equity and debt securities, to record dividends on stock investments, and to record interest received or accrued on bond investments remain the same as shown previously for trading securities. Differences occur for (1) end-of-period valuation and (2) subsequent sales of the securities. To illustrate the differences for available-for-sale securities, we will use the previous example for Nike's assumed investments in Coca-Cola and Wendy's common stocks.

Valuation and Subsequent Sale of Available-for-Sale Securities

FASB Statement No. 115 requires that we show investments in available-for-sale securities at market value on the balance sheet. Assume that Nike, Inc. has two short-term investments in stocks(Coca-Cola and Wendy's). The only difference now is that we assume the stocks are available-for-sale instead of trading securities. Valuation information for the two investments in stocks at December 31, 2007, is:

Short-term Investments (Available-for-Sale Securities), December 31, 2007

Security	Acquisition Cost	Market Value	Unrealized Gain (Loss)
Coca-Cola Common Stock	$ 80,000	$ 86,000	$ 6,000
Wendy's Common Stock	60,000	58,000	(2,000)
Total	$140,000	$144,000	$ 4,000

The difference between the total cost of $140,000 and the total current market of $144,000 is a $4,000 net *unrealized gain on investments*. Under *FASB Statement No. 115*, we recognize both unrealized gains and losses on *available-for-sale* securities as part of Accumulated Other Comprehensive Income, which is a *separate component of stockholders' equity*. The account we use is **Unrealized Gain (Loss) on Available-for-Sale Securities.** We record the following entry on December 31, 2007, to revalue the available-for-sale securities to market and to show the net unrealized gain:

2007					
Dec.	31	Short-term Investments (Available-for-Sale) Coca-Cola Stock		6,000	
		Short-term Investments (Available-for-Sale) Wendy's Stock			2,000
		Unrealized Gain (Loss) on Available-for-Sale Securities			4,000
		To revalue available-for-sale securities to market value and record a net unrealized gain in a separate stockholders' equity account.			

The balance sheet as of December 31, 2007, will report the available-for-sale securities at current market value, $144,000. We show the net unrealized gain of $4,000 as part of Accumulated Other Comprehensive Income, a separate component of stockholders' equity. The following illustrates this with assumed amounts for other stockholders' equity accounts:

Stockholders' Equity

Paid-in capital	$ 300,000
Retained earnings	400,000
Total paid-in capital and retained earnings	$ 700,000
Accumulated Other Comprehensive Income	4,000
Total stockholders' equity	$ 704,000

Assume that on January 10, 2008, Nike sells all of the Coca-Cola shares for $84,000 and all of the Wendy's shares for $59,000, net of commissions. In the entries, note that we compute the realized gain or loss on original acquisition cost. Essentially, we *cancel previous unrealized* gains/losses and *record realized* gains/losses in the entries. The entries to record the two sales are:

2008

Jan.	10	Cash		84,000	
		Unrealized Gain (Loss) on Available-for-Sale Securities		6,000	
		Short-term Investments (Available-for-Sale)			
		Coca-Cola Stock			86,000
		Realized Gain on Investments			4,000
		To record the sale of Coca-Cola common stock which originally cost $80,000 for $84,000, net of commissions.			
	10	Cash		59,000	
		Realized Loss on Investments		1,000	
		Short-term Investments (Available-for-Sale)			
		Wendy's Stock			58,000
		Unrealized Gain (Loss) on Available-for-Sale Securities			2,000
		To record the sale of Wendy's common stock which originally cost $60,000 for $59,000, net of commissions.			

LONG-TERM INVESTMENTS IN STOCKS WITH SIGNIFICANT INFLUENCE

Long-term investments are securities that management intends to hold for longer than one year. We refer to the buyer as the **investor** and the issuer of stock as the **investee**. One company may buy shares of voting capital stock in another company as a long-term investment for a number of reasons. One motivation may be to receive cash dividends. A second reason is the hope that the price of the stock of the investee company will increase and that the investor can ultimately sell the investment at a gain. A third reason may be to develop sources of supply for key materials or components or to gain access to new areas of business.

The accounting for long-term investments in voting capital stock generally depends on the percentage of ownership. Exhibit 14.3 presents an overview of the accounting methods used to account for long-term investments in voting capital stock. When the percentage of ownership is less than 20%, we use the *market value method*. We have already illustrated the market value method for equity securities that qualify under *FASB Statement No. 115* as available-for-sale securities. When the percentage of ownership is between 20% and 50%, we assume the investor can exert *significant influence* over the investee. Therefore, we use a new approach called the *equity* method. For percentage ownership over 50%, we prepare *consolidated financial statements*. In this section, we discuss the use of the equity method for percentage ownership between 20% and 50%. Chapter 17 discusses consolidated statements.

THE EQUITY METHOD OF ACCOUNTING FOR LONG-TERM INVESTMENTS IN STOCKS

Learning Goal 5   Apply the equity method to account for long-term investments in stocks where there is significant influence.

Sometimes a corporation's investment in voting shares is large enough that the investor can exercise significant influence over the investee. In these cases, the investor can affect investee decisions on such matters as dividend distributions, product lines, and sources of supply. Under GAAP, we view

Percentage of Ownership Interest Guidelines	Accounting Method	Overview of Income Statement and Balance Sheet Effects
Own less than 20% of voting stock	Market value method	Record the investment account at acquisition cost. Record dividends we receive as revenue on the income statement. Value the investment in available-for-sale securities at fair market value on the balance sheet. Report changes in unrealized gains and losses as a separate component in stockholders' equity.
Own 20-50% of voting stock	Equity method	Record the investment account initially at the acquisition cost of the investment. Record the investor's share of investee net income or net loss as revenue or loss on the investor income statement. Increase the investment account by the investor's share of investee net income and decrease it by the investor's share of investee net losses and dividends.
Own more than 50% of voting stock	Prepare consolidated financial statements	Combine income statement and balance sheet accounts of investee and investor companies. (Chapter 17 discusses this method.)

EXHIBIT **14.3**

Overview of Intercompany Long-term Investments in Voting Shares of Stock

ownership of 20% and up to 50% of the voting stock as evidence of significant influence.[2] In these cases, we use the equity method to account for the investment.

Under the **equity method**, we recognize the investor's share of the investee's income or loss in the income statement instead of dividends we receive. We record the initial purchase of stock at cost plus any brokerage fees as before. After the initial acquisition, the accounting changes. We debit the investment account and credit an income account for the investor's share of investee net income. We debit Cash and credit the investment account for the investor's share of investee dividend distributions.

To illustrate the equity method, assume that Nike, Inc., purchases 80,000 shares of Shoelace Company common stock on January 1, 2008. Shoelace Company has a total of 200,000 common shares outstanding. The total price including brokerage fees is $400,000. Assume that the price paid equals the book value (proportionate share of stockholders' equity) of the Shoelace stock. This simplifies the illustration since there is no excess paid above book value. After the purchase, Nike, Inc., has a 40% (80,000 shares held ÷ 200,000 shares outstanding) interest in Shoelace Corporation. Since this falls between 20% and 50%, we use the equity method to account for the investment. Shoelace Corporation reports the following results for 2008 and 2009:

December 31, 2008	Shoelace Corporation reports a net income of $100,000 for 2008.
March 1, 2009	Shoelace Corporation declares and pays a total cash dividend of $20,000.
December 31, 2009	Shoelace Corporation reports a net loss of $30,000 for 2009.

---

[2] *Accounting Principles Board Opinion No. 18*, "The Equity Method of Accounting for Investments in Common Stock" (New York: AICPA, March 1971), paragraph 17.

In some cases, investor companies may own less than 20% of the voting shares and still use the equity method if they can show that they have significant influence over the investee company. This topic is covered in more advanced accounting courses.

We record the initial investment in Shoelace and the subsequent transactions in 2008 and 2009 on the books of Nike, Inc. by the equity method as follows:

2008			
Jan.	1	Long-term Investment in Stocks—Common Stock of Shoelace Corporation	400,000
		Cash		400,000
		To record purchase of 40% of the stock of Shoelace Corporation.	
Dec.	31	Long-term Investment in Stocks—Common Stock of Shoelace Corporation	40,000
		Equity in Investee Income		40,000
		To record investor's share of reported net income (40% × $100,000).	
2009			
Mar.	1	Cash	8,000
		Long-term Investment in Stocks—Common Stock of Shoelace Corporation		8,000
		To record receipt of dividend from the Shoelace Corporation (40% × $20,000).	
Dec.	31	Equity in Investee Loss	12,000
		Long-term Investment in Stocks—Common Stock of Shoelace Corporation		12,000
		To record investor's share of reported net loss (40% × $30,000).	

After we post these entries, the Long-term Investment in Stocks account will appear as follows:

Long-term Investment in Stocks

Date		Explanation	PR	Debit	Credit	Balance Debit	Balance Credit
2008							
Jan.	1	Initial cost of 40% of stock of Shoelace		400,000		400,000	
Dec.	31	Share of Shoelace's net income for 2008		40,000		440,000	
2009							
Mar.	1	Receipt of share of Shoelace's dividends			8,000	432,000	
Dec.	31	Share of Shoelace's net loss for 2009			12,000	420,000	

Using the equity method, an investor corporation recognizes the *economic* relationship between the two companies. Income and losses of the investee are essentially part of the investor corporation's own income and losses since they can influence the investee's operating policies. We use the **Equity in Investee Income** and **Equity in Investee Loss** accounts to indicate the investor's share of net income or net loss of an investee under the equity method of accounting. They appear in the income statement of the investor company. We consider the receipt of dividends a realization in cash of previously recorded investee earnings. We record the receipt of cash dividends from the investee by debiting the Cash account and crediting the investment account.

INVESTMENTS IN BONDS HELD-TO-MATURITY

Learning Goal 6   Account for investments in bonds held-to-maturity purchased at a premium and a discount.

The law prohibits certain types of companies from buying common stock. Organizations such as banks, insurance companies, some trusts, and pension funds may acquire bonds as investments. Industrial companies also frequently buy bonds, either for the interest revenue or for business connections. For bonds to classify as **held-to-maturity securities**, *FASB Statement No. 115* states that there must not be any foreseeable intent or need to sell the bonds before the maturity date.

If the *stated interest rate* on bonds is the same as the prevailing *market interest rate* for the particular grade of bonds, the bonds should sell for face value. If there is a difference between the stated bond interest rate and the prevailing market rate, the investor will buy the bonds at a *premium* or a *discount*. Accounting by the purchaser of bonds held-to-maturity is almost the opposite of accounting by the issuer of bonds. We emphasize this point by using Chapter 13 examples to illustrate accounting for investments in bonds held-to-maturity.

Bonds Purchased at a Premium

In Chapter 13 Mankato Corporation issued $100,000 of bonds for $107,732 on July 1, 2007. The stated interest rate is 12% with interest payable on June 30 and December 31. The issue price at a premium results in an effective interest rate of 10%. Assume that Trio Corporation purchases all of the Mankato Corporation bonds for $107,732 on July 1, 2007. Trio Corporation intends to hold the bonds to maturity. Since the bonds mature in 2012, Trio classifies the bonds as a long-term investment on the balance sheet. To simplify the example, assume that there are no brokerage fees.

Recording Purchases

The entry to record the purchase on July 1, 2007, is as follows:

2007					
Jul.	1	Long-term Investments (Held-to-Maturity) Mankato Bonds	107,732	
		Cash		107,732
		To record purchase of 12%, $100,000 Mankato Corporation bonds due June 30, 2009.		

The investor does not separately record a premium or discount account. Instead, we include the premium in the investment account.

Recording Interest

For long-term investments in bonds, we must amortize any premium or discount amount. GAAP requires the effective interest method, which provides a constant rate of return over the term in the investment. However, investors may use the straight-line method of amortization if the results are not materially different.

Straight-line Method of Amortization

Under the straight-line amortization method, we record *equal amounts of bond interest revenue* each period. Exhibit 13.4 shows a bond interest table for the Mankato bond using straight-line amortization. The total amount of the bond premium is $7,732 ($107,732 - $100,000). The entry to record interest revenue for the first six-month period ending December 31, 2007, is as follows:

2007
Dec.   31   Cash   6,000
                    Interest Revenue   5,227
                    Long-term Investments (Held-to-Maturity) Mankato
                        Bonds   773
                To record the semiannual interest receipt and amortization.
                    Cash: $100,000 × 0.12 × 6/12 = $6,000.
                    Amortization: $7,732 ÷ 10 = $773.
                    Interest revenue: $6,000 - $773 = $5,227.

We include the premium as part of the balance in the investment account. The credit to the Long-term Investment (Held-to-Maturity) Mankato Bonds account amortizes a portion of the premium each interest period. The premium amortization decreases the amount of interest revenue the investor records. After the last amortization entry, the balance in the investment account equals the face or maturity value of the bonds ($100,000). At this point, the investor debits Cash and credits Long-term Investment (Held-to-Maturity) Mankato Bonds for $100,000 to record receipt of the maturity value.

Effective Interest Method of Amortization

Under the effective interest method of amortization, we measure interest revenue using a *constant effective interest rate*. Exhibit 13.5 shows a bond interest table for the Mankato bond using the effective interest method. The entries to record interest revenue for the first two six-month periods ending December 31, 2007, and June 30, 2008, are as follows:

2007
Dec.   31   Cash   6,000
                    Interest Revenue   5,387
                    Long-term Investments (Held-to-Maturity) Mankato Bonds   613
                To record the semiannual interest receipt and amortization.
                    Cash: $100,000 × 0.12 × 6/12 = $6,000.
                    Interest revenue: $107,732 × 0.05 = $5,387.
                    Amortization: $6,000 - $5,387 = $613.

2008
Jun.   30   Cash   6,000
                    Interest Revenue   5,356
                    Long-term Investments (Held-to-Maturity) Mankato Bonds   644
                To record the semiannual interest receipt and amortization.
                    Cash: $100,000 × 0.12 × 6/12 = $6,000.
                    Interest revenue: $107,732 - $613 = $107,119.
                                           $107,119 × 0.05 = $5,356.
                    Amortization: $6,000 - $5,356 = $644.

Using the effective interest method, the amount of interest revenue decreases each period as the bond investment balance decreases. This results in a constant effective interest rate on a decreasing investment balance.

Bonds Purchased at a Discount

In Chapter 13 Hastings Corporation issued $100,000 of bonds for $92,944 on July 1, 2007. The stated interest rate is 12% with interest payable on June 30 and December 31. The issue price at a discount gives an effective interest rate of 14%. Assume that Trio Corporation purchases all of the Hastings Corporation bonds for $92,944 on July 1, 2007. To simplify the example, assume that there are no brokerage fees.

Recording Purchases

```
2007
Jul.    1  Long-term Investments (Held-to-Maturity) Hastings Bonds    92,944
              Cash                                                                 92,944
           To record purchase of 12%, $100,000 Hastings
           Corporation bonds due June 30, 2012.
```

We include the discount in the investment account.

Straight-line Method of Amortization

Exhibit 13.8 shows the bond interest table for the Hastings Corporation bond using straight-line depreciation. The total amount of the bond discount is $7,056 ($100,000-$92,944). The entry to record interest revenue for the first six-month period ending December 31, 2007, is as follows:

```
2007
Dec.    31  Cash                                                        6,000
               Long-term Investments (Held-to-Maturity) Hastings Bonds    706
               Interest Revenue                                                    6,706
            To record the semiannual interest receipt and amortization.
               Cash: $100,000 × 0.12 × 6/12 = $6,000.
               Amortization: $7,056 ÷ 10 = $706.
               Interest revenue: $6,000 + $706 = $6,706.
```

Effective Interest Method of Amortization

Exhibit 13.9 shows the bond interest table for the Hastings Corporation bonds using the effective interest method of amortization. The entries to record interest revenue for the first two six-month periods ending December 31, 2007, and June 30, 2008, are as follows:

```
2007
Dec.    31  Cash                                                        6,000
               Long-term Investments (Held-to-Maturity) Hastings Bonds    506
               Interest Revenue                                                    6,506
            To record the semiannual interest receipt and amortization.
               Cash: $100,000 × 0.12 × 6/12 = $6,000.
               Interest revenue: $92,944 × 0.07  = $6,506.
               Amortization: $6,506 - $6,000 = $506.


2008
Jun.    30  Cash                                                        6,000
               Long-term Investments (Held-to-Maturity) Hastings Bonds    542
               Interest Revenue                                                    6,542
            To record the semiannual interest receipt and amortization.
               Cash: $100,000 × 0.12 × 6/12 = $6,000.
               Interest revenue:   $92,944 + $506 = $93,450.
                                   $93,450 × 0.07  = $6,542.
               Amortization:  $6,542 - $6,000 = $542.
```

Using the effective interest method of amortization, the amount of interest revenue increases each period as the bond investment balance increases. This results in a constant effective interest rate on an increasing investment balance.

Bonds Purchased Between Interest Dates

Learning Goal 7   Record bonds purchased between interest dates.

When investors purchase bonds between interest dates, the investor must also pay for the interest accrued since the last interest date. Assume TennTech authorized issuance of $100,000 in 12% bonds on June 30, 2007. Interest is payable June 30 and December 31. The bonds mature June 30, 2012. Assume that Trio Corporation purchases all of the bonds on September 1, 2007. Therefore, the remaining life of the bonds is 58 months [(5 years × 12 months) - 2 months = 58]. They sold for 105 plus accrued interest. We show the entries to record the purchase and the receipt of interest on December 31, 2007, as follows. We illustrate only the straight-line amortization method.

2007					
Sep.	1	Long-term Investments (Held-to-Maturity) TennTech Bonds	105,000	
		Interest Receivable	2,000	
		Cash		107,000

To record purchase of 12%, $100,000 TennTech
Corporation bonds due June 30, 2009.
Investment: $100,000 × 1.05 = $105,000.
Interest Receivable: $100,000 × 0.12 × 2/12
= $2,000.
Cash: $105,000 + $2,000.

Nov.	1	Cash	6,000	
		Interest Receivable		2,000
		Interest Revenue		3,655
		Long-term Investments (Held-to-Maturity) TennTech Bonds		345

To record the semiannual interest receipt and
amortization.
Cash: $100,000 × 0.12 × 6/12 = $6,000.
Amortization: $5,000 ÷ 58 months = $86.21.
$86.21 × 4 months = $345.
Interest revenue: $6,000 - ($2,000 + $345) = $3,655.

The important accounting issues in accounting for the TennTech bond purchased between accounting periods are as follows:

1. Two assets are purchased on September 1, 2007: the bonds at 105 and the accrued interest of $2,000.

2. The amortization period begins on the date of purchase, September 1, 2007. It ends on the maturity date, June 30, 2012. Therefore, the amortization period totals 58 months. The monthly amortization is $86.21 ($5,000 ÷ 58 months).

3. The receipt of interest on December 31, 2007, represents four months' interest earned and the collection of the interest receivable for two months. Also, we must record four months of premium amortization for 2007.

Valuation of Investments in Bonds (Held-to-Maturity)

Under *FASB Statement No. 115*, we value investments in held-to-maturity bonds and other debt securities at amortized cost. Since the investor intends to hold the debt securities to maturity, amortized cost is more relevant than current market value. Therefore, we do *not* record changes in market value. We do not sell these bonds before the maturity date. Therefore, we do *not* recognize any realized or unrealized gains and losses on held-to-maturity bonds.

ANALYZING INFORMATION

Learning Goal 8   Analyze financial statement information for real-life companies.

Exhibit 14.5 shows a partial balance sheet and disclosures on marketable securities for Starbucks Coffee Company. Starbucks shows cash and cash equivalents of $299.1 million, current marketable securities of $54.3 million, and noncurrent marketable securities of $135.2 million on September 30, 2004. Starbucks has large amounts of cash inflows from its coffee products and services. In order to maximize income, the Company must invest these cash inflows.

STARBUCKS COFFEE COMPANY
PARTIAL BALANCE SHEET
SEPTEMBER 30, 2004 AND 2003
(in millions)

	2004	2003
Current assets		
Cash and cash equivalents	$ 299.1	$ 200.9
Marketable securities	353.9	148.1
Accounts receivable, less allowance for doubtful accounts		
of 2.2 and 4.8	131.0	114.1
Inventories	422.7	342.9
Prepaid expenses	152.5	116.5
Total current assets	$ 1,359.3	$ 924.0
Investments		
Investments in marketable securities	$ 135.2	$ 136.2
Total assets	$ 3,319.0	$ 2,729.7

Partial Notes to Financial Statements: Marketable Securities
Marketable securities at September 30, 2004, are classified as trading and available-for-sale. Trading securities are current and total $24.8 and $20.2 million in 2004 and 2003. The available for sale securities are carried at market value with unrealized gains and losses included in stockholders' equity. The amortized cost and market value of available-for-sale marketable securities at September 30, 2004, are:

Current:	Gross Amortized Cost	Gross Unrealized Gains	Unrealized Losses	Market Value
Municipal bonds and notes	$310.0	$ 0	$ 0.5	$ 309.5
U.S. Government obligations and other	19.6	0	0	19.6
Subtotal	$329.6	$ 0	$ 0.5	$ 329.1
Noncurrent:				
Municipal bonds	$130.8	$ 0	$ .3	$ 130.5
Mortgage trusts and Corporate Debt	4.7	0	0	4.7
Subtotal	$135.5	$ 0	$ 0.3	$ 135.2
Total	$165.1	$ 0	$ 0.3	$ 464.3

*differences may be due to rounding

EXHIBIT **14.5**

Current and Noncurrent Investments in Securities: Starbucks

The note to the financial statements states that most current and all noncurrent marketable securities are classified as *available-for-sale*. This means that: (1) the securities will be shown on the balance sheet at market value, (2) unrealized gains and losses will appear as part of Accumulated Other Comprehensive Income, a separate component of stockholders' equity, and (3) realized gains and losses when the securities are actually sold will appear in the income statement. The note shows cost and market values for both current and noncurrent securities. Starbucks also discloses the total amounts of securities maturing within one year, one to five years, and after five years through ten years.

Question. Overall, the statement user wants to assess the extent and type of investments, past success in generating investment income, current valuation for the investments, and relative maturity dates for the investments. The following questions are important to raise: (1) What is the overall percent of total assets invested in current and noncurrent securities? (2) What is the mix of trading, available-for-sale, and held-to-maturity investments? (3) How does the current market value and cost of the securities compare?

Answer. (1) Starbucks has a significant investment in securities. As of September 30, 2004, 10.7% of total assets are invested in current marketable securities and 4.1% of total assets are invested in noncurrent marketable securities. (2) Almost all marketable securities are classified as available-for-sale. This means that unrealized gains and losses will be shown in stockholders' equity instead of on the income statement. (3) As of September 30, 2004, the total market value ($464.3 million) is slightly lower than the amortized cost ($465.1 million).

LEARNING GOALS REVIEW

1. Define *short-term investments* and explain what types of securities are included in this classification.

Investments must meet two criteria to qualify as a short-term investment: (1) the securities must be readily saleable and (2) management must intend to sell them within one year. The primary goal in short-term investing is to preserve the amount originally invested. Many companies invest in U.S. government securities as short-term investments.

2. Account for short-term investments in stocks (trading securities).

We initially record short-term investments in stocks (trading securities) at cost, which includes the stock price plus any brokerage fees. We record cash dividends as revenue when the company receives them. At the end of each accounting period, we value trading securities at market value and report unrealized gains or losses in the income statement. When we sell trading securities, we show a realized gain or loss for the difference between the selling price and adjusted cost.

3. Account for short-term investments in bonds (trading securities).

We initially record short-term investments in bonds (trading securities) at cost plus any brokerage fees. The investor does not use a separate premium or discount account. Since interest on bonds is a contractual obligation, companies should accrue interest at the end of each accounting period. We do not amortize premiums and discounts on short-term investments because we will not hold the bonds to maturity. At the end of each accounting period, we value trading securities at market value and report unrealized gains or losses in the income statement. When we sell trading securities, we show a realized gain or loss for the difference between the selling price and adjusted cost.

4. Account for investments in available-for-sale securities.

Available-for-sale securities are debt and equity securities which are not classified as held-to-maturity or trading securities. At the end of each accounting period, we value available-for-sale securities at market value and report unrealized gains or losses in the balance sheet as part of Accumulated Other Comprehensive Income, which is a separate component of stockholders' equity. When we sell available-for-sale securities, we show a realized gain or loss for the difference between the selling price and original cost.

5. **Apply the equity method for long-term investments in stock where there is significant influence.**
We use the equity method for long-term investments in stock when the investor can exert significant influence over the investee. As a guideline, companies should generally use the equity method when they own 20-50% of the voting shares. We record long-term investments in stock at cost, which includes the stock price plus any brokerage fees. Under the equity method, we debit the investment account and credit Equity in Investee Income to record the investor's share of investee net income. We debit Equity in Investee Loss and credit the investment account to record the investor's share of investee net loss. We record cash dividends as a debit to Cash and a credit to the investment account. The balance in the investment account under the equity method equals the following:
    Original cost at acquisition date

Add:	Investor share of investee income since acquisition
Deduct:	Investor share of investee losses since acquisition
Deduct:	Investor share of investee dividends since acquisition.

The share is the dollar amount based on the percentage of the investee's voting shares the investor owns. We report this carrying value on the balance sheet as the value for the long-term investment in stocks.

6. **Account for investments in bonds held-to-maturity purchased at a premium and a discount.**
We debit investment in bonds for the full cost of the bonds including any premium or discount. We must amortize the premium or discount on long-term bond investments. Under the straight-line method, we amortize the premium or discount over the number of periods remaining in the bond life. Under the effective interest method, we credit Interest Revenue for the bond carrying value times the effective interest rate. The difference between the cash we receive and the interest revenue is a debit or credit to the bond investment account. This amortizes the premium or discount. We show investments in bonds held-to-maturity on the balance sheet at amortized cost.

7. **Record bonds purchased between interest dates.**
When we purchase bonds between interest dates, we debit the amount we pay for accrued interest to Interest Receivable. We do not record it as part of the bond investment. When we receive the first interest payment, we debit Cash for the full amount received. We credit Interest Receivable for the amount accrued. We credit the remainder of the interest receipt to Interest Revenue.

8. **Analyze financial statement information for real-life companies.**
Overall, the statement user wants to assess the extent and type of investments, past success in generating investment income, current valuation for the investments, and relative maturity dates for the investments. This information is contained in the notes to the financial statements.

DEMONSTRATION PROBLEM

Journal Entries to Record Investment Transactions

Miami Corporation had the following transactions involving investments during 2007:

2007

Jun.	10	Purchased 300 shares of the 20,000 shares outstanding of Schoff Corporation $3 par value common stock at $10.50 per share as a short-term investment (trading securities). Brokerage fees were $150.
Feb.	3	Purchased 10,000 shares of the 40,000 shares outstanding of Collins Corporation $5 par value common stock at its current book value per share of $8 as a long-term investment. Brokerage fees were $1,100.
Sep.	1	Purchased Tolland Corporation 12% bonds with a face value of $200,000 and a maturity date of December 31, 2009, as a long-term investment. The bonds were purchased in the open market at 94 plus accrued interest. Interest on the bonds is paid semiannually on June 30 and December 31. Miami Corporation intends to hold the bonds until the maturity date. The straight-line method of amortization is used.
	5	Collins Corporation declared and paid a cash dividend of $0.30 per share on common shares outstanding.
Nov.	8	Schoff Corporation declared and paid a cash dividend of $0.20 per share on its common shares outstanding.
Dec.	31	Received the semiannual interest on the Tolland Corporation bonds and amortized the discount.
	31	Collins Corporation reported a net loss for 2007 of $20,000.
	31	As of December 31, 2007, the Schoff Corporation stock was selling for $12 per share, the Collins Corporation stock was selling for $7.50 per share, and the Tolland Corporation bonds were selling at 95.

REQUIRED

Prepare journal entries to record these transactions (**LG 1, 2, 5, 6, 7**).

SOLUTION

Solution Approach

Security	Type of Investment	Accounting Method
Schoff common stock	Short-term(Trading Security)	Record at cost. Recognize dividends received as revenue. Value investment at market as of December 31, 2007.
Collins common stock	Long-term(Equity Method)	Record at cost. Use equity method since ownership interest is 25% and significant influence is assumed. Recognize share of investee income or loss in investor income statement. Deduct dividends from the investment account.
Tolland bonds	Long-term (Held-to-Maturity)	Record at cost. Amortize discount on bonds ($12,000) over remaining life of bonds (40 months), since the bonds will be held to maturity.

2007

Jan.	10	Short-term Investments (Trading Securities) Schoff Stock	3,300	
		Cash		3,300
		To record the purchase of 300 shares of Schoff Corporation common stock at $10.50 per share plus brokerage fees of $150.		
Feb.	3	Long-term Investment in Stocks—Common Stock of Collins Corporation	81,100	
		Cash		81,100
		To record the purchase of 10,000 shares of Collins Corporation common stock at $8 per share plus brokerage fees of $1,100.		
Sep.	1	Long-term Investments (Held-to-Maturity) Tolland Bonds	188,000	
		Interest Receivable	4,000	
		Cash		192,000
		To record the purchase of Tolland Corporation bonds at 94 plus accrued interest.		

Solution Approach

The computation of cash paid is as follows:

Purchase price: $200,000 × 0.94	$188,000
Accrued interest: $200,000 × 0.12 × 2/12	4,000
Total cash paid	$192,000

2007

Sep. 5 Cash 3,000
    Long-term Investments in Stock—Common Stock of
      Collins Corporation 3,000
    To record the receipt of the dividend from Collins
    Corporation (10,000 shares × $.30).

Nov. 8 Cash 60
    Dividend Revenue 60
    To record the receipt of the dividend from Schoff Corporation
    (300 shares × $.20).

Dec. 31 Cash 12,000
    Long-term Investments (Held-to-Maturity) Tolland Bonds ... 1,200
      Interest Revenue 9,200
      Interest Receivable 4,000
    To record the receipt of semiannual interest from Tolland
    Corporation and to record amortization of the discount
    element of the bond investment.

Solution Approach

Cash received: $200,000 × 0.12 × 6/21 = $12,000
Discount amortization: ($12,000 ÷ 40 months) × 4 months = $1,200

2007

Dec. 31 Equity in Investee Loss 5,000
    Long-term Investments in Stock—Common Stock of
      Collins Corporation 5,000
    To record investor's share of reported net loss (25% × $20,000).

Dec. 31 Short-term Investments (Trading Securities) Schoff Stock ... 300
    Unrealized Gain on Investments 300
    To revalue trading securities to market value and recognize
    holding gain in income. ($12 × 300 shares = $3,600 - $3,300 = $300).

Explanations of valuation:

- Schoff common stock increased in value from $10.50 to $12 per share. We show the increase in market value on trading securities as an unrealized gain on the income statement.

- Collins common stock decreased in value from $8 to $7.50. We do not record the decrease in market value for this long-term investment since we are using the equity method to account for the investment.

- Tolland bonds increased in value from 94 to 95. We do not record changes in the value of investments in bonds held-to-maturity. We show these investments at amortized cost.

GLOSSARY

available-for-sale securities Equity and debt securities that are neither trading securities nor held-to-maturity securities. We report unrealized gains and losses on these securities as a separate component of stockholders' equity. When we actually sell these securities, the realized gain or loss is the difference between selling price and adjusted cost.

cost In stock and bond investment, the stock or bond price plus the brokerage fee as well as other incidental costsof acquisition.

Dividend Revenue A revenue account representing the receipt of dividends on investments in stock.

Equity in Investee Income A revenue account used to record the investor's share of investee's net income underthe equity method.

Equity in Investee Loss An expense or loss account used to record the investor's share of investee's net loss underthe equity method.

equity method An accounting method for long-term stock investments with significant influence that adjusts thecost of the investment by the investor's share of the net income or net loss of the investee and decreases the investment account for receipt of dividends.

held-to-maturity securities Bonds and other debt securities the investor will hold to maturity. We show them atamortized cost on the balance sheet.

investee A corporation whose stock is partially or fully owned by another corporation, the investor company.

investor A corporation owning stock in another corporation, the investee company.

Long-term investments Debt and equity securities management intends to hold for longer than one year.

Realized Gain (loss) on Investments An income statement account whose balance is the difference between actual selling price at the time of sale and the carrying value of investments.

short-term investments Investments in readily saleable debt and equity securities that management intends to hold for less than one year. These are classified as current assets on the balance sheet.

trading securities Securities we purchase and sell for short-term profit potential. We value these at market value on the balance sheet and show unrealized gains and losses on the income statement.

Unrealized Gain (loss) on Investments An income statement account whose balance is the difference between market value on a balance sheet date and the carrying value of trading securities.

Unrealized Gain (loss) on Available-for-Sale Securities A balance sheet account included as part of Accumulated Other Comprehensive Income, which is a component of stockholders' equity. This shows the difference between market value on a balance sheet date and the carrying value of available-for-sale securities.

QUESTIONS FOR GROUP LEARNING

Q14-1. What are short-term investments? How do we classify them on the balance sheet?

Q14-2. List some types of investments that may qualify as short-term investments.

Q14-3. Under *FASB Statement No. 115*, what are the three categories for investment securities? Is market value used to value all three classes of securities on the balance sheet? Briefly explain.

Q14-4. Explain the difference in financial statement presentation for unrealized gains and losses for trading securities versus available-for-sale securities.

Q14-5. When we sell trading securities and available-for-sale securities, what do we use as the basis for computing the realized gain or loss for each security category?

Q14-6. Your classmate Frank states that trading securities are always classified as short-term investments on the balance sheet and that available-for-sale securities are always classified as long-term. Is he correct? Briefly explain.

Q14-7. State the main differences in accounting for short-term investments in (1) stocks and (2) bonds held as trading securities.

Q14-8. When do we use the equity method to account for investments in stocks? How do we treat the receipt of dividends under the equity method?

Q14-9. What is a stock split? Discuss the accounting for a stock split from the point of view of the investor. Would there be any difference in the accounting for a stock dividend and for a stock split on the investor's books? Explain.

Q14-10. Why is the effective interest method theoretically preferable to the straight-line method of amortization?

Q14-11. Discuss the following statement: "Generally speaking, accounting for investment in bonds held-to-maturity is the mirror image of accounting for the issuance of bonds." In your discussion, state the differences and similarities in the accounting for each.

Q14-12. Assume you are in a period of increasing interest rates. In analyzing investments in marketable securities for a company, would you generally feel more comfortable or less comfortable if contractual maturity dates for available-for-sale debt securities were (1) mostly within one year or (2) after one year through five years? Briefly explain.

EXERCISES

NOTE: In order to clearly show areas of similarity and difference between investment valuation methods, the following exercises use common data: (E14-13 and 14) (E14-15, 16, and 17) (E14-20 and 21).

E14-13. **Recording short-term investments in stocks (trading securities) (LG 2)** On October 8, 2007, Bridgeport Company acquired 200 shares of McDonald's Corporation common stock for a total cost of $6,000. It also acquired 300 shares of General Electric common stock for a total cost of $15,000. Management intends to sell all of the shares within the next year and lists the securities as a short-term investment in stocks(trading securities). Bridgeport received cash dividends of $.60 per share from General Electric on December 10, 2007. On December 31, 2007, McDonald's Corporation stock is selling for $25 per share and General Electric stock is selling for $51 per share. Bridgeport sells all of its shares of McDonald's Corporation stock on February 3, 2008, for $5,800. Bridgeport sells all of its shares of General Electric stock on February 6, 2008, for $14,900.

Prepare journal entries to: record the stock purchases on October 8, 2007; the receipt of dividends on December 10, 2007; the valuation at market on December 31, 2007; the sale of McDonald's Corporation stock on February 3, 2008; and the sale of General Electric stock on February 6, 2008.

E14-14.   **Recording short-term investments in stocks (available-for-sale securities) (LG 4)**
Assume the same information in Exercise 14-13 with the exception that the common stocks are *available-for-sale* instead of trading securities. The stocks are still held as a short-term investment. Prepare all of the entries listed in Exercise 14-13 under the new assumption.

E14-15.   **Recording short-term investments in bonds (trading securities) (LG 3)** On July 1, 2007, Clay Company purchased 14% bonds of Deere Corporation with a face value of $500,000 at 103 as a short-term investment (trading securities). The bonds pay interest on July 1 and January 1 and mature in six years. On December 31, 2007, the bonds were selling for 102. After receiving the interest payment on January 1, 2008, Clay sold all of the bonds at 102 less a brokerage fee of $1,000.

Prepare journal entries to: record the bond purchase on July 1, 2007; the accrual of interest on a December 31, 2007; the valuation at market on December 31, 2007; the receipt of interest on January 1, 2008; and the sale of the bonds on January 1, 2008.

E14-16.   **Recording short-term investments in bonds (available-for-sale securities) (LG 4)**
Assume the same information in Exercise 14-15 with the exception that the bonds are *available-for-sale* instead of trading securities. The bonds are still held as a short-term investment.

Prepare journal entries to: record the bond purchase on July 1, 2007; the accrual of interest on December 31, 2007; the valuation at market on December 31, 2007; the receipt of interest on January 1, 2008; and the sale of the bonds on January 1, 2008.

E14-17.   **Recording long-term investments in bonds (held-to-maturity securities) (LG 6)**
Assume the same information in Exercise 14-15 with the exception that the bonds are *held-to-maturity* instead of trading securities. Assume that the bonds are not sold on January 1, 2008. The bonds are now held-to-maturity as a long-term investment.

Prepare journal entries to: record the bond purchase on July 1, 2007; the accrual of interest and the amortization of the bond premium on December 31, 2007 (assume straight-line amortization); and the receipt of interest on January 1, 2008.

E14-18.   **Integration of trading, available-for-sale, and held-to-maturity securities (LG 2, 3, 4, 6)** Listed below are descriptions of four investments in securities held by Jose Company. For each security, (a) identify the investment category: trading, available-for-sale, or held-to-maturity, (b) state whether each security would appear as a current or noncurrent asset on the balance sheet, (c) state the value it would be shown at on the balance sheet on December 31, 2007, (d) state the amount of any unrealized gain or loss on the securities, and (e) state which financial statement the gain or loss in part (d) would appear.

1. On December 15, 2007, Jose purchased $300,000 of 8% IBM bonds which mature in the year 2009. Management intends to hold the bonds for less than one month and sell the bonds at a profit. Juan paid $303,000 for the bonds. The market value on December 31, 2007, is $303,800.

2. On December 20, 2007, Jose purchased $200,000 of 9% Wal-Mart bonds which mature in 2009. Management intends to hold the bonds to maturity. The bonds were purchased at face value and have a market value of $200,900 on December 31, 2007.

3. On November 12, 2007, Jose purchased 1,000 shares of General Electric common stock for $70,000. Management intends to hold the securities for more than one year and sell them when they hopefully double in price next year. At December 31, 2007, the total market value of the stock is $73,400

4. On December 1, 2007, Juan purchased $200,000 of 6% Ford Motor bonds at face value. Management intends to hold the bonds to maturity. The bonds mature in July 2010. At December 31, 2007, the bonds have a market value of $198,900.

E14-19. **Accounting for long-term investment in stock by equity method (LG 5)** Allen Company acquired 6,000 of the 20,000 shares of Iverson stock at book value for $420,000 on January 1, 2007. During 2007, Iverson paid total cash dividends of $40,000 ($10,000 on July 11 and $30,000 on November 14) and reported a net income of $80,000. Record all necessary journal entries for 2007 on the books of Allen Corporation.

E14-20. **Investment in bonds held-to-maturity: straight-line amortization of premium (LG 6)** On January 1, 2007, Bugs Corporation purchased as a long-term investment 12% bonds of Bunny Corporation with a face value of $100,000 at 102. The bonds have a maturity date of January 1, 2017. Bugs will hold the bonds to maturity. The bonds pay interest on January 1 and July 1. Record (a) the purchase of the bonds by Bugs Corporation and (b) all the necessary remaining entries for 2007. Use the straight-line method of amortization.

E14-21. **Investment in bonds held-to-maturity: straight-line amortization of discount (LG 6)** Assume the same information as in Exercise 14-20 except that Bugs Corporation purchased the Bunny Corporation bonds at 99 instead of 102. Prepare all the required entries for 2007. Use the straight-line method of amortization.

E14-22. **Investment in bonds held-to-maturity: effective interest method of amortization (LG 6)** On July 1, 2007, Vegas Corporation purchased as a long-term investment 11%, 10-year bonds of O'Shea Company with a face value of $300,000 for $318,693, which is a price to yield 10% (5% each six months). The bonds pay interest on June 30 and December 31. Maturity date of the bonds is June 30, 2017. Vegas will hold the bonds to maturity. Record the purchase of the bonds on the books of Vegas Corporation. Record the receipt of interest on December 31, 2007, and June 30, 2008, and the amortization of the premium, using the effective interest method.

E14-23. **Investment in bonds held-to-maturity: effective interest method of amortization (LG 6)** On February 1, 2007, the date of authorization, Halifax Corporation acquired as a long-term investment 10-year, 11% bonds of Detroit Company for $678,048, which is a price to yield 9%. The bonds pay interest on February 1 and August 1. The face amount of the bonds is $600,000. Halifax will hold the bonds to maturity.

1. For 2007, prepare journal entries to record: the acquisition of the bonds; receipt of interest on August 1, including amortization of the premium by the effective interest method; and any necessary adjusting entries on December 31 (year-end).

2. For 2008, prepare journal entries to record the receipt of semiannual interest including amortization of the premium by the effective interest method.

E14-24. **Investment in bonds held-to-maturity: purchased between interest dates-straight-line amortization (LG 7)** Rizzo Corporation acquired as a long-term investment on March 1, 2007, Kennedy Company bonds for $130,365 plus accrued interest. The date of authorization is January 1, 2007. The bonds of Kennedy Company have a face value of $150,000 with an interest rate of 12%. The maturity date is January 1, 2027. The bonds pay interest on January 1 and July 1. Rizzo will hold the bonds to maturity.

1. For 2007, record: the acquisition of the bonds; receipt of the interest on July 1, including amortization of the discount by the straight-line method; and any necessary adjusting entries on December 31, 2007 (year-end).

2. For 2008, record receipt of the semiannual interest, including amortization of the discount by the straight-line method.

PROBLEMS

NOTE: In order to clearly show areas of similarity and difference between investment valuation methods, the following problems use common data: (P14-25 and 26) (P14-27 and 28) (P14-29 and 30).

P14-25. **Record and value short-term investments in stocks (trading securities) (LG 2) (See P14-26 for same data as available-for-sale securities)** Tasty Company has a seasonal business that involves baking and selling fruitcakes. The fruitcakes are sold on a national mail-order basis from September through December each year. The company has large amounts of cash to invest on a short-term basis from January through July. It has large uses of cash from August through December. Tasty had the following selected transactions involving short-term investments held as *trading securities* during 2007:

2007		
Feb.	1	Purchased 1,000 shares of Monsanto Company common stock at $50 per share plus a brokerage fee of $500. Management classifies the shares as trading securities.
	9	Purchased 1,500 shares of Pfizer common stock at $60 per share plus a brokerage fee of $800. Management classifies the shares as trading securities.
Mar.	31	The company prepared financial statements for the quarter ending March 31. As of March 31, 2007, Monsanto Company is selling for $46 per share and Pfizer Corporation is selling for $63 per share. Value the securities at market.
Apr.	2	Received cash dividend from Pfizer Corporation of $1.20 per share.
May	21	Sold all of the shares of Pfizer Corporation at $68 less a brokerage fee of $500.
Jun.	30	The company prepared financial statements for the quarter ending June 30. As of June 30, 2007, Monsanto Company is selling for $56 per share. Value the securities at market.

REQUIRED

1. Journalize the transactions on the books of Tasty Company.

2. Compute the total amount of net investment revenue on the short-term investments for the first six months of 2007.

P14-26. **Record and value short-term investments in stocks (available-for-sale securities) (LG 4) (See P14-25 for same data as trading securities)** Assume the same information as in Problem 14-25 with the exception that the common stocks are *available-for-sale* securities instead of trading securities.

REQUIRED

1. Journalize the transactions on the books of Tasty Company.

2. Compute the total amount of net investment revenue on the short-term investments for the first six months of 2007.

P14-27. **Record and value short-term investments in bonds (trading securities) (LG 3) (See P14-28 for same data as available-for-sale securities)** North Philly Company had the following transactions in short-term investments in bonds held as *trading securities* during 2007 and 2008:

2007

Jul.	1	Purchased 12% bonds of Boeing Company with a face value of $800,000 at 96 as a short-term investment. The bonds pay interest on July 1 and January 1 and mature in eight years. Brokerage fees were $2,000. Management classifies the bonds as trading securities.
Dec.	31	Accrued interest on the bonds for six months.
	31	On December 31, 2007, the bonds were selling for 98. Prepare any necessary adjusting entry.

2008

Jan.	1	Recorded receipt of interest for six months.
Feb.	1	Sold all of the bonds for 99 plus accrued interest less a commission of $2,000.

REQUIRED

Journalize the transactions on the books of North Philly Company.

P14-28. **Record and value short-term investments in bonds (available-for-sale securities) (LG 4) (See P14-27 for same data as trading securities)** Assume the same data as in Problem 14-27 except that the bonds are classified as *available-for-sale* securities instead of trading securities.

REQUIRED

Journalize the transactions on the books of North Philly Company.

P14-29. **Record and value long-term investments in stock (equity method) (LG 5) (See P14-30 for same data as market value method)** Larry Company had the following transactions involving long-term investment in the voting common stock of Brown Company in 2007. Larry Company uses the *equity method* to account for the securities.

2007

Jan.	1	Purchased 30,000 of the 100,000 outstanding shares of $5 par value common stock of Brown Company at a total price of $62 per share.
Mar.	5	Received a cash dividend of $2.00 per share on the stock of Brown Company.
Dec.	31	Brown Company common stock is selling for $67 per share on December 31, 2007. For 2007, Brown Company reports a net income of $700,000. Prepare any necessary entries to properly account for the securities under the equity method.

REQUIRED

1. Journalize the transactions on the books of Larry Company.

2. Show how Larry Company should report all accounts related to its long-term investment in Brown Company stock on its 2007 income statement and balance sheet as of December 31, 2007 (both location and amounts).

P14-30. **Record and value long-term investments in stock (market value method) (LG 4) (See P14-29 for same data as equity method)** Assume the same data as in Problem 14-29 except that Larry Company now owns 10% of the voting common stock of Brown Company. Larry Company uses the *market value method* to account for the available-for-sale securities.

2007

Jan.	1	Purchased 10,000 of the 100,000 outstanding shares of $5 par value common stock of Brown Company at a total price of $62 per share.
Mar.	5	Received a cash dividend of $6.00 per share on the stock of Brown Company.
Dec.	31	Brown Company common stock is selling for $67 per share on December 31, 2007. For 2007, Brown Company reports a net income of $900,000. Prepare any necessary entries to properly account for the securities under the market value method. The securities are classified by management as available-for-sale.

REQUIRED

1. Journalize the transactions on the books of Larry Company.

2. Show how Larry Company should report all accounts related to its long-term investment in Brown Company stock on its 2007 income statement and balance sheet as of December 31, 2007 (both location and amounts).

P14-31. **Investment in bonds held-to-maturity: straight-line method of amortization of premium (LG 6)** On June 30, 2007, Tomato Corporation purchased as a long-term investment 10% bonds of Onion Corporation for $378,506, which is a price to yield 9%. The bonds pay interest on June 30 and December 31. The bonds mature on June 30, 2022. The face amount of the bonds purchased is $350,000. Management intends to hold the bonds to maturity.

REQUIRED

Prepare all entries for 2007 and 2008 on the books of Tomato Corporation, except closing entries, using the straight-line method of amortization.

P14-32. **Investment in bonds held-to-maturity: effective interest method of amortization of discount (LG 6)** On February 1, 2007, the date of authorization, Blue Corporation acquired as a long-term investment 20-year, 10% bonds of White Company for $679,629, which is a price to yield 12%. The bonds pay interest on February 1 and August 1, and their face amount is $800,000. Management intends to hold the bonds to maturity.

REQUIRED

Prepare all entries for 2007 and 2008, including adjusting entries December 31 of each year on the books of White Corporation. Do not prepare closing entries. Blue Corporation uses the effective interest method of amortization.

P14-33. **Analyzing information (proper accounting for investments) (LG 8)** You are a loan officer for Bronx Bank considering a loan request from Yankee Company. A partial balance sheet and disclosures on investment securities for Yankee Company are shown below.

YANKEE COMPANY
PARTIAL BALANCE SHEET
DECEMBER 31, 2007
(*in thousands*)

Current assets	Dec. 31, 2007
Cash (including certificates of deposit of $72,000)	$ 80,000
Marketable securities	220,000
Accounts receivable (at gross amount)	346,000
Total current assets	$ 646,000
Investments	
Investments in marketable securities	80,000
Property, plant, and equipment (net of depreciation)	400,000
Total assets	$1,126,000

Notes to Financial Statements: Investment Securities (1) As of December 31, 2007, all certificates of deposit included in "cash and cash equivalents" are held at one local savings bank. The certificates mature in May 2009. There is a significant penalty for early withdrawal. (2) All marketable securities listed as current assets consist of shares of common stock in ChocoChip Company. The shares represent 10% of the total shares outstanding in ChocoChip. The shares were purchased on December 31, 2006, for $220,000. At December 31, 2007, the shares have a market value of $70,000. We intend to sell the shares when the price recovers. The shares are carried at cost because we believe the drop in market value is only temporary. (3) All marketable securities listed as long-term consist of debt securities (available-for-sale). The securities were purchased for $60,000 on March 1, 2007. These securities are carried at market value with unrealized gains and losses included in the income statement for 2007.

REQUIRED

1. As shown, what is the overall percent of total assets held as investments as of December 31, 2007? Do the investments represent a significant portion of total assets?
2. Comment on each specific item involving investments where you believe incorrect accounting or footnote disclosure has occurred. As you identify the problem, briefly explain the correct accounting method or procedure.
3. Prepare a revised partial balance sheet and notes to correct for the errors you observe in part (2).

PRACTICE CASE

Short-term and long-term investments (LG 1-3, 5, 7) Zeppelin Company had the following transactions involving short-term and long-term investments during 2007:

2007

Jan.	1	Purchased 16,000 shares of the 40,000 shares outstanding of Led Company $4 par value common stock at its current book value per share of $7. Brokerage fees were $900. Management intends to hold the shares as a long-term investment and uses the equity method.
Mar.	11	Purchased 400 shares of the 30,000 shares outstanding of Plant Company $2 par value common stock at $11 per share as a short-term investment (trading securities). Brokerage fees were $135.
Jun.	30	Purchased Page Company 12% bonds with a face value of $400,000 and a maturity date of December 31, 2007. The bonds were purchased in the open market at 102 on an interest date. Interest on the bonds is paid semiannually on June 30 and December 31. Zeppelin Company intends to sell the bonds within the next year and considers the bonds as available-for-sale securities.
Nov.	22	Led Company declared and distributed a cash dividend of $0.60 per share on its common shares outstanding.
	27	Plant Company declared and distributed a cash dividend of $0.50 per share on its common shares outstanding.

Dec.	31	Received the semiannual interest on the Page Company bonds.
	31	Led Company reported a net income for 2007 of $50,000. Plant Company reported a net income for 2007 of $30,000.
	31	As of December 31, 2007, the Led Company stock was selling for $8 per share, the Plant company stock was selling for $10 per share, and the Page Company bonds were selling at 103.

Required

Prepare the journal entries to record these transactions.

1. Describe how each of the three investments should be accounted for.

2. Journalize the transactions on the books of Zeppelin Company.

3. Compute the total amount of net investment revenue on the investments for 2007.

BUSINESS DECISION AND COMMUNICATION PROBLEM

Interpretation of equity method for Dow Jones (LG 5, 8) One of your English professors is aware that you are taking an accounting course. Assume that he shows you the following income data and disclosures based on information about Dow Jones (in thousands).

	2007	2006	2005
Income from continuing operations before income taxes and equity in operations of forest products group	$148,364	$223,863	$260,745
Income taxes	64,267	91,830	122,471
Income from continuing operations before equity in operations of forest products group	84,097	132,033	138,274
Equity in operations of forest products group	(15,922)	28,928	17,990
Income from continuing operations	68,175	160,961	156,264

Note 6: Investment in Forest Products Group

The Company has equity interests in three Canadian newsprint companies and a paper manufacturing company operating as a partnership. The equity interests in the three Canadian newsprint companies are: Donohue Malbaie Inc. (49%); Gaspesia Pulp and Paper Company Ltd. (47%); and Spruce Falls Power and Paper Company, Limited (49.5%).

Your professor, Dr. John Papers, asks you to explain what "equity in operations of forest product group" is. Specifically, he wants to know why the equity item is positive in 2005 and 2006, and negative in 2007. Also, he wants to know if equity earnings represent cash receipts for the investor.

REQUIRED

Write a memo to Dr. Papers addressing his questions about the use of the equity method by Dow Jones.

ETHICAL DILEMMA

Valuation of investments (LG 5, 8) You are the chief accountant of Ocean Company. For 2007, the Company faces a projected loss of $2,000,000. Ocean Company owns 10% of the voting common stock of River Company. Ocean Company has been using the market value method to account for the investment in River. Ocean Company lists the shares as a long-term investment in available-for-sale securities. The cost of the securities and the market value has remained stable for the past two years. River does not pay any cash dividends. However, it is highly profitable and expects 2007 income to be $7,000,000.

The president of Ocean Company suggests that it would be more appropriate to use the equity method to account for the investment in River Company. He requests that you change to this method immediately.

REQUIRED

In terms of reported net income or loss for Ocean Company for 2007, what would be the impact of changing to the equity method? Do you feel the equity method is appropriate in this case? Justify your answer.

COMPREHENSIVE ANALYSIS CASE GENERAL MILLS, INC.

Analyzing General Mills, Inc. for the Period 2004-2002 General Mills, Inc. is one of the largest food products companies in the world. Brand items include Bugles, Cheerios, Gold Medal flour, Wheaties, and Betty Crocker cake mixes. Listed below are comparative income statements and balance sheets with common-size percents for 2004-2002 (in millions). Also included are selected ratio statistics. Please provide a brief explanation for your answer to each question.

REQUIRED

Income statement questions:

1. Are total revenues higher or lower over the three-year period?

2. What is the percent change in total revenues from 2002 to 2004?

3. Is the percent of cost of goods sold to total revenues increasing or decreasing over the three-year period? As a result, is the gross margin percent increasing or decreasing?

4. Is the percent of total operating expenses to total revenues increasing or decreasing over the three-year period? As a result, is the operating income percent increasing or decreasing?

5. Is the percent of net income to total revenue increasing or decreasing over the three-year period?

Balance sheet questions:

6. Are total assets higher or lower over the three-year period?

7. What is the percent change in total assets from 2002 to 2004?

8. What are the largest asset investments for the company over the three-year period?

9. Are the largest asset investments increasing faster or slower than the percent change in total revenues?

10. Is the percent of total liabilities to total liabilities + owners' equity increasing or decreasing? As a result, is there more or less risk that the company could not pay its debts?

Integrative income statement and balance sheet question:

11. Is the company operating more or less efficiently by using the least amount of asset investment to generate a given level of total revenues? Note that the "total asset turnover" ratio is computed and included in the "ratio analysis summary."

Ratio analysis questions:

12. Is the *current ratio* better or worse in the most current year compared to prior years?

13. Is the *quick ratio* better or worse in the most current year compared to prior years?

14. Is the *accounts receivable turnover ratio 1* (based on *average* receivables) better or worse in the most current year compared to prior years?

15. Is the 2004 *accounts receivable turnover ratio 2* (based on *year-end* receivables) better or worse than the 2004 ratio based on an *average*?

16. Is the *inventory turnover ratio 1* (based on *average* inventory) better or worse in the most current year compared to prior years?

17. Is the 2004 *inventory turnover ratio 2* (based on *year-end* inventory) better or worse than the 2004 ratio based on an *average*?

18. Is the *return on total assets (ROA) ratio* better or worse in the most current year compared to prior years

GENERAL MILLS, INC.
COMPARATIVE COMMON-SIZE INCOME STATEMENTS
For The Years Ended May 31, 2004, 2003, 2002
(in millions)

	2004 $	2004 %	2003 $	2003 %	2002 $	2002 %
Revenues	$ 11,070.0	100.0%	$ 10,506.0	100.0%	$ 7,949.0	100.0%
Cost of goods sold	$ 6,584.0	59.5%	$ 6,109.0	58.1%	$ 4,662.0	58.6%
Gross margin	$ 4,486.0	40.5%	$ 4,397.0	41.9%	$ 3,287.0	41.4%
Operating expenses:						
Selling, general, and administrative	$ 2,443.0	22.1%	$ 2,472.0	23.5%	$ 2,070.0	26.0%
Other expense	$ 26.0	0.2%	$ 62.0	0.6%	$ 134.0	1.7%
Total operating expenses	$ 2,469.0	22.3%	$ 2,534.0	24.1%	$ 2,204.0	27.7%
Operating income	$ 2,017.0	18.2%	$ 1,863.0	17.7%	$ 1,083.0	13.6%
Net interest expense (income)	$ 508.0	4.6%	$ 547.0	5.2%	$ 416.0	5.2%
Other expense (income), net	$ (74.0)	-0.7%	$ (61.0)	-0.6%	$ (33.0)	-0.4%
Income before income taxes	$ 1,583.0	14.3%	$ 1,377.0	13.1%	$ 700.0	8.8%
Income taxes	$ 528.0	4.8%	$ 460.0	4.4%	$ 239.0	3.0%
Net income (loss) before unusual items	$ 1,055.0	9.5%	$ 917.0	8.7%	$ 461.0	5.8%
Other losses (gains) net of tax	$ -	0.0%	$ -	0.0%	$ -	0.0%
Net income (loss)	$ 1,055.0	9.5%	$ 917.0	8.7%	$ 461.0	5.8%

GENERAL MILLS, INC.
COMPARATIVE COMMON-SIZE BALANCE SHEETS
May 31, 2004, 2003, 2002
(in millions)

	2004 $	2004 %	2003 $	2003 %	2002 $	2002 %
ASSETS						
Current:						
Cash & cash equivalents	$ 751.0	4.1%	$ 703.0	3.9%	$ 975.0	5.9%
Accounts receivable, net	$ 1,010.0	5.5%	$ 980.0	5.4%	$ 1,010.0	6.1%
Inventory	$ 1,063.0	5.8%	$ 1,082.0	5.9%	$ 1,055.0	6.4%
Deferred Income Taxes	$ 169.0	0.9%	$ 230.0	1.3%	$ -	0.0%
Other current assets	$ 222.0	1.2%	$ 184.0	1.0%	$ 397.0	2.4%
Total current assets	$ 3,215.0	17.4%	$ 3,179.0	17.4%	$ 3,437.0	20.8%
Fixed:						
Land, Buildings, and Equipment at cost, net	$ 3,111.0	16.9%	$ 2,980.0	16.3%	$ 2,764.0	16.7%
Intangibles & goodwill	$ 10,325.0	56.0%	$ 10,272.0	56.4%	$ 8,563.0	51.8%
Other assets	$ 1,797.0	9.7%	$ 1,796.0	9.9%	$ 1,776.0	10.7%
Total assets	$ 18,448.0	100.0%	$ 18,227.0	100.0%	$ 16,540.0	100.0%
LIABILITIES						
Current:						
Accounts payable	$ 1,145.0	6.2%	$ 1,303.0	7.1%	$ 1,217.0	7.4%
Current Portion of long-term debt	$ 233.0	1.3%	$ 105.0	0.6%	$ 248.0	1.5%
Notes Payable	$ 583.0	3.2%	$ 1,236.0	6.8%	$ 3,600.0	21.8%
Other current liabilities	$ 796.0	4.3%	$ 800.0	4.4%	$ 682.0	4.1%
Total current liabilities	$ 2,757.0	14.9%	$ 3,444.0	18.9%	$ 5,747.0	34.7%
Long-term debt	$ 7,410.0	40.2%	$ 7,516.0	41.2%	$ 5,591.0	33.8%
Deferred Income Taxes	$ 1,773.0	9.6%	$ 1,661.0	9.1%	$ 407.0	2.5%
Other long-term liabilities	$ 1,260.0	6.8%	$ 1,431.0	7.9%	$ 1,219.0	7.4%
Total liabilities	$ 13,200.0	71.6%	$ 14,052.0	77.1%	$ 12,964.0	78.4%
OWNERS' EQUITY						
Total owners' equity	$ 5,248.0	28.4%	$ 4,175.0	22.9%	$ 3,576.0	21.6%
Total liabilities and owners' equity	$ 18,448.0	100.0%	$ 18,227.0	100.0%	$ 16,540.0	100.0%

(Note: percents may not add to 100 due to rounding)

GENERAL MILLS, INC.
RATIO ANALYSIS SUMMARY
For The Years Ended May 31, 2004, 2003, 2002

	2004	2003	2002
SHORT-TERM LIQUIDITY RATIOS			
Current Ratio (Current Assets/Current Liabilities)	1.17	0.92	0.60
Quick Ratio (Cash + Short-term Investments + Accounts Receivable)/Current Liabilities	0.64	0.49	0.35
Accounts Receivable Turnover 1 (Revenues/Average Accounts Receivable)	11.13	10.56	
Accounts Receivable Turnover 2 (Revenues/Year-end Accounts Receivable)	10.96	10.72	7.87
Inventory Turnover 1 (Cost Goods Sold/Average Inventory)	6.14	5.72	
Inventory Turnover 2 (Cost Goods Sold/Year-end Inventory)	6.19	5.65	4.42
LONG-TERM SOLVENCY (LEVERAGE) RATIO			
Total Debt Ratio (Total Liabilities/Total Assets)	71.55%	77.09%	78.38%
PROFITABILITY RATIOS			
Gross Profit Margin (Gross Margin/Revenues)	40.52%	41.85%	41.35%
Operating Profit Margin (Operating Income/Revenues)	18.22%	17.73%	13.62%
Net Profit Margin (Return on Sales) (ROS) (Net Income/Revenues)	9.53%	8.73%	5.80%
Total Asset Turnover (Revenues/Average Total Assets)	0.60	0.60	
Return on Total Assets (ROA) (Net Income/Average Total Assets)	5.75%	5.28%	

PART

four

REPORTING AND ANALYSIS ISSUES

STATEMENT OF CASH FLOWS

"A goal is a dream with a deadline."

Napoleon Hill

LEARNING GOALS

After studying Chapter 15, you should be able to:

1. Explain the purpose of the statement of cash flows.

2. Classify cash receipts and cash payments as operating, investing, or financing activities in the statement of cash flows.

3. Analyze business transactions to determine their cash flows.

4. Compute the amount of net cash provided by (used in) operating activities using the direct method.

5. Compute the amount of net cash provided by (used in) operating activities using the indirect method.

6. Explain the steps used to prepare a statement of cash flows.

7. Prepare a statement of cash flows using the direct method to report cash provided by (used in) operating activities.

8. Interpret information in the statement of cash flows to assess management performance.

9. Prepare a statement of cash flows using the indirect method to report cash provided by (used in) operating activities.

UNDERSTANDING BUSINESS ISSUES

In the preceding chapters we emphasize only three of the four basic financial statements. The income statement shows the results of operations for a period of time. The statement of retained earnings reconciles the beginning balance of retained earnings to the ending balance. The balance sheet shows the status of the financial resources of the company and the claims on those resources as of a specific date. However, these three financial statements do not explain all of the changes in the financial resources of the firm during a period of time.

To keep operating, a business spends and receives cash in three basic ways: (1) operating activities (selling goods or providing services), (2) investing activities (such as acquiring and selling plant assets), and (3) financial activities (such as borrowing money and issuing stock). The **statement of cash flows**, a fourth major financial statement, reports the cash provided and used by these *operating*, *investing*, and *financing* activities.

Having information about the cash receipts and cash payments of an entity during a period of time is important to users of financial statements. Information about a firm's cash inflows and outflows helps investors, creditors, and others to do the following:

1. Assess its ability to generate operating cash flows.

2. Assess its sources and uses of cash from investing transactions.

3. Assess its ability to pay bills as they come due, pay dividends, and obtain additional financing.

Chapter 15 begins with a description of the purpose and content of the statement of cash flows. Then we illustrate the steps needed to prepare this statement. In addition, we *interpret* the information contained in the statement to point out its managerial uses.

THE STATEMENT OF CASH FLOWS: ITS PURPOSE AND CONTENT

Learning Goal 1   Explain the purpose of the statement of cash flows.

The primary purpose of a statement of cash flows is to provide information about the cash receipts and cash payments of an entity during a period of time.[1] The statement of cash flows also helps us to see how the financial position (shown in the balance sheet) *changes* during an accounting period. Exhibit 15.1 shows how the statement of cash flows fits in with the other financial statements. The statement of cash flows uses the information shown in the other financial statements. However, it is the only statement that collects and shows in one statement the causes of changes in cash during a financial reporting period.

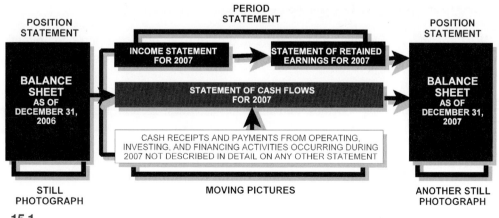

EXHIBIT **15.1**

Relationship Among the Major Financial Statements

---

[1] *Statement of Financial Accounting Standards (SFAS) No. 95*, "Statement of Cash Flows" (Norwalk, Conn.: Financial Accounting Standards Board, November 1987), paragraph 4.

We use the information shown on the statement of cash flows to assess the *cash flows* of the entity's activities. The following questions are examples of situations where information about cash flows would be helpful:

1. Why is there a difference between net income on the income statement (computed on an accrual accounting basis) and net cash flow from operating activities?

2. How has the firm generated the cash necessary to pay dividends?

3. How has the firm financed the purchase of plant assets?

4. In what ways has the firm obtained external financing?

5. Why has the balance in cash increased or decreased from one balance sheet date to another?

Cash And Cash Equivalents

One of the goals in preparing the statement of cash flows is to explain the increase or decrease in cash during the accounting period. Generally accepted accounting principles (GAAP) require that a statement of cash flows explain the change during the period in *cash and cash equivalents*. **Cash** includes not only currency on hand but also *demand deposits* with banks and other financial institutions. **Cash equivalents** are short-term, highly liquid investments that have *both* of the following features:

1. They must be readily convertible to known amounts of cash.

2. They must be so near their maturity that they are not likely to change in value due to changes in interest rates.[2]

Generally, only investments a company purchases with maturities of three months or less at the time of purchase are cash equivalents. For example, a three-year Treasury note we purchase as an investment three months from maturity qualifies as a cash equivalent. However, a Treasury note we purchase as an investment three years ago does *not* become a cash equivalent when its remaining maturity reaches three months.

Classification of Cash Receipts and Cash Payments

Learning Goal 2   Classify cash receipts and cash payments as operating, investing, or financing activities in the statement of cash flows.

The statement of cash flows classifies cash receipts and cash payments into three categories: operating activities, investing activities, and financing activities. Exhibit 15.2 contains guidelines for classifying cash flows and examples of each kind of activity.

Operating activities include producing or delivering goods for sale and providing services. Cash flows from operating activities generally include the cash receipts and payments from transactions that are part of net income.

Investing activities include (1) acquiring and selling plant assets, (2) acquiring and selling securities not considered cash equivalents, and (3) lending money and collecting on the principal amount of these loans. It is important to note that *FASB Statement No. 95* specifies that we must show interest and dividend receipts and interest payments as operating activities instead of investing activities. The reason for this is that we use these cash flows to

---

[2] *SFAS No. 95*, paragraph 8.

help determine net income on the income statement. Therefore, we classify them as operating activities.

Financing activities include (1) obtaining resources from owners and providing them with a return on their investment (dividend payments) and a return *of* their investment (buying treasury stock), and (2) obtaining resources from creditors and repaying the principal amounts borrowed. Unlike interest payments to creditors, dividend payments to owners do not appear on the income statement. Thus, we classify them as a financing activity rather than an operating activity.

Activity	Guidelines	Examples
Operating	Transactions that generally involve producing and delivering goods and providing services.	Cash *inflows* from: selling goods, providing services, dividend revenue, interest revenue. Cash *outflows* for: inventory, salary expense, tax expense, interest expense, other expenses.
Investing	1. Buying and selling plant assets. 2. Buying and selling securities that are not cash equivalents. 3. Making loans and collecting on them.	Cash *inflows* from: sale of plant assets, sale of investment securities, collection of loans made by the entity. Cash *outflows* for: purchasing plant assets, purchasing investment securities, lending funds to others.
Financing	1. Obtaining resources from owners and providing a return. 2. Obtaining resources from creditors and repaying principal amounts owed.	Cash *inflows* from: selling stock; issuing bonds, notes, mortgages; and other short-term and long-term borrowing. Cash *outflows* for: purchasing treasury stock, repaying principal on borrowings, cash dividends.

EXHIBIT **15.2**

Classification of Activities in the Statement of Cash Flows

Gross And Net Cash Flows

Generally, information about the *gross* amounts of cash receipts and cash payments is more relevant than information about the *net* amounts. Therefore, we report *separately* the investing and financing activities that provide *both* cash receipts and cash payments. For example, a company may issue new long-term debt to retire maturing debt. Under financing activities we report the cash proceeds from new issuances of long-term debt separately from cash payments for maturing debt issues.

Noncash Investing And Financing Activities

Some investing and financing activities affect assets or liabilities on the balance sheet but do not result in cash receipts or cash payments. We call these items **noncash investing and financing activities**. Examples of such transactions include acquiring plant assets by issuing notes payable to the seller of the plant asset and converting bonds payable into common stock. To show *all* investing and financing activities, we need to disclose *noncash transactions*. We may report noncash transactions either as notes or as a supplemental schedule to the statement of cash flows.

INTRODUCTION TO PREPARING AND INTERPRETING STATEMENTS OF CASH FLOWS

Accountants use different methods to obtain the information that appears in the statement of cash flows. To introduce the preparation of the statement of cash flows, this section analyzes the summary transactions of Expo Company during its first year of operations. We will prepare the income statement, the statement of retained earnings, the balance sheet, and the statement of cash flows at the end of the first year. Our focus will be on the *relationships* between these four financial statements.

Transactions of Expo Company During 2007

Expo Company began operations on January 1, 2007. Summary transactions for the year ended December 31, 2007, are as follows:

1. Issued for cash on January 1, 2007, 50,000 shares of $5 par value stock at $5 per share.

2. Rented a building on January 1, 2007. Paid rent in advance for the next 18 months. The monthly rental fee is $3,000.

3. Purchased machinery costing $80,000 on January 1, 2007, for cash. The machinery has an estimated useful life of eight years, and there is no estimated residual value. Expo uses the straight-line depreciation method.

4. Purchased merchandise inventory on account during 2007 totaling $200,000. Expo Company uses a perpetual inventory system. Payments on account during the year total $130,000.

5. Sold merchandise on account during 2007 totaling $280,000. The cost of the merchandise was $150,000. Collections of trade accounts receivable during 2007 totaled $100,000.

6. Salaries expense for 2007 totaled $50,000. Of this amount, Expo paid $46,000 in cash during 2007.

7. Paid income taxes of $12,000 in cash during 2007.

8. Declared and paid a cash dividend of $5,000 on the common stock during 2007.

Journal Entries to Record Expo Company Transactions

Exhibit 15.3 shows the journal entries to record the summary transactions for Expo Company during 2007. Adjusting entries, where necessary, follow the related transaction item.

2007

1.	Cash		250,000	
	Common Stock			250,000
	To record the issuance of 50,000 shares of $5 par value stock at $5 per share.			
2a.	Prepaid Rent		54,000	
	Cash			54,000
	To record payment in advance for rent of $3,000 per month for 18 months.			
b.	Rent Expense		36,000	
	Prepaid Rent			36,000
	To record expiration of rent for 12 months.			
3a.	Machinery		80,000	
	Cash			80,000
	To record purchase of machinery for cash.			
b.	Depreciation Expense—Machinery		10,000	
	Accumulated Depreciation—Machinery			10,000
	To record depreciation for 12 months.			
4a.	Merchandise Inventory		200,000	
	Accounts Payable			200,000
	To record purchase of merchandise on account.			
b.	Accounts Payable		130,000	
	Cash			130,000
	To record payment of accounts payable.			
5a.	Accounts Receivable		280,000	
	Sales			280,000
	To record sales of merchandise on account.			
b.	Cost of Goods Sold		150,000	
	Merchandise Inventory			150,000
	To record cost of merchandise sold.			
c.	Cash		100,000	
	Accounts Receivable			100,000
	To record collections of accounts receivable.			
6a.	Salaries Expense		50,000	
	Salaries Payable			50,000
	To record salary expense for the year.			
b.	Salaries Payable		46,000	
	Cash			46,000
	To record payment of salaries.			
7.	Income Tax Expense		12,000	
	Cash			12,000
	To record payment of income tax expense.			
8.	Dividends—Common Stock		5,000	
	Cash			5,000
	To record declaration and payment of cash dividend.			

EXHIBIT **15.3**

General Journal of Expo Company: Summary of Entites for the Year Ended December 31, 2007

Cash Flow Analysis of Transactions

Learning Goal 3 Analyze business transactions to determine their cash flows.

Exhibit 15.4 shows the cash flow impact of each transaction of Expo Company. It also classifies each transaction as an operating, investing, or financing activity. As you study each journal entry, ask yourself, "What is the impact on cash?" For example, transaction 1 involves the sale of common stock. It results in an *inflow* of cash of $250,000. We classify this transaction as a financing activity on the statement of cash flows.

The cash flow analysis of transaction 2 shows a cash *outflow* of $54,000 for prepayment of rent. Therefore, $54,000 will appear as a cash outflow under operating activities on the statement of cash flows. This is in contrast to how much rent expired ($36,000), which appears as an expense on the income statement.

The purchase of the machinery in transaction 3a involves a cash *outflow* of $80,000. The statement of cash flows will show this transaction as an investing activity. Transaction 3b shows the recording of

Transaction	Cost Flow Impact	Classification
1.	Cash *inflow* of $250,000 from sale of common stock.	Financing activity
2.	Cash *outflow* of $54,000 for rent payment for 18 months.	Operating activity (operating expense)
3.	Cash *outflow* of $80,000 for purchase of machinery.	Investing activity
	Depreciation is an operating expense that does not result in a cash outflow.	Does not affect cash
4.	Cash *outflow* of $130,000 for payments to suppliers.	Operating activity (cost of sales)
5.	Cash *inflow* of $100,000 from collections from customers.	Operating activity (sales revenue)
6.	Cash *outflow* of $46,000 for salaries paid.	Operating activity (operating expense)
7.	Cash *outflow* of $12,000 for income taxes paid.	Operating activity (operating expense)
8.	Cash *outflow* of $5,000 for cash dividends paid.	Financing activity (return to owners)

EXHIBIT **15.4**

Cash Flow Analysis of Transactions for Expo Company for 2007

$10,000 of depreciation expense. Depreciation expense is an example of a *noncash expense*. Recognizing this expense does not involve an outflow of cash, as entry 3b makes clear. This amount appears as a deduction on the income statement to compute net income. However, we do not deduct it to compute net cash from operating activities, since there is no inflow or outflow of cash from the company. The cash outflow for the machinery occurs when we buy the asset. Carefully study each event journalized in Exhibit 15.3. Relate each transaction to the cash flow analysis in Exhibit 15.4

Preparing The Financial Statements

Exhibit 15.5 shows all of Expo Company's financial statements for 2007. Since Expo Company began operations on January 1, 2007, all beginning balance sheet balances would be zero. Thus, the balances on the December 31, 2007, balance sheet also represent *changes in the accounts* during 2007. This will be important when we analyze cash flows during 2007 in the next section. We show interconnecting arrowsand keyed items in Exhibit 15.5 to point out these relationships. We discuss these in the next section. During its first year of operations, Expo Company earned a net income of $22,000 (computed on an accrual accounting basis). We transfer the net income to retained earnings (arrow **A**). After deducting cash dividends of $5,000, the ending balance in retained earnings is $17,000. We show this amount on the statement of retained earnings and on the ending balance sheet (arrow **B**). As of December 31, 2007, the total assets and total liabilities and stockholders' equity on the balance sheet are each $341,000.

Analysis of Expo Company's Cash Flows

We have keyed the explanations of the cash flows of Expo Company to the numbered arrows in Exhibit 15.5. We also show journal entry reference numbers from Exhibit 15.3. At this point in the chapter, the easiest way to see the cash flow effect of a transaction is simply to look at the debit or credit to Cash in the journal entry. In the following cash flow explanations, we also show the cash flow effects by discussing the relationship between income statement and balance sheet accounts.

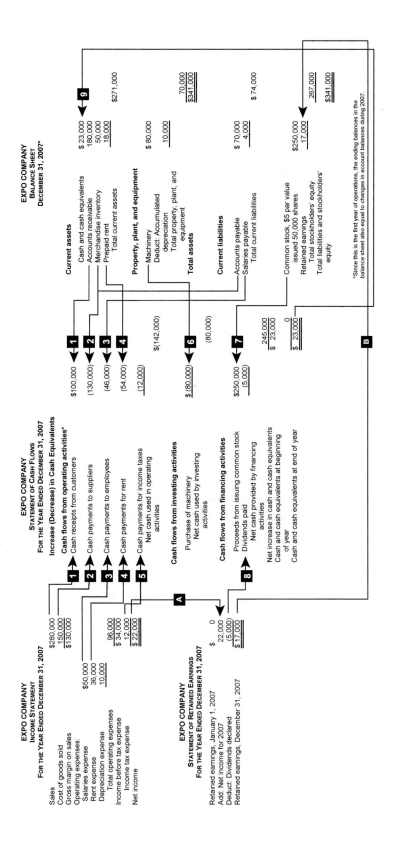

EXPO COMPANY
INCOME STATEMENT
FOR THE YEAR ENDED DECEMBER 31, 2007

Sales		$280,000
Cost of goods sold		150,000
Gross margin on sales		$130,000
Operating expenses:		
Salaries expense	$50,000	
Rent expense	36,000	
Depreciation expense	10,000	
Total operating expenses		96,000
Income before tax expense		$ 34,000
Income tax expense		12,000
Net income		$ 22,000

EXPO COMPANY
STATEMENT OF RETAINED EARNINGS
FOR THE YEAR ENDED DECEMBER 31, 2007

Retained earnings, January 1, 2007	$ 0
Add: Net income for 2007	22,000
Deduct: Dividends declared	(5,000)
Retained earnings, December 31, 2007	$17,000

EXPO COMPANY
STATEMENT OF CASH FLOWS
FOR THE YEAR ENDED DECEMBER 31, 2007

Increase (Decrease) in Cash Equivalents

Cash flows from operating activities*

Cash receipts from customers		$100,000
Cash payments to suppliers		(130,000)
Cash payments to employees		(46,000)
Cash payments for rent		(54,000)
Cash payments for income taxes		(12,000)
Net cash used in operating activities		$(142,000)

Cash flows from investing activities

Purchase of machinery		$ (80,000)
Net cash used by investing activities		(80,000)

Cash flows from financing activities

Proceeds from issuing common stock		$250,000
Dividends paid		(5,000)
Net cash provided by financing activities		245,000
Net increase in cash and cash equivalents		$ 23,000
Cash and cash equivalents at beginning of year		0
Cash and cash equivalents at end of year		$ 23,000

EXPO COMPANY
BALANCE SHEET
DECEMBER 31, 2007*

Current assets

Cash and cash equivalents		$ 23,000
Accounts receivable		180,000
Merchandise inventory		50,000
Prepaid rent		18,000
Total current assets		$271,000

Property, plant, and equipment

Machinery	$ 80,000	
Deduct: Accumulated depreciation	10,000	
Total property, plant, and equipment		70,000
Total assets		$341,000

Current liabilities

Accounts payable		$ 70,000
Salaries payable		4,000
Total current liabilities		$ 74,000
Common stock, $5 par value issued 50,000 shares		$250,000
Retained earnings		17,000
Total stockholders' equity		267,000
Total liabilities and stockholders' equity		$341,000

*Since this is the first year of operations, the ending balances in the balance sheet also equal to changes in account balances during 2007.

Cash Flows from Operating Activities

Accrual Income Effect	Cash Flow Effect
1 Sales are $280,000 *(transaction 5a)*.	Cash receipts from customers are $100,000 *(transaction 5c)*.
	Accounts receivable increased from $0 to $180,000. This increase means that Expo Company did not collect $180,000 of its sales. Thus, the cash receipts from customers for 2007 are only $100,000 ($280,000 - $180,000). The uncollected accounts receivable appear on the ending balance sheet.
2 Cost of goods sold is $150,000 *(transaction 5b)*.	Cash payments to suppliers are $130,000 *(transaction 4b)*.
	To get cash payments to suppliers, we must combine changes in Merchandise Inventory and Accounts Payable with cost of goods sold. Since Merchandise Inventory increased from $0 to $50,000 we bought $50,000 more than we sold. However, since Accounts Payable increased from $0 to $70,000, we did not pay for all of the purchases. Thus, cash payments to suppliers are $130,000 ($150,000 + 50,000 - $70,000).
3 Salaries expense is $50,000 *(transaction 6a)*.	Cash payments to employees are $46,000 *(transaction 6b)*.
	Salaries payable increased from $0 to $4,000. This means that Expo incurred but did not pay $4,000 of salaries. Thus cash payments to employees are $46,000 ($50,000 - $4,000).
4 Rent expense is $36,000 *(transaction 2b)*.	Cash payments for rent are $54,000 *(transaction 2a)*.
	Prepaid rent increased from $0 to $18,000. This means that in addition to the rent expense of $36,000, Expo Company paid $18,000 in cash for rent during 2007.
5 Income tax expense is $12,000 *(transaction 7)*.	Cash payments for income taxes are $12,000 *(transaction 7)*.
	Expo Company's income tax expense for 2007 was equal to the amount paid in cash.

Cash Flows from Investing Activities

6 Purchases of machinery *(transaction 3a)*.	During 2007, Expo made an investing cash outflow of $80,000 for the purchase of new machinery. The depreciation of the machinery during 2007 ($10,000) is a noncash expense. Thus, the depreciation entry in transaction 3b has no effect on cash.

Cash Flows from Financing Activities

7 Proceeds from issuing common stock *(transaction 1)*.	During 2007, the issue of stock provided a financing cash inflow of $250,000.
8 Payment of cash dividend *(transaction 8)*.	The payment of the cash dividend was a financing cash outflow of $5,000.

Cash and Cash Equivalents at End of Year

9 Since there was no beginning cash balance, the ending cash balance is equal to the net increase in cash of $23,000 during 2007. This net increase in cash was a result of (1) net cash *used in* operating activities of $142,000 (2) net cash *used in* operating activities of $142,000, (2) net cash *used by* investing activities of $80,000, and (3) net cash *provided by* financing activities of $245,000.

Interpreting the Statement of Cash Flows

Question. Overall, how successful has management been in generating and investing cash flows during the year? Specifically: (1) How does accrual basis net income compare with cash basis net income? (2) What cash uses have been made for investing activities and to what extent has cash from operations been sufficient to pay for these investments? (3) What sources and uses have been generated from financing activities?

Answer. Expo Company reported a net income on its income statement of $22,000 during 2007. However, the statement of cash flows shows that net cash *used* in operating activities is $142,000. This points out the high demand for cash during Expo's start-up period. These demands came from the need to finance increases in accounts receivable, prepaid expenses, and the initial investment in merchandise inventory. The investment in machinery during 2007 caused an additional cash out-flow. Many new companies fail during this critical time because they do not have enough cash to get through the start-up period.

Expo financed operating and investing activities during 2007 by the sale of common stock, which provided a cash inflow of $250,000. Dividend payments decreased this amount by $5,000. The excess of the net cash provided by financing activities ($245,000) over the net cash used in operating and investing activities ($222,000) resulted in a net increase of $23,000 in the cash balance at the end of 2007.

Expo Company survived its first year of operations. However, it will need to monitor its cash inflows and outflows carefully during 2008. Expo should be concerned that it collected only $100,000 of the $280,000 in sales during 2007. The timely collection of the $180,000 of accounts receivable on the balance sheet is important to the survival of the company. Management should examine credit and sales terms of the company.

At this point in Chapter 15, your instructor may assign Exercises E15-18 through E15-20 and Problems P15-32 and P15-33. These exercises and problems will reinforce your understanding of key cash flow concepts *before* we explain in detail how to prepare the statement of cash flows. Three end-of-chapter Business Decision and Communication problems focus on interpreting cash flows for Microsoft, Nike, and Oracle.

DIRECT VERSUS INDIRECT METHODS OF REPORTING CASH FLOWS FROM OPERATING ACTIVITIES

FASB Statement No. 95 permits companies to use either the direct method or the indirect method to report cash from operating activities. We explain both methods in this section.

The Direct Method

Learning Goal 4   Compute the amount of net cash provided by (used in) operating activities using the direct method.

Exhibit 15.5 shows the net cash flows from operating activities during 2007 for Expo Company using the direct method. Under the **direct method**, we show the major classes of gross cash receipts (for example, cash receipts from customers) and gross cash payments (for example, cash payments to suppliers) under cash flows from operating activities. The difference is the net cash provided by, or used in, operating activities.

FASB Statement No. 95 encourages, but does not require, companies to use the direct method to report cash flows from operating activities. Companies that choose not to use the direct method should determine and report the cash provided by (used in) operating activities by the *indirect* method, discussed later.

Illustration of the Direct Method

The goal of the direct method is to convert each income statement item from an accrual-basis amount to a cash-basis amount. The steps in this process are as follows:

1. Identify the balance sheet account(s) that relate to each item on the income statement.

2. Combine the *change* in these related balance sheet accounts during the period with the income statement item to find the cash flow.

The balance sheet accounts that relate to income statement items are current assets and current liabilities. For example, the change in Accounts Receivable relates to the Sales account. If Accounts Receivable increases during the period, the company did not collect all of this period's sales. Thus, cash receipts from customers (cash-basis sales revenue) is less than accrual-basis sales revenue.

Exhibit 15.6 shows the general approach to computing the cash flows from each income statement item. The exhibit summarizes the methods that we used in the Expo Company example in the previous section. For example, look at cash receipts from customers. It is equal to:

$$\text{Sales} \begin{cases} + \text{ Decrease in accounts receivable} \\ \\ - \text{ Increase in accounts receivable} \end{cases}$$

For Expo Company, sales for 2007 were $280,000 and accounts receivable increased by $180,000. Therefore, the cash receipts from customers during 2007 are as follows:

Sales	-	Increase in Accounts Receivable	=	Cash Receipts from Customers
$280,000	-	$180,000	=	$100,000

We can also use a T account for Accounts Receivable to show the computation of cash receipts from customers as follows (The bold face shows the amount that we need to solve for and is unknown to start out.):

Accounts Receivable			
Balance, 1/1/07	0		
Sales, 2007	280,000	**Cash receipts from customers, 2007**	**100,000**
Balance, 12/31/07	180,000		

We can find the cash payments to suppliers in a similar way. Here we need to know the cost of goods sold and information on changes in two balance sheet accounts, Merchandise Inventory and Accounts Payable. For Expo Company, cost of goods sold for 2007 was $150,000. Merchandise Inventory increased by $50,000 and Accounts Payable increased by $70,000. From the formula in Exhibit 15.6 cash payments to suppliers are as follows:

Cost of Goods Sold	+	Increase in Inventory	-	Increase in Accounts Payable	=	Cash payments to Suppliers
$150,000	+	$50,000	-	$70,000	=	$130,000

We can use T accounts to show the computation of cash payments to suppliers in a two-step process. First, we compute purchases of merchandise during 2007 by looking at the Merchandise Inventory account as follows:

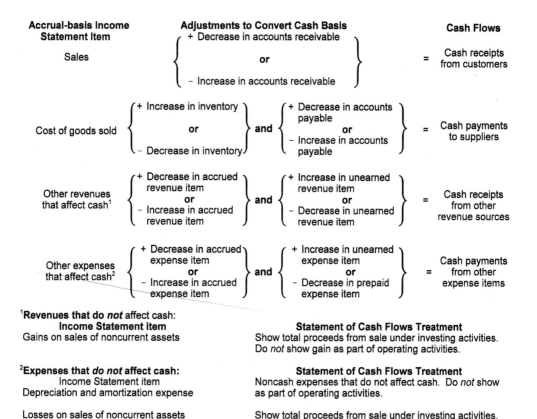

Accrual-basis Income Statement Item	Adjustments to Convert Cash Basis		Cash Flows
Sales	+ Decrease in accounts receivable or − Increase in accounts receivable		= Cash receipts from customers
Cost of goods sold	+ Increase in inventory or − Decrease in inventory	and	+ Decrease in accounts payable or − Increase in accounts payable	= Cash payments to suppliers
Other revenues that affect cash[1]	+ Decrease in accrued revenue item or − Increase in accrued revenue item	and	+ Increase in unearned revenue item or − Decrease in unearned revenue item	= Cash receipts from other revenue sources
Other expenses that affect cash[2]	+ Decrease in accrued expense item or − Increase in accrued expense item	and	+ Increase in unearned expense item or − Decrease in prepaid expense item	= Cash payments from other expense items

[1]**Revenues that do *not* affect cash:**

Income Statement item	Statement of Cash Flows Treatment
Gains on sales of noncurrent assets	Show total proceeds from sale under investing activities. Do *not* show gain as part of operating activities.

[2]**Expenses that *do not* affect cash:**

Income Statement item	Statement of Cash Flows Treatment
Depreciation and amortization expense	Noncash expenses that do not affect cash. Do *not* show as part of operating activities.
Losses on sales of noncurrent assets	Show total proceeds from sale under investing activities. Do *not* show loss as part of operating activities.

EXHIBIT **15.6**

Direct Method:General Approach Computing Cash Provided by (Used in) Operating Activites

Merchandise Inventory			
Balance, 1/1/07	0		
Purchases, 2007	**200,000**	Cost of goods sold, 2007	150,000
Balance, 12/31/07	50,000		

Here, inventory increased during 2007. Therefore, Expo purchased more goods than it sold. We add the increase in inventory to cost of goods sold to compute purchases.

Second, we compute cash payments to suppliers by using the purchases amount to reconstruct the Accounts Payable account as follows:

Accounts Payable			
		Balance, 1/1/07	0
Cash payments to		Purchases, 2007,	
suppliers, 2007	**130,000**	from above	200,000
		Balance, 12/31/07	70,000

Since accounts payable increased, cash payments to suppliers by Expo Company were less than the purchases amount. We subtract the increase in accounts payable from purchases to compute cash payments.

We compute the cash flows of other revenues and expenses in a similar manner using Exhibit 15.6 as a guide. Exhibit 15.6 also shows the treatment of revenue and expense items that do not affect cash. Exhibit 15.7 uses the general approach in Exhibit 15.6 to compute the cash flows of

Accrual-basis Income Statement Item		Adjustments to Convert to Cash Basis			Cash Flows	
Sales	$ 280,000	– $180,000	(Increase in accounts receivable)	=	$ 100,000	Cash receipts from customers
Cost of goods sold	$ 150,000	+ $ 50,000 – $ 70,000	(Increase in inventory) (Increase in accounts payable)	=	$ 130,000	Cash payments to suppliers
Salaries expense	50,000	– $ 4,000	(Increase in salaries payable)	=	46,000	Cash payments to employees
Rent expense	36,000	+ $ 18,000	(Increase in prepaid rent)	=	54,000	Cash payment for rent
Depreciation expense	10,000		Noncash expense	=	0	
Tax expense	12,000		No change in related balance sheet account.	=	12,000	Cash payments for income taxes
Total expenses	$ 258,000				$ 242,000	
Net income	$ 22,000				$ (142,000)	Net cash used in operating activities

EXHIBIT 15.7

Direct Method: Computation of Net Cash Used in Operating Activities for Expo Company for 2007

---

each revenue and expense item for Expo Company for 2007. The amount of cash used in operating activities ($142,000) is the same amount shown in Exhibit 15.5

Indirect Method

Learning Goal 5   Compute the amount of net cash provided by (used in) operating activities using the indirect method.

The **indirect method** starts with net income or net loss on the income statement. It then adjusts it for revenues and expenses that did not cause changes in cash in the current period. The resulting figure is net cash provided by (used in) operating activities.

Both the direct and indirect methods result in the same total for net cash provided by (used in) operating activities. The direct method is easy to understand and shows each source and use of operating cash flow individually. Under the indirect method, the financial statement user can see the process that we use to reconcile net income to net cash flow from operations.

The FASB encourages the use of the direct method. However, it believes that the reconciliation of net income to net cash flow from operating activities is useful information. Therefore, if companies use the direct method of reporting net operating cash flow, they must also show the indirect method reconciliation.[3] This section on the indirect method has two purposes: to show (1) how we can use the indirect method alone if needed and (2) how to use the indirect method for the reconciliation included on the direct-method statement of cash flows as required by the FASB.

Illustration of the Indirect Method

The objective of the indirect method is to reconcile accrual net income to net cash provided by (used in) operating activities. Two steps are necessary in this reconciliation:

1. Adjust accrual net income for *noncash charges and credits to operations*.

2. Adjust accrual net income for changes in *operating current assets and liabilities that provide or require cash* Exhibit 15.8 illustrates the general approach for the indirect method.

Step 1.   Adjustments For Noncash Charges And Credits
Noncash charges to operations and **noncash credits to operations** are deductions or additions on the income statement that do not cause a cash inflow or outflow. For example,

---

[3] *SFAS No. 95*, paragraph 29.

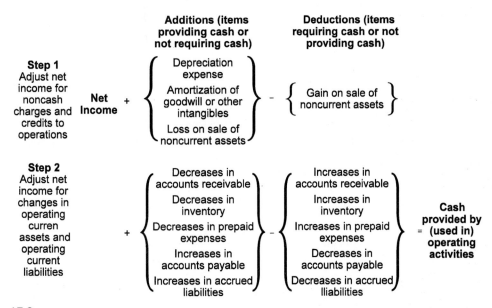

EXHIBIT 15.8

Indirect Method: General Approach-Reconciling Net Income to Cash Provided by (Used in) Operating Activities

depreciation expense is a deduction on the income statement. However, it does not require any payment of cash. Instead, the company pays cash when it acquires the asset.

For Expo Company in 2007, the only noncash charge is the $10,000 depreciation expense. We deducted this amount in computing net income of $22,000. Since deducting depreciation on the income statement reduces net income but does not require the use of cash, we add it back to net income in the indirect method. This simply reverses the effect of deducting it on the income statement.

Step 2. Adjustments For Operating Current Assets And Operating Current Liabilities

Operating current assets and **operating current liabilities** are current asset and current liability accounts that *relate* to revenues and expenses shown on the income statement. Expo Company has the following changes in current asset and current liability accounts other than cash and cash equivalents during 2007:

Account	Changes in Account Balance	
	Increase	Decrease
Accounts Receivable	$180,000	
Merchandise inventory	50,000	
Prepaid Rent	18,000	
Accounts Payable	70,000	
Salaries Payable	4,000	

We analyze the cash effects of the changes in each current asset and current liability account as follows:

Accounts Receivable

The increase in accounts receivable during 2007 means that cash collections from customers were less than accrual-basis sales revenue. This means that cash income is less than accrual income.

Therefore, the increase in accounts receivable represents an item not providing cash. We deduct the $180,000 from net income to convert it to a cash basis.

Merchandise Inventory

The increase in the Merchandise Inventory account means that we used some purchases to increase ending inventory instead of selling them. Therefore, purchases were greater than cost of goods sold on the accrual-basis income statement. The increase in Merchandise Inventory requires the use of cash. We deduct the $50,000 from net income to convert it to a cash basis.

Prepaid Rent

The increase in Prepaid Rent means that the cash payments for rent were greater than accrual-basis rent expense. Therefore, the increase in Prepaid Rent represents an item requiring the use of cash. We deduct the $18,000 from net income to convert it to a cash basis.

Accounts Payable

The increase in Accounts Payable means that cash payments for merchandise purchased were less than accrual-basis purchases. Therefore, the increase in Accounts Payable represents an item not requiring cash. We add the $70,000 to net income to convert it to a cash basis.

Salaries Payable

The increase in Salaries Payable means that cash payments for salaries were less than accrual-basis salaries expense. Therefore, the increase in Salaries Payable represents an item not requiring cash. We add the $4,000 to net income to convert it to a cash basis.

Indirect Method For Expo Company For 2007

Exhibit 15.9 illustrates the reconciliation of net income to net cash provided by (used in) operating activities for Expo Company using the indirect method. The amount of net cash used in operating activities under the indirect method ($142,000) is the same as under the direct method. At this point, you should compare the direct method (Exhibit 15.7 with the indirect method (Exhibit 15.9).

Cash flows from operating activities		
Net income		$ 22,000
Add: Items providing cash or not requiring cash:		
Depreciation expense (*noncash expense*)	$ 10,000	
Increase in accounts payable (*cash payments for purchases less than accrual-basis purchases*)	70,000	
Increase in salaries payable (*cash payment for salaries less than accrual-basis expense*)	4,000	
Deduct: Items requiring cash or not providing cash:		
Increase in accounts receivable (*cash collections less than accrual-basis sales revenue*)	(180,000)	
Increase in merchandise inventory (*purchases on an accrual-basis greater than cost of goods sold*)	(50,000)	
Increase in prepaid rent (*cash payments for rent greater than accrual-basis expense*)	(18,000)	
Total adjustments		(164,000)
Net cash used in operating activities		$(142,000)

EXHIBIT **15.9**

Indirect Method: Reconciliation of Net Income to Net Cash Used in Operating Activities, Expo Company, 2007

STEPS IN PREPARING THE STATEMENT OF CASH FLOWS

Learning Goal 6   Explain the steps used to prepare a statement of cash flows.

In this section, we show step-by-step how to prepare the statement of cash flows. We will use data for Expo Company during its second year of operations. By analyzing the changes in account balances from two **comparative balance sheets** (balance sheets prepared as of the end of two succeeding periods), we will determine the sources and uses of cash.

Gathering the Information: Income Statement and Comparative Balance Sheet Accounts For Expo Company

Exhibit 15.10 shows the income statement for the second year of operations (2008) for Expo Company. Sales revenue in 2008 is $360,000 and net income is $34,000. Exhibit 15.11 shows comparative balance sheet account balances as of December 31, 2008 and 2007, and additional information concerning changes in account balances.

Step 1. **Compute the Net Change in Cash and Cash Equivalents** The first step in preparing the statement of cash flows is to find the net change in cash and cash equivalents during the first year. From the comparative balance sheets in Exhibit 15.11 we can see that, as of December 31, 2008, the balance in cash and cash equivalents is $76,000. This is an increase of $53,000 from the December 31, 2007, balance. One goal of the statement of cash flows is to explain the reasons for the increase.

Step 2. **Compute the Amount of Net Cash Provided by (Used in) Operating Activities by the Direct Method** Exhibit 15.12 shows the cash flow for each accrual-basis revenue and expense item for Expo Company in 2008. We use the general approach for the direct method from Exhibit 15.6 For 2008, net cash provided by operations is $71,000. The increase in cash provided by operating activities in 2008 is mainly due to an increase in collections of receivables. Therefore, sales on cash basis ($404,000) is greater than sales on an accrual basis ($360,000). This is a positive sign for the firm's management.

EXPO COMPANY
INCOME STATEMENT
FOR THE YEAR ENDED DECEMBER 31, 2008

Sales		$ 360,000
Cost of goods sold		193,000
Gross margin on sales		$ 167,000
Operating expenses:		
Salaries expense	$ 70,000	
Rent expense	36,000	
Depreciation expense	10,000	
Total operating expenses		116,000
Net operating income		$ 51,000
Other expenses:		
Loss on sale of machinery		1,000
Net income before tax expense		$ 50,000
Income tax expense		16,000
Net income		$ 34,000

EXHIBIT **15.10**

Income statement For Expo Company For 2008

EXPO COMPANY
COMPARATIVE BALANCE SHEET ACCOUNTS
DECEMBER 31, 2008 AND 2007

	December 31		Increase or
Debit Accounts	**2008**	**2007**	**(Decrease)**
Cash and Cash Equivalents	$ 76,000	$ 23,000	$ 53,000
Accounts Receivable	136,000	180,000	(44,000)
Merchandise Inventory	70,000	50,000	20,000
Prepaid Rent	9,000	18,000	(9,000)
Land	122,000	0	122,000
Machinery	110,000	80,000	30,000
Totals	$ 523,000	$ 351,000	$ 172,000
Credit Accounts			
Accumulated Depreciation—Machinery	$ 15,000	$ 10,000	$ 5,000
Accounts Payable	60,000	70,000	(10,000)
Salaries Payable	7,000	4,000	3,000
12% Bonds Payable	100,000	0	100,000
Common Stock, $5 par	300,000	250,000	50,000
Retained Earnings	41,000	17,000	24,000
Totals	$ 523,000	$ 351,000	$ 172,000

Additional Information

a. During 2008, purchased land for $122,000 in cash for use as a future plant site. Construction will begin in 2009.

b. On December 31, 2008, sold for $14,000 machinery costing $20,000 with accumulated depreciation of $5,000.

c. On December 31, 2008, purchased machinery for $50,000 by issuing 10,000 shares of common stock at par value.

d. Depreciation expense for 2008 is $10,000.

e. Declared and paid cash dividends of $10,000 on the common stock during 2008.

f. On December 31, 2008, issued for cash 12% bonds at 100 with a face value of $100,000. The bonds mature in 10 years. The bonds pay interest annually on December 31.

g. Net income for 2008 is $34,000.

EXHIBIT **15.11**

Comparative Balance Sheet Accounts and Additional Information for Expo Company for 2008

Accrual-basis Income Statement Item		Adjustments to Convert to Cash Basis		Cash Flows	
Sales	$ 360,000	+ $ 44,000 (Decrease in accounts receivable)	=	$ 404,000	Cash receipts from customers
Cost of goods sold	$ 193,000	+ $ 20,000 (Increase in inventory) + $ 10,000 (Decrease in accounts payable)	=	$ 223,000	Cash payments to suppliers
Salaries expense	70,000	– $ 3,000 (Increase in salaries payable)	=	67,000	Cash payments to employees
Rent expense	36,000	– $ 18,000 (Decrease in prepaid rent)	=	27,000	Cash payment for rent
Depreciation expense	10,000	Noncash expense	=	0	
Loss on sale of machinery	1,000	Noncash expense	=	0	
Tax expense	16,000	No change in related balance sheet account	=	16,000	Cash payments for income taxes
Total expenses	$ 326,000			$ 333,000	
Net income	$ 34,000			$ 71,000	Net cash used in operating activities

EXHIBIT **15.12**

Direct Method: Computations of Net Cash Provided by Operating Activities for Expo Company for 2008

Step 3. Prepare the Reconciliation of Net Income to Net Cash Provided by (Used In) Operating Activities by the Indirect Method

Exhibit 15.13 shows the computation of net cash provided by operations for Expo Company for 2008 using the indirect method. Under the indirect method we start with the net income figure and convert it to cash provided by (used in) operating activities. We use the general approach illustrated in Exhibit 15.8 for the indirect method. (You may wish to refer back to that exhibit.) We show explanatory comments in Exhibit 15.13 to help your understanding. The cash provided by operating activities ($71,000) is the same as for the direct approach in Exhibit 15.12.

Cash flows from operating activities

Net income		$ 34,000
Add: Items providing cash or not requiring cash:		
Depreciation expense (*noncash expense*)	$ 10,000	
Loss on sale of machinery (*noncash charge to operations*)	1,000	
Decrease in accounts receivable (*cash collections greater than accrual-basis revenue*)	44,000	
Decrease in prepaid rent (*cash payments for rent less than accrual-basis expense*)	9,000	
Increase in salaries payable (*cash payments for salaries less than accrual-basis expense*)	3,000	
Deduct: Items requiring cash or not providing cash:		
Increase in merchandise inventory (*purchases on accrual-basis greater than cost of goods sold*)	(20,000)	
Decrease in accounts payable (*cash payments for purchases greater than accrual-basis purchases*)	(10,000)	
Total adjustments		37,000
Net cash provided by operating activities		$ 71,000

EXHIBIT **15.13**

Indirect Method: Reconciliation of Net Cash Provided by Operating Activities for Expo Company for 2008

Step 4.   Compute the Amount of Net Cash Provided by (Used By) Investing and Financing Activities

To find the net cash provided by (used by) investing and financing activities, we must analyze all changes in remaining balance sheet accounts. For Expo Company in 2008, we did not explain the following changes in account balances as a part of cash flows from operating activities:

	Changes in Account Balance	
Account	**Increase**	**Decrease**
Land	$122,000	
Machinery	30,000	
Accumulated Depreciation—Machinery	5,000	
12% Bonds Payable	100,000	
Common Stock, $5 par	50,000	
Retained Earnings	24,000	

Notice that the accounts remaining are noncurrent. We have already explained the changes in the current accounts in computing cash from operating activities. We now analyze the reasons for changes to each noncurrent account to calculate the cash flow impact of each item.

Exhibit 15.14 shows the analysis of noncurrent accounts. We key the explanations of additional information to the lettered items in Exhibit 15.11. As we analyze the change in each noncurrent account, we determine its cash flow impact. For example, the increase in the Land account during 2008 is due to an investing cash outflow of $122,000 to purchase a future plant site.

Analyzing the cash impact of sales of noncurrent assets at gains or losses is sometimes difficult. The journal entry recording the sale provides a helpful hint. The entry for item (b) is as follows:

2008				
Dec.	31	Cash	14,000	
		Accumulated Depreciation—Machinery	5,000	
		Loss on Sale of Machinery	1,000	
		Machinery		20,000
		To record sale of machinery with a book value of $15,000 ($20,000 - $5,000) for cash proceeds of $14,000.		

Noncurrent Account			Cash Flow Impact		
	Increase	Decrease	Account Change	Cash Inflow/Outflow	Classification
Land	$ 122,000		(a) + $ 122,000	Cash *outflow* of $122,000 to purchase land.	Investing activity
Machinery	30,000		(b) − $ 20,000	Cash *inflow* for machinery sold equal to $14,000 proceeds on sale.	Investing activity
			(c) + $ 50,000	Purchase of machinery by exchange of common stock.	Noncash investing and financing activity
Accumulated Depreciation— Machinery		5,000	(b) − $ 5,000	Decrease due to write-off accompanying sale. *No cash flow impact.*	Does not affect cash
			(d) + $ 10,000	Increase by depreciation expense for 2008. *No cash flow impact.*	Does not affect cash
12% Bonds Payable	100,000		(f) + $ 100,000	Cash *inflow* of $100,000 from issuing bonds.	Financing activity
Common Stock, $5 par	50,000		(c) + $ 50,000	Issue common stock in exchange for machinery.	Noncash investing and financing activity
Retained Earnings	24,000		(e) − $ 10,000	Cash *outflow* of $10,000 for payment of dividends.	Financing activity
			(g) + $ 34,000	Net income for 2008.	Already used to compute cash from operating activities

EXHIBIT **15.14**

Cash Flow Analysis of Noncurrent Accounts: Expo Company for 2008

Step 5. Preparing The Statement of Cash Flows

Learning Goal 7   Prepare a statement of cash flows using the direct method to report cash provided by (used in) operating activities.

We combine the cash flows from operating, investing, and financing activities to form the statement of cash flows. Exhibit 15.15 shows this statement. We show a reconciliation of

EXPO COMPANY
STATEMENT OF CASH FLOWS
FOR THE YEAR ENDED DECEMBER 31, 2008

Increase (Decrease) in Cash and Cash Equivalents

Cash flows from operating activities:		
Cash receipts from customers	$ 404,000	
Cash payments to suppliers	(223,000)	
Cash payments to employees	(67,000)	
Cash payment for rent	(27,000)	
Cash payments for income taxes	(16,000)	
Net cash provided by operating activities		$ 71,000
Cash flows from investing activities:		
Purchase of land	$ (122,000)	
Proceeds from sale of machinery	14,000	
Net cash used by investing activities		(108,000)
Cash flows from financing activities:		
Proceeds of bonds payable	$ 100,000	
Dividends paid	(10,000)	
Net cash provided by financing activities		90,000
Net increase in cash and cash equivalents		$ 53,000
Cash and cash equivalents at beginning of year		23,000
Cash and cash equivalents at end of year		$ 76,000
Reconciliation of net income to net cash provided by operating activities		
Net income		$ 34,000
Add: Items providing cash or not requiring cash:		
Depreciation expense	$ 10,000	
Loss on sale of machinery	1,000	
Decrease in accounts receivable	44,000	
Decrease in prepaid rent	9,000	
Increase in salaries payable	3,000	
Deduct: Items requiring cash or not providing cash:		
Increase in merchandise inventory	(20,000)	
Decrease in accounts payable	(10,000)	
Total adjustments		37,000
Net cash provide by operating activities		$ 71,000
Supplemental schedule of noncash investing and financing activities		
Common stock issued for machinery acquired		$ 50,000

EXHIBIT **15.15**

Statement of Cash Flows for Expo Company (Direct Method Used to Compute Cash Flows from Operating Activities)

net income to cash provided by operating activities using the indirect method in a supplemental schedule. The issuance of common stock for machinery is a noncash investing and financing activity. We show this separately at the bottom of the statement of cash flows.

Analysis of the 2008 Statement of Cash Flows for Expo Company

Exhibit 15.16 shows the relationships between the financial statements for 2008. The explanations are keyed to the numbered items in Exhibit 15.16.

1. Sales for 2008 on an accrual basis were $360,000. The decrease of $44,000 in accounts receivable during 2008 means that cash collections from customers were greater than sales on an accrual basis. Therefore, the operating cash *inflow* from sales on a cash basis for 2008 was $404,000.

2. Cost of goods sold on an accrual basis was $193,000. However, cash payments to suppliers were $30,000 greater due to the use of $20,000 of cash to increase the ending merchandise inventory balance and $10,000 to decrease the ending balance in accounts payable. Therefore, the operating cash *outflow* for purchases of merchandise inventory in 2008 was $223,000.

3. Salaries expense on an accrual basis was $70,000 during 2008. The increase in salaries payable of $3,000 during the year means that we paid out less cash for salaries than we recognized as expense. Therefore, the operating cash *outflow* for salaries during 2008 was $67,000.

4. Rent expense on an accrual basis was $36,000 during 2008. Since the balance in Prepaid Rent decreased by $9,000 during the year, Expo paid out less cash for rent than it recognized as rent expense. Therefore, the operating cash *outflow* for rent during 2008 was $27,000.

5. Income tax expense on an accrual basis was $16,000 during 2008. Since Expo paid this amount in cash, the operating cash *outflow* for income taxes in 2008 was $16,000.

6. During 2008, Expo made an investing cash *outflow* of $122,000 to purchase land.

7. During 2008, Expo sold machinery with a book value of $15,000 at a loss of $1,000. The cash received is an investing cash *inflow* of $14,000.

8. During 2008, the issuance of bonds provided a financing cash *inflow* of $100,000.

9. During 2008, Expo made a financing cash *outflow* of $10,000 for cash dividend payments to owners.

10. The net increase in cash and cash equivalents of $53,000 during 2008 is a result of (1) net cash provided by operating activities of $71,000, (2) net cash used by investing activities of $108,000, and (3) net cash provided by financing activities of $90,000.

11. The common stock Expo issued is for machinery, a noncash investing and financing activity. The statement of cash flows shows this in a separate schedule at the bottom.

Interpretation of the 2008 Statement of Cash Flows for Expo Company

Learning Goal 8   Interpret information in the statement of cash flows to assess management performance.

Question. Overall, how successful has management been in generating and investing cash flows during the year? Specifically: (1) How does accrual basis net income compare with cash basis net income? (2) What cash uses have been made for investing activities and to what extent has cash from operations been sufficient to pay for these investments? (3) What sources and uses have been generated from financing activities?

Answer. A comparison of the income statements for Expo Company for 2007 and 2008 reveals increases in sales and gross margin on sales of 29%. These results show that the company was able not only to increase sales revenue but also control cost of goods sold. The increase in net income was 55%.

The statement of cash flows for 2008, in Exhibit 15.15, shows that net cash provided by operating activities was $71,000, compared to accrual net income of $34,000. The excess of operating cash flows over reported net income in 2008 is in contrast to the results for 2007. In 2007, income was $22,000 and net cash used in operating activities was ($142,000). The increase in operating cash flows in 2008 is primarily because Expo reduced its balance in Accounts Receivable from $180,000 to $136,000 during the year. Overall, the results reveal that Expo Company was able to increase sales and net income during 2008. Expo also made progress toward reducing levels of accounts receivable.

In addition to a cash flow from operating activities in 2008, the major source of cash was the proceeds obtained from the issuance of bonds payable, $100,000. During 2008, the major use of cash was the $122,000 for the acquisition of land. The excess of net cash inflows from operating and financing activities ($71,000 + $90,000) over net cash outflows from investing activities ($108,000) resulted in a net increase in cash and cash equivalents of $53,000.

Although Expo Company has made progress in reducing levels of accounts receivable during 2008, the balance outstanding still is large (about four months' sales). Expo should monitor and speed up collections even further. Additional cash concerns include the cash necessary for construction of a plant scheduled to start in 2009 and the payment of annual bond interest expense on bonds issued in 2008.

INDIRECT METHOD OF REPORTING CASH FLOWS FROM OPERATING ACTIVITIES ILLUSTRATED FOR EXPO COMPANY

Learning Goal 9   Prepare a statement of cash flows using the indirect method to report cash provided by (used in) operating activities.

As discussed previously, the FASB allows companies to report cash provided by (used in) operating activities under either the direct or indirect methods. The statement of cash flows for 2008 for Expo Company in Exhibit 15.15 uses the direct method. Exhibit 15.17 shows the complete statement of cash flows using the indirect method for operating activities. The difference between the direct method and indirect method is the format used to compute net cash provided by (used in) operating activities. The *total* amounts shown from operating, investing, and financing activities and the format for investing and financing activities remains the same. When companies report the net cash flows from operating activities using the indirect method, a supplemental reconciliation of net income to net cash provided by operating activities is not necessary. The statement itself serves as the reconciliation.

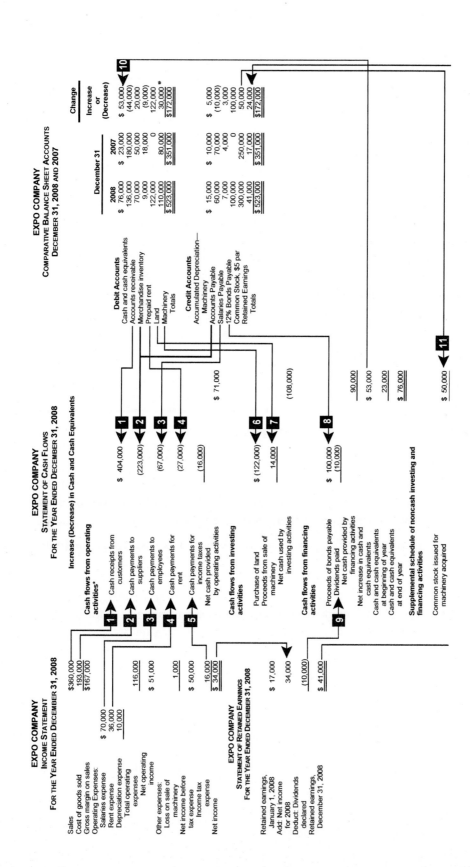

EXPO COMPANY
INCOME STATEMENT
FOR THE YEAR ENDED DECEMBER 31, 2008

Sales		$360,000
Cost of goods sold		193,000
Gross margin on sales		$167,000
Operating Expenses:		
Salaries expense	$ 70,000	
Rent expense	36,000	
Depreciation expense	10,000	
Total operating expenses		116,000
Net operating income		$ 51,000
Other expenses:		
Loss on sale of machinery		1,000
Net income before tax expense		$ 50,000
Income tax expense		16,000
Net income		$ 34,000

EXPO COMPANY
STATEMENT OF RETAINED EARNINGS
FOR THE YEAR ENDED DECEMBER 31, 2008

Retained earnings, January 1, 2008		$ 17,000
Add: Net income for 2008		34,000
Deduct: Dividends declared		(10,000)
Retained earnings, December 31, 2008		$ 41,000

EXPO COMPANY
STATEMENT OF CASH FLOWS
FOR THE YEAR ENDED DECEMBER 31, 2008

Increase (Decrease) in Cash and Cash Equivalents

Cash flows from operating activities*		
Cash receipts from customers	$ 404,000	
Cash payments to suppliers	(223,000)	
Cash payments to employees	(67,000)	
Cash payments for rent	(27,000)	
Cash payments for income taxes	(16,000)	
Net cash provided by operating activities		$ 71,000
Cash flows from investing activities		
Purchase of land	$ (122,000)	
Proceeds from sale of machinery	14,000	
Net cash used by investing activities		(108,000)
Cash flows from financing activities		
Proceeds of bonds payable	$ 100,000	
Dividends paid	(10,000)	
Net cash provided by financing activities		90,000
Net increase in cash and cash equivalents		$ 53,000
Cash and cash equivalents at beginning of year		23,000
Cash and cash equivalents at end of year		$ 76,000

Supplemental schedule of noncash investing and financing activities

Common stock issued for machinery acquired	$ 50,000

EXPO COMPANY
COMPARATIVE BALANCE SHEET ACCOUNTS
DECEMBER 31, 2008 AND 2007

	December 31		Change Increase or (Decrease)
	2008	**2007**	
Debit Accounts			
Cash and cash equivalents	$ 76,000	$ 23,000	$ 53,000
Accounts receivable	136,000	180,000	(44,000)
Merchandise inventory	70,000	50,000	20,000
Prepaid rent	9,000	18,000	(9,000)
Land	122,000	0	122,000
Machinery	110,000	80,000	30,000 *
Totals	$ 523,000	$ 351,000	$172,000
Credit Accounts			
Accumulated Depreciation— Machinery	$ 15,000	$ 10,000	$ 5,000
Accounts Payable	60,000	70,000	(10,000)
Salaries Payable	7,000	4,000	3,000
12% Bonds Payable	100,000	0	100,000
Common Stock, $5 par	300,000	250,000	50,000
Retained Earnings	41,000	17,000	24,000
Totals	$ 523,000	$ 351,000	$172,000

EXPO COMPANY
STATEMENT OF CASH FLOWS
FOR THE YEAR ENDED DECEMBER 31, 2008
Increase (Decrease) in Cash and Cash Equivalents

Cash flows from operating activities:		
Net income		$ 34,000
Add: Items providing cash or not requiring cash:		
Depreciation expense	$ 10,000	
Loss on sale of machinery	1,000	
Decrease in accounts receivable	44,000	
Decrease in prepaid rent	9,000	
Increase in salaries payable	3,000	
Deduct: Items requiring cash or not providing cash:		
Increase in merchandise inventory	(20,000)	
Decrease in accounts payable	(10,000)	
Total adjustments		37,000
Net cash provided by operating activities		$ 71,000
Cash flows from investing activities:		
Purchase of land	$ (122,000)	
Proceeds from sale of machinery	14,000	
Net cash used by investing activities		(108,000)
Cash flows from financing activities:		
Proceeds of bonds payable	$ 100,000	
Dividends paid	(10,000)	
Net cash provided by financing activities		90,000
Net increase in cash and cash equivalents		$ 53,000
Cash and cash equivalents at beginning of year		23,000
Cash and cash equivalents at end of year		$ 76,000
Supplemental schedule of noncash investing and financing activities		
Common stock issued for machinery acquired		$ 50,000

EXHIBIT **15.17**

Statement of Cash Flows for Expo Company (Indirect Method Used to Compute Cash Flows from Operating Activities)

LEARNING GOALS REVIEW

1. Explain the purpose of the statement of cash flows.

The primary purpose of a statement of cash flows is to provide relevant information about the cash receipts and payments of an entity during a period of time. The statement also shows how the financial position of the entity has changed during the accounting period. It is the only financial statement that shows the causes of changes in cash during a reporting period. It helps users assess the cash consequences of the entity's activities.

2. Classify cash receipts and cash payments as operating, investing, or financing activities in the statement of cash flows.

Operating activities include producing or delivering goods for sale and providing services. Related cash inflows include payments for selling goods and providing services, dividend income, and interest income. Related cash outflows include payments for inventories, salaries, taxes, and interest.

Investing activities include acquiring and selling plant assets, acquiring and selling securities not considered cash equivalents, and lending money and collecting on the principal amount of the loans. Related cash inflows come from the sale of plant assets or investment securities and the collection of loans made by the entity. Related cash outflows go for the purchase of plant assets and investment securities, and loans made by the entity.

Financing activities include obtaining resources from owners and providing them with a return on and of their investment, and obtaining resources from creditors and repaying the principal amounts borrowed. Related cash inflows come from the sale of capital stock and the issuance of bonds, notes, mortgages, and other borrowings. Related cash outflows go to purchase treasury stock, repay the principal on borrowings, and pay cash dividends.

3. Analyze business transactions to determine their cash flows.

We analyze each transaction to determine (1) whether it is an inflow or outflow of cash and

(2) whether it is an operating, investing, or financing activity. We must analyze transactions involving revenues and expenses to determine the cash flows of each transaction as opposed to the accrual-based revenue or expense amount. Expenses such as depreciation do not involve an outflow of cash. We do not include them in the computation of cash flows from operating activities. We illustrate a cash flow analysis of individual business transactions in Exhibits 15-3 and 15-4.

4. **Compute the amount of net cash provided by (used in) operating activities using the direct method.**

   Under the direct method, we show the major classes of gross cash receipts and gross cash payments under cash flows from operating activities. The difference between these receipts and payments is the net cash provided by or used in operating activities. We adjust each income statement item to convert it to the cash basis. Sales must be increased by any decrease in accounts receivable or decreased by any increase in accounts receivable. Cost of goods sold requires two adjustments. First, it is increased by increases in inventory or decreased by decreases. Second, it is increased by decreases in accounts payable or decreased by increases. Exhibit 15.6 shows a generalized approach for the direct method.

5. **Compute the amount of net cash provided by (used in) operating activities using the indirect method.**

   The indirect method starts with net income or net loss as reported on the income statement. We then adjust it for revenues and expenses that did not cause changes in cash in the current period. The first step is to make adjustments for noncash charges and credits. The next step is to make adjustments for changes in operating current assets and operating current liabilities. The resulting figure is net cash provided by (used in) operating activities. Exhibit 15.8 shows a general approach for the indirect method.

6. **Explain the steps used to prepare a statement of cash flows.**

   The first step in preparing a statement of cash flows is to compute the net change in cash and cash equivalents. Second, using the direct method, we compute the amount of net cash provided by (used in) operating activities. The third step is to use the indirect method to prepare the reconciliation of net income to net cash provided by (used in) operating activities. Fourth, we compute the amounts of net cash provided by (used by) investing and financing activities. This requires analyzing all remaining changes in balance sheet accounts that an operating activity did not explain. The last step is to prepare the statement of cash flows.

7. **Prepare a statement of cash flows using the direct method to report cash provided by (used in) operating activities.**

   The first part of the statement of cash flows shows the items causing the increase (or decrease) in cash and cash equivalents. This includes the cash flows from operating activities, the cash flows from investing activities, and the cash flows from financing activities. We compute the net increase (or decrease) in cash and cash equivalents. Then we add the cash and cash equivalents at the beginning of the accounting period to compute the cash and cash equivalents at the end of the accounting period. The next part of the statement of cash flows contains a reconciliation of net income to net cash provided by operating activities using the indirect method. A supplemental schedule shows any noncash investing and financing activities.

8. **Interpret information in the statement of cash flows to assess management performance.**

   Specific questions we may ask are: (1) How does accrual basis net income compare with cash basis net income? (2) What cash uses have been made for investing activities and to what extent has cash from operations been sufficient to pay for these investments? (3) What sources and uses have been generated from financing activities?

9. **Prepare a statement of cash flows using the indirect method to report cash provided by (used in) operating activities.**

The indirect method is the same as the direct method except for the way we show net cash provided by (used in) operating activities. The format for the indirect method starts with net income or loss and then adjusts it to net cash provided by operating activities. Because this method serves as a reconciliation of net income to net cash provided by operating activities, it requires no supplemental reconciliation.

DEMONSTRATION PROBLEM

Statement of Cash Flows

Data of Morrison Company follow:

MORRISON COMPANY
COMPARATIVE BALANCE SHEET ACCOUNTS
DECEMBER 31, 2007 AND 2006

	December 31	
Debit Accounts	**2007**	**2006**
Cash and Cash Equivalents	$ 48,000	$ 52,000
Accounts Receivable	92,000	55,000
Merchandise Inventory	42,000	46,000
Land	15,000	0
Machinery	90,000	74,000
Totals	$ 287,000	$ 227,000
Credit Accounts		
Accumulated Depreciation—Machinery	$ 18,000	$ 10,000
Accounts Payable	35,000	29,000
Rent Payable	4,000	6,000
Bonds Payable (due 2010)	50,000	0
Common Stock ($1 par value)	115,000	100,000
Retained Earnings	65,000	82,000
Totals	$ 287,000	$ 227,000

MORRISON COMPANY
INCOME STATEMENT
FOR THE YEAR ENDED DECEMBER 31, 2007

Sales		$300,000
Cost of goods sold		180,000
Gross margin on sales		$120,000
Operating expenses:		
Salaries expense	$74,000	
Rent expense	45,000	
Depreciation expense—machinery	12,000	
Total operating expenses		131,000
Net operating loss		$ (11,000)
Other income:		
Gain on sale of machinery		2,000
Net loss		$ (9,000)

Additional Information

a. Morrison Company sold machinery that cost $8,000, on which $4,000 in depreciation had accumulated, for $6,000.

b. Additional purchases of machinery for $24,000 during the year were for cash.

c. Depreciation expense for 2007 was $12,000.

d. On December 31, 2007, Morrison issued bonds payable at par value in the amount of $50,000 for cash.

e. On December 31, 2007, Morrison issued additional shares of common stock at par value in exchange for land valued at $15,000.

f. Cash dividends declared and paid during the year were $8,000.

g. Morrison had a net loss of $9,000 for 2007.

REQUIRED

1. (LG 2-7) Prepare a statement of cash flows for 2007. Use the direct method to report cash provided by (used in) operations within the statement of cash flows. Include a reconciliation of net income to net cash provided by (used in) operating activities by the indirect method. Use the following steps:

- **Step 1: Compute the net change in cash and cash equivalents.**

- **Step 2: Compute the amount of net cash provided by (used in) operating activities by the direct method.**

- **Step 3: Prepare the reconciliation of net income to net cash provided by (used in) operating activities by the indirect method.**

- **Step 4: Compute the amount of net cash provided by (used by) investing and financing activities.**

- **Step 5: Prepare the statement of cash flows.**

2. (LG 9) Prepare a statement of cash flows for 2007 using the indirect approach to report cash provided by (used in) operations.

3. (LG 8) Prepare a brief interpretation of the statement of cash flows for 2007 that comments on the major sources and uses of cash.

SOLUTION

Requirement 1
Step 1

Solution Approach

During 2007, cash and cash equivalents decreased by $4,000. One of the objectives of the statement of cash flows is to explain the reasons for this decrease.

	December 31		Changes in Cash and Cash Equivalents	
	2007	**2006**	**Increase**	**Decrease**
Cash and cash equivalents	$48,000	$52,000		$4,000

Step 2

Solution Approach

This step involves converting each income statement item from an accrual basis to a cash basis. A general approach for this process is presented in Exhibit 15.6. The following schedule follows the calculation format in Exhibit 15.12. It shows the computation of the cash flows of each revenue and expense item on the income statement.

DIRECT METHOD: COMPUTATION OF NET CASH PROVIDED BY (USED IN) OPERATING ACTIVITIES

Accrual-basis Income Statement Item		Adjustments to Convert to Cash Basis		Cash Flows	
Sales	$300,000	− $ 37,000	(Increase in accounts receivable)	= $263,000	Cash receipts from customers
Cost of goods sold	$180,000	− $ 4,000	(Decrease in inventory)	= $170,000	Cash payments to suppliers
		− $ 6,000	(Increase in accounts payable)		
Salaries expense	74,000		No change in related Balance sheet account.	= 74,000	Cash payments to employees
Rent expense	45,000	+ $ 2,000	(Decrease in rent payable)	= 47,000	Cash payments for rent
Depreciation expense	12,000		Noncash expense	= 0	
Gain on sale of machinery	(2,000)		Noncash revenue	= 0	
Total expenses	$309,000			$291,000	Net cash used in
Net loss	$ (9,000)			$ (28,000)	operating activities

Computation of Cash Provided by (used in) Operating Activities
Cash flows from operating activities

Cash receipts from customers	$ 263,000
Cash payments to suppliers	(170,000)
Cash payments to employees	(74,000)
Cash payments for rent	(47,000)
Net cash used in operating activities	$ (28,000)

Step 3

Solution Approach

When we use the direct method to report cash provided by (used in) operating activities, *FASB Statement No. 95* requires that we show a reconciliation of net income to net cash flow from operations. We use the indirect method to convert net income from an accrual basis to a cash basis. We present a general approach for this process in Exhibit 15.8 In the computation below, note that the amount of cash used in operations ($28,000) is the same as the amount under the direct method. The indirect method can serve as a useful check on the computation of cash from operating activities.

Reconciliation of Net Income in Net Cash Provided by Operating Activities

Net loss		$ (9,000)
Add: Items providing cash or not requiring cash		
Depreciation expense—machinery	$ 12,000	
Decrease in merchandise inventory	4,000	
Increase in accounts payable	6,000	
Deduct: Items requiring cash or not providing cash:		
Gain or sale of machinery	(2,000)	
Increase in accounts receivable	(37,000)	
Decrease in rent payable	(2,000)	
Total adjustments		(19,000)
Net cash used in operating activities		$ (28,000)

Step 4

Solution Approach

To determine the cash flows from investing and financing activities, we must explain all remaining changes in balance sheet accounts that have not been explained in Step 2. The following changes in account balances were *not* explained as a part of cash flow from operating activities in Step 2:

Account	Changes in Account Balance	
	Increase	Decrease
Land	$ 15,000	
Machinery	16,000	
Accumulated Depreciation—Machinery	8,000	
Bonds Payable	50,000	
Common Stock ($1 par)	15,000	
Retained Earnings		$ 17,000

Solution Approach

The following schedule presents an analysis of each noncurrent account change in order to determine its treatment on the statement of cash flows.

CASH FLOW ANALYSIS OF NONCURRENT ACCOUNTS

Noncurrent Account			Cash Flow Impact*		Classification
	Increase	Decrease	Account Change	Cash inflow/Outflow	
Land	$ 15,000		(e) + $ 15,000	Purchase land in exchange For common stock	Noncash investing and financing activity
Machinery	16,000		(a) – $ 8,000	Cash *inflow* for machinery sold equal to $6,000 proceeds on sale.	Investing activity
			(b) + $ 24,000	Cash *outflow* to purchase machinery	Investing activity
Accumulated Depreciation— Machinery	8,000		(a) – $ 4,000	Decrease due to write-off accompanying sale. No cash flow impact.	Does not affect cash
			(c) + $ 12,000	Increase by depreciation expense for 2007. No cash flow impact.	Does not affect cash
Bonds Payable (Due 2010)	50,000		(d) + $ 50,000	Cash *inflow* of $50,000 from issuing bonds.	Financing activity
Common Stock ($1 par value)	15,000		(e) + $ 15,000	Issue common stock in exchange for land.	Noncash investing and financing activity.
Retained Earnings		$ 17,000	(f) – $ 8,000	Cash *outflow* of $8,000 for payment of dividends.	Financing activity
			(g) – $ 9,000	Net loss for 2007.	Already used to compute cash from operating activities.

*Explanations are keyed to additional information in demonstration problem.

Summary of Cash Flows from Investing and Financing Activities

Cash flows from investing activities
Purchase of machinery ... $ (24,000)
Proceeds from sale of machinery ... 6,000
Net cash used by investing activities ... $ (18,000)

Cash flows from financing activities
Proceeds from issuance of bonds ... $ 50,000
Dividends paid ... (8,000)
Net cash provided by financing activities ... $ 42,000

Noncash investing and financing activity
Common stock issued for land ... $ 15,000

Step 5

Solution Approach

The cash flows from operating, investing, and financing activities are combined to form a statement of cash flows. Noncash investing and financing activities are shown in a separate schedule.

MORRISON COMPANY
STATEMENT OF CASH FLOWS
FOR THE YEAR ENDED DECEMBER 31, 2007

Increase (Decrease) in Cash and Cash Equivalents

Cash flows from operating activities		
Cash receipts from customers	$ 263,000	
Cash payments to suppliers	(170,000)	
Cash payments to employees	(74,000)	
Cash payments for rent	(47,000)	
Net cash used in operating activities		$ (28,000)
Cash flows from investing activities		
Purchase of machinery	$ (24,000)	
Proceeds from sale of machinery	6,000	
Net cash used by investing activities		$ (18,000)
Cash flows from financing activities		
Proceeds from issuance of bonds	$ 50,000	
Dividends paid	(8,000)	
Net cash provided by financing activities		42,000
Net decrease in cash and cash equivalents		$ (4,000)
Cash and cash equivalents at beginning of year		52,000
Cash and cash equivalents at end of year		$ 48,000
Reconciliation of Net Income to Net Cash Provided by Operating Activities		
Net loss		$ (9,000)
Add: Items providing cash or not requiring cash:		
Depreciation expense—machinery	$ 12,000	
Decrease in merchandise inventory	4,000	
Increase in accounts payable	6,000	
Deduct: Items requiring cash or not providing cash:		
Gain on sale of machinery	(2,000)	
Increase in accounts receivable	(37,000)	
Decrease in rent payable	(2,000)	
Total adjustments		(19,000)
Net cash used in operating activities		$ (28,000)
Supplemental Schedule of Noncash Investing and Financing Activities		
Common stock issued in exchange for land		$ 15,000

Requirement 2

Solution Approach

The indirect and direct methods are the same except for the format we use to show net cash provided by (used in) operating activities. The format for the indirect method starts with the net loss and then adjusts it to cash from operating activities. This reconciliation is the same as that computed in step 3 of requirement 1 in this demonstration problem.

MORRISON COMPANY
STATEMENT OF CASH FLOWS
FOR THE YEAR ENDED DECEMBER 31, 2007

Increase (Decrease) in Cash and Cash Equivalents

Cash flows from operating activities		
Net loss		$ (9,000)
Add: Items providing cash or not requiring cash:		
Depreciation expense—machinery	$ 12,000	
Decrease in merchandise inventory	4,000	
Increase in accounts payable	6,000	
Deduct: Items requiring cash or not providing cash:		
Gain on sale of machinery	(2,000)	
Increase in accounts receivable	(37,000)	
Decrease in rent payable	(2,000)	
Total adjustments		(19,000)
Net cash used in operating activities		$ (28,000)
Cash flows from investing activities		
Purchase of machinery	$ (24,000)	
Proceeds from sale of machinery	6,000	
Net cash used by investing activities		(18,000)
Cash flows from financing activities		
Proceeds from issuance of bonds	$ 50,000	
Dividends paid	(8,000)	
Net cash provided by financing activities		42,000
Net decrease in cash and cash equivalents		$ (4,000)
Cash and cash equivalents at beginning of year		52,000
Cash and cash equivalents at end of year		$ 48,000
Supplemental Schedule of Noncash Investing and Financing Activities		
Common stock issued in exchange for land		$ 15,000

Requirement 3

Operating Activities: For the year ended December 31, 2007, Morrison Company reported a net loss of $9,000 on its income statement. For the same period, net cash of $28,000 was used in operations. The primary reason for the difference between the accrual basis net loss and the operating cash outflow for 2007 was the increase of $37,000 in accounts receivable, which represented a decrease in the amount of cash collected from customers.

Investing Activities: Morrison used $24,000 cash to acquire new machinery. The sale of used machinery for $6,000 partially offset this cash outflow.

Financing Activities: The major source of cash inflow for 2007 was through the issuance of $50,000 of bonds payable that mature in 2010. This one source of cash was used to finance the amounts of cash used for operating and investing activities, and also to pay $8,000 of cash dividends.

GLOSSARY

cash Currency on hand and demand deposits with banks and other financial institutions.

cash equivalents Short-term, highly liquid investments that are both (1) readily convertible to known amounts of cash and (2) so near their maturity that they present insignificant risk of changes in value because of changes in interest rates.

comparative balance sheets The balance sheet as of a given date compared with one or more immediately preceding balance sheets.

direct method A method of reporting cash provided by (used in) operating activities by listing the major classes of gross cash receipts and the gross cash payments from operations.

financing activities Cash receipts and cash payments from these activities: (1) Obtaining resources from owners and providing them with a return on and of their investment and (2) obtaining resources from creditors and repaying the principal amounts borrowed.

indirect method A method of reporting cash provided by (used in) operating activities by starting with the net income or net loss as reported on the income statement and adjusting it for revenues and expenses that did not cause changes in cash in the current period.

investing activities Cash receipts and cash payments from these activities: (1) Acquiring and selling plant assets, (2) acquiring and selling securities not considered to be cash equivalents, and (3) lending money and collecting the principal amount of these loans.

noncash charges to operations Deductions on the income statement in computing net income that do not require a cash outflow.

noncash credits to operations Additions on the income statement in computing net income that do not result in a cash inflow.

noncash investing and financing activities Investing and financing activities of an entity during a period of time that affect assets or liabilities on the balance sheet but that do not result in cash receipts or cash payments in the period.

operating activities Producing and delivering goods for sale and providing services. Cash flows from operating activities include cash receipts and cash payments from transactions that are part of net income.

operating current assets Current asset accounts on the balance sheet that relate to revenue and expense accounts on the income statement.

operating current liabilities Current liability accounts on the balance sheet that relate to revenue and expense accounts on the income statement.

statement of cash flows A major financial statement prepared to report the cash provided by and used in operating, investing, and financing activities and the aggregate effect of these activities on the cash balance during a period of time.

QUESTIONS FOR GROUP LEARNING

Q15-1. What is the purpose of the statement of cash flows?

Q15-2. Student A argues that net income is generally the same as the amount of cash provided by (used in) operations. Student B says that the amount of cash provided by (used in) operations is generally less than the net income amount. Which student is right? State why.

Q15-3. What are cash equivalents?

Q15-4. Give two examples each of cash receipts and cash payments that are classified as (a) operating activities, (b) investing activities, and (c) financing activities on the statement of cash flows.

Q15-5. Discuss how interest payments and dividends paid are classified on the statement of cash flows. Why is the classification for the two items different?

Q15-6. The acquisition of land by issuing shares of common stock does not result in a net cash outflow or inflow. Discuss whether this transaction must be shown in the statement of cash flows under generally accepted accounting principles.

Q15-7. A firm declares a cash dividend on common stock of $19,000 in 2007. Of this amount, it pays $12,000 in September 2007 and will pay $7,000 in January 2008. Discuss the impact of the cash dividend on (a) the balance in retained earnings as of December 31, 2007, and (b) the amount of cash outflow for dividends shown in the statement of cash flows for 2007.

Q15-8. Is it possible for a company to have a net loss on the income statement for an accounting period and yet have a positive amount for cash provided by operations? Explain.

Q15-9. If a company is in a period of rapid growth, is it likely to show cash provided by or used in operating activities? Discuss and justify your conclusions.

Q15-10. Briefly explain the difference between the direct and indirect methods used to report cash provided by (used in) operating activities. What are the advantages of both methods from the point of view of the financial statement user?

Q15-11. Under the indirect method used to report cash provided by (used in) operating activities, list five items each that would be (a) additions to and (b) deductions from net income.

Q15-12. What are operating current assets and operating current liabilities? Give two examples of each.

Q15-13. During 2007, a company reported net sales of $400,000. Its beginning and ending balances in accounts receivable during 2007 were $60,000 and $320,000, respectively. What is the amount of cash collections from customers during 2007? Discuss the extent to which the company could remain in business with this type of situation.

Q15-14. Depreciation is a deduction on the income statement in computing net income or net loss. Yet it is an addition in computing cash provided by (used in) operating activities under the indirect method. Discuss why this is true.

Q15-15. Discuss the steps needed to adjust cost of sales on an accrual basis to cash payments to suppliers.

Q15-16. During 2007, a company sold machinery with a cost of $40,000 and a book value of $17,000 for $26,000. Discuss what items would appear in the income statement and in the statement of cash flows for this transaction.

Q15-17. Discuss the impact on the statement of cash flows of the declaration and payment of (a) a cash dividend and (b) a stock dividend.

EXERCISES

E15-18. Classifying cash receipts and cash payments on the statement of cash flows (LG 2) For each of the following items, state whether the item would be shown on the statement of cash flows as an operating, investing, or financing activity. If the item would not be shown on the statement of cash flows, indicate no effect.

    a. Salary payments to employees.

    b. Cash to acquire new computers for use in the business.

    c. Cash proceeds from sale of common stock at more than par value.

    d. Cash dividends declared and paid on common stock.

    e. Stock dividends declared and distributed on common stock.

    f. Interest paid during the year.

g. Cash used to pay dividends declared last year but payable this year.

h. Cash used to purchase long-term investments in common stock of another company.

i. Cash to pay bonds payable at the maturity date.

j. Cash payments for income taxes.

E15-19.   **Computing and identifying cash flows for transactions (LG 3)** For each of the following transactions, (1) compute the net cash inflow or outflow and (2) indicate whether the item would be shown on the statement of cash flows for 2007 as an operating, investing, or financing activity.

    a. Issued 40,000 shares of $2 par value stock at $6 per share on June 1, 2007.

    b. Sales of merchandise during 2007 on account were $200,000. The balance in the Accounts Receivable account decreased by $50,000 during the year.

    c. Declared a cash dividend on common stock of $6,000 during 2007. Paid one-half of the dividend in 2007 and will pay one-half in 2008.

    d. Sold machinery on August 1, 2007, for $39,000. The machinery cost $65,000 and had an accumulated depreciation balance of $22,000.

    e. Salaries expense for 2007 was $32,000. The balance in the Salaries Payable account increased by $1,600 during 2007.

    f. Cost of sales for 2007 was $90,000. During 2007, the balance in the Accounts Payable account decreased by $5,000 and the balance in the Merchandise Inventory account increased by $9,000.

    g. Used $10,000 cash to purchase shares of the company's own common stock during 2007.

    h. Accrued and paid income taxes of $13,000 during 2007.

E15-20.   **Statement of cash flows: classification of operating, investing, and financing activities (LG 2)** The accounting records of R2D2 Company reveal the following information for the year ended December 31, 2007:

Cash and cash equivalents, January 1, 2007	$ 10,000
Cash payments for employee salaries	60,000
Cash receipts from customers	280,000
Cash payments to purchase equipment used in the business	50,000
Depreciation expense for 2007	32,000
Cash payments for rent	20,000
Cash paid for dividends to stockholders	5,000
Cash received from issuance of common stock	100,000
Cash payments to suppliers	150,000
Cash payments for income taxes	9,000

Prepare a statement of cash flows for the year ended December 31, 2007. Use the format for the statement of cash flows shown in Exhibit 15.5.

E15-21. Computing cash flows from operating activities using the direct method (LG 4)
In each of the following cases, use the information for 2007 provided to compute the cash flow indicated.

a. Compute cash receipts from customers:

Sales revenue for 2007	$530,000
Accounts receivable, January 1, 2007	60,000
Accounts receivable, December 31, 2007	25,000

b. Compute cash payments to suppliers:

Cost of goods sold for 2007	$380,000
Inventory, January 1, 2007	60,000
Inventory, December 31, 2007	40,000
Accounts payable, January 1, 2007	35,000
Accounts payable, December 31, 2007	20,000

c. Compute cash payments to employees:

Salaries expense for 2007	$90,000
Salaries payable, January 1, 2007	12,000
Salaries payable, December 31, 2007	5,000

d. Compute cash payments for rent:

Rent expense for 2007	$21,000
Prepaid rent, January 1, 2007	11,000
Prepaid rent, December 31, 2007	5,000

e. Compute cash payments for income taxes:

Income tax expense for 2007	$50,000
Income taxes payable, January 1, 2007	5,000
Income taxes payable, December 31, 2007	12,000

E15-22. Compute cash flows from operating activities using the direct method (LG 4) In each of the following cases, use the information for 2007 provided to compute the cash flow indicated.

a. Compute cash receipts from customers:

Sales revenue for 2007	$700,000
Accounts receivable, January 1, 2007	60,000
Accounts receivable, December 31, 2007	82,000

b. Compute cash payments to suppliers:

Cost of goods sold for 2007	$300,000
Inventory, January 1, 2007	45,000
Inventory, December 31, 2007	62,000
Accounts payable, January 1, 2007	25,000
Accounts payable, December 31, 2007	34,000

c. Compute cash payments to employees:

Salaries expense for 2007	$60,000
Salaries payable, January 1, 2007	3,000
Salaries payable, December 31, 2007	7,000

d. Compute cash payments for rent:

Rent expense for 2007	$45,000
Rent payable, January 1, 2007	8,000
Rent payable, December 31, 2007	1,000

e. Compute receipts for consulting revenue:

Consulting revenue for 2007	$135,000
Unearned consulting revenue, January 1, 2007	12,000
Unearned consulting revenue, December 31, 2007	8,000

E15-23. Accrual-basis and cash-basis accounting (LG 4) The following selected account balances are taken from the accounting records of Trusty Accounting Service:

Balance Sheet Accounts	December 31, 2007	December 31, 2006
Cash	$ 10,000	$ 12,000
Accounts Receivable	200,000	170,000
Merchandise Inventory	68,000	78,000
Prepaid Insurance	25,000	14,000
Salaries Payable	50,000	56,000
Accounts Payable	25,000	20,000

You are provided with the following accrual basis income statement for Excel Accounting Service for the year ended December 31, 2007. Compute the blank amounts in the cash income statement and enter them in the appropriate spaces.

Income Statement Accounts	Accrual Basis	Cash Basis
Sales revenue	$ 600,000	$_____
Less expenses:		
Cost of goods sold	(200,000)	(_____)
Salaries expense	(180,000)	(_____)
Insurance expense	(50,000)	(_____)
Net income	$ 170,000	$_____

E15-24. Converting income statement accounts from an accrual basis to a cash basis (LG 4) The following data are taken from the accounts of Frog Company for the year ended December 31, 2007:

	For the Year 2007	End of Year	Beginning of Year
Accounts receivable (net)		$85,000	$70,000
Merchandise inventories		55,000	80,000
Prepaid expenses		12,000	5,000
Accounts payable (trade)		50,000	30,000
Accrued payables		7,000	9,000
Net sales	$500,000		
Cost of goods sold	290,000		
Operating expenses (including depre. of $56,000)	140,000		

Compute each of the following:

1. Cash receipts from customers during 2007.

2. Net purchases of merchandise during 2007.

3. Cash payments for merchandise during 2007.

4. Cash payments for operating expenses during 2007.

E15-25. Computing cash provided by (used in) operating activities using the indirect method (LG 5) For each of the independent cases below, compute the amount of cash provided by (used in) operating activities using the indirect method.

	Case A	Case B	Case C	Case D
Net Income (Loss)	$ 200	$ 20	$ (90)	$ 40
Depreciation Expense	20	11	110	15
Gain (Loss) on Sale of Noncurrent Assets	50	20	(80)	9
Increase (decrease) in:				
Merchandise Inventory	55	15	35	(20)
Accounts Payable	(10)	15	20	(15)
Accounts Receivable	85	20	35	(5)
Income Taxes Payable	25	(17)	2	(13)
Salaries Payable	(32)	16	13	6
Prepaid Expenses	8	3	(12)	7

E15-26. Computing cash provided by (used in) operating activities: direct and indirect methods (LG 4, 5) The following selected data are taken from the accounts of the Owens Company for the year ended December 31, 2007:

	For the Year 2007	End of Year	Beginning of Year
Merchandise inventories		$42,000	$35,000
Accounts payable		22,000	16,000
Accounts receivable		34,000	24,000
Salaries payable		2,000	7,000
Income taxes payable		9,000	6,000
Net sales	$170,000		
Cost of goods sold	90,000		
Salaries expense	26,000		
Depreciation expense	8,000		
Tax expense	7,000		

1. Prepare the cash provided by (used in) operations section of the statement of cash flows using the direct method.

2. Prepare the cash provided by (used in) operations section of the statement of cash flows using the indirect method.

E15-27. Preparing the statement of cash flows: direct method (LG 7) True Company had cash and cash equivalents on January 1, 2007, of $11,000. Data of True Company for the year ended December 31, 2007, follow:

Cash Inflows

Collections from customers	$80,000
Proceeds from sale of equipment	40,000
Proceeds from sale of common stock	60,000

Cash Outflows

Cash payments for taxes	$12,000
Cash paid to suppliers	45,000
Cash paid for new equipment	30,000
Dividends declared and paid	8,000
Interest expense paid	5,000

Prepare a statement of cash flows for the year ended December 31, 2007. Use the direct method to show cash provided by (used in) operations.

E15-28. **Computing cash flows from investing activities (LG 6, 7)** For the year ended December 31, 2007, Zar Company had the following transactions involving machinery:

a. Zar Company sold machinery that cost $5,000, on which $2,000 in depreciation had accumulated, for $3,000.

b. Zar purchased additional machinery for $38,000.

c. Depreciation expense for 2007 was $16,000.

Account balances for Zar's Machinery and Accumulated Depreciation accounts are as follows:

	December 31	
	2007	**2006**
Machinery	$233,000	$200,000
Accumulated Depreciation—Machinery	74,000	60,000

1. Prepare the journal entries required to record each of the transactions a-c above.

2. Use a format like that shown in Exhibit 15.14 to determine the cash flow impact and classification of each of the three transactions a-c.

E15-29. **Computing cash flows from financing activities (LG 6, 7)** For the year ended December 31, 2007, First Company had the following transactions involving financing activities:

a. Net income for 2007 was $60,000.

b. First Company declared and paid cash dividends of $10,000 during the year.

c. During 2007, First sold 50,000 shares of $1 par value stock for $4 per share.

d. During 2007, First retired bonds at their face value by paying cash of $200,000.

Selected account balances are as follows:

	December 31	
	2007	**2006**
Bonds Payable	$300,000	$500,000
Common Stock, ($1 par value)	650,000	600,000
Paid-in Capital—Excess Over Par Value, Common	450,000	300,000
Retained Earnings	750,000	700,000

1. Prepare the journal entries required to record each of the transactions a-d. (For transaction a, close the net income to retained earnings.)

2. Use a format like that shown in Exhibit 15.14 to determine the cash flow impact and classification of each of the four transactions a-d.

E15-30. Preparing statement of cash flows: direct method (LG 7) Data of Texas Company follow:

TEXAS COMPANY
COMPARATIVE BALANCE SHEET ACCOUNTS
DECEMBER 31, 2007 AND 2006

	December 31	
Debit Accounts	**2007**	**2006**
Cash and Cash Equivalents	$ 7,000	$ 6,000
Accounts Receivable	12,000	5,000
Merchandise Inventory	7,000	8,000
Machinery	15,000	10,000
Totals	$41,000	$29,000
Credit Accounts		
Accumulated Depreciation—Machinery	$ 7,000	$ 1,000
Accounts Payable	6,000	9,000
Salaries Payable	4,000	2,000
Common Stock ($1 par value)	14,000	12,000
Retained Earnings	10,000	5,000
Totals	$41,000	$29,000

TEXAS COMPANY
INCOME STATEMENT
FOR THE YEAR ENDED DECEMBER 31, 2007

Sales		$94,000
Cost of goods sold		50,000
Gross margin on sales		$44,000
Operating expenses:		
Salaries expense	$28,000	
Depreciation expense—machinery	6,000	
Total operating expenses		34,000
Net income		$10,000

Additional Data

a. Texas declared and paid cash dividends of $5,000 during 2007.

b. Purchased additional machinery for cash during the year.

c. Issued 2,000 shares of common stock at par value during 2007.

Prepare a statement of cash flows for 2007. Use the direct method to report cash provided by (used in) operations within the statement of cash flows. Include a reconciliation of net income to net cash provided by (used in) operating activities by the indirect method.

E15-31. Preparing the statement of cash flows: indirect method (LG 9) Assume the same information for Texas Company in E15-30. Prepare a statement of cash flows using the indirect method to report cash provided by (used in) operating activities.

PROBLEMS

P15-32. **Statement of cash flows: classifying operating, investing, and financing activities of cash flows (LG 2)** Star Company began operations on January 1, 2007. The accounting records of Star Company reveal the following transactions for the year ended December 31, 2007:

    a. Cash proceeds received from sale of common stock were $325,000.

    b. Cash payments to suppliers for merchandise inventory purchases were $195,000.

    c. Dividends on common stock declared and paid were $50,000.

    d. Notes payable (long-term) issued for cash during the year were $35,000.

    e. Interest payments on notes payable amounted to $2,000.

    f. Cash collections from customers were $245,000.

    g. Cash proceeds from sale of machinery were $46,000.

    h. Salaries paid to employees were $54,000.

    i. Purchases of investment securities totaled $65,000.

    j. Dividend revenue received totaled $3,000.

    k. Purchased shares of our own common stock for $30,000.

    l. Payments for insurance were $6,000.

REQUIRED
Prepare a statement of cash flows for the year ended December 31, 2007. Use the direct method (format shown in Exhibit 15.5 to determine cash provided by (used in) operating activities.

P15-33. **Statement of cash flows: analysis of transactions and classification of cash receipts and cash payments (LG 3)** The summary transactions for Freedom Company during its first year of operations follow:

    a. Issued for cash on January 1, 2007, 50,000 shares of $5 par value stock at $8 per share.

    b. Rented a building on January 1, 2007, and paid rent in advance for the next 18 months. The monthly rental fee is $1,000.

    c. Purchased store fixtures costing $80,000 on January 1, 2007, for cash. The store fixtures have an estimated useful life of 10 years, they have no estimated residual value, and the straight-line depreciation method is used.

    d. Purchased merchandise inventory on account during 2007 totaling $160,000. Payments on account during 2007 were $150,000.

    e. Sold merchandise inventory on account during 2007 totaling $250,000. The cost of the merchandise sold was $130,000. The balance in accounts receivable increased by $60,000 in 2007.

    f. During 2007, received an advance payment of $3,000 from a customer for merchandise to be delivered during May 2008.

g. Had salaries expense for 2007 totaling $60,000, of which $51,000 was paid in cash and $9,000 was accrued as of December 31, 2007.

h. Paid income taxes amounting to $25,000 in cash during 2007.

i. Declared and paid a cash dividend of $5,000 on the common stock during 2007.

REQUIRED

1. Assuming an accrual basis of accounting, prepare an income statement for 2007.

2. Prepare a statement of cash flows for the year ended December 31, 2007. Use the direct method (format shown in Exhibit 15.5 to determine cash provided by (used in) operating activities.

3. What are the major reasons why net income computed on an accrual accounting basis is more or less than cash provided by (used in) operating activities for Freedom Company during 2007?

P15-34. **Computation of cash provided by (used in) operating activities: direct and indirect methods (LG 4, 5)** The following selected data are taken from the accounts of Marines Company for the year ended December 31, 2007:

	For the Year 2007	End of Year	Beginning of Year
Cash		$35,000	$40,000
Merchandise inventories		155,000	70,000
Accounts payable		38,000	30,000
Prepaid rent		8,000	13,000
Land		190,000	230,000
Accounts receivable		98,000	24,000
Salaries payable		9,000	14,000
Common stock		300,000	250,000
Income taxes payable		9,000	4,000
Net sales	$520,000		
Cost of goods sold	240,000		
Salaries expense	86,000		
Depreciation expense	60,000		
Rent expense	36,000		
Loss on sale of land	2,000		
Income tax expense	28,000		
Dividend declared and paid	15,000		

REQUIRED

1. Prepare the cash provided by (used in) operating activities section of the statement of cash flows using the direct method.

2. Prepare the cash provided by (used in) operating activities section of the statement of cash flows using the indirect method.

3. What are the major reasons why net income computed on an accrual accounting basis is more or less than cash provided by (used in) operating activities for Marines Company during 2007?

P15-35. **Statement of cash flows: direct or indirect method (LG 7, 8)** Data of USA Company follow:

USA COMPANY
COMPARATIVE BALANCE SHEET ACCOUNTS
DECEMBER 31, 2007 AND 2006

Debit Accounts	December 31 2007	2006
Cash and Cash Equivalents	$ 35,500	$ 34,000
Accounts Receivable	52,000	76,000
Merchandise Inventory	35,000	25,000
Investments (long-term)	20,500	37,500
Land	41,500	20,000
Buildings	67,500	46,000
Machinery	30,000	18,000
Totals	$ 282,000	$ 256,500
Credit Accounts		
Accumulated Depreciation—Buildings	$ 13,500	$ 9,000
Accumulated Depreciation—Machinery	5,600	2,300
Accounts Payable	32,000	24,500
Salaries Payable	4,900	7,000
Bonds Payable (due 2012)	35,000	70,000
Common Stock ($1 par value)	157,000	137,000
Retained Earnings	34,000	6,700
Totals	$ 282,000	$ 256,500

USA COMPANY
INCOME STATEMENT
FOR THE YEAR ENDED DECEMBER 31, 2007

Sales		$ 275,000
Cost of goods sold		165,000
Gross margin on sales		$ 110,000
Operating expenses:		
Salaries expense	$ 32,000	
Depreciation expense—buildings	4,500	
Depreciation expense—machinery	4,800	
Total operating expenses		41,300
Net operating income		$ 68,700
Other expenses:		
Interest expense	$ 4,400	
Loss on sale of machinery	1,000	
Total other expenses		5,400
Income before tax expense		$ 63,300
Income tax expense		20,000
Net income		$ 43,300

Additional Data

a. During 2007, USA Company sold long-term investments that cost $17,000 for $17,000.

b. Made additional purchases of land during the year for cash.

c. Made additional purchases of buildings during the year for cash. Sold no buildings during the year.

d. Sold machinery that cost $7,500, on which $1,500 in depreciation had accumulated, for $5,000.

e. Purchased additional machinery costing $19,500 for cash.

f. Depreciation expense on the buildings for 2007 was $4,500.

g. Depreciation expense on the machinery for 2007 was $4,800.

h. Retired bonds payable in the amount of $35,000 for cash during 2007.

i. Sold additional shares of common stock for par value.

j. Declared and paid cash dividends in the amount of $16,000 during the year.

REQUIRED

(Do either requirement 1 or requirement 2 as directed by your instructor.)

1. Prepare a statement of cash flows for 2007. Use the direct method to report cash provided by (used in) operating activities within the statement of cash flows. Include a reconciliation of net income to net cash provided by (used in) operating activities by the indirect method. You may wish to use a supporting calculations form like Exhibit 15.7 to compute cash from operating activities and a supporting calculations form like Exhibit 15.14 for the cash flows analysis of noncurrent accounts.

2. Prepare a statement of cash flows for 2007. Use the indirect method to report cash provided by (used in) operating activities within the statement of cash flows. You may wish to use a supporting calculations form like Exhibit 15.14 for the cash flows analysis of noncurrent accounts.

PRACTICE CASE

Statement of cash flows: direct and indirect methods (LG 7, 9) Data for Jump Company follow:

JUMP COMPANY
COMPARATIVE BALANCE SHEET ACCOUNTS
DECEMBER 31, 2007 AND 2006

	December 31	
Debit Accounts	**2007**	**2006**
Cash and Cash Equivalents	$ 89,000	$ 50,000
Accounts Receivable	52,000	65,000
Merchandise Inventory	59,000	46,000
Land	35,000	0
Machinery	92,000	67,000
Totals	$ 327,000	$228,000
Credit Accounts		
Accumulated Depreciation—Machinery	$ 17,000	$ 15,000
Accounts Payable	21,000	10,000
Salaries Payable	8,000	2,000
Bonds Payable (due 2012)	40,000	0
Common Stock ($2 par value)	125,000	90,000
Retained Earnings	116,000	111,000
Totals	$ 327,000	$228,000

JUMP COMPANY
INCOME STATEMENT
FOR THE YEAR ENDED DECEMBER 31, 2007

Sales		$390,000
Cost of goods sold		260,000
Gross margin on sales		$130,000
Operating expenses:		
Salaries expense	$ 54,000	
Rent expense	38,000	
Depreciation expense—machinery	4,000	
Total operating expenses		96,000
Net operating income		$ 34,000
Other expense:		
Loss on sale of machinery		2,000
Income before tax		32,000
Income tax expense		12,000
Net income		$ 20,000

Additional Data

a. On September 1, 2007, Jump Company issued additional shares of common stock at par value in exchange for land worth $35,000.

b. Sold machinery that cost $10,000, on which $2,000 in depreciation had accumulated, for $6,000.

c. Purchased additional machinery costing $35,000 for cash.

d. Depreciation expense on the machinery for 2007 was $4,000.

e. Issued bonds payable in the amount of $40,000 for cash during 2007.

f. Declared and paid cash dividends in the amount of $15,000 during the year.

REQUIRED

1. Prepare a statement of cash flows for 2007. Use the direct method to report cash provided by (used in) operating activities within the statement of cash flows. Include a reconciliation of net income to net cash provided by (used in) operating activities by the indirect method.

2. Prepare a statement of cash flows for 2007. Use the indirect method to report cash provided by (used in) operating activities within the statement of cash flows.

3. Prepare a brief interpretation of the statement of cash flows for 2007 that comments on the major sources and uses of cash.

BUSINESS DECISION AND COMMUNICATION PROBLEM 1

Analyzing cash flows for Microsoft Corporation (LG 8) Microsoft is a leading producer of software. The Company ends its fiscal year on June 30. Assume that total revenues and total net income in millions for the years ended June 30, 2007, 2006, and 2005 are:

	2007	2006	2005
Revenues	$25,296	$22,965	$19,747
Net income	7,346	9,421	7,785

Cash flow statement information for 2007, 2006, and 2005 is:

	2007	2006	2005
Cash flows from operating activities			
Net income	$ 7,346	$ 9,421	$ 7,785
Depreciation	1,536	748	1,010
Adjustments to net income	4,843	5,956	1,191
Change in accounts receivable	(418)	(944)	(687)
Change in inventory	0	0	0
Change in liabilities	927	(445)	966
Changes in other operating activities	(812)	(775)	(235)
Cash flows from operating activities	$13,422	$ 13,961	$ 10,030
Cash flows from investing activities			
Capital expenditures	$ (1,103)	$ (879)	$ (583)
Investments	(7,631)	(11,048)	(10,687)
Other cash flows from investing activities			79
Cash flows from investing activities	$ (8,734)	$(11,927)	$(11,191)
Cash flows from financing activities			
Dividends paid	$ 0	$ (13)	$ (28)
Sale (purchase of stock)	(5,821)	(2,179)	2,273
Net borrowings	0	0	0
Other cash flows from financing activities	(235)	0	0
Cash flows from financing activities	$ (5,586)	$ (2,192)	$ 2,245
Effect of exchange rate	$ (26)	$ 0	$ 0
Change in cash and cash equivalents	$ (924)	$ (158)	$ 1,084

REQUIRED

Your supervisor, Sandy Tomany, has asked you to comment on cash flows for Microsoft. Prepare a memo which responds to the following questions:

1. What is the trend in gross revenues over the three year period? Has the company been able to increase its revenue base?

2. What is the trend in accrual basis net income over the three year period? Was the company more or less profitable in 2007 than in past years?

3. In 2007, what were the main reasons why accrual basis net income was $7,346 million and cash provided by operations was $13,422 million.

4. In 2007, why do you think the change in accounts receivable of $418 million was subtracted from income to determine cash from operating activities?

5. What cash uses have been made for investing activities over the three year period and to what extent has cash from operations been sufficient to pay for these investments?

6. What is the most significant (a) source of cash and (b) use of cash from financing activities in 2007?

7. Comment on the dividend policy for the company over the three year period. Considering the levels of net income and operating cash flows, do you feel dividends are too high, too large, or just right? Explain.

8. List any overall cash flow concerns or questions you would want to ask management at the end of 2007. Note: Microsoft's balance sheet shows cash and short-term investments at the end of fiscal 2001 are $31,600 million compared to total assets of $59,257 million.

BUSINESS DECISION AND COMMUNICATION PROBLEM 2

Analyzing cash flows for Nike, Inc. (LG 8) Nike is a leading producer of footwear. The Company ends its fiscal year on May 31. Assume that total revenues and total net income in millions for the years ended May 31, 2007, 2006, and 2005 are:

	2007	2006	2005
Revenues	$9,448.8	$8,995.1	$ 8,776.9
Net income	589.7	579.1	451.4

Cash flow statement information for 2007, 2006, and 2005 is:

	2007	2006	2005
Cash flows from operating activities			
Net income	$ 589.7	$ 579.1	$ 451.4
Depreciation	214.1	223.6	228.8
Adjustments to net income	112.2	36.8	65.9
Change in accounts receivable	(141.4)	(27.1)	134.3
Change in inventory	(16.7)	(275.4)	197.3
Change in liabilities	(179.4)	157.3	(170.4)
Changes in other operating activities	78.0	65.6	(53.7)
Cash flows from operating activities	$ 656.0	$ 759.9	$ 961.0
Cash flows from investing activities			
Capital expenditures	$ (317.6)	$ (419.9)	$ (384.1)
Investments	0	0	0
Other cash flows from investing activities	(24.7)	(20.1)	(32.4)
Cash flows from investing activities	$ (342.3)	$ (440.0)	(416.5)
Cash flows from financing activities			
Dividends paid	$ (129.70)	$ (133.1)	$ (136.2)
Sale (purchase of stock)	(101.0)	(622.4)	(245.4)
Net borrowings	(119.2)	503.4	(62.5)
Other cash flows from financing activities	0	0	0
Cash flows from financing activities	$ (349.9)	$ (252.1)	$ (444.1)
Effect of exchange rate	85.4	(11.6)	(10.9)
Change in cash and cash equivalents	$ 49.7	$ 56.2	$ 89.5

REQUIRED

Your supervisor, Ralph Cramden, has asked you to comment on cash flows for Nike. Prepare a memo which responds to the following questions:

1. What is the trend in gross revenues over the three year period? Has the company been able to increase its revenue base?

2. What is the trend in accrual basis net income over the three year period? Was the company more or less profitable in 2007 than in past years?

3. In 2007, what were the main reasons why accrual basis net income was $589.7 million and cash provided by operations was $656.5 million.

4. In 2006, what were the main reasons why accrual basis net income was $579.1 million and cash provided by operations was $759.9 million.

5. What cash uses have been made for investing activities over the three year period and to what extent has cash from operations been sufficient to pay for these investments?

6. What is the most significant (a) source of cash and (b) use of cash from financing activities in 2007?

7. Comment on the dividend policy for the company over the three year period. Considering the levels of net income and operating cash flows, do you feel dividends are too high, too large, or just right? Explain.

8. List any overall cash flow concerns or questions you would want to ask management at the end of 2007.

BUSINESS DECISION AND COMMUNICATION PROBLEM 3

Analyzing cash flows for Oracle Corp. (LG 8) Oracle Corp. is a leading computer networking company. The company ends its fiscal year on May 31. Assume that total revenues and total net income in millions for the years ended May 31, 2007, 2006, and 2005 are:

	2007	2006	2005
Revenues	$10,859.7	$10,130.1	$8,827.3
Net income	2,561.1	6,296.8	1,289.7

Cash flow statement information for 2007, 2006, and 2005 is:

	2007	2006	2005
Cash flows from operating activities			
Net income	$ 2,561.1	$ 6,296.8	$1,289.7
Depreciation	346.9	390.9	375.4
Adjustments to net income	272.7	(6,801.6)	72.5
Change in accounts receivable	(199.0)	(412.5)	(486.4)
Change in inventory	0	0	0
Change in liabilities	(678.1)	3,415.9	658.4
Changes in other operating activities	(124.5)	43.1	(102.5)
Cash flows from operating activities	$ 2,179.1	$ 2,923.6	$1,807.1
Cash flows from investing activities			
Capital expenditures	$ (313.3)	$ (263.4)	$ (346.6)
Investments	(858.6)	7,631.1	(194.6)
Other cash flows from investing activities	(82.8)	(474.6)	(261.1)
Cash flows from investing activities	$(1,254.7)	$ 6,893.1	$ (802.3)
Cash flows from financing activities			
Dividends paid	$ 0	$ 0	$ 0
Sale (purchase of stock)	(3,804.9)	(4,178.4)	(484.7)
Net borrowings	(0.1)	(4.8)	0
Other cash flows from financing activities	0	0	0
Cash flows from financing activities	$(3,805.0)	$(4,183.2)	$ (484.7)
Effect of exchange rate	$ (99.4)	$ 10.1	$ (8.1)
Change in cash and cash equivalents	$(2,980.0)	$ 5,643.6	$ 512.0

REQUIRED

Your supervisor, Barney Rubble, has asked you to comment on cash flows for Oracle. Prepare a memo which responds to the following questions:

1. What is the trend in gross revenues over the three year period? Has the company been able to increase its revenue base?

2. What is the trend in accrual basis net income over the three year period? Was the company more or less profitable in 2007 than in past years?

3. In 2006, what were the main reasons why accrual basis net income was $6,296.8 million and cash provided by operations was $2,923.6 million.

4. In 2006, what were the main reasons why cash provided by investing activities was $6,893.1 million?

5. What is the most significant (a) source of cash and (b) use of cash from financing activities in 2007?

6. Comment on the dividend policy for the company over the three year period. Considering the levels of net income and operating cash flows, do you feel dividends are too high, too large, or just right? Explain.

7. List any overall cash flow concerns or questions you would want to ask management at the end of 2007.

ETHICAL DILEMMA

Year-end loan to improve cash position on balance sheet Randy Rancher, chief accountant of Great Flix Sales, desires to report a higher cash balance on the ending balance sheet. His purpose is to show a more liquid financial position to suppliers from whom he hopes to purchase more goods on account. To accomplish this, he is negotiating a 10-day bank loan of $100,000. This will substantially increase the cash amount on the balance sheet from its current balance of $15,000. Frank, a friend of yours, has asked your opinion of this action.

REQUIRED

Briefly discuss whether suppliers will believe that the 10-day bank loan has provided the company with improved liquidity.

COMPREHENSIVE ANALYSIS CASE PHILIPS ELECTRONICS

Analyzing Philips Electronics for the Period 2004-2002 Philips, a Netherlands-based company, is one of the largest producers of leading home and business electronics. Listed below are comparative income statements and balance sheets with common-size percents for 2004-2002 (in millions). Also included are selected ratio statistics. Please provide a brief explanation for your answer to each question.

REQUIRED

Income statement questions:

1. Are total revenues higher or lower over the three-year period?

2. What is the percent change in total revenues from 2002 to 2004?

3. Is the percent of sales, general and administrative expense to total revenues increasing or decreasing over the three-year period? As a result, is the operating income percent increasing or decreasing?

4. Is the percent of total operating expenses to total revenues increasing or decreasing over the three-year period? As a result, is the operating income percent increasing or decreasing?

5. Is the percent of net income to total revenue increasing or decreasing over the three-year period?

Balance sheet questions:

6. Are total assets higher or lower over the three-year period?

7. What is the percent change in total assets from 2002 to 2004?

8. What are the largest asset investments for the company over the three-year period?

9. Are the largest asset investments increasing faster or slower than the percent change in total revenues?

10. Is the percent of total liabilities to total liabilities + owners' equity increasing or decreasing? As a result, is there more or less risk that the company could not pay its debts?

PHILIPS ELECTRONICS
COMPARATIVE COMMON-SIZE INCOME STATEMENTS
For The Years Ended December 31, 2004, 2003, 2002
(in millions)

	2004	2004	2003	2003	2002	2002
	$	%	$	%	$	%
Revenues	$ 30,319.0	100.0%	$ 29,037.0	100.0%	$ 31,820.0	100.0%
Cost of goods sold	$ 20,155.0	66.5%	$ 19,558.0	67.4%	$ 21,722.0	68.3%
Gross margin	$ 10,164.0	33.5%	$ 9,479.0	32.6%	$ 10,098.0	31.7%
Operating expenses:						
Selling, general, and administrative	$ 5,852.0	19.3%	$ 6,067.0	20.9%	$ 6,605.0	20.8%
Research and Development	$ 2,534.0	8.4%	$ 2,617.0	9.0%	$ 3,043.0	9.6%
Other expense	$ 171.0	0.6%	$ 307.0	1.1%	$ 30.0	0.1%
Total operating expenses	$ 8,557.0	28.2%	$ 8,991.0	31.0%	$ 9,678.0	30.4%
Operating income	$ 1,607.0	5.3%	$ 488.0	1.7%	$ 420.0	1.3%
Other expense (income), net	$ (216.0)	-0.7%	$ 244.0	0.8%	$ 2,227.0	7.0%
Income before income taxes	$ 1,823.0	6.0%	$ 244.0	0.8%	$ (1,807.0)	-5.7%
Income taxes	$ 358.0	1.2%	$ (15.0)	-0.1%	$ 27.0	0.1%
Other Extraordinary Items	$ 1,371.0	4.5%	$ 436.0	1.5%	$ 1,372.0	4.3%
Net income (loss)	$ 2,836.0	9.4%	$ 695.0	2.4%	$ (3,206.0)	-10.1%

PHILIPS ELECTRONICS
COMPARATIVE COMMON-SIZE BALANCE SHEETS
December 31, 2004, 2003, 2002
(in millions)

	2004	2004	2003	2003	2002	2002
	$	%	$	%	$	%
ASSETS						
Current:						
Cash & cash equivalents	$ 4,349.0	14.2%	$ 3,072.0	10.4%	$ 1,858.0	5.8%
Accounts receivable, net	$ 4,528.0	14.7%	$ 4,628.0	15.7%	$ 5,068.0	15.7%
Inventory	$ 3,230.0	10.5%	$ 3,204.0	10.9%	$ 3,522.0	10.9%
Other current assets	$ 1,216.0	4.0%	$ 1,010.0	3.4%	$ 603.0	1.9%
Total current assets	$ 13,323.0	43.4%	$ 11,914.0	40.5%	$ 11,051.0	34.2%
Fixed:						
Property & equipment, net	$ 4,997.0	16.3%	$ 4,879.0	16.6%	$ 6,137.0	19.0%
Long Term Investments	$ 5,670.0	18.5%	$ 4,841.0	16.5%	$ 6,089.0	18.9%
Intangibles & goodwill	$ 2,807.0	9.1%	$ 3,765.0	12.8%	$ 4,934.0	15.3%
Other assets	$ 3,926.0	12.8%	$ 4,012.0	13.6%	$ 4,078.0	12.6%
Total assets	$ 30,723.0	100.0%	$ 29,411.0	100.0%	$ 32,289.0	100.0%
LIABILITIES						
Current:						
Short-term debt	$ 1,742.0	5.7%	$ 2,809.0	9.6%	$ 1,893.0	5.9%
Accounts payable	$ 3,499.0	11.4%	$ 3,205.0	10.9%	$ 3,228.0	10.0%
Accrued Liabilities	$ 3,307.0	10.8%	$ 3,165.0	10.8%	$ 3,314.0	10.3%
Other Current Liabilities	$ 627.0	2.0%	$ 649.0	2.2%	$ 691.0	2.1%
Total current liabilities	$ 9,175.0	29.9%	$ 9,828.0	33.4%	$ 9,126.0	28.3%
Long-term debt	$ 5,669.0	18.5%	$ 5,992.0	20.4%	$ 8,462.0	26.2%
Other long-term liabilities	$ 1,019.0	3.3%	$ 828.0	2.8%	$ 782.0	2.4%
Total liabilities	$ 15,863.0	51.6%	$ 16,648.0	56.6%	$ 18,370.0	56.9%
OWNERS' EQUITY						
Total owners' equity	$ 14,860.0	48.4%	$ 12,763.0	43.4%	$ 13,919.0	43.1%
Total liabilities and owners' equity	$ 30,723.0	100.0%	$ 29,411.0	100.0%	$ 32,289.0	100.0%

(Note: percents may not add to 100 due to rounding)

PHILIPS ELECTRONICS
RATIO ANALYSIS SUMMARY
For The Years Ended December 31, 2004, 2003, 2002

	2004	2003	2002
SHORT-TERM LIQUIDITY RATIOS			
Current Ratio (Current Assets/Current Liabilities)	1.45	1.21	1.21
Quick Ratio (Cash + Short-term Investments + Accounts Receivable)/Current Liabilities	0.97	0.78	0.76
Accounts Receivable Turnover 1 (Revenues/Average Accounts Receivable)	6.62	5.99	
Accounts Receivable Turnover 2 (Revenues/Year-end Accounts Receivable)	6.70	6.27	6.28
Inventory Turnover 1 (Cost Goods Sold/Average Inventory)	6.27	5.82	
Inventory Turnover 2 (Cost Goods Sold/Year-end Inventory)	6.24	6.10	6.17
LONG-TERM SOLVENCY (LEVERAGE) RATIO			
Total Debt Ratio (Total Liabilities/Total Assets)	51.63%	56.60%	56.89%
PROFITABILITY RATIOS			
Gross Profit Margin (Gross Margin/Revenues)	33.52%	32.64%	31.73%
Operating Profit Margin (Operating Income/Revenues)	5.30%	1.68%	1.32%
Net Profit Margin (Return on Sales) (ROS] (Net Income/Revenues)	9.35%	2.39%	-10.08%
Total Asset Turnover (Revenues/Average Total Assets)	1.01	0.94	1.00
Return on Total Assets (ROA] (Net Income/Average Total Assets)	9.43%	2.25%	2.39%

Integrative income statement and balance sheet question:

11. Is the company operating more or less efficiently by using the least amount of asset investment to generate a given level of total revenues? Note that the "total asset turnover" ratio is computed and included in the "ratio analysis summary."

Ratio analysis questions:

12. Is the current ratio better or worse in the most current year compared to prior years?

13. Is the *quick ratio* better or worse in the most current year compared to prior years?

14. Is the *accounts receivable turnover ratio 1* (based on *average* receivables) better or worse in the most current year compared to prior years?

15. Is the 2004 *accounts receivable turnover ratio 2* (based on *year-end* receivables) better or worse than the 2004 ratio based on an *average*?

16. Is the *return on total assets (ROA) ratio* better or worse in the most current year compared to prior years?

ANALYSIS AND INTERPRETATION OF FINANCIAL STATEMENTS

"Diamonds are nothing more than chunks of coal that stuck to their jobs."

Malcolm S.Forbes

LEARNING GOALS

After studying Chapter 16, you should be able to:

1. State the objectives and describe the process of financial statement analysis.

2. Describe the sources of information for financial statement analysis.

3. Prepare and interpret a horizontal analysis of financial statements.

4. Prepare and interpret a vertical analysis of financial statements.

5. Calculate and interpret ratios used to evaluate short-term liquidity, long-term solvency, profitability, and market performance.

6. Identify the limitations of financial statement analysis.

UNDERSTANDING BUSINESS ISSUES

The purpose of accounting is to provide information useful for making decisions. In previous chapters you have learned about accounting concepts, methods, and applications. Each chapter in the text so far has a section focusing on analyzing information for real-life companies. In this chapter, we both review concepts you have already used and introduce some new analysis techniques. At the end of the chapter, we present an overview of major financial statement limitations. Our goal in this chapter is to provide an overall summary of ways to analyze and interpret financial statement information.

OBJECTIVES AND PROCESS OF FINANCIAL STATEMENT ANALYSIS

Learning Goal 1   State the objectives and describe the process of financial statement analysis.

Users of accounting information wish to predict the future financial results of an organization. Managers, who are *internal users*, want to predict next year's revenues to plan operations and decide where to invest the company's assets. *External* users—persons outside the firm's management—have different goals. Union leaders want to predict the company's income to negotiate wage increase requests. Lenders want to predict which applicants for loans will be able to repay them. Investors want to predict which stocks will go up in value. The overall **objective of financial statement analysis** is to make predictions about an organization as an aid in decision making.

Management can request any information it wishes about the company's operations for decision making. For example, many companies attempt to operate more efficiently by decreasing costs. Management may request information such as sales per salesperson. It may use this data to make difficult decisions about which employees to retain. Our primary focus in this chapter is not on the special reports accountants prepare for management. Rather, we focus on the information needs of persons outside the firm. External users rely on the **general-purpose financial statements** companies publish. These include an income statement, a statement of retained earnings or stockholders' equity, a balance sheet, and a statement of cash flows. The explanatory notes that accompany the statements are an integral part of the statements.

When analyzing the general-purpose statements, users highlight important *trends* or changes in the operations and financial position of a company. **Financial statement analysis** is the application of analytical tools and techniques to financial statement data. It allows users to focus on how the numbers are related and how they have changed over time.

EVALUATING RISK AND RETURN

In making investment and lending decisions, users constantly try to evaluate and balance the *risk* of an investment with its expected *return*. Generally, the greater the risk, the higher the return. For example, suppose you are in charge of making business loans at a bank. Currently, two companies are requesting loans of $1,000,000. IBM Corporation presents a loan request to open up a local service center for its computer equipment. Sunshine Company, a recently formed company with no operating history, presents a loan request to open up a chain of tanning salons. The IBM loan has less risk than the Sunshine Company loan. IBM has a long history of successful performance, large resources, and proven demand for its products. Sunshine Company has no past performance history, limited resources, and is opening a business with unproven customer demand. Therefore, the interest rate on the IBM loan should be lower than on the Sunshine Company loan. The risk with the Sunshine Company may be so great that even the highest return could not compensate the bank for the possibility of losing both interest and principal if the business fails.

Financial statement users perform financial statement analysis as one source of information for assessing the risk and potential return of an investment or lending proposal. Accounting information provides a history of past performance for a company. Financial statement users analyze these historical results to estimate future results and risk. Outstanding past performance does not guarantee future success. However, frequently it is the best information available to a user. Exhibit 16.1 shows an overview of financial statement users, the decisions they make, and accounting information they use.

Financial Statement User	Financial Statement Decisions	Accounting Information Needs
INTERNAL		
Management	Make planning and operating decisions that require timely and specific information.	Special-purpose reports.
	Evaluate periodic information the company presents to external users of accounting information. Management must do this to view the company as other users do.	General-purpose financial statements and related notes.
	Compare overall operating results and financial position of company to their competitors.	General-purpose financial statements and related notes.
EXTERNAL		
Short-term credit grantors (suppliers, banks, lenders)	Evaluate the company's ability to pay accounts payable or short-term notes payable plus any accompanying interest.	Current resources on the balance sheet and cash flows from operations.
Long-term credit grantor (banks, lenders, insurance companies, other companies)	Evaluate prospects for future earnings, since repayment will come from future profits. Also evaluate the firm's *capital structure* for its use of debt and equity financing to assess risk.	Profitability shown on income statement. Relative percentages of debt and equity shown on balance sheet. Ability of company to pay current debts.
Stockholders	Evaluate the company's future earnings prospects and dividend policies. Evaluate the firm's use of debt and equity financing to assess risk. Evaluate current stock price in relation to estimated future price of stock.	Profitability shown on income statement. Dividend distributions. Relative percentages of debt and equity shown on balance sheet. Forecast of future profitability and comparison to current stock price.

EXHIBIT **16.1**

Overview of Decisions and Information Needs of Financial Statement Users

SOURCES OF EXTERNAL INFORMATION

Learning Goal 2   Describe the sources of information for financial statement analysis.

Financial information about a firm can come from a variety of sources. Following are the primary sources of financial information about publicly owned companies (those with stock the general public may purchase):

- Published reports.

- Government reports.

- Financial service information.

- Financial newspapers and periodicals.

Published Reports

Public companies must publish an annual financial report. This report is for stockholders and other interested parties. The major sections of an annual report are as follows:

1. *Letter to stockholders.* The chief executive officer of the company reviews the past year and discusses future plans.

2. *Financial statements.* Companies show two years of comparative data in the balance sheet and three years in the income statement and statement of cash flows.

3. *Explanatory notes.* The notes specify accounting methods the company uses and provide additional information about financial statement items.

4. *Management's discussion and analysis (MDA).* Management explains reasons for changes in operations and financial position and comments on the ability of the company to meet its financial obligations. This section helps users gain perspective on management's decision making and the long-term prospects for the company.

5. *Report of independent accountants.* The public accountant expresses an opinion on the fairness of the presentation in the financial statements. Management is responsible for the information contained in the annual report.

Public companies also release quarterly reports known as **interim reports**. Interim reports contain summarized financial information about the most recent quarter and the year-to-date. Today, most companies make their annual and interim reports available on their world-wide-web sites.

Government Reports

The Securities and Exchange Commission (SEC) requires periodic reports of public companies. The primary reports are an annual report (Form 10-K), quarterly reports (Form 10-Q), and special events reports (Form 8-K). These reports sometimes contain more detailed information than the published reports. Some companies prepare a combined report, which they issue to both external users and the SEC. The SEC website (www.sec.gov) houses a large library of these reports in the EDGAR database.

Financial Service Information

Financial statement analysis is more meaningful if users can compare the information with that of other firms in similar lines of business and with industry norms. Moody's Investors Service and Standard & Poor's are firms that provide information on individual companies and industries. Dun and Bradstreet, Inc., publishes *Key Business Ratios*, which contain information for specific industries such as retailing, communications, and insurance. Robert Morris Associates publishes *Annual Statement Studies*, which provide condensed financial statement data and ratios for more than 200 industries. Standard and Poor's *Industry Surveys* contain background descriptions on the nature and economic outlook for different industries in addition to company statistics.

Financial Newspapers and Periodicals

Financial statement users must be knowledgeable about current developments in business. Information companies present in their published reports is dated. Newspapers such as *The Wall Street Journal* and *Barron's* report current information about companies. Business periodicals such as *Forbes, Fortune, Business Week*, and *The Economist* are sources of current information about individual companies and the economy in general.

FINANCIAL ANALYSIS TOOLS AND TECHNIQUES

We illustrate three categories of financial analysis tools and techniques: (1) *horizontal analysis*, (2) *vertical analysis*, and (3) *ratio analysis*. Evaluating financial statements is more meaningful when we compare data for several periods to look for trends. **Comparative financial statements** show two or more years of data in parallel columns. In this section we will use the 2007 and 2006 comparative financial statements for Amy Company to illustrate these three categories of analysis.

Horizontal Analysis

Learning Goal 3   Prepare and interpret a horizontal analysis of financial statements.

A common question statement users have is whether specific financial statement items increased or decreased from the previous year. For example, users may ask, "Are current sales larger or smaller than sales were at this time last year?" **Horizontal analysis** measures the dollar amount and the percent of change in each financial statement item from a previous year.

Computing Amounts and Percentages of Change

To begin horizontal analysis, we first compute an *amount change* for a financial statement item by subtracting a prior-year amount from the current-year amount. For example, if sales for 2007 and 2006 are $800,000 and $700,000, respectively, the amount of change in 2007 is an increase of $100,000 ($800,000 - $700,000). We refer to the prior year from which we compute changes as the **base year**. We compute each *percent change* as follows:

$$\text{Percent change} = 100 \times \frac{\text{Dollar Amount of Change}}{\text{Dollar Amount for Base Year}}$$

If the base year is zero or a negative number, we cannot calculate the percent change. In this textbook, we round the percent change to the nearest tenth of a percent. The following percent change computations illustrate horizontal analysis in which we compute changes in each item from the previous year (dollar amounts are in thousands):

| | Years Ended December 31 | | | Increase (Decrease) | | | |
| | | | | During 2007 | | During 2006 | |
	2007	2006	2005	Amount	Percent	Amount	Percent
Sales	$ 800	$700	$600	$ 100	14.3%	$ 100	16.7%
Total expenses	900	400	500	500	125.0	(100)	(20.0)
Net income (loss)	$ (100)	$300	$100	$ (400)	(133.3)	$ 200	200.0

To compute the percent increase in sales from 2006 (the base year) to 2007:

$$100 \times \frac{\$100^*}{\$700} = 14.3\%$$

$$^*\$800 - \$700$$

Note that sales increases by $100 in both 2006 and 2007. However, the percent increase in 2006 is greater than in 2007. This is because the 2006 percent increase uses a smaller base-year amount ($600) than 2007 ($700).

Analysis of Comparative Statements

Exhibit 16.2 shows comparative balance sheets and percentage changes for Amy Company using 2006 as a base year. Exhibit 16.3 shows Amy's comparative income statements. To analyze comparative statements, we identify the largest dollar or percent changes (indicated here by bold numbers). Then we try to explain the changes and identify whether they are favorable or unfavorable.

CHAPTER 16

AMY COMPANY
COMPARATIVE BALANCE SHEETS
DECEMBER 31, 2007 AND 2006

	December 31 2007	December 31 2006	Increase (Decrease) Amount	Increase (Decrease) Percentage
Assets				
Current assets				
Cash	$ 36,000	$ 33,000	$ 3,000	9.1%
Accounts receivable (net)	80,600	60,000	20,600	34.3
Inventories	115,000	80,000	35,000	43.8
Total current assets	$ 231,600	$ 173,000	$ 58,600	33.9
Property, plant, equipment				
Land	$ 125,000	$ 125,000	$ 0	0.0
Building (net)	150,000	83,000	67,000	80.7
Store equipment (net)	36,000	25,000	11,000	44.0
Office equipment (net)	28,000	30,000	(2,000)	(6.7)
Total property, plant, and equipment	$ 339,000	$ 263,000	$ 76,000	28.9
Total assets	$ 570,600	$ 436,000	$134,600	30.9
Liabilities				
Current liabilities				
Accounts payable	$ 83,000	$ 70,000	$ 13,000	18.6
Notes payable	15,000	17,000	(2,000)	(11.8)
Wages payable	4,000	3,000	1,000	33.3
Total current liabilities	$ 102,000	$ 90,000	$ 12,000	13.3
Long-term liabilities				
Note payable (due 2011)	80,000	20,000	60,000	300.0
Total liabilities	$ 182,000	$ 110,000	$ 72,000	65.5
Owners' Equity				
Common stock, $1 par value	$ 100,000	$ 100,000	$ 0	0.0
Additional paid-in capital	90,000	90,000	0	0.0
Retained earnings	198,600	136,000	62,600	46.0
Total owners' equity	$ 388,600	$ 326,000	$ 62,600	19.2
Total liabilities and owners' equity	$ 570,600	$ 436,000	$ 134,600	30.9

EXHIBIT **16.2**

Comparative Balance Sheets for Amy Company: Horizontal Analysis

---

Our analysis for Amy Company is as follows:

Significant Changes Balance Sheets (EXHIBIT 16.2)	Explanations
1 Increases in long-term notes payable, building, store equipment.	Amy Company invested in plant assets and financed part of the purchase by issuing long-term notes payable.
2 Increases in accounts receivable and inventories.	Possible problem if Amy cannot collect receivables and cannot sell its inventory increase.
3 Increase in retained earnings.	Excess of income over dividends declared

Income Statements (EXHIBIT 16.3)	
4 Increases in interest expense and depreciation expense.	Amy issued long-term notes payable and purchased plant assets.
5 Equal percent increases in sales and cost of goods sold	Favorable. Amy increased sales and maintained gross margin percent by having a similar increase in cost of goods sold.
6 Percent increases in most operating expenses other than depreciation are less than the 16.2% increase in gross margin.	Favorable. Lower percentage increase in operating expenses resulted in net income increase of 19.5%.

AMY COMPANY
COMPARATIVE INCOME STATEMENTS
FOR THE YEARS ENDED DECEMBER 31, 2007 AND 2006

	Years Ended December 31		Increase (Decrease)	
	2007	2006	Amount	Percentage
Sales (net)	$ 940,000	$ 810,000	$ 130,000	16.0%
Cost of goods sold	545,000	470,000	75,000	16.0
Gross margin on sales	$ 395,000	$ 340,000	$ 55,000	16.2
Operating expenses:				
Selling expenses:				
Sales salaries expense	$ 170,000	$ 150,000	$ 20,000	13.3
Advertising expense	14,000	12,000	2,000	16.7
Depreciation expense—store equipment	3,600	2,500	1,100	44.0
Depreciation expense—building	1,800	1,800	0	0.0
Total selling expenses	$ 189,400	$ 166,300	$ 23,100	13.9
General and administrative expenses:				
General salaries expense	$ 62,000	$ 59,000	$ 3,000	5.1
Office expense	6,000	5,600	400	7.1
Depreciation expense—office equipment	2,000	2,000	0	0.0
Depreciation expense—building	5,300	2,200	3,100	140.9
Total general and administrative expenses	$ 75,300	$ 68,800	$ 6,500	9.4
Total operating expenses	$ 264,700	$ 235,100	$ 29,600	12.6
Net operating income	$ 130,300	$ 104,900	$ 25,400	24.2
Interest expense	9,500	3,700	5,800	156.8
Net income before income taxes	$ 120,800	$ 101,200	$ 19,600	19.4
Income taxes	36,200	30,400	5,800	19.1
Net income	$ 84,600	$ 70,800	$ 13,800	19.5
Earnings per share	$.85	$.71	$.14	19.7

Total cash dividends declared and paid for each year were $22,000.

EXHIBIT **16.3**

Comparative Income Statements for Amy Company: Horizontal Analysis

---

Overall, Amy Company's investment in additional plant assets provided additional capacity to increase 2007 sales by 16%. By maintaining the same 16% increase in cost of goods sold as in sales, the gross margin increases by a similar percent (16.2%). As we saw in Chapter 5, *gross margin* is the difference between the net sales revenue and cost of goods sold. By keeping down the percent increases in most operating expenses, Amy raises net income by 19.5%. Areas of possible concern are the large increases in accounts receivable (34.3%) and inventories (43.8%).

Trend Percentages

Computing **trend percentages** is another form of horizontal analysis. First we set all amounts in the base year at 100%. Then we compute percentages for a number of years by dividing each statement amount by the related amount in the base year. Therefore, we express all years after the base year as a percentage of the base year. This lets us observe trends in data over a longer period such as five to ten years.

To illustrate, assume we have collected the following income statement data for Bent Company for a seven-year period (all amounts are in thousands of dollars):

	2007	2006	2005	2004	2003	2002	2001
Sales	$850	$790	$730	$690	$610	$640	$650
Cost of goods sold	612	537	475	428	366	384	390
Gross margin	$238	$253	$255	$262	$244	$256	$260

We compute trend percentages for sales, cost of goods sold, and gross margin by dividing the amount in each year by the base-year (2001) amount. The trend percentages for Bent Company are as follows:

	2007	2006	2005	2004	2003	2002	2001
Sales	131%	122%	112%	106%	94%	98%	100%
Cost of goods sold	157	138	122	110	94	98	100
Gross margin	92	97	98	101	94	98	100

From the preceding trend percentages, we can make the following observations:

1. Bent Company's sales decreased in 2002 and 2003 and then increased each year from 2004 through 2007.

2. Cost of goods sold changed uniformly with sales during 2002 and 2003. However, beginning with 2004, cost of goods sold increased at a faster rate than sales. This is unfavorable and means that Bent Company is paying an increasing amount for the products it purchases for resale.

3. As a result of the increase in cost of goods sold, the gross margin percent decreased in 2005, 2006, and 2007.

Trend percentages show the degree of increase or decrease in individual statement items. By comparing the trends in related items, we can explain changes in operating performance. For example, an unfavorable trend would be a decrease in sales accompanied by increases in accounts receivable and inventories. A favorable trend would be an increase in sales accompanied by decreases in cost of goods sold and operating expenses.

Vertical Analysis

Learning Goal 4   Prepare and interpret a vertical analysis of financial statements.

Vertical analysis shows how each item in a financial statement compares to the total for that statement. In a balance sheet, we set both total assets and total equities at 100%. Using total assets as an example, we then compute the percentage of each asset amount to total assets. In an income statement, we set net sales at 100%. We refer to the statement percentages we compute in vertical analysis as **common-size statements**.

Exhibit 16.4 shows comparative common-size balance sheets for Amy Company. Exhibit 16.5 shows Amy's comparative common-size income statements. To analyze these financial statements, we look for percent changes in individual items from year to year. We identify the most significant dollar or percentage changes. Then we try to explain the changes and identify whether they are favorable or unfavorable. In some cases, comparative common-size percentages for items that remain the same may be either favorable or unfavorable. Our analysis for Amy Company's comparative common-size financial statements is as follows:

Significant Changes Balance Sheets (EXHIBIT 16.4)	Explanations
1 Increases in long-term liabilities as building, store equipment.a	Amy Company invested in plant assets and financed part of the purchase by issuing long-term notes payable. Interest payments and repayment of principal at maturity will result in cash outflows company must plan for.
2 Increases in building and store equipment.	Result of additions to plant assets.

3 Decrease in owners' equity as a source of capital.

The decrease is due to the issuance of long-term notes. Amy Company increased its use of debt as a source of capital. A favorable sign is that retained earnings increases as a result of profitable operations.

4 Increases in accounts receivable and inventories.

Possible problem if Amy cannot collect receivables and its inventory increase is excessive.

Income Statements (EXHIBIT 16.5)

Explanations

5 Constant cost of goods sold as percentage of net sales.

Favorable. Amy increased dollar sales and maintained gross margin percent by maintaining cost of goods sold percent. We should also compare this percent to those of competing firms

6 Decreases in most operating expense percentages. Sales salaries expense as a percent of sales decreased from 18.5% to 18.0%. General salaries expense decreased from 7.3% to 6.6%.

Favorable. Shows management's ability to control costs while increasing sales revenues. Overall result is an increase in net income as a percent of sales from 8.7% to 9%.

7 Increases in interest expense and depreciation expense.

Amy issued long-term notes payable and purchased plant assets.

AMY COMPANY
COMPARATIVE COMMON-SIZE BALANCE SHEETS
DECEMBER 31, 2007 AND 2006

	December 31 2007	December 31 2006	Common-size Percentages 2007	Common-size Percentages 2006
Assets				
Current assets				
Cash	$ 36,000	$ 33,000	6.3%	7.6%
Accounts receivable (net)	80,600	60,000	14.1 ◄4	13.8
Inventories	115,000	80,000	20.2 ◄	18.3
Total current assets	$ 231,600	$ 173,000	40.6	39.7
Property, plant, equipment				
Land	$ 125,000	$ 125,000	21.9	28.7
Building (net)	150,000	83,000	26.3 ◄2	19.0
Store equipment (net)	36,000	25,000	6.3 ◄	5.7
Office equipment (net)	28,000	30,000	4.9	6.9
Total property, plant, and equipment	$ 339,000	$ 263,000	59.4	60.3
Total assets	$ 570,600	$ 436,000	100.0	100.0
Liabilities				
Current liabilities				
Accounts payable	$ 83,000	$ 70,000	14.6*	16.0*
Notes payable	15,000	17,000	2.6	3.9
Wages payable	4,000	3,000	0.7	0.7
Total current liabilities	$ 102,000	$ 90,000	17.9	20.6
Long-term liabilities				
Note payable (due 2011)	80,000	20,000	14.0 ◄1	4.6
Total liabilities	$ 182,000	$ 110,000	31.9	25.2
Owners' Equity				
Common stock, $1 par value	$ 100,000	$ 100,000	17.5	22.9
Additional paid-in capital	90,000	90,000	15.8	20.7*
Retained earnings	198,600	136,000	34.8	31.2
Total owners' equity	$ 388,600	$ 326,000	68.1 ◄3	74.8
Total liabilities and owners' equity	$ 570,600	$ 436,000	100.0	100.0

*Total results are rounded so that major subtotals are the correct percentage.

EXHIBIT **16.4**

Comparative Balance Sheets for Amy Company: Vertical Analysis

AMY COMPANY
COMPARATIVE COMMON-SIZE INCOME STATEMENTS
FOR THE YEARS ENDED DECEMBER 31, 2007 AND 2006

	Years Ended December 31		Common-size Percentages	
	2007	2006	2007	2006
Sales (net)	$ 940,000	$ 810,000	100.0%	100.0%
Cost of goods sold	545,000	470,000	58.0 ◄ 5	58.0
Gross margin on sales	$ 395,000	$ 340,000	42.0	42.0
Operating expenses:				
Selling expenses:				
Sales salaries expense	$ 170,000	$ 150,000	18.0* ◄	18.5
Advertising expense	14,000	12,000	1.5	1.5
Depreciation expense—store equipment	3,600	2,500	0.4	0.3
Depreciation expense—building	1,800	1,800	0.2	0.2
Total selling expenses	$ 189,400	$ 166,300	20.1	20.5
General and administrative expenses:				
General salaries expense	$ 62,000	$ 59,000	6.6 ◄	7.3
Office expense	6,000	5,600	0.6	0.7
Depreciation expense—office equipment	2,000	2,000	0.2	0.2
Depreciation expense—building	5,300	2,200	0.6 ◄ 7	0.3
Total general and administrative expenses	$ 75,300	$ 68,800	8.0	8.5
Total operating expenses	$ 264,700	$ 235,100	28.1*	29.0
Net operating income	$ 130,300	$ 104,900	13.9	13.0
Interest expense	9,500	3,700	1.0 ◄ 7	0.5
Net income before income taxes	$ 120,800	$ 101,200	12.9	12.5
Income taxes	36,200	30,400	3.9	3.8
Net income	$ 84,600	$ 70,800	9.0	8.7
Earnings per share	$.85	$.71		

*These results are rounded so that major subtotals are the correct percentage.

EXHIBIT **16.5**

Comparative Income Statements for Amy Company: Vertical Analysis

Overall, Amy Company is increasing its use of debt financing. This is acceptable so long as the company can meet the debt payments and earn a favorable rate of return on the invested funds. It looks as though this is the case, because sales increases and operating expense reductions increased net income as a percent of sales in 2007.

Note that horizontal analysis and vertical analysis work together to explain changes in comparative financial statements. The results of horizontal analysis point out trends in statement items over time. The results of vertical analysis point out changes in how statement items fit together. Both analytical tools highlight areas of the company that require investigation and explanation.

RATIO ANALYSIS

Learning Goal 5 Calculate and interpret ratios used to evaluate short-term liquidity, long-term solvency, profitability, and market performance.

Ratio analysis shows the relative size of one financial statement component to another. We cannot make financial decisions by looking at one isolated ratio. Financial ratios are effective only when we use them in combination with other ratios, analyses, and information. A primary limitation of ratio analysis is that the results depend on the accounting methods the company uses. We will calculate and interpret ratios to evaluate (1) short-term liquidity, (2) long-term solvency, (3) profitability, and (4) market performance.

Evaluation of Short-term Liquidity

Short-term liquidity means a company can pay current liabilities as they come due. Ratios that measure liquidity generally involve current assets and current liabilities. **Working capital** refers to the excess of current assets over current liabilities. We compute working capital by subtracting total current liabilities from total current assets. Following are the working capital ratios we use to evaluate short-term liquidity:

1. Current ratio.

2. Quick ratio.

3. Accounts receivable turnover.

4. Days' sales in receivables.

5. Inventory turnover.

Current Ratio

We compute the **current ratio** by dividing current assets by current liabilities. The current ratio is a common measure of liquidity. The current ratios for Amy Company at December 31, 2007, and 2006 are as follows:

CURRENT RATIO

Formula	For Amy Company 2007	For Amy Company 2006
$\dfrac{\text{Current Assets}}{\text{Current Liabilities}}$	$\dfrac{\$231,600}{\$102,000} = 2.27$	$\dfrac{\$173,000}{\$90,000} = 1.92$

This ratio means that as of December 31, 2007, Amy Company had approximately $2.27 for every $1 of current liabilities. Users frequently read the 2007 ratio as 2.27:1, sometimes seen as "2.27 to 1." The increase in Amy's current ratio in 2007 indicates an increase in liquidity. However, we need to combine these results with other ratios before making a final evaluation of liquidity.

What is a satisfactory current ratio? As a rule of thumb, many financial statement users consider a current ratio of 2:1 as adequate. However, we must consider other factors such as the nature of the company's business and the composition of the current assets. For example, if 90% of the current assets consist of old, unsaleable merchandise inventory, a 2:1 current ratio would be unfavorable. In contrast, if 90% of the current assets consist of cash and marketable securities, we would consider a 2:1 current ratio as excellent.

In some cases, an unusually high current ratio in comparison with other firms in the same industry may be unfavorable. It may mean that the company is missing long-term investment opportunities by keeping too much of its funds in current assets. We must compare the company's data with industry norms to see if its current ratio is out of line.

Quick Ratio

The **quick ratio** (sometimes called the *acid-test ratio*) is a more strict measure of short-term liquidity. To compute the quick ratio, we add cash, short-term investments, and receivables (net of allowance for doubtful accounts) and divide the total by current liabilities. By excluding inventories and prepaid expenses from current assets, the ratio better reflects liquid assets available to pay liabilities. The quick ratios for Amy Company as of December 31, 2007 and 2006, are as follows:

QUICK RATIO

Formula	For Amy Company 2007	For Amy Company 2006
$\dfrac{\text{Cash + Short-term Investments + Net Current Receivables}}{\text{Current Liabilities}}$	$\dfrac{\$36,000 + \$0 + \$80,600}{\$102,000} = 1.14$	$\dfrac{\$33,000 + \$0 + \$60,000}{\$90,000} = 1.03$

A rule of thumb for an adequate quick ratio is 1:1. However, once again this would depend on industry norms and the types of assets the company owns. For Amy Company this ratio improved in 2007, from 1.03 to 1.14. Most of the improvement is due to an increase in accounts receivable. Since a large portion of the numerator consists of accounts receivable ($80,600 in 2007), the quality of this ratio depends largely on how much of these receivables Amy Company can actually collect.

Accounts Receivable Turnover

Accounts receivable turnover measures how many times we turn receivables into cash during a period. We calculate accounts receivable turnover by dividing net sales by average net accounts receivable. We compute average net accounts receivable by adding the beginning and ending net receivable balances and dividing by 2. Amy Company's accounts receivable turnover for 2007 is as follows:

ACCOUNTS RECEIVABLE TURNOVER

Formula	For Amy Company for 2007
$\dfrac{\text{Net Sales}}{\text{Average Net Accounts Receivable}}$	$\dfrac{\$940,000}{(\$60,000 + \$80,600) \div 2} = 13.37 \text{ times}$

This ratio means that Amy Company is collecting its average balance in accounts receivable 13.37 times per year. A high accounts receivable turnover ratio means that a company is more successful in collecting cash from its credit customers. We can compare this ratio to industry norms, or to past ratios for the company, to decide if it is favorable or unfavorable.

To obtain the most meaningful results, we should use credit sales instead of net sales in the numerator. However, companies do not generally show separate figures for cash and credit sales. Also, if receivable balances are larger or smaller than normal at the balance sheet date, the ratio will not reflect actual collections during the year. Many companies end their financial reporting year at a low point of business activity. Therefore, the balance in receivables may be at a low level. In this case, we may wish to use the average monthly balance in receivables during the year in calculating the ratio.

Days' Sales in Receivables

Days' sales in receivables shows how many days' sales remain uncollected in accounts receivable. This tells us the average collection period. We compute the days' sales in receivables by a two-step process:

1. Compute net sales per day.

2. Divide average accounts receivable by net sales per day.

Amy Company's days' sales in receivables for 2007 is as follows:

DAYS' SALES IN RECEIVABLES

Formula	For Amy Company for 2007
1 Net sales per day: $\dfrac{\text{Net Sales}}{365 \text{ Days}}$	$\dfrac{\$940,000}{365} = \$2,575$
2 Days' sales in receivables: $\dfrac{\text{Average Net Accounts Receivable}}{\text{Net Sales per Day}}$	$\dfrac{(\$60,000 + \$80,600) \div 2}{\$2,575} = 27.3 \text{ days}$

An alternate way to compute days' sales in receivables is to divide 365 days by the accounts receivable turnover ratio. In this case, the computation is as follows:

$$\frac{365 \text{ Days}}{\text{Accounts Receivable Turnover Ratio}} = \frac{365}{13.37} = 27.3 \text{ days}$$

This means that Amy Company has to wait an average of 27.3 days to collect a credit sale. A low number of days' sales in receivables is favorable. It indicates that the company waits less time to collect cash. We should compare this ratio with industry norms and past experience for the company. Average collection periods vary with the industry and a firm's sales terms. Wholesalers of shoes may average 45 days, while grocery wholesalers may average 15 days. The ability to turn receivables into cash on a timely basis is a key factor in assessing a company's liquidity.

Inventory Turnover

Holding inventory results in financing and storage costs. Thus companies should try to carry as little inventory as possible without losing the ability to service customers. The length of time a company holds inventory before selling it has a great impact on its investment in working capital. **Inventory turnover** measures the number of times the company sells and replaces its inventory in a period. We calculate inventory turnover by dividing cost of goods sold by average merchandise inventory. We compute average merchandise inventory by adding the beginning and ending inventory balances and dividing by 2. Amy Company's inventory turnover for 2007 is as follows:

INVENTORY TURNOVER

Formula	For Amy Company for 2007
$\dfrac{\text{Cost of Goods Sold}}{\text{Average Inventory}}$	$\dfrac{\$545,000}{(\$80,000 + \$115,000) \div 2} = 5.59$ times

This ratio means that Amy Company sold and replaced its inventory 5.59 times in 2007. A high inventory turnover ratio means a company is operating with a smaller investment in inventory. This is favorable so long as the company can still satisfy customer demand. Inventory turnover varies by industry. A wholesaler of automobile parts may average five inventory turnovers per year. A wholesaler of perishables such as meat and poultry may average 35 or more. High-volume, low-margin businesses such as fast-food chains have high inventory turnover. Computer manufacturers typically hold low levels of inventory to avoid the risk of components' obsolescence. Low-volume, high-margin businesses such as jewelry stores have low turnover. Once again, we can compare this ratio to industry norms or to past ratios for the company to decide if it is favorable or unfavorable. In cases where the beginning and ending inventory balances are lower or higher than normal, we may wish to use a monthly average for the year.

Evaluation of Long-term Solvency

Long-term solvency is the ability of a company to operate for a long time. Our primary concern is to assess if the company can remain a going concern and avoid bankruptcy. When analyzing a firm's long-term solvency, we use ratios that focus on the proportion of debt the firm uses. Long-term solvency also means the ability to meet fixed interest payments. Following are the two ratios we use to evaluate long-term solvency (we number the ratios consecutively for easy review using Exhibit 16.6 later in the chapter):

6. Debt ratio.

7. Times interest earned ratio.

Debt Ratio

Both creditors and investors are interested in the portion of total assets creditors contribute. Higher levels of debt financing mean that a company has a higher risk of not meeting fixed interest and principal payments. This could force the company into bankruptcy, in which creditors and investors could lose part or all of their investments. The **debt ratio** shows the amount of total assets creditors provide. We calculate the debt ratio by dividing total liabilities by total assets at the end of a year. Amy Company's debt ratios for the years ended December 31, 2007 and 2006, are as follows:

DEBT RATIO

For Amy Company

Formula	2007	2006
$\dfrac{\text{Total Liabilities}}{\text{Total Assets}}$	$\dfrac{\$182,000}{\$570,600} = 31.9\%$	$\dfrac{\$110,000}{\$436,000} = 25.2\%$

This ratio means that for Amy Company, creditors provide 31.9% of the financing for total assets at December 31, 2007. This is an increase from the debt ratio of 25.2% in 2006. A higher debt ratio means that a company is financing more of its assets with debt. This involves more risk. If Amy Company can invest the borrowed funds successfully, the increase in debt is manageable. Based on the previous comparative statement analysis, this seems to be the case. Exhibit 16.5 shows that despite the higher amounts of depreciation and interest expense in 2007, net income was 9% of sales in 2007 versus 8.7% in 2006. We should also make comparisons with industry norms.

Times Interest Earned Ratio

Fixed interest payments on debt are an obligation companies must meet each year. Creditors want to know the firm's ability to pay annual interest charges. The **times interest earned ratio** calculates the number of times the company earned interest expense with current income. Some people also call this the *interest coverage ratio*. We compute this ratio by dividing income before interest and income taxes by interest expense. Amy Company's times interest earned ratios for the years ended December 31, 2007 and 2006, are as follows:

TIMES INTEREST EARNED

For Amy Company

Formula	2007	2006
$\dfrac{\text{Net Income} + \text{Income Tax Expense} + \text{Interest Expense}}{\text{Interest Expense}}$	$\dfrac{\$84,600 + \$36,200 + \$9,500}{\$9,500} = 13.72 \text{ times}$	$\dfrac{\$70,800 + \$30,400 + \$3,700}{\$3,700} = 28.35 \text{ times}$

This ratio means that Amy Company earned its total interest expense 13.72 times in 2007. This is a decrease from 28.35 times in 2006. A higher ratio for times interest earned is more favorable. The decrease in the ratio reflects the increase in Amy Company's use of debt. It is important to compare company ratios with industry norms. The average range of interest coverage ratios for most U.S. nonfinancial businesses is 2.0 to 3.0 times. Therefore, the interest coverage for Amy Company of 13.72 times in 2007 appears very strong.

Evaluation of Profitability

The primary objective of a business is to earn a profit for its owners. As a result, financial statement users have an interest in measures that assist in evaluating profitability. We have introduced many of these ratios in previous chapters. In this chapter we show five profitability ratios:

8. Profit margin.

9. Total asset turnover.

10. Return on total assets.

11. Return on owners' equity.

12. Earnings per share.

Profit Margin

Profit margin is the percentage each sales dollar contributes to net income. We compute profit margin by dividing net income by net sales. Amy Company's profit margin percentages for 2007 and 2006 are as follows:

PROFIT MARGIN
For Amy Company

Formula	2007	2006
$\dfrac{\text{Net Income}}{\text{Net Sales}}$	$\dfrac{\$84,600}{\$940,000} = 9.0\%$	$\dfrac{\$70,800}{\$810,000} = 8.7\%$

Amy Company's profit margin percent increased in 2007. In our previous vertical analysis of Amy's comparative financial statements, we computed all income statement items as a percent of sales. The reasons for the 2007 profit margin increase were that management held the cost of goods percent constant in 2007 and decreased most percentages for operating expenses. Profit margins vary by industry. Following are 2003 fiscal year operating revenues and profit margin percents for some well-known companies:

Company	Industry	Total Revenues(millions)	Net Income %
Coca-Cola	Softdrinks	$21,962.0	22.9%
PepsiCo	Softdrinks	29,261.0	14.4
H. J. Heinz	Foods	8,414.5	9.6
Hershey	Foods	4,429.2	13.3
Nike	Footwear	12,253.1	7.7
Reebok	Footwear	3,785.3	5.1
Home Depot	Retail	64,816.0	6.6
Best Buy	Retail	24,547.0	2.9

Total Asset Turnover

Total asset turnover measures the *efficiency* of the company in using its investment in assets to generate sales. We calculate total asset turnover by dividing net sales by average total assets. Amy Company's total asset turnover for 2007 is as follows:

TOTAL ASSET TURNOVER
For Amy Company for 2007

Formula	
$\dfrac{\text{Net Sales}}{\text{Average Total Assets}}$	$\dfrac{\$940,000}{(\$570,600 + \$436,000) \div 2} = 1.87 \text{ times}$

This means that Amy Company generated $1.87 in sales for each dollar of investment in assets. A higher number indicates a company is using its assets more efficiently. Generally, manufacturing firms with heavy investments in plant assets have a lower total asset turnover ratio than a retailer. For example, Boeing Company had a recent total asset turnover ratio of 1.3 compared to 3.9 for Best Buy Stores.

Return on Total Assets

Investors frequently use return on total assets as an overall measure of profitability. **Return on total assets** measures the amount a company earns on each dollar of investment. All of us can relate to this since it is a common concern when we invest our own money. We compute return on total assets by dividing net income by average total assets. Amy Company's return on total assets for 2007 is as follows:

RETURN ON TOTAL ASSETS

Formula	For Amy Company for 2007
$\dfrac{\text{Net Income}}{\text{Average Total Assets}}$	$\dfrac{\$84,600}{(\$570,600 + \$436,000) \div 2} = 16.8\%$

Comparison with industry norms is important. Following are 2003 average total assets and return on assets percents for some well-known companies:

Company	Industry	Average Total Assets (millions)	Return on Assets %
Coca-Cola	Softdrinks	$27,332.0	17.7
PepsiCo	Softdrinks	26,657	15.8
H. J. Heinz	Foods	9,551.0	8.4
Hershey	Foods	3,690.0	16.0
Nike	Footwear	7,356.4	12.9
Reebok	Footwear	2,215.2	8.7
Home Depot	Retail	32,224.0	13.4
Best Buy	Retail	8,157.5	8.2

Return on Owners' Equity

Return on total assets measures the return on assets provided by both creditors and owners. **Return on owners' equity** measures the return on the owners' investment in the company. We compute return on owners' equity by dividing net income by average owners' equity. Amy Company's return on owners' equity for 2007 is:

RETURN ON OWNERS' EQUITY

Formula	For Amy Company for 2007
$\dfrac{\text{Net Income - Preferred Dividends}}{\text{Average Owners' Equity}}$	$\dfrac{\$84,600 - \$0}{(\$388,600 + \$326,000) \div 2} = 23.7\%$

Earnings per Share

One of the most widely quoted financial statistics is earnings per share. In a simple situation, we calculate **earnings per share (EPS)** by dividing net income less any preferred dividends by the weighted average number of common shares outstanding during the year. We discussed more complex EPS calculations in Chapter 16. Amy Company's earnings per share for 2007 and 2006 are as follows:

EARNINGS PER SHARE

Formula	For Amy Company 2007	For Amy Company 2006
$\dfrac{\text{Net Income - Preferred Dividends}}{\text{Average Number of Common Shares Outstanding during the year}}$	$\dfrac{\$84,600}{\$100,000} = \$.85$	$\dfrac{\$70,800}{\$100,000} = \$.71$

Evaluation of Market Performance

The market price of a stock reflects investors' expectations about the future earnings prospects for a company. We will discuss two common ratios investors watch:

13. Price/earnings (P/E) ratio.

14. Dividend yield.

Price/Earnings (P/E) Ratio

The **price/earnings (P/E) ratio** is the number of times earnings per share the stock is currently selling for. We compute the price/earnings ratio by dividing the stock market price per share by the earnings per share. Assume that Amy Company common stock is selling for $15 as of December 31, 2007. Its price/earnings ratio is as follows:

PRICE/EARNINGS RATIO

Formula	For Amy Company for 2007
$\dfrac{\text{Market Price per Share of Common Stock}}{\text{Earnings per Share}}$	$\dfrac{\$15}{\$.85} = 17.6$ times

Amy Company's common stock is selling at 17.6 times earnings as of December 31, 2007. Price/earnings ratios vary by industry. For example, on April 1, 2005, Wal-Mart had a price/earnings ratio of 40 times on its common stock. At the same date, The Coca-Cola Company (soft drink industry) had a price/earnings ratio of 33 times. This means that investors have higher future earnings expectations for Wal-Mart than for Coca-Cola Company. As a result, they are willing to pay a higher times earnings price for Wal-Mart.

Dividend Yield

Investors buy stocks for two reasons: (1) to receive cash dividends and (2) to sell the stock at a higher price in the market. Not all companies pay dividends. Investors match their own investment goals with the dividend policy and stock appreciation potential of individual companies. **Dividend yield** is a measure of the dividend-paying performance of a company. We calculate dividend yield by dividing the yearly dividend per share of common stock by the current market price per share. In 2007, Amy Company paid total cash dividends of $22,000, or $.22 per share ($22,000 ÷ 100,000 shares). Amy's dividend yield is as follows:

DIVIDEND YIELD

Formula	For Amy Company for 2007
$\dfrac{\text{Dividend per Share}}{\text{Market Price per Share}}$	$\dfrac{\$.22}{\$15} = 0.015$, or 1.5%

Dividend yields vary by company. Generally, high-growth companies tend to have a lower dividend yield. This is because these companies invest most of the profits back into the business instead of using cash to pay large dividends. Investors buy growth stocks primarily for their rising stock price, not their dividend yield. Following are dividend yields and price/earnings (P/E) ratios as of April 1, 2005, for some well-known companies:

Company	Industry	Dividend Yield %	Price/Earnings (P/E) Ratio
Coca-Cola	Softdrinks	2.70%	21 times
PepsiCo	Softdrinks	1.70	22 times
H. J. Heinz	Foods	3.10	17 times
Hershey	Foods	1.50	26 times
Nike	Footwear	1.20	19 times
Reebok	Footwear	0.70	15 times
Home Depot	Retail	1.10	17 times
Best Buy	Retail	0.90	19 times

Exhibit 16.6 summarizes all of the ratios we present in this chapter. Use this summary exhibit as a reference when doing end-of-chapter exercises and problems.

Ratio	Computation	Information Provided
Evaluation of short-term liquidity		
1. Current ratio	$\dfrac{\text{Current Assets}}{\text{Current Liabilities}}$	Shows current assets available to pay current liabilities.
2. Quick Ratio	$\dfrac{\text{Cash + Short-term Investments + Net Current Receivables}}{\text{Current Liabilities}}$	Shows liquid assets available to pay current liabilities.
3. Accounts receivable turnover	$\dfrac{\text{Net Sales}}{\text{Average Net Accounts Receivable}}$	The number of times receivables are turned into cash during a period.
4. Days' sales in receivables	$\dfrac{\text{Average Net Accounts Receivable}}{\text{Net Sales per Day}}$	Shows how many days' sales remain uncollected in accounts receivable.
5. Inventory turnover	$\dfrac{\text{Cost of Goods Sold}}{\text{Average Inventory}}$	Measures the number of times inventory turns over in an accounting period.
Evaluation of long-term solvency		
6. Debt ratio	$\dfrac{\text{Total Liabilities}}{\text{Total Assets}}$	Shows the percent of total assets creditors provide.
7. Times interest earned ratio	$\dfrac{\text{Net Income + Income Tax Expense + Interest Expense}}{\text{Interest Expense}}$	Measures the coverage of interest expense by current operating income.
Evaluation of profitability		
8. Profit margin	$\dfrac{\text{Net Income}}{\text{Net Sales}}$	The percentage a sales dollar contributes to net income.
9. Total asset turnover	$\dfrac{\text{Net Sales}}{\text{Average Total Assets}}$	Measures the efficiency of asset use.
10. Return on total assets	$\dfrac{\text{Net Income}}{\text{Average Total Assets}}$	Measures the amount a firm earns on a dollar of investment in assets.
11. Return on owners' equity	$\dfrac{\text{Net Income—Preferred Dividends}}{\text{Average Owners' Equity}}$	Measures the return on the owners' investment in the firm.
12. Earnings per share	$\dfrac{\text{Net Income—Preferred Dividends}}{\text{Weighted Average Number of Common Shares Outstanding during Year}}$	The amount of earnings per share the stock sells for.
Evaluation of market performance		
13. Price/earnings (P/E) ratio	$\dfrac{\text{Market Price per Share of Common Stock}}{\text{Earnings per Share}}$	The number of times earnings per share the stock sells for.
14. Dividend yield	$\dfrac{\text{Dividend per Share}}{\text{Market Price per Share}}$	Measures dividend-paying performance of a company.

EXHIBIT **16.6**

Summary of Financial Analysis Ratios

LIMITATIONS OF FINANCIAL ANALYSIS TOOLS AND TECHNIQUES

Learning Goal 6   Identify the limitations of financial statement analysis.

When using the financial analysis comparisons and ratios, it is important to be aware of their limitations. Making business decisions involves considering all related information. Financial trends and ratio analysis are only one part of this information. Users should always remember the following limitations:

1. *The historical nature of accounting information.* Trends and ratios using accounting information reflect the past. Decisions affect the future. Although the past can be a useful guide in estimating future results, remember that it is not a guarantee of future performance.

2. *Changing economic conditions.* When we compare ratios for different periods, we must consider changes in economic conditions. For example, an acceptable level of debt financing when the economy and consumer demand is strong may be unacceptable when we face a recession. Ratio analysis is a useful screening device. However, awareness of changes in consumer demand, interest rates, and competition is equally important in making lending and investing decisions.

3. *Comparisons with industry averages.* Throughout our discussion of ratio analysis, we say that users should compare company ratios to industry norms. Yet there may be situations in which departure from industry norms is acceptable and even desirable. For example, a decrease in inventory turnover is normally a bad sign that a company is accumulating excess inventory. However, if the company expects its inventory to increase in price, the buildup may result in a competitive advantage for the company.

4. *Seasonal factors.* We compute balance sheet ratios as of a moment in time. Account balances at that date that are higher or lower than normal will distort the ratio. Ask yourself if the account balances you use to calculate a ratio represent normal activity.

5. *The quality of reported net income.* Reported net income is a key item of interest to financial statement users. By this time in your study of accounting, you should be aware that the accounting methods a company uses affect the net income it reports. For example, Company A using LIFO and double-declining balance depreciation will most likely report a lower net income than Company B using FIFO and straight-line depreciation. In this case, accountants would call Company A's net income number "higher quality." It uses accounting methods that tend to minimize reported net income.

Evaluating the underlying accounting methods and estimates a company uses is an important part of interpreting financial statement trends and ratios. Exhibit 16.7 presents a summary of various accounting methods and their usual effect on reported net income. We recommend that you use it as a review of financial accounting methods and a useful reference when evaluating financial statement information.

LEARNING GOALS REVIEW

1. **State the objective and describe the process of financial statement analysis.**
   Financial statement analysis helps users make decisions about an organization. The process of financial statement analysis involves applying tools and techniques to financial statement data. This enables users to study relationships and trends to assess the risk and return of an investment or lending proposal.

Choices Involving Accounting Methods	Alternative Methods	Method that Generally Produces lower (More Conservative) Net Income Number	Refer to Chapter
Bad debts	Allowance versus direct write-off	Allowance method	Chapter 7
Inventories	LIFO versus FIFO	LIFO in a period of inflation	Chapter 9
Long-term assets	Accelerated versus straight-line depreciation	Accelerated depreciation methods (double-declining balance or sum-of-the-years'-digits).	Chapter 10
Bonds and long-term liabilities	Effective interest versus straight-line amortization	Effective interest method results in more correct determination of interest expense.	Chapter 13

Choices Involving Accounting Estimates	Management Decision	Estimate that Generally Produces lower (More Conservative) Net Income Number	Refer to Chapter
End-of-period adjusting entries: Accruals and deferrals	Recognize all appropriate revenues and expenses	Careful analysis of all accounts to properly reflect revenues earned and expenses incurred.	Chapter 3
Bad debts	Choice of estimation percentage	Careful aging of accounts receivable to determine net realizable value.	Chapter 7
Inventories	Lower-of-cost-or-market valuation	Recognizing declines in inventory value in the period they occur.	Chapter 9
Long-lived assets	Estimate of asset life	Using shorter rather than longer estimate of useful life within the range of possible estimates.	Chapter 10

EXHIBIT **16.7**

Summary of Accounting Methods and Estimates and Their Usual Effect on Reported Net Income

2. Describe the sources of information for financial statement analysis.

Sources of financial statement analysis information for publicly held companies include: published reports, government reports, financial service information, and financial newspapers and periodicals. Exhibit 16.1 shows a summary of statement users, the decisions they face, and their information needs.

3. Prepare and interpret a horizontal analysis of financial statements.

Horizontal analysis shows trends in individual financial statement items over time. We prepare horizontal analyses by measuring the percentage change in each financial statement item from a previous year. Trend percentages are a form of horizontal analysis in which we set base-year amounts at 100%. Interpretation of horizontal analysis involves identifying major dollar or percentage changes in individual statement items and deciding whether they are favorable or unfavorable.

4. Prepare and interpret a vertical analysis of financial statements.

Vertical analysis shows changes in the relationship of individual financial statement items to a statement total. We call the resulting statement percentages common-size statements. Vertical analysis interpretation involves identifying changes in financial statement relationships and determining whether they are favorable or unfavorable. For example, an increase in cost of goods sold as a percentage of sales would be unfavorable.

5. Calculate and interpret ratios used to evaluate short-term liquidity, long-term solvency, profitability, and market performance.

Exhibit 16.6 presents a summary of all the ratios we discuss in the chapter.

6. Identify the limitations of financial statement analysis.

The limitations of financial statement analysis include: the historical nature of accounting information, changing economic conditions, comparisons with industry averages, seasonal factors, and the quality of reported net income. Factors that affect the quality of reported net income are the company's choice of accounting methods and its estimates. We show a summary of choices in accounting methods and estimates in Exhibit 16.7.

DEMONSTRATION PROBLEM

Analyzing and Interpreting Financial Statements

Following are the income statement for the year ended December 31, 2007, and balance sheets for December 31, 2007 and 2006, for Denim, Inc.:

DENIM, INC.
INCOME STATEMENT
FOR THE YEAR ENDED DECEMBER 31, 2007

Sales	$ 50,000
Cost of goods sold	35,000
Gross margin on sales	$ 15,000
Operating expenses	7,000
Net operating income	$ 8,000
Interest expense	1,000
Net income before income taxes	$ 7,000
Income taxes	2,500
Net income	$ 4,500

DENIM, INC.
COMPARATIVE BALANCE SHEETS
DECEMBER 31, 2007 AND 2006

	December 31	
Assets	**2007**	**2006**
Current assets		
Cash	$ 3,000	$ 2,000
Accounts receivable	12,000	10,000
Merchandise inventory	14,000	12,000
Total current assets	$ 29,000	$ 24,000
Property, plant, and equipment		
Land	$ 20,000	$ 20,000
Buildings (net of depreciation)	39,000	40,000
Total property, plant, and equipment	$ 59,000	$ 60,000
Total assets	$ 88,000	$ 84,000
Liabilities		
Current liabilities		
Accounts payable	$ 10,000	$ 9,000
Interest payable	500	0
Total current liabilities	$ 10,500	$ 9,000
Long-term liabilities		
Mortgage payable	12,500	13,000
Total liabilities	$ 23,000	$ 22,000
Owners' Equity		
Common stock	$ 40,000	$ 40,000
Retained earnings	25,000	22,000
Total owners' equity	$ 65,000	$ 62,000
Total liabilities and owners' equity	$ 88,000	$ 84,000

REQUIRED

1. **(LG 3)** Calculate the amount of change and percentage change in accounts receivable, buildings, and interest payable.

2. **(LG 4)** Calculate the percentage that would appear in a 2007 common-size income statement for cost of goods sold and net income before taxes. Calculate a 2007 common-size balance sheet percentage for merchandise inventory, and a 2006 common-size balance sheet percentage for mortgage payable.

3. **(LG 5)** Calculate the following ratios for 2007: (a) current ratio. (b) quick ratio. (c) accounts receivable turnover. (d) inventory turnover. (e) debt ratio. (f) times interest earned ratio. (g) total asset turnover. (h) return on total assets. (I) return on owners' equity.

SOLUTION

Requirement 1

> ### Solution Approach
> The amount of change and percentage change are calculated from data for two periods. The earlier period is the base period. In this case, 2006 will be the base for comparison. To calculate the amount of change, subtract the amount for the later year from the amount for the earlier year. Calculate the percentage change by dividing the amount of change by the amount for the earlier year. Remember that percentage change is only calculated if the base year is positive.

Accounts receivable:

$$\$12,000 - \$10,000 = \$2,000$$
$$\frac{\$2,000}{\$10,000} = .20, \text{ or } 20\%$$

Buildings:

$$\$39,000 - \$40,000 = \$(1,000)$$
$$\frac{\$(1,000)}{\$40,000} = (.025), \text{ or } (2.5)\%$$

Interest payable:

$$\$500 - \$0 = \$500$$

We cannot calculate the percentage change for interest payable because for the base year it is zero.

Requirement 2

> ### Solution Approach
> To calculate the percentage for a common-size income statement, use net sales as the base. For the balance sheet, total assets or total liabilities and stockholders' equity is the base.

Cost of goods sold:

$$\frac{\$35,000}{\$50,000} = .70, \text{ or } 70\%$$

Net income before taxes:

$$\frac{\$7,000}{\$50,000} = .14, \text{ or } 14\%$$

Merchandise inventory:

$$\frac{\$14,000}{\$88,000} = .159, \text{ or } 15.9\%$$

Mortgage payable:

$$\frac{\$13,000}{\$84,000} = .155, \text{ of } 15.5\%$$

Requirement 3

Solution Approach

Calculate each of the ratios by identifying the appropriate formula and plugging the appropriate number from the financial statements into the formula. Remember that often the name of the ratio provides a clue as to what the formula is. In all turnover ratios, an amount from the income statement is the numerator and an average of the beginning and end-of-the-period related amounts from the balance sheet is the denominator. For example, sales is related to accounts receivable, and cost of goods sold is related to inventory. Also, in any ratio that involves an amount from the income statement and an amount from the balance sheet, the amount from the balance sheet must be an average of the beginning and end-of-period amounts.

a. Current ratio:
$$\frac{\$29,000}{\$10,500} = 2.76$$

b. Quick ratio:
$$\frac{\$15,000}{\$10,500} = 1.43$$

c. Accounts receivable turnover:
$$\frac{\$50,000}{(\$12,000 + \$10,000) \div 2} = 4.55 \text{ times}$$

d. Inventory turnover:
$$\frac{\$35,000}{(\$14,000 + \$12,000) \div 2} = 2.69 \text{ times}$$

e. Debt ratio:
$$\frac{\$23,000}{\$88,000} = .261, \text{ or } 26.1\%$$

f. Times interest earned:
$$\frac{\$4,500 + \$2,500 + \$1,000}{\$1,000} = 8 \text{ times}$$

g. Total asset turnover:
$$\frac{\$50,000}{(\$88,000 + \$84,000) \div 2} = .58 \text{ times}$$

h. Return on total assets:
$$\frac{\$4,500}{(\$88,000 + \$84,000) \div 2} = .052, \text{ or } 5.2\%$$

i. Return on owners' equity:
$$\frac{\$4,500 - \$0}{(\$65,000 + \$62,000) \div 2} = .071, \text{ or } 7.1\%$$

GLOSSARY

accounts receivable turnover The number of times a company collects receivables during a period.

base year The first year in a series of years to which all other years are compared.

common-size statements Financial statements in which the dollar amounts are converted to percentages of the total for vertical analysis.

comparative financial statements Current and past financial statements shown in parallel columns.

current ratio Current assets divided by current liabilities, a measure of the ability of a firm to pay its current debts.

days' sales in receivables A ratio that indicates the average collection period by showing how many days' sales are uncollected in accounts receivable.

debt ratio The division of total liabilities by total assets: it indicates the percent of total assets provided by creditors.

dividend yield A measure of the dividend-paying performance of a firm; it is derived by dividing the yearly dividend per share of common stock by the market price per share.

earnings per share (EPS) Net income (less preferred dividends) divided by the weighted average number of common shares outstanding during the year.

financial statement analysis Applying tools and techniques to financial statement data to identify how the numbers are related and how they have changed over time.

general-purpose financial statements Financial statements for external users that include the income statement, the statement of retained earnings or stockholders' equity, the balance sheet, and the statement of cash flows.

horizontal analysis Current and past financial statements of a company that show dollar and percent changes for each financial statement item for the periods shown.

interim reports Quarterly reports that contain summarized financial information about the most recent quarter and the year to date.

inventory turnover The number of times the company sells and replaces its inventory during a period.

objective of financial statement analysis To make predictions about an organization as an aid in decision making.

price/earnings (P/E) ratio The number of times earnings per share the stock is selling for: the division of the stock price by the earnings per share.

profit margin The percentage contribution of a sales dollar to net income; it is derived by dividing net income by net sales.

quick ratio The sum of cash, short-term investments, and receivables (less doubtful accounts) divided by current liabilities; it is a more strict measure of short-term liquidity than the current ratio.

ratio analysis Shows the relative size of one financial statement item to another by converting the dollar amounts to a percentage, a decimal, or a fraction.

return on owners' equity Net income as a percentage of average owners' equity; it measures the return on the owners' investment in the company.

return on total assets The measure of the amount a firm earns on each dollar it invests; it shows net income as a percentage of average total assets.

times interest earned ratio The division of income before interest expense and income taxes by interest expense; it indicates a firm's ability to pay its annual interest expense. Also called the interest coverage ratio.

total asset turnover The division of net sales by average total assets; it indicates a firm's ability to use assets efficiently to generate sales.

trend percentages A form of horizontal analysis in which we set all amounts in the base year equal to 100%. Each statement item in subsequent years is divided by the corresponding amount in the base year.

vertical analysis A form of financial statement analysis that portrays each financial statement item in relation to a financial statement total. We set net sales at 100% in the income statement. We set both total assets and total equities at 100% in the balance sheet.

working capital The excess of current assets over current liabilities.

QUESTIONS FOR GROUP LEARNING

Q16-1. What limitations do external users of financial statements face when obtaining information in order to analyze a company?

Q16-2. What roles do risk and return play in investment decisions?

Q16-3. Discuss the differences in the accounting information needs of a short-term creditor versus an investor.

Q16-4. Discuss the sources of financial statement analysis information for publicly held companies. As an external user of financial information, what is the purpose of the independent accountant?

Q16-5. Name the three major categories of financial tools and techniques we discuss in this chapter. Should financial users select one of the tools to use or should they use a combination of the methods?

Q16-6. Discuss the basic difference between horizontal and vertical analysis.

Q16-7. What is a base year? Is it used in horizontal or vertical analysis?

Q16-8. What is the purpose of ratio analysis? Should financial decisions be made by looking at isolated ratios?

Q16-9. Is a current ratio of 4:1 always good? Briefly explain your answer.

Q16-10. Explain how you would determine each of the following:

    a. company's earning power.

    b. The extent to which credit has been used to finance a company's assets.

    c. The ability of a company to meet its annual interest payments.

    d. How fast accounts receivable are collected.

    e. The ability of a business to pay current debts as they come due.

Q16-11. What ratios or analytical devices help in answering each of the following questions?

    a. "Are the assets used efficiently?"

    b. "How is the business being financed?"

    c. "Are earnings adequate?"

    d. "Are costs and expenses too high?"

Q16-12. List the ratios useful in evaluating the following aspects of a company.

    a. Short-term liquidity.

    b. Long-term solvency.

    c. Profitability.

    d. Stock as an investment.

Q16-13. Two companies have the same market price per common share. Would investors feel both companies have the same growth potential?

Q16-14. Charlie Company has a debt ratio of 30%. All competing companies in the industry have debt ratios of 50%. Discuss how this may be a favorable indicator for Charlie Company. Discuss how it may be unfavorable.

Q16-15. What does the term earnings quality mean? What items are indicators of the quality of earnings?

EXERCISES

E16-16. **Horizontal analysis: computing percentage changes (LG 3)** The following data are for two companies as of December 31, 2007 and 2006, for the years then ended:

	Company A		Company B	
	2007	**2006**	**2007**	**2006**
Sales	$ 68,200	$ 52,100	$ 131,500	$ 143,000
Cost of goods sold	44,000	38,200	78,900	88,040
Operating expenses	11,000	8,800	26,300	25,560
Interest expense	3,100	8,000	9,200	6,300
Net income (loss)	10,100	(2,900)	17,100	23,100

Compute the percentage of increase or decrease for each item (where possible).

E16-17. **Horizontal analysis: computing trend percentages (LG 3)** Following are selected data for three years for Motel Company:

	2007	**2006**	**2005**
Net sales	$ 150,000	$ 140,000	$ 120,000
Cost of goods sold	96,768	89,208	75,600
Operating expenses	30,240	28,224	25,200
Net income	22,992	22,568	19,200
Current assets at end of year	20,444	22,596	21,520
Current liabilities at end of year	9,790	10,780	11,000
Property, plant, and equipment at end of year	60,264	54,432	48,600

Compute trend percentages for all items, rounding to the nearest tenth of a percent where necessary. Use 2005 as a base year. Which grew more over the three-year period, net sales or net income? Which decreased more over the three-year period, current assets or current liabilities?

E16-18. **Vertical analysis: preparing common-size income statements (LG 4)** Following are selected data for two years for AAA Company:

	2007	2006
Sales	$ 152,000	$ 125,000
Cost of goods sold	94,240	92,950
Operating expenses	27,360	21,450
Interest expense	11,400	6,500
Net income	19,000	4,100

Compute common-size percentages rounded to the nearest tenth of a percent. What is the major reason why net income as a percentage of sales increased from 2006 to 2007?

E16-19. **Vertical analysis: preparing common-size balance sheets (LG 4)** Following are condensed comparative balance sheet data for Anthony Company:

	December 31	
	2007	2006
Current assets	$ 100,848	$ 91,324
Investments	42,402	21,804
Property, plant, and equipment (net)	238,750	202,872
Total assets	$ 382,000	$ 316,000
Current liabilities	$ 44,132	$ 33,812
Long-term liabilities	163,878	125,768
Common stock	137,520	113,760
Retained earnings	36,470	42,660
Total liabilities and stockholders' equity	$ 382,000	$ 316,000

Compute common-size percentages rounded to the nearest tenth of a percent. Over the two-year period, did Anthony Company increase or decrease its percentage use of total debt as a source of financing?

E16-20. **Vertical analysis: evaluating comparative data (LG 4)** The following data are available for Tolland Company:

TOLLAND COMPANY
COMPARATIVE TREND PERCENTAGES FOR THE YEARS ENDED OCTOBER 31

	2007	2006	2005	2004
Sales (net)	125%	115%	109%	100%
Cost of goods sold	128	118	112	100
Gross margin on sales	120	112	105	100
Net income	108	103	101	100
Accounts receivable	136	121	120	100
Merchandise inventory	130	121	114	100

Point out the favorable and unfavorable trends and suggest some areas for management study.

E16-21. **Evaluating short-term liquidity (LG 5)** Income statement and balance sheet data for Racer Company follow as of December 31, 2007, 2006, and 2005, for the years then ended:

INCOME STATEMENTS

	2007	2006	2005
Net sales	$ 628,000	$ 600,000	$ 540,000
Cost of goods sold	389,360	381,000	349,600
Gross margin	$ 238,640	$ 219,000	$ 190,400
Operating expenses	138,440	121,000	109,550
Net operating income	$ 100,200	$ 98,000	$ 80,850
Interest expense	6,000	10,000	12,000
Net income before income taxes	$ 94,200	$ 88,000	$ 68,850
Income taxes	37,680	35,200	27,540
Net income	$ 56,520	$ 52,800	$ 41,310

BALANCE SHEETS

Assets

Cash	$ 17,600	$ 12,260	$ 18,800
Short-term investments	12,800	16,200	10,500
Accounts receivable	52,400	50,500	44,600
Merchandise inventory	64,800	63,200	58,600
Property, plant, and equipment (net)	122,400	123,840	127,500
Total assets	$ 270,000	$ 266,000	$ 260,000

Liabilities and Owners' Equity

Current liabilities	$ 78,000	$ 83,000	$ 92,100
Long-term liabilities	2,680	20,200	27,900
Common stock, $1 par	80,000	80,000	80,000
Retained earnings*	109,320	82,800	60,000
Total liabilities and owners' equity	$ 270,000	$ 266,000	$ 260,000

*Racer Company declared and paid cash dividends of $30,000 each year.

Compute and briefly comment on changes between 2006 and 2007 for the following:

a. Current ratio for December 31, 2007 and 2006.

b. Quick ratio for December 31, 2007 and 2006.

c. Accounts receivable turnover and days' sales in receivables for 2007 and 2006.

d. Inventory turnover for 2007 and 2006.

E16-22. **Evaluating long-term solvency (data from E16-21) (LG 5)** Using the data in E16-21, compute the following ratios. Briefly comment on changes in the ratios between 2006 and 2007.

a. Debt ratio for December 31, 2007 and 2006.

b. Times interest earned ratio for 2007 and 2006.

E16-23. **Evaluating profitability (data from E16-21) (LG 5)** Using the data in E16-21, compute the following ratios. Briefly comment on changes in the ratios between 2006 and 2007.

a. Profit margin for 2007 and 2006.

b. Total asset turnover for 2007 and 2006.

c. Return on total assets for 2007 and 2006.

d. Return on owners' equity for 2007 and 2006.

E16-24. **Evaluating reasons for changes in profitability using vertical analysis (data from E16-21) (LG 4)** Using the income and expense data in E16-21, prepare common-size income statements for 2007, 2006, and 2005. Round to the nearest tenth of a percent. Explain reasons for changes in profitability over the three-year period.

E16-25. **Evaluating the reasons for changes in financial position using vertical analysis (data from E16-21) (LG 4)** Using the asset, liability, and owners' equity data in E16-21, prepare common-size balance sheets for 2007, 2006, and 2005. Round to the nearest tenth of a percent. Explain reasons for changes in financial position over the three-year period.

E16-26. **Evaluating stocks as investments (LG 5)** You are interested in investing in the common stocks of one of two competing companies in the same industry. Both companies currently pay a cash dividend of $1.50 per share each year. You collect the following information on both companies:

	Company X	Company Y
Total assets	$18,000,000	$10,000,000
Total liabilities	8,000,000	2,000,000
Total stockholders' equity	10,000,000	8,000,000
Net income	1,800,000	1,500,000
Earnings per share	$1.80	$1.50
Market price of common stock	$27	$22.50

Compute the following ratios for both companies and briefly comment on the results. Based only on this limited information, which company would you recommend?

a. Price/earnings (P/E) ratio

b. Dividend yield.

c. Debt ratio.

E16-27. **Limitations of financial statement analysis (LG 6)** North Video Company and South Video Company both operate chains of video rental stores. Both companies face an economy in which prices have been rising steadily. All income taxes have been paid in cash. Following are the accounting policies for both companies:

	North Video	South Video
Inventory cost flow assumption	FIFO	LIFO
Depreciation method	Straight-line	Double declining-balance
Estimated depreciable life for building and fixtures	40 years	10 years
Estimated amortization life for videos purchased for rental	60 months	18 months

For each of the following ratios, state which company should report the higher amount. Briefly explain your answer.

a. Current ratio.

b. Inventory turnover.

c. Quick ratio.

d. Profit margin.

E16-28. **Evaluating inventory turnover (LG 6)** One of your coworkers has calculated the inventory turnover of two alternative companies for possible investment. The inventory turnover is 5.8 times for Company C and was 10 times for Company D. The footnotes to the company's annual reports reveal that Company C uses FIFO and Company D uses LIFO. For many years, the industry has faced steadily rising costs for its products. Comment on the relative strengths and positions of the companies.

PROBLEMS

P16-29.   Horizontal analysis: computing change amounts and percentages (LG 3) Following are the condensed comparative income statements and balance sheets for Cinema Company:

CAVALIER COMPANY
COMPARATIVE INCOME STATEMENTS
FOR THE YEARS ENDED DECEMBER 31, 2007 AND 2006

	Years Ended December 31	
	2007	2006
Sales (net)	$ 900,000	$ 750,000
Cost of goods sold	562,500	450,000
Gross margin on sales	$ 337,500	$ 300,000
Operating expenses:		
Selling expenses	$ 120,000	$ 100,000
General and administrative expenses	100,000	90,000
Total operating expenses	$ 220,000	$ 190,000
Net operating income	$ 117,500	$ 110,000
Interest expense	10,000	10,000
Net income before income taxes	$ 107,500	$ 100,000
Income taxes	25,500	30,000
Net income	$ 82,000	$ 70,000

Total cash dividends declared and paid each year were $30,000.

CAVALIER COMPANY
COMPARATIVE BALANCE SHEETS
DECEMBER 31, 2007 AND 2006

	December 31	
	2007	2006
Assets		
Current assets		
Cash	$ 10,000	$ 20,000
Accounts receivable (net)	90,000	50,000
Inventories	90,000	70,000
Total current assets	$ 190,000	$ 140,000
Property, plant, and equipment		
Land	$ 150,000	$ 150,000
Building (net)	190,000	200,000
Equipment (net)	50,000	60,000
Total property, plant, and equipment	$ 390,000	$ 410,000
Total assets	$ 580,000	$ 550,000
Liabilities		
Current liabilities		
Accounts payable	$ 66,000	$ 70,000
Notes payable	10,000	15,000
Wages payable	2,000	3,000
Total current liabilities	$ 78,000	$ 88,000
Long-term liabilities		
Note payable (due 2009)	60,000	70,000
Total liabilities	$ 138,000	$ 158,000
Owners' Equity		
Common stock, $1 par value	$ 100,000	$ 100,000
Additional-paid-in capital	150,000	150,000
Retained earnings	192,000	142,000
Total owners' equity	$ 442,000	$ 392,000
Total liabilities and owners' equity	$ 580,000	$ 550,000

REQUIRED

1. Prepare comparative balance sheets showing the amounts of change and the percentage increase or decrease during 2007.

2. Prepare comparative income statements showing the amounts of change and the percentage increase or decrease during 2007.

3. Write a brief report stating whether the changes in financial position and operating results are favorable or unfavorable.

Round to the nearest tenth of a percent.

P16-30. **Vertical analysis: preparing common-size statements (data from P16-29) (LG 4)** Use the condensed income statements and balance sheets in P16-29 to prepare a vertical analysis of Cavalier Company.

REQUIRED

1. Prepare common-size balance sheets for 2007 and 2006.

2. Prepare common-size income statements for 2007 and 2006.

3. Write a brief report stating whether the changes in financial position and operations are favorable or unfavorable.

Round to the nearest tenth of a percent.

P16-31. **Calculating short-term liquidity, long-term solvency, and profitability ratios (data from P16-29) (LG 5)** Use the condensed income statements and balance sheets in P16-29 to calculate ratios for Cavalier Company. Round computations to the nearest tenth of a percent. When you have computed ratios for both years, briefly indicate whether changes in ratios from 2006 to 2007 are favorable or unfavorable.

REQUIRED

Compute the following:

1. Current ratio for December 31, 2007 and 2006.

2. Quick ratio for December 31, 2007 and 2006.

3. Accounts receivable turnover for 2007.

4. Days' sales in receivables for 2007.

5. Inventory turnover for 2007.

6. Debt ratio for December 31, 2007 and 2006.

7. Times interest earned for 2007 and 2006.

8. Profit margin for 2007 and 2006.

9. Total asset turnover for 2007.

10. Return on total assets for 2007.

11. Return on owners' equity for 2007.

12. Earnings per share for 2007 and 2006 (assume 200,000 shares are outstanding throughout both years).

P16-32. **Horizontal analysis: trend percentages and interpretation of results (LG 3)** Following are condensed comparative balance sheets for A1 Company. The statements show the base-year (2005) dollar amounts. For 2006 and 2007, trend percentages as a percentage of the base year 2005 amounts are as follows:

A1 COMPANY
COMPARATIVE BALANCE SHEETS
DECEMBER 31, 2007, 2006, AND 2005
(IN THOUSANDS OF DOLLARS)

	December 31		
	2007	**2006**	**2005**
Assets			
Current assets	120%	110%	$ 400
Long-term investments	140	120	300
Property, plant, and equipment	50	75	1,200
Total assets	79	89	$1,900
Liabilities			
Current liabilities	50	50	$ 200
Long-term liabilities	50	80	800
Owners' Equity			
Common stock, $1 par value	100	100	300
Retained earnings	117	110	600
Total liabilities and owners' equity	79	89	$1,900

REQUIRED

1. Prepare comparative balance sheets for 2007, 2006, and 2005 showing dollar amounts.

2. Prepare a brief explanation of trends in the distribution of assets, liabilities, and owners' equity over the three-year period.

P16-33. **Common-size statements with evaluation (LG 4)** Following are the common-size financial statements of Rose Company:

ROSE COMPANY
COMPARATIVE COMMON-SIZE INCOME STATEMENTS
FOR THE YEARS ENDED DECEMBER 31, 2007 AND 2006

	Years Ended December 31	
	2007	**2006**
Sales (net)	$900,000	$850,000
Cost of goods sold	60.0%	55.3%
Gross margin on sales	40.0	44.7
Operating expenses:		
Selling expenses	22.8	18.8
General and administrative expenses	12.0	9.7
Total operating expenses	34.8	28.5
Net income	5.2	16.2

ROSE COMPANY
COMPARATIVE COMMON-SIZE BALANCE SHEETS
DECEMBER 31, 2007 AND 2006

		December 31	
		2007	2006
Assets			
Current assets		26%	30%
Property, plant, and equipment		74	70
Total assets		100.0	100.0
Liabilities			
Current liabilities		22	45
Long-term liabilities		34	20
Total liabilities		56	65
Owners' Equity			
Common stock		30	15
Retained earnings		14	20
Total owners' equity		44	35
Total liabilities and owners' equity		$870,000	$780,000

REQUIRED

1. Prepare:

    a. A comparative balance sheet showing dollar amounts.

    b. A comparative income statement showing dollar amounts.

2. Discuss the financial condition and operating results of the company, emphasizing favorable and unfavorable trends.

Round amounts to the nearest dollar.

P16-34. **Effect of accounting methods, estimates, and transactions on ratios (LG 6)**
Indicate the effect of each accounting method, estimate, or transaction on the following ratios. Briefly explain the reasons for your choice.

Accounting Method, Estimate, or Transaction	Ratio	Effect on Ratio Increase	Decrease	No Effect
1. Use FIFO in a period of rising prices versus LIFO.	Profit margin			
2. Made adjusting entry recognizing large increase in allowance for doubtful accounts.	Quick ratio			
3. Using the allowance method, wrote off accounts as uncollectible.	Current ratio			
4. Use double declining-balance depreciation versus straight-line.	Total asset turnover			
5. Declared a large cash dividend on common stock.	Return on owners' equity			
6. Write down inventories to lower-of-cost-or-market.	Inventory turnover			
7. Use estimate of 5 years to amortize intangible asset instead of 20 years.	Times interest earned			
8. Sold large amounts of merchandise on account at year-end.	Quick ratio			
9. Use the direct write-off method for bad debts versus the allowance method.	Current ratio			
10. Issue large amount of new shares of common stock.	Debt ratio			

P16-35. **Analysis and interpretation of financial statements for General Mills and Starbucks (LG 5)** Assume that selected information from the 2004 fiscal year of General Mills and Starbucks are shown below. General Mills is a major food company. Starbucks is a growing retailer and distributor of coffee products. All numbers are in millions.

Income Statement	General Mills	Starbucks
Net sales	$11,070.0	$ 5,294.0
Cost of goods sold	6,584.0	2,199.0
Gross margin	$ 4,486.0	$ 3,095.0
Operating expenses	$ 2,469.0	$ 2,546.0
Interest expense (Income)	434.0	(75.0)
Income before taxes	$ 1,583.0	$ 624.0
Income taxes	528.0	232.0
Net income	$ 1,055.0	$ 392.0
Balance Sheet		
Current assets:		
Cash and cash equivalents	$ 751.0	$ 299.0
Trade accounts receivable (net)	1,010.0	131.0
Inventories	1,063.0	423.0
Other current assets	391.0	506.0
Total current assets	$ 3,215.0	$ 1,359.0
Noncurrent assets	15,233.0	1,659.0
Total assets	$18,448.0	$ 3,018.0
Current liabilities	$ 2,757.0	$ 774.0
Long-term liabilities	10,443.0	59.0
Total liabilities	$13,200.0	$ 833.0
Total owners' equity	5,248.0	2,185.0
Total liabilities and owners' equity	$18,448.0	$ 3,018.0

REQUIRED

1. Compute the following ratios rounding computations to the nearest tenth of a percent.

   a. Current ratio for the end of fiscal 2004.

   b. Quick ratio for the end of fiscal 2004. Starbucks held $354.0 of short-term investment at the end of fiscal 2004.

   c. Accounts receivable turnover ratio for 2004. (Accounts receivable at the end of fiscal 2003: General Mills $980.0, Starbucks $114.0)

   d. Inventory turnover ratio for 2004. (Inventory at the end of fiscal 2003: General Mills $1082.0, Starbucks $343.0)

   e. Debt ratio for the end of fiscal 2004.

   f. Gross profit margin for fiscal 2004.

   g. Profit margin for fiscal 2004.

   h. Total asset turnover for fiscal 2004. (Total assets at the end of fiscal 2003: General Mills $18,227.0, Starbucks $2,729.0)

   i. Return on total assets for fiscal 2004.

2. Based on the ratios you computed in requirement 1, which of the two companies would you recommend as an investment? Briefly explain.

PRACTICE CASE

Analysis and interpretation of financial statements (LG 5) Assume that selected information from the 2007 annual reports of two major retailers, A Mart and All Mart are shown below. All numbers are in millions.

Income Statement	A Mart	All Mart
Net sales	$ 37,028.0	$193,295.0
Cost of goods sold	29,658.0	150,255.0
Gross margin	$ 7,370.0	$ 43,040.0
Operating expenses	$ 7,461.0	$ 31,679.0
Interest expense	287.0	1,374.0
Income before taxes	$ (378.0)	$ 9,987.0
Income taxes	(134.0)	3,692.0
Net income (loss)	$ (244.0)	$ 6,295.0
Balance Sheet		
Current assets:		
Cash and cash equivalents	$ 401.0	$ 2,054.0
Trade accounts receivable (net)	0.0	1,768.0
Inventories	6,412.0	21,442.0
Other current assets	811.0	1,291.0
Total current assets	$ 7,624.0	$ 26,555.0
Noncurrent assets	7,006.0	51,575.0
Total assets	$ 14,630.0	$ 78,130.0
Current liabilities	$ 3,799.0	$ 28,949.0
Long-term liabilities	3,861.0	17,838.0
Total liabilities	$ 7,660.0	$ 46,787.0
Total owners' equity	6,970.0	31,343.0
Total liabilities and owners' equity	$ 14,630.0	$ 78,130.0

REQUIRED

1. Compute the following ratios rounding computations to the nearest tenth of a percent.

   a. Current ratio for the end of fiscal 2007.

   b. Quick ratio for the end of fiscal 2007.

   c. Accounts receivable turnover ratio for 2007. (Accounts receivable at the end of fiscal 2006: A Mart $0.0, All Mart $1,341.0)

   d. Inventory turnover ratio for 2007. (Inventory at the end of fiscal 2006: A Mart $7,101.0, All Mart $19,793.0)

   e. Debt ratio for the end of fiscal 2007.

   f. Times interest earned for 2007.

   g. Gross profit margin for fiscal 2007.

   h. Profit margin for fiscal 2007.

   i. Total asset turnover for fiscal 2007. (Total assets at the end of fiscal 2006: A Mart $15,140.0, All Mart $70,349.0)

   j. Return on total assets for fiscal 2007.

2. Based on the ratios you computed in requirement 1, which of the two companies would you recommend as an investment? Briefly explain.

BUSINESS DECISION AND COMMUNICATION PROBLEM

Preparing an investment recommendation (LG 4) The soft drink company you work for desires to invest $800,000 in the common stock of a company that makes glass and metal recycling equipment. You narrow the list to two companies: Once Again Company and Evergreen Company. Both companies had net sales of $50 million in 2007. The following information for both companies is provided to you for the year ended December 31, 2007:

	Once Again Company	Evergreen Company
Common-size Income Statements		
Net sales	100%	100%
Cost of goods sold	51	49
Gross margin	49	51
Selling and administrative expenses	34	28
Interest expense	5	17
Total selling, administrative, and interest expense	39	45
Income before income taxes	10	6
Income taxes	4	2
Net income	6	4
Common-size Balance Sheets		
Current assets	35%	70%
Plant, property, and equipment	65	30
Total assets	100	100
Current liabilities	30	30
Long-term liabilities	10	45
Common stock	20	15
Retained earnings	40	10
Total liabilities and stockholders' equity	100	100

REQUIRED

Based only on the information provided, prepare a memo to your supervisor, Jen Glass, recommending which stock to purchase. Your memo should include an explanation of the reasons that support your recommendation.

ETHICAL DILEMMA

Releasing preliminary financial data to the press You have been recently employed by Meddle Company to serve in its external communications department. Ben Meddle, president of Meddle Company, has prepared a draft of a press announcement concerning expected operating results for the first quarter of 2007. In the press release, Meddle points out that sales have increased by 30% compared to the first quarter in 2006. He also emphasizes that investment in manufacturing capacity has increased by 100%. The press release fails to mention that long-term debt and interest expense have both increased by 50%. In addition, cost of goods sold and operating expenses have increased significantly. The result is that the company expects a net loss for the first quarter.

REQUIRED

Part of your job is to review information before it is released to the press. How would you respond to the draft? Is it ethical?

COMPREHENSIVE ANALYSIS CASE ABBOTT LABORATORIES

Analyzing Abbott Laboratories for the Period 2004-2002 Abbott is one of the largest drug manufacturers in the country. Listed below are comparative income statements and balance sheets with common-size percents for 2004-2002 (in millions). Also included are selected ratio statistics. Please provide a brief explanation for your answer to each question.

REQUIRED

Income statement questions:

1. Are total revenues higher or lower over the three-year period?

2. What is the percent change in total revenues from 2002 to 2004?

3. Is the percent of cost of goods sold to total revenues increasing or decreasing over the three-year period? As a result, is the gross margin percent increasing or decreasing?

4. Is the percent of total operating expenses to total revenues increasing or decreasing over the three-year period? As a result, is the operating income percent increasing or decreasing?

5. Is the percent of net income to total revenue increasing or decreasing over the three-year period?

Balance sheet questions:

6. Are total assets higher or lower over the three-year period?

7. What is the percent change in total assets from 2002 to 2004?

8. What are the largest asset investments for the company over the three-year period?

9. Are the largest asset investments increasing faster or slower than the percent change in total revenues?

10. Is the percent of total liabilities to total liabilities + owners' equity increasing or decreasing? As a result, is there more or less risk that the company could not pay its debts?

Integrative income statement and balance sheet question:

11. Is the company operating more or less efficiently by using the least amount of asset investment to generate a given level of total revenues? Note that the "total asset turnover" ratio is computed and included in the "ratio analysis summary."

Ratio analysis questions:

12. Is the *current ratio* better or worse in the most current year compared to prior years?

13. Is the *quick ratio* better or worse in the most current year compared to prior years?

14. Is the *accounts receivable turnover ratio 1* (based on *average* receivables) better or worse in the most current year compared to prior years?

15. Is the 2004 *accounts receivable turnover ratio 2* (based on *year-end* receivables) better or worse than the 2004 ratio based on an *average*?

16. Is the *inventory turnover ratio 1* (based on *average* inventory) better or worse in the most current year compared to prior years?

17. Is the 2004 *inventory turnover ratio 2* (based on *year-end* inventory) better or worse than the 2004 ratio based on an *average*?

18. Is the *return on total assets (ROA) ratio* better or worse in the most current year compared to prior years?

ABBOT LABS
COMPARATIVE COMMON-SIZE INCOME STATEMENTS
For The Years Ended December 31, 2004, 2003, 2002
(in millions)

	2004	2004	2003	2003	2002	2002
	$	%	$	%	$	%
Revenues	$ 19,680.0	100.0%	$ 17,280.0	100.0%	$ 15,280.0	100.0%
Cost of goods sold	$ 8,884.0	45.1%	$ 7,774.0	45.0%	$ 6,821.0	44.6%
Gross margin	$ 10,796.0	54.9%	$ 9,506.0	55.0%	$ 8,459.0	55.4%
Operating expenses:						
Selling, general, and administrative	$ 4,922.0	25.0%	$ 4,808.0	27.8%	$ 3,725.0	24.4%
Research and development	$ 1,976.0	10.0%	$ 1,724.0	10.0%	$ 1,583.0	10.4%
Other expense	$ -	0.0%	$ -	0.0%	$ -	0.0%
Total operating expenses	$ 6,898.0	35.1%	$ 6,532.0	37.8%	$ 5,308.0	34.7%
Operating income	$ 3,898.0	19.8%	$ 2,974.0	17.2%	$ 3,151.0	20.6%
Net interest expense (income)	$ 149.0	0.8%	$ 146.0	0.8%	$ 205.0	1.3%
Net Foreign Exchange (gain) loss	$ 29.0	0.1%	$ 57.0	0.3%	$ 71.0	0.5%
Other expense (income), net	$ (405.0)	-2.1%	$ (617.0)	-3.6%	$ (446.0)	-2.9%
Income before income taxes	$ 4,125.0	21.0%	$ 3,388.0	19.6%	$ 3,321.0	21.7%
Income taxes	$ 950.0	4.8%	$ 882.0	5.1%	$ 774.0	5.1%
Net income (loss) before unusual items	$ 3,175.0	16.1%	$ 2,506.0	14.5%	$ 2,547.0	16.7%
Earnings from Discontinued Operations	$ 60.0	0.3%	$ 249.0	1.4%	$ 247.0	1.6%
Other losses (gains) net of tax	$ -	0.0%	$ -	0.0%	$ -	0.0%
Net income (loss)	$ 3,235.0	16.4%	$ 2,755.0	15.9%	$ 2,794.0	18.3%

ABBOT LABS
COMPARATIVE COMMON-SIZE BALANCE SHEETS
December 31, 2004, 2003, 2002
(in millions)

	2004	2004	2003	2003	2002	2002
	$	%	$	%	$	%
ASSETS						
Current:						
Cash & cash equivalents	$ 1,226.0	4.3%	$ 995.0	3.8%	$ 704.0	3.0%
Short-term investments	$ 833.0	2.9%	$ 291.0	1.1%	$ 262.0	1.1%
Accounts receivable, net	$ 3,696.0	12.8%	$ 3,313.0	12.7%	$ 2,927.0	12.4%
Inventory	$ 2,620.0	9.1%	$ 2,739.0	10.5%	$ 2,441.0	10.3%
Deferred Income Taxes	$ 1,032.0	3.6%	$ 1,165.0	4.5%	$ 1,023.0	4.3%
Other current assets	$ 1,327.0	4.6%	$ 1,111.0	4.3%	$ 1,098.0	4.7%
Total current assets	$ 10,734.0	37.3%	$ 9,614.0	36.9%	$ 8,455.0	35.8%
Fixed:						
Property & equipment, net	$ 6,008.0	20.9%	$ 6,282.0	24.1%	$ 5,828.0	24.7%
Long-term investments	$ 146.0	0.5%	$ 406.0	1.6%	$ 251.0	1.1%
Intangibles & goodwill	$ 10,857.0	37.7%	$ 8,539.0	32.8%	$ 7,652.0	32.4%
Other assets	$ 1,023.0	3.6%	$ 1,197.0	4.6%	$ 1,407.0	6.0%
Total assets	$ 28,768.0	100.0%	$ 26,038.0	100.0%	$ 23,593.0	100.0%
LIABILITIES						
Current:						
Short-term debt	$ 1,837.0	6.4%	$ 828.0	3.2%	$ 1,928.0	8.2%
Accounts payable	$ 1,054.0	3.7%	$ 1,078.0	4.1%	$ 995.0	4.2%
Accrued salaries, benefits, and Commissions	$ 637.0	2.2%	$ 626.0	2.4%	$ 580.0	2.5%
Dividends Payable	$ 406.0	1.4%	$ 383.0	1.5%	$ 367.0	1.6%
Income Tax Payable	$ 156.0	0.5%	$ 159.0	0.6%	$ 42.0	0.2%
Other current liabilities	$ 2,735.0	9.5%	$ 3,889.0	14.9%	$ 2,423.0	10.3%
Total current liabilities	$ 6,825.0	23.7%	$ 6,963.0	26.7%	$ 6,335.0	26.9%
Long-term debt	$ 4,788.0	16.6%	$ 3,452.0	13.3%	$ 4,274.0	18.1%
Deferred Income Taxes	$ 220.0	0.8%	$ -	0.0%	$ -	0.0%
Other long-term liabilities	$ 2,608.0	9.1%	$ 2,551.0	9.8%	$ 2,318.0	9.8%
Total liabilities	$ 14,441.0	50.2%	$ 12,966.0	49.8%	$ 12,927.0	54.8%
OWNERS' EQUITY						
Total owners' equity	$ 14,327.0	49.8%	$ 13,072.0	50.2%	$ 10,666.0	45.2%
Total liabilities and owners' equity	$ 28,768.0	100.0%	$ 26,038.0	100.0%	$ 23,593.0	100.0%

(Note: percents may not add to 100 due to rounding)

ABBOT LABS
RATIO ANALYSIS SUMMARY
For The Years Ended December 31, 2004, 2003, 2002

	2004	2003	2002
SHORT-TERM LIQUIDITY RATIOS			
Current Ratio (Current Assets/Current Liabilities)	1.57	1.38	1.33
Quick Ratio (Cash + Short-term Investments + Accounts Receivable)/Current Liabilities	0.84	0.66	0.61
Accounts Receivable Turnover 1 (Revenues/Average Accounts Receivable)	5.62	5.54	
Accounts Receivable Turnover 2 (Revenues/Year-end Accounts Receivable)	5.32	5.22	5.22
Inventory Turnover 1 (Cost Goods Sold/Average Inventory)	3.32	3.00	
Inventory Turnover 2 (Cost Goods Sold/Year-end Inventory)	3.39	2.84	2.79
LONG-TERM SOLVENCY (LEVERAGE) RATIO			
Total Debt Ratio (Total Liabilities/Total Assets)	50.20%	49.80%	54.79%
PROFITABILITY RATIOS			
Gross Profit Margin (Gross Margin/Revenues)	54.86%	55.01%	55.36%
Operating Profit Margin (Operating Income/Revenues)	19.81%	17.21%	20.62%
Net Profit Margin (Return on Sales) (ROS) (Net Income/Revenues)	16.44%	15.94%	18.29%
Total Asset Turnover (Revenues/Average Total Assets)	0.72	0.70	
Return on Total Assets (ROA) (Net Income/Average Total Assets)	11.81%	11.10%	

BUSINESS CONSOLIDATIONS

CHAPTER

17

Chapter Thought

"The ultimate measure of a man is not where he stands in moments of comfort, but where he stands at times of challenge and controversy."

MartinLuther King, Jr.

LEARNING GOALS

After studying Chapter 17, you should be able to:

1. Describe the parent/subsidiary relationship and explain when to prepare consolidated financial statements.

2. Prepare a consolidated balance sheet at acquisition date for companies purchased at book value.

3. Prepare a consolidated balance sheet at acquisition date for companies purchased for more than book value.

4. Prepare a consolidated balance sheet after the acquisition date.

5. Explain why we eliminate intercompany transactions in preparing consolidated financial statements.

6. Prepare a consolidated income statement.

UNDERSTANDING BUSINESS ISSUES

Companies purchase other companies for a variety of reasons. Sometimes, competing in a given industry requires significant resources. Only large companies can survive. Some large deals in 2004 were:

• Wachovia Bank bought South Trust for $14 billion.

• General Electric bought Invision Technologies for $433 million.

• Manulife's stockholders approved the acquisition of John Hancock for $10.8 billion.

Some companies also decide that breaking up into smaller parts makes good business sense. In 2004, Bayer spun off its chemical division, Lanxess Corporation.

Accounting principles require *consolidated financial statements* when a parent company owns more than 50% of a subsidiary company. In this chapter, we explain how to prepare consolidated statements for parent/subsidiary companies.

BUSINESS CONSOLIDATIONS

As a corporate strategy, many large companies diversify into different product areas. Frequently, companies choose to operate companies they acquire as separate legal entities. However, from a financial reporting point of view, statement users want to see the results of the entire economic entity. To do this, the companies *consolidate* or combine the financial results of the separate companies. Companies combine in two basic ways. One company may purchase part or all of the voting stock of another company. The purchased company continues to exist as a separate legal entity. We call this an *acquisition*. Or, one company may purchase all of the voting stock of another company and eliminate the purchased company. We call this a *merger*. Our focus in this chapter is on the acquisition form of business combination.

PARENT AND SUBSIDIARY CORPORATIONS

Learning Goal 1   Describe the parent/subsidiary relationship and explain when to prepare consolidated financial statements.

Chapter 14 discussed the equity method of accounting for long-term investments in stocks. Under generally accepted accounting principles (GAAP), we view ownership of 20% up to 50% of voting stock as evidence of *significant influence*. In these cases, the investor company should use the equity method to account for the investment.

When an investor owns more than 50% of the voting stock of another company, we assume it has the ability to control rather than just exert significant influence. At this point, we view the investor as a **parent company** and the investee as a **subsidiary company**. When a parent/subsidiary relationship exists, we refer to the companies as **affiliates** or **affiliated companies**. The parent company can use its voting shares to elect members of the subsidiary's board of directors. In this way, the parent company can control the activities of the subsidiary company.

GAAP requires the use of "purchase" accounting when a parent acquires an interest in a subsidiary. Under purchase accounting, we value assets and liabilities of the subsidiary at their fair market value as of the acquisition date. The examples in this chapter all assume payment in cash and use the purchase method.

Consolidated Financial Statements

Although a parent company and a subsidiary company may be separate legal entities, for reporting we view them as a single *economic* entity. In these cases, financial statements of the combined economic entity are more meaningful than separate statements of the legal entities. **Consolidated financial statements** show the financial position and operating results of the combined companies. The result is a set of financial statements that show all of the individual companies under the parent's control as a single economic unit.

Exhibit 17.1 shows the relationship between the separate legal entities and the consolidated economic entity. Each separate legal entity still prepares its own set of financial statements. However, in reporting to external users, we only report the combined results of the consolidated entity. Financial statement users want to see the operating results and financial position of the combined economic entity. Therefore, the consolidated income statement shows the combined revenues and expenses of the parent and subsidiary companies. The balance sheet shows the combined assets and liabilities of the parent and subsidiary companies.

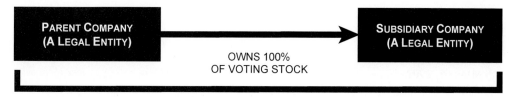

THE ECONOMIC ENTITY
CONSOLIDATED FINANCIAL STATEMENTS

EXHIBIT **17.1**

Relationship Between Separate Legal Entities and the Consolidated Entity

---

FASB Statement No. 94 requires that we prepare consolidated financial statements for external reporting when a parent has a controlling interest.[1] The statement defines a controlling interest as the ownership of more than 50% of the voting stock of a subsidiary company. Before the release of *FASB Statement No. 94* there were several exceptions to the general rule of consolidation of more than 50%-owned companies. However, currently the only exceptions under which we do not prepare consolidated statements are as follows:

1. When control is temporary.

2. When control does not rest with the majority owners (as often happens when the organization is in the hands of a trustee for reorganization or bankruptcy).

Thus, under current GAAP, we must consolidate nearly all majority-owned subsidiary companies with the financial statements of the parent company for external reporting purposes.

Consolidated Balance Sheet

In this section we illustrate the preparation of a consolidated balance sheet using work sheets. Before starting our discussion, we first need to explain the nature of reciprocal accounts.

Reciprocal Accounts

In preparing a consolidated balance sheet, we combine similar accounts from the separate financial statements of the parent and subsidiary companies. In combining the separate accounts, we must eliminate reciprocal accounts. **Reciprocal accounts** are accounts in two separate sets of books that represent a common element and will cancel each other when we combine the two sets of books. For example, assume that on January 1, 2007, Par Company acquires 100% of the voting common stock of Sub Company at its book value of $100,000. The entry on the books of Par Company to record the acquisition is as follows:

2007					
Jan.	1	Investment in Sub Company		100,000	
		Cash			100,000
		To record the purchase of 100% of the common stock of Sub Company at book value.			

---

[1] Statements of the Financial Accounting Standards Board (SFAS) No. 94, "Consolidation of All Majority Owned Subsidiaries (Norwalk, Conn.: FASB, October 1987).

SEPARATE BALANCE SHEETS: PARENT AND SUBSIDIARY

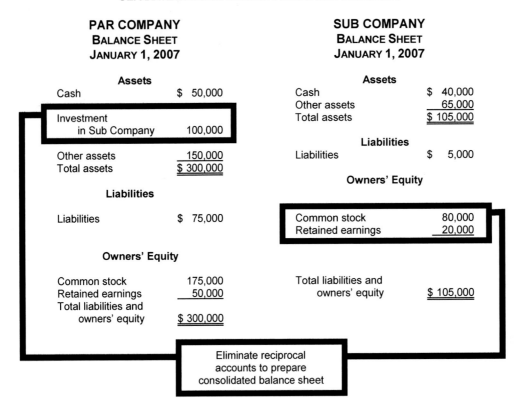

CONSOLIDATED BALANCE SHEET (RECIPROCAL ACCOUNTS ELIMINATED)

PAR COMPANY AND SUB COMPANY
CONSOLIDATED BALANCE SHEET
JANUARY 1, 2007

Assets

Cash ($50,000 + $40,000)	$ 90,000
Other assets ($150,000 + $65,000)	215,000
Total assets	$ 305,000

Liabilities

| Liabilities ($75,000 + $5,000) | $ 80,000 |

Owners' Equity

Common stock (parent only)	175,000
Retained earnings (parent only)	50,000
Total liabilities and owners' equity	$ 305,000

EXHIBIT **17.2**

Elimination of Reciprocal Accounts and Preparation of Consolidated Balance Sheet

---

Par purchases the shares of Sub's stock directly from the Sub Company stockholders. Sub does not receive any of the cash from the stock purchase. Thus, there is no entry on Sub's books to record this purchase. The top part of Exhibit 17.2 shows how we link the following reciprocal accounts immediately after the acquisition:

- The investment account on Par Company's books.

- The owners' equity accounts on Sub Company's books.

The parent shows its investment in the voting shares of the subsidiary on its books as an asset. This investment represents the parent's interest (here 100%) in the owners' equity of the subsidiary company. In preparing a consolidated balance sheet, we must eliminate the investment on the parent's books against the owners' equity accounts on the subsidiary's books. If we do not eliminate these reciprocal accounts, we would count the investment twice. We would count it once as an asset on the books of the parent, and we would count it a second time as net assets (assets - liabilities) on the books of the subsidiary.

The lower part of Exhibit 17.2 shows the consolidated balance sheet as of the acquisition date. After we eliminate the reciprocal accounts, we combine the remaining assets and liabilities of both companies. The owners' equity accounts consist of only those of the parent company. This is because we have eliminated the owners' equity accounts of the subsidiary.

Acquisition of 100% of Subsidiary at Book Value

Learning Goal 2   Prepare a consolidated balance sheet at acquisition date for companies purchased at book value.

Using the previous example, assume again that on January 1, 2007, Par Company acquires 100% of the voting common stock of Sub Company at its book value of $100,000. The journal entry to record the acquisition on Par Company's books is the same as that shown above.

In preparing consolidated financial statements, the use of work sheets allows us to organize the data. Exhibit 17.3 shows a consolidated work sheet at the acquisition date for the purchase of 100% of a subsidiary at book value. We took the separate company balances for Par Company and Sub Company from Exhibit 17.2 In the eliminations columns, we make an entry to eliminate the reciprocal accounts. We must make an **elimination entry** on the worksheet to remove all reciprocal items in the parent and subsidiary financial statements. *We do not journalize or post the work sheet elimination entry in the accounting records of either the parent or subsidiary company.* It is a work sheet entry only. Its purpose is to remove the reciprocal accounts before we prepare a consolidated balance sheet. We add the work sheet amounts horizontally to compute the amounts in the consolidated balance sheet. The formal consolidated balance sheet is the same as the one shown in Exhibit 17.2

PAR COMPANY AND SUB COMPANY
WORK SHEET FOR CONSOLIDATED BALANCE SHEET
JANUARY 1, 2007

Account Title	Par Company	Sub Company	Eliminations Debit	Eliminations Credit	Consolidated Balance Sheet
Debit Accounts					
Cash	50,000	40,000			90,000
Investment in Sub Company	100,000	0		(a) 100,000	0
Property, Plant, and Equipment (net)	150,000	65,000			215,000
Totals	300,000	105,000			305,000
Credit Accounts					
Liabilities	75,000	5,000			80,000
Common Stock	175,000	80,000	(a) 80,000		175,000
Retained Earnings	50,000	20,000	(a) 20,000		50,000
Totals	300,000	105,000	100,000	100,000	305,000

(a) To eliminate reciprocal investment and owners' equity accounts.

EXHIBIT **17.3**

Consolidated Work Sheet: Purchase of 100% of Subsidiary at Book Value at Acquisition Date

Acquisition of less than 100% of Subsidiary at Book Value

To control a subsidiary, a parent only needs to purchase more than 50% of the voting stock. Assume that on January 1, 2007, Par Company acquires 80% of the voting common stock of Sub Company at its book value of $80,000 ($100,000 × 0.80). The entry on the books of Par Company to record the acquisition is as follows:

```
2007
Jan.   1   Investment in Sub Company              80,000
               Cash                                        80,000
           To record the purchase of 80% of the common stock
           of Sub Company at book value.
```

Exhibit 17.4 shows a consolidated work sheet at the acquisition date. Here, Par Company acquired 80% of a subsidiary at book value on the acquisition date. In the separate accounts of Par Company, cash is higher than in the previous example by $20,000. This is because Par used only $80,000 to purchase its 80% interest in the Sub Company instead of $100,000 for 100% as previously. In the elimination entry, we still debit the owners' equity accounts of the Sub Company for 100% of their amounts ($80,000 + $20,000). We credit Investment in Sub Company for its balance of $80,000. We then credit a new account called Minority Interest for $20,000. A **minority interest** is the ownership interest of the remaining owners in the assets of the subsidiary company. Here, the remaining owners still own 20% of the shares outstanding. On the formal consolidated balance sheet, many companies show minority interest as a separate item between liabilities and owners' equity.

Acquisition of 100% of Subsidiary at More than Book Value

Learning Goal 3   Prepare a consolidated balance sheet at acquisition date for companies purchased for more than book value.

In Exhibit 17.3 we assumed that Par Company purchased 100% of the voting stock of Sub Company at its book value of $100,000. Assume instead that Par Company pays $110,000

PAR COMPANY AND SUB COMPANY
WORK SHEET FOR CONSOLIDATED BALANCE SHEET
JANUARY 1, 2007

Account Title	Par Company	Sub Company	Eliminations Debit	Eliminations Credit	Consolidated Balance Sheet
Debit Accounts					
Cash	70,000	40,000			110,000
Investment in Sub Company	80,000	0		(a) 80,000	0
Property, Plant, and Equipment (net)	150,000	65,000			215,000
Totals	300,000	105,000			325,000
Credit Accounts					
Liabilities	75,000	5,000			80,000
Common Stock	175,000	80,000	(a) 80,000		175,000
Retained Earnings	50,000	20,000	(a) 20,000		50,000
Minority Interest				(a) 20,000	20,000
Totals	300,000	105,000	100,000	100,000	325,000

(a) To eliminate reciprocal investment and owners' equity accounts.

EXHIBIT **17.4**

Consolidated Work Sheet: Purchase of 80% of Subsidiary at Book Value at Acquisition Date

($10,000 more than book value) for 100% of the voting shares. The entry on the books of Par Company to record the acquisition is as follows:

```
2007
Jan.    1    Investment in Sub Company                           110,000
                 Cash                                                            110,000
                 To record the purchase of 100% of the common stock
                 of Sub Company at $10,000 above book value.
```

In real life, companies frequently pay more than book value when they acquire a controlling interest in another company. The excess they pay may be due to undervalued assets or overvalued liabilities on the books of the subsidiary. In such cases, we assign the excess to increase an asset or decrease a liability of the subsidiary company. Another reason the acquiring company may pay an excess is that the subsidiary company has a record of above-normal earnings. We assign the excess paid to a new account called *Goodwill*.

When a company pays more than book value, GAAP requires that we first assign any excess to undervalued assets or overvalued liabilities. After we adjust the assets and liabilities to fair value, we show any remaining excess of cost over book value as goodwill.[2] In a few cases, a company may pay less than book value to acquire a controlling interest in another company. We discuss this topic in advanced accounting classes.

Exhibit 17.5 shows a consolidated work sheet at the acquisition date. Here, Par Company acquired 100% of a subsidiary at $10,000 above book value at the acquisition date. We assume that the assets and liabilities of Sub Company are fairly valued. Therefore, we show the excess above book value as goodwill on the consolidated balance sheet. We classify goodwill as an intangible asset. We calculate the excess over book value as follows:

Purchase price		$110,000
Share of Sub Company book value:		
Common stock	$ 80,000	
Retained earnings	20,000	
Total book value	$100,000	
Times parent's share	× 1.00	100,000
Amount paid above book value		$ 10,000
Allocation of excess paid:		
Goodwill		$ 10,000

Preparing the Consolidated Balance Sheet after the Acquisition Date

Learning Goal 4   Prepare a consolidated balance sheet after the acquisition date.

After the acquisition date, the preparation of a consolidated balance sheet must take into account changes in the parent's investment account under the equity method and the subsidiary's owners' equity. After the acquisition, entries under the equity method on the parent's books have the following effects:

1. They increase the investment account for the parent's share of subsidiary income.

2. They decrease the investment account for the parent's share of subsidiary loss.

3. They decrease the investment account for the parent's share of subsidiary dividends.

---

[2] *Opinions of the Accounting Principles Board (APB) No. 16,* "Business Combinations" (New York: AICPA, 1970), paragraph 87.

PAR COMPANY AND SUB COMPANY
WORK SHEET FOR CONSOLIDATED BALANCE SHEET
JANUARY 1, 2007

Account Title	Par Company	Sub Company	Eliminations Debit	Eliminations Credit	Consolidated Balance Sheet
Debit Accounts					
Cash	40,000	40,000			80,000
Investment in Sub Company	110,000	0		(a) 110,000	0
Property, Plant, and Equipment (net)	150,000	65,000			215,000
Goodwill			(a) 10,000		10,000
Totals	300,000	105,000			305,000
Credit Accounts					
Liabilities	75,000	5,000			80,000
Common Stock	175,000	80,000	(a) 80,000		175,000
Retained Earnings	50,000	20,000	(a) 20,000		50,000
Totals	300,000	105,000	110,000	110,000	305,000

(a) To eliminate reciprocal investment and owners' equity accounts.

EXHIBIT **17.5**

Consolidated Work Sheet: Purchase of 100% of Subsidiary at $10,000 above Book Value at Acquisition Date

Assume again that on January 1, 2007, Par Company acquires 100% of the voting stock of Sub Company at its book value of $100,000. The entry on the books of Par Company to record the acquisition is as follows:

```
2007
Jan.    1   Investment in Sub Company                           100,000
                Cash                                                        100,000
                To record the purchase of 100% of the common stock
                of Sub Company at book value.
```

Assume that Sub Company earns $40,000 during 2007 and pays out $10,000 in dividends at the end of the year. To account for these events, the entries under the equity method on the books of Par Company during 2007 are as follows:

```
2007
Dec.    31  Investment in Sub Company                            40,000
                Equity in Sub Company Income                               40,000
                To record parent's share of Sub Company's net
                income.

        31  Cash                                                 10,000
                Investment in Sub Company                                  10,000
                To record receipt of dividends from Sub Company.
```

The work sheet in Exhibit 17.3 previously showed the individual company and consolidated balance sheets at the acquisition date, January 1, 2007. Exhibit 17.6 shows a consolidated work sheet at the end of the first year after acquisition. Par Company acquired 100% of Sub Company at

PAR COMPANY AND SUB COMPANY
Work Sheet for Consolidated Balance Sheet
December 31, 2007

Account Title	Par Company	Sub Company	Eliminations Debit	Eliminations Credit	Consolidated Balance Sheet
Debit Accounts					
Cash	60,000	70,000			130,000
Investment in Sub Company	130,000	0		(a) 130,000	0
Property, Plant, and Equipment (net)	150,000	65,000			215,000
Totals	340,000	135,000			345,000
Credit Accounts					
Liabilities	75,000	5,000			80,000
Common Stock	175,000	80,000	(a) 80,000		175,000
Retained Earnings	90,000	50,000	(a) 50,000		90,000
Totals	340,000	135,000	130,000	130,000	345,000

(a) To eliminate reciprocal investment and owners' equity accounts.

EXHIBIT **17.6**

Consolidated Work Sheet: Acquisition of 100% of Subsidiary at Book Value One Year After Acquisition Date

book value. To keep the example simple, we assume that Par Company's only transactions during 2007 are to record its equity in Sub Company's income and dividends. During 2007, the accounts of Par Company and Sub Company have changed from the balances shown in the work sheet in Exhibit 17.3 as follows:

	Balances (Jan. 1, 2007)	Changes	Balances (Dec. 31, 2007)
Par Company:			
Cash	$ 50,000	+ $ 10,000 (Sub Co. dividends)	$ 60,000
Investment in Sub Co.	100,000	+ 40,000 (Sub Co. income) − 10,000 (Sub Co. dividends)	130,000
Retained Earnings	50,000	+ 40,000 (Sub Co. income)	90,000

	Balances (Jan. 1, 2007)	Changes	Balances (Dec. 31, 2007)
Sub Company:			
Cash	$ 40,000	+ $ 40,000 (net income) − 10,000 (dividends paid)	$ 70,000
Retained Earnings	20,000	+ 40,000 (net income) − 10,000 (dividends paid)	50,000

Under the equity method, the investment account changes in proportion to the owners' equity of the 100%-owned subsidiary. Therefore, during 2007 the investment account on Par Company's books and the owners' equity accounts of Sub Company both increase by $30,000. In the elimination entry, we cancel the new balances in the reciprocal investment and owners' equity accounts at December 31, 2007, to prepare a consolidated balance sheet.

Intercompany Transactions

Learning Goal 5   Explain why we eliminate intercompany transactions in preparing consolidated financial statements.

Often, parent and subsidiary companies have transactions between themselves, such as intercompany loans or sales. When such events occur between a parent and a subsidiary, we call them **intercompany transactions**. In preparing consolidated financial statements, we must eliminate the intercompany transactions in order not to double-count revenues, expenses, assets, and liabilities. Typical examples of intercompany transactions are:

Intercompany receivables and payables. For example, loans between parent and subsidiary would inflate both consolidated assets and liabilities. The consolidated work sheet elimination entry debits a payable account and credits a receivable account.

Intercompany revenues and expenses. For example, interest on loans between parent and subsidiary that would inflate both consolidated revenues and expenses. The consolidated work sheet elimination entry debits a revenue account and credits an expense account.

The demonstration problem at the end of the chapter shows a comprehensive situation involving intercompany transactions, goodwill, and minority interest.

Consolidated Income Statement

Learning Goal 6   Prepare a consolidated income statement.

We prepare consolidated income statements by combining revenues and expenses of the parent and subsidiary companies. We must eliminate all amounts resulting from intercompany transactions such as interest revenue and expense between parent and subsidiary. Sometimes, these eliminations are extensive. To illustrate a simple example, assume Pop Company purchases 100% of the voting stock of Son Company on January 1, 2007, at book value. For the year ended December 31, 2007, Pop Company and Son Company report the following separate operating results:

INCOME STATEMENT
FOR THE YEAR ENDED DECEMBER 31, 2007

	Pop Company*	Son Company
Revenues		
Sales	$500,000	$200,000
Interest revenue	10,000	0
Total revenues	$510,000	$200,000
Expenses		
Cost of goods sold	$300,000	$120,000
Operating expenses	100,000	40,000
Interest expense	0	10,000
Total expenses	$400,000	$170,000
Net income	$110,000	$ 30,000

*Pop Company has not yet made entries to record its share of Son's 2007 net income under the equity method.

The following intercompany transactions took place during 2007:

1. Pop Company sold merchandise costing $60,000 to Son Company. Son Company then sold all of the goods to other companies during 2007.

POP COMPANY AND SON COMPANY
WORK SHEET FOR CONSOLIDATED INCOME STATEMENT
FOR YEAR ENDED DECEMBER 31, 2007

| Account Title | Pop Company | Son Company | Eliminations | | Consolidated Income Statement |
			Debit	Credit	
Revenues					
Sales	500,000	200,000	(a) 60,000		640,000
Interest Revenue	10,000	0	(b) 10,000		0
Total Revenues	510,000	200,000			640,000
Expenses					
Cost of Goods Sold	300,000	120,000		(a) 60,000	360,000
Operating Expenses	100,000	40,000			140,000
Interest Expense	0	10,000		(b) 10,000	0
Total Expenses	400,000	170,000			500,000
Net Income	110,000	30,000	70,000	70,000	140,000

(a) To eliminate intercompany sales and purchases.
(b) To eliminate intercompany interest revenue and expense.

EXHIBIT **17.7**

Consolidated Work Sheet: Eliminations to Prepare Consolidated Income Statement

---

2. Pop Company received $10,000 from Son Company for interest on a loan made by Pop Company to Son Company.

3. During 2007, Son Company did not declare or pay any cash dividends to Pop Company. Pop Company did not make an entry under the equity method to record its share of Son Company's 2007 income yet.

Exhibit 17.7 shows a consolidated work sheet with the eliminations necessary to prepare a consolidated income statement. The overall objective is to show the results of Pop Company and Son Company as a single economic entity. Elimination entry (a) removes the intercompany sales Pop Company made to Son Company. The effect of entry (a) is to show only total sales and total cost of goods sold to companies outside the consolidated entity. Elimination entry (b) removes intercompany interest revenue and expense. If we did not make the elimination entries, we would overstate total revenues and total expenses on the consolidated income statement.

ANALYZING INFORMATION

In reviewing financial statements for affiliated companies, the user should ask the following questions:

1. For companies that have recorded goodwill as a result of a purchase combination, has there been an impairment of the goodwill? Under GAAP, when there has been an impairment of the goodwill, the company must write down the goodwill and show an expense.

2. If a majority owned company has not been consolidated for some reason, what is the financial statement impact of consolidation? In many cases, consolidation of subsidiaries will significantly increase the total debt as a percent of assets on the balance sheet. The Business Decision and Communication at the end of this chapter raises this issue for General Motors and General Motors Acceptance Corporation (GMAC).

3. For companies using the equity method for 20%–50% owned companies, how much cash dividends are actually being received? Under the equity method, the investor recognizes its share of investee income on the investor's income statement. The problem is that if the investee does not pay dividends, the share of income recognized by the investor does not result in any actual cash inflows. Essentially, the equity income represents a noncash income item.

LEARNING GOALS REVIEW

1. Describe the parent/subsidiary relationship and explain when to prepare consolidated statements.
   When an investor holds more than 50% of the voting stock of another company, we presume it has the ability to control the company. We call the investor a parent company and the investee a subsidiary company. Minority interest refers to any share of the subsidiary the parent does not own. Frequently, the subsidiary operates as a separate legal entity. We must prepare consolidated statements which show the combined entity as a single economic unit when the parent owns more than 50% of the voting stock.

2. Prepare a consolidated balance sheet at acquisition date for companies purchased at book value.
   First we enter the separate company balances on a consolidated work sheet. In the elimination columns, we make an elimination entry to remove the reciprocal investment account on the parent's books and the owners' equity accounts on the subsidiary's books. We then add the work sheet amounts horizontally to compute the amounts in the consolidated balance sheet.

3. Prepare a consolidated balance sheet at acquisition date for companies purchased for more than book value.
   If the excess paid over book value is due to undervalued assets or overvalued liabilities on the books of the subsidiary, we assign the excess to these items in the consolidated work sheet. If the excess is due to above normal earnings, we assign the excess paid to goodwill.

4. Prepare a consolidated balance sheet after the acquisition date.
   After the acquisition date, the parent's investment account and the subsidiary owners' equity accounts change because of subsidiary income, losses, and dividends. In the elimination entry, we must cancel the new balances in the reciprocal accounts to prepare a consolidated balance sheet.

5. Explain why we eliminate intercompany transactions in preparing consolidated financial statements.
   Examples of intercompany transactions are intercompany receivables and payables and intercompany revenues and expenses. We must eliminate these intercompany transactions in order not to double-count revenues, expenses, assets, and liabilities.

6. Prepare a consolidated income statement.
   We prepare consolidated income statements by adding revenues and expenses of the parent and subsidiary companies. In doing so, we must eliminate all amounts resulting from intercompany transactions such as sales of merchandise and interest between affiliates.

DEMONSTRATION PROBLEM

Consolidated Statements

DeMac Company acquired 80% of the voting stock of Boone Company on January 1, 2007, for $170,000 in cash. The individual financial statements of the two companies as of the acquisition date are as follows:

	DeMac Company	Boone Company
Assets		
Cash	$ 50,000	$ 30,000
Accounts receivable	70,000	20,000
Notes receivable (current)	10,000	0
Merchandise inventory	100,000	60,000
Investment in Boone Company	170,000	0
Land	90,000	40,000
Buildings (net)	210,000	80,000
Total assets	$ 700,000	$ 230,000
Liabilities and Owners' Equity		
Accounts payable	$ 40,000	$ 30,000
Notes payable (current)	0	10,000
Common stock	300,000	100,000
Retained earnings	360,000	90,000
Total liabilities and owners' equity	$ 700,000	$ 230,000

ADDITIONAL INFORMATION:

1. On January 1, 2007, Boone Company borrowed $10,000 from DeMac Company. The note is payable at the end of six months.

2. Of the excess paid above book value, $10,000 is for undervalued land for Boone Company and the rest is for goodwill.

REQUIRED

1. (**LG 1**) Identify the reciprocal accounts and intercompany transactions.

2. (**LG 3, 5**) Prepare a work sheet for a consolidated balance sheet as of the acquisition date.

3. (**LG 3**) Prepare a classified consolidated balance sheet as of January 1, 2007.

SOLUTION

Requirement 1

Solution Approach

Reciprocal accounts are accounts measuring a common element that appear on two different sets of books and have opposite balances. Intercompany transactions are transactions between parent and subsidiary.

The investment account on DeMac's books is reciprocal to the Common Stock and Retained Earnings accounts on the books of Boone. The two companies had one intercompany transaction: the intercompany loan between the affiliates.

Requirement 2

Solution Approach

Set up a work sheet using Exhibits 17.4 and 17.5 as a guide. Compute the total amount paid above book value by comparing purchase price with the parent's share of the subsidiary's book value, as follows:

Purchase price		$170,000
Share of Boone Company book value:		
Common stock	$100,000	
Retained earnings	90,000	
Total book value	$190,000	
Times parent's share	× 0.80	152,000
Amount paid above book value		$ 18,000
Allocation of excess paid:		
Land		$ 10,000
Goodwill		8,000
Total allocated		$ 18,000

First, eliminate the investment against the common stock and retained earnings of Boone Company. Recognize the interest of the minority owners in the owners' equity accounts of Boone Company. Assign $10,000 of the excess paid above book value to Land and $8,000 to Goodwill. Eliminate the intercompany note receivable and note payable.

DEMAC COMPANY AND BOONE COMPANY
WORK SHEET FOR CONSOLIDATED STATEMENTS
JANUARY 1, 2007

Account Titles	DeMac Company	Boone Company	Eliminations Debit	Eliminations Credit	Consolidated Balance Sheet
Debit Accounts					
Cash	50,000	30,000			80,000
Accounts Receivable	70,000	20,000			90,000
Notes Receivable	10,000	0		(b) 10,000	0
Merchandise Inventory	100,000	60,000			160,000
Investment in Boone Company	170,000	0		(a) 170,000	0
Land	90,000	40,000	(a) 10,000		140,000
Buildings (net)	210,000	80,000			290,000
Goodwill	0	0	(a) 8,000		8,000
Totals	700,000	230,000			768,000
Credit Accounts					
Accounts Payable	40,000	30,000			70,000
Notes Payable	0	10,000	(b) 10,000		0
Common Stock	300,000	100,000	(a) 100,000		300,000
Retained Earnings	360,000	90,000	(a) 90,000		360,000
Minority Interest	0	0		(a) 38,000	38,000
Totals	700,000	230,000	218,000	218,000	768,000

(a) To eliminate reciprocal investment and owners' equity accounts. Minority interest is 20% ($100,000 +$90,000).
(b) To eliminate intercompany note receivable and note payable.

Requirement 3

Solution Approach

Construct the formal consolidated balance sheet directly from the work sheet.

DEMAC COMPANY AND BOONE COMPANY
CONSOLIDATED BALANCE SHEET
JANUARY 1, 2007

Assets

Current Assets

Cash		$ 80,000
Accounts receivable		90,000
Merchandise inventory		160,000
Total current assets		$ 330,000

Property, plant and equipment

Land	$ 140,000	
Buildings (net)	290,000	
Total property, plant, and equipment		430,000

Intangible assets

Goodwill		8,000
Total assets		$ 768,000

Liabilities

Current liabilities

Accounts payable		$ 70,000
Total liabilities		$ 70,000
Minority interest		38,000

Owners' Equity

Common stock	$ 300,000	
Retained earnings	360,000	
Total owners' equity		660,000
Total liabilities and owners' equity		$ 768,000

GLOSSARY

affiliates (or affiliated companies) Companies that have a parent/subsidiary relationship with one another.

consolidated financial statements Financial reports in which the assets, liabilities, revenues, and expenses of subsidiary companies are combined with those of the parent company.

elimination entry An entry on the consolidated statement work sheet that removes duplicate items in subsidiary and parent financial statements from the consolidated amount.

intercompany transactions Transactions that take place between affiliated companies.

minority interest The portion of a subsidiary corporation's ownership (its owners' equity) held by owners other than the parent company.

parent company A company that owns a controlling interest (more than 50%) in the voting stock of another company.

reciprocal accounts Accounts in two sets of books that offset each other and would cause double counting if combined into a consolidated total.

subsidiary company A company controlled by another corporation that holds a controlling interest (more than 50%) in its voting stock.

QUESTIONS FOR GROUP LEARNING

Q17-1.   In accounting for intercompany investments, what is the difference between ownership in a company with "significant influence" and control?

Q17-2. Would investors in stock of Newell, which owns Rubbermaid, be more interested in the financial statements of the consolidated entity or the separate entities? Explain your answer.

Q17-3. If a parent owns more than 50% of a subsidiary, must the parent prepare consolidated financial statements? Explain your answer.

Q17-4. Explain what reciprocal accounts are. In preparing consolidated financial statements, what must we do with them?

Q17-5. In a recent annual report, Gearhart Industries, Inc., reported that it had issued 150,000 shares valued at $4,344,000 to acquire the outstanding minority interest of a consolidated subsidiary. Does this make Gearhart a parent company, or was it already one? Explain your answer.

Q17-6. Some corporations report that they are accounting for investments in other companies by the equity method. What does this tell you about the percentage of ownership? Why do you think a company would benefit from having ownership in this proportion?

Q17-7. Is a parent company an investor company? Is an investor company always a parent company? Explain.

Q17-8. What is required for a group of companies to be called "affiliated"?

Q17-9. What is the minority interest? Do the investors holding the minority interest have voting rights? Do they receive dividends? Explain.

Q17-10. What are consolidated financial statements? When is it appropriate to use them in reporting to owners and to the public?

Q17-11. What is an intercompany transaction? Give three examples. How do they fit into consolidated statements? Why?

EXERCISES

E17-12. **When to prepare consolidated financial statements (LG 1)** As of December 31, 2007 West Company has the following five investments in other companies:

1. Ownership of 600,000 shares out of 600,000 voting shares of North Computer Company.

2. Ownership of 30,000 shares out of 100,000 voting shares of East Company.

3. Ownership of 80,000 shares out of 100,000 voting shares of South Company, which is in the hands of a trustee for bankruptcy.

4. Ownership of 104,000 shares out of 200,000 voting shares of Ocean Company.

5. Ownership of 324,000 shares out of 360,000 shares of nonvoting preferred stock of Easy Street Company.

Of the five companies, which would you include with West Company in consolidated financial statements? Briefly explain your answer.

E17-13. **Income tax effect of organization (LG 1)** Chester Health Care, Inc., owns 100% of the stock in three companies. The affiliates had net incomes before income tax in 2007 as follows:

Chester Health Care, Inc.	$60,000
Shady Rest Home	24,000
Yellow River Bestcare, Inc.	60,000
Colonial Village, Inc.	52,000

Assume corporate federal income tax rates to be as follows:

Taxable Income	Rate
$0 to $50,000	15%
$50,000 to $75,000	25
Over $75,000	34

Compute the income tax expense of the affiliated group filing tax returns as individual corporations. Then compute the income tax expense if all the corporate identities were merged into the parent company and a single tax return was filed. Which do you recommend? (Assume that the income tax rates apply uniformly to individual companies and the consolidated group.)

E17-14. **Exceptions to consolidated statements (LG 1)** Orlando Company (a machine manufacturer) owns 100% of the voting stock in three other corporations: (1) Gull Point Company, a producer of parts used in Orlando's assembly operations; (2) Warrington Finance Company, which provides loans to purchasers of Orlando's products; and (3) Santa Rosa Company, a company in the hands of a trustee during bankruptcy proceedings. Which of these affiliates should be combined in the consolidated financial statements? Give reasons if you decide that any should not.

E17-15. **Eliminating reciprocal accounts: 100% ownership (LG 2)** On January 1, 2007, Queens Corporation purchased 100% of Kings Company. Immediately after the acquisition, the following accounts were in the separate company books:

Account Titles	Queens Corporation	Kings Company
Investment in Kings Company	$1,450,000	$ 0
Common Stock $5 Par Value	600,000	500,000
Paid-in Capital—Excess over Par Value, Common	2,600,000	675,000
Retained Earnings	1,565,000	275,000

What is the amount of each account to be shown in the consolidated balance sheet?

E17-16. **Eliminating reciprocal accounts: 80% ownership (LG 2)** On January 1, 2007, Alan Corporation purchased 80% of Fred Company. Immediately after the acquisition, the following accounts were in the separate company books:

Account Titles	Alan Corporation	Fred Company
Investment in Fred Company	$1,160,000	$ 0
Common Stock, $5 Par Value	700,000	600,000
Paid-in Capital—Excess over Par Value, Common	2,600,000	675,000
Retained Earnings	1,565,000	175,000

What is the amount of each account to be shown in the consolidated balance sheet?

E17-17. **Consolidated balance sheet at acquisition date: 100% ownership at book value (LG 2)** On January 1, 2007, Sim Company purchased 100% of the voting stock of Pal Company at its book value of $200,000. Immediately after the acquisition, the separate company account balances were as follows:

Account Titles	Sim Company	Pal Company
Assets		
Cash	$ 100,000	$ 40,000
Accounts Receivable	80,000	30,000
Investment in Pal Company	200,000	0
Property, Plant, and Equipment (net)	340,000	150,000
Total assets	$ 720,000	$ 220,000
Liabilities and Owners' Equity		
Accounts Payable	$ 70,000	$ 20,000
Common Stock	150,000	75,000
Retained Earnings	500,000	125,000
Total liabilities and owners' equity	$ 720,000	$ 220,000

Prepare a work sheet for the consolidated balance sheet at the acquisition date.

E17-18. **Consolidated balance sheet at acquisition date: 80% ownership at book value (LG 2)** Assume that on January 1, 2007, Tim Company purchased 80% of the voting stock of Hal Company at its book value of $160,000. Immediately after the acquisition, the separate company account balances were as follows:

Account Titles	Tim Company	Hal Company
Assets		
Cash	$ 140,000	$ 40,000
Accounts Receivable	80,000	30,000
Investment in Pal Company	160,000	0
Property, Plant, and Equipment (net)	340,000	150,000
Total assets	$ 720,000	$ 220,000
Liabilities and Owners' Equity		
Accounts Payable	$ 70,000	$ 20,000
Common Stock	150,000	75,000
Retained Earnings	500,000	125,000
Total liabilities and owners' equity	$ 720,000	$ 220,000

Prepare a work sheet for the consolidated balance sheet at the acquisition date.

E17-19.   **Consolidated balance sheet at acquisition date: 100% ownership at more than book value (LG 3)** Assume that on January 1, 2007, Sim Company purchased 100%-of the voting stock of Pal Company for $240,000. Of the excess paid over book value, $12,000 is due to undervalued property, plant, and equipment on the books of Pal Company and the remainder is payment for goodwill. Immediately after the acquisition, the separate company account balances were as follows:

Account Titles	Sim Company	Pal Company
Assets		
Cash	$ 70,000	$ 40,000
Accounts Receivable	80,000	30,000
Investment in Pal Company	240,000	0
Property, Plant, and Equipment (net)	330,000	150,000
Total assets	$ 720,000	$ 220,000
Liabilities and Owners' Equity		
Accounts Payable	$ 70,000	$ 20,000
Common Stock	150,000	75,000
Retained Earnings	500,000	125,000
Total liabilities and owners' equity	$ 720,000	$ 220,000

Prepare a work sheet for the consolidated balance sheet at the acquisition date.

E17-20.   **Review of equity method (LG 4)** On January 1, 2007, Val Company purchased 35,000 of the 50,000 outstanding voting shares of Brown Company at its book value of $24 per share. On December 31, 2007, Brown Company reported a net income for 2007 of $80,000 and paid a cash dividend of $0.20 per share. Record these events on the books of Val Company in general journal form.

E17-21.   **Consolidated balance sheet after acquisition date: 100% ownership at book value (LG 4)** Assume that on January 1, 2007, Sim Company purchased 100% of the voting stock of Pal Company at its book value of $200,000. Assume that the only transactions that occurred during 2007 were the following:

Pal Company reported net income of $60,000.

Pal Company paid cash dividends of $15,000.

During 2007, Sim Company made entries to update the investment account using the equity method. After closing the books, the separate company account balances on December 31, 2007, were as follows:

Account Titles	Sim Company	Pal Company
Assets		
Cash	$ 115,000	$ 85,000
Accounts Receivable	80,000	30,000
Investment in Pal Company	245,000	0
Property, Plant, and Equipment (net)	330,000	150,000
Total assets	$ 770,000	$ 265,000
Liabilities and Owners' Equity		
Accounts Payable	$ 70,000	$ 20,000
Common Stock	150,000	75,000
Retained Earnings	550,000	170,000
Total liabilities and owners' equity	$ 770,000	$ 265,000

1. Journalize the entries Sim Company made on its books during 2007 to record investment under the equity method.

2. Prepare a work sheet for the consolidated balance sheet as of December 31, 2007.

E17-22. **Work sheet involving intercompany transactions (LG 5)** On December 31, 2007, the accounts of Bear Corporation and its 100% wholly owned subsidiary, Bryant Corporation, showed the following balances:

Account Titles	Bear Corporation	Bryant Corporation
Cash	$ 90,000	$ 50,000
Accounts Receivable from Bryant	25,600	0
Accounts Receivable—Other	60,500	32,180
Investment in Bryant Corporation	173,930	0
Property, Plant, and Equipment	182,250	135,600
Accounts Payable to Bear	0	25,600
Accounts Payable—Other	41,500	18,250
Common Stock	400,000	125,000
Retained Earnings	90,780	48,930

Enter the balances on a work sheet to prepare consolidated financial statements, complete the work sheet, and prepare a consolidated balance sheet.

E17-23. **Consolidated income statement (LG 6)** Paul Company purchased 100% of Gene Company on January 1, 2007, at its book value. For the year ended December 31, 2007, Paul and Gene report the following separate operating results:

	Paul Company*	Gene Company
Revenues		
Sales	$ 320,000	$ 140,000
Interest revenue	8,000	0
Total revenue	$ 328,000	$ 140,000
Expenses		
Cost of goods sold	$ 180,000	$ 72,000
Operating expenses	90,000	48,000
Interest expense	0	8,000
Total expenses	$ 270,000	$ 128,000
Net income	$ 58,000	$ 12,000

*Paul Company has not yet made entries to record its share of Gene Company's 2007 net income under the equity method.

Information on intercompany transactions during 2007 is as follows:

1. Gene Company sold merchandise costing $50,000 to Paul Company. Paul then sold all of the goods to other companies during 2007.

2. Paul Company received $8,000 from Gene Company for interest on a loan Paul made to Gene.

3. During 2007, Gene Company did not declare or pay any cash dividends to Paul Company. Paul has not yet made an entry under the equity method to record its share of Gene's 2007 income.

Prepare a work sheet for a consolidated income statement for the year ended December 31, 2007.

PROBLEMS

P17-24. Eliminating reciprocal accounts (LG 2) Joe Corporation and its wholly owned subsidiary, Paterno, Inc., have the following items in their trial balances on December 1, 2007, immediately after Joe made the investment at book value:

Account Titles	Joe Corporation	Paterno Inc.
Investment in Paterno, Inc.	$ 559,000	$ 0
Common Stock, $1 Par Value	450,000	0
Common Stock, $2 Par Value	0	250,000
Paid-in Capital—Excess Par Value, Common	311,600	122,000
Retained Earnings	195,000	187,000

REQUIRED

Enter the balances on a work sheet for consolidated statements, make the necessary eliminations, and carry the consolidated amounts to the proper column.

P17-25. Consolidated balance sheet at acquisition date: 100% ownership at book value (LG 2) On January 1, 2007, Jane's Muffin Company purchased 100% of the voting stock of Bert's Import Coffee for cash at its book value of $375,000. Immediately after the acquisition, the separate company account balances were as follows:

Account Titles	Jane's Muffin Company	Bert's Import Coffee
Assets		
Cash	$ 125,000	$ 55,000
Accounts Receivable	60,000	25,000
Notes Receivable (current)	15,000	0
Merchandise Inventory	155,000	70,000
Investment in Bert's Import Coffee	375,000	0
Property, Plant, and Equipment (net)	240,000	320,000
Total assets	$ 970,000	$ 470,000
Liabilities and Owners' Equity		
Accounts Payable	$ 100,000	$ 20,000
Notes Payable (current)	140,000	75,000
Common Stock	300,000	100,000
Retained Earnings	430,000	275,000
Total liabilities and owners' equity	$ 970,000	$ 470,000

REQUIRED

1. Prepare a work sheet for the consolidated balance sheet at the acquisition date.

2. Prepare a classified consolidated balance sheet as of January 1, 2007.

P17-26. Consolidated balance sheet at acquisition date: 100% ownership at more than book value (LG 3) Assume that on January 1, 2007, Jane's Muffin Company purchased 100% of the voting stock of Bert's Import Coffee for cash in the amount of $405,000. Of the excess paid over book value, $14,000 is due to undervalued property, plant, and equipment on the books of Bert's Import Coffee, and the remainder is goodwill. Immediately after the acquisition, the separate company account balances were as follows:

Account Titles	Jane's Muffin Company	Bert's Import Coffee
Assets		
Cash	$ 85,000	$ 55,000
Accounts Receivable	60,000	35,000
Notes Receivable (current)	15,000	0
Merchandise Inventory	165,000	70,000
Investment in Bert's Import Coffee	405,000	0
Property, Plant, and Equipment (net)	240,000	310,000
Total assets	$970,000	$470,000
Liabilities and Owners' Equity		
Accounts Payable	$100,000	$ 20,000
Notes Payable (current)	140,000	75,000
Common Stock	300,000	100,000
Retained Earnings	430,000	275,000
Total liabilities and owners' equity	$970,000	$470,000

REQUIRED

1. Compute the amount of the excess paid over book value and show the allocation of the excess to the appropriate accounts.

2. Prepare a work sheet for the consolidated balance sheet at the acquisition date.

3. Prepare a classified consolidated balance sheet as of January 1, 2007.

P17-27. Consolidated balance sheet after acquisition date: 100% ownership at book value (LG 4, 5) Assume that on January 1, 2007, Jane's Muffin Company purchased 100% of the voting stock of Bert's Import Coffee for cash at its book value of $375,000. Assume that the following were the only transactions that occurred during 2007:

Bert's Import Coffee reported net income of $50,000.
Bert's Import Coffee paid cash dividends of $10,000.

During 2007, Jane's Muffin Company made entries to update its investment account using the equity method. After closing the books, the separate company balances on December 31, 2007, were as follows:

Account Titles	Jane's Muffin Company	Bert's Import Coffee
Assets		
Cash	$ 115,000	$ 95,000
Accounts Receivable	60,000	35,000
Notes Receivable (current)	15,000	0
Merchandise Inventory	165,000	70,000
Investment in Bert's Import Coffee	415,000	0
Property, Plant, and Equipment (net)	240,000	310,000
Total assets	$1,010,000	$500,000
Liabilities and Owners' Equity		
Accounts Payable	$ 100,000	$ 20,000
Notes Payable (current)	140,000	75,000
Common Stock	300,000	100,000
Retained Earnings	470,000	315,000
Total liabilities and owners' equity	$1,010,000	$500,000

Additional Information: Of the notes outstanding on December 31, 2007, $10,000 is a loan to Bert's Import Coffee from Jane's Muffin Company. The notes mature within the next 12 months.

REQUIRED

1. Journalize the entries that Jane's Muffin Company made on its books during 2007 to record investment entries under the equity method.

2. Prepare a work sheet for the consolidated balance sheet at December 31, 2007.

P17-28. **Eliminating intercompany payables and receivables (LG 5)** Hartford Corporation and its wholly owned subsidiary, Whaler, Inc., have the following items in their trial balances on June 30, 2007, the end of the fiscal year of both companies:

Account Titles	Hartford Corporation	Whaler, Inc.
Accounts Receivable—General Customers	$ 237,500	$ 69,000
Accounts Receivable—Affiliate	21,250	15,825
Notes Receivable—Affiliate	41,500	0
Accounts Payable—General Creditors	93,375	43,335
Accounts Payable—Affiliate	15,825	21,250
Notes Payable to Bank	75,000	0
Notes Payable to Affiliate	0	41,500

REQUIRED

Enter the balances on a work sheet for consolidated balance sheet, make the necessary eliminations, and carry the consolidated amounts to the proper column.

P17-29. **Consolidated income statement (LG 6)** Long Company purchased 100% of Life Company on January 1, 2007, at its book value. For the year ended December 31, 2007, Long Company and Life Company report the following separate operating results:

	Long Company*	Life Company
Revenues		
Sales	$ 600,000	$ 220,000
Interest revenue	8,000	0
Consulting fee revenue	0	7,000
Total revenues	$ 608,000	$ 227,000
Expenses		
Cost of goods sold	$ 320,000	$ 120,000
Operating expenses	110,000	60,000
Interest expense	12,000	10,000
Total expenses	$ 442,000	$ 190,000
Net income	$ 166,000	$ 37,000

*Long Company has not yet made entries to record its share of Life Company's 2007 net income under the equity method.

Information on intercompany transactions during 2007 is as follows:

1. Long Company sold merchandise costing $50,000 to Life Company. Life then sold all of the goods to other companies during 2007.

2. Life Company sold merchandise costing $20,000 to Long Company. Long then sold all of the goods to other companies during 2007.

3. Long Company received $4,000 from Life Company for interest on a loan that Long made to Life.

4. Life Company received $7,000 from Long Company for a consulting project. The consulting expense is included in operating expenses on Long's books.

5. During 2007, Life Company did not declare or pay any cash dividends to Long Company. Long did not yet make an entry under the equity method to record its share of Life's 2007 income.

REQUIRED

Prepare a work sheet for a consolidated income statement for the year ended December 31, 2007.

PRACTICE CASE

Preparing consolidated balance sheets (LG 3, 5) Sinc Company and Porch Company both produce and release recorded music. Sinc Company acquired 70% of the voting stock of Porch Company on January 1, 2007, for $289,000 in cash. The individual financial statements of the two companies as of the acquisition date are as follows:

Account Titles	Sinc Company	Porch Company
Assets		
Cash	$ 25,000	$ 45,000
Accounts Receivable	55,000	35,000
Notes Receivable (current)	40,000	0
Record Inventory	70,000	50,000
Investment in Porch Company	289,000	0
Recording equipment (net)	200,000	300,000
Total assets	$679,000	$430,000
Liabilities and Owners' Equity		
Accounts Payable	$ 50,000	$ 10,000
Notes Payable (current)	0	20,000
Common Stock	250,000	150,000
Retained Earnings	379,000	250,000
Total liabilities and owners' equity	$679,000	$430,000

Additional information:

1. On January 1, 2007, Porch Company borrowed $20,000 from Sinc Company. All notes mature within the next 12 months.

2. The excess Sinc Company paid above book value is due to goodwill.

REQUIRED

1. Compute the amount of excess over book value.

2. Prepare a work sheet for a consolidated balance sheet as of the acquisition date.

3. Prepare a classified consolidated balance sheet as of January 1, 2007.

BUSINESS DECISION AND COMMUNICATION PROBLEM

Consolidation of finance subsidiary by General Motors Corporation (LG 4, 5) General Motors Corporation owns 100% of a finance subsidiary called General Motors Acceptance Corporation (GMAC). It has owned 100% of GMAC since it was formed, and it accounts for the investment using the equity method. The purpose of GMAC is to provide customer financing for the purchase of General Motors automobiles. At the end of 2004, the separate balance sheet subtotals of both General Motors Corporation and GMAC are assumed as follows (in millions):

Balance Sheet Subtotals	General Motors Corporation	GMAC
Assets		
Assets (excluding GMAC notes and investment)	$114,710	$192,202
Notes Receivable from General Motors Corporation	0	1,557
Investment in Stocks—GMAC	15,500	0
Total assets	$130,210	$193,759
Liabilities and Owners' Equity		
Liabilities (excluding GMAC notes)	$124,614	$178,259
Notes Payable to GMAC	1,557	0
Owners' Equity	4,039	15,500
Total liabilities and owners' equity	$130,210	$193,759

REQUIRED

Assume you are a financial analyst. Your supervisor, Tom Morrison, asks you if, under current GAAP, General Motors Corporation is required to consolidate its investment in GMAC when it prepares financial statements. Tom asks you to prepare a consolidated balance sheet for General Motors Corporation and GMAC based on the preceding information. Which statements provide a more complete picture of the firm, the separate or the consolidated financial statements?

ETHICAL DILEMMA

Intercompany transactions (LG 1, 5) Plastic Company supplies Plastic products to a variety of furniture companies. It also owns 90% of the voting stock of Chair Company. Recently, Plastic has informed Chair that Chair must use it as its sole supplier of Plastic for the chairs it produces. Previously, Chair Company has been able to purchase some of its Plastic materials at lower prices elsewhere than from Plastic Company.

REQUIRED

Is the demand by Plastic Company ethical? Does it represent sound business judgement?

COMPREHENSIVE ANALYSIS CASE SAFEWAY, INC.

Analyzing Safeway, Inc. for the Period 2004-2002 Safeway, Inc. is one of the largest food retailers in the country. Listed below are comparative income statements and balance sheets with common-size percents for 2004-2002 (in millions). Also included are selected ratio statistics. Please provide a brief explanation for your answer to each question.

SAFEWAY
COMPARATIVE COMMON-SIZE INCOME STATEMENTS
For The Years Ended December 31, 2004, 2003, 2002
(*in millions*)

	2004 $	2004 %	2003 $	2003 %	2002 $	2002 %
Revenues	$ 35,823.0	100.0%	$ 35,553.0	100.0%	$ 34,768.0	100.0%
Cost of goods sold	$ 25,228.0	70.4%	$ 25,019.0	70.4%	$ 23,956.0	68.9%
Gross margin	$ 10,595.0	29.6%	$ 10,534.0	29.6%	$ 10,812.0	31.1%
Operating expenses:						
Operating and administrative	$ 9,423.0	26.3%	$ 9,231.0	26.0%	$ 8,576.0	24.7%
Other expense	$ -	0.0%	$ 729.0	2.1%	$ 1,288.0	3.7%
Total operating expenses	$ 9,423.0	26.3%	$ 9,960.0	28.0%	$ 9,864.0	28.4%
Operating income	$ 1,172.0	3.3%	$ 574.0	1.6%	$ 948.0	2.7%
Net interest expense (income)	$ 411.0	1.1%	$ 442.0	1.2%	$ 431.0	1.2%
Other expense (income), net	$ (33.0)	-0.1%	$ (10.0)	0.0%	$ (16.0)	0.0%
Income before income taxes	$ 794.0	2.2%	$ 142.0	0.4%	$ 533.0	1.5%
Income taxes	$ 234.0	0.7%	$ 311.0	0.9%	$ 660.0	1.9%
Net income (loss) before unusual items	$ 560.0	1.6%	$ (169.0)	-0.5%	$ (127.0)	-0.4%
Cumulative effect of accounting change	$ -	0.0%	$ -	0.0%	$ (700.0)	-2.0%
Net income (loss)	$ 560.0	1.6%	$ (169.0)	-0.5%	$ (827.0)	-2.4%

SAFEWAY
COMPARATIVE COMMON-SIZE BALANCE SHEETS
December 31, 2004, 2003, 2002
(*in millions*)

	2004 $	2004 %	2003 $	2003 %	2002 $	2002 %
ASSETS						
Current:						
Cash & cash equivalents	$ 267.0	1.7%	$ 175.0	1.2%	$ 76.0	0.5%
Accounts receivable, net	$ 339.0	2.2%	$ 383.0	2.5%	$ 432.0	2.7%
Inventory	$ 2,741.0	17.8%	$ 2,642.0	17.5%	$ 2,718.0	16.9%
Other current assets	$ 251.0	1.6%	$ 308.0	2.0%	$ 233.0	1.5%
Total current assets	$ 3,598.0	23.4%	$ 3,508.0	23.2%	$ 3,459.0	21.6%
Fixed:						
Property & equipment, net	$ 8,689.0	56.5%	$ 8,406.0	55.7%	$ 8,531.0	53.2%
Long-term investments	$ 188.0	1.2%	$ 192.0	1.3%	$ 208.0	1.3%
Goodwill	$ 2,406.0	15.6%	$ 2,405.0	15.9%	$ 3,126.0	19.5%
Other assets	$ 496.0	3.2%	$ 586.0	3.9%	$ 723.0	4.5%
Total assets	$ 15,377.0	100.0%	$ 15,097.0	100.0%	$ 16,047.0	100.0%
LIABILITIES						
Current:						
Short-term debt	$ 640.0	4.2%	$ 751.0	5.0%	$ 824.0	5.1%
Accounts payable	$ 3,152.0	20.5%	$ 1,510.0	10.0%	$ 1,812.0	11.3%
Accrued salaries and benefits	$ -	0.0%	$ 406.0	2.7%	$ 401.0	2.5%
Other current liabilities	$ -	0.0%	$ 799.0	5.3%	$ 757.0	4.7%
Total current liabilities	$ 3,792.0	24.7%	$ 3,466.0	23.0%	$ 3,794.0	23.6%
Long-term debt	$ 6,124.0	39.8%	$ 7,072.0	46.8%	$ 7,613.0	47.4%
Deferred Income Taxes	$ 464.0	3.0%	$ 422.0	2.8%	$ 578.0	3.6%
Other long-term liabilities	$ 691.0	4.5%	$ 494.0	3.3%	$ 437.0	2.7%
Total liabilities	$ 11,071.0	72.0%	$ 11,454.0	75.9%	$ 12,422.0	77.4%
OWNERS' EQUITY						
Total owners' equity	$ 4,306.0	28.0%	$ 3,643.0	24.1%	$ 3,625.0	22.6%
Total liabilities and owners' equity	$ 15,377.0	100.0%	$ 15,097.0	100.0%	$ 16,047.0	100.0%

(Note: percents may not add to 100 due to rounding)

SAFEWAY
RATIO ANALYSIS SUMMARY
For The Years Ended December 31, 2004, 2003, 2002

	2004	2003	2002
SHORT-TERM LIQUIDITY RATIOS			
Current Ratio (Current Assets/Current Liabilities)	0.95	1.01	0.91
Quick Ratio (Cash + Short-term Investments + Accounts Receivable)/Current Liabilities	0.16	0.16	0.13
Accounts Receivable Turnover 1 (Revenues/Average Accounts Receivable)	99.23	87.25	
Accounts Receivable Turnover 2 (Revenues/Year-end Accounts Receivable)	105.67	92.83	80.48
Inventory Turnover 1 (Cost Goods Sold/Average Inventory)	9.37	9.34	
Inventory Turnover 2 (Cost Goods Sold/Year-end Inventory)	9.20	9.47	8.81
LONG-TERM SOLVENCY (LEVERAGE) RATIO			
Total Debt Ratio (Total Liabilities/Total Assets)	72.00%	75.87%	77.41%
PROFITABILITY RATIOS			
Gross Profit Margin (Gross Margin/Revenues)	29.58%	29.63%	31.10%
Operating Profit Margin (Operating Income/Revenues)	3.27%	1.61%	2.73%
Net Profit Margin (Return on Sales) (ROS) (Net Income/Revenues)	1.56%	-0.48%	-2.38%
Total Asset Turnover (Revenues/Average Total Assets)	2.35	2.28	
Return on Total Assets (ROA) (Net Income/Average Total Assets)	3.68%	-1.09%	

REQUIRED

Income statement questions:

1. Are total revenues higher or lower over the three-year period?

2. What is the percent change in total revenues from 2002 to 2004?

3. Is the percent of cost of goods sold to total revenues increasing or decreasing over the three-year period? As a result, is the gross margin percent increasing or decreasing?

4. Is the percent of total operating expenses to total revenues increasing or decreasing over the three-year period? As a result, is the operating income percent increasing or decreasing?

5. Is the percent of net income to total revenue increasing or decreasing over the three-year period?

Balance sheet questions:

6. Are total assets higher or lower over the three-year period?

7. What is the percent change in total assets from 2002 to 2004?

8. What are the largest asset investments for the company over the three-year period?

9. Are the largest asset investments increasing faster or slower than the percent change in total revenues?

10. Is the percent of total liabilities to total liabilities + owners' equity increasing or decreasing? As a result, is there more or less risk that the company could not pay its debts?

Integrative income statement and balance sheet question:

11. Is the company operating more or less efficiently by using the least amount of asset investment to generate a given level of total revenues? Note that the "total asset turnover" ratio is computed and included in the "ratio analysis summary."

Ratio analysis questions:

12. Is the *current ratio* better or worse in the most current year compared to prior years?

13. Is the *quick ratio* better or worse in the most current year compared to prior years?

14. Is the *accounts receivable turnover ratio 1* (based on *average* receivables) better or worse in the most current year compared to prior years?

15. Is the 2004 *accounts receivable turnover ratio 2* (based on *year-end* receivables) better or worse than the 2004 ratio based on an *average*?

16. Is the *inventory turnover ratio 1* (based on *average* inventory) better or worse in the most current year compared to prior years?

17. Is the 2004 *inventory turnover ratio 2* (based on *year-end* inventory) better or worse than the 2004 ratio based on an *average*?

18. Is the *return on total assets (ROA) ratio* better or worse in the most current year compared to prior years?

INTERNATIONAL ACCOUNTING AND FINANCIAL REPORTING ISSUES

"The real measure of your wealth is how much you'd be worth if you lost all of your money."

Anonymous

LEARNING GOALS

After studying Chapter 18, you should be able to:

1. Describe the primary issues in accounting for international operations.

2. Describe the financial reporting issues that arise from international transactions.

3. Describe the process of translating foreign currency financial statements.

4. Define hedging strategies used to manage changes in currency exchange rates.

5. Discuss accounting standard setting and the basic generally accepted accounting principles (GAAP).

6. Describe the conceptual framework of accounting.

7. Describe the effects of inflation on financial statement information.

UNDERSTANDING BUSINESS ISSUES

In recent years, the global economy has grown tremendously. Today firms now conduct business across borders and with many nations around the world. Many well-known U.S. companies (Coca-Cola, Motorola, and Nike) rely on international business for a major percentage of their sales revenue. Likewise, many non-U.S. firms (Sony, Toyota, and Philips Electronics) sell large amounts of their products in the United States and even issue their common stock in the U.S. stock market.

The use of different currencies, varied accounting principles and legal differences raise many financial reporting issues related to international trade. As the global economy becomes more fluid and better integrated in the 21st Century, these issues will continue to gain importance. Throughout this book, we have examined how business transactions affect corporate financial accounting and reporting.

We have assumed the U.S. dollar to be the standard monetary unit for all measurement. In this chapter, we will examine how the complexity of international business affects accounting and financial reporting.

We will discuss the primary issues in accounting for international operations. We will examine some examples of how accounting practices differ across the globe. We will focus on accounting for foreign currency exchange transactions and how companies translate foreign subsidiary financial statements to home country currency. Last, we discuss the impact of inflation on financial reporting.

INTERNATIONAL ACCOUNTING

Learning Goal 1   Describe the primary issues in accounting for international operations.

Many companies in the United States but business throughout the world. For example, you can buy a Big Mac not only in Philadelphia but in London, Tokyo, or Moscow. In 2004, 65.7% of total revenues and 38.3% of operating income for McDonald's Corporation came from operations outside the U.S. The Coca-Cola Company sells soft-drink products in nearly 200 countries throughout the world. In 2004, 69.8% of total revenue and 71.9% of operating income came from operations outside of North America.

There are two major factors that complicate accounting for international operations:

1. Accounting standards differ around the world.

2. The exchange rates between different currencies change frequently.

Accounting standards differ throughout the world. In the United States, accounting standards come from the Financial Accounting Standards Board which is a private-sector body as opposed to a government agency. In countries with strongly socialized economies, such as Germany, accounting standards are set by governmental agencies. The *International Accounting Standards Committee (IASC)* was formed in 1973 with the goal of reducing differences in accounting methods throughout the world. Because the IASC is a private organization, compliance with IASC standards is voluntary. Generally, IASC pronouncements to date have limited the range of choice instead of recommending a single accounting method for a specific accounting issue. Therefore, one issue in accounting for international operations involves recognizing the impact of different accounting methods on reported results. Exhibit 18.1 compares selected accounting practices for the United States, United Kingdom, and Japan. The ongoing movement towards International Financial Reporting Standards (IFRS) is intended to minimize these differences.

Accounting in United States	Accounting in Japan	Accounting in United Kingdom
➤ **Inventory costing:** Different methods allowed	Different methods allowed	Mostly first-in, first-out (FIFO)
➤ **Depreciation:** Mostly straight-line	Accelerated method	Straight-line
➤ **Business Combinations:** Mostly purchase method	Purchase method by many	Purchase method by many
➤ **Goodwill:** Capitalized & written off if impaired	Capitalized & amortized over 5-10 years.	Written off immediately
➤ **Assets in balance sheet:** Arranged by decreasing liquidity order	Arranged by decreasing liquidity order.	Arranged by increasing liquidity order.
➤ **Term for revenue:** Sales revenue	Sales revenue	Turnover

EXHIBIT **18.1**

Selected Accounting Practices: International Perspective

Exchange Rates Between Currencies

A country's currency is its standard form of paying all debts. We actively trade currencies from different countries on organized currency exchange markets each day. The **foreign exchange rate** is the price of one currency stated in terms of another currency. These prices change each day based on the supply of and demand for individual currencies. For example, on April 1, 2005, and April 3, 2002, the prices of selected foreign currencies stated in terms of U.S. dollars were as follows:

Country	Foreign Currency in U.S. Dollars April 1, 2005	Foreign Currency in U.S. Dollars April 3, 2002
Britain (pound)	$1.881	$1.4361
Canada (dollar)	.8243	.6290
Hong Kong (dollar)	.1282	.1282
Japan (yen)	.009323	.007537
Mexico (peso)	.08942	.1107
Switzerland (franc)	.8303	.6028
Euro	1.289	.8811

For example, on April 1, 2005, we could exchange one Euro for $1.289 U.S. dollars. On April 3, 2002, one Euro was worth $.8811 U.S. dollars. In this case, the Euro increased in value relative to the U.S. dollar between April 2002 and April 2005.

When a seller in the United States makes a sale to a buyer in England, the seller normally expects to end up with U.S. dollars when the buyer makes payment. If the buyer pays in British pounds, the seller must use these British pounds to purchase U.S. dollars. A **foreign currency exchange** is a transaction when we use one currency to purchase another. If the relative values of the U.S. dollar and the British pound remain constant from sale to collection and exchange, there is no problem. However, if the value of the British pound changes compared with the U.S. dollar, the seller will have a gain or loss on the exchange.

Financial Reporting Issues

Two basic financial reporting issues arise when international transactions involve dealings in more than one national currency:

1. Accounting for foreign currency exchange transactions.

2. Translation of foreign subsidiary financial statements from a foreign currency to a reporting currency.

The first issue arises when exchange rates change while a transaction is in process. The second issue arises at the end of an accounting period when we prepare consolidated financial statements.

Accounting for Foreign Currency Exchange Transactions

Learning Goal 2   Describe the financial reporting issues that arise from international transactions.

Assume that Alabama Corporation is a U.S. company that has many foreign operations. Its basic reporting currency is the U.S. dollar. Alabama closes the books annually each December 31. On December 16, 2007, it made a sale to a company in Mexico and agreed to receive 2 million pesos in 30 days. The exchange rate was $0.15 per peso on December 16, 2007. On Alabama Corporation's books, we record the sale in the U.S. dollar equivalent as follows:

2007
Dec.   16   Accounts Receivable   300,000
                    Sales   300,000
                    To record a sale for 2,000,000 pesos at an exchange
                    rate of $0.15, n/30.

With an exchange rate of $0.15, the dollar translation on the date of sale is $300,000 (2,000,000 × $0.15). Assume that when Alabama Corporation closed its books on December 31, 2007, the exchange rate had risen to $0.18 per peso. Since we measure payment in pesos, the 2 million pesos Alabama will collect now have a dollar value of $360,000 (2,000,000 × $0.18). We must recognize the exchange gain of $60,000 ($360,000 - $300,000). We record it as follows:

2007
Dec.   31   Accounts Receivable   60,000
                    Foreign Currency Exchange Gain   60,000
                    To recognize gain from translation of asset receivable
                    in foreign currency.

The exchange gain is a part of Alabama Corporation's net income in 2007. We report the gain in the other revenues section of the income statement.

Assume further that, on the date of collection, the new exchange rate is $0.17 per peso. The 2 million pesos Alabama Corporation receives will now buy only $340,000. Since the accounts receivable show $360,000, Alabama Corporation has lost due to fluctuations in the currencies since December 31, 2007. The journal entry to record the collection of the receivable and to recognize the exchange loss is as follows:

2008
Jan.   15   Cash   340,000
              Foreign Currency Exchange Loss   20,000
                    Accounts Receivable   360,000
                    To record collection of 2,000,000 pesos at an
                    exchange rate of $0.17.

The exchange loss is a part of 2008 net income. We report it in the other expenses section of the income statement. We use the same methods to account for other foreign exchange transactions, such as purchases and accounts payable.

Translation of Foreign Currency Statements

Learning Goal 3   Describe the process of translating foreign currency financial statements.

When we consolidate financial statements of foreign subsidiaries with statements of the U.S. parent company, we must *translate* the foreign currency amounts into dollars. In recent years, considerable controversy has existed over (1) the exchange rate used to translate income statement and balance sheet items and (2) the treatment of any gains or losses resulting from the translation.

In December 1981, the Financial Accounting Standards Board (FASB) issued revised guidelines for translating the financial statements of foreign subsidiaries into U.S. dollars.[1] In that issuance, the FASB introduced the concept of the **functional currency**. Normally, the functional currency is the currency of the primary economic environment in which the foreign entity generates revenue and expends cash. Determining the functional currency is a critical management decision. We apply different translation methods depending on whether the functional currency is the local currency of the environment in which the foreign subsidiary operates or the reporting currency of the parent.[2]

When the functional currency is the local currency of the particular country of the foreign subsidiary, we follow the *current rate method* of translation. We measure all elements of the financial statements first in the functional (local) currency. We then use the current exchange rate to translate all assets and liabilities from the functional currency to the reporting currency (U.S. dollars). We generally translate revenues and expenses at the weighted average exchange rate for the period. We do not include gains and losses from these translations in net income. Instead, we accumulate them and show them as a separate component of owners' equity on the balance sheet. The commonly accepted method of doing this is to *report the item between paid-in capital and retained earnings* in the owners' equity section of the balance sheet as part of an account called Accumulated Other Comprehensive Income.

When the functional currency is the reporting currency of the U.S. parent company, we follow the *current/historical rate method* of translation. We translate monetary assets and liabilities (items with fixed dollar balances such as cash, receivables, current payables, and long-term debt) at the current exchange rate. We translate all other assets, liabilities, and owners' equity at the exchange rate in effect when we initially recorded these balances (the historical exchange rate). We translate revenues and expenses incurred evenly throughout a period at weighted average exchange rates for the period. We translate expenses related to specific balance sheet items (mainly cost of sales and depreciation) at the same historical rates as the balance sheet item. Gains and losses resulting from translation do not appear directly on the income statement. Once we have translated the statements of the foreign subsidiary into U.S. dollars, we consolidate them with those of the parent company. These do not affect the income statement until the subsidiary is sold.

As companies expand international operations, these translation adjustments can quickly become material items on the balance sheet. For example, as January 31, 2002, the foreign currency translation adjustment on Wal-Mart's balance sheet reduced owners' equity of $39 billion by $1.1 billion. As of January 31, 2005, the foreign currency adjustment reduced owners' equity of $49.4 billion by $2.1 billion.

Translation Illustration

As discussed earlier, when generating consolidated financial statements, firms must convert the financial statements of foreign subsidiaries to the home currency. In the following example, we will use the *current rate method* of translation. This method assumes the *functional currency* is the local currency of the foreign subsidiary. To consolidate financial statements, U.S. firms are required to convert the assets and liabilities of the foreign subsidiary at the exchange rate on the balance sheet date. The owners' equity section is converted using historical rates. Stock is converted using the rate at the time in which the subsidiary was acquired. Retained earnings is converted using the average exchange over the reporting period.

---

[1] *Statement of Financial Accounting Standards (SFAS) No. 52*, "Foreign Currency Translation" (Norwalk, Conn.: Financial Accounting Standards Board, December 1981).

[2] *SFAS No. 52* provides guidance on determining whether the functional currency is the local currency or the reporting currency. These specific requirements are complex and are not necessary to understand the concepts presented here.

Any change in currency exchange will give rise to a situation where the difference between assets and liabilities does not equal owners' equity. To reconcile this difference, the parent must report a **foreign currency translation adjustment**. This adjustment is the amount necessary to balance the assets and equities. The foreign currency translation adjustment appears as part of Accumulated Other Comprehensive Income of the parent's owners' equity section on the balance sheet. A positive balance represents gains related to stronger foreign currencies relative to the home currency. A negative balance means that the foreign currencies have devalued relative to the home currency.

Consider the following example. Assume that California Foods own Tijuana Tastes, a Mexican subsidiary. When California Foods acquired the subsidiary the Mexican peso was valued at $.13. Assume that in 2007, the average price of the peso was $.10 and on December 31, 2007 the value of the peso was $.09. On December 31, 2007, Tijuana Tastes has assets of 1,000,000 pesos and liabilities of 800,000 pesos. Their owners' equity section consists of common stock and retained earnings listed at 100,000 pesos each.

The parent must convert the subsidiary's financial statement to the currency of the parent (U.S. dollars). We make this conversion and calculate the foreign currency translation adjustment in Exhibit 18.2.

TIJUANA TASTES
BALANCE SHEET
DECEMBER 31, 2007

	Pesos	Conversion Rate	U.S. Dollars
Assets	1,000,000	.09 (current)	$90,000
Liabilities	800,000	.09 (current)	$72,000
Owners' equity			
Common stock	100,000	.13 (historical)	$13,000
Retained earnings	100,000	.10 (average)	10,000
Accumulated Other Comprehensive Income	-------		**(5,000)**
Total owners' equity	200,000		$18,000
Total liabilities and owners' equity	1,000,000		$90,000

EXHIBIT **18.2**

Converting Tijuana Tastes' Balance Sheet from Pesos to U. S. Dollars

California Foods will show a $5,000 negative Accumulated Other Comprehensive Income adjustment in its owners' equity section. The negative balance reflects the devaluation of the Mexican peso over time.

Hedging Strategies

Learning Goal 4   Define hedging strategies used to manage changes in currency exchange rates.

Companies have ways to limit or avoid losses arising from changes in currency exchange rates. There are two primary alternatives. First, the company may enter into transactions of equal value to counter-balance existing receivables or payables. For example, a company with a receivable in Japanese yen may enter into a transaction that creates a payable due in Japanese yen in an equal amount at a similar time. This approach negates the risk of any devaluation of Japanese yen in relation to the home currency. Many times this approach is difficult to pursue. There may not be appropriate suppliers or it may be difficult to align the timing and amounts of transactions.

A second approach is to enter into hedging contracts. Hedging contracts essentially allow companies to buy insurance against declines in currency values. For example, suppose a U.S. firm sells its product to a customer in Belgium. The U.S. firm sells the product on the transaction date and expects to collect the receivable in Belgian francs at some point in the future. If the company expects the franc to decline in value, collecting that sum would be worth some amount smaller than the dollar value of the receivable.

To offset this expected loss, the U.S. firm may enter into a transaction to buy the foreign currency at the current exchange rate at the collection date. This *forward contract* creates a payable to offset the receivable. Companies with payables due in foreign currencies may enter into contracts to sell currency in the future.

GENERALLY ACCEPTED ACCOUNTING PRINCIPLES (GAAP)

Learning Goal 5   Discuss accounting standard setting and the basic generally accepted accounting principles (GAAP).

As business transactions become more complicated and are conducted across national borders, it is important to develop financial reporting practices that keep pace with these changes. The chapters in this book have used many basic concepts that make up generally accepted accounting principles (GAAP). GAAP are an evolving set of standards that guide the preparation and reporting of financial information.

Users of accounting information are more effective if they understand the accounting standards and alternative reporting methods that underlie the preparation of financial statements. In this section, we discuss the development of GAAP and present the conceptual framework that enables standard setters to continually develop new principles to meet users' changing needs.

Sources of GAAP

Over the years, the accounting profession has developed GAAP. GAAP arise from two broad sources: (1) authoritative pronouncements of a recognized standard-setting body and (2) those principles that have gained general acceptance through widespread use.

The American Institute of Certified Public Accountants (AICPA) took the lead in setting accounting standards from 1937 to 1973. Through its Committee on Accounting Procedure, the AICPA issued 51 *Accounting Research Bulletins (ARBs)* that gave guidance to accountants for more than two decades. In 1959, the Accounting Principles Board (APB) replaced the Committee on Accounting Procedure. From 1959 to 1973 the APB published 31 pronouncements called *Opinions of the Accounting Principles Board (APB Opinions)*. In mid-1973, an *independent* private body, the Financial Accounting Standards Board (FASB), replaced the APB and began issuing financial accounting standards. Since then, the FASB has issued two main types of guidance to accountants. *Statements of Financial Accounting Standards (SFAS)* help to solve specific accounting questions, such as how to account for computer software development costs. *Statements of Financial Accounting Concepts (SFAC)* are a basic conceptual framework for accounting.

In addition to the private sector standard-setting bodies, the Securities and Exchange Commission (SEC), created in 1934, is an independent federal agency with the legal power to set accounting methods for firms that sell securities to the investing public on stock exchanges. The SEC has left the task of issuing detailed accounting rules to the accounting profession. However, it still influences the standard-setting process where necessary. Typically, the SEC has required publicly held companies to disclose additional information in external financial reports. Both public and nonpublic firms have adopted the accounting releases issued by the SEC that require additional disclosures in annual reports. Thus, the SEC's releases have become GAAP through general acceptance.

Basic GAAP

This section reviews some of the basic generally accepted accounting principles.

Entity

The **entity concept** requires that we must keep a separate set of records for each business enterprise of its owners. The financial reports of a business must report only the resources of that business, claims to those resources, and changes in those resources. We must guard against intermingling the transactions of businesses with the personal transactions of the owners and managers.

Going Concern

We assume that an entity is a **going concern**—that it will continue in operation indefinitely—unless there is evidence to the contrary. Because of the going concern assumption, the accountant discloses plant assets at their book value (cost less accumulated depreciation) and not at their current market value. Using current market value assumes that the company may need to sell these assets soon to liquidate the business. We report long-term debts at their face value and not at the amount that creditors would receive if the company went out of business.

Consistency

Previous chapters explain several acceptable alternative methods that we may use in accounting records. Once we have made a choice, the principle of **consistency** requires that we follow the same procedure in all future periods. This is so that statements covering different time periods will be comparable. This principle does not mean that we cannot make a change to a better method. If there is sufficient reason to change an accounting method, we may do so if we disclose it in the financial reports.

Conservatism

Where there are several acceptable methods of accounting for an item, the method we should choose is that which produces the *least favorable* immediate result on the financial statements. The principle of **conservatism** aims to avoid favorable exaggeration in accounting reports. Reporting inventories at lower-of-cost-or-market is an example of this principle.

Periodicity

We prepare financial statements at regular specified time periods during the lifetime of a firm. The principle of **periodicity** states that we allocate expenses and revenues to time periods so that we properly match them for determining income. This is why we make adjusting entries. The *accrual concept* is essential to this standard.

Objective Evidence

As much as possible, we should base the amounts we use in recording events on **objective evidence** rather than subjective judgment. Sales invoices, receipts, and other *source documents* provide such evidence. We may still have to estimate some items, however. For example, in calculating depreciation expense, estimating useful life and residual value are necessary. When such estimates are necessary, we should base them on experience or another logical base that we use consistently from year to year.

Materiality

An item is *immaterial* (that is, not material) when it is too small to influence a decision based on the financial statements. Accounting treatments for immaterial items do not have to follow prescribed accounting standards. **Materiality** depends on the size and the nature of the item compared with the size of the business. In a very small business, an inventory error of $300 may be large enough to influence the decision of the user of the financial statements. On the other hand, an error of $300 in valuation of inventories of a multimillion-dollar company would most likely be immaterial.

Full Disclosure

Financial statements should report all significant financial and economic information relating to an entity. Financial statements that show this information practice **full disclosure**. If the accounting system does not automatically capture some specific item of significance, we should include it in a note to the accounting statements. The SEC insists on full disclosure in financial reports.

Historical Cost

The **historical cost** principle states that the actual incurred cost—arrived at through agreement by two independent entities—is the appropriate amount we use to record the value of a newly acquired asset.

Stable Dollar

The **stable dollar concept** assumes that the dollar is sufficiently free from changes in purchasing power. Therefore, we can use the dollar as the basic unit of measure in accounting without adjustment for price-level changes. Many accountants challenge the general use of this principle because it does not reflect changing prices over time.

Revenue Realization

Under accrual accounting, we *realize* revenue when we earn it, but when do we earn revenue? When we do something to the product to add value? When the product changes hands? Or when we collect the cash?

With certain exceptions, GAAP requires that we realize revenue at the *point of sale* (the method used in this textbook). For a business that deals with a product, we define the point of sale to be the delivery of the merchandise. For a service business, we normally agree that the time we render the service is the point of sale. Thus, we earn revenue in the accounting period in which the sale takes place. Two other revenue realization methods are acceptable under specific circumstances: the collection method and the percentage of completion method.

Under the **collection method**, we defer the realization of revenue until we collect the cash. We may apply this method using either the cost recovery basis or the installment basis. With the **cost recovery basis**, we view all collections first as recoveries of the cost of the product sold. We recognize profit only after we recover the total cost. This method is appropriate when there is a high probability that we will not receive total payment. It is a very conservative method.

Under the **installment basis**, we consider each dollar we collect to be a proportionate return of the cost of the merchandise and a realization of the gross margin. For example, assume that a company sells a television set that cost $300 for $400. We would view each dollar the company collects as a return of $0.75 ($300 ÷ $400) of the cost of the set and a $0.25 [($400 - $300) ÷ $400] realization of the gross margin from the sale. If in a given month the customer makes a $100 installment payment, the company realizes $25 in gross margin. We use the installment basis when cash collections are uncertain.

The other alternative to point of sale is the **percentage of completion method**. This method is useful for large construction projects requiring more than one accounting period to complete, such as a high-rise office building. Under these circumstances, use of the point of sale method of revenue realization could significantly distort income reporting. This is because several periods might go by with no expense or revenue shown. Then in the period that we complete the project, the company would record a large amount of expense or revenue. We can avoid this distortion by realizing part of the gross margin from the project during each period in which the work on the project is done. We allocate the gross margin to each accounting period based on how much of the project we estimate has been completed. This estimated percentage of completion is the ratio of the current year's actual costs to the total estimated costs. In the final period, we recognize the remaining actual gross margin.

For example, assume that a construction company enters a contract to build a high-rise condominium building at a price of $4 million. Also, assume that it estimates that the total cost of the building is $3 million. This gives a gross margin of $1 million on the project. If the actual incurred costs were as shown in the following schedule, the gross margin recognized by the company each year would be as follows:

Year	Actual Incurred Cost	Percentage of Completion	×	Total Gross Margin	=	Gross Margin Recognized
1	$ 900,000	$900,000 ÷ $3,000,000		$1,000,000		$ 300,000
2	1,200,000	$1,200,000 ÷ $3,000,000		$1,000,000		400,000
3	1,000,000					200,000*
	$3,100,000					$ 900,000

*Balance of gross margin: ($4,000,000 - $3,100,000) - ($300,000 + $400,000) = $200,000.

If at the end of an accounting period a loss on the project becomes apparent, we should show the loss in that period.

Matching Expenses and Revenues

The **matching principle** states that we match expenses we incur in the generation of revenues against those revenues in determining income. Examples are recording advertising expense in the period that the advertisement to produce the sale appears or using the allowance method to determine bad debts expense. We achieve proper matching of revenue and expense by using accrual accounting methods.

Other Concepts

As research and study continue, accountants will review certain standards and they will issue new ones. We design accounting systems to meet changing user needs. These needs continue to increase in scope and complexity as changes occur in the environment in which users make economic decisions. It is the ongoing task of the rule-making bodies to develop and publish new and revised accounting standards that will keep pace with these changes.

The Conceptual Framework

Learning Goal 6   Describe the conceptual framework of accounting.

Though these generally accepted accounting principles exist, debate continues on the basic concepts of accounting. This debate has led to the FASB's issuance of a series of *Statements of Financial Accounting Concepts (SFAC)*. They are an attempt to develop a *conceptual framework* within which we form new accounting standards. Important accounting topics discussed in the concepts statements have included: (1) the objectives of financial reporting, (2) the *qualitative* aspects of accounting information, and (3) the elements of financial statements.

Objectives of Financial Reporting

The FASB's first concepts statement, "Objectives of Financial Reporting by Business Enterprises," presents the overall objectives of financial reporting. The objectives focus on the users of financial statements and financial information. *SFAC No. 1* lists three basic objectives of financial reporting:

1. It should provide information useful in making investment and credit decisions.

2. It should provide information useful in judging the amounts, timing, and certainty of future cash flows.

3. It should provide information about the resources of the business, the claims on the resources, and the changes in the resources during an accounting period.[3]

We should present this information so that it is understandable to people who have a reasonable knowledge of business and economics. Overall, information we present to financial statement users must have *decision usefulness*.

Qualitative Characteristics

SFAC No. 2 is titled "Qualitative Characteristics of Accounting Information." Its purpose is to examine what qualities make accounting information useful. We can view accounting information as having several levels, called a *hierarchy*, of qualities. Usefulness for decision making is the most important quality. Exhibit 18.3 shows this hierarchy of accounting qualities. Note that although decision usefulness is the most important quality, understandability is above it in the diagram. This is because accounting information must be in a form users can understand before it can be useful to them. The diagram is from *SFAC No. 2*.

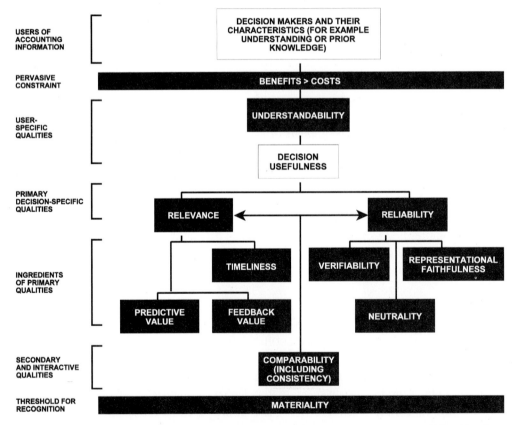

Source: *Statement of Financial Accounting Concepts No. 2*, "Qualitative Characteristics of Accounting Information: (Norwalk, Conn.: FASB, 1980), p. 15.

EXHIBIT **18.3**

A Hierarchy of Accounting Qualities

---

[3] *Statement of Financial Accounting Concepts (SFAC) No. 1*, "Objectives of Financial Reporting by Business Enterprises" (Norwalk, Conn.: Financial Accounting Standards Board, 1978).

The diagram shows overall *constraints* at the top and bottom. The constraints define the limits within which we report accounting information. The "pervasive" constraint on top specifies that the benefits of providing the information must be greater than the cost of gathering and reporting the information. This means that we should report information only if the benefits are greater than the costs. The "threshold for recognition" constraint at the bottom of the diagram specifies that we report information only if it is material. This means that we should report information only if it would have an impact on or change the decision of users.

The "user-specific qualities" specify that the accounting information we report should be understandable and be useful in making decisions. The two primary qualities that make accounting information useful for decision making are relevance and reliability. *SFAC No. 2* divides each of these primary decision-specific qualities into three components, or ingredients. Accounting information is *relevant* if it (1) is timely, (2) helps users form predictions about the future, and (3) provides feedback about the results of decisions. Information is *reliable* if it (1) is verifiable, (2) is neutral, and (3) has representational faithfulness. The latter means that an accounting measure or description closely resembles what it represents. Comparability and consistency are other qualities that join relevance and reliability to make information more useful.

Elements of Financial Statements

SFAC No. 6 contains definitions of interrelated elements that are directly related to measuring the performance and status of a business. These elements include: assets, liabilities, owners' equity, income, revenues, gains, expenses, and losses.[4] We introduced, explained, and discussed these elements throughout this textbook.

IMPACT OF INFLATION ON ACCOUNTING INFORMATION

Learning Goal 7   Describe the effects of inflation on financial statement information.

We use *historical cost* as the primary basis for valuing assets. Because of the effects of inflation, some accountants worry about the information value of traditional historical cost-based financial statements. For example, if a company's profit increases by 5% during a year in which general prices increase by 10%, the company has not kept up with inflation.

The methods of accounting we present in this textbook are generally based on the historical cost principle. We should record each asset or expense at the cost when we purchase the asset or incur the expense. Recording at cost will cause no problem with the reported financial results *if the value of the dollar does not change.* However, if the value of the dollar is changing, we may report misleading results.

During the late 1970s and early 1980s (a period of high inflation in the United States), the FASB required large companies to present supplemental inflation adjusted information in the annual report. Since this time, inflation has been much lower. As a result, the requirement for inflation adjusted information was abandoned in 1987. However, the financial statement user needs to recognize the potential for inflation distortions when using financial statement information. Companies also adjust financial statements when conducting business in nations with hyper-inflationary economies.

---

[4] *SFAC No. 6*, "Elements of Financial Statements' (Norwalk, Conn.: Financial Accounting Standards Board, 1985).

Impact of Inflation on the Balance Sheet

If a company purchased a piece of land in 1998 for $50,000, it would record the land at $50,000 using the historical cost principle. If the company purchased an identical piece of land in 2007, it would record the second parcel at the amount it paid in 2007, say $200,000. Under the stable dollar assumption used in conventional financial statements, we assume that each of the recorded land costs represents dollars of equal purchasing power. Therefore, we add the individual land costs to arrive at a total for land of $250,000 on the balance sheet. If the pieces of land are identical, the total historical cost for land on the balance sheet does not reflect the total current asset value in 2007 ($200,000 × 2 pieces of land = $400,000). Over time, adding assets we acquire during periods of different purchasing power results in an asset total on the balance sheet that is hard to interpret. From a financial statement user point of view, it is important to:

1. Understand that most assets in the balance sheet are stated at historical cost and do not reflect current market values.

2. In making decisions which require information on asset values (for example, a loan decision where an asset is pledged as security), independent appraisals of current asset values may be necessary to make informed decisions.

Impact of Inflation on the Income Statement

Assume that in 2001 a company purchased a delivery truck for $10,000 with an estimated life of 10 years and no residual value. Depreciation expense computed using the straight-line method would be $1,000 per year. If the company purchased an identical delivery truck in 2007, it would record this second purchase at the amount it paid in 2007, say $20,000. Depreciation expense using the straight-line method on the second delivery truck would be $2,000 per year. For 2007, total depreciation expense on the two identical trucks would be $3,000 ($1,000 + $2,000). When we match current revenues and historical cost-based depreciation expense on the 2007 income statement, we will overstate net income in terms of current purchasing power. This is because the depreciation expense on the 2001 delivery truck does not reflect current replacement cost.

For a company to continue in business, it must replace assets as it consumes them. In a period of inflation, each new asset costs more than the one it replaces. Depreciation expense on the older, lower-cost assets is lower. Thus, net income is higher, and we may not recover the current costs to replace existing assets through depreciation deductions based on historical cost. From a financial statement user perspective, it is important to:

1. Understand that some expenses in the income statement (depreciation and amortization) may reflect historical cost versus current cost.

2. In assessing profitability for a company with a large investment in fixed assets, we should consider the relative age of the assets and the impact on expense recognition and profitability. In some cases, independent appraisals of the cost to replace aging and outdated long-term assets may be necessary to make informed assessments of future profitability.

LEARNING GOALS REVIEW

1. Describe the primary issues in accounting for international operations.
The global economy is growing every year. Accounting issues arise because accounting principles and currencies differ from country to country. In evaluating reported results, it is important to consider differences in accounting principles when comparing companies in different countries.

Because international transactions involve different currencies, currency exchange is necessary. When companies engage in transactions that involve different currencies they must convert these transactions to prepare home currency based financial statements.

2. **Describe the financial reporting issues that arise from international transactions.**

There are two primary financial reporting issues that arise from international transactions. First, companies must account for changes in currency rates between the transaction date, statement date, and settlement date. Second, companies must translate the financial statements of foreign subsidiaries to their home country.

3. **Describe the process of translating foreign currency financial statements.**

To consolidate financial statements using the *current rate method*, U.S. firms are required to convert the assets and liabilities of the subsidiary at the exchange rate on the balance sheet date. The owners' equity section is converted using historical rates. Stock is converted using the rate at the time in which the subsidiary was acquired. Retained earnings is converted using the average exchange rate over the reporting period. The parent company must report a foreign currency translation adjustment as part of Accumulated Other Comprehensive Income to reconcile any difference between assets, liabilities, and owners' equity.

4. **Define hedging strategies used to manage changes in currency exchange rates.**

Companies adopt hedging strategies to avoid or limit losses from foreign currency transactions. There are two primary hedging approaches. First, companies may enter into transactions to counterbalance receivables or payables. Second, companies may enter into a contract to buy or sell a fixed amount of a foreign currency at the current rate at some point in the future.

5. **Discuss accounting standard setting and the basic generally accepted accounting principles (GAAP).**

As business transactions are becoming more complicated and commerce is conducted across borders, accounting standards need to evolve over time to keep pace with these changes. Over the past several decades, private sector bodies (i.e. the FASB) and the Securities and Exchange Commission have offered pronouncements that have resulted in generally accepted accounting principles (GAAP). GAAP are important because they allow financial statement users to interpret financial reports and to understand the impact of differences in alternative reporting methods.

GAAP are based on several fundamental concepts. The *entity concept* specifies that we must keep a separate set of records for each business enterprise of an owner. We should assume that an entity is a *going concern* unless there is evidence to the contrary. We must follow *consistent* procedures for entries so that statements covering different time periods will be comparable. In a choice among alternatives, we should select the most *conservative* alternative. We should allocate expense and revenue items to regularly specified time periods so that expenses and revenues can be *matched* to determine income. As much as possible, we should base the amounts used in recording events on *objective evidence*. The accounting treatment of *immaterial items* need not follow prescribed accounting standards. Financial statements should report all significant financial and economic information related to an entity. The appropriate amount to use in recording the value of a newly acquired asset is the actual incurred cost. We assume that the dollar is free enough from changes in purchasing power to be used as the basic unit of measure without adjustment.

We *realize revenue* at the point of sale. Under certain circumstances, we may recognize revenue after or before the point of sale. Under the *collection method*, we defer realization of revenue until we actually collect the cash. Under the *percentage of completion method*, we allocate revenue to each accounting period based on the amount of work completed on the project. Completion is measured by the proportion of estimated total costs that the project has incurred.

6. Describe the conceptual framework of accounting.

The overall objectives of financial reporting are that it should provide: information useful in makings investment and credit decisions; information useful in judging the amounts, timing, and certainty of future cash flows; and information about the resources of the business, the claims on the resources, and the changes in the resources during an accounting period. We must present this information so that it is understandable to people with a reasonable knowledge of business and economic activities. To contribute to decision usefulness, information should have benefits greater than cost and it should meet the test of materiality. To be useful, information should be relevant, reliable, comparable, and consistent. The conceptual framework of accounting also includes the definitions of assets, liabilities, owners' equity, income, revenues, gains, expenses, and losses.

7. Describe the effects of inflation on financial statement information.

Changes in price levels may affect the value of the dollar. The declining ability of the dollar to purchase goods and services is called inflation. The opposite is deflation. It is important to remember that most assets on the balance sheet and many expenses on the income statement do not reflect current market values. In cases where changes in price levels have been significant, supplemental current value information may be necessary to make informed decisions.

DEMONSTRATION PROBLEM

Assume that Washington Lumber Company owns Hong Kong Furniture Maker, a Hong Kong subsidiary. When Washington Lumber acquired the subsidiary the Hong Kong dollar was valued at $.14 (U.S. dollars). Assume that in 2007, the average price of the Hong Kong Dollar was $.12 and on December 31, 2007 the value of the Hong Kong dollar was $.10. On December 31, 2007, Hong Kong Furniture Maker has assets of 2,000,000 Hong Kong Dollars and liabilities of 1,200,000 Hong Kong Dollars. The subsidiary's owners' equity section consists of common stock 300,000 Hong Kong Dollars and retained earnings listed of 500,000 Hong Kong Dollars.

REQUIRED

1. **(LG 3)** Convert Hong Kong Furniture Maker's financial statements to U.S. dollars using the current rate method.

2. **(LG 3)** Calculate any foreign currency translation adjustment that Washington Lumber must report. Will this increase or decrease the parent's owners' equity? Has the U.S. dollar increased or decreased in value against the Hong Kong Dollar?

SOLUTION

Requirement 1

Solution Approach

To consolidate financial statements using the *current rate method*, U.S. firms are required to convert the assets and liabilities of the subsidiary at the exchange rate on the balance sheet date. The owners' equity section is converted using historical rates. Stock is converted using the rate at the time when the subsidiary was acquired. Retained earnings is converted using the average exchange rate over the reporting period. The parent company must report a foreign currency translation adjustment as part of Accumulated Other Comprehensive Income to reconcile any difference between assets, liabilities, and owners' equity.

HONG KONG FURNITURE MAKER
BALANCE SHEET
DECEMBER 31, 2007

Assets	Hong Kong Dollars	Conversion Rate	U.S. Dollars
	2,000,000	.10 (current)	$200,000
Liabilities	1,200,000	.10 (current)	$120,000
Owners' equity			
Common stock	300,000	.14 (historical)	$ 42,000
Retained earnings	500,000	.12 (average)	60,000
Accumulated Other Comprehensive Income	---------		(22,000)
Total owners' equity	800,000		$ 80,000
Total liabilities and owners' equity	2,000,000		$200,000

Requirement 2

Solution Approach

Any change in currency exchange will give rise to a situation where the difference between assets and liabilities does not equal owners' equity. To reconcile this difference, the parent must report a foreign currency translation adjustment. This adjustment is the amount necessary to balance the assets and equities. The foreign currency translation adjustment appears as part of Accumulated Other Comprehensive Income on the parent's owners' equity section on the balance sheet. A positive balance represents gains related to stronger foreign currencies relative to the home currency. A negative balance means that the foreign currencies have devalued relative tot he home currency.

In this case, Washington Lumber must report a negative foreign currency translation adjustment of $22,000 as part of Accumulated Other Comprehensive Income. This entry will decrease the Washington Lumber owners' equity section of the balance sheet. This indicates that the value of the U.S. dollar has increased in value against the Hong Kong Dollar. Thus, Washington's holdings in its Hong Kong subsidiary have declined in value in terms of U.S. dollars.

GLOSSARY

collection method A method of revenue recognition in which we defer the realization of revenue until we collect cash.

conservatism The principle that where acceptable alternatives exist, we should choose one that produces the least favorable immediate result.

consistency The principle that once we choose a method of recording over an alternative, we must use the chosen method consistently from year to year.

cost recovery basis A method of revenue recognition in which we first consider all collections to be a recovery of cost before recognizing income.

entity concept The principle that the focus of a set of accounting records must be on a single enterprise.

foreign currency A transaction in which a company uses one currency to purchase another.

foreign currency rate The price of one currency stated in terms of another.

full disclosure The principle that requires an organization to reveal in its financial reports all significant economic and financial information relating to it.

functional currency The currency of the primary economic environment in which the foreign entity generates revenues and expends cash.

generally accepted accounting principles(GAAP) Accounting principles (standards) that have arisen from wide acceptance in the past or are contained in authoritative pronouncements.

going concern The principle or assumption that an enterprise will continue to operate indefinitely unless there is evidence to the contrary.

historical cost The principle that we should record an asset at the actual cost of obtaining it. We arrive at the actual cost through agreement with another independent entity.

installment basis A method of revenue recognition in which we consider each dollar collected to be a proportionate return of cost and the realization of gross margin.

matching principle A principle in which we should match expenses incurred in generating revenue against that revenue to determine income.

materiality The principle that we must give an item a prescribed accounting treatment only if it is significant enough to influence a decision by a user of the accounting information.

objective evidence The principle that recording accounting events is based on some type of document that supports the amount and method of recording.

percentage of completion method A method of revenue recognition in which the amount of estimated gross margin earned is proportional to the percentage of completion of a long-term contract.

periodicity The principle that we allocate items of revenue and expense to a time period to determine net income for that period.

purchasing power gains and losses Gains and losses arising out of holding monetary items during periods of inflation and deflation; the difference between the monetary items based on historical cost and the same items adjusted for changes in price levels.

replacement cost The current cost of replacing one specific asset with another asset of equivalent capacity.

specific price-level change A change in the value of the dollar that results from changes in the value of a specific good or service.

stable dollar concept The principle or assumption that historical cost dollars of different years are comparable.

translation adjustment An adjustment to a parent's owners' equity section (Accumulated Other Comprehensive Income) of the balance sheet to reflect changes in the value of the assets and equities of a foreign subsidiary.

QUESTIONS FOR GROUP LEARNING

Q18-1. Why do exchange gains and losses occur in import/export transactions?

Q18-2. Define currency exchange rate.

Q18-3. Define functional currency.

Q18-4. Assume that an American company has a subsidiary in Mexico. If the peso devalued this year with respect to the dollar, will the company have a positive or negative foreign currency translation adjustment on its balance sheet?

Q18-5. In a recent annual report, Wal-Mart reported a negative foreign currency translation adjustment. Does this indicate that foreign currencies were stronger or weaker than the U. S. dollar in the years covered by their report?

Q18-6. What was the role of the American Institute of Certified Public Accountants (AICPA) in the development of financial reporting standards prior to the formation of the Financial Accounting Standards Board (FASB)?

Q18-7. What financial reporting standards were issued by the AICPA from 1937 to 1973?

Q18-8. What is the purpose of the FASB? What are the reporting standards the FASB issues called?

Q18-9. Describe how the Securities and Exchange Commission (SEC) influences the development of financial reporting standards.

Q18-10. What are generally accepted accounting principles (GAAP)? What are the sources of GAAP? Explain the importance of GAAP to users of financial statements.

Q18-11. Under GAAP, we recognize revenue at the point of sale. Briefly describe alternative revenue recognition methods.

Q18-12. What are the three objectives of financial reporting stated in *SFAC No. 1*?

Q18-13. Discuss the primary decision-specific qualities of accounting information. What are the ingredients of each of the primary qualities?

Q18-14. What are the overall constraints on qualitative characteristics of accounting information?

Q18-15. What are the major reasons to consider changing price levels in financial reports?

Q18-16. Give three illustrations of distortions or inaccuracies in conventional financial statements resulting from a period of high inflation.

Q18-17. Clarke Company constructed a plant in 1993 at a cost of $2 million and a second, similar plant in 2007 at a cost of $5 million. The 2007 report has a current appraised value of $12 million. What will be the gross plant cost in conventional financial statements? Is this a fair report? Why?

Q18-18. What is the effect of adjusting depreciation expenses for changes in prices so often much more pronounced than adjusting other expenses?

EXERCISES

E18-19. **International financial reporting (LG 1)** Accounting reporting standards can vary from country to country. Identify at least one major difference in the reporting standards between the United States, Japan and the United Kingdom.

E18-20. **Computing foreign currency exchange gains or losses (LG 2)** On December 10, 2007, Iowa Grain Company sold a shipment to German Importers for 920,000 Euros when the exchange rate in New York was $.80 = 1 Euro. The invoice carries terms of n/ 30 and is to be paid in euros. On December 31, when Iowa Grain closed its books to prepare year-end consolidated statements, the Euro closed on the foreign exchange market at $.82 = 1 Euro. On January 9, 2008, Iowa Grain collected the bill when the euro closed on the foreign exchange market at $.795 = 1 Euro. Prepare journal entries on Iowa Grain Company's books to record the sale, closing of the books, and collection.

E18-21. **Foreign currency transactions (LG 2)** Tolland Company sells soups worldwide and is based in Tolland, Connecticut. A sale of goods resulted in a $10,000 receivable denominated in Japanese yen. The receivable is due sixty days after the sale. At the time of the sale, the Japanese yen was valued at $.008 per yen. After sixty days the price of the yen fell to $.007 per yen.

1. Does the decrease in the value of the yen represent a gain or loss to Tolland?

2. Calculate the foreign currency transaction gain or loss associated with this transaction.

E18-22. **Foreign currency transactions (LG 2)** Winter Company imports radio transistors into the United States. A recent purchase of goods resulted in a $10,000 payable denominated in Hong Kong dollars. The payable is due sixty days after the sale. At the time of the sale, the Hong Kong dollar was valued at $.12 per HK$. After sixty days the price of the HK$ rose to $.14 per HK$.

1. Does the increase in the price of HK$ represent a gain or loss to Summers?

2. Calculate the foreign currency transaction gain or loss associated with this transaction.

E18-23. **Hedging strategies (LG 4)** Global Games Company is headquartered in Cape May, New Jersey. The company sells board games to customers around the world. This year the company has developed a large client base in France. Nearly 40% of their receivables are from French customers and due in about 90 days. The president of the company expects the value of the Euro to decline in relation to the U.S. dollar in the next few months. She wants to hedge this risk through hedging contracts. Should she enter into a futures contract to buy or sell Euros in 90 days?

E18-24. **Accounting standards (LG 5)** What accounting principle is involved in each of the following cases and why?

a. The accountant does not count the paper clips in office desk drawers as part of the inventory of office supplies.

b. At the end of each accounting period, a company makes an adjustment to the Prepaid Insurance account to recognize the amount of insurance applicable to that period.

c. In the preparation of financial statements, the accountant follows the same procedures used in previous periods.

d. The accountant, to the extent possible, uses source documents in recording transactions.

E18-25. **Installment basis (LG 5)** On January 19, 2007, Mo Appliance sells a refrigerator that cost $245 for $350. Following is a partial list of the payments Central received from the customer during 2007:

Date	Amount
January	$40
February	60
March	80

Calculate the dollar amount of cost recovered and the gross margins recognized each month by the installment basis.

E18-26. **Percentage of completion method of revenue recognition (LG 5)** Sharp Contractors, using the percentage of completion method of revenue recognition, has a contract to build a dormitory for State University at a price of $15,000,000. Total costs to build the dormitory are expected to be $11,500,000. By the end of 2007, the first year of construction, construction costs of $9,200,000 had been incurred. Compute the amount of gross margin on this contract to be recognized in 2007.

E18-27. **Adjustment of income for inflation (LG 7)** Brad Company reported net income of $700,000 for 2007. The president observed that physical levels of inventory had been nearly the same, the income statement showed merchandise inventory with an increase of $25,000. He noted that the balance sheet reported property plant and equipment at $3,000,000, whereas it would cost $6,000,000 to replace it. Depreciation expense was 10% of property, plant and equipment. The president questioned the accuracy of reported income. Comment.

PROBLEMS

P18-28. **Foreign currency transactions (LG 2)** Global Exporting Company engaged in the following transactions during December 2007:

2007

Dec.	5	Sold merchandise at a price of 20,000 Euros to Hamburg Company of Germany ($0.70 = 1 euro). Payment will be in euros.
	9	Sold $5,000 in merchandise to North Hampton Importers of Great Britain ($1.40 = 1 pound). The transaction called for payment to be made in British pounds.
	15	Sold merchandise at a price of 50,000 pesos to Mexico-American of Mexico ($0.10 = 1 peso). Payment will be in pesos.
	28	Received 20,000 Euros from the Hamburg Company in full payment of its account ($0.75 = 1 euro).
	31	The closing foreign exchange rates were as follows:

$0.73 = 1 euro

$1.45 = 1 pound

$0.09 = 1 peso

REQUIRED

Journalize the transactions and any necessary year-end adjustments in general journal form.

P18-29. **Foreign currency transactions (LG 2)** Corn Exporting Company engaged in the following transactions during December 2007:

2007

Dec.	8	Sold 5,000 bushels of grain at a price of 5 euros per bushel to Banhoff Bakers of Germany ($0.70 = 1 euro).
	12	Sold 20,000 bushels of grain to Tokyo Exchange of Japan at a price of 350 yen per bushel ($0.0075 = 1 yen).
	20	Sold 2,000 bushels of grain to Pastries of Montreal at a price of $2.50 Canadian per bushel ($.63 = $1 Canadian).
	29	Received 7,000,000 yen from the Tokyo Exchange in full payment of its account ($0.0070 = 1 yen).
	31	The closing foreign exchange rates were as follows:

$0.68 = 1 euro

$0.65 = 1 Canadian dollar

$ .008 = 1 yen

REQUIRED

Journalize the transactions and any necessary year-end adjustments in general journal form.

P18-30. **Translating foreign currency statements (LG 3)** Consider the following example. Assume that Cal Company owns Baja Nuts and Bolts, a Mexican subsidiary. When Cal Company acquired the subsidiary the Mexican peso was valued at $.14. Assume that in 2004, the average price of the peso was $.08 and on December 31, 2007 the value of the peso was $.10. On December 31, 2007, Baja Nuts and Bolts has assets of 1,800,000 pesos and liabilities of 400,000 pesos. Their owners' equity section consists of common stock and retained earnings listed at 900,000 pesos each.

REQUIRED

1. Convert Baja Nuts and Bolts financial statements to U.S. dollars using the current rate method.

2. Calculate the foreign currency translation adjustment that Cal Company must report.

3. Has the U.S. dollar increased or decreased in value against the Mexican peso?

P18-31. **Identifying GAAP (LG 5)** Following is a list of generally accepted accounting principles or concepts discussed in this chapter. Also following are statements (a) through (g) about Scott Sales Company.

Principle or Concept (Not all of the following choices are illustrated in this problem. In some cases, more than one principle or concept may apply.)

Conservatism	Materiality
Consistency	Objectivity
Entity	Periodicity
Full disclosure	Revenue realization
Going concern	Historical cost
Stable dollar	Matching

a. Scott Sales Company maintains separate checking accounts from the personal checking account of the company president.

b. The company president believes that the only time a business' financial success can be accurately measured is when the business ends its existence and liquidates. Therefore, she thinks the preparation of yearly financial statements is not necessary. The only time she prepares financial statements for Scott Sales is when the company needs to present them to a bank for a loan request.

c. When it prepares financial statements, the company provides for estimates of uncollectible accounts receivable by a debit to Bad Debts Expense.

d. The company recognizes sales revenue at the time a customer makes a verbal statement that he or she intends to purchase merchandise.

e. When Scott Sales does prepare a balance sheet, it lists all assets at fair market value. It recognizes increases in asset value as revenues on the income statement, and recognizes decreases in asset value as losses.

f. In a period of inflation, the company has consistently used FIFO. The company president thinks using this cost flow assumption has produced the most representative figures for net income on the income statement and inventory on the balance sheet.

g. The company expenses all expenditures of less than $50 even if they benefit more than one accounting period.

REQUIRED

From the generally accepted accounting principles or concepts listed, indicate the principle or concept followed or not followed in statements (a) through (g). Briefly explain the reason for your answer to each part. If the application of accounting principles is incorrect, state the change needed to conform to GAAP.

P18-32. Identifying violations of GAAP (LG 5) The following accounting practices violate generally accepted accounting principles:

a. Gibbs Company capitalizes the costs of minor items such as wastebaskets and depreciates them over their expected useful lives. The cost of maintaining these records each year is significant.

b. Vest Company recognizes 100% of the sales price of land as revenue when customers place refundable deposits to purchase parcels of land at a vacation housing development. Generally, Vest requires a $100 deposit. The sales price of each land parcel is $10,000.

c. Bizz Company records no depreciation expense for the first two years of an asset's life. It then uses the double declining-balance method for the remainder of the asset life.

d. The accountants at Process Company have devised a game to play in estimating the lives over which to depreciate plant assets. They pick a numbered ball from a drum containing many numbered balls to select the estimated life. All the accountants take chances as to what number will be selected.

e. In order to obtain a bank loan, the president of a company temporarily includes personal investments and assets on the balance sheet of the company. She does not disclose the temporary nature or source of the investment.

f. Key Company shows all assets in its balance sheet at their current market value. It shows increases in value during the year on the income statement.

g. Ness Company changes accounting methods for inventory valuation and depreciation each year in order to show desired amounts of reported net income. Ness does not include notes explaining the company's accounting methods with the financial statements it gives external users.

REQUIRED

For each case, state the accounting principle(s) or concept(s) violated.

P18-33. Evaluating financial statements to conform to GAAP (LG 5) Kearney Company was incorporated on January 1, 2007. The income statement, statement of owners' equity, balance sheet, and selected notes to the financial statements for Kearney Company for 2007 are as follows:

KEARNEY COMPANY
INCOME STATEMENT
FOR THE YEAR ENDED DECEMBER 31, 2007

Revenues
Sales revenue (cash basis)		$ 510,000
Sales revenue (accrual basis)		150,000
Total revenues		$ 660,000

Expenses
Cost of goods sold	$ 280,000	
Selling expenses	40,000	
General and administrative expenses	50,000	
Delivery truck expense	100,000	
Total expenses		470,000
Net income		$ 190,000

KEARNEY COMPANY
STATEMENT OF OWNERS' EQUITY
FOR THE YEAR ENDED DECEMBER 31, 2007

Common stock, January 1, 2007	$ 0	
Additional investments by owners	200,000	
Common stock, December 31, 2007		$ 200,000
Retained earnings, January 1, 2007	$ 0	
Add: Net income	190,000	
Deduct: Dividends	(10,000)	
Retained earnings, December 31, 2007		180,000
Owners' equity, December 31, 2007		$ 380,000

KEARNEY COMPANY
BALANCE SHEET
DECEMBER 31, 2007
Assets

Cash		$ 115,000
Merchandise inventory (LIFO)		160,000
Research and development costs		50,000
Accounts receivable		150,000
Total assets		$ 475,000

Liabilities and Owners' Equity

Liabilities
Accounts payable	$ 25,000	
Notes payable, due 2009	50,000	
Expenses payable	20,000	
Total liabilities		$ 95,000

Owners' Equity
Common stock	$ 200,000	
Retained earnings	180,000	
Total owners' equity		380,000
Total liabilities and owners' equity		$ 475,000

SELECTED NOTES TO FINANCIAL STATEMENTS:

1. Kearney Company recognizes revenue under two methods:

   a. Most customers pay cash on the delivery of merchandise.

   b. Accrual-basis revenues represent the total sales value of orders placed by customers during the month of December 2007. The merchandise is on order and will most likely be received by the company and delivered to customers in February 2008. No cash from customers has been received and the orders may be canceled by the customers.

2. The company purchased four delivery trucks on January 1, 2007, for a total cost of $100,000. To be conservative, the company expensed the cost of the four delivery trucks during 2007. The trucks have an estimated useful life of four years and no residual value. The company had used the straight-line method for plant assets.

3. Research and development expenditures for 2007 resulted from the company's own attempts to develop a new refrigeration process. Carla Kearney, the director of research, thinks that the company will develop a successful process in 2008.

4. During 2006, the company used FIFO as an inventory cost flow assumption. During 2007, it changed to LIFO. For 2008, the company is planning to change to average cost.

   REQUIRED

   Prepare a corrected income statement, statement of owners' equity, and balance sheet for Kearney Company in good form and in accordance with generally accepted accounting principles. Include revised selected notes to the financial statements. Comment on inappropriate changes in accounting principles.

P18-34. **Interpreting information for Starbucks Corporation (LG 7)** In a recent annual report, Starbucks Corporation states that the use of LIFO for a significant portion of costs of products it sells helps to reduce the impact of inflation.

   1. Describe how the use of LIFO helps protect Starbucks against the effects of inflation in a period of rising prices.

   2. Describe a situation in which the use of LIFO would not benefit Starbucks in its fight against inflation.

PRACTICE CASE

Preparing corrected financial statements (LG 5) The income statement, statement of owners' equity, balance sheet, selected notes to the financial statements, and report of the independent accountant for Cycle Company are as follows:

CYCLE COMPANY
INCOME STATEMENT
FOR THE YEAR ENDED DECEMBER 31, 2007

Revenues		
Sales revenue		$ 800,000
Expenses		
Cost of goods sold	$ 560,000	
Selling expenses	90,000	
General and administrative expenses	44,000	
Patent expense	30,000	
Depreciation expense	19,000	
Total expenses		743,000
Net income		$ 57,000

CYCLE COMPANY
STATEMENT OF OWNERS' EQUITY
FOR THE YEAR ENDED DECEMBER 31, 2007

Common stock, January 1, 2007	$ 120,000	
Additional investments by owners	10,000	
Common stock, December 31, 2007		$ 130,000
Retained earnings, January 1, 2007	$ 100,000	
Add: Net income	57,000	
Retained earnings, December 31, 2007		157,000
Owners' equity, December 31, 2007		$ 287,000

CYCLE COMPANY
BALANCE SHEET
DECEMBER 31, 2007
Assets

Cash		$ 100,000
Accounts receivable		70,000
Merchandise inventory (LIFO)		85,000
Machinery	$ 150,000	
Deduct: Accumulated depreciation	50,000	100,000
Total assets		$ 355,000
Liabilities		
Accounts payable	$ 28,000	
Notes payable, due 2008	70,000	
Expenses payable	10,000	
Total liabilities		$ 108,000
Owners' Equity		
Common stock	$ 130,000	
Retained earnings	157,000	
Deduct: Loss on decrease in machinery to fair market value	40,000	
Total owners' equity		247,000
Total liabilities and owners' equity		$ 355,000

SELECTED NOTES TO FINANCIAL STATEMENTS:

1. The company shows the machinery at its fair market value as of December 31, 2007, of $150,000. It shows the difference between the cost of the machinery ($190,000) and its fair market value ($150,000) as a loss in the owners' equity section of the balance sheet. The company has based depreciation to date on original cost.

2. The company has expensed expenditures to acquire a patent in the amount of $30,000 incurred on January 1, 2007. It believes that the patent will have an estimated useful life to the company of three years before competing patents are issued. The firm based its decision to expense the cost of the patents during 2007 on an attempt to be conservative.

Report of Independent Accountant

To the Creditors of Cycle Company:

We have audited the accompanying balance sheet of Cycle Company as of December 31, 2007, and the related statements of earnings and owners' equity.

In our opinion, the financial statements referred to above present approximately the financial position of the company at December 31, 2007.

Avery & Avery   January 30, 2008

REQUIRED

1. Prepare a corrected income statement, statement of owners' equity, and balance sheet for the Cycle Company in good form and in accordance with generally accepted accounting principles.

2. Prepare revised selected notes to the financial statements.

3. Comment on deficiencies in the report of the independent accountant and prepare a corrected report.

BUSINESS DECISION AND COMMUNICATION PROBLEM

Are dividends in order? (LG 3) You are the chief accountant for Super Supply Company. The company reported net income for 2007 of $360,000. The president has asked your advice regarding the payment of dividends of $300,000 for 2007, saying that the retention of $60,000 in the business should be sufficient for the planned growth he has in mind.

The business was founded in 2001, when almost all of the property, plant, and equipment was purchased. Relatively few plant assets have been purchased since 2001. Total depreciation expense each year is approximately $125,000. Assume that the average rate of inflation has been 6% per year from 2001 through 2006. During 2007, it dropped to 4% and is expected to stay there for the near future.

REQUIRED

Prepare a memo to the president in which you either support his position or attempt to convince him of any error he may have made in his reasoning regarding dividend payments. Include any supporting computations you believe necessary.

ETHICAL DILEMMA

Hextall Company is headquartered in Somerset, New Jersey. They have recently acquired a foreign subsidiary in Halifax, Nova Scotia. Year-end has come and it is time to prepare consolidated financial statements. During the year, the Canadian dollar has devalued with respect to the U.S. dollar. The company president has realized that this will result in a negative foreign currency translation adjustment on its balance sheet. The company controller realizes that this will reduce assets and shareholders' equity. He has suggested that the company should sell future contracts at a value that will create a receivable to offset this deficit. He argues that this offset would net to zero and the company would not need to report its foreign holdings on the balance sheet. He has relied on consultants' reports and is absolutely convinced that the currency will turn around this year.

REQUIRED

Prepare a memo to the controller that states and explains your opinion of the plan.

STARBUCKS
COMPARATIVE COMMON-SIZE INCOME STATEMENTS
For The Years Ended October 3, 2004, 2003, 2002
(*in millions*)

	2004 $	2004 %	2003 $	2003 %	2002 $	2002 %
Revenues	$ 5,294.0	100.0%	$ 4,075.0	100.0%	$ 3,289.0	100.0%
Cost of goods sold	$ 2,199.0	41.5%	$ 1,686.0	41.4%	$ 1,350.0	41.0%
Gross margin	$ 3,095.0	58.5%	$ 2,389.0	58.6%	$ 1,939.0	59.0%
Operating expenses:						
Store operating expenses	$ 1,790.0	33.8%	$ 1,380.0	33.9%	$ 1,110.0	33.7%
General and administrative	$ 304.0	5.7%	$ 245.0	6.0%	$ 235.0	7.1%
Other expenses	$ 452.0	8.5%	$ 378.0	9.3%	$ 311.0	9.5%
Total operating expenses	$ 2,546.0	48.1%	$ 2,003.0	49.2%	$ 1,656.0	50.3%
Operating income	$ 549.0	10.4%	$ 386.0	9.5%	$ 283.0	8.6%
Net interest expense (income)	$ (14.0)	-0.3%	$ (12.0)	-0.3%	$ (9.0)	-0.3%
(Gain) on sale of investment	$ -	0.0%	$ -	0.0%	$ (13.0)	-0.4%
Other expense (income), net	$ (61.0)	-1.2%	$ (38.0)	-0.9%	$ (33.0)	-1.0%
Income before income taxes	$ 624.0	11.8%	$ 436.0	10.7%	$ 338.0	10.3%
Income taxes	$ 232.0	4.4%	$ 168.0	4.1%	$ 126.0	3.8%
Net income (loss)	$ 392.0	7.4%	$ 268.0	6.6%	$ 212.0	6.4%

STARBUCKS
COMPARATIVE COMMON-SIZE BALANCE SHEETS
December 3, 2004, 2003, 2002
(*in millions*)

	2004 $	2004 %	2003 $	2003 %	2002 $	2002 %
ASSETS						
Current:						
Cash & cash equivalents	$ 299.0	9.0%	$ 201.0	7.4%	$ 100.0	4.5%
Short-term investments	$ 354.0	10.7%	$ 150.0	5.5%	$ 226.0	10.2%
Accounts receivable, net	$ 131.0	3.9%	$ 114.0	4.2%	$ 98.0	4.4%
Inventory	$ 423.0	12.7%	$ 343.0	12.6%	$ 263.0	11.9%
Deferred Income Taxes	$ 81.0	2.4%	$ 61.0	2.2%	$ 42.0	1.9%
Other current assets	$ 71.0	2.1%	$ 55.0	2.0%	$ 42.0	1.9%
Total current assets	$ 1,359.0	41.0%	$ 924.0	33.9%	$ 771.0	34.8%
Fixed:						
Property, plant & equipment, net	$ 1,471.0	44.3%	$ 1,385.0	50.8%	$ 1,266.0	57.2%
Long-term investments	$ 306.0	9.2%	$ 280.0	10.3%	$ 103.0	4.7%
Intangibles & goodwill	$ 96.0	2.9%	$ 88.0	3.2%	$ 30.0	1.4%
Other assets	$ 86.0	2.6%	$ 52.0	1.9%	$ 44.0	2.0%
Total assets	$ 3,318.0	100.0%	$ 2,729.0	100.0%	$ 2,214.0	100.0%
LIABILITIES						
Current:						
Accounts payable	$ 192.0	5.8%	$ 169.0	6.2%	$ 136.0	6.1%
Accrued expenses	$ 460.0	13.9%	$ 366.0	13.4%	$ 283.0	12.8%
Deferred revenue	$ 121.0	3.6%	$ 73.0	2.7%	$ 42.0	1.9%
Other current liabilities	$ 1.0	0.0%	$ 1.0	0.0%	$ 1.0	0.0%
Total current liabilities	$ 774.0	23.3%	$ 609.0	22.3%	$ 462.0	20.9%
Long-term debt	$ 4.0	0.1%	$ 4.0	0.1%	$ 5.0	0.2%
Deferred Income Taxes	$ 47.0	1.4%	$ 33.0	1.2%	$ 22.0	1.0%
Other long-term liabilities	$ 8.0	0.2%	$ 1.0	0.0%	$ 1.0	0.0%
Total liabilities	$ 833.0	25.1%	$ 647.0	23.7%	$ 490.0	22.1%
OWNERS' EQUITY						
Total owners' equity	$ 2,485.0	74.9%	$ 2,082.0	76.3%	$ 1,724.0	77.9%
Total liabilities and owners' equity	$ 3,318.0	100.0%	$ 2,729.0	100.0%	$ 2,214.0	100.0%

(Note: percents may not add to 100 due to rounding)

STARBUCKS
RATIO ANALYSIS SUMMARY
For The Years Ended October 3, 2004, 2003, 2002

	2004	2003	2002
SHORT-TERM LIQUIDITY RATIOS			
Current Ratio (Current Assets/Current Liabilities)	1.76	1.52	1.67
Quick Ratio (Cash + Short-term Investments + Accounts Receivable)/Current Liabilities	1.01	0.76	0.92
Accounts Receivable Turnover 1 (Revenues/Average Accounts Receivable)	43.22	38.44	
Accounts Receivable Turnover 2 (Revenues/Year-end Accounts Receivable)	40.41	35.75	33.56
Inventory Turnover 1 (Cost Goods Sold/Average Inventory)	5.74	5.56	
Inventory Turnover 2 (Cost Goods Sold/Year-end Inventory)	5.20	4.92	5.13
LONG-TERM SOLVENCY (LEVERAGE) RATIO			
Total Debt Ratio (Total Liabilities/Total Assets)	25.11%	23.71%	22.13%
PROFITABILITY RATIOS			
Gross Profit Margin (Gross Margin/Revenues)	58.46%	58.63%	58.95%
Operating Profit Margin (Operating Income/Revenues)	10.37%	9.47%	8.60%
Net Profit Margin (Return on Sales) (ROS) (Net Income/Revenues)	7.40%	6.58%	6.45%
Total Asset Turnover (Revenues/Average Total Assets)	1.75	1.65	
Return on Total Assets (ROA) (Net Income/Average Total Assets)	12.97%	10.84%	

COMPREHENSIVE ANALYSIS CASE STARBUCKS CORPORATION

Analyzing Starbucks Corporation for the Period 2004-2002 Starbucks is one of the largest coffee retailers in the country. Listed below are comparative income statements and balance sheets with common-size percents for 2004-2002 (in millions). Also included are selected ratio statistics. Please provide a brief explanation for your answer to each question.

REQUIRED
Income statement questions:

1. Are total revenues higher or lower over the three-year period?

2. What is the percent change in total revenues from 2002 to 2004?

3. Is the percent of cost of goods sold to total revenues increasing or decreasing over the three-year period? As a result, is the gross margin percent increasing or decreasing?

4. Is the percent of total operating expenses to total revenues increasing or decreasing over the three-year period? As a result, is the operating income percent increasing or decreasing?

5. Is the percent of net income to total revenue increasing or decreasing over the three-year period?

Balance sheet questions:

6. Are total assets higher or lower over the three-year period?

7. What is the percent change in total assets from 2002 to 2004?

8. What are the largest asset investments for the company over the three-year period?

9. Are the largest asset investments increasing faster or slower than the percent change in total revenues?

10. Is the percent of total liabilities to total liabilities + owners' equity increasing or decreasing? As a result, is there more or less risk that the company could not pay its debts?

Integrative income statement and balance sheet question:

11. Is the company operating more or less efficiently by using the least amount of asset investment to generate a given level of total revenues? Note that the "total asset turnover" ratio is computed and included in the "ratio analysis summary."

Ratio analysis questions:

12. Is the *current ratio* better or worse in the most current year compared to prior years?

13. Is the *quick ratio* better or worse in the most current year compared to prior years?

14. Is the *accounts receivable turnover ratio 1* (based on *average* receivables) better or worse in the most current year compared to prior years?

15. Is the 2004 *accounts receivable turnover ratio 2* (based on *year-end* receivables) better or worse than the 2004 ratio based on an *average*?

16. Is the *inventory turnover ratio 1* (based on *average* inventory) better or worse in the most current year compared to prior years?

17. Is the 2004 *inventory turnover ratio 2* (based on *year-end* inventory) better or worse than the 2004 ratio based on an *average*?

18. Is the *return on total assets (ROA) ratio* better or worse in the most current year compared to prior years?

APPENDICES

FEDERAL INCOME TAXES

APPENDIX

A

Chapter Thought

LEARNING GOALS

After studying Appendix A, you should be able to:

1. Identify the items that enter the calculation of gross income and adjusted gross income for an individual taxpayer.

2. Explain the difference between standard deductions and itemized personal deductions for an individual taxpayer.

3. Describe the personal exemptions, filing status, and tax credits available to an individual taxpayer.

4. Explain basic differences between the corporate income tax and the individual income tax.

5. Identify the reason for differences between financial accounting income and taxable income.

UNDERSTANDING BUSINESS ISSUES

Since its origin in 1913, the Congress of the United States has changed the federal income tax law frequently. Examples of recent changes are the *Economic Recovery Tax Act of 1981* (ERTA), the *Tax Equity and Fiscal Responsibility Act of 1982* (TEFRA), and the *Tax Reform Act of 1984*. Such acts amend the basic Internal Revenue Code. In August 1986, the House and Senate tax conferees agreed to a sweeping revision of the tax code. This revision is the largest and most important in the 73-year history of the nation's income tax. Called the *Tax Reform Act of 1986*, it touches the lives of all Americans. There also have been several other Congressional acts affecting the tax laws in recent years. This appendix is a broad overview of federal income taxes based on the *Tax Reform Act of 1986*. We include this broad overview in the textbook to explain:

1. The taxation of income for individuals and corporations.

2. The tax requirements of partnerships.

692

3. Some of the differences between business income and taxable income needed to introduce interperiod income tax allocation.

CLASSES OF TAXPAYERS

Four separate kinds of entities are subject to federal income tax: individuals, corporations, estates, and some trusts. Two of these—estates and trusts—need a brief description. When an individual dies and leaves income-producing assets, those assets (and liabilities) form his or her estate. Until the executor distributes these assets to the heirs, they will remain in the estate for a certain period of time and will produce taxable income. A trust, created by a contract or will, transfers assets to a trustee to be managed for the specific purpose named in the trust document.

Each of these entities must submit a calculation of the income tax on the specified type of tax return to the Internal Revenue Service. We call this submission the filing of the tax return. We call the entity filing the return the **filer**. In addition to filing a return, each entity must pay a tax, if applicable, on its taxable income.[1] Single proprietorships and partnerships are not taxed as separate business entities. Instead, the single proprietor reports business income on Schedule C of Form 1040, the U.S. Individual Income Tax Return. The partnership files a separate informational return, Form 1065. Each partner includes his or her share of partnership net income, with the personal nonpartnership income, on Form 1040.

TAX ACCOUNTING METHODS

The Internal Revenue Code sets forth the law, the Treasury Department establishes regulations, and the Internal Revenue Services issues *Revenue Rulings* for the inclusion and exclusion of revenue and expense items. These regulations and rulings also establish the use of certain methods and procedures in computing taxable income. The Internal Revenue Code, however, permits taxpayers to select certain options. Among them is the alternative of choosing the cash or the accrual basis of computing net income under certain circumstances. The taxpayer should choose the method permitted under the law that will postpone and avoid taxes (**tax avoidance**). This will conserve cash and achieve the taxpayer's goal of the lowest long-term tax cost. On the other hand, the taxpayer should not illegally attempt to evade the payment of taxes (**tax evasion**) by not reporting income or by over-reporting expenses.

Cash Basis

Under the **cash basis**, we recognize income when we receive cash. We incur expenses when we make cash payments. For financial reporting purposes, the cash basis is usually not a satisfactory way of measuring net business income for a company. For tax purposes, however, it is well suited for professionals such as doctors and lawyers. In the latter case, calculating net income by the cash

---

[1] For some trusts, all of the income goes to beneficiaries. These trusts file tax returns for information purposes only. The individual beneficiaries should report the income received from these trusts on their individual tax returns. Under these circumstances, the trust would not pay any income taxes.

method may approximate the accrual basis. An individual whose only income is salary must use the cash basis.

For income tax purposes, we modify the cash basis in two ways. First, we cannot deduct the cost of long-term assets, such as machinery or a truck, in the year of purchase when we pay cash. The taxpayer must treat these items as assets and allocate their cost over their useful service lives. Second, we recognize revenue when we constructively receive it—that is, when the revenue is in the control of the taxpayer. For example, a taxpayer constructively receives interest credited to a savings account, though the cash is not yet in the hands of the taxpayer.

Accrual Basis

Under the **accrual basis** of measuring income, we recognize revenue in the period when we make a sale or render a service. We recognize expenses in the period when we use services or goods in the production of revenue. Income tax rules require the accrual basis for those entities in which production, purchases, and sales of merchandise are significant factors. Under these circumstances, the Internal Revenue Code requires the accrual basis. Any taxpayer (other than a person whose only income is salary) who maintains a set of accounting records may elect to use the accrual basis.

INDIVIDUAL INCOME TAX

We will introduce the formula for computing the federal income tax (as reported on the U.S. Individual Income Tax Return, Form 1040) in a series of steps. First, we present a broad general formula to show the direction of the calculation. Then we break down the formula into sections that reveal variations in the tax formula approach of various taxpayers.

Exhibit A.1 shows a general formula that an individual taxpayer must use to determine the additional or net tax payable (remaining tax due) to the Internal Revenue Service or the tax refund expected because of an overpayment of taxes.

Determining Gross Income

Learning Goal 1   Identify the items that enter the calculation of gross income and adjusted gross income for an individual taxpayer.

We will now consider the various parts of this formula in more detail. Exhibit A.2 shows an expanded version of the first three items to determine gross income that is legally subject to the income tax.

Income Broadly Conceived

A starting point for determining income tax is to consider income in its broadest context. It would include all receipts or claims against entities for receipts arising out of an earning process. This excludes receipts from borrowing, the sales of assets for no profit, the withdrawal of funds from savings accounts, and other similar nonrevenue receipt sources. We do not include some items of the broadly conceived income, called exclusions, in legal gross income that is subject to tax.

Exclusions

Those items that do not qualify as gross income are **exclusions**. Law, U.S. Treasury regulations, or court decisions specifically exclude them. Among others, these include the items shown in Exhibit A.2.

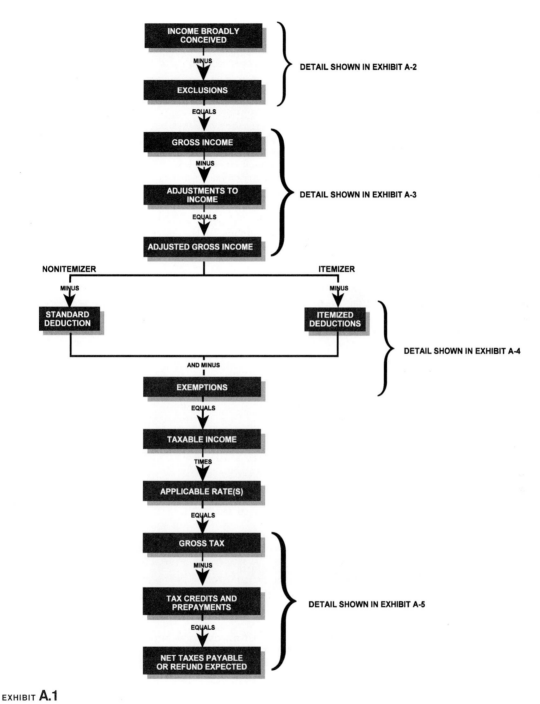

EXHIBIT **A.1**

General Income Tax Formula for Individuals

Adjustments to Income

Adjusted gross income is the amount remaining after the adjustments to income shown in Exhibit A.3. Usually, the deductions are self-explanatory. A brief word about a few is necessary. Employees may deduct only reimbursed expenses. We deduct all other employee-related expenses as miscellaneous itemized deductions (see Exhibit A.4).

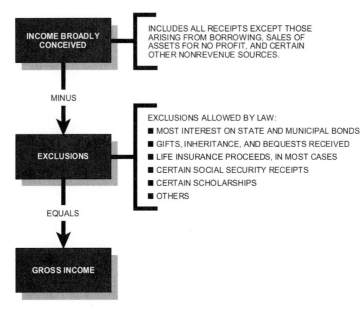

EXHIBIT **A.2**

Tax Formula for Determining Gross Income

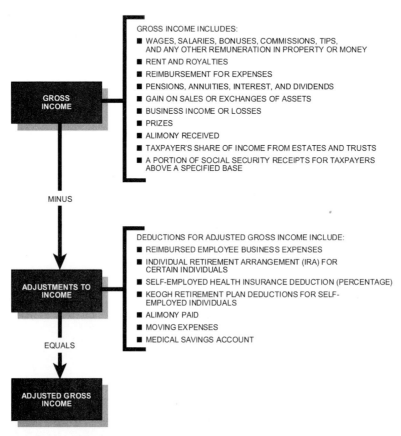

EXHIBIT **A.3**

Tax Formula for Adjusted Gross Income

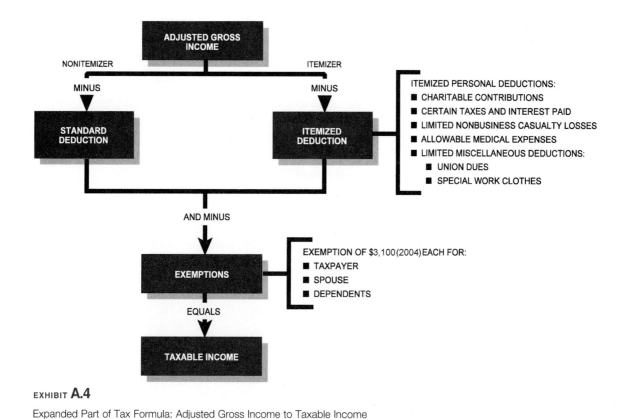

Expanded Part of Tax Formula: Adjusted Gross Income to Taxable Income

A special type of deduction for adjusted gross income is contributions to an **Individual Retirement Arrangement (IRA)**. The *Economic Recovery Tax Act of 1981* liberalized tax laws regarding IRAs as a way to boost savings. Under the *Tax Reform Act of 1986* and the *1997 Taxpayer Relief Act*, taxpayers with no employer pension coverage and whose income exceeds $4,000 are allowed to set aside $3,000 per year in an IRA. We deduct such amounts from the current year's tax return. They are part of taxable income when the taxpayer receives them after age 59½. If an employer pension plan covers a taxpayer, we phase out deductions for IRAs for adjusted gross incomes between $65,000 and $75,000 for joint returns and between $45,000 and $55,000 for single returns. Therefore, a married worker covered by an employer pension plan with a family income of $55,000 is not allowed to take an IRA deduction. Self-employed individuals are also allowed to establish their own retirement plan, called a *Keogh plan*.

A GENERALIZED APPROACH FOR DETERMINING INCOME TAX FOR INDIVIDUALS

Learning Goal 2   Explain the difference between standard deductions and itemized personal deductions for an individual taxpayer.

Exhibit A.4 shows an expanded version of that part of the tax formula from adjusted gross income to taxable income. Under the tax law, we subtract a standard deduction from income before we calculate taxes. However, if a filer (either a single taxpayer or married taxpayers filing one tax return) has enough allowable personal deductions, it is an advantage to itemize them (list and deduct them individually). A taxpayer who itemizes allowable personal deductions is an **itemizer taxpayer**; one who does not is a **nonitemizer taxpayer**.

Standard Deduction

The Internal Revenue Code provides standard deduction amounts. For 2004, these were as follows:

Standard Deduction	Applicable to Following Taxpayers
$9,700	Married persons filing joint returns and certain qualifying surviving spouses who are allowed to file joint returns
4,850	Married persons filing separately
7,150	Heads of households
4,850	Single persons

Standard deduction amounts for years following 1998 are adjusted for inflation, or *indexed*, each year. The standard deduction applies unless the taxpayer's itemized deductions exceed the standard deduction. In this case the taxpayer takes the itemized deductions instead of the standard deduction.

Personal Deductions

Exhibit A.4 shows some common allowable itemized personal deductions. Many of these have restrictions and limits.

Charitable Contributions

For an *itemizer taxpayer*, allowable contributions to recognized charitable, religious, and educational organizations are limited to a percentage that may vary from 20% to 50% of adjusted gross income. An itemizer may deduct the full amount of contributions up to 50% of adjusted gross income actually paid to religious, educational, Community Chest, and other charitable organizations that derive their funds from the public. Deductions for contributions to certain other charities—particularly nonoperating private foundations—may, under certain conditions, be limited to 20% of adjusted gross income.

Deductible Taxes

Taxes that we may deduct in calculating the federal income tax fall into four general categories: state and local income taxes, real estate taxes, personal property taxes (including intangible property tax), and a few other specialized taxes. Sales taxes and gasoline taxes are not allowable itemized deductions.

Nonbusiness Casualty Losses

A portion of large casualty losses not compensated by insurance, such as damage done by storms or wrecks, is deductible. We determine the amount allowable in a two-step calculation:

1. The gross loss for each casualty is the amount that exceeds $100.

2. Sum the gross casualty losses. The deductible portion is the amount that exceeds 10% of adjusted gross income.

Gross Medical and Dental Expenses

Gross medical and dental expenses include unreimbursed doctor, hospital, and dental fees; the unreimbursed amount paid for prescription drugs and medicines; travel to receive medical treatment; and medical and hospital insurance premiums. Deductible medical and dental expenses consist of total unreimbursed medical and dental expenses in excess of 7½% of adjusted gross income.

Miscellaneous Personal Deductions

These include: (1) various *employee expenses*, such as union dues, safety equipment, protective clothing, and dues to professional organizations, and (2) *expenses of producing income*, such as tax return preparation fee, safe deposit box rental, and clerical help in excess of 2% of adjusted gross income.

Exemptions

Learning Goal 3   Describe the personal exemptions, filing status, and tax credits available to an individual taxpayer.

The code allows a personal **exemption** of $3,100 in 2004 for the taxpayer, for the spouse if the taxpayer files a joint return, and for each person who qualifies as a dependent of the taxpayer. This exemption amount increases annually for inflation. Personal exemptions are decreased when income exceeds a specified amount. For example, for a single person the personal exemption begins to decrease for taxable income greater than $142,700. It decreases by 2% for each $2,500 of income over $142,700 until the exemption is $0. For a married person, the exemption begins to decrease at $214,050.

Under the law, a **dependent** is a person who receives over half of his or her support from the taxpayer; who is closely related to the taxpayer or lives in the taxpayer's home for the entire year; who has received less in gross income during the year than the amount of the personal exemption (unless the dependent is a child of the taxpayer under 19 years old or a full-time student); and who has not filed a joint return and is a citizen or resident of the United States, Canada, or Mexico.

Filing Status of Taxpayers

After we determine taxable income (see Exhibit A.4), we then compute the tax due. The tax rates depend on the filing status of taxpayers. Different tax rates apply to (1) a single person who does not qualify as a head of household, (2) an individual who does qualify as head of household, (3) a married couple filing a joint return, and (4) married taxpayers filing separate returns. We determine marital status as of December 31 of a given taxable year. For example, a couple that married on December 31, 2004, would qualify to file a joint return for 2004.

The special tax rates for single heads of households are to help compensate for the additional family burden. Persons who qualify as a **head of household** must be unmarried (or separated) at the end of the taxable year. Also, they must have paid more than half the cost of maintaining a principal residence that for more than half the year has been the residence of a child or specified dependent of the taxpayer.

Calculating Remaining Income Tax Due or Refund Expected

After we determine the gross income tax before tax credits, we must take additional steps to determine whether any remaining tax is due or whether a refund is expected. Exhibit A.5 shows the steps we must take to complete the requirements for filing Form 1040 (and appropriate schedules to Form 1040). The next step is to determine whether the filer has any available income tax credits.

Tax Credits

We may deduct certain **tax credits** from the gross income tax in computing the amount of the net tax liability currently outstanding. The code typically allows tax credits for the items discussed below.

Credit for the Elderly and Permanently Disabled

This credit was previously called the retirement income credit. Elderly and disabled persons are entitled to the credit. Congress has frequently changed the amount of this tax credit. It also depends on the taxpayer's adjusted gross income and Social Security income.

Child and Dependent Care Credit

Within certain limitations, taxpayers who pay someone to care for their child or dependent so that they can work or look for work may take a limited amount as a credit against their tax. The amount of this credit is determined by a formula specified by the Internal Revenue Code.

Earned Income Credit

The earned income credit applies to low-income workers who have an *earned income*—wages, salaries, and earnings from self-employment. This credit includes a negative income tax element.

Adoption Credit

Persons adopting a child may take a credit of up to $10,000 for qualified adoption expenses. The law allows the credit in the year the adoption is finalized.

Miscellaneous Tax Credits

A few other tax credits are allowed. For example, credits are allowed for taxes paid to foreign countries on income that is also taxed by the United States, for alcohol used as fuel, and for certain other items. There are also credits allowed for certain lifetime learning and adoption costs.

Calculation of Net Tax Liability and Remaining Tax Due or Refund Expected

We total the tax credits and subtract the total from the gross income tax. The difference is the **net tax liability**. As shown in Exhibit A.5, the taxpayer must subtract any prepayments to determine if

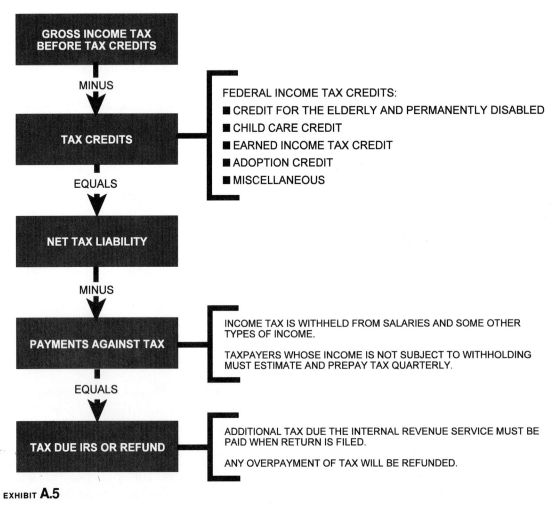

EXHIBIT A.5

Remaining Steps Necessary to Complete the Income Tax Model

additional tax is due or if a refund is forthcoming. These prepayments take two forms: (1) income taxes withheld by employers from the salaries of all employees and possibly from certain interest and dividend payments, and (2) income tax prepaid in quarterly installments by taxpayers who have income not subject to withholding and who estimate the tax for the year.

Taxpayers whose prepayments exceed the income tax liability may claim a refund or apply the excess to the following year. Taxpayers who owe additional tax pay the tax due.

REPORTING PARTNERSHIP INCOME

The code does not tax partnerships as separate taxable entities. We report the relevant revenues and expenses of the partnership on an information return, Form 1065. The individual partners report their respective shares of operating income, dividends received, contributions, tax-exempt income, and any other items that require special treatment on their own individual income tax returns.

CORPORATE INCOME TAXES

Learning Goal 4   Explain basic differences between the corporate income tax and the individual income tax.

The income of a business corporation is subject to a separate income tax based on the amount of taxable income shown on the Corporate Income Tax Return, Form 1120. The stockholders are also taxed on any dividends received from the corporation. Yet the corporation is not allowed to deduct any of these dividends paid to stockholders. Corporate taxable income is subject to tax under the following eight-bracket graduated rate system.

If Taxable Income is Over	But not Over			of the Tax Rate	Amount Over
$ 0	$ 50,000			15%	$ 0
50,000	75,000	$ 7,500	+	25%	50,000
75,000	100,000	13,750	+	34%	75,000
100,000	335,000	22,250	+	39%	100,000
335,000	10,000,000	113,900	+	34%	335,000
10,000,000	15,000,000	3,400,000	+	35%	10,000,000
15,000,000	18,333,333	5,150,000	+	38%	15,000,000
18,333,000	—	6,416,667	+	35%	18,333,333

In general, the taxable income of a corporation is computed in the same manner as that of an individual. Among the exceptions is the fact that a corporation may not itemize certain personal deductions allowed to individuals. For example, a corporation is not entitled to personal exemptions, the standard deduction amount, or such personal deductions as medical expenses. Personal deductions and the concept of adjusted gross income are not applicable to the corporation.

Normally, corporations may deduct from gross income up to 80% of dividends received from domestic corporations. Under certain conditions, when a parent files a return for itself and those companies that it owns, the affiliated group may, in effect, deduct 100% of dividends members of the group receive from each other (that is, 100% of the intercompany dividend amount).

In any one year, a corporation's charitable contributions are deductible up to a maximum limit of 10% of net income figured without regard to the contribution deduction. The corporation may carry over any contribution in excess of this limit to the five succeeding years and deduct it, provided the total contributions including the carried-over amounts are within the 10% limit of the appropriate years.

Differences Between Financial Accounting Income and Taxable Income

Learning Goal 5 Identify the reason for differences between financial accounting income and taxable income.

We must compute *accounting income* for financial reporting purposes using the generally accepted accounting principles discussed in this textbook. In contrast, we must compute *taxable income* in accordance with federal statutes and administrative regulations established by Congress and the Treasury. Tax rules change over time as Congress attempts to balance the federal budget and accomplish public goals. Using different methods of computing accounting income and taxable income frequently results in differences between the two net income figures. The differences between accounting income and taxable income fall into two classes: (1) those that tend to result in a *permanent* difference between accounting and taxable income and (2) those that cancel each other out over a period of time (*temporary* differences).

Permanent Differences

Permanent differences occur when an item affects the determination of accounting income or taxable income, but not both. For example, we include interest income on municipal bonds in accounting income but not in taxable income because it is exempt from tax by law. A second example of a permanent difference is 50% of meals and entertainment expense. We deduct this as an expense in computing accounting income, but it is not an allowable deduction for computing taxable income. Permanent differences affect the determination of accounting income or taxable income *in the current period only* and do not have future tax consequences. As a result, we do not need special procedures to account for permanent differences.

Temporary Differences

Temporary differences occur when revenues or expenses enter into the determination of accounting income and taxable income in *different accounting periods*, and where the differences "reverse" or "turn around" over time. One of the most common temporary differences for most corporations is depreciation. Most corporations compute depreciation for financial accounting purposes by using the straight-line method. For federal income tax purposes, corporations generally use the modified accelerated cost recovery system (MACRS). This permits accelerated deductions in the early years of an asset's life. Over time, the total depreciation deductions for financial reporting and tax purposes should be the same as the temporary differences reverse. However, in any given year, the depreciation deductions for computing accounting income and taxable income will most likely be different. For temporary differences, **interperiod income tax allocation** procedures are necessary to match a proper amount in income tax expense with accounting income each year.

An illustration of the issues involved in accounting for temporary differences using depreciation as an example is provided in Exhibit A.6. Part 1 of Exhibit A.6 shows the computation of accounting

1. Accounting Income before Tax

	2006	2007	2008	2009	Total
Income before depreciation	$ 50,000	$ 50,000	$ 50,000	$ 50,000	$ 200,000
Depreciation—SL ($100,000 ÷ 4 years)	25,000	25,000	25,000	25,000	100,000
Accounting income before tax	$ 25,000	$ 25,000	$ 25,000	$ 25,000	$ 100,000

2. MACRS Deduction, Income before Tax, and Income Tax Payable

	2006	2007	2008	2009	Total
Income before MACRS deduction	$ 50,000	$ 50,000	$ 50,000	$ 50,000	$ 200,000
MACRS deduction					
(33.33%, 44.45%, 14.81%, 7.41%)	33,330	44,450	14,810	7,410	100,000
Income before tax	$ 16,670	$ 5,550	$ 35,190	$ 42,590	$ 100,000
Income tax payable (15%)	$ 2,500	$ 832	$ 5,279	$ 6,389	$ 15,000

3. Accounting Income after Tax without Tax Allocation

	2006	2007	2008	2009	Total
Accounting income before tax	$ 25,000	$ 25,000	$ 25,000	$ 25,000	$ 100,000
Income tax based on taxable income	2,500	832	5,279	6,389	15,000
Net income	$ 22,500	$ 24,168	$ 19,721	$ 18,611	$ 85,000

4. Accounting Income after Tax with Tax Allocation

	2006	2007	2008	2009	Total
Accounting income before tax	$ 25,000	$ 25,000	$ 25,000	$ 25,000	$ 100,000
Income tax based on accounting income (15%)	3,750	3,750	3,750	3,750	15,000
Net income	$ 21,250	$ 21,250	$ 21,250	$ 21,250	$ 85,000

EXHIBIT **A.6**

Illustration of Interperiod Tax Allocation Results

income before tax over a four-year period. We assume that income before depreciation expense is constant at $50,000 per year. Depreciation expense on an asset with a cost of $100,000, a four-year estimated life, and no residual value is $25,000 each year. Therefore, accounting income before tax is a constant $25,000 for each of the four years 2006 through 2009.

We assume for income tax purposes that the MACRS tables show a three-year life for the asset. The MACRS system sets the lives of various classes of assets. For personal property used in a trade or business, MACRS provides lives of 3, 5, 7, 10, 15, and 20 years. In addition, MACRS permits only one-half year's depreciation in the first year. Thus, we need an additional year to recover the entire cost. These tables provide us with the following percentages to compute depreciation for a three-year-life asset:

2006	33.33%
2007	44.45
2008	14.81
2009	7.41

This results in accelerated depreciation deductions for tax purposes shown in Part 2 of Exhibit A.6. Using a 15% corporate income tax rate applicable for taxable income up to $50,000, the income tax amounts payable are $2,500 in 2006, $832 in 2007, $5,279 in 2008, and $6,389 in 2009, for a total tax payable of $15,000 over the four-year period.

Part 3 of Exhibit A.6 shows the accounting net income results if we did *not* use income tax allocation procedures. In this case, the income tax payable for tax purposes would be the amount of income tax expense deducted to determine accounting net income for financial reporting purposes. When we match income tax based on taxable income with accounting income before tax, net income varies over the four-year period despite the fact that accounting income before tax is constant. The reason for the variation is the improper matching of tax payable (based on MACRS depreciation deductions) and pretax accounting income (based on straight-line depreciation deductions).

Part 4 of Exhibit A.6 shows the results obtained when we match accounting income before tax with an appropriate amount of income tax expense computed at 15% per year. A constant amount of accounting income before tax ($25,000) is matched with an appropriate amount of income tax expense each year ($3,750) to report a constant amount of net income each year ($21,250). The Financial Accounting Standards Board has concluded that we must allocate income tax expense among relevant periods using interperiod income tax allocation procedures to account for temporary differences.

JOURNAL ENTRIES FOR INTERPERIOD INCOME TAX ALLOCATION

The difference between income tax expense based on accounting income and income tax payable based on taxable income is an allocation of income taxes from one year to another. We debit or credit this difference to Deferred Income Taxes. For the temporary difference due to depreciation illustrated in Exhibit A.6, we prepare the following journal entries to record income taxes at the end of each year:

2006					
Dec.	31	Income Tax Expense		3,750	
		Income Taxes Payable			2,500
		Deferred Income Taxes			1,250
		To record estimated federal income taxes for 2006.			

2007					
Dec.	31	Income Tax Expense		3,750	
		Income Taxes Payable			832
		Deferred Income Taxes			2,918
		To record estimated federal income taxes for 2007.			

2008					
Dec.	31	Income Tax Expense		3,750	
		Deferred Income Taxes		1,529	
		Income Taxes Payable			5,279
		To record estimated federal income taxes for 2008.			

2009					
Dec.	31	Income Tax Expense		3,750	
		Deferred Income Taxes		2,639	
		Income Taxes Payable			6,389
		To record estimated federal income taxes for 2009.			

The debit to Income Tax Expense each year results in an expense for taxes on the income statement for financial reporting that appropriately matches tax expense with accounting income. The credit to Income Taxes Payable each year establishes the liability for estimated taxes owed to the federal government. The credits to Deferred Income Taxes in 2006 and 2007 reconcile the fact that tax expense based on accounting income is greater than taxes payable based on taxable income.

We would show the balance in Deferred Income Taxes as a liability in the balance sheets prepared as of December 31, 2006 and 2007. In 2008 and 2009, the temporary difference due to depreciation reverses as MACRS deductions become less than straight-line depreciation amounts. As a result, we debit the Deferred Income Taxes account each year, reducing the credit balance. At the end of 2009, the temporary difference has completely reversed and the balance in Deferred Income Taxes would be zero.

Deferred income taxes can be a liability or an asset on the balance sheet depending on the nature of the temporary difference. The recognition of deferred tax assets has more restrictions than does deferred tax liabilities. Therefore, it is less common in financial reporting practice. In the depreciation example illustrated in Exhibit A.6, we assumed income tax rates were constant over the four-year period. If tax rates are changing, accounting rules require that we establish the Deferred Income Taxes account using the tax rate *expected in the period when the temporary difference reverses*. Also, existing balances in deferred income taxes must be adjusted for changes in income tax rates. More advanced accounting courses cover these additional tax reporting issues.

LEARNING GOALS REVIEW

1. **Identify the items that enter the calculation of gross income and adjusted gross income for an individual taxpayer.**

   Income broadly conceived includes all receipts or claims for receipts arising out of an earning process. Gross income is income broadly defined minus exclusions. Exclusions are items excluded from gross income by law, Treasury regulations, or court decisions. Adjusted gross income is gross income minus adjustments to income. Adjustments to income include reimbursed expenses of an employee, self-employed health insurance deductions, alimony paid, and certain funds saved for retirement.

2. **Explain the difference between standard deductions and itemized personal deductions for an individual taxpayer.**

   A nonitemizer taxpayer subtracts the standard deduction, which is a defined amount specified by the Internal Revenue Code for each class of taxpayer. An itemizer computes personal deductions, which include the taxpayer's charitable contributions, certain taxes and interest paid, limited nonbusiness casualty losses, allowable medical expenses, and limited miscellaneous deductions.

3. **Describe the personal exemptions, filing status, and tax credits available to an individual taxpayer.**

   The personal exemptions are deductions of a flat amount for the taxpayer, taxpayer's spouse, and any dependents. The amount of the exemption is $3,100 in 2004. The filing status of the taxpayer may be a single person who is not head of household, an individual head of household, a married couple filing a joint return, or a married person filing a separate return. To qualify as a single head of household, the taxpayer must be unmarried or separated at the end of the taxable year and must have paid more than half the cost of maintaining a principal residence that for more than half the year has been the residence of a child or specified dependent of the taxpayer. Tax credits are deducted from the gross income tax in computing net tax liability. Tax credits available to individuals include a credit for the elderly and permanently disabled, a child and dependent care credit, an earned income credit for low-income workers, a targeted job tax credit, and miscellaneous tax credits.

4. **Explain basic differences between the corporate income tax and the individual income tax.**

   A corporation may not itemize certain personal deductions allowed to individuals, notably personal exemptions and the standard deduction. Itemized personal deductions and the concept of adjusted gross income do not apply to the corporation. Unlike individuals, corporations may deduct from gross income 80% of dividends received from domestic corporations. Under certain conditions, a consolidated group may in effect deduct 100% of intercompany dividends. A corporation's charitable contributions are deductible up to a limit of 10% of net income. Excess contributions may be carried forward five years.

5. **Identify the reason for differences between financial accounting income and taxable income.**

   Financial accounting income and taxable income differ because they are computed in accordance with different standards. Financial accounting income should be based on generally accepted accounting principles. Taxable income must be computed in accordance with federal statutes and administrative regulations.

GLOSSARY

accrual basis The basis of measuring income that assumes that revenue is realized at the time of the sale of goods or services, regardless of when the cash is received; expenses are recognized at the time the services are received and used or an asset is consumed in the production of revenue, regardless of when payment for these services or assets is made.

adjusted gross income Gross income less allowable deductions (including business-related and revenue-producing expenses).

cash basis An accounting basis that measures net income by offsetting paid expenses against collected revenue for a given period (modified versions of this basis are usually found in practice).

dependent Under the law, a person who receives over one-half of his or her support from the taxpayer; is closely related to the taxpayer or lives in the taxpayer's home for the entire year; has received less in gross income during the year than the personal exemption amount for the taxable year (unless the dependent is a child of the taxpayer under 19 years old or a full-time student); has not filed a joint return; and is a U.S., Canadian or Mexican citizen or resident.

exclusions Items of income broadly conceived that are not required by law to be reported as gross income.

exemption Deduction allowed by law for each taxpayer, spouse, and dependent.

filer An entity—individual, married couple filing a joint return, married couple filing separate returns, estate or trust, or head of household-filing the tax return.

gross income Income required by law to be reported on the tax return and subject to the income tax.

head of household A single individual who pays more than half the cost of maintaining a residence for over half the year. The household must contain a child or dependent persons. Special tax schedules are provided for heads of households to partially compensate them for the additional family burden they must carry.

Individual Retirement Arrangement (IRA) A plan under which a taxpayer pays into a personal retirement plan an annual amount that can be deducted from gross income. All returns from such plans are taxable when the taxpayer receives them at age 59½ or later.

interperiod income tax allocation The allocation of income tax expense among periods to compensate for a temporary difference between reported book income and taxable income.

itemizer taxpayer A taxpayer who elects to itemize personal deductions.

net tax liability The amount of tax after tax credits have been deducted. This amount must be paid to the Internal Revenue Service.

nonitemizer taxpayer A taxpayer who elects to take the standard deduction.

permanent difference Difference that occurs when an item affects the determination of accounting income or taxable income, but not both.

tax avoidance A legal method of postponing taxes or preventing a tax liability from coming into existence.

tax credits Credits that are allowed to be subtracted from the income tax itself. Examples are credit for the elderly and permanently disabled, child care credit, and earned income credits.

tax evasion Illegal tax reporting, failure to report taxes, or nonpayment of taxes.

temporary difference Difference that occurs when revenues or expenses enter into the determination of accounting income and taxable income in different accounting periods and where the difference reverses over time.

QUESTIONS FOR GROUP LEARNING

QA-1. (a) Distinguish between the cash and accrual bases of accounting. (b) What is a modified cash basis?

QA-2. (a) Define the term *gross income* from an individual income tax point of view. (b) List six items that are reported as gross income. (c) List four items that are excludable from gross income.

QA-3. (a) Define the term *adjusted gross income* from an individual income tax point of view. (b) List four items that are deductions from gross income in computing adjusted gross income.

QA-4. Differentiate between an itemizer taxpayer and a nonitemizer taxpayer.

QA-5. (a) What is the individual income tax standard deduction? (b) State the 2004 standard deduction amounts applicable to all kinds of individual taxpayers.

QA-6. Ray Ross and Diane Casio were married on December 31, 2004. Can they file a joint tax return for the 2004 tax year?

QA-7. List four special tax credits that may be deducted from gross income tax in computing the net tax liability.

QA-8. Jose Garcia, age 21, is attending the state university. During the summer of 2004, he worked as a construction laborer and earned $2,300. His parents contributed more than one-half of his support in 2004. Can Garcia's parents claim him as an exemption?

QA-9. John and Susan Adams own some shares of stock. During 2004, they received $700 in dividends. John received dividends of $610 on stock he himself owned. Susan received $90 on stock she owned. What would be the dividends included in gross income on a joint return?

QA-10. List and briefly discuss the differences in computing the individual income tax and the corporate income tax.

QA-11. Is the amount for income tax expense shown on the income statement for a corporation always equal to the income tax liability on the tax return for a given year? Briefly explain.

QA-12. State ways that traditional business income may differ from taxable income as a result of both permanent and temporary differences.

PROBLEMS

Instructor's Note: The following problems may be used as class demonstration problems or assigned as outside work.

PA-1. Calculating adjusted gross income (LG 1) Rob and Sandra Lincoln had the following income and related information for 2004:

Salary to Rob Alter	$60,000
Dividends on stock owned by Rob Lincoln	2,000
Dividends on stock owned by Sandra Lincoln	3,000
On May 15, 2004, Sandra Lincoln sold some stock she had acquired on April 1, 2003, at a gain of	4,000

REQUIRED

Compute the adjusted gross income subject to tax on a joint return filed by Rob and Sandra Lincoln.

PA-2. Calculating comprehensive individual taxable income (LG 1, 2, 3) Adam Carter, 50 years old, is married to Sara Carter, who is 46. They have two children: John, 16; and Susan, 20, who is attending a university. The Carters furnish over half the support for both their children. Susan works as a sales clerk in the summer and earned $1,250 in 2004. Carter owns and operates a service station under the name of Carter Service Station. Sara Carter did not have any earned income in 2004. Relevant business and personal information for the family follows:

Cash receipts:	
Gross revenue from Carter Service Station	$250,200
Interest on corporate industrial bonds	1,000
Interest on State of Virginia bonds	3,800
Dividends on stock jointly owned	3,600
Cash prize won in state lottery	10,000
Gains on sales of securities:	
Sale of 200 shares of National Fruit Company common stock:	

Date Acquired	Date Sold	Cost	Selling Price
March 4, 2004	May 2, 2004	$24,000	$28,000

Sale of 100 shares of United Fusbits Company common stock:

Date Acquired	Date Sold	Cost	Selling Price
April 2, 2004	June 10, 2004	$10,000	$10,600

Expenditures:	
Cost of goods sold ($155,000) and operating expenses ($35,000) of	
Carter Service Station	$190,000
Contributions to church and university	4,000
Contributions to Community Chest	800
Property taxes paid:	
Sales tax	160
State income tax	5,200
Family medical expenses:	
Doctor and hospital fees	650
Prescription drugs and medicine	118
Keogh Retirement Plan payments for 2004	6,000

REQUIRED

In an orderly schedule form, compute the taxable income for 2004, assuming that the Carters file a joint return.

PA-3. Calculating comprehensive individual taxable income (LG 1, 2, 3) Al Wilson is single and is 56 years old. He has the following receipts and expenditures:

Cash receipts:	
Salary received from Belvedere University	$67,500
Interest received on school district bonds	1,500
Royalty income on textbook	6,100
Expenditures:	
Contributions to church and university	6,000
Contribution to The Human Fund	500
Personal property taxes	1,000
Insurance on residence	200
Automobile license plates	24
State income taxes	4,560
State sales taxes	150
Medical expenses:	
Prescription medications	380
Doctor and hospital bills	6,850

REQUIRED

Compute the taxable income for 2004 for Al Wilson.

PA-4. Calculating corporation income tax (LG 4) Eagle Corporation reported the following information for 2004:

Sales	$2,180,000
Cost of goods sold	980,000
Operating expenses other than charitable contributions	580,000
Charitable contributions	81,000

REQUIRED

Compute the corporate income tax for 2004.

PA-5. Accounting for temporary differences (LG 5) USA Company purchased a plant asset for $300,000 on January 1, 2006. The asset has an estimated life of four years and no residual value. USA uses straight-line depreciation for financial reporting purposes. Assume MACRS deductions allowed in each of the four years from 2006 through 2009 are 33.33%, 44.45%, 14.81%, and 7.41%, respectively. Assume that total revenues each year are $900,000, that total expenses other than depreciation are $200,000 each year, and that the applicable income tax rate is 34% for all four years.

REQUIRED

1. Compute accounting income after income taxes each year assuming that USA does not use interperiod income tax procedures.

2. Compute accounting income after income taxes each year assuming that USA uses interperiod income tax procedures.

UNDERSTANDING PUBLISHED ANNUAL FINANCIAL REPORTS

APPENDIX

B

LEARNING GOAL

After studying Appendix B, you should be able to:

1. Explain information contained in a realistic annual financial report using the accounting concepts and methods discussed in this book.

UNDERSTANDING BUSINESS ISSUES

An ultimate goal of this textbook is to enable readers to use the accounting concepts and methods we discuss to understand company financial reports. In most of the chapter introductions, we use a real-life company example to highlight the relevance and importance of the accounting topic to the statement user. Real-life examples in the chapters, excerpts from business journal articles, and real-life end-of-chapter problems continue this important theme. This appendix contains a summary review of the accounting concepts presented in this textbook. We illustrate a hypothetical set of financial statements and accompanying notes for a consumer products company called Starr Home Products Company. We show boxed references to the statements and notes to provide a review of concepts learned throughout the textbook.

FINANCIAL STATEMENTS ILLUSTRATED AND EXPLAINED

Learning Goal 1   Explain information contained in a realistic annual financial report using the accounting concepts and methods discussed in this book.

The Starr Home Products Company illustrations provide a review of the basic financial concepts presented in this textbook. We present the income statement, statement of retained earnings, balance sheet, statement of cash flows, notes to the financial statements, and report of the independent accountant for Starr Home Products Company. We have simplified the financial statements and notes to present a clear and concise review and summary. Boxed references highlight important items and explain their significance. Use these hypothetical financial statements and boxed explanations as a summary review of how the accounting concepts discussed in the textbook translate into an actual set of published financial statements.

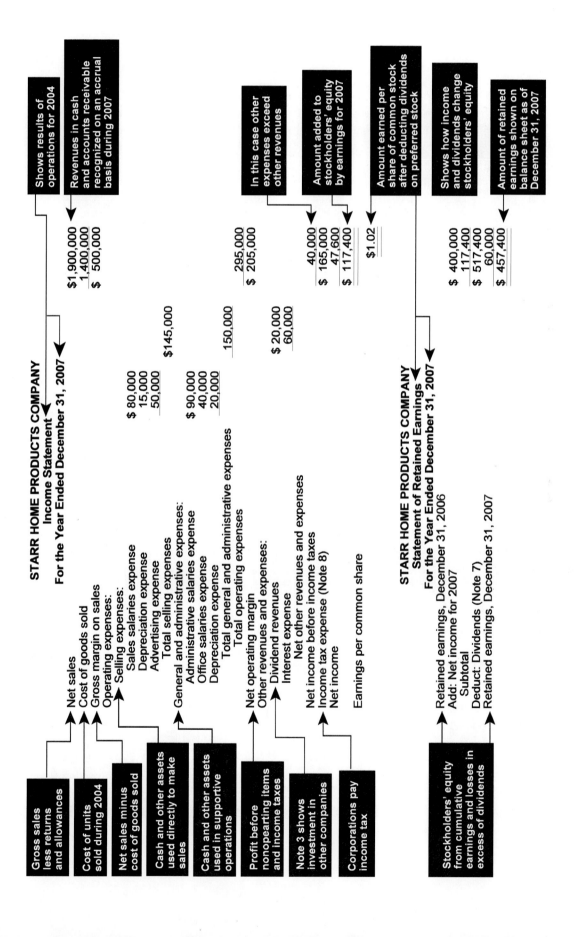

STARR HOME PRODUCTS COMPANY
Income Statement
For the Year Ended December 31, 2007

Net sales			$1,900,000
Cost of goods sold			1,400,000
Gross margin on sales			$ 500,000
Operating expenses:			
Selling expenses:			
Sales salaries expense	$ 80,000		
Depreciation expense	15,000		
Advertising expense	50,000		
Total selling expenses		$145,000	
General and administrative expenses:			
Administrative salaries expense	$ 90,000		
Office salaries expense	40,000		
Depreciation expense	20,000		
Total general and administrative expenses		150,000	
Total operating expenses			295,000
Net operating margin			$ 205,000
Other revenues and expenses:			
Dividend revenues	$ 20,000		
Interest expense	60,000		
Net other revenues and expenses			40,000
Net income before income taxes			$ 165,000
Income tax expense (Note 8)			47,600
Net income			$ 117,400
Earnings per common share			$1.02

STARR HOME PRODUCTS COMPANY
Statement of Retained Earnings
For the Year Ended December 31, 2007

Retained earnings, December 31, 2006	$ 400,000
Add: Net income for 2007	117,400
Subtotal	$ 517,400
Deduct: Dividends (Note 7)	60,000
Retained earnings, December 31, 2007	$ 457,400

Callout labels:

- Shows results of operations for 2004
- Revenues in cash and accounts receivable recognized on an accrual basis during 2007
- In this case other expenses exceed other revenues
- Amount added to stockholders' equity by earnings for 2007
- Amount earned per share of common stock after deducting dividends on preferred stock
- Shows how income and dividends change stockholders' equity
- Amount of retained earnings shown on balance sheet as of December 31, 2007
- Gross sales less returns and allowances
- Cost of units sold during 2004
- Net sales minus cost of goods sold
- Cash and other assets used directly to make sales
- Cash and other assets used in supportive operations
- Profit before nonoperating items and income taxes
- Note 3 shows investment in other companies
- Corporations pay income tax
- Stockholders' equity from cumulative earnings and losses in excess of dividends

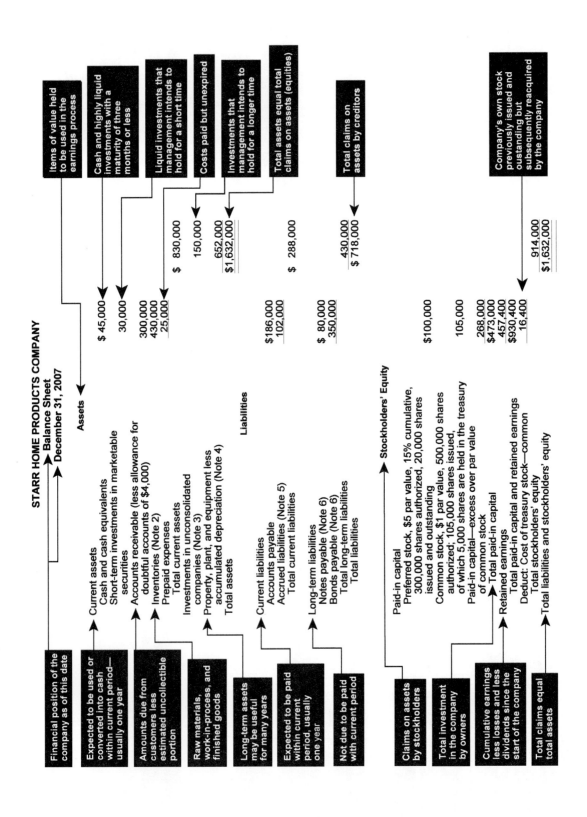

STARR HOME PRODUCTS COMPANY
Balance Sheet
December 31, 2007

Assets

Current assets		
Cash and cash equivalents	$ 45,000	
Short-term investments in marketable securities	30,000	
Accounts receivable (less allowance for doubtful accounts of **$4,000**)	300,000	
Inventories (Note 2)	430,000	
Prepaid expenses	25,000	
Total current assets		$ 830,000
Investments in unconsolidated companies (Note 3)		150,000
Property, plant, and equipment less accumulated depreciation (Note 4)		652,000
Total assets		$1,632,000

Liabilities

Current liabilities		
Accounts payable	$186,000	
Accrued liabilities (Note 5)	102,000	
Total current liabilities		$ 288,000
Long-term liabilities		
Notes payable (Note 6)	$ 80,000	
Bonds payable (Note 6)	350,000	
Total long-term liabilities		430,000
Total liabilities		$ 718,000

Stockholders' Equity

Paid-in capital		
Preferred stock, $5 par value, 15% cumulative, 300,000 shares authorized, 20,000 shares issued and outstanding	$100,000	
Common stock, $1 par value, 500,000 shares authorized; 105,000 shares issued, of which 5,000 shares are held in the treasury	105,000	
Paid-in capital—excess over par value of common stock	268,000	
Total paid-in capital	$473,000	
Retained earnings	457,400	
Total paid-in capital and retained earnings	$930,400	
Deduct: Cost of treasury stock—common	16,400	
Total stockholders' equity		914,000
Total liabilities and stockholders' equity		$1,632,000

Callout boxes (left/assets side, top to bottom):
- Financial position of the company as of this date
- Expected to be used or converted into cash within current period—usually one year
- Amounts due from customers less estimated uncollectible portion
- Raw materials, work-in-process, and finished goods
- Long-term assets may be useful for many years
- Expected to be paid within current period, usually one year
- Not due to be paid with current period

Callout boxes (right/top side, top to bottom):
- Items of value held to be used in the earnings process
- Cash and highly liquid investments with a maturity of three months or less
- Liquid investments that management intends to hold for a short time
- Costs paid but unexpired
- Investments that management intends to hold for a longer time
- Total assets equal total claims on assets (equities)
- Total claims on assets by creditors
- Company's own stock previously issued and outstanding but subsequently reacquired by the company

Callout boxes (bottom, stockholders' equity):
- Claims on assets by stockholders
- Total investment in the company by owners
- Cumulative earnings less losses and less dividends since the start of the company
- Total claims equal total assets

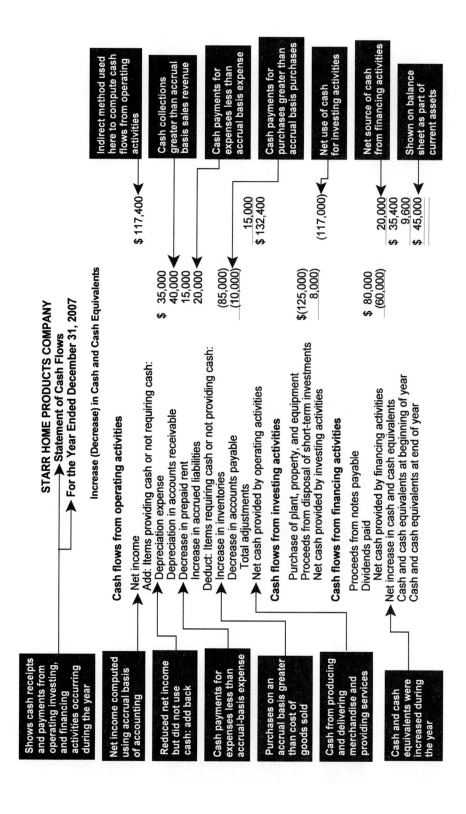

STARR HOME PRODUCTS COMPANY
Statement of Cash Flows
For the Year Ended December 31, 2007

Increase (Decrease) in Cash and Cash Equivalents

Cash flows from operating activities

Net income		$ 117,400
Add: Items providing cash or not requiring cash:		
Depreciation expense	$ 35,000	
Depreciation in accounts receivable	40,000	
Decrease in prepaid rent	15,000	
Increase in accrued liabilities	20,000	
Deduct: Items requiring cash or not providing cash:		
Increase in inventories	(85,000)	
Decrease in accounts payable	(10,000)	
Total adjustments		15,000
Net cash provided by operating activities		$ 132,400

Cash flows from investing activities

Purchase of plant, property, and equipment	$(125,000)	
Proceeds from disposal of short-term investments	8,000	
Net cash provided by investing activities		(117,000)

Cash flows from financing activities

Proceeds from notes payable	$ 80,000	
Dividends paid	(60,000)	
Net cash provided by financing activities		20,000
Net increase in cash and cash equivalents		35,400
Cash and cash equivalents at beginning of year		9,600
Cash and cash equivalents at end of year		$ 45,000

Callout labels:

- Shows cash receipts and payments from operating, investing, and financing activities occurring during the year
- Net income computed using accrual basis of accounting
- Reduced net income but did not use cash: add back
- Cash payments for expenses less than accrual-basis expense
- Purchases on an accrual basis greater than cost of goods sold
- Cash from producing and delivering merchandise and providing services
- Cash and cash equivalents were increased during the year
- Indirect method used here to compute cash flows from operating activities
- Cash collections greater than accrual basis sales revenue
- Cash payments for expenses less than accrual basis expense
- Cash payments for purchases greater than accrual basis purchases
- Net use of cash for investing activities
- Net source of cash from financing activities
- Shown on balance sheet as part of current assets

NOTES TO FINANCIAL STATEMENTS

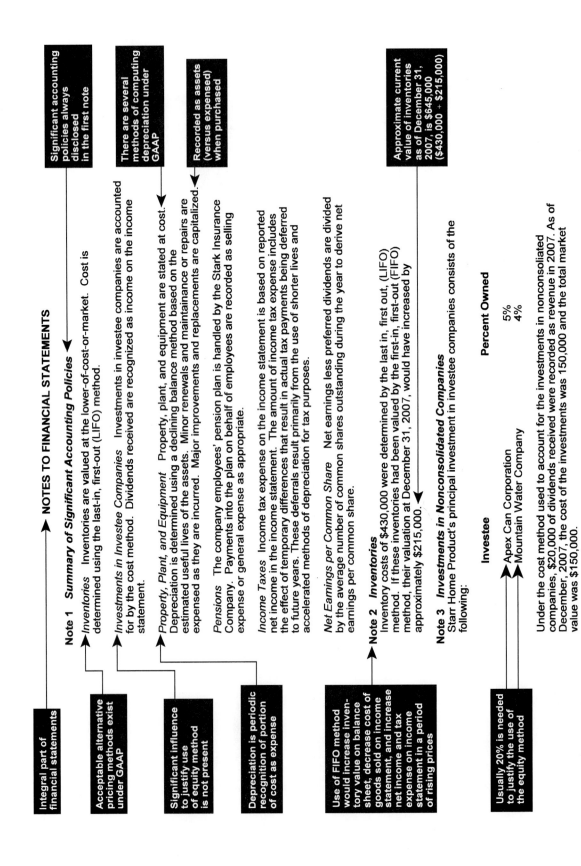

Significant accounting policies always disclosed in the first note

There are several methods of computing depreciation under GAAP

Recorded as assets (versus expensed) when purchased

Approximate current value of inventories as of December 31, 2007, is $645,000 ($430,000 + $215,000)

Integral part of financial statements

Acceptable alternative pricing methods exist under GAAP

Significant influence to justify use of equity method is not present

Depreciation is periodic recognition of portion of cost as expense

Use of FIFO method would increase inventory value on balance sheet, decrease cost of goods sold on income statement, and increase net income and tax expense on income statement in a period of rising prices

Usually 20% is needed to justify the use of the equity method

Note 1   *Summary of Significant Accounting Policies*

Inventories   Inventories are valued at the lower-of-cost-or-market.   Cost is determined using the last-in, first-out (LIFO) method.

Investments in Investee Companies   Investments in investee companies are accounted for by the cost method.   Dividends received are recognized as income on the income statement.

Property, Plant, and Equipment   Property, plant, and equipment are stated at cost. Depreciation is determined using a declining balance method based on the estimated useful lives of the assets.   Minor renewals and maintainance or repairs are expensed as they are incurred.   Major improvements and replacements are capitalized.

Pensions   The company employees' pension plan is handled by the Stark Insurance Company.   Payments into the plan on behalf of employees are recorded as selling expense or general expense as appropriate.

Income Taxes   Income tax expense on the income statement is based on reported net income in the income statement.   The amount of income tax expense includes the effect of temporary differences that result in actual tax payments being deferred to future years.   These deferrals result primarily from the use of shorter lives and accelerated methods of depreciation for tax purposes.

Net Earnings per Common Share   Net earnings less preferred dividends are divided by the average number of common shares outstanding during the year to derive net earnings per common share.

Note 2   *Inventories*
Inventory costs of $430,000 were determined by the last in, first out, (LIFO) method.   If these inventories had been valued by the first-in, first-out (FIFO) method, their valuation at December 31, 2007, would have increased by approximately $215,000.

Note 3   *Investments in Nonconsolidated Companies*
Starr Home Product's principal investment in investee companies consists of the following:

Investee	Percent Owned
Apex Can Corporation	5%
Mountain Water Company	4%

Under the cost method used to account for the investments in nonconsoliated companies, $20,000 of dividends received were recorded as revenue in 2007. As of December, 2007, the cost of the investments was 150,000 and the total market value was $150,000.

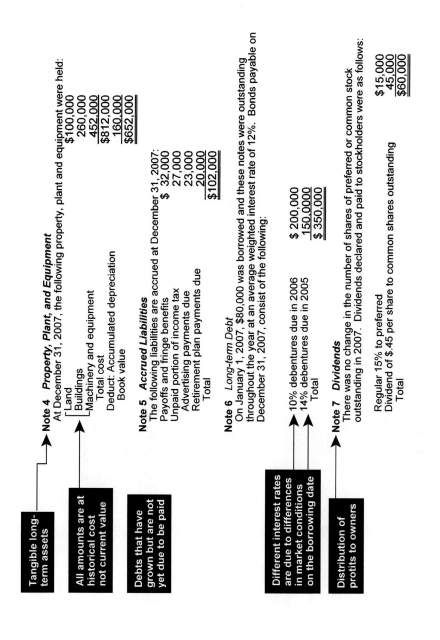

Tangible long-term assets

All amounts are at historical cost not current value

Debts that have grown but are not yet due to be paid

Different interest rates are due to differences in market conditions on the borrowing date

Distribution of profits to owners

Note 4   *Property, Plant, and Equipment*
At December 31, 2007, the following property, plant and equipment were held:

Land	$100,000
Buildings	260,000
Machinery and equipment	452,000
Total cost	$812,000
Deduct: Accumulated depreciation	160,000
Book value	$652,000

Note 5   *Accrued Liabilities*
The following liabilities are accrued at December 31, 2007:

Payoffs and fringe benefits	$ 32,000
Unpaid portion of income tax	27,000
Advertising payments due	23,000
Retirement plan payments due	20,000
Total	$102,000

Note 6   *Long-term Debt*
On January 1, 2007, $80,000 was borrowed and these notes were outstanding throughout the year at an average weighted interest rate of 12%. Bonds payable on December 31, 2007, consist of the following:

10% debentures due in 2006	$ 200,000
14% debentures due in 2005	150,0000
Total	$ 350,000

Note 7   *Dividends*
There was no change in the number of shares of preferred or common stock outstanding in 2007. Dividends declared and paid to stockholders were as follows:

Regular 15% to preferred	$15,000
Dividend of $.45 per share to common shares outstanding	45,000
Total	$60,000

Note 8 *Income Tax Expense*

In this illustration, there are no deferred income taxes. If there were deferred income taxes, the current and deferred (as a result of temporary differences) components of income tax expense would be shown as follows:

Current	$XXX
Deferred	XXX
Total income tax expense shown on income statement	$XXX

Note 9 *Litigation and Claims*

Various legal actions and government proceedings are pending against the Company relating to product quality and safety. The Company is providing suitable defense in all cases. Management believes that these proceedings will not materially affectt the data contained in these financial statements.

REPORT OF INDEPENDENT ACCOUNTANT

To the Stockholders and Board of Directors of Starr Home Products Company:

We have audited the accompanying balance sheet of Starr Home Products Company as of December 31, 2007, and the related statements of earnings, retained earnings, and cash flows for the year ended December 31, 2007. These financial statements are the responsibility of the company's management. Our responsibility is to express an opinion on these financial statements based on our audits.

We conducted our audits in accordance with generally accepted auditing standards. Those standards require that we plan and perform the audits to obtain reasonable assurance about whether the financial statements are free from material misstatement. An audit includes examining, on a test basis, evidence supporting the amounts and disclosures in the financial statements. An audit also includes assessing the accounting principles used and significant estimates made by management, as well as evaluating the overall financial statement presentation. We believe that our audits provide a reasonable basis for our opinion.

In our opinion, the financial statements referred to above present fairly, in all material respects, the financial position of the company at December 31, 2007, and the results of its operations and cash flows for the year ending December 31, 2007 in conformity with generally accepted accounting principles.

Clarke & Snider

Clarke & Snider
Houston, Texas

March 1, 2008

Callout boxes:

- Difference between income tax expense and income tax payable due to temporary difference caused by the use of different methods for financial reporting and income tax purposes
- Contingencies not included in any statement amount
- Annual audit of publicly owned companies required
- Statements examined in the audit
- Management is ultimately responsible for the information in the statements
- Description of what an audit is
- Opinion of auditors: statements are fairly presented
- Independent public accounting firm
- Date audit report submitted to cover 2007 statements

APPLICATION OF COMPOUND INTEREST AND TABLES

APPEN

C

LEARNING GOALS

After studying Appendix C, you should be able to:

1. Contrast simple interest and compound interest.

2. Calculate and use the future amount of a single sum at compound interest.

3. Calculate and use the present value of a single sum due in the future.

4. Calculate and use the future amount of an ordinary annuity.

5. Calculate and use the present value of an ordinary annuity.

6. Calculate and use the present value of an annuity due.

UNDERSTANDING BUSINESS ISSUES

Managers must understand the calculation of both simple and compound interest to make many types of decisions. For example, in decisions on short-term borrowing, a manager must be able to compute the cost of obtaining money—simple interest. Many decisions, such as long-term borrowing and acquisition of property, plant, and equipment, involve understanding compound interest. We use compound interest concepts in (1) accounting for installment receivables and payables, (2) accounting for notes used for the purchase of equipment, (3) computing the issue price of bonds, and (4) determining the present value of future cash flows in capital expenditure decisions. This appendix explains how to use compound interest computations.

NOTE: The exact point in a beginning principles course at which you might study this appendix is up to the instructor. Although you may omit it entirely, certain exercises and problems in Chapter 13 require a knowledge of present value concepts. The interest rates used in this chapter and throughout the book range from 9% to 20%. We do not mean these rates to represent interest rates in 2007, the year used most often in this textbook.

A COMPARISON OF SIMPLE INTEREST AND COMPOUND INTEREST

Learning Goal 1   Contrast simple interest and compound interest.

Simple interest is interest computed on the original principal (face value) of a note. Assume that Kevin Wait gives Don Orlando a 12% note that has a principal amount of $10,000. The simple interest calculations for two different terms follow.

1. If the note has a term of one year, the simple interest would be as follows:

$$\$10,000 \times 0.12 \times 360/360 = \$1,200$$

2. If the note has a term of 90 days, the simple interest would be as follows:

$$\$10,000 \times 0.12 \times 90/360 = \$300$$

Compound interest is interest earned on a principal sum that we increase at the end of each period by the interest for that period. To contrast simple and compound interest, compare the simple interest of $1,200 for one year on the Wait note with compound interest. Suppose we compound the 12% interest quarterly for one year. The total compound interest would be $1,255.09, as shown in Exhibit C.1. In Exhibit C.1, the accumulated amount at the end of each quarter becomes the principal for computing the interest for the next period. The $11,255.09 accumulated at the end of the specified period—in this case, one year—is the future amount of a single sum.

COMPOUND INTEREST TECHNIQUES

We use compound interest for computing the information needed to solve many modern business problems. Following are the five basic types of compound interest computations:

1. Future amount of a single sum.

2. Present value of a single sum due in the future.

3. Future amount of an ordinary annuity.

4. Present value of an ordinary annuity.

5. Present value of an annuity due.

Period	Accumulated Amount at Beginning of Quarter (Principal)	×	Rate	×	Compound Time	=	Interest	Accumulated Amount at End of Quarter
1st quarter	$10,000.00		0.12		3/12		$ 300.00	$ 10,300.00
2nd quarter	10,300.00		0.12		3/12		309.00	10,609.00
3rd quarter	10,609.00		0.12		3/12		318.27	10,927.27
4th quarter	10,927.27		0.12		3/12		327.82	11,255.09

Compound interest on $10,000 at 12% compounded quarterly
for one year $ 1,255.09

EXHIBIT **C.1**

Compound Interest Computation

Future Amount of a Single Sum

Learning Goal 2   Calculate and use the future amount of a single sum at compound interest.

The **future amount of a single sum** is the original sum plus the compound interest earned up to a specific future date. We also call it the future value of a single sum. In Exhibit C.1, we illustrated the computation of the future amount of $10,000 at the end of one year with 12% interest compounded quarterly. We multiply the accumulated amount at the beginning of each quarter by the periodic interest rate successively for a number of periods. This mathematical process is the same as multiplying the single invested sum (p) by the future amount of $1 at the compound interest rate (i) for the designated periods (n).

Using the designated symbols, mathematicians provide the following formula for the future amount (f) of $1:

$$f = 1(1 + i)^n.$$

We have constructed tables for the future amount of $1 for varying interest rates and numbers of periods. Exhibit C.2 shows the future value of $1 table factors for 9% and 12% and 1, 2, 3, 4, and 40 periods. Tables show the amounts without dollar signs and could be the future amount of 1 of any monetary unit. More complete tables appear at the end of this appendix.

The table factors in Exhibit C.2 and Table C.1 of the compound interest tables at the end of this appendix are values of the formula $1(1 + i)^n$, the future amount of $1. We can find the future amount f for any given single sum p by the following formula:

$$f = p \times (\text{table factor or furture amount of } \$1)$$

Assume we want to calculate how an investment of $10,000 will accumulate in four years at 12% compounded annually. First we look up the table factor for the future amount of $1 for four time periods at 12%. It is 1.573519 **Note:** *In this appendix, we use more decimal places than shown in the tables to avoid rounding errors. If you use a business calculator instead of tables, you will also avoid the rounding errors.* Each $1 in the $10,000 will have a future amount of $1.573519 (the table factor). Then we can calculate the future amount of all 10,000 of these dollars by multiplying the $10,000 times this table factor, as follows:

$$f = \$10,000 \times (1.573519) = \$15,735.19$$

Periods (n)	9%	12%
1	1.090	1.120
2	1.188	1.254
3	1.295	1.405
4	1.412	1.574
.		
.		
.		
40	31.409	93.051

EXHIBIT C.2

Future Amount of $1 = $1(1 + i)^n$

We can show this to be the correct amount if we do the calculations for each of the four times:

Period	Accumulated Amount at Beginning of Year	×	Rate	×	Time	=	Compound Interest	Accumulated Amount at End of Year
1st year	$10,000.00		0.12		1		$1,200.00	$11,200.00
2nd year	11,200.00		0.12		1		1,344.00	12,544.00
3rd year	12,544.00		0.12		1		1,505.28	14,049.28
4th year	14,049.28		0.12		1		1,685.91	15,735.19

Assume the problem had instead asked for the sum in four years at 12% compounded *semiannually*. We would have had to determine the number of compounding periods in four years and the interest rate for one compounding period. Since there would be two compounding periods in each of the four years, there would be eight periods. And since the annual interest rate is 12%, the interest rate for half of one year would be 6%. Therefore, in the future amount of a single sum table, we would look up the factor for eight periods at 6%.

We calculate the future amount of $10,000 at the end of four years with interest compounded semiannually at the annual rate of 12%, as follows:

$$f = \$10,000 \times 1.594 = \$15,940$$

Note that with semiannual compounding the future value is higher than with annual compounding.

Present Value of a Single Sum

Learning Goal 3   Calculate and use the present value of a single sum due in the future.

We saw that $10,000 is worth $15,735.19 when it is left at 12% interest compounded annually for four years. Then a cash flow of $15,735.19 four years from now should be worth $10,000 at the present time if the interest rate is 12% compounded annually. That is, $10,000 is the *present value* of $15,735.19 discounted back to the present time for four years at 12%. The **present value of a single sum** is the amount that must be invested at **time period zero**, today, to produce the known future value.

We can confirm the present value amount by calculating the present value of $15,735.19 discounted for four years at 12% compounded annually. We can show this problem graphically as follows:

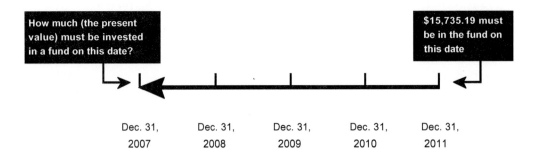

The interest rate is 12% compounded annually.

Mathematicians have developed tables for different interest rates (i) and for different numbers of time periods (n) for the present value of a single sum of $1 ($p$ value of $1). Following is the formula for these table values:

$$p = \frac{\$1}{(1+i)^n}$$

Precalculated table factors for selected interest rates for time periods 1 through 40 are in compound interest Table C.2. Following is the generalized table approach for finding the present value of any future sum:

$$p = f \times (\text{table factor for present value of } \$1)$$

Assume we want to calculate the present value of $15,735.19 discounted at 12% compounded annually for four years. First we look up the value in the present-value-of-$1 table for $n = 4, i = 12\%$. It is 0.635518 (Remember, we are using more detailed tables to avoid rounding errors.) Then we multiply the $15,735.19 future amount by that table factor to determine the present value amount of $10,000, as shown below:

$$p = \$15,735.19 \times 0.635518 = \$10,000$$

If the compounding periods were semiannual, we would use the table factor for an n of 8 and an i of 6%.

Future Amount of an Ordinary Annuity

Learning Goal 4   Calculate and use the future amount of an ordinary annuity.

An **annuity** is a series of equal payments (deposits, receipts, or withdrawals) made at regular intervals with interest compounded at a certain rate. We call these payments **rents**. The equal intervals between payments may be any time period: a year, a month, six months, or three months. But they must be equal in length to the compounding period. In a straightforward situation, the following features must be present in the calculation of the future amount of an ordinary annuity. (1) The periodic rents must be equal in amount. (2) The time periods between rents must be of the same length. (3) The interest rate for each time period must be constant. (4) The interest rate must be compounded at the end of each time period.

When we calculate the future amount of a series of deposits (rents) *immediately after the last deposit*, the calculation is the **future amount of an ordinary annuity**. Assume that we must calculate the future amount of four rents of $10,000 each with interest compounded annually at 12%. The first deposit is on December 31, 2007, and the last deposit is on December 31, 2010. We can present this information graphically as follows below. (The time graphs from this point in the appendix deal with annuities and use asterisks rather than vertical lines. The lines in the earlier graphs represented time periods, whereas the asterisks here represent rents.)

Mathematicians start with the general formula for the future amount of an ordinary annuity. They develop tables for different interest rates and for different numbers of rents of $1 each. The formula for these table values is as follows:

$$F_0 = \frac{(1+i)^n - 1}{i}$$

where F_0 = The future amount of an ordinary annuity of rents of $1.

n = The number of rents (*not time periods*; remember that for the future value of an ordinary annuity there is always one more rent than there are time periods).

i = The interest rate *per time period*.

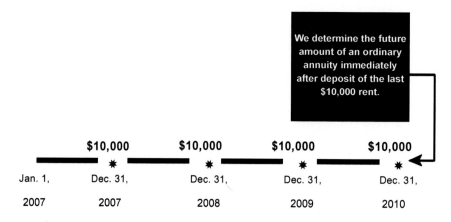

We determine the future amount of an ordinary annuity immediately after deposit of the last $10,000 rent.

	$10,000	$10,000	$10,000	$10,000
Jan. 1,	Dec. 31,	Dec. 31,	Dec. 31,	Dec. 31,
2007	2007	2008	2009	2010

Interest rate is 12% compounded each year.

Table factors for selected interest rates and for rents of $1 each for 1 through 40 rents have been precalculated in Table C.3 of the compound interest tables. Turn to this table and note the following from these precalculations:

1. The numbers in the first column (n) are the number of rents, not the number of time periods.

2. The future amount values are always equal to or greater than the number of rents. For example, the future value of three rents of $1 each at 14% is 3.440. This figure comprises two elements: (a) the three rents of $1 each without any interest, and (b) the compound interest on the rents. In an ordinary annuity the last rent in the series does not earn any interest.

We can state the generalized table approach as follows:

$$F_0 = R \times \text{(table factor for future amount of an annuity of \$1)}$$

R is equal to the amount of each rent. It becomes a simple matter to calculate the future amount of an ordinary annuity of four annual rents of $10,000 each at 12% compounded annually. First, look up the table factor. That table factor is 4.779328. Second, multiply the $10,000 by this table factor as follows:

$$F_0 = \$10,000 \times 4.779328 = \$47,793.28$$

In other words, assume you deposited $10,000 at the end of each year for four years in an account that earned 12% compounded annually. There would be $47,793.28 in the account immediately after the last deposit. We can show this to be true in the following table. At the end of 2007, we deposit $10,000 in an account earning 12% compounded annually.

Period	Beginning-of-the-Year Balance	Period's Interest	End-of-the-Year Deposit	End-of-the-Year Balance
2007	$ 0.00	$ 0.00	$10,000.00	$10,000.00
2008	10,000.00	1,200.00	10,000.00	21,200.00
2009	21,200.00	2,544.00	10,000.00	33,744.00
2010	33,744.00	4,049.28	10,000.00	47,793.28

We have included this table to help you understand the concept of the future value of an annuity. You should work problems using the table factors as shown in the earlier calculation.

Present Value of an Ordinary Annuity

Learning Goal 5   Calculate and use the present value of an ordinary annuity.

The **present value of an annuity** is the present value of a series of withdrawals or payments (rents) discounted at compound interest. In other words, it is the amount that we must invest now at compound interest to provide for a withdrawal of equal rents at regular intervals. We make the last withdrawal on the final date. Over time, the balance increases periodically for interest and decreases periodically for the withdrawal of each rent. The last withdrawal (rent) in the series exhausts the balance on deposit.

We frequently use the present value of an annuity concept in accounting. We use it to measure and report: (1) notes payable and notes receivable when the interest rate differs from the current market rate, (2) the carrying value of investment in bonds and the bonds payable liability, (3) the receivable or debt under installment contracts, and (4) the desirability of capital investment projects.

When we calculate the present value of the series of rents one period *before* the withdrawal of the first rent, the series of rents is the **present value of an ordinary annuity**. For this illustration, assume that we want to calculate the present value on January 1, 2007, of four yearly withdrawals of $10,000 discounted at 12%. We will make the first withdrawal on December 31, 2007. We compute the present value of the flows on January 1, 2007, one period before the first withdrawal. We would be answering the question, "How much would I have to deposit today to withdraw $10,000 each year for the next four years, with the first withdrawal one year from today?" We can present this information graphically as follows:

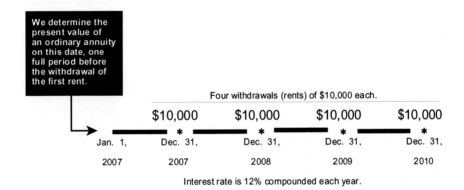

Four withdrawals (rents) of $10,000 each.

| | $10,000 | $10,000 | $10,000 | $10,000 |

We determine the present value of an ordinary annuity on this date, one full period before the withdrawal of the first rent.

Jan. 1, 2007   Dec. 31, 2007   Dec. 31, 2008   Dec. 31, 2009   Dec. 31, 2010

Interest rate is 12% compounded each year.

Again, mathematicians develop tables for different interest rates and for different numbers of rents of $1 each. They use the following formula for the present value of an ordinary annuity:

$$P_0 = \frac{1 - \frac{1}{(1+i)^n}}{i}$$

where P_0 = The present value of an ordinary annuity of a series of rents of $1.

n = The number of rents (*not time periods*; it happens that for present value of an ordinary annuity there are the same number of rents as there are time periods).

i = The interest rate *per time period*.

Table C.4 shows table factors for selected interest rates and for rents of $1 each for 1 through 40 rents. Turn to this table and observe the following:

1. The numbers in the first column (n) represent the number of rents of $1 each.

2. The present value amounts are *always smaller* than the number of rents of $1. For example, the present value of three rents of $1 at 14% is 2.322.

Since Table C.4 shows the precalculation of P_O values of $1, we can express a generalized table approach as follows:

$$P_0 = R \times \text{(table factor for present value of an ordinary annuity of \$1)}$$

R is equal to the amount of a rent. Assume we are calculating the present value on January 1, 2007, of four rents of $10,000 discounted at 12% with the first rent withdrawn on December 31, 2007. First we look up the factor in the table for the present value of an ordinary annuity of $1. This value is 3.037349 (Again, we use a more detailed table to avoid rounding errors). Then we multiply this factor by $10,000 to calculate the present value figure of $30,373.49, as shown below:

$$P_0 = \$10,000 \times 3.037349 = \$30,373.49$$

We can show that this amount is correct by the following table. At the beginning of 2007, $30,373.49 is in a savings account (the present value). The account earns interest on that amount for the year, and we make a $10,000 withdrawal (the rent) at the end of the year. We repeat this pattern for three more periods. (Again, we show this table to help you understand the concept, not for calculating the present value of an annuity.)

Period	Beginning-of-the-year Balance	Period's Interest	End-of-the-Year Withdrawal	End-of-the-Year Balance
2007	$30,373.49	$3,644.82	$10,000.00	$24,018.31
2008	24,018.31	2,882.20	10,000.00	16,900.51
2009	16,900.51	2,028.06	10,000.00	8,928.57
2010	8,928.57	1,071.43	10,000.00	0.00

Being able to distinguish between different compound interest applications is important. Some situations require future value and some require present value computations. Some situations are for single sums and some are for annuities. To distinguish between single-sum and annuity situations, we need to ask whether we will exchange one single amount or equal amounts at regular intervals. For example, assume we were asking the question, "How much must I deposit today to make one withdrawal in five years?" It involves a single amount. Therefore, we would be working with a single-sum situation. Assume the question had been, "How much must I deposit today to make equal withdrawals at the end of each of the next five years?" This involves a series of equal withdrawals. Thus, we would have been working with an annuity.

To distinguish between future value and present value, we must identify when we will exchange the unknown amount (or the amount calculated). For example, assume that we are asking the question, "How much must I invest today at 10% compounded annually to have $25,000 five years from now?" We know the future amount, but the value of that amount today, the present value, is unknown. Therefore, we are trying to calculate the present value and would use a present value table. On the other hand, assume we are asking, "I have $12,000 today. How much will I have five years from now at 9% compounded annually?" We know the value today (the present value), but the value in the future is the unknown. Therefore, we would try to calculate the future value and would use the future value table.

Present Value of an Annuity Due

Learning Goal 6   Calculate and use the present value of an annuity due.

With an ordinary annuity, each withdrawal or payment (rent) occurs at the end of the period. If the withdrawal or payment occurs at the beginning of the period, it is an annuity due. We calculate the **present value of an annuity due** immediately before the first rent. The following diagram compares an ordinary annuity and an annuity due.

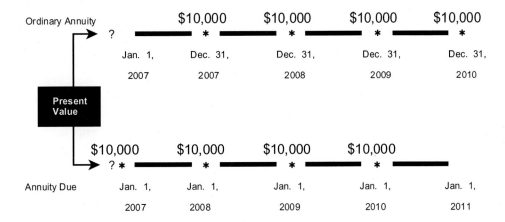

Each is an annuity of four rents. In an ordinary annuity, the first rent occurs one period after the calculation of the present value. In an annuity due, the first rent occurs immediately after the calculation of the present value. Thus, in an ordinary annuity the initial sum earns interest for one period before the first rent. In an annuity due, the initial sum earns no interest before the first rent. The present value of an annuity due of one $1 rent is $1. The last rent in an annuity due also occurs one period before the last rent in an ordinary annuity.

We can find the present value factor for an annuity due by using the present value of an ordinary annuity table, Table C.4. The present value of an annuity due of four rents of $1 is equal to the present value of an ordinary annuity of three rents of $1 plus $1. This is true because the first rent does not earn any interest. The present value of the first rent of $1 is equal to $1.

Assume that we are calculating the present value of the annuity due shown in the preceding chart. We wish to know the present value on January 1, 2007, of an annuity due of four rents of $10,000 discounted at 12%. We will withdraw the first rent on January 1, 2007. We use the table factor for an ordinary annuity of three rents, not four, at 12% and add one to it. The factor is 2.401831. The factor for an annuity due of four rents at 12% is then 3.401831 (2.401831 + 1.000000). We calculate the present value as follows:

$$\$10,000 \times 3.401831 = \$34,018.31$$

We can show that this amount is correct with the following table. At the beginning of 2007, $34,018.31 is in a savings account (present value). Immediately we make the first withdrawal of $10,000. The account then earns interest for one year, and we make the second withdrawal. We repeat this pattern for two more withdrawals.

Period	Beginning-of-the-Year Balance	Beginning-of-the-Year Withdrawal	Period's Interest	End-of-the-Year Balance
2007	$34,018.31	$10,000.00	$2,882.20	$26,900.51
2008	26,900.51	10,000.00	2,028.06	18,928.57
2009	18,928.57	10,000.00	1,071.43	10,000.00
2010	10,000.00	10,000.00	0.00	0.00

Being able to distinguish between ordinary annuities and annuities due is important. The distinction is when the first rent occurs. In an ordinary annuity the first rent occurs one period after the calculation of the present value. In an annuity due the first rent occurs immediately after the calculation of the present value.

COMPOUNDING PERIODS OF LESS THAN ONE YEAR

The examples used in this appendix have been for annual periods. Many actual accounting situations involve monthly, quarterly, or semiannual periods. For example, we may be purchasing as in investment a bond paying interest semiannually. To value this investment, we would need to calculate the present value of the semiannual interest payments plus the principal.

Although the tables in this appendix are for annual periods, we can still use them with a straightforward adjustment. When the period for compounding is less than one year, we need to know the interest rate for each compounding period and the number of compounding periods. To use the tables, we divide the annual interest rate by the number of compounding periods in one year. Then we multiply the number of years by the number of compounding periods per year.

For example, assume that we want to find the future value of $2,000 for 5 years at 10% compounded semiannually. Remember that we always state interest rates as annual rates. Thus, 10% compounded semiannually is 10% per year compounded twice each year. Semiannual means that there are two compounding periods each year. To find the factor to solve this problem, we would use an i of 5% (10% ÷ 2) and an n of 10 periods (5 years × 2 periods per year) in the future value of a single sum table (C.1). Looking up that factor in the table, we find 1.629. The future value of $2,000 for 5 years at 10% compounded semiannually is $3,258 ($2,000 × 1.629).

The future value of $2,000 for 5 years at 10% compounded annually is $3,222 ($2,000 × 1.611). Note that the future value compounded semiannually is more than compounded annually. This is because the interest is calculated and added to the amount twice each year instead of once each year.

Let us practice with one more example. Assume that we desire to calculate the present value of an ordinary annuity of $500 per month for two years at 18% compounded monthly. First, with an annuity, the frequency of the rents and the compounding period's length must be the same. In this case, the rents are monthly and the compounding is monthly. Since there are 12 compounding periods in one year, we divide the interest rate of 18% by 12 giving an i of 1.5%. Then, we multiply the two years by 12 giving an n of 24. Using Table C.4, we have a factor of 20.030. Thus, the present value of an ordinary annuity of $500 per month for two years at 18% compounded monthly is $10,015 ($500 × 20.030).

APPLICATIONS OF COMPOUND INTEREST TECHNIQUES

Accountants use compound interest techniques in many areas. We will examine two applications in this appendix: accounting for noninterest-bearing notes and market price of a long-term bond.

Using Present Values to Calculate Implied Interest

If a note is noninterest-bearing or the interest rate is lower than the prevailing market rate, the accountant must calculate the implied interest. In *Opinion No. 21*, the Accounting Principles Board required that we discount these notes to their present value using the current borrowing rate for the firm.[1]

To illustrate, assume that on December 31, 2006, Vanna Company buys a computer from Office Products Company. The seller agrees to take a one-year, noninterest-bearing note for $4,561. Assume that Vanna Company's current interest rate for borrowing is 14%. The $4,561 to be paid on December 31, 2007, includes interest and is therefore worth less than $4,561 on December 31, 2006. Using the provisions of *APB Opinion No. 21*, we must discount the $4,561 at 14% for one year. This determines the implied present value of the note and thus the fair market value of the computer.

In Table C.2 of the compound interest tables, the present value of $1 at 14% for one year is 0.877. Then the present value of $4,561 discounted at 14% for one year is $4,000, calculated as follows:

$$\$4,561 \times 0.877 = \$4,000$$

Thus, according to *Opinion No. 21*, Vanna is buying a computer at a cost of $4,000 and signing a note that will have interest expense of $561. The journal entry on Vanna's books to record the purchase of the equipment is as follows:

```
2006
Dec.   31   Office Equipment                                    4,000
            Discount on Notes Payable                             561
                 Notes Payable                                          4,561
            To record the purchase of a computer and the issuance of a
            one-year note that does not bear any interest on the face
            amount.
```

When the note matures on December 31, 2007, we make two entries: (1) an entry for the payment of the note, and (2) an entry to record the implied interest expense in the transaction. These would be as follows:

```
2007
Dec.   31   Notes Payable                                       4,561
                 Cash                                                   4,561
            To record payment of note to Office Products Company.
```

```
2007
Dec.   31   Interest Expense                                      561
                 Discount on Notes Payable                                561
            To record implied interest expense on the Office Products
            note.
```

---

[1] Accounting Principles Board (APB) Opinion No. 21, "Interest on Receivables and Payables" (New York: AICPA, 1971), paragraph 12.

Using Present Values to Calculate the Exact Market Price of Bonds to Yield a Given Rate

We can calculate the exact price that an investor must pay for a bond to yield a given rate using present values. To illustrate the computation, assume that a company will issue five-year, 12% bonds with a face value of $100,000. The bonds pay interest semiannually. Thus, there will be 10 interest periods. Assume the company issues the bonds at a price to yield 10% (or 5% every six months). The calculation of the issue price involves the determination of the present value at the issue date of two separate cash flows: (1) the face amount of the bonds discounted at the market rate, and (2) the interest payments discounted at the market rate. This calculation is as follows:

1. **Present value of face amount of $100,000**
   $100,000 (a single sum) will be paid in 10 periods
   at a market rate of 5% ($100,000 × 0.614) $ 61,400
2. **Present value of 10 interest payments of $6,000**
   Ten $6,000 interest payments (an annuity) at a
   market rate of 5% ($6,000 × 7.722)   46,332
   Total price to yield 10% annually to maturity $107,732

The following comments explain the calculation of the sales price of the bond:

- It helps to decide whether the selling price will be above or below par before calculating the sales price. Here, the stated interest rate on the bonds is 12% compared to a market interest rate of 10%. Since the stated interest rate is greater than the current market interest rate, investors will pay a premium for the bonds.

- The interest rate used to calculate the sales price of a bond is always the market interest rate. Here the annual market interest rate is 10%. Since interest payments on the bonds are semiannual, we use the semiannual market rate of 5%. Since the rate is on a semiannual basis, we must state the number of time periods the same way. Therefore, we use 10 semiannual periods to calculate the sales price.

- There are two cash flows that the bondholders will receive on the bond. They will receive the face value of the bond, $100,000, when the bond matures at the end of five years (10 semiannual periods). This is a single flow of cash. We find the present value factor of 0.614 by looking up the present value of a single sum of $1 for 10 periods at 5% in Table C.2.

- The second flow of cash that the bondholders will receive consists of the ten semiannual interest payments of $6,000. They will receive these payments at the end of each of the ten semiannual periods. This is an ordinary annuity. We find the present value factor of 7.722 by looking up the present value of an ordinary annuity of $1 for 10 periods at 5% in Table C.4 in Appendix C.

- The sum of the two present values ($107,732) is the sales price of the bonds that will yield a market rate of return on the bonds of 10% (or 5% every six months).

Accountants use compound interest techniques in many other areas. We discuss some of these in Chapter 13.

Use of a Calculator for Compound Interest

The appendix presented compound interest calculations using a table approach. In this method, we look up a precalculated value for the future value or present value of $1. We then multiply that factor by the number of dollars involved. Using a calculator to solve this requires that we enter the amount that we desire to find the future or present value of, touching the multiplication (x) key, entering the factor, and touching the equals (=) key. The table approach does not require any skills different from those required to multiply any two numbers together.

Many calculators today have compound interest capabilities built into the calculator. Thus, compound interest tables are not necessary. The specific techniques depend on the brand and model of the calculator. Usually, we enter the interest rate per compounding period and touch the key indicating that we have entered the interest rate. Then we enter the number of periods and touch the appropriate key. If we are calculating the present or future value of a single sum, we enter the single sum and then press either the present value key or the future value key (PV and FV, respectively, on some models). If we are calculating the present or future value of an ordinary annuity, we would enter the amount of one rent and then press the appropriate key. Some models of calculators can also determine the amount of rent given the future or present value of the annuity.

If we do not have a compound interest calculator or tables, we can use a simple calculator to calculate the factor using the appropriate formula. For example, we can calculate the present value of an ordinary annuity factor for $n = 4$ and $i = 12\%$ using the formula:

$$p = \frac{1}{(1+i)^n}$$

Using the calculator, we would enter 1 and touch the plus key (+). Then we would enter 0.12 and touch =. We then store this in memory by touching the memory enter (M + on some models) or equivalent key. Then we touch × and =. We have now calculated 1.12^2. We need 1.12^4. So we touch × and recall the contents of memory, 1.12 (using the RM key in some models), and then =. We now have 1.12^3. We repeat the last step one more time to get 1.12^4, or 1.5735193. Now clear memory and store this amount in memory. Then enter 1, ÷ , RM, and =. The display now shows 0.635518. This is the same factor that we would get (rounded) if we looked up the present value of $1 for four periods at 12% in Table C.2.

LEARNING GOALS REVIEW

1. Contrast simple interest and compound interest.

Simple interest is interest computed on the original principal of a note. Compound interest is interest earned on a principal sum that is increased at the end of each period by the interest for that period. The future accumulated amount at the end of each period becomes the principal sum for purposes of computing the interest for the next period.

2. Calculate and use the future amount of a single sum at compound interest.

The future amount of a single sum is calculated as follows:

$$f = p \times (\text{table factor for future amount of \$1})$$

where p equals the principal amount. Compound interest tables show factors for various interest rates and time periods. Thus, we calculate the future amount of a single sum by multiplying the single sum by the appropriate factor from the "future value of a single sum" table (Table C.1).

3. Calculate and use the present value of a single sum due in the future.

The present value of a single sum due in the future is calculated as follows:

$$p = f \times (\text{table factor for present value of \$ 1})$$

where f equals the future known amount. Compound interest tables show factors for various interest rates and time periods. Using tables, we calculate the present value of a single sum by multiplying the known future amount by the appropriate factor from a "present value of a single sum" table (Table C.2).

4. **Calculate and use the future amount of an ordinary annuity.**
   The future amount of an ordinary annuity is calculated as follows:

   $$F_0 = R \times \text{(table factor for future amount of an annuity value of \$ 1)}$$

   where R is equal to the amount of each rent. We calculate the future value by multiplying the amount of the rent by the appropriate factor from a "future value of an annuity" table (Table C.3).

5. **Calculate and use the present value of an ordinary annuity.**
   The present value of an ordinary annuity is

   $$P_0 = R \times \text{(table factor for present value of an ordinary annuity of \$ 1)}$$

   where R is equal to the amount of a rent. We use this formula to calculate what sum of money we must invest now so that a series of withdrawals of a given size and frequency will exhaust the fund by a given date in the future. We calculate the present value by multiplying the amount of the rent by the appropriate factor from a "present value of an annuity" table (Table C.4). Common applications of this formula include measuring notes payable and receivable when the interest rate differs from the current market rate, the carrying value of investment in bonds and the bonds payable liability, and the desirability of capital investment projects.

6. **Calculate and use the present value of an annuity due.**
   An annuity due is an annuity in which the withdrawal or payment occurs at the beginning of the period. We calculate the present value of an annuity due immediately before the first payment. The present value is equal to the value of one rent times the present value of an annuity due factor. We find the annuity due factor by using the present value of an ordinary annuity table (Table C.4). It is equal to the present value of an ordinary annuity of n - 1 rents of \$1 plus \$1.

GLOSSARY

annuity A series of equal payments-deposits, receipts, or withdrawals-made at regular intervals with interest compounded at a certain rate.

compound interest Interest computed not only on the principal but also on any interest that has been earned in the past but not yet paid. This term also refers to the difference between the future compound amount and the original principal.

future amount of an ordinary annuity The future amount of a series of equal rents at equal intervals plus interest compounded at a certain rate, with the future amount being determined immediately after the last rent in the series is made.

future amount of a single sum This is also called future compound amount or amount of a single sum; the amount of a single investment plus compound interest thereon for a given number of periods.

present value of an annuity The present value of a series of equal withdrawals or rents discounted at a given rate of interest.

present value of an annuity due Present value immediately before withdrawal of the first rent of a series of equal rents made at equal intervals of time in the future.

present value of an ordinary annuity Present value one period before withdrawal of the first rent of a series of equal rents made at equal intervals of time in the future.

present value of a single sum Present value at time period zero of a single future investment.

rent The amount of each of a series of equal annuity deposits or withdrawals.

simple interest Interest computed on the original principal (face value) of a note.

time period zero The date at which the present value is determined.

QUESTIONS FOR GROUP LEARNING

QC-1. Some people consider that interest is a form of rent. Do you agree? Why or why not?

QC-2. Distinguish between simple interest and compound interest.

QC-3. Distinguish between the future amount of $1 and the present value of $1.

QC-4. Distinguish between the present value of $1 and the present value of an ordinary annuity of $1.

QC-5. Distinguish between the future amount of $1 and the future amount of an ordinary annuity of $1.

QC-6. Distinguish between the present value of an annuity of $1 and the future amount of an annuity of $1.

QC-7. What are i and n for two years in each of the following: a. 20% compounded semiannually? b. 16% compounded quarterly? c. 18 % compounded monthly?

QC-8. What are some uses of compound interest concepts in business?

EXERCISES

EC-9. **Compound interest concepts (LG 2, 3)** Choose the correct response to complete the sentences below by indicating either a, b, or c to mean:

  a. greater than ($>$)

  b. less than ($<$)

  c. equal to ($=$)

      1. The present value of an amount on date zero should be (a, b, c) the amount desired on future date X.

      2. The future value of an amount should be (a, b, c) the amount invested on date zero.

      3. The table factor for the future amount of a single sum should be (a, b, c) 1.

      4. The table factor for the present value of a single sum should be (a, b, c) 1.

EC-10.   **Future amount of a single investment (LG 2)** Using the future-amount-of-a-single-sum tables, solve the following problems:

1. What is the future amount on January 1, 2012, of $16,000 invested on January 1, 2007, to earn interest at 12% compounded annually?

2. What is the future amount on January 1, 2008, of $5,250 invested on January 1, 2007, to earn interest at 10% compounded semiannually?

3. What is the future amount on January 1, 2013, of $16,000 invested on January 1, 2007, to earn interest at 16% compounded quarterly?

EC-11.   **Present value of a single sum (LG 3)** Using the present-value-of-a-single-sum tables, solve the following problems:

1. What is the present value on January 1, 2007, of $19,450 due to be paid on January 1, 2010, discounted at 9% compounded annually?

2. What is the present value on January 1, 2007, of $9,000 due to be paid on July 1, 2009, discounted at 10% compounded quarterly?

3. What is the present value on July 1, 2007, of $15,000 due to be paid on July 1, 2017, discounted at 14% compounded annually?

EC-12.   **Future amount of an annuity (LG 4)** What is the future amount on April 1, 2012, of 20 equal quarterly rents of $500 beginning on July 1, 2007, compounded quarterly at a 10% annual rate?

EC-13.   **Present value of an annuity (LG 5)** (a) What is the present value on January 1, 2007, of five equal annual rents of $2,500 beginning on January 1, 2008, compounded annually at 10%? (b) of $600 compounded semiannually at an annual rate of 11%?

EC-14.   **Future amount issue (LG 2)** David West deposited $60,000 in a special investment that provides for interest at the annual rate of 18% compounded monthly if the investment is maintained for three years. Calculate the balance of the savings account at the end of the three-year period.

EC-15.   **Calculating future amount (LG 2)** On September 1, 2007, Jo Wan puts her hotel bill of $560 on a charge account. The stipulated annual interest rate is 18% compounded monthly. How much will she owe at the end of three months? six months? one year?

EC-16.   **Calculating required current deposit (LG 3)** Pat Holmes is interested in purchasing a new car when he graduates from college in four years. Based on his estimates of the price of cars, he desires to have $40,000 at the time he graduates. He has located an investment that will earn 10% compounded quarterly. How much must he put in that investment today to have the $25,000 available at the end of the fourth year?

EC-17.   **Calculating required investment for retirement (LG 3)** Fred Boulder is interested in determining how much he would have to put into an investment today to be a millionaire when he retires. He will make a single investment today and plans to retire at the end of 40 years. He has located an investment that will earn 8% compounded annually for the 40 years. How much must he put in that investment now if he is to be a millionaire when he retires? If he could earn 10%, how much must he invest?

EC-18.   **Use of future amount of $1 tables to calculate needed present value factors (LG 2, 3)** While taking a test, Lea Waters, a student, realizes that she has failed to bring her present-value-of a-single-sum tables, although she does have her future-value-of-a-single-sum tables.

She needs to answer the following: "How much needs to be invested now in order to have $8,000 at the end of three years at 1 ½% monthly interest?"

1. Can the student use the future-amount-of-a-single-sum tables to solve this problem? Explain.
2. If the future-amount-of-a-single-sum table factor for 1 1/2% for 36 months is 1.709, how much needs to be invested now in order to have $8,000 at the end of three years?

EC-19. **Calculating future amount of an annuity (LG 4)** John Long is depositing his annual bonus in a special fund. Long receives a $6,000 bonus each year. Assume that he will continue to receive this amount and that he deposits these bonuses each December 31 in a fund that will earn 9% compounded annually. Also assume that the first deposit was made on December 31, 2007. What amount will be in the fund after the deposit on December 31, 2011?

EC-20. **Saving to make a major purchase (LG 4)** Randy Molander is considering the purchase of a car. Instead of borrowing the money to buy the car, he has decided to start a savings program. He will make regular semiannual deposits of $6,000 for five years into an account that will earn 9% annually. How much will he have available to spend on the car immediately after that last deposit?

EC-21. **Retiring a debt (LG 4)** Delta Corporation has a $900,000 long-term bond outstanding. It plans to make annual cash deposits at the start of each year into a fund that earns 8% compounded annually. If it must pay off the bond in 12 years, how much must it deposit in the fund each year to have the $800,000 available immediately after the last deposit?

EC-22. **College living expenses (LG 5)** Susie Oh will be starting college. Her father has offered to put money in an account that she can draw on to pay her living expenses at school. She desires to make withdrawals at the end of every two months for the 4 years that she will be away at school. Her father has identified an account that pays 9% compounded every two months. How much must he deposit to the account today so that she can make regular withdrawals of $500 every two months, beginning in two months?

EC-23. **College tuition (LG 6)** Jim Hauser's father has offered to establish a fund to pay for Jim's college tuition. The tuition at Northwest State will be $10,000 each of the four years. Jim must pay for all of his other expenses. Jim's father will make the deposit into the fund immediately before Jim must make the first year's tuition payment. The fund will earn interest at 8% compounded annually. Jim will make a withdrawal each year to pay his tuition. How much must Jim's father deposit in the fund?

EC-24. **Retirement planning (LG 5)** Your father has asked for your help in planning his retirement. He believes that he will need an annual income of $45,000 during retirement. To be safe, he would plan on having that income for 25 years after he retires. He has located an investment that earns 10% compounded annually and permits equal annual withdrawals. How much must he put into the investment when he retires to be able to withdraw $45,000 at the end of each of 25 years?

EC-25. **Preretirement planning (LG 3, 5)** Although you have just begun your career, retirement is very appealing. You have decided that when you retire you would like to purchase an investment that allows you to withdraw $50,000 each year as an income. In order to do this, you have decided to make an annual deposit at the beginning of each year to a fund that you will use to purchase the desired investment immediately after the last deposit when you retire. You have located a fund into which you can make your annual deposits that earns 9 % compounded annually for the 40 years until you retire. You estimate that you will be able to purchase an investment when you retire that will earn 10% compounded annually. To be safe, you would like to provide for a retirement income for 30 years. How much must you deposit annually to be able to withdraw $50,000 at the end of each of 30 years?

PRACTICE CASES

1. **Determining which gift to accept (LG 3,5)** As a graduation gift, your family offers you a choice from among the following:

   a. $14,000 cash now.

   b. $3,200 at the end of each year for five years.

   c. $20,000 at the end of five years.

   REQUIRED
   1. Based on the highest present value, which gift should you choose? Determine by assuming an annual discount factor of 14% and then ranking the choices in order of preference.

   2. If the discount factor were 7%, would your choice be different? Again rank the choices in order of your preference (based on the highest present value).

   3. If your answer to requirement 2 is different from your answer to requirement 1, explain why.

2. **Determining which gift to accept (LG 3,5)** Assume that you have a wealthy uncle. He has discussed three methods of sharing his estate with you. These alternatives are listed as follows:

   a. A gift of $18,000 in cash made at the present time.

   b. A gift of $45,000 to be made 10 years from now when some bonds that the uncle owns mature.

   c. A bequest in the uncle's will leaving you $50,000 in cash. Assume that the uncle is likely to live 12 more years.

   REQUIRED
   If the time value of money is 12% compounded annually, what offer would be the most beneficial for you to accept? Discuss why. If the first offer turns out to be impossible, what method would be the next most beneficial? Why? Which method is the least beneficial? Why?

COMPOUND INTEREST
TABLES

Table C-1 Future Amount of a Single Sum of $1

n	1.5%	2.5%	4.0%	4.5%	5.0%	5.5%	6.0%	6.5%
1	1.015	1.025	1.040	1.045	1.050	1.055	1.060	1.065
2	1.030	1.051	1.082	1.092	1.103	1.113	1.124	1.134
3	1.046	1.077	1.125	1.141	1.158	1.174	1.191	1.208
4	1.061	1.104	1.170	1.193	1.216	1.239	1.262	1.286
5	1.077	1.131	1.217	1.246	1.276	1.307	1.338	1.370
6	1.093	1.160	1.265	1.302	1.340	1.379	1.419	1.459
7	1.110	1.189	1.316	1.361	1.407	1.455	1.504	1.554
8	1.126	1.218	1.369	1.422	1.477	1.535	1.594	1.655
9	1.143	1.249	1.423	1.486	1.551	1.619	1.689	1.763
10	1.161	1.280	1.480	1.553	1.629	1.708	1.791	1.877
11	1.178	1.312	1.539	1.623	1.710	1.802	1.898	1.999
12	1.196	1.345	1.601	1.696	1.796	1.901	2.012	2.129
13	1.214	1.379	1.665	1.772	1.886	2.006	2.133	2.267
14	1.232	1.413	1.732	1.852	1.980	2.116	2.261	2.415
15	1.250	1.448	1.801	1.935	2.079	2.232	2.397	2.572
16	1.269	1.485	1.873	2.022	2.183	2.355	2.540	2.739
17	1.288	1.522	1.948	2.113	2.292	2.485	2.693	2.917
18	1.307	1.560	2.026	2.208	2.407	2.621	2.854	3.107
19	1.327	1.599	2.107	2.308	2.527	2.766	3.026	3.309
20	1.347	1.639	2.191	2.412	2.653	2.918	3.207	3.524
21	1.367	1.680	2.279	2.520	2.786	3.078	3.400	3.753
22	1.388	1.722	2.370	2.634	2.925	3.248	3.604	3.997
23	1.408	1.765	2.465	2.752	3.072	3.426	3.820	4.256
24	1.430	1.809	2.563	2.876	3.225	3.615	4.049	4.533
25	1.451	1.854	2.666	3.005	3.386	3.813	4.292	4.828
26	1.473	1.900	2.772	3.141	3.556	4.023	4.549	5.141
27	1.495	1.948	2.883	3.282	3.733	4.244	4.822	5.476
28	1.517	1.996	2.999	3.430	3.920	4.478	5.112	5.832
29	1.540	2.046	3.119	3.584	4.116	4.724	5.418	6.211
30	1.563	2.098	3.243	3.745	4.322	4.984	5.743	6.614
31	1.587	2.150	3.373	3.914	4.538	5.258	6.088	7.044
32	1.610	2.204	3.508	4.090	4.765	5.547	6.453	7.502
33	1.634	2.259	3.648	4.274	5.003	5.852	6.841	7.990
34	1.659	2.315	3.794	4.466	5.253	6.174	7.251	8.509
35	1.684	2.373	3.946	4.667	5.516	6.514	7.686	9.062
36	1.709	2.433	4.104	4.877	5.792	6.872	8.147	9.651
37	1.735	2.493	4.268	5.097	6.081	7.250	8.636	10.279
38	1.761	2.556	4.439	5.326	6.385	7.649	9.154	10.947
39	1.787	2.620	4.616	5.566	6.705	8.069	9.704	11.658
40	1.814	2.685	4.801	5.816	7.040	8.513	10.286	12.416

Table C-1 Future Amount of a Single Sum of $1

n	7.0%	8.0%	9.0%	10.0%	12.0%	14.0%	16.0%	2.00%
1	1.070	1.080	1.090	1.100	1.120	1.140	1.160	1.200
2	1.145	1.166	1.188	1.210	1.254	1.300	1.346	1.440
3	1.225	1.260	1.295	1.331	1.405	1.482	1.561	1.728
4	1.311	1.360	1.412	1.464	1.574	1.689	1.811	2.074
5	1.403	1.469	1.539	1.611	1.762	1.925	2.100	2.488
6	1.501	1.587	1.677	1.772	1.974	2.195	2.436	2.986
7	1.606	1.714	1.828	1.949	2.211	2.502	2.826	3.583
6	1.718	1.851	1.993	2.144	2.476	2.853	3.278	4.300
9	1.838	1.999	2.172	2.358	2.773	3.252	3.803	5.160
10	1.967	2.159	2.367	2.594	3.106	3.707	4.411	6.192
11	2.105	2.332	2.580	2.853	3.479	4.226	5.117	7.430
12	2.252	2.518	2.813	3.138	3.896	4.818	5.936	8.916
13	2.410	2.720	3.066	3.452	4.363	5.492	6.886	10.699
14	2.579	2.937	3.342	3.797	4.887	6.261	7.988	12.839
15	2.759	3.172	3.642	4.177	5.474	7.138	9.266	15.407
16	2.952	3.426	3.970	4.595	6.130	8.137	10.748	18.488
17	3.159	3.700	4.328	5.054	6.666	9.276	12.468	22.186
18	3.380	3.996	4.717	5.560	7.690	10.575	14.463	26.623
19	3.617	4.316	5.142	6.116	8.613	12.056	16.777	31.948
20	3.870	4.661	5.604	6.727	9.646	13.743	19.461	38.338
21	4.141	5.034	6.109	7.400	10.804	15.668	22.574	46.005
22	4.430	5.437	6.659	8.140	12.100	17.861	26.186	55.206
23	4.741	5.871	7.258	8.954	13.552	20.362	30.376	66.247
24	5.072	6.341	7.911	9.850	15.179	23.212	35.236	79.497
25	5.427	6.848	8.623	10.835	17.000	26.462	40.874	95.396
26	5.807	7.396	9.399	11.918	19.040	30.167	47.414	114.475
27	6.214	7.988	10.245	13.110	21.325	34.390	55.000	137.371
28	6.649	8.627	11.167	14.421	23.884	39.204	63.800	164.845
29	7.114	9.317	12.172	15.863	26.750	44.693	74.009	197.814
30	7.612	10.063	13.268	17.449	29.960	50.950	85.850	237.376
31	8.145	10.868	14.462	19.194	33.555	58.083	99.586	284.852
32	8.715	11.737	15.763	21.114	37.582	66.215	115.520	341.822
33	9.325	12.676	17.182	23.225	42.092	75.485	134.003	410.186
34	9.978	13.690	18.728	25.548	47.143	86.053	155.443	492.224
35	10.677	14.785	20.414	28.102	52.600	98.100	180.314	590.668
36	11.424	15.968	22.251	30.913	59.136	111.834	209.164	708.802
37	12.224	17.246	24.254	34.004	66.232	127.491	242.631	850.562
38	13.079	18.625	26.437	37.404	74.180	145.340	281.452	1020.675
39	13.995	20.115	28.816	41.145	83.081	165.687	326.484	1224.810
40	14.974	21.725	31.409	45.259	93.051	188.884	378.721	1469.772

Table C-2 Present Value of a Single Sum of $1

n	1.50%	2.50%	4.0%	4.50%	5.00%	5.50%	6.00%	6.50%
1	0.985	0.976	0.962	0.957	0.952	0.948	0.943	0.939
2	0.971	0.952	0.925	0.916	0.907	0.898	0.890	0.882
3	0.956	0.929	0.889	0.876	0.864	0.852	0.840	0.828
4	0.942	0.906	0.855	0.839	0.823	0.807	0.792	0.777
5	0.928	0.884	0.822	0.802	0.784	0.765	0.747	0.730
6	0.915	0.862	0.790	0.768	0.746	0.725	0.705	0.685
7	0.901	0.841	0.760	0.735	0.711	0.687	0.665	0.644
8	0.888	0.821	0.731	0.703	0.677	0.652	0.627	0.604
9	0.875	0.801	0.703	0.673	0.645	0.618	0.592	0.567
10	0.862	0.781	0.676	0.644	0.614	0.585	0.558	0.533
11	0.849	0.762	0.650	0.616	0.585	0.555	0.527	0.500
12	0.836	0.744	0.625	0.590	0.557	0.526	0.497	0.470
13	0.824	0.725	0.601	0.564	0.530	0.499	0.469	0.441
14	0.812	0.708	0.577	0.540	0.505	0.473	0.442	0.414
15	0.800	0.690	0.555	0.517	0.481	0.448	0.417	0.389
16	0.788	0.674	0.534	0.494	0.458	0.425	0.394	0.365
17	0.776	0.657	0.513	0.473	0.436	0.402	0.371	0.343
18	0.765	0.641	0.494	0.453	0.416	0.381	0.350	0.322
19	0.754	0.626	0.475	0.433	0.396	0.362	0.331	0.302
20	0.742	0.610	0.456	0.415	0.377	0.343	0.312	0.284
21	0.731	0.595	0.439	0.397	0.359	0.325	0.294	0.266
22	0.721	0.581	0.422	0.380	0.342	0.308	0.278	0.250
23	0.710	0.567	0.406	0.363	0.326	0.292	0.262	0.235
24	0.700	0.553	0.390	0.348	0.310	0.277	0.247	0.221
25	0.689	0.539	0.375	0.333	0.295	0.262	0.233	0.207
26	0.679	0.526	0.361	0.318	0.281	0.249	0.220	0.194
27	0.669	0.513	0.347	0.305	0.268	0.236	0.207	0.183
28	0.659	0.501	0.333	0.292	0.255	0.223	0.196	0.171
29	0.649	0.489	0.321	0.279	0.243	0.212	0.185	0.161
30	0.640	0.477	0.308	0.267	0.231	0.201	0.174	0.151
31	0.630	0.465	0.296	0.256	0.220	0.190	0.164	0.142
32	0.621	0.454	0.285	0.244	0.210	0.180	0.155	0.133
33	0.612	0.443	0.274	0.234	0.200	0.171	0.146	0.125
34	0.603	0.432	0.264	0.224	0.190	0.162	0.138	0.118
35	0.594	0.421	0.253	0.214	0.181	0.154	0.130	0.110
36	0.585	0.411	0.244	0.205	0.173	0.146	0.123	0.104
37	0.576	0.401	0.234	0.196	0.164	0.138	0.116	0.097
38	0.568	0.391	0.225	0.188	0.157	0.131	0.109	0.091
39	0.560	0.382	0.217	0.180	0.149	0.124	0.103	0.086
40	0.551	0.372	0.208	0.172	0.142	0.117	0.097	0.081

Table C-2 Present Value of a Single Sum of $1

n	7.00%	8.00%	9.00%	10.00%	12.00%	14.00%	16.00%	20.00%
1	0.935	0.926	0.917	0.909	0.893	0.877	0.862	0.833
2	0.873	0.857	0.842	0.826	0.797	0.769	0.743	0.694
3	0.816	0.794	0.772	0.751	0.712	0.675	0.641	0.579
4	0.763	0.735	0.708	0.683	0.636	0.592	0.552	0.482
5	0.713	0.681	0.650	0.621	0.567	0.519	0.476	0.402
6	0.666	0.630	0.596	0.564	0.507	0.456	0.410	0.335
7	0.623	0.583	0.547	0.513	0.452	0.400	0.354	0.279
8	0.582	0.540	0.502	0.467	0.404	0.351	0.305	0.233
9	0.544	0.500	0.460	0.424	0.361	0.308	0.263	0.194
10	0.508	0.463	0.422	0.386	0.322	0.270	0.227	0.162
11	0.475	0.429	0.388	0.350	0.287	0.237	0.195	0.135
12	0.444	0.397	0.356	0.319	0.257	0.208	0.168	0.112
13	0.415	0.368	0.326	0.290	0.229	0.182	0.145	0.093
14	0.388	0.340	0.299	0.263	0.205	0.160	0.125	0.078
15	0.362	0.315	0.275	0.239	0.183	0.140	0.108	0.065
16	0.339	0.292	0.252	0.218	0.163	0.123	0.093	0.054
17	0.317	0.270	0.231	0.198	0.146	0.108	0.080	0.045
18	0.296	0.250	0.212	0.180	0.130	0.095	0.069	0.038
19	0.277	0.232	0.194	0.164	0.116	0.083	0.060	0.031
20	0.258	0.215	0.178	0.149	0.104	0.073	0.051	0.026
21	0.242	0.199	0.164	0.135	0.093	0.064	0.044	0.022
22	0.226	0.184	0.150	0.123	0.083	0.056	0.038	0.018
23	0.211	0.170	0.138	0.112	0.074	0.049	0.033	0.015
24	0.197	0.158	0.126	0.102	0.066	0.043	0.028	0.013
25	0.184	0.146	0.116	0.092	0.059	0.038	0.024	0.010
26	0.172	0.135	0.106	0.084	0.053	0.033	0.021	0.009
27	0.161	0.125	0.098	0.076	0.047	0.029	0.018	0.007
28	0.150	0.116	0.090	0.069	0.042	0.026	0.016	0.006
29	0.141	0.107	0.082	0.063	0.037	0.022	0.014	0.005
30	0.131	0.099	0.075	0.057	0.033	0.020	0.012	0.004
31	0.123	0.092	0.069	0.052	0.030	0.017	0.010	0.004
32	0.115	0.085	0.063	0.047	0.027	0.015	0.009	0.003
33	0.107	0.079	0.058	0.043	0.024	0.013	0.007	0.002
34	0.100	0.073	0.053	0.039	0.021	0.012	0.006	0.002
35	0.094	0.068	0.049	0.036	0.019	0.010	0.006	0.002
36	0.088	0.063	0.045	0.032	0.017	0.009	0.005	0.001
37	0.082	0.058	0.041	0.029	0.015	0.008	0.004	0.001
38	0.076	0.054	0.038	0.027	0.013	0.007	0.004	0.001
39	0.071	0.050	0.035	0.024	0.012	0.006	0.003	0.001
40	0.067	0.046	0.032	0.022	0.011	0.005	0.003	0.001

Table C-3 Future Amount of an Ordinary Annuity of $1

n	1.5%	2.5%	4.0%	4.5%	5.0%	5.5%	6.0%	6.5%
1	1.000	1.000	1.000	1.000	1.000	1.000	1.000	1.000
2	2.015	2.025	2.040	2.045	2.050	2.055	2.060	2.065
3	3.045	3.076	3.122	3.137	3.153	3.168	1.184	3.199
4	4.091	4.153	4.246	4.278	4.310	4.342	4.375	4.407
5	5.152	5.256	5.416	5.471	5.526	5.581	5.637	5.694
6	6.230	6.388	6.633	6.717	6.802	6.888	6.975	7.064
7	7.323	7.547	7.898	8.019	8.142	8.267	8.394	8.523
8	8.433	8.736	9.214	9.380	9.549	9.722	9.897	10.077
9	9.559	9.955	10.583	10.802	11.027	11.256	11.491	11.732
10	10.703	11.203	12.006	12.288	12.578	12.875	13.181	13.494
11	11.863	12.483	13.486	13.841	14.207	14.583	14.972	15.372
12	13.041	13.796	15.026	15.464	15.917	16.386	16.870	17.371
13	14.237	15.140	16.627	17.160	17.713	18.287	18.882	19.500
14	15.450	16.519	18.292	18.932	19.599	20.293	21.015	21.767
15	16.682	17.932	20.024	20.784	21.579	22.409	23.276	24.182
16	17.932	19.360	21.825	22.719	23.657	24.641	25.673	26.754
17	19.201	20.865	23.698	24.742	25.840	26.996	28.213	29.493
18	20.489	22.386	25.645	26.855	28.132	29.481	30.906	32.410
19	21.797	23.946	27.671	29.064	30.539	32.103	33.760	35.517
20	23.124	25.545	29.778	31.371	33.066	34.868	36.786	38.825
21	24.471	27.183	31.969	33.783	35.719	37.786	39.993	42.349
22	25.838	28.863	34.248	36.303	38.505	40.864	43.392	46.102
23	27.225	30.584	36.618	38.937	41.430	44.112	46.996	50.098
24	28.634	32.349	39.083	41.689	44.502	47.538	50.816	54.355
25	30.063	34.158	41.646	44.565	47.727	51.153	54.865	58.888
26	31.514	36.012	44.312	47.571	51.113	54.966	59.156	63.715
27	32.987	37.912	47.084	50.711	54.669	58.989	63.706	68.857
28	34.481	39.860	49.968	53.993	58.403	63.234	66.528	74.333
29	35.999	41.856	52.966	57.423	62.323	67.711	73.640	80.164
30	37.539	43.903	56.085	61.007	66.439	72.435	79.058	86.375
31	39.102	46.000	59.328	64.752	70.761	77.419	84.802	92.989
32	40.688	48.150	62.701	68.666	75.299	82.677	90.890	100.034
33	42.299	50.354	66.210	72.756	80.064	88.225	97.343	107.536
34	43.933	52.613	69.658	77.030	85.067	94.077	104.184	115.526
35	45.592	54.928	73.652	81.497	90.320	100.251	111.435	124.035
36	47.276	57.301	77.598	86.164	95.836	106.765	119.121	133.097
37	48.985	59.734	81.702	91.041	101.628	113.637	127.268	142.748
38	50.720	62.227	85.970	96.138	107.710	120.887	135.904	153.027
39	52.481	64.783	90.409	101.464	114.095	128.536	145.058	163.974
40	54.268	67.403	95.026	107.030	120.800	136.606	154.762	175.632

Table C-3 Future Amount of an Ordinary Annuity of $1

n	7.0%	8.0%	9.0%	10.0%	12.0%	14.0%	16.0%	20.0%
1	1.000	1.000	1.000	1.000	1.000	1.000	1.000	1.000
2	2.070	2.080	2.090	2.100	2.120	2.140	2.160	2.200
3	3.215	3.246	3.278	3.310	3.374	3.440	3.506	3.640
4	4.440	4.506	4.573	4.641	4.779	4.921	5.066	5.368
5	5.751	5.867	5.985	6.105	6.353	6.610	6.877	7.442
6	7.153	7.336	7.523	7.716	8.115	8.536	8.977	9.930
7	8.654	8.923	9.200	9.487	10.089	10.730	11.414	12.916
8	10.260	10.637	11.028	11.436	12.300	13.233	14.240	16.499
9	11.978	12.488	13.021	13.579	14.776	16.085	17.519	20.799
10	13.816	14.487	15.193	15.937	17.549	19.337	21.321	25.959
11	15.784	16.645	17.560	18.531	20.655	23.045	25.733	32.150
12	17.888	18.977	20.141	21.384	24.133	27.271	30.850	39.581
13	20.141	21.495	22.953	24.523	28.029	32.089	36.786	48.497
14	22.550	24.215	26.019	27.975	32.393	37.581	43.672	59.196
15	25.129	27.152	29.361	31.772	37.280	43.842	51.660	72.035
16	27.888	30.324	33.003	35.950	42.753	50.980	60.925	87.442
17	30.840	33.750	36.974	40.545	48.884	59.118	71.673	105.931
18	33.999	37.450	41.301	45.599	55.750	68.394	84.141	128.117
19	37.379	41.446	46.018	51.159	63.440	78.969	98.603	154.740
20	40.995	45.762	51.160	57.275	72.052	91.025	115.380	186.688
21	44.865	50.423	56.765	64.002	81.699	104.768	134.841	225.026
22	49.006	55.457	62.873	71.403	92.503	120.436	157.415	271.031
23	53.436	60.893	69.532	79.543	104.603	138.297	183.601	326.237
24	58.177	66.765	76.790	88.497	118.155	158.659	213.978	392.484
25	63.249	73.106	84.701	98.347	133.334	181.871	249.214	471.981
26	68.676	79.954	93.324	109.182	150.334	208.333	290.088	567.377
27	74.484	87.351	102.723	121.100	169.374	238.499	337.502	681.853
28	80.698	95.339	112.968	134.210	190.699	272.889	392.503	819.223
29	87.347	103.966	124.135	148.631	214.583	312.094	456.303	984.068
30	94.461	113.283	136.308	164.494	241.333	356.787	530.312	1181.882
31	102.073	123.346	149.575	181.943	271.293	407.737	616.162	1419.258
32	110.218	134.214	164.037	201.138	304.848	465.820	715.747	1704.109
33	118.933	145.951	179.800	222.252	342.429	532.035	831.267	2045.931
34	128.259	158.627	196.982	245.477	384.521	607.520	965.270	2456.118
35	138.237	172.317	215.711	271.024	431.663	693.573	1120.713	2948.341
36	148.913	187.102	236.125	299.127	484.463	791.673	1301.027	3539.009
37	160.337	203.070	258.376	330.039	543.599	903.507	1510.191	4247.811
38	172.561	220.316	282.630	364.043	609.831	1030.998	1752.822	5098.373
39	185.640	238.941	309.066	401.448	684.010	1176.338	2034.273	6119.048
40	199.635	259.057	337.882	442.593	767.091	1342.025	2360.757	7343.858

Table C-4 Present Value of an Ordinary Annuity of $1

n	1.5%	2.5 %	4.0 %	4.5 %	5.0 %	5.5 %	6.0 %	6.5 %
1	0.985	0.976	0.962	0.957	0.952	0.948	0.943	0.939
2	1.956	1.927	1.886	1.873	1.859	1.846	1.833	1.821
3	2.912	2.856	2.775	2.749	2.723	2.698	2.673	2.648
4	3.854	3.762	3.630	3.588	3.546	3.505	3.465	3.426
5	4.783	4.646	4.452	4.390	4.329	4.270	4.212	4.156
6	5.697	5.508	5.242	5.158	5.076	4.996	4.917	4.841
7	6.598	6.349	6.002	5.893	5.786	5.683	5.582	5.485
8	7.486	7.170	6.733	6.596	6.463	6.335	6.210	6.089
9	8.361	7.971	7.435	7.269	7.108	6.952	6.802	6.656
10	9.222	8.752	8.111	7.913	7.722	7.538	7.360	7.189
11	10.071	9.514	8.760	8.529	8.306	8.093	7.887	7.689
12	10.908	10.258	9.385	9.119	8.863	8.619	8.384	8.159
13	11.732	10.983	9.986	9.683	9.394	9.117	8.853	8.600
14	12.543	11.691	10.563	10.223	9.899	9.590	9.295	9.014
15	13.343	12.381	11.118	10.740	10.380	10.038	9.712	9.403
16	14.131	13.055	11.652	11.234	10.838	10.462	10.106	9.768
17	14.908	13.712	12.166	11.707	11.274	10.865	10.477	10.111
18	15.673	14.353	12.659	12.160	11.690	11.246	10.828	10.432
19	16.426	14.979	13.134	12.593	12.085	11.608	11.158	10.735
20	17.169	15.589	13.590	13.008	12.462	11.950	11.470	11.019
21	17.900	16.185	14.029	13.405	12.821	12.275	11.764	11.285
22	18.621	16.765	14.451	13.784	13.163	12.583	12.042	11.535
23	19.331	17.332	14.857	14.148	13.489	12.875	12.303	11.770
24	20.030	17.885	15.247	14.495	13.799	13.152	12.550	11.991
25	20.720	18.424	15.622	14.828	14.094	13.414	12.783	12.198
26	21.399	18.951	15.983	15.147	14.375	13.662	13.003	12.392
27	22.068	19.464	16.330	15.451	14.643	13.898	13.211	12.575
28	22.727	19.965	16.663	15.743	14.898	14.121	13.406	12.746
29	23.376	20.454	16.984	16.022	15.141	14.333	13.591	12.907
30	24.016	20.930	17.292	16.289	15.372	14.534	13.765	13.059
31	24.646	21.395	17.588	16.544	15.593	14.724	13.929	13.201
32	25.267	21.849	17.874	16.789	15.803	14.904	14.084	13.334
33	25.879	22.292	18.148	17.023	16.003	15.075	14.230	13.459
34	26.482	22.724	18.411	17.247	16.193	15.237	14.368	13.577
35	27.076	23.145	18.665	17.461	16.374	15.391	14.498	13.687
36	27.661	23.556	18.908	17.666	16.547	15.536	14.621	13.791
37	28.237	23.957	19.143	17.862	16.711	15.674	14.737	13.888
38	28.805	24.349	19.368	18.050	16.868	15.805	14.846	13.979
39	29.365	24.730	19.584	18.230	17.017	15.929	14.949	14.065
40	29.916	25.103	19.793	18.402	17.159	16.046	15.046	14.146

Table C-4 Present Value of an Ordinary Annuity of $1

n	7.0%	8.0%	9.0%	10.0%	12.0%	14.0%	16.0%	20.0%
1	0.935	0.926	0.917	0.909	0.893	0.877	0.862	0.833
2	1.808	1.783	1.759	1.736	1.690	1.647	1.605	1.528
3	2.624	2.577	2.531	2.487	2.402	2.322	2.246	2.106
4	3.387	3.312	3.240	3.170	3.037	2.914	2.798	2.589
5	4.100	3.993	3.890	3.791	3.605	3.433	3.274	2.991
6	4.767	4.623	4.486	4.355	4.111	3.889	3.685	3.326
7	5.389	5.206	5.033	4.868	4.564	4.288	4.039	3.605
8	5.971	5.747	5.535	5.335	4.968	4.639	4.344	3.837
9	6.515	6.247	5.995	5.759	5.328	4.946	4.607	4.031
10	7.024	6.710	6.418	6.145	5.650	5.216	4.833	4.192
11	7.499	7.139	6.805	6.495	5.938	5.453	5.029	4.327
12	7.943	7.536	7.161	6.814	6.194	5.660	5.197	4.439
13	8.358	7.904	7.487	7.103	6.424	5.842	5.342	4.533
14	8.745	8.244	7.786	7.367	6.628	6.002	5.468	4.611
15	9.108	8.559	8.061	7.606	6.811	6.142	5.575	4.675
16	9.447	8.851	8.313	7.824	6.974	6.265	5.668	4.730
17	9.763	9.122	8.544	8.022	7.120	6.373	5.749	4.775
18	10.059	9.372	8.756	8.201	7.250	6.467	5.818	4.812
19	10.336	9.604	8.950	8.365	7.366	6.550	5.877	4.843
20	10.594	9.818	9.129	8.514	7.469	6.623	5.929	4.870
21	10.836	10.017	9.292	8.649	7.562	6.687	5.973	4.891
22	11.061	10.201	9.442	6.772	7.645	6.743	6.011	4.909
23	11.272	10.371	9.580	8.883	7.718	6.792	6.044	4.925
24	11.469	10.529	9.707	8.985	7.784	6.835	6.073	4.937
25	11.654	10.675	9.823	9.077	7.843	6.873	6.097	4.948
26	11.826	10.810	9.929	9.161	7.896	6.906	6.118	4.956
27	11.987	10.935	10.027	9.237	7.943	6.935	6.136	4.964
28	12.137	11.051	10.116	9.307	7.984	6.961	6.152	4.970
29	12.278	11.158	10.198	9.370	8.022	6.983	6.166	4.975
30	12.409	11.258	10.274	9.427	8.055	7.003	6.177	4.979
31	12.532	11.350	10.343	9.479	8.085	7.020	6.187	4.982
32	12.647	11.435	10.406	9.526	8.112	7.035	6.196	4.985
33	12.754	11.514	10.464	9.569	8.135	7.048	6.203	4.988
34	12.854	11.587	10.518	9.609	8.157	7.060	6.210	4.990
35	12.948	11.655	10.567	9.644	8.176	7.070	6.215	4.992
36	13.035	11.717	10.612	9.677	8.192	7.079	6.220	4.993
37	13.117	11.775	10.653	9.706	8.208	7.087	6.224	4.994
38	13.193	11.829	10.691	9.733	8.221	7.094	6.228	4.995
39	13.265	11.879	10.726	9.757	8.233	7.100	6.231	4.996
40	13.332	11.925	10.757	9.779	8.244	7.105	6.233	4.997

INDEX